DRG Expert

A comprehensive guidebook to the DRG classification system

Changes effective with discharges on or after October 1, 2005

2006

22nd Edition

Disclaimer

Acknowledgments

Sharon Powell, RHIA, *Product Manager*
Sheri Poe Bernard, CPC, CPC-H, CPC-P, *Senior Director, Product Management*
Lynn Speirs, *Senior Director, Editorial/Desktop Publishing*
Karen Schmidt, BSN, *Technical Director*
Stacy Perry, *Manager, Desktop Publishing*
Lisa Singley, *Project Manager*
Shelley Ramsdell, MPA, RHIA, *Technical Editor*
Kerrie Hornsby, *Desktop Publishing Specialist*
Kate Holden, *Project Editor*

Our Commitment to Accuracy

Ingenix is committed to producing accurate and reliable materials. To report corrections, please visit www.ingenixonline.com/accuracy or email accuracy@ingenix.com. You can also reach customer service by calling 1.800.INGENIX (464.3649), option 1.

About the Technical Editors

Karen Schmidt, BSN, *Technical Director*

Ms. Schmidt has more than 20 years of health care experience beginning with a strong clinical background in critical care nursing and later functioning as director of case management including the components of quality assurance, utilization management, concurrent coding, case-mix analysis, and discharge planning. Her areas of expertise include ICD-9-CM/DRG coding, physician documentation education, implementation of concurrent coding methodology, outpatient observation audits, billing compliance audits, strategic planning, and APC implementation.

Shelley Ramsdell, MPA, RHIA, *Technical Editor*

Ms. Ramsdell has over 20 years in the health care field. She has supervised inpatient, ER and outpatient coding staff; directed information management; worked with patient accounts departments to resolve billing issues and has extensive experience analyzing and reporting health care data. Ms. Ramsdell holds a BA from the College of St. Scholastica and a Master's degree from University of New Haven in public administration with a concentration in health care management. She is an active member of the American Heath Information Management Association (AHIMA).

Continuing Education Units for AAPC Certified Members

This publication has prior approval by the American Academy of Professional Coders for continuing education units. Granting of prior approval in no way constitutes endorsement by AAPC of the publication content nor the publisher. Instructions to submit CEUs are available at www.aapc.com/education/CEUs/ceus.htm

Printed in the United States of America.

ISBN 1-56337-718-7

Summary of Changes

FISCAL YEAR 2006

New Format

The *DRG Expert* contains the same information in a new format that should be easier to use and understand. No longer will you see color over text. Ingenix has added new symbols to this book to make it easier for you to locate and identify,

S Surgical DRGs;

M Medical DRGs;

CC DRGs with CCs;

A Age restrictions; and,

SP Postacute care special pay transfer DRGs.

Available on CD

The *DRG Expert* is now available on CD for your convenience. The CD version of *DRG Expert* contains a complete copy of this book, appendices and all, and may be purchased separately.

DRG EXPERT WEBSITE

Ingenix now maintains a website to accompany the *DRG Expert*. Ingenix will post special reports, CMS information, and updated data files on this website so that the information is available before the next book update. This website address is:

www.ingenixonline.com/content/drg/resources.asp

This website is available only to customers who purchase the DRG Expert. The following password is needed to access this site:

drgres06

The password will change annually and Ingenix will supply customers with the new password when it changes.

DRG and ICD-9-CM Coding Changes

- A new DRG was created that identifies embolic stroke combined with tPA treatment, DRG 559 Acute Ischemic Stroke with Use of Thrombolytic Agent
- A new list of major cardiovascular conditions (MCVs) was defined and newly created DRGs in MDC 5 will be differentiated by the MCVs.
- Twelve new DRGs were created in MDC 5 based on the presence or absence of an MCV condition and will replace DRGs 107, 109, 115, 116, 478, 516, 517, 526, and 527 (please see DRG Conversion Table on the following page)
- Code 37.26 (Cardiac electrophysiologic stimulation and recording studies) was removed from the list of cardiac catheterizations for DRGs 535 (Cardiac Defibrillator Implant with Cardiac Catheterization with Acute Myocardial Infarction, Heart Failure, or Shock) and 536 (Cardiac Defibrillator Implant with Cardiac Catheterization without Acute Myocardial Infarction, Heart Failure, or Shock) and reassigned to DRG 515 (Cardiac Defibrillator Implant without Cardiac Catheterization)
- There are four new ICD-9-CM codes that identify multiple stent insertion (codes 00.45, 00.46, 00.47, and 00.48) and four new codes that identify multiple vessel treatment (codes 00.40, 00.41, 00.42, and 00.43
- Procedure code 35.52 (Repair of atrial septal defect with prosthesis, closed technique) was moved from DRG 108 (Other Cardiothoracic Procedures) and reassigned to DRG 518 (Percutaneous Cardiovascular Procedures without Acute Myocardial Infarction without Coronary Artery Stent Implant)

- DRG 103 was revised to include 37.65 (Implant of external heart assist system) and 37.64 (Removal of heart assist system)
- The title of DRG 541 was revised to ECMO or Tracheostomy with Mechanical Ventilation 96+ Hours or Principal Diagnosis Except Face, Mouth and Neck with Major O.R. and for consistency purposes the title of DRG 542 was revised to Tracheostomy with Mechanical Ventilation 96+ Hours or Principal Diagnosis Except Face, Mouth and Neck without Major O.R.
- Procedure code 39.65 (Extracorporeal membrane oxygenation [ECMO]) was removed from DRGs 104 and 105 and reassigned to DRG 541
- DRG 209 (Major Joint and Limb Reattachment Procedures of Lower Extremity) was deleted
- Three new DRGs were created in MDC 8, DRG 544 (Major Joint Replacement or Reattachment of Lower Extremity), DRG 545 (Revision of Hip or Knee Replacement) and DRG 546 (Spinal Fusions Except Cervical with Curvature of the Spine or Malignancy)
- Principal diagnosis codes for curvature of the spine or malignancy were removed from DRG 497 (Spinal Fusion Except Cervical with CC) and DRG 498 (Spinal Fusion Except Cervical without CC) and reassigned to DRG 546
- Procedure code 26.12 (Open biopsy of salivary gland or duct) was removed from DRG 468 to DRG 477
- CMS restructured four edits in the Medicare Code Editor (MCE): edit 4 (age conflict), edit 5 (sex conflict), edit 8 (questionable admission), and edit 11 (noncovered procedure)
- The surgical hierarchies for MDC 5 Diseases and Disorders of the Circulatory System and MDC 8 Diseases and Disorders of the Musculoskeletal System and Connective Tissue were revised
- 173 new diagnosis codes and 37 procedure codes were added
- New diagnosis codes were added to the complications and comorbidities (CC) list
- DRG relative weights were recalibrated as required by the Social Security Act
- The criteria used to determine whether a DRG qualifies for inclusion in the postacute care transfer policy was revised. There are now approximately 182 DRGs that are categorized as postacute care transfers and 13 DRGs that are categorized as postacute care special pay transfers.

DRG Conversion Table

Invalid DRG	MDC	DRG Title	Replacement DRG	DRG Title	Relative Weight
107	5	Coronary Bypass with Cardiac Catheterization	547	Coronary Bypass with Cardiac Catheterization with Major Cardiovascular Diagnosis	6.1948
			548	Coronary Bypass with Cardiac Catheterization without Major Cardiovascular Diagnosis	4.7198
109	5	Coronary Bypass without Cardiac Catheterization	549	Coronary Bypass without Cardiac Catheterization with Major Cardiovascular Diagnosis	5.098
			550	Coronary Bypass without Cardiac Catheterization without Major Cardiovascular Diagnosis	3.6151

Invalid DRG	MDC	DRG Title	Replacement DRG	DRG Title	Relative Weight
115	5	Permanent Cardiac Pacemaker Implant with AMI, Heart Failure or Shock or AICD Lead or Generator Procedure	551	Permanent Cardiac Pacemaker Implant with Major Cardiovascular Diagnosis or AICD Lead or Generator	3.1007
116	5	Other Permanent Cardiac Pacemaker Implantation	552	Other Permanent Cardiac Pacemaker Implant without Major Cardiovascular Diagnosis	2.0996
209	8	Major Joint and Limb Reattachment Procedures of Lower Extremity	544	Major Joint Replacement or Reattachment of Lower Extremity	1.9643
			545	Revision of Hip or Knee Replacement	2.4827
478	5	Other Vascular Procedures with CC	553	Other Vascular Procedures with CC with Major Cardiovascular Diagnosis	3.0957
			554	Other Vascular Procedures with CC without Major Cardiovascular Diagnosis	2.0721
516	5	Percutaneous Cardiovascular Procedures with AMI	555	Percutaneous Cardiovascular Procedure with Major Cardiovascular Diagnosis	2.4315
517	5	Percutaneous Cardiovascular Procedure with Non Drug-Eluting Stent without AMI	556	Percutaneous Cardiovascular Procedure with Non Drug-Eluting Stent without Major Cardiovascular Diagnosis	1.9132
526	5	Percutaneous Cardiovascular Procedure with Drug-Eluting Stent with AMI	557	Percutaneous Cardiovascular Procedure with Drug-Eluting Stent with Major Cardiovascular Diagnosis	2.8717
527	5	Percutaneous Cardiovascular Procedure with Drug-Eluting Stent without AMI	558	Percutaneous Cardiovascular Procedure with Drug-Eluting Stent without Major Cardiovascular Diagnosis	2.2108

Invalid DRG	MDC	DRG Title	Replacement DRG	DRG Title	Relative Weight
	1		*559	Acute Ischemic Stroke with Use of Thrombolytic Agent	2.2473
	8		**546	Spinal Fusion Except Cervical With Curvature of the Spine or Malignancy	5.0739

* New DRG 559 does not replace an existing DRG

** New DRG 546 does not replace an existing DRG

Contents

Numeric Listing of DRGs viii
DRG Listing by Major Diagnostic Category xx
Introduction
- Source of Information .... Introduction — 1
- Basic Characteristics of DRG Classification .... Introduction — 1
- DRG Assignment Process .... Introduction — 2
- Complications and Comorbidities .... Introduction — 2
- Postacute Care Transfer Policy .... Introduction — 3
- Long Term Acute Care Hospital Prospective Payment System (LTCH PPS) .... Introduction — 4
- Keys to a Financially Successful DRG Program .... Introduction — 5
- The Physician's Role .... Introduction — 5
- *DRG Expert* Organization .... Introduction — 5
- Instructions for Using *DRG Expert* .... Introduction — 6
- Important Protocols of *DRG Expert* .... Introduction — 7
- Changes in the DRG System for 2005 .... Introduction — 8
- Glossary of DRG Terms .... Introduction — 9

Definitions of the DRGs Organized by MDC
- MDC 1: Diseases and Disorders of the Nervous System 1
- MDC 2: Diseases and Disorders of the Eye 18
- MDC 3: Diseases and Disorders of the Ear, Nose, Mouth and Throat 27
- MDC 4: Diseases and Disorders of the Respiratory System 39
- MDC 5: Diseases and Disorders of the Circulatory System 49
- MDC 6: Diseases and Disorders of the Digestive System 92
- MDC 7: Diseases and Disorders of the Hepatobiliary System and Pancreas 106
- MDC 8: Diseases and Disorders of the Musculoskeletal System and Connective Tissue 112
- MDC 9: Diseases and Disorders of the Skin, Subcutaneous Tissue and Breast 136
- MDC 10: Endocrine, Nutritional and Metabolic Diseases and Disorders 149
- MDC 11: Diseases and Disorders of the Kidney and Urinary Tract 157
- MDC 12: Diseases and Disorders of the Male Reproductive System 167
- MDC 13: Diseases and Disorders of the Female Reproductive System 174
- MDC 14: Pregnancy, Childbirth and the Puerperium 185
- MDC 15: Newborns and Other Neonates with Conditions Originating in the Perinatal Period 215
- MDC 16: Diseases and Disorders of the Blood and Blood-Forming Organs and Immunological Disorders 233
- MDC 17: Myeloproliferative Diseases and Disorders and Poorly Differentiated Neoplasms 236
- MDC 18: Infectious and Parasitic Diseases 245
- MDC 19: Mental Diseases and Disorders 250
- MDC 20: Alcohol/Drug Use and Alcohol/Drug-Induced Organic Mental Disorders 254
- MDC 21: Injury, Poisoning and Toxic Effects of Drugs 256
- MDC 22: Burns 276
- MDC 23: Factors Influencing Health Status and Other Contacts with Health Services 285
- MDC 24: Multiple Significant Trauma 290
- MDC 25: Human Immunodeficiency Virus Infections 307
- DRGs Associated with All MDCs and the Pre-MDC 311

Alphabetic Index to Diseases 325
Numeric Index to Diseases 423
Alphabetic Index to Procedures 521
Numeric Index to Procedures 553
Appendix A — Invalid DRG Conversion Table .... Appendix — 1
Appendix B — DRG Surgical Hierarchy Table .... Appendix — 31
Appendix C — LTC-DRG Crosswalk .... Appendix — 39
Appendix D — National Average Payment Table .... Appendix — 57

Numeric Listing of DRGs

DRG	Description	MDC	Page
001	Craniotomy, Age Greater than 17 with CC	1	1
002	Craniotomy, Age Greater than 17 without CC	1	1
003	Craniotomy, Age 0-17	1	2
004	No Longer Valid	1	2
005	No Longer Valid	1	2
006	Carpal Tunnel Release	1	2
007	Peripheral and Cranial Nerve and Other Nervous System Procedures with CC	1	3
008	Peripheral and Cranial Nerve and Other Nervous System Procedures without CC	1	5
009	Spinal Disorders and Injuries	1	9
010	Nervous System Neoplasms with CC	1	9
011	Nervous System Neoplasms without CC	1	9
012	Degenerative Nervous System Disorders	1	9
013	Multiple Sclerosis and Cerebellar Ataxia	1	10
014	Intracranial Hemorrhage or Cerebral Infarction	1	10
015	Nonspecific Cerebrovascular and Precerebral Occlusion without Infarction	1	10
016	Nonspecific Cerebrovascular Disorders with CC	1	11
017	Nonspecific Cerebrovascular Disorders without CC	1	11
018	Cranial and Peripheral Nerve Disorders with CC	1	11
019	Cranial and Peripheral Nerve Disorders without CC	1	12
020	Nervous System Infection Except Viral Meningitis	1	12
021	Viral Meningitis	1	13
022	Hypertensive Encephalopathy	1	13
023	Nontraumatic Stupor and Coma	1	13
024	Seizure and Headache, Age Greater than 17 with CC	1	13
025	Seizure and Headache, Age Greater than 17 without CC	1	14
026	Seizure and Headache, Age 0-17	1	14
027	Traumatic Stupor and Coma, Coma Greater than One Hour	1	14
028	Traumatic Stupor and Coma, Coma Less than One Hour, Age Greater than 17 with CC	1	14
029	Traumatic Stupor and Coma, Coma Less than One Hour, Age Greater than 17 without CC	1	14
030	Traumatic Stupor and Coma, Coma Less than One Hour, Age 0-17	1	14
031	Concussion, Age Greater than 17 with CC	1	14
032	Concussion, Age Greater than 17 without CC	1	14
033	Concussion, Age 0-17	1	15
034	Other Disorders of Nervous System with CC	1	15
035	Other Disorders of Nervous System without CC	1	17
036	Retinal Procedures	2	18
037	Orbital Procedures	2	18
038	Primary Iris Procedures	2	18
039	Lens Procedures with or without Vitrectomy	2	19
040	Extraocular Procedures Except Orbit, Age Greater than 17	2	19
041	Extraocular Procedures Except Orbit, Age 0-17	2	19
042	Intraocular Procedures Except Retina, Iris and Lens	2	19
043	Hyphema	2	21
044	Acute Major Eye Infections	2	21
045	Neurological Eye Disorders	2	21
046	Other Disorders of the Eye, Age Greater than 17 with CC	2	22
047	Other Disorders of the Eye, Age Greater than 17 without CC	2	26

DRG	Description	MDC	Page
048	Other Disorders of the Eye, Age 0-17	2	26
049	Major Head and Neck Procedures	3	27
050	Sialoadenectomy	3	27
051	Salivary Gland Procedures Except Sialoadenectomy	3	27
052	Cleft Lip and Palate Repair	3	27
053	Sinus and Mastoid Procedures, Age Greater than 17	3	27
054	Sinus and Mastoid Procedures, Age 0-17	3	28
055	Miscellaneous Ear, Nose, Mouth and Throat Procedures	3	28
056	Rhinoplasty	3	29
057	Tonsillectomy and Adenoidectomy Procedures Except Tonsillectomy and/or Adenoidectomy Only, Age Greater than 17	3	29
058	Tonsillectomy and Adenoidectomy Procedures Except Tonsillectomy and/or Adenoidectomy Only, Age 0-17	3	29
059	Tonsillectomy and/or Adenoidectomy Only, Age Greater than 17	3	29
060	Tonsillectomy and/or Adenoidectomy Only, Age 0-17	3	29
061	Myringotomy with Tube Insertion, Age Greater than 17	3	29
062	Myringotomy with Tube Insertion, Age 0-17	3	29
063	Other Ear, Nose, Mouth and Throat O.R. Procedures	3	30
064	Ear, Nose, Mouth and Throat Malignancy	3	33
065	Dysequilibrium	3	33
066	Epistaxis	3	33
067	Epiglottitis	3	33
068	Otitis Media and URI, Age Greater than 17 with CC	3	34
069	Otitis Media and URI, Age Greater than 17 without CC	3	34
070	Otitis Media and URI, Age 0-17	3	34
071	Laryngotracheitis	3	35
072	Nasal Trauma and Deformity	3	35
073	Other Ear, Nose, Mouth and Throat Diagnoses, Age Greater than 17	3	35
074	Other Ear, Nose, Mouth and Throat Diagnoses, Age 0-17	3	37
075	Major Chest Procedures	4	39
076	Other Respiratory System O.R. Procedures with CC	4	40
077	Other Respiratory System O.R. Procedures without CC	4	41
078	Pulmonary Embolism	4	42
079	Respiratory Infections and Inflammations, Age Greater than 17 with CC	4	42
080	Respiratory Infections and Inflammations, Age Greater than 17 without CC	4	43
081	Respiratory Infections and Inflammations, Age 0-17	4	43
082	Respiratory Neoplasms	4	43
083	Major Chest Trauma with CC	4	43
084	Major Chest Trauma without CC	4	44
085	Pleural Effusion with CC	4	44
086	Pleural Effusion without CC	4	44
087	Pulmonary Edema and Respiratory Failure	4	44
088	Chronic Obstructive Pulmonary Disease	4	44
089	Simple Pneumonia and Pleurisy, Age Greater than 17	4	45
090	Simple Pneumonia and Pleurisy, Age Greater than 17 without CC	4	45
091	Simple Pneumonia and Pleurisy, Age 0-17	4	45
092	Interstitial Lung Disease with CC	4	45
093	Interstitial Lung Disease without CC	4	45
094	Pneumothorax with CC	4	46
095	Pneumothorax without CC	4	46
096	Bronchitis and Asthma, Age Greater than 17 with CC	4	46
097	Bronchitis and Asthma, Age Greater than 17 without CC	4	46

DRG	Description	MDC	Page
098	Bronchitis and Asthma, Age 0-17	4	46
099	Respiratory Signs and Symptoms with CC	4	46
100	Respiratory Signs and Symptoms without CC	4	46
101	Other Respiratory System Diagnoses with CC	4	47
102	Other Respiratory System Diagnoses without CC	4	47
103	Heart Transplant or Implant of Heart Assist System	Pre	317
104	Cardiac Valve Procedures and Other Major Cardiothoracic Procedures with Cardiac Catheterization	5	49
105	Cardiac Valve Procedures and Other Major Cardiothoracic Procedures without Cardiac Catheterization	5	49
106	Coronary Bypass with PTCA	5	49
107	No Longer Valid	5	49
108	Other Cardiothoracic Procedures	5	49
109	No Longer Valid	5	50
110	Major Cardiovascular Procedures with CC	5	50
111	Major Cardiovascular Procedures without CC	5	51
112	No Longer Valid	5	51
113	Amputation for Circulatory System Disorders Except Upper Limb and Toe	5	51
114	Upper Limb and Toe Amputation for Circulatory System Disorders	5	52
115	No Longer Valid	5	52
116	No Longer Valid	5	52
117	Cardiac Pacemaker Revision Except Device Replacement	5	52
118	Cardiac Pacemaker Device Replacement	5	52
119	Vein Ligation and Stripping	5	52
120	Other Circulatory System O.R. Procedures	5	52
121	Circulatory Disorders with Acute Myocardial Infarction and Major Complications, Discharged Alive	5	82
122	Circulatory Disorders with Acute Myocardial Infarction without Major Complications, Discharged Alive	5	83
123	Circulatory Disorders with Acute Myocardial Infarction, Expired	5	84
124	Circulatory Disorders Except Acute Myocardial Infarction with Cardiac Catheterization and Complex Diagnosis	5	84
125	Circulatory Disorders Except Acute Myocardial Infarction with Cardiac Catheterization without Complex Diagnosis	5	85
126	Acute and Subacute Endocarditis	5	85
127	Heart Failure and Shock	5	85
128	Deep Vein Thrombophlebitis	5	86
129	Cardiac Arrest, Unexplained	5	86
130	Peripheral Vascular Disorders with CC	5	86
131	Peripheral Vascular Disorders without CC	5	87
132	Atherosclerosis with CC	5	87
133	Atherosclerosis without CC	5	87
134	Hypertension	5	87
135	Cardiac Congenital and Valvular Disorders, Age Greater than 17 with CC	5	88
136	Cardiac Congenital and Valvular Disorders, Age Greater than 17 without CC	5	89
137	Cardiac Congenital and Valvular Disorders, Age 0-17	5	89
138	Cardiac Arrhythmia and Conduction Disorders with CC	5	89
139	Cardiac Arrhythmia and Conduction Disorders without CC	5	89
140	Angina Pectoris	5	89
141	Syncope and Collapse with CC	5	89
142	Syncope and Collapse without CC	5	90
143	Chest Pain	5	90
144	Other Circulatory System Diagnoses with CC	5	90
145	Other Circulatory System Diagnoses without CC	5	91

DRG	Description	MDC	Page
146	Rectal Resection with CC	6	92
147	Rectal Resection without CC	6	92
148	Major Small and Large Bowel Procedures with CC	6	92
149	Major Small and Large Bowel Procedures without CC	6	93
150	Peritoneal Adhesiolysis with CC	6	93
151	Peritoneal Adhesiolysis without CC	6	93
152	Minor Small and Large Bowel Procedures with CC	6	93
153	Minor Small and Large Bowel Procedures without CC	6	93
154	Stomach, Esophageal and Duodenal Procedures, Age Greater than 17 with CC	6	93
155	Stomach, Esophageal and Duodenal Procedures, Age Greater than 17 without CC	6	95
156	Stomach, Esophageal and Duodenal Procedures, Age 0-17	6	95
157	Anal and Stomal Procedures with CC	6	95
158	Anal and Stomal Procedures without CC	6	95
159	Hernia Procedures Except Inguinal and Femoral, Age Greater than 17 with CC	6	95
160	Hernia Procedures Except Inguinal and Femoral, Age Greater than 17 without CC	6	95
161	Inguinal and Femoral Hernia Procedures, Age Greater than 17 with CC	6	96
162	Inguinal and Femoral Hernia Procedures, Age Greater than 17 without CC	6	96
163	Hernia Procedures, Age 0-17	6	96
164	Appendectomy with Complicated Principal Diagnosis with CC	6	96
165	Appendectomy with Complicated Principal Diagnosis without CC	6	96
166	Appendectomy without Complicated Principal Diagnosis with CC	6	96
167	Appendectomy without Complicated Principal Diagnosis without CC	6	97
168	Mouth Procedures with CC	3	32
169	Mouth Procedures without CC	3	32
170	Other Digestive System O.R. Procedures with CC	6	97
171	Other Digestive System O.R. Procedures without CC	6	98
172	Digestive Malignancy with CC	6	99
173	Digestive Malignancy without CC	6	99
174	GI Hemorrhage with CC	6	99
175	GI Hemorrhage without CC	6	100
176	Complicated Peptic Ulcer	6	100
177	Uncomplicated Peptic Ulcer with CC	6	101
178	Uncomplicated Peptic Ulcer without CC	6	101
179	Inflammatory Bowel Disease	6	101
180	GI Obstruction with CC	6	101
181	GI Obstruction without CC	6	101
182	Esophagitis, Gastroenteritis and Miscellaneous Digestive Disorders, Age Greater than 17 with CC	6	101
183	Esophagitis, Gastroenteritis and Miscellaneous Digestive Disorders, Age Greater than 17 without CC	6	103
184	Esophagitis, Gastroenteritis and Miscellaneous Digestive Disorders, Age 0-17	6	103
185	Dental and Oral Diseases Except Extractions and Restorations, Age Greater than 17	3	37
186	Dental and Oral Diseases Except Extractions and Restorations, Age 0-17	3	38
187	Dental Extractions and Restorations	3	38
188	Other Digestive System Diagnoses, Age Greater than 17 with CC	6	103
189	Other Digestive System Diagnoses, Age Greater than 17 without CC	6	105
190	Other Digestive System Diagnoses, Age 0-17	6	105
191	Pancreas, Liver and Shunt Procedures with CC	7	106
192	Pancreas, Liver and Shunt Procedures without CC	7	106
193	Biliary Tract Procedures Except Only Cholecystectomy with or without Common Duct Exploration with CC	7	106

DRG	Description	MDC	Page
194	Biliary Tract Procedures Except Only Cholecystectomy with or without Common Duct Exploration without CC	7	107
195	Cholecystectomy with Common Duct Exploration with CC	7	107
196	Cholecystectomy with Common Duct Exploration without CC	7	107
197	Cholecystectomy Except by Laparoscope without Common Duct Exploration with CC	7	107
198	Cholecystectomy Except by Laparoscope without Common Duct Exploration without CC	7	107
199	Hepatobiliary Diagnostic Procedure for Malignancy	7	107
200	Hepatobiliary Diagnostic Procedure for Nonmalignancy	7	108
201	Other Hepatobiliary or Pancreas O.R. Procedures	7	108
202	Cirrhosis and Alcoholic Hepatitis	7	110
203	Malignancy of Hepatobiliary System or Pancreas	7	110
204	Disorders of Pancreas Except Malignancy	7	110
205	Disorders of Liver Except Malignancy, Cirrhosis and Alcoholic Hepatitis with CC	7	110
206	Disorders of Liver Except Malignancy, Cirrhosis and Alcoholic Hepatitis without CC	7	111
207	Disorders of the Biliary Tract with CC	7	111
208	Disorders of the Biliary Tract without CC	7	111
209	No Longer Valid	8	112
210	Hip and Femur Procedures Except Major Joint Procedures, Age Greater than 17 with CC	8	112
211	Hip and Femur Procedures Except Major Joint Procedures, Age Greater than 17 without CC	8	112
212	Hip and Femur Procedures Except Major Joint Procedures, Age 0-17	8	113
213	Amputation for Musculoskeletal System and Connective Tissue Disorders	8	113
214	No Longer Valid	8	113
215	No Longer Valid	8	113
216	Biopsies of Musculoskeletal System and Connective Tissue	8	113
217	Wound Debridement and Skin Graft Except Hand for Musculoskeletal and Connective Tissue Disorders Greater than 17 with CC	8	114
218	Lower Extremity and Humerus Procedures Except Hip, Foot and Femur, Age Greater than 17 with CC	8	114
219	Lower Extremity and Humerus Procedures Except Hip, Foot and Femur, Age Greater than 17 without CC	8	115
220	Lower Extremity and Humerus Procedures Except Hip, Foot and Femur, Age 0-17	8	115
221	No Longer Valid	8	115
222	No Longer Valid	8	115
223	Major Shoulder/Elbow Procedures or Other Upper Extremity Procedures with CC	8	115
224	Shoulder, Elbow or Forearm Procedures Except Major Joint Procedures without CC	8	116
225	Foot Procedures	8	116
226	Soft Tissue Procedures with CC	8	117
227	Soft Tissue Procedures without CC	8	117
228	Major Thumb or Joint Procedures or Other Hand or Wrist Procedures with CC	8	118
229	Hand or Wrist Procedures Except Major Joint Procedures without CC	8	119
230	Local Excision and Removal of Internal Fixation Devices of Hip and Femur	8	119
231	No Longer Valid	8	119
232	Arthroscopy	8	119
233	Other Musculoskeletal System and Connective Tissue O.R. Procedures with CC	8	119
234	Other Musculoskeletal System and Connective Tissue O.R. Procedures without CC	8	122
235	Fractures of Femur	8	127
236	Fractures of Hip and Pelvis	8	127
237	Sprains, Strains and Dislocations of Hip, Pelvis and Thigh	8	127

DRG	Description	MDC	Page
238	Osteomyelitis	8	127
239	Pathological Fractures and Musculoskeletal and Connective Tissue Malignancy	8	127
240	Connective Tissue Disorders with CC	8	128
241	Connective Tissue Disorders without CC	8	128
242	Septic Arthritis	8	128
243	Medical Back Problems	8	129
244	Bone Diseases and Specific Arthropathies with CC	8	129
245	Bone Diseases and Specific Arthropathies without CC	8	130
246	Nonspecific Arthropathies	8	130
247	Signs and Symptoms of Musculoskeletal System and Connective Tissue	8	130
248	Tendonitis, Myositis and Bursitis	8	131
249	Aftercare, Musculoskeletal System and Connective Tissue	8	131
250	Fractures, Sprains, Strains and Dislocations of Forearm, Hand and Foot, Age Greater than 17 with CC	8	132
251	Fractures, Sprains, Strains and Dislocations of Forearm, Hand and Foot, Age Greater than 17 without CC	8	132
252	Fractures, Sprains, Strains and Dislocations of Forearm, Hand and Foot, Age 0-17	8	132
253	Fractures, Sprains, Strains and Dislocations of Upper Arm and Lower Leg Except Foot, Age Greater than 17 with CC	8	132
254	Fractures, Sprains, Strains and Dislocations of Upper Arm and Lower Leg Except Foot, Age Greater than 17 without CC	8	133
255	Fractures, Sprains, Strains and Dislocations of Upper Arm and Lower Leg Except Foot, Age 0-17	8	133
256	Other Musculoskeletal System and Connective Tissue Diagnoses	8	133
257	Total Mastectomy for Malignancy with CC	9	136
258	Total Mastectomy for Malignancy without CC	9	136
259	Subtotal Mastectomy for Malignancy with CC	9	136
260	Subtotal Mastectomy for Malignancy without CC	9	136
261	Breast Procedure for Nonmalignancy Except Biopsy and Local Excision	9	137
262	Breast Biopsy and Local Excision for Nonmalignancy	9	137
263	Skin Graft and/or Debridement for Skin Ulcer or Cellulitis with CC	9	137
264	Skin Graft and/or Debridement for Skin Ulcer or Cellulitis without CC	9	138
265	Skin Graft and/or Debridement Except for Skin Ulcer or Cellulitis with CC	9	138
266	Skin Graft and/or Debridement Except for Skin Ulcer or Cellulitis without CC	9	138
267	Perianal and Pilonidal Procedures	9	138
268	Skin, Subcutaneous Tissue and Breast Plastic Procedures	9	138
269	Other Skin, Subcutaneous Tissue and Breast Procedures with CC	9	139
270	Other Skin, Subcutaneous Tissue and Breast Procedures without CC	9	141
271	Skin Ulcers	9	142
272	Major Skin Disorders with CC	9	142
273	Major Skin Disorders without CC	9	142
274	Malignant Breast Disorders with CC	9	142
275	Malignant Breast Disorders without CC	9	143
276	Nonmalignant Breast Disorders	9	143
277	Cellulitis, Age Greater than 17 with CC	9	143
278	Cellulitis, Age Greater than 17 without CC	9	144
279	Cellulitis, Age 0-17	9	144
280	Trauma to Skin, Subcutaneous Tissue and Breast, Age Greater than 17 with CC	9	144
281	Trauma to Skin, Subcutaneous Tissue and Breast, Age Greater than 17 without CC	9	146
282	Trauma to Skin, Subcutaneous Tissue and Breast, Age 0-17	9	146
283	Minor Skin Disorders with CC	9	146
284	Minor Skin Disorders without CC	9	148

DRG	Description	MDC	Page
285	Amputation of Lower Limb for Endocrine, Nutritional and Metabolic Disorders	10	149
286	Adrenal and Pituitary Procedures	10	149
287	Skin Grafts and Wound Debridement for Endocrine, Nutritional and Metabolic Disorders	10	149
288	O.R. Procedures for Obesity	10	150
289	Parathyroid Procedures	10	150
290	Thyroid Procedures	10	150
291	Thyroglossal Procedures	10	150
292	Other Endocrine, Nutritional and Metabolic O.R. Procedures with CC	10	150
293	Other Endocrine, Nutritional and Metabolic O.R. Procedures without CC	10	153
294	Diabetes, Age Greater than 35	10	154
295	Diabetes, Age 0-35	10	154
296	Nutritional and Miscellaneous Metabolic Disorders, Age Greater than 17 with CC	10	154
297	Nutritional and Miscellaneous Metabolic Disorders, Age Greater than 17 without CC	10	155
298	Nutritional and Miscellaneous Metabolic Disorders, Age 0-17	10	155
299	Inborn Errors of Metabolism	10	155
300	Endocrine Disorders with CC	10	155
301	Endocrine Disorders without CC	10	156
302	Kidney Transplant	11	157
303	Kidney, Ureter and Major Bladder Procedures for Neoplasm	11	157
304	Kidney, Ureter and Major Bladder Procedures for Non-neoplasms with CC	11	158
305	Kidney, Ureter and Major Bladder Procedures for Non-neoplasms without CC	11	158
306	Prostatectomy with CC	11	158
307	Prostatectomy without CC	11	158
308	Minor Bladder Procedures with CC	11	158
309	Minor Bladder Procedures without CC	11	159
310	Transurethral Procedures with CC	11	159
311	Transurethral Procedures without CC	11	159
312	Urethral Procedures, Age Greater than 17 with CC	11	159
313	Urethral Procedures, Age Greater than 17 without CC	11	159
314	Urethral Procedures, Age 0-17	11	159
315	Other Kidney and Urinary Tract O.R. Procedures	11	160
316	Renal Failure	11	162
317	Admission for Renal Dialysis	11	162
318	Kidney and Urinary Tract Neoplasms with CC	11	162
319	Kidney and Urinary Tract Neoplasms without CC	11	162
320	Kidney and Urinary Tract Infections, Age Greater than 17 with CC	11	163
321	Kidney and Urinary Tract Infections, Age Greater than 17 without CC	11	163
322	Kidney and Urinary Tract Infections, Age 0-17	11	163
323	Urinary Stones with CC and/or ESW Lithotripsy	11	163
324	Urinary Stones without CC	11	164
325	Kidney and Urinary Tract Signs and Symptoms, Age Greater than 17 with CC	11	164
326	Kidney and Urinary Tract Signs and Symptoms, Age Greater than 17 without CC	11	164
327	Kidney and Urinary Tract Signs and Symptoms, Age 0-17	11	164
328	Urethral Stricture, Age Greater than 17 with CC	11	164
329	Urethral Stricture, Age Greater than 17 without CC	11	164
330	Urethral Stricture, Age 0-17	11	164
331	Other Kidney and Urinary Tract Diagnoses, Age Greater than 17 with CC	11	164
332	Other Kidney and Urinary Tract Diagnoses, Age Greater than 17 without CC	11	166
333	Other Kidney and Urinary Tract Diagnoses, Age 0-17	11	166

DRG	Description	MDC	Page
334	Major Male Pelvic Procedures with CC	12	167
335	Major Male Pelvic Procedures without CC	12	167
336	Transurethral Prostatectomy with CC	12	167
337	Transurethral Prostatectomy without CC	12	167
338	Testes Procedures for Malignancy	12	167
339	Testes Procedures for Nonmalignancy, Age Greater than 17	12	168
340	Testes Procedures for Nonmalignancy, Age 0-17	12	168
341	Penis Procedures	12	168
342	Circumcision, Age Greater than 17	12	169
343	Circumcision, Age 0-17	12	169
344	Other Male Reproductive System O.R. Procedures for Malignancy	12	169
345	Other Male Reproductive System O.R. Procedures Except for Malignancy	12	170
346	Malignancy of Male Reproductive System with CC	12	171
347	Malignancy of Male Reproductive System without CC	12	171
348	Benign Prostatic Hypertrophy with CC	12	171
349	Benign Prostatic Hypertrophy without CC	12	171
350	Inflammation of the Male Reproductive System	12	171
351	Sterilization, Male	12	172
352	Other Male Reproductive System Diagnoses	12	172
353	Pelvic Evisceration, Radical Hysterectomy and Radical Vulvectomy	13	174
354	Uterine and Adnexa Procedures for Nonovarian/Adnexal Malignancy with CC	13	174
355	Uterine and Adnexa Procedures for Nonovarian/Adnexal Malignancy without CC	13	175
356	Female Reproductive System Reconstructive Procedures	13	175
357	Uterine and Adnexa Procedures for Ovarian or Adnexal Malignancy	13	175
358	Uterine and Adnexa Procedures for Nonmalignancy with CC	13	176
359	Uterine and Adnexa Procedures for Nonmalignancy without CC	13	178
360	Vagina, Cervix and Vulva Procedures	13	178
361	Laparoscopy and Incisional Tubal Interruption	13	179
362	Endoscopic Tubal Interruption	13	179
363	D and C, Conization and Radio-Implant for Malignancy	13	179
364	D and C, Conization Except for Malignancy	13	180
365	Other Female Reproductive System O.R. Procedures	13	180
366	Malignancy of Female Reproductive System with CC	13	182
367	Malignancy of Female Reproductive System without CC	13	182
368	Infections of Female Reproductive System	13	182
369	Menstrual and Other Female Reproductive System Disorders	13	183
370	Cesarean Section with CC	14	185
371	Cesarean Section without CC	14	193
372	Vaginal Delivery with Complicating Diagnoses	14	195
373	Vaginal Delivery without Complicating Diagnoses	14	197
374	Vaginal Delivery with Sterilization and/or D and C	14	193
375	Vaginal Delivery with O.R. Procedure Except Sterilization and/or D and C	14	193
376	Postpartum and Postabortion Diagnoses without O.R. Procedure	14	203
377	Postpartum and Postabortion Diagnoses with O.R. Procedure	14	194
378	Ectopic Pregnancy	14	205
379	Threatened Abortion	14	205
380	Abortion without D and C	14	206
381	Abortion with D and C, Aspiration Curettage or Hysterotomy	14	194
382	False Labor	14	206
383	Other Antepartum Diagnoses with Medical Complications	14	206
384	Other Antepartum Diagnoses without Medical Complications	14	211

DRG	Description	MDC	Page
385	Neonates, Died or Transferred to Another Acute Care Facility	15	215
386	Extreme Immaturity or Respiratory Distress Syndrome of Neonate	15	215
387	Prematurity with Major Problems	15	215
388	Prematurity without Major Problems	15	222
389	Full Term Neonate with Major Problems	15	222
390	Neonate with Other Significant Problems	15	229
391	Normal Newborn	15	229
392	Splenectomy, Age Greater than 17	16	233
393	Splenectomy, Age 0-17	16	233
394	Other O.R. Procedures of the Blood and Blood-Forming Organs	16	233
395	Red Blood Cell Disorders, Age Greater than 17	16	234
396	Red Blood Cell Disorders, Age 0-17	16	234
397	Coagulation Disorders	16	234
398	Reticuloendothelial and Immunity Disorders with CC	16	234
399	Reticuloendothelial and Immunity Disorders without CC	16	235
400	No Longer Valid	17	236
401	Lymphoma and Nonacute Leukemia with Other O.R. Procedure with CC	17	236
402	Lymphoma and Nonacute Leukemia with Other O.R. Procedure without CC	17	236
403	Lymphoma and Nonacute Leukemia with CC	17	242
404	Lymphoma and Nonacute Leukemia without CC	17	242
405	Acute Leukemia without Major O.R. Procedure, Age 0-17	17	242
406	Myeloproliferative Disorders or Poorly Differentiated Neoplasms with Major O.R. Procedures with CC	17	236
407	Myeloproliferative Disorders or Poorly Differentiated Neoplasms with Major O.R. Procedures without CC	17	237
408	Myeloproliferative Disorders or Poorly Differentiated Neoplasms with Other O.R. Procedures	17	237
409	Radiotherapy	17	242
410	Chemotherapy without Acute Leukemia as Secondary Diagnosis	17	242
411	History of Malignancy without Endoscopy	17	242
412	History of Malignancy with Endoscopy	17	242
413	Other Myeloproliferative Disorders or Poorly Differentiated Neoplasm Diagnoses with CC	17	244
414	Other Myeloproliferative Disorders or Poorly Differentiated Neoplasm Diagnoses without CC	17	244
415	O.R. Procedure for Infectious and Parasitic Diseases	18	245
416	Septicemia, Age Greater than 17	18	246
417	Septicemia, Age 0-17	18	246
418	Postoperative and Posttraumatic Infections	18	246
419	Fever of Unknown Origin, Age Greater than 17 with CC	18	246
420	Fever of Unknown Origin, Age Greater than 17 without CC	18	246
421	Viral Illness, Age Greater than 17	18	246
422	Viral Illness and Fever of Unknown Origin, Age 0-17	18	247
423	Other Infectious and Parasitic Diseases Diagnoses	18	247
424	O.R. Procedure with Principal Diagnosis of Mental Illness	19	250
425	Acute Adjustment Reactions and Psychosocial Dysfunction	19	251
426	Depressive Neuroses	19	251
427	Neuroses Except Depressive	19	251
428	Disorders of Personality and Impulse Control	19	252
429	Organic Disturbances and Mental Retardation	19	252
430	Psychoses	19	252
431	Childhood Mental Disorders	19	253
432	Other Mental Disorder Diagnoses	19	253

Numeric Listing of DRGs

DRG	Description	MDC	Page
433	Alcohol/Drug Abuse or Dependence, Left Against Medical Advice	20	254
434	No Longer Valid	20	254
435	No Longer Valid	20	254
436	No Longer Valid	20	254
437	No Longer Valid	20	254
438	No Longer Valid	20	254
439	Skin Grafts for Injuries	21	256
440	Wound Debridements for Injuries	21	256
441	Hand Procedures for Injuries	21	256
442	Other O.R. Procedures for Injuries with CC	21	257
443	Other O.R. Procedures for Injuries without CC	21	271
444	Traumatic Injury, Age Greater than 17 with CC	21	272
445	Traumatic Injury, Age Greater than 17 without CC	21	273
446	Traumatic Injury, Age 0-17	21	273
447	Allergic Reactions, Age Greater than 17	21	273
448	Allergic Reactions, Age 0-17	21	273
449	Poisoning and Toxic Effects of Drugs, Age Greater than 17 with CC	21	273
450	Poisoning and Toxic Effects of Drugs, Age Greater than 17 without CC	21	274
451	Poisoning and Toxic Effects of Drugs, Age 0-17	21	274
452	Complications of Treatment with CC	21	274
453	Complications of Treatment without CC	21	274
454	Other Injury, Poisoning and Toxic Effect Diagnoses with CC	21	274
455	Other Injury, Poisoning and Toxic Effect Diagnoses without CC	21	275
456	No Longer Valid	22	280
457	No Longer Valid	22	280
458	No Longer Valid	22	276
459	No Longer Valid	22	276
460	No Longer Valid	22	280
461	O.R. Procedure with Diagnosis of Other Contact with Health Services	23	285
462	Rehabilitation	23	286
463	Signs and Symptoms with CC	23	286
464	Signs and Symptoms without CC	23	286
465	Aftercare with History of Malignancy as Secondary Diagnosis	23	286
466	Aftercare without History of Malignancy as Secondary Diagnosis	23	287
467	Other Factors Influencing Health Status	23	287
468	Extensive O.R. Procedure Unrelated to Principal Diagnosis	All	311
469	Principal Diagnosis Invalid as Discharge Diagnosis	14	211
469	Principal Diagnosis Invalid as Discharge Diagnosis	15	232
469	Principal Diagnosis Invalid as Discharge Diagnosis	All	311
470	Ungroupable	All	311
471	Bilateral or Multiple Major Joint Procedures of Lower Extremity	8	122
472	No Longer Valid	22	276
473	Acute Leukemia without Major O.R. Procedure, Age Greater than 17	17	244
474	No Longer Valid	4	41
475	Respiratory System Diagnosis with Ventilator Support	4	48
476	Prostatic O.R. Procedure Unrelated to Principal Diagnosis	All	311
477	Nonextensive O.R. Procedure Unrelated to Principal Diagnosis	All	311
478	No Longer Valid	5	54
479	Other Vascular Procedures without CC	5	54
480	Liver Transplant and/or Intestinal Transplant	Pre	317
481	Bone Marrow Transplant	Pre	318
482	Tracheostomy for Face, Mouth and Neck Diagnoses	Pre	318

DRG	Description	MDC	Page
483	No Longer Valid	Pre	321
484	Craniotomy for Multiple Significant Trauma	24	290
485	Limb Reattachment, Hip and Femur Procedures for Multiple Significant Trauma	24	291
486	Other O.R. Procedures for Multiple Significant Trauma	24	292
487	Other Multiple Significant Trauma	24	293
488	HIV with Extensive O.R. Procedure	25	307
489	HIV with Major Related Condition	25	308
490	HIV with or without Other Related Condition	25	309
491	Major Joint and Limb Reattachment Procedures of Upper Extremity	8	122
492	Chemotherapy with Acute Leukemia as Secondary Diagnosis or with Use of High-Dose Chemotherapy Agent	17	244
493	Laparoscopic Cholecystectomy without Common Duct Exploration with CC	7	109
494	Laparoscopic Cholecystectomy without Common Duct Exploration without CC	7	109
495	Lung Transplant	Pre	321
496	Combined Anterior/Posterior Spinal Fusion	8	122
497	Spinal Fusion Except Cervical with CC	8	123
498	Spinal Fusion Except Cervical without CC	8	123
499	Back and Neck Procedures Except Spinal Fusion with CC	8	123
500	Back and Neck Procedures Except Spinal Fusion without CC	8	123
501	Knee Procedures with Principal Diagnosis of Infection with CC	8	123
502	Knee Procedures with Principal Diagnosis of Infection without CC	8	124
503	Knee Procedures without Principal Diagnosis of Infection	8	124
504	Extensive Burns or Full Thickness Burns with Mechanical Ventilation 96+ Hours with Skin Graft	22	276
505	Extensive Burns or Full Thickness Burns with Mechanical Ventilation 96+ Hours without Skin Graft	22	280
506	Full Thickness Burn with Skin Graft or Inhalation Injury with CC or Significant Trauma	22	278
507	Full Thickness Burn with Skin Graft or Inhalation Injury without CC or Significant Trauma	22	279
508	Full Thickness Burn without Skin Graft or Inhalation Injury with CC or Significant Trauma	28	282
509	Full Thickness Burn without Skin Graft or Inhalation Injury without CC or Significant Trauma	22	282
510	Nonextensive Burns with CC or Significant Trauma	22	282
511	Nonextensive Burns without CC or Significant Trauma	22	284
512	Simultaneous Pancreas/Kidney Transplant	Pre	321
513	Pancreas Transplant	Pre	322
514	No Longer Valid	5	55
515	Cardiac Defibrillator Implant without Cardiac Catheterization	5	55
516	No Longer Valid	5	56
517	No Longer Valid	5	56
518	Percutaneous Cardiovascular Procedures without Acute Myocardial Infarction without Coronary Artery Stent Implant	5	56
519	Cervical Spinal Fusion with CC	8	124
520	Cervical Spinal Fusion without CC	8	124
521	Alcohol/Drug Abuse or Dependence with CC	20	254
522	Alcohol/Drug Abuse or Dependence with Rehabilitation Therapy without CC	20	255
523	Alcohol/Drug Abuse or Dependence without Rehabilitation Therapy without CC	20	255
524	Transient Ischemia	1	17
525	Other Heart Assist System Implant	5	56
526	No Longer Valid	5	56
527	No Longer Valid	5	56
528	Intracranial Vascular Procedure with Principal Diagnosis of Hemorrhage	1	5

DRG	Description	MDC	Page
529	Ventricular Shunt Procedures with CC	1	5
530	Ventricular Shunt Procedures without CC	1	5
531	Spinal Procedures with CC	1	5
532	Spinal Procedures without CC	1	6
533	Extracranial Vascular Procedures with CC	1	6
534	Extracranial Vascular Procedures without CC	1	6
535	Cardiac Defibrillator Implant with Cardiac Catheterization with Acute Myocardial Infarction, Heart Failure, or Shock	5	56
536	Cardiac Defibrillator Implant with Cardiac Catheterization without Acute Myocardial Infarction, Heart Failure, or Shock	5	58
537	Local Excision and Removal of Internal Fixation Devices Except Hip and Femur with CC	8	125
538	Local Excision and Removal of Internal Fixation Devices Except Hip and Femur without CC	8	125
539	Lymphoma and Leukemia with Major O.R. Procedure with CC	17	237
540	Lymphoma and Leukemia with Major O.R. Procedure without CC	17	241
▲ 541	ECMO or Tracheostomy with Mechanical Ventilation 96+ Hours or Principal Diagnosis Except Face, Mouth, and Neck with Major O.R.	Pre	323
▲ 542	Tracheostomy with Mechanical Ventilation 96+ Hours or Principal Diagnosis Except Face, Mouth, and Neck without Major O.R.	Pre	323
543	Craniotomy with Implantation of Chemotherapeutic Agent or Acute Complex Central Nervous System Principal Diagnosis	1	6
● 544	Major Joint Replacement or Reattachment of Lower Extremity	8	126
● 545	Revision of Hip or Knee Replacement	8	126
● 546	Spinal Fusions Except Cervical With Curvature of the Spine or Malignancy	8	126
● 547	Coronary Bypass with Cardiac Catheterization with MCV Diagnosis	5	58
● 548	Coronary Bypass with Cardiac Catheterization without MCV Diagnosis	5	60
● 549	Coronary Bypass without Cardiac Catheterization with MCV Diagnosis	5	61
● 550	Coronary Bypass without Cardiac Catheterization without MCV Diagnosis	5	63
● 551	Permanent Cardiac Pacemaker Implant with MCV Diagnosis or AICD Lead or Generator	5	63
● 552	Other Permanent Cardiac Pacemaker Implant without MCV Diagnosis	5	69
● 553	Other Vascular Procedures with CC with MCV Diagnosis	5	72
● 554	Other Vascular Procedures with CC without MCV Diagnosis	5	75
● 555	Percutaneous Cardiovascular Procedure with MCV Diagnosis	5	76
● 556	Percutaneous Cardiovascular Procedure with Non Drug-Eluting Stent without MCV Diagnosis	5	78
● 557	Percutaneous Cardiovascular Procedure with Drug-Eluting Stent with MCV Diagnosis	5	78
● 558	Percutaneous Cardiovascular Procedure with Drug-Eluting Stent without MCV Diagnosis	5	81
● 559	Acute Ischemic Stroke with Use of Thrombolytic Agent	1	17

DRG Listing by Major Diagnostic Category

MDC 1 DISEASES AND DISORDERS OF THE NERVOUS SYSTEM

Surgical

DRG	DRG Description	Page
001	Craniotomy, Age Greater than 17 with CC	1
002	Craniotomy, Age Greater than 17 without CC	1
003	Craniotomy, Age 0-17	2
004	No Longer Valid	2
005	No Longer Valid	2
006	Carpal Tunnel Release	2
007	Peripheral and Cranial Nerve and Other Nervous System Procedures with CC	3
008	Peripheral and Cranial Nerve and Other Nervous System Procedures without CC	5
528	Intracranial Vascular Procedure with Principal Diagnosis of Hemorrhage	5
529	Ventricular Shunt Procedures with CC	5
530	Ventricular Shunt Procedures without CC	5
531	Spinal Procedures with CC	5
532	Spinal Procedures without CC	6
533	Extracranial Vascular Procedures with CC	6
534	Extracranial Vascular Procedures without CC	6
543	Craniotomy with Implantation of Chemotherapeutic Agent or Acute Complex Central Nervous System Principal Diagnosis	6

Medical

DRG	DRG Description	Page
009	Spinal Disorders and Injuries	9
010	Nervous System Neoplasms with CC	9
011	Nervous System Neoplasms without CC	9
012	Degenerative Nervous System Disorders	9
013	Multiple Sclerosis and Cerebellar Ataxia	10
014	Intracranial Hemorrhage or Cerebral Infarction	10
015	Nonspecific Cerebrovascular and Precerebral Occlusion without Infarction	10
016	Nonspecific Cerebrovascular Disorders with CC	11
017	Nonspecific Cerebrovascular Disorders without CC	11
018	Cranial and Peripheral Nerve Disorders with CC	11
019	Cranial and Peripheral Nerve Disorders without CC	12
020	Nervous System Infection Except Viral Meningitis	12
021	Viral Meningitis	13
022	Hypertensive Encephalopathy	13
023	Nontraumatic Stupor and Coma	13
024	Seizure and Headache, Age Greater than 17 with CC	13
025	Seizure and Headache, Age Greater than 17 without CC	14
026	Seizure and Headache, Age 0-17	14
027	Traumatic Stupor and Coma, Coma Greater than One Hour	14
028	Traumatic Stupor and Coma, Coma Less than One Hour, Age Greater than 17 with CC	14
029	Traumatic Stupor and Coma, Coma Less than One Hour, Age Greater than 17 without CC	14
030	Traumatic Stupor and Coma, Coma Less than One Hour, Age 0-17	14
031	Concussion, Age Greater than 17 with CC	14
032	Concussion, Age Greater than 17 without CC	14
033	Concussion, Age 0-17	15
034	Other Disorders of Nervous System with CC	15
035	Other Disorders of Nervous System without CC	17
524	Transient Ischemia	17
● 559	Acute Ischemic Stroke with Use of Thrombolytic Agent	17

MDC 2 DISEASES AND DISORDERS OF THE EYE

Surgical

DRG	DRG Description	Page
036	Retinal Procedures	18
037	Orbital Procedures	18
038	Primary Iris Procedures	18
039	Lens Procedures with or without Vitrectomy	19
040	Extraocular Procedures Except Orbit, Age Greater than 17	19
041	Extraocular Procedures Except Orbit, Age 0-17	19
042	Intraocular Procedures Except Retina, Iris and Lens	19

MDC 2 — continued

Medical

DRG	DRG Description	Page
043	Hyphema	21
044	Acute Major Eye Infections	21
045	Neurological Eye Disorders	21
046	Other Disorders of the Eye, Age Greater than 17 with CC	22
047	Other Disorders of the Eye, Age Greater than 17 without CC	26
048	Other Disorders of the Eye, Age 0-17	26

MDC 3 DISEASES AND DISORDERS OF THE EAR, NOSE, MOUTH AND THROAT

Surgical

DRG	DRG Description	Page
049	Major Head and Neck Procedures	27
050	Sialoadenectomy	27
051	Salivary Gland Procedures Except Sialoadenectomy	27
052	Cleft Lip and Palate Repair	27
053	Sinus and Mastoid Procedures, Age Greater than 17	27
054	Sinus and Mastoid Procedures, Age 0-17	28
055	Miscellaneous Ear, Nose, Mouth and Throat Procedures	28
056	Rhinoplasty	29
057	Tonsillectomy and Adenoidectomy Procedures Except Tonsillectomy and/or Adenoidectomy Only, Age Greater than 17	29
058	Tonsillectomy and Adenoidectomy Procedures Except Tonsillectomy and/or Adenoidectomy Only, Age 0-17	29
059	Tonsillectomy and/or Adenoidectomy Only, Age Greater than 17	29
060	Tonsillectomy and/or Adenoidectomy Only, Age 0-17	29
061	Myringotomy with Tube Insertion, Age Greater than 17	29
062	Myringotomy with Tube Insertion, Age 0-17	29
063	Other Ear, Nose, Mouth and Throat O.R. Procedures	30
168	Mouth Procedures with CC	32
169	Mouth Procedures without CC	32

Medical

DRG	DRG Description	Page
064	Ear, Nose, Mouth and Throat Malignancy	33
065	Dysequilibrium	33
066	Epistaxis	33
067	Epiglottitis	33
068	Otitis Media and URI, Age Greater than 17 with CC	34
069	Otitis Media and URI, Age Greater than 17 without CC	34
070	Otitis Media and URI, Age 0-17	34
071	Laryngotracheitis	35
072	Nasal Trauma and Deformity	35
073	Other Ear, Nose, Mouth and Throat Diagnoses, Age Greater than 17	35
074	Other Ear, Nose, Mouth and Throat Diagnoses, Age 0-17	37
185	Dental and Oral Diseases Except Extractions and Restorations, Age Greater than 17	37
186	Dental and Oral Diseases Except Extractions and Restorations, Age 0-17	38
187	Dental Extractions and Restorations	38

MDC 4 DISEASES AND DISORDERS OF THE RESPIRATORY SYSTEM

Surgical

DRG	DRG Description	Page
075	Major Chest Procedures	39
076	Other Respiratory System O.R. Procedures with CC	40
077	Other Respiratory System O.R. Procedures without CC	41
474	No Longer Valid	41

Medical

DRG	DRG Description	Page
078	Pulmonary Embolism	42
079	Respiratory Infections and Inflammations, Age Greater than 17 with CC	42
080	Respiratory Infections and Inflammations, Age Greater than 17 without CC	43
081	Respiratory Infections and Inflammations, Age 0-17	43
082	Respiratory Neoplasms	43
083	Major Chest Trauma with CC	43
084	Major Chest Trauma without CC	44
085	Pleural Effusion with CC	44
086	Pleural Effusion without CC	44
087	Pulmonary Edema and Respiratory Failure	44
088	Chronic Obstructive Pulmonary Disease	44
089	Simple Pneumonia and Pleurisy, Age Greater than 17	45

MDC 4 — continued

Medical — continued

090 Simple Pneumonia and Pleurisy, Age Greater than 17 without CC ... 45
091 Simple Pneumonia and Pleurisy, Age 0-17 ... 45
092 Interstitial Lung Disease with CC ... 45
093 Interstitial Lung Disease without CC ... 45
094 Pneumothorax with CC ... 46
095 Pneumothorax without CC ... 46
096 Bronchitis and Asthma, Age Greater than 17 with CC ... 46
097 Bronchitis and Asthma, Age Greater than 17 without CC ... 46
098 Bronchitis and Asthma, Age 0-17 ... 46
099 Respiratory Signs and Symptoms with CC ... 46
100 Respiratory Signs and Symptoms without CC ... 46
101 Other Respiratory System Diagnoses with CC ... 47
102 Other Respiratory System Diagnoses without CC ... 47
475 Respiratory System Diagnosis with Ventilator Support ... 48

MDC 5 DISEASES AND DISORDERS OF THE CIRCULATORY SYSTEM

Surgical

DRG **DRG Description** **Page**
104 Cardiac Valve Procedures and Other Major Cardiothoracic Procedures with Cardiac Catheterization ... 49
105 Cardiac Valve Procedures and Other Major Cardiothoracic Procedures without Cardiac Catheterization ... 49
106 Coronary Bypass with PTCA ... 49
107 No Longer Valid ... 49
108 Other Cardiothoracic Procedures ... 49
109 No Longer Valid ... 50
110 Major Cardiovascular Procedures with CC ... 50
111 Major Cardiovascular Procedures without CC ... 51
112 No Longer Valid ... 51
113 Amputation for Circulatory System Disorders Except Upper Limb and Toe ... 51
114 Upper Limb and Toe Amputation for Circulatory System Disorders ... 52
115 No Longer Valid ... 52
116 No Longer Valid ... 52
117 Cardiac Pacemaker Revision Except Device Replacement ... 52
118 Cardiac Pacemaker Device Replacement ... 52
119 Vein Ligation and Stripping ... 52
120 Other Circulatory System O.R. Procedures ... 52
478 No Longer Valid ... 54
479 Other Vascular Procedures without CC ... 54
514 No Longer Valid ... 55
515 Cardiac Defibrillator Implant without Cardiac Catheterization ... 55
516 No Longer Valid ... 56
517 No Longer Valid ... 56
518 Percutaneous Cardiovascular Procedures without Acute Myocardial Infarction without Coronary Artery Stent Implant ... 56
525 Other Heart Assist System Implant ... 56
526 No Longer Valid ... 56
527 No Longer Valid ... 56
535 Cardiac Defibrillator Implant with Cardiac Catheterization with Acute Myocardial Infarction, Heart Failure, or Shock ... 56
536 Cardiac Defibrillator Implant with Cardiac Catheterization without Acute Myocardial Infarction, Heart Failure, or Shock ... 58
● 547 Coronary Bypass with Cardiac Catheterization with MCV Diagnosis ... 60
● 548 Coronary Bypass with Cardiac Catheterization without MCV Diagnosis ... 60
● 549 Coronary Bypass without Cardiac Catheterization with MCV Diagnosis ... 61
● 550 Coronary Bypass without Cardiac Catheterization without MCV Diagnosis ... 63
● 551 Permanent Cardiac Pacemaker Implant with MCV Diagnosis or AICD Lead or Generator .. 63
● 552 Other Permanent Cardiac Pacemaker Implant without MCV Diagnosis ... 69
● 553 Other Vascular Procedures with CC with MCV Diagnosis ... 72
● 554 Other Vascular Procedures with CC without MCV Diagnosis ... 75
● 555 Percutaneous Cardiovascular Procedure with MCV Diagnosis ... 76
● 556 Percutaneous Cardiovascular Procedure with Non Drug-Eluting Stent without Major Cardiovascular Diagnosis ... 78
● 557 Percutaneous Cardiovascular Procedure with Drug-Eluting Stent with Major Cardiovascular Diagnosis ... 78
● 558 Percutaneous Cardiovascular Procedure with Drug-Eluting Stent without Major Cardiovascular Diagnosis ... 81

MDC 5 — continued

Medical

DRG	DRG Description	Page
121	Circulatory Disorders with Acute Myocardial Infarction and Major Complications, Discharged Alive	82
122	Circulatory Disorders with Acute Myocardial Infarction without Major Complications, Discharged Alive	83
123	Circulatory Disorders with Acute Myocardial Infarction, Expired	84
124	Circulatory Disorders Except Acute Myocardial Infarction with Cardiac Catheterization and Complex Diagnosis	84
125	Circulatory Disorders Except Acute Myocardial Infarction with Cardiac Catheterization without Complex Diagnosis	85
126	Acute and Subacute Endocarditis	85
127	Heart Failure and Shock	85
128	Deep Vein Thrombophlebitis	86
129	Cardiac Arrest, Unexplained	86
130	Peripheral Vascular Disorders with CC	86
131	Peripheral Vascular Disorders without CC	87
132	Atherosclerosis with CC	87
133	Atherosclerosis without CC	87
134	Hypertension	87
135	Cardiac Congenital and Valvular Disorders, Age Greater than 17 with CC	88
136	Cardiac Congenital and Valvular Disorders, Age Greater than 17 without CC	89
137	Cardiac Congenital and Valvular Disorders, Age 0-17	89
138	Cardiac Arrhythmia and Conduction Disorders with CC	89
139	Cardiac Arrhythmia and Conduction Disorders without CC	89
140	Angina Pectoris	89
141	Syncope and Collapse with CC	89
142	Syncope and Collapse without CC	90
143	Chest Pain	90
144	Other Circulatory System Diagnoses with CC	90
145	Other Circulatory System Diagnoses without CC	91

MDC 6 DISEASES AND DISORDERS OF THE DIGESTIVE SYSTEM

Surgical

DRG	DRG Description	Page
146	Rectal Resection with CC	92
147	Rectal Resection without CC	92
148	Major Small and Large Bowel Procedures with CC	92
149	Major Small and Large Bowel Procedures without CC	93
150	Peritoneal Adhesiolysis with CC	93
151	Peritoneal Adhesiolysis without CC	93
152	Minor Small and Large Bowel Procedures with CC	93
153	Minor Small and Large Bowel Procedures without CC	93
154	Stomach, Esophageal and Duodenal Procedures, Age Greater than 17 with CC	93
155	Stomach, Esophageal and Duodenal Procedures, Age Greater than 17 without CC	95
156	Stomach, Esophageal and Duodenal Procedures, Age 0-17	95
157	Anal and Stomal Procedures with CC	95
158	Anal and Stomal Procedures without CC	95
159	Hernia Procedures Except Inguinal and Femoral, Age Greater than 17 with CC	95
160	Hernia Procedures Except Inguinal and Femoral, Age Greater than 17 without CC	95
161	Inguinal and Femoral Hernia Procedures, Age Greater than 17 with CC	96
162	Inguinal and Femoral Hernia Procedures, Age Greater than 17 without CC	96
163	Hernia Procedures, Age 0-17	96
164	Appendectomy with Complicated Principal Diagnosis with CC	96
165	Appendectomy with Complicated Principal Diagnosis without CC	96
166	Appendectomy without Complicated Principal Diagnosis with CC	96
167	Appendectomy without Complicated Principal Diagnosis without CC	97
170	Other Digestive System O.R. Procedures with CC	97
171	Other Digestive System O.R. Procedures without CC	98

Medical

DRG	DRG Description	Page
172	Digestive Malignancy with CC	99
173	Digestive Malignancy without CC	99
174	GI Hemorrhage with CC	99
175	GI Hemorrhage without CC	100
176	Complicated Peptic Ulcer	100
177	Uncomplicated Peptic Ulcer with CC	101
178	Uncomplicated Peptic Ulcer without CC	101
179	Inflammatory Bowel Disease	101
180	GI Obstruction with CC	101

MDC 6 — continued

Medical – continued

DRG	DRG Description	Page
181	GI Obstruction without CC	101
182	Esophagitis, Gastroenteritis and Miscellaneous Digestive Disorders, Age Greater than 17 with CC	101
183	Esophagitis, Gastroenteritis and Miscellaneous Digestive Disorders, Age Greater than 17 without CC	103
184	Esophagitis, Gastroenteritis and Miscellaneous Digestive Disorders, Age 0-17	103
188	Other Digestive System Diagnoses, Age Greater than 17 with CC	103
189	Other Digestive System Diagnoses, Age Greater than 17 without CC	105
190	Other Digestive System Diagnoses, Age 0-17	105

MDC 7 DISEASES AND DISORDERS OF THE HEPATOBILIARY SYSTEM AND PANCREAS

Surgical

DRG	DRG Description	Page
191	Pancreas, Liver and Shunt Procedures with CC	106
192	Pancreas, Liver and Shunt Procedures without CC	106
193	Biliary Tract Procedures Except Only Cholecystectomy with or without Common Duct Exploration with CC	106
194	Biliary Tract Procedures Except Only Cholecystectomy with or without Common Duct Exploration without CC	107
195	Cholecystectomy with Common Duct Exploration with CC	107
196	Cholecystectomy with Common Duct Exploration without CC	107
197	Cholecystectomy Except by Laparoscope without Common Duct Exploration with CC	107
198	Cholecystectomy Except by Laparoscope without Common Duct Exploration without CC	107
199	Hepatobiliary Diagnostic Procedure for Malignancy	107
200	Hepatobiliary Diagnostic Procedure for Nonmalignancy	108
201	Other Hepatobiliary or Pancreas O.R. Procedures	108
493	Laparoscopic Cholecystectomy without Common Duct Exploration with CC	109
494	Laparoscopic Cholecystectomy without Common Duct Exploration without CC	109

Medical

DRG	DRG Description	Page
202	Cirrhosis and Alcoholic Hepatitis	110
203	Malignancy of Hepatobiliary System or Pancreas	110
204	Disorders of Pancreas Except Malignancy	110
205	Disorders of Liver Except Malignancy, Cirrhosis and Alcoholic Hepatitis with CC	110
206	Disorders of Liver Except Malignancy, Cirrhosis and Alcoholic Hepatitis without CC	111
207	Disorders of the Biliary Tract with CC	111
208	Disorders of the Biliary Tract without CC	111

MDC 8 DISEASES AND DISORDERS OF THE MUSCULOSKELETAL SYSTEM AND CONNECTIVE TISSUE

Surgical

DRG	DRG Description	Page
209	No Longer Valid	112
210	Hip and Femur Procedures Except Major Joint Procedures, Age Greater than 17 with CC	112
211	Hip and Femur Procedures Except Major Joint Procedures, Age Greater than 17 without CC	112
212	Hip and Femur Procedures Except Major Joint Procedures, Age 0-17	113
213	Amputation for Musculoskeletal System and Connective Tissue Disorders	113
214	No Longer Valid	113
215	No Longer Valid	113
216	Biopsies of Musculoskeletal System and Connective Tissue	113
217	Wound Debridement and Skin Graft Except Hand for Musculoskeletal and Connective Tissue Disorders	114
218	Lower Extremity and Humerus Procedures Except Hip, Foot and Femur, Age Greater than 17 with CC	114
219	Lower Extremity and Humerus Procedures Except Hip, Foot and Femur, Age Greater than 17 without CC	115
220	Lower Extremity and Humerus Procedures Except Hip, Foot and Femur, Age 0-17	115
221	No Longer Valid	115
222	No Longer Valid	115
223	Major Shoulder/Elbow Procedures or Other Upper Extremity Procedures with CC	115
224	Shoulder, Elbow or Forearm Procedures Except Major Joint Procedures without CC	116
225	Foot Procedures	116
226	Soft Tissue Procedures with CC	117

MDC 8 — continued

Surgical — continued

DRG	DRG Description	Page
227	Soft Tissue Procedures without CC	117
228	Major Thumb or Joint Procedures or Other Hand or Wrist Procedures with CC	118
229	Hand or Wrist Procedures Except Major Joint Procedures without CC	119
230	Local Excision and Removal of Internal Fixation Devices of Hip and Femur	119
231	No Longer Valid	119
232	Arthroscopy	119
233	Other Musculoskeletal System and Connective Tissue O.R. Procedures with CC	119
234	Other Musculoskeletal System and Connective Tissue O.R. Procedures without CC	122
471	Bilateral or Multiple Major Joint Procedures of Lower Extremity	122
491	Major Joint and Limb Reattachment Procedures of Upper Extremity	122
496	Combined Anterior/Posterior Spinal Fusion	122
497	Spinal Fusion Except Cervical with CC	123
498	Spinal Fusion Except Cervical without CC	123
499	Back and Neck Procedures Except Spinal Fusion with CC	123
500	Back and Neck Procedures Except Spinal Fusion without CC	123
501	Knee Procedures with Principal Diagnosis of Infection with CC	123
502		124
503	Knee Procedures without Principal Diagnosis of Infection	124
519	Cervical Spinal Fusion with CC	124
520	Cervical Spinal Fusion without CC	124
537	Local Excision and Removal of Internal Fixation Devices Except Hip and Femur with CC	125
538	Local Excision and Removal of Internal Fixation Devices Except Hip and Femur without CC	125
● 544	Major Joint Replacement or Reattachment of Lower Extremity	126
● 545	Revision of Hip or Knee Replacement	126
● 546	Spinal Fusions Except Cervical With Curvature of the Spine or Malignancy	126

Medical

DRG	DRG Description	Page
235	Fractures of Femur	127
236	Fractures of Hip and Pelvis	127
237	Sprains, Strains and Dislocations of Hip, Pelvis and Thigh	127
238	Osteomyelitis	127
239	Pathological Fractures and Musculoskeletal and Connective Tissue Malignancy	127
240	Connective Tissue Disorders with CC	128
241	Connective Tissue Disorders without CC	128
242	Septic Arthritis	128
243	Medical Back Problems	129
244	Bone Diseases and Specific Arthropathies with CC	129
245	Bone Diseases and Specific Arthropathies without CC	130
246	Nonspecific Arthropathies	130
247	Signs and Symptoms of Musculoskeletal System and Connective Tissue	130
248	Tendonitis, Myositis and Bursitis	131
249	Aftercare, Musculoskeletal System and Connective Tissue	131
250	Fractures, Sprains, Strains and Dislocations of Forearm, Hand and Foot, Age Greater than 17 with CC	132
251	Fractures, Sprains, Strains and Dislocations of Forearm, Hand and Foot, Age Greater than 17 without CC	132
252	Fractures, Sprains, Strains and Dislocations of Forearm, Hand and Foot, Age 0-17	132
253	Fractures, Sprains, Strains and Dislocations of Upper Arm and Lower Leg Except Foot, Age Greater than 17 with CC	132
254	Fractures, Sprains, Strains and Dislocations of Upper Arm and Lower Leg Except Foot, Age Greater than 17 without CC	133
255	Fractures, Sprains, Strains and Dislocations of Upper Arm and Lower Leg Except Foot, Age 0-17	133
256	Other Musculoskeletal System and Connective Tissue Diagnoses	133

MDC 9 DISEASES AND DISORDERS OF THE SKIN, SUBCUTANEOUS TISSUE AND BREAST

Surgical

DRG	DRG Description	Page
257	Total Mastectomy for Malignancy with CC	136
258	Total Mastectomy for Malignancy without CC	136
259	Subtotal Mastectomy for Malignancy with CC	136
260	Subtotal Mastectomy for Malignancy without CC	136
261	Breast Procedure for Nonmalignancy Except Biopsy and Local Excision	137
262	Breast Biopsy and Local Excision for Nonmalignancy	137
263	Skin Graft and/or Debridement for Skin Ulcer or Cellulitis with CC	137

MDC 9 — continued

Surgical — continued

DRG	DRG Description	Page
264	Skin Graft and/or Debridement for Skin Ulcer or Cellulitis without CC	138
265	Skin Graft and/or Debridement Except for Skin Ulcer or Cellulitis with CC	138
266	Skin Graft and/or Debridement Except for Skin Ulcer or Cellulitis without CC	138
267	Perianal and Pilonidal Procedures	138
268	Skin, Subcutaneous Tissue and Breast Plastic Procedures	138
269	Other Skin, Subcutaneous Tissue and Breast Procedures with CC	139
270	Other Skin, Subcutaneous Tissue and Breast Procedures without CC	141

Medical

DRG	DRG Description	Page
271	Skin Ulcers	142
272	Major Skin Disorders with CC	142
273	Major Skin Disorders without CC	142
274	Malignant Breast Disorders with CC	142
275	Malignant Breast Disorders without CC	143
276	Nonmalignant Breast Disorders	143
277	Cellulitis, Age Greater than 17 with CC	143
278	Cellulitis, Age Greater than 17 without CC	144
279	Cellulitis, Age 0-17	144
280	Trauma to Skin, Subcutaneous Tissue and Breast, Age Greater than 17 with CC	144
281	Trauma to Skin, Subcutaneous Tissue and Breast, Age Greater than 17 without CC	146
282	Trauma to Skin, Subcutaneous Tissue and Breast, Age 0-17	146
283	Minor Skin Disorders with CC	146
284	Minor Skin Disorders without CC	148

MDC 10 ENDOCRINE, NUTRITIONAL AND METABOLIC DISEASES AND DISORDERS

Surgical

DRG	DRG Description	Page
285	Amputation of Lower Limb for Endocrine, Nutritional and Metabolic Disorders	149
286	Adrenal and Pituitary Procedures	149
287	Skin Grafts and Wound Debridement for Endocrine, Nutritional and Metabolic Disorders	149
288	O.R. Procedures for Obesity	150
289	Parathyroid Procedures	150
290	Thyroid Procedures	150
291	Thyroglossal Procedures	150
292	Other Endocrine, Nutritional and Metabolic O.R. Procedures with CC	150
293	Other Endocrine, Nutritional and Metabolic O.R. Procedures without CC	153

Medical

DRG	DRG Description	Page
294	Diabetes, Age Greater than 35	154
295	Diabetes, Age 0-35	154
296	Nutritional and Miscellaneous Metabolic Disorders, Age Greater than 17 with CC	154
297	Nutritional and Miscellaneous Metabolic Disorders, Age Greater than 17 without CC	155
298	Nutritional and Miscellaneous Metabolic Disorders, Age 0-17	155
299	Inborn Errors of Metabolism	155
300	Endocrine Disorders with CC	155
301	Endocrine Disorders without CC	156

MDC 11 DISEASES AND DISORDERS OF THE KIDNEY AND URINARY TRACT

Surgical

DRG	DRG Description	Page
302	Kidney Transplant	157
303	Kidney, Ureter and Major Bladder Procedures for Neoplasm	157
304	Kidney, Ureter and Major Bladder Procedures for Non-neoplasms with CC	158
305	Kidney, Ureter and Major Bladder Procedures for Non-neoplasms without CC	158
306	Prostatectomy with CC	158
307	Prostatectomy without CC	158
308	Minor Bladder Procedures with CC	158
309	Minor Bladder Procedures without CC	159
310	Transurethral Procedures with CC	159
311	Transurethral Procedures without CC	159
312	Urethral Procedures, Age Greater than 17 with CC	159
313	Urethral Procedures, Age Greater than 17 without CC	159
314	Urethral Procedures, Age 0-17	159
315	Other Kidney and Urinary Tract O.R. Procedures	160

MDC 11 — continued

Medical

DRG	DRG Description	Page
316	Renal Failure	162
317	Admission for Renal Dialysis	162
318	Kidney and Urinary Tract Neoplasms with CC	162
319	Kidney and Urinary Tract Neoplasms without CC	162
320	Kidney and Urinary Tract Infections, Age Greater than 17 with CC	163
321	Kidney and Urinary Tract Infections, Age Greater than 17 without CC	163
322	Kidney and Urinary Tract Infections, Age 0-17	163
323	Urinary Stones with CC and/or ESW Lithotripsy	163
324	Urinary Stones without CC	164
325	Kidney and Urinary Tract Signs and Symptoms, Age Greater than 17 with CC	164
326	Kidney and Urinary Tract Signs and Symptoms, Age Greater than 17 without CC	164
327	Kidney and Urinary Tract Signs and Symptoms, Age 0-17	164
328	Urethral Stricture, Age Greater than 17 with CC	164
329	Urethral Stricture, Age Greater than 17 without CC	164
330	Urethral Stricture, Age 0-17	164
331	Other Kidney and Urinary Tract Diagnoses, Age Greater than 17 with CC	164
332	Other Kidney and Urinary Tract Diagnoses, Age Greater than 17 without CC	166
333	Other Kidney and Urinary Tract Diagnoses, Age 0-17	166

MDC 12 DISEASES AND DISORDERS OF THE MALE REPRODUCTIVE SYSTEM

Surgical

DRG	DRG Description	Page
334	Major Male Pelvic Procedures with CC	167
335	Major Male Pelvic Procedures without CC	167
336	Transurethral Prostatectomy with CC	167
337	Transurethral Prostatectomy without CC	167
338	Testes Procedures for Malignancy	167
339	Testes Procedures for Nonmalignancy, Age Greater than 17	168
340	Testes Procedures for Nonmalignancy, Age 0-17	168
341	Penis Procedures	168
342	Circumcision, Age Greater than 17	169
343	Circumcision, Age 0-17	169
344	Other Male Reproductive System O.R. Procedures for Malignancy	169
345	Other Male Reproductive System O.R. Procedures Except for Malignancy	170

Medical

DRG	DRG Description	Page
346	Malignancy of Male Reproductive System with CC	171
347	Malignancy of Male Reproductive System without CC	171
348	Benign Prostatic Hypertrophy with CC	171
349	Benign Prostatic Hypertrophy without CC	171
350	Inflammation of the Male Reproductive System	171
351	Sterilization, Male	172
352	Other Male Reproductive System Diagnoses	172

MDC 13 DISEASES AND DISORDERS OF THE FEMALE REPRODUCTIVE SYSTEM

Surgical

DRG	DRG Description	Page
353	Pelvic Evisceration, Radical Hysterectomy and Radical Vulvectomy	174
354	Uterine and Adnexa Procedures for Nonovarian/Adnexal Malignancy with CC	174
355	Uterine and Adnexa Procedures for Nonovarian/Adnexal Malignancy without CC	175
356	Female Reproductive System Reconstructive Procedures	175
357	Uterine and Adnexa Procedures for Ovarian or Adnexal Malignancy	175
358	Uterine and Adnexa Procedures for Nonmalignancy with CC	176
359	Uterine and Adnexa Procedures for Nonmalignancy without CC	178
360	Vagina, Cervix and Vulva Procedures	178
361	Laparoscopy and Incisional Tubal Interruption	179
362	Endoscopic Tubal Interruption	179
363	D and C, Conization and Radio-Implant for Malignancy	179
364	D and C, Conization Except for Malignancy	180
365	Other Female Reproductive System O.R. Procedures	180

Medical

DRG	DRG Description	Page
366	Malignancy of Female Reproductive System with CC	182
367	Malignancy of Female Reproductive System without CC	182
368	Infections of Female Reproductive System	182
369	Menstrual and Other Female Reproductive System Disorders	183

MDC 14 PREGNANCY, CHILDBIRTH AND THE PUERPERIUM

Surgical

DRG	DRG Description	Page
370	Cesarean Section with CC	185
371	Cesarean Section without CC	193
374	Vaginal Delivery with Sterilization and/or D and C	193
375	Vaginal Delivery with O.R. Procedure Except Sterilization and/or D and C	193
377	Postpartum and Postabortion Diagnoses with O.R. Procedure	194
381	Abortion with D and C, Aspiration Curettage or Hysterotomy	194

Medical

DRG	DRG Description	Page
372	Vaginal Delivery with Complicating Diagnoses	195
373	Vaginal Delivery without Complicating Diagnoses	197
376	Postpartum and Postabortion Diagnoses without O.R. Procedure	203
378	Ectopic Pregnancy	205
379	Threatened Abortion	205
380	Abortion without D and C	206
382	False Labor	206
383	Other Antepartum Diagnoses with Medical Complications	206
384	Other Antepartum Diagnoses without Medical Complications	211
469	Principal Diagnosis Invalid as Discharge Diagnosis	211

MDC 15 NEWBORNS AND OTHER NEONATES WITH CONDITIONS ORIGINATING IN THE PERINATAL PERIOD

Medical

DRG	DRG Description	Page
385	Neonates, Died or Transferred to Another Acute Care Facility	215
386	Extreme Immaturity or Respiratory Distress Syndrome of Neonate	215
387	Prematurity with Major Problems	215
388	Prematurity without Major Problems	222
389	Full Term Neonate with Major Problems	222
390	Neonate with Other Significant Problems	229
391	Normal Newborn	229
469	Principal Diagnosis Invalid as Discharge Diagnosis	232

MDC 16 DISEASES AND DISORDERS OF THE BLOOD AND BLOOD-FORMING ORGANS AND IMMUNOLOGICAL DISORDERS

Surgical

DRG	DRG Description	Page
392	Splenectomy, Age Greater than 17	233
393	Splenectomy, Age 0-17	233
394	Other O.R. Procedures of the Blood and Blood-Forming Organs	233

Medical

DRG	DRG Description	Page
395	Red Blood Cell Disorders, Age Greater than 17	234
396	Red Blood Cell Disorders, Age 0-17	234
397	Coagulation Disorders	234
398	Reticuloendothelial and Immunity Disorders with CC	234
399	Reticuloendothelial and Immunity Disorders without CC	235

MDC 17 MYELOPROLIFERATIVE DISEASES AND DISORDERS AND POORLY DIFFERENTIATED NEOPLASMS

Surgical

DRG	DRG Description	Page
400	No Longer Valid	236
401	Lymphoma and Nonacute Leukemia with Other O.R. Procedure with CC	236
402	Lymphoma and Nonacute Leukemia with Other O.R. Procedure without CC	236
406	Myeloproliferative Disorders or Poorly Differentiated Neoplasms with Major O.R. Procedures with CC	236
407	Myeloproliferative Disorders or Poorly Differentiated Neoplasms with Major O.R. Procedures without CC	237
408	Myeloproliferative Disorders or Poorly Differentiated Neoplasms with Other O.R. Procedures	237
539	Lymphoma and Leukemia with Major O.R. Procedure with CC	237
540	Lymphoma and Leukemia with Major O.R. Procedure without CC	241

Medical

DRG	DRG Description	Page
403	Lymphoma and Nonacute Leukemia with CC	242
404	Lymphoma and Nonacute Leukemia without CC	242

 ● *New DRG* ▲ *Revised DRG Title*

MDC 17 — continued

Medical — continued

DRG	DRG Description	Page
405	Acute Leukemia without Major O.R. Procedure, Age 0-17	242
409	Radiotherapy	242
410	Chemotherapy without Acute Leukemia as Secondary Diagnosis	242
411	History of Malignancy without Endoscopy	242
412	History of Malignancy with Endoscopy	242
413	Other Myeloproliferative Disorders or Poorly Differentiated Neoplasm Diagnoses with CC	244
414	Other Myeloproliferative Disorders or Poorly Differentiated Neoplasm Diagnoses without CC	244
473	Acute Leukemia without Major O.R. Procedure, Age Greater than 17	244
492	Chemotherapy with Acute Leukemia as Secondary Diagnosis or with Use of High-Dose Chemotherapy Agent	244

MDC 18 INFECTIOUS AND PARASITIC DISEASES

Surgical

DRG	DRG Description	Page
415	O.R. Procedure for Infectious and Parasitic Diseases	245

Medical

DRG	DRG Description	Page
416	Septicemia, Age Greater than 17	246
417	Septicemia, Age 0-17	246
418	Postoperative and Posttraumatic Infections	246
419	Fever of Unknown Origin, Age Greater than 17 with CC	246
420	Fever of Unknown Origin, Age Greater than 17 without CC	246
421	Viral Illness, Age Greater than 17	246
422	Viral Illness and Fever of Unknown Origin, Age 0-17	247
423	Other Infectious and Parasitic Diseases Diagnoses	247

MDC 19 MENTAL DISEASES AND DISORDERS

Surgical

DRG	DRG Description	Page
424	O.R. Procedure with Principal Diagnosis of Mental Illness	250

Medical

DRG	DRG Description	Page
425	Acute Adjustment Reactions and Psychosocial Dysfunction	251
426	Depressive Neuroses	251
427	Neuroses Except Depressive	251
428	Disorders of Personality and Impulse Control	252
429	Organic Disturbances and Mental Retardation	252
430	Psychoses	252
431	Childhood Mental Disorders	253
432	Other Mental Disorder Diagnoses	253

MDC 20 ALCOHOL/DRUG USE AND ALCOHOL/DRUG-INDUCED ORGANIC MENTAL DISORDERS

Medical

DRG	DRG Description	Page
433	Alcohol/Drug Abuse or Dependence, Left Against Medical Advice	254
434	No Longer Valid	254
435	No Longer Valid	254
436	No Longer Valid	254
437	No Longer Valid	254
438	No Longer Valid	254
521	Alcohol/Drug Abuse or Dependence with CC	254
522	Alcohol/Drug Abuse or Dependence with Rehabilitation Therapy without CC	255
523	Alcohol/Drug Abuse or Dependence without Rehabilitation Therapy without CC	255

MDC 21 INJURY, POISONING AND TOXIC EFFECTS OF DRUGS

Surgical

DRG	DRG Description	Page
439	Skin Grafts for Injuries	256
440	Wound Debridements for Injuries	256
441	Hand Procedures for Injuries	256
442	Other O.R. Procedures for Injuries with CC	257
443	Other O.R. Procedures for Injuries without CC	271

MDC 21 — continued

Medical

DRG	DRG Description	Page
444	Traumatic Injury, Age Greater than 17 with CC	272
445	Traumatic Injury, Age Greater than 17 without CC	273
446	Traumatic Injury, Age 0-17	273
447	Allergic Reactions, Age Greater than 17	273
448	Allergic Reactions, Age 0-17	273
449	Poisoning and Toxic Effects of Drugs, Age Greater than 17 with CC	273
450	Poisoning and Toxic Effects of Drugs, Age Greater than 17 without CC	274
451	Poisoning and Toxic Effects of Drugs, Age 0-17	274
452	Complications of Treatment with CC	274
453	Complications of Treatment without CC	274
454	Other Injury, Poisoning and Toxic Effect Diagnoses with CC	274
455	Other Injury, Poisoning and Toxic Effect Diagnoses without CC	275

MDC 22 BURNS

Surgical

DRG	DRG Description	Page
458	No Longer Valid	276
459	No Longer Valid	276
472	No Longer Valid	276
504	Extensive Burns or Full Thickness Burns with Mechanical Ventilation 96+ Hours with Skin Graft	276
506	Full Thickness Burn with Skin Graft or Inhalation Injury with CC or Significant Trauma	278
507	Full Thickness Burn with Skin Graft or Inhalation Injury without CC or Significant Trauma	279

Medical

DRG	DRG Description	Page
456	No Longer Valid	280
457	No Longer Valid	280
460	No Longer Valid	280
505	Extensive Burns or Full Thickness Burns with Mechanical Ventilation 96+ Hours without Skin Graft	280
508	Full Thickness Burn without Skin Graft or Inhalation Injury with CC or Significant Trauma	282
509	Full Thickness Burn without Skin Graft or Inhalation Injury without CC or Significant Trauma	282
510	Nonextensive Burns with CC or Significant Trauma	282
511	Nonextensive Burns without CC or Significant Trauma	284

MDC 23 FACTORS INFLUENCING HEALTH STATUS AND OTHER CONTACTS WITH HEALTH SERVICES

Surgical

DRG	DRG Description	Page
461	O.R. Procedure with Diagnosis of Other Contact with Health Services	285

Medical

DRG	DRG Description	Page
462	Rehabilitation	286
463	Signs and Symptoms with CC	286
464	Signs and Symptoms without CC	286
465	Aftercare with History of Malignancy as Secondary Diagnosis	286
466	Aftercare without History of Malignancy as Secondary Diagnosis	287
467	Other Factors Influencing Health Status	287

MDC 24 MULTIPLE SIGNIFICANT TRAUMA

Surgical

DRG	DRG Description	Page
484	Craniotomy for Multiple Significant Trauma	290
485	Limb Reattachment, Hip and Femur Procedures for Multiple Significant Trauma	291
486	Other O.R. Procedures for Multiple Significant Trauma	292

Medical

DRG	DRG Description	Page
487	Other Multiple Significant Trauma	293

MDC 25 HUMAN IMMUNODEFICIENCY VIRUS INFECTIONS

Surgical

DRG	DRG Description	Page
488	HIV with Extensive O.R. Procedure	307

Medical

DRG	DRG Description	Page
489	HIV with Major Related Condition	308
490	HIV with or without Other Related Condition	309

DRGs Associated with All MDCs and Pre-MDC

DRG	DRG Description	Page
469	Principal Diagnosis Invalid as Discharge Diagnosis	311
470	Ungroupable	311

Surgical

DRG	DRG Description	Page
468	Extensive O.R. Procedure Unrelated to Principal Diagnosis	311
476	Prostatic O.R. Procedure Unrelated to Principal Diagnosis	311
477	Nonextensive O.R. Procedure Unrelated to Principal Diagnosis	311

Pre MDC

Surgical

DRG	DRG Description	Page
103	Heart Transplant or Implant of Heart Assist System	317
480	Liver Transplant and/or Intestinal Transplant	317
481	Bone Marrow Transplant	318
482	Tracheostomy for Face, Mouth and Neck Diagnoses	318
483	No Longer Valid	321
495	Lung Transplant	321
512	Simultaneous Pancreas/Kidney Transplant	321
513	Pancreas Transplant	322
▲ 541	ECMO or Tracheostomy with Mechanical Ventilation 96+ Hours or Principal Diagnosis Except Face, Mouth, and Neck with Major O.R.	323
▲ 542	Tracheostomy with Mechanical Ventilation 96+ Hours or Principal Diagnosis Except Face, Mouth, and Neck without Major O.R.	323

Introduction

The diagnosis-related group (DRG) system organizes ICD-9-CM diagnosis and procedure codes into a complex, comprehensive system based on a few simple principles.

Understanding how the DRG system works enables providers to recover the appropriate payment for inpatient services rendered in an acute care hospital facility, which is consistent with the intent of the federal government when the DRG system was devised. The *DRG Expert* helps providers understand DRGs, thus ensuring appropriate payment.

Note: For information concerning the DRG classification system for long-term acute care hospitals (LTCHs), refer to the section titled "Long Term Acute Care Hospital Prospective Payment System (LTCH PPS)" on page Introduction — 4.

SOURCE OF INFORMATION

Information in the book is taken from the official data published by the Centers for Medicare and Medicaid Services (CMS) in the *Federal Register*, Vol. 70, no. 155, dated August 12, 2005, pages 47278 - 47482 ("Medicare Program; Changes to the Hospital Inpatient Prospective Payment Systems and Fiscal Year 2006 Rates; Final Rule"). The information presented is consistent with the fiscal 2006 Grouper version 23.0.

BASIC CHARACTERISTICS OF DRG CLASSIFICATION

A DRG is one of 559 currently valid groups that classify patients into clinically cohesive groups that demonstrate similar consumption of hospital resources and length-of-stay patterns. In 1983, Congress mandated a national inpatient prospective payment system (IPPS) for all Medicare inpatients. The following types of hospitals are excluded from the IPPS:

- Psychiatric hospitals and units
- Rehabilitation hospitals and units
- Children's hospitals
- Long-term care hospitals
- Cancer hospitals

This IPPS uses DRGs to determine hospital reimbursement. CMS administers the IPPS and issues all rules and changes with regard to DRGs.

In addition to calculating reimbursement, DRGs have two major functions. The first is to help evaluate the quality of care. Not only are critical pathways designed around DRGs, but benchmarking and outcomes analysis can be launched using the DRG clinical framework, and quality reviews can be performed to assess coding practices and physician documentation. Ongoing education of physicians, coders, nurses, and utilization review personnel can be guided by the results of DRG analysis.

Second, DRGs assist in evaluating utilization of services. Each DRG represents the average resources needed to treat patients grouped to that DRG relative to the national average of resources used to treat all Medicare patients. The DRG assigned to each hospital inpatient stay also relates to the hospital case mix (i.e., the types of patients the hospital treats). The hospital case-mix index (CMI) is determined by dividing the sum of all DRG relative weights for every DRG used by Medicare patients (counting each patient populating the DRG separately) by the total number of Medicare inpatient cases for the hospital.

Medicare computes the case-mix adjustment for each fiscal year for all hospitals based upon the case-mix data received. This CMI is then used to adjust the hospital base rate, which is a factor in computing the total hospital payment under IPPS.

The formula for computing the hospital payment for each DRG is as follows:

DRG Relative Weight x Hospital Base Rate = Hospital Payment

The hospital case mix complexity includes the following patient attributes:

- Severity of illness — the level of loss of function or mortality associated with disease
- Prognosis — defined as probable outcome of illness
- Treatment difficulty — patient management problems
- Need for intervention — severity of illness that would result due to lack of immediate or continuing care
- Resource intensity — volume and types of services required for patient management

The DRG system was developed to relate case mix to resource utilization. Reimbursement is adjusted to reflect the resource utilization and does not take into consideration severity of illness, prognosis, treatment difficulty, or need for intervention.

Case mix and complexity can be analyzed and monitored in relation to cost and utilization of services. In addition, high-volume conditions and services can be identified and monitored, and DRG trend analysis can aid in forecasting future staff and facility requirements. One important operating parameter is the CMI, which measures the cost of a hospital's Medicare patient mix in relation to the cost of all Medicare patients. A low case mix may indicate unnecessary revenue loss.

DRG ASSIGNMENT PROCESS

DRGs are assigned using the principal diagnosis; up to eight additional diagnoses; the principal procedure and up to five additional procedure codes; and age, sex, and discharge status. One DRG is assigned to each inpatient stay. Diagnoses and procedures are designated by ICD-9-CM codes. The following describes the typical decision process used to assign a DRG to a case.

A case is assigned to one of 25 major diagnostic categories (MDCs), which are mutually exclusive groups based on principal diagnosis. DRG assignment is based upon the following considerations:

- Principal and secondary diagnosis and procedure codes
- Sex
- Age
- Discharge status
- Presence or absence of complications and comorbidities (CCs)
- Birth weight for neonates

Each MDC is organized into one of two sections — surgical or medical. The surgical section classifies all surgical conditions based upon operating room procedures. The medical section classifies all diagnostic conditions based upon diagnosis codes. The majority of MDCs are organized by major body system and/or are associated with a particular medical specialty.

There are two groups of DRGs that are not assigned to MDCs. First, there is the group that may be associated with all MDCs. This group includes DRGs created specifically to report admissions into a facility that have been assigned invalid principal diagnoses (DRG 469), have O.R. procedures unrelated to a principal diagnosis (DRGs 468, 476, and 477), or are ungroupable principal diagnoses (DRG 470). Although the scope is too broad for clinical analysis, the DRGs encompass clinically coherent cases.

Another group not assigned to MDCs are called pre-MDC DRGs, which consist of cases that are grouped by surgical procedure rather than principal diagnosis. The pre-MDC DRG group includes bone marrow and organ transplant cases as well as tracheostomy cases.

Further sorting of medical classifications is performed by principal diagnosis type and/or surgical classifications by type of surgery. Finally, the case is analyzed for age and/or the presence of CCs as indicated by ICD-9-CM diagnosis codes, and a DRG is assigned.

Each year, effective October 1 through September 30, DRG assignments are adjusted based on relative weight (RW), arithmetic mean length of stay (AMLOS), and geometric mean length of stay (GMLOS). Annually, new ICD-9-CM codes are also incorporated into the existing DRGs or new DRGs are added for the next fiscal year.

The information contained in this manual reflects the DRG classification system for fiscal 2006, Grouper version 23.0.

Grouper Version	Effective Time Period
CMS 23.0	10/01/2005 – 09/30/2006
CMS 22.0	10/01/2004 – 09/30/2005
CMS 21.0	10/01/2003 – 09/30/2004
CMS 20.0	10/01/2002 – 09/30/2003
CMS 19.0	10/01/2001 – 09/30/2002
CMS 18.0	10/01/2000 – 09/30/2001
CMS 17.0	10/01/1999 – 09/30/2000
CMS 16.0	10/01/1998 – 09/30/1999
CMS 15.0	10/01/1997 – 09/30/1998
CMS 14.0	10/01/1996 – 09/30/1997
CMS 13.0	10/01/1995 – 09/30/1996
CMS 12.0	10/01/1994 – 09/30/1995
CMS 11.0	10/01/1993 – 09/30/1994
CMS 10.0	10/01/1992 – 09/30/1993
CMS 9.0	10/01/1991 – 09/30/1992
CMS 8.0	10/01/1990 – 09/30/1991
CMS 7.0	10/01/1989 – 09/30/1990
CMS 6.0	10/01/1988 – 09/30/1989
CMS 5.0	10/01/1987 – 09/30/1988
CMS 4.0	10/01/1986 – 09/30/1987
CMS 3.0	05/01/1986 – 09/30/1986
CMS 2.0	10/01/1983 – 04/30/1986

COMPLICATIONS AND COMORBIDITIES

CMS developed a standard list of diagnoses that are recognized as CCs for DRGs. When a CC is present as a secondary diagnosis, it may affect DRG assignment.

Examples of the most commonly missed CCs are:

- Alcoholism
- Anemia due to blood loss, acute/chronic
- Angina pectoris
- Atrial fibrillation/flutter
- Atelectasis
- Cachexia
- Cardiogenic shock
- Cardiomyopathy
- Cellulitis
- Congestive heart failure (CHF)
- Chronic obstructive pulmonary disease (COPD)
- Decubitus ulcer
- Dehydration
- Diabetes mellitus
- Furuncles
- Hematuria
- Hematemesis
- Hypertensive heart disease with CHF
- Hyponatremia
- Malnutrition
- Melena
- Pleural effusion
- Pneumothorax
- Renal failure, acute/chronic
- Respiratory failure
- Urinary retention
- Urinary tract infection

For certain principal diagnoses, conditions generally considered CCs are not seen as such because a closely related condition deemed a CC would result in duplicative or inconsistent coding. The following parameters determine those secondary diagnoses that are excluded from the CC list:

- Chronic and acute manifestations of the same condition should not be considered CCs for one another.
- Specific and nonspecific diagnosis codes for the same condition should not be considered CCs for one another.
- Conditions that may not coexist such as partial/total, unilateral/bilateral, obstructed/unobstructed, and benign/malignant should not be considered CCs for one another.
- The same condition in anatomically proximal sites should not be considered CCs for one another.
- Closely related conditions should not be considered CCs for one another.

POSTACUTE CARE TRANSFER POLICY

Transfers are defined in two different ways in, Section 412.4(b) defines transfers from one acute care hospital to another and Section 412.4(c) defines transfers to certain postacute care providers.

The purpose of the transfer payment policy is to avoid providing an incentive for a hospital to transfer patients to another hospital early in the patients' stay to minimize costs and still receive the full DRG payment. The transfer policy adjusts the payments to approximate the reduced costs of transfer cases. Effective for discharges occurring on or after October 1, 2005, CMS adopted new criteria to expand the application of the postacute care transfer policy. The new criteria to determine which DRGs should be included is as follows:

- The DRG has at least 2,050 postacute care transfer cases;
- At least 5.5 percent of the cases in the DRG are discharged to postacute care prior to the geometric mean length of stay for the DRG;
- The DRG has a geometric mean length of stay of at least 3.0 days; and,
- If the DRG is one of a paired set of DRGs based on the presence or absence of a comorbidity or complication, both paired DRGs are included if either one meets the first three criteria.

There are approximately 182 DRGs that meet the new postacute care transfer DRG criteria. These DRGs are identified throughout *DRG Expert* with the symbol T.

For those DRGs that are subject to the special payment methodology, CMS compared the average charges for all cases with a length of stay of one day to the average charges of all cases in a particular DRG. To qualify for the special payment methodology the average charges of the one day discharge cases must be at least 50 percent of the average charges for all cases in the DRG. This methodology is only applied to those DRGs that have a mean length of stay that is greater than four days because cases with a shorter average length of stay will receive the full DRG payment on the second day of the stay anyway. It should also be noted, if a DRG is a corresponding part of a paired set of DRGs, with and without CC, meets the criteria for being included in the postacute care transfer policy and qualifies for the special payment methodology both DRGs are included in the special payment methodology.

The following DRGs are included under the special payment methodology. These DRGs are identified throughout *DRG Expert* with the symbol SP.

007	Peripheral and Cranial Nerve and Other Nervous System Procedures with CC
008	Peripheral and Cranial Nerve and Other Nervous System Procedures without CC
210	Hip and Femur Procedures Except Major Joint Procedures, Age Greater than 17 with CC
211	Hip and Femur Procedures Except Major Joint Procedures, Age Greater than 17 without CC
233	Other Musculoskeletal System and Connective Tissue O.R. Procedures with CC
234	Other Musculoskeletal System and Connective Tissue O.R. Procedures without CC
471	Bilateral or Multiple Major Joint Procedures of Lower Extremity
497	Spinal Fusion Except Cervical with CC
498	Spinal Fusion Except Cervical without CC
544	Major Joint Replacement or Reattachment of Lower Extremity
545	Revision of Hip or Knee Replacement
549	Coronary Bypass without Cardiac Catheterization with Major Cardiovascular Diagnosis
550	Coronary Bypass without Cardiac Catheterization without Major Cardiovascular Diagnosis

LONG TERM ACUTE CARE HOSPITAL PROSPECTIVE PAYMENT SYSTEM (LTCH PPS)

Use of postacute care services has grown rapidly in recent years since the implementation of the acute care hospital inpatient prospective payment system. The average length of stay in acute care hospitals has decreased, and patients are increasingly being discharged to postacute care settings such as long term care hospitals (LTCHs), skilled nursing facilities (SNFs), home health agencies (HHAs), and inpatient rehabilitation facilities (IRFs) to complete their course of treatment. The increased use of postacute care providers, including hospitals excluded from the acute care hospital inpatient PPS, has resulted in the rapid growth in Medicare payments to these hospitals in recent years.

Under the provisions of the Balanced Budget Refinement Act of 1999 and the Medicare, Medicaid, and SCHIP Benefits Improvement and Protection Act of 2000, over a five-year period LTCHs are being transitioned from a blend of reasonable cost-based reimbursement to prospective payment rates beginning October 1, 2002. LTCHs are defined as facilities that have an average length of stay greater than 25 days. As of November 2001, there were 270 designated LTCHs.

The LTC-DRG system is based on the current DRG system under the acute care hospital inpatient PPS (CMS-DRGs). The LTC-DRGs model uses the existing hospital inpatient DRG classification system with weights calibrated to account for the difference in resource use by patients exhibiting the case complexity and multiple medical problems characteristic of LTCHs. The existing CMS-DRGs were regrouped into 184 classification groups (179 DRG-based and 5 charge-based payment groups) based on patient data called case-mix groups (CMGs).

After screening through the Medicare Code Editor, each claim will be classified into the appropriate LTC-DRG by the Medicare LTCH Grouper. The LTCH Grouper is specialized computer software based on the Grouper used by the acute care hospital inpatient PPS, which was developed as a means of classifying each case into a DRG on the basis of diagnosis and procedure codes and other demographic information (age, sex, and discharge status). Following the LTC-DRG assignment, the Medicare fiscal intermediary determines the prospective payment by using the Medicare Pricer program, which accounts for hospital-specific adjustments.

CMS modified the DRGs for the LTCH PPS by developing LTCH-specific relative weights to account for the fact that LTCHs generally treat patients with multiple medical problems. Therefore, CMS developed a crosswalk of IPPS-DRG to LTC-DRG data, including relative weight (RW), GMLOS, and 5/6 GMLOS for short stay outlier case payment adjustment.

The LTC-DRG is linked to the recalibration and reclassification of the CMS-DRGs under the IPPS to be effective with discharges occurring on or after October 1 through September 30 each year.

Appendix C of this manual is the LTC-DRG crosswalk based upon the Grouper version 23.0.

KEYS TO A FINANCIALLY SUCCESSFUL DRG PROGRAM

CMS assigns each DRG a relative weight based upon charge data for all Medicare inpatient hospital discharges. Each hospital has a customized base rate that adjusts payment commensurate with the hospital's cost of providing services. The type of hospital and the wage index for the geographic area determines the hospital base rate. DRG relative weights and hospital base rates are adjusted yearly (effective October 1 through September 30) to reflect changes in health care resource consumption as well as economic factors. Payment is determined by multiplying the DRG relative weight by the hospital base rate. The DRG with the highest relative weight is the highest-paying DRG. Regardless of actual costs incurred, the hospital receives only the calculated payment.

The DRG payment system is based on averages. Payment is determined by the resource needs of the average Medicare patient for a given set of diseases or disorders. These resources include the length of stay and the number and intensity of services provided. Therefore, the more efficiently a provider delivers care, the greater the operating margin will be.

The keys to a financially successful DRG program are:

- Decreased length of stay
- Decreased resource utilization (tests and procedures)
- Increased intensity of case-management services resulting in optimal length of stay for the patient and facility
- Increased preadmission testing
- Improved medical record documentation

THE PHYSICIAN'S ROLE

Proper DRG assignment requires a complete and thorough accounting of the following:

- Principal diagnosis
- Procedures
- Complications
- Comorbidities (all relevant pre-existing conditions)
- Signs and symptoms when diagnoses are not established
- Discharge status

Because DRG assignment is based on documentation in the medical record, the record should:

- Be comprehensive and complete
- Include all diagnoses, procedures, complications, and comorbidities, as well as abnormal test results documented by the physician. It should also include any suspected conditions and what was done to investigate or evaluate them.
- Be timely

All dictation, signatures, etc., should be completed in the medical record as patient care is provided and must be:

- Legible
- Well documented

The information should be documented properly. With complete information in the medical record, coders can effectively analyze, code, and report the required information. This ensures that proper payment is received. For example, if the physician documents that a patient with a skull fracture was in a coma for less than one hour, DRG 28 is assigned. If the physician documents that the coma lasted for more than one hour, DRG 27 is assigned, with a resulting payment difference.

DRG EXPERT ORGANIZATION

Numeric DRG Listing

This section is a numeric listing of all DRGs with MDC, medical/surgical partitioning, and page reference.

DRG Listing by Major Diagnostic Category

The "MDC List" section is a numerical listing of the MDCs with the category title. Each MDC then is separated into a surgical DRG list and medical DRG list for the MDC. Also, the page reference for each DRG is noted.

Changes to the DRG System

As a special feature, a summary of all the important changes in the DRG system for the current year is presented in this section.

Glossary of DRG Terms

This section of the introduction contains definitions of terms associated with the DRG classification system.

Definitions of the DRG

The book contains a list of the 25 MDCs divided into surgical and medical sections (when appropriate). Listed in each section are the applicable DRGs and their associated diagnosis and/or procedure codes. Beside each DRG title is its GMLOS, AMLOS, and

RW. Under each DRG is a list of diagnosis and/or procedure codes that determine assignment of the case to that DRG.

Indexes

Your *DRG Expert* allows you to locate a DRG by searching alphabetically (code narrative) or numerically (ICD-9-CM codes) by either disease or procedure.

The indexes are arranged in the following order at the back of the book:

- Alphabetic Index to Diseases
- Numeric Index to Diseases
- Alphabetic Index to Procedures
- Numeric Index to Procedures

Appendix A, Invalid DRG Conversion Table

Periodically, the annual adjustments to the DRG system require reclassification and that results in invalidation of some DRGs. The table in this section lists the reclassification of the diagnosis and procedure codes to the new DRGs once the previously assigned DRG has become invalid.

Appendix B, DRG Surgical Hierarchy Table

Since patients may be assigned to only one DRG per admission, a tool was necessary to enable the evaluation of the relative resource consumption for cases involving multiple surgeries that individually group to different surgical DRGs within an MDC. The surgical hierarchy table in this section reflects the relative resource requirements of the various surgical procedures of each MDC. Arranging the surgical DRGs in this manner helps you assign the DRG that accurately reflects the resource utilization for multiple surgery cases and, thereby, assign the case to the highest surgical DRG.

Appendix C, LTC-DRG Crosswalk

CMS modified the DRGs for the LTCH PPS by developing LTCH-specific relative weights to account for the fact that LTCHs generally treat patients with multiple medical problems. Therefore, CMS developed a crosswalk of IPPS-DRG to LTC-DRG data, including RW, GMLOS, and 5/6 GMLOS. Appendix C of this manual is the LTC-DRG based upon the Grouper version 23.0.

Appendix D, National Average Payment Table

This section lists all DRGs in numerical order. Each DRG is listed with the DRG title, MDC number, average national payment, and the book reference page number.

The national average payment for each DRG is calculated by multiplying the current RW of the DRG and the estimated national average hospital Medicare base rate. That estimated average hospital Medicare base rate is adjusted yearly using information gathered by Ingenix, Inc., and information published in the *Federal Register* ("Medicare Program: Changes to the Hospital Inpatient Prospective Payment Systems and Fiscal Year 2006 Rates; Final Rule").

INSTRUCTIONS FOR USING *DRG EXPERT*

If the DRG is known, use the "Numeric DRG Listing." The DRGs are numerically ordered in this section. Locate the designated DRG and check the DRG title, the MDC into which the DRG falls, and the reference page number. Turn to the referenced page for a complete list of codes that group to the DRG, as well as the reimbursement data for the DRG. Scan the list for codes with an asterisk (*). The asterisk indicates a sequence or range of codes, and all codes within that code category or subcategory are represented. See the ICD-9-CM code book for specific codes.

If the MDC to which the case groups is known but the specific DRG is not, use the "DRG Listed by Major Diagnostic Category" to locate potential DRG selections. Find the MDC, determine whether the case is surgical or medical, scan the DRG and title list, and then turn to the referenced page for further information.

If the DRG is not known, follow the steps below to determine DRG assignment:

1. Determine whether the case had an operating room procedure (certain operating room procedures do not qualify and do not appear in this book). If so, refer to either the alphabetic or numeric procedure index to locate all potential DRG assignments.

   Look for the specific code or search by main term with qualifier, then body site and qualifier. Main terms are listed as specific operative procedures.

   Example: 57.79 Cystectomy, other, total

   Use the main term "Operation" when the procedure is unspecified.

   Example: 07.59 Operation, other, pineal gland

   To locate a diagnostic procedure, look for the specific code under "Procedure, diagnostic" and the body site, in that order.

   Example: *67.1 Procedure, diagnostic, cervix

Introduction

Note: An asterisk denotes an incomplete code that represents a sequence or range of codes. Refer to the ICD-9-CM code book for the specific codes.

2. If the case lacks an operating room procedure, look up the diagnosis by using either the alphabetic or numeric diagnosis index.

   To locate a diagnosis, look for the specific code or the condition, qualifier, then body site and qualifier, in that order.

   Example: 807.5 Fracture, closed, larynx and trachea

3. In some cases it is necessary to scan the list of codes in the index for both the category code (three-digit code) and the subcategory (four-digit code) level of the code, listed in the index with an asterisk. Note the pages referenced for the DRG to which the category code and the subcategory code ranges are assigned. Turn to the page or pages and review the DRG descriptions to determine the correct DRG to assign to the case.

   Example: In the index, code 263.0 Malnutrition, degree, moderate, directs the coder to DRG 387 Prematurity with Major Problem. Code 263.0 is listed as a principal or secondary diagnosis of major problem. However, this DRG assignment is appropriate only for newborns and other neonates. The category level, *263, refers the coder to DRG 296 Nutritional and Miscellaneous Metabolic Disorders, Age 17 with CC, and to DRG 490 HIV with or without Other Related Conditions. The coder must make the final determination of the correct DRG assignment using these DRG choices.

4. Turn to the page(s) and review the DRG descriptions. Determine which is the correct DRG.

   Often a diagnosis or procedure code is assigned to more than one DRG. Not every DRG entry has a full list of the codes that group to the particular DRG, but refers to a DRG entry that does contain the full list. As in the example above for 807.5 Fracture, closed, larynx and trachea, the index sends you to DRG 073 Other Ear, Nose, Mouth and Throat Diagnosis, Age Greater than 17, as well as, DRG 487 Multiple Significant Trauma, and DRG 482 Tracheostomy for Face, Mouth, and Neck. However, DRG 073 and DRG 074 are considered "paired" DRGs. The only difference in the assignment of either of the DRGs is the age factor. In the guidebook a note appears under DRG 074 that says "Select principal diagnosis listed under DRG 073." That means that code 807.5 groups to either DRG 073 or 074 depending on the patient's age. Be careful to examine all possible potential DRG assignments when the DRG title includes qualifiers such as "with CC" versus. "without CC" and age. These qualifiers are highlighted in the title as an alert to the coder.

   Also note those codes listed with an asterisk (*). The asterisk indicates a sequence or range of codes, and all codes within that code category or subcategory are represented. See ICD-9-CM code book for specific codes.

5. Examine the medical record closely for the following considerations: principal and secondary diagnosis and procedure codes, sex, age, discharge status, presence or absence of CCs, and birth weight for neonates. Documentation must support selection of the final DRG.

IMPORTANT PROTOCOLS OF *DRG EXPERT*

More than one DRG: Many diagnosis and procedure codes group to more than one DRG. Be sure to check every DRG referred to.

Asterisks: Some codes are preceded by an asterisk, which indicates that the ICD-9-CM code is incomplete and represents a sequence or range of codes. Refer to the ICD-9-CM code book for the specific codes included in the code range.

A complete DRG title is necessary to understand the nature of the cases the DRG comprises.

Example:

DRG 320 Kidney and Urinary Tract Infections, Age Greater than 17 with CC

DRG 321 Kidney and Urinary Tract Infections, Age Greater than 17 without CC

DRG 322 Kidney and Urinary Tract Infections, Age 0-17

A complete review of the DRG title is necessary to understand that correct DRG assignment depends on two factors — the patient's age and the presence/absence of a CC. Review DRGs that precede or follow the target DRG, and determine how their narrative descriptions differ. It is possible another DRG with a higher relative weight may be assigned appropriately.

The symbol T indicates a DRG selected as a qualified discharge that may be paid as a transfer case.

The symbol SP indicates a DRG that is subject to the special payment methodology.

The symbol ▽ indicates that the DRG is one of the targeted pairs of DRGs identified as a DRG having the potential for "upcoding" or "DRG creep." These DRGs should be considered as probable targets of an audit. The symbol reminds the coder to carefully consider the documentation that supports the DRG assignment.

The ☑ indicates that there is the potential for assigning a more appropriate, higher-paying DRG. The coder should review the medical documentation to identify all the major factors that might justify assigning the case to a higher-paying DRG.

The ● indicates a new DRG.

The ▲ indicates a revised DRG title.

The S indicates a surgical DRG.

The M indicates a medical DRG.

The CC indicates DRGs with or without CCs.

The A indicates the age category associated with the DRG.

The terms principal or secondary diagnosis indicates DRGs that are based on specific principal or secondary diagnosis requirements.

Bold text OR, AND, WITH, and WITHOUT alerts the user to those complex DRGs that have additional diagnosis or procedure qualifications.

CHANGES IN THE DRG SYSTEM FOR 2006

The Centers for Medicare and Medicaid Services (CMS) issued it's final rule on changes to the hospital inpatient prospective payment system (IPPS) and fiscal year (FY) rates in the *Federal Register* dated August 12, 2005. These changes become effective with discharges on or after October 1, 2005.

Summary of DRG and Coding Changes

- A new DRG was created that identifies embolic stroke combined with tPA treatment, DRG 559 Acute Ischemic Stroke with Use of Thrombolytic Agent.
- A new list of major cardiovascular conditions (MCVs) was defined and newly created DRGs in MDC 5 will be differentiated by the MCVs
- Twelve new DRGs were created in MDC 5 based on the presence or absence of an MCV condition and will replace DRGs 107, 109, 115, 116, 478, 516, 517, 526, and 527
- Code 37.26 (Cardiac electrophysiologic stimulation and recording studies) was removed from the list of cardiac catheterizations for DRGs 535 (Cardiac Defibrillator Implant with Cardiac Catheterization with Acute Myocardial Infarction, Heart Failure, or Shock) and 536 (Cardiac Defibrillator Implant with Cardiac Catheterization without Acute Myocardial Infarction, Heart Failure, or Shock) and reassigned to DRG 515 (Cardiac Defibrillator Implant without Cardiac Catheterization)
- There are four new ICD-9-CM codes that identify multiple stent insertion (codes 00.45, 00.46, 00.47, and 00.48) and four new codes that identify multiple vessel treatment (codes 00.40, 00.41, 00.42, and 00.43
- Procedure code 35.52 (Repair of atrial septal defect with prosthesis, closed technique) was moved from DRG 108 (Other Cardiothoracic Procedures) and reassigned to DRG 518 (Percutaneous Cardiovascular Procedures without Acute Myocardial Infarction without Coronary Artery Stent Implant)
- DRG 103 was revised to include 37.65 (Implant of external heart assist system) and 37.64 (Removal of heart assist system)
- The title of DRG 541 was revised to ECMO or Tracheostomy with Mechanical Ventilation 96+ Hours or Principal Diagnosis Except Face, Mouth and Neck with Major O.R. and for consistency purposes the title of DRG 542 was revised to Tracheostomy with Mechanical Ventilation 96+ Hours or Principal Diagnosis Except Face, Mouth and Neck without Major O.R.
- Procedure code 39.65 (Extracorporeal membrane oxygenation [ECMO]) was removed from DRGs 104 and 105 and reassigned to DRG 541
- DRG 209 (Major Joint and Limb Reattachment Procedures of Lower Extremity) was deleted
- Three new DRGs were created in MDC 8, DRG 544 (Major Joint Replacement or Reattachment of Lower Extremity), DRG 545 (Revision of Hip or Knee Replacement) and DRG 546 (Spinal Fusions Except Cervical with Curvature of the Spine or Malignancy)
- Principal diagnosis codes for curvature of the spine or malignancy were removed from DRG 497 (Spinal Fusion Except Cervical with CC) and DRG 498 (Spinal Fusion Except Cervical without CC) and reassigned to DRG 546
- Procedure code 26.12 (Open biopsy of salivary gland or duct) was removed from DRG 468 to DRG 477

- CMS restructured four edits in the Medicare Code Editor (MCE): edit 4 (age conflict), edit 5 (sex conflict), edit 8 (questionable admission), and edit 11 (noncovered procedure)
- The surgical hierarchies for MDC 5 Diseases and Disorders of the Circulatory System and MDC 8 Diseases and Disorders of the Musculoskeletal System and Connective Tissue were revised
- 173 new diagnosis codes and 37 procedure codes were added
- New diagnosis codes were added to the complications and comorbidities (CC) list
- DRG relative weights were recalibrated as required by the Social Security Act
- The criteria used to determine whether a DRG qualifies for inclusion in the postacute care transfer policy was revised. There are now approximately 182 DRGs that are categorized as postacute care transfers and 13 DRGs that are categorized as postacute care special pay transfers.

GLOSSARY OF DRG TERMS

against medical advice: The discharge status of patients who leave the hospital after signing a form that releases the hospital from responsibility, or who leave the hospital premises without notifying hospital personnel.

arithmetic mean length of stay (AMLOS): The average number of days patients within a given DRG stay in the hospital, also referred to as the average length of stay. The AMLOS is used to determine payment for outlier cases.

base rate: A number assigned to a hospital that is used to calculate DRG reimbursement. Base rates vary from hospital to hospital. The base rate adjusts reimbursement to allow for such individual characteristics of the hospital as geographic location, status (urban/rural, teaching), and local labor costs.

case-mix index (CMI): The sum of all DRG relative weights, divided by the number of Medicare cases. A low CMI may denote DRG assignments that do not adequately reflect the resources used to treat Medicare patients.

CC: Complication or comorbid condition.

charges: The dollar amount of hospital bills.

comorbidity: Pre-existing condition that, because of its presence with a specific diagnosis, causes an increase in length of stay by at least one day in approximately 75 percent of the cases.

complication: A condition that arises during the hospital stay that prolongs the length of stay by at least one day in approximately 75 percent of the cases.

diagnosis-related group (DRG): One of the 526 valid classifications of diagnoses in which patients demonstrate similar resource consumption and length-of-stay patterns.

discharge: A situation in which the patient leaves an acute care (prospective payment) hospital after receiving complete acute care treatment.

discharge status: Disposition of the patient at discharge (for example: left against medical advice, discharged home, transferred to an acute care hospital, expired).

geometric mean length of stay (GMLOS): Used to compute reimbursement, the GMLOS is a statistically adjusted value for all cases for a given DRG, allowing for the outliers, transfer cases, and negative outlier cases that would normally skew the data. The GMLOS is used to determine payment only for transfer cases — i.e., the per diem rate.

Grouper: The software program that assigns DRGs.

homogeneous: Adjective describing patients who consume similar types and amounts of hospital resources.

major diagnostic category (MDC): Broad classification of diagnoses typically grouped by body system.

nonoperating room procedure: A procedure that does not normally require the use of the operating room and that can affect DRG assignment.

operating room (OR) procedure: A procedure that falls into a defined group of procedures that normally require the use of an operating room.

other diagnosis (*see also* **comorbidity** and **complication**). All conditions (secondary) that exist at the time of admission or that develop subsequently that affect the treatment received and/or the length of stay. Diagnoses that relate to an earlier episode and that have no bearing on the current hospital stay are not to be reported.

outliers: There are two types of outliers: day and cost outliers. Payment for day outliers was eliminated with discharges occurring on or after October 1, 1997. A cost outlier is a case in which the costs for treating the patient are extraordinarily high in relation to the costs for other patients in the DRG. An increase in cost outlier payments compensates for the elimination of day outlier payments. Hospital-specific cost-to-charge ratios are applied to the covered charges (operating and capital costs computed separately) for the case to determine whether the costs of the case exceed the fixed loss outlier threshold.

per diem rate: Payment made to the hospital from which a patient is transferred for each day of stay. Per diem rate is determined by dividing the full DRG payment by the GMLOS for the DRG. The payment rate for the first day of stay is twice the per diem rate, and subsequent days are paid at the per diem rate up to the full DRG amount.

PMDC (pre-MDC): There are nine DRGs to which cases are directly assigned based upon procedure codes. Cases are assigned to these DRGs before classification to an MDC. The PMDC includes DRGs for heart, liver, bone marrow, simultaneous pancreas/kidney transplant, pancreas transplant, lung transplant, and three DRGs for tracheostomies. These DRGs are listed in the section of this manual entitled "DRGs Associated with All MDCs and Pre-MDCs."

principal diagnosis: The condition established after study to be chiefly responsible for occasioning the admission of the patient to the hospital for care.

principal procedure: A procedure performed for definitive treatment rather than diagnostic or exploratory purposes, or that was necessary to treat a complication. The principal procedure usually is related to the principal diagnosis.

relative weight (RW): An assigned weight that is intended to reflect the relative resource consumption associated with each DRG. The higher the relative weight, the greater the payment to the hospital. The relative weights are calculated by CMS and published in the final PPS rule.

surgical hierarchy: Surgical hierarchy is defined as an ordering of surgical cases from most to least resource intensive. Application of this decision rule is necessary when patient stays involve multiple surgical procedures, each one of which, occurring by itself, could result in assignment to a different DRG. All patients must be assigned to only one DRG per admission.

transfer: A situation in which the patient is transferred to another acute care hospital for related care.

volume: The number of patients in each DRG.

MDC 1
DISEASES AND DISORDERS OF THE NERVOUS SYSTEM

The complete and up-to-date listing of ICD-9-CM diagnosis codes assigned to this MDC can be found online at www.ingenixonline.com/content/drg/resources.asp.

SURGICAL

[S] DRG 001 Craniotomy, Age Greater than 17 with CC

GMLOS 7.6 AMLOS 10.1 RW 3.4347 ☑ [T] [CC] [A]

Operating Room Procedures

01.12	Open biopsy of cerebral meninges
01.14	Open biopsy of brain
01.15	Biopsy of skull
01.18	Other diagnostic procedures on brain and cerebral meninges
01.19	Other diagnostic procedures on skull
*01.2	Craniotomy and craniectomy
*01.3	Incision of brain and cerebral meninges
*01.4	Operations on thalamus and globus pallidus
*01.5	Other excision or destruction of brain and meninges
01.6	Excision of lesion of skull
*02.0	Cranioplasty
*02.1	Repair of cerebral meninges
02.2	Ventriculostomy
02.91	Lysis of cortical adhesions
02.92	Repair of brain
02.93	Implantation or replacement of intracranial neurostimulator lead(s)
02.94	Insertion or replacement of skull tongs or halo traction device
02.99	Other operations on skull, brain, and cerebral meninges
04.01	Excision of acoustic neuroma
04.41	Decompression of trigeminal nerve root
07.13	Biopsy of pituitary gland, transfrontal approach
07.14	Biopsy of pituitary gland, transsphenoidal approach
07.15	Biopsy of pituitary gland, unspecified approach
07.17	Biopsy of pineal gland
*07.5	Operations on pineal gland
*07.6	Hypophysectomy
*07.7	Other operations on hypophysis
29.92	Division of glossopharyngeal nerve
38.01	Incision of intracranial vessels
38.11	Endarterectomy of intracranial vessels
38.31	Resection of intracranial vessels with anastomosis
38.41	Resection of intracranial vessels with replacement
38.51	Ligation and stripping of varicose veins of intracranial vessels
38.61	Other excision of intracranial vessels
38.81	Other surgical occlusion of intracranial vessels
39.28	Extracranial-intracranial (EC-IC) vascular bypass
39.51	Clipping of aneurysm
39.52	Other repair of aneurysm
39.53	Repair of arteriovenous fistula
39.72	Endovascular repair or occlusion of head and neck vessels
39.79	Other endovascular repair (of aneurysm) of other vessels

[S] DRG 002 Craniotomy, Age Greater than 17 without CC

GMLOS 3.5 AMLOS 4.6 RW 1.9587 ☑ [T] [A]

Select operating room procedures listed under DRG 001

S DRG 003 Craniotomy, Age 0-17

GMLOS 12.7 AMLOS 12.7 RW 1.9860 ☑ A

Operating Room Procedures

01.12	Open biopsy of cerebral meninges
01.14	Open biopsy of brain
01.15	Biopsy of skull
01.18	Other diagnostic procedures on brain and cerebral meninges
01.19	Other diagnostic procedures on skull
*01.2	Craniotomy and craniectomy
*01.3	Incision of brain and cerebral meninges
*01.4	Operations on thalamus and globus pallidus
*01.5	Other excision or destruction of brain and meninges
01.6	Excision of lesion of skull
*02.0	Cranioplasty
*02.1	Repair of cerebral meninges
02.2	Ventriculostomy
*02.3	Extracranial ventricular shunt
02.42	Replacement of ventricular shunt
02.43	Removal of ventricular shunt
02.91	Lysis of cortical adhesions
02.92	Repair of brain
02.93	Implantation or replacement of intracranial neurostimulator lead(s)
02.94	Insertion or replacement of skull tongs or halo traction device
02.99	Other operations on skull, brain, and cerebral meninges
04.01	Excision of acoustic neuroma
04.41	Decompression of trigeminal nerve root
07.13	Biopsy of pituitary gland, transfrontal approach
07.14	Biopsy of pituitary gland, transsphenoidal approach
07.15	Biopsy of pituitary gland, unspecified approach
07.17	Biopsy of pineal gland
*07.5	Operations on pineal gland
*07.6	Hypophysectomy
*07.7	Other operations on hypophysis
29.92	Division of glossopharyngeal nerve
38.01	Incision of intracranial vessels
38.11	Endarterectomy of intracranial vessels
38.31	Resection of intracranial vessels with anastomosis
38.41	Resection of intracranial vessels with replacement
38.51	Ligation and stripping of varicose veins of intracranial vessels
38.61	Other excision of intracranial vessels
38.81	Other surgical occlusion of intracranial vessels
39.28	Extracranial-intracranial (EC-IC) vascular bypass
39.51	Clipping of aneurysm
39.52	Other repair of aneurysm
39.53	Repair of arteriovenous fistula
39.72	Endovascular repair or occlusion of head and neck vessels
39.79	Other endovascular repair (of aneurysm) of other vessels

DRG 004 No Longer Valid

GMLOS 0.0 AMLOS 0.0 RW 0.0000

Omitted in October 2003 grouper version

DRG 005 No Longer Valid

GMLOS 0.0 AMLOS 0.0 RW 0.0000

Omitted in October 2003 grouper version

S DRG 006 Carpal Tunnel Release

GMLOS 2.2 AMLOS 3.0 RW 0.7878

Operating Room Procedure

04.43	Release of carpal tunnel

S Surgical *M Medical* *CC CC Indicator* *A Age Restriction* *● New DRG* *▲ Revised DRG Title*

[S] DRG 007 Peripheral and Cranial Nerve and Other Nervous System Procedures with CC

GMLOS 6.7 AMLOS 9.7 RW 2.6978 [SP] [CC]

Operating Room Procedures

04.02	Division of trigeminal nerve
04.03	Division or crushing of other cranial and peripheral nerves
04.04	Other incision of cranial and peripheral nerves
04.05	Gasserian ganglionectomy
04.06	Other cranial or peripheral ganglionectomy
04.07	Other excision or avulsion of cranial and peripheral nerves
04.12	Open biopsy of cranial or peripheral nerve or ganglion
04.19	Other diagnostic procedures on cranial and peripheral nerves and ganglia
04.3	Suture of cranial and peripheral nerves
04.42	Other cranial nerve decompression
04.44	Release of tarsal tunnel
04.49	Other peripheral nerve or ganglion decompression or lysis of adhesions
04.5	Cranial or peripheral nerve graft
04.6	Transposition of cranial and peripheral nerves
*04.7	Other cranial or peripheral neuroplasty
*04.9	Other operations on cranial and peripheral nerves
05.0	Division of sympathetic nerve or ganglion
*05.1	Diagnostic procedures on sympathetic nerves or ganglia
*05.2	Sympathectomy
*05.8	Other operations on sympathetic nerves or ganglia
05.9	Other operations on nervous system
07.19	Other diagnostic procedures on adrenal glands, pituitary gland, pineal gland, and thymus
*07.8	Thymectomy
*08.5	Other adjustment of lid position
27.62	Correction of cleft palate
27.69	Other plastic repair of palate
29.4	Plastic operation on pharynx
29.59	Other repair of pharynx
37.74	Insertion or replacement of epicardial lead (electrode) into epicardium
37.75	Revision of lead (electrode)
37.76	Replacement of transvenous atrial and/or ventricular lead(s) (electrode(s))
37.77	Removal of lead(s) (electrodes) without replacement
37.79	Revision or relocation of cardiac device pocket
37.80	Insertion of permanent pacemaker, initial or replacement, type of device not specified
37.85	Replacement of any type of pacemaker device with single-chamber device, not specified as rate responsive
37.86	Replacement of any type of pacemaker device with single-chamber device, rate responsive
37.87	Replacement of any type of pacemaker device with dual-chamber device
37.89	Revision or removal of pacemaker device
38.02	Incision of other vessels of head and neck
38.21	Biopsy of blood vessel
38.42	Resection of other vessels of head and neck with replacement
38.7	Interruption of the vena cava
38.82	Other surgical occlusion of other vessels of head and neck
40.11	Biopsy of lymphatic structure
44.00	Vagotomy, not otherwise specified
54.95	Incision of peritoneum
81.71	Arthroplasty of metacarpophalangeal and interphalangeal joint with implant
81.72	Arthroplasty of metacarpophalangeal and interphalangeal joint without implant
81.74	Arthroplasty of carpocarpal or carpometacarpal joint with implant
81.75	Arthroplasty of carpocarpal or carpometacarpal joint without implant
81.79	Other repair of hand, fingers, and wrist
*82.5	Transplantation of muscle and tendon of hand
*82.6	Reconstruction of thumb
*82.7	Plastic operation on hand with graft or implant
*82.8	Other plastic operations on hand
83.13	Other tenotomy

DRG 007 — continued

83.14	Fasciotomy
83.19	Other division of soft tissue
83.21	Biopsy of soft tissue
83.41	Excision of tendon for graft
83.43	Excision of muscle or fascia for graft
83.45	Other myectomy
83.49	Other excision of soft tissue
*83.7	Reconstruction of muscle and tendon
83.81	Tendon graft
83.82	Graft of muscle or fascia
83.83	Tendon pulley reconstruction on muscle, tendon, and fascia
83.85	Other change in muscle or tendon length
83.87	Other plastic operations on muscle
83.88	Other plastic operations on tendon
83.89	Other plastic operations on fascia
83.92	Insertion or replacement of skeletal muscle stimulator
83.93	Removal of skeletal muscle stimulator
84.11	Amputation of toe
84.12	Amputation through foot
84.13	Disarticulation of ankle
84.14	Amputation of ankle through malleoli of tibia and fibula
84.15	Other amputation below knee
84.16	Disarticulation of knee
84.17	Amputation above knee
86.06	Insertion of totally implantable infusion pump
86.22	Excisional debridement of wound, infection, or burn
86.4	Radical excision of skin lesion
86.60	Free skin graft, not otherwise specified
86.61	Full-thickness skin graft to hand
86.62	Other skin graft to hand
86.63	Full-thickness skin graft to other sites
86.65	Heterograft to skin
86.66	Homograft to skin
86.67	Dermal regenerative graft
86.69	Other skin graft to other sites
86.70	Pedicle or flap graft, not otherwise specified
86.71	Cutting and preparation of pedicle grafts or flaps
86.72	Advancement of pedicle graft
86.74	Attachment of pedicle or flap graft to other sites
86.75	Revision of pedicle or flap graft
86.81	Repair for facial weakness
86.91	Excision of skin for graft
86.93	Insertion of tissue expander
86.94	Insertion or replacement of single array neurostimulator pulse generator, not specified as rechargeable
86.95	Insertion or replacement of dual array neurostimulator pulse generator, not specified as rechargeable
86.96	Insertion or replacement of other neurostimulator pulse generator
86.97	Insertion or replacement of single array rechargeable neurostimulator pulse generator
86.98	Insertion or replacement of dual array rechargeable neurostimulator pulse generator
92.27	Implantation or insertion of radioactive elements

OR

Any of the following procedure combinations

37.70	Initial insertion of lead (electrode), not otherwise specified (must be in combination with 37.80, 37.81, 37.82, 37.85, 37.86, or 37.87)
37.71	Initial insertion of transvenous lead (electrode) into ventricle (must be in combination with 37.80, 37.81, 37.82, 37.85, 37.86, or 37.87)
37.72	Initial insertion of transvenous leads (electrodes) into atrium and ventricle (must be in combination with 37.80 or 37.83)
37.73	Initial insertion of transvenous lead (electrode) into atrium (must be in combination with 37.80, 37.81, 37.82, 37.83, 37.85, 37.86, or 37.87)

37.74	Insertion or replacement of epicardial lead (electrode) into epicardium (must be in combination with 37.80, 37.85, 37.86 or 37.87)
37.76	Replacement of transvenous atrial and/or ventricular lead(s) (electrode(s)) (must be in combination with 37.80, 37.81, 37.82, 37.85, 37.86, or 37.87)

OR

Nonoperating Room Procedures

*92.3	Stereotactic radiosurgery

S DRG 008 Peripheral and Cranial Nerve and Other Nervous System Procedures without CC

GMLOS 2.0 AMLOS 3.0 RW 1.5635 ☑ SP

Select operating or nonoperating room procedures listed under DRG 007

S DRG 528 Intracranial Vascular Procedure with Principal Diagnosis of Hemorrhage

GMLOS 13.8 AMLOS 17.2 RW 7.0505

Principal Diagnosis

094.87	Syphilitic ruptured cerebral aneurysm
430	Subarachnoid hemorrhage
431	Intracerebral hemorrhage
*432	Other and unspecified intracranial hemorrhage

Operating Room Procedures

02.13	Ligation of meningeal vessel
38.01	Incision of intracranial vessels
38.11	Endarterectomy of intracranial vessels
38.31	Resection of intracranial vessels with anastomosis
38.41	Resection of intracranial vessels with replacement
38.51	Ligation and stripping of varicose veins of intracranial vessels
38.61	Other excision of intracranial vessels
38.81	Other surgical occlusion of intracranial vessels
39.28	Extracranial-intracranial (EC-IC) vascular bypass
39.51	Clipping of aneurysm
39.52	Other repair of aneurysm
39.53	Repair of arteriovenous fistula
39.72	Endovascular repair or occlusion of head and neck vessels
39.79	Other endovascular repair (of aneurysm) of other vessels

S DRG 529 Ventricular Shunt Procedures with CC

GMLOS 5.3 AMLOS 8.3 RW 2.3160 ☑ T CC

Note: For age less than 17 see DRG 003

Operating Room Procedures

*02.3	Extracranial ventricular shunt
02.42	Replacement of ventricular shunt
02.43	Removal of ventricular shunt

S DRG 530 Ventricular Shunt Procedures without CC

GMLOS 2.4 AMLOS 3.1 RW 1.2041 ☑ T

Note: For age less than 17 see DRG 003

Select operating room procedures listed under DRG 529

S DRG 531 Spinal Procedures with CC

GMLOS 6.5 AMLOS 9.6 RW 3.1279 T CC

Operating Room Procedures

*03.0	Exploration and decompression of spinal canal structures
03.1	Division of intraspinal nerve root
*03.2	Chordotomy

** Code Range* ☑ *Optimization Potential* *Targeted Potential* T *Transfer DRG* SP *Special Payment*

DRG 531 — continued

03.32	Biopsy of spinal cord or spinal meninges
03.39	Other diagnostic procedures on spinal cord and spinal canal structures
03.4	Excision or destruction of lesion of spinal cord or spinal meninges
*03.5	Plastic operations on spinal cord structures
03.6	Lysis of adhesions of spinal cord and nerve roots
*03.7	Shunt of spinal theca
03.93	Implantation or replacement of spinal neurostimulator lead(s)
03.94	Removal of spinal neurostimulator lead(s)
03.97	Revision of spinal thecal shunt
03.98	Removal of spinal thecal shunt
03.99	Other operations on spinal cord and spinal canal structures
77.81	Other partial ostectomy of scapula, clavicle, and thorax (ribs and sternum)
77.91	Total ostectomy of scapula, clavicle, and thorax (ribs and sternum)
80.50	Excision or destruction of intervertebral disc, unspecified
80.51	Excision of intervertebral disc
80.59	Other destruction of intervertebral disc
*81.0	Spinal fusion
*81.3	Refusion of spine
84.58	Implantation of interspinous process decompression device
84.59	Insertion of other spinal devices
*84.6	Replacement of spinal disc

S DRG 532 Spinal Procedures without CC

GMLOS 2.8 AMLOS 3.7 RW 1.4195 ☑ T

Select operating room procedures listed under DRG 531

S DRG 533 Extracranial Vascular Procedures with CC

GMLOS 2.4 AMLOS 3.8 RW 1.5767 ☑ CC

Operating Room Procedures

00.61	Percutaneous angioplasty or atherectomy of precerebral (extracranial) vessel(s)
00.62	Percutaneous angioplasty or atherectomy of intracranial vessel(s)
38.10	Endarterectomy, unspecified site
38.12	Endarterectomy of other vessels of head and neck
38.32	Resection of other vessels of head and neck with anastomosis
38.62	Other excision of other vessels of head and neck
39.22	Aorta-subclavian-carotid bypass
39.29	Other (peripheral) vascular shunt or bypass
*39.3	Suture of vessel
39.50	Angioplasty or atherectomy of other non-coronary vessel(s)
39.56	Repair of blood vessel with tissue patch graft
39.57	Repair of blood vessel with synthetic patch graft
39.58	Repair of blood vessel with unspecified type of patch graft
39.59	Other repair of vessel
39.8	Operations on carotid body and other vascular bodies
39.92	Injection of sclerosing agent into vein

S DRG 534 Extracranial Vascular Procedures without CC

GMLOS 1.5 AMLOS 1.8 RW 1.0201 ☑

Select operating room procedure listed under DRG 533

S DRG 543 Craniotomy with Implantation of Chemotherapeutic Agent or Acute Complex Central Nervous System Principal Diagnosis

GMLOS 8.5 AMLOS 12.3 RW 4.4184 ☑ T

Operating Room Procedures

01.12	Open biopsy of cerebral meninges
01.14	Open biopsy of brain
01.15	Biopsy of skull

01.18	Other diagnostic procedures on brain and cerebral meninges
01.19	Other diagnostic procedures on skull
*01.2	Craniotomy and craniectomy
*01.3	Incision of brain and cerebral meninges
*01.4	Operations on thalamus and globus pallidus
*01.5	Other excision or destruction of brain and meninges
01.6	Excision of lesion of skull
*02.0	Cranioplasty
*02.1	Repair of cerebral meninges
02.2	Ventriculostomy
02.91	Lysis of cortical adhesions
02.92	Repair of brain
02.93	Implantation or replacement of intracranial neurostimulator lead(s)
02.94	Insertion or replacement of skull tongs or halo traction device
02.99	Other operations on skull, brain, and cerebral meninges
04.01	Excision of acoustic neuroma
04.41	Decompression of trigeminal nerve root
07.13	Biopsy of pituitary gland, transfrontal approach
07.14	Biopsy of pituitary gland, transsphenoidal approach
07.15	Biopsy of pituitary gland, unspecified approach
07.17	Biopsy of pineal gland
*07.5	Operations on pineal gland
*07.6	Hypophysectomy
*07.7	Other operations on hypophysis
29.92	Division of glossopharyngeal nerve
38.01	Incision of intracranial vessels
38.11	Endarterectomy of intracranial vessels
38.31	Resection of intracranial vessels with anastomosis
38.41	Resection of intracranial vessels with replacement
38.51	Ligation and stripping of varicose veins of intracranial vessels
38.61	Other excision of intracranial vessels
38.81	Other surgical occlusion of intracranial vessels
39.28	Extracranial-intracranial (EC-IC) vascular bypass
39.51	Clipping of aneurysm
39.52	Other repair of aneurysm
39.53	Repair of arteriovenous fistula
39.72	Endovascular repair or occlusion of head and neck vessels
39.79	Other endovascular repair (of aneurysm) of other vessels

AND

00.10	Implantation of chemotherapeutic agent

OR

Principal Diagnosis

003.21	Salmonella meningitis
006.5	Amebic brain abscess
*013	Tuberculosis of meninges and central nervous system
036.0	Meningococcal meningitis
036.1	Meningococcal encephalitis
*045.0	Acute paralytic poliomyelitis specified as bulbar
*045.1	Acute poliomyelitis with other paralysis
*045.9	Acute unspecified poliomyelitis
054.3	Herpetic meningoencephalitis
054.72	Herpes simplex meningitis
055.0	Postmeasles encephalitis
*062	Mosquito-borne viral encephalitis
*063	Tick-borne viral encephalitis
064	Viral encephalitis transmitted by other and unspecified arthropods
066.2	Venezuelan equine fever
071	Rabies
072.1	Mumps meningitis
072.2	Mumps encephalitis
091.81	Early syphilis, acute syphilitic meningitis (secondary)

DRG 543 — continued

094.2	Syphilitic meningitis
094.81	Syphilitic encephalitis
098.82	Gonococcal meningitis
*100.8	Other specified leptospiral infections
112.83	Candidal meningitis
114.2	Coccidioidal meningitis
115.01	Histoplasma capsulatum meningitis
115.11	Histoplasma duboisii meningitis
115.91	Unspecified Histoplasmosis meningitis
130.0	Meningoencephalitis due to toxoplasmosis
*320	Bacterial meningitis
321.0	Cryptococcal meningitis
321.1	Meningitis in other fungal diseases
321.2	Meningitis due to viruses not elsewhere classified
321.3	Meningitis due to trypanosomiasis
323.0	Encephalitis in viral diseases classified elsewhere
323.1	Encephalitis in rickettsial diseases classified elsewhere
323.2	Encephalitis in protozoal diseases classified elsewhere
323.4	Other encephalitis due to infection classified elsewhere
323.5	Encephalitis following immunization procedures
323.6	Postinfectious encephalitis
323.7	Toxic encephalitis
323.8	Other causes of encephalitis
323.9	Unspecified cause of encephalitis
*324	Intracranial and intraspinal abscess
325	Phlebitis and thrombophlebitis of intracranial venous sinuses
430	Subarachnoid hemorrhage
431	Intracerebral hemorrhage
432.9	Unspecified intracranial hemorrhage
433.01	Occlusion and stenosis of basilar artery with cerebral infarction
433.11	Occlusion and stenosis of carotid artery with cerebral infarction
433.21	Occlusion and stenosis of vertebral artery with cerebral infarction
433.31	Occlusion and stenosis of multiple and bilateral precerebral arteries with cerebral infarction
433.81	Occlusion and stenosis of other specified precerebral artery with cerebral infarction
433.91	Occlusion and stenosis of unspecified precerebral artery with cerebral infarction
434.01	Cerebral thrombosis with cerebral infarction
434.11	Cerebral embolism with cerebral infarction
434.91	Unspecified cerebral artery occlusion with cerebral infarction
*851.1	Cortex (cerebral) contusion with open intracranial wound
*851.2	Cortex (cerebral) laceration without mention of open intracranial wound
*851.3	Cortex (cerebral) laceration with open intracranial wound
*851.5	Cerebellar or brain stem contusion with open intracranial wound
*851.6	Cerebellar or brain stem laceration without mention of open intracranial wound
*851.7	Cerebellar or brain stem laceration with open intracranial wound
*851.8	Other and unspecified cerebral laceration and contusion, without mention of open intracranial wound
*851.9	Other and unspecified cerebral laceration and contusion, with open intracranial wound
*852.0	Subarachnoid hemorrhage following injury without mention of open intracranial wound
*852.1	Subarachnoid hemorrhage following injury, with open intracranial wound
*852.3	Subdural hemorrhage following injury, with open intracranial wound
*853.0	Other and unspecified intracranial hemorrhage following injury, without mention of open intracranial wound
*853.1	Other and unspecified intracranial hemorrhage following injury with open intracranial wound
*854.1	Intracranial injury of other and unspecified nature with open intracranial wound

MDC 1
DISEASES AND DISORDERS OF THE NERVOUS SYSTEM

The complete and up-to-date listing of ICD-9-CM diagnosis codes assigned to this MDC can be found online at www.ingenixonline.com/content/drg/resources.asp.

MEDICAL

M DRG 009 Spinal Disorders and Injuries

GMLOS 4.5 AMLOS 6.4 RW 1.4045 ☑

Principal Diagnosis

343.0	Diplegic infantile cerebral palsy
343.1	Hemiplegic infantile cerebral palsy
343.2	Quadriplegic infantile cerebral palsy
343.4	Infantile hemiplegia
*344.0	Quadriplegia and quadriparesis
344.1	Paraplegia
344.2	Diplegia of upper limbs
*806	Fracture of vertebral column with spinal cord injury
907.2	Late effect of spinal cord injury
*952	Spinal cord injury without evidence of spinal bone injury

M DRG 010 Nervous System Neoplasms with CC

GMLOS 4.6 AMLOS 6.2 RW 1.2222 T CC

Principal Diagnosis

*191	Malignant neoplasm of brain
*192	Malignant neoplasm of other and unspecified parts of nervous system
194.4	Malignant neoplasm of pineal gland
194.5	Malignant neoplasm of carotid body
194.6	Malignant neoplasm of aortic body and other paraganglia
198.3	Secondary malignant neoplasm of brain and spinal cord
198.4	Secondary malignant neoplasm of other parts of nervous system
*225	Benign neoplasm of brain and other parts of nervous system
227.4	Benign neoplasm of pineal gland
227.5	Benign neoplasm of carotid body
227.6	Benign neoplasm of aortic body and other paraganglia
237.1	Neoplasm of uncertain behavior of pineal gland
237.3	Neoplasm of uncertain behavior of paraganglia
237.5	Neoplasm of uncertain behavior of brain and spinal cord
237.6	Neoplasm of uncertain behavior of meninges
237.9	Neoplasm of uncertain behavior of other and unspecified parts of nervous system
239.6	Neoplasm of unspecified nature of brain

M DRG 011 Nervous System Neoplasms without CC

GMLOS 2.9 AMLOS 3.8 RW 0.8736 ☑ T

Select principal diagnosis listed under DRG 010

M DRG 012 Degenerative Nervous System Disorders

GMLOS 4.3 AMLOS 5.5 RW 0.8998 T

Principal Diagnosis

*046	Slow virus infection of central nervous system
094.0	Tabes dorsalis
094.1	General paresis
094.82	Syphilitic Parkinsonism
094.85	Syphilitic retrobulbar neuritis
094.89	Other specified neurosyphilis

** Code Range ☑ Optimization Potential Targeted Potential T Transfer DRG SP Special Payment*

DRG 012 — continued

094.9	Unspecified neurosyphilis
*330	Cerebral degenerations usually manifest in childhood
331.0	Alzheimer's disease
*331.1	Pick's disease
331.2	Senile degeneration of brain
331.3	Communicating hydrocephalus
331.4	Obstructive hydrocephalus
331.7	Cerebral degeneration in diseases classified elsewhere
331.82	Dementia with Lewy bodies
331.89	Other cerebral degeneration
331.9	Unspecified cerebral degeneration
*332	Parkinson's disease
333.0	Other degenerative diseases of the basal ganglia
333.4	Huntington's chorea
333.5	Other choreas
333.6	Idiopathic torsion dystonia
333.7	Symptomatic torsion dystonia
333.90	Unspecified extrapyramidal disease and abnormal movement disorder
333.99	Other extrapyramidal disease and abnormal movement disorder
*335	Anterior horn cell disease
336.0	Syringomyelia and syringobulbia
*342	Hemiplegia and hemiparesis
*358.0	Myasthenia gravis
358.1	Myasthenic syndromes in diseases classified elsewhere
379.45	Argyll Robertson pupil, atypical
*438	Late effects of cerebrovascular disease

M DRG 013 Multiple Sclerosis and Cerebellar Ataxia

GMLOS 4.0 AMLOS 5.0 RW 0.8575 ☑ T

Principal Diagnosis

*334	Spinocerebellar disease
340	Multiple sclerosis
*341	Other demyelinating diseases of central nervous system

M DRG 014 Intracranial Hemorrhage or Cerebral Infarction

GMLOS 4.5 AMLOS 5.8 RW 1.2456 ☑ T YIELD

Principal Diagnosis

430	Subarachnoid hemorrhage
431	Intracerebral hemorrhage
*432	Other and unspecified intracranial hemorrhage
433.01	Occlusion and stenosis of basilar artery with cerebral infarction
433.11	Occlusion and stenosis of carotid artery with cerebral infarction
433.21	Occlusion and stenosis of vertebral artery with cerebral infarction
433.31	Occlusion and stenosis of multiple and bilateral precerebral arteries with cerebral infarction
433.81	Occlusion and stenosis of other specified precerebral artery with cerebral infarction
433.91	Occlusion and stenosis of unspecified precerebral artery with cerebral infarction
434.01	Cerebral thrombosis with cerebral infarction
434.11	Cerebral embolism with cerebral infarction
434.91	Unspecified cerebral artery occlusion with cerebral infarction

M DRG 015 Nonspecific Cerebrovascular and Precerebral Occlusion without Infarction

GMLOS 3.7 AMLOS 4.6 RW 0.9421 ☑ T YIELD

Principal Diagnosis

433.00	Occlusion and stenosis of basilar artery without mention of cerebral infarction
433.10	Occlusion and stenosis of carotid artery without mention of cerebral infarction
433.20	Occlusion and stenosis of vertebral artery without mention of cerebral infarction
433.30	Occlusion and stenosis of multiple and bilateral precerebral arteries without mention of cerebral infarction

433.80	Occlusion and stenosis of other specified precerebral artery without mention of cerebral infarction
433.90	Occlusion and stenosis of unspecified precerebral artery without mention of cerebral infarction
434.00	Cerebral thrombosis without mention of cerebral infarction
434.10	Cerebral embolism without mention of cerebral infarction
434.90	Unspecified cerebral artery occlusion without mention of cerebral infarction
436	Acute, but ill-defined, cerebrovascular disease

M DRG 016 Nonspecific Cerebrovascular Disorders with CC

GMLOS 5.0 AMLOS 6.5 RW 1.3351 ☑ T CC

Principal Diagnosis

*348.3	Unspecified encephalopathy
348.8	Other conditions of brain
348.9	Unspecified condition of brain
349.89	Other specified disorder of nervous system
349.9	Unspecified disorders of nervous system
437.0	Cerebral atherosclerosis
437.7	Transient global amnesia
437.8	Other ill-defined cerebrovascular disease
437.9	Unspecified cerebrovascular disease

M DRG 017 Nonspecific Cerebrovascular Disorders without CC

GMLOS 2.5 AMLOS 3.2 RW 0.7229 ☑ T

Select principal diagnosis listed under DRG 016

M DRG 018 Cranial and Peripheral Nerve Disorders with CC

GMLOS 4.1 AMLOS 5.3 RW 0.9903 T CC

Principal Diagnosis

053.10	Herpes zoster with unspecified nervous system complication
053.11	Geniculate herpes zoster
053.12	Postherpetic trigeminal neuralgia
053.13	Postherpetic polyneuropathy
053.19	Other herpes zoster with nervous system complications
056.00	Unspecified rubella neurological complication
072.72	Mumps polyneuropathy
*250.6	Diabetes with neurological manifestations
*337	Disorders of the autonomic nervous system
344.60	Cauda equina syndrome without mention of neurogenic bladder
*350	Trigeminal nerve disorders
*351	Facial nerve disorders
*352	Disorders of other cranial nerves
*353	Nerve root and plexus disorders
*354	Mononeuritis of upper limb and mononeuritis multiplex
*355	Mononeuritis of lower limb and unspecified site
356.0	Hereditary peripheral neuropathy
356.1	Peroneal muscular atrophy
356.2	Hereditary sensory neuropathy
356.4	Idiopathic progressive polyneuropathy
356.8	Other specified idiopathic peripheral neuropathy
356.9	Unspecified hereditary and idiopathic peripheral neuropathy
357.1	Polyneuropathy in collagen vascular disease
357.2	Polyneuropathy in diabetes
357.3	Polyneuropathy in malignant disease
357.4	Polyneuropathy in other diseases classified elsewhere
357.5	Alcoholic polyneuropathy
357.6	Polyneuropathy due to drugs
357.7	Polyneuropathy due to other toxic agents
*357.8	Other inflammatory and toxic neuropathy
357.9	Unspecified inflammatory and toxic neuropathy
358.2	Toxic myoneural disorders

DRG 018 — continued

358.8	Other specified myoneural disorders
358.9	Unspecified myoneural disorders
723.2	Cervicocranial syndrome
723.3	Cervicobrachial syndrome (diffuse)
723.4	Brachial neuritis or radiculitis nos
729.2	Unspecified neuralgia, neuritis, and radiculitis
736.05	Wrist drop (acquired)
736.06	Claw hand (acquired)
736.07	Club hand, acquired
736.74	Claw foot, acquired
951.0	Injury to oculomotor nerve
951.1	Injury to trochlear nerve
951.2	Injury to trigeminal nerve
951.3	Injury to abducens nerve
951.4	Injury to facial nerve
951.6	Injury to accessory nerve
951.7	Injury to hypoglossal nerve
951.8	Injury to other specified cranial nerves
951.9	Injury to unspecified cranial nerve
*953	Injury to nerve roots and spinal plexus
*954	Injury to other nerve(s) of trunk, excluding shoulder and pelvic girdles
*955	Injury to peripheral nerve(s) of shoulder girdle and upper limb
*956	Injury to peripheral nerve(s) of pelvic girdle and lower limb
*957	Injury to other and unspecified nerves

Ⓜ DRG 019 Cranial and Peripheral Nerve Disorders without CC

GMLOS 2.7 AMLOS 3.5 RW 0.7077 ☑🅃

Select principal diagnosis listed under DRG 018

Ⓜ DRG 020 Nervous System Infection Except Viral Meningitis

GMLOS 8.0 AMLOS 10.4 RW 2.7865 ☑🅃

Principal Diagnosis

003.21	Salmonella meningitis
006.5	Amebic brain abscess
*013	Tuberculosis of meninges and central nervous system
036.0	Meningococcal meningitis
036.1	Meningococcal encephalitis
*045.0	Acute paralytic poliomyelitis specified as bulbar
*045.1	Acute poliomyelitis with other paralysis
*045.9	Acute unspecified poliomyelitis
049.8	Other specified non-arthropod-borne viral diseases of central nervous system
049.9	Unspecified non-arthropod-borne viral disease of central nervous system
052.0	Postvaricella encephalitis
054.3	Herpetic meningoencephalitis
055.0	Postmeasles encephalitis
056.01	Encephalomyelitis due to rubella
056.09	Other neurological rubella complications
*062	Mosquito-borne viral encephalitis
*063	Tick-borne viral encephalitis
064	Viral encephalitis transmitted by other and unspecified arthropods
066.2	Venezuelan equine fever
071	Rabies
072.2	Mumps encephalitis
*090.4	Juvenile neurosyphilis
091.81	Early syphilis, acute syphilitic meningitis (secondary)
094.2	Syphilitic meningitis
094.3	Asymptomatic neurosyphilis
094.81	Syphilitic encephalitis
098.82	Gonococcal meningitis
*100.8	Other specified leptospiral infections

MDC 1: Nervous System — Medical

112.83	Candidal meningitis
114.2	Coccidioidal meningitis
115.01	Histoplasma capsulatum meningitis
115.11	Histoplasma duboisii meningitis
115.91	Unspecified Histoplasmosis meningitis
130.0	Meningoencephalitis due to toxoplasmosis
*320	Bacterial meningitis
*321	Meningitis due to other organisms
*322	Meningitis of unspecified cause
323.0	Encephalitis in viral diseases classified elsewhere
323.1	Encephalitis in rickettsial diseases classified elsewhere
323.2	Encephalitis in protozoal diseases classified elsewhere
323.4	Other encephalitis due to infection classified elsewhere
323.5	Encephalitis following immunization procedures
323.6	Postinfectious encephalitis
323.8	Other causes of encephalitis
323.9	Unspecified cause of encephalitis
*324	Intracranial and intraspinal abscess
357.0	Acute infective polyneuritis

M DRG 021 Viral Meningitis

GMLOS 4.9 AMLOS 6.3 RW 1.4451 ☑

Principal Diagnosis

*047	Meningitis due to enterovirus
048	Other enterovirus diseases of central nervous system
049.0	Lymphocytic choriomeningitis
049.1	Meningitis due to adenovirus
053.0	Herpes zoster with meningitis
054.72	Herpes simplex meningitis
072.1	Mumps meningitis

M DRG 022 Hypertensive Encephalopathy

GMLOS 4.0 AMLOS 5.2 RW 1.1304 ☑

Principal Diagnosis

437.2	Hypertensive encephalopathy

M DRG 023 Nontraumatic Stupor and Coma

GMLOS 3.0 AMLOS 3.9 RW 0.7712 ☑

Principal Diagnosis

348.4	Compression of brain
348.5	Cerebral edema
780.01	Coma
780.03	Persistent vegetative state
780.09	Other alteration of consciousness

M DRG 024 Seizure and Headache, Age Greater than 17 with CC

GMLOS 3.6 AMLOS 4.8 RW 0.9970 ☑ T CC A

Principal Diagnosis

307.81	Tension headache
310.2	Postconcussion syndrome
*345	Epilepsy
*346	Migraine
348.2	Benign intracranial hypertension
349.0	Reaction to spinal or lumbar puncture
437.4	Cerebral arteritis
*780.3	Convulsions
784.0	Headache

MDC 1: Nervous System — Medical

Code Range ☑ *Optimization Potential* *Targeted Potential* T *Transfer DRG* SP *Special Payment*

Ⓜ DRG 025 Seizure and Headache, Age Greater than 17 without CC

GMLOS 2.5 AMLOS 3.1 RW 0.6180 ☑Ⓣ Ⓐ

Select principal diagnosis listed under DRG 024

Ⓜ DRG 026 Seizure and Headache, Age 0-17

GMLOS 3.4 AMLOS 6.3 RW 1.8191 ☑Ⓐ

Select principal diagnosis listed under DRG 024

Ⓜ DRG 027 Traumatic Stupor and Coma, Coma Greater than One Hour

GMLOS 3.2 AMLOS 5.2 RW 1.3531 ☑

Principal Diagnosis of Traumatic Stupor and Coma

*800	Fracture of vault of skull
*801	Fracture of base of skull
*803	Other and unqualified skull fractures
*804	Multiple fractures involving skull or face with other bones
*851	Cerebral laceration and contusion
*852	Subarachnoid, subdural, and extradural hemorrhage, following injury
*853	Other and unspecified intracranial hemorrhage following injury
*854	Intracranial injury of other and unspecified nature

AND

Principal or Secondary Diagnosis of Coma > 1 hour

Above listed diagnoses with a description of loss of consciousness greater than one hour or of unspecified duration

Ⓜ DRG 028 Traumatic Stupor and Coma, Coma Less than One Hour, Age Greater than 17 with CC

GMLOS 4.4 AMLOS 5.9 RW 1.3353 ☑Ⓣ Ⓒ Ⓐ

Select principal diagnosis listed under DRG 027 excluding those with loss of consciousness of greater than one hour or of unspecified duration

Ⓜ DRG 029 Traumatic Stupor and Coma, Coma Less than One Hour, Age Greater than 17 without CC

GMLOS 2.6 AMLOS 3.4 RW 0.7212 ☑Ⓣ Ⓐ

Select principal diagnosis listed under DRG 027 excluding those with loss of consciousness of greater than one hour or of unspecified duration

Ⓜ DRG 030 Traumatic Stupor and Coma, Coma Less than One Hour, Age 0-17

GMLOS 2.0 AMLOS 2.0 RW 0.3359 ☑Ⓐ

Select principal diagnosis listed under DRG 027 excluding those with loss of consciousness of greater than one hour or of unspecified duration

Ⓜ DRG 031 Concussion, Age Greater than 17 with CC

GMLOS 3.0 AMLOS 4.0 RW 0.9567 ☑Ⓒ Ⓐ

Principal Diagnosis

*850 Concussion

Ⓜ DRG 032 Concussion, Age Greater than 17 without CC

GMLOS 1.9 AMLOS 2.4 RW 0.6194 ☑Ⓐ

Principal Diagnosis

*850 Concussion

Ⓜ DRG 033 Concussion, Age 0-17

GMLOS 1.6 AMLOS 1.6 RW 0.2109 ☑Ⓐ

Principal Diagnosis

*850 Concussion

Ⓜ DRG 034 Other Disorders of Nervous System with CC

GMLOS 3.7 AMLOS 4.8 RW 1.0062 ☑Ⓣ🅲🅲

Principal Diagnosis

078.81 Epidemic vertigo
094.87 Syphilitic ruptured cerebral aneurysm
137.1 Late effects of central nervous system tuberculosis
138 Late effects of acute poliomyelitis
139.0 Late effects of viral encephalitis
228.02 Hemangioma of intracranial structures
237.70 Neurofibromatosis, unspecified
237.71 Neurofibromatosis, Type 1 (von Recklinghausen's disease)
237.72 Neurofibromatosis, Type 2 (acoustic neurofibromatosis)
*307.2 Tics
323.7 Toxic encephalitis
325 Phlebitis and thrombophlebitis of intracranial venous sinuses
326 Late effects of intracranial abscess or pyogenic infection
327.21 Primary central sleep apnea
327.25 Congenital central alveolar hypoventilation syndrome
327.27 Central sleep apnea in conditions classified elsewhere
*327.3 Circadian rhythm sleep disorder
327.41 Confusional arousals
327.43 Recurrent isolated sleep paralysis
327.51 Periodic limb movement disorder
327.52 Sleep related leg cramps
331.81 Reye's syndrome
333.1 Essential and other specified forms of tremor
333.2 Myoclonus
333.3 Tics of organic origin
333.82 Orofacial dyskinesia
333.83 Spasmodic torticollis
333.84 Organic writers' cramp
333.89 Other fragments of torsion dystonia
333.91 Stiff-man syndrome
333.92 Neuroleptic malignant syndrome
333.93 Benign shuddering attacks
336.1 Vascular myelopathies
336.2 Subacute combined degeneration of spinal cord in diseases classified elsewhere
336.3 Myelopathy in other diseases classified elsewhere
336.8 Other myelopathy
336.9 Unspecified disease of spinal cord
343.3 Monoplegic infantile cerebral palsy
343.8 Other specified infantile cerebral palsy
343.9 Unspecified infantile cerebral palsy
*344.3 Monoplegia of lower limb
*344.4 Monoplegia of upper limb
344.5 Unspecified monoplegia
*344.8 Other specified paralytic syndromes
344.9 Unspecified paralysis
*347 Cataplexy and narcolepsy
348.0 Cerebral cysts
348.1 Anoxic brain damage
349.1 Nervous system complications from surgically implanted device
349.2 Disorders of meninges, not elsewhere classified
349.81 Cerebrospinal fluid rhinorrhea
349.82 Toxic encephalopathy
356.3 Refsum's disease

DRG 034 — continued

*359	Muscular dystrophies and other myopathies
377.00	Unspecified papilledema
377.01	Papilledema associated with increased intracranial pressure
377.04	Foster-Kennedy syndrome
*377.5	Disorders of optic chiasm
*377.6	Disorders of other visual pathways
*377.7	Disorders of visual cortex
377.9	Unspecified disorder of optic nerve and visual pathways
378.86	Internuclear ophthalmoplegia
388.61	Cerebrospinal fluid otorrhea
437.3	Cerebral aneurysm, nonruptured
437.5	Moyamoya disease
437.6	Nonpyogenic thrombosis of intracranial venous sinus
*740	Anencephalus and similar anomalies
*741	Spina bifida
*742	Other congenital anomalies of nervous system
747.81	Congenital anomaly of cerebrovascular system
747.82	Congenital spinal vessel anomaly
756.17	Spina bifida occulta
759.5	Tuberous sclerosis
779.7	Periventricular leukomalacia
780.51	Insomnia with sleep apnea, unspecified
780.53	Hypersomnia with sleep apnea, unspecified
780.57	Unspecified sleep apnea
781.0	Abnormal involuntary movements
781.1	Disturbances of sensation of smell and taste
781.2	Abnormality of gait
781.3	Lack of coordination
781.4	Transient paralysis of limb
781.6	Meningismus
781.8	Neurological neglect syndrome
781.91	Loss of height
781.92	Abnormal posture
781.94	Facial weakness
781.99	Other symptoms involving nervous and musculoskeletal systems
782.0	Disturbance of skin sensation
784.3	Aphasia
784.5	Other speech disturbance
792.0	Nonspecific abnormal finding in cerebrospinal fluid
793.0	Nonspecific abnormal findings on radiological and other examination of skull and head
*794.0	Nonspecific abnormal results of function study of brain and central nervous system
794.10	Nonspecific abnormal response to unspecified nerve stimulation
794.19	Other nonspecific abnormal result of function study of peripheral nervous system and special senses
796.1	Abnormal reflex
798.0	Sudden infant death syndrome
905.0	Late effect of fracture of skull and face bones
907.0	Late effect of intracranial injury without mention of skull fracture
907.1	Late effect of injury to cranial nerve
907.3	Late effect of injury to nerve root(s), spinal plexus(es), and other nerves of trunk
907.4	Late effect of injury to peripheral nerve of shoulder girdle and upper limb
907.5	Late effect of injury to peripheral nerve of pelvic girdle and lower limb
907.9	Late effect of injury to other and unspecified nerve
950.1	Injury to optic chiasm
950.2	Injury to optic pathways
950.3	Injury to visual cortex
950.9	Injury to unspecified optic nerve and pathways
996.2	Mechanical complication of nervous system device, implant, and graft
996.63	Infection and inflammatory reaction due to nervous system device, implant, and graft
996.75	Other complications due to nervous system device, implant, and graft
*997.0	Nervous system complications
*V53.0	Fitting and adjustment of devices related to nervous system and special senses

Ⓜ DRG 035 Other Disorders of Nervous System without CC

GMLOS 2.4 AMLOS 3.0 RW 0.6241 ☑ T

Select principal diagnosis listed under DRG 034

Ⓜ DRG 524 Transient Ischemia

GMLOS 2.6 AMLOS 3.2 RW 0.7288 ☑

Principal Diagnosis

*435	Transient cerebral ischemia
437.1	Other generalized ischemic cerebrovascular disease

● Ⓜ DRG 559 Acute Ischemic Stroke with Use of Thrombolytic Agent

GMLOS 5.8 AMLOS 7.2 RW 2.2473

Principal Diagnosis

433.01	Occlusion and stenosis of basilar artery with cerebral infarction
433.11	Occlusion and stenosis of carotid artery with cerebral infarction
433.21	Occlusion and stenosis of vertebral artery with cerebral infarction
433.31	Occlusion and stenosis of multiple and bilateral precerebral arteries with cerebral infarction
433.81	Occlusion and stenosis of other specified precerebral artery with cerebral infarction
433.91	Occlusion and stenosis of unspecified precerebral artery with cerebral infarction
434.01	Cerebral thrombosis with cerebral infarction
434.11	Cerebral embolism with cerebral infarction
434.91	Unspecified cerebral artery occlusion with cerebral infarction

AND

Nonoperating Room Procedure

99.10	Injection or infusion of thrombolytic agent

MDC 2
DISEASES AND DISORDERS OF THE EYE

The complete and up-to-date listing of ICD-9-CM diagnosis codes assigned to this MDC can be found online at www.ingenixonline.com/content/drg/resources.asp.

SURGICAL

S DRG 036 Retinal Procedures
GMLOS 1.3 AMLOS 1.6 RW 0.7288 ☑

Operating Room Procedures

14.21	Destruction of chorioretinal lesion by diathermy
14.22	Destruction of chorioretinal lesion by cryotherapy
14.26	Destruction of chorioretinal lesion by radiation therapy
14.27	Destruction of chorioretinal lesion by implantation of radiation source
14.29	Other destruction of chorioretinal lesion
14.31	Repair of retinal tear by diathermy
14.32	Repair of retinal tear by cryotherapy
14.39	Other repair of retinal tear
*14.4	Repair of retinal detachment with scleral buckling and implant
*14.5	Other repair of retinal detachment
14.9	Other operations on retina, choroid, and posterior chamber

S DRG 037 Orbital Procedures
GMLOS 2.7 AMLOS 4.2 RW 1.1858

Operating Room Procedures

*16.0	Orbitotomy
16.22	Diagnostic aspiration of orbit
16.23	Biopsy of eyeball and orbit
16.29	Other diagnostic procedures on orbit and eyeball
*16.3	Evisceration of eyeball
*16.4	Enucleation of eyeball
*16.5	Exenteration of orbital contents
*16.6	Secondary procedures after removal of eyeball
*16.7	Removal of ocular or orbital implant
*16.8	Repair of injury of eyeball and orbit
16.92	Excision of lesion of orbit
16.98	Other operations on orbit
76.46	Other reconstruction of other facial bone
76.79	Other open reduction of facial fracture
76.91	Bone graft to facial bone
76.92	Insertion of synthetic implant in facial bone

S DRG 038 Primary Iris Procedures
GMLOS 2.5 AMLOS 3.5 RW 0.6975

Operating Room Procedures

*12.1	Iridotomy and simple iridectomy
12.22	Biopsy of iris
12.31	Lysis of goniosynechiae
12.32	Lysis of other anterior synechiae
12.33	Lysis of posterior synechiae
12.40	Removal of lesion of anterior segment of eye, not otherwise specified
12.41	Destruction of lesion of iris, nonexcisional
12.42	Excision of lesion of iris
12.55	Cyclodialysis
12.59	Other facilitation of intraocular circulation
*12.7	Other procedures for relief of elevated intraocular pressure
12.97	Other operations on iris

[S] DRG 039 Lens Procedures with or without Vitrectomy

GMLOS 1.7 AMLOS 2.4 RW 0.7108 ☑

Operating Room Procedures

*12.0	Removal of intraocular foreign body from anterior segment of eye
*13	Operations on lens

WITH OR WITHOUT

Operating Room Procedures

12.91	Therapeutic evacuation of anterior chamber
12.92	Injection into anterior chamber
*14.7	Operations on vitreous

[S] DRG 040 Extraocular Procedures Except Orbit, Age Greater than 17

GMLOS 3.0 AMLOS 4.1 RW 0.9627 ☑ [A]

Operating Room Procedures

08.11	Biopsy of eyelid
*08.2	Excision or destruction of lesion or tissue of eyelid
*08.3	Repair of blepharoptosis and lid retraction
*08.4	Repair of entropion or ectropion
*08.5	Other adjustment of lid position
*08.6	Reconstruction of eyelid with flaps or grafts
*08.7	Other reconstruction of eyelid
*08.9	Other operations on eyelids
*09	Operations on lacrimal system
*10	Operations on conjunctiva
11.0	Magnetic removal of embedded foreign body from cornea
*11.2	Diagnostic procedures on cornea
*11.3	Excision of pterygium
*11.4	Excision or destruction of tissue or other lesion of cornea
11.61	Lamellar keratoplasty with autograft
11.62	Other lamellar keratoplasty
11.71	Keratomileusis
11.72	Keratophakia
11.74	Thermokeratoplasty
11.76	Epikeratophakia
11.91	Tattooing of cornea
12.84	Excision or destruction of lesion of sclera
12.87	Scleral reinforcement with graft
12.88	Other scleral reinforcement
12.89	Other operations on sclera
14.6	Removal of surgically implanted material from posterior segment of eye
*15	Operations on extraocular muscles
16.93	Excision of lesion of eye, unspecified structure
16.99	Other operations on eyeball
38.21	Biopsy of blood vessel
86.22	Excisional debridement of wound, infection, or burn
86.4	Radical excision of skin lesion
95.04	Eye examination under anesthesia

[S] DRG 041 Extraocular Procedures Except Orbit, Age 0-17

GMLOS 1.6 AMLOS 1.6 RW 0.3419 ☑ [A]

Select operating room procedures listed under DRG 040

[S] DRG 042 Intraocular Procedures Except Retina, Iris and Lens

GMLOS 2.0 AMLOS 2.8 RW 0.7852 ☑

Operating Room Procedures

11.1	Incision of cornea
*11.5	Repair of cornea
11.60	Corneal transplant, not otherwise specified

** Code Range* ☑ *Optimization Potential* *Targeted Potential* [T] *Transfer DRG* [SP] *Special Payment*

DRG 042 — continued

11.63	Penetrating keratoplasty with autograft
11.64	Other penetrating keratoplasty
11.69	Other corneal transplant
11.73	Keratoprosthesis
11.75	Radial keratotomy
11.79	Other reconstructive surgery on cornea
11.92	Removal of artificial implant from cornea
11.99	Other operations on cornea
12.21	Diagnostic aspiration of anterior chamber of eye
12.29	Other diagnostic procedures on iris, ciliary body, sclera, and anterior chamber
12.34	Lysis of corneovitreal adhesions
12.35	Coreoplasty
12.39	Other iridoplasty
12.43	Destruction of lesion of ciliary body, nonexcisional
12.44	Excision of lesion of ciliary body
12.51	Goniopuncture without goniotomy
12.52	Goniotomy without goniopuncture
12.53	Goniotomy with goniopuncture
12.54	Trabeculotomy ab externo
*12.6	Scleral fistulization
12.81	Suture of laceration of sclera
12.82	Repair of scleral fistula
12.83	Revision of operative wound of anterior segment, not elsewhere classified
12.85	Repair of scleral staphyloma with graft
12.86	Other repair of scleral staphyloma
12.93	Removal or destruction of epithelial downgrowth from anterior chamber
12.98	Other operations on ciliary body
12.99	Other operations on anterior chamber
*14.0	Removal of foreign body from posterior segment of eye
*14.1	Diagnostic procedures on retina, choroid, vitreous, and posterior chamber
16.1	Removal of penetrating foreign body from eye, not otherwise specified

OR

Operating Room Procedures

12.91	Therapeutic evacuation of anterior chamber
12.92	Injection into anterior chamber
*14.7	Operations on vitreous

MDC 2: Eye — Surgical

MDC 2
DISEASES AND DISORDERS OF THE EYE

The complete and up-to-date listing of ICD-9-CM diagnosis codes assigned to this MDC can be found online at www.ingenixonline.com/content/drg/resources.asp.

MEDICAL

[M] DRG 043 Hyphema

GMLOS 2.4 AMLOS 3.1 RW 0.6141 ☑

Principal Diagnosis

364.41	Hyphema
921.1	Contusion of eyelids and periocular area
921.3	Contusion of eyeball

[M] DRG 044 Acute Major Eye Infections

GMLOS 3.9 AMLOS 4.8 RW 0.6874 ☑

Principal Diagnosis

360.00	Unspecified purulent endophthalmitis
360.01	Acute endophthalmitis
360.02	Panophthalmitis
360.04	Vitreous abscess
360.13	Parasitic endophthalmitis NOS
360.19	Other endophthalmitis
370.00	Unspecified corneal ulcer
370.03	Central corneal ulcer
370.04	Hypopyon ulcer
370.05	Mycotic corneal ulcer
370.06	Perforated corneal ulcer
370.55	Corneal abscess
375.01	Acute dacryoadenitis
375.31	Acute canaliculitis, lacrimal
375.32	Acute dacryocystitis
376.01	Orbital cellulitis
376.02	Orbital periostitis
376.03	Orbital osteomyelitis
376.04	Orbital tenonitis

[M] DRG 045 Neurological Eye Disorders

GMLOS 2.5 AMLOS 3.1 RW 0.7474

Principal Diagnosis

036.81	Meningococcal optic neuritis
*362.3	Retinal vascular occlusion
365.12	Low tension open-angle glaucoma
367.52	Total or complete internal ophthalmoplegia
368.11	Sudden visual loss
368.12	Transient visual loss
368.2	Diplopia
368.40	Unspecified visual field defect
368.41	Scotoma involving central area in visual field
368.43	Sector or arcuate defects in visual field
368.44	Other localized visual field defect
368.45	Generalized contraction or constriction in visual field
368.46	Homonymous bilateral field defects in visual field
368.47	Heteronymous bilateral field defects in visual field
368.55	Acquired color vision deficiencies
374.30	Unspecified ptosis of eyelid
374.31	Paralytic ptosis
374.32	Myogenic ptosis

*Code Range ☑ Optimization Potential [YIELD] Targeted Potential [T] Transfer DRG [SP] Special Payment

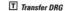

DRG 045 — continued

374.45	Other sensorimotor disorders of eyelid
376.34	Intermittent exophthalmos
376.35	Pulsating exophthalmos
376.36	Lateral displacement of globe of eye
376.82	Myopathy of extraocular muscles
377.10	Unspecified optic atrophy
377.11	Primary optic atrophy
377.12	Postinflammatory optic atrophy
377.15	Partial optic atrophy
377.16	Hereditary optic atrophy
377.21	Drusen of optic disc
377.24	Pseudopapilledema
*377.3	Optic neuritis
*377.4	Other disorders of optic nerve
*378.5	Paralytic strabismus
378.72	Progressive external ophthalmoplegia
378.73	Strabismus in other neuromuscular disorders
378.87	Other dissociated deviation of eye movements
379.40	Unspecified abnormal pupillary function
379.41	Anisocoria
379.42	Miosis (persistent), not due to miotics
379.43	Mydriasis (persistent), not due to mydriatics
379.46	Tonic pupillary reaction
379.49	Other anomaly of pupillary function
379.50	Unspecified nystagmus
379.52	Latent nystagmus
379.54	Nystagmus associated with disorders of the vestibular system
379.55	Dissociated nystagmus
379.57	Nystagmus with deficiencies of saccadic eye movements
379.58	Nystagmus with deficiencies of smooth pursuit movements

M DRG 046 Other Disorders of the Eye, Age Greater than 17 with CC

GMLOS 3.2 AMLOS 4.2 RW 0.7524 CC A

Principal Diagnosis

*017.3	Tuberculosis of eye
032.81	Conjunctival diphtheria
*053.2	Herpes zoster with ophthalmic complications
*054.4	Herpes simplex with ophthalmic complications
055.71	Measles keratoconjunctivitis
*076	Trachoma
*077	Other diseases of conjunctiva due to viruses and Chlamydiae
090.3	Syphilitic interstitial keratitis
*091.5	Early syphilis, uveitis due to secondary syphilis
094.83	Syphilitic disseminated retinochoroiditis
094.84	Syphilitic optic atrophy
095.0	Syphilitic episcleritis
*098.4	Gonococcal infection of eye
098.81	Gonococcal keratosis (blennorrhagica)
115.02	Histoplasma capsulatum retinitis
115.12	Histoplasma duboisii retinitis
115.92	Unspecified Histoplasmosis retinitis
130.1	Conjunctivitis due to toxoplasmosis
130.2	Chorioretinitis due to toxoplasmosis
139.1	Late effects of trachoma
172.1	Malignant melanoma of skin of eyelid, including canthus
173.1	Other malignant neoplasm of skin of eyelid, including canthus
*190	Malignant neoplasm of eye
216.1	Benign neoplasm of eyelid, including canthus
*224	Benign neoplasm of eye
228.03	Hemangioma of retina
232.1	Carcinoma in situ of eyelid, including canthus

234.0	Carcinoma in situ of eye
*250.5	Diabetes with ophthalmic manifestations
264.0	Vitamin A deficiency with conjunctival xerosis
264.1	Vitamin A deficiency with conjunctival xerosis and Bitot's spot
264.2	Vitamin A deficiency with corneal xerosis
264.3	Vitamin A deficiency with corneal ulceration and xerosis
264.4	Vitamin A deficiency with keratomalacia
264.5	Vitamin A deficiency with night blindness
264.6	Vitamin A deficiency with xerophthalmic scars of cornea
264.7	Other ocular manifestations of vitamin A deficiency
333.81	Blepharospasm
360.03	Chronic endophthalmitis
360.11	Sympathetic uveitis
360.12	Panuveitis
360.14	Ophthalmia nodosa
*360.2	Degenerative disorders of globe
*360.3	Hypotony of eye
*360.4	Degenerated conditions of globe
*360.5	Retained (old) intraocular foreign body, magnetic
*360.6	Retained (old) intraocular foreign body, nonmagnetic
*360.8	Other disorders of globe
360.9	Unspecified disorder of globe
*361.0	Retinal detachment with retinal defect
*361.1	Retinoschisis and retinal cysts
361.2	Serous retinal detachment
*361.3	Retinal defects without detachment
*361.8	Other forms of retinal detachment
361.9	Unspecified retinal detachment
*362.0	Diabetic retinopathy
*362.1	Other background retinopathy and retinal vascular changes
*362.2	Other proliferative retinopathy
*362.4	Separation of retinal layers
*362.5	Degeneration of macula and posterior pole of retina
*362.6	Peripheral retinal degenerations
*362.7	Hereditary retinal dystrophies
*362.8	Other retinal disorders
362.9	Unspecified retinal disorder
*363	Chorioretinal inflammations, scars, and other disorders of choroid
*364.0	Acute and subacute iridocyclitis
*364.1	Chronic iridocyclitis
*364.2	Certain types of iridocyclitis
364.3	Unspecified iridocyclitis
364.42	Rubeosis iridis
*364.5	Degenerations of iris and ciliary body
*364.6	Cysts of iris, ciliary body, and anterior chamber
*364.7	Adhesions and disruptions of iris and ciliary body
364.8	Other disorders of iris and ciliary body
364.9	Unspecified disorder of iris and ciliary body
*365.0	Borderline glaucoma (glaucoma suspect)
365.10	Unspecified open-angle glaucoma
365.11	Primary open-angle glaucoma
365.13	Pigmentary open-angle glaucoma
365.14	Open-angle glaucoma of childhood
365.15	Residual stage of open angle glaucoma
*365.2	Primary angle-closure glaucoma
*365.3	Corticosteroid-induced glaucoma
*365.4	Glaucoma associated with congenital anomalies, dystrophies, and systemic syndromes
*365.5	Glaucoma associated with disorders of the lens
*365.6	Glaucoma associated with other ocular disorders
*365.8	Other specified forms of glaucoma
365.9	Unspecified glaucoma
*366	Cataract
367.0	Hypermetropia

DRG 046 — continued

367.1	Myopia
*367.2	Astigmatism
*367.3	Anisometropia and aniseikonia
367.4	Presbyopia
367.51	Paresis of accommodation
367.53	Spasm of accommodation
*367.8	Other disorders of refraction and accommodation
367.9	Unspecified disorder of refraction and accommodation
*368.0	Amblyopia ex anopsia
368.10	Unspecified subjective visual disturbance
368.13	Visual discomfort
368.14	Visual distortions of shape and size
368.15	Other visual distortions and entoptic phenomena
368.16	Psychophysical visual disturbances
*368.3	Other disorders of binocular vision
368.42	Scotoma of blind spot area in visual field
368.51	Protan defect in color vision
368.52	Deutan defect in color vision
368.53	Tritan defect in color vision
368.54	Achromatopsia
368.59	Other color vision deficiencies
*368.6	Night blindness
368.8	Other specified visual disturbances
368.9	Unspecified visual disturbance
*369	Blindness and low vision
370.01	Marginal corneal ulcer
370.02	Ring corneal ulcer
370.07	Mooren's ulcer
*370.2	Superficial keratitis without conjunctivitis
*370.3	Certain types of keratoconjunctivitis
*370.4	Other and unspecified keratoconjunctivitis
370.50	Unspecified interstitial keratitis
370.52	Diffuse interstitial keratitis
370.54	Sclerosing keratitis
370.59	Other interstitial and deep keratitis
*370.6	Corneal neovascularization
370.8	Other forms of keratitis
370.9	Unspecified keratitis
*371	Corneal opacity and other disorders of cornea
*372	Disorders of conjunctiva
*373	Inflammation of eyelids
*374.0	Entropion and trichiasis of eyelid
*374.1	Ectropion
*374.2	Lagophthalmos
374.33	Mechanical ptosis
374.34	Blepharochalasis
374.41	Eyelid retraction or lag
374.43	Abnormal innervation syndrome of eyelid
374.44	Sensory disorders of eyelid
374.46	Blepharophimosis
374.50	Unspecified degenerative disorder of eyelid
374.52	Hyperpigmentation of eyelid
374.53	Hypopigmentation of eyelid
374.54	Hypertrichosis of eyelid
374.55	Hypotrichosis of eyelid
374.56	Other degenerative disorders of skin affecting eyelid
*374.8	Other disorders of eyelid
374.9	Unspecified disorder of eyelid
375.00	Unspecified dacryoadenitis
375.02	Chronic dacryoadenitis
375.03	Chronic enlargement of lacrimal gland
*375.1	Other disorders of lacrimal gland

*375.2	Epiphora
375.30	Unspecified dacryocystitis
375.33	Phlegmonous dacryocystitis
*375.4	Chronic inflammation of lacrimal passages
*375.5	Stenosis and insufficiency of lacrimal passages
*375.6	Other changes of lacrimal passages
*375.8	Other disorders of lacrimal system
375.9	Unspecified disorder of lacrimal system
376.00	Unspecified acute inflammation of orbit
*376.1	Chronic inflammatory disorders of orbit
*376.2	Endocrine exophthalmos
376.30	Unspecified exophthalmos
376.31	Constant exophthalmos
376.32	Orbital hemorrhage
376.33	Orbital edema or congestion
*376.4	Deformity of orbit
*376.5	Enophthalmos
376.6	Retained (old) foreign body following penetrating wound of orbit
376.81	Orbital cysts
376.89	Other orbital disorder
376.9	Unspecified disorder of orbit
377.02	Papilledema associated with decreased ocular pressure
377.03	Papilledema associated with retinal disorder
377.13	Optic atrophy associated with retinal dystrophies
377.14	Glaucomatous atrophy (cupping) of optic disc
377.22	Crater-like holes of optic disc
377.23	Coloboma of optic disc
*378.0	Esotropia
*378.1	Exotropia
*378.2	Intermittent heterotropia
*378.3	Other and unspecified heterotropia
*378.4	Heterophoria
*378.6	Mechanical strabismus
378.71	Duane's syndrome
378.81	Palsy of conjugate gaze
378.82	Spasm of conjugate gaze
378.83	Convergence insufficiency or palsy in binocular eye movement
378.84	Convergence excess or spasm in binocular eye movement
378.85	Anomalies of divergence in binocular eye movement
378.9	Unspecified disorder of eye movements
*379.0	Scleritis and episcleritis
*379.1	Other disorders of sclera
*379.2	Disorders of vitreous body
*379.3	Aphakia and other disorders of lens
379.51	Congenital nystagmus
379.53	Visual deprivation nystagmus
379.56	Other forms of nystagmus
379.59	Other irregularities of eye movements
379.8	Other specified disorders of eye and adnexa
*379.9	Unspecified disorder of eye and adnexa
694.61	Benign mucous membrane pemphigoid with ocular involvement
*743	Congenital anomalies of eye
794.11	Nonspecific abnormal retinal function studies
794.12	Nonspecific abnormal electro-oculogram (EOG)
794.13	Nonspecific abnormal visually evoked potential
794.14	Nonspecific abnormal oculomotor studies
802.6	Orbital floor (blow-out), closed fracture
802.7	Orbital floor (blow-out), open fracture
*870	Open wound of ocular adnexa
*871	Open wound of eyeball
*918	Superficial injury of eye and adnexa
921.0	Black eye, not otherwise specified
921.2	Contusion of orbital tissues

**** Code Range*** ☑ ***Optimization Potential*** ▽ ***Targeted Potential*** 🅃 ***Transfer DRG*** SP ***Special Payment***

DRG 046 — continued

921.9	Unspecified contusion of eye
*930	Foreign body on external eye
*940	Burn confined to eye and adnexa
941.02	Burn of unspecified degree of eye (with other parts of face, head, and neck)
941.12	Erythema due to burn (first degree) of eye (with other parts face, head, and neck)
941.22	Blisters, with epidermal loss due to burn (second degree) of eye (with other parts of face, head, and neck)
941.32	Full-thickness skin loss due to burn (third degree nos) of eye (with other parts of face, head, and neck)
941.42	Deep necrosis of underlying tissues due to burn (deep third degree) of eye (with other parts of face, head, and neck), without mention of loss of a body part
941.52	Deep necrosis of underlying tissues due to burn (deep third degree) of eye (with other parts of face, head, and neck), with loss of a body part
950.0	Optic nerve injury
976.5	Poisoning by eye anti-infectives and other eye drugs
996.51	Mechanical complication due to corneal graft
996.53	Mechanical complication due to ocular lens prosthesis
998.82	Cataract fragments in eye following surgery
V42.5	Cornea replaced by transplant
V43.0	Eye globe replaced by other means
V43.1	Lens replaced by other means
V45.78	Acquired absence of organ, eye

M DRG 047 Other Disorders of the Eye, Age Greater than 17 without CC

GMLOS 2.3 AMLOS 2.9 RW 0.5203 ☑A

Select principal diagnosis listed under DRG 046

M DRG 048 Other Disorders of the Eye, Age 0-17

GMLOS 2.9 AMLOS 2.9 RW 0.3012 ☑A

Select principal diagnosis listed under DRG 046

MDC 2: Eye — Medical

MDC 3
DISEASES AND DISORDERS OF THE EAR, NOSE, MOUTH AND THROAT

The complete and up-to-date listing of ICD-9-CM diagnosis codes assigned to this MDC can be found online at www.ingenixonline.com/content/drg/resources.asp.

SURGICAL

S DRG 049 Major Head and Neck Procedures

GMLOS 3.1 AMLOS 4.4 RW 1.6361 ☑

Operating Room Procedures

20.96	Implantation or replacement of cochlear prosthetic device, not otherwise specified
20.97	Implantation or replacement of cochlear prosthetic device, single channel
20.98	Implantation or replacement of cochlear prosthetic device, multiple channel
25.3	Complete glossectomy
25.4	Radical glossectomy
27.32	Wide excision or destruction of lesion or tissue of bony palate
30.1	Hemilaryngectomy
30.29	Other partial laryngectomy
40.40	Radical neck dissection, not otherwise specified
40.41	Radical neck dissection, unilateral
40.42	Radical neck dissection, bilateral
40.50	Radical excision of lymph nodes, not otherwise specified
40.59	Radical excision of other lymph nodes
76.31	Partial mandibulectomy
76.41	Total mandibulectomy with synchronous reconstruction
76.42	Other total mandibulectomy

S DRG 050 Sialoadenectomy

GMLOS 1.5 AMLOS 1.8 RW 0.8690 ☑

Operating Room Procedures

*26.3	Sialoadenectomy

S DRG 051 Salivary Gland Procedures Except Sialoadenectomy

GMLOS 1.9 AMLOS 2.8 RW 0.8809

Operating Room Procedures

26.12	Open biopsy of salivary gland or duct
*26.2	Excision of lesion of salivary gland
*26.4	Repair of salivary gland or duct
26.99	Other operations on salivary gland or duct

S DRG 052 Cleft Lip and Palate Repair

GMLOS 1.5 AMLOS 1.9 RW 0.8348

Operating Room Procedures

27.54	Repair of cleft lip
27.62	Correction of cleft palate
27.63	Revision of cleft palate repair
27.69	Other plastic repair of palate

S DRG 053 Sinus and Mastoid Procedures, Age Greater than 17

GMLOS 2.4 AMLOS 3.9 RW 1.3269 A

Operating Room Procedures

20.21	Incision of mastoid
20.22	Incision of petrous pyramid air cells
*20.4	Mastoidectomy

** Code Range ☑ Optimization Potential ▽ Targeted Potential T Transfer DRG SP Special Payment*

DRG 053 — continued

20.92	Revision of mastoidectomy
22.12	Open biopsy of nasal sinus
*22.3	External maxillary antrotomy
*22.4	Frontal sinusotomy and sinusectomy
*22.5	Other nasal sinusotomy
*22.6	Other nasal sinusectomy
*22.7	Repair of nasal sinus
22.9	Other operations on nasal sinuses

S DRG 054 Sinus and Mastoid Procedures, Age 0-17

GMLOS 3.2 AMLOS 3.2 RW 0.4882 A

Select operating room procedures listed under DRG 053

S DRG 055 Miscellaneous Ear, Nose, Mouth and Throat Procedures

GMLOS 2.0 AMLOS 3.1 RW 0.9597

Operating Room Procedures

06.09	Other incision of thyroid field
09.12	Biopsy of lacrimal sac
09.19	Other diagnostic procedures on lacrimal system
09.44	Intubation of nasolacrimal duct
09.81	Dacryocystorhinostomy (DCR)
09.99	Other operations on lacrimal system
18.21	Excision of preauricular sinus
*18.3	Other excision of external ear
18.5	Surgical correction of prominent ear
18.6	Reconstruction of external auditory canal
*18.7	Other plastic repair of external ear
18.9	Other operations on external ear
*19	Reconstructive operations on middle ear
20.23	Incision of middle ear
20.32	Biopsy of middle and inner ear
20.39	Other diagnostic procedures on middle and inner ear
*20.5	Other excision of middle ear
*20.6	Fenestration of inner ear
*20.7	Incision, excision, and destruction of inner ear
20.91	Tympanosympathectomy
20.93	Repair of oval and round windows
20.95	Implantation of electromagnetic hearing device
20.99	Other operations on middle and inner ear
21.4	Resection of nose
21.5	Submucous resection of nasal septum
*21.6	Turbinectomy
21.72	Open reduction of nasal fracture
21.82	Closure of nasal fistula
21.89	Other repair and plastic operations on nose
21.99	Other operations on nose
*30.0	Excision or destruction of lesion or tissue of larynx
30.22	Vocal cordectomy
31.3	Other incision of larynx or trachea
31.45	Open biopsy of larynx or trachea
31.5	Local excision or destruction of lesion or tissue of trachea
*31.6	Repair of larynx
31.91	Division of laryngeal nerve
31.98	Other operations on larynx

S DRG 056 Rhinoplasty

GMLOS 1.8 AMLOS 2.6 RW 0.8711 ☑

Operating Room Procedures

21.83	Total nasal reconstruction
21.84	Revision rhinoplasty
21.85	Augmentation rhinoplasty
21.86	Limited rhinoplasty
21.87	Other rhinoplasty
21.88	Other septoplasty

S DRG 057 Tonsillectomy and Adenoidectomy Procedures Except Tonsillectomy and/or Adenoidectomy Only, Age Greater than 17

GMLOS 2.3 AMLOS 3.6 RW 1.0428 ☑ A

Operating Room Procedures

28.0	Incision and drainage of tonsil and peritonsillar structures
*28.1	Diagnostic procedures on tonsils and adenoids
28.4	Excision of tonsil tag
28.5	Excision of lingual tonsil
28.7	Control of hemorrhage after tonsillectomy and adenoidectomy
*28.9	Other operations on tonsils and adenoids

OR

Operating Room Procedures

28.2	Tonsillectomy without adenoidectomy
28.3	Tonsillectomy with adenoidectomy
28.6	Adenoidectomy without tonsillectomy

AND

Any other operating room procedure

S DRG 058 Tonsillectomy and Adenoidectomy Procedures Except Tonsillectomy and/or Adenoidectomy Only, Age 0-17

GMLOS 1.5 AMLOS 1.5 RW 0.2772 ☑ A

Select operating room procedures listed under DRG 057

S DRG 059 Tonsillectomy and/or Adenoidectomy Only, Age Greater than 17

GMLOS 1.8 AMLOS 2.6 RW 0.8082 ☑ A

Operating Room Procedures

28.2	Tonsillectomy without adenoidectomy
28.3	Tonsillectomy with adenoidectomy
28.6	Adenoidectomy without tonsillectomy

S DRG 060 Tonsillectomy and/or Adenoidectomy Only, Age 0-17

GMLOS 1.5 AMLOS 1.5 RW 0.2110 ☑ A

Select operating room procedure listed under DRG 059

S DRG 061 Myringotomy with Tube Insertion, Age Greater than 17

GMLOS 3.3 AMLOS 5.4 RW 1.2867 A

Operating Room Procedure

20.01	Myringotomy with insertion of tube

S DRG 062 Myringotomy with Tube Insertion, Age 0-17

GMLOS 1.3 AMLOS 1.3 RW 0.2989 ☑ A

Select operating room procedures listed under DRG 061

S DRG 063 Other Ear, Nose, Mouth and Throat O.R. Procedures

GMLOS 3.0 AMLOS 4.5 RW 1.3983 ☑

Operating Room Procedures

*04.0	Incision, division, and excision of cranial and peripheral nerves
04.12	Open biopsy of cranial or peripheral nerve or ganglion
04.19	Other diagnostic procedures on cranial and peripheral nerves and ganglia
04.41	Decompression of trigeminal nerve root
04.42	Other cranial nerve decompression
04.49	Other peripheral nerve or ganglion decompression or lysis of adhesions
04.71	Hypoglossal-facial anastomosis
04.72	Accessory-facial anastomosis
04.73	Accessory-hypoglossal anastomosis
04.74	Other anastomosis of cranial or peripheral nerve
04.75	Revision of previous repair of cranial and peripheral nerves
04.76	Repair of old traumatic injury of cranial and peripheral nerves
04.92	Implantation or replacement of peripheral neurostimulator lead(s)
04.93	Removal of peripheral neurostimulator lead(s)
04.99	Other operations on cranial and peripheral nerves
05.21	Sphenopalatine ganglionectomy
05.22	Cervical sympathectomy
06.6	Excision of lingual thyroid
06.7	Excision of thyroglossal duct or tract
09.43	Probing of nasolacrimal duct
16.52	Exenteration of orbit with therapeutic removal of orbital bone
16.65	Secondary graft to exenteration cavity
16.66	Other revision of exenteration cavity
16.98	Other operations on orbit
21.04	Control of epistaxis by ligation of ethmoidal arteries
21.05	Control of epistaxis by (transantral) ligation of the maxillary artery
21.06	Control of epistaxis by ligation of the external carotid artery
21.07	Control of epistaxis by excision of nasal mucosa and skin grafting of septum and lateral nasal wall
21.09	Control of epistaxis by other means
29.0	Pharyngotomy
29.2	Excision of branchial cleft cyst or vestige
*29.3	Excision or destruction of lesion or tissue of pharynx
29.4	Plastic operation on pharynx
*29.5	Other repair of pharynx
29.92	Division of glossopharyngeal nerve
29.99	Other operations on pharynx
30.21	Epiglottidectomy
*31.7	Repair and plastic operations on trachea
31.92	Lysis of adhesions of trachea or larynx
31.99	Other operations on trachea
34.22	Mediastinoscopy
38.00	Incision of vessel, unspecified site
38.02	Incision of other vessels of head and neck
38.12	Endarterectomy of other vessels of head and neck
38.21	Biopsy of blood vessel
38.32	Resection of other vessels of head and neck with anastomosis
38.42	Resection of other vessels of head and neck with replacement
38.62	Other excision of other vessels of head and neck
38.82	Other surgical occlusion of other vessels of head and neck
39.98	Control of hemorrhage, not otherwise specified
39.99	Other operations on vessels
*40.1	Diagnostic procedures on lymphatic structures
40.21	Excision of deep cervical lymph node
40.23	Excision of axillary lymph node
40.29	Simple excision of other lymphatic structure
40.3	Regional lymph node excision
40.9	Other operations on lymphatic structures
*42.0	Esophagotomy

S *Surgical* M *Medical* CC *CC Indicator* A *Age Restriction* ● *New DRG* ▲ *Revised DRG Title*

*42.1	Esophagostomy
42.21	Operative esophagoscopy by incision
42.25	Open biopsy of esophagus
42.31	Local excision of esophageal diverticulum
42.32	Local excision of other lesion or tissue of esophagus
42.39	Other destruction of lesion or tissue of esophagus
*42.4	Excision of esophagus
*42.5	Intrathoracic anastomosis of esophagus
*42.6	Antesternal anastomosis of esophagus
42.7	Esophagomyotomy
42.82	Suture of laceration of esophagus
42.83	Closure of esophagostomy
42.84	Repair of esophageal fistula, not elsewhere classified
42.86	Production of subcutaneous tunnel without esophageal anastomosis
42.87	Other graft of esophagus
42.89	Other repair of esophagus
50.12	Open biopsy of liver
*76.0	Incision of facial bone without division
*76.1	Diagnostic procedures on facial bones and joints
76.2	Local excision or destruction of lesion of facial bone
76.39	Partial ostectomy of other facial bone
76.43	Other reconstruction of mandible
76.44	Total ostectomy of other facial bone with synchronous reconstruction
76.45	Other total ostectomy of other facial bone
76.46	Other reconstruction of other facial bone
76.5	Temporomandibular arthroplasty
*76.6	Other facial bone repair and orthognathic surgery
76.70	Reduction of facial fracture, not otherwise specified
76.72	Open reduction of malar and zygomatic fracture
76.74	Open reduction of maxillary fracture
76.76	Open reduction of mandibular fracture
76.77	Open reduction of alveolar fracture
76.79	Other open reduction of facial fracture
76.91	Bone graft to facial bone
76.92	Insertion of synthetic implant in facial bone
76.94	Open reduction of temporomandibular dislocation
76.97	Removal of internal fixation device from facial bone
76.99	Other operations on facial bones and joints
77.19	Other incision of other bone, except facial bones, without division
77.30	Other division of bone, unspecified site
77.40	Biopsy of bone, unspecified site
77.49	Biopsy of other bone, except facial bones
77.69	Local excision of lesion or tissue of other bone, except facial bones
77.79	Excision of other bone for graft, except facial bones
77.89	Other partial ostectomy of other bone, except facial bones
77.99	Total ostectomy of other bone, except facial bones
79.29	Open reduction of fracture of other specified bone, except facial bones, without internal fixation
79.39	Open reduction of fracture of other specified bone, except facial bones, with internal fixation
79.69	Debridement of open fracture of other specified bone, except facial bones
83.02	Myotomy
83.39	Excision of lesion of other soft tissue
83.49	Other excision of soft tissue
86.22	Excisional debridement of wound, infection, or burn
86.4	Radical excision of skin lesion
86.63	Full-thickness skin graft to other sites
86.66	Homograft to skin
86.67	Dermal regenerative graft
86.69	Other skin graft to other sites
86.70	Pedicle or flap graft, not otherwise specified
86.71	Cutting and preparation of pedicle grafts or flaps
86.72	Advancement of pedicle graft
86.74	Attachment of pedicle or flap graft to other sites

DRG 063 — continued

86.75	Revision of pedicle or flap graft
86.81	Repair for facial weakness
86.82	Facial rhytidectomy
86.84	Relaxation of scar or web contracture of skin
86.89	Other repair and reconstruction of skin and subcutaneous tissue
86.91	Excision of skin for graft
86.93	Insertion of tissue expander
92.27	Implantation or insertion of radioactive elements

S DRG 168 Mouth Procedures with CC

GMLOS 3.3 AMLOS 4.9 RW 1.2662 ☑ CC

Operating Room Procedures

24.2	Gingivoplasty
24.4	Excision of dental lesion of jaw
24.5	Alveoloplasty
25.02	Open biopsy of tongue
25.1	Excision or destruction of lesion or tissue of tongue
25.2	Partial glossectomy
25.59	Other repair and plastic operations on tongue
25.94	Other glossotomy
25.99	Other operations on tongue
27.0	Drainage of face and floor of mouth
27.1	Incision of palate
27.21	Biopsy of bony palate
27.22	Biopsy of uvula and soft palate
27.31	Local excision or destruction of lesion or tissue of bony palate
27.42	Wide excision of lesion of lip
27.43	Other excision of lesion or tissue of lip
27.49	Other excision of mouth
27.53	Closure of fistula of mouth
27.55	Full-thickness skin graft to lip and mouth
27.56	Other skin graft to lip and mouth
27.57	Attachment of pedicle or flap graft to lip and mouth
27.59	Other plastic repair of mouth
27.61	Suture of laceration of palate
*27.7	Operations on uvula
27.92	Incision of mouth, unspecified structure
27.99	Other operations on oral cavity

S DRG 169 Mouth Procedures without CC

GMLOS 1.8 AMLOS 2.3 RW 0.7297 ☑

Select operating room procedures listed under DRG 168

MDC 3
DISEASES AND DISORDERS OF THE EAR, NOSE, MOUTH AND THROAT

The complete and up-to-date listing of ICD-9-CM diagnosis codes assigned to this MDC can be found online at www.ingenixonline.com/content/drg/resources.asp.

MEDICAL

M DRG 064 Ear, Nose, Mouth and Throat Malignancy
GMLOS 4.1 AMLOS 6.1 RW 1.1663 ☑

Principal Diagnosis

*140	Malignant neoplasm of lip
*141	Malignant neoplasm of tongue
*142	Malignant neoplasm of major salivary glands
*143	Malignant neoplasm of gum
*144	Malignant neoplasm of floor of mouth
*145	Malignant neoplasm of other and unspecified parts of mouth
*146	Malignant neoplasm of oropharynx
*147	Malignant neoplasm of nasopharynx
*148	Malignant neoplasm of hypopharynx
*149	Malignant neoplasm of other and ill-defined sites within the lip, oral cavity, and pharynx
*160	Malignant neoplasm of nasal cavities, middle ear, and accessory sinuses
*161	Malignant neoplasm of larynx
165.0	Malignant neoplasm of upper respiratory tract, part unspecified
176.2	Kaposi's sarcoma of palate
195.0	Malignant neoplasm of head, face, and neck
230.0	Carcinoma in situ of lip, oral cavity, and pharynx
231.0	Carcinoma in situ of larynx
235.0	Neoplasm of uncertain behavior of major salivary glands
235.1	Neoplasm of uncertain behavior of lip, oral cavity, and pharynx
235.6	Neoplasm of uncertain behavior of larynx

M DRG 065 Dysequilibrium
GMLOS 2.3 AMLOS 2.8 RW 0.5991 ☑

Principal Diagnosis

*386.0	Meniere's disease
*386.1	Other and unspecified peripheral vertigo
386.2	Vertigo of central origin
*386.3	Labyrinthitis
*386.5	Labyrinthine dysfunction
386.8	Other disorders of labyrinth
386.9	Unspecified vertiginous syndromes and labyrinthine disorders
780.4	Dizziness and giddiness
994.6	Motion sickness

M DRG 066 Epistaxis
GMLOS 2.4 AMLOS 3.1 RW 0.5958 ☑

Principal Diagnosis

784.7	Epistaxis

M DRG 067 Epiglottitis
GMLOS 2.9 AMLOS 3.7 RW 0.7725

Principal Diagnosis

*464.3	Acute epiglottitis

** Code Range ☑ Optimization Potential ▽ Targeted Potential T Transfer DRG SP Special Payment*

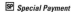

Ⓜ DRG 068 Otitis Media and URI, Age Greater than 17 with CC

GMLOS 3.2 AMLOS 4.0 RW 0.6611 ☑ CC A

Principal Diagnosis

034.0	Streptococcal sore throat
055.2	Postmeasles otitis media
074.0	Herpangina
098.6	Gonococcal infection of pharynx
099.51	Chlamydia trachomatis infection of pharynx
101	Vincent's angina
380.00	Unspecified perichondritis of pinna
*381.0	Acute nonsuppurative otitis media
*381.1	Chronic serous otitis media
*381.2	Chronic mucoid otitis media
381.3	Other and unspecified chronic nonsuppurative otitis media
381.4	Nonsuppurative otitis media, not specified as acute or chronic
*381.5	Eustachian salpingitis
*382	Suppurative and unspecified otitis media
*383.0	Acute mastoiditis
383.1	Chronic mastoiditis
*383.2	Petrositis
383.9	Unspecified mastoiditis
*384.0	Acute myringitis without mention of otitis media
384.1	Chronic myringitis without mention of otitis media
460	Acute nasopharyngitis (common cold)
*461	Acute sinusitis
462	Acute pharyngitis
463	Acute tonsillitis
464.00	Acute laryngitis, without mention of obstruction
464.01	Acute laryngitis, with obstruction
464.50	Unspecified supraglottis, without mention of obstruction
464.51	Unspecified supraglottis, with obstruction
*465	Acute upper respiratory infections of multiple or unspecified sites
*472	Chronic pharyngitis and nasopharyngitis
*473	Chronic sinusitis
474.00	Chronic tonsillitis
474.01	Chronic adenoiditis
474.02	Chronic tonsillitis and adenoiditis
475	Peritonsillar abscess
*476	Chronic laryngitis and laryngotracheitis
*477	Allergic rhinitis
478.21	Cellulitis of pharynx or nasopharynx
478.22	Parapharyngeal abscess
478.24	Retropharyngeal abscess
478.71	Cellulitis and perichondritis of larynx
478.8	Upper respiratory tract hypersensitivity reaction, site unspecified
478.9	Other and unspecified diseases of upper respiratory tract
487.1	Influenza with other respiratory manifestations
993.0	Barotrauma, otitic
993.1	Barotrauma, sinus

Ⓜ DRG 069 Otitis Media and URI, Age Greater than 17 without CC

GMLOS 2.5 AMLOS 3.0 RW 0.4850 ☑ A

Select principal diagnosis listed under DRG 068

Ⓜ DRG 070 Otitis Media and URI, Age 0-17

GMLOS 2.1 AMLOS 2.3 RW 0.4210 ☑ A

Select principal diagnosis listed under DRG 068

M DRG 071 Laryngotracheitis

GMLOS 3.2 AMLOS 4.0 RW 0.7524 ☑

Principal Diagnosis

*464.2	Acute laryngotracheitis
464.4	Croup

M DRG 072 Nasal Trauma and Deformity

GMLOS 2.6 AMLOS 3.4 RW 0.7449 ☑

Principal Diagnosis

470	Deviated nasal septum
738.0	Acquired deformity of nose
802.0	Nasal bones, closed fracture
802.1	Nasal bones, open fracture
873.20	Open wound of nose, unspecified site, without mention of complication
932	Foreign body in nose

M DRG 073 Other Ear, Nose, Mouth and Throat Diagnoses, Age Greater than 17

GMLOS 3.3 AMLOS 4.4 RW 0.8527 ☑ T A

Principal Diagnosis

*012.3	Tuberculous laryngitis
*015.6	Tuberculosis of mastoid
*017.4	Tuberculosis of ear
032.0	Faucial diphtheria
032.1	Nasopharyngeal diphtheria
032.2	Anterior nasal diphtheria
032.3	Laryngeal diphtheria
053.71	Otitis externa due to herpes zoster
054.73	Herpes simplex otitis externa
094.86	Syphilitic acoustic neuritis
102.5	Gangosa due to yaws
112.82	Candidal otitis externa
210.2	Benign neoplasm of major salivary glands
210.5	Benign neoplasm of tonsil
210.6	Benign neoplasm of other parts of oropharynx
210.7	Benign neoplasm of nasopharynx
210.8	Benign neoplasm of hypopharynx
210.9	Benign neoplasm of pharynx, unspecified
212.0	Benign neoplasm of nasal cavities, middle ear, and accessory sinuses
212.1	Benign neoplasm of larynx
327.20	Organic sleep apnea, unspecified
327.23	Obstructive sleep apnea (adult) (pediatric)
327.24	Idiopathic sleep related nonobstructive alveolar hypoventilation
327.26	Sleep related hypoventilation/hypoxemia in conditions classifiable elsewhere
327.29	Other organic sleep apnea
327.40	Organic parasomnia, unspecified
327.42	REM sleep behavior disorder
327.44	Parasomnia in conditions classified elsewhere
327.49	Other organic parasomnia
327.53	Sleep related bruxism
327.59	Other organic sleep related movement disorders
327.8	Other organic sleep disorders
*380.1	Infective otitis externa
*380.2	Other otitis externa
*380.3	Noninfectious disorders of pinna
380.4	Impacted cerumen
*380.5	Acquired stenosis of external ear canal
*380.8	Other disorders of external ear
380.9	Unspecified disorder of external ear
*381.6	Obstruction of Eustachian tube

DRG 073 — continued

381.7	Patulous Eustachian tube
*381.8	Other disorders of Eustachian tube
381.9	Unspecified Eustachian tube disorder
*383.3	Complications following mastoidectomy
*383.8	Other disorders of mastoid
*384.2	Perforation of tympanic membrane
*384.8	Other specified disorders of tympanic membrane
384.9	Unspecified disorder of tympanic membrane
*385	Other disorders of middle ear and mastoid
*386.4	Labyrinthine fistula
*387	Otosclerosis
*388.0	Degenerative and vascular disorders of ear
*388.1	Noise effects on inner ear
388.2	Unspecified sudden hearing loss
*388.3	Tinnitus
*388.4	Other abnormal auditory perception
388.5	Disorders of acoustic nerve
388.60	Unspecified otorrhea
388.69	Other otorrhea
*388.7	Otalgia
388.8	Other disorders of ear
388.9	Unspecified disorder of ear
*389	Hearing loss
*471	Nasal polyps
*474.1	Hypertrophy of tonsils and adenoids
474.2	Adenoid vegetations
474.8	Other chronic disease of tonsils and adenoids
474.9	Unspecified chronic disease of tonsils and adenoids
478.0	Hypertrophy of nasal turbinates
478.1	Other diseases of nasal cavity and sinuses
478.20	Unspecified disease of pharynx
478.25	Edema of pharynx or nasopharynx
478.26	Cyst of pharynx or nasopharynx
478.29	Other disease of pharynx or nasopharynx
*478.3	Paralysis of vocal cords or larynx
478.4	Polyp of vocal cord or larynx
478.5	Other diseases of vocal cords
478.6	Edema of larynx
478.70	Unspecified disease of larynx
478.74	Stenosis of larynx
478.75	Laryngeal spasm
478.79	Other diseases of larynx
*527	Diseases of the salivary glands
738.7	Cauliflower ear
*744.0	Congenital anomalies of ear causing impairment of hearing
744.1	Congenital anomalies of accessory auricle
*744.2	Other specified congenital anomalies of ear
744.3	Unspecified congenital anomaly of ear
*744.4	Congenital branchial cleft cyst or fistula; preauricular sinus
744.89	Other specified congenital anomaly of face and neck
748.0	Congenital choanal atresia
748.1	Other congenital anomaly of nose
748.2	Congenital web of larynx
748.3	Other congenital anomaly of larynx, trachea, and bronchus
750.21	Congenital absence of salivary gland
750.22	Congenital accessory salivary gland
750.23	Congenital atresia, salivary duct
750.24	Congenital fistula of salivary gland
750.27	Congenital diverticulum of pharynx
750.29	Other specified congenital anomaly of pharynx
784.1	Throat pain
*784.4	Voice disturbance

784.8	Hemorrhage from throat
784.9	Other symptoms involving head and neck
792.4	Nonspecific abnormal finding in saliva
794.15	Nonspecific abnormal auditory function studies
794.16	Nonspecific abnormal vestibular function studies
807.5	Closed fracture of larynx and trachea
807.6	Open fracture of larynx and trachea
*872	Open wound of ear
873.21	Open wound of nasal septum, without mention of complication
873.22	Open wound of nasal cavity, without mention of complication
873.23	Open wound of nasal sinus, without mention of complication
873.29	Open wound of nose, multiple sites, without mention of complication
*873.3	Open wound of nose, complicated
874.00	Open wound of larynx with trachea, without mention of complication
874.01	Open wound of larynx, without mention of complication
874.10	Open wound of larynx with trachea, complicated
874.11	Open wound of larynx, complicated
874.4	Open wound of pharynx, without mention of complication
874.5	Open wound of pharynx, complicated
931	Foreign body in ear
*933	Foreign body in pharynx and larynx
947.0	Burn of mouth and pharynx
951.5	Injury to acoustic nerve

M DRG 074 Other Ear, Nose, Mouth and Throat Diagnoses, Age 0-17

GMLOS 2.1 AMLOS 2.1 RW 0.3398 ☑ A

Select principal diagnosis listed under DRG 073

M DRG 185 Dental and Oral Diseases Except Extractions and Restorations, Age Greater than 17

GMLOS 3.2 AMLOS 4.5 RW 0.8702 A

Principal Diagnosis

054.2	Herpetic gingivostomatitis
112.0	Candidiasis of mouth
210.0	Benign neoplasm of lip
210.1	Benign neoplasm of tongue
210.3	Benign neoplasm of floor of mouth
210.4	Benign neoplasm of other and unspecified parts of mouth
213.1	Benign neoplasm of lower jaw bone
*520	Disorders of tooth development and eruption
*521	Diseases of hard tissues of teeth
*522	Diseases of pulp and periapical tissues
*523	Gingival and periodontal diseases
*524	Dentofacial anomalies, including malocclusion
*525	Other diseases and conditions of the teeth and supporting structures
*526	Diseases of the jaws
*528	Diseases of the oral soft tissues, excluding lesions specific for gingiva and tongue
*529	Diseases and other conditions of the tongue
744.81	Macrocheilia
744.82	Microcheilia
744.83	Macrostomia
744.84	Microstomia
*749	Cleft palate and cleft lip
750.0	Tongue tie
*750.1	Other congenital anomalies of tongue
750.25	Congenital fistula of lip
750.26	Other specified congenital anomalies of mouth
*802.2	Mandible, closed fracture
*802.3	Mandible, open fracture
802.4	Malar and maxillary bones, closed fracture
802.5	Malar and maxillary bones, open fracture

DRG 185 — continued

*830	Dislocation of jaw
848.1	Sprain and strain of jaw
873.43	Open wound of lip, without mention of complication
873.44	Open wound of jaw, without mention of complication
873.53	Open wound of lip, complicated
873.54	Open wound of jaw, complicated
*873.6	Open wound of internal structures of mouth, without mention of complication
*873.7	Open wound of internal structure of mouth, complicated
935.0	Foreign body in mouth

M DRG 186 Dental and Oral Diseases Except Extractions and Restorations, Age 0-17

GMLOS 2.9 AMLOS 2.9 RW 0.3253 ☑ A

Select principal diagnosis listed under DRG 185

M DRG 187 Dental Extractions and Restorations

GMLOS 3.1 AMLOS 4.2 RW 0.8363

Select principal diagnosis listed under DRG 185

AND

Nonoperating Room Procedures

*23	Removal and restoration of teeth

MDC 4
DISEASES AND DISORDERS OF THE RESPIRATORY SYSTEM

The complete and up-to-date listing of ICD-9-CM diagnosis codes assigned to this MDC can be found online at www.ingenixonline.com/content/drg/resources.asp.

SURGICAL

S DRG 075 Major Chest Procedures

GMLOS 7.6 AMLOS 9.9 RW 3.0732 ☑ T

Operating Room Procedures

07.16	Biopsy of thymus
*07.8	Thymectomy
*07.9	Other operations on thymus
31.73	Closure of other fistula of trachea
31.75	Reconstruction of trachea and construction of artificial larynx
31.79	Other repair and plastic operations on trachea
32.09	Other local excision or destruction of lesion or tissue of bronchus
32.1	Other excision of bronchus
32.21	Plication of emphysematous bleb
32.22	Lung volume reduction surgery
32.29	Other local excision or destruction of lesion or tissue of lung
32.3	Segmental resection of lung
32.4	Lobectomy of lung
32.5	Complete pneumonectomy
32.6	Radical dissection of thoracic structures
32.9	Other excision of lung
33.0	Incision of bronchus
33.1	Incision of lung
33.25	Open biopsy of bronchus
33.28	Open biopsy of lung
33.34	Thoracoplasty
33.39	Other surgical collapse of lung
*33.4	Repair and plastic operation on lung and bronchus
33.92	Ligation of bronchus
33.98	Other operations on bronchus
33.99	Other operations on lung
34.02	Exploratory thoracotomy
34.03	Reopening of recent thoracotomy site
34.27	Biopsy of diaphragm
34.3	Excision or destruction of lesion or tissue of mediastinum
*34.5	Pleurectomy
34.6	Scarification of pleura
34.73	Closure of other fistula of thorax
34.74	Repair of pectus deformity
*34.8	Operations on diaphragm
34.93	Repair of pleura
37.12	Pericardiotomy
37.24	Biopsy of pericardium
37.31	Pericardiectomy
37.91	Open chest cardiac massage
38.05	Incision of other thoracic vessels
38.15	Endarterectomy of other thoracic vessels
38.35	Resection of other thoracic vessels with anastomosis
38.45	Resection of other thoracic vessels with replacement
38.55	Ligation and stripping of varicose veins of other thoracic vessel
38.65	Other excision of other thoracic vessel
38.85	Other surgical occlusion of other thoracic vessel
39.54	Re-entry operation (aorta)

*** Code Range** ☑ **Optimization Potential** ▽ **Targeted Potential** T **Transfer DRG** SP **Special Payment**

DRG 075 — continued

39.98	Control of hemorrhage, not otherwise specified
40.22	Excision of internal mammary lymph node
40.52	Radical excision of periaortic lymph nodes
*40.6	Operations on thoracic duct
53.7	Repair of diaphragmatic hernia, abdominal approach
*53.8	Repair of diaphragmatic hernia, thoracic approach

S DRG 076 Other Respiratory System O.R. Procedures with CC

GMLOS 8.4 AMLOS 11.1 RW 2.8830 ☑ T CC

Operating Room Procedures

30.01	Marsupialization of laryngeal cyst
30.09	Other excision or destruction of lesion or tissue of larynx
30.1	Hemilaryngectomy
*30.2	Other partial laryngectomy
31.3	Other incision of larynx or trachea
31.45	Open biopsy of larynx or trachea
31.5	Local excision or destruction of lesion or tissue of trachea
*31.6	Repair of larynx
31.71	Suture of laceration of trachea
31.72	Closure of external fistula of trachea
31.74	Revision of tracheostomy
31.91	Division of laryngeal nerve
31.92	Lysis of adhesions of trachea or larynx
31.98	Other operations on larynx
31.99	Other operations on trachea
33.27	Closed endoscopic biopsy of lung
33.29	Other diagnostic procedures on lung or bronchus
33.93	Puncture of lung
34.1	Incision of mediastinum
34.21	Transpleural thoracoscopy
34.22	Mediastinoscopy
34.26	Open biopsy of mediastinum
34.28	Other diagnostic procedures on chest wall, pleura, and diaphragm
34.29	Other diagnostic procedures on mediastinum
34.4	Excision or destruction of lesion of chest wall
34.79	Other repair of chest wall
34.99	Other operations on thorax
38.21	Biopsy of blood vessel
38.7	Interruption of the vena cava
39.29	Other (peripheral) vascular shunt or bypass
39.31	Suture of artery
39.50	Angioplasty or atherectomy of other non-coronary vessel(s)
39.8	Operations on carotid body and other vascular bodies
39.99	Other operations on vessels
40.11	Biopsy of lymphatic structure
40.19	Other diagnostic procedures on lymphatic structures
40.21	Excision of deep cervical lymph node
40.23	Excision of axillary lymph node
40.24	Excision of inguinal lymph node
40.29	Simple excision of other lymphatic structure
40.3	Regional lymph node excision
*40.4	Radical excision of cervical lymph nodes
40.50	Radical excision of lymph nodes, not otherwise specified
40.59	Radical excision of other lymph nodes
50.12	Open biopsy of liver
54.11	Exploratory laparotomy
77.01	Sequestrectomy of scapula, clavicle, and thorax (ribs and sternum)
77.11	Other incision of scapula, clavicle, and thorax (ribs and sternum) without division
77.21	Wedge osteotomy of scapula, clavicle, and thorax (ribs and sternum)
77.31	Other division of scapula, clavicle, and thorax (ribs and sternum)
77.41	Biopsy of scapula, clavicle, and thorax (ribs and sternum)

77.49	Biopsy of other bone, except facial bones
77.61	Local excision of lesion or tissue of scapula, clavicle, and thorax (ribs and sternum)
77.71	Excision of scapula, clavicle, and thorax (ribs and sternum) for graft
77.81	Other partial ostectomy of scapula, clavicle, and thorax (ribs and sternum)
77.91	Total ostectomy of scapula, clavicle, and thorax (ribs and sternum)
78.01	Bone graft of scapula, clavicle, and thorax (ribs and sternum)
78.11	Application of external fixator device, scapula, clavicle, and thorax [ribs and sternum]
78.41	Other repair or plastic operations on scapula, clavicle, and thorax (ribs and sternum)
78.51	Internal fixation of scapula, clavicle, and thorax (ribs and sternum) without fracture reduction
78.61	Removal of implanted device from scapula, clavicle, and thorax (ribs and sternum)
78.71	Osteoclasis of scapula, clavicle, and thorax (ribs and sternum)
78.81	Diagnostic procedures on scapula, clavicle, and thorax (ribs and sternum) not elsewhere classified
78.91	Insertion of bone growth stimulator into scapula, clavicle and thorax (ribs and sternum)
83.21	Biopsy of soft tissue
86.06	Insertion of totally implantable infusion pump
86.22	Excisional debridement of wound, infection, or burn
86.69	Other skin graft to other sites
92.27	Implantation or insertion of radioactive elements

S DRG 077 Other Respiratory System O.R. Procedures without CC

GMLOS 3.3 AMLOS 4.7 RW 1.1857 ☑ T

Select operating room procedures listed under DRG 076

DRG 474 No Longer Valid

GMLOS 0.0 AMLOS 0.0 RW 0.0000

Omitted in the October 1990 grouper revision

MDC 4: Respiratory System — Surgical

** Code Range* ☑ *Optimization Potential* *Targeted Potential* T *Transfer DRG* SP *Special Payment*

MDC 4
DISEASES AND DISORDERS OF THE RESPIRATORY SYSTEM

The complete and up-to-date listing of ICD-9-CM diagnosis codes assigned to this MDC can be found online at www.ingenixonline.com/content/drg/resources.asp.

MEDICAL

[M] DRG 078 Pulmonary Embolism
GMLOS 5.4 AMLOS 6.4 RW 1.2427 ☑ [T]

Principal Diagnosis

*415.1	Pulmonary embolism and infarction
958.0	Air embolism as an early complication of trauma
958.1	Fat embolism as an early complication of trauma
999.1	Air embolism as complication of medical care, not elsewhere classified

[M] DRG 079 Respiratory Infections and Inflammations, Age Greater than 17 with CC
GMLOS 6.7 AMLOS 8.5 RW 1.6238 ☑ [T] [YIELD] [CC] [A]

Principal Diagnosis

003.22	Salmonella pneumonia
006.4	Amebic lung abscess
*010	Primary tuberculous infection
*011	Pulmonary tuberculosis
*012.0	Tuberculous pleurisy
*012.1	Tuberculosis of intrathoracic lymph nodes
*012.2	Isolated tracheal or bronchial tuberculosis
*012.8	Other specified respiratory tuberculosis
020.3	Primary pneumonic plague
020.4	Secondary pneumonic plague
020.5	Pneumonic plague, unspecified
021.2	Pulmonary tularemia
022.1	Pulmonary anthrax
031.0	Pulmonary diseases due to other mycobacteria
039.1	Pulmonary actinomycotic infection
052.1	Varicella (hemorrhagic) pneumonitis
055.1	Postmeasles pneumonia
073.0	Ornithosis with pneumonia
095.1	Syphilis of lung
112.4	Candidiasis of lung
114.0	Primary coccidioidomycosis (pulmonary)
114.4	Chronic pulmonary coccidioidomycosis
114.5	Unspecified pulmonary coccidioidomycosis
115.05	Histoplasma capsulatum pneumonia
115.15	Histoplasma duboisii pneumonia
115.95	Unspecified Histoplasmosis pneumonia
121.2	Paragonimiasis
122.1	Echinococcus granulosus infection of lung
130.4	Pneumonitis due to toxoplasmosis
136.3	Pneumocystosis
277.02	Cystic fibrosis with pulmonary manifestations
482.0	Pneumonia due to Klebsiella pneumoniae
482.1	Pneumonia due to Pseudomonas
*482.4	Pneumonia due to Staphylococcus
*482.8	Pneumonia due to other specified bacteria
*484	Pneumonia in infectious diseases classified elsewhere
*507	Pneumonitis due to solids and liquids

*510	Empyema
511.1	Pleurisy with effusion, with mention of bacterial cause other than tuberculosis
*513	Abscess of lung and mediastinum
519.2	Mediastinitis
795.5	Nonspecific reaction to tuberculin skin test without active tuberculosis
V71.2	Observation for suspected tuberculosis

M DRG 080 Respiratory Infections and Inflammations, Age Greater than 17 without CC

GMLOS 4.4 AMLOS 5.5 RW 0.8947 ☑ T A

Select principal diagnosis listed under DRG 079

M DRG 081 Respiratory Infections and Inflammations, Age 0-17

GMLOS 6.1 AMLOS 6.1 RW 1.5383 ☑ A

Select principal diagnosis listed under DRG 079

M DRG 082 Respiratory Neoplasms

GMLOS 5.1 AMLOS 6.8 RW 1.3936 ☑ T

Principal Diagnosis

*162	Malignant neoplasm of trachea, bronchus, and lung
*163	Malignant neoplasm of pleura
164.2	Malignant neoplasm of anterior mediastinum
164.3	Malignant neoplasm of posterior mediastinum
164.8	Malignant neoplasm of other parts of mediastinum
164.9	Malignant neoplasm of mediastinum, part unspecified
165.8	Malignant neoplasm of other sites within the respiratory system and intrathoracic organs
165.9	Malignant neoplasm of ill-defined sites within the respiratory system
176.4	Kaposi's sarcoma of lung
195.1	Malignant neoplasm of thorax
197.0	Secondary malignant neoplasm of lung
197.1	Secondary malignant neoplasm of mediastinum
197.2	Secondary malignant neoplasm of pleura
197.3	Secondary malignant neoplasm of other respiratory organs
212.2	Benign neoplasm of trachea
212.3	Benign neoplasm of bronchus and lung
212.4	Benign neoplasm of pleura
212.5	Benign neoplasm of mediastinum
212.8	Benign neoplasm of other specified sites of respiratory and intrathoracic organs
212.9	Benign neoplasm of respiratory and intrathoracic organs, site unspecified
213.3	Benign neoplasm of ribs, sternum, and clavicle
214.2	Lipoma of intrathoracic organs
231.1	Carcinoma in situ of trachea
231.2	Carcinoma in situ of bronchus and lung
231.8	Carcinoma in situ of other specified parts of respiratory system
231.9	Carcinoma in situ of respiratory system, part unspecified
235.7	Neoplasm of uncertain behavior of trachea, bronchus, and lung
235.8	Neoplasm of uncertain behavior of pleura, thymus, and mediastinum
235.9	Neoplasm of uncertain behavior of other and unspecified respiratory organs
239.1	Neoplasm of unspecified nature of respiratory system
795.1	Nonspecific abnormal Papanicolaou smear of other site

M DRG 083 Major Chest Trauma with CC

GMLOS 4.2 AMLOS 5.3 RW 0.9828 ☑ T CC

Principal Diagnosis

807.03	Closed fracture of three ribs
807.04	Closed fracture of four ribs
807.05	Closed fracture of five ribs
807.06	Closed fracture of six ribs
807.07	Closed fracture of seven ribs

MDC 4: Respiratory System — Medical

Code Range ☑ *Optimization Potential* *Targeted Potential* T *Transfer DRG* SP *Special Payment*

DRG 083 — continued

807.08	Closed fracture of eight or more ribs
807.09	Closed fracture of multiple ribs, unspecified
*807.1	Open fracture of rib(s)
807.2	Closed fracture of sternum
807.3	Open fracture of sternum
807.4	Flail chest
839.61	Closed dislocation, sternum
839.71	Open dislocation, sternum
861.22	Lung laceration without mention of open wound into thorax
861.32	Lung laceration with open wound into thorax
862.0	Diaphragm injury without mention of open wound into cavity
862.1	Diaphragm injury with open wound into cavity
862.21	Bronchus injury without mention of open wound into cavity
862.31	Bronchus injury with open wound into cavity
874.02	Open wound of trachea, without mention of complication
874.12	Open wound of trachea, complicated

M DRG 084 Major Chest Trauma without CC

GMLOS 2.6 AMLOS 3.2 RW 0.5799 ☑T

Select principal diagnosis listed under DRG 083

M DRG 085 Pleural Effusion with CC

GMLOS 4.8 AMLOS 6.3 RW 1.2405 ☑T CC

Principal Diagnosis

511.8	Pleurisy with other specified forms of effusion, except tuberculous
511.9	Unspecified pleural effusion

M DRG 086 Pleural Effusion without CC

GMLOS 2.8 AMLOS 3.6 RW 0.6974 ☑T

Select principal diagnosis listed under DRG 085

M DRG 087 Pulmonary Edema and Respiratory Failure

GMLOS 4.9 AMLOS 6.4 RW 1.3654 ☑ YIELD

Principal Diagnosis

506.1	Acute pulmonary edema due to fumes and vapors
514	Pulmonary congestion and hypostasis
518.4	Unspecified acute edema of lung
518.5	Pulmonary insufficiency following trauma and surgery
518.81	Acute respiratory failure
518.83	Chronic respiratory failure
518.84	Acute and chronic respiratory failure

M DRG 088 Chronic Obstructive Pulmonary Disease

GMLOS 4.0 AMLOS 4.9 RW 0.8778 ☑ YIELD

Principal Diagnosis

491.1	Mucopurulent chronic bronchitis
*491.2	Obstructive chronic bronchitis
491.8	Other chronic bronchitis
491.9	Unspecified chronic bronchitis
492.0	Emphysematous bleb
492.8	Other emphysema
493.20	Chronic obstructive asthma, unspecified
493.21	Chronic obstructive asthma with status asthmaticus
493.22	Chronic obstructive asthma, with (acute) exacerbation
*494	Bronchiectasis
496	Chronic airway obstruction, not elsewhere classified
506.4	Chronic respiratory conditions due to fumes and vapors

506.9	Unspecified respiratory conditions due to fumes and vapors
748.61	Congenital bronchiectasis

M DRG 089 Simple Pneumonia and Pleurisy, Age Greater than 17 with CC

GMLOS 4.7 AMLOS 5.7 RW 1.0320 ☑ T ▽ CC A

Principal Diagnosis

074.1	Epidemic pleurodynia
*480	Viral pneumonia
481	Pneumococcal pneumonia (streptococcus pneumoniae pneumonia)
482.2	Pneumonia due to Hemophilus influenzae (H. influenzae)
*482.3	Pneumonia due to Streptococcus
482.9	Unspecified bacterial pneumonia
*483	Pneumonia due to other specified organism
485	Bronchopneumonia, organism unspecified
486	Pneumonia, organism unspecified
487.0	Influenza with pneumonia
511.0	Pleurisy without mention of effusion or current tuberculosis

M DRG 090 Simple Pneumonia and Pleurisy, Age Greater than 17 without CC

GMLOS 3.2 AMLOS 3.8 RW 0.6104 ☑ T A

Select principal diagnosis listed under DRG 089

M DRG 091 Simple Pneumonia and Pleurisy, Age 0-17

GMLOS 3.4 AMLOS 4.4 RW 0.8124 ☑ A

Select principal diagnosis listed under DRG 089

M DRG 092 Interstitial Lung Disease with CC

GMLOS 4.8 AMLOS 6.1 RW 1.1853 ☑ T CC

Principal Diagnosis

135	Sarcoidosis
137.0	Late effects of respiratory or unspecified tuberculosis
*495	Extrinsic allergic alveolitis
500	Coal workers' pneumoconiosis
501	Asbestosis
502	Pneumoconiosis due to other silica or silicates
503	Pneumoconiosis due to other inorganic dust
504	Pneumonopathy due to inhalation of other dust
505	Unspecified pneumoconiosis
508.1	Chronic and other pulmonary manifestations due to radiation
515	Postinflammatory pulmonary fibrosis
*516	Other alveolar and parietoalveolar pneumonopathy
517.1	Rheumatic pneumonia
517.2	Lung involvement in systemic sclerosis
517.3	Acute chest syndrome
517.8	Lung involvement in other diseases classified elsewhere
518.3	Pulmonary eosinophilia
518.6	Allergic bronchopulmonary aspergillosis
714.81	Rheumatoid lung
770.7	Chronic respiratory disease arising in the perinatal period

M DRG 093 Interstitial Lung Disease without CC

GMLOS 3.1 AMLOS 3.9 RW 0.7150 ☑ T

Select principal diagnosis listed under DRG 092

Ⓜ DRG 094 Pneumothorax with CC

GMLOS 4.6 AMLOS 6.2 RW 1.1354 ☑ CC

Principal Diagnosis

512.0	Spontaneous tension pneumothorax
512.1	Iatrogenic pneumothroax
512.8	Other spontaneous pneumothorax
518.1	Interstitial emphysema
*860	Traumatic pneumothorax and hemothorax
958.7	Traumatic subcutaneous emphysema

Ⓜ DRG 095 Pneumothorax without CC

GMLOS 2.9 AMLOS 3.6 RW 0.6035 ☑

Select principal diagnosis listed under DRG 094

Ⓜ DRG 096 Bronchitis and Asthma, Age Greater than 17 with CC

GMLOS 3.6 AMLOS 4.4 RW 0.7303 ☑ YIELD CC A

Principal Diagnosis

*033	Whooping cough
*464.1	Acute tracheitis
*466	Acute bronchitis and bronchiolitis
490	Bronchitis, not specified as acute or chronic
491.0	Simple chronic bronchitis
*493.0	Extrinsic asthma
*493.1	Intrinsic asthma
*493.8	Other forms of asthma
*493.9	Unspecified asthma
519.1	Other diseases of trachea and bronchus, not elsewhere classified

Ⓜ DRG 097 Bronchitis and Asthma, Age Greater than 17 without CC

GMLOS 2.8 AMLOS 3.4 RW 0.5364 ☑ A

Select principal diagnosis listed under DRG 096

Ⓜ DRG 098 Bronchitis and Asthma, Age 0-17

GMLOS 3.7 AMLOS 3.7 RW 0.5560 ☑ A

Select principal diagnosis listed under DRG 096

Ⓜ DRG 099 Respiratory Signs and Symptoms with CC

GMLOS 2.4 AMLOS 3.1 RW 0.7094 ☑ CC

Principal Diagnosis

327.22	High altitude periodic breathing
518.82	Other pulmonary insufficiency, not elsewhere classified
*786.0	Dyspnea and respiratory abnormalities
786.1	Stridor
786.2	Cough
786.3	Hemoptysis
786.4	Abnormal sputum
786.52	Painful respiration
786.6	Swelling, mass, or lump in chest
786.7	Abnormal chest sounds
786.8	Hiccough
786.9	Other symptoms involving respiratory system and chest
793.1	Nonspecific abnormal findings on radiological and other examination of lung field

Ⓜ DRG 100 Respiratory Signs and Symptoms without CC

GMLOS 1.7 AMLOS 2.1 RW 0.5382 ☑

Select principal diagnosis listed under DRG 099

M DRG 101 Other Respiratory System Diagnoses with CC

GMLOS 3.3 AMLOS 4.3 RW 0.8733 ☑ T CC

Principal Diagnosis

306.1	Respiratory malfunction arising from mental factors
506.0	Bronchitis and pneumonitis due to fumes and vapors
506.2	Upper respiratory inflammation due to fumes and vapors
506.3	Other acute and subacute respiratory conditions due to fumes and vapors
508.0	Acute pulmonary manifestations due to radiation
508.8	Respiratory conditions due to other specified external agents
508.9	Respiratory conditions due to unspecified external agent
518.0	Pulmonary collapse
518.2	Compensatory emphysema
518.89	Other diseases of lung, not elsewhere classified
*519.0	Tracheostomy complications
519.3	Other diseases of mediastinum, not elsewhere classified
519.4	Disorders of diaphragm
519.8	Other diseases of respiratory system, not elsewhere classified
519.9	Unspecified disease of respiratory system
733.6	Tietze's disease
748.4	Congenital cystic lung
748.5	Congenital agenesis, hypoplasia, and dysplasia of lung
748.60	Unspecified congenital anomaly of lung
748.69	Other congenital anomaly of lung
748.8	Other specified congenital anomaly of respiratory system
748.9	Unspecified congenital anomaly of respiratory system
754.81	Pectus excavatum
754.82	Pectus carinatum
756.3	Other congenital anomaly of ribs and sternum
756.6	Congenital anomaly of diaphragm
781.5	Clubbing of fingers
794.2	Nonspecific abnormal results of pulmonary system function study
*799.0	Asphyxia and hypoxemia
799.1	Respiratory arrest
807.00	Closed fracture of rib(s), unspecified
807.01	Closed fracture of one rib
807.02	Closed fracture of two ribs
848.3	Sprain and strain of ribs
*848.4	Sprain and strain of sternum
861.20	Unspecified lung injury without mention of open wound into thorax
861.21	Lung contusion without mention of open wound into thorax
861.30	Unspecified lung injury with open wound into thorax
861.31	Lung contusion with open wound into thorax
862.29	Injury to other specified intrathoracic organs without mention of open wound into cavity
862.39	Injury to other specified intrathoracic organs with open wound into cavity
908.0	Late effect of internal injury to chest
934.0	Foreign body in trachea
934.1	Foreign body in main bronchus
934.8	Foreign body in other specified parts of trachea, bronchus, and lung
934.9	Foreign body in respiratory tree, unspecified
947.1	Burn of larynx, trachea, and lung
996.84	Complications of transplanted lung
997.3	Respiratory complications
V42.6	Lung replaced by transplant
V45.76	Acquired absence of organ, lung
V55.0	Attention to tracheostomy

M DRG 102 Other Respiratory System Diagnoses without CC

GMLOS 2.0 AMLOS 2.5 RW 0.5402 ☑ T

Select principal diagnosis listed under DRG 101

Ⓜ DRG 475 Respiratory System Diagnosis with Ventilator Support

GMLOS 8.1 AMLOS 11.3 RW 3.6091 ☑ⓉⓋ

Nonoperating Room Procedure

*96.7 Other continuous mechanical ventilation

MDC 5
DISEASES AND DISORDERS OF THE CIRCULATORY SYSTEM

The complete and up-to-date listing of ICD-9-CM diagnosis codes assigned to this MDC can be found online at www.ingenixonline.com/content/drg/resources.asp.

SURGICAL

S DRG 104 Cardiac Valve Procedures and Other Major Cardiothoracic Procedures with Cardiac Catheterization
GMLOS 12.7 AMLOS 14.9 RW 8.2201 T

Operating Room Procedures

*35.1	Open heart valvuloplasty without replacement
*35.2	Replacement of heart valve
35.33	Annuloplasty
37.68	Insertion of percutaneous external heart assist device

AND

Nonoperating Room Procedures

37.21	Right heart cardiac catheterization
37.22	Left heart cardiac catheterization
37.23	Combined right and left heart cardiac catheterization
37.26	Cardiac electrophysiologic stimulation and recording studies
88.52	Angiocardiography of right heart structures
88.53	Angiocardiography of left heart structures
88.54	Combined right and left heart angiocardiography
88.55	Coronary arteriography using single catheter
88.56	Coronary arteriography using two catheters
88.57	Other and unspecified coronary arteriography
88.58	Negative-contrast cardiac roentgenography

S DRG 105 Cardiac Valve Procedures and Other Major Cardiothoracic Procedures without Cardiac Catheterization
GMLOS 8.4 AMLOS 10.2 RW 6.0192 ☑ T

Select operating room procedure listed under DRG 104

S DRG 106 Coronary Bypass with PTCA
GMLOS 9.5 AMLOS 11.2 RW 7.0346

Operating Room Procedures

*36.1	Bypass anastomosis for heart revascularization

AND

Operating Room Procedures

00.66	Percutaneous transluminal coronary angioplasty [PTCA] or coronary atherectomy
35.96	Percutaneous valvuloplasty

DRG 107 No Longer Valid
GMLOS 0.0 AMLOS 0.0 RW 0.0000

Omitted in the October 2005 grouper version

S DRG 108 Other Cardiothoracic Procedures
GMLOS 8.6 AMLOS 11.0 RW 5.8789 ☑ T

Operating Room Procedures

35.31	Operations on papillary muscle
35.32	Operations on chordae tendineae

** Code Range* ☑ *Optimization Potential* ▽ *Targeted Potential* T *Transfer DRG* SP *Special Payment*

DRG 108 — continued

35.34	Infundibulectomy
35.35	Operations on trabeculae carneae cordis
35.39	Operations on other structures adjacent to valves of heart
35.42	Creation of septal defect in heart
35.50	Repair of unspecified septal defect of heart with prosthesis
35.51	Repair of atrial septal defect with prosthesis, open technique
35.53	Repair of ventricular septal defect with prosthesis
35.54	Repair of endocardial cushion defect with prosthesis
*35.6	Repair of atrial and ventricular septa with tissue graft
*35.7	Other and unspecified repair of atrial and ventricular septa
*35.8	Total repair of certain congenital cardiac anomalies
35.91	Interatrial transposition of venous return
35.92	Creation of conduit between right ventricle and pulmonary artery
35.93	Creation of conduit between left ventricle and aorta
35.94	Creation of conduit between atrium and pulmonary artery
35.95	Revision of corrective procedure on heart
35.98	Other operations on septa of heart
35.99	Other operations on valves of heart
36.03	Open chest coronary artery angioplasty
36.2	Heart revascularization by arterial implant
*36.3	Other heart revascularization
*36.9	Other operations on vessels of heart
37.10	Incision of heart, not otherwise specified
37.11	Cardiotomy
37.32	Excision of aneurysm of heart
37.33	Excision or destruction of other lesion or tissue of heart, open approach
37.35	Partial ventriculectomy

OR

The following procedure combination

38.44 Resection of abdominal aorta with replacement

and

38.45 Resection of other thoracic vessels with replacement

DRG 109 No Longer Valid

GMLOS 0.0 AMLOS 0.0 RW 0.0000

Omitted in the October 2005 grouper version

S DRG 110 Major Cardiovascular Procedures with CC

GMLOS 5.7 AMLOS 8.4 RW 3.8417 ☑CC

Operating Room Procedures

*35.0	Closed heart valvotomy
37.12	Pericardiotomy
37.24	Biopsy of pericardium
37.31	Pericardiectomy
*37.4	Repair of heart and pericardium
37.61	Implant of pulsation balloon
37.64	Removal of heart assist system
37.67	Implantation of cardiomyostimulation system
37.91	Open chest cardiac massage
37.99	Other operations on heart and pericardium
38.04	Incision of aorta
38.05	Incision of other thoracic vessels
38.06	Incision of abdominal arteries
38.07	Incision of abdominal veins
38.14	Endarterectomy of aorta
38.15	Endarterectomy of other thoracic vessels
38.16	Endarterectomy of abdominal arteries
38.34	Resection of aorta with anastomosis
38.35	Resection of other thoracic vessels with anastomosis

S *Surgical* M *Medical* CC *CC Indicator* A *Age Restriction* ● *New DRG* ▲ *Revised DRG Title*

38.36	Resection of abdominal arteries with anastomosis
38.37	Resection of abdominal veins with anastomosis
38.44	Resection of abdominal aorta with replacement
38.45	Resection of other thoracic vessels with replacement
38.46	Resection of abdominal arteries with replacement
38.47	Resection of abdominal veins with replacement
38.55	Ligation and stripping of varicose veins of other thoracic vessel
38.64	Other excision of abdominal aorta
38.65	Other excision of other thoracic vessel
38.66	Other excision of abdominal arteries
38.67	Other excision of abdominal veins
38.84	Other surgical occlusion of abdominal aorta
38.85	Other surgical occlusion of other thoracic vessel
38.86	Other surgical occlusion of abdominal arteries
38.87	Other surgical occlusion of abdominal veins
39.0	Systemic to pulmonary artery shunt
39.1	Intra-abdominal venous shunt
39.21	Caval-pulmonary artery anastomosis
39.22	Aorta-subclavian-carotid bypass
39.23	Other intrathoracic vascular shunt or bypass
39.24	Aorta-renal bypass
39.25	Aorta-iliac-femoral bypass
39.26	Other intra-abdominal vascular shunt or bypass
39.52	Other repair of aneurysm
39.54	Re-entry operation (aorta)
39.71	Endovascular implantation of graft in abdominal aorta
39.72	Endovascular repair or occlusion of head and neck vessels
39.73	Endovascular implantation of graft in thoracic aorta
39.79	Other endovascular repair (of aneurysm) of other vessels

[S] DRG 111 Major Cardiovascular Procedures without CC

GMLOS 2.6 AMLOS 3.4 RW 2.4840 ☑

Select operating room procedure listed under DRG 110

DRG 112 No Longer Valid

GMLOS 0.0 AMLOS 0.0 RW 0.0000

Omitted in the October 2001 grouper version

[S] DRG 113 Amputation for Circulatory System Disorders Except Upper Limb and Toe

GMLOS 10.8 AMLOS 13.7 RW 3.1682 [T]

Operating Room Procedures

84.10	Lower limb amputation, not otherwise specified
84.12	Amputation through foot
84.13	Disarticulation of ankle
84.14	Amputation of ankle through malleoli of tibia and fibula
84.15	Other amputation below knee
84.16	Disarticulation of knee
84.17	Amputation above knee
84.18	Disarticulation of hip
84.19	Abdominopelvic amputation
84.91	Amputation, not otherwise specified

[S] DRG 114 Upper Limb and Toe Amputation for Circulatory System Disorders

GMLOS 6.7 AMLOS 8.9 RW 1.7354 ☑ [T]

Operating Room Procedures

*84.0	Amputation of upper limb
84.11	Amputation of toe
84.3	Revision of amputation stump

DRG 115 No Longer Valid

GMLOS 0.0 AMLOS 0.0 RW 0.0000

Omitted in the October 2005 grouper version

DRG 116 No Longer Valid

GMLOS 0.0 AMLOS 0.0 RW 0.0000

Omitted in the October 2005 grouper version

[S] DRG 117 Cardiac Pacemaker Revision Except Device Replacement

GMLOS 2.6 AMLOS 4.2 RW 1.3223 ☑

Operating Room Procedures

37.74	Insertion or replacement of epicardial lead (electrode) into epicardium (must be in combination with 37.80, 37.81, 37.82, 37.83, 37.85, 37.86, or 37.87)
37.75	Revision of lead (electrode) (must be in combination with 37.80, 37.85, 37.86 or 37.87)
37.76	Replacement of transvenous atrial and/or ventricular lead(s) (electrode(s))
37.77	Removal of lead(s) (electrodes) without replacement
37.79	Revision or relocation of cardiac device pocket
37.89	Revision or removal of pacemaker device

[S] DRG 118 Cardiac Pacemaker Device Replacement

GMLOS 2.1 AMLOS 3.0 RW 1.6380 ☑

Operating Room Procedures

00.53	Implantation or replacement of cardiac resynchronization pacemaker pulse generator only (CRT-P)
37.80	Insertion of permanent pacemaker, initial or replacement, type of device not specified
37.85	Replacement of any type of pacemaker device with single-chamber device, not specified as rate responsive
37.86	Replacement of any type of pacemaker device with single-chamber device, rate responsive
37.87	Replacement of any type of pacemaker device with dual-chamber device

[S] DRG 119 Vein Ligation and Stripping

GMLOS 3.3 AMLOS 5.5 RW 1.3456

Operating Room Procedures

38.09	Incision of lower limb veins
38.39	Resection of lower limb veins with anastomosis
38.49	Resection of lower limb veins with replacement
38.50	Ligation and stripping of varicose veins, unspecified site
38.53	Ligation and stripping of varicose veins of upper limb vessels
38.59	Ligation and stripping of lower limb varicose veins
38.69	Other excision of lower limb veins
38.89	Other surgical occlusion of lower limb veins
39.32	Suture of vein
39.92	Injection of sclerosing agent into vein

[S] DRG 120 Other Circulatory System O.R. Procedures

GMLOS 5.9 AMLOS 9.2 RW 2.3853 [T]

Operating Room Procedures

05.0	Division of sympathetic nerve or ganglion
*05.2	Sympathectomy

05.89	Other operations on sympathetic nerves or ganglia
21.04	Control of epistaxis by ligation of ethmoidal arteries
21.05	Control of epistaxis by (transantral) ligation of the maxillary artery
21.06	Control of epistaxis by ligation of the external carotid artery
21.07	Control of epistaxis by excision of nasal mucosa and skin grafting of septum and lateral nasal wall
21.09	Control of epistaxis by other means
25.1	Excision or destruction of lesion or tissue of tongue
31.72	Closure of external fistula of trachea
31.74	Revision of tracheostomy
33.27	Closed endoscopic biopsy of lung
33.28	Open biopsy of lung
34.02	Exploratory thoracotomy
34.03	Reopening of recent thoracotomy site
34.1	Incision of mediastinum
34.21	Transpleural thoracoscopy
34.22	Mediastinoscopy
34.26	Open biopsy of mediastinum
34.29	Other diagnostic procedures on mediastinum
39.27	Arteriovenostomy for renal dialysis
39.42	Revision of arteriovenous shunt for renal dialysis
39.43	Removal of arteriovenous shunt for renal dialysis
39.93	Insertion of vessel-to-vessel cannula
39.98	Control of hemorrhage, not otherwise specified
*40.1	Diagnostic procedures on lymphatic structures
40.21	Excision of deep cervical lymph node
40.23	Excision of axillary lymph node
40.24	Excision of inguinal lymph node
40.29	Simple excision of other lymphatic structure
40.3	Regional lymph node excision
41.5	Total splenectomy
43.6	Partial gastrectomy with anastomosis to duodenum
43.7	Partial gastrectomy with anastomosis to jejunum
43.89	Other partial gastrectomy
43.99	Other total gastrectomy
44.38	Laparoscopic gastroenterostomy
45.61	Multiple segmental resection of small intestine
45.62	Other partial resection of small intestine
45.72	Cecectomy
45.73	Right hemicolectomy
45.74	Resection of transverse colon
45.75	Left hemicolectomy
45.79	Other partial excision of large intestine
45.8	Total intra-abdominal colectomy
45.93	Other small-to-large intestinal anastomosis
46.03	Exteriorization of large intestine
46.13	Permanent colostomy
47.09	Other appendectomy
48.25	Open biopsy of rectum
48.35	Local excision of rectal lesion or tissue
48.62	Anterior resection of rectum with synchronous colostomy
48.63	Other anterior resection of rectum
48.69	Other resection of rectum
50.12	Open biopsy of liver
54.0	Incision of abdominal wall
54.11	Exploratory laparotomy
54.19	Other laparotomy
54.93	Creation of cutaneoperitoneal fistula
54.95	Incision of peritoneum
55.91	Decapsulation of kidney
86.06	Insertion of totally implantable infusion pump
86.22	Excisional debridement of wound, infection, or burn
86.4	Radical excision of skin lesion

***** Code Range** ☑ ***Optimization Potential*** ***Targeted Potential*** T ***Transfer DRG*** SP ***Special Payment***

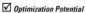

DRG 120 — continued

86.60	Free skin graft, not otherwise specified
86.61	Full-thickness skin graft to hand
86.62	Other skin graft to hand
86.63	Full-thickness skin graft to other sites
86.65	Heterograft to skin
86.66	Homograft to skin
86.67	Dermal regenerative graft
86.69	Other skin graft to other sites
86.70	Pedicle or flap graft, not otherwise specified
86.71	Cutting and preparation of pedicle grafts or flaps
86.72	Advancement of pedicle graft
86.74	Attachment of pedicle or flap graft to other sites
86.75	Revision of pedicle or flap graft
86.91	Excision of skin for graft
86.93	Insertion of tissue expander
92.27	Implantation or insertion of radioactive elements

DRG 478 No Longer Valid

GMLOS 0.0 AMLOS 0.0 RW 0.0000

Omitted in the October 2005 grouper version

S DRG 479 Other Vascular Procedures without CC

GMLOS 2.1 AMLOS 2.8 RW 1.4434 ☑

Operating Room Procedures

00.61	Percutaneous angioplasty or atherectomy of precerebral (extracranial) vessel(s)
00.62	Percutaneous angioplasty or atherectomy of intracranial vessel(s)
38.00	Incision of vessel, unspecified site
38.02	Incision of other vessels of head and neck
38.03	Incision of upper limb vessels
38.08	Incision of lower limb arteries
38.10	Endarterectomy, unspecified site
38.12	Endarterectomy of other vessels of head and neck
38.13	Endarterectomy of upper limb vessels
38.18	Endarterectomy of lower limb arteries
38.21	Biopsy of blood vessel
38.29	Other diagnostic procedures on blood vessels
38.30	Resection of vessel with anastomosis, unspecified site
38.32	Resection of other vessels of head and neck with anastomosis
38.33	Resection of upper limb vessels with anastomosis
38.38	Resection of lower limb arteries with anastomosis
38.40	Resection of vessel with replacement, unspecified site
38.42	Resection of other vessels of head and neck with replacement
38.43	Resection of upper limb vessels with replacement
38.48	Resection of lower limb arteries with replacement
38.52	Ligation and stripping of varicose veins of other vessels of head and neck
38.57	Ligation and stripping of abdominal varicose veins
38.60	Other excision of vessels, unspecified site
38.62	Other excision of other vessels of head and neck
38.63	Other excision of upper limb vessels
38.68	Other excision of lower limb arteries
38.7	Interruption of the vena cava
38.80	Other surgical occlusion of vessels, unspecified site
38.82	Other surgical occlusion of other vessels of head and neck
38.83	Other surgical occlusion of upper limb vessels
38.88	Other surgical occlusion of lower limb arteries
39.29	Other (peripheral) vascular shunt or bypass
39.30	Suture of unspecified blood vessel
39.31	Suture of artery
39.41	Control of hemorrhage following vascular surgery
39.49	Other revision of vascular procedure

39.50	Angioplasty or atherectomy of other non-coronary vessel(s)
39.51	Clipping of aneurysm
39.53	Repair of arteriovenous fistula
39.55	Reimplantation of aberrant renal vessel
39.56	Repair of blood vessel with tissue patch graft
39.57	Repair of blood vessel with synthetic patch graft
39.58	Repair of blood vessel with unspecified type of patch graft
39.59	Other repair of vessel
39.8	Operations on carotid body and other vascular bodies
39.91	Freeing of vessel
39.94	Replacement of vessel-to-vessel cannula
39.99	Other operations on vessels

DRG 514 No Longer Valid

GMLOS 0.0 AMLOS 0.0 RW 0.0000

Omitted in the October 2003 grouper version

S DRG 515 Cardiac Defibrillator Implant without Cardiac Catheterization

GMLOS 2.6 AMLOS 4.3 RW 5.5205 ☑

Operating Room Procedures

00.51	Implantation of cardiac resynchronization defibrillator, total system (CRT-D)
37.94	Implantation or replacement of automatic cardioverter/ defibrillator, total system (AICD)

OR

Any of the following procedure combinations

00.52 Implantation or replacement of transvenous lead (electrode) into left ventricular coronary venous system

and

00.54 Implantation or replacement of cardiac resynchronization defibrillator pulse generator device only (CRT-D)

OR

37.95 Implantation of automatic cardioverter/defibrillator leads(s) only

and

00.54 Implantation or replacement of cardiac resynchronization defibrillator pulse generator device only (CRT-D)

OR

37.97 Replacement of automatic cardioverter/defibrillator leads(s) only

and

00.54 Implantation or replacement of cardiac resynchronization defibrillator pulse generator device only (CRT-D)

OR

37.95 Implantation of automatic cardioverter/defibrillator leads(s) only

and

37.96 Implantation of automatic cardioverter/defibrillator pulse generator only

OR

37.97 Replacement of automatic cardioverter/defibrillator leads(s) only

and

37.98 Replacement of automatic cardioverter/defibrillator pulse generator only

OR

Nonoperating Room Procedure

37.26 Cardiac electrophysiologic stimulation and recording studies

DRG 516 No Longer Valid

GMLOS 0.0 AMLOS 0.0 RW 0.0000

Omitted in the October 2005 grouper version

DRG 517 No Longer Valid

GMLOS 0.0 AMLOS 0.0 RW 0.0000

Omitted in the October 2005 grouper version

S DRG 518 Percutaneous Cardiovascular Procedures without Acute Myocardial Infarction without Coronary Artery Stent Implant

GMLOS 1.8 AMLOS 2.5 RW 1.6544 ☑

Operating Room Procedures

00.66	Percutaneous transluminal coronary angioplasty [PTCA] or coronary atherectomy
35.52	Repair of atrial septal defect with prosthesis, closed technique
35.96	Percutaneous valvuloplasty
36.09	Other removal of coronary artery obstruction
37.34	Excision or destruction of other lesion or tissue of heart, other approach

OR

Nonoperating Room Procedures

37.26	Cardiac electrophysiologic stimulation and recording studies
37.27	Cardiac mapping
37.90	Insertion of left atrial appendage device

S DRG 525 Other Heart Assist System Implant

GMLOS 7.2 AMLOS 13.6 RW 11.4282

Operating Room Procedures

37.52	Implantation of total replacement heart system
37.53	Replacement or repair of thoracic unit of total replacement heart system
37.54	Replacement or repair of other implantable component of total replacement heart system
37.62	Insertion of non-implantable heart assist system
37.63	Repair of heart assist system
37.65	Implant of external heart assist system

DRG 526 No Longer Valid

GMLOS 0.0 AMLOS 0.0 RW 0.0000

Omitted in the October 2005 grouper version

DRG 527 No Longer Valid

GMLOS 0.0 AMLOS 0.0 RW 0.0000

Omitted in the October 2005 grouper version

S DRG 535 Cardiac Defibrillator Implant with Cardiac Catheterization with Acute Myocardial Infarction, Heart Failure, or Shock

GMLOS 7.9 AMLOS 10.3 RW 7.9738 ☑

Principal Diagnosis

398.91	Rheumatic heart failure (congestive)
402.01	Malignant hypertensive heart disease with heart failure
402.11	Benign hypertensive heart disease with heart failure
402.91	Unspecified hypertensive heart disease with heart failure
404.01	Hypertensive heart and kidney disease, malignant, with heart failure

404.03	Hypertensive heart and kidney disease, malignant, with heart failure and chronic kidney disease
404.11	Hypertensive heart and kidney disease, benign, with heart failure
404.13	Hypertensive heart and kidney disease, benign, with heart failure and chronic kidney disease
404.91	Hypertensive heart and kidney disease, unspecified, with heart failure
404.93	Hypertensive heart and kidney disease, unspecified, with heart failure and chronic kidney disease
410.01	Acute myocardial infarction of anterolateral wall, initial episode of care
410.11	Acute myocardial infarction of other anterior wall, initial episode of care
410.21	Acute myocardial infarction of inferolateral wall, initial episode of care
410.31	Acute myocardial infarction of inferoposterior wall, initial episode of care
410.41	Acute myocardial infarction of other inferior wall, initial episode of care
410.51	Acute myocardial infarction of other lateral wall, initial episode of care
410.61	Acute myocardial infarction, true posterior wall infarction, initial episode of care
410.71	Acute myocardial infarction, subendocardial infarction, initial episode of care
410.81	Acute myocardial infarction of other specified sites, initial episode of care
410.91	Acute myocardial infarction, unspecified site, initial episode of care
428.0	Congestive heart failure, unspecified
428.1	Left heart failure
*428.2	Systolic heart failure
*428.3	Diastolic heart failure
*428.4	Combined systolic and diastolic heart failure
428.9	Unspecified heart failure
785.50	Unspecified shock
785.51	Cardiogenic shock

AND

Operating Room Procedures

00.51	Implantation of cardiac resynchronization defibrillator, total system (CRT-D)
37.94	Implantation or replacement of automatic cardioverter/ defibrillator, total system (AICD)

OR

Any of the following procedure combinations

00.52 Implantation or replacement of transvenous lead (electrode) into left ventricular coronary venous system

and

00.54 Implantation or replacement of cardiac resynchronization defibrillator pulse generator device only (CRT-D)

OR

37.95 Implantation of automatic cardioverter/defibrillator leads(s) only

and

37.96 Implantation of automatic cardioverter/defibrillator pulse generator only

OR

37.95 Implantation of automatic cardioverter/defibrillator leads(s) only

and

00.54 Implantation or replacement of cardiac resynchronization defibrillator pulse generator device only (CRT-D)

OR

37.97 Replacement of automatic cardioverter/defibrillator leads(s) only

and

00.54 Implantation or replacement of cardiac resynchronization defibrillator pulse generator device only (CRT-D)

DRG 535 — continued

OR

37.97	Replacement of automatic cardioverter/defibrillator leads(s) only
	and
37.98	Replacement of automatic cardioverter/defibrillator pulse generator only

AND

Nonoperating Room Procedures

37.21	Right heart cardiac catheterization
37.22	Left heart cardiac catheterization
37.23	Combined right and left heart cardiac catheterization
88.52	Angiocardiography of right heart structures
88.53	Angiocardiography of left heart structures
88.54	Combined right and left heart angiocardiography
88.55	Coronary arteriography using single catheter
88.56	Coronary arteriography using two catheters
88.57	Other and unspecified coronary arteriography
88.58	Negative-contrast cardiac roentgenography

S DRG 536 Cardiac Defibrillator Implant with Cardiac Catheterization without Acute Myocardial Infarction, Heart Failure, or Shock

GMLOS 5.9 AMLOS 7.6 RW 6.9144 ☑

Select any principal diagnosis listed under MDC 5 excluding acute myocardial infarction, heart failure and shock

Select any operating room procedure or combinations and nonoperating room procedures listed under DRG 535

● S DRG 547 Coronary Bypass with Cardiac Catheterization with Major Cardiovascular Diagnosis

GMLOS 10.8 AMLOS 12.3 RW 6.1948 T

Principal or Secondary Diagnosis of Major Cardiovascular Condition (MCV)

398.91	Rheumatic heart failure (congestive)
402.01	Malignant hypertensive heart disease with heart failure
402.11	Benign hypertensive heart disease with heart failure
402.91	Unspecified hypertensive heart disease with heart failure
404.01	Hypertensive heart and kidney disease, malignant, with heart failure
404.03	Hypertensive heart and kidney disease, malignant, with heart failure and chronic kidney disease
404.11	Hypertensive heart and kidney disease, benign, with heart failure
404.13	Hypertensive heart and kidney disease, benign, with heart failure and chronic kidney disease
404.91	Hypertensive heart and kidney disease, unspecified, with heart failure
404.93	Hypertensive heart and kidney disease, unspecified, with heart failure and chronic kidney disease
410.01	Acute myocardial infarction of anterolateral wall, initial episode of care
410.11	Acute myocardial infarction of other anterior wall, initial episode of care
410.21	Acute myocardial infarction of inferolateral wall, initial episode of care
410.31	Acute myocardial infarction of inferoposterior wall, initial episode of care
410.41	Acute myocardial infarction of other inferior wall, initial episode of care
410.51	Acute myocardial infarction of other lateral wall, initial episode of care
410.61	Acute myocardial infarction, true posterior wall infarction, initial episode of care
410.71	Acute myocardial infarction, subendocardial infarction, initial episode of care
410.81	Acute myocardial infarction of other specified sites, initial episode of care
410.91	Acute myocardial infarction, unspecified site, initial episode of care
411.0	Postmyocardial infarction syndrome
414.10	Aneurysm of heart
414.11	Aneurysm of coronary vessels
414.12	Dissection of coronary artery

414.19	Other aneurysm of heart
415.0	Acute cor pulmonale
420.0	Acute pericarditis in diseases classified elsewhere
420.90	Unspecified acute pericarditis
420.91	Acute idiopathic pericarditis
420.99	Other acute pericarditis
421.0	Acute and subacute bacterial endocarditis
421.1	Acute and subacute infective endocarditis in diseases classified elsewhere
421.9	Unspecified acute endocarditis
422.92	Septic myocarditis
423.0	Hemopericardium
424.90	Endocarditis, valve unspecified, unspecified cause
426.0	Atrioventricular block, complete
426.53	Other bilateral bundle branch block
426.54	Trifascicular block
427.1	Paroxysmal ventricular tachycardia
427.41	Ventricular fibrillation
427.5	Cardiac arrest
428.0	Congestive heart failure, unspecified
428.1	Left heart failure
428.20	Unspecified systolic heart failure
428.21	Acute systolic heart failure
428.22	Chronic systolic heart failure
428.23	Acute on chronic systolic heart failure
428.30	Unspecified diastolic heart failure
428.31	Acute diastolic heart failure
428.32	Chronic diastolic heart failure
428.33	Acute on chronic diastolic heart failure
428.40	Unspecified combined systolic and diastolic heart failure
428.41	Acute combined systolic and diastolic heart failure
428.42	Chronic combined systolic and diastolic heart failure
428.43	Acute on chronic combined systolic and diastolic heart failure
428.9	Unspecified heart failure
429.5	Rupture of chordae tendineae
429.6	Rupture of papillary muscle
429.71	Acquired cardiac septal defect
429.79	Other certain sequelae of myocardial infarction, not elsewhere classified
429.81	Other disorders of papillary muscle
441.00	Dissecting aortic aneurysm (any part), unspecified site
441.01	Dissecting aortic aneurysm (any part), thoracic
441.02	Dissecting aortic aneurysm (any part), abdominal
441.03	Dissecting aortic aneurysm (any part), thoracoabdominal
441.1	Thoracic aneurysm, ruptured
441.3	Abdominal aneurysm, ruptured
441.5	Aortic aneurysm of unspecified site, ruptured
441.6	Thoracoabdominal aneurysm, ruptured
443.22	Dissection of iliac artery
443.29	Dissection of other artery
444.0	Embolism and thrombosis of abdominal aorta
444.1	Embolism and thrombosis of thoracic aorta
453.2	Embolism and thrombosis of vena cava
785.50	Unspecified shock
785.51	Cardiogenic shock
861.02	Heart laceration without penetration of heart chambers or mention of open wound into thorax
861.03	Heart laceration with penetration of heart chambers, without mention of open wound into thorax
861.10	Unspecified injury to heart with open wound into thorax
861.11	Heart contusion with open wound into thorax
861.12	Heart laceration without penetration of heart chambers, with open wound into thorax
861.13	Heart laceration with penetration of heart chambers and open wound into thorax
996.61	Infection and inflammatory reaction due to cardiac device, implant, and graft
996.62	Infection and inflammatory reaction due to other vascular device, implant, and graft

MDC 5: Circulatory System — Surgical

DRG 547 — continued

996.72	Other complications due to other cardiac device, implant, and graft
996.83	Complications of transplanted heart

OR

Secondary Diagnosis of Major Cardiovascular Condition (MCV)

415.11	Iatrogenic pulmonary embolism and infarction
415.19	Other pulmonary embolism and infarction
430	Subarachnoid hemorrhage
431	Intracerebral hemorrhage
432.0	Nontraumatic extradural hemorrhage
432.1	Subdural hemorrhage
432.9	Unspecified intracranial hemorrhage
433.01	Occlusion and stenosis of basilar artery with cerebral infarction
433.11	Occlusion and stenosis of carotid artery with cerebral infarction
433.21	Occlusion and stenosis of vertebral artery with cerebral infarction
433.31	Occlusion and stenosis of multiple and bilateral precerebral arteries with cerebral infarction
433.81	Occlusion and stenosis of other specified precerebral artery with cerebral infarction
433.91	Occlusion and stenosis of unspecified precerebral artery with cerebral infarction
434.00	Cerebral thrombosis without mention of cerebral infarction
434.01	Cerebral thrombosis with cerebral infarction
434.10	Cerebral embolism without mention of cerebral infarction
434.11	Cerebral embolism with cerebral infarction
434.90	Unspecified cerebral artery occlusion without mention of cerebral infarction
434.91	Unspecified cerebral artery occlusion with cerebral infarction
436	Acute, but ill-defined, cerebrovascular disease
445.81	Atheroembolism of kidney
862.9	Injury to multiple and unspecified intrathoracic organs with open wound into cavity

AND

Operating Room Procedures

*36.1	Bypass anastomosis for heart revascularization

AND

Nonoperating Room Procedures

37.21	Right heart cardiac catheterization
37.22	Left heart cardiac catheterization
37.23	Combined right and left heart cardiac catheterization
88.52	Angiocardiography of right heart structures
88.53	Angiocardiography of left heart structures
88.54	Combined right and left heart angiocardiography
88.55	Coronary arteriography using single catheter
88.56	Coronary arteriography using two catheters
88.57	Other and unspecified coronary arteriography
88.58	Negative-contrast cardiac roentgenography

● S DRG 548 Coronary Bypass with Cardiac Catheterization without Major Cardiovascular Diagnosis

GMLOS 8.2 AMLOS 9.0 RW 4.7198 T

Operating Room Procedures

*36.1	Bypass anastomosis for heart revascularization

AND

Nonoperating Room Procedures

37.21	Right heart cardiac catheterization
37.22	Left heart cardiac catheterization
37.23	Combined right and left heart cardiac catheterization
88.52	Angiocardiography of right heart structures
88.53	Angiocardiography of left heart structures
88.54	Combined right and left heart angiocardiography
88.55	Coronary arteriography using single catheter
88.56	Coronary arteriography using two catheters

88.57 Other and unspecified coronary arteriography
88.58 Negative-contrast cardiac roentgenography

● S DRG 549 Coronary Bypass without Cardiac Catheterization with Major Cardiovascular Diagnosis

GMLOS 8.7 AMLOS 10.3 RW 5.0980 T

Principal or Secondary Diagnosis of Major Cardiovascular Condition (MCV)

398.91	Rheumatic heart failure (congestive)
402.01	Malignant hypertensive heart disease with heart failure
402.11	Benign hypertensive heart disease with heart failure
402.91	Unspecified hypertensive heart disease with heart failure
404.01	Hypertensive heart and kidney disease, malignant, with heart failure
404.03	Hypertensive heart and kidney disease, malignant, with heart failure and chronic kidney disease
404.11	Hypertensive heart and kidney disease, benign, with heart failure
404.13	Hypertensive heart and kidney disease, benign, with heart failure and chronic kidney disease
404.91	Hypertensive heart and kidney disease, unspecified, with heart failure
404.93	Hypertensive heart and kidney disease, unspecified, with heart failure and chronic kidney disease
410.01	Acute myocardial infarction of anterolateral wall, initial episode of care
410.11	Acute myocardial infarction of other anterior wall, initial episode of care
410.21	Acute myocardial infarction of inferolateral wall, initial episode of care
410.31	Acute myocardial infarction of inferoposterior wall, initial episode of care
410.41	Acute myocardial infarction of other inferior wall, initial episode of care
410.51	Acute myocardial infarction of other lateral wall, initial episode of care
410.61	Acute myocardial infarction, true posterior wall infarction, initial episode of care
410.71	Acute myocardial infarction, subendocardial infarction, initial episode of care
410.81	Acute myocardial infarction of other specified sites, initial episode of care
410.91	Acute myocardial infarction, unspecified site, initial episode of care
411.0	Postmyocardial infarction syndrome
414.10	Aneurysm of heart
414.11	Aneurysm of coronary vessels
414.12	Dissection of coronary artery
414.19	Other aneurysm of heart
415.0	Acute cor pulmonale
420.0	Acute pericarditis in diseases classified elsewhere
420.90	Unspecified acute pericarditis
420.91	Acute idiopathic pericarditis
420.99	Other acute pericarditis
421.0	Acute and subacute bacterial endocarditis
421.1	Acute and subacute infective endocarditis in diseases classified elsewhere
421.9	Unspecified acute endocarditis
422.92	Septic myocarditis
423.0	Hemopericardium
424.90	Endocarditis, valve unspecified, unspecified cause
426.0	Atrioventricular block, complete
426.53	Other bilateral bundle branch block
426.54	Trifascicular block
427.1	Paroxysmal ventricular tachycardia
427.41	Ventricular fibrillation
427.5	Cardiac arrest
428.0	Congestive heart failure, unspecified
428.1	Left heart failure
428.20	Unspecified systolic heart failure
428.21	Acute systolic heart failure
428.22	Chronic systolic heart failure
428.23	Acute on chronic systolic heart failure
428.30	Unspecified diastolic heart failure
428.31	Acute diastolic heart failure
428.32	Chronic diastolic heart failure
428.33	Acute on chronic diastolic heart failure
428.40	Unspecified combined systolic and diastolic heart failure

DRG 549 — continued

428.41	Acute combined systolic and diastolic heart failure
428.42	Chronic combined systolic and diastolic heart failure
428.43	Acute on chronic combined systolic and diastolic heart failure
428.9	Unspecified heart failure
429.5	Rupture of chordae tendineae
429.6	Rupture of papillary muscle
429.71	Acquired cardiac septal defect
429.79	Other certain sequelae of myocardial infarction, not elsewhere classified
429.81	Other disorders of papillary muscle
441.00	Dissecting aortic aneurysm (any part), unspecified site
441.01	Dissecting aortic aneurysm (any part), thoracic
441.02	Dissecting aortic aneurysm (any part), abdominal
441.03	Dissecting aortic aneurysm (any part), thoracoabdominal
441.1	Thoracic aneurysm, ruptured
441.3	Abdominal aneurysm, ruptured
441.5	Aortic aneurysm of unspecified site, ruptured
441.6	Thoracoabdominal aneurysm, ruptured
443.22	Dissection of iliac artery
443.29	Dissection of other artery
444.0	Embolism and thrombosis of abdominal aorta
444.1	Embolism and thrombosis of thoracic aorta
453.2	Embolism and thrombosis of vena cava
785.50	Unspecified shock
785.51	Cardiogenic shock
861.02	Heart laceration without penetration of heart chambers or mention of open wound into thorax
861.03	Heart laceration with penetration of heart chambers, without mention of open wound into thorax
861.10	Unspecified injury to heart with open wound into thorax
861.11	Heart contusion with open wound into thorax
861.12	Heart laceration without penetration of heart chambers, with open wound into thorax
861.13	Heart laceration with penetration of heart chambers and open wound into thorax
996.61	Infection and inflammatory reaction due to cardiac device, implant, and graft
996.62	Infection and inflammatory reaction due to other vascular device, implant, and graft
996.72	Other complications due to other cardiac device, implant, and graft
996.83	Complications of transplanted heart

OR

Secondary Diagnosis of Major Cardiovascular Condition (MCV)

415.11	Iatrogenic pulmonary embolism and infarction
415.19	Other pulmonary embolism and infarction
430	Subarachnoid hemorrhage
431	Intracerebral hemorrhage
432.0	Nontraumatic extradural hemorrhage
432.1	Subdural hemorrhage
432.9	Unspecified intracranial hemorrhage
433.01	Occlusion and stenosis of basilar artery with cerebral infarction
433.11	Occlusion and stenosis of carotid artery with cerebral infarction
433.21	Occlusion and stenosis of vertebral artery with cerebral infarction
433.31	Occlusion and stenosis of multiple and bilateral precerebral arteries with cerebral infarction
433.81	Occlusion and stenosis of other specified precerebral artery with cerebral infarction
433.91	Occlusion and stenosis of unspecified precerebral artery with cerebral infarction
434.00	Cerebral thrombosis without mention of cerebral infarction
434.01	Cerebral thrombosis with cerebral infarction
434.10	Cerebral embolism without mention of cerebral infarction
434.11	Cerebral embolism with cerebral infarction
434.90	Unspecified cerebral artery occlusion without mention of cerebral infarction
434.91	Unspecified cerebral artery occlusion with cerebral infarction
436	Acute, but ill-defined, cerebrovascular disease
445.81	Atheroembolism of kidney
862.9	Injury to multiple and unspecified intrathoracic organs with open wound into cavity

AND

Operating Room Procedures

*36.1	Bypass anastomosis for heart revascularization

● S DRG 550 Coronary Bypass without Cardiac Catheterization without Major Cardiovascular Diagnosis

GMLOS 6.2 AMLOS 6.9 RW 3.6151 T

Operating Room Procedures

*36.1	Bypass anastomosis for heart revascularization

● S DRG 551 Permanent Cardiac Pacemaker Implant with Major Cardiovascular Diagnosis or AICD Lead or Generator

GMLOS 4.4 AMLOS 6.4 RW 3.1007 ☑

Principal or Secondary Diagnosis of Major Cardiovascular Condition (MCV)

398.91	Rheumatic heart failure (congestive)
402.01	Malignant hypertensive heart disease with heart failure
402.11	Benign hypertensive heart disease with heart failure
402.91	Unspecified hypertensive heart disease with heart failure
404.01	Hypertensive heart and kidney disease, malignant, with heart failure
404.03	Hypertensive heart and kidney disease, malignant, with heart failure and chronic kidney disease
404.11	Hypertensive heart and kidney disease, benign, with heart failure
404.13	Hypertensive heart and kidney disease, benign, with heart failure and chronic kidney disease
404.91	Hypertensive heart and kidney disease, unspecified, with heart failure
404.93	Hypertensive heart and kidney disease, unspecified, with heart failure and chronic kidney disease
410.01	Acute myocardial infarction of anterolateral wall, initial episode of care
410.11	Acute myocardial infarction of other anterior wall, initial episode of care
410.21	Acute myocardial infarction of inferolateral wall, initial episode of care
410.31	Acute myocardial infarction of inferoposterior wall, initial episode of care
410.41	Acute myocardial infarction of other inferior wall, initial episode of care
410.51	Acute myocardial infarction of other lateral wall, initial episode of care
410.61	Acute myocardial infarction, true posterior wall infarction, initial episode of care
410.71	Acute myocardial infarction, subendocardial infarction, initial episode of care
410.81	Acute myocardial infarction of other specified sites, initial episode of care
410.91	Acute myocardial infarction, unspecified site, initial episode of care
411.0	Postmyocardial infarction syndrome
411.1	Intermediate coronary syndrome
411.81	Acute coronary occlusion without myocardial infarction
414.10	Aneurysm of heart
414.11	Aneurysm of coronary vessels
414.12	Dissection of coronary artery
414.19	Other aneurysm of heart
415.0	Acute cor pulmonale
420.0	Acute pericarditis in diseases classified elsewhere
420.90	Unspecified acute pericarditis
420.91	Acute idiopathic pericarditis
420.99	Other acute pericarditis
421.0	Acute and subacute bacterial endocarditis
421.1	Acute and subacute infective endocarditis in diseases classified elsewhere
421.9	Unspecified acute endocarditis
422.92	Septic myocarditis
423.0	Hemopericardium
424.90	Endocarditis, valve unspecified, unspecified cause
427.1	Paroxysmal ventricular tachycardia
427.41	Ventricular fibrillation
427.5	Cardiac arrest
428.0	Congestive heart failure, unspecified
428.1	Left heart failure
428.20	Unspecified systolic heart failure

MDC 5: Circulatory System – Surgical

** Code Range* ☑ *Optimization Potential* *Targeted Potential* T *Transfer DRG* *Special Payment*

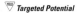

DRG 551 — continued

428.21	Acute systolic heart failure
428.22	Chronic systolic heart failure
428.23	Acute on chronic systolic heart failure
428.30	Unspecified diastolic heart failure
428.31	Acute diastolic heart failure
428.32	Chronic diastolic heart failure
428.33	Acute on chronic diastolic heart failure
428.40	Unspecified combined systolic and diastolic heart failure
428.41	Acute combined systolic and diastolic heart failure
428.42	Chronic combined systolic and diastolic heart failure
428.43	Acute on chronic combined systolic and diastolic heart failure
428.9	Unspecified heart failure
429.5	Rupture of chordae tendineae
429.6	Rupture of papillary muscle
429.71	Acquired cardiac septal defect
429.79	Other certain sequelae of myocardial infarction, not elsewhere classified
429.81	Other disorders of papillary muscle
441.00	Dissecting aortic aneurysm (any part), unspecified site
441.01	Dissecting aortic aneurysm (any part), thoracic
441.02	Dissecting aortic aneurysm (any part), abdominal
441.03	Dissecting aortic aneurysm (any part), thoracoabdominal
441.1	Thoracic aneurysm, ruptured
441.3	Abdominal aneurysm, ruptured
441.5	Aortic aneurysm of unspecified site, ruptured
441.6	Thoracoabdominal aneurysm, ruptured
443.22	Dissection of iliac artery
443.29	Dissection of other artery
444.0	Embolism and thrombosis of abdominal aorta
444.1	Embolism and thrombosis of thoracic aorta
453.2	Embolism and thrombosis of vena cava
785.50	Unspecified shock
785.51	Cardiogenic shock
861.02	Heart laceration without penetration of heart chambers or mention of open wound into thorax
861.03	Heart laceration with penetration of heart chambers, without mention of open wound into thorax
861.10	Unspecified injury to heart with open wound into thorax
861.11	Heart contusion with open wound into thorax
861.12	Heart laceration without penetration of heart chambers, with open wound into thorax
861.13	Heart laceration with penetration of heart chambers and open wound into thorax
996.61	Infection and inflammatory reaction due to cardiac device, implant, and graft
996.62	Infection and inflammatory reaction due to other vascular device, implant, and graft
996.72	Other complications due to other cardiac device, implant, and graft
996.83	Complications of transplanted heart

OR

Secondary Diagnosis of Major Cardiovascular Condition (MCV)

415.11	Iatrogenic pulmonary embolism and infarction
415.19	Other pulmonary embolism and infarction
430	Subarachnoid hemorrhage
431	Intracerebral hemorrhage
432.0	Nontraumatic extradural hemorrhage
432.1	Subdural hemorrhage
432.9	Unspecified intracranial hemorrhage
433.01	Occlusion and stenosis of basilar artery with cerebral infarction
433.11	Occlusion and stenosis of carotid artery with cerebral infarction
433.21	Occlusion and stenosis of vertebral artery with cerebral infarction
433.31	Occlusion and stenosis of multiple and bilateral precerebral arteries with cerebral infarction
433.81	Occlusion and stenosis of other specified precerebral artery with cerebral infarction
433.91	Occlusion and stenosis of unspecified precerebral artery with cerebral infarction
434.00	Cerebral thrombosis without mention of cerebral infarction
434.01	Cerebral thrombosis with cerebral infarction
434.10	Cerebral embolism without mention of cerebral infarction

434.11	Cerebral embolism with cerebral infarction
434.90	Unspecified cerebral artery occlusion without mention of cerebral infarction
434.91	Unspecified cerebral artery occlusion with cerebral infarction
436	Acute, but ill-defined, cerebrovascular disease
445.81	Atheroembolism of kidney
862.9	Injury to multiple and unspecified intrathoracic organs with open wound into cavity

AND

Operating Room Procedure

00.50 Implantation of cardiac resynchronization pacemaker without mention of defibrillation, total system (CRT-P)

OR

Any of the following procedure combinations

00.52 Implantation or replacement of transvenous lead (electrode) into left ventricular coronary venous system

and

00.53 Implantation or replacement of cardiac resynchronization pacemaker pulse generator only (CRT-P)

OR

37.70 Initial insertion of lead (electrode), not otherwise specified

and

00.53 Implantation or replacement of cardiac resynchronization pacemaker pulse generator only (CRT-P)

OR

37.70 Initial insertion of lead (electrode), not otherwise specified

and

37.80 Insertion of permanent pacemaker, initial or replacement, type of device not specified

OR

37.70 Initial insertion of lead (electrode), not otherwise specified

and

37.81 Initial insertion of single-chamber device, not specified as rate responsive

OR

37.70 Initial insertion of lead (electrode), not otherwise specified

and

37.82 Initial insertion of single-chamber device, rate responsive

OR

37.70 Initial insertion of lead (electrode), not otherwise specified

and

37.85 Replacement of any type of pacemaker device with single-chamber device, not specified as rate responsive

OR

37.70 Initial insertion of lead (electrode), not otherwise specified

and

37.86 Replacement of any type of pacemaker device with single-chamber device, rate responsive

OR

37.70 Initial insertion of lead (electrode), not otherwise specified

and

37.87 Replacement of any type of pacemaker device with dual-chamber device

DRG 551 — continued

OR

37.71	Initial insertion of transvenous lead (electrode) into ventricle
	and
00.53	Implantation or replacement of cardiac resynchronization pacemaker pulse generator only (CRT-P)

OR

37.71	Initial insertion of transvenous lead (electrode) into ventricle
	and
37.80	Insertion of permanent pacemaker, initial or replacement, type of device not specified

OR

37.71	Initial insertion of transvenous lead (electrode) into ventricle
	and
37.81	Initial insertion of single-chamber device, not specified as rate responsive

OR

37.71	Initial insertion of transvenous lead (electrode) into ventricle
	and
37.82	Initial insertion of single-chamber device, rate responsive

OR

37.71	Initial insertion of transvenous lead (electrode) into ventricle
	and
37.85	Replacement of any type of pacemaker device with single-chamber device, not specified as rate responsive

OR

37.71	Initial insertion of transvenous lead (electrode) into ventricle
	and
37.86	Replacement of any type of pacemaker device with single-chamber device, rate responsive

OR

37.71	Initial insertion of transvenous lead (electrode) into ventricle
	and
37.87	Replacement of any type of pacemaker device with dual-chamber device

OR

37.72	Initial insertion of transvenous leads (electrodes) into atrium and ventricle
	and
00.53	Implantation or replacement of cardiac resynchronization pacemaker pulse generator only (CRT-P)

OR

37.72	Initial insertion of transvenous leads (electrodes) into atrium and ventricle
	and
37.80	Insertion of permanent pacemaker, initial or replacement, type of device not specified

OR

37.72	Initial insertion of transvenous leads (electrodes) into atrium and ventricle
	and
37.83	Initial insertion of dual-chamber device

OR

37.73	Initial insertion of transvenous lead (electrode) into atrium
	and
00.53	Implantation or replacement of cardiac resynchronization pacemaker pulse generator only (CRT-P)

OR

37.73 Initial insertion of transvenous lead (electrode) into atrium

and

37.80 Insertion of permanent pacemaker, initial or replacement, type of device not specified

OR

37.73 Initial insertion of transvenous lead (electrode) into atrium

and

37.81 Initial insertion of single-chamber device, not specified as rate responsive

OR

37.73 Initial insertion of transvenous lead (electrode) into atrium

and

37.82 Initial insertion of single-chamber device, rate responsive

OR

37.73 Initial insertion of transvenous lead (electrode) into atrium

and

37.85 Replacement of any type of pacemaker device with single-chamber device, not specified as rate responsive

OR

37.73 Initial insertion of transvenous lead (electrode) into atrium

and

37.86 Replacement of any type of pacemaker device with single-chamber device, rate responsive

OR

37.73 Initial insertion of transvenous lead (electrode) into atrium

and

37.87 Replacement of any type of pacemaker device with dual-chamber device

OR

37.74 Insertion or replacement of epicardial lead (electrode) into epicardium

and

00.53 Implantation or replacement of cardiac resynchronization pacemaker pulse generator only (CRT-P)

OR

37.74 Insertion or replacement of epicardial lead (electrode) into epicardium

and

37.80 Insertion of permanent pacemaker, initial or replacement, type of device not specified

OR

37.74 Insertion or replacement of epicardial lead (electrode) into epicardium

and

37.81 Initial insertion of single-chamber device, not specified as rate responsive

OR

37.74 Insertion or replacement of epicardial lead (electrode) into epicardium

and

37.82 Initial insertion of single-chamber device, rate responsive

OR

37.74 Insertion or replacement of epicardial lead (electrode) into epicardium

and

37.83 Initial insertion of dual-chamber device

DRG 551 — continued

OR

37.74 Insertion or replacement of epicardial lead (electrode) into epicardium

and

37.85 Replacement of any type of pacemaker device with single-chamber device, not specified as rate responsive

OR

37.74 Insertion or replacement of epicardial lead (electrode) into epicardium

and

37.86 Replacement of any type of pacemaker device with single-chamber device, rate responsive

OR

37.74 Insertion or replacement of epicardial lead (electrode) into epicardium

and

37.87 Replacement of any type of pacemaker device with dual-chamber device

OR

37.76 Replacement of transvenous atrial and/or ventricular lead(s) (electrode(s))

and

00.53 Implantation or replacement of cardiac resynchronization pacemaker pulse generator only (CRT-P)

OR

37.76 Replacement of transvenous atrial and/or ventricular lead(s) (electrode(s))

and

37.80 Insertion of permanent pacemaker, initial or replacement, type of device not specified

OR

37.76 Replacement of transvenous atrial and/or ventricular lead(s) (electrode(s))

and

37.85 Replacement of any type of pacemaker device with single-chamber device, not specified as rate responsive

OR

37.76 Replacement of transvenous atrial and/or ventricular lead(s) (electrode(s))

and

37.86 Replacement of any type of pacemaker device with single-chamber device, rate responsive

OR

37.76 Replacement of transvenous atrial and/or ventricular lead(s) (electrode(s))

and

37.87 Replacement of any type of pacemaker device with dual-chamber device

OR

Select any principal diagnosis from MDC 5

AND

Operating Room Procedures (occurring singly, not in pairs)

00.54 Implantation or replacement of cardiac resynchronization defibrillator pulse generator device only (CRT-D)
37.95 Implantation of automatic cardioverter/defibrillator leads(s) only
37.96 Implantation of automatic cardioverter/defibrillator pulse generator only
37.97 Replacement of automatic cardioverter/defibrillator leads(s) only
37.98 Replacement of automatic cardioverter/defibrillator pulse generator only

OR

Operating Room Procedure

00.52 Implantation or replacement of transvenous lead (electrode) into left ventricular coronary venous system

● S DRG 552 Other Permanent Cardiac Pacemaker Implant without Major Cardiovascular Diagnosis

GMLOS 2.5 AMLOS 3.5 RW 2.0996 ☑

Operating Room Procedure

00.50 Implantation of cardiac resynchronization pacemaker without mention of defibrillation, total system (CRT-P)

OR

Any of the following procedure combinations

00.52 Implantation or replacement of transvenous lead (electrode) into left ventricular coronary venous system

and

00.53 Implantation or replacement of cardiac resynchronization pacemaker pulse generator only (CRT-P)

OR

37.70 Initial insertion of lead (electrode), not otherwise specified

and

00.53 Implantation or replacement of cardiac resynchronization pacemaker pulse generator only (CRT-P)

OR

37.70 Initial insertion of lead (electrode), not otherwise specified

and

37.80 Insertion of permanent pacemaker, initial or replacement, type of device not specified

OR

37.70 Initial insertion of lead (electrode), not otherwise specified

and

37.81 Initial insertion of single-chamber device, not specified as rate responsive

OR

37.70 Initial insertion of lead (electrode), not otherwise specified

and

37.82 Initial insertion of single-chamber device, rate responsive

OR

37.70 Initial insertion of lead (electrode), not otherwise specified

and

37.85 Replacement of any type of pacemaker device with single-chamber device, not specified as rate responsive

OR

37.70 Initial insertion of lead (electrode), not otherwise specified

and

37.86 Replacement of any type of pacemaker device with single-chamber device, rate responsive

OR

37.70 Initial insertion of lead (electrode), not otherwise specified

and

37.87 Replacement of any type of pacemaker device with dual-chamber device

OR

37.71 Initial insertion of transvenous lead (electrode) into ventricle

and

00.53 Implantation or replacement of cardiac resynchronization pacemaker pulse generator only (CRT-P)

DRG 552 — continued

OR

37.71 Initial insertion of transvenous lead (electrode) into ventricle

and

37.80 Insertion of permanent pacemaker, initial or replacement, type of device not specified

OR

37.71 Initial insertion of transvenous lead (electrode) into ventricle

and

37.81 Initial insertion of single-chamber device, not specified as rate responsive

OR

37.71 Initial insertion of transvenous lead (electrode) into ventricle

and

37.82 Initial insertion of single-chamber device, rate responsive

OR

37.71 Initial insertion of transvenous lead (electrode) into ventricle

and

37.85 Replacement of any type of pacemaker device with single-chamber device, not specified as rate responsive

OR

37.71 Initial insertion of transvenous lead (electrode) into ventricle

and

37.86 Replacement of any type of pacemaker device with single-chamber device, rate responsive

OR

37.71 Initial insertion of transvenous lead (electrode) into ventricle

and

37.87 Replacement of any type of pacemaker device with dual-chamber device

OR

37.72 Initial insertion of transvenous leads (electrodes) into atrium and ventricle

and

00.53 Implantation or replacement of cardiac resynchronization pacemaker pulse generator only (CRT-P)

OR

37.72 Initial insertion of transvenous leads (electrodes) into atrium and ventricle

and

37.80 Insertion of permanent pacemaker, initial or replacement, type of device not specified

OR

37.72 Initial insertion of transvenous leads (electrodes) into atrium and ventricle

and

37.83 Initial insertion of dual-chamber device

OR

37.73 Initial insertion of transvenous lead (electrode) into atrium

and

00.53 Implantation or replacement of cardiac resynchronization pacemaker pulse generator only (CRT-P)

OR

37.73 Initial insertion of transvenous lead (electrode) into atrium

and

37.80 Insertion of permanent pacemaker, initial or replacement, type of device not specified

OR

37.73 Initial insertion of transvenous lead (electrode) into atrium

and

37.81 Initial insertion of single-chamber device, not specified as rate responsive

OR

37.73 Initial insertion of transvenous lead (electrode) into atrium

and

37.82 Initial insertion of single-chamber device, rate responsive

OR

37.73 Initial insertion of transvenous lead (electrode) into atrium

and

37.85 Replacement of any type of pacemaker device with single-chamber device, not specified as rate responsive

OR

37.73 Initial insertion of transvenous lead (electrode) into atrium

and

37.86 Replacement of any type of pacemaker device with single-chamber device, rate responsive

OR

37.73 Initial insertion of transvenous lead (electrode) into atrium

and

37.87 Replacement of any type of pacemaker device with dual-chamber device

OR

37.74 Insertion or replacement of epicardial lead (electrode) into epicardium

and

00.53 Implantation or replacement of cardiac resynchronization pacemaker pulse generator only (CRT-P)

OR

37.74 Insertion or replacement of epicardial lead (electrode) into epicardium

and

37.80 Insertion of permanent pacemaker, initial or replacement, type of device not specified

OR

37.74 Insertion or replacement of epicardial lead (electrode) into epicardium

and

37.81 Initial insertion of single-chamber device, not specified as rate responsive

OR

37.74 Insertion or replacement of epicardial lead (electrode) into epicardium

and

37.82 Initial insertion of single-chamber device, rate responsive

OR

37.74 Insertion or replacement of epicardial lead (electrode) into epicardium

and

37.83 Initial insertion of dual-chamber device

OR

37.74 Insertion or replacement of epicardial lead (electrode) into epicardium

and

37.85 Replacement of any type of pacemaker device with single-chamber device, not specified as rate responsive

DRG 552 — continued

OR

37.74 Insertion or replacement of epicardial lead (electrode) into epicardium
and
37.86 Replacement of any type of pacemaker device with single-chamber device, rate responsive

OR

37.74 Insertion or replacement of epicardial lead (electrode) into epicardium
and
37.87 Replacement of any type of pacemaker device with dual-chamber device

OR

37.76 Replacement of transvenous atrial and/or ventricular lead(s) (electrode(s))
and
00.53 Implantation or replacement of cardiac resynchronization pacemaker pulse generator only (CRT-P)

OR

37.76 Replacement of transvenous atrial and/or ventricular lead(s) (electrode(s))
and
37.80 Insertion of permanent pacemaker, initial or replacement, type of device not specified

OR

37.76 Replacement of transvenous atrial and/or ventricular lead(s) (electrode(s))
and
37.85 Replacement of any type of pacemaker device with single-chamber device, not specified as rate responsive

OR

37.76 Replacement of transvenous atrial and/or ventricular lead(s) (electrode(s))
and
37.86 Replacement of any type of pacemaker device with single-chamber device, rate responsive

OR

37.76 Replacement of transvenous atrial and/or ventricular lead(s) (electrode(s))
and
37.87 Replacement of any type of pacemaker device with dual-chamber device

● S DRG 553 Other Vascular Procedures with CC with Major Cardiovascular Diagnosis

GMLOS 6.6 AMLOS 9.7 RW 3.0957 ☑ T CC

Principal or Secondary Diagnosis of Major Cardiovascular Condition (MCV)

398.91	Rheumatic heart failure (congestive)
402.01	Malignant hypertensive heart disease with heart failure
402.11	Benign hypertensive heart disease with heart failure
402.91	Unspecified hypertensive heart disease with heart failure
404.01	Hypertensive heart and kidney disease, malignant, with heart failure
404.03	Hypertensive heart and kidney disease, malignant, with heart failure and chronic kidney disease
404.11	Hypertensive heart and kidney disease, benign, with heart failure
404.13	Hypertensive heart and kidney disease, benign, with heart failure and chronic kidney disease
404.91	Hypertensive heart and kidney disease, unspecified, with heart failure
404.93	Hypertensive heart and kidney disease, unspecified, with heart failure and chronic kidney disease
410.01	Acute myocardial infarction of anterolateral wall, initial episode of care
410.11	Acute myocardial infarction of other anterior wall, initial episode of care
410.21	Acute myocardial infarction of inferolateral wall, initial episode of care
410.31	Acute myocardial infarction of inferoposterior wall, initial episode of care
410.41	Acute myocardial infarction of other inferior wall, initial episode of care
410.51	Acute myocardial infarction of other lateral wall, initial episode of care

S *Surgical* M *Medical* CC *CC Indicator* A *Age Restriction* ● *New DRG* ▲ *Revised DRG Title*

410.61	Acute myocardial infarction, true posterior wall infarction, initial episode of care
410.71	Acute myocardial infarction, subendocardial infarction, initial episode of care
410.81	Acute myocardial infarction of other specified sites, initial episode of care
410.91	Acute myocardial infarction, unspecified site, initial episode of care
411.0	Postmyocardial infarction syndrome
414.10	Aneurysm of heart
414.11	Aneurysm of coronary vessels
414.12	Dissection of coronary artery
414.19	Other aneurysm of heart
415.0	Acute cor pulmonale
420.0	Acute pericarditis in diseases classified elsewhere
420.90	Unspecified acute pericarditis
420.91	Acute idiopathic pericarditis
420.99	Other acute pericarditis
421.0	Acute and subacute bacterial endocarditis
421.1	Acute and subacute infective endocarditis in diseases classified elsewhere
421.9	Unspecified acute endocarditis
422.92	Septic myocarditis
423.0	Hemopericardium
424.90	Endocarditis, valve unspecified, unspecified cause
426.0	Atrioventricular block, complete
426.53	Other bilateral bundle branch block
426.54	Trifascicular block
427.1	Paroxysmal ventricular tachycardia
427.41	Ventricular fibrillation
427.5	Cardiac arrest
428.0	Congestive heart failure, unspecified
428.1	Left heart failure
428.20	Unspecified systolic heart failure
428.21	Acute systolic heart failure
428.22	Chronic systolic heart failure
428.23	Acute on chronic systolic heart failure
428.30	Unspecified diastolic heart failure
428.31	Acute diastolic heart failure
428.32	Chronic diastolic heart failure
428.33	Acute on chronic diastolic heart failure
428.40	Unspecified combined systolic and diastolic heart failure
428.41	Acute combined systolic and diastolic heart failure
428.42	Chronic combined systolic and diastolic heart failure
428.43	Acute on chronic combined systolic and diastolic heart failure
428.9	Unspecified heart failure
429.5	Rupture of chordae tendineae
429.6	Rupture of papillary muscle
429.71	Acquired cardiac septal defect
429.79	Other certain sequelae of myocardial infarction, not elsewhere classified
429.81	Other disorders of papillary muscle
441.00	Dissecting aortic aneurysm (any part), unspecified site
441.01	Dissecting aortic aneurysm (any part), thoracic
441.02	Dissecting aortic aneurysm (any part), abdominal
441.03	Dissecting aortic aneurysm (any part), thoracoabdominal
441.1	Thoracic aneurysm, ruptured
441.3	Abdominal aneurysm, ruptured
441.5	Aortic aneurysm of unspecified site, ruptured
441.6	Thoracoabdominal aneurysm, ruptured
443.22	Dissection of iliac artery
443.29	Dissection of other artery
444.0	Embolism and thrombosis of abdominal aorta
444.1	Embolism and thrombosis of thoracic aorta
453.2	Embolism and thrombosis of vena cava
785.50	Unspecified shock
785.51	Cardiogenic shock
861.02	Heart laceration without penetration of heart chambers or mention of open wound into thorax

MDC 5: Circulatory System — Surgical

DRG 553 — continued

861.03	Heart laceration with penetration of heart chambers, without mention of open wound into thorax
861.10	Unspecified injury to heart with open wound into thorax
861.11	Heart contusion with open wound into thorax
861.12	Heart laceration without penetration of heart chambers, with open wound into thorax
861.13	Heart laceration with penetration of heart chambers and open wound into thorax
996.61	Infection and inflammatory reaction due to cardiac device, implant, and graft
996.62	Infection and inflammatory reaction due to other vascular device, implant, and graft
996.72	Other complications due to other cardiac device, implant, and graft
996.83	Complications of transplanted heart

OR

Secondary Diagnosis of Major Cardiovascular Condition (MCV)

415.11	Iatrogenic pulmonary embolism and infarction
415.19	Other pulmonary embolism and infarction
430	Subarachnoid hemorrhage
431	Intracerebral hemorrhage
432.0	Nontraumatic extradural hemorrhage
432.1	Subdural hemorrhage
432.9	Unspecified intracranial hemorrhage
433.01	Occlusion and stenosis of basilar artery with cerebral infarction
433.11	Occlusion and stenosis of carotid artery with cerebral infarction
433.21	Occlusion and stenosis of vertebral artery with cerebral infarction
433.31	Occlusion and stenosis of multiple and bilateral precerebral arteries with cerebral infarction
433.81	Occlusion and stenosis of other specified precerebral artery with cerebral infarction
433.91	Occlusion and stenosis of unspecified precerebral artery with cerebral infarction
434.00	Cerebral thrombosis without mention of cerebral infarction
434.01	Cerebral thrombosis with cerebral infarction
434.10	Cerebral embolism without mention of cerebral infarction
434.11	Cerebral embolism with cerebral infarction
434.90	Unspecified cerebral artery occlusion without mention of cerebral infarction
434.91	Unspecified cerebral artery occlusion with cerebral infarction
436	Acute, but ill-defined, cerebrovascular disease
445.81	Atheroembolism of kidney
862.9	Injury to multiple and unspecified intrathoracic organs with open wound into cavity

AND

Operating Room Procedures

00.61	Percutaneous angioplasty or atherectomy of precerebral (extracranial) vessel(s)
00.62	Percutaneous angioplasty or atherectomy of intracranial vessel(s)
38.00	Incision of vessel, unspecified site
38.02	Incision of other vessels of head and neck
38.03	Incision of upper limb vessels
38.08	Incision of lower limb arteries
38.10	Endarterectomy, unspecified site
38.12	Endarterectomy of other vessels of head and neck
38.13	Endarterectomy of upper limb vessels
38.18	Endarterectomy of lower limb arteries
38.21	Biopsy of blood vessel
38.29	Other diagnostic procedures on blood vessels
38.30	Resection of vessel with anastomosis, unspecified site
38.32	Resection of other vessels of head and neck with anastomosis
38.33	Resection of upper limb vessels with anastomosis
38.38	Resection of lower limb arteries with anastomosis
38.40	Resection of vessel with replacement, unspecified site
38.42	Resection of other vessels of head and neck with replacement
38.43	Resection of upper limb vessels with replacement
38.48	Resection of lower limb arteries with replacement
38.52	Ligation and stripping of varicose veins of other vessels of head and neck
38.57	Ligation and stripping of abdominal varicose veins
38.60	Other excision of vessels, unspecified site
38.62	Other excision of other vessels of head and neck

38.63	Other excision of upper limb vessels
38.68	Other excision of lower limb arteries
38.7	Interruption of the vena cava
38.80	Other surgical occlusion of vessels, unspecified site
38.82	Other surgical occlusion of other vessels of head and neck
38.83	Other surgical occlusion of upper limb vessels
38.88	Other surgical occlusion of lower limb arteries
39.29	Other (peripheral) vascular shunt or bypass
39.30	Suture of unspecified blood vessel
39.31	Suture of artery
39.41	Control of hemorrhage following vascular surgery
39.49	Other revision of vascular procedure
39.50	Angioplasty or atherectomy of other non-coronary vessel(s)
39.51	Clipping of aneurysm
39.53	Repair of arteriovenous fistula
39.55	Reimplantation of aberrant renal vessel
39.56	Repair of blood vessel with tissue patch graft
39.57	Repair of blood vessel with synthetic patch graft
39.58	Repair of blood vessel with unspecified type of patch graft
39.59	Other repair of vessel
39.8	Operations on carotid body and other vascular bodies
39.91	Freeing of vessel
39.94	Replacement of vessel-to-vessel cannula
39.99	Other operations on vessels

● S DRG 554 Other Vascular Procedures with CC without Major Cardiovascular Diagnosis

GMLOS 4.0 AMLOS 5.9 RW 2.0721 ☑ T CC

Operating Room Procedures

00.61	Percutaneous angioplasty or atherectomy of precerebral (extracranial) vessel(s)
00.62	Percutaneous angioplasty or atherectomy of intracranial vessel(s)
38.00	Incision of vessel, unspecified site
38.02	Incision of other vessels of head and neck
38.03	Incision of upper limb vessels
38.08	Incision of lower limb arteries
38.10	Endarterectomy, unspecified site
38.12	Endarterectomy of other vessels of head and neck
38.13	Endarterectomy of upper limb vessels
38.18	Endarterectomy of lower limb arteries
38.21	Biopsy of blood vessel
38.29	Other diagnostic procedures on blood vessels
38.30	Resection of vessel with anastomosis, unspecified site
38.32	Resection of other vessels of head and neck with anastomosis
38.33	Resection of upper limb vessels with anastomosis
38.38	Resection of lower limb arteries with anastomosis
38.40	Resection of vessel with replacement, unspecified site
38.42	Resection of other vessels of head and neck with replacement
38.43	Resection of upper limb vessels with replacement
38.48	Resection of lower limb arteries with replacement
38.52	Ligation and stripping of varicose veins of other vessels of head and neck
38.57	Ligation and stripping of abdominal varicose veins
38.60	Other excision of vessels, unspecified site
38.62	Other excision of other vessels of head and neck
38.63	Other excision of upper limb vessels
38.68	Other excision of lower limb arteries
38.7	Interruption of the vena cava
38.80	Other surgical occlusion of vessels, unspecified site
38.82	Other surgical occlusion of other vessels of head and neck
38.83	Other surgical occlusion of upper limb vessels
38.88	Other surgical occlusion of lower limb arteries
39.29	Other (peripheral) vascular shunt or bypass
39.30	Suture of unspecified blood vessel

** Code Range* ☑ *Optimization Potential* *Targeted Potential* T *Transfer DRG* SP *Special Payment*

DRG 554 — continued

39.31	Suture of artery
39.41	Control of hemorrhage following vascular surgery
39.49	Other revision of vascular procedure
39.50	Angioplasty or atherectomy of other non-coronary vessel(s)
39.51	Clipping of aneurysm
39.53	Repair of arteriovenous fistula
39.55	Reimplantation of aberrant renal vessel
39.56	Repair of blood vessel with tissue patch graft
39.57	Repair of blood vessel with synthetic patch graft
39.58	Repair of blood vessel with unspecified type of patch graft
39.59	Other repair of vessel
39.8	Operations on carotid body and other vascular bodies
39.91	Freeing of vessel
39.94	Replacement of vessel-to-vessel cannula
39.99	Other operations on vessels

● S DRG 555 Percutaneous Cardiovascular Procedure with Major Cardiovascular Diagnosis

GMLOS 3.4 AMLOS 4.7 RW 2.4315 ☑

Principal or Secondary Diagnosis of Major Cardiovascular Condition (MCV)

398.91	Rheumatic heart failure (congestive)
402.01	Malignant hypertensive heart disease with heart failure
402.11	Benign hypertensive heart disease with heart failure
402.91	Unspecified hypertensive heart disease with heart failure
404.01	Hypertensive heart and kidney disease, malignant, with heart failure
404.03	Hypertensive heart and kidney disease, malignant, with heart failure and chronic kidney disease
404.11	Hypertensive heart and kidney disease, benign, with heart failure
404.13	Hypertensive heart and kidney disease, benign, with heart failure and chronic kidney disease
404.91	Hypertensive heart and kidney disease, unspecified, with heart failure
404.93	Hypertensive heart and kidney disease, unspecified, with heart failure and chronic kidney disease
410.01	Acute myocardial infarction of anterolateral wall, initial episode of care
410.11	Acute myocardial infarction of other anterior wall, initial episode of care
410.21	Acute myocardial infarction of inferolateral wall, initial episode of care
410.31	Acute myocardial infarction of inferoposterior wall, initial episode of care
410.41	Acute myocardial infarction of other inferior wall, initial episode of care
410.51	Acute myocardial infarction of other lateral wall, initial episode of care
410.61	Acute myocardial infarction, true posterior wall infarction, initial episode of care
410.71	Acute myocardial infarction, subendocardial infarction, initial episode of care
410.81	Acute myocardial infarction of other specified sites, initial episode of care
410.91	Acute myocardial infarction, unspecified site, initial episode of care
411.0	Postmyocardial infarction syndrome
414.10	Aneurysm of heart
414.11	Aneurysm of coronary vessels
414.12	Dissection of coronary artery
414.19	Other aneurysm of heart
415.0	Acute cor pulmonale
420.0	Acute pericarditis in diseases classified elsewhere
420.90	Unspecified acute pericarditis
420.91	Acute idiopathic pericarditis
420.99	Other acute pericarditis
421.0	Acute and subacute bacterial endocarditis
421.1	Acute and subacute infective endocarditis in diseases classified elsewhere
421.9	Unspecified acute endocarditis
422.92	Septic myocarditis
423.0	Hemopericardium
424.90	Endocarditis, valve unspecified, unspecified cause
426.0	Atrioventricular block, complete
426.53	Other bilateral bundle branch block

426.54	Trifascicular block
427.1	Paroxysmal ventricular tachycardia
427.41	Ventricular fibrillation
427.5	Cardiac arrest
428.0	Congestive heart failure, unspecified
428.1	Left heart failure
428.20	Unspecified systolic heart failure
428.21	Acute systolic heart failure
428.22	Chronic systolic heart failure
428.23	Acute on chronic systolic heart failure
428.30	Unspecified diastolic heart failure
428.31	Acute diastolic heart failure
428.32	Chronic diastolic heart failure
428.33	Acute on chronic diastolic heart failure
428.40	Unspecified combined systolic and diastolic heart failure
428.41	Acute combined systolic and diastolic heart failure
428.42	Chronic combined systolic and diastolic heart failure
428.43	Acute on chronic combined systolic and diastolic heart failure
428.9	Unspecified heart failure
429.5	Rupture of chordae tendineae
429.6	Rupture of papillary muscle
429.71	Acquired cardiac septal defect
429.79	Other certain sequelae of myocardial infarction, not elsewhere classified
429.81	Other disorders of papillary muscle
441.00	Dissecting aortic aneurysm (any part), unspecified site
441.01	Dissecting aortic aneurysm (any part), thoracic
441.02	Dissecting aortic aneurysm (any part), abdominal
441.03	Dissecting aortic aneurysm (any part), thoracoabdominal
441.1	Thoracic aneurysm, ruptured
441.3	Abdominal aneurysm, ruptured
441.5	Aortic aneurysm of unspecified site, ruptured
441.6	Thoracoabdominal aneurysm, ruptured
443.22	Dissection of iliac artery
443.29	Dissection of other artery
444.0	Embolism and thrombosis of abdominal aorta
444.1	Embolism and thrombosis of thoracic aorta
453.2	Embolism and thrombosis of vena cava
785.50	Unspecified shock
785.51	Cardiogenic shock
861.02	Heart laceration without penetration of heart chambers or mention of open wound into thorax
861.03	Heart laceration with penetration of heart chambers, without mention of open wound into thorax
861.10	Unspecified injury to heart with open wound into thorax
861.11	Heart contusion with open wound into thorax
861.12	Heart laceration without penetration of heart chambers, with open wound into thorax
861.13	Heart laceration with penetration of heart chambers and open wound into thorax
996.61	Infection and inflammatory reaction due to cardiac device, implant, and graft
996.62	Infection and inflammatory reaction due to other vascular device, implant, and graft
996.72	Other complications due to other cardiac device, implant, and graft
996.83	Complications of transplanted heart

OR

Secondary Diagnosis of Major Cardiovascular Condition (MCV)

415.11	Iatrogenic pulmonary embolism and infarction
415.19	Other pulmonary embolism and infarction
430	Subarachnoid hemorrhage
431	Intracerebral hemorrhage
432.0	Nontraumatic extradural hemorrhage
432.1	Subdural hemorrhage
432.9	Unspecified intracranial hemorrhage
433.01	Occlusion and stenosis of basilar artery with cerebral infarction
433.11	Occlusion and stenosis of carotid artery with cerebral infarction
433.21	Occlusion and stenosis of vertebral artery with cerebral infarction

*** Code Range** ☑ **Optimization Potential** ▽ **Targeted Potential** 🅃 **Transfer DRG** SP **Special Payment**

DRG 555 — continued

433.31	Occlusion and stenosis of multiple and bilateral precerebral arteries with cerebral infarction
433.81	Occlusion and stenosis of other specified precerebral artery with cerebral infarction
433.91	Occlusion and stenosis of unspecified precerebral artery with cerebral infarction
434.00	Cerebral thrombosis without mention of cerebral infarction
434.01	Cerebral thrombosis with cerebral infarction
434.10	Cerebral embolism without mention of cerebral infarction
434.11	Cerebral embolism with cerebral infarction
434.90	Unspecified cerebral artery occlusion without mention of cerebral infarction
434.91	Unspecified cerebral artery occlusion with cerebral infarction
436	Acute, but ill-defined, cerebrovascular disease
445.81	Atheroembolism of kidney
862.9	Injury to multiple and unspecified intrathoracic organs with open wound into cavity

AND

Operating Room Procedures

00.66	Percutaneous transluminal coronary angioplasty [PTCA] or coronary atherectomy
35.96	Percutaneous valvuloplasty
36.09	Other removal of coronary artery obstruction
37.34	Excision or destruction of other lesion or tissue of heart, other approach

OR

Nonoperating Room Procedures

37.26	Cardiac electrophysiologic stimulation and recording studies
37.27	Cardiac mapping

● Ⓢ DRG 556 Percutaneous Cardiovascular Procedure with Non Drug-Eluting Stent without Major Cardiovascular Diagnosis

GMLOS 1.6 AMLOS 2.1 RW 1.9132 ☑

Operating Room Procedures

00.66	Percutaneous transluminal coronary angioplasty [PTCA] or coronary atherectomy
35.96	Percutaneous valvuloplasty
36.09	Other removal of coronary artery obstruction
37.34	Excision or destruction of other lesion or tissue of heart, other approach

OR

Nonoperating Room Procedures

37.26	Cardiac electrophysiologic stimulation and recording studies
37.27	Cardiac mapping

AND

Operating Room Procedure

92.27	Implantation or insertion of radioactive elements

OR

Nonoperating Room Procedure

36.06	Insertion of non-drug-eluting coronary artery stent(s)

● Ⓢ DRG 557 Percutaneous Cardiovascular Procedure with Drug-Eluting Stent with Major Cardiovascular Diagnosis

GMLOS 3.0 AMLOS 4.1 RW 2.8717 ☑

Principal or Secondary Diagnosis of Major Cardiovascular Condition (MCV)

398.91	Rheumatic heart failure (congestive)
402.01	Malignant hypertensive heart disease with heart failure
402.11	Benign hypertensive heart disease with heart failure
402.91	Unspecified hypertensive heart disease with heart failure
404.01	Hypertensive heart and kidney disease, malignant, with heart failure
404.03	Hypertensive heart and kidney disease, malignant, with heart failure and chronic kidney disease
404.11	Hypertensive heart and kidney disease, benign, with heart failure
404.13	Hypertensive heart and kidney disease, benign, with heart failure and chronic kidney disease

404.91	Hypertensive heart and kidney disease, unspecified, with heart failure
404.93	Hypertensive heart and kidney disease, unspecified, with heart failure and chronic kidney disease
410.01	Acute myocardial infarction of anterolateral wall, initial episode of care
410.11	Acute myocardial infarction of other anterior wall, initial episode of care
410.21	Acute myocardial infarction of inferolateral wall, initial episode of care
410.31	Acute myocardial infarction of inferoposterior wall, initial episode of care
410.41	Acute myocardial infarction of other inferior wall, initial episode of care
410.51	Acute myocardial infarction of other lateral wall, initial episode of care
410.61	Acute myocardial infarction, true posterior wall infarction, initial episode of care
410.71	Acute myocardial infarction, subendocardial infarction, initial episode of care
410.81	Acute myocardial infarction of other specified sites, initial episode of care
410.91	Acute myocardial infarction, unspecified site, initial episode of care
411.0	Postmyocardial infarction syndrome
414.10	Aneurysm of heart
414.11	Aneurysm of coronary vessels
414.12	Dissection of coronary artery
414.19	Other aneurysm of heart
415.0	Acute cor pulmonale
420.0	Acute pericarditis in diseases classified elsewhere
420.90	Unspecified acute pericarditis
420.91	Acute idiopathic pericarditis
420.99	Other acute pericarditis
421.0	Acute and subacute bacterial endocarditis
421.1	Acute and subacute infective endocarditis in diseases classified elsewhere
421.9	Unspecified acute endocarditis
422.92	Septic myocarditis
423.0	Hemopericardium
424.90	Endocarditis, valve unspecified, unspecified cause
426.0	Atrioventricular block, complete
426.53	Other bilateral bundle branch block
426.54	Trifascicular block
427.1	Paroxysmal ventricular tachycardia
427.41	Ventricular fibrillation
427.5	Cardiac arrest
428.0	Congestive heart failure, unspecified
428.1	Left heart failure
428.20	Unspecified systolic heart failure
428.21	Acute systolic heart failure
428.22	Chronic systolic heart failure
428.23	Acute on chronic systolic heart failure
428.30	Unspecified diastolic heart failure
428.31	Acute diastolic heart failure
428.32	Chronic diastolic heart failure
428.33	Acute on chronic diastolic heart failure
428.40	Unspecified combined systolic and diastolic heart failure
428.41	Acute combined systolic and diastolic heart failure
428.42	Chronic combined systolic and diastolic heart failure
428.43	Acute on chronic combined systolic and diastolic heart failure
428.9	Unspecified heart failure
429.5	Rupture of chordae tendineae
429.6	Rupture of papillary muscle
429.71	Acquired cardiac septal defect
429.79	Other certain sequelae of myocardial infarction, not elsewhere classified
429.81	Other disorders of papillary muscle
441.00	Dissecting aortic aneurysm (any part), unspecified site
441.01	Dissecting aortic aneurysm (any part), thoracic
441.02	Dissecting aortic aneurysm (any part), abdominal
441.03	Dissecting aortic aneurysm (any part), thoracoabdominal
441.1	Thoracic aneurysm, ruptured
441.3	Abdominal aneurysm, ruptured
441.5	Aortic aneurysm of unspecified site, ruptured
441.6	Thoracoabdominal aneurysm, ruptured

DRG 557 — continued

443.22	Dissection of iliac artery
443.29	Dissection of other artery
444.0	Embolism and thrombosis of abdominal aorta
444.1	Embolism and thrombosis of thoracic aorta
453.2	Embolism and thrombosis of vena cava
785.50	Unspecified shock
785.51	Cardiogenic shock
861.02	Heart laceration without penetration of heart chambers or mention of open wound into thorax
861.03	Heart laceration with penetration of heart chambers, without mention of open wound into thorax
861.10	Unspecified injury to heart with open wound into thorax
861.11	Heart contusion with open wound into thorax
861.12	Heart laceration without penetration of heart chambers, with open wound into thorax
861.13	Heart laceration with penetration of heart chambers and open wound into thorax
996.61	Infection and inflammatory reaction due to cardiac device, implant, and graft
996.62	Infection and inflammatory reaction due to other vascular device, implant, and graft
996.72	Other complications due to other cardiac device, implant, and graft
996.83	Complications of transplanted heart

OR

Secondary Diagnosis of Major Cardiovascular Condition (MCV)

415.11	Iatrogenic pulmonary embolism and infarction
415.19	Other pulmonary embolism and infarction
430	Subarachnoid hemorrhage
431	Intracerebral hemorrhage
432.0	Nontraumatic extradural hemorrhage
432.1	Subdural hemorrhage
432.9	Unspecified intracranial hemorrhage
433.01	Occlusion and stenosis of basilar artery with cerebral infarction
433.11	Occlusion and stenosis of carotid artery with cerebral infarction
433.21	Occlusion and stenosis of vertebral artery with cerebral infarction
433.31	Occlusion and stenosis of multiple and bilateral precerebral arteries with cerebral infarction
433.81	Occlusion and stenosis of other specified precerebral artery with cerebral infarction
433.91	Occlusion and stenosis of unspecified precerebral artery with cerebral infarction
434.00	Cerebral thrombosis without mention of cerebral infarction
434.01	Cerebral thrombosis with cerebral infarction
434.10	Cerebral embolism without mention of cerebral infarction
434.11	Cerebral embolism with cerebral infarction
434.90	Unspecified cerebral artery occlusion without mention of cerebral infarction
434.91	Unspecified cerebral artery occlusion with cerebral infarction
436	Acute, but ill-defined, cerebrovascular disease
445.81	Atheroembolism of kidney
862.9	Injury to multiple and unspecified intrathoracic organs with open wound into cavity

AND

Operating Room Procedures

00.66	Percutaneous transluminal coronary angioplasty [PTCA] or coronary atherectomy
35.96	Percutaneous valvuloplasty
36.09	Other removal of coronary artery obstruction
37.34	Excision or destruction of other lesion or tissue of heart, other approach

OR

Nonoperating Room Procedures

37.26	Cardiac electrophysiologic stimulation and recording studies
37.27	Cardiac mapping

AND

Nonoperating Room Procedure

36.07	Insertion of drug-eluting coronary artery stent(s)

● Ⓢ DRG 558 Percutaneous Cardiovascular Procedure with Drug-Eluting Stent without Major Cardiovascular Diagnosis

GMLOS 1.5 AMLOS 1.9 RW 2.2108 ☑

Operating Room Procedures

00.66	Percutaneous transluminal coronary angioplasty [PTCA] or coronary atherectomy
35.96	Percutaneous valvuloplasty
36.09	Other removal of coronary artery obstruction
37.34	Excision or destruction of other lesion or tissue of heart, other approach

OR

Nonoperating Room Procedures

37.26	Cardiac electrophysiologic stimulation and recording studies
37.27	Cardiac mapping

AND

Nonoperating Room Procedure

36.07	Insertion of drug-eluting coronary artery stent(s)

MDC 5
DISEASES AND DISORDERS OF THE CIRCULATORY SYSTEM

The complete and up-to-date listing of ICD-9-CM diagnosis codes assigned to this MDC can be found online at www.ingenixonline.com/content/drg/resources.asp.

MEDICAL

M DRG 121 Circulatory Disorders with Acute Myocardial Infarction and Major Complications, Discharged Alive

GMLOS 5.3 AMLOS 6.6 RW 1.6136

Principal or Secondary Diagnosis

410.01	Acute myocardial infarction of anterolateral wall, initial episode of care
410.11	Acute myocardial infarction of other anterior wall, initial episode of care
410.21	Acute myocardial infarction of inferolateral wall, initial episode of care
410.31	Acute myocardial infarction of inferoposterior wall, initial episode of care
410.41	Acute myocardial infarction of other inferior wall, initial episode of care
410.51	Acute myocardial infarction of other lateral wall, initial episode of care
410.61	Acute myocardial infarction, true posterior wall infarction, initial episode of care
410.71	Acute myocardial infarction, subendocardial infarction, initial episode of care
410.81	Acute myocardial infarction of other specified sites, initial episode of care
410.91	Acute myocardial infarction, unspecified site, initial episode of care

AND

Principal or Secondary Diagnosis

398.91	Rheumatic heart failure (congestive)
402.01	Malignant hypertensive heart disease with heart failure
402.11	Benign hypertensive heart disease with heart failure
402.91	Unspecified hypertensive heart disease with heart failure
404.01	Hypertensive heart and kidney disease, malignant, with heart failure
404.03	Hypertensive heart and kidney disease, malignant, with heart failure and chronic kidney disease
404.11	Hypertensive heart and kidney disease, benign, with heart failure
404.13	Hypertensive heart and kidney disease, benign, with heart failure and chronic kidney disease
404.91	Hypertensive heart and kidney disease, unspecified, with heart failure
404.93	Hypertensive heart and kidney disease, unspecified, with heart failure and chronic kidney disease
411.0	Postmyocardial infarction syndrome
*414.1	Aneurysm and dissection of heart
416.0	Primary pulmonary hypertension
426.0	Atrioventricular block, complete
426.10	Unspecified atrioventricular block
426.12	Mobitz (type) II atrioventricular block
426.13	Other second degree atrioventricular block
426.3	Other left bundle branch block
426.51	Right bundle branch block and left posterior fascicular block
426.52	Right bundle branch block and left anterior fascicular block
426.53	Other bilateral bundle branch block
426.54	Trifascicular block
427.0	Paroxysmal supraventricular tachycardia
427.1	Paroxysmal ventricular tachycardia
427.2	Unspecified paroxysmal tachycardia
*427.3	Atrial fibrillation and flutter
*427.4	Ventricular fibrillation and flutter
427.5	Cardiac arrest
*428	Heart failure
429.5	Rupture of chordae tendineae
429.6	Rupture of papillary muscle

429.81	Other disorders of papillary muscle
*441.0	Dissection of aorta
458.8	Other specified hypotension
458.9	Unspecified hypotension
785.50	Unspecified shock
785.51	Cardiogenic shock
996.62	Infection and inflammatory reaction due to other vascular device, implant, and graft
996.72	Other complications due to other cardiac device, implant, and graft

OR

Secondary Diagnosis

*415.1	Pulmonary embolism and infarction
430	Subarachnoid hemorrhage
431	Intracerebral hemorrhage
432.0	Nontraumatic extradural hemorrhage
432.1	Subdural hemorrhage
432.9	Unspecified intracranial hemorrhage
433.01	Occlusion and stenosis of basilar artery with cerebral infarction
433.11	Occlusion and stenosis of carotid artery with cerebral infarction
433.21	Occlusion and stenosis of vertebral artery with cerebral infarction
433.31	Occlusion and stenosis of multiple and bilateral precerebral arteries with cerebral infarction
433.81	Occlusion and stenosis of other specified precerebral artery with cerebral infarction
433.91	Occlusion and stenosis of unspecified precerebral artery with cerebral infarction
*434	Occlusion of cerebral arteries
436	Acute, but ill-defined, cerebrovascular disease
481	Pneumococcal pneumonia (streptococcus pneumoniae pneumonia)
*482	Other bacterial pneumonia
*483	Pneumonia due to other specified organism
*484	Pneumonia in infectious diseases classified elsewhere
485	Bronchopneumonia, organism unspecified
486	Pneumonia, organism unspecified
487.0	Influenza with pneumonia
*507	Pneumonitis due to solids and liquids
518.0	Pulmonary collapse
518.5	Pulmonary insufficiency following trauma and surgery
518.81	Acute respiratory failure
518.83	Chronic respiratory failure
518.84	Acute and chronic respiratory failure
584.5	Acute renal failure with lesion of tubular necrosis
584.6	Acute renal failure with lesion of renal cortical necrosis
584.7	Acute renal failure with lesion of renal medullary (papillary) necrosis
584.8	Acute renal failure with other specified pathological lesion in kidney
584.9	Unspecified acute renal failure
*707.0	Decubitus ulcer

M DRG 122 Circulatory Disorders with Acute Myocardial Infarction without Major Complications, Discharged Alive

GMLOS 2.8 AMLOS 3.5 RW 0.9847 ☑ ▽

Principal or Secondary Diagnosis

410.01	Acute myocardial infarction of anterolateral wall, initial episode of care
410.11	Acute myocardial infarction of other anterior wall, initial episode of care
410.21	Acute myocardial infarction of inferolateral wall, initial episode of care
410.31	Acute myocardial infarction of inferoposterior wall, initial episode of care
410.41	Acute myocardial infarction of other inferior wall, initial episode of care
410.51	Acute myocardial infarction of other lateral wall, initial episode of care
410.61	Acute myocardial infarction, true posterior wall infarction, initial episode of care
410.71	Acute myocardial infarction, subendocardial infarction, initial episode of care
410.81	Acute myocardial infarction of other specified sites, initial episode of care
410.91	Acute myocardial infarction, unspecified site, initial episode of care

Code Range** ☑ ***Optimization Potential ▽ ***Targeted Potential*** T ***Transfer DRG*** SP ***Special Payment***

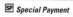

Ⓜ DRG 123 Circulatory Disorders with Acute Myocardial Infarction, Expired

GMLOS 2.9 AMLOS 4.8 RW 1.5407 ☑

Principal or Secondary Diagnosis

410.01	Acute myocardial infarction of anterolateral wall, initial episode of care
410.11	Acute myocardial infarction of other anterior wall, initial episode of care
410.21	Acute myocardial infarction of inferolateral wall, initial episode of care
410.31	Acute myocardial infarction of inferoposterior wall, initial episode of care
410.41	Acute myocardial infarction of other inferior wall, initial episode of care
410.51	Acute myocardial infarction of other lateral wall, initial episode of care
410.61	Acute myocardial infarction, true posterior wall infarction, initial episode of care
410.71	Acute myocardial infarction, subendocardial infarction, initial episode of care
410.81	Acute myocardial infarction of other specified sites, initial episode of care
410.91	Acute myocardial infarction, unspecified site, initial episode of care

Ⓜ DRG 124 Circulatory Disorders Except Acute Myocardial Infarction with Cardiac Catheterization and Complex Diagnosis

GMLOS 3.3 AMLOS 4.4 RW 1.4425 ☑ YIELD

Principal or Secondary Diagnosis

398.91	Rheumatic heart failure (congestive)
402.01	Malignant hypertensive heart disease with heart failure
402.11	Benign hypertensive heart disease with heart failure
402.91	Unspecified hypertensive heart disease with heart failure
404.01	Hypertensive heart and kidney disease, malignant, with heart failure
404.03	Hypertensive heart and kidney disease, malignant, with heart failure and chronic kidney disease
404.11	Hypertensive heart and kidney disease, benign, with heart failure
404.13	Hypertensive heart and kidney disease, benign, with heart failure and chronic kidney disease
404.91	Hypertensive heart and kidney disease, unspecified, with heart failure
404.93	Hypertensive heart and kidney disease, unspecified, with heart failure and chronic kidney disease
*411	Other acute and subacute forms of ischemic heart disease
415.0	Acute cor pulmonale
420.0	Acute pericarditis in diseases classified elsewhere
*420.9	Other and unspecified acute pericarditis
*421	Acute and subacute endocarditis
*422	Acute myocarditis
423.0	Hemopericardium
424.90	Endocarditis, valve unspecified, unspecified cause
424.91	Endocarditis in diseases classified elsewhere
425.2	Obscure cardiomyopathy of Africa
425.3	Endocardial fibroelastosis
425.4	Other primary cardiomyopathies
425.5	Alcoholic cardiomyopathy
425.7	Nutritional and metabolic cardiomyopathy
425.8	Cardiomyopathy in other diseases classified elsewhere
425.9	Unspecified secondary cardiomyopathy
427.1	Paroxysmal ventricular tachycardia
427.5	Cardiac arrest
*428	Heart failure
429.4	Functional disturbances following cardiac surgery
429.5	Rupture of chordae tendineae
429.6	Rupture of papillary muscle
429.71	Acquired cardiac septal defect
429.79	Other certain sequelae of myocardial infarction, not elsewhere classified
429.81	Other disorders of papillary muscle
429.82	Hyperkinetic heart disease
785.50	Unspecified shock
785.51	Cardiogenic shock

OR

Secondary Diagnosis Only

*415.1	Pulmonary embolism and infarction

AND

Nonoperating Room Procedures

37.21	Right heart cardiac catheterization
37.22	Left heart cardiac catheterization
37.23	Combined right and left heart cardiac catheterization
88.52	Angiocardiography of right heart structures
88.53	Angiocardiography of left heart structures
88.54	Combined right and left heart angiocardiography
88.55	Coronary arteriography using single catheter
88.56	Coronary arteriography using two catheters
88.57	Other and unspecified coronary arteriography
88.58	Negative-contrast cardiac roentgenography

M DRG 125 Circulatory Disorders Except Acute Myocardial Infarction with Cardiac Catheterization without Complex Diagnosis

GMLOS 2.1 AMLOS 2.7 RW 1.0948 ☑ YIELD

Principal Diagnosis

Select any principal diagnosis listed under MDC 5 excluding AMI and excluding any principal or secondary diagnosis listed under DRG 124

AND

Select nonoperating room procedure listed under DRG 124

M DRG 126 Acute and Subacute Endocarditis

GMLOS 9.4 AMLOS 12.0 RW 2.7440 T

Principal Diagnosis

036.42	Meningococcal endocarditis
093.20	Unspecified syphilitic endocarditis of valve
098.84	Gonococcal endocarditis
112.81	Candidal endocarditis
115.04	Histoplasma capsulatum endocarditis
115.14	Histoplasma duboisii endocarditis
115.94	Unspecified Histoplasmosis endocarditis
421.0	Acute and subacute bacterial endocarditis
421.1	Acute and subacute infective endocarditis in diseases classified elsewhere
421.9	Unspecified acute endocarditis

M DRG 127 Heart Failure and Shock

GMLOS 4.1 AMLOS 5.2 RW 1.0345 ☑ T YIELD

Principal Diagnosis

398.91	Rheumatic heart failure (congestive)
402.01	Malignant hypertensive heart disease with heart failure
402.11	Benign hypertensive heart disease with heart failure
402.91	Unspecified hypertensive heart disease with heart failure
404.01	Hypertensive heart and kidney disease, malignant, with heart failure
404.03	Hypertensive heart and kidney disease, malignant, with heart failure and chronic kidney disease
404.11	Hypertensive heart and kidney disease, benign, with heart failure
404.13	Hypertensive heart and kidney disease, benign, with heart failure and chronic kidney disease
404.91	Hypertensive heart and kidney disease, unspecified, with heart failure
404.93	Hypertensive heart and kidney disease, unspecified, with heart failure and chronic kidney disease
*428	Heart failure
785.50	Unspecified shock
785.51	Cardiogenic shock

** Code Range* ☑ *Optimization Potential* YIELD *Targeted Potential* T *Transfer DRG* SP *Special Payment*

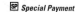

M DRG 128 Deep Vein Thrombophlebitis

GMLOS 4.4 AMLOS 5.2 RW 0.6949

Principal Diagnosis

*451.1	Phlebitis and thrombophlebitis of deep veins of lower extremities
451.2	Phlebitis and thrombophlebitis of lower extremities, unspecified
451.81	Phlebitis and thrombophlebitis of iliac vein
453.2	Embolism and thrombosis of vena cava

M DRG 129 Cardiac Arrest, Unexplained

GMLOS 1.7 AMLOS 2.6 RW 1.0404

Principal Diagnosis

427.5	Cardiac arrest
798.1	Instantaneous death
798.2	Death occurring in less than 24 hours from onset of symptoms, not otherwise explained

M DRG 130 Peripheral Vascular Disorders with CC

GMLOS 4.4 AMLOS 5.5 RW 0.9425

Principal Diagnosis

*250.7	Diabetes with peripheral circulatory disorders
440.0	Atherosclerosis of aorta
*440.2	Atherosclerosis of native arteries of the extremities
*440.3	Atheroslerosis of bypass graft of extremities
440.8	Atherosclerosis of other specified arteries
440.9	Generalized and unspecified atherosclerosis
*441.0	Dissection of aorta
441.1	Thoracic aneurysm, ruptured
441.2	Thoracic aneurysm without mention of rupture
441.3	Abdominal aneurysm, ruptured
441.4	Abdominal aneurysm without mention of rupture
441.5	Aortic aneurysm of unspecified site, ruptured
441.6	Thoracoabdominal aneurysm, ruptured
441.7	Thoracoabdominal aneurysm without mention of rupture
441.9	Aortic aneurysm of unspecified site without mention of rupture
442.0	Aneurysm of artery of upper extremity
442.2	Aneurysm of iliac artery
442.3	Aneurysm of artery of lower extremity
*442.8	Aneurysm of other specified artery
442.9	Other aneurysm of unspecified site
443.1	Thromboangiitis obliterans (Buerger's disease)
443.21	Dissection of carotid artery
443.22	Dissection of iliac artery
443.24	Dissection of vertebral artery
443.29	Dissection of other artery
*443.8	Other specified peripheral vascular diseases
443.9	Unspecified peripheral vascular disease
444.0	Embolism and thrombosis of abdominal aorta
444.1	Embolism and thrombosis of thoracic aorta
*444.2	Embolism and thrombosis of arteries of the extremities
*444.8	Embolism and thrombosis of other specified artery
444.9	Embolism and thrombosis of unspecified artery
*445.0	Atheroembolism of extremities
445.89	Atheroembolism of other site
447.0	Arteriovenous fistula, acquired
447.1	Stricture of artery
447.2	Rupture of artery
447.5	Necrosis of artery
447.8	Other specified disorders of arteries and arterioles
447.9	Unspecified disorders of arteries and arterioles
448.0	Hereditary hemorrhagic telangiectasia
448.9	Other and unspecified capillary diseases

451.0	Phlebitis and thrombophlebitis of superficial vessels of lower extremities
451.82	Phlebitis and thrombophlebitis of superficial veins of upper extremities
451.83	Phlebitis and thrombophlebitis of deep veins of upper extremities
451.84	Phlebitis and thrombophlebitis of upper extremities, unspecified
451.89	Phlebitis and thrombophlebitis of other site
451.9	Phlebitis and thrombophlebitis of unspecified site
453.1	Thrombophlebitis migrans
*453.4	Venous embolism and thrombosis of deep vessels of lower extremity
453.8	Embolism and thrombosis of other specified veins
453.9	Embolism and thrombosis of unspecified site
454.0	Varicose veins of lower extremities with ulcer
454.1	Varicose veins of lower extremities with inflammation
454.2	Varicose veins of lower extremities with ulcer and inflammation
454.8	Varicose veins of the lower extremities with other complications
454.9	Asymptomatic varicose veins
456.3	Sublingual varices
456.8	Varices of other sites
*459.1	Postphlebitic syndrome
459.2	Compression of vein
*459.3	Chronic venous hypertension
459.81	Unspecified venous (peripheral) insufficiency
747.5	Congenital absence or hypoplasia of umbilical artery
*747.6	Other congenital anomaly of peripheral vascular system
747.89	Other specified congenital anomaly of circulatory system
747.9	Unspecified congenital anomaly of circulatory system
785.4	Gangrene
908.3	Late effect of injury to blood vessel of head, neck, and extremities
908.4	Late effect of injury to blood vessel of thorax, abdomen, and pelvis
997.2	Peripheral vascular complications
997.79	Vascular complications of other vessels

M DRG 131 Peripheral Vascular Disorders without CC

GMLOS 3.2 AMLOS 3.9 RW 0.5566 ☑ T

Select principal diagnosis listed under DRG 130

M DRG 132 Atherosclerosis with CC

GMLOS 2.2 AMLOS 2.8 RW 0.6273 ☑ ▽ CC

Principal Diagnosis

412	Old myocardial infarction
*414.0	Coronary atherosclerosis
414.8	Other specified forms of chronic ischemic heart disease
414.9	Unspecified chronic ischemic heart disease
429.2	Unspecified cardiovascular disease
429.3	Cardiomegaly
429.89	Other ill-defined heart disease
429.9	Unspecified heart disease
459.89	Other specified circulatory system disorders
459.9	Unspecified circulatory system disorder
793.2	Nonspecific abnormal findings on radiological and other examination of other intrathoracic organs

M DRG 133 Atherosclerosis without CC

GMLOS 1.8 AMLOS 2.2 RW 0.5337 ☑

Select principal diagnosis listed under DRG 132

M DRG 134 Hypertension

GMLOS 2.4 AMLOS 3.1 RW 0.6068 ☑

Principal Diagnosis

401.0	Essential hypertension, malignant
401.1	Essential hypertension, benign

DRG 134 — continued

401.9	Unspecified essential hypertension
402.00	Malignant hypertensive heart disease without heart failure
402.10	Benign hypertensive heart disease without heart failure
402.90	Unspecified hypertensive heart disease without heart failure
404.00	Hypertensive heart and kidney disease, malignant, without heart failure or chronic kidney disease
404.10	Hypertensive heart and kidney disease, benign, without heart failure or chronic kidney disease
404.90	Hypertensive heart and kidney disease, unspecified, without heart failure or chronic kidney disease
*405	Secondary hypertension

M DRG 135 Cardiac Congenital and Valvular Disorders, Age Greater than 17 with CC

GMLOS 3.2 AMLOS 4.3 RW 0.8917 ☑ CC A

Principal Diagnosis

074.22	Coxsackie endocarditis
093.0	Aneurysm of aorta, specified as syphilitic
093.1	Syphilitic aortitis
093.21	Syphilitic endocarditis, mitral valve
093.22	Syphilitic endocarditis, aortic valve
093.23	Syphilitic endocarditis, tricuspid valve
093.24	Syphilitic endocarditis, pulmonary valve
391.1	Acute rheumatic endocarditis
*394	Diseases of mitral valve
*395	Diseases of aortic valve
*396	Diseases of mitral and aortic valves
*397	Diseases of other endocardial structures
*424	Other diseases of endocardium
429.5	Rupture of chordae tendineae
429.6	Rupture of papillary muscle
429.81	Other disorders of papillary muscle
745.0	Bulbus cordis anomalies and anomalies of cardiac septal closure, common truncus
*745.1	Transposition of great vessels
745.2	Tetralogy of Fallot
745.3	Bulbus cordis anomalies and anomalies of cardiac septal closure, common ventricle
745.4	Ventricular septal defect
745.5	Ostium secundum type atrial septal defect
745.60	Unspecified type congenital endocardial cushion defect
745.61	Ostium primum defect
745.69	Other congenital endocardial cushion defect
745.7	Cor biloculare
745.8	Other bulbus cordis anomalies and anomalies of cardiac septal closure
745.9	Unspecified congenital defect of septal closure
*746.0	Congenital anomalies of pulmonary valve
746.1	Congenital tricuspid atresia and stenosis
746.2	Ebstein's anomaly
746.3	Congenital stenosis of aortic valve
746.4	Congenital insufficiency of aortic valve
746.5	Congenital mitral stenosis
746.6	Congenital mitral insufficiency
746.7	Hypoplastic left heart syndrome
746.81	Congenital subaortic stenosis
746.82	Cor triatriatum
746.83	Congenital infundibular pulmonic stenosis
746.84	Congenital obstructive anomalies of heart, not elsewhere classified
746.85	Congenital coronary artery anomaly
746.87	Congenital malposition of heart and cardiac apex
746.89	Other specified congenital anomaly of heart
746.9	Unspecified congenital anomaly of heart
747.0	Patent ductus arteriosus

*747.1	Coarctation of aorta
*747.2	Other congenital anomaly of aorta
747.3	Congenital anomalies of pulmonary artery
*747.4	Congenital anomalies of great veins
759.82	Marfan's syndrome
785.2	Undiagnosed cardiac murmurs
996.02	Mechanical complication due to heart valve prosthesis

M DRG 136 Cardiac Congenital and Valvular Disorders, Age Greater than 17 without CC

GMLOS 2.2 AMLOS 2.8 RW 0.6214 ☑ A

Select principal diagnosis listed under DRG 135

M DRG 137 Cardiac Congenital and Valvular Disorders, Age 0-17

GMLOS 3.3 AMLOS 3.3 RW 0.8288 ☑ A

Select principal diagnosis listed under DRG 135

M DRG 138 Cardiac Arrhythmia and Conduction Disorders with CC

GMLOS 3.0 AMLOS 3.9 RW 0.8287 ☑ YIELD CC

Principal Diagnosis

*426	Conduction disorders
427.0	Paroxysmal supraventricular tachycardia
427.1	Paroxysmal ventricular tachycardia
427.2	Unspecified paroxysmal tachycardia
*427.3	Atrial fibrillation and flutter
*427.4	Ventricular fibrillation and flutter
*427.6	Premature beats
*427.8	Other specified cardiac dysrhythmias
427.9	Unspecified cardiac dysrhythmia
746.86	Congenital heart block
785.0	Unspecified tachycardia
785.1	Palpitations
996.01	Mechanical complication due to cardiac pacemaker (electrode)
996.04	Mechanical complication due to automatic implantable cardiac defibrillator

M DRG 139 Cardiac Arrhythmia and Conduction Disorders without CC

GMLOS 2.0 AMLOS 2.4 RW 0.5227 ☑

Select principal diagnosis listed under DRG 138

M DRG 140 Angina Pectoris

GMLOS 2.0 AMLOS 2.4 RW 0.5116 ☑ YIELD

Principal Diagnosis

411.1	Intermediate coronary syndrome
411.81	Acute coronary occlusion without myocardial infarction
411.89	Other acute and subacute form of ischemic heart disease
413.0	Angina decubitus
413.1	Prinzmetal angina
413.9	Other and unspecified angina pectoris

M DRG 141 Syncope and Collapse with CC

GMLOS 2.7 AMLOS 3.5 RW 0.7521 ☑ CC

Principal Diagnosis

458.0	Orthostatic hypotension
*458.2	Iatrogenic hypotension
780.2	Syncope and collapse

Ⓜ DRG 142 Syncope and Collapse without CC

GMLOS 2.0 AMLOS 2.5 RW 0.5852 ☑

Select principal diagnosis listed under DRG 141

Ⓜ DRG 143 Chest Pain

GMLOS 1.7 AMLOS 2.1 RW 0.5659 ☑

Principal Diagnosis

786.50	Unspecified chest pain
786.51	Precordial pain
786.59	Other chest pain
V71.7	Observation for suspected cardiovascular disease

Ⓜ DRG 144 Other Circulatory System Diagnoses with CC

GMLOS 4.1 AMLOS 5.8 RW 1.2761 ☑ T CC

Principal Diagnosis

032.82	Diphtheritic myocarditis
036.40	Meningococcal carditis, unspecified
036.41	Meningococcal pericarditis
036.43	Meningococcal myocarditis
074.20	Coxsackie carditis, unspecified
074.21	Coxsackie pericarditis
074.23	Coxsackie myocarditis
086.0	Chagas' disease with heart involvement
*093.8	Other specified cardiovascular syphilis
093.9	Unspecified cardiovascular syphilis
098.83	Gonococcal pericarditis
098.85	Other gonococcal heart disease
115.03	Histoplasma capsulatum pericarditis
115.13	Histoplasma duboisii pericarditis
115.93	Unspecified Histoplasmosis pericarditis
130.3	Myocarditis due to toxoplasmosis
164.1	Malignant neoplasm of heart
212.7	Benign neoplasm of heart
228.00	Hemangioma of unspecified site
228.09	Hemangioma of other sites
306.2	Cardiovascular malfunction arising from mental factors
391.0	Acute rheumatic pericarditis
391.2	Acute rheumatic myocarditis
391.8	Other acute rheumatic heart disease
391.9	Unspecified acute rheumatic heart disease
*392	Rheumatic chorea
393	Chronic rheumatic pericarditis
398.0	Rheumatic myocarditis
398.90	Unspecified rheumatic heart disease
398.99	Other and unspecified rheumatic heart diseases
410.00	Acute myocardial infarction of anterolateral wall, episode of care unspecified
410.02	Acute myocardial infarction of anterolateral wall, subsequent episode of care
410.10	Acute myocardial infarction of other anterior wall, episode of care unspecified
410.12	Acute myocardial infarction of other anterior wall, subsequent episode of care
410.20	Acute myocardial infarction of inferolateral wall, episode of care unspecified
410.22	Acute myocardial infarction of inferolateral wall, subsequent episode of care
410.30	Acute myocardial infarction of inferoposterior wall, episode of care unspecified
410.32	Acute myocardial infarction of inferoposterior wall, subsequent episode of care
410.40	Acute myocardial infarction of other inferior wall, episode of care unspecified
410.42	Acute myocardial infarction of other inferior wall, subsequent episode of care
410.50	Acute myocardial infarction of other lateral wall, episode of care unspecified
410.52	Acute myocardial infarction of other lateral wall, subsequent episode of care
410.60	Acute myocardial infarction, true posterior wall infarction, episode of care unspecified
410.62	Acute myocardial infarction, true posterior wall infarction, subsequent episode of care
410.70	Acute myocardial infarction, subendocardial infarction, episode of care unspecified

410.72	Acute myocardial infarction, subendocardial infarction, subsequent episode of care
410.80	Acute myocardial infarction of other specified sites, episode of care unspecified
410.82	Acute myocardial infarction of other specified sites, subsequent episode of care
410.90	Acute myocardial infarction, unspecified site, episode of care unspecified
410.92	Acute myocardial infarction, unspecified site, subsequent episode of care
411.0	Postmyocardial infarction syndrome
*414.1	Aneurysm and dissection of heart
415.0	Acute cor pulmonale
*416	Chronic pulmonary heart disease
*417	Other diseases of pulmonary circulation
*420	Acute pericarditis
*422	Acute myocarditis
*423	Other diseases of pericardium
*425	Cardiomyopathy
429.0	Unspecified myocarditis
429.1	Myocardial degeneration
429.4	Functional disturbances following cardiac surgery
429.71	Acquired cardiac septal defect
429.79	Other certain sequelae of myocardial infarction, not elsewhere classified
429.82	Hyperkinetic heart disease
458.1	Chronic hypotension
458.8	Other specified hypotension
458.9	Unspecified hypotension
459.0	Unspecified hemorrhage
785.3	Other abnormal heart sounds
785.9	Other symptoms involving cardiovascular system
794.30	Nonspecific abnormal unspecified cardiovascular function study
794.31	Nonspecific abnormal electrocardiogram (ecg) (ekg)
794.39	Other nonspecific abnormal cardiovascular system function study
796.2	Elevated blood pressure reading without diagnosis of hypertension
796.3	Nonspecific low blood pressure reading
*861.0	Heart injury, without mention of open wound into thorax
*861.1	Heart injury, with open wound into thorax
996.00	Mechanical complication of unspecified cardiac device, implant, and graft
996.03	Mechanical complication due to coronary bypass graft
996.09	Mechanical complication of cardiac device, implant, and graft, other
996.1	Mechanical complication of other vascular device, implant, and graft
996.61	Infection and inflammatory reaction due to cardiac device, implant, and graft
996.62	Infection and inflammatory reaction due to other vascular device, implant, and graft
996.71	Other complications due to heart valve prosthesis
996.72	Other complications due to other cardiac device, implant, and graft
996.73	Other complications due to renal dialysis device, implant, and graft
996.74	Other complications due to other vascular device, implant, and graft
996.83	Complications of transplanted heart
997.1	Cardiac complications
999.2	Other vascular complications of medical care, not elsewhere classified
V42.1	Heart replaced by transplant
V42.2	Heart valve replaced by transplant
*V43.2	Heart replaced by other means
V43.3	Heart valve replaced by other means
V43.4	Blood vessel replaced by other means
*V53.3	Fitting and adjustment of cardiac device

M DRG 145 Other Circulatory System Diagnoses without CC

GMLOS 2.1 AMLOS 2.6 RW 0.5835 ☑ T

Select principal diagnosis listed under DRG 144

MDC 6
DISEASES AND DISORDERS OF THE DIGESTIVE SYSTEM

The complete and up-to-date listing of ICD-9-CM diagnosis codes assigned to this MDC can be found online at www.ingenixonline.com/content/drg/resources.asp.

SURGICAL

S DRG 146 Rectal Resection with CC
GMLOS 8.6 AMLOS 10.0 RW 2.6621 ☑ T CC

Operating Room Procedures

*48.4	Pull-through resection of rectum
48.5	Abdominoperineal resection of rectum
*48.6	Other resection of rectum
49.75	Implantation or revision of artificial anal sphincter
49.76	Removal of artificial anal sphincter
68.8	Pelvic evisceration

S DRG 147 Rectal Resection without CC
GMLOS 5.2 AMLOS 5.8 RW 1.4781 ☑ T

Select operating room procedures listed under DRG 146

S DRG 148 Major Small and Large Bowel Procedures with CC
GMLOS 10.0 AMLOS 12.3 RW 3.4479 ☑ T CC

Operating Room Procedures

*45.5	Isolation of intestinal segment
*45.6	Other excision of small intestine
*45.7	Partial excision of large intestine
45.8	Total intra-abdominal colectomy
*45.9	Intestinal anastomosis
*46.0	Exteriorization of intestine
46.10	Colostomy, not otherwise specified
46.11	Temporary colostomy
46.13	Permanent colostomy
46.20	Ileostomy, not otherwise specified
46.21	Temporary ileostomy
46.22	Continent ileostomy
46.23	Other permanent ileostomy
46.73	Suture of laceration of small intestine, except duodenum
46.74	Closure of fistula of small intestine, except duodenum
46.75	Suture of laceration of large intestine
46.76	Closure of fistula of large intestine
46.79	Other repair of intestine
46.80	Intra-abdominal manipulation of intestine, not otherwise specified
46.81	Intra-abdominal manipulation of small intestine
46.82	Intra-abdominal manipulation of large intestine
46.91	Myotomy of sigmoid colon
46.92	Myotomy of other parts of colon
46.93	Revision of anastomosis of small intestine
46.94	Revision of anastomosis of large intestine
46.99	Other operations on intestines
47.92	Closure of appendiceal fistula
48.1	Proctostomy
48.71	Suture of laceration of rectum
48.72	Closure of proctostomy
48.74	Rectorectostomy
48.75	Abdominal proctopexy

48.76 Other proctopexy
70.52 Repair of rectocele
70.72 Repair of colovaginal fistula
70.73 Repair of rectovaginal fistula
70.74 Repair of other vaginoenteric fistula

S DRG 149 Major Small and Large Bowel Procedures without CC

GMLOS 5.4 AMLOS 6.0 RW 1.4324 ☑ T

Select operating room procedure listed under DRG 148

S DRG 150 Peritoneal Adhesiolysis with CC

GMLOS 8.9 AMLOS 11.0 RW 2.8061 T CC

Operating Room Procedure

*54.5 Lysis of peritoneal adhesions

S DRG 151 Peritoneal Adhesiolysis without CC

GMLOS 4.0 AMLOS 5.1 RW 1.2641 ☑ T

Select operating room procedure listed under DRG 150

S DRG 152 Minor Small and Large Bowel Procedures with CC

GMLOS 6.7 AMLOS 8.0 RW 1.8783 ☑ CC

Operating Room Procedures

45.00 Incision of intestine, not otherwise specified
45.02 Other incision of small intestine
45.03 Incision of large intestine
45.11 Transabdominal endoscopy of small intestine
45.15 Open biopsy of small intestine
45.21 Transabdominal endoscopy of large intestine
45.26 Open biopsy of large intestine
45.34 Other destruction of lesion of small intestine, except duodenum
45.49 Other destruction of lesion of large intestine
*46.5 Closure of intestinal stoma
*46.6 Fixation of intestine
47.91 Appendicostomy
48.0 Proctotomy
48.21 Transabdominal proctosigmoidoscopy
48.25 Open biopsy of rectum
56.84 Closure of other fistula of ureter
57.83 Repair of fistula involving bladder and intestine
69.42 Closure of fistula of uterus
70.75 Repair of other fistula of vagina
71.72 Repair of fistula of vulva or perineum

S DRG 153 Minor Small and Large Bowel Procedures without CC

GMLOS 4.5 AMLOS 5.0 RW 1.0821 ☑

Select operating room procedures listed under DRG 152

S DRG 154 Stomach, Esophageal and Duodenal Procedures, Age Greater than 17 with CC

GMLOS 9.9 AMLOS 13.3 RW 4.0399 T CC A

Operating Room Procedures

*29.3 Excision or destruction of lesion or tissue of pharynx
31.73 Closure of other fistula of trachea
38.05 Incision of other thoracic vessels
38.35 Resection of other thoracic vessels with anastomosis
38.45 Resection of other thoracic vessels with replacement
38.65 Other excision of other thoracic vessel
38.85 Other surgical occlusion of other thoracic vessel

MDC 6: Digestive System — Surgical

** Code Range* ☑ *Optimization Potential* *Targeted Potential* T *Transfer DRG* SP *Special Payment*

DRG 154 — continued

39.1	Intra-abdominal venous shunt
42.01	Incision of esophageal web
42.09	Other incision of esophagus
*42.1	Esophagostomy
42.21	Operative esophagoscopy by incision
42.25	Open biopsy of esophagus
42.31	Local excision of esophageal diverticulum
42.32	Local excision of other lesion or tissue of esophagus
42.39	Other destruction of lesion or tissue of esophagus
*42.4	Excision of esophagus
*42.5	Intrathoracic anastomosis of esophagus
*42.6	Antesternal anastomosis of esophagus
42.7	Esophagomyotomy
42.82	Suture of laceration of esophagus
42.83	Closure of esophagostomy
42.84	Repair of esophageal fistula, not elsewhere classified
42.85	Repair of esophageal stricture
42.86	Production of subcutaneous tunnel without esophageal anastomosis
42.87	Other graft of esophagus
42.89	Other repair of esophagus
42.91	Ligation of esophageal varices
43.0	Gastrotomy
43.3	Pyloromyotomy
43.42	Local excision of other lesion or tissue of stomach
43.49	Other destruction of lesion or tissue of stomach
43.5	Partial gastrectomy with anastomosis to esophagus
43.6	Partial gastrectomy with anastomosis to duodenum
43.7	Partial gastrectomy with anastomosis to jejunum
*43.8	Other partial gastrectomy
*43.9	Total gastrectomy
*44.0	Vagotomy
44.11	Transabdominal gastroscopy
44.15	Open biopsy of stomach
44.21	Dilation of pylorus by incision
44.29	Other pyloroplasty
*44.3	Gastroenterostomy without gastrectomy
44.40	Suture of peptic ulcer, not otherwise specified
44.41	Suture of gastric ulcer site
44.42	Suture of duodenal ulcer site
44.5	Revision of gastric anastomosis
44.61	Suture of laceration of stomach
44.63	Closure of other gastric fistula
44.64	Gastropexy
44.65	Esophagogastroplasty
44.66	Other procedures for creation of esophagogastric sphincteric competence
44.67	Laparoscopic procedures for creation of esophagogastric sphincteric competence
44.68	Laparoscopic gastroplasty
44.69	Other repair of stomach
44.91	Ligation of gastric varices
44.92	Intraoperative manipulation of stomach
44.99	Other operations on stomach
45.01	Incision of duodenum
45.31	Other local excision of lesion of duodenum
45.32	Other destruction of lesion of duodenum
46.71	Suture of laceration of duodenum
46.72	Closure of fistula of duodenum
51.82	Pancreatic sphincterotomy
51.83	Pancreatic sphincteroplasty
52.7	Radical pancreaticoduodenectomy
53.7	Repair of diaphragmatic hernia, abdominal approach
*53.8	Repair of diaphragmatic hernia, thoracic approach

[S] DRG 155 Stomach, Esophageal and Duodenal Procedures, Age Greater than 17 without CC

GMLOS 3.1 AMLOS 4.1 RW 1.2889 ☑ [T] [A]

Select operating room procedures listed under DRG 154

[S] DRG 156 Stomach, Esophageal and Duodenal Procedures, Age 0-17

GMLOS 6.0 AMLOS 6.0 RW 0.8535 ☑ [A]

Select operating room procedures listed under DRG 154

[S] DRG 157 Anal and Stomal Procedures with CC

GMLOS 4.1 AMLOS 5.8 RW 1.3356 ☑ [T] [CC]

Operating Room Procedures

45.33	Local excision of lesion or tissue of small intestine, except duodenum
45.41	Excision of lesion or tissue of large intestine
*46.4	Revision of intestinal stoma
48.35	Local excision of rectal lesion or tissue
48.73	Closure of other rectal fistula
48.79	Other repair of rectum
*48.8	Incision or excision of perirectal tissue or lesion
*48.9	Other operations on rectum and perirectal tissue
49.01	Incision of perianal abscess
49.02	Other incision of perianal tissue
49.04	Other excision of perianal tissue
*49.1	Incision or excision of anal fistula
49.39	Other local excision or destruction of lesion or tissue of anus
49.44	Destruction of hemorrhoids by cryotherapy
49.45	Ligation of hemorrhoids
49.46	Excision of hemorrhoids
49.49	Other procedures on hemorrhoids
*49.5	Division of anal sphincter
49.6	Excision of anus
49.71	Suture of laceration of anus
49.72	Anal cerclage
49.73	Closure of anal fistula
49.79	Other repair of anal sphincter
*49.9	Other operations on anus

[S] DRG 158 Anal and Stomal Procedures without CC

GMLOS 2.1 AMLOS 2.6 RW 0.6657 ☑ [T]

Select operating room procedures listed under DRG 157

[S] DRG 159 Hernia Procedures Except Inguinal and Femoral, Age Greater than 17 with CC

GMLOS 3.8 AMLOS 5.1 RW 1.4081 ☑ [CC] [A]

Operating Room Procedures

*53.4	Repair of umbilical hernia
*53.5	Repair of other hernia of anterior abdominal wall (without graft or prosthesis)
*53.6	Repair of other hernia of anterior abdominal wall with graft or prosthesis
53.9	Other hernia repair
54.71	Repair of gastroschisis
54.72	Other repair of abdominal wall

[S] DRG 160 Hernia Procedures Except Inguinal and Femoral, Age Greater than 17 without CC

GMLOS 2.2 AMLOS 2.7 RW 0.8431 ☑ [A]

Select operating room procedures listed under DRG 159

MDC 6: Digestive System — Surgical

** Code Range* ☑ *Optimization Potential* [YIELD] *Targeted Potential* [T] *Transfer DRG* [SP] *Special Payment*

Ⓢ DRG 161 Inguinal and Femoral Hernia Procedures, Age Greater than 17 with CC

GMLOS 3.1 AMLOS 4.4 RW 1.1931 ☑ CC A

Operating Room Procedures

*53.0	Unilateral repair of inguinal hernia
*53.1	Bilateral repair of inguinal hernia
*53.2	Unilateral repair of femoral hernia
*53.3	Bilateral repair of femoral hernia

Ⓢ DRG 162 Inguinal and Femoral Hernia Procedures, Age Greater than 17 without CC

GMLOS 1.7 AMLOS 2.1 RW 0.6785 ☑ A

Select operating room procedures listed under DRG 161

Ⓢ DRG 163 Hernia Procedures, Age 0-17

GMLOS 2.2 AMLOS 2.9 RW 0.6723 ☑ A

Operating Room Procedures

*53.0	Unilateral repair of inguinal hernia
*53.1	Bilateral repair of inguinal hernia
*53.2	Unilateral repair of femoral hernia
*53.3	Bilateral repair of femoral hernia
*53.4	Repair of umbilical hernia
*53.5	Repair of other hernia of anterior abdominal wall (without graft or prosthesis)
*53.6	Repair of other hernia of anterior abdominal wall with graft or prosthesis
53.9	Other hernia repair
54.71	Repair of gastroschisis
54.72	Other repair of abdominal wall

Ⓢ DRG 164 Appendectomy with Complicated Principal Diagnosis with CC

GMLOS 6.6 AMLOS 8.0 RW 2.2476 ☑ CC

Principal Diagnosis

153.5	Malignant neoplasm of appendix
540.0	Acute appendicitis with generalized peritonitis
540.1	Acute appendicitis with peritoneal abscess

Operating Room Procedures

*47.0	Appendectomy
47.2	Drainage of appendiceal abscess
47.99	Other operations on appendix

Ⓢ DRG 165 Appendectomy with Complicated Principal Diagnosis without CC

GMLOS 3.6 AMLOS 4.2 RW 1.1868 ☑

Select principal diagnosis and operating room procedures listed under DRG 164

Ⓢ DRG 166 Appendectomy without Complicated Principal Diagnosis with CC

GMLOS 3.3 AMLOS 4.5 RW 1.4521 ☑ CC

Operating Room Procedures

*47.0	Appendectomy
47.2	Drainage of appendiceal abscess
47.99	Other operations on appendix

☒ DRG 167 Appendectomy without Complicated Principal Diagnosis without CC

GMLOS 1.9 AMLOS 2.2 RW 0.8929 ☑

Select operating room procedures listed under DRG 166

☒ DRG 170 Other Digestive System O.R. Procedures with CC

GMLOS 7.8 AMLOS 11.0 RW 2.9612 T CC

Operating Room Procedures

38.04	Incision of aorta
38.06	Incision of abdominal arteries
38.07	Incision of abdominal veins
38.14	Endarterectomy of aorta
38.16	Endarterectomy of abdominal arteries
38.34	Resection of aorta with anastomosis
38.36	Resection of abdominal arteries with anastomosis
38.37	Resection of abdominal veins with anastomosis
38.46	Resection of abdominal arteries with replacement
38.47	Resection of abdominal veins with replacement
38.57	Ligation and stripping of abdominal varicose veins
38.64	Other excision of abdominal aorta
38.66	Other excision of abdominal arteries
38.67	Other excision of abdominal veins
38.7	Interruption of the vena cava
38.84	Other surgical occlusion of abdominal aorta
38.86	Other surgical occlusion of abdominal arteries
38.87	Other surgical occlusion of abdominal veins
39.26	Other intra-abdominal vascular shunt or bypass
39.27	Arteriovenostomy for renal dialysis
39.49	Other revision of vascular procedure
39.50	Angioplasty or atherectomy of other non-coronary vessel(s)
39.91	Freeing of vessel
39.98	Control of hemorrhage, not otherwise specified
39.99	Other operations on vessels
*40.1	Diagnostic procedures on lymphatic structures
40.21	Excision of deep cervical lymph node
40.23	Excision of axillary lymph node
40.24	Excision of inguinal lymph node
40.29	Simple excision of other lymphatic structure
40.3	Regional lymph node excision
*40.5	Radical excision of other lymph nodes
40.9	Other operations on lymphatic structures
41.5	Total splenectomy
49.74	Gracilis muscle transplant for anal incontinence
50.12	Open biopsy of liver
50.19	Other diagnostic procedures on liver
50.29	Other destruction of lesion of liver
51.03	Other cholecystostomy
51.13	Open biopsy of gallbladder or bile ducts
51.19	Other diagnostic procedures on biliary tract
51.22	Cholecystectomy
51.23	Laparoscopic cholecystectomy
*51.3	Anastomosis of gallbladder or bile duct
51.59	Incision of other bile duct
51.62	Excision of ampulla of Vater (with reimplantation of common duct)
51.63	Other excision of common duct
51.69	Excision of other bile duct
51.81	Dilation of sphincter of Oddi
52.12	Open biopsy of pancreas
52.19	Other diagnostic procedures on pancreas
52.92	Cannulation of pancreatic duct
52.99	Other operations on pancreas

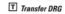

DRG 170 — continued

54.0	Incision of abdominal wall
*54.1	Laparotomy
54.21	Laparoscopy
54.22	Biopsy of abdominal wall or umbilicus
54.23	Biopsy of peritoneum
54.29	Other diagnostic procedures on abdominal region
54.3	Excision or destruction of lesion or tissue of abdominal wall or umbilicus
54.4	Excision or destruction of peritoneal tissue
*54.6	Suture of abdominal wall and peritoneum
54.73	Other repair of peritoneum
54.74	Other repair of omentum
54.75	Other repair of mesentery
54.92	Removal of foreign body from peritoneal cavity
54.93	Creation of cutaneoperitoneal fistula
54.94	Creation of peritoneovascular shunt
54.95	Incision of peritoneum
70.50	Repair of cystocele and rectocele
86.06	Insertion of totally implantable infusion pump
86.22	Excisional debridement of wound, infection, or burn
86.60	Free skin graft, not otherwise specified
86.63	Full-thickness skin graft to other sites
86.65	Heterograft to skin
86.66	Homograft to skin
86.67	Dermal regenerative graft
86.69	Other skin graft to other sites
86.70	Pedicle or flap graft, not otherwise specified
86.71	Cutting and preparation of pedicle grafts or flaps
86.72	Advancement of pedicle graft
86.74	Attachment of pedicle or flap graft to other sites
86.75	Revision of pedicle or flap graft
86.93	Insertion of tissue expander
92.27	Implantation or insertion of radioactive elements

S DRG 171 Other Digestive System O.R. Procedures without CC

GMLOS 3.1 AMLOS 4.1 RW 1.1905 ☑ T

Select operating room procedures listed under DRG 170

MDC 6
DISEASES AND DISORDERS OF THE DIGESTIVE SYSTEM

The complete and up-to-date listing of ICD-9-CM diagnosis codes assigned to this MDC can be found online at www.ingenixonline.com/content/drg/resources.asp.

MEDICAL

M DRG 172 Digestive Malignancy with CC

GMLOS 5.1 AMLOS 7.0 RW 1.4125 ☑ T CC

Principal Diagnosis

*150	Malignant neoplasm of esophagus
*151	Malignant neoplasm of stomach
*152	Malignant neoplasm of small intestine, including duodenum
*153	Malignant neoplasm of colon
*154	Malignant neoplasm of rectum, rectosigmoid junction, and anus
158.8	Malignant neoplasm of specified parts of peritoneum
158.9	Malignant neoplasm of peritoneum, unspecified
159.0	Malignant neoplasm of intestinal tract, part unspecified
159.8	Malignant neoplasm of other sites of digestive system and intra-abdominal organs
159.9	Malignant neoplasm of ill-defined sites of digestive organs and peritoneum
176.3	Kaposi's sarcoma of gastrointestinal sites
195.2	Malignant neoplasm of abdomen
197.4	Secondary malignant neoplasm of small intestine including duodenum
197.5	Secondary malignant neoplasm of large intestine and rectum
197.6	Secondary malignant neoplasm of retroperitoneum and peritoneum
197.8	Secondary malignant neoplasm of other digestive organs and spleen
230.1	Carcinoma in situ of esophagus
230.2	Carcinoma in situ of stomach
230.3	Carcinoma in situ of colon
230.4	Carcinoma in situ of rectum
230.5	Carcinoma in situ of anal canal
230.6	Carcinoma in situ of anus, unspecified
230.7	Carcinoma in situ of other and unspecified parts of intestine
230.9	Carcinoma in situ of other and unspecified digestive organs
235.2	Neoplasm of uncertain behavior of stomach, intestines, and rectum
235.4	Neoplasm of uncertain behavior of retroperitoneum and peritoneum
235.5	Neoplasm of uncertain behavior of other and unspecified digestive organs
239.0	Neoplasm of unspecified nature of digestive system

M DRG 173 Digestive Malignancy without CC

GMLOS 2.7 AMLOS 3.6 RW 0.7443 ☑ T

Select principal diagnosis listed under DRG 172

M DRG 174 GI Hemorrhage with CC

GMLOS 3.8 AMLOS 4.7 RW 1.0060 ☑ YIELD CC

Principal Diagnosis

456.0	Esophageal varices with bleeding
530.7	Gastroesophageal laceration-hemorrhage syndrome
530.82	Esophageal hemorrhage
*531.0	Acute gastric ulcer with hemorrhage
*531.2	Acute gastric ulcer with hemorrhage and perforation
*531.4	Chronic or unspecified gastric ulcer with hemorrhage
*531.6	Chronic or unspecified gastric ulcer with hemorrhage and perforation
*532.0	Acute duodenal ulcer with hemorrhage
*532.2	Acute duodenal ulcer with hemorrhage and perforation
*532.4	Chronic or unspecified duodenal ulcer with hemorrhage

** Code Range* ☑ *Optimization Potential* YIELD *Targeted Potential* T *Transfer DRG* SP *Special Payment*

DRG 174 — continued

*532.6	Chronic or unspecified duodenal ulcer with hemorrhage and perforation
*533.0	Acute peptic ulcer, unspecified site, with hemorrhage
*533.2	Acute peptic ulcer, unspecified site, with hemorrhage and perforation
*533.4	Chronic or unspecified peptic ulcer, unspecified site, with hemorrhage
*533.6	Chronic or unspecified peptic ulcer, unspecified site, with hemorrhage and perforation
*534.0	Acute gastrojejunal ulcer with hemorrhage
*534.2	Acute gastrojejunal ulcer with hemorrhage and perforation
*534.4	Chronic or unspecified gastrojejunal ulcer with hemorrhage
*534.6	Chronic or unspecified gastrojejunal ulcer with hemorrhage and perforation
535.01	Acute gastritis with hemorrhage
535.11	Atrophic gastritis with hemorrhage
535.21	Gastric mucosal hypertrophy with hemorrhage
535.31	Alcoholic gastritis with hemorrhage
535.41	Other specified gastritis with hemorrhage
535.51	Unspecified gastritis and gastroduodenitis with hemorrhage
535.61	Duodenitis with hemorrhage
537.83	Angiodysplasia of stomach and duodenum with hemorrhage
537.84	Dieulafoy lesion (hemorrhagic) of stomach and duodenum
562.02	Diverticulosis of small intestine with hemorrhage
562.03	Divertulitis of small intestine with hemorrhage
562.12	Diverticulosis of colon with hemorrhage
562.13	Diverticulitis of colon with hemorrhage
569.3	Hemorrhage of rectum and anus
569.85	Angiodysplasia of intestine with hemorrhage
*578	Gastrointestinal hemorrhage

M DRG 175 GI Hemorrhage without CC

GMLOS 2.4 AMLOS 2.9 RW 0.5646 ☑

Select principal diagnosis listed under DRG 174

M DRG 176 Complicated Peptic Ulcer

GMLOS 4.1 AMLOS 5.2 RW 1.1246 ☑ T

Principal Diagnosis

251.5	Abnormality of secretion of gastrin
*530.2	Ulcer of esophagus
530.85	Barrett's esophagus
*531.1	Acute gastric ulcer with perforation
531.31	Acute gastric ulcer without mention of hemorrhage or perforation, with obstruction
*531.5	Chronic or unspecified gastric ulcer with perforation
531.71	Chronic gastric ulcer without mention of hemorrhage or perforation, with obstruction
531.91	Gastric ulcer, unspecified as acute or chronic, without mention of hemorrhage or perforation, with obstruction
*532.1	Acute duodenal ulcer with perforation
532.31	Acute duodenal ulcer without mention of hemorrhage or perforation, with obstruction
*532.5	Chronic or unspecified duodenal ulcer with perforation
532.71	Chronic duodenal ulcer without mention of hemorrhage or perforation, with obstruction
532.91	Duodenal ulcer, unspecified as acute or chronic, without mention of hemorrhage or perforation, with obstruction
*533.1	Acute peptic ulcer, unspecified site, with perforation
533.31	Acute peptic ulcer, unspecified site, without mention of hemorrhage and perforation, with obstruction
*533.5	Chronic or unspecified peptic ulcer, unspecified site, with perforation
533.71	Chronic peptic ulcer of unspecified site without mention of hemorrhage or perforation, with obstruction
533.91	Peptic ulcer, unspecified site, unspecified as acute or chronic, without mention of hemorrhage or perforation, with obstruction
*534.1	Acute gastrojejunal ulcer with perforation
*534.3	Acute gastrojejunal ulcer without mention of hemorrhage or perforation
*534.5	Chronic or unspecified gastrojejunal ulcer with perforation
*534.7	Chronic gastrojejunal ulcer without mention of hemorrhage or perforation

S Surgical M Medical CC CC Indicator A Age Restriction ● New DRG ▲ Revised DRG Title

*534.9	Gastrojejunal ulcer, unspecified as acute or chronic, without mention of hemorrhage or perforation
537.0	Acquired hypertrophic pyloric stenosis
537.3	Other obstruction of duodenum
751.0	Meckel's diverticulum

Ⓜ DRG 177 Uncomplicated Peptic Ulcer with CC

GMLOS 3.6 AMLOS 4.4 RW 0.9166 ☑ CC

Principal Diagnosis

531.30	Acute gastric ulcer without mention of hemorrhage, perforation, or obstruction
531.70	Chronic gastric ulcer without mention of hemorrhage, perforation, without mention of obstruction
531.90	Gastric ulcer, unspecified as acute or chronic, without mention of hemorrhage, perforation, or obstruction
532.30	Acute duodenal ulcer without mention of hemorrhage, perforation, or obstruction
532.70	Chronic duodenal ulcer without mention of hemorrhage, perforation, or obstruction
532.90	Duodenal ulcer, unspecified as acute or chronic, without hemorrhage, perforation, or obstruction
533.30	Acute peptic ulcer, unspecified site, without mention of hemorrhage, perforation, or obstruction
533.70	Chronic peptic ulcer, unspecified site, without mention of hemorrhage, perforation, or obstruction
533.90	Peptic ulcer, unspecified site, unspecified as acute or chronic, without mention of hemorrhage, perforation, or obstruction

Ⓜ DRG 178 Uncomplicated Peptic Ulcer without CC

GMLOS 2.6 AMLOS 3.1 RW 0.7013 ☑

Select principal diagnosis listed under DRG 177

Ⓜ DRG 179 Inflammatory Bowel Disease

GMLOS 4.5 AMLOS 5.9 RW 1.0911 ☑

Principal Diagnosis

*555	Regional enteritis
*556	Ulcerative colitis

Ⓜ DRG 180 GI Obstruction with CC

GMLOS 4.2 AMLOS 5.4 RW 0.9784 ☑ T ▽ CC

Principal Diagnosis

*560	Intestinal obstruction without mention of hernia

Ⓜ DRG 181 GI Obstruction without CC

GMLOS 2.8 AMLOS 3.3 RW 0.5614 ☑ T

Select principal diagnosis listed under DRG 180

Ⓜ DRG 182 Esophagitis, Gastroenteritis and Miscellaneous Digestive Disorders, Age Greater than 17 with CC

GMLOS 3.4 AMLOS 4.4 RW 0.8413 ☑ ▽ CC A

Principal Diagnosis

*001	Cholera
003.0	Salmonella gastroenteritis
*004	Shigellosis
005.0	Staphylococcal food poisoning
005.2	Food poisoning due to Clostridium perfringens (C. welchii)
005.3	Food poisoning due to other Clostridia
005.4	Food poisoning due to Vibrio parahaemolyticus
*005.8	Other bacterial food poisoning
005.9	Unspecified food poisoning
006.0	Acute amebic dysentery without mention of abscess

*** Code Range** ☑ **Optimization Potential** ▽ **Targeted Potential** T **Transfer DRG** SP **Special Payment**

DRG 182 — continued

006.1	Chronic intestinal amebiasis without mention of abscess
006.2	Amebic nondysenteric colitis
*007	Other protozoal intestinal diseases
*008	Intestinal infections due to other organisms
*009	Ill-defined intestinal infections
078.82	Epidemic vomiting syndrome
112.84	Candidiasis of the esophagus
112.85	Candidiasis of the intestine
*123	Other cestode infection
*126	Ancylostomiasis and necatoriasis
127.0	Ascariasis
127.1	Anisakiasis
127.2	Strongyloidiasis
127.3	Trichuriasis
127.4	Enterobiasis
127.5	Capillariasis
127.6	Trichostrongyliasis
127.7	Other specified intestinal helminthiasis
127.9	Unspecified intestinal helminthiasis
129	Unspecified intestinal parasitism
228.04	Hemangioma of intra-abdominal structures
271.2	Hereditary fructose intolerance
271.3	Intestinal disaccharidase deficiencies and disaccharide malabsorption
306.4	Gastrointestinal malfunction arising from mental factors
447.4	Celiac artery compression syndrome
530.0	Achalasia and cardiospasm
*530.1	Esophagitis
530.3	Stricture and stenosis of esophagus
530.4	Perforation of esophagus
530.5	Dyskinesia of esophagus
530.6	Diverticulum of esophagus, acquired
530.81	Esophageal reflux
530.83	Esophageal leukoplakia
530.84	Tracheoesophageal fistula
530.89	Other specified disorder of the esophagus
530.9	Unspecified disorder of esophagus
535.00	Acute gastritis without mention of hemorrhage
535.10	Atrophic gastritis without mention of hemorrhage
535.20	Gastric mucosal hypertrophy without mention of hemorrhage
535.30	Alcoholic gastritis without mention of hemorrhage
535.40	Other specified gastritis without mention of hemorrhage
535.50	Unspecified gastritis and gastroduodenitis without mention of hemorrhage
535.60	Duodenitis without mention of hemorrhage
536.0	Achlorhydria
536.1	Acute dilatation of stomach
536.2	Persistent vomiting
536.3	Gastroparesis
536.8	Dyspepsia and other specified disorders of function of stomach
536.9	Unspecified functional disorder of stomach
537.1	Gastric diverticulum
537.2	Chronic duodenal ileus
537.4	Fistula of stomach or duodenum
537.5	Gastroptosis
537.6	Hourglass stricture or stenosis of stomach
537.81	Pylorospasm
537.82	Angiodysplasia of stomach and duodenum (without mention of hemorrhage)
537.89	Other specified disorder of stomach and duodenum
537.9	Unspecified disorder of stomach and duodenum
552.3	Diaphragmatic hernia with obstruction
553.3	Diaphragmatic hernia without mention of obstruction or gangrene
558.3	Gastroenteritis and colitis, allergic
558.9	Other and unspecified noninfectious gastroenteritis and colitis

562.00	Diverticulosis of small intestine (without mention of hemorrhage)
562.01	Diverticulitis of small intestine (without mention of hemorrhage)
562.10	Diverticulosis of colon (without mention of hemorrhage)
562.11	Diverticulitis of colon (without mention of hemorrhage)
*564.0	Constipation
564.1	Irritable bowel syndrome
564.2	Postgastric surgery syndromes
564.3	Vomiting following gastrointestinal surgery
564.4	Other postoperative functional disorders
564.5	Functional diarrhea
564.6	Anal spasm
*564.8	Other specified functional disorders of intestine
564.9	Unspecified functional disorder of intestine
*579	Intestinal malabsorption
617.5	Endometriosis of intestine
*787	Symptoms involving digestive system
*789.0	Abdominal pain
*789.3	Abdominal or pelvic swelling, mass, or lump
*789.6	Abdominal tenderness
789.9	Other symptoms involving abdomen and pelvis
792.1	Nonspecific abnormal finding in stool contents
793.4	Nonspecific abnormal findings on radiological and other examination of gastrointestinal tract
793.6	Nonspecific abnormal findings on radiological and other examination of abdominal area, including retroperitoneum

M DRG 183 Esophagitis, Gastroenteritis and Miscellaneous Digestive Disorders, Age Greater than 17 without CC

GMLOS 2.3 AMLOS 2.9 RW 0.5848 ☑ A

Select principal diagnosis listed under DRG 182

M DRG 184 Esophagitis, Gastroenteritis and Miscellaneous Digestive Disorders, Age 0-17

GMLOS 2.5 AMLOS 3.3 RW 0.5663 ☑ A

Select principal diagnosis listed under DRG 182

M DRG 188 Other Digestive System Diagnoses, Age Greater than 17 with CC

GMLOS 4.2 AMLOS 5.6 RW 1.1290 ☑ T YIELD CC A

Principal Diagnosis

*014	Tuberculosis of intestines, peritoneum, and mesenteric glands
*017.8	Tuberculosis of esophagus
021.1	Enteric tularemia
022.2	Gastrointestinal anthrax
032.83	Diphtheritic peritonitis
039.2	Abdominal actinomycotic infection
040.2	Whipple's disease
054.71	Visceral herpes simplex
091.1	Primary anal syphilis
091.69	Early syphilis, secondary syphilis of other viscera
095.2	Syphilitic peritonitis
098.7	Gonococcal infection of anus and rectum
098.86	Gonococcal peritonitis
099.52	Chlamydia trachomatis infection of anus and rectum
099.56	Chlamydia trachomatis infection of peritoneum
211.0	Benign neoplasm of esophagus
211.1	Benign neoplasm of stomach
211.2	Benign neoplasm of duodenum, jejunum, and ileum
211.3	Benign neoplasm of colon
211.4	Benign neoplasm of rectum and anal canal
211.8	Benign neoplasm of retroperitoneum and peritoneum

DRG 188 — continued

211.9	Benign neoplasm of other and unspecified site of the digestive system
214.3	Lipoma of intra-abdominal organs
277.03	Cystic fibrosis with gastrointestinal manifestations
289.2	Nonspecific mesenteric lymphadenitis
*455	Hemorrhoids
456.1	Esophageal varices without mention of bleeding
*456.2	Esophageal varices in diseases classified elsewhere
530.86	Infection of esophagostomy
530.87	Mechanical complication of esophagostomy
*536.4	Gastrostomy complications
*540	Acute appendicitis
541	Appendicitis, unqualified
542	Other appendicitis
*543	Other diseases of appendix
*550	Inguinal hernia
*551	Other hernia of abdominal cavity, with gangrene
*552.0	Femoral hernia with obstruction
552.1	Umbilical hernia with obstruction
*552.2	Ventral hernia with obstruction
552.8	Hernia of other specified site, with obstruction
552.9	Hernia of unspecified site, with obstruction
*553.0	Femoral hernia without mention of obstruction or gangrene
553.1	Umbilical hernia without mention of obstruction or gangrene
*553.2	Ventral hernia without mention of obstruction or gangrene
553.8	Hernia of other specified sites of abdominal cavity without mention of obstruction or gangrene
553.9	Hernia of unspecified site of abdominal cavity without mention of obstruction or gangrene
*557	Vascular insufficiency of intestine
558.1	Gastroenteritis and colitis due to radiation
558.2	Toxic gastroenteritis and colitis
564.7	Megacolon, other than Hirschsprung's
*565	Anal fissure and fistula
566	Abscess of anal and rectal regions
*567	Peritonitis and retroperitoneal infections
*568	Other disorders of peritoneum
569.0	Anal and rectal polyp
569.1	Rectal prolapse
569.2	Stenosis of rectum and anus
*569.4	Other specified disorders of rectum and anus
569.5	Abscess of intestine
*569.6	Colostomy and enterostomy complications
569.81	Fistula of intestine, excluding rectum and anus
569.82	Ulceration of intestine
569.83	Perforation of intestine
569.84	Angiodysplasia of intestine (without mention of hemorrhage)
569.86	Dieulafoy lesion (hemorrhagic) of intestine
569.89	Other specified disorder of intestines
569.9	Unspecified disorder of intestine
619.1	Digestive-genital tract fistula, female
750.3	Congenital tracheoesophageal fistula, esophageal atresia and stenosis
750.4	Other specified congenital anomaly of esophagus
750.5	Congenital hypertrophic pyloric stenosis
750.6	Congenital hiatus hernia
750.7	Other specified congenital anomalies of stomach
750.8	Other specified congenital anomalies of upper alimentary tract
750.9	Unspecified congenital anomaly of upper alimentary tract
751.1	Congenital atresia and stenosis of small intestine
751.2	Congenital atresia and stenosis of large intestine, rectum, and anal canal
751.3	Hirschsprung's disease and other congenital functional disorders of colon
751.4	Congenital anomalies of intestinal fixation
751.5	Other congenital anomalies of intestine
751.8	Other specified congenital anomalies of digestive system
751.9	Unspecified congenital anomaly of digestive system

*756.7	Congenital anomaly of abdominal wall
759.3	Situs inversus
759.4	Conjoined twins
*789.4	Abdominal rigidity
862.22	Esophagus injury without mention of open wound into cavity
862.32	Esophagus injury with open wound into cavity
863.0	Stomach injury without mention of open wound into cavity
863.1	Stomach injury with open wound into cavity
*863.2	Small intestine injury without mention of open wound into cavity
*863.3	Small intestine injury with open wound into cavity
*863.4	Colon or rectal injury without mention of open wound into cavity
*863.5	Injury to colon or rectum with open wound into cavity
863.80	Gastrointestinal tract injury, unspecified site, without mention of open wound into cavity
863.85	Appendix injury without mention of open wound into cavity
863.89	Injury to other and unspecified gastrointestinal sites without mention of open wound into cavity
863.90	Gastrointestinal tract injury, unspecified site, with open wound into cavity
863.95	Appendix injury with open wound into cavity
863.99	Injury to other and unspecified gastrointestinal sites with open wound into cavity
868.00	Injury to unspecified intra-abdominal organ without mention of open wound into cavity
868.03	Peritoneum injury without mention of open wound into cavity
868.10	Injury to unspecified intra-abdominal organ, with open wound into cavity
868.13	Peritoneum injury with open wound into cavity
908.1	Late effect of internal injury to intra-abdominal organs
935.1	Foreign body in esophagus
935.2	Foreign body in stomach
936	Foreign body in intestine and colon
937	Foreign body in anus and rectum
938	Foreign body in digestive system, unspecified
947.2	Burn of esophagus
947.3	Burn of gastrointestinal tract
997.4	Digestive system complication
997.71	Vascular complications of mesenteric artery
V53.5	Fitting and adjustment of other intestinal appliance
V55.1	Attention to gastrostomy
V55.2	Attention to ileostomy
V55.3	Attention to colostomy
V55.4	Attention to other artificial opening of digestive tract

M DRG 189 Other Digestive System Diagnoses, Age Greater than 17 without CC

GMLOS 2.4 AMLOS 3.1 RW 0.6064 ☑ T A

Select principal diagnosis listed under DRG 188

M DRG 190 Other Digestive System Diagnoses, Age 0-17

GMLOS 3.1 AMLOS 4.4 RW 0.6179 ☑ A

Select principal diagnosis listed under DRG 188

MDC 7
DISEASES AND DISORDERS OF THE HEPATOBILIARY SYSTEM AND PANCREAS

The complete and up-to-date listing of ICD-9-CM diagnosis codes assigned to this MDC can be found online at www.ingenixonline.com/content/drg/resources.asp.

SURGICAL

S DRG 191 Pancreas, Liver and Shunt Procedures with CC

GMLOS 9.0 AMLOS 12.9 RW 3.9680 T CC

Operating Room Procedures

39.1	Intra-abdominal venous shunt
50.0	Hepatotomy
50.21	Marsupialization of lesion of liver
50.22	Partial hepatectomy
50.29	Other destruction of lesion of liver
50.3	Lobectomy of liver
50.4	Total hepatectomy
50.61	Closure of laceration of liver
50.69	Other repair of liver
51.43	Insertion of choledochohepatic tube for decompression
51.82	Pancreatic sphincterotomy
51.83	Pancreatic sphincteroplasty
*52.0	Pancreatotomy
52.22	Other excision or destruction of lesion or tissue of pancreas or pancreatic duct
52.3	Marsupialization of pancreatic cyst
52.4	Internal drainage of pancreatic cyst
*52.5	Partial pancreatectomy
52.6	Total pancreatectomy
52.7	Radical pancreaticoduodenectomy
*52.8	Transplant of pancreas
52.92	Cannulation of pancreatic duct
52.95	Other repair of pancreas
52.96	Anastomosis of pancreas
52.99	Other operations on pancreas
54.94	Creation of peritoneovascular shunt

S DRG 192 Pancreas, Liver and Shunt Procedures without CC

GMLOS 4.3 AMLOS 5.7 RW 1.6793 ☑ T

Select operating room procedures listed under DRG 191

S DRG 193 Biliary Tract Procedures Except Only Cholecystectomy with or without Common Duct Exploration with CC

GMLOS 9.9 AMLOS 12.1 RW 3.2818 CC

Operating Room Procedures

51.02	Trocar cholecystostomy
51.03	Other cholecystostomy
51.04	Other cholecystotomy
*51.3	Anastomosis of gallbladder or bile duct
51.49	Incision of other bile ducts for relief of obstruction
51.59	Incision of other bile duct
51.61	Excision of cystic duct remnant
51.62	Excision of ampulla of Vater (with reimplantation of common duct)
51.63	Other excision of common duct
51.69	Excision of other bile duct
*51.7	Repair of bile ducts
51.81	Dilation of sphincter of Oddi

51.89 Other operations on sphincter of Oddi
51.91 Repair of laceration of gallbladder
51.92 Closure of cholecystostomy
51.93 Closure of other biliary fistula
51.94 Revision of anastomosis of biliary tract
51.95 Removal of prosthetic device from bile duct
51.99 Other operations on biliary tract

WITH OR WITHOUT

Operating Room Procedures

51.41 Common duct exploration for removal of calculus
51.42 Common duct exploration for relief of other obstruction
51.51 Exploration of common bile duct

WITH OR WITHOUT

Operating Room Procedures

*51.2 Cholecystectomy

S DRG 194 Biliary Tract Procedures Except Only Cholecystectomy with or without Common Duct Exploration without CC

GMLOS 5.6 AMLOS 6.7 RW 1.5748 ☑

Select operating room procedures listed under DRG 193

S DRG 195 Cholecystectomy with Common Duct Exploration with CC

GMLOS 8.8 AMLOS 10.6 RW 3.0530 ☑ CC

Operating Room Procedures

51.41 Common duct exploration for removal of calculus
51.42 Common duct exploration for relief of other obstruction
51.51 Exploration of common bile duct

AND

Operating Room Procedures

*51.2 Cholecystectomy

S DRG 196 Cholecystectomy with Common Duct Exploration without CC

GMLOS 4.9 AMLOS 5.7 RW 1.6031 ☑

Select operating room procedures listed under DRG 195

S DRG 197 Cholecystectomy Except by Laparoscope without Common Duct Exploration with CC

GMLOS 7.5 AMLOS 9.2 RW 2.5425 ☑ T CC

Operating Room Procedures

51.21 Other partial cholecystectomy
51.22 Cholecystectomy

S DRG 198 Cholecystectomy Except by Laparoscope without Common Duct Exploration without CC

GMLOS 3.7 AMLOS 4.3 RW 1.1604 ☑ T

Select operating room procedure listed under DRG 197

S DRG 199 Hepatobiliary Diagnostic Procedure for Malignancy

GMLOS 6.8 AMLOS 9.5 RW 2.4073 ☑

Principal Diagnosis

*155 Malignant neoplasm of liver and intrahepatic bile ducts
*156 Malignant neoplasm of gallbladder and extrahepatic bile ducts
*157 Malignant neoplasm of pancreas

** Code Range* ☑ *Optimization Potential* *Targeted Potential* T *Transfer DRG* SP *Special Payment*

DRG 199 — continued

197.7	Secondary malignant neoplasm of liver
230.8	Carcinoma in situ of liver and biliary system
235.3	Neoplasm of uncertain behavior of liver and biliary passages

WITH

Operating Room Procedures

44.11	Transabdominal gastroscopy
50.12	Open biopsy of liver
50.19	Other diagnostic procedures on liver
51.13	Open biopsy of gallbladder or bile ducts
51.19	Other diagnostic procedures on biliary tract
52.12	Open biopsy of pancreas
52.19	Other diagnostic procedures on pancreas
54.11	Exploratory laparotomy
54.19	Other laparotomy
54.21	Laparoscopy
54.23	Biopsy of peritoneum
54.29	Other diagnostic procedures on abdominal region
87.53	Intraoperative cholangiogram

S DRG 200 Hepatobiliary Diagnostic Procedure for Nonmalignancy

GMLOS 6.5 AMLOS 9.8 RW 2.7868

Select operating room procedures listed under DRG 199

S DRG 201 Other Hepatobiliary or Pancreas O.R. Procedures

GMLOS 9.9 AMLOS 13.7 RW 3.7339

Operating Room Procedures

*03.2	Chordotomy
38.7	Interruption of the vena cava
39.26	Other intra-abdominal vascular shunt or bypass
39.29	Other (peripheral) vascular shunt or bypass
39.49	Other revision of vascular procedure
39.50	Angioplasty or atherectomy of other non-coronary vessel(s)
39.98	Control of hemorrhage, not otherwise specified
40.11	Biopsy of lymphatic structure
42.91	Ligation of esophageal varices
43.0	Gastrotomy
43.42	Local excision of other lesion or tissue of stomach
44.32	Percutaneous [endoscopic] gastrojejunostomy
44.38	Laparoscopic gastroenterostomy
44.39	Other gastroenterostomy without gastrectomy
44.63	Closure of other gastric fistula
44.91	Ligation of gastric varices
44.92	Intraoperative manipulation of stomach
45.01	Incision of duodenum
45.31	Other local excision of lesion of duodenum
45.32	Other destruction of lesion of duodenum
46.80	Intra-abdominal manipulation of intestine, not otherwise specified
46.81	Intra-abdominal manipulation of small intestine
46.82	Intra-abdominal manipulation of large intestine
46.97	Transplant of intestine
46.99	Other operations on intestines
54.0	Incision of abdominal wall
54.12	Reopening of recent laparotomy site
54.4	Excision or destruction of peritoneal tissue
*54.5	Lysis of peritoneal adhesions
54.61	Reclosure of postoperative disruption of abdominal wall
54.62	Delayed closure of granulating abdominal wound
54.64	Suture of peritoneum
54.72	Other repair of abdominal wall

54.73 Other repair of peritoneum
54.74 Other repair of omentum
54.75 Other repair of mesentery
54.93 Creation of cutaneoperitoneal fistula
54.95 Incision of peritoneum
86.06 Insertion of totally implantable infusion pump
86.22 Excisional debridement of wound, infection, or burn

S DRG 493 Laparoscopic Cholecystectomy without Common Duct Exploration with CC

GMLOS 4.5 AMLOS 6.1 RW 1.8333 ☑ CC

Operating room procedures

51.23 Laparoscopic cholecystectomy
51.24 Laparoscopic partial cholecystectomy

S DRG 494 Laparoscopic Cholecystectomy without Common Duct Exploration without CC

GMLOS 2.1 AMLOS 2.7 RW 1.0285 ☑

Select operating room procedures listed under DRG 493

MDC 7
DISEASES AND DISORDERS OF THE HEPATOBILIARY SYSTEM AND PANCREAS

The complete and up-to-date listing of ICD-9-CM diagnosis codes assigned to this MDC can be found online at www.ingenixonline.com/content/drg/resources.asp.

MEDICAL

M DRG 202 Cirrhosis and Alcoholic Hepatitis
GMLOS 4.7 AMLOS 6.2 RW 1.3318 ☑

Principal Diagnosis

571.1	Acute alcoholic hepatitis
571.2	Alcoholic cirrhosis of liver
571.3	Unspecified alcoholic liver damage
571.5	Cirrhosis of liver without mention of alcohol
571.6	Biliary cirrhosis

M DRG 203 Malignancy of Hepatobiliary System or Pancreas
GMLOS 4.9 AMLOS 6.5 RW 1.3552 ☑

Principal Diagnosis

*155	Malignant neoplasm of liver and intrahepatic bile ducts
*156	Malignant neoplasm of gallbladder and extrahepatic bile ducts
*157	Malignant neoplasm of pancreas
197.7	Secondary malignant neoplasm of liver
230.8	Carcinoma in situ of liver and biliary system
235.3	Neoplasm of uncertain behavior of liver and biliary passages

M DRG 204 Disorders of Pancreas Except Malignancy
GMLOS 4.2 AMLOS 5.6 RW 1.1249 ☑

Principal Diagnosis

072.3	Mumps pancreatitis
211.6	Benign neoplasm of pancreas, except islets of Langerhans
*577	Diseases of pancreas
751.7	Congenital anomalies of pancreas
863.81	Pancreas head injury without mention of open wound into cavity
863.82	Pancreas body injury without mention of open wound into cavity
863.83	Pancreas tail injury without mention of open wound into cavity
863.84	Pancreas injury, multiple and unspecified sites, without mention of open wound into cavity
863.91	Pancreas head injury with open wound into cavity
863.92	Pancreas body injury with open wound into cavity
863.93	Pancreas tail injury with open wound into cavity
863.94	Pancreas injury, multiple and unspecified sites, with open wound into cavity
996.86	Complications of transplanted pancreas
V42.83	Pancreas replaced by transplant

M DRG 205 Disorders of Liver Except Malignancy, Cirrhosis and Alcoholic Hepatitis with CC
GMLOS 4.4 AMLOS 6.0 RW 1.2059 ☑ T CC

Principal Diagnosis

006.3	Amebic liver abscess
*070	Viral hepatitis
072.71	Mumps hepatitis
091.62	Early syphilis, secondary syphilitic hepatitis
095.3	Syphilis of liver
120.1	Schistosomiasis due to schistosoma mansoni
121.0	Opisthorchiasis

121.1	Clonorchiasis
121.3	Fascioliasis
121.4	Fasciolopsiasis
122.0	Echinococcus granulosus infection of liver
122.5	Echinococcus multilocularis infection of liver
122.8	Unspecified echinococcus of liver
130.5	Hepatitis due to toxoplasmosis
211.5	Benign neoplasm of liver and biliary passages
277.4	Disorders of bilirubin excretion
452	Portal vein thrombosis
453.0	Budd-Chiari syndrome
570	Acute and subacute necrosis of liver
571.0	Alcoholic fatty liver
*571.4	Chronic hepatitis
571.8	Other chronic nonalcoholic liver disease
571.9	Unspecified chronic liver disease without mention of alcohol
*572	Liver abscess and sequelae of chronic liver disease
*573	Other disorders of liver
751.62	Congenital cystic disease of liver
751.69	Other congenital anomaly of gallbladder, bile ducts, and liver
782.4	Jaundice, unspecified, not of newborn
789.1	Hepatomegaly
791.4	Biliuria
794.8	Nonspecific abnormal results of liver function study
*864	Injury to liver
996.82	Complications of transplanted liver
*V02.6	Carrier or suspected carrier of viral hepatitis
V42.7	Liver replaced by transplant
V59.6	Liver donor

Ⓜ DRG 206 Disorders of Liver Except Malignancy, Cirrhosis and Alcoholic Hepatitis without CC

GMLOS 3.0 AMLOS 3.9 RW 0.7292 ☑ T

Select principal diagnosis listed under DRG 205

Ⓜ DRG 207 Disorders of the Biliary Tract with CC

GMLOS 4.1 AMLOS 5.3 RW 1.1746 ☑ CC

Principal Diagnosis

*574	Cholelithiasis
*575	Other disorders of gallbladder
*576	Other disorders of biliary tract
751.60	Unspecified congenital anomaly of gallbladder, bile ducts, and liver
751.61	Congenital biliary atresia
793.3	Nonspecific abnormal findings on radiological and other examination of biliary tract
868.02	Bile duct and gallbladder injury without mention of open wound into cavity
868.12	Bile duct and gallbladder injury, with open wound into cavity

Ⓜ DRG 208 Disorders of the Biliary Tract without CC

GMLOS 2.3 AMLOS 2.9 RW 0.6895 ☑

Select principal diagnosis listed under DRG 207

MDC 8
DISEASES AND DISORDERS OF THE MUSCULOSKELETAL SYSTEM AND CONNECTIVE TISSUE

The complete and up-to-date listing of ICD-9-CM diagnosis codes assigned to this MDC can be found online at www.ingenixonline.com/content/drg/resources.asp.

SURGICAL

DRG 209 No Longer Valid

GMLOS 0.0 AMLOS 0.0 RW 0.0000

Omitted in the October 2005 grouper version

S DRG 210 Hip and Femur Procedures Except Major Joint Procedures, Age Greater than 17 with CC

GMLOS 6.1 AMLOS 6.9 RW 1.9059 ☑ SP CC A

Operating Room Procedures

77.05	Sequestrectomy of femur
77.25	Wedge osteotomy of femur
77.35	Other division of femur
77.85	Other partial ostectomy of femur
77.95	Total ostectomy of femur
78.05	Bone graft of femur
78.15	Application of external fixator device, femur
78.25	Limb shortening procedures, femur
78.35	Limb lengthening procedures, femur
78.45	Other repair or plastic operations on femur
78.55	Internal fixation of femur without fracture reduction
78.75	Osteoclasis of femur
78.95	Insertion of bone growth stimulator into femur
79.15	Closed reduction of fracture of femur with internal fixation
79.25	Open reduction of fracture of femur without internal fixation
79.35	Open reduction of fracture of femur with internal fixation
79.45	Closed reduction of separated epiphysis of femur
79.55	Open reduction of separated epiphysis of femur
79.65	Debridement of open fracture of femur
79.85	Open reduction of dislocation of hip
79.95	Unspecified operation on bone injury of femur
80.05	Arthrotomy for removal of prosthesis of hip
80.15	Other arthrotomy of hip
80.45	Division of joint capsule, ligament, or cartilage of hip
80.75	Synovectomy of hip
80.95	Other excision of hip joint
81.21	Arthrodesis of hip
81.40	Repair of hip, not elsewhere classified
83.12	Adductor tenotomy of hip

S DRG 211 Hip and Femur Procedures Except Major Joint Procedures, Age Greater than 17 without CC

GMLOS 4.4 AMLOS 4.7 RW 1.2690 ☑ SP A

Select operating room procedures listed under DRG 210

S DRG 212 Hip and Femur Procedures Except Major Joint Procedures, Age 0-17

GMLOS 2.4 AMLOS 2.9 RW 1.2877 ☑ A

Select operating room procedures listed under DRG 210

S DRG 213 Amputation for Musculoskeletal System and Connective Tissue Disorders

GMLOS 7.2 AMLOS 9.7 RW 2.0428 ☑ T

Operating Room Procedures

84.00	Upper limb amputation, not otherwise specified
84.03	Amputation through hand
84.04	Disarticulation of wrist
84.05	Amputation through forearm
84.06	Disarticulation of elbow
84.07	Amputation through humerus
84.08	Disarticulation of shoulder
84.09	Interthoracoscapular amputation
84.10	Lower limb amputation, not otherwise specified
84.12	Amputation through foot
84.13	Disarticulation of ankle
84.14	Amputation of ankle through malleoli of tibia and fibula
84.15	Other amputation below knee
84.16	Disarticulation of knee
84.17	Amputation above knee
84.18	Disarticulation of hip
84.19	Abdominopelvic amputation
84.3	Revision of amputation stump
84.91	Amputation, not otherwise specified

DRG 214 No Longer Valid

GMLOS 0.0 AMLOS 0.0 RW 0.0000

Omitted in the October 1997 grouper revision

DRG 215 No Longer Valid

GMLOS 0.0 AMLOS 0.0 RW 0.0000

Omitted in the October 1997 grouper revision

S DRG 216 Biopsies of Musculoskeletal System and Connective Tissue

GMLOS 3.3 AMLOS 5.8 RW 1.9131 T

Operating Room Procedures

01.15	Biopsy of skull
01.19	Other diagnostic procedures on skull
*76.1	Diagnostic procedures on facial bones and joints
*77.4	Biopsy of bone
78.80	Diagnostic procedures on bone, not elsewhere classified, unspecified site
78.81	Diagnostic procedures on scapula, clavicle, and thorax (ribs and sternum) not elsewhere classified
78.82	Diagnostic procedures on humerus, not elsewhere classified
78.83	Diagnostic procedures on radius and ulna, not elsewhere classified
78.85	Diagnostic procedures on femur, not elsewhere classified
78.86	Diagnostic procedures on patella, not elsewhere classified
78.87	Diagnostic procedures on tibia and fibula, not elsewhere classified
78.89	Diagnostic procedures on other bone, except facial bones, not elsewhere classified
81.98	Other diagnostic procedures on joint structures

MDC 8: Musculoskeletal System — Surgical

Ⓢ DRG 217 Wound Debridement and Skin Graft Except Hand for Musculoskeletal and Connective Tissue Disorders

GMLOS 9.3 AMLOS 13.2 RW 3.0596 Ⓣ

Operating Room Procedures

86.22	Excisional debridement of wound, infection, or burn
86.60	Free skin graft, not otherwise specified
86.63	Full-thickness skin graft to other sites
86.65	Heterograft to skin
86.66	Homograft to skin
86.67	Dermal regenerative graft
86.69	Other skin graft to other sites
86.70	Pedicle or flap graft, not otherwise specified
86.71	Cutting and preparation of pedicle grafts or flaps
86.72	Advancement of pedicle graft
86.74	Attachment of pedicle or flap graft to other sites
86.75	Revision of pedicle or flap graft
86.93	Insertion of tissue expander

Ⓢ DRG 218 Lower Extremity and Humerus Procedures Except Hip, Foot and Femur, Age Greater than 17 with CC

GMLOS 4.4 AMLOS 5.6 RW 1.6648 ☑ Ⓣ CC A

Operating Room Procedures

77.02	Sequestrectomy of humerus
77.07	Sequestrectomy of tibia and fibula
77.22	Wedge osteotomy of humerus
77.27	Wedge osteotomy of tibia and fibula
77.32	Other division of humerus
77.37	Other division of tibia and fibula
77.82	Other partial ostectomy of humerus
77.87	Other partial ostectomy of tibia and fibula
77.92	Total ostectomy of humerus
77.97	Total ostectomy of tibia and fibula
78.02	Bone graft of humerus
78.07	Bone graft of tibia and fibula
78.12	Application of external fixator device, humerus
78.17	Application of external fixator device, tibia and fibula
78.22	Limb shortening procedures, humerus
78.27	Limb shortening procedures, tibia and fibula
78.32	Limb lengthening procedures, humerus
78.37	Limb lengthening procedures, tibia and fibula
78.42	Other repair or plastic operation on humerus
78.47	Other repair or plastic operations on tibia and fibula
78.52	Internal fixation of humerus without fracture reduction
78.57	Internal fixation of tibia and fibula without fracture reduction
78.72	Osteoclasis of humerus
78.77	Osteoclasis of tibia and fibula
78.92	Insertion of bone growth stimulator into humerus
78.97	Insertion of bone growth stimulator into tibia and fibula
79.11	Closed reduction of fracture of humerus with internal fixation
79.16	Closed reduction of fracture of tibia and fibula with internal fixation
79.21	Open reduction of fracture of humerus without internal fixation
79.26	Open reduction of fracture of tibia and fibula without internal fixation
79.31	Open reduction of fracture of humerus with internal fixation
79.36	Open reduction of fracture of tibia and fibula with internal fixation
79.41	Closed reduction of separated epiphysis of humerus
79.46	Closed reduction of separated epiphysis of tibia and fibula
79.51	Open reduction of separated epiphysis of humerus
79.56	Open reduction of separated epiphysis of tibia and fibula
79.61	Debridement of open fracture of humerus
79.66	Debridement of open fracture of tibia and fibula

79.87	Open reduction of dislocation of ankle
79.91	Unspecified operation on bone injury of humerus
79.96	Unspecified operation on bone injury of tibia and fibula
79.97	Unspecified operation on bone injury of tarsals and metatarsals
80.17	Other arthrotomy of ankle
80.47	Division of joint capsule, ligament, or cartilage of ankle
80.77	Synovectomy of ankle
80.87	Other local excision or destruction of lesion of ankle joint
80.97	Other excision of ankle joint
80.99	Other excision of joint of other specified site
81.11	Ankle fusion
81.12	Triple arthrodesis
81.49	Other repair of ankle
84.48	Implantation of prosthetic device of leg

S DRG 219 Lower Extremity and Humerus Procedures Except Hip, Foot and Femur, Age Greater than 17 without CC

GMLOS 2.6 AMLOS 3.1 RW 1.0443 ☑ T A

Select operating room procedures listed under DRG 218

S DRG 220 Lower Extremity and Humerus Procedures Except Hip, Foot and Femur, Age 0-17

GMLOS 5.3 AMLOS 5.3 RW 0.5913 ☑ A

Select operating room procedures listed under DRG 218

DRG 221 No Longer Valid

GMLOS 0.0 AMLOS 0.0 RW 0.0000

Omitted in the October 1997 grouper revision

DRG 222 No Longer Valid

GMLOS 0.0 AMLOS 0.0 RW 0.0000

Omitted in the October 1997 grouper revision

S DRG 223 Major Shoulder/Elbow Procedures or Other Upper Extremity Procedures with CC

GMLOS 2.3 AMLOS 3.2 RW 1.1164 ☑ CC

Operating Room Procedures

Major joint procedures

80.11	Other arthrotomy of shoulder
80.12	Other arthrotomy of elbow
81.23	Arthrodesis of shoulder
81.24	Arthrodesis of elbow
81.83	Other repair of shoulder
81.85	Other repair of elbow

OR

Operating Room Procedures

77.03	Sequestrectomy of radius and ulna
77.23	Wedge osteotomy of radius and ulna
77.33	Other division of radius and ulna
77.83	Other partial ostectomy of radius and ulna
77.93	Total ostectomy of radius and ulna
78.03	Bone graft of radius and ulna
78.13	Application of external fixator device, radius and ulna
78.23	Limb shortening procedures, radius and ulna
78.33	Limb lengthening procedures, radius and ulna
78.43	Other repair or plastic operations on radius and ulna
78.53	Internal fixation of radius and ulna without fracture reduction

DRG 223 — continued

78.73	Osteoclasis of radius and ulna
78.93	Insertion of bone growth stimulator into radius and ulna
79.12	Closed reduction of fracture of radius and ulna with internal fixation
79.22	Open reduction of fracture of radius and ulna without internal fixation
79.32	Open reduction of fracture of radius and ulna with internal fixation
79.42	Closed reduction of separated epiphysis of radius and ulna
79.52	Open reduction of separated epiphysis of radius and ulna
79.62	Debridement of open fracture of radius and ulna
79.81	Open reduction of dislocation of shoulder
79.82	Open reduction of dislocation of elbow
79.92	Unspecified operation on bone injury of radius and ulna
80.41	Division of joint capsule, ligament, or cartilage of shoulder
80.42	Division of joint capsule, ligament, or cartilage of elbow
80.71	Synovectomy of shoulder
80.72	Synovectomy of elbow
80.91	Other excision of shoulder joint
80.92	Other excision of elbow joint
81.82	Repair of recurrent dislocation of shoulder
81.93	Suture of capsule or ligament of upper extremity
83.63	Rotator cuff repair
84.44	Implantation of prosthetic device of arm

S DRG 224 Shoulder, Elbow or Forearm Procedures Except Major Joint Procedures without CC

GMLOS 1.6 AMLOS 1.9 RW 0.8185 ☑

Select operating room procedures listed under DRG 223, except major joint procedures

S DRG 225 Foot Procedures

GMLOS 3.7 AMLOS 5.2 RW 1.2251 ☑T

Operating Room Procedures

04.44	Release of tarsal tunnel
77.08	Sequestrectomy of tarsals and metatarsals
77.18	Other incision of tarsals and metatarsals without division
77.28	Wedge osteotomy of tarsals and metatarsals
77.38	Other division of tarsals and metatarsals
*77.5	Excision and repair of bunion and other toe deformities
77.68	Local excision of lesion or tissue of tarsals and metatarsals
77.78	Excision of tarsals and metatarsals for graft
77.88	Other partial ostectomy of tarsals and metatarsals
77.98	Total ostectomy of tarsals and metatarsals
78.08	Bone graft of tarsals and metatarsals
78.18	Application of external fixator device, tarsals and metatarsals
78.28	Limb shortening procedures, tarsals and metatarsals
78.38	Limb lengthening procedures, tarsals and metatarsals
78.48	Other repair or plastic operations on tarsals and metatarsals
78.58	Internal fixation of tarsals and metatarsals without fracture reduction
78.78	Osteoclasis of tarsals and metatarsals
78.88	Diagnostic procedures on tarsals and metatarsals, not elsewhere classified
78.98	Insertion of bone growth stimulator into tarsals and metatarsals
79.17	Closed reduction of fracture of tarsals and metatarsals with internal fixation
79.18	Closed reduction of fracture of phalanges of foot with internal fixation
79.27	Open reduction of fracture of tarsals and metatarsals without internal fixation
79.28	Open reduction of fracture of phalanges of foot without internal fixation
79.37	Open reduction of fracture of tarsals and metatarsals with internal fixation
79.38	Open reduction of fracture of phalanges of foot with internal fixation
79.67	Debridement of open fracture of tarsals and metatarsals
79.68	Debridement of open fracture of phalanges of foot
79.88	Open reduction of dislocation of foot and toe
79.98	Unspecified operation on bone injury of phalanges of foot

80.18	Other arthrotomy of foot and toe
80.48	Division of joint capsule, ligament, or cartilage of foot and toe
80.78	Synovectomy of foot and toe
80.88	Other local excision or destruction of lesion of joint of foot and toe
80.98	Other excision of joint of foot and toe
81.13	Subtalar fusion
81.14	Midtarsal fusion
81.15	Tarsometatarsal fusion
81.16	Metatarsophalangeal fusion
81.17	Other fusion of foot
81.57	Replacement of joint of foot and toe
81.94	Suture of capsule or ligament of ankle and foot
83.11	Achillotenotomy
83.84	Release of clubfoot, not elsewhere classified
84.11	Amputation of toe
84.25	Toe reattachment

S DRG 226 Soft Tissue Procedures with CC

GMLOS 4.5 AMLOS 6.5 RW 1.5884 ☑ T CC

Operating Room Procedures

54.3	Excision or destruction of lesion or tissue of abdominal wall or umbilicus
80.70	Synovectomy, unspecified site
80.79	Synovectomy of other specified site
81.95	Suture of capsule or ligament of other lower extremity
*83.0	Incision of muscle, tendon, fascia, and bursa
83.13	Other tenotomy
83.14	Fasciotomy
83.19	Other division of soft tissue
*83.2	Diagnostic procedures on muscle, tendon, fascia, and bursa, including that of hand
*83.3	Excision of lesion of muscle, tendon, fascia, and bursa
*83.4	Other excision of muscle, tendon, and fascia
83.5	Bursectomy
83.61	Suture of tendon sheath
83.62	Delayed suture of tendon
83.64	Other suture of tendon
83.65	Other suture of muscle or fascia
*83.7	Reconstruction of muscle and tendon
83.81	Tendon graft
83.82	Graft of muscle or fascia
83.83	Tendon pulley reconstruction on muscle, tendon, and fascia
83.85	Other change in muscle or tendon length
83.86	Quadricepsplasty
83.87	Other plastic operations on muscle
83.88	Other plastic operations on tendon
83.89	Other plastic operations on fascia
83.91	Lysis of adhesions of muscle, tendon, fascia, and bursa
83.92	Insertion or replacement of skeletal muscle stimulator
83.93	Removal of skeletal muscle stimulator
83.99	Other operations on muscle, tendon, fascia, and bursa
86.4	Radical excision of skin lesion
86.81	Repair for facial weakness

S DRG 227 Soft Tissue Procedures without CC

GMLOS 2.1 AMLOS 2.6 RW 0.8311 ☑ T

Select operating room procedures listed under DRG 226

S DRG 228 Major Thumb or Joint Procedures or Other Hand or Wrist Procedures with CC

GMLOS 2.8 AMLOS 4.1 RW 1.1459 ☑CC

Operating Room Procedures

04.43	Release of carpal tunnel
77.04	Sequestrectomy of carpals and metacarpals
77.14	Other incision of carpals and metacarpals without division
77.24	Wedge osteotomy of carpals and metacarpals
77.34	Other division of carpals and metacarpals
77.44	Biopsy of carpals and metacarpals
77.64	Local excision of lesion or tissue of carpals and metacarpals
77.74	Excision of carpals and metacarpals for graft
77.84	Other partial ostectomy of carpals and metacarpals
77.94	Total ostectomy of carpals and metacarpals
78.04	Bone graft of carpals and metacarpals
78.14	Application of external fixator device, carpals and metacarpals
78.24	Limb shortening procedures, carpals and metacarpals
78.34	Limb lengthening procedures, carpals and metacarpals
78.44	Other repair or plastic operations on carpals and metacarpals
78.54	Internal fixation of carpals and metacarpals without fracture reduction
78.74	Osteoclasis of carpals and metacarpals
78.84	Diagnostic procedures on carpals and metacarpals, not elsewhere classified
78.94	Insertion of bone growth stimulator into carpals and metacarpals
79.13	Closed reduction of fracture of carpals and metacarpals with internal fixation
79.14	Closed reduction of fracture of phalanges of hand with internal fixation
79.23	Open reduction of fracture of carpals and metacarpals without internal fixation
79.24	Open reduction of fracture of phalanges of hand without internal fixation
79.33	Open reduction of fracture of carpals and metacarpals with internal fixation
79.34	Open reduction of fracture of phalanges of hand with internal fixation
79.63	Debridement of open fracture of carpals and metacarpals
79.64	Debridement of open fracture of phalanges of hand
79.83	Open reduction of dislocation of wrist
79.84	Open reduction of dislocation of hand and finger
79.93	Unspecified operation on bone injury of carpals and metacarpals
79.94	Unspecified operation on bone injury of phalanges of hand
80.43	Division of joint capsule, ligament, or cartilage of wrist
80.44	Division of joint capsule, ligament, or cartilage of hand and finger
80.73	Synovectomy of wrist
80.74	Synovectomy of hand and finger
80.83	Other local excision or destruction of lesion of wrist joint
80.84	Other local excision or destruction of lesion of joint of hand and finger
80.93	Other excision of wrist joint
80.94	Other excision of joint of hand and finger
81.25	Carporadial fusion
81.26	Metacarpocarpal fusion
81.27	Metacarpophalangeal fusion
81.28	Interphalangeal fusion
82.01	Exploration of tendon sheath of hand
82.02	Myotomy of hand
82.03	Bursotomy of hand
82.09	Other incision of soft tissue of hand
*82.1	Division of muscle, tendon, and fascia of hand
*82.2	Excision of lesion of muscle, tendon, and fascia of hand
*82.3	Other excision of soft tissue of hand
*82.4	Suture of muscle, tendon, and fascia of hand
*82.5	Transplantation of muscle and tendon of hand
*82.7	Plastic operation on hand with graft or implant
*82.8	Other plastic operations on hand
82.91	Lysis of adhesions of hand
82.99	Other operations on muscle, tendon, and fascia of hand
84.01	Amputation and disarticulation of finger

84.02 Amputation and disarticulation of thumb
84.21 Thumb reattachment
84.22 Finger reattachment
86.61 Full-thickness skin graft to hand
86.62 Other skin graft to hand
86.73 Attachment of pedicle or flap graft to hand
86.85 Correction of syndactyly

OR

Operating Room Procedures

Major joint procedures

80.13 Other arthrotomy of wrist
80.14 Other arthrotomy of hand and finger
*81.7 Arthroplasty and repair of hand, fingers, and wrist
*82.6 Reconstruction of thumb

S DRG 229 Hand or Wrist Procedures Except Major Joint Procedures without CC

GMLOS 1.9 AMLOS 2.5 RW 0.6976 ☑

Select operating room procedures listed under DRG 228 except major joint procedures

S DRG 230 Local Excision and Removal of Internal Fixation Devices of Hip and Femur

GMLOS 3.7 AMLOS 5.6 RW 1.3174

Operating Room Procedures

77.15 Other incision of femur without division
77.65 Local excision of lesion or tissue of femur
77.75 Excision of femur for graft
78.65 Removal of implanted device from femur
80.85 Other local excision or destruction of lesion of hip joint

DRG 231 No Longer Valid

GMLOS 0.0 AMLOS 0.0 RW 0.0000

Omitted in the October 2003 grouper version

S DRG 232 Arthroscopy

GMLOS 1.8 AMLOS 2.8 RW 0.9702

Operating Room Procedures

*80.2 Arthroscopy

S DRG 233 Other Musculoskeletal System and Connective Tissue O.R. Procedures with CC

GMLOS 4.6 AMLOS 6.8 RW 1.9184 ☑ SP CC

Operating Room Procedures

01.25 Other craniectomy
*02.0 Cranioplasty
02.94 Insertion or replacement of skull tongs or halo traction device
02.99 Other operations on skull, brain, and cerebral meninges
04.03 Division or crushing of other cranial and peripheral nerves
04.04 Other incision of cranial and peripheral nerves
04.06 Other cranial or peripheral ganglionectomy
04.07 Other excision or avulsion of cranial and peripheral nerves
04.12 Open biopsy of cranial or peripheral nerve or ganglion
04.19 Other diagnostic procedures on cranial and peripheral nerves and ganglia
04.49 Other peripheral nerve or ganglion decompression or lysis of adhesions
04.92 Implantation or replacement of peripheral neurostimulator lead(s)
04.93 Removal of peripheral neurostimulator lead(s)

** Code Range* ☑ *Optimization Potential* *Targeted Potential* T *Transfer DRG* SP *Special Payment*

DRG 233 — continued

04.99	Other operations on cranial and peripheral nerves
06.13	Biopsy of parathyroid gland
06.19	Other diagnostic procedures on thyroid and parathyroid glands
16.51	Exenteration of orbit with removal of adjacent structures
16.59	Other exenteration of orbit
21.72	Open reduction of nasal fracture
21.83	Total nasal reconstruction
21.84	Revision rhinoplasty
21.85	Augmentation rhinoplasty
21.86	Limited rhinoplasty
21.87	Other rhinoplasty
21.88	Other septoplasty
21.89	Other repair and plastic operations on nose
22.62	Excision of lesion of maxillary sinus with other approach
33.28	Open biopsy of lung
34.74	Repair of pectus deformity
34.79	Other repair of chest wall
34.81	Excision of lesion or tissue of diaphragm
38.21	Biopsy of blood vessel
38.7	Interruption of the vena cava
39.50	Angioplasty or atherectomy of other non-coronary vessel(s)
39.98	Control of hemorrhage, not otherwise specified
*40.1	Diagnostic procedures on lymphatic structures
40.21	Excision of deep cervical lymph node
40.23	Excision of axillary lymph node
40.24	Excision of inguinal lymph node
40.29	Simple excision of other lymphatic structure
40.3	Regional lymph node excision
40.51	Radical excision of axillary lymph nodes
40.52	Radical excision of periaortic lymph nodes
40.53	Radical excision of iliac lymph nodes
40.54	Radical groin dissection
40.59	Radical excision of other lymph nodes
41.43	Partial splenectomy
41.5	Total splenectomy
50.12	Open biopsy of liver
55.24	Open biopsy of kidney
59.00	Retroperitoneal dissection, not otherwise specified
62.41	Removal of both testes at same operative episode
76.01	Sequestrectomy of facial bone
76.31	Partial mandibulectomy
76.39	Partial ostectomy of other facial bone
*76.4	Excision and reconstruction of facial bones
76.5	Temporomandibular arthroplasty
*76.6	Other facial bone repair and orthognathic surgery
76.70	Reduction of facial fracture, not otherwise specified
76.72	Open reduction of malar and zygomatic fracture
76.74	Open reduction of maxillary fracture
76.76	Open reduction of mandibular fracture
76.77	Open reduction of alveolar fracture
76.79	Other open reduction of facial fracture
76.91	Bone graft to facial bone
76.92	Insertion of synthetic implant in facial bone
76.94	Open reduction of temporomandibular dislocation
76.99	Other operations on facial bones and joints
77.00	Sequestrectomy, unspecified site
77.01	Sequestrectomy of scapula, clavicle, and thorax (ribs and sternum)
77.09	Sequestrectomy of other bone, except facial bones
77.20	Wedge osteotomy, unspecified site
77.21	Wedge osteotomy of scapula, clavicle, and thorax (ribs and sternum)
77.29	Wedge osteotomy of other bone, except facial bones
77.30	Other division of bone, unspecified site

77.31	Other division of scapula, clavicle, and thorax (ribs and sternum)
77.39	Other division of other bone, except facial bones
77.80	Other partial ostectomy, unspecified site
77.81	Other partial ostectomy of scapula, clavicle, and thorax (ribs and sternum)
77.89	Other partial ostectomy of other bone, except facial bones
77.90	Total ostectomy, unspecified site
77.91	Total ostectomy of scapula, clavicle, and thorax (ribs and sternum)
77.99	Total ostectomy of other bone, except facial bones
78.00	Bone graft, unspecified site
78.01	Bone graft of scapula, clavicle, and thorax (ribs and sternum)
78.09	Bone graft of other bone, except facial bones
78.10	Application of external fixator device, unspecified site
78.11	Application of external fixator device, scapula, clavicle, and thorax [ribs and sternum]
78.13	Application of external fixator device, radius and ulna
78.19	Application of external fixator device, other
78.20	Limb shortening procedures, unspecified site
78.29	Limb shortening procedures, other
78.30	Limb lengthening procedures, unspecified site
78.39	Other limb lengthening procedures
78.40	Other repair or plastic operations on bone, unspecified site
78.41	Other repair or plastic operations on scapula, clavicle, and thorax (ribs and sternum)
78.49	Other repair or plastic operations on other bone, except facial bones
78.50	Internal fixation of bone without fracture reduction, unspecified site
78.51	Internal fixation of scapula, clavicle, and thorax (ribs and sternum) without fracture reduction
78.59	Internal fixation of other bone, except facial bones, without fracture reduction
78.70	Osteoclasis, unspecified site
78.71	Osteoclasis of scapula, clavicle, and thorax (ribs and sternum)
78.79	Osteoclasis of other bone, except facial bones
78.90	Insertion of bone growth stimulator, unspecified site
78.91	Insertion of bone growth stimulator into scapula, clavicle and thorax (ribs and sternum)
78.99	Insertion of bone growth stimulator into other bone
79.10	Closed reduction of fracture with internal fixation, unspecified site
79.19	Closed reduction of fracture of other specified bone, except facial bones, with internal fixation
79.20	Open reduction of fracture without internal fixation, unspecified site
79.29	Open reduction of fracture of other specified bone, except facial bones, without internal fixation
79.30	Open reduction of fracture with internal fixation, unspecified site
79.39	Open reduction of fracture of other specified bone, except facial bones, with internal fixation
79.40	Closed reduction of separated epiphysis, unspecified site
79.49	Closed reduction of separated epiphysis of other specified bone
79.50	Open reduction of separated epiphysis, unspecified site
79.59	Open reduction of separated epiphysis of other specified bone
79.60	Debridement of open fracture, unspecified site
79.69	Debridement of open fracture of other specified bone, except facial bones
79.80	Open reduction of dislocation of unspecified site
79.89	Open reduction of dislocation of other specified site, except temporomandibular
79.90	Unspecified operation on bone injury, unspecified site
79.99	Unspecified operation on bone injury of other specified bone
80.10	Other arthrotomy, unspecified site
80.19	Other arthrotomy of other specified site
80.40	Division of joint capsule, ligament, or cartilage, unspecified site
80.49	Division of joint capsule, ligament, or cartilage of other specified site
80.90	Other excision of joint, unspecified site
81.18	Subtalar joint arthroereisis
81.20	Arthrodesis of unspecified joint
81.29	Arthrodesis of other specified joint
81.59	Revision of joint replacement of lower extremity, not elsewhere classified
81.65	Vertebroplasty
81.66	Kyphoplasty
81.96	Other repair of joint
81.97	Revision of joint replacement of upper extremity
81.99	Other operations on joint structures
84.29	Other reattachment of extremity

DRG 233 — continued

84.40	Implantation or fitting of prosthetic limb device, not otherwise specified
84.92	Separation of equal conjoined twins
84.93	Separation of unequal conjoined twins
84.99	Other operations on musculoskeletal system
86.06	Insertion of totally implantable infusion pump

S DRG 234 Other Musculoskeletal System and Connective Tissue O.R. Procedures without CC

GMLOS 2.0 AMLOS 2.8 RW 1.2219 ☑ SP

Select operating room procedures listed under DRG 233

S DRG 471 Bilateral or Multiple Major Joint Procedures of Lower Extremity

GMLOS 4.5 AMLOS 5.1 RW 3.1391 SP

Any combination of two or more of the following procedures

*00.7	Other hip procedures
*00.8	Other knee procedures
81.51	Total hip replacement
81.52	Partial hip replacement
81.53	Revision of hip replacement, not otherwise specified
81.54	Total knee replacement
81.55	Revision of knee replacement, not otherwise specified
81.56	Total ankle replacement

S DRG 491 Major Joint and Limb Reattachment Procedures of Upper Extremity

GMLOS 2.6 AMLOS 3.1 RW 1.6780 ☑

Operating Room Procedures

81.73	Total wrist replacement
81.80	Total shoulder replacement
81.81	Partial shoulder replacement
81.84	Total elbow replacement
84.23	Forearm, wrist, or hand reattachment
84.24	Upper arm reattachment

S DRG 496 Combined Anterior/Posterior Spinal Fusion

GMLOS 6.4 AMLOS 8.8 RW 6.0932

Operating Room Procedures

81.02	Other cervical fusion, anterior technique
81.04	Dorsal and dorsolumbar fusion, anterior technique
81.06	Lumbar and lumbosacral fusion, anterior technique
81.32	Refusion of other cervical spine, anterior technique
81.34	Refusion of dorsal and dorsolumbar spine, anterior technique
81.36	Refusion of lumbar and lumbosacral spine, anterior technique

AND

Operating Room Procedures

81.03	Other cervical fusion, posterior technique
81.05	Dorsal and dorsolumbar fusion, posterior technique
81.07	Lumbar and lumbosacral fusion, lateral transverse process technique
81.08	Lumbar and lumbosacral fusion, posterior technique
81.33	Refusion of other cervical spine, posterior technique
81.35	Refusion of dorsal and dorsolumbar spine, posterior technique
81.37	Refusion of lumbar and lumbosacral spine, lateral transverse process technique
81.38	Refusion of lumbar and lumbosacral spine, posterior technique

S DRG 497 Spinal Fusion Except Cervical with CC

GMLOS 5.0 AMLOS 5.9 RW 3.6224 ☑ SP CC

Includes any of the following procedure codes, as long as any combination of procedure codes would not otherwise result in assignment to DRG 496

81.00	Spinal fusion, not otherwise specified
81.04	Dorsal and dorsolumbar fusion, anterior technique
81.05	Dorsal and dorsolumbar fusion, posterior technique
81.06	Lumbar and lumbosacral fusion, anterior technique
81.07	Lumbar and lumbosacral fusion, lateral transverse process technique
81.08	Lumbar and lumbosacral fusion, posterior technique
81.30	Refusion of spine, not otherwise specified
81.34	Refusion of dorsal and dorsolumbar spine, anterior technique
81.35	Refusion of dorsal and dorsolumbar spine, posterior technique
81.36	Refusion of lumbar and lumbosacral spine, anterior technique
81.37	Refusion of lumbar and lumbosacral spine, lateral transverse process technique
81.38	Refusion of lumbar and lumbosacral spine, posterior technique
81.39	Refusion of spine, not elsewhere classified

S DRG 498 Spinal Fusion Except Cervical without CC

GMLOS 3.4 AMLOS 3.8 RW 2.7791 ☑ SP

Select operating room procedures listed under DRG 497

S DRG 499 Back and Neck Procedures Except Spinal Fusion with CC

GMLOS 3.1 AMLOS 4.3 RW 1.3831 ☑ CC

Operating Room Procedures

03.02	Reopening of laminectomy site
03.09	Other exploration and decompression of spinal canal
03.1	Division of intraspinal nerve root
03.32	Biopsy of spinal cord or spinal meninges
03.39	Other diagnostic procedures on spinal cord and spinal canal structures
03.4	Excision or destruction of lesion of spinal cord or spinal meninges
03.53	Repair of vertebral fracture
03.59	Other repair and plastic operations on spinal cord structures
03.6	Lysis of adhesions of spinal cord and nerve roots
03.93	Implantation or replacement of spinal neurostimulator lead(s)
03.94	Removal of spinal neurostimulator lead(s)
03.97	Revision of spinal thecal shunt
03.98	Removal of spinal thecal shunt
03.99	Other operations on spinal cord and spinal canal structures
80.50	Excision or destruction of intervertebral disc, unspecified
80.51	Excision of intervertebral disc
80.59	Other destruction of intervertebral disc
84.58	Implantation of interspinous process decompression device
84.59	Insertion of other spinal devices
*84.6	Replacement of spinal disc

S DRG 500 Back and Neck Procedures Except Spinal Fusion without CC

GMLOS 1.8 AMLOS 2.2 RW 0.9046 ☑

Select operating room procedures listed under DRG 499

S DRG 501 Knee Procedures with Principal Diagnosis of Infection with CC

GMLOS 8.5 AMLOS 10.4 RW 2.6462 T CC

Principal Diagnosis

711.06	Pyogenic arthritis, lower leg
730.06	Acute osteomyelitis, lower leg
730.16	Chronic osteomyelitis, lower leg

** Code Range* ☑ *Optimization Potential* ▽ *Targeted Potential* T *Transfer DRG* SP *Special Payment*

DRG 501 — continued

730.26	Unspecified osteomyelitis, lower leg
996.66	Infection and inflammatory reaction due to internal joint prosthesis
996.67	Infection and inflammatory reaction due to other internal orthopedic device, implant, and graft

Operating Room Procedures

77.06	Sequestrectomy of patella
77.26	Wedge osteotomy of patella
77.36	Other division of patella
77.86	Other partial ostectomy of patella
77.96	Total ostectomy of patella
78.06	Bone graft of patella
78.16	Application of external fixator device, patella
78.46	Other repair or plastic operations on patella
78.56	Internal fixation of patella without fracture reduction
78.76	Osteoclasis of patella
78.96	Insertion of bone growth stimulator into patella
79.86	Open reduction of dislocation of knee
80.16	Other arthrotomy of knee
80.46	Division of joint capsule, ligament, or cartilage of knee
80.6	Excision of semilunar cartilage of knee
80.76	Synovectomy of knee
80.96	Other excision of knee joint
81.22	Arthrodesis of knee
81.42	Five-in-one repair of knee
81.43	Triad knee repair
81.44	Patellar stabilization
81.45	Other repair of the cruciate ligaments
81.46	Other repair of the collateral ligaments
81.47	Other repair of knee

S DRG 502 Knee Procedures with Principal Diagnosis of Infection without CC

GMLOS 4.9 AMLOS 5.9 RW 1.4462 ☑ T

Select principal diagnosis and operating room procedures listed under DRG 501

S DRG 503 Knee Procedures without Principal Diagnosis of Infection

GMLOS 2.9 AMLOS 3.8 RW 1.2038 ☑

Select only operating room procedures listed under DRG 501

S DRG 519 Cervical Spinal Fusion with CC

GMLOS 3.0 AMLOS 4.8 RW 2.4695 CC

Operating Room Procedures

81.01	Atlas-axis spinal fusion
81.02	Other cervical fusion, anterior technique
81.03	Other cervical fusion, posterior technique
81.31	Refusion of Atlas-axis spine
81.32	Refusion of other cervical spine, anterior technique
81.33	Refusion of other cervical spine, posterior technique

S DRG 520 Cervical Spinal Fusion without CC

GMLOS 1.6 AMLOS 2.0 RW 1.6788 ☑

Select operating room procedures listed under DRG 519

S DRG 537 Local Excision and Removal of Internal Fixation Devices Except Hip and Femur with CC

GMLOS 4.8 AMLOS 6.9 RW 1.8360 T CC

Operating Room Procedures

01.6	Excision of lesion of skull
34.4	Excision or destruction of lesion of chest wall
76.09	Other incision of facial bone
76.2	Local excision or destruction of lesion of facial bone
76.97	Removal of internal fixation device from facial bone
77.10	Other incision of bone without division, unspecified site
77.11	Other incision of scapula, clavicle, and thorax (ribs and sternum) without division
77.12	Other incision of humerus without division
77.13	Other incision of radius and ulna without division
77.16	Other incision of patella without division
77.17	Other incision of tibia and fibula without division
77.19	Other incision of other bone, except facial bones, without division
77.60	Local excision of lesion or tissue of bone, unspecified site
77.61	Local excision of lesion or tissue of scapula, clavicle, and thorax (ribs and sternum)
77.62	Local excision of lesion or tissue of humerus
77.63	Local excision of lesion or tissue of radius and ulna
77.66	Local excision of lesion or tissue of patella
77.67	Local excision of lesion or tissue of tibia and fibula
77.69	Local excision of lesion or tissue of other bone, except facial bones
77.70	Excision of bone for graft, unspecified site
77.71	Excision of scapula, clavicle, and thorax (ribs and sternum) for graft
77.72	Excision of humerus for graft
77.73	Excision of radius and ulna for graft
77.76	Excision of patella for graft
77.77	Excision of tibia and fibula for graft
77.79	Excision of other bone for graft, except facial bones
78.60	Removal of implanted device, unspecified site
78.61	Removal of implanted device from scapula, clavicle, and thorax (ribs and sternum)
78.62	Removal of implanted device from humerus
78.63	Removal of implanted device from radius and ulna
78.64	Removal of implanted device from carpals and metacarpals
78.66	Removal of implanted device from patella
78.67	Removal of implanted device from tibia and fibula
78.68	Removal of implanted device from tarsal and metatarsals
78.69	Removal of implanted device from other bone
80.00	Arthrotomy for removal of prosthesis, unspecified site
80.01	Arthrotomy for removal of prosthesis of shoulder
80.02	Arthrotomy for removal of prosthesis of elbow
80.03	Arthrotomy for removal of prosthesis of wrist
80.04	Arthrotomy for removal of prosthesis of hand and finger
80.06	Arthrotomy for removal of prosthesis of knee
80.07	Arthrotomy for removal of prosthesis of ankle
80.08	Arthrotomy for removal of prosthesis of foot and toe
80.09	Arthrotomy for removal of prosthesis of other specified site
80.80	Other local excision or destruction of lesion of joint, unspecified site
80.81	Other local excision or destruction of lesion of shoulder joint
80.82	Other local excision or destruction of lesion of elbow joint
80.86	Other local excision or destruction of lesion of knee joint
80.89	Other local excision or destruction of lesion of joint of other specified site

S DRG 538 Local Excision and Removal of Internal Fixation Devices Except Hip and Femur without CC

GMLOS 2.1 AMLOS 2.8 RW 0.9833 ☑ T

Select operating room procedure listed under DRG 537

● S DRG 544 Major Joint Replacement or Reattachment of Lower Extremity

GMLOS 4.1 AMLOS 4.5 RW 1.9643

Operating Room Procedures

81.51	Total hip replacement
81.52	Partial hip replacement
81.54	Total knee replacement
81.56	Total ankle replacement
84.26	Foot reattachment
84.27	Lower leg or ankle reattachment
84.28	Thigh reattachment

● S DRG 545 Revision of Hip or Knee Replacement

GMLOS 4.5 AMLOS 5.2 RW 2.4827

Operating Room Procedures

00.70	Revision of hip replacement, both acetabular and femoral components
00.71	Revision of hip replacement, acetabular component
00.72	Revision of hip replacement, femoral component
00.73	Revision of hip replacement, acetabular liner and/or femoral head only
*00.8	Other knee procedures
81.53	Revision of hip replacement, not otherwise specified
81.55	Revision of knee replacement, not otherwise specified

● S DRG 546 Spinal Fusions Except Cervical With Curvature of the Spine or Malignancy

GMLOS 7.1 AMLOS 8.8 RW 5.0739

Includes any of the following procedure codes, and a principal or secondary diagnosis of curvature of the spine or a principal diagnosis of a malignancy

81.00	Spinal fusion, not otherwise specified
81.04	Dorsal and dorsolumbar fusion, anterior technique
81.05	Dorsal and dorsolumbar fusion, posterior technique
81.06	Lumbar and lumbosacral fusion, anterior technique
81.07	Lumbar and lumbosacral fusion, lateral transverse process technique
81.08	Lumbar and lumbosacral fusion, posterior technique
81.30	Refusion of spine, not otherwise specified
81.34	Refusion of dorsal and dorsolumbar spine, anterior technique
81.35	Refusion of dorsal and dorsolumbar spine, posterior technique
81.36	Refusion of lumbar and lumbosacral spine, anterior technique
81.37	Refusion of lumbar and lumbosacral spine, lateral transverse process technique
81.38	Refusion of lumbar and lumbosacral spine, posterior technique
81.39	Refusion of spine, not elsewhere classified

MDC 8
DISEASES AND DISORDERS OF THE MUSCULOSKELETAL SYSTEM AND CONNECTIVE TISSUE

The complete and up-to-date listing of ICD-9-CM diagnosis codes assigned to this MDC can be found online at www.ingenixonline.com/content/drg/resources.asp.

MEDICAL

M DRG 235 Fractures of Femur
GMLOS 3.8 AMLOS 4.8 RW 0.7768 ☑ T

Principal Diagnosis

*821	Fracture of other and unspecified parts of femur

M DRG 236 Fractures of Hip and Pelvis
GMLOS 3.8 AMLOS 4.6 RW 0.7407 ☑ T

Principal Diagnosis

*808	Fracture of pelvis
*820	Fracture of neck of femur

M DRG 237 Sprains, Strains and Dislocations of Hip, Pelvis and Thigh
GMLOS 3.0 AMLOS 3.7 RW 0.6090 ☑

Principal Diagnosis

*835	Dislocation of hip
*843	Sprains and strains of hip and thigh
848.5	Pelvic sprain and strains

M DRG 238 Osteomyelitis
GMLOS 6.7 AMLOS 8.7 RW 1.4401 ☑ T

Principal Diagnosis

003.24	Salmonella osteomyelitis
*015.0	Tuberculosis of vertebral column
*015.5	Tuberculosis of limb bones
*015.7	Tuberculosis of other specified bone
091.61	Early syphilis, secondary syphilitic periostitis
095.5	Syphilis of bone
098.53	Gonococcal spondylitis
*730.0	Acute osteomyelitis
*730.1	Chronic osteomyelitis
*730.2	Unspecified osteomyelitis
*730.8	Other infections involving bone in diseases classified elsewhere
*730.9	Unspecified infection of bone

M DRG 239 Pathological Fractures and Musculoskeletal and Connective Tissue Malignancy
GMLOS 5.0 AMLOS 6.2 RW 1.0767 T YIELD

Principal Diagnosis

*170	Malignant neoplasm of bone and articular cartilage
*171	Malignant neoplasm of connective and other soft tissue
198.5	Secondary malignant neoplasm of bone and bone marrow
238.0	Neoplasm of uncertain behavior of bone and articular cartilage
446.3	Lethal midline granuloma
446.4	Wegener's granulomatosis
*733.1	Pathologic fracture

** Code Range* ☑ *Optimization Potential* YIELD *Targeted Potential* T *Transfer DRG* SP *Special Payment*

DRG 239 — continued

733.93	Stress fracture of tibia or fibula
733.94	Stress fracture of the metatarsals
733.95	Stress fracture of other bone

M DRG 240 Connective Tissue Disorders with CC

GMLOS 5.0 AMLOS 6.7 RW 1.4051 T CC

Principal Diagnosis

099.3	Reiter's disease
136.1	Behcet's syndrome
277.3	Amyloidosis
279.4	Autoimmune disease, not elsewhere classified
390	Rheumatic fever without mention of heart involvement
443.0	Raynaud's syndrome
446.0	Polyarteritis nodosa
446.1	Acute febrile mucocutaneous lymph node syndrome (MCLS)
*446.2	Hypersensitivity angiitis
446.5	Giant cell arteritis
446.6	Thrombotic microangiopathy
446.7	Takayasu's disease
447.6	Unspecified arteritis
696.0	Psoriatic arthropathy
*710	Diffuse diseases of connective tissue
*711.1	Arthropathy associated with Reiter's disease and nonspecific urethritis
*711.2	Arthropathy in Behcet's syndrome
714.0	Rheumatoid arthritis
714.1	Felty's syndrome
714.2	Other rheumatoid arthritis with visceral or systemic involvement
*714.3	Juvenile chronic polyarthritis
714.89	Other specified inflammatory polyarthropathies
720.0	Ankylosing spondylitis
725	Polymyalgia rheumatica
795.6	False positive serological test for syphilis

M DRG 241 Connective Tissue Disorders without CC

GMLOS 3.0 AMLOS 3.7 RW 0.6629 ☑ T

Select principal diagnosis listed under DRG 240

M DRG 242 Septic Arthritis

GMLOS 5.1 AMLOS 6.7 RW 1.1504 ☑

Principal Diagnosis

003.23	Salmonella arthritis
*015.1	Tuberculosis of hip
*015.2	Tuberculosis of knee
*015.8	Tuberculosis of other specified joint
*015.9	Tuberculosis of unspecified bones and joints
036.82	Meningococcal arthropathy
098.50	Gonococcal arthritis
098.51	Gonococcal synovitis and tenosynovitis
098.52	Gonococcal bursitis
098.59	Other gonococcal infection of joint
102.6	Bone and joint lesions due to yaws
*711.0	Pyogenic arthritis
*711.4	Arthropathy associated with other bacterial diseases
*711.6	Arthropathy associated with mycoses
*711.7	Arthropathy associated with helminthiasis
*711.8	Arthropathy associated with other infectious and parasitic diseases
*711.9	Unspecified infective arthritis

DRG 243 Medical Back Problems

GMLOS 3.6 AMLOS 4.5 RW 0.7658

Principal Diagnosis

720.1	Spinal enthesopathy
720.2	Sacroiliitis, not elsewhere classified
*720.8	Other inflammatory spondylopathies
720.9	Unspecified inflammatory spondylopathy
*721	Spondylosis and allied disorders
*722	Intervertebral disc disorders
723.0	Spinal stenosis in cervical region
723.1	Cervicalgia
723.5	Torticollis, unspecified
723.7	Ossification of posterior longitudinal ligament in cervical region
723.8	Other syndromes affecting cervical region
723.9	Unspecified musculoskeletal disorders and symptoms referable to neck
*724	Other and unspecified disorders of back
*737	Curvature of spine
738.4	Acquired spondylolisthesis
738.5	Other acquired deformity of back or spine
739.1	Nonallopathic lesion of cervical region, not elsewhere classified
739.2	Nonallopathic lesion of thoracic region, not elsewhere classified
739.3	Nonallopathic lesion of lumbar region, not elsewhere classified
739.4	Nonallopathic lesion of sacral region, not elsewhere classified
756.10	Congenital anomaly of spine, unspecified
756.11	Congenital spondylolysis, lumbosacral region
756.12	Congenital spondylolisthesis
756.13	Congenital absence of vertebra
756.14	Hemivertebra
756.15	Congenital fusion of spine (vertebra)
756.19	Other congenital anomaly of spine
781.93	Ocular torticollis
*805	Fracture of vertebral column without mention of spinal cord injury
*839.0	Closed dislocation, cervical vertebra
*839.1	Open dislocation, cervical vertebra
*839.2	Closed dislocation, thoracic and lumbar vertebra
*839.3	Open dislocation, thoracic and lumbar vertebra
*839.4	Closed dislocation, other vertebra
*839.5	Open dislocation, other vertebra
*846	Sprains and strains of sacroiliac region
*847	Sprains and strains of other and unspecified parts of back
905.1	Late effect of fracture of spine and trunk without mention of spinal cord lesion

DRG 244 Bone Diseases and Specific Arthropathies with CC

GMLOS 3.6 AMLOS 4.5 RW 0.7200

Principal Diagnosis

056.71	Arthritis due to rubella
268.0	Rickets, active
268.1	Rickets, late effect
268.2	Osteomalacia, unspecified
274.0	Gouty arthropathy
*274.8	Gout with other specified manifestations
274.9	Gout, unspecified
*711.3	Postdysenteric arthropathy
*711.5	Arthropathy associated with other viral diseases
*712	Crystal arthropathies
*713	Arthropathy associated with other disorders classified elsewhere
714.4	Chronic postrheumatic arthropathy
714.9	Unspecified inflammatory polyarthropathy
*715	Osteoarthrosis and allied disorders
*716.0	Kaschin-Beck disease
*716.1	Traumatic arthropathy

*** Code Range** ☑ *Optimization Potential* *Targeted Potential* T *Transfer DRG* SP *Special Payment*

DRG 244 — continued

*716.2	Allergic arthritis
*716.3	Climacteric arthritis
*718.5	Ankylosis of joint
*719.1	Hemarthrosis
*719.2	Villonodular synovitis
*719.3	Palindromic rheumatism
730.30	Periostitis, without mention of osteomyelitis, unspecified site
730.31	Periostitis, without mention of osteomyelitis, shoulder region
730.32	Periostitis, without mention of osteomyelitis, upper arm
730.33	Periostitis, without mention of osteomyelitis, forearm
730.34	Periostitis, without mention of osteomyelitis, hand
730.35	Periostitis, without mention of osteomyelitis, pelvic region and thigh
730.36	Periostitis, without mention of osteomyelitis, lower leg
*731	Osteitis deformans and osteopathies associated with other disorders classified elsewhere
*732	Osteochondropathies
*733.0	Osteoporosis
*733.2	Cyst of bone
*733.4	Aseptic necrosis of bone
733.5	Osteitis condensans
733.92	Chondromalacia

M DRG 245 Bone Diseases and Specific Arthropathies without CC

GMLOS 2.5 AMLOS 3.1 RW 0.4583 ☑ T

Select principal diagnosis listed under DRG 244

M DRG 246 Nonspecific Arthropathies

GMLOS 2.8 AMLOS 3.6 RW 0.5932 ☑

Principal Diagnosis

*716.4	Transient arthropathy
*716.5	Unspecified polyarthropathy or polyarthritis
*716.6	Unspecified monoarthritis
*716.8	Other specified arthropathy
*716.9	Unspecified arthropathy

M DRG 247 Signs and Symptoms of Musculoskeletal System and Connective Tissue

GMLOS 2.6 AMLOS 3.3 RW 0.5795 ☑

Principal Diagnosis

*719.4	Pain in joint
*719.5	Stiffness of joint, not elsewhere classified
*719.6	Other symptoms referable to joint
719.7	Difficulty in walking
*719.8	Other specified disorders of joint
*719.9	Unspecified disorder of joint
728.85	Spasm of muscle
728.87	Muscle weakness (generalized)
729.0	Rheumatism, unspecified and fibrositis
729.1	Unspecified myalgia and myositis
729.5	Pain in soft tissues of limb
729.81	Swelling of limb
729.82	Cramp of limb
729.89	Other musculoskeletal symptoms referable to limbs
729.9	Other and unspecified disorders of soft tissue
739.0	Nonallopathic lesion of head region, not elsewhere classified
739.5	Nonallopathic lesion of pelvic region, not elsewhere classified
739.6	Nonallopathic lesion of lower extremities, not elsewhere classified
739.7	Nonallopathic lesion of upper extremities, not elsewhere classified
739.8	Nonallopathic lesion of rib cage, not elsewhere classified
739.9	Nonallopathic lesion of abdomen and other sites, not elsewhere classified

Ⓜ DRG 248 Tendonitis, Myositis and Bursitis
GMLOS 3.8 AMLOS 4.8 RW 0.8554

Principal Diagnosis

040.81	Tropical pyomyositis
095.6	Syphilis of muscle
095.7	Syphilis of synovium, tendon, and bursa
306.0	Musculoskeletal malfunction arising from mental factors
726.0	Adhesive capsulitis of shoulder
*726.1	Rotator cuff syndrome of shoulder and allied disorders
726.2	Other affections of shoulder region, not elsewhere classified
*726.3	Enthesopathy of elbow region
726.4	Enthesopathy of wrist and carpus
726.5	Enthesopathy of hip region
*726.6	Enthesopathy of knee
726.70	Unspecified enthesopathy of ankle and tarsus
726.71	Achilles bursitis or tendinitis
726.72	Tibialis tendinitis
726.79	Other enthesopathy of ankle and tarsus
726.8	Other peripheral enthesopathies
*726.9	Unspecified enthesopathy
727.00	Unspecified synovitis and tenosynovitis
727.01	Synovitis and tenosynovitis in diseases classified elsewhere
727.03	Trigger finger (acquired)
727.04	Radial styloid tenosynovitis
727.05	Other tenosynovitis of hand and wrist
727.06	Tenosynovitis of foot and ankle
727.09	Other synovitis and tenosynovitis
727.2	Specific bursitides often of occupational origin
727.3	Other bursitis disorders
*727.4	Ganglion and cyst of synovium, tendon, and bursa
*727.5	Rupture of synovium
*727.6	Rupture of tendon, nontraumatic
*727.8	Other disorders of synovium, tendon, and bursa
727.9	Unspecified disorder of synovium, tendon, and bursa
*728	Disorders of muscle, ligament, and fascia
729.4	Unspecified fasciitis

Ⓜ DRG 249 Aftercare, Musculoskeletal System and Connective Tissue
GMLOS 2.7 AMLOS 3.9 RW 0.7095

Principal Diagnosis

905.2	Late effect of fracture of upper extremities
905.3	Late effect of fracture of neck of femur
905.4	Late effect of fracture of lower extremities
905.5	Late effect of fracture of multiple and unspecified bones
905.8	Late effect of tendon injury
905.9	Late effect of traumatic amputation
*996.4	Mechanical complication of internal orthopedic device, implant, and graft
996.66	Infection and inflammatory reaction due to internal joint prosthesis
996.67	Infection and inflammatory reaction due to other internal orthopedic device, implant, and graft
996.77	Other complications due to internal joint prosthesis
996.78	Other complications due to other internal orthopedic device, implant, and graft
*996.9	Complications of reattached extremity or body part
V52.0	Fitting and adjustment of artificial arm (complete) (partial)
V52.1	Fitting and adjustment of artificial leg (complete) (partial)
V53.7	Fitting and adjustment of orthopedic device
*V54.0	Aftercare involving removal of fracture plate or other internal fixation device
*V54.1	Aftercare for healing traumatic fracture
*V54.2	Aftercare for healing pathologic fracture
*V54.8	Other orthopedic aftercare
V54.9	Unspecified orthopedic aftercare

M DRG 250 Fractures, Sprains, Strains and Dislocations of Forearm, Hand and Foot, Age Greater than 17 with CC

GMLOS 3.2 AMLOS 3.9 RW 0.6974 ☑ T CC A

Principal Diagnosis

718.03	Articular cartilage disorder, forearm
718.04	Articular cartilage disorder, hand
718.20	Pathological dislocation of joint, site unspecified
718.23	Pathological dislocation of forearm joint
718.24	Pathological dislocation of hand joint
718.33	Recurrent dislocation of forearm joint
718.34	Recurrent dislocation of hand joint
*813	Fracture of radius and ulna
*814	Fracture of carpal bone(s)
*815	Fracture of metacarpal bone(s)
*816	Fracture of one or more phalanges of hand
*817	Multiple fractures of hand bones
*825.2	Closed fracture of other tarsal and metatarsal bones
*825.3	Open fracture of other tarsal and metatarsal bones
*826	Fracture of one or more phalanges of foot
*829	Fracture of unspecified bones
*833	Dislocation of wrist
*834	Dislocation of finger
*838	Dislocation of foot
839.69	Closed dislocation, other location
839.79	Open dislocation, other location
839.8	Closed dislocation, multiple and ill-defined sites
839.9	Open dislocation, multiple and ill-defined sites
*841	Sprains and strains of elbow and forearm
*842	Sprains and strains of wrist and hand
*845.1	Foot sprain and strain
848.8	Other specified sites of sprains and strains
848.9	Unspecified site of sprain and strain
905.6	Late effect of dislocation
905.7	Late effect of sprain and strain without mention of tendon injury

M DRG 251 Fractures, Sprains, Strains and Dislocations of Forearm, Hand and Foot, Age Greater than 17 without CC

GMLOS 2.3 AMLOS 2.8 RW 0.4749 ☑ T A

Select principal diagnosis listed under DRG 250

M DRG 252 Fractures, Sprains, Strains and Dislocations of Forearm, Hand and Foot, Age 0-17

GMLOS 1.8 AMLOS 1.8 RW 0.2567 ☑ A

Select principal diagnosis listed under DRG 250

M DRG 253 Fractures, Sprains, Strains and Dislocations of Upper Arm and Lower Leg Except Foot, Age Greater than 17 with CC

GMLOS 3.8 AMLOS 4.6 RW 0.7747 ☑ T CC A

Principal Diagnosis

717.0	Old bucket handle tear of medial meniscus
717.1	Derangement of anterior horn of medial meniscus
717.2	Derangement of posterior horn of medial meniscus
717.3	Other and unspecified derangement of medial meniscus
*717.4	Derangement of lateral meniscus
717.5	Derangement of meniscus, not elsewhere classified
717.7	Chondromalacia of patella
*717.8	Other internal derangement of knee
717.9	Unspecified internal derangement of knee
718.01	Articular cartilage disorder, shoulder region

S Surgical M Medical CC CC Indicator A Age Restriction ● New DRG ▲ Revised DRG Title

718.02	Articular cartilage disorder, upper arm
718.07	Articular cartilage disorder, ankle and foot
718.21	Pathological dislocation of shoulder joint
718.22	Pathological dislocation of upper arm joint
718.26	Pathological dislocation of lower leg joint
718.27	Pathological dislocation of ankle and foot joint
718.31	Recurrent dislocation of shoulder joint
718.32	Recurrent dislocation of upper arm joint
718.36	Recurrent dislocation of lower leg joint
718.37	Recurrent dislocation of ankle and foot joint
754.41	Congenital dislocation of knee (with genu recurvatum)
*810	Fracture of clavicle
811.00	Closed fracture of unspecified part of scapula
811.01	Closed fracture of acromial process of scapula
811.02	Closed fracture of coracoid process of scapula
811.03	Closed fracture of glenoid cavity and neck of scapula
811.10	Open fracture of unspecified part of scapula
811.11	Open fracture of acromial process of scapula
811.12	Open fracture of coracoid process
811.13	Open fracture of glenoid cavity and neck of scapula
*812	Fracture of humerus
*818	Ill-defined fractures of upper limb
*822	Fracture of patella
*823	Fracture of tibia and fibula
*824	Fracture of ankle
825.0	Closed fracture of calcaneus
825.1	Open fracture of calcaneus
*827	Other, multiple, and ill-defined fractures of lower limb
*831	Dislocation of shoulder
*832	Dislocation of elbow
*836	Dislocation of knee
*837	Dislocation of ankle
*840	Sprains and strains of shoulder and upper arm
*844	Sprains and strains of knee and leg
*845.0	Ankle sprain and strain

M DRG 254 Fractures, Sprains, Strains and Dislocations of Upper Arm and Lower Leg Except Foot, Age Greater than 17 without CC

GMLOS 2.6 AMLOS 3.1 RW 0.4588 ☑ T A

Select principal diagnosis listed under DRG 253

M DRG 255 Fractures, Sprains, Strains and Dislocations of Upper Arm and Lower Leg Except Foot, Age 0-17

GMLOS 2.9 AMLOS 2.9 RW 0.2990 ☑ A

Select principal diagnosis listed under DRG 253

M DRG 256 Other Musculoskeletal System and Connective Tissue Diagnoses

GMLOS 3.9 AMLOS 5.1 RW 0.8509 ☑ T

Principal Diagnosis

137.3	Late effects of tuberculosis of bones and joints
213.0	Benign neoplasm of bones of skull and face
213.2	Benign neoplasm of vertebral column, excluding sacrum and coccyx
213.4	Benign neoplasm of scapula and long bones of upper limb
213.5	Benign neoplasm of short bones of upper limb
213.6	Benign neoplasm of pelvic bones, sacrum, and coccyx
213.7	Benign neoplasm of long bones of lower limb
213.8	Benign neoplasm of short bones of lower limb
213.9	Benign neoplasm of bone and articular cartilage, site unspecified

DRG 256 — continued

*215	Other benign neoplasm of connective and other soft tissue
238.1	Neoplasm of uncertain behavior of connective and other soft tissue
239.2	Neoplasms of unspecified nature of bone, soft tissue, and skin
380.01	Acute perichondritis of pinna
380.02	Chronic perichondritis of pinna
380.03	Chondritis of pinna
717.6	Loose body in knee
718.00	Articular cartilage disorder, site unspecified
718.05	Articular cartilage disorder, pelvic region and thigh
718.08	Articular cartilage disorder, other specified site
718.09	Articular cartilage disorder, multiple sites
*718.1	Loose body in joint
718.25	Pathological dislocation of pelvic region and thigh joint
718.28	Pathological dislocation of joint of other specified site
718.29	Pathological dislocation of joint of multiple sites
718.30	Recurrent dislocation of joint, site unspecified
718.35	Recurrent dislocation of pelvic region and thigh joint
718.38	Recurrent dislocation of joint of other specified site
718.39	Recurrent dislocation of joint of multiple sites
*718.4	Contracture of joint
718.60	Unspecified intrapelvic protrusion of acetabulum, site unspecified
718.65	Unspecified intrapelvic protrusion acetabulum, pelvic region and thigh
*718.7	Developmental dislocation of joint
*718.8	Other joint derangement, not elsewhere classified
*718.9	Unspecified derangement of joint
*719.0	Effusion of joint
726.73	Calcaneal spur
727.02	Giant cell tumor of tendon sheath
727.1	Bunion
729.6	Residual foreign body in soft tissue
730.37	Periostitis, without mention of osteomyelitis, ankle and foot
730.38	Periostitis, without mention of osteomyelitis, other specified sites
730.39	Periostitis, without mention of osteomyelitis, multiple sites
*730.7	Osteopathy resulting from poliomyelitis
733.3	Hyperostosis of skull
733.7	Algoneurodystrophy
*733.8	Malunion and nonunion of fracture
733.90	Disorder of bone and cartilage, unspecified
733.91	Arrest of bone development or growth
733.99	Other disorders of bone and cartilage
734	Flat foot
*735	Acquired deformities of toe
736.00	Unspecified deformity of forearm, excluding fingers
736.01	Cubitus valgus (acquired)
736.02	Cubitus varus (acquired)
736.03	Valgus deformity of wrist (acquired)
736.04	Varus deformity of wrist (acquired)
736.09	Other acquired deformities of forearm, excluding fingers
736.1	Mallet finger
*736.2	Other acquired deformities of finger
*736.3	Acquired deformities of hip
*736.4	Genu valgum or varum (acquired)
736.5	Genu recurvatum (acquired)
736.6	Other acquired deformities of knee
736.70	Unspecified deformity of ankle and foot, acquired
736.71	Acquired equinovarus deformity
736.72	Equinus deformity of foot, acquired
736.73	Cavus deformity of foot, acquired
736.75	Cavovarus deformity of foot, acquired
736.76	Other acquired calcaneus deformity
736.79	Other acquired deformity of ankle and foot
*736.8	Acquired deformities of other parts of limbs

736.9	Acquired deformity of limb, site unspecified
*738.1	Other acquired deformity of head
738.2	Acquired deformity of neck
738.3	Acquired deformity of chest and rib
738.6	Acquired deformity of pelvis
738.8	Acquired musculoskeletal deformity of other specified site
738.9	Acquired musculoskeletal deformity of unspecified site
754.0	Congenital musculoskeletal deformities of skull, face, and jaw
754.1	Congenital musculoskeletal deformity of sternocleidomastoid muscle
754.2	Congenital musculoskeletal deformity of spine
*754.3	Congenital dislocation of hip
754.40	Congenital genu recurvatum
754.42	Congenital bowing of femur
754.43	Congenital bowing of tibia and fibula
754.44	Congenital bowing of unspecified long bones of leg
*754.5	Congenital varus deformities of feet
*754.6	Congenital valgus deformities of feet
*754.7	Other congenital deformity of feet
754.89	Other specified nonteratogenic anomalies
*755	Other congenital anomalies of limbs
756.0	Congenital anomalies of skull and face bones
756.16	Klippel-Feil syndrome
756.2	Cervical rib
756.4	Chondrodystrophy
*756.5	Congenital osteodystrophies
*756.8	Other specified congenital anomalies of muscle, tendon, fascia, and connective tissue
756.9	Other and unspecified congenital anomaly of musculoskeletal system
759.7	Multiple congenital anomalies, so described
759.81	Prader-Willi syndrome
759.89	Other specified multiple congenital anomalies, so described
793.7	Nonspecific abnormal findings on radiological and other examination of musculoskeletal system
794.17	Nonspecific abnormal electromyogram (EMG)
802.8	Other facial bones, closed fracture
802.9	Other facial bones, open fracture
809.0	Fracture of bones of trunk, closed
809.1	Fracture of bones of trunk, open
811.09	Closed fracture of other part of scapula
811.19	Open fracture of other part of scapula
848.0	Sprain and strain of septal cartilage of nose
848.2	Sprain and strain of thyroid region
*880.2	Open wound of shoulder and upper arm, with tendon involvement
*881.2	Open wound of elbow, forearm, and wrist, with tendon involvement
882.2	Open wound of hand except finger(s) alone, with tendon involvement
883.2	Open wound of finger(s), with tendon involvement
884.2	Multiple and unspecified open wound of upper limb, with tendon involvement
890.2	Open wound of hip and thigh, with tendon involvement
891.2	Open wound of knee, leg (except thigh), and ankle, with tendon involvement
892.2	Open wound of foot except toe(s) alone, with tendon involvement
893.2	Open wound of toe(s), with tendon involvement
894.2	Multiple and unspecified open wound of lower limb, with tendon involvement
958.6	Volkmann's ischemic contracture
*997.6	Amputation stump complication
V42.4	Bone replaced by transplant
*V43.6	Joint replaced by other means
V43.7	Limb replaced by other means
V59.2	Bone donor

MDC 9
DISEASES AND DISORDERS OF THE SKIN, SUBCUTANEOUS TISSUE AND BREAST

The complete and up-to-date listing of ICD-9-CM diagnosis codes assigned to this MDC can be found online at www.ingenixonline.com/content/drg/resources.asp.

SURGICAL

S DRG 257 Total Mastectomy for Malignancy with CC
GMLOS 2.0 AMLOS 2.6 RW 0.8967 CC

Principal or Secondary Diagnosis

*174	Malignant neoplasm of female breast
*175	Malignant neoplasm of male breast
198.2	Secondary malignant neoplasm of skin
198.81	Secondary malignant neoplasm of breast
233.0	Carcinoma in situ of breast
238.3	Neoplasm of uncertain behavior of breast

Operating Room Procedures

*85.3	Reduction mammoplasty and subcutaneous mammectomy
*85.4	Mastectomy
85.7	Total reconstruction of breast

S DRG 258 Total Mastectomy for Malignancy without CC
GMLOS 1.5 AMLOS 1.7 RW 0.7138 ☑

Select principal or secondary diagnosis and operating room procedures listed under DRG 257

S DRG 259 Subtotal Mastectomy for Malignancy with CC
GMLOS 1.8 AMLOS 2.8 RW 0.9671 CC

Select principal or secondary diagnosis listed under DRG 257

AND

Operating Room Procedures

85.12	Open biopsy of breast
*85.2	Excision or destruction of breast tissue
85.50	Augmentation mammoplasty, not otherwise specified
85.53	Unilateral breast implant
85.54	Bilateral breast implant
85.6	Mastopexy
85.86	Transposition of nipple
85.87	Other repair or reconstruction of nipple
85.89	Other mammoplasty
85.93	Revision of implant of breast
85.94	Removal of implant of breast
85.95	Insertion of breast tissue expander
85.96	Removal of breast tissue expander (s)
85.99	Other operations on the breast

S DRG 260 Subtotal Mastectomy for Malignancy without CC
GMLOS 1.2 AMLOS 1.4 RW 0.7032 ☑

Select principal or secondary diagnosis and operating room procedures listed under DRG 259

[S] DRG 261 Breast Procedure for Nonmalignancy Except Biopsy and Local Excision

GMLOS 1.6 AMLOS 2.2 RW 0.9732

Operating Room Procedures

85.22	Resection of quadrant of breast
85.23	Subtotal mastectomy
85.24	Excision of ectopic breast tissue
85.25	Excision of nipple
*85.3	Reduction mammoplasty and subcutaneous mammectomy
*85.4	Mastectomy
85.50	Augmentation mammoplasty, not otherwise specified
85.53	Unilateral breast implant
85.54	Bilateral breast implant
85.6	Mastopexy
85.7	Total reconstruction of breast
85.86	Transposition of nipple
85.87	Other repair or reconstruction of nipple
85.89	Other mammoplasty
85.93	Revision of implant of breast
85.94	Removal of implant of breast
85.95	Insertion of breast tissue expander
85.96	Removal of breast tissue expander (s)
85.99	Other operations on the breast

[S] DRG 262 Breast Biopsy and Local Excision for Nonmalignancy

GMLOS 3.3 AMLOS 4.8 RW 0.9766 ☑

Operating Room Procedures

85.12	Open biopsy of breast
85.20	Excision or destruction of breast tissue, not otherwise specified
85.21	Local excision of lesion of breast

[S] DRG 263 Skin Graft and/or Debridement for Skin Ulcer or Cellulitis with CC

GMLOS 8.6 AMLOS 11.4 RW 2.1130 [T] [CC]

Principal Diagnosis

*681	Cellulitis and abscess of finger and toe
*682	Other cellulitis and abscess
*707	Chronic ulcer of skin

Operating Room Procedures

85.82	Split-thickness graft to breast
85.83	Full-thickness graft to breast
85.84	Pedicle graft to breast
85.85	Muscle flap graft to breast
86.22	Excisional debridement of wound, infection, or burn
86.4	Radical excision of skin lesion
86.60	Free skin graft, not otherwise specified
86.61	Full-thickness skin graft to hand
86.62	Other skin graft to hand
86.63	Full-thickness skin graft to other sites
86.65	Heterograft to skin
86.66	Homograft to skin
86.67	Dermal regenerative graft
86.69	Other skin graft to other sites
*86.7	Pedicle grafts or flaps
86.91	Excision of skin for graft
86.93	Insertion of tissue expander

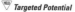

[S] DRG 264 Skin Graft and/or Debridement for Skin Ulcer or Cellulitis without CC

GMLOS 5.0 AMLOS 6.5 RW 1.0635 ☑[T]

Select principal diagnosis and operating room procedures listed under DRG 263

[S] DRG 265 Skin Graft and/or Debridement Except for Skin Ulcer or Cellulitis with CC

GMLOS 4.4 AMLOS 6.8 RW 1.6593 [T][CC]

Select operating room procedures listed under DRG 263

[S] DRG 266 Skin Graft and/or Debridement Except for Skin Ulcer or Cellulitis without CC

GMLOS 2.3 AMLOS 3.2 RW 0.8637 ☑[T]

Select operating room procedures listed under DRG 263

[S] DRG 267 Perianal and Pilonidal Procedures

GMLOS 2.8 AMLOS 4.2 RW 0.8962

Operating Room Procedures

49.01	Incision of perianal abscess
49.02	Other incision of perianal tissue
49.04	Other excision of perianal tissue
49.11	Anal fistulotomy
49.39	Other local excision or destruction of lesion or tissue of anus
49.75	Implantation or revision of artificial anal sphincter
49.76	Removal of artificial anal sphincter
49.79	Other repair of anal sphincter
86.21	Excision of pilonidal cyst or sinus

[S] DRG 268 Skin, Subcutaneous Tissue and Breast Plastic Procedures

GMLOS 2.4 AMLOS 3.5 RW 1.1326

Operating Room Procedures

08.38	Correction of lid retraction
*08.5	Other adjustment of lid position
*08.6	Reconstruction of eyelid with flaps or grafts
*08.7	Other reconstruction of eyelid
18.5	Surgical correction of prominent ear
18.6	Reconstruction of external auditory canal
18.71	Construction of auricle of ear
18.79	Other plastic repair of external ear
21.83	Total nasal reconstruction
21.84	Revision rhinoplasty
21.85	Augmentation rhinoplasty
21.86	Limited rhinoplasty
21.87	Other rhinoplasty
21.88	Other septoplasty
21.89	Other repair and plastic operations on nose
21.99	Other operations on nose
27.55	Full-thickness skin graft to lip and mouth
27.56	Other skin graft to lip and mouth
27.69	Other plastic repair of palate
82.89	Other plastic operations on hand
86.25	Dermabrasion
86.81	Repair for facial weakness
86.82	Facial rhytidectomy
86.83	Size reduction plastic operation
86.84	Relaxation of scar or web contracture of skin
86.85	Correction of syndactyly
86.89	Other repair and reconstruction of skin and subcutaneous tissue

[S] Surgical *[M] Medical* *[CC] CC Indicator* *[A] Age Restriction* *● New DRG* *▲ Revised DRG Title*

S DRG 269 Other Skin, Subcutaneous Tissue and Breast Procedures with CC

GMLOS 6.2 AMLOS 8.6 RW 1.8352 ☑ T CC

Operating Room Procedures

06.09	Other incision of thyroid field
07.22	Unilateral adrenalectomy
07.3	Bilateral adrenalectomy
07.63	Partial excision of pituitary gland, unspecified approach
07.64	Total excision of pituitary gland, transfrontal approach
07.65	Total excision of pituitary gland, transsphenoidal approach
07.68	Total excision of pituitary gland, other specified approach
07.69	Total excision of pituitary gland, unspecified approach
07.72	Incision of pituitary gland
07.79	Other operations on hypophysis
08.20	Removal of lesion of eyelid, not otherwise specified
08.22	Excision of other minor lesion of eyelid
08.23	Excision of major lesion of eyelid, partial-thickness
08.24	Excision of major lesion of eyelid, full-thickness
08.25	Destruction of lesion of eyelid
08.44	Repair of entropion or ectropion with lid reconstruction
08.99	Other operations on eyelids
09.73	Repair of canaliculus
16.93	Excision of lesion of eye, unspecified structure
18.21	Excision of preauricular sinus
*18.3	Other excision of external ear
18.9	Other operations on external ear
21.4	Resection of nose
21.72	Open reduction of nasal fracture
27.0	Drainage of face and floor of mouth
27.42	Wide excision of lesion of lip
27.43	Other excision of lesion or tissue of lip
27.54	Repair of cleft lip
27.57	Attachment of pedicle or flap graft to lip and mouth
27.59	Other plastic repair of mouth
27.63	Revision of cleft palate repair
27.92	Incision of mouth, unspecified structure
29.2	Excision of branchial cleft cyst or vestige
29.52	Closure of branchial cleft fistula
31.72	Closure of external fistula of trachea
31.74	Revision of tracheostomy
34.4	Excision or destruction of lesion of chest wall
34.79	Other repair of chest wall
37.79	Revision or relocation of cardiac device pocket
39.25	Aorta-iliac-femoral bypass
39.29	Other (peripheral) vascular shunt or bypass
39.31	Suture of artery
39.50	Angioplasty or atherectomy of other non-coronary vessel(s)
39.59	Other repair of vessel
39.98	Control of hemorrhage, not otherwise specified
40.0	Incision of lymphatic structures
*40.1	Diagnostic procedures on lymphatic structures
*40.2	Simple excision of lymphatic structure
40.3	Regional lymph node excision
*40.4	Radical excision of cervical lymph nodes
*40.5	Radical excision of other lymph nodes
40.9	Other operations on lymphatic structures
48.35	Local excision of rectal lesion or tissue
48.73	Closure of other rectal fistula
*48.8	Incision or excision of perirectal tissue or lesion
49.12	Anal fistulectomy
49.71	Suture of laceration of anus

*** Code Range** ☑ ***Optimization Potential*** ▽ ***Targeted Potential*** T ***Transfer DRG*** SP ***Special Payment***

DRG 269 — continued

49.72	Anal cerclage
49.73	Closure of anal fistula
50.12	Open biopsy of liver
50.19	Other diagnostic procedures on liver
54.0	Incision of abdominal wall
54.11	Exploratory laparotomy
54.21	Laparoscopy
54.22	Biopsy of abdominal wall or umbilicus
54.3	Excision or destruction of lesion or tissue of abdominal wall or umbilicus
54.63	Other suture of abdominal wall
54.72	Other repair of abdominal wall
59.00	Retroperitoneal dissection, not otherwise specified
64.11	Biopsy of penis
64.2	Local excision or destruction of lesion of penis
64.49	Other repair of penis
*65.5	Bilateral oophorectomy
65.61	Other removal of both ovaries and tubes at same operative episode
65.63	Laparoscopic removal of both ovaries and tubes at same operative episode
*67.1	Diagnostic procedures on cervix
67.39	Other excision or destruction of lesion or tissue of cervix
70.24	Vaginal biopsy
70.33	Excision or destruction of lesion of vagina
70.71	Suture of laceration of vagina
71.09	Other incision of vulva and perineum
*71.1	Diagnostic procedures on vulva
71.24	Excision or other destruction of Bartholin's gland (cyst)
71.3	Other local excision or destruction of vulva and perineum
71.62	Bilateral vulvectomy
71.71	Suture of laceration of vulva or perineum
76.43	Other reconstruction of mandible
77.28	Wedge osteotomy of tarsals and metatarsals
*77.4	Biopsy of bone
80.83	Other local excision or destruction of lesion of wrist joint
82.09	Other incision of soft tissue of hand
82.21	Excision of lesion of tendon sheath of hand
82.29	Excision of other lesion of soft tissue of hand
82.39	Other excision of soft tissue of hand
82.45	Other suture of other tendon of hand
82.72	Plastic operation on hand with graft of muscle or fascia
82.79	Plastic operation on hand with other graft or implant
82.91	Lysis of adhesions of hand
83.02	Myotomy
83.09	Other incision of soft tissue
83.14	Fasciotomy
83.21	Biopsy of soft tissue
83.32	Excision of lesion of muscle
83.39	Excision of lesion of other soft tissue
83.44	Other fasciectomy
83.45	Other myectomy
83.49	Other excision of soft tissue
83.65	Other suture of muscle or fascia
83.71	Advancement of tendon
83.82	Graft of muscle or fascia
83.87	Other plastic operations on muscle
83.88	Other plastic operations on tendon
83.89	Other plastic operations on fascia
*84.0	Amputation of upper limb
*84.1	Amputation of lower limb
84.3	Revision of amputation stump
84.91	Amputation, not otherwise specified
86.06	Insertion of totally implantable infusion pump

86.86 Onychoplasty
92.27 Implantation or insertion of radioactive elements

OR

Nonoperating Room Procedures

86.07 Insertion of totally implantable vascular access device (VAD)
86.09 Other incision of skin and subcutaneous tissue
86.3 Other local excision or destruction of lesion or tissue of skin and subcutaneous tissue

S DRG 270 Other Skin, Subcutaneous Tissue and Breast Procedures without CC

GMLOS 2.7 AMLOS 3.9 RW 0.8313 ☑ T

Select procedures listed under DRG 269

MDC 9
DISEASES AND DISORDERS OF THE SKIN, SUBCUTANEOUS TISSUE AND BREAST

The complete and up-to-date listing of ICD-9-CM diagnosis codes assigned to this MDC can be found online at www.ingenixonline.com/content/drg/resources.asp.

MEDICAL

M DRG 271 Skin Ulcers
GMLOS 5.6 AMLOS 7.1 RW 1.0195 ☑T

Principal Diagnosis

*707	Chronic ulcer of skin

M DRG 272 Major Skin Disorders with CC
GMLOS 4.5 AMLOS 5.9 RW 0.9860 T CC

Principal Diagnosis

*017.1	Erythema nodosum with hypersensitivity reaction in tuberculosis
053.9	Herpes zoster without mention of complication
172.0	Malignant melanoma of skin of lip
172.2	Malignant melanoma of skin of ear and external auditory canal
172.3	Malignant melanoma of skin of other and unspecified parts of face
172.4	Malignant melanoma of skin of scalp and neck
172.5	Malignant melanoma of skin of trunk, except scrotum
172.6	Malignant melanoma of skin of upper limb, including shoulder
172.7	Malignant melanoma of skin of lower limb, including hip
172.8	Malignant melanoma of other specified sites of skin
172.9	Melanoma of skin, site unspecified
694.4	Pemphigus
694.5	Pemphigoid
694.60	Benign mucous membrane pemphigoid without mention of ocular involvement
694.8	Other specified bullous dermatosis
694.9	Unspecified bullous dermatosis
695.0	Toxic erythema
695.1	Erythema multiforme
695.2	Erythema nodosum
695.4	Lupus erythematosus
695.81	Ritter's disease
696.1	Other psoriasis and similar disorders
696.2	Parapsoriasis

M DRG 273 Major Skin Disorders without CC
GMLOS 2.9 AMLOS 3.7 RW 0.5539 ☑T

Select principal diagnosis listed under DRG 272

M DRG 274 Malignant Breast Disorders with CC
GMLOS 4.7 AMLOS 6.3 RW 1.1294 ☑CC

Principal Diagnosis

*174	Malignant neoplasm of female breast
*175	Malignant neoplasm of male breast
198.2	Secondary malignant neoplasm of skin
198.81	Secondary malignant neoplasm of breast
233.0	Carcinoma in situ of breast
238.3	Neoplasm of uncertain behavior of breast

M DRG 275 Malignant Breast Disorders without CC

GMLOS 2.4 AMLOS 3.3 RW 0.5340 ☑

Select principal diagnosis listed under DRG 274

M DRG 276 Nonmalignant Breast Disorders

GMLOS 3.5 AMLOS 4.5 RW 0.6892 ☑

Principal Diagnosis

239.3	Neoplasm of unspecified nature of breast
457.0	Postmastectomy lymphedema syndrome
*610	Benign mammary dysplasias
*611	Other disorders of breast
757.6	Specified congenital anomalies of breast
793.80	Unspecified abnormal mammogram
793.81	Mammographic microcalcification
793.89	Other abnormal findings on radiological examination of breast
996.54	Mechanical complication due to breast prosthesis
V50.41	Prophylactic breast removal

M DRG 277 Cellulitis, Age Greater than 17 with CC

GMLOS 4.6 AMLOS 5.6 RW 0.8676 ☑ T CC A

Principal Diagnosis

035	Erysipelas
457.2	Lymphangitis
*680	Carbuncle and furuncle
*681	Cellulitis and abscess of finger and toe
*682	Other cellulitis and abscess
684	Impetigo
*685	Pilonidal cyst
*686	Other local infection of skin and subcutaneous tissue
910.1	Face, neck, and scalp except eye, abrasion or friction burn, infected
910.5	Face, neck, and scalp except eye, insect bite, nonvenomous,infected
910.7	Face, neck, and scalp except eye, superficial foreign body (splinter), without major open wound, infected
910.9	Other and unspecified superficial injury of face, neck, and scalp, infected
911.1	Trunk abrasion or friction burn, infected
911.3	Trunk blister, infected
911.5	Trunk, insect bite, nonvenomous, infected
911.7	Trunk, superficial foreign body (splinter), without major open wound, infected
911.9	Other and unspecified superficial injury of trunk, infected
912.1	Shoulder and upper arm, abrasion or friction burn, infected
912.3	Shoulder and upper arm, blister, infected
912.5	Shoulder and upper arm, insect bite, nonvenomous, infected
912.7	Shoulder and upper arm, superficial foreign body (splinter), without major open wound, infected
912.9	Other and unspecified superficial injury of shoulder and upper arm, infected
913.1	Elbow, forearm, and wrist, abrasion or friction burn, infected
913.3	Elbow, forearm, and wrist, blister infected
913.5	Elbow, forearm, and wrist, insect bite, nonvenomous, infected
913.7	Elbow, forearm, and wrist, superficial foreign body (splinter), without major open wound, infected
913.9	Other and unspecified superficial injury of elbow, forearm, and wrist, infected
914.1	Hand(s) except finger(s) alone, abrasion or friction burn, infected
914.3	Hand(s) except finger(s) alone, blister, infected
914.5	Hand(s) except finger(s) alone, insect bite, nonvenomous, infected
914.7	Hand(s) except finger(s) alone, superficial foreign body (splinter) without major open wound, infected
914.9	Other and unspecified superficial injury of hand(s) except finger(s) alone, infected
915.1	Finger, abrasion or friction burn, infected
915.3	Finger, blister, infected
915.5	Finger, insect bite, nonvenomous, infected

*** Code Range** ☑ ***Optimization Potential*** ▽ ***Targeted Potential*** T ***Transfer DRG*** SP ***Special Payment***

DRG 277 — continued

915.7 Finger, superficial foreign body (splinter), without major open wound, infected
915.9 Other and unspecified superficial injury of finger, infected
916.1 Hip, thigh, leg, and ankle, abrasion or friction burn, infected
916.3 Hip, thigh, leg, and ankle, blister, infected
916.5 Hip, thigh, leg, and ankle, insect bite, nonvenomous, infected
916.7 Hip, thigh, leg, and ankle, superficial foreign body (splinter), without major open wound, infected
916.9 Other and unspecified superficial injury of hip, thigh, leg, and ankle, infected
917.1 Foot and toe(s), abrasion or friction burn, infected
917.3 Foot and toe(s), blister, infected
917.5 Foot and toe(s), insect bite, nonvenomous, infected
917.7 Foot and toe(s), superficial foreign body (splinter), without major open wound, infected
917.9 Other and unspecified superficial injury of foot and toes, infected
919.1 Other, multiple, and unspecified sites, abrasion or friction burn, infected
919.3 Other, multiple, and unspecified sites, blister, infected
919.5 Other, multiple, and unspecified sites, insect bite, nonvenomous, infected
919.7 Other, multiple, and unspecified sites, superficial foreign body (splinter), without major open wound, infected
919.9 Other and unspecified superficial injury of other, multiple, and unspecified sites, infected

M DRG 278 Cellulitis, Age Greater than 17 without CC

GMLOS 3.4 AMLOS 4.1 RW 0.5391 ☑ T A

Select principal diagnosis listed under DRG 277

M DRG 279 Cellulitis, Age 0-17

GMLOS 4.2 AMLOS 4.2 RW 0.7822 ☑ A

Select principal diagnosis listed under DRG 277

M DRG 280 Trauma to Skin, Subcutaneous Tissue and Breast, Age Greater than 17 with CC

GMLOS 3.2 AMLOS 4.1 RW 0.7313 ☑ T CC A

Principal Diagnosis

873.0 Open wound of scalp, without mention of complication
873.1 Open wound of scalp, complicated
873.40 Open wound of face, unspecified site, without mention of complication
873.41 Open wound of cheek, without mention of complication
873.42 Open wound of forehead, without mention of complication
873.49 Open wound of face, other and multiple sites, without mention of complication
873.50 Open wound of face, unspecified site, complicated
873.51 Open wound of cheek, complicated
873.52 Open wound of forehead, complicated
873.59 Open wound of face, other and multiple sites, complicated
873.8 Other and unspecified open wound of head without mention of complication
873.9 Other and unspecified open wound of head, complicated
874.8 Open wound of other and unspecified parts of neck, without mention of complication
874.9 Open wound of other and unspecified parts of neck, complicated
875.0 Open wound of chest (wall), without mention of complication
*876 Open wound of back
*877 Open wound of buttock
879.0 Open wound of breast, without mention of complication
879.1 Open wound of breast, complicated
879.2 Open wound of abdominal wall, anterior, without mention of complication
879.4 Open wound of abdominal wall, lateral, without mention of complication
879.6 Open wound of other and unspecified parts of trunk, without mention of complication
879.8 Open wound(s) (multiple) of unspecified site(s), without mention of complication
*880.0 Open wound of shoulder and upper arm, without mention of complication
*881.0 Open wound of elbow, forearm, and wrist, without mention of complication
882.0 Open wound of hand except finger(s) alone, without mention of complication
883.0 Open wound of finger(s), without mention of complication

884.0	Multiple and unspecified open wound of upper limb, without mention of complication
890.0	Open wound of hip and thigh, without mention of complication
891.0	Open wound of knee, leg (except thigh), and ankle, without mention of complication
892.0	Open wound of foot except toe(s) alone, without mention of complication
893.0	Open wound of toe(s), without mention of complication
894.0	Multiple and unspecified open wound of lower limb, without mention of complication
*906	Late effects of injuries to skin and subcutaneous tissues
910.0	Face, neck, and scalp, except eye, abrasion or friction burn, without mention of infection
910.6	Face, neck, and scalp, except eye, superficial foreign body (splinter), without major open wound or mention of infection
910.8	Other and unspecified superficial injury of face, neck, and scalp, without mention of infection
911.0	Trunk abrasion or friction burn, without mention of infection
911.6	Trunk, superficial foreign body (splinter), without major open wound and without mention of infection
911.8	Other and unspecified superficial injury of trunk, without mention of infection
912.0	Shoulder and upper arm, abrasion or friction burn, without mention of infection
912.2	Shoulder and upper arm, blister, without mention of infection
912.6	Shoulder and upper arm, superficial foreign body (splinter), without major open wound and without mention of infection
912.8	Other and unspecified superficial injury of shoulder and upper arm, without mention of infection
913.0	Elbow, forearm, and wrist, abrasion or friction burn, without mention of infection
913.6	Elbow, forearm, and wrist, superficial foreign body (splinter), without major open wound and without mention of infection
913.8	Other and unspecified superficial injury of elbow, forearm, and wrist, without mention of infection
914.0	Hand(s) except finger(s) alone, abrasion or friction burn, without mention of infection
914.6	Hand(s) except finger(s) alone, superficial foreign body (splinter), without major open wound and without mention of infection
914.8	Other and unspecified superficial injury of hand(s) except finger(s) alone, without mention of infection
915.0	Abrasion or friction burn of finger, without mention of infection
915.6	Finger, superficial foreign body (splinter), without major open wound and without mention of infection
915.8	Other and unspecified superficial injury of finger without mention of infection
916.0	Hip, thigh, leg, and ankle, abrasion or friction burn, without mention of infection
916.6	Hip, thigh, leg, and ankle, superficial foreign body (splinter), without major open wound and without mention of infection
916.8	Other and unspecified superficial injury of hip, thigh, leg, and ankle, without mention of infection
917.0	Abrasion or friction burn of foot and toe(s), without mention of infection
917.6	Foot and toe(s), superficial foreign body (splinter), without major open wound and without mention of infection
917.8	Other and unspecified superficial injury of foot and toes, without mention of infection
919.0	Abrasion or friction burn of other, multiple, and unspecified sites, without mention of infection
919.6	Other, multiple, and unspecified sites, superficial foreign body (splinter), without major open wound and without mention of infection
919.8	Other and unspecified superficial injury of other, multiple, and unspecified sites, without mention of infection
920	Contusion of face, scalp, and neck except eye(s)
922.0	Contusion of breast
922.1	Contusion of chest wall
922.2	Contusion of abdominal wall
*922.3	Contusion of trunk
922.8	Contusion of multiple sites of trunk
922.9	Contusion of unspecified part of trunk
*923	Contusion of upper limb
*924	Contusion of lower limb and of other and unspecified sites

M DRG 281 Trauma to Skin, Subcutaneous Tissue and Breast, Age Greater than 17 without CC

GMLOS 2.3 AMLOS 2.9 RW 0.4913 ☑ T A

Select principal diagnosis listed under DRG 280

M DRG 282 Trauma to Skin, Subcutaneous Tissue and Breast, Age 0-17

GMLOS 2.2 AMLOS 2.2 RW 0.2600 ☑ A

Select principal diagnosis listed under DRG 280

M DRG 283 Minor Skin Disorders with CC

GMLOS 3.5 AMLOS 4.6 RW 0.7423 ☑ T CC

Principal Diagnosis

006.6	Amebic skin ulceration
*017.0	Tuberculosis of skin and subcutaneous cellular tissue
022.0	Cutaneous anthrax
031.1	Cutaneous diseases due to other mycobacteria
032.85	Cutaneous diphtheria
039.0	Cutaneous actinomycotic infection
039.3	Cervicofacial actinomycotic infection
039.4	Madura foot
051.1	Pseudocowpox
051.2	Contagious pustular dermatitis
054.0	Eczema herpeticum
054.6	Herpetic whitlow
054.9	Herpes simplex without mention of complication
078.0	Molluscum contagiosum
*078.1	Viral warts
085.1	Cutaneous leishmaniasis, urban
085.2	Cutaneous leishmaniasis, Asian desert
085.3	Cutaneous leishmaniasis, Ethiopian
085.4	Cutaneous leishmaniasis, American
085.5	Mucocutaneous leishmaniasis, (American)
091.3	Secondary syphilis of skin or mucous membranes
091.82	Early syphilis, syphilitic alopecia
102.0	Initial lesions of yaws
102.1	Multiple papillomata and wet crab yaws due to yaws
102.2	Other early skin lesions due to yaws
102.3	Hyperkeratosis due to yaws
102.4	Gummata and ulcers due to yaws
103.0	Primary lesions of pinta
103.1	Intermediate lesions of pinta
103.3	Mixed lesions of pinta
*110	Dermatophytosis
*111	Dermatomycosis, other and unspecified
112.3	Candidiasis of skin and nails
114.1	Primary extrapulmonary coccidioidomycosis
120.3	Cutaneous schistosomiasis
*132	Pediculosis and phthirus infestation
*133	Acariasis
*134	Other infestation
173.0	Other malignant neoplasm of skin of lip
173.2	Other malignant neoplasm of skin of ear and external auditory canal
173.3	Other malignant neoplasm of skin of other and unspecified parts of face
173.4	Other malignant neoplasm of scalp and skin of neck
173.5	Other malignant neoplasm of skin of trunk, except scrotum
173.6	Other malignant neoplasm of skin of upper limb, including shoulder
173.7	Other malignant neoplasm of skin of lower limb, including hip
173.8	Other malignant neoplasm of other specified sites of skin
173.9	Other malignant neoplasm of skin, site unspecified
176.0	Kaposi's sarcoma of skin

176.1	Kaposi's sarcoma of soft tissue
176.8	Kaposi's sarcoma of other specified sites
176.9	Kaposi's sarcoma of unspecified site
214.0	Lipoma of skin and subcutaneous tissue of face
214.1	Lipoma of other skin and subcutaneous tissue
214.8	Lipoma of other specified sites
214.9	Lipoma of unspecified site
216.0	Benign neoplasm of skin of lip
216.2	Benign neoplasm of ear and external auditory canal
216.3	Benign neoplasm of skin of other and unspecified parts of face
216.4	Benign neoplasm of scalp and skin of neck
216.5	Benign neoplasm of skin of trunk, except scrotum
216.6	Benign neoplasm of skin of upper limb, including shoulder
216.7	Benign neoplasm of skin of lower limb, including hip
216.8	Benign neoplasm of other specified sites of skin
216.9	Benign neoplasm of skin, site unspecified
217	Benign neoplasm of breast
228.01	Hemangioma of skin and subcutaneous tissue
232.0	Carcinoma in situ of skin of lip
232.2	Carcinoma in situ of skin of ear and external auditory canal
232.3	Carcinoma in situ of skin of other and unspecified parts of face
232.4	Carcinoma in situ of scalp and skin of neck
232.5	Carcinoma in situ of skin of trunk, except scrotum
232.6	Carcinoma in situ of skin of upper limb, including shoulder
232.7	Carcinoma in situ of skin of lower limb, including hip
232.8	Carcinoma in situ of other specified sites of skin
232.9	Carcinoma in situ of skin, site unspecified
238.2	Neoplasm of uncertain behavior of skin
306.3	Skin malfunction arising from mental factors
374.51	Xanthelasma of eyelid
448.1	Nevus, non-neoplastic
457.1	Other noninfectious lymphedema
617.6	Endometriosis in scar of skin
*690	Erythematosquamous dermatosis
*691	Atopic dermatitis and related conditions
*692	Contact dermatitis and other eczema
*693	Dermatitis due to substances taken internally
694.0	Dermatitis herpetiformis
694.1	Subcorneal pustular dermatosis
694.2	Juvenile dermatitis herpetiformis
694.3	Impetigo herpetiformis
695.3	Rosacea
695.89	Other specified erythematous condition
695.9	Unspecified erythematous condition
696.3	Pityriasis rosea
696.4	Pityriasis rubra pilaris
696.5	Other and unspecified pityriasis
696.8	Other psoriasis and similar disorders
*697	Lichen
698.0	Pruritus ani
698.2	Prurigo
698.3	Lichenification and lichen simplex chronicus
698.4	Dermatitis factitia (artefacta)
698.8	Other specified pruritic conditions
698.9	Unspecified pruritic disorder
700	Corns and callosities
*701	Other hypertrophic and atrophic conditions of skin
*702	Other dermatoses
*703	Diseases of nail
*704	Diseases of hair and hair follicles
*705	Disorders of sweat glands
*706	Diseases of sebaceous glands
*708	Urticaria

DRG 283 — continued

*709	Other disorders of skin and subcutaneous tissue
723.6	Panniculitis specified as affecting neck
*729.3	Unspecified panniculitis
744.5	Congenital webbing of neck
744.9	Unspecified congenital anomaly of face and neck
757.0	Hereditary edema of legs
757.1	Ichthyosis congenita
757.2	Dermatoglyphic anomalies
757.31	Congenital ectodermal dysplasia
757.32	Congenital vascular hamartomas
757.33	Congenital pigmentary anomaly of skin
757.39	Other specified congenital anomaly of skin
757.4	Specified congenital anomalies of hair
757.5	Specified congenital anomalies of nails
757.8	Other specified congenital anomalies of the integument
757.9	Unspecified congenital anomaly of the integument
780.8	Generalized hyperhidrosis
782.1	Rash and other nonspecific skin eruption
782.2	Localized superficial swelling, mass, or lump
782.8	Changes in skin texture
782.9	Other symptoms involving skin and integumentary tissues
784.2	Swelling, mass, or lump in head and neck
910.2	Face, neck, and scalp except eye, blister, without mention of infection
910.3	Face, neck, and scalp except eye, blister, infected
910.4	Face, neck, and scalp except eye, insect bite, nonvenomous, without mention of infection
911.2	Trunk blister, without mention of infection
911.4	Trunk, insect bite, nonvenomous, without mention of infection
912.4	Shoulder and upper arm, insect bite, nonvenomous, without mention of infection
913.2	Elbow, forearm, and wrist, blister, without mention of infection
913.4	Elbow, forearm, and wrist, insect bite, nonvenomous, without mention of infection
914.2	Hand(s) except finger(s) alone, blister, without mention of infection
914.4	Hand(s) except finger(s) alone, insect bite, nonvenomous, without mention of infection
915.2	Finger, blister, without mention of infection
915.4	Finger, insect bite, nonvenomous, without mention of infection
916.2	Hip, thigh, leg, and ankle, blister, without mention of infection
916.4	Hip, thigh, leg, and ankle, insect bite, nonvenomous, without mention of infection
917.2	Foot and toe(s), blister, without mention of infection
917.4	Foot and toe(s), insect bite, nonvenomous, without mention of infection
919.2	Other, multiple, and unspecified sites, blister, without mention of infection
919.4	Other, multiple, and unspecified sites, insect bite, nonvenomous, without mention of infection
V42.3	Skin replaced by transplant
V50.0	Elective hair transplant for purposes other than remedying health states
V50.1	Other plastic surgery for unacceptable cosmetic appearance
V51	Aftercare involving the use of plastic surgery
V59.1	Skin donor

M DRG 284 Minor Skin Disorders without CC

GMLOS 2.4 AMLOS 3.0 RW 0.4563 ☑ T

Select principal diagnosis listed under DRG 283

MDC 10
ENDOCRINE, NUTRITIONAL AND METABOLIC DISEASES AND DISORDERS

The complete and up-to-date listing of ICD-9-CM diagnosis codes assigned to this MDC can be found online at www.ingenixonline.com/content/drg/resources.asp.

SURGICAL

S DRG 285 Amputation of Lower Limb for Endocrine, Nutritional and Metabolic Disorders

GMLOS 8.2 AMLOS 10.5 RW 2.1831 ☑ T

Operating Room Procedures

84.10	Lower limb amputation, not otherwise specified
84.11	Amputation of toe
84.12	Amputation through foot
84.13	Disarticulation of ankle
84.14	Amputation of ankle through malleoli of tibia and fibula
84.15	Other amputation below knee
84.16	Disarticulation of knee
84.17	Amputation above knee

S DRG 286 Adrenal and Pituitary Procedures

GMLOS 4.0 AMLOS 5.5 RW 1.9390

Operating Room Procedures

*07.0	Exploration of adrenal field
07.12	Open biopsy of adrenal gland
07.13	Biopsy of pituitary gland, transfrontal approach
07.14	Biopsy of pituitary gland, transsphenoidal approach
07.15	Biopsy of pituitary gland, unspecified approach
07.17	Biopsy of pineal gland
07.19	Other diagnostic procedures on adrenal glands, pituitary gland, pineal gland, and thymus
*07.2	Partial adrenalectomy
07.3	Bilateral adrenalectomy
*07.4	Other operations on adrenal glands, nerves, and vessels
*07.5	Operations on pineal gland
*07.6	Hypophysectomy
*07.7	Other operations on hypophysis

S DRG 287 Skin Grafts and Wound Debridement for Endocrine, Nutritional and Metabolic Disorders

GMLOS 7.8 AMLOS 10.4 RW 1.9470 T

Operating Room Procedures

84.3	Revision of amputation stump
86.22	Excisional debridement of wound, infection, or burn
86.60	Free skin graft, not otherwise specified
86.63	Full-thickness skin graft to other sites
86.67	Dermal regenerative graft
86.69	Other skin graft to other sites
86.70	Pedicle or flap graft, not otherwise specified
86.71	Cutting and preparation of pedicle grafts or flaps
86.72	Advancement of pedicle graft
86.74	Attachment of pedicle or flap graft to other sites
86.75	Revision of pedicle or flap graft
86.91	Excision of skin for graft
86.93	Insertion of tissue expander

** Code Range* ☑ *Optimization Potential* *Targeted Potential* T *Transfer DRG* SP *Special Payment*

S DRG 288 O.R. Procedures for Obesity

GMLOS 3.2 AMLOS 4.1 RW 2.0384

Operating Room Procedures

*44.3	Gastroenterostomy without gastrectomy
44.5	Revision of gastric anastomosis
44.68	Laparoscopic gastroplasty
44.69	Other repair of stomach
44.95	Laparoscopic gastric restrictive procedure
44.96	Laparoscopic revision of gastric restrictive procedure
44.97	Laparoscopic removal of gastric restrictive device(s)
44.98	(Laparoscopic) adjustment of size of adjustable gastric restrictive device
44.99	Other operations on stomach
45.90	Intestinal anastomosis, not otherwise specified
45.91	Small-to-small intestinal anastomosis
85.31	Unilateral reduction mammoplasty
85.32	Bilateral reduction mammoplasty
86.83	Size reduction plastic operation
86.89	Other repair and reconstruction of skin and subcutaneous tissue

S DRG 289 Parathyroid Procedures

GMLOS 1.7 AMLOS 2.6 RW 0.9315

Operating Room Procedures

06.13	Biopsy of parathyroid gland
*06.8	Parathyroidectomy
06.99	Other operations on parathyroid glands

S DRG 290 Thyroid Procedures

GMLOS 1.6 AMLOS 2.1 RW 0.8891 ☑

Operating Room Procedures

06.02	Reopening of wound of thyroid field
06.09	Other incision of thyroid field
06.12	Open biopsy of thyroid gland
06.19	Other diagnostic procedures on thyroid and parathyroid glands
06.2	Unilateral thyroid lobectomy
*06.3	Other partial thyroidectomy
06.4	Complete thyroidectomy
*06.5	Substernal thyroidectomy
06.6	Excision of lingual thyroid
06.91	Division of thyroid isthmus
06.92	Ligation of thyroid vessels
06.93	Suture of thyroid gland
06.94	Thyroid tissue reimplantation
06.95	Parathyroid tissue reimplantation
06.98	Other operations on thyroid glands

S DRG 291 Thyroglossal Procedures

GMLOS 1.6 AMLOS 2.8 RW 1.0877

Operating Room Procedure

06.7	Excision of thyroglossal duct or tract

S DRG 292 Other Endocrine, Nutritional and Metabolic O.R. Procedures with CC

GMLOS 7.3 AMLOS 10.3 RW 2.6395 ☑ T CC

Operating Room Procedures

*00.7	Other hip procedures
01.15	Biopsy of skull
07.16	Biopsy of thymus
*07.8	Thymectomy

S *Surgical* M *Medical* CC *CC Indicator* A *Age Restriction* ● *New DRG* ▲ *Revised DRG Title*

*07.9	Other operations on thymus
08.20	Removal of lesion of eyelid, not otherwise specified
08.38	Correction of lid retraction
08.70	Reconstruction of eyelid, not otherwise specified
12.64	Trabeculectomy ab externo
12.72	Cyclocryotherapy
12.79	Other glaucoma procedures
*13.1	Intracapsular extraction of lens
13.59	Other extracapsular extraction of lens
14.49	Other scleral buckling
14.54	Repair of retinal detachment with laser photocoagulation
14.6	Removal of surgically implanted material from posterior segment of eye
14.72	Other removal of vitreous
14.74	Other mechanical vitrectomy
16.99	Other operations on eyeball
34.26	Open biopsy of mediastinum
34.3	Excision or destruction of lesion or tissue of mediastinum
34.4	Excision or destruction of lesion of chest wall
38.00	Incision of vessel, unspecified site
38.02	Incision of other vessels of head and neck
38.03	Incision of upper limb vessels
38.08	Incision of lower limb arteries
38.12	Endarterectomy of other vessels of head and neck
38.13	Endarterectomy of upper limb vessels
38.18	Endarterectomy of lower limb arteries
38.21	Biopsy of blood vessel
38.29	Other diagnostic procedures on blood vessels
38.30	Resection of vessel with anastomosis, unspecified site
38.33	Resection of upper limb vessels with anastomosis
38.38	Resection of lower limb arteries with anastomosis
38.43	Resection of upper limb vessels with replacement
38.48	Resection of lower limb arteries with replacement
38.55	Ligation and stripping of varicose veins of other thoracic vessel
38.60	Other excision of vessels, unspecified site
38.63	Other excision of upper limb vessels
38.68	Other excision of lower limb arteries
38.7	Interruption of the vena cava
38.83	Other surgical occlusion of upper limb vessels
38.88	Other surgical occlusion of lower limb arteries
39.25	Aorta-iliac-femoral bypass
39.27	Arteriovenostomy for renal dialysis
39.29	Other (peripheral) vascular shunt or bypass
39.31	Suture of artery
39.41	Control of hemorrhage following vascular surgery
39.42	Revision of arteriovenous shunt for renal dialysis
39.49	Other revision of vascular procedure
39.50	Angioplasty or atherectomy of other non-coronary vessel(s)
39.56	Repair of blood vessel with tissue patch graft
39.57	Repair of blood vessel with synthetic patch graft
39.58	Repair of blood vessel with unspecified type of patch graft
39.59	Other repair of vessel
39.91	Freeing of vessel
39.93	Insertion of vessel-to-vessel cannula
39.98	Control of hemorrhage, not otherwise specified
*40.1	Diagnostic procedures on lymphatic structures
40.21	Excision of deep cervical lymph node
40.29	Simple excision of other lymphatic structure
40.3	Regional lymph node excision
*40.4	Radical excision of cervical lymph nodes
40.52	Radical excision of periaortic lymph nodes
40.53	Radical excision of iliac lymph nodes
43.0	Gastrotomy
43.42	Local excision of other lesion or tissue of stomach

Code Range** ☑ ***Optimization Potential ***Targeted Potential*** T ***Transfer DRG*** SP ***Special Payment***

DRG 292 — continued

43.7	Partial gastrectomy with anastomosis to jejunum
44.92	Intraoperative manipulation of stomach
45.41	Excision of lesion or tissue of large intestine
45.62	Other partial resection of small intestine
45.75	Left hemicolectomy
45.93	Other small-to-large intestinal anastomosis
45.94	Large-to-large intestinal anastomosis
50.12	Open biopsy of liver
52.12	Open biopsy of pancreas
52.19	Other diagnostic procedures on pancreas
52.22	Other excision or destruction of lesion or tissue of pancreas or pancreatic duct
*52.5	Partial pancreatectomy
52.80	Pancreatic transplant, not otherwise specified
52.82	Homotransplant of pancreas
52.83	Heterotransplant of pancreas
54.11	Exploratory laparotomy
54.3	Excision or destruction of lesion or tissue of abdominal wall or umbilicus
54.4	Excision or destruction of peritoneal tissue
54.59	Other lysis of peritoneal adhesions
62.7	Insertion of testicular prosthesis
65.22	Wedge resection of ovary
65.24	Laparoscopic wedge resection of ovary
77.27	Wedge osteotomy of tibia and fibula
77.38	Other division of tarsals and metatarsals
*77.4	Biopsy of bone
77.61	Local excision of lesion or tissue of scapula, clavicle, and thorax (ribs and sternum)
77.68	Local excision of lesion or tissue of tarsals and metatarsals
77.69	Local excision of lesion or tissue of other bone, except facial bones
77.88	Other partial ostectomy of tarsals and metatarsals
77.89	Other partial ostectomy of other bone, except facial bones
78.65	Removal of implanted device from femur
79.35	Open reduction of fracture of femur with internal fixation
80.10	Other arthrotomy, unspecified site
80.12	Other arthrotomy of elbow
80.16	Other arthrotomy of knee
80.26	Arthroscopy of knee
80.6	Excision of semilunar cartilage of knee
80.82	Other local excision or destruction of lesion of elbow joint
80.88	Other local excision or destruction of lesion of joint of foot and toe
80.98	Other excision of joint of foot and toe
81.11	Ankle fusion
81.23	Arthrodesis of shoulder
81.52	Partial hip replacement
81.53	Revision of hip replacement, not otherwise specified
82.21	Excision of lesion of tendon sheath of hand
82.33	Other tenonectomy of hand
83.13	Other tenotomy
83.31	Excision of lesion of tendon sheath
83.39	Excision of lesion of other soft tissue
83.65	Other suture of muscle or fascia
83.75	Tendon transfer or transplantation
83.79	Other muscle transposition
85.12	Open biopsy of breast
85.21	Local excision of lesion of breast
86.06	Insertion of totally implantable infusion pump
92.27	Implantation or insertion of radioactive elements

OR

Nonoperating Room Procedures

*92.3	Stereotactic radiosurgery

S DRG 293 Other Endocrine, Nutritional and Metabolic O.R. Procedures without CC

GMLOS 3.2 AMLOS 4.5 RW 1.3472 ☑ T

Select operating or nonoperating room procedures listed under DRG 292

MDC 10
ENDOCRINE, NUTRITIONAL AND METABOLIC DISEASES AND DISORDERS

The complete and up-to-date listing of ICD-9-CM diagnosis codes assigned to this MDC can be found online at www.ingenixonline.com/content/drg/resources.asp.

MEDICAL

M DRG 294 Diabetes, Age Greater than 35
GMLOS 3.3 AMLOS 4.3 RW 0.7652 ☑ T A

Principal Diagnosis

*250.0	Diabetes mellitus without mention of complication
*250.1	Diabetes with ketoacidosis
*250.2	Diabetes with hyperosmolarity
*250.3	Diabetes with other coma
*250.8	Diabetes with other specified manifestations
*250.9	Diabetes with unspecified complication
791.5	Glycosuria

M DRG 295 Diabetes, Age 0-35
GMLOS 2.8 AMLOS 3.7 RW 0.7267 ☑ A

Select principal diagnosis listed under DRG 294

M DRG 296 Nutritional and Miscellaneous Metabolic Disorders, Age Greater than 17 with CC
GMLOS 3.7 AMLOS 4.8 RW 0.8187 ☑ T ▽ CC A

Principal Diagnosis

251.0	Hypoglycemic coma
251.2	Hypoglycemia, unspecified
251.3	Postsurgical hypoinsulinemia
260	Kwashiorkor
261	Nutritional marasmus
262	Other severe protein-calorie malnutrition
*263	Other and unspecified protein-calorie malnutrition
264.8	Other manifestations of vitamin A deficiency
264.9	Unspecified vitamin A deficiency
*265	Thiamine and niacin deficiency states
*266	Deficiency of B-complex components
267	Ascorbic acid deficiency
268.9	Unspecified vitamin D deficiency
*269	Other nutritional deficiencies
275.2	Disorders of magnesium metabolism
*275.4	Disorders of calcium metabolism
*276	Disorders of fluid, electrolyte, and acid-base balance
277.00	Cystic fibrosis without mention of meconium ileus
277.09	Cystic fibrosis with other manifestations
*278	Overweight, obesity and other hyperalimentation
781.7	Tetany
*783	Symptoms concerning nutrition, metabolism, and development
*790.2	Abnormal glucose tolerance test
791.6	Acetonuria
V85.4	Body Mass Index 40 and over, adult

M DRG 297 Nutritional and Miscellaneous Metabolic Disorders, Age Greater than 17 without CC

GMLOS 2.5 AMLOS 3.1 RW 0.4879 ☑ T A

Select principal diagnosis listed under DRG 296

M DRG 298 Nutritional and Miscellaneous Metabolic Disorders, Age 0-17

GMLOS 2.5 AMLOS 3.9 RW 0.5486 ☑ A

Select principal diagnosis listed under DRG 296

M DRG 299 Inborn Errors of Metabolism

GMLOS 3.7 AMLOS 5.2 RW 1.0329

Principal Diagnosis

*270	Disorders of amino-acid transport and metabolism
271.0	Glycogenosis
271.1	Galactosemia
271.4	Renal glycosuria
271.8	Other specified disorders of carbohydrate transport and metabolism
271.9	Unspecified disorder of carbohydrate transport and metabolism
*272	Disorders of lipoid metabolism
273.4	Alpha-1-antitrypsin deficiency
275.0	Disorders of iron metabolism
275.1	Disorders of copper metabolism
275.3	Disorders of phosphorus metabolism
275.8	Other specified disorders of mineral metabolism
275.9	Unspecified disorder of mineral metabolism
277.1	Disorders of porphyrin metabolism
277.2	Other disorders of purine and pyrimidine metabolism
277.5	Mucopolysaccharidosis
277.6	Other deficiencies of circulating enzymes
277.7	Dysmetabolic Syndrome X
*277.8	Other specified disorders of metabolism
277.9	Unspecified disorder of metabolism

M DRG 300 Endocrine Disorders with CC

GMLOS 4.6 AMLOS 6.0 RW 1.0922 ☑ T CC

Principal Diagnosis

*017.5	Tuberculosis of thyroid gland
*017.6	Tuberculosis of adrenal glands
122.2	Echinococcus granulosus infection of thyroid
193	Malignant neoplasm of thyroid gland
194.0	Malignant neoplasm of adrenal gland
194.1	Malignant neoplasm of parathyroid gland
194.3	Malignant neoplasm of pituitary gland and craniopharyngeal duct
194.8	Malignant neoplasm of other endocrine glands and related structures
194.9	Malignant neoplasm of endocrine gland, site unspecified
198.7	Secondary malignant neoplasm of adrenal gland
211.7	Benign neoplasm of islets of Langerhans
226	Benign neoplasm of thyroid glands
227.0	Benign neoplasm of adrenal gland
227.1	Benign neoplasm of parathyroid gland
227.3	Benign neoplasm of pituitary gland and craniopharyngeal duct (pouch)
227.8	Benign neoplasm of other endocrine glands and related structures
227.9	Benign neoplasm of endocrine gland, site unspecified
237.0	Neoplasm of uncertain behavior of pituitary gland and craniopharyngeal duct
237.2	Neoplasm of uncertain behavior of adrenal gland
237.4	Neoplasm of uncertain behavior of other and unspecified endocrine glands
239.7	Neoplasm of unspecified nature of endocrine glands and other parts of nervous system
*240	Simple and unspecified goiter

***** Code Range* ☑ *Optimization Potential* *Targeted Potential* T *Transfer DRG* SP *Special Payment*

DRG 300 — continued

*241	Nontoxic nodular goiter
*242	Thyrotoxicosis with or without goiter
243	Congenital hypothyroidism
*244	Acquired hypothyroidism
*245	Thyroiditis
*246	Other disorders of thyroid
251.1	Other specified hypoglycemia
251.4	Abnormality of secretion of glucagon
251.8	Other specified disorders of pancreatic internal secretion
251.9	Unspecified disorder of pancreatic internal secretion
*252	Disorders of parathyroid gland
*253	Disorders of the pituitary gland and its hypothalamic control
*255	Disorders of adrenal glands
*257	Testicular dysfunction
*258	Polyglandular dysfunction and related disorders
*259	Other endocrine disorders
306.6	Endocrine malfunction arising from mental factors
759.1	Congenital anomalies of adrenal gland
759.2	Congenital anomalies of other endocrine glands
794.5	Nonspecific abnormal results of thyroid function study
794.6	Nonspecific abnormal results of other endocrine function study
794.7	Nonspecific abnormal results of basal metabolism function study
868.01	Adrenal gland injury without mention of open wound into cavity
868.11	Adrenal gland injury, with open wound into cavity
874.2	Open wound of thyroid gland, without mention of complication
874.3	Open wound of thyroid gland, complicated

M DRG 301 Endocrine Disorders without CC

GMLOS 2.7 AMLOS 3.4 RW 0.6118 ☑ T

Select principal diagnosis listed under DRG 300

MDC 11
DISEASES AND DISORDERS OF THE KIDNEY AND URINARY TRACT

The complete and up-to-date listing of ICD-9-CM diagnosis codes assigned to this MDC can be found online at www.ingenixonline.com/content/drg/resources.asp.

SURGICAL

SP DRG 302 Kidney Transplant
GMLOS 7.0 AMLOS 8.2 RW 3.1679

Operating Room Procedure

55.69	Other kidney transplantation

SP DRG 303 Kidney, Ureter and Major Bladder Procedures for Neoplasm
GMLOS 5.8 AMLOS 7.4 RW 2.2183

Principal Diagnosis

*188	Malignant neoplasm of bladder
*189	Malignant neoplasm of kidney and other and unspecified urinary organs
198.0	Secondary malignant neoplasm of kidney
198.1	Secondary malignant neoplasm of other urinary organs
*223	Benign neoplasm of kidney and other urinary organs
233.7	Carcinoma in situ of bladder
233.9	Carcinoma in situ of other and unspecified urinary organs
236.7	Neoplasm of uncertain behavior of bladder
*236.9	Neoplasm of uncertain behavior of other and unspecified urinary organs
239.4	Neoplasm of unspecified nature of bladder
239.5	Neoplasm of unspecified nature of other genitourinary organs

Operating Room Procedures

39.24	Aorta-renal bypass
39.26	Other intra-abdominal vascular shunt or bypass
39.55	Reimplantation of aberrant renal vessel
40.52	Radical excision of periaortic lymph nodes
40.53	Radical excision of iliac lymph nodes
40.54	Radical groin dissection
40.59	Radical excision of other lymph nodes
*55.0	Nephrotomy and nephrostomy
*55.1	Pyelotomy and pyelostomy
55.24	Open biopsy of kidney
55.29	Other diagnostic procedures on kidney
*55.3	Local excision or destruction of lesion or tissue of kidney
55.4	Partial nephrectomy
*55.5	Complete nephrectomy
55.61	Renal autotransplantation
55.7	Nephropexy
*55.8	Other repair of kidney
55.91	Decapsulation of kidney
55.97	Implantation or replacement of mechanical kidney
55.98	Removal of mechanical kidney
55.99	Other operations on kidney
56.1	Ureteral meatotomy
56.2	Ureterotomy
56.34	Open biopsy of ureter
56.39	Other diagnostic procedures on ureter
*56.4	Ureterectomy
*56.5	Cutaneous uretero-ileostomy
*56.6	Other external urinary diversion
*56.7	Other anastomosis or bypass of ureter

DRG 303 — continued

*56.8	Repair of ureter
56.92	Implantation of electronic ureteral stimulator
56.93	Replacement of electronic ureteral stimulator
56.94	Removal of electronic ureteral stimulator
56.95	Ligation of ureter
56.99	Other operations on ureter
*57.7	Total cystectomy
57.87	Reconstruction of urinary bladder
59.00	Retroperitoneal dissection, not otherwise specified
59.02	Other lysis of perirenal or periureteral adhesions
59.03	Laparoscopic lysis of perirenal or periureteral adhesions
59.09	Other incision of perirenal or periureteral tissue

S DRG 304 Kidney, Ureter and Major Bladder Procedures for Non-neoplasms with CC

GMLOS 6.1 AMLOS 8.6 RW 2.3761 ☑ T CC

Select operating room procedures listed under DRG 303

S DRG 305 Kidney, Ureter and Major Bladder Procedures for Non-neoplasms without CC

GMLOS 2.6 AMLOS 3.2 RW 1.1595 ☑ T

Select operating room procedures listed under DRG 303

S DRG 306 Prostatectomy with CC

GMLOS 3.6 AMLOS 5.5 RW 1.2700 CC

Operating Room Procedures

*60.2	Transurethral prostatectomy
60.3	Suprapubic prostatectomy
60.4	Retropubic prostatectomy
60.5	Radical prostatectomy
60.62	Perineal prostatectomy
60.69	Other prostatectomy
60.96	Transurethral destruction of prostate tissue by microwave thermotherapy
60.97	Other transurethral destruction of prostate tissue by other thermotherapy

S DRG 307 Prostatectomy without CC

GMLOS 1.7 AMLOS 2.1 RW 0.6202 ☑

Select operating room procedures listed under DRG 306

S DRG 308 Minor Bladder Procedures with CC

GMLOS 3.9 AMLOS 6.1 RW 1.6349 ☑ CC

Operating Room Procedures

57.12	Lysis of intraluminal adhesions with incision into bladder
57.18	Other suprapubic cystostomy
57.19	Other cystotomy
*57.2	Vesicostomy
57.34	Open biopsy of bladder
57.39	Other diagnostic procedures on bladder
*57.5	Other excision or destruction of bladder tissue
57.6	Partial cystectomy
57.81	Suture of laceration of bladder
57.82	Closure of cystostomy
57.83	Repair of fistula involving bladder and intestine
57.84	Repair of other fistula of bladder
57.85	Cystourethroplasty and plastic repair of bladder neck
57.86	Repair of bladder exstrophy
57.88	Other anastomosis of bladder

57.89	Other repair of bladder
57.91	Sphincterotomy of bladder
57.93	Control of (postoperative) hemorrhage of bladder
57.96	Implantation of electronic bladder stimulator
57.97	Replacement of electronic bladder stimulator
57.98	Removal of electronic bladder stimulator
57.99	Other operations on bladder
58.93	Implantation of artificial urinary sphincter (AUS)
*59.1	Incision of perivesical tissue
*59.2	Diagnostic procedures on perirenal and perivesical tissue
59.3	Plication of urethrovesical junction
59.4	Suprapubic sling operation
59.5	Retropubic urethral suspension
59.6	Paraurethral suspension
59.71	Levator muscle operation for urethrovesical suspension
59.79	Other repair of urinary stress incontinence
59.91	Excision of perirenal or perivesical tissue
59.92	Other operations on perirenal or perivesical tissue
70.50	Repair of cystocele and rectocele
70.51	Repair of cystocele
70.77	Vaginal suspension and fixation

S DRG 309 Minor Bladder Procedures without CC

GMLOS 1.6 AMLOS 2.0 RW 0.9085 ☑

Select operating room procedures listed under DRG 308

S DRG 310 Transurethral Procedures with CC

GMLOS 3.0 AMLOS 4.5 RW 1.1898 ☑ CC

Operating Room Procedures

56.0	Transurethral removal of obstruction from ureter and renal pelvis
57.33	Closed (transurethral) biopsy of bladder
*57.4	Transurethral excision or destruction of bladder tissue
60.12	Open biopsy of prostate
60.95	Transurethral balloon dilation of the prostatic urethra

S DRG 311 Transurethral Procedures without CC

GMLOS 1.5 AMLOS 1.9 RW 0.6432 ☑

Select operating room procedures listed under DRG 310

S DRG 312 Urethral Procedures, Age Greater than 17 with CC

GMLOS 3.2 AMLOS 4.8 RW 1.1159 ☑ CC A

Operating Room Procedures

58.0	Urethrotomy
58.1	Urethral meatotomy
*58.4	Repair of urethra
58.5	Release of urethral stricture
58.91	Incision of periurethral tissue
58.92	Excision of periurethral tissue
58.99	Other operations on urethra and periurethral tissue

S DRG 313 Urethral Procedures, Age Greater than 17 without CC

GMLOS 1.7 AMLOS 2.2 RW 0.6783 ☑ A

Select operating room procedures listed under DRG 312

S DRG 314 Urethral Procedures, Age 0-17

GMLOS 2.3 AMLOS 2.3 RW 0.5012 ☑ A

Select operating room procedures listed under DRG 312

** Code Range* ☑ *Optimization Potential* *Targeted Potential* T *Transfer DRG* SP *Special Payment*

S DRG 315 Other Kidney and Urinary Tract O.R. Procedures
GMLOS 3.6 AMLOS 6.8 RW 2.0823

Operating Room Procedures

03.93	Implantation or replacement of spinal neurostimulator lead(s)
03.94	Removal of spinal neurostimulator lead(s)
04.92	Implantation or replacement of peripheral neurostimulator lead(s)
*06.8	Parathyroidectomy
33.28	Open biopsy of lung
34.02	Exploratory thoracotomy
38.06	Incision of abdominal arteries
38.07	Incision of abdominal veins
38.16	Endarterectomy of abdominal arteries
38.21	Biopsy of blood vessel
38.36	Resection of abdominal arteries with anastomosis
38.37	Resection of abdominal veins with anastomosis
38.46	Resection of abdominal arteries with replacement
38.47	Resection of abdominal veins with replacement
38.66	Other excision of abdominal arteries
38.67	Other excision of abdominal veins
38.7	Interruption of the vena cava
38.86	Other surgical occlusion of abdominal arteries
38.87	Other surgical occlusion of abdominal veins
39.27	Arteriovenostomy for renal dialysis
39.42	Revision of arteriovenous shunt for renal dialysis
39.43	Removal of arteriovenous shunt for renal dialysis
39.49	Other revision of vascular procedure
39.50	Angioplasty or atherectomy of other non-coronary vessel(s)
39.52	Other repair of aneurysm
39.56	Repair of blood vessel with tissue patch graft
39.57	Repair of blood vessel with synthetic patch graft
39.58	Repair of blood vessel with unspecified type of patch graft
39.59	Other repair of vessel
39.71	Endovascular implantation of graft in abdominal aorta
39.72	Endovascular repair or occlusion of head and neck vessels
39.73	Endovascular implantation of graft in thoracic aorta
39.79	Other endovascular repair (of aneurysm) of other vessels
39.93	Insertion of vessel-to-vessel cannula
39.94	Replacement of vessel-to-vessel cannula
39.98	Control of hemorrhage, not otherwise specified
40.11	Biopsy of lymphatic structure
40.19	Other diagnostic procedures on lymphatic structures
40.24	Excision of inguinal lymph node
40.29	Simple excision of other lymphatic structure
40.3	Regional lymph node excision
40.50	Radical excision of lymph nodes, not otherwise specified
40.9	Other operations on lymphatic structures
50.12	Open biopsy of liver
50.19	Other diagnostic procedures on liver
54.0	Incision of abdominal wall
*54.1	Laparotomy
54.21	Laparoscopy
*54.5	Lysis of peritoneal adhesions
54.92	Removal of foreign body from peritoneal cavity
54.93	Creation of cutaneoperitoneal fistula
54.95	Incision of peritoneum
64.0	Circumcision
64.95	Insertion or replacement of non-inflatable penile prosthesis
64.96	Removal of internal prosthesis of penis
64.97	Insertion or replacement of inflatable penile prosthesis
*77.4	Biopsy of bone
86.06	Insertion of totally implantable infusion pump
86.22	Excisional debridement of wound, infection, or burn

92.27	Implantation or insertion of radioactive elements

OR

Nonoperating Room Procedures

52.84	Autotransplantation of cells of islets of Langerhans
52.85	Allotransplantation of cells of islets of Langerhans

OR

Principal Diagnosis

403.01	Hypertensive kidney disease, malignant, with chronic kidney disease
403.11	Hypertensive kidney disease, benign, with chronic kidney disease
403.91	Hypertensive kidney disease, unspecified, with chronic kidney disease
404.02	Hypertensive heart and kidney disease, malignant, with chronic kidney disease
404.12	Hypertensive heart and kidney disease, benign, with chronic kidney disease
404.92	Hypertensive heart and kidney disease, unspecified, with chronic kidney disease
584.5	Acute renal failure with lesion of tubular necrosis
584.6	Acute renal failure with lesion of renal cortical necrosis
584.7	Acute renal failure with lesion of renal medullary (papillary) necrosis
584.8	Acute renal failure with other specified pathological lesion in kidney
584.9	Unspecified acute renal failure
*585	Chronic kidney disease (CKD)
586	Unspecified renal failure
788.5	Oliguria and anuria
958.5	Traumatic anuria

AND

Nonoperating Room Procedure

86.07	Insertion of totally implantable vascular access device (VAD)

MDC 11
DISEASES AND DISORDERS OF THE KIDNEY AND URINARY TRACT

The complete and up-to-date listing of ICD-9-CM diagnosis codes assigned to this MDC can be found online at www.ingenixonline.com/content/drg/resources.asp.

MEDICAL

Ⓜ DRG 316 Renal Failure
GMLOS 4.9 AMLOS 6.4 RW 1.2692 ☑ T ▽

Principal Diagnosis

403.01	Hypertensive kidney disease, malignant, with chronic kidney disease
403.11	Hypertensive kidney disease, benign, with chronic kidney disease
403.91	Hypertensive kidney disease, unspecified, with chronic kidney disease
404.02	Hypertensive heart and kidney disease, malignant, with chronic kidney disease
404.12	Hypertensive heart and kidney disease, benign, with chronic kidney disease
404.92	Hypertensive heart and kidney disease, unspecified, with chronic kidney disease
584.5	Acute renal failure with lesion of tubular necrosis
584.6	Acute renal failure with lesion of renal cortical necrosis
584.7	Acute renal failure with lesion of renal medullary (papillary) necrosis
584.8	Acute renal failure with other specified pathological lesion in kidney
584.9	Unspecified acute renal failure
*585	Chronic kidney disease (CKD)
586	Unspecified renal failure
788.5	Oliguria and anuria
958.5	Traumatic anuria

Ⓜ DRG 317 Admission for Renal Dialysis
GMLOS 2.4 AMLOS 3.5 RW 0.7942 ☑

Principal Diagnosis

*V56	Encounter for dialysis and dialysis catheter care

Ⓜ DRG 318 Kidney and Urinary Tract Neoplasms with CC
GMLOS 4.2 AMLOS 5.8 RW 1.1539 ☑ CC

Principal Diagnosis

*188	Malignant neoplasm of bladder
*189	Malignant neoplasm of kidney and other and unspecified urinary organs
198.0	Secondary malignant neoplasm of kidney
198.1	Secondary malignant neoplasm of other urinary organs
*223	Benign neoplasm of kidney and other urinary organs
233.7	Carcinoma in situ of bladder
233.9	Carcinoma in situ of other and unspecified urinary organs
236.7	Neoplasm of uncertain behavior of bladder
*236.9	Neoplasm of uncertain behavior of other and unspecified urinary organs
239.4	Neoplasm of unspecified nature of bladder
239.5	Neoplasm of unspecified nature of other genitourinary organs

Ⓜ DRG 319 Kidney and Urinary Tract Neoplasms without CC
GMLOS 2.1 AMLOS 2.8 RW 0.6385 ☑

Select principal diagnosis listed under DRG 318

M DRG 320 Kidney and Urinary Tract Infections, Age Greater than 17 with CC

GMLOS 4.2 AMLOS 5.2 RW 0.8658 ☑ T YIELD CC A

Principal Diagnosis

*016.0	Tuberculosis of kidney
*016.1	Tuberculosis of bladder
*016.2	Tuberculosis of ureter
*016.3	Tuberculosis of other urinary organs
*016.9	Genitourinary tuberculosis, unspecified
032.84	Diphtheritic cystitis
078.6	Hemorrhagic nephrosonephritis
095.4	Syphilis of kidney
098.11	Gonococcal cystitis (acute)
098.30	Chronic gonococcal infection of upper genitourinary tract, site unspecified
098.31	Gonococcal cystitis, chronic
099.54	Chlamydia trachomatis infection of other genitourinary sites
120.0	Schistosomiasis due to schistosoma haematobium
137.2	Late effects of genitourinary tuberculosis
*590	Infections of kidney
593.3	Stricture or kinking of ureter
595.0	Acute cystitis
595.1	Chronic interstitial cystitis
595.2	Other chronic cystitis
595.3	Trigonitis
595.4	Cystitis in diseases classified elsewhere
595.81	Cystitis cystica
595.89	Other specified types of cystitis
595.9	Unspecified cystitis
*597	Urethritis, not sexually transmitted, and urethral syndrome
599.0	Urinary tract infection, site not specified

M DRG 321 Kidney and Urinary Tract Infections, Age Greater than 17 without CC

GMLOS 3.0 AMLOS 3.6 RW 0.5652 ☑ T A

Select principal diagnosis listed under DRG 320

M DRG 322 Kidney and Urinary Tract Infections, Age 0-17

GMLOS 2.9 AMLOS 3.4 RW 0.5498 ☑ A

Select principal diagnosis listed under DRG 320

M DRG 323 Urinary Stones with CC and/or ESW Lithotripsy

GMLOS 2.3 AMLOS 3.1 RW 0.8214 ☑ CC

Principal Diagnosis

274.11	Uric acid nephrolithiasis
591	Hydronephrosis
*592	Calculus of kidney and ureter
593.4	Other ureteric obstruction
593.5	Hydroureter
594.1	Other calculus in bladder
594.2	Calculus in urethra
594.8	Other lower urinary tract calculus
594.9	Unspecified calculus of lower urinary tract
788.0	Renal colic

WITH OR WITHOUT

Nonoperating Room Procedure

98.51	Extracorporeal shockwave lithotripsy (ESWL) of the kidney, ureter and/or bladder

*** Code Range** ☑ ***Optimization Potential*** YIELD ***Targeted Potential*** T ***Transfer DRG*** SP ***Special Payment***

Ⓜ DRG 324 Urinary Stones without CC

GMLOS 1.6 AMLOS 1.9 RW 0.5050 ☑

Select principal diagnosis listed under DRG 323

Ⓜ DRG 325 Kidney and Urinary Tract Signs and Symptoms, Age Greater than 17 with CC

GMLOS 2.9 AMLOS 3.7 RW 0.6436 ☑ CC A

Principal Diagnosis

599.7	Hematuria
788.1	Dysuria
*788.2	Retention of urine
*788.3	Urinary incontinence
*788.4	Frequency of urination and polyuria
*788.6	Other abnormality of urination
788.7	Urethral discharge
788.8	Extravasation of urine
788.9	Other symptoms involving urinary system
791.0	Proteinuria
791.1	Chyluria
791.2	Hemoglobinuria
791.7	Other cells and casts in urine
791.9	Other nonspecific finding on examination of urine
793.5	Nonspecific abnormal findings on radiological and other examination of genitourinary organs
794.4	Nonspecific abnormal results of kidney function study
794.9	Nonspecific abnormal results of other specified function study

Ⓜ DRG 326 Kidney and Urinary Tract Signs and Symptoms, Age Greater than 17 without CC

GMLOS 2.1 AMLOS 2.6 RW 0.4391 ☑ A

Select principal diagnosis listed under DRG 325

Ⓜ DRG 327 Kidney and Urinary Tract Signs and Symptoms, Age 0-17

GMLOS 3.1 AMLOS 3.1 RW 0.3748 ☑ A

Select principal diagnosis listed under DRG 325

Ⓜ DRG 328 Urethral Stricture, Age Greater than 17 with CC

GMLOS 2.6 AMLOS 3.5 RW 0.7079 ☑ CC A

Principal Diagnosis

*598	Urethral stricture

Ⓜ DRG 329 Urethral Stricture, Age Greater than 17 without CC

GMLOS 1.5 AMLOS 1.8 RW 0.4701 ☑ A

Select principal diagnosis listed under DRG 328

Ⓜ DRG 330 Urethral Stricture, Age 0-17

GMLOS 1.6 AMLOS 1.6 RW 0.3227 ☑ A

Select principal diagnosis listed under DRG 328

Ⓜ DRG 331 Other Kidney and Urinary Tract Diagnoses, Age Greater than 17 with CC

GMLOS 4.1 AMLOS 5.5 RW 1.0619 ☑ T ▽ CC A

Principal Diagnosis

*250.4	Diabetes with renal manifestations
274.10	Gouty nephropathy, unspecified
274.19	Other gouty nephropathy
306.50	Psychogenic genitourinary malfunction, unspecified

306.53	Psychogenic dysuria
306.59	Other genitourinary malfunction arising from mental factors
344.61	Cauda equina syndrome with neurogenic bladder
403.00	Hypertensive kidney disease, malignant, without chronic kidney disease
403.10	Hypertensive kidney disease, benign, without chronic kidney disease
403.90	Hypertensive kidney disease, unspecified, without chronic kidney disease
440.1	Atherosclerosis of renal artery
442.1	Aneurysm of renal artery
443.23	Dissection of renal artery
445.81	Atheroembolism of kidney
447.3	Hyperplasia of renal artery
453.3	Embolism and thrombosis of renal vein
*580	Acute glomerulonephritis
*581	Nephrotic syndrome
*582	Chronic glomerulonephritis
*583	Nephritis and nephropathy, not specified as acute or chronic
587	Unspecified renal sclerosis
*588	Disorders resulting from impaired renal function
*589	Small kidney of unknown cause
593.0	Nephroptosis
593.1	Hypertrophy of kidney
593.2	Acquired cyst of kidney
593.6	Postural proteinuria
*593.7	Vesicoureteral reflux
*593.8	Other specified disorders of kidney and ureter
593.9	Unspecified disorder of kidney and ureter
594.0	Calculus in diverticulum of bladder
595.82	Irradiation cystitis
*596	Other disorders of bladder
599.1	Urethral fistula
599.2	Urethral diverticulum
599.3	Urethral caruncle
599.4	Urethral false passage
599.5	Prolapsed urethral mucosa
*599.6	Urinary obstruction
*599.8	Other specified disorder of urethra and urinary tract
599.9	Unspecified disorder of urethra and urinary tract
*753	Congenital anomalies of urinary system
*866	Injury to kidney
867.0	Bladder and urethra injury without mention of open wound into cavity
867.1	Bladder and urethra injury with open wound into cavity
867.2	Ureter injury without mention of open wound into cavity
867.3	Ureter injury with open wound into cavity
868.04	Retroperitoneum injury without mention of open wound into cavity
868.14	Retroperitoneum injury with open wound into cavity
939.0	Foreign body in bladder and urethra
939.9	Foreign body in unspecified site in genitourinary tract
996.30	Mechanical complication of unspecified genitourinary device, implant, and graft
996.31	Mechanical complication due to urethral (indwelling) catheter
996.39	Mechanical complication of genitourinary device, implant, and graft, other
996.64	Infection and inflammatory reaction due to indwelling urinary catheter
996.65	Infection and inflammatory reaction due to other genitourinary device, implant, and graft
996.76	Other complications due to genitourinary device, implant, and graft
996.81	Complications of transplanted kidney
997.5	Urinary complications
997.72	Vascular complications of renal artery
V42.0	Kidney replaced by transplant
V43.5	Bladder replaced by other means
V45.74	Acquired absence of organ, other parts of urinary tract
V53.6	Fitting and adjustment of urinary device
V55.5	Attention to cystostomy
V55.6	Attention to other artificial opening of urinary tract
V59.4	Kidney donor

***** Code Range ☑ **Optimization Potential** ▽ **Targeted Potential** T **Transfer DRG** SP **Special Payment**

Ⓜ DRG 332 Other Kidney and Urinary Tract Diagnoses, Age Greater than 17 without CC

GMLOS 2.4 AMLOS 3.1 RW 0.6160 ☑ Ⓣ Ⓐ

Select principal diagnosis listed under DRG 331

Ⓜ DRG 333 Other Kidney and Urinary Tract Diagnoses, Age 0-17

GMLOS 3.5 AMLOS 5.3 RW 0.9669 ☑ Ⓐ

Select principal diagnosis listed under DRG 331

MDC 12
DISEASES AND DISORDERS OF THE MALE REPRODUCTIVE SYSTEM

The complete and up-to-date listing of ICD-9-CM diagnosis codes assigned to this MDC can be found online at www.ingenixonline.com/content/drg/resources.asp.

SURGICAL

SP DRG 334 Major Male Pelvic Procedures with CC
GMLOS 3.5 AMLOS 4.3 RW 1.4368 ☑ CC

Operating Room Procedures

40.52	Radical excision of periaortic lymph nodes
40.53	Radical excision of iliac lymph nodes
40.54	Radical groin dissection
40.59	Radical excision of other lymph nodes
48.69	Other resection of rectum
54.11	Exploratory laparotomy
57.6	Partial cystectomy
*57.7	Total cystectomy
59.00	Retroperitoneal dissection, not otherwise specified
60.3	Suprapubic prostatectomy
60.4	Retropubic prostatectomy
60.5	Radical prostatectomy
60.62	Perineal prostatectomy
60.69	Other prostatectomy

SP DRG 335 Major Male Pelvic Procedures without CC
GMLOS 2.4 AMLOS 2.7 RW 1.1004 ☑

Select operating room procedures listed under DRG 334

SP DRG 336 Transurethral Prostatectomy with CC
GMLOS 2.5 AMLOS 3.3 RW 0.8425 ☑ CC

Operating Room Procedure

*60.2	Transurethral prostatectomy
60.96	Transurethral destruction of prostate tissue by microwave thermotherapy
60.97	Other transurethral destruction of prostate tissue by other thermotherapy

SP DRG 337 Transurethral Prostatectomy without CC
GMLOS 1.7 AMLOS 1.9 RW 0.5747 ☑

Select operating room procedure listed under DRG 336

SP DRG 338 Testes Procedures for Malignancy
GMLOS 3.9 AMLOS 6.2 RW 1.3772

Principal Diagnosis

185	Malignant neoplasm of prostate
*186	Malignant neoplasm of testis
*187	Malignant neoplasm of penis and other male genital organs
195.3	Malignant neoplasm of pelvis
198.82	Secondary malignant neoplasm of genital organs
233.4	Carcinoma in situ of prostate
233.5	Carcinoma in situ of penis
233.6	Carcinoma in situ of other and unspecified male genital organs
236.4	Neoplasm of uncertain behavior of testis
236.5	Neoplasm of uncertain behavior of prostate
236.6	Neoplasm of uncertain behavior of other and unspecified male genital organs

DRG 338 — continued

AND

Operating Room Procedures

61.2	Excision of hydrocele (of tunica vaginalis)
61.42	Repair of scrotal fistula
61.49	Other repair of scrotum and tunica vaginalis
61.92	Excision of lesion of tunica vaginalis other than hydrocele
61.99	Other operations on scrotum and tunica vaginalis
62.0	Incision of testis
62.12	Open biopsy of testis
62.19	Other diagnostic procedures on testes
62.2	Excision or destruction of testicular lesion
62.3	Unilateral orchiectomy
*62.4	Bilateral orchiectomy
62.5	Orchiopexy
*62.6	Repair of testes
62.7	Insertion of testicular prosthesis
62.99	Other operations on testes
63.09	Other diagnostic procedures on spermatic cord, epididymis, and vas deferens
63.1	Excision of varicocele and hydrocele of spermatic cord
63.2	Excision of cyst of epididymis
63.3	Excision of other lesion or tissue of spermatic cord and epididymis
63.4	Epididymectomy
63.51	Suture of laceration of spermatic cord and epididymis
63.53	Transplantation of spermatic cord
63.59	Other repair of spermatic cord and epididymis
63.81	Suture of laceration of vas deferens and epididymis
63.82	Reconstruction of surgically divided vas deferens
63.83	Epididymovasostomy
63.85	Removal of valve from vas deferens
63.89	Other repair of vas deferens and epididymis
63.92	Epididymotomy
63.93	Incision of spermatic cord
63.94	Lysis of adhesions of spermatic cord
63.95	Insertion of valve in vas deferens
63.99	Other operations on spermatic card, epididymis, and vas deferens

S DRG 339 Testes Procedures for Nonmalignancy, Age Greater than 17

GMLOS 3.2 AMLOS 5.1 RW 1.1866 ☑ A

Select operating room procedures listed under DRG 338

S DRG 340 Testes Procedures for Nonmalignancy, Age 0-17

GMLOS 2.4 AMLOS 2.4 RW 0.2868 ☑ A

Select operating room procedures listed under DRG 338

S DRG 341 Penis Procedures

GMLOS 1.9 AMLOS 3.2 RW 1.2622

Operating Room Procedures

58.43	Closure of other fistula of urethra
58.45	Repair of hypospadias or epispadias
58.46	Other reconstruction of urethra
58.49	Other repair of urethra
58.5	Release of urethral stricture
64.11	Biopsy of penis
64.2	Local excision or destruction of lesion of penis
64.3	Amputation of penis
*64.4	Repair and plastic operation on penis
64.5	Operations for sex transformation, not elsewhere classified
64.92	Incision of penis
64.93	Division of penile adhesions

64.95	Insertion or replacement of non-inflatable penile prosthesis
64.96	Removal of internal prosthesis of penis
64.97	Insertion or replacement of inflatable penile prosthesis
64.98	Other operations on penis
64.99	Other operations on male genital organs

S DRG 342 Circumcision, Age Greater than 17

GMLOS 2.5 AMLOS 3.4 RW 0.8737 A

Operating Room Procedure

64.0	Circumcision

S DRG 343 Circumcision, Age 0-17

GMLOS 1.7 AMLOS 1.7 RW 0.1559 ☑ A

Select operating room procedure listed under DRG 342

S DRG 344 Other Male Reproductive System O.R. Procedures for Malignancy

GMLOS 1.7 AMLOS 2.7 RW 1.2475

Principal Diagnosis

185	Malignant neoplasm of prostate
*186	Malignant neoplasm of testis
*187	Malignant neoplasm of penis and other male genital organs
195.3	Malignant neoplasm of pelvis
198.82	Secondary malignant neoplasm of genital organs
233.4	Carcinoma in situ of prostate
233.5	Carcinoma in situ of penis
233.6	Carcinoma in situ of other and unspecified male genital organs
236.4	Neoplasm of uncertain behavior of testis
236.5	Neoplasm of uncertain behavior of prostate
236.6	Neoplasm of uncertain behavior of other and unspecified male genital organs

Operating Room Procedures

03.93	Implantation or replacement of spinal neurostimulator lead(s)
03.94	Removal of spinal neurostimulator lead(s)
04.92	Implantation or replacement of peripheral neurostimulator lead(s)
04.93	Removal of peripheral neurostimulator lead(s)
38.7	Interruption of the vena cava
39.98	Control of hemorrhage, not otherwise specified
*40.1	Diagnostic procedures on lymphatic structures
40.24	Excision of inguinal lymph node
40.29	Simple excision of other lymphatic structure
40.3	Regional lymph node excision
40.50	Radical excision of lymph nodes, not otherwise specified
40.9	Other operations on lymphatic structures
50.12	Open biopsy of liver
56.41	Partial ureterectomy
*56.5	Cutaneous uretero-ileostomy
*56.6	Other external urinary diversion
56.71	Urinary diversion to intestine
56.72	Revision of ureterointestinal anastomosis
56.73	Nephrocystanastomosis, not otherwise specified
56.75	Transureteroureterostomy
56.83	Closure of ureterostomy
56.84	Closure of other fistula of ureter
57.18	Other suprapubic cystostomy
*57.2	Vesicostomy
57.33	Closed (transurethral) biopsy of bladder
57.34	Open biopsy of bladder
57.39	Other diagnostic procedures on bladder
57.49	Other transurethral excision or destruction of lesion or tissue of bladder
*57.5	Other excision or destruction of bladder tissue

** Code Range ☑ Optimization Potential ▽ Targeted Potential T Transfer DRG SP Special Payment*

DRG 344 — continued

57.82	Closure of cystostomy
57.83	Repair of fistula involving bladder and intestine
57.84	Repair of other fistula of bladder
57.88	Other anastomosis of bladder
58.1	Urethral meatotomy
58.47	Urethral meatoplasty
58.99	Other operations on urethra and periurethral tissue
59.02	Other lysis of perirenal or periureteral adhesions
59.03	Laparoscopic lysis of perirenal or periureteral adhesions
59.09	Other incision of perirenal or periureteral tissue
*59.1	Incision of perivesical tissue
*59.2	Diagnostic procedures on perirenal and perivesical tissue
59.91	Excision of perirenal or perivesical tissue
59.92	Other operations on perirenal or perivesical tissue
60.0	Incision of prostate
60.12	Open biopsy of prostate
60.14	Open biopsy of seminal vesicles
60.15	Biopsy of periprostatic tissue
60.18	Other diagnostic procedures on prostate and periprostatic tissue
60.19	Other diagnostic procedures on seminal vesicles
60.61	Local excision of lesion of prostate
60.72	Incision of seminal vesicle
60.73	Excision of seminal vesicle
60.79	Other operations on seminal vesicles
*60.8	Incision or excision of periprostatic tissue
60.93	Repair of prostate
60.94	Control of (postoperative) hemorrhage of prostate
60.95	Transurethral balloon dilation of the prostatic urethra
60.99	Other operations on prostate
*77.4	Biopsy of bone
86.06	Insertion of totally implantable infusion pump
86.22	Excisional debridement of wound, infection, or burn
92.27	Implantation or insertion of radioactive elements

S DRG 345 Other Male Reproductive System O.R. Procedures Except for Malignancy

GMLOS 3.1 AMLOS 4.8 RW 1.1472 ☑

Select operating room procedures listed under DRG 344

MDC 12
DISEASES AND DISORDERS OF THE MALE REPRODUCTIVE SYSTEM

The complete and up-to-date listing of ICD-9-CM diagnosis codes assigned to this MDC can be found online at www.ingenixonline.com/content/drg/resources.asp.

MEDICAL

M DRG 346 Malignancy of Male Reproductive System with CC

GMLOS 4.2 AMLOS 5.7 RW 1.0441 ☑ CC

Principal Diagnosis

185	Malignant neoplasm of prostate
*186	Malignant neoplasm of testis
*187	Malignant neoplasm of penis and other male genital organs
195.3	Malignant neoplasm of pelvis
198.82	Secondary malignant neoplasm of genital organs
233.4	Carcinoma in situ of prostate
233.5	Carcinoma in situ of penis
233.6	Carcinoma in situ of other and unspecified male genital organs
236.4	Neoplasm of uncertain behavior of testis
236.5	Neoplasm of uncertain behavior of prostate
236.6	Neoplasm of uncertain behavior of other and unspecified male genital organs

M DRG 347 Malignancy of Male Reproductive System without CC

GMLOS 2.2 AMLOS 3.1 RW 0.6104 ☑

Select principal diagnosis listed under DRG 346

M DRG 348 Benign Prostatic Hypertrophy with CC

GMLOS 3.2 AMLOS 4.1 RW 0.7188 ☑ CC

Principal Diagnosis

*600	Hyperplasia of prostate

M DRG 349 Benign Prostatic Hypertrophy without CC

GMLOS 1.9 AMLOS 2.4 RW 0.4210 ☑

Select principal diagnosis listed under DRG 348

M DRG 350 Inflammation of the Male Reproductive System

GMLOS 3.5 AMLOS 4.5 RW 0.7289 ☑

Principal Diagnosis

*016.4	Tuberculosis of epididymis
*016.5	Tuberculosis of other male genital organs
054.10	Unspecified genital herpes
054.13	Herpetic infection of penis
054.19	Other genital herpes
072.0	Mumps orchitis
091.0	Genital syphilis (primary)
098.0	Gonococcal infection (acute) of lower genitourinary tract
098.10	Gonococcal infection (acute) of upper genitourinary tract, site unspecified
098.12	Gonococcal prostatitis (acute)
098.13	Gonococcal epididymo-orchitis (acute)
098.14	Gonococcal seminal vesiculitis (acute)
098.19	Other gonococcal infections (acute) of upper genitourinary tract
098.2	Gonococcal infections, chronic, of lower genitourinary tract
098.32	Gonococcal prostatitis, chronic
098.33	Gonococcal epididymo-orchitis, chronic

DRG 350 — continued

098.34	Gonococcal seminal vesiculitis, chronic
098.39	Other chronic gonococcal infections of upper genitourinary tract
099.0	Chancroid
099.1	Lymphogranuloma venereum
099.2	Granuloma inguinale
*099.4	Other nongonococcal urethritis (NGU)
099.50	Chlamydia trachomatis infection of unspecified site
099.53	Chlamydia trachomatis infection of lower genitourinary sites
099.55	Chlamydia trachomatis infection of unspecified genitourinary site
099.59	Chlamydia trachomatis infection of other specified site
099.8	Other specified venereal diseases
099.9	Unspecified venereal disease
112.2	Candidiasis of other urogenital sites
131.00	Unspecified urogenital trichomoniasis
131.02	Trichomonal urethritis
131.03	Trichomonal prostatitis
131.09	Other urogenital trichomoniasis
*601	Inflammatory diseases of prostate
603.1	Infected hydrocele
*604	Orchitis and epididymitis
605	Redundant prepuce and phimosis
607.1	Balanoposthitis
607.2	Other inflammatory disorders of penis
607.81	Balanitis xerotica obliterans
608.0	Seminal vesiculitis
608.4	Other inflammatory disorder of male genital organs
V50.2	Routine or ritual circumcision

M DRG 351 Sterilization, Male

GMLOS 1.3 AMLOS 1.3 RW 0.2392

Principal Diagnosis

V25.2	Sterilization

M DRG 352 Other Male Reproductive System Diagnoses

GMLOS 2.9 AMLOS 4.0 RW 0.7360 ☑

Principal Diagnosis

214.4	Lipoma of spermatic cord
*222	Benign neoplasm of male genital organs
456.4	Scrotal varices
456.5	Pelvic varices
*602	Other disorders of prostate
603.0	Encysted hydrocele
603.8	Other specified type of hydrocele
603.9	Unspecified hydrocele
*606	Male infertility
607.0	Leukoplakia of penis
607.3	Priapism
607.82	Vascular disorders of penis
607.83	Edema of penis
607.84	Impotence of organic origin
607.85	Peyronie's disease
607.89	Other specified disorder of penis
607.9	Unspecified disorder of penis
608.1	Spermatocele
608.2	Torsion of testis
608.3	Atrophy of testis
*608.8	Other specified disorder of male genital organs
608.9	Unspecified disorder of male genital organs
698.1	Pruritus of genital organs
*752.5	Undescended and retractile testicle

*752.6	Hypospadias and epispadias and other penile anomalies
752.7	Indeterminate sex and pseudohermaphroditism
*752.8	Other specified congenital anomalies of genital organs
752.9	Unspecified congenital anomaly of genital organs
758.6	Gonadal dysgenesis
758.7	Klinefelter's syndrome
*758.8	Other conditions due to chromosome anomalies
792.2	Nonspecific abnormal finding in semen
867.6	Injury to other specified pelvic organs without mention of open wound into cavity
867.7	Injury to other specified pelvic organs with open wound into cavity
867.8	Injury to unspecified pelvic organ without mention of open wound into cavity
867.9	Injury to unspecified pelvic organ with open wound into cavity
878.0	Open wound of penis, without mention of complication
878.1	Open wound of penis, complicated
878.2	Open wound of scrotum and testes, without mention of complication
878.3	Open wound of scrotum and testes, complicated
878.8	Open wound of other and unspecified parts of genital organs, without mention of complication
878.9	Open wound of other and unspecified parts of genital organs, complicated
908.2	Late effect of internal injury to other internal organs
922.4	Contusion of genital organs
926.0	Crushing injury of external genitalia
939.3	Foreign body in penis
V26.0	Tuboplasty or vasoplasty after previous sterilization
V45.77	Acquired absence of organ, genital organs

MDC 13
DISEASES AND DISORDERS OF THE FEMALE REPRODUCTIVE SYSTEM

The complete and up-to-date listing of ICD-9-CM diagnosis codes assigned to this MDC can be found online at www.ingenixonline.com/content/drg/resources.asp.

SURGICAL

S DRG 353 Pelvic Evisceration, Radical Hysterectomy and Radical Vulvectomy

GMLOS 4.7 AMLOS 6.3 RW 1.8504

Operating Room Procedures

40.50	Radical excision of lymph nodes, not otherwise specified
40.52	Radical excision of periaortic lymph nodes
40.53	Radical excision of iliac lymph nodes
40.54	Radical groin dissection
40.59	Radical excision of other lymph nodes
68.6	Radical abdominal hysterectomy
68.7	Radical vaginal hysterectomy
68.8	Pelvic evisceration
71.5	Radical vulvectomy

S DRG 354 Uterine and Adnexa Procedures for Nonovarian/Adnexal Malignancy with CC

GMLOS 4.6 AMLOS 5.7 RW 1.5135 ☑ CC

Principal Diagnosis

179	Malignant neoplasm of uterus, part unspecified
*180	Malignant neoplasm of cervix uteri
181	Malignant neoplasm of placenta
*182	Malignant neoplasm of body of uterus
*184	Malignant neoplasm of other and unspecified female genital organs
195.3	Malignant neoplasm of pelvis
198.82	Secondary malignant neoplasm of genital organs
233.1	Carcinoma in situ of cervix uteri
233.2	Carcinoma in situ of other and unspecified parts of uterus
233.3	Carcinoma in situ of other and unspecified female genital organs
236.0	Neoplasm of uncertain behavior of uterus
236.1	Neoplasm of uncertain behavior of placenta
236.3	Neoplasm of uncertain behavior of other and unspecified female genital organs

Operating Room Procedures

*65	Operations on ovary
*66.0	Salpingotomy
*66.1	Diagnostic procedures on fallopian tubes
66.4	Total unilateral salpingectomy
*66.5	Total bilateral salpingectomy
66.61	Excision or destruction of lesion of fallopian tube
66.62	Salpingectomy with removal of tubal pregnancy
66.69	Other partial salpingectomy
*66.7	Repair of fallopian tube
66.92	Unilateral destruction or occlusion of fallopian tube
66.93	Implantation or replacement of prosthesis of fallopian tube
66.94	Removal of prosthesis of fallopian tube
66.96	Dilation of fallopian tube
66.97	Burying of fimbriae in uterine wall
66.99	Other operations on fallopian tubes
68.0	Hysterotomy
68.13	Open biopsy of uterus

68.14	Open biopsy of uterine ligaments
68.19	Other diagnostic procedures on uterus and supporting structures
68.23	Endometrial ablation
68.29	Other excision or destruction of lesion of uterus
*68.3	Subtotal abdominal hysterectomy
68.4	Total abdominal hysterectomy
*68.5	Vaginal hysterectomy
68.9	Other and unspecified hysterectomy
69.19	Other excision or destruction of uterus and supporting structures
69.3	Paracervical uterine denervation
*69.4	Uterine repair

S DRG 355 Uterine and Adnexa Procedures for Nonovarian/Adnexal Malignancy without CC

GMLOS 2.8 AMLOS 3.1 RW 0.8824 ☑

Select principal diagnosis with operating room procedure listed under DRG 354

S DRG 356 Female Reproductive System Reconstructive Procedures

GMLOS 1.7 AMLOS 1.9 RW 0.7428

Operating Room Procedures

57.85	Cystourethroplasty and plastic repair of bladder neck
59.4	Suprapubic sling operation
59.5	Retropubic urethral suspension
59.6	Paraurethral suspension
59.71	Levator muscle operation for urethrovesical suspension
59.79	Other repair of urinary stress incontinence
64.5	Operations for sex transformation, not elsewhere classified
*69.2	Repair of uterine supporting structures
69.98	Other operations on supporting structures of uterus
70.4	Obliteration and total excision of vagina
*70.5	Repair of cystocele and rectocele
*70.6	Vaginal construction and reconstruction
70.77	Vaginal suspension and fixation
70.8	Obliteration of vaginal vault

S DRG 357 Uterine and Adnexa Procedures for Ovarian or Adnexal Malignancy

GMLOS 6.5 AMLOS 8.1 RW 2.2237

Principal Diagnosis

*183	Malignant neoplasm of ovary and other uterine adnexa
198.6	Secondary malignant neoplasm of ovary
236.2	Neoplasm of uncertain behavior of ovary

Operating Room Procedures

*65	Operations on ovary
*66.0	Salpingotomy
*66.1	Diagnostic procedures on fallopian tubes
66.4	Total unilateral salpingectomy
*66.5	Total bilateral salpingectomy
66.61	Excision or destruction of lesion of fallopian tube
66.62	Salpingectomy with removal of tubal pregnancy
66.69	Other partial salpingectomy
*66.7	Repair of fallopian tube
66.92	Unilateral destruction or occlusion of fallopian tube
66.93	Implantation or replacement of prosthesis of fallopian tube
66.94	Removal of prosthesis of fallopian tube
66.96	Dilation of fallopian tube
66.97	Burying of fimbriae in uterine wall
66.99	Other operations on fallopian tubes
68.0	Hysterotomy

DRG 357 — continued

68.13	Open biopsy of uterus
68.14	Open biopsy of uterine ligaments
68.19	Other diagnostic procedures on uterus and supporting structures
68.23	Endometrial ablation
68.29	Other excision or destruction of lesion of uterus
*68.3	Subtotal abdominal hysterectomy
68.4	Total abdominal hysterectomy
*68.5	Vaginal hysterectomy
68.9	Other and unspecified hysterectomy
69.19	Other excision or destruction of uterus and supporting structures
69.3	Paracervical uterine denervation
*69.4	Uterine repair

S DRG 358 Uterine and Adnexa Procedures for Nonmalignancy with CC

GMLOS 3.2 AMLOS 4.0 RW 1.1448 ☑ CC

Principal Diagnosis

*016.6	Tuberculous oophoritis and salpingitis
*016.7	Tuberculosis of other female genital organs
054.10	Unspecified genital herpes
054.11	Herpetic vulvovaginitis
054.12	Herpetic ulceration of vulva
054.19	Other genital herpes
091.0	Genital syphilis (primary)
098.0	Gonococcal infection (acute) of lower genitourinary tract
098.10	Gonococcal infection (acute) of upper genitourinary tract, site unspecified
098.15	Gonococcal cervicitis (acute)
098.16	Gonococcal endometritis (acute)
098.17	Gonococcal salpingitis, specified as acute
098.19	Other gonococcal infections (acute) of upper genitourinary tract
098.2	Gonococcal infections, chronic, of lower genitourinary tract
098.35	Gonococcal cervicitis, chronic
098.36	Gonococcal endometritis, chronic
098.37	Gonococcal salpingitis (chronic)
098.39	Other chronic gonococcal infections of upper genitourinary tract
099.0	Chancroid
099.1	Lymphogranuloma venereum
099.2	Granuloma inguinale
*099.4	Other nongonococcal urethritis (NGU)
099.50	Chlamydia trachomatis infection of unspecified site
099.53	Chlamydia trachomatis infection of lower genitourinary sites
099.55	Chlamydia trachomatis infection of unspecified genitourinary site
099.59	Chlamydia trachomatis infection of other specified site
099.8	Other specified venereal diseases
099.9	Unspecified venereal disease
112.1	Candidiasis of vulva and vagina
112.2	Candidiasis of other urogenital sites
131.00	Unspecified urogenital trichomoniasis
131.01	Trichomonal vulvovaginitis
131.02	Trichomonal urethritis
131.09	Other urogenital trichomoniasis
*218	Uterine leiomyoma
*219	Other benign neoplasm of uterus
220	Benign neoplasm of ovary
*221	Benign neoplasm of other female genital organs
*256	Ovarian dysfunction
306.51	Psychogenic vaginismus
306.52	Psychogenic dysmenorrhea
456.5	Pelvic varices
456.6	Vulval varices

*614	Inflammatory disease of ovary, fallopian tube, pelvic cellular tissue, and peritoneum
*615	Inflammatory diseases of uterus, except cervix
616.0	Cervicitis and endocervicitis
*616.1	Vaginitis and vulvovaginitis
616.2	Cyst of Bartholin's gland
616.3	Abscess of Bartholin's gland
616.4	Other abscess of vulva
*616.5	Ulceration of vulva
616.8	Other specified inflammatory disease of cervix, vagina, and vulva
616.9	Unspecified inflammatory disease of cervix, vagina, and vulva
617.0	Endometriosis of uterus
617.1	Endometriosis of ovary
617.2	Endometriosis of fallopian tube
617.3	Endometriosis of pelvic peritoneum
617.4	Endometriosis of rectovaginal septum and vagina
617.8	Endometriosis of other specified sites
617.9	Endometriosis, site unspecified
*618	Genital prolapse
619.0	Urinary-genital tract fistula, female
619.2	Genital tract-skin fistula, female
619.8	Other specified fistula involving female genital tract
619.9	Unspecified fistula involving female genital tract
*620	Noninflammatory disorders of ovary, fallopian tube, and broad ligament
*621	Disorders of uterus, not elsewhere classified
*622	Noninflammatory disorders of cervix
*623	Noninflammatory disorders of vagina
*624	Noninflammatory disorders of vulva and perineum
*625	Pain and other symptoms associated with female genital organs
*626	Disorders of menstruation and other abnormal bleeding from female genital tract
*627	Menopausal and postmenopausal disorders
*628	Female infertility
*629	Other disorders of female genital organs
698.1	Pruritus of genital organs
752.0	Congenital anomalies of ovaries
752.10	Unspecified congenital anomaly of fallopian tubes and broad ligaments
752.11	Embryonic cyst of fallopian tubes and broad ligaments
752.19	Other congenital anomaly of fallopian tubes and broad ligaments
752.2	Congenital doubling of uterus
752.3	Other congenital anomaly of uterus
752.40	Unspecified congenital anomaly of cervix, vagina, and external female genitalia
752.41	Embryonic cyst of cervix, vagina, and external female genitalia
752.42	Imperforate hymen
752.49	Other congenital anomaly of cervix, vagina, and external female genitalia
752.7	Indeterminate sex and pseudohermaphroditism
752.89	Other specified anomalies of genital organs
752.9	Unspecified congenital anomaly of genital organs
758.6	Gonadal dysgenesis
*758.8	Other conditions due to chromosome anomalies
*795.0	Abnormal Papanicolaou smear of cervix and cervical HPV
867.4	Uterus injury without mention of open wound into cavity
867.5	Uterus injury with open wound into cavity
867.6	Injury to other specified pelvic organs without mention of open wound into cavity
867.7	Injury to other specified pelvic organs with open wound into cavity
867.8	Injury to unspecified pelvic organ without mention of open wound into cavity
867.9	Injury to unspecified pelvic organ with open wound into cavity
878.4	Open wound of vulva, without mention of complication
878.5	Open wound of vulva, complicated
878.6	Open wound of vagina, without mention of complication
878.7	Open wound of vagina, complicated
878.8	Open wound of other and unspecified parts of genital organs, without mention of complication
878.9	Open wound of other and unspecified parts of genital organs, complicated
908.2	Late effect of internal injury to other internal organs
922.4	Contusion of genital organs

DRG 358 — continued

926.0	Crushing injury of external genitalia
939.1	Foreign body in uterus, any part
939.2	Foreign body in vulva and vagina
947.4	Burn of vagina and uterus
996.32	Mechanical complication due to intrauterine contraceptive device
V25.2	Sterilization
V25.3	Menstrual extraction
V26.0	Tuboplasty or vasoplasty after previous sterilization
V45.77	Acquired absence of organ, genital organs
V50.42	Prophylactic ovary removal
V55.7	Attention to artificial vagina
V61.5	Multiparity

Operating Room Procedures

*65	Operations on ovary
*66.0	Salpingotomy
*66.1	Diagnostic procedures on fallopian tubes
66.4	Total unilateral salpingectomy
*66.5	Total bilateral salpingectomy
66.61	Excision or destruction of lesion of fallopian tube
66.62	Salpingectomy with removal of tubal pregnancy
66.69	Other partial salpingectomy
*66.7	Repair of fallopian tube
66.92	Unilateral destruction or occlusion of fallopian tube
66.93	Implantation or replacement of prosthesis of fallopian tube
66.94	Removal of prosthesis of fallopian tube
66.96	Dilation of fallopian tube
66.97	Burying of fimbriae in uterine wall
66.99	Other operations on fallopian tubes
68.0	Hysterotomy
68.13	Open biopsy of uterus
68.14	Open biopsy of uterine ligaments
68.19	Other diagnostic procedures on uterus and supporting structures
68.23	Endometrial ablation
68.29	Other excision or destruction of lesion of uterus
*68.3	Subtotal abdominal hysterectomy
68.4	Total abdominal hysterectomy
*68.5	Vaginal hysterectomy
68.9	Other and unspecified hysterectomy
69.19	Other excision or destruction of uterus and supporting structures
69.3	Paracervical uterine denervation
*69.4	Uterine repair

S DRG 359 Uterine and Adnexa Procedures for Nonmalignancy without CC

GMLOS 2.2 AMLOS 2.4 RW 0.7948 ☑

Select principal diagnosis and operating room procedure listed under DRG 358

S DRG 360 Vagina, Cervix and Vulva Procedures

GMLOS 2.0 AMLOS 2.6 RW 0.8582

Operating Room Procedures

48.73	Closure of other rectal fistula
57.18	Other suprapubic cystostomy
57.21	Vesicostomy
*67.3	Other excision or destruction of lesion or tissue of cervix
67.4	Amputation of cervix
67.51	Transabdominal cerclage of cervix
67.59	Other repair of cervical os
*67.6	Other repair of cervix
69.95	Incision of cervix

MDC 13: Female Reproductive System — Surgical

69.97 Removal of other penetrating foreign body from cervix
70.13 Lysis of intraluminal adhesions of vagina
70.14 Other vaginotomy
70.23 Biopsy of cul-de-sac
70.24 Vaginal biopsy
70.29 Other diagnostic procedures on vagina and cul-de-sac
*70.3 Local excision or destruction of vagina and cul-de-sac
70.71 Suture of laceration of vagina
70.72 Repair of colovaginal fistula
70.73 Repair of rectovaginal fistula
70.74 Repair of other vaginoenteric fistula
70.75 Repair of other fistula of vagina
70.76 Hymenorrhaphy
70.79 Other repair of vagina
*70.9 Other operations on vagina and cul-de-sac
*71.0 Incision of vulva and perineum
*71.1 Diagnostic procedures on vulva
71.22 Incision of Bartholin's gland (cyst)
71.23 Marsupialization of Bartholin's gland (cyst)
71.24 Excision or other destruction of Bartholin's gland (cyst)
71.29 Other operations on Bartholin's gland
71.3 Other local excision or destruction of vulva and perineum
71.4 Operations on clitoris
*71.6 Other vulvectomy
*71.7 Repair of vulva and perineum
71.8 Other operations on vulva

S DRG 361 Laparoscopy and Incisional Tubal Interruption

GMLOS 2.2 AMLOS 3.0 RW 1.0847

Operating Room Procedures

54.21 Laparoscopy
*66.3 Other bilateral destruction or occlusion of fallopian tubes
66.63 Bilateral partial salpingectomy, not otherwise specified
68.15 Closed biopsy of uterine ligaments

S DRG 362 Endoscopic Tubal Interruption

GMLOS 1.4 AMLOS 1.4 RW 0.3057 ☑

Operating Room Procedures

*66.2 Bilateral endoscopic destruction or occlusion of fallopian tubes

S DRG 363 D and C, Conization and Radio-Implant for Malignancy

GMLOS 2.7 AMLOS 3.8 RW 0.9728

Principal Diagnosis

179 Malignant neoplasm of uterus, part unspecified
*180 Malignant neoplasm of cervix uteri
181 Malignant neoplasm of placenta
*182 Malignant neoplasm of body of uterus
*183 Malignant neoplasm of ovary and other uterine adnexa
*184 Malignant neoplasm of other and unspecified female genital organs
195.3 Malignant neoplasm of pelvis
198.6 Secondary malignant neoplasm of ovary
198.82 Secondary malignant neoplasm of genital organs
233.1 Carcinoma in situ of cervix uteri
233.2 Carcinoma in situ of other and unspecified parts of uterus
233.3 Carcinoma in situ of other and unspecified female genital organs
236.0 Neoplasm of uncertain behavior of uterus
236.1 Neoplasm of uncertain behavior of placenta
236.2 Neoplasm of uncertain behavior of ovary

DRG 363 — continued

236.3	Neoplasm of uncertain behavior of other and unspecified female genital organs

Operating Room Procedures

*67.1	Diagnostic procedures on cervix
67.2	Conization of cervix
68.16	Closed biopsy of uterus
68.21	Division of endometrial synechiae
68.22	Incision or excision of congenital septum of uterus
69.09	Other dilation and curettage of uterus
92.27	Implantation or insertion of radioactive elements

S DRG 364 D and C, Conization Except for Malignancy

GMLOS 3.0 AMLOS 4.2 RW 0.8709 ☑

Select operating room procedures listed under DRG 363

S DRG 365 Other Female Reproductive System O.R. Procedures

GMLOS 5.3 AMLOS 7.7 RW 2.0408

Operating Room Procedures

03.93	Implantation or replacement of spinal neurostimulator lead(s)
03.94	Removal of spinal neurostimulator lead(s)
04.92	Implantation or replacement of peripheral neurostimulator lead(s)
04.93	Removal of peripheral neurostimulator lead(s)
05.24	Presacral sympathectomy
38.7	Interruption of the vena cava
39.98	Control of hemorrhage, not otherwise specified
40.11	Biopsy of lymphatic structure
40.24	Excision of inguinal lymph node
40.29	Simple excision of other lymphatic structure
40.3	Regional lymph node excision
*47.1	Incidental appendectomy
50.12	Open biopsy of liver
*54.1	Laparotomy
54.23	Biopsy of peritoneum
54.29	Other diagnostic procedures on abdominal region
54.4	Excision or destruction of peritoneal tissue
*54.5	Lysis of peritoneal adhesions
54.61	Reclosure of postoperative disruption of abdominal wall
54.62	Delayed closure of granulating abdominal wound
56.41	Partial ureterectomy
*56.5	Cutaneous uretero-ileostomy
*56.6	Other external urinary diversion
56.71	Urinary diversion to intestine
56.72	Revision of ureterointestinal anastomosis
56.73	Nephrocystanastomosis, not otherwise specified
56.75	Transureteroureterostomy
56.83	Closure of ureterostomy
56.84	Closure of other fistula of ureter
57.22	Revision or closure of vesicostomy
57.33	Closed (transurethral) biopsy of bladder
57.34	Open biopsy of bladder
*57.5	Other excision or destruction of bladder tissue
57.6	Partial cystectomy
*57.7	Total cystectomy
57.82	Closure of cystostomy
57.83	Repair of fistula involving bladder and intestine
57.84	Repair of other fistula of bladder
57.89	Other repair of bladder
58.0	Urethrotomy
58.43	Closure of other fistula of urethra
58.49	Other repair of urethra
58.5	Release of urethral stricture

58.99	Other operations on urethra and periurethral tissue
59.00	Retroperitoneal dissection, not otherwise specified
59.02	Other lysis of perirenal or periureteral adhesions
59.03	Laparoscopic lysis of perirenal or periureteral adhesions
59.09	Other incision of perirenal or periureteral tissue
*59.1	Incision of perivesical tissue
66.95	Insufflation of therapeutic agent into fallopian tubes
69.99	Other operations on cervix and uterus
70.12	Culdotomy
71.9	Other operations on female genital organs
86.06	Insertion of totally implantable infusion pump
86.22	Excisional debridement of wound, infection, or burn

MDC 13
DISEASES AND DISORDERS OF THE FEMALE REPRODUCTIVE SYSTEM

The complete and up-to-date listing of ICD-9-CM diagnosis codes assigned to this MDC can be found online at www.ingenixonline.com/content/drg/resources.asp.

MEDICAL

M DRG 366 Malignancy of Female Reproductive System with CC

GMLOS 4.8 AMLOS 6.6 RW 1.2348 ☑ CC

Select principal diagnosis listed under DRG 363

M DRG 367 Malignancy of Female Reproductive System without CC

GMLOS 2.3 AMLOS 3.0 RW 0.5728 ☑

Select principal diagnosis listed under DRG 363

M DRG 368 Infections of Female Reproductive System

GMLOS 5.2 AMLOS 6.7 RW 1.1684

Principal Diagnosis

*016.6	Tuberculous oophoritis and salpingitis
*016.7	Tuberculosis of other female genital organs
054.10	Unspecified genital herpes
054.11	Herpetic vulvovaginitis
054.12	Herpetic ulceration of vulva
054.19	Other genital herpes
091.0	Genital syphilis (primary)
098.0	Gonococcal infection (acute) of lower genitourinary tract
098.10	Gonococcal infection (acute) of upper genitourinary tract, site unspecified
098.15	Gonococcal cervicitis (acute)
098.16	Gonococcal endometritis (acute)
098.17	Gonococcal salpingitis, specified as acute
098.19	Other gonococcal infections (acute) of upper genitourinary tract
098.2	Gonococcal infections, chronic, of lower genitourinary tract
098.35	Gonococcal cervicitis, chronic
098.36	Gonococcal endometritis, chronic
098.37	Gonococcal salpingitis (chronic)
098.39	Other chronic gonococcal infections of upper genitourinary tract
099.0	Chancroid
099.1	Lymphogranuloma venereum
099.2	Granuloma inguinale
*099.4	Other nongonococcal urethritis (NGU)
099.50	Chlamydia trachomatis infection of unspecified site
099.53	Chlamydia trachomatis infection of lower genitourinary sites
099.55	Chlamydia trachomatis infection of unspecified genitourinary site
099.59	Chlamydia trachomatis infection of other specified site
099.8	Other specified venereal diseases
099.9	Unspecified venereal disease
112.1	Candidiasis of vulva and vagina
112.2	Candidiasis of other urogenital sites
131.00	Unspecified urogenital trichomoniasis
131.01	Trichomonal vulvovaginitis
131.02	Trichomonal urethritis
131.09	Other urogenital trichomoniasis
614.0	Acute salpingitis and oophoritis
614.1	Chronic salpingitis and oophoritis
614.2	Salpingitis and oophoritis not specified as acute, subacute, or chronic
614.3	Acute parametritis and pelvic cellulitis

614.4	Chronic or unspecified parametritis and pelvic cellulitis
614.5	Acute or unspecified pelvic peritonitis, female
614.7	Other chronic pelvic peritonitis, female
614.8	Other specified inflammatory disease of female pelvic organs and tissues
614.9	Unspecified inflammatory disease of female pelvic organs and tissues
*615	Inflammatory diseases of uterus, except cervix
616.0	Cervicitis and endocervicitis
*616.1	Vaginitis and vulvovaginitis
616.3	Abscess of Bartholin's gland
616.4	Other abscess of vulva
616.8	Other specified inflammatory disease of cervix, vagina, and vulva
616.9	Unspecified inflammatory disease of cervix, vagina, and vulva
698.1	Pruritus of genital organs

M DRG 369 Menstrual and Other Female Reproductive System Disorders

GMLOS 2.4 AMLOS 3.3 RW 0.6310 ☑

Principal Diagnosis

*218	Uterine leiomyoma
*219	Other benign neoplasm of uterus
220	Benign neoplasm of ovary
*221	Benign neoplasm of other female genital organs
*256	Ovarian dysfunction
306.51	Psychogenic vaginismus
306.52	Psychogenic dysmenorrhea
456.5	Pelvic varices
456.6	Vulval varices
614.6	Pelvic peritoneal adhesions, female (postoperative) (postinfection)
616.2	Cyst of Bartholin's gland
*616.5	Ulceration of vulva
617.0	Endometriosis of uterus
617.1	Endometriosis of ovary
617.2	Endometriosis of fallopian tube
617.3	Endometriosis of pelvic peritoneum
617.4	Endometriosis of rectovaginal septum and vagina
617.8	Endometriosis of other specified sites
617.9	Endometriosis, site unspecified
*618	Genital prolapse
619.0	Urinary-genital tract fistula, female
619.2	Genital tract-skin fistula, female
619.8	Other specified fistula involving female genital tract
619.9	Unspecified fistula involving female genital tract
*620	Noninflammatory disorders of ovary, fallopian tube, and broad ligament
*621	Disorders of uterus, not elsewhere classified
*622	Noninflammatory disorders of cervix
*623	Noninflammatory disorders of vagina
*624	Noninflammatory disorders of vulva and perineum
*625	Pain and other symptoms associated with female genital organs
*626	Disorders of menstruation and other abnormal bleeding from female genital tract
*627	Menopausal and postmenopausal disorders
*628	Female infertility
*629	Other disorders of female genital organs
752.0	Congenital anomalies of ovaries
*752.1	Congenital anomalies of fallopian tubes and broad ligaments
752.2	Congenital doubling of uterus
752.3	Other congenital anomaly of uterus
*752.4	Congenital anomalies of cervix, vagina, and external female genitalia
752.7	Indeterminate sex and pseudohermaphroditism
752.89	Other specified anomalies of genital organs
752.9	Unspecified congenital anomaly of genital organs
758.6	Gonadal dysgenesis
*758.8	Other conditions due to chromosome anomalies

MDC 13: Female Reproductive System — Medical

** Code Range* ☑ *Optimization Potential* *Targeted Potential* T *Transfer DRG* SP *Special Payment*

DRG 369 — continued

*795.0	Abnormal Papanicolaou smear of cervix and cervical HPV
867.4	Uterus injury without mention of open wound into cavity
867.5	Uterus injury with open wound into cavity
867.6	Injury to other specified pelvic organs without mention of open wound into cavity
867.7	Injury to other specified pelvic organs with open wound into cavity
867.8	Injury to unspecified pelvic organ without mention of open wound into cavity
867.9	Injury to unspecified pelvic organ with open wound into cavity
878.4	Open wound of vulva, without mention of complication
878.5	Open wound of vulva, complicated
878.6	Open wound of vagina, without mention of complication
878.7	Open wound of vagina, complicated
878.8	Open wound of other and unspecified parts of genital organs, without mention of complication
878.9	Open wound of other and unspecified parts of genital organs, complicated
908.2	Late effect of internal injury to other internal organs
922.4	Contusion of genital organs
926.0	Crushing injury of external genitalia
939.1	Foreign body in uterus, any part
939.2	Foreign body in vulva and vagina
947.4	Burn of vagina and uterus
996.32	Mechanical complication due to intrauterine contraceptive device
V25.2	Sterilization
V25.3	Menstrual extraction
V26.0	Tuboplasty or vasoplasty after previous sterilization
V45.77	Acquired absence of organ, genital organs
V50.42	Prophylactic ovary removal
V55.7	Attention to artificial vagina
V61.5	Multiparity

MDC 14
PREGNANCY, CHILDBIRTH AND THE PUERPERIUM

The complete and up-to-date listing of ICD-9-CM diagnosis codes assigned to this MDC can be found online at www.ingenixonline.com/content/drg/resources.asp.

SURGICAL

S DRG 370 Cesarean Section with CC

GMLOS 4.1 AMLOS 5.2 RW 0.8974 CC

Principal Diagnosis

640.01	Threatened abortion, delivered
640.81	Other specified hemorrhage in early pregnancy, delivered
640.91	Unspecified hemorrhage in early pregnancy, delivered
641.01	Placenta previa without hemorrhage, with delivery
641.11	Hemorrhage from placenta previa, with delivery
641.21	Premature separation of placenta, with delivery
641.31	Antepartum hemorrhage associated with coagulation defects, with delivery
641.81	Other antepartum hemorrhage, with delivery
641.91	Unspecified antepartum hemorrhage, with delivery
642.01	Benign essential hypertension with delivery
642.02	Benign essential hypertension, with delivery, with current postpartum complication
642.11	Hypertension secondary to renal disease, with delivery
642.12	Hypertension secondary to renal disease, with delivery, with current postpartum complication
642.21	Other pre-existing hypertension, with delivery
642.22	Other pre-existing hypertension, with delivery, with current postpartum complication
642.31	Transient hypertension of pregnancy, with delivery
642.32	Transient hypertension of pregnancy, with delivery, with current postpartum complication
642.41	Mild or unspecified pre-eclampsia, with delivery
642.42	Mild or unspecified pre-eclampsia, with delivery, with current postpartum complication
642.51	Severe pre-eclampsia, with delivery
642.52	Severe pre-eclampsia, with delivery, with current postpartum complication
642.61	Eclampsia, with delivery
642.62	Eclampsia, with delivery, with current postpartum complication
642.71	Pre-eclampsia or eclampsia superimposed on pre-existing hypertension, with delivery
642.72	Pre-eclampsia or eclampsia superimposed on pre-existing hypertension, with delivery, with current postpartum complication
642.91	Unspecified hypertension, with delivery
642.92	Unspecified hypertension, with delivery, with current postpartum complication
643.01	Mild hyperemesis gravidarum, delivered
643.11	Hyperemesis gravidarum with metabolic disturbance, delivered
643.21	Late vomiting of pregnancy, delivered
643.81	Other vomiting complicating pregnancy, delivered
643.91	Unspecified vomiting of pregnancy, delivered
644.21	Early onset of delivery, delivered, with or without mention of antepartum condition
645.11	Post term pregnancy, delivered, with or without mention of antepartum condition
645.21	Prolonged pregnancy, delivered, with or without mention of antepartum condition
646.00	Papyraceous fetus, unspecified as to episode of care
646.01	Papyraceous fetus, delivered, with or without mention of antepartum condition
646.11	Edema or excessive weight gain in pregnancy, with delivery, with or without mention of antepartum complication
646.12	Edema or excessive weight gain in pregnancy, with delivery, with current postpartum complication
646.21	Unspecified renal disease in pregnancy, with delivery
646.22	Unspecified renal disease in pregnancy, with delivery, with current postpartum complication
646.31	Pregnancy complication, habitual aborter with or without mention of antepartum condition
646.41	Peripheral neuritis in pregnancy, with delivery
646.42	Peripheral neuritis in pregnancy, with delivery, with current postpartum complication
646.51	Asymptomatic bacteriuria in pregnancy, with delivery
646.52	Asymptomatic bacteriuria in pregnancy, with delivery, with current postpartum complication

*** Code Range** ☑ ***Optimization Potential*** ***Targeted Potential*** T ***Transfer DRG*** SP ***Special Payment***

DRG 370 — continued

646.61	Infections of genitourinary tract in pregnancy, with delivery
646.62	Infections of genitourinary tract in pregnancy, with delivery, with current postpartum complication
646.71	Liver disorders in pregnancy, with delivery
646.81	Other specified complication of pregnancy, with delivery
646.82	Other specified complications of pregnancy, with delivery, with current postpartum complication
646.91	Unspecified complication of pregnancy, with delivery
647.01	Maternal syphilis, complicating pregnancy, with delivery
647.02	Maternal syphilis, complicating pregnancy, with delivery, with current postpartum complication
647.11	Maternal gonorrhea with delivery
647.12	Maternal gonorrhea, with delivery, with current postpartum complication
647.21	Other maternal venereal diseases with delivery
647.22	Other maternal venereal diseases with delivery, with current postpartum complication
647.31	Maternal tuberculosis with delivery
647.32	Maternal tuberculosis with delivery, with current postpartum complication
647.41	Maternal malaria with delivery
647.42	Maternal malaria with delivery, with current postpartum complication
647.51	Maternal rubella with delivery
647.52	Maternal rubella with delivery, with current postpartum complication
647.61	Other maternal viral disease with delivery
647.62	Other maternal viral disease with delivery, with current postpartum complication
647.81	Other specified maternal infectious and parasitic disease with delivery
647.82	Other specified maternal infectious and parasitic disease with delivery, with current postpartum complication
647.91	Unspecified maternal infection or infestation with delivery
647.92	Unspecified maternal infection or infestation with delivery, with current postpartum complication
648.01	Maternal diabetes mellitus with delivery
648.02	Maternal diabetes mellitus with delivery, with current postpartum complication
648.11	Maternal thyroid dysfunction with delivery, with or without mention of antepartum condition
648.12	Maternal thyroid dysfunction with delivery, with current postpartum complication
648.21	Maternal anemia, with delivery
648.22	Maternal anemia with delivery, with current postpartum complication
648.31	Maternal drug dependence, with delivery
648.32	Maternal drug dependence, with delivery, with current postpartum complication
648.41	Maternal mental disorders, with delivery
648.42	Maternal mental disorders, with delivery, with current postpartum complication
648.51	Maternal congenital cardiovascular disorders, with delivery
648.52	Maternal congenital cardiovascular disorders, with delivery, with current postpartum complication
648.61	Other maternal cardiovascular diseases, with delivery
648.62	Other maternal cardiovascular diseases, with delivery, with current postpartum complication
648.71	Bone and joint disorders of maternal back, pelvis, and lower limbs, with delivery
648.72	Bone and joint disorders of maternal back, pelvis, and lower limbs, with delivery, with current postpartum complication
648.81	Abnormal maternal glucose tolerance, with delivery
648.82	Abnormal maternal glucose tolerance, with delivery, with current postpartum complication
648.91	Other current maternal conditions classifiable elsewhere, with delivery
648.92	Other current maternal conditions classifiable elsewhere, with delivery, with current postpartum complication
650	Normal delivery
651.01	Twin pregnancy, delivered
651.11	Triplet pregnancy, delivered
651.21	Quadruplet pregnancy, delivered
651.31	Twin pregnancy with fetal loss and retention of one fetus, delivered
651.41	Triplet pregnancy with fetal loss and retention of one or more, delivered
651.51	Quadruplet pregnancy with fetal loss and retention of one or more, delivered
651.61	Other multiple pregnancy with fetal loss and retention of one or more fetus(es), delivered
651.71	Multiple gestation following (elective) fetal reduction, delivered, with or without mention of antepartum condition

651.81	Other specified multiple gestation, delivered
651.91	Unspecified multiple gestation, delivered
652.01	Unstable lie of fetus, delivered
652.11	Breech or other malpresentation successfully converted to cephalic presentation, delivered
652.21	Breech presentation without mention of version, delivered
652.31	Transverse or oblique fetal presentation, delivered
652.41	Fetal face or brow presentation, delivered
652.51	High fetal head at term, delivered
652.61	Multiple gestation with malpresentation of one fetus or more, delivered
652.71	Prolapsed arm of fetus, delivered
652.81	Other specified malposition or malpresentation of fetus, delivered
652.91	Unspecified malposition or malpresentation of fetus, delivered
653.01	Major abnormality of bony pelvis, not further specified, delivered
653.11	Generally contracted pelvis in pregnancy, delivered
653.21	Inlet contraction of pelvis in pregnancy, delivered
653.31	Outlet contraction of pelvis in pregnancy, delivered
653.41	Fetopelvic disproportion, delivered
653.51	Unusually large fetus causing disproportion, delivered
653.61	Hydrocephalic fetus causing disproportion, delivered
653.71	Other fetal abnormality causing disproportion, delivered
653.81	Fetal disproportion of other origin, delivered
653.91	Unspecified fetal disproportion, delivered
654.01	Congenital abnormalities of pregnant uterus, delivered
654.02	Congenital abnormalities of pregnant uterus, delivered, with mention of postpartum complication
654.11	Tumors of body of uterus, delivered
654.12	Tumors of body of uterus, delivered, with mention of postpartum complication
654.21	Previous cesarean delivery, delivered, with or without mention of antepartum condition
654.31	Retroverted and incarcerated gravid uterus, delivered
654.32	Retroverted and incarcerated gravid uterus, delivered, with mention of postpartum complication
654.41	Other abnormalities in shape or position of gravid uterus and of neighboring structures, delivered
654.42	Other abnormalities in shape or position of gravid uterus and of neighboring structures, delivered, with mention of postpartum complication
654.51	Cervical incompetence, delivered
654.52	Cervical incompetence, delivered, with mention of postpartum complication
654.61	Other congenital or acquired abnormality of cervix, with delivery
654.62	Other congenital or acquired abnormality of cervix, delivered, with mention of postpartum complication
654.71	Congenital or acquired abnormality of vagina, with delivery
654.72	Congenital or acquired abnormality of vagina, delivered, with mention of postpartum complication
654.81	Congenital or acquired abnormality of vulva, with delivery
654.82	Congenital or acquired abnormality of vulva, delivered, with mention of postpartum complication
654.91	Other and unspecified abnormality of organs and soft tissues of pelvis, with delivery
654.92	Other and unspecified abnormality of organs and soft tissues of pelvis, delivered, with mention of postpartum complication
655.01	Central nervous system malformation in fetus, with delivery
655.11	Chromosomal abnormality in fetus, affecting management of mother, with delivery
655.21	Hereditary disease in family possibly affecting fetus, affecting management of mother, with delivery
655.31	Suspected damage to fetus from viral disease in mother, affecting management of mother, with delivery
655.41	Suspected damage to fetus from other disease in mother, affecting management of mother, with delivery
655.51	Suspected damage to fetus from drugs, affecting management of mother, delivered
655.61	Suspected damage to fetus from radiation, affecting management of mother, delivered
655.71	Decreased fetal movements, affecting management of mother, delivered
655.81	Other known or suspected fetal abnormality, not elsewhere classified, affecting management of mother, delivery
655.91	Unspecified fetal abnormality affecting management of mother, delivery

DRG 370 — continued

656.01	Fetal-maternal hemorrhage, with delivery
656.11	Rhesus isoimmunization affecting management of mother, delivered
656.21	Isoimmunization from other and unspecified blood-group incompatibility, affecting management of mother, delivered
656.30	Fetal distress affecting management of mother, unspecified as to episode of care
656.31	Fetal distress affecting management of mother, delivered
656.40	Intrauterine death affecting management of mother, unspecified as to episode of care
656.41	Intrauterine death affecting management of mother, delivered
656.51	Poor fetal growth, affecting management of mother, delivered
656.61	Excessive fetal growth affecting management of mother, delivered
656.71	Other placental conditions affecting management of mother, delivered
656.81	Other specified fetal and placental problems affecting management of mother, delivered
656.91	Unspecified fetal and placental problem affecting management of mother, delivered
657.01	Polyhydramnios, with delivery
658.01	Oligohydramnios, delivered
658.10	Premature rupture of membranes in pregnancy, unspecified as to episode of care
658.11	Premature rupture of membranes in pregnancy, delivered
658.20	Delayed delivery after spontaneous or unspecified rupture of membranes, unspecified as to episode of care
658.21	Delayed delivery after spontaneous or unspecified rupture of membranes, delivered
658.30	Delayed delivery after artificial rupture of membranes, unspecified as to episode of care
658.31	Delayed delivery after artificial rupture of membranes, delivered
658.40	Infection of amniotic cavity, unspecified as to episode of care
658.41	Infection of amniotic cavity, delivered
658.81	Other problem associated with amniotic cavity and membranes, delivered
658.91	Unspecified problem associated with amniotic cavity and membranes, delivered
659.00	Failed mechanical induction of labor, unspecified as to episode of care
659.01	Failed mechanical induction of labor, delivered
659.10	Failed medical or unspecified induction of labor, unspecified as to episode of care
659.11	Failed medical or unspecified induction of labor, delivered
659.20	Unspecified maternal pyrexia during labor, unspecified as to episode of care
659.21	Unspecified maternal pyrexia during labor, delivered
659.30	Generalized infection during labor, unspecified as to episode of care
659.31	Generalized infection during labor, delivered
659.41	Grand multiparity, delivered, with or without mention of antepartum condition
659.50	Elderly primigravida, unspecified as to episode of care
659.51	Elderly primigravida, delivered
659.60	Elderly multigravida, unspecified as to episode of care or not applicable
659.61	Elderly multigravida, delivered, with mention of antepartum condition
659.70	Abnormality in fetal heart rate or rhythm, unspecified as to episode of care or not applicable
659.71	Abnormality in fetal heart rate or rhythm, delivered, with or without mention of antepartum condition
659.80	Other specified indication for care or intervention related to labor and delivery, unspecified as to episode of care
659.81	Other specified indication for care or intervention related to labor and delivery, delivered
659.90	Unspecified indication for care or intervention related to labor and delivery, unspecified as to episode of care
659.91	Unspecified indication for care or intervention related to labor and delivery, delivered
660.00	Obstruction caused by malposition of fetus at onset of labor, unspecified as to episode of care
660.01	Obstruction caused by malposition of fetus at onset of labor, delivered
660.10	Obstruction by bony pelvis during labor and delivery, unspecified as to episode of care
660.11	Obstruction by bony pelvis during labor and delivery, delivered
660.20	Obstruction by abnormal pelvic soft tissues during labor and delivery, unspecified as to episode of care
660.21	Obstruction by abnormal pelvic soft tissues during laborand delivery, delivered
660.30	Deep transverse arrest and persistent occipitoposterior position during labor and delivery, unspecified as to episode of care
660.31	Deep transverse arrest and persistent occipitoposterior position during labor and deliver, delivered
660.40	Shoulder (girdle) dystocia during labor and delivery, unspecified as to episode of care
660.41	Shoulder (girdle) dystocia during labor and deliver, delivered
660.50	Locked twins during labor and delivery, unspecified as to episode of care in pregnancy

660.51	Locked twins, delivered
660.60	Unspecified failed trial of labor, unspecifed as to episode
660.61	Unspecified failed trial of labor, delivered
660.70	Unspecified failed forceps or vacuum extractor, unspecified as to episode of care
660.71	Unspecified failed forceps or vacuum extractor, delivered
660.80	Other causes of obstructed labor, unspecified as to episode of care
660.81	Other causes of obstructed labor, delivered
660.90	Unspecified obstructed labor, unspecified as to episode of care
660.91	Unspecified obstructed labor, with delivery
661.00	Primary uterine inertia, unspecified as to episode of care
661.01	Primary uterine inertia, with delivery
661.10	Secondary uterine inertia, unspecified as to episode of care
661.11	Secondary uterine inertia, with delivery
661.20	Other and unspecified uterine inertia, unspecified as to episode of care
661.21	Other and unspecified uterine inertia, with delivery
661.30	Precipitate labor, unspecified as to episode of care
661.31	Precipitate labor, with delivery
661.40	Hypertonic, incoordinate, or prolonged uterine contractions, unspecified as to episode of care
661.41	Hypertonic, incoordinate, or prolonged uterine contractions, with delivery
661.90	Unspecified abnormality of labor, unspecified as to episode of care
661.91	Unspecified abnormality of labor, with delivery
662.00	Prolonged first stage of labor, unspecified as to episode of care
662.01	Prolonged first stage of labor, delivered
662.10	Unspecified prolonged labor, unspecified as to episode of care
662.11	Unspecified prolonged labor, delivered
662.20	Prolonged second stage of labor, unspecified as to episode of care
662.21	Prolonged second stage of labor, delivered
662.30	Delayed delivery of second twin, triplet, etc., unspecified as to episode of care
662.31	Delayed delivery of second twin, triplet, etc., delivered
663.00	Prolapse of cord, complicating labor and delivery, unspecified as to episode of care
663.01	Prolapse of cord, complicating labor and delivery, delivered
663.10	Cord around neck, with compression, complicating labor and delivery, unspecified as to episode of care
663.11	Cord around neck, with compression, complicating labor and delivery, delivered
663.20	Other and unspecified cord entanglement, with compression, complicating labor and delivery, unspecified as to episode of care
663.21	Other and unspecified cord entanglement, with compression, complicating labor and delivery, delivered
663.30	Other and unspecified cord entanglement, without mention of compression, complicating labor and delivery, unspecified as to episode of care
663.31	Other and unspecified cord entanglement, without mention of compression, complicating labor and delivery, delivered
663.40	Short cord complicating labor and delivery, unspecified as to episode of care
663.41	Short cord complicating labor and delivery, delivered
663.50	Vasa previa complicating labor and delivery, unspecified as to episode of care
663.51	Vasa previa complicating labor and delivery, delivered
663.60	Vascular lesions of cord complicating labor and delivery, unspecified as to episode of care
663.61	Vascular lesions of cord complicating labor and delivery, delivered
663.80	Other umbilical cord complications during labor and delivery, unspecified as to episode of care
663.81	Other umbilical cord complications during labor and delivery, delivered
663.90	Unspecified umbilical cord complication during labor and delivery, unspecified as to episode of care
663.91	Unspecified umbilical cord complication during labor and delivery, delivered
664.00	First-degree perineal laceration, unspecified as to episode of care in pregnancy
664.01	First-degree perineal laceration, with delivery
664.10	Second-degree perineal laceration, unspecified as to episode of care in pregnancy
664.11	Second-degree perineal laceration, with delivery
664.20	Third-degree perineal laceration, unspecified as to episode of care in pregnancy
664.21	Third-degree perineal laceration, with delivery
664.30	Fourth-degree perineal laceration, unspecified as to episode of care in pregnancy
664.31	Fourth-degree perineal laceration, with delivery
664.40	Unspecified perineal laceration, unspecified as to episode of care in pregnancy
664.41	Unspecified perineal laceration, with delivery

DRG 370 — continued

664.50	Vulvar and perineal hematoma, unspecified as to episode of care in pregnancy
664.51	Vulvar and perineal hematoma, with delivery
664.80	Other specified trauma to perineum and vulva, unspecified as to episode of care in pregnancy
664.81	Other specified trauma to perineum and vulva, with delivery
664.90	Unspecified trauma to perineum and vulva, unspecified as to episode of care in pregnancy
664.91	Unspecified trauma to perineum and vulva, with delivery
665.00	Rupture of uterus before onset of labor, unspecified as to episode of care
665.01	Rupture of uterus before onset of labor, with delivery
665.10	Rupture of uterus during labor, unspecified as to episode
665.11	Rupture of uterus during labor, with delivery
665.20	Inversion of uterus, unspecified as to episode of care in pregnancy
665.22	Inversion of uterus, delivered with postpartum complication
665.30	Laceration of cervix, unspecified as to episode of care in pregnancy
665.31	Laceration of cervix, with delivery
665.40	High vaginal laceration, unspecified as to episode of care in pregnancy
665.41	High vaginal laceration, with delivery
665.50	Other injury to pelvic organs, unspecified as to episode of care in pregnancy
665.51	Other injury to pelvic organs, with delivery
665.60	Damage to pelvic joints and ligaments, unspecified as to episode of care in pregnancy
665.61	Damage to pelvic joints and ligaments, with delivery
665.70	Pelvic hematoma, unspecified as to episode of care
665.71	Pelvic hematoma, with delivery
665.72	Pelvic hematoma, delivered with postpartum complication
665.80	Other specified obstetrical trauma, unspecified as to episode of care
665.81	Other specified obstetrical trauma, with delivery
665.82	Other specified obstetrical trauma, delivered, with postpartum
665.90	Unspecified obstetrical trauma, unspecified as to episode of care
665.91	Unspecified obstetrical trauma, with delivery
665.92	Unspecified obstetrical trauma, delivered, with postpartum complication
666.02	Third-stage postpartum hemorrhage, with delivery
666.12	Other immediate postpartum hemorrhage, with delivery
666.22	Delayed and secondary postpartum hemorrhage, with delivery
666.32	Postpartum coagulation defects, with delivery
667.02	Retained placenta without hemorrhage, with delivery, with mention of postpartum complication
667.12	Retained portions of placenta or membranes, without hemorrhage, delivered, with mention of postpartum complication
668.00	Pulmonary complications of the administration of anesthesia or other sedation in labor and delivery, unspecified as to episode of care
668.01	Pulmonary complications of the administration of anesthesia or other sedation in labor and delivery, delivered
668.02	Pulmonary complications of the administration of anesthesia or other sedation in labor and delivery, delivered, with mention of postpartum complication
668.10	Cardiac complications of the administration of anesthesia or other sedation in labor and delivery, unspecified as to episode of care
668.11	Cardiac complications of the administration of anesthesia or other sedation in labor and delivery, delivered
668.12	Cardiac complications of the administration of anesthesia or other sedation in labor and delivery, delivered, with mention of postpartum complication
668.20	Central nervous system complications of the administration of anesthesia or other sedation in labor and delivery, unspecified as to episode of care
668.21	Central nervous system complications of the administration of anesthesia or other sedation in labor and delivery, delivered
668.22	Central nervous system complications of the administration of anesthesia or other sedation in labor and delivery, delivered, with mention of postpartum complication
668.80	Other complications of the administration of anesthesia or other sedation in labor and delivery, unspecified as to episode of care
668.81	Other complications of the administration of anesthesia or other sedation in labor and delivery, delivered
668.82	Other complications of the administration of anesthesia or other sedation in labor and delivery, delivered, with mention of postpartum complication

668.90	Unspecified complication of the administration of anesthesia or other sedation in labor and delivery, unspecified as to episode of care
668.91	Unspecified complication of the administration of anesthesia or other sedation in labor and delivery, delivered
668.92	Unspecified complication of the administration of anesthesia or other sedation in labor and delivery, delivered, with mention of postpartum complication
669.00	Maternal distress complicating labor and delivery, unspecified as to episode of care
669.01	Maternal distress, with delivery, with or without mention of antepartum condition
669.02	Maternal distress, with delivery, with mention of postpartum complication
669.10	Shock during or following labor and delivery, unspecified as to episode of care
669.11	Shock during or following labor and delivery, with delivery, with or without mention of antepartum condition
669.12	Shock during or following labor and delivery, with delivery, with mention of postpartum complication
669.20	Maternal hypotension syndrome complicating labor and delivery, unspecified as to episode of care
669.21	Maternal hypotension syndrome, with delivery, with or without mention of antepartum condition
669.22	Maternal hypotension syndrome, with delivery, with mention of postpartum complication
669.30	Acute renal failure following labor and delivery, unspecified as to episode of care
669.32	Acute renal failure with delivery, with mention of postpartum complication
669.40	Other complications of obstetrical surgery and procedures, unspecified as to episode of care
669.41	Other complications of obstetrical surgery and procedures, with delivery, with or without mention of antepartum condition
669.42	Other complications of obstetrical surgery and procedures, with delivery, with mention of postpartum complication
669.50	Forceps or vacuum extractor delivery without mention of indication, unspecified as to episode of care
669.51	Forceps or vacuum extractor delivery without mention of indication, delivered, with or without mention of antepartum condition
669.60	Breech extraction, without mention of indication, unspecified as to episode of care
669.61	Breech extraction, without mention of indication, delivered, with or without mention of antepartum condition
669.70	Cesarean delivery, without mention of indication, unspecified as to episode of care
669.71	Cesarean delivery, without mention of indication, delivered, with or without mention of antepartum condition
669.80	Other complication of labor and delivery, unspecified as to episode of care
669.81	Other complication of labor and delivery, delivered, with or without mention of antepartum condition
669.82	Other complication of labor and delivery, delivered, with mention of postpartum complication
669.90	Unspecified complication of labor and delivery, unspecified as to episode of care
669.91	Unspecified complication of labor and delivery, with delivery, with or without mention of antepartum condition
669.92	Unspecified complication of labor and delivery, with delivery, with mention of postpartum complication
670.02	Major puerperal infection, delivered, with mention of postpartum complication
671.01	Varicose veins of legs, with delivery, with or without mention of antepartum condition
671.02	Varicose veins of legs, with delivery, with mention of postpartum complication
671.11	Varicose veins of vulva and perineum, with delivery, with or without mention of antepartum condition
671.12	Varicose veins of vulva and perineum, with delivery, with mention of postpartum complication
671.21	Superficial thrombophlebitis with delivery, with or without mention of antepartum condition
671.22	Superficial thrombophlebitis with delivery, with mention of postpartum complication
671.31	Deep phlebothrombosis, antepartum, with delivery
671.42	Deep phlebothrombosis, postpartum, with delivery
671.51	Other phlebitis and thrombosis with delivery, with or without mention of antepartum condition
671.52	Other phlebitis and thrombosis with delivery, with mention of postpartum complication
671.81	Other venous complication, with delivery, with or without mention of antepartum condition
671.82	Other venous complication, with delivery, with mention of postpartum complication
671.91	Unspecified venous complication, with delivery, with or without mention of antepartum condition
671.92	Unspecified venous complication, with delivery, with mention of postpartum complication

*** Code Range** ☑ **Optimization Potential** **Targeted Potential** **T Transfer DRG** **SP Special Payment**

DRG 370 — continued

672.02	Puerperal pyrexia of unknown origin, delivered, with mention of postpartum complication
673.01	Obstetrical air embolism, with delivery, with or without mention of antepartum condition
673.02	Obstetrical air embolism, with delivery, with mention of postpartum complication
673.11	Amniotic fluid embolism, with delivery, with or without mention of antepartum condition
673.12	Amniotic fluid embolism, with delivery, with mention of postpartum complication
673.21	Obstetrical blood-clot embolism, with delivery, with or without mention of antepartum condition
673.22	Obstetrical blood-clot embolism, with mention of postpartum complication
673.31	Obstetrical pyemic and septic embolism, with delivery, with or without mention of antepartum condition
673.32	Obstetrical pyemic and septic embolism, with delivery, with mention of postpartum complicaton
673.81	Other obstetrical pulmonary embolism, with delivery, with or without mention of antepartum condition
673.82	Other obstetrical pulmonary embolism, with delivery, with mention of postpartum complication
674.01	Cerebrovascular disorder, with delivery, with or without mention of antepartum condition
674.02	Cerebrovascular disorder, with delivery, with mention of postpartum complication
674.12	Disruption of cesarean wound, with delivery, with mention of postpartum complication
674.22	Disruption of perineal wound, with delivery, with mention of postpartum complicaton
674.32	Other complication of obstetrical surgical wounds, with delivery, with mention of postpartum complication
674.42	Placental polyp, with delivery, with mention of postpartum complication
674.51	Peripartum cardiomyopathy, delivered, with or without mention of antepartum condition
674.52	Peripartum cardiomyopathy, delivered, with mention of postpartum condition
674.82	Other complication of puerperium, with delivery, with mention of postpartum complication
674.92	Unspecified complications of puerperium, with delivery, with mention of postpartum complication
675.01	Infection of nipple associated with childbirth, delivered, with or without mention of antepartum condition
675.02	Infection of nipple associated with childbirth, delivered with mention of postpartum complication
675.11	Abscess of breast associated with childbirth, delivered, with or without mention of antepartum condition
675.12	Abscess of breast associated with childbirth, delivered, with mention of postpartum complication
675.21	Nonpurulent mastitis, delivered, with or without mention of antepartum condition
675.22	Nonpurulent mastitis, delivered, with mention of postpartum complication
675.81	Other specified infection of the breast and nipple associated with childbirth, delivered, with or without mention of antepartum condition
675.82	Other specified infection of the breast and nipple associated with childbirth, delivered, with mention of postpartum complication
675.91	Unspecified infection of the breast and nipple, delivered, with or without mention of antepartum condition
675.92	Unspecified infection of the breast and nipple, delivered, with mention of postpartum complication
676.01	Retracted nipple, delivered, with or without mention of antepartum condition
676.02	Retracted nipple, delivered, with mention of postpartum complication
676.11	Cracked nipple, delivered, with or without mention of antepartum condition
676.12	Cracked nipple, delivered, with mention of postpartum complication
676.21	Engorgement of breasts, delivered, with or without mention of antepartum condition
676.22	Engorgement of breasts, delivered, with mention of postpartum complication
676.31	Other and unspecified disorder of breast associated with childbirth, delivered, with or without mention of antepartum condition
676.32	Other and unspecified disorder of breast associated with childbirth, delivered, with mention of postpartum complication
676.41	Failure of lactation, with delivery, with or without mention of antepartum condition
676.42	Failure of lactation, with delivery, with mention of postpartum complication
676.51	Suppressed lactation, with delivery, with or without mention of antepartum condition
676.52	Suppressed lactation, with delivery, with mention of postpartum complication
676.61	Galactorrhea, with delivery, with or without mention of antepartum condition
676.62	Galactorrhea, with delivery, with mention of postpartum complication

676.81	Other disorder of lactation, with delivery, with or without mention of antepartum condition
676.82	Other disorder of lactation, with delivery, with mention of postpartum complication
676.91	Unspecified disorder of lactation, with delivery, with or without mention of antepartum condition
676.92	Unspecified disorder of lactation, with delivery, with mention of postpartum complication

Operating Room Procedures

74.0	Classical cesarean section
74.1	Low cervical cesarean section
74.2	Extraperitoneal cesarean section
74.4	Cesarean section of other specified type
74.99	Other cesarean section of unspecified type

S DRG 371 Cesarean Section without CC

GMLOS 3.1 AMLOS 3.4 RW 0.6066 ☑

Select principal diagnosis and operating room procedure listed under DRG 370

S DRG 374 Vaginal Delivery with Sterilization and/or D and C

GMLOS 2.5 AMLOS 2.8 RW 0.6712

Select principal diagnosis listed under DRG 370

Operating Room Procedures

*66.2	Bilateral endoscopic destruction or occlusion of fallopian tubes
*66.3	Other bilateral destruction or occlusion of fallopian tubes
66.4	Total unilateral salpingectomy
*66.5	Total bilateral salpingectomy
66.63	Bilateral partial salpingectomy, not otherwise specified
66.69	Other partial salpingectomy
66.92	Unilateral destruction or occlusion of fallopian tube
66.97	Burying of fimbriae in uterine wall
69.02	Dilation and curettage following delivery or abortion
69.09	Other dilation and curettage of uterus
69.52	Aspiration curettage following delivery or abortion

S DRG 375 Vaginal Delivery with O.R. Procedure Except Sterilization and/or D and C

GMLOS 4.4 AMLOS 4.4 RW 0.5837

Select principal diagnosis listed under DRG 370

Operating Room Procedures

38.7	Interruption of the vena cava
39.98	Control of hemorrhage, not otherwise specified
39.99	Other operations on vessels
40.24	Excision of inguinal lymph node
40.3	Regional lymph node excision
48.79	Other repair of rectum
49.46	Excision of hemorrhoids
54.11	Exploratory laparotomy
54.21	Laparoscopy
66.62	Salpingectomy with removal of tubal pregnancy
*67.1	Diagnostic procedures on cervix
67.2	Conization of cervix
*67.3	Other excision or destruction of lesion or tissue of cervix
67.62	Repair of fistula of cervix
68.0	Hysterotomy
*68.3	Subtotal abdominal hysterectomy
68.4	Total abdominal hysterectomy
*68.5	Vaginal hysterectomy
68.6	Radical abdominal hysterectomy
68.7	Radical vaginal hysterectomy
68.9	Other and unspecified hysterectomy
69.41	Suture of laceration of uterus

*** Code Range** ☑ ***Optimization Potential*** ***Targeted Potential*** **T** ***Transfer DRG*** **SP** ***Special Payment***

DRG 375 — continued

69.49	Other repair of uterus
69.95	Incision of cervix
70.12	Culdotomy
70.23	Biopsy of cul-de-sac
70.29	Other diagnostic procedures on vagina and cul-de-sac
70.32	Excision or destruction of lesion of cul-de-sac
71.22	Incision of Bartholin's gland (cyst)
71.23	Marsupialization of Bartholin's gland (cyst)
71.24	Excision or other destruction of Bartholin's gland (cyst)
71.29	Other operations on Bartholin's gland
73.94	Pubiotomy to assist delivery
74.3	Removal of extratubal ectopic pregnancy
75.36	Correction of fetal defect
75.52	Repair of current obstetric laceration of corpus uteri
75.93	Surgical correction of inverted uterus
75.99	Other obstetric operations

S DRG 377 Postpartum and Postabortion Diagnoses with O.R. Procedure

GMLOS 2.9 AMLOS 4.5 RW 1.6996

Select principal diagnosis listed under DRG 376 with any operating room procedure

S DRG 381 Abortion with D and C, Aspiration Curettage or Hysterotomy

GMLOS 1.6 AMLOS 2.2 RW 0.6034

Select principal diagnosis listed under DRG 380

Operating Room Procedures

*69.0	Dilation and curettage of uterus
69.51	Aspiration curettage of uterus for termination of pregnancy
69.52	Aspiration curettage following delivery or abortion
74.91	Hysterotomy to terminate pregnancy

MDC 14
PREGNANCY, CHILDBIRTH AND THE PUERPERIUM

The complete and up-to-date listing of ICD-9-CM diagnosis codes assigned to this MDC can be found online at www.ingenixonline.com/content/drg/resources.asp.

MEDICAL

M DRG 372 Vaginal Delivery with Complicating Diagnoses
GMLOS 2.5 AMLOS 3.2 RW 0.5027 ☑

Select principal diagnosis listed under DRG 370

AND

Principal or Secondary Diagnosis Complicating Delivery

641.01	Placenta previa without hemorrhage, with delivery
641.11	Hemorrhage from placenta previa, with delivery
641.21	Premature separation of placenta, with delivery
641.31	Antepartum hemorrhage associated with coagulation defects, with delivery
641.81	Other antepartum hemorrhage, with delivery
641.91	Unspecified antepartum hemorrhage, with delivery
642.01	Benign essential hypertension with delivery
642.02	Benign essential hypertension, with delivery, with current postpartum complication
642.11	Hypertension secondary to renal disease, with delivery
642.12	Hypertension secondary to renal disease, with delivery, with current postpartum complication
642.21	Other pre-existing hypertension, with delivery
642.22	Other pre-existing hypertension, with delivery, with current postpartum complication
642.41	Mild or unspecified pre-eclampsia, with delivery
642.42	Mild or unspecified pre-eclampsia, with delivery, with current postpartum complication
642.51	Severe pre-eclampsia, with delivery
642.52	Severe pre-eclampsia, with delivery, with current postpartum complication
642.61	Eclampsia, with delivery
642.62	Eclampsia, with delivery, with current postpartum complication
642.71	Pre-eclampsia or eclampsia superimposed on pre-existing hypertension, with delivery
642.72	Pre-eclampsia or eclampsia superimposed on pre-existing hypertension, with delivery, with current postpartum complication
642.91	Unspecified hypertension, with delivery
642.92	Unspecified hypertension, with delivery, with current postpartum complication
647.01	Maternal syphilis, complicating pregnancy, with delivery
647.02	Maternal syphilis, complicating pregnancy, with delivery, with current postpartum complication
647.11	Maternal gonorrhea with delivery
647.12	Maternal gonorrhea, with delivery, with current postpartum complication
647.21	Other maternal venereal diseases with delivery
647.22	Other maternal venereal diseases with delivery, with current postpartum complication
647.31	Maternal tuberculosis with delivery
647.32	Maternal tuberculosis with delivery, with current postpartum complication
647.41	Maternal malaria with delivery
647.42	Maternal malaria with delivery, with current postpartum complication
647.51	Maternal rubella with delivery
647.52	Maternal rubella with delivery, with current postpartum complication
647.61	Other maternal viral disease with delivery
647.62	Other maternal viral disease with delivery, with current postpartum complication
647.81	Other specified maternal infectious and parasitic disease with delivery
647.82	Other specified maternal infectious and parasitic disease with delivery, with current postpartum complication
647.91	Unspecified maternal infection or infestation with delivery
647.92	Unspecified maternal infection or infestation with delivery, with current postpartum complication
648.01	Maternal diabetes mellitus with delivery
648.02	Maternal diabetes mellitus with delivery, with current postpartum complication
648.51	Maternal congenital cardiovascular disorders, with delivery

*** Code Range** ☑ **Optimization Potential** **Targeted Potential** T **Transfer DRG** SP **Special Payment**

DRG 372 — continued

648.52	Maternal congenital cardiovascular disorders, with delivery, with current postpartum complication
648.61	Other maternal cardiovascular diseases, with delivery
648.62	Other maternal cardiovascular diseases, with delivery, with current postpartum complication
659.21	Unspecified maternal pyrexia during labor, delivered
659.31	Generalized infection during labor, delivered
666.02	Third-stage postpartum hemorrhage, with delivery
666.12	Other immediate postpartum hemorrhage, with delivery
666.22	Delayed and secondary postpartum hemorrhage, with delivery
666.32	Postpartum coagulation defects, with delivery
667.02	Retained placenta without hemorrhage, with delivery, with mention of postpartum complication
667.12	Retained portions of placenta or membranes, without hemorrhage, delivered, with mention of postpartum complication
668.01	Pulmonary complications of the administration of anesthesia or other sedation in labor and delivery, delivered
668.02	Pulmonary complications of the administration of anesthesia or other sedation in labor and delivery, delivered, with mention of postpartum complication
668.11	Cardiac complications of the administration of anesthesia or other sedation in labor and delivery, delivered
668.12	Cardiac complications of the administration of anesthesia or other sedation in labor and delivery, delivered, with mention of postpartum complication
668.21	Central nervous system complications of the administration of anesthesia or other sedation in labor and delivery, delivered
668.22	Central nervous system complications of the administration of anesthesia or other sedation in labor and delivery, delivered, with mention of postpartum complication
668.81	Other complications of the administration of anesthesia or other sedation in labor and delivery, delivered
668.82	Other complications of the administration of anesthesia or other sedation in labor and delivery, delivered, with mention of postpartum complication
668.91	Unspecified complication of the administration of anesthesia or other sedation in labor and delivery, delivered
668.92	Unspecified complication of the administration of anesthesia or other sedation in labor and delivery, delivered, with mention of postpartum complication
669.11	Shock during or following labor and delivery, with delivery, with or without mention of antepartum condition
669.12	Shock during or following labor and delivery, with delivery, with mention of postpartum complication
669.32	Acute renal failure with delivery, with mention of postpartum complication
669.41	Other complications of obstetrical surgery and procedures, with delivery, with or without mention of antepartum condition
669.42	Other complications of obstetrical surgery and procedures, with delivery, with mention of postpartum complication
670.02	Major puerperal infection, delivered, with mention of postpartum complication
671.31	Deep phlebothrombosis, antepartum, with delivery
671.42	Deep phlebothrombosis, postpartum, with delivery
671.51	Other phlebitis and thrombosis with delivery, with or without mention of antepartum condition
671.52	Other phlebitis and thrombosis with delivery, with mention of postpartum complication
672.02	Puerperal pyrexia of unknown origin, delivered, with mention of postpartum complication
673.01	Obstetrical air embolism, with delivery, with or without mention of antepartum condition
673.02	Obstetrical air embolism, with delivery, with mention of postpartum complication
673.11	Amniotic fluid embolism, with delivery, with or without mention of antepartum condition
673.12	Amniotic fluid embolism, with delivery, with mention of postpartum complication
673.21	Obstetrical blood-clot embolism, with delivery, with or without mention of antepartum condition
673.22	Obstetrical blood-clot embolism, with mention of postpartum complication
673.31	Obstetrical pyemic and septic embolism, with delivery, with or without mention of antepartum condition
673.32	Obstetrical pyemic and septic embolism, with delivery, with mention of postpartum complicaton

673.81 Other obstetrical pulmonary embolism, with delivery, with or without mention of antepartum condition
673.82 Other obstetrical pulmonary embolism, with delivery, with mention of postpartum complication
674.01 Cerebrovascular disorder, with delivery, with or without mention of antepartum condition
674.02 Cerebrovascular disorder, with delivery, with mention of postpartum complication
674.12 Disruption of cesarean wound, with delivery, with mention of postpartum complication
674.22 Disruption of perineal wound, with delivery, with mention of postpartum complicaton
674.32 Other complication of obstetrical surgical wounds, with delivery, with mention of postpartum complication
674.82 Other complication of puerperium, with delivery, with mention of postpartum complication
675.01 Infection of nipple associated with childbirth, delivered, with or without mention of antepartum condition
675.02 Infection of nipple associated with childbirth, delivered with mention of postpartum complication
675.11 Abscess of breast associated with childbirth, delivered, with or without mention of antepartum condition
675.12 Abscess of breast associated with childbirth, delivered, with mention of postpartum complication
675.21 Nonpurulent mastitis, delivered, with or without mention of antepartum condition
675.22 Nonpurulent mastitis, delivered, with mention of postpartum complication

AND

Only Operating Room Procedures

48.71 Suture of laceration of rectum
49.59 Other anal sphincterotomy
67.51 Transabdominal cerclage of cervix
67.59 Other repair of cervical os
67.61 Suture of laceration of cervix
67.69 Other repair of cervix
70.13 Lysis of intraluminal adhesions of vagina
70.14 Other vaginotomy
70.24 Vaginal biopsy
70.31 Hymenectomy
70.33 Excision or destruction of lesion of vagina
70.71 Suture of laceration of vagina
70.79 Other repair of vagina
*71.0 Incision of vulva and perineum
*71.1 Diagnostic procedures on vulva
71.3 Other local excision or destruction of vulva and perineum
71.71 Suture of laceration of vulva or perineum
71.79 Other repair of vulva and perineum
73.99 Other operations to assist delivery
75.50 Repair of current obstetric laceration of uterus, not otherwise specified
75.51 Repair of current obstetric laceration of cervix
75.61 Repair of current obstetric laceration of bladder and urethra

M DRG 373 Vaginal Delivery without Complicating Diagnoses

GMLOS 2.0 AMLOS 2.2 RW 0.3556 ☑

Principal Diagnosis

640.01 Threatened abortion, delivered
640.81 Other specified hemorrhage in early pregnancy, delivered
640.91 Unspecified hemorrhage in early pregnancy, delivered
642.31 Transient hypertension of pregnancy, with delivery
642.32 Transient hypertension of pregnancy, with delivery, with current postpartum complication
643.01 Mild hyperemesis gravidarum, delivered
643.11 Hyperemesis gravidarum with metabolic disturbance, delivered
643.21 Late vomiting of pregnancy, delivered
643.81 Other vomiting complicating pregnancy, delivered
643.91 Unspecified vomiting of pregnancy, delivered
644.21 Early onset of delivery, delivered, with or without mention of antepartum condition
645.11 Post term pregnancy, delivered, with or without mention of antepartum condition

DRG 373 — continued

645.21	Prolonged pregnancy, delivered, with or without mention of antepartum condition
646.00	Papyraceous fetus, unspecified as to episode of care
646.01	Papyraceous fetus, delivered, with or without mention of antepartum condition
646.11	Edema or excessive weight gain in pregnancy, with delivery, with or without mention of antepartum complication
646.12	Edema or excessive weight gain in pregnancy, with delivery, with current postpartum complication
646.21	Unspecified renal disease in pregnancy, with delivery
646.22	Unspecified renal disease in pregnancy, with delivery, with current postpartum complication
646.31	Pregnancy complication, habitual aborter with or without mention of antepartum condition
646.41	Peripheral neuritis in pregnancy, with delivery
646.42	Peripheral neuritis in pregnancy, with delivery, with current postpartum complication
646.51	Asymptomatic bacteriuria in pregnancy, with delivery
646.52	Asymptomatic bacteriuria in pregnancy, with delivery, with current postpartum complication
646.61	Infections of genitourinary tract in pregnancy, with delivery
646.62	Infections of genitourinary tract in pregnancy, with delivery, with current postpartum complication
646.71	Liver disorders in pregnancy, with delivery
646.81	Other specified complication of pregnancy, with delivery
646.82	Other specified complications of pregnancy, with delivery, with current postpartum complication
646.91	Unspecified complication of pregnancy, with delivery
648.11	Maternal thyroid dysfunction with delivery, with or without mention of antepartum condition
648.12	Maternal thyroid dysfunction with delivery, with current postpartum complication
648.21	Maternal anemia, with delivery
648.22	Maternal anemia with delivery, with current postpartum complication
648.31	Maternal drug dependence, with delivery
648.32	Maternal drug dependence, with delivery, with current postpartum complication
648.41	Maternal mental disorders, with delivery
648.42	Maternal mental disorders, with delivery, with current postpartum complication
648.71	Bone and joint disorders of maternal back, pelvis, and lower limbs, with delivery
648.72	Bone and joint disorders of maternal back, pelvis, and lower limbs, with delivery, with current postpartum complication
648.81	Abnormal maternal glucose tolerance, with delivery
648.82	Abnormal maternal glucose tolerance, with delivery, with current postpartum complication
648.91	Other current maternal conditions classifiable elsewhere, with delivery
648.92	Other current maternal conditions classifiable elsewhere, with delivery, with current postpartum complication
650	Normal delivery
651.01	Twin pregnancy, delivered
651.11	Triplet pregnancy, delivered
651.21	Quadruplet pregnancy, delivered
651.31	Twin pregnancy with fetal loss and retention of one fetus, delivered
651.41	Triplet pregnancy with fetal loss and retention of one or more, delivered
651.51	Quadruplet pregnancy with fetal loss and retention of one or more, delivered
651.61	Other multiple pregnancy with fetal loss and retention of one or more fetus(es), delivered
651.71	Multiple gestation following (elective) fetal reduction, delivered, with or without mention of antepartum condition
651.81	Other specified multiple gestation, delivered
651.91	Unspecified multiple gestation, delivered
652.01	Unstable lie of fetus, delivered
652.11	Breech or other malpresentation successfully converted to cephalic presentation, delivered
652.21	Breech presentation without mention of version, delivered
652.31	Transverse or oblique fetal presentation, delivered
652.41	Fetal face or brow presentation, delivered
652.51	High fetal head at term, delivered
652.61	Multiple gestation with malpresentation of one fetus or more, delivered
652.71	Prolapsed arm of fetus, delivered
652.81	Other specified malposition or malpresentation of fetus, delivered
652.91	Unspecified malposition or malpresentation of fetus, delivered
653.01	Major abnormality of bony pelvis, not further specified, delivered
653.11	Generally contracted pelvis in pregnancy, delivered

653.21	Inlet contraction of pelvis in pregnancy, delivered
653.31	Outlet contraction of pelvis in pregnancy, delivered
653.41	Fetopelvic disproportion, delivered
653.51	Unusually large fetus causing disproportion, delivered
653.61	Hydrocephalic fetus causing disproportion, delivered
653.71	Other fetal abnormality causing disproportion, delivered
653.81	Fetal disproportion of other origin, delivered
653.91	Unspecified fetal disproportion, delivered
654.01	Congenital abnormalities of pregnant uterus, delivered
654.02	Congenital abnormalities of pregnant uterus, delivered, with mention of postpartum complication
654.11	Tumors of body of uterus, delivered
654.12	Tumors of body of uterus, delivered, with mention of postpartum complication
654.21	Previous cesarean delivery, delivered, with or without mention of antepartum condition
654.31	Retroverted and incarcerated gravid uterus, delivered
654.32	Retroverted and incarcerated gravid uterus, delivered, with mention of postpartum complication
654.41	Other abnormalities in shape or position of gravid uterus and of neighboring structures, delivered
654.42	Other abnormalities in shape or position of gravid uterus and of neighboring structures, delivered, with mention of postpartum complication
654.51	Cervical incompetence, delivered
654.52	Cervical incompetence, delivered, with mention of postpartum complication
654.61	Other congenital or acquired abnormality of cervix, with delivery
654.62	Other congenital or acquired abnormality of cervix, delivered, with mention of postpartum complication
654.71	Congenital or acquired abnormality of vagina, with delivery
654.72	Congenital or acquired abnormality of vagina, delivered, with mention of postpartum complication
654.81	Congenital or acquired abnormality of vulva, with delivery
654.82	Congenital or acquired abnormality of vulva, delivered, with mention of postpartum complication
654.91	Other and unspecified abnormality of organs and soft tissues of pelvis, with delivery
654.92	Other and unspecified abnormality of organs and soft tissues of pelvis, delivered, with mention of postpartum complication
655.01	Central nervous system malformation in fetus, with delivery
655.11	Chromosomal abnormality in fetus, affecting management of mother, with delivery
655.21	Hereditary disease in family possibly affecting fetus, affecting management of mother, with delivery
655.31	Suspected damage to fetus from viral disease in mother, affecting management of mother, with delivery
655.41	Suspected damage to fetus from other disease in mother, affecting management of mother, with delivery
655.51	Suspected damage to fetus from drugs, affecting management of mother, delivered
655.61	Suspected damage to fetus from radiation, affecting management of mother, delivered
655.71	Decreased fetal movements, affecting management of mother, delivered
655.81	Other known or suspected fetal abnormality, not elsewhere classified, affecting management of mother, delivery
655.91	Unspecified fetal abnormality affecting management of mother, delivery
656.01	Fetal-maternal hemorrhage, with delivery
656.11	Rhesus isoimmunization affecting management of mother, delivered
656.21	Isoimmunization from other and unspecified blood-group incompatibility, affecting management of mother, delivered
656.30	Fetal distress affecting management of mother, unspecified as to episode of care
656.31	Fetal distress affecting management of mother, delivered
656.40	Intrauterine death affecting management of mother, unspecified as to episode of care
656.41	Intrauterine death affecting management of mother, delivered
656.51	Poor fetal growth, affecting management of mother, delivered
656.61	Excessive fetal growth affecting management of mother, delivered
656.71	Other placental conditions affecting management of mother, delivered
656.81	Other specified fetal and placental problems affecting management of mother, delivered
656.91	Unspecified fetal and placental problem affecting management of mother, delivered
657.01	Polyhydramnios, with delivery

*** Code Range** ☑ ***Optimization Potential*** ***Targeted Potential*** 🅃 ***Transfer DRG*** SP ***Special Payment***

DRG 373 — continued

658.01	Oligohydramnios, delivered
658.10	Premature rupture of membranes in pregnancy, unspecified as to episode of care
658.11	Premature rupture of membranes in pregnancy, delivered
658.20	Delayed delivery after spontaneous or unspecified rupture of membranes, unspecified as to episode of care
658.21	Delayed delivery after spontaneous or unspecified rupture of membranes, delivered
658.30	Delayed delivery after artificial rupture of membranes, unspecified as to episode of care
658.31	Delayed delivery after artificial rupture of membranes, delivered
658.40	Infection of amniotic cavity, unspecified as to episode of care
658.41	Infection of amniotic cavity, delivered
658.81	Other problem associated with amniotic cavity and membranes, delivered
658.91	Unspecified problem associated with amniotic cavity and membranes, delivered
659.00	Failed mechanical induction of labor, unspecified as to episode of care
659.01	Failed mechanical induction of labor, delivered
659.10	Failed medical or unspecified induction of labor, unspecified as to episode of care
659.11	Failed medical or unspecified induction of labor, delivered
659.20	Unspecified maternal pyrexia during labor, unspecified as to episode of care
659.30	Generalized infection during labor, unspecified as to episode of care
659.41	Grand multiparity, delivered, with or without mention of antepartum condition
659.50	Elderly primigravida, unspecified as to episode of care
659.51	Elderly primigravida, delivered
659.60	Elderly multigravida, unspecified as to episode of care or not applicable
659.61	Elderly multigravida, delivered, with mention of antepartum condition
659.70	Abnormality in fetal heart rate or rhythm, unspecified as to episode of care or not applicable
659.71	Abnormality in fetal heart rate or rhythm, delivered, with or without mention of antepartum condition
659.80	Other specified indication for care or intervention related to labor and delivery, unspecified as to episode of care
659.81	Other specified indication for care or intervention related to labor and delivery, delivered
659.90	Unspecified indication for care or intervention related to labor and delivery, unspecified as to episode of care
659.91	Unspecified indication for care or intervention related to labor and delivery, delivered
660.00	Obstruction caused by malposition of fetus at onset of labor, unspecified as to episode of care
660.01	Obstruction caused by malposition of fetus at onset of labor, delivered
660.10	Obstruction by bony pelvis during labor and delivery, unspecified as to episode of care
660.11	Obstruction by bony pelvis during labor and delivery, delivered
660.20	Obstruction by abnormal pelvic soft tissues during labor and delivery, unspecified as to episode of care
660.21	Obstruction by abnormal pelvic soft tissues during laborand delivery, delivered
660.30	Deep transverse arrest and persistent occipitoposterior position during labor and delivery, unspecified as to episode of care
660.31	Deep transverse arrest and persistent occipitoposterior position during labor and deliver, delivered
660.40	Shoulder (girdle) dystocia during labor and delivery, unspecified as to episode of care
660.41	Shoulder (girdle) dystocia during labor and deliver, delivered
660.50	Locked twins during labor and delivery, unspecified as to episode of care in pregnancy
660.51	Locked twins, delivered
660.60	Unspecified failed trial of labor, unspecifed as to episode
660.61	Unspecified failed trial of labor, delivered
660.70	Unspecified failed forceps or vacuum extractor, unspecified as to episode of care
660.71	Unspecified failed forceps or vacuum extractor, delivered
660.80	Other causes of obstructed labor, unspecified as to episode of care
660.81	Other causes of obstructed labor, delivered
660.90	Unspecified obstructed labor, unspecified as to episode of care
660.91	Unspecified obstructed labor, with delivery
661.00	Primary uterine inertia, unspecified as to episode of care
661.01	Primary uterine inertia, with delivery
661.10	Secondary uterine inertia, unspecified as to episode of care
661.11	Secondary uterine inertia, with delivery
661.20	Other and unspecified uterine inertia, unspecified as to episode of care
661.21	Other and unspecified uterine inertia, with delivery
661.30	Precipitate labor, unspecified as to episode of care

661.31	Precipitate labor, with delivery
661.40	Hypertonic, incoordinate, or prolonged uterine contractions, unspecified as to episode of care
661.41	Hypertonic, incoordinate, or prolonged uterine contractions, with delivery
661.90	Unspecified abnormality of labor, unspecified as to episode of care
661.91	Unspecified abnormality of labor, with delivery
662.00	Prolonged first stage of labor, unspecified as to episode of care
662.01	Prolonged first stage of labor, delivered
662.10	Unspecified prolonged labor, unspecified as to episode of care
662.11	Unspecified prolonged labor, delivered
662.20	Prolonged second stage of labor, unspecified as to episode of care
662.21	Prolonged second stage of labor, delivered
662.30	Delayed delivery of second twin, triplet, etc., unspecified as to episode of care
662.31	Delayed delivery of second twin, triplet, etc., delivered
663.00	Prolapse of cord, complicating labor and delivery, unspecified as to episode of care
663.01	Prolapse of cord, complicating labor and delivery, delivered
663.10	Cord around neck, with compression, complicating labor and delivery, unspecified as to episode of care
663.11	Cord around neck, with compression, complicating labor and delivery, delivered
663.20	Other and unspecified cord entanglement, with compression, complicating labor and delivery, unspecified as to episode of care
663.21	Other and unspecified cord entanglement, with compression, complicating labor and delivery, delivered
663.30	Other and unspecified cord entanglement, without mention of compression, complicating labor and delivery, unspecified as to episode of care
663.31	Other and unspecified cord entanglement, without mention of compression, complicating labor and delivery, delivered
663.40	Short cord complicating labor and delivery, unspecified as to episode of care
663.41	Short cord complicating labor and delivery, delivered
663.50	Vasa previa complicating labor and delivery, unspecified as to episode of care
663.51	Vasa previa complicating labor and delivery, delivered
663.60	Vascular lesions of cord complicating labor and delivery, unspecified as to episode of care
663.61	Vascular lesions of cord complicating labor and delivery, delivered
663.80	Other umbilical cord complications during labor and delivery, unspecified as to episode of care
663.81	Other umbilical cord complications during labor and delivery, delivered
663.90	Unspecified umbilical cord complication during labor and delivery, unspecified as to episode of care
663.91	Unspecified umbilical cord complication during labor and delivery, delivered
664.00	First-degree perineal laceration, unspecified as to episode of care in pregnancy
664.01	First-degree perineal laceration, with delivery
664.10	Second-degree perineal laceration, unspecified as to episode of care in pregnancy
664.11	Second-degree perineal laceration, with delivery
664.20	Third-degree perineal laceration, unspecified as to episode of care in pregnancy
664.21	Third-degree perineal laceration, with delivery
664.30	Fourth-degree perineal laceration, unspecified as to episode of care in pregnancy
664.31	Fourth-degree perineal laceration, with delivery
664.40	Unspecified perineal laceration, unspecified as to episode of care in pregnancy
664.41	Unspecified perineal laceration, with delivery
664.50	Vulvar and perineal hematoma, unspecified as to episode of care in pregnancy
664.51	Vulvar and perineal hematoma, with delivery
664.80	Other specified trauma to perineum and vulva, unspecified as to episode of care in pregnancy
664.81	Other specified trauma to perineum and vulva, with delivery
664.90	Unspecified trauma to perineum and vulva, unspecified as to episode of care in pregnancy
664.91	Unspecified trauma to perineum and vulva, with delivery
665.00	Rupture of uterus before onset of labor, unspecified as to episode of care
665.01	Rupture of uterus before onset of labor, with delivery
665.10	Rupture of uterus during labor, unspecified as to episode
665.11	Rupture of uterus during labor, with delivery
665.20	Inversion of uterus, unspecified as to episode of care in pregnancy
665.22	Inversion of uterus, delivered with postpartum complication
665.30	Laceration of cervix, unspecified as to episode of care in pregnancy
665.31	Laceration of cervix, with delivery
665.40	High vaginal laceration, unspecified as to episode of care in pregnancy
665.41	High vaginal laceration, with delivery

MDC 14: Pregnancy, Childbirth and the Puerperium — Medical

DRG 373 — continued

665.50	Other injury to pelvic organs, unspecified as to episode of care in pregnancy
665.51	Other injury to pelvic organs, with delivery
665.60	Damage to pelvic joints and ligaments, unspecified as to episode of care in pregnancy
665.61	Damage to pelvic joints and ligaments, with delivery
665.70	Pelvic hematoma, unspecified as to episode of care
665.71	Pelvic hematoma, with delivery
665.72	Pelvic hematoma, delivered with postpartum complication
665.80	Other specified obstetrical trauma, unspecified as to episode of care
665.81	Other specified obstetrical trauma, with delivery
665.82	Other specified obstetrical trauma, delivered, with postpartum
665.90	Unspecified obstetrical trauma, unspecified as to episode of care
665.91	Unspecified obstetrical trauma, with delivery
665.92	Unspecified obstetrical trauma, delivered, with postpartum complication
668.00	Pulmonary complications of the administration of anesthesia or other sedation in labor and delivery, unspecified as to episode of care
668.10	Cardiac complications of the administration of anesthesia or other sedation in labor and delivery, unspecified as to episode of care
668.20	Central nervous system complications of the administration of anesthesia or other sedation in labor and delivery, unspecified as to episode of care
668.80	Other complications of the administration of anesthesia or other sedation in labor and delivery, unspecified as to episode of care
668.90	Unspecified complication of the administration of anesthesia or other sedation in labor and delivery, unspecified as to episode of care
669.00	Maternal distress complicating labor and delivery, unspecified as to episode of care
669.01	Maternal distress, with delivery, with or without mention of antepartum condition
669.02	Maternal distress, with delivery, with mention of postpartum complication
669.10	Shock during or following labor and delivery, unspecified as to episode of care
669.20	Maternal hypotension syndrome complicating labor and delivery, unspecified as to episode of care
669.21	Maternal hypotension syndrome, with delivery, with or without mention of antepartum condition
669.22	Maternal hypotension syndrome, with delivery, with mention of postpartum complication
669.30	Acute renal failure following labor and delivery, unspecified as to episode of care
669.40	Other complications of obstetrical surgery and procedures, unspecified as to episode of care
669.50	Forceps or vacuum extractor delivery without mention of indication, unspecified as to episode of care
669.51	Forceps or vacuum extractor delivery without mention of indication, delivered, with or without mention of antepartum condition
669.60	Breech extraction, without mention of indication, unspecified as to episode of care
669.61	Breech extraction, without mention of indication, delivered, with or without mention of antepartum condition
669.70	Cesarean delivery, without mention of indication, unspecified as to episode of care
669.71	Cesarean delivery, without mention of indication, delivered, with or without mention of antepartum condition
669.80	Other complication of labor and delivery, unspecified as to episode of care
669.81	Other complication of labor and delivery, delivered, with or without mention of antepartum condition
669.82	Other complication of labor and delivery, delivered, with mention of postpartum complication
669.90	Unspecified complication of labor and delivery, unspecified as to episode of care
669.91	Unspecified complication of labor and delivery, with delivery, with or without mention of antepartum condition
669.92	Unspecified complication of labor and delivery, with delivery, with mention of postpartum complication
671.01	Varicose veins of legs, with delivery, with or without mention of antepartum condition
671.02	Varicose veins of legs, with delivery, with mention of postpartum complication
671.11	Varicose veins of vulva and perineum, with delivery, with or without mention of antepartum condition
671.12	Varicose veins of vulva and perineum, with delivery, with mention of postpartum complication
671.21	Superficial thrombophlebitis with delivery, with or without mention of antepartum condition
671.22	Superficial thrombophlebitis with delivery, with mention of postpartum complication
671.81	Other venous complication, with delivery, with or without mention of antepartum condition
671.82	Other venous complication, with delivery, with mention of postpartum complication

671.91	Unspecified venous complication, with delivery, with or without mention of antepartum condition
671.92	Unspecified venous complication, with delivery, with mention of postpartum complication
674.42	Placental polyp, with delivery, with mention of postpartum complication
674.92	Unspecified complications of puerperium, with delivery, with mention of postpartum complication
675.81	Other specified infection of the breast and nipple associated with childbirth, delivered, with or without mention of antepartum condition
675.82	Other specified infection of the breast and nipple associated with childbirth, delivered, with mention of postpartum complication
675.91	Unspecified infection of the breast and nipple, delivered, with or without mention of antepartum condition
675.92	Unspecified infection of the breast and nipple, delivered, with mention of postpartum complication
676.01	Retracted nipple, delivered, with or without mention of antepartum condition
676.02	Retracted nipple, delivered, with mention of postpartum complication
676.11	Cracked nipple, delivered, with or without mention of antepartum condition
676.12	Cracked nipple, delivered, with mention of postpartum complication
676.21	Engorgement of breasts, delivered, with or without mention of antepartum condition
676.22	Engorgement of breasts, delivered, with mention of postpartum complication
676.31	Other and unspecified disorder of breast associated with childbirth, delivered, with or without mention of antepartum condition
676.32	Other and unspecified disorder of breast associated with childbirth, delivered, with mention of postpartum complication
676.41	Failure of lactation, with delivery, with or without mention of antepartum condition
676.42	Failure of lactation, with delivery, with mention of postpartum complication
676.51	Suppressed lactation, with delivery, with or without mention of antepartum condition
676.52	Suppressed lactation, with delivery, with mention of postpartum complication
676.61	Galactorrhea, with delivery, with or without mention of antepartum condition
676.62	Galactorrhea, with delivery, with mention of postpartum complication
676.81	Other disorder of lactation, with delivery, with or without mention of antepartum condition
676.82	Other disorder of lactation, with delivery, with mention of postpartum complication
676.91	Unspecified disorder of lactation, with delivery, with or without mention of antepartum condition
676.92	Unspecified disorder of lactation, with delivery, with mention of postpartum complication

AND

Only operating room procedures listed under DRG 372

OR

No operating room procedures

Ⓜ DRG 376 Postpartum and Postabortion Diagnoses without O.R. Procedure

GMLOS 2.6 AMLOS 3.4 RW 0.5242 ☑

Principal Diagnosis

*639	Complications following abortion or ectopic and molar pregnancies
642.04	Benign essential hypertension, previous postpartum complication
642.14	Hypertension secondary to renal disease, previous postpartum condition
642.24	Other pre-existing hypertension, previous postpartum condition
642.34	Transient hypertension of pregnancy, previous postpartum condition
642.44	Mild or unspecified pre-eclampsia, previous postpartum condition
642.54	Severe pre-eclampsia, previous postpartum condition
642.64	Eclampsia, previous postpartum condition
642.74	Pre-eclampsia or eclampsia superimposed on pre-existing hypertension, postpartum
642.94	Unspecified hypertension, previous postpartum condition
646.14	Edema or excessive weight gain, previous postpartum condition
646.24	Unspecified renal disease, previous postpartum condition
646.44	Peripheral neuritis, previous postpartum condition
646.54	Asymptomatic bacteriuria, previous postpartum condition
646.64	Infections of genitourinary tract, previous postpartum condition
646.84	Other specified complications, previous postpartum condition

** Code Range* ☑ *Optimization Potential* *Targeted Potential* 🅃 *Transfer DRG* *SP Special Payment*

DRG 376 — continued

647.04	Maternal syphilis, previous postpartum condition
647.14	Maternal gonorrhea, previous postpartum condition
647.24	Other postpartum venereal diseases
647.34	Maternal tuberculosis, previous postpartum condition
647.44	Maternal malaria, previous postpartum condition
647.54	Maternal rubella, previous postpartum condition
647.64	Other maternal viral disease, previous postpartum condition
647.84	Other specified maternal infectious and parasitic disease, previous postpartum condition
647.94	Unspecified maternal infection or infestation, previous postpartum condition
648.04	Maternal diabetes mellitus, previous postpartum condition
648.14	Maternal thyroid dysfunction, previous postpartum condition or complication
648.24	Maternal anemia, previous postpartum condition
648.34	Maternal drug dependence, previous postpartum condition
648.44	Maternal mental disorders, previous postpartum condition
648.54	Maternal congenital cardiovascular disorders, previous postpartum condition
648.64	Other maternal cardiovascular diseases, previous postpartum condition
648.74	Bone and joint disorders of maternal back, pelvis, and lower limbs, previous postpartum condition
648.84	Abnormal maternal glucose tolerance, previous postpartum condition
648.94	Other current maternal conditions classifiable elsewhere, previous postpartum condition
654.04	Congenital abnormalities of pregnant uterus
654.14	Tumors of body of uterus, postpartum condition or complication
654.34	Retroverted and incarcerated gravid uterus, postpartum
654.44	Other abnormalities in shape or position of gravid uterus and of neighboring structures, postpartum
654.54	Cervical incompetence, postpartum condition or complication
654.64	Other congenital or acquired abnormality of cervix, postpartum condition or complication
654.74	Congenital or acquired abnormality of vagina, postpartum condition or complication
654.84	Congenital or acquired abnormality of vulva, postpartum condition or complication
654.94	Other and unspecified abnormality of organs and soft tissues of pelvis, postpartum condition or complication
664.04	First-degree perineal laceration, postpartum
664.14	Second-degree perineal laceration, postpartum
664.24	Third-degree perineal laceration, postpartum
664.34	Fourth-degree perineal laceration, postpartum
664.44	Unspecified perineal laceration, postpartum
664.54	Vulvar and perineal hematoma, postpartum
664.84	Other specified trauma to perineum and vulva, postpartum
664.94	Unspecified trauma to perineum and vulva, postpartum
665.24	Inversion of uterus, postpartum
665.34	Laceration of cervix, postpartum
665.44	High vaginal laceration, postpartum
665.54	Other injury to pelvic organs, postpartum
665.64	Damage to pelvic joints and ligaments, postpartum
665.74	Pelvic hematoma, postpartum
665.84	Other specified obstetrical trauma, postpartum
665.94	Unspecified obstetrical trauma, postpartum
666.04	Third-stage postpartum hemorrhage, postpartum
666.14	Other immediate postpartum hemorrhage, postpartum
666.24	Delayed and secondary postpartum hemorrhage, postpartum
666.34	Postpartum coagulation defects, postpartum
667.04	Retained placenta without hemorrhage, postpartum condition or complication
667.14	Retained portions of placenta or membranes, without hemorrhage, postpartum condition or complication
668.04	Pulmonary complications of the administration of anesthesia or other sedation in labor and delivery, postpartum
668.14	Cardiac complications of the administration of anesthesia or other sedation in labor and delivery, postpartum
668.24	Central nervous system complications of the administration of anesthesia or other sedation in labor and delivery, postpartum
668.84	Other complications of the administration of anesthesia or other sedation in labor and delivery, postpartum

668.94	Unspecified complication of the administration of anesthesia or other sedation in labor and delivery, postpartum
669.04	Maternal distress complicating labor and delivery, postpartum condition or complication
669.14	Shock during or following labor and delivery, postpartum shock
669.24	Maternal hypotension syndrome, postpartum
669.34	Acute renal failure following labor and delivery, postpartum condition or complication
669.44	Other complications of obstetrical surgery and procedures, postpartum condition or complication
669.84	Other complication of labor and delivery, postpartum condition or complication
669.94	Unspecified complication of labor and delivery, postpartum condition or complication
670.04	Major puerperal infection, postpartum
671.04	Varicose veins of legs, postpartum
671.14	Varicose veins of vulva and perineum, postpartum
671.24	Superficial thrombophlebitis, postpartum
671.44	Deep phlebothrombosis, postpartum
671.54	Other postpartum phlebitis and thrombosis
671.84	Other venous complication, postpartum
671.94	Unspecified venous complication, postpartum
672.04	Puerperal pyrexia of unknown origin, postpartum
673.04	Obstetrical air embolism, postpartum condition or complication
673.14	Amniotic fluid embolism, postpartum condition or complication
673.24	Obstetrical blood-clot embolism, postpartum
673.34	Obstetrical pyemic and septic embolism, postpartum
673.84	Other obstetrical pulmonary embolism, postpartum
674.04	Cerebrovascular disorder, postpartum
674.14	Disruption of cesarean wound, postpartum
674.24	Disruption of perineal wound, postpartum
674.34	Other complication of obstetrical surgical wounds, postpartum condition or complication
674.44	Placental polyp, postpartum
674.54	Peripartum cardiomyopathy, postpartum condition or complication
674.84	Other complication of puerperium
674.94	Unspecified complications of puerperium
675.04	Infection of nipple, postpartum
675.14	Abscess of breast, postpartum
675.24	Nonpurulent mastitis, postpartum
675.84	Other specified infection of the breast and nipple, postpartum
675.94	Unspecified infection of the breast and nipple, postpartum
676.04	Retracted nipple, postpartum condition or complication
676.14	Cracked nipple, postpartum condition or complication
676.24	Engorement of breast, postpartum
676.34	Other and unspecified disorder of breast associated with childbirth, postpartum condition or complication
676.44	Failure of lactation, postpartum condition or complication
676.54	Suppressed lactation, postpartum condition or complication
676.64	Galactorrhea, postpartum condition or complication
676.84	Other disorder of lactation, postpartum condition or complication
676.94	Unspecified disorder of lactation, postpartum condition or complication
V24.0	Postpartum care and examination immediately after delivery

M DRG 378 Ectopic Pregnancy

GMLOS 1.9 AMLOS 2.3 RW 0.7472

Principal Diagnosis

*633	Ectopic pregnancy

M DRG 379 Threatened Abortion

GMLOS 2.0 AMLOS 2.8 RW 0.3578 ☑

Principal Diagnosis

640.00	Threatened abortion, unspecified as to episode of care
640.03	Threatened abortion, antepartum
640.80	Other specified hemorrhage in early pregnancy, unspecified as to episode of care
640.83	Other specified hemorrhage in early pregnancy, antepartum

DRG 379 — continued

640.90	Unspecified hemorrhage in early pregnancy, unspecified as to episode of care
640.93	Unspecified hemorrhage in early pregnancy, antepartum
644.00	Threatened premature labor, unspecified as to episode of care
644.03	Threatened premature labor, antepartum

Ⓜ DRG 380 Abortion without D and C

GMLOS 1.6 AMLOS 2.1 RW 0.3925 ☑

Principal Diagnosis

632	Missed abortion
*634	Spontaneous abortion
*635	Legally induced abortion
*636	Illegally induced abortion
*637	Legally unspecified abortion
*638	Failed attempted abortion
V61.7	Other unwanted pregnancy

Ⓜ DRG 382 False Labor

GMLOS 1.3 AMLOS 1.4 RW 0.2070 ☑

Principal Diagnosis

644.10	Other threatened labor, unspecified as to episode of care
644.13	Other threatened labor, antepartum

Ⓜ DRG 383 Other Antepartum Diagnoses with Medical Complications

GMLOS 2.6 AMLOS 3.7 RW 0.5053

Principal Diagnosis

630	Hydatidiform mole
631	Other abnormal product of conception
641.03	Placenta previa without hemorrhage, antepartum
641.13	Hemorrhage from placenta previa, antepartum
641.23	Premature separation of placenta, antepartum
641.33	Antepartum hemorrhage associated with coagulation defect, antepartumm
641.83	Other antepartum hemorrhage, antepartum
641.93	Unspecified antepartum hemorrhage, antepartum
642.03	Benign essential hypertension antepartum
642.13	Hypertension secondary to renal disease, antepartum
642.23	Other pre-existing hypertension, antepartum
642.33	Transient hypertension of pregnancy, antepartum
642.43	Mild or unspecified pre-eclampsia, antepartum
642.53	Severe pre-eclampsia, antepartum
642.63	Eclampsia, antepartum
642.73	Pre-eclampsia or eclampsia superimposed on pre-existing hypertension, antepartum
642.93	Unspecified hypertension antepartum
643.03	Mild hyperemesis gravidarum, antepartum
643.13	Hyperemesis gravidarum with metabolic disturbance, antepartum
643.23	Late vomiting of pregnancy, antepartum
643.83	Other vomiting complicating pregnancy, antepartum
643.93	Unspecified vomiting of pregnancy, antepartum
644.20	Early onset of delivery, unspecified as to episode of care
645.13	Post term pregnancy, antepartum condition or complication
645.23	Prolonged pregnancy, delivered, antepartum condition or complication
646.03	Papyraceous fetus, antepartum
646.13	Edema or excessive weight gain, antepartum
646.23	Unspecified antepartum renal disease
646.33	Habitual aborter, antepartum condition or complication
646.43	Peripheral neuritis antepartum
646.53	Asymptomatic bacteriuria antepartum
646.63	Infections of genitourinary tract antepartum
646.73	Liver disorders antepartum
646.83	Other specifed complication, antepartum

646.93	Unspecified complication of pregnancy, antepartum
647.03	Maternal syphilis, antepartum
647.13	Maternal gonorrhea, antepartum
647.23	Other antepartum maternal venereal disease, previous postpartum condition
647.33	Maternal tuberculosis, antepartum
647.43	Maternal malaria, antepartum
647.53	Maternal rubella, antepartum
647.63	Other maternal viral disease, antepartum
647.83	Other specified maternal infectious and parasitic disease, antepartum
647.93	Unspecified maternal infection or infestation, antepartum
648.03	Maternal diabetes mellitus, antepartum
648.13	Maternal thyroid dysfunction, antepartum condition or complication
648.23	Maternal anemia, antepartum
648.33	Maternal drug dependence, antepartum
648.43	Maternal mental disorders, antepartum
648.53	Maternal congenital cardiovascular disorders, antepartum
648.63	Other maternal cardiovascular diseases, antepartum
648.73	Bone and joint disorders of maternal back, pelvis, and lower limbs, antepartum
648.83	Abnormal maternal glucose tolerance, antepartum
648.93	Other current maternal conditions classifiable elsewhere, antepartum
651.03	Twin pregnancy, antepartum
651.13	Triplet pregnancy, antepartum
651.23	Quadruplet pregnancy, antepartum
651.33	Twin pregnancy with fetal loss and retention of one fetus, antepartum
651.43	Triplet pregnancy with fetal loss and retention of one or more, antepartum
651.53	Quadruplet pregnancy with fetal loss and retention of one or more, antepartum
651.63	Other multiple pregnancy with fetal loss and retention of one or more fetus(es), antepartum
651.73	Multiple gestation following (elective) fetal reduction, antepartum condition or complication
651.83	Other specified multiple gestation, antepartum
651.93	Unspecified multiple gestation, antepartum
652.03	Unstable lie of fetus, antepartum
652.13	Breech or other malpresentation successfully converted to cephalic presentation, antepartum
652.23	Breech presentation without mention of version, antepartum
652.33	Transverse or oblique fetal presentation, antepartum
652.43	Fetal face or brow presentation, antepartum
652.53	High fetal head at term, antepartum
652.63	Multiple gestation with malpresentation of one fetus or more, antepartum
652.73	Prolapsed arm of fetus, antepartum condition or complication
652.83	Other specified malposition or malpresentation of fetus, antepartum
652.93	Unspecified malposition or malpresentation of fetus, antepartum
653.03	Major abnormality of bony pelvis, not further specified, antepartum
653.13	Generally contracted pelvis in pregnancy, antepartum
653.23	Inlet contraction of pelvis in pregnancy, antepartum
653.33	Outlet contraction of pelvis in pregnancy, antepartum
653.43	Fetopelvic disproportion, antepartum
653.53	Unusually large fetus causing disproportion, antepartum
653.63	Hydrocephalic fetus causing disproportion, antepartum
653.73	Other fetal abnormality causing disproportion, antepartum
653.83	Fetal disproportion of other origin, antepartum
653.93	Unspecified fetal disproportion, antepartum
654.03	Congenital abnormalities of pregnant uterus, antepartum
654.13	Tumors of body of uterus, antepartum condition or complication
654.23	Previous cesarean delivery, antepartum condition or complication
654.33	Retroverted and incarcerated gravid uterus, antepartum
654.43	Other abnormalities in shape or position of gravid uterus and of neighboring structures, antepartum
654.53	Cervical incompetence, antepartum condition or complication
654.63	Other congenital or acquired abnormality of cervix, antepartum condition or complication
654.73	Congenital or acquired abnormality of vagina, antepartum condition or complication
654.83	Congenital or acquired abnormality of vulva, antepartum condition or complication
654.93	Other and unspecified abnormality of organs and soft tissues of pelvis, antepartum condition or complication
655.03	Central nervous system malformation in fetus, antepartum

DRG 383 — continued

655.13	Chromosomal abnormality in fetus, affecting management of mother, antepartum
655.23	Hereditary disease in family possibly affecting fetus, affecting management of mother, antepartum condition or complication
655.33	Suspected damage to fetus from viral disease in mother, affecting management of mother, antepartum condition or complication
655.43	Suspected damage to fetus from other disease in mother, affecting management of mother, antepartum condition or complication
655.53	Suspected damage to fetus from drugs, affecting management of mother, antepartum
655.63	Suspected damage to fetus from radiation, affecting management of mother, antepartum condition or complication
655.73	Decreased fetal movements, affecting management of mother, antepartum condition or complication
655.83	Other known or suspected fetal abnormality, not elsewhere classified, affecting management of mother, antepartum condition or complication
655.93	Unspecified fetal abnormality affecting management of mother, antepartum condition or complication
656.03	Fetal-maternal hemorrhage, antepartum condition or complication
656.13	Rhesus isoimmunization affecting management of mother, antepartum condition
656.23	Isoimmunization from other and unspecified blood-group incompatibility, affecting management of mother, antepartum
656.33	Fetal distress affecting management of mother, antepartum
656.43	Intrauterine death affecting management of mother, antepartum
656.53	Poor fetal growth, affecting management of mother, antepartum condition or complication
656.63	Excessive fetal growth affecting management of mother, antepartum
656.73	Other placental conditions affecting management of mother, antepartum
656.83	Other specified fetal and placental problems affecting management of mother, antepartum
656.93	Unspecified fetal and placental problem affecting management of mother, antepartum
657.03	Polyhydramnios, antepartum complication
658.03	Oligohydramnios, antepartum
658.13	Premature rupture of membranes in pregnancy, antepartum
658.23	Delayed delivery after spontaneous or unspecified rupture of membranes, antepartum
658.33	Delayed delivery after artificial rupture of membranes, antepartum
658.43	Infection of amniotic cavity, antepartum
658.83	Other problem associated with amniotic cavity and membranes, antepartum
658.93	Unspecified problem associated with amniotic cavity and membranes, antepartum
659.03	Failed mechanical induction of labor, antepartum
659.13	Failed medical or unspecified induction of labor, antepartum
659.23	Unspecified maternal pyrexia, antepartum
659.33	Generalized infection during labor, antepartum
659.43	Grand multiparity with current pregnancy, antepartum
659.53	Elderly primigravida, antepartum
659.63	Elderly multigravida, with antepartum condition or complication
659.73	Abnormality in fetal heart rate or rhythm, antepartum condition or complication
659.83	Other specified indication for care or intervention related to labor and delivery, antepartum
659.93	Unspecified indication for care or intervention related to labor and delivery, antepartum
660.03	Obstruction caused by malposition of fetus at onset of labor, antepartum
660.13	Obstruction by bony pelvis during labor and delivery, antepartum
660.23	Obstruction by abnormal pelvic soft tissues during labor and delivery, antepartum
660.33	Deep transverse arrest and persistent occipitoposterior position during labor and delivery, antepartum
660.43	Shoulder (girdle) dystocia during labor and delivery, antepartum
660.53	Locked twins, antepartum
660.63	Unspecified failed trial of labor, antepartum
660.73	Failed forceps or vacuum extractor, unspecified, antepartum
660.83	Other causes of obstructed labor, antepartum
660.93	Unspecified obstructed labor, antepartum
661.03	Primary uterine inertia, antepartum
661.13	Secondary uterine inertia, antepartum
661.23	Other and unspecified uterine inertia, antepartum
661.33	Precipitate labor, antepartum
661.43	Hypertonic, incoordinate, or prolonged uterine contractions, antepartum
661.93	Unspecified abnormality of labor, antepartum

662.03	Prolonged first stage of labor, antepartum
662.13	Unspecified prolonged labor, antepartum
662.23	Prolonged second stage of labor, antepartum
662.33	Delayed delivery of second twin, triplet, etc., antepartum
663.03	Prolapse of cord, complicating labor and delivery, antepartum
663.13	Cord around neck, with compression, complicating labor and delivery, antepartum
663.23	Other and unspecified cord entanglement, with compression, complicating labor and delivery, antepartum
663.33	Other and unspecified cord entanglement, without mention of compression, complicating labor and delivery, antepartum
663.43	Short cord complicating labor and delivery, antepartum
663.53	Vasa previa complicating labor and delivery, antepartum
663.63	Vascular lesions of cord complicating labor and delivery, antepartum
663.83	Other umbilical cord complications during labor and delivery, antepartum
663.93	Unspecified umbilical cord complication during labor and delivery, antepartum
665.03	Rupture of uterus before onset of labor, antepartum
665.83	Other specified obstetrical trauma, antepartum
665.93	Unspecified obstetrical trauma, antepartum
668.03	Pulmonary complications of the administration of anesthesia or other sedation in labor and delivery, antepartum
668.13	Cardiac complications of the administration of anesthesia or other sedation in labor and delivery, antepartum
668.23	Central nervous system complications of the administration of anesthesia or other sedation in labor and delivery, antepartum
668.83	Other complications of the administration of anesthesia or other sedation in labor and delivery, antepartum
668.93	Unspecified complication of the administration of anesthesia or other sedation in labor and delivery, antepartum
669.03	Maternal distress complicating labor and delivery, antepartum condition or complication
669.13	Shock during or following labor and delivery, antepartum shock
669.23	Maternal hypotension syndrome, antepartum
669.43	Other complications of obstetrical surgery and procedures, antepartum condition or complication
669.83	Other complication of labor and delivery, antepartum condition or complication
669.93	Unspecified complication of labor and delivery, antepartum condition or complication
671.03	Varicose veins of legs, antepartum
671.13	Varicose veins of vulva and perineum, antepartum
671.23	Superficial thrombophlebitis, antepartum
671.33	Deep phlebothrombosis, antepartum
671.53	Other antepartum phlebitis and thrombosis
671.83	Other venous complication, antepartum
671.93	Unspecified venous complication, antepartum
673.03	Obstetrical air embolism, antepartum condition or complication
673.13	Amniotic fluid embolism, antepartum condition or complication
673.23	Obstetrical blood-clot embolism, antepartum
673.33	Obstetrical pyemic and septic embolism, antepartum
673.83	Other obstetrical pulmonary embolism, antepartum
674.03	Cerebrovascular disorder, antepartum
674.53	Peripartum cardiomyopathy, antepartum condition or complication
675.03	Infection of nipple, antepartum
675.13	Abscess of breast, antepartum
675.23	Nonpurulent mastitis, antepartum
675.83	Other specified infection of the breast and nipple, antepartum
675.93	Unspecified infection of the breast and nipple, antepartum
676.03	Retracted nipple, antepartum condition or complication
676.13	Cracked nipple, antepartum condition or complication
676.23	Engorgement of breast, antepartum
676.33	Other and unspecified disorder of breast associated with childbirth, antepartum condition or complication
676.43	Failure of lactation, antepartum condition or complication
676.53	Suppressed lactation, antepartum condition or complication
676.63	Galactorrhea, antepartum condition or complication
676.83	Other disorder of lactation, antepartum condition or complication

DRG 383 — continued

676.93	Unspecified disorder of lactation, antepartum condition or complication
792.3	Nonspecific abnormal finding in amniotic fluid
796.5	Abnormal finding on antenatal screening
V28.0	Screening for chromosomal anomalies by amniocentesis
V28.1	Screening for raised alpha-fetoprotein levels in amniotic fluid
V28.2	Other antenatal screening based on amniocentesis
V61.6	Illegitimacy or illegitimate pregnancy

AND

Principal or Secondary Diagnosis

641.30	Antepartum hemorrhage associated with coagulation defects, unspecified as to episode of care
641.33	Antepartum hemorrhage associated with coagulation defect, antepartumm
642.03	Benign essential hypertension antepartum
642.13	Hypertension secondary to renal disease, antepartum
642.23	Other pre-existing hypertension, antepartum
642.43	Mild or unspecified pre-eclampsia, antepartum
642.50	Severe pre-eclampsia, unspecified as to episode of care
642.53	Severe pre-eclampsia, antepartum
642.60	Eclampsia complicating pregnancy, childbirth or the puerperium, unspecified as to episode of care
642.63	Eclampsia, antepartum
642.70	Pre-eclampsia or eclampsia superimposed on pre-existing hypertension, complicating pregnancy, childbirth, or the puerperium, unspecified as to episode of care
642.73	Pre-eclampsia or eclampsia superimposed on pre-existing hypertension, antepartum
642.93	Unspecified hypertension antepartum
643.00	Mild hyperemesis gravidarum, unspecified as to episode of care
643.03	Mild hyperemesis gravidarum, antepartum
643.10	Hyperemesis gravidarum with metabolic disturbance, unspecified as to episode of care
643.13	Hyperemesis gravidarum with metabolic disturbance, antepartum
643.20	Late vomiting of pregnancy, unspecified as to episode of care
643.23	Late vomiting of pregnancy, antepartum
643.80	Other vomiting complicating pregnancy, unspecified as to episode of care
643.83	Other vomiting complicating pregnancy, antepartum
643.90	Unspecified vomiting of pregnancy, unspecified as to episode of care
643.93	Unspecified vomiting of pregnancy, antepartum
646.10	Edema or excessive weight gain in pregnancy, unspecified as to episode of care
646.13	Edema or excessive weight gain, antepartum
646.20	Unspecified renal disease in pregnancy, unspecified as to episode of care
646.23	Unspecified antepartum renal disease
646.43	Peripheral neuritis antepartum
646.60	Infections of genitourinary tract in pregnancy, unspecified as to episode of care
646.63	Infections of genitourinary tract antepartum
646.70	Liver disorders in pregnancy, unspecified as to episode of care
646.73	Liver disorders antepartum
646.80	Other specified complication of pregnancy, unspecified as to episode of care
646.83	Other specifed complication, antepartum
647.03	Maternal syphilis, antepartum
647.13	Maternal gonorrhea, antepartum
647.23	Other antepartum maternal venereal disease, previous postpartum condition
647.33	Maternal tuberculosis, antepartum
647.43	Maternal malaria, antepartum
647.53	Maternal rubella, antepartum
647.63	Other maternal viral disease, antepartum
647.83	Other specified maternal infectious and parasitic disease, antepartum
647.93	Unspecified maternal infection or infestation, antepartum
648.03	Maternal diabetes mellitus, antepartum
648.13	Maternal thyroid dysfunction, antepartum condition or complication
648.23	Maternal anemia, antepartum
648.33	Maternal drug dependence, antepartum
648.43	Maternal mental disorders, antepartum
648.53	Maternal congenital cardiovascular disorders, antepartum
648.63	Other maternal cardiovascular diseases, antepartum

648.73	Bone and joint disorders of maternal back, pelvis, and lower limbs, antepartum
648.83	Abnormal maternal glucose tolerance, antepartum
648.93	Other current maternal conditions classifiable elsewhere, antepartum

Ⓜ DRG 384 Other Antepartum Diagnoses without Medical Complications

GMLOS 1.8 AMLOS 2.6 RW 0.3225 ☑

Select principal diagnosis listed under DRG 383 excluding principal or secondary diagnoses

Ⓜ DRG 469 Principal Diagnosis Invalid as Discharge Diagnosis

GMLOS 0.0 AMLOS 0.0 RW 0.0000

Principal diagnoses listed for MDC 14 considered invalid as discharge diagnosis

641.00	Placenta previa without hemorrhage, unspecified as to episode of care
641.10	Hemorrhage from placenta previa, unspecified as to episode of care
641.20	Premature separation of placenta, unspecified as to episode of care
641.30	Antepartum hemorrhage associated with coagulation defects, unspecified as to episode of care
641.80	Other antepartum hemorrhage, unspecified as to episode of care
641.90	Unspecified antepartum hemorrhage, unspecified as to episode of care
642.00	Benign essential hypertension complicating pregnancy, childbirth, and the puerperium, unspecified as to episode of care
642.10	Hypertension secondary to renal disease, complicating pregnancy, childbirth, and the puerperium, unspecified as to episode of care
642.20	Other pre-existing hypertension complicating pregnancy, childbirth, and the puerperium, unspecified as to episode of care
642.30	Transient hypertension of pregnancy, unspecified as to episode of care
642.40	Mild or unspecified pre-eclampsia, unspecified as to episode of care
642.50	Severe pre-eclampsia, unspecified as to episode of care
642.60	Eclampsia complicating pregnancy, childbirth or the puerperium, unspecified as to episode of care
642.70	Pre-eclampsia or eclampsia superimposed on pre-existing hypertension, complicating pregnancy, childbirth, or the puerperium, unspecified as to episode of care
642.90	Unspecified hypertension complicating pregnancy, childbirth, or the puerperium, unspecified as to episode of care
643.00	Mild hyperemesis gravidarum, unspecified as to episode of care
643.10	Hyperemesis gravidarum with metabolic disturbance, unspecified as to episode of care
643.20	Late vomiting of pregnancy, unspecified as to episode of care
643.80	Other vomiting complicating pregnancy, unspecified as to episode of care
643.90	Unspecified vomiting of pregnancy, unspecified as to episode of care
645.10	Post term pregnancy, unspecified as to episode of care or not applicable
645.20	Prolonged pregnancy, unspecified as to episode of care or not applicable
646.10	Edema or excessive weight gain in pregnancy, unspecified as to episode of care
646.20	Unspecified renal disease in pregnancy, unspecified as to episode of care
646.30	Pregnancy complication, habitual aborter unspecified as to episode of care
646.40	Peripheral neuritis in pregnancy, unspecified as to episode of care
646.50	Asymptomatic bacteriuria in pregnancy, unspecified as to episode of care
646.60	Infections of genitourinary tract in pregnancy, unspecified as to episode of care
646.70	Liver disorders in pregnancy, unspecified as to episode of care
646.80	Other specified complication of pregnancy, unspecified as to episode of care
646.90	Unspecified complication of pregnancy, unspecified as to episode of care
647.00	Maternal syphilis, complicating pregnancy, childbirth, or the puerperium, unspecified as to episode of care
647.10	Maternal gonorrhea complicating pregnancy, childbirth, or the puerperium, unspecified as to episode of care
647.20	Other maternal venereal diseases, complicating pregnancy, childbirth, or the puerperium, unspecified as to episode of care
647.30	Maternal tuberculosis complicating pregnancy, childbirth, or the puerperium, unspecified as to episode of care
647.40	Maternal malaria complicating pregnancy, childbirth or the puerperium, unspecified as to episode of care

DRG 469 — continued

647.50	Maternal rubella complicating pregnancy, childbirth, or the puerperium, unspecified as to episode of care
647.60	Other maternal viral disease complicating pregnancy, childbirth, or the puerperium, unspecified as to episode of care
647.80	Other specified maternal infectious and parasitic disease complicating pregnancy, childbirth, or the puerperium, unspecified as to episode of care
647.90	Unspecified maternal infection or infestation complicating pregnancy, childbirth, or the puerperium, unspecified as to episode of care
648.00	Maternal diabetes mellitus, complicating pregnancy, childbirth, or the puerperium, unspecified as to episode of care
648.10	Maternal thyroid dysfunction complicating pregnancy, childbirth, or the puerperium, unspecified as to episode of care or not applicable
648.20	Maternal anemia of mother, complicating pregnancy, childbirth, or the puerperium, unspecified as to episode of care
648.30	Maternal drug dependence complicating pregnancy, childbirth, or the puerperium, unspecified as to episode of care
648.40	Maternal mental disorders, complicating pregnancy, childbirth, or the puerperium, unspecified as to episode of care
648.50	Maternal congenital cardiovascular disorders, complicating pregnancy, childbirth, or the puerperium, unspecified as to episode of care
648.60	Other maternal cardiovascular diseases complicating pregnancy, childbirth, or the puerperium, unspecified as to episode of care
648.70	Bone and joint disorders of maternal back, pelvis, and lower limbs, complicating pregnancy, childbirth, or the puerperium, unspecified as to episode of care
648.80	Abnormal maternal glucose tolerance, complicating pregnancy, childbirth, or the puerperium, unspecified as to episode of care
648.90	Other current maternal conditions classifiable elsewhere, complicating pregnancy, childbirth, or the puerperium, unspecified as to episode of care
651.00	Twin pregnancy, unspecified as to episode of care
651.10	Triplet pregnancy, unspecified as to episode of care
651.20	Quadruplet pregnancy, unspecified as to episode of care
651.30	Twin pregnancy with fetal loss and retention of one fetus, unspecified as to episode of care or not applicable
651.40	Triplet pregnancy with fetal loss and retention of one or more, unspecified as to episode of care or not applicable
651.50	Quadruplet pregnancy with fetal loss and retention of one or more, unspecified as to episode of care or not applicable
651.60	Other multiple pregnancy with fetal loss and retention of one or more fetus(es), unspecified as to episode of care or not applicable
651.70	Multiple gestation following (elective) fetal reduction, unspecified as to episode of care or not applicable
651.80	Other specified multiple gestation, unspecified as to episode of care
651.90	Unspecified multiple gestation, unspecified as to episode of care
652.00	Unstable lie of fetus, unspecified as to episode of care
652.10	Breech or other malpresentation successfully converted to cephalic presentation, unspecified as to episode of care
652.20	Breech presentation without mention of version, unspecified as to episode of care
652.30	Transverse or oblique fetal presentation, unspecified as to episode of care
652.40	Fetal face or brow presentation, unspecified as to episode of care
652.50	High fetal head at term, unspecified as to episode of care
652.60	Multiple gestation with malpresentation of one fetus or more, unspecified as to episode of care
652.70	Prolapsed arm of fetus, unspecified as to episode of care
652.80	Other specified malposition or malpresentation of fetus, unspecified as to episode of care
652.90	Unspecified malposition or malpresentation of fetus, unspecified as to episode of care
653.00	Major abnormality of bony pelvis, not further specified in pregnancy, unspecified as to episode of care
653.10	Generally contracted pelvis in pregnancy, unspecified as to episode of care in pregnancy
653.20	Inlet contraction of pelvis in pregnancy, unspecified as to episode of care in pregnancy
653.30	Outlet contraction of pelvis in pregnancy, unspecified as to episode of care in pregnancy
653.40	Fetopelvic disproportion, unspecified as to episode of care
653.50	Unusually large fetus causing disproportion, unspecified as to episode of care
653.60	Hydrocephalic fetus causing disproportion, unspecified as to episode of care

653.70	Other fetal abnormality causing disproportion, unspecified as to episode of care
653.80	Fetal disproportion of other origin, unspecified as to episode of care
653.90	Unspecified fetal disproportion, unspecified as to episode of care
654.00	Congenital abnormalities of pregnant uterus, unspecified as to episode of care
654.10	Tumors of body of pregnant uterus, unspecified as to episode of care in pregnancy
654.20	Previous cesarean delivery, unspecified as to episode of care or not applicable
654.30	Retroverted and incarcerated gravid uterus, unspecified as to episode of care
654.40	Other abnormalities in shape or position of gravid uterus and of neighboring structures, unspecified as to episode of care
654.50	Cervical incompetence, unspecified as to episode of care in pregnancy
654.60	Other congenital or acquired abnormality of cervix, unspecified as to episode of care in pregnancy
654.70	Congenital or acquired abnormality of vagina, unspecified as to episode of care in pregnancy
654.80	Congenital or acquired abnormality of vulva, unspecified as to episode of care in pregnancy
654.90	Other and unspecified abnormality of organs and soft tissues of pelvis, unspecified as to episode of care in pregnancy
655.00	Central nervous system malformation in fetus, unspecified as to episode of care in pregnancy
655.10	Chromosomal abnormality in fetus, affecting management of mother, unspecified as to episode of care in pregnancy
655.20	Hereditary disease in family possibly affecting fetus, affecting management of mother, unspecified as to episode of care in pregnancy
655.30	Suspected damage to fetus from viral disease in mother, affecting management of mother, unspecified as to episode of care in pregnancy
655.40	Suspected damage to fetus from other disease in mother, affecting management of mother, unspecified as to episode of care in pregnancy
655.50	Suspected damage to fetus from drugs, affecting management of mother, unspecified as to episode of care
655.60	Suspected damage to fetus from radiation, affecting management of mother, unspecified as to episode of care
655.70	Decreased fetal movements, unspecified as to episode of care
655.80	Other known or suspected fetal abnormality, not elsewhere classified, affecting management of mother, unspecified as to episode of care
655.90	Unspecified fetal abnormality affecting management of mother, unspecified as to episode of care
656.00	Fetal-maternal hemorrhage, unspecified as to episode of care in pregnancy
656.10	Rhesus isoimmunization unspecified as to episode of care in pregnancy
656.20	Isoimmunization from other and unspecified blood-group incompatibility, unspecified as to episode of care in pregnancy
656.50	Poor fetal growth, affecting management of mother, unspecified as to episode of care
656.60	Excessive fetal growth affecting management of mother, unspecified as to episode of care
656.70	Other placental conditions affecting management of mother, unspecified as to episode of care
656.80	Other specified fetal and placental problems affecting management of mother, unspecified as to episode of care
656.90	Unspecified fetal and placental problem affecting management of mother, unspecified as to episode of care
657.00	Polyhydramnios, unspecified as to episode of care
658.00	Oligohydramnios, unspecified as to episode of care
658.80	Other problem associated with amniotic cavity and membranes, unspecified as to episode of care
658.90	Unspecified problem associated with amniotic cavity and membranes, unspecified as to episode of care
659.40	Grand multiparity with current pregnancy, unspecified as to episode of care
666.00	Third-stage postpartum hemorrhage, unspecified as to episode of care
666.10	Other immediate postpartum hemorrhage, unspecified as to episode of care
666.20	Delayed and secondary postpartum hemorrhage, unspecified as to episode of care
666.30	Postpartum coagulation defects, unspecified as to episode of care
667.00	Retained placenta without hemorrhage, unspecified as to episode of care
667.10	Retained portions of placenta or membranes, without hemorrhage, unspecified as to episode of care
670.00	Major puerperal infection, unspecified as to episode of care
671.00	Varicose veins of legs complicating pregnancy and the puerperium, unspecified as to episode of care

DRG 469 — continued

671.10	Varicose veins of vulva and perineum complicating pregnancy and the puerperium, unspecified as to episode of care
671.20	Superficial thrombophlebitis complicating pregnancy and the puerperium, unspecified as to episode of care
671.30	Deep phlebothrombosis, antepartum, unspecified as to episode of care
671.40	Deep phlebothrombosis, postpartum, unspecified as to episode of care
671.50	Other phlebitis and thrombosis complicating pregnancy and the puerperium, unspecified as to episode of care
671.80	Other venous complication of pregnancy and the puerperium, unspecified as to episode of care
671.90	Unspecified venous complication of pregnancy and the puerperium, unspecified as to episode of care
672.00	Puerperal pyrexia of unknown origin, unspecified as to episode of care
673.00	Obstetrical air embolism, unspecified as to episode of care
673.10	Amniotic fluid embolism, unspecified as to episode of care
673.20	Obstetrical blood-clot embolism, unspecified as to episode of care
673.30	Obstetrical pyemic and septic embolism, unspecified as to episode of care
673.80	Other obstetrical pulmonary embolism, unspecified as to episode of care
674.00	Cerebrovascular disorder occurring in pregnancy, childbirth, or the puerperium, unspecified as to episode of care
674.10	Disruption of cesarean wound, unspecified as to episode of care
674.20	Disruption of perineal wound, unspecified as to episode of care in pregnancy
674.30	Other complication of obstetrical surgical wounds, unspecified as to episode of care
674.40	Placental polyp, unspecified as to episode of care
674.50	Peripartum cardiomyopathy, unspecified as to episode of care or not applicable
674.80	Other complication of puerperium, unspecified as to episode of care
674.90	Unspecified complications of puerperium, unspecified as to episode of care
675.00	Infection of nipple associated with childbirth, unspecified as to episode of care
675.10	Abscess of breast associated with childbirth, unspecified as to episode of care
675.20	Nonpurulent mastitis, unspecified as to episode of prenatal or postnatal care
675.80	Other specified infection of the breast and nipple associated with childbirth, unspecified as to episode of care
675.90	Unspecified infection of the breast and nipple, unspecified as to prenatal or postnatal episode of care
676.00	Retracted nipple, unspecified as to prenatal or postnatal episode of care
676.10	Cracked nipple, unspecified as to prenatal or postnatal episode of care
676.20	Engorgement of breasts, unspecified as to prenatal or postnatal episode of care
676.30	Other and unspecified disorder of breast associated with childbirth, unspecified as to episode of care
676.40	Failure of lactation, unspecified as to episode of care
676.50	Suppressed lactation, unspecified as to episode of care
676.60	Galactorrhea associated with childbirth, unspecified as to episode of care
676.80	Other disorder of lactation, unspecified as to episode of care
676.90	Unspecified disorder of lactation, unspecified as to episode of care
677	Late effect of complication of pregnancy, childbirth, and the puerperium
V23.0	Pregnancy with history of infertility
V23.1	Pregnancy with history of trophoblastic disease
V23.2	Pregnancy with history of abortion
V23.3	Pregnancy with grand multiparity
*V23.4	Pregnancy with other poor obstetric history
V23.5	Pregnancy with other poor reproductive history
V23.7	Insufficient prenatal care
*V23.8	Other high-risk pregnancy
V23.9	Unspecified high-risk pregnancy

MDC 15
NEWBORNS AND OTHER NEONATES WITH CONDITIONS ORIGINATING IN THE PERINATAL PERIOD

The complete and up-to-date listing of ICD-9-CM diagnosis codes assigned to this MDC can be found online at www.ingenixonline.com/content/drg/resources.asp.

MEDICAL

M DRG 385 Neonates, Died or Transferred to Another Acute Care Facility
GMLOS 1.8 AMLOS 1.8 RW 1.3930

Discharge status of transfer to an acute care facility or expired

Assign newborns transferred to other than acute care facilities to DRGs 386-391 as appropriate

M DRG 386 Extreme Immaturity or Respiratory Distress Syndrome of Neonate
GMLOS 17.9 AMLOS 17.9 RW 4.5935

Principal or Secondary Diagnosis

765.01	Extreme fetal immaturity, less than 500 grams
765.02	Extreme fetal immaturity, 500-749 grams
765.03	Extreme fetal immaturity, 750-999 grams
765.04	Extreme fetal immaturity, 1,000-1,249 grams
765.05	Extreme fetal immaturity, 1,250-1,499 grams
765.21	Less than 24 completed weeks of gestation
765.22	24 completed weeks of gestation
765.23	25-26 completed weeks of gestation
769	Respiratory distress syndrome in newborn

M DRG 387 Prematurity with Major Problems
GMLOS 13.3 AMLOS 13.3 RW 3.1372 ☑

Principal or Secondary Diagnosis of Prematurity

765.00	Extreme fetal immaturity, unspecified (weight)
765.06	Extreme fetal immaturity, 1,500-1,749 grams
765.07	Extreme fetal immaturity, 1,750-1,999 grams
765.08	Extreme fetal immaturity, 2,000-2,499 grams
*765.1	Other preterm infants
765.24	27-28 completed weeks of gestation
765.25	29-30 completed weeks of gestation
765.26	31-32 completed weeks of gestation
765.27	33-34 completed weeks of gestation
765.28	35-36 completed weeks of gestation

AND

Principal or Secondary Diagnosis of Major Problem

*276.5	Volume depletion
277.01	Cystic fibrosis with meconium ileus
*567.2	Other suppurative peritonitis
*567.3	Retroperitoneal infections
*567.8	Other specified peritonitis
747.83	Persistent fetal circulation
763.4	Fetus or newborn affected by cesarean delivery
764.11	"Light-for-dates" with signs of fetal malnutrition, less than 500 grams
764.12	"Light-for-dates" with signs of fetal malnutrition, 500-749 grams
764.13	"Light-for-dates" with signs of fetal malnutrition, 750-999 grams

** Code Range* ☑ *Optimization Potential* *Targeted Potential* *T Transfer DRG* *SP Special Payment*

DRG 387 — continued

764.14	"Light-for-dates" with signs of fetal malnutrition, 1,000-1,249 grams
764.15	"Light-for-dates" with signs of fetal malnutrition, 1,250-1,499 grams
764.16	"Light-for-dates" with signs of fetal malnutrition, 1,500-1,749 grams
764.17	"Light-for-dates" with signs of fetal malnutrition, 1,750-1,999 grams
764.18	"Light-for-dates" with signs of fetal malnutrition, 2,000-2,499 grams
764.21	Fetal malnutrition without mention of "light-for-dates," less than 500 grams
764.22	Fetal malnutrition without mention of "light-for-dates," 500-749 grams
764.23	Fetal malnutrition without mention of "light-for-dates," 750-999 grams
764.24	Fetal malnutrition without mention of "light-for-dates", 1,000-1,249 grams
764.25	Fetal malnutrition without mention of "light-for-dates," 1,250-1,499 grams
764.26	Fetal malnutrition without mention of "light-for-dates," 1,500-1,749 grams
764.27	Fetal malnutrition without mention of "light-for-dates", 1,750-1,999 grams
764.28	Fetal malnutrition without mention of "light-for-dates", 2,000-2,499 grams
767.0	Subdural and cerebral hemorrhage, birth trauma
767.11	Birth trauma, Epicranial subaponeurotic hemorrhage (massive)
767.4	Injury to spine and spinal cord, birth trauma
767.7	Other cranial and peripheral nerve injuries, birth trauma
768.5	Severe birth asphyxia
770.0	Congenital pneumonia
*770.1	Fetal and newborn aspiration
770.2	Interstitial emphysema and related conditions of newborn
770.3	Pulmonary hemorrhage of fetus or newborn
770.4	Primary atelectasis of newborn
770.84	Respiratory failure of newborn
771.0	Congenital rubella
771.1	Congenital cytomegalovirus infection
771.2	Other congenital infection specific to the perinatal period
771.4	Omphalitis of the newborn
771.5	Neonatal infective mastitis
*771.8	Other infection specific to the perinatal period
772.0	Fetal blood loss
*772.1	Intraventricular hemorrhage
772.2	Fetal and neonatal subarachnoid hemorrhage of newborn
772.4	Fetal and neonatal gastrointestinal hemorrhage
772.5	Fetal and neonatal adrenal hemorrhage
773.2	Hemolytic disease due to other and unspecified isoimmunization of fetus or newborn
773.3	Hydrops fetalis due to isoimmunization
773.4	Kernicterus due to isoimmunization of fetus or newborn
773.5	Late anemia due to isoimmunization of fetus or newborn
774.4	Perinatal jaundice due to hepatocellular damage
774.7	Kernicterus of fetus or newborn not due to isoimmunization
775.1	Neonatal diabetes mellitus
775.2	Neonatal myasthenia gravis
775.3	Neonatal thyrotoxicosis
775.4	Hypocalcemia and hypomagnesemia of newborn
775.5	Other transitory neonatal electrolyte disturbances
775.6	Neonatal hypoglycemia
775.7	Late metabolic acidosis of newborn
776.0	Hemorrhagic disease of newborn
776.1	Transient neonatal thrombocytopenia
776.2	Disseminated intravascular coagulation in newborn
776.3	Other transient neonatal disorders of coagulation
776.6	Anemia of neonatal prematurity
777.1	Fetal and newborn meconium obstruction
777.2	Neonatal intestinal obstruction due to inspissated milk
777.5	Necrotizing enterocolitis in fetus or newborn
777.6	Perinatal intestinal perforation
778.0	Hydrops fetalis not due to isoimmunization
779.0	Convulsions in newborn
779.1	Other and unspecified cerebral irritability in newborn
779.2	Cerebral depression, coma, and other abnormal cerebral signs in fetus or newborn

779.4	Drug reactions and intoxications specific to newborn
779.5	Drug withdrawal syndrome in newborn

OR

Secondary Diagnosis of Major Problem

036.3	Waterhouse-Friderichsen syndrome, meningococcal
*036.4	Meningococcal carditis
036.81	Meningococcal optic neuritis
036.82	Meningococcal arthropathy
037	Tetanus
*038	Septicemia
040.0	Gas gangrene
046.2	Subacute sclerosing panencephalitis
*052	Chickenpox
*053	Herpes zoster
054.0	Eczema herpeticum
054.2	Herpetic gingivostomatitis
054.3	Herpetic meningoencephalitis
*054.4	Herpes simplex with ophthalmic complications
054.5	Herpetic septicemia
*054.7	Herpes simplex with other specified complications
054.8	Unspecified herpes simplex complication
055.0	Postmeasles encephalitis
055.1	Postmeasles pneumonia
055.2	Postmeasles otitis media
*055.7	Measles, with other specified complications
055.8	Unspecified measles complication
*056.0	Rubella with neurological complications
*056.7	Rubella with other specified complications
056.8	Unspecified rubella complications
*070.2	Viral hepatitis B with hepatic coma
*070.3	Viral hepatitis B without mention of hepatic coma
*070.4	Other specified viral hepatitis with hepatic coma
*070.5	Other specified viral hepatitis without mention of hepatic coma
070.6	Unspecified viral hepatitis with hepatic coma
070.9	Unspecified viral hepatitis without mention of hepatic coma
072.0	Mumps orchitis
072.1	Mumps meningitis
072.2	Mumps encephalitis
072.3	Mumps pancreatitis
*072.7	Mumps with other specified complications
072.8	Unspecified mumps complication
079.6	Respiratory syncytial virus (RSV)
112.4	Candidiasis of lung
112.5	Disseminated candidiasis
112.81	Candidal endocarditis
112.82	Candidal otitis externa
112.83	Candidal meningitis
112.84	Candidiasis of the esophagus
112.85	Candidiasis of the intestine
114.2	Coccidioidal meningitis
114.3	Other forms of progressive coccidioidomycosis
115.01	Histoplasma capsulatum meningitis
115.02	Histoplasma capsulatum retinitis
115.03	Histoplasma capsulatum pericarditis
115.04	Histoplasma capsulatum endocarditis
115.05	Histoplasma capsulatum pneumonia
115.11	Histoplasma duboisii meningitis
115.12	Histoplasma duboisii retinitis
115.13	Histoplasma duboisii pericarditis
115.14	Histoplasma duboisii endocarditis
115.15	Histoplasma duboisii pneumonia
115.91	Unspecified Histoplasmosis meningitis

*** Code Range** ☑ ***Optimization Potential*** ▽ ***Targeted Potential*** T ***Transfer DRG*** SP ***Special Payment***

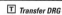

DRG 387 — continued

115.92	Unspecified Histoplasmosis retinitis
115.93	Unspecified Histoplasmosis pericarditis
115.94	Unspecified Histoplasmosis endocarditis
115.95	Unspecified Histoplasmosis pneumonia
116.0	Blastomycosis
116.1	Paracoccidioidomycosis
117.3	Aspergillosis
117.4	Mycotic mycetomas
117.5	Cryptococcosis
117.6	Allescheriosis (Petriellidosis)
117.7	Zygomycosis (Phycomycosis or Mucormycosis)
118	Opportunistic mycoses
130.0	Meningoencephalitis due to toxoplasmosis
130.1	Conjunctivitis due to toxoplasmosis
130.2	Chorioretinitis due to toxoplasmosis
130.3	Myocarditis due to toxoplasmosis
130.4	Pneumonitis due to toxoplasmosis
130.5	Hepatitis due to toxoplasmosis
130.7	Toxoplasmosis of other specified sites
130.8	Multisystemic disseminated toxoplasmosis
136.3	Pneumocystosis
251.0	Hypoglycemic coma
252.1	Hypoparathyroidism
253.5	Diabetes insipidus
254.1	Abscess of thymus
261	Nutritional marasmus
262	Other severe protein-calorie malnutrition
263.0	Malnutrition of moderate degree
263.1	Malnutrition of mild degree
263.8	Other protein-calorie malnutrition
263.9	Unspecified protein-calorie malnutrition
*276	Disorders of fluid, electrolyte, and acid-base balance
277.01	Cystic fibrosis with meconium ileus
*282.4	Thalassemias
*283.1	Non-autoimmune hemolytic anemias
283.2	Hemoglobinuria due to hemolysis from external causes
283.9	Acquired hemolytic anemia, unspecified
285.1	Acute posthemorrhagic anemia
286.6	Defibrination syndrome
287.4	Secondary thrombocytopenia
292.0	Drug withdrawal
*320	Bacterial meningitis
*321	Meningitis due to other organisms
322.0	Nonpyogenic meningitis
322.1	Eosinophilic meningitis
322.9	Unspecified meningitis
*324	Intracranial and intraspinal abscess
348.1	Anoxic brain damage
349.0	Reaction to spinal or lumbar puncture
349.1	Nervous system complications from surgically implanted device
349.81	Cerebrospinal fluid rhinorrhea
349.82	Toxic encephalopathy
377.00	Unspecified papilledema
377.01	Papilledema associated with increased intracranial pressure
377.02	Papilledema associated with decreased ocular pressure
383.01	Subperiosteal abscess of mastoid
383.81	Postauricular fistula
398.91	Rheumatic heart failure (congestive)
402.01	Malignant hypertensive heart disease with heart failure
402.11	Benign hypertensive heart disease with heart failure
402.91	Unspecified hypertensive heart disease with heart failure
404.01	Hypertensive heart and kidney disease, malignant, with heart failure

404.03	Hypertensive heart and kidney disease, malignant, with heart failure and chronic kidney disease
404.11	Hypertensive heart and kidney disease, benign, with heart failure
404.13	Hypertensive heart and kidney disease, benign, with heart failure and chronic kidney disease
404.91	Hypertensive heart and kidney disease, unspecified, with heart failure
404.93	Hypertensive heart and kidney disease, unspecified, with heart failure and chronic kidney disease
414.10	Aneurysm of heart
*415	Acute pulmonary heart disease
420.0	Acute pericarditis in diseases classified elsewhere
*421	Acute and subacute endocarditis
422.0	Acute myocarditis in diseases classified elsewhere
422.92	Septic myocarditis
423.0	Hemopericardium
*424.9	Endocarditis, valve unspecified
425.8	Cardiomyopathy in other diseases classified elsewhere
426.0	Atrioventricular block, complete
426.53	Other bilateral bundle branch block
426.54	Trifascicular block
426.7	Anomalous atrioventricular excitation
426.89	Other specified conduction disorder
427.1	Paroxysmal ventricular tachycardia
*427.3	Atrial fibrillation and flutter
*427.4	Ventricular fibrillation and flutter
427.5	Cardiac arrest
428.0	Congestive heart failure, unspecified
428.1	Left heart failure
*428.2	Systolic heart failure
*428.3	Diastolic heart failure
*428.4	Combined systolic and diastolic heart failure
428.9	Unspecified heart failure
429.4	Functional disturbances following cardiac surgery
429.81	Other disorders of papillary muscle
429.82	Hyperkinetic heart disease
430	Subarachnoid hemorrhage
431	Intracerebral hemorrhage
*432	Other and unspecified intracranial hemorrhage
433.01	Occlusion and stenosis of basilar artery with cerebral infarction
433.11	Occlusion and stenosis of carotid artery with cerebral infarction
433.21	Occlusion and stenosis of vertebral artery with cerebral infarction
433.31	Occlusion and stenosis of multiple and bilateral precerebral arteries with cerebral infarction
433.81	Occlusion and stenosis of other specified precerebral artery with cerebral infarction
433.91	Occlusion and stenosis of unspecified precerebral artery with cerebral infarction
*434	Occlusion of cerebral arteries
436	Acute, but ill-defined, cerebrovascular disease
440.24	Atherosclerosis of native arteries of the extremities with gangrene
*444	Arterial embolism and thrombosis
*451.1	Phlebitis and thrombophlebitis of deep veins of lower extremities
451.2	Phlebitis and thrombophlebitis of lower extremities, unspecified
451.81	Phlebitis and thrombophlebitis of iliac vein
453.2	Embolism and thrombosis of vena cava
457.2	Lymphangitis
459.0	Unspecified hemorrhage
478.22	Parapharyngeal abscess
478.24	Retropharyngeal abscess
*478.3	Paralysis of vocal cords or larynx
478.75	Laryngeal spasm
481	Pneumococcal pneumonia (streptococcus pneumoniae pneumonia)
*482	Other bacterial pneumonia
*483	Pneumonia due to other specified organism
485	Bronchopneumonia, organism unspecified
486	Pneumonia, organism unspecified
493.01	Extrinsic asthma with status asthmaticus

** Code Range* ☑ *Optimization Potential* *Targeted Potential* T *Transfer DRG* SP *Special Payment*

DRG 387 — continued

493.11	Intrinsic asthma with status asthmaticus
493.91	Unspecified asthma, with status asthmaticus
507.0	Pneumonitis due to inhalation of food or vomitus
507.8	Pneumonitis due to other solids and liquids
508.0	Acute pulmonary manifestations due to radiation
*510	Empyema
511.1	Pleurisy with effusion, with mention of bacterial cause other than tuberculosis
511.8	Pleurisy with other specified forms of effusion, except tuberculous
511.9	Unspecified pleural effusion
*513	Abscess of lung and mediastinum
518.0	Pulmonary collapse
518.1	Interstitial emphysema
518.4	Unspecified acute edema of lung
518.5	Pulmonary insufficiency following trauma and surgery
519.2	Mediastinitis
530.4	Perforation of esophagus
530.84	Tracheoesophageal fistula
536.1	Acute dilatation of stomach
550.00	Inguinal hernia with gangrene, unilateral or unspecified, (not specified as recurrent)
550.02	Inguinal hernia with gangrene, bilateral
550.10	Inguinal hernia with obstruction, without mention of gangrene, unilateral or unspecified, (not specified as recurrent)
550.12	Inguinal hernia with obstruction, without mention gangrene, bilateral, (not specified as recurrent)
551.00	Femoral hernia with gangrene, unilateral or unspecified (not specified as recurrent)
551.02	Femoral hernia with gangrene, bilateral, (not specified as recurrent)
551.1	Umbilical hernia with gangrene
*551.2	Ventral hernia with gangrene
551.3	Diaphragmatic hernia with gangrene
551.8	Hernia of other specified sites, with gangrene
551.9	Hernia of unspecified site, with gangrene
552.00	Unilateral or unspecified femoral hernia with obstruction
552.02	Bilateral femoral hernia with obstruction
552.1	Umbilical hernia with obstruction
*552.2	Ventral hernia with obstruction
552.3	Diaphragmatic hernia with obstruction
552.8	Hernia of other specified site, with obstruction
552.9	Hernia of unspecified site, with obstruction
557.0	Acute vascular insufficiency of intestine
558.2	Toxic gastroenteritis and colitis
560.0	Intussusception
560.1	Paralytic ileus
560.2	Volvulus
560.30	Unspecified impaction of intestine
560.39	Other impaction of intestine
560.89	Other specified intestinal obstruction
560.9	Unspecified intestinal obstruction
566	Abscess of anal and rectal regions
*567	Peritonitis and retroperitoneal infections
568.81	Hemoperitoneum (nontraumatic)
569.3	Hemorrhage of rectum and anus
569.83	Perforation of intestine
570	Acute and subacute necrosis of liver
572.0	Abscess of liver
572.1	Portal pyemia
572.2	Hepatic coma
572.4	Hepatorenal syndrome
573.3	Unspecified hepatitis
573.4	Hepatic infarction
576.1	Cholangitis
577.0	Acute pancreatitis
577.2	Cyst and pseudocyst of pancreas

*578	Gastrointestinal hemorrhage
579.3	Other and unspecified postsurgical nonabsorption
*580	Acute glomerulonephritis
*584	Acute renal failure
*590.1	Acute pyelonephritis
590.2	Renal and perinephric abscess
590.3	Pyeloureteritis cystica
*590.8	Other pyelonephritis or pyonephrosis, not specified as acute or chronic
590.9	Unspecified infection of kidney
591	Hydronephrosis
593.5	Hydroureter
595.0	Acute cystitis
595.4	Cystitis in diseases classified elsewhere
595.81	Cystitis cystica
595.89	Other specified types of cystitis
595.9	Unspecified cystitis
596.0	Bladder neck obstruction
596.1	Intestinovesical fistula
596.2	Vesical fistula, not elsewhere classified
596.4	Atony of bladder
596.6	Nontraumatic rupture of bladder
596.7	Hemorrhage into bladder wall
597.0	Urethral abscess
599.0	Urinary tract infection, site not specified
*599.6	Urinary obstruction
599.7	Hematuria
619.1	Digestive-genital tract fistula, female
619.8	Other specified fistula involving female genital tract
620.7	Hematoma of broad ligament
*682	Other cellulitis and abscess
683	Acute lymphadenitis
693.0	Dermatitis due to drugs and medicines taken internally
695.0	Toxic erythema
708.0	Allergic urticaria
*733.1	Pathologic fracture
*740	Anencephalus and similar anomalies
*741	Spina bifida
*742	Other congenital anomalies of nervous system
745.4	Ventricular septal defect
759.4	Conjoined twins
*770.1	Fetal and newborn aspiration
779.7	Periventricular leukomalacia
780.01	Coma
780.03	Persistent vegetative state
*780.3	Convulsions
781.7	Tetany
785.0	Unspecified tachycardia
785.4	Gangrene
785.50	Unspecified shock
*788.2	Retention of urine
790.7	Bacteremia
791.1	Chyluria
799.1	Respiratory arrest
*820	Fracture of neck of femur
*821.0	Closed fracture of shaft or unspecified part of femur
*821.1	Open fracture of shaft or unspecified part of femur
*860	Traumatic pneumothorax and hemothorax
*865	Injury to spleen
*900.0	Injury to carotid artery
900.1	Internal jugular vein injury
900.81	External jugular vein injury
901.0	Thoracic aorta injury
901.1	Innominate and subclavian artery injury

DRG 387 — continued

901.2	Superior vena cava injury
901.3	Innominate and subclavian vein injury
901.41	Pulmonary artery injury
901.42	Pulmonary vein injury
902.0	Abdominal aorta injury
902.10	Unspecified inferior vena cava injury
953.4	Injury to brachial plexus
958.0	Air embolism as an early complication of trauma
958.1	Fat embolism as an early complication of trauma
958.2	Secondary and recurrent hemorrhage as an early complication of trauma
958.3	Posttraumatic wound infection not elsewhere classified
958.4	Traumatic shock
958.5	Traumatic anuria
958.7	Traumatic subcutaneous emphysema
995.2	Unspecified adverse effect of drug medicinal and biological substance, not elsewhere classified
995.4	Shock due to anesthesia not elsewhere classified
*997.0	Nervous system complications
997.1	Cardiac complications
997.2	Peripheral vascular complications
997.3	Respiratory complications
997.4	Digestive system complication
997.5	Urinary complications
997.71	Vascular complications of mesenteric artery
997.72	Vascular complications of renal artery
997.79	Vascular complications of other vessels
*998	Other complications of procedures, not elsewhere classified
999.1	Air embolism as complication of medical care, not elsewhere classified
999.2	Other vascular complications of medical care, not elsewhere classified
999.3	Other infection due to medical care, not elsewhere classified
999.4	Anaphylactic shock due to serum, not elsewhere classified
999.5	Other serum reaction, not elsewhere classified
999.6	Abo incompatibility reaction, not elsewhere classified
999.7	Rh incompatibility reaction, not elsewhere classified
999.8	Other transfusion reaction, not elsewhere classified

M DRG 388 Prematurity without Major Problems

GMLOS 8.6 AMLOS 8.6 RW 1.8929 ☑

Principal or Secondary Diagnosis of Prematurity

765.00	Extreme fetal immaturity, unspecified (weight)
765.06	Extreme fetal immaturity, 1,500-1,749 grams
765.07	Extreme fetal immaturity, 1,750-1,999 grams
765.08	Extreme fetal immaturity, 2,000-2,499 grams
*765.1	Other preterm infants
765.24	27-28 completed weeks of gestation
765.25	29-30 completed weeks of gestation
765.26	31-32 completed weeks of gestation
765.27	33-34 completed weeks of gestation
765.28	35-36 completed weeks of gestation

M DRG 389 Full Term Neonate with Major Problems

GMLOS 4.7 AMLOS 4.7 RW 3.2226 ☑

Principal or Secondary Diagnosis of Major Problem

277.01	Cystic fibrosis with meconium ileus
*567.2	Other suppurative peritonitis
*567.3	Retroperitoneal infections
*567.8	Other specified peritonitis
747.83	Persistent fetal circulation
763.4	Fetus or newborn affected by cesarean delivery
764.11	"Light-for-dates" with signs of fetal malnutrition, less than 500 grams
764.12	"Light-for-dates" with signs of fetal malnutrition, 500-749 grams

764.13	"Light-for-dates" with signs of fetal malnutrition, 750-999 grams
764.14	"Light-for-dates" with signs of fetal malnutrition, 1,000-1,249 grams
764.15	"Light-for-dates" with signs of fetal malnutrition, 1,250-1,499 grams
764.16	"Light-for-dates" with signs of fetal malnutrition, 1,500-1,749 grams
764.17	"Light-for-dates" with signs of fetal malnutrition, 1,750-1,999 grams
764.18	"Light-for-dates" with signs of fetal malnutrition, 2,000-2,499 grams
764.21	Fetal malnutrition without mention of "light-for-dates," less than 500 grams
764.22	Fetal malnutrition without mention of "light-for-dates," 500-749 grams
764.23	Fetal malnutrition without mention of "light-for-dates," 750-999 grams
764.24	Fetal malnutrition without mention of "light-for-dates", 1,000-1,249 grams
764.25	Fetal malnutrition without mention of "light-for-dates," 1,250-1,499 grams
764.26	Fetal malnutrition without mention of "light-for-dates," 1,500-1,749 grams
764.27	Fetal malnutrition without mention of "light-for-dates", 1,750-1,999 grams
764.28	Fetal malnutrition without mention of "light-for-dates", 2,000-2,499 grams
767.0	Subdural and cerebral hemorrhage, birth trauma
767.11	Birth trauma, Epicranial subaponeurotic hemorrhage (massive)
767.4	Injury to spine and spinal cord, birth trauma
767.7	Other cranial and peripheral nerve injuries, birth trauma
768.5	Severe birth asphyxia
770.0	Congenital pneumonia
*770.1	Fetal and newborn aspiration
770.2	Interstitial emphysema and related conditions of newborn
770.3	Pulmonary hemorrhage of fetus or newborn
770.4	Primary atelectasis of newborn
770.84	Respiratory failure of newborn
771.0	Congenital rubella
771.1	Congenital cytomegalovirus infection
771.2	Other congenital infection specific to the perinatal period
771.4	Omphalitis of the newborn
771.5	Neonatal infective mastitis
*771.8	Other infection specific to the perinatal period
772.0	Fetal blood loss
*772.1	Intraventricular hemorrhage
772.2	Fetal and neonatal subarachnoid hemorrhage of newborn
772.4	Fetal and neonatal gastrointestinal hemorrhage
772.5	Fetal and neonatal adrenal hemorrhage
773.2	Hemolytic disease due to other and unspecified isoimmunization of fetus or newborn
773.3	Hydrops fetalis due to isoimmunization
773.4	Kernicterus due to isoimmunization of fetus or newborn
773.5	Late anemia due to isoimmunization of fetus or newborn
774.4	Perinatal jaundice due to hepatocellular damage
774.7	Kernicterus of fetus or newborn not due to isoimmunization
775.1	Neonatal diabetes mellitus
775.2	Neonatal myasthenia gravis
775.3	Neonatal thyrotoxicosis
775.4	Hypocalcemia and hypomagnesemia of newborn
775.5	Other transitory neonatal electrolyte disturbances
775.6	Neonatal hypoglycemia
775.7	Late metabolic acidosis of newborn
776.0	Hemorrhagic disease of newborn
776.1	Transient neonatal thrombocytopenia
776.2	Disseminated intravascular coagulation in newborn
776.3	Other transient neonatal disorders of coagulation
776.6	Anemia of neonatal prematurity
777.1	Fetal and newborn meconium obstruction
777.2	Neonatal intestinal obstruction due to inspissated milk
777.5	Necrotizing enterocolitis in fetus or newborn
777.6	Perinatal intestinal perforation
778.0	Hydrops fetalis not due to isoimmunization
779.0	Convulsions in newborn
779.1	Other and unspecified cerebral irritability in newborn
779.2	Cerebral depression, coma, and other abnormal cerebral signs in fetus or newborn

DRG 389 — continued

779.4	Drug reactions and intoxications specific to newborn
779.5	Drug withdrawal syndrome in newborn

OR

Secondary Diagnosis of Major Problem

036.3	Waterhouse-Friderichsen syndrome, meningococcal
*036.4	Meningococcal carditis
036.81	Meningococcal optic neuritis
036.82	Meningococcal arthropathy
037	Tetanus
*038	Septicemia
040.0	Gas gangrene
046.2	Subacute sclerosing panencephalitis
*052	Chickenpox
*053	Herpes zoster
054.0	Eczema herpeticum
054.2	Herpetic gingivostomatitis
054.3	Herpetic meningoencephalitis
*054.4	Herpes simplex with ophthalmic complications
054.5	Herpetic septicemia
*054.7	Herpes simplex with other specified complications
054.8	Unspecified herpes simplex complication
055.0	Postmeasles encephalitis
055.1	Postmeasles pneumonia
055.2	Postmeasles otitis media
*055.7	Measles, with other specified complications
055.8	Unspecified measles complication
*056.0	Rubella with neurological complications
*056.7	Rubella with other specified complications
056.8	Unspecified rubella complications
*070.2	Viral hepatitis B with hepatic coma
*070.3	Viral hepatitis B without mention of hepatic coma
*070.4	Other specified viral hepatitis with hepatic coma
*070.5	Other specified viral hepatitis without mention of hepatic coma
070.6	Unspecified viral hepatitis with hepatic coma
070.9	Unspecified viral hepatitis without mention of hepatic coma
072.0	Mumps orchitis
072.1	Mumps meningitis
072.2	Mumps encephalitis
072.3	Mumps pancreatitis
*072.7	Mumps with other specified complications
072.8	Unspecified mumps complication
079.6	Respiratory syncytial virus (RSV)
112.4	Candidiasis of lung
112.5	Disseminated candidiasis
112.81	Candidal endocarditis
112.82	Candidal otitis externa
112.83	Candidal meningitis
112.84	Candidiasis of the esophagus
112.85	Candidiasis of the intestine
114.2	Coccidioidal meningitis
114.3	Other forms of progressive coccidioidomycosis
115.01	Histoplasma capsulatum meningitis
115.02	Histoplasma capsulatum retinitis
115.03	Histoplasma capsulatum pericarditis
115.04	Histoplasma capsulatum endocarditis
115.05	Histoplasma capsulatum pneumonia
115.11	Histoplasma duboisii meningitis
115.12	Histoplasma duboisii retinitis
115.13	Histoplasma duboisii pericarditis
115.14	Histoplasma duboisii endocarditis
115.15	Histoplasma duboisii pneumonia

115.91	Unspecified Histoplasmosis meningitis
115.92	Unspecified Histoplasmosis retinitis
115.93	Unspecified Histoplasmosis pericarditis
115.94	Unspecified Histoplasmosis endocarditis
115.95	Unspecified Histoplasmosis pneumonia
116.0	Blastomycosis
116.1	Paracoccidioidomycosis
117.3	Aspergillosis
117.4	Mycotic mycetomas
117.5	Cryptococcosis
117.6	Allescheriosis (Petriellidosis)
117.7	Zygomycosis (Phycomycosis or Mucormycosis)
118	Opportunistic mycoses
130.0	Meningoencephalitis due to toxoplasmosis
130.1	Conjunctivitis due to toxoplasmosis
130.2	Chorioretinitis due to toxoplasmosis
130.3	Myocarditis due to toxoplasmosis
130.4	Pneumonitis due to toxoplasmosis
130.5	Hepatitis due to toxoplasmosis
130.7	Toxoplasmosis of other specified sites
130.8	Multisystemic disseminated toxoplasmosis
136.3	Pneumocystosis
251.0	Hypoglycemic coma
252.1	Hypoparathyroidism
253.5	Diabetes insipidus
254.1	Abscess of thymus
261	Nutritional marasmus
262	Other severe protein-calorie malnutrition
263.0	Malnutrition of moderate degree
263.1	Malnutrition of mild degree
263.8	Other protein-calorie malnutrition
263.9	Unspecified protein-calorie malnutrition
*276	Disorders of fluid, electrolyte, and acid-base balance
*282.4	Thalassemias
*283.1	Non-autoimmune hemolytic anemias
283.2	Hemoglobinuria due to hemolysis from external causes
283.9	Acquired hemolytic anemia, unspecified
285.1	Acute posthemorrhagic anemia
286.6	Defibrination syndrome
287.4	Secondary thrombocytopenia
292.0	Drug withdrawal
*320	Bacterial meningitis
*321	Meningitis due to other organisms
322.0	Nonpyogenic meningitis
322.1	Eosinophilic meningitis
322.9	Unspecified meningitis
*324	Intracranial and intraspinal abscess
348.1	Anoxic brain damage
349.0	Reaction to spinal or lumbar puncture
349.1	Nervous system complications from surgically implanted device
349.81	Cerebrospinal fluid rhinorrhea
349.82	Toxic encephalopathy
377.00	Unspecified papilledema
377.01	Papilledema associated with increased intracranial pressure
377.02	Papilledema associated with decreased ocular pressure
383.01	Subperiosteal abscess of mastoid
383.81	Postauricular fistula
398.91	Rheumatic heart failure (congestive)
402.01	Malignant hypertensive heart disease with heart failure
402.11	Benign hypertensive heart disease with heart failure
402.91	Unspecified hypertensive heart disease with heart failure
404.01	Hypertensive heart and kidney disease, malignant, with heart failure

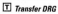

DRG 389 — continued

404.03	Hypertensive heart and kidney disease, malignant, with heart failure and chronic kidney disease
404.11	Hypertensive heart and kidney disease, benign, with heart failure
404.13	Hypertensive heart and kidney disease, benign, with heart failure and chronic kidney disease
404.91	Hypertensive heart and kidney disease, unspecified, with heart failure
404.93	Hypertensive heart and kidney disease, unspecified, with heart failure and chronic kidney disease
414.10	Aneurysm of heart
*415	Acute pulmonary heart disease
420.0	Acute pericarditis in diseases classified elsewhere
*421	Acute and subacute endocarditis
422.0	Acute myocarditis in diseases classified elsewhere
422.92	Septic myocarditis
423.0	Hemopericardium
*424.9	Endocarditis, valve unspecified
425.8	Cardiomyopathy in other diseases classified elsewhere
426.0	Atrioventricular block, complete
426.53	Other bilateral bundle branch block
426.54	Trifascicular block
426.7	Anomalous atrioventricular excitation
426.89	Other specified conduction disorder
427.1	Paroxysmal ventricular tachycardia
*427.3	Atrial fibrillation and flutter
*427.4	Ventricular fibrillation and flutter
427.5	Cardiac arrest
428.0	Congestive heart failure, unspecified
428.1	Left heart failure
*428.2	Systolic heart failure
*428.3	Diastolic heart failure
*428.4	Combined systolic and diastolic heart failure
428.9	Unspecified heart failure
429.4	Functional disturbances following cardiac surgery
429.81	Other disorders of papillary muscle
429.82	Hyperkinetic heart disease
430	Subarachnoid hemorrhage
431	Intracerebral hemorrhage
*432	Other and unspecified intracranial hemorrhage
433.01	Occlusion and stenosis of basilar artery with cerebral infarction
433.11	Occlusion and stenosis of carotid artery with cerebral infarction
433.21	Occlusion and stenosis of vertebral artery with cerebral infarction
433.31	Occlusion and stenosis of multiple and bilateral precerebral arteries with cerebral infarction
433.81	Occlusion and stenosis of other specified precerebral artery with cerebral infarction
433.91	Occlusion and stenosis of unspecified precerebral artery with cerebral infarction
*434	Occlusion of cerebral arteries
436	Acute, but ill-defined, cerebrovascular disease
440.24	Atherosclerosis of native arteries of the extremities with gangrene
*444	Arterial embolism and thrombosis
*451.1	Phlebitis and thrombophlebitis of deep veins of lower extremities
451.2	Phlebitis and thrombophlebitis of lower extremities, unspecified
451.81	Phlebitis and thrombophlebitis of iliac vein
453.2	Embolism and thrombosis of vena cava
457.2	Lymphangitis
459.0	Unspecified hemorrhage
478.22	Parapharyngeal abscess
478.24	Retropharyngeal abscess
*478.3	Paralysis of vocal cords or larynx
478.75	Laryngeal spasm
481	Pneumococcal pneumonia (streptococcus pneumoniae pneumonia)
*482	Other bacterial pneumonia
*483	Pneumonia due to other specified organism
485	Bronchopneumonia, organism unspecified
486	Pneumonia, organism unspecified

493.01	Extrinsic asthma with status asthmaticus
493.11	Intrinsic asthma with status asthmaticus
493.91	Unspecified asthma, with status asthmaticus
507.0	Pneumonitis due to inhalation of food or vomitus
507.8	Pneumonitis due to other solids and liquids
508.0	Acute pulmonary manifestations due to radiation
*510	Empyema
511.1	Pleurisy with effusion, with mention of bacterial cause other than tuberculosis
511.8	Pleurisy with other specified forms of effusion, except tuberculous
511.9	Unspecified pleural effusion
*513	Abscess of lung and mediastinum
518.0	Pulmonary collapse
518.1	Interstitial emphysema
518.4	Unspecified acute edema of lung
518.5	Pulmonary insufficiency following trauma and surgery
519.2	Mediastinitis
530.4	Perforation of esophagus
530.84	Tracheoesophageal fistula
536.1	Acute dilatation of stomach
550.00	Inguinal hernia with gangrene, unilateral or unspecified, (not specified as recurrent)
550.02	Inguinal hernia with gangrene, bilateral
550.10	Inguinal hernia with obstruction, without mention of gangrene, unilateral or unspecified, (not specified as recurrent)
550.12	Inguinal hernia with obstruction, without mention gangrene, bilateral, (not specified as recurrent)
551.00	Femoral hernia with gangrene, unilateral or unspecified (not specified as recurrent)
551.02	Femoral hernia with gangrene, bilateral, (not specified as recurrent)
551.1	Umbilical hernia with gangrene
*551.2	Ventral hernia with gangrene
551.3	Diaphragmatic hernia with gangrene
551.8	Hernia of other specified sites, with gangrene
551.9	Hernia of unspecified site, with gangrene
552.00	Unilateral or unspecified femoral hernia with obstruction
552.02	Bilateral femoral hernia with obstruction
552.1	Umbilical hernia with obstruction
*552.2	Ventral hernia with obstruction
552.3	Diaphragmatic hernia with obstruction
552.8	Hernia of other specified site, with obstruction
552.9	Hernia of unspecified site, with obstruction
557.0	Acute vascular insufficiency of intestine
558.2	Toxic gastroenteritis and colitis
560.0	Intussusception
560.1	Paralytic ileus
560.2	Volvulus
560.30	Unspecified impaction of intestine
560.39	Other impaction of intestine
560.89	Other specified intestinal obstruction
560.9	Unspecified intestinal obstruction
566	Abscess of anal and rectal regions
*567	Peritonitis and retroperitoneal infections
568.81	Hemoperitoneum (nontraumatic)
569.3	Hemorrhage of rectum and anus
569.83	Perforation of intestine
570	Acute and subacute necrosis of liver
572.0	Abscess of liver
572.1	Portal pyemia
572.2	Hepatic coma
572.4	Hepatorenal syndrome
573.3	Unspecified hepatitis
573.4	Hepatic infarction
576.1	Cholangitis
577.0	Acute pancreatitis
577.2	Cyst and pseudocyst of pancreas

*** Code Range** ☑ ***Optimization Potential*** ***Targeted Potential*** T ***Transfer DRG*** SP ***Special Payment***

DRG 389 — continued

*578	Gastrointestinal hemorrhage
579.3	Other and unspecified postsurgical nonabsorption
*580	Acute glomerulonephritis
*584	Acute renal failure
*590.1	Acute pyelonephritis
590.2	Renal and perinephric abscess
590.3	Pyeloureteritis cystica
*590.8	Other pyelonephritis or pyonephrosis, not specified as acute or chronic
590.9	Unspecified infection of kidney
591	Hydronephrosis
593.5	Hydroureter
595.0	Acute cystitis
595.4	Cystitis in diseases classified elsewhere
595.81	Cystitis cystica
595.89	Other specified types of cystitis
595.9	Unspecified cystitis
596.0	Bladder neck obstruction
596.1	Intestinovesical fistula
596.2	Vesical fistula, not elsewhere classified
596.4	Atony of bladder
596.6	Nontraumatic rupture of bladder
596.7	Hemorrhage into bladder wall
597.0	Urethral abscess
599.0	Urinary tract infection, site not specified
*599.6	Urinary obstruction
599.7	Hematuria
619.1	Digestive-genital tract fistula, female
619.8	Other specified fistula involving female genital tract
620.7	Hematoma of broad ligament
*682	Other cellulitis and abscess
683	Acute lymphadenitis
693.0	Dermatitis due to drugs and medicines taken internally
695.0	Toxic erythema
708.0	Allergic urticaria
*733.1	Pathologic fracture
*740	Anencephalus and similar anomalies
*741	Spina bifida
*742	Other congenital anomalies of nervous system
745.4	Ventricular septal defect
759.4	Conjoined twins
779.7	Periventricular leukomalacia
780.01	Coma
780.03	Persistent vegetative state
*780.3	Convulsions
781.7	Tetany
785.0	Unspecified tachycardia
785.4	Gangrene
785.50	Unspecified shock
*788.2	Retention of urine
790.7	Bacteremia
791.1	Chyluria
799.1	Respiratory arrest
*820	Fracture of neck of femur
*821.0	Closed fracture of shaft or unspecified part of femur
*821.1	Open fracture of shaft or unspecified part of femur
*860	Traumatic pneumothorax and hemothorax
*865	Injury to spleen
*900.0	Injury to carotid artery
900.1	Internal jugular vein injury
900.81	External jugular vein injury
901.0	Thoracic aorta injury
901.1	Innominate and subclavian artery injury

901.2	Superior vena cava injury
901.3	Innominate and subclavian vein injury
901.41	Pulmonary artery injury
901.42	Pulmonary vein injury
902.0	Abdominal aorta injury
902.10	Unspecified inferior vena cava injury
953.4	Injury to brachial plexus
958.0	Air embolism as an early complication of trauma
958.1	Fat embolism as an early complication of trauma
958.2	Secondary and recurrent hemorrhage as an early complication of trauma
958.3	Posttraumatic wound infection not elsewhere classified
958.4	Traumatic shock
958.5	Traumatic anuria
958.7	Traumatic subcutaneous emphysema
995.2	Unspecified adverse effect of drug medicinal and biological substance, not elsewhere classified
995.4	Shock due to anesthesia not elsewhere classified
*997.0	Nervous system complications
997.1	Cardiac complications
997.2	Peripheral vascular complications
997.3	Respiratory complications
997.4	Digestive system complication
997.5	Urinary complications
997.71	Vascular complications of mesenteric artery
997.72	Vascular complications of renal artery
997.79	Vascular complications of other vessels
*998	Other complications of procedures, not elsewhere classified
999.1	Air embolism as complication of medical care, not elsewhere classified
999.2	Other vascular complications of medical care, not elsewhere classified
999.3	Other infection due to medical care, not elsewhere classified
999.4	Anaphylactic shock due to serum, not elsewhere classified
999.5	Other serum reaction, not elsewhere classified
999.6	Abo incompatibility reaction, not elsewhere classified
999.7	Rh incompatibility reaction, not elsewhere classified
999.8	Other transfusion reaction, not elsewhere classified

M DRG 390 Neonate with Other Significant Problems

GMLOS 3.4 AMLOS 3.4 RW 1.1406 ☑

Principal or secondary diagnosis of newborn or neonate with other significant problems, not assigned to DRGs 385-389, 391 or 469

M DRG 391 Normal Newborn

GMLOS 3.1 AMLOS 3.1 RW 0.1544 ☑

Principal Diagnosis

762.4	Fetus or newborn affected by prolapsed cord
762.5	Fetus or newborn affected by other compression of umbilical cord
762.6	Fetus or newborn affected by other and unspecified conditions of umbilical cord
763.0	Fetus or newborn affected by breech delivery and extraction
763.1	Fetus or newborn affected by other malpresentation, malposition, and disproportion during labor and delivery
763.2	Fetus or newborn affected by forceps delivery
763.3	Fetus or newborn affected by delivery by vacuum extractor
763.6	Fetus or newborn affected by precipitate delivery
763.9	Unspecified complication of labor and delivery affecting fetus or newborn
764.08	"Light-for-dates" without mention of fetal malnutrition, 2,000-2,499 grams
764.09	"Light-for-dates" without mention of fetal malnutrition, 2,500 or more grams
764.98	Unspecified fetal growth retardation, 2,000-2,499 grams
764.99	Unspecified fetal growth retardation, 2,500 or more grams
765.20	Unspecified weeks of gestation
765.29	37 or more completed weeks of gestation
766.0	Exceptionally large baby relating to long gestation
766.1	Other "heavy-for-dates" infants not related to gestation period

** Code Range ☑ Optimization Potential Targeted Potential T Transfer DRG SP Special Payment*

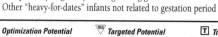

DRG 391 — continued

*766.2	Late infant, not "heavy-for-dates"
767.19	Birth trauma, Other injuries to scalp
768.6	Mild or moderate birth asphyxia
772.6	Fetal and neonatal cutaneous hemorrhage
*774.3	Neonatal jaundice due to delayed conjugation from other causes
774.5	Perinatal jaundice from other causes
774.6	Unspecified fetal and neonatal jaundice
778.8	Other specified condition involving the integument of fetus and newborn
779.3	Feeding problems in newborn
779.83	Delayed separation of umbilical cord
V30.00	Single liveborn, born in hospital, delivered without mention of cesarean delivery
V30.01	Single liveborn, born in hospital, delivered by cesarean delivery
V30.1	Single liveborn, born before admission to hospital
V31.00	Twin, mate liveborn, born in hospital, delivered without mention of cesarean delivery
V31.01	Twin, mate liveborn, born in hospital, delivered by cesarean delivery
V31.1	Twin birth, mate liveborn, born before admission to hospital
V32.00	Twin, mate stillborn, born in hospital, delivered without mention of cesarean delivery
V32.01	Twin, mate stillborn, born in hospital, delivered by cesarean delivery
V32.1	Twin birth, mate stillborn, born before admission to hospital
V33.00	Twin, unspecified whether mate stillborn or liveborn, born in hospital, delivered without mention of cesarean delivery
V33.01	Twin, unspecified whether mate stillborn or liveborn, born in hospital, delivered by cesarean delivery
V33.1	Twin birth, unspecified whether mate liveborn or stillborn, born before admission to hospital
V34.00	Other multiple, mates all liveborn, born in hospital, delivered without mention of cesarean delivery
V34.01	Other multiple, mates all liveborn, born in hospital, delivered by cesarean delivery
V34.1	Other multiple birth (three or more), mates all liveborn, born before admission to hospital
V35.00	Other multiple, mates all stillborn, born in hospital, delivered without mention of cesarean delivery
V35.01	Other multiple, mates all stillborn, born in hospital, delivered by cesarean delivery
V35.1	Other multiple birth (three or more), mates all stillborn, born before admission to hospital
V36.00	Other multiple, mates liveborn and stillborn, born in hospital, delivered without mention of cesarean delivery
V36.01	Other multiple, mates liveborn and stillborn, born in hospital, delivered by cesarean delivery
V36.1	Other multiple birth (three or more), mates liveborn and stillborn, born before admission to hospital
V37.00	Other multiple, unspecified whether mates stillborn or liveborn, born in hospital, delivered without mention of cesarean delivery
V37.01	Other multiple, unspecified whether mates stillborn or liveborn, born in hospital, delivered by cesarean delivery
V37.1	Other multiple birth (three or more), unspecified whether mates liveborn or stillborn, born before admission to hospital
V39.00	Liveborn infant, unspecified whether single, twin, or multiple, born in hospital, delivered without mention of cesarean delivery
V39.01	Liveborn infant, unspecified whether single, twin, or multiple, born in hospital, delivered by cesarean
V39.1	Liveborn, unspecified whether single, twin or multiple, born before admission to hospital

AND

No Secondary Diagnosis

OR

Only Secondary Diagnosis

478.1	Other diseases of nasal cavity and sinuses
520.6	Disturbances in tooth eruption
605	Redundant prepuce and phimosis
623.8	Other specified noninflammatory disorder of vagina
686.9	Unspecified local infection of skin and subcutaneous tissue
691.0	Diaper or napkin rash
*709	Other disorders of skin and subcutaneous tissue
744.1	Congenital anomalies of accessory auricle

*752.5	Undescended and retractile testicle
754.61	Congenital pes planus
757.33	Congenital pigmentary anomaly of skin
757.39	Other specified congenital anomaly of skin
762.4	Fetus or newborn affected by prolapsed cord
762.5	Fetus or newborn affected by other compression of umbilical cord
762.6	Fetus or newborn affected by other and unspecified conditions of umbilical cord
763.0	Fetus or newborn affected by breech delivery and extraction
763.1	Fetus or newborn affected by other malpresentation, malposition, and disproportion during labor and delivery
763.2	Fetus or newborn affected by forceps delivery
763.3	Fetus or newborn affected by delivery by vacuum extractor
763.6	Fetus or newborn affected by precipitate delivery
763.9	Unspecified complication of labor and delivery affecting fetus or newborn
764.08	"Light-for-dates" without mention of fetal malnutrition, 2,000-2,499 grams
764.09	"Light-for-dates" without mention of fetal malnutrition, 2,500 or more grams
764.98	Unspecified fetal growth retardation, 2,000-2,499 grams
764.99	Unspecified fetal growth retardation, 2,500 or more grams
765.20	Unspecified weeks of gestation
765.29	37 or more completed weeks of gestation
766.0	Exceptionally large baby relating to long gestation
766.1	Other "heavy-for-dates" infants not related to gestation period
*766.2	Late infant, not "heavy-for-dates"
767.19	Birth trauma, Other injuries to scalp
768.6	Mild or moderate birth asphyxia
772.6	Fetal and neonatal cutaneous hemorrhage
*774.3	Neonatal jaundice due to delayed conjugation from other causes
774.5	Perinatal jaundice from other causes
774.6	Unspecified fetal and neonatal jaundice
778.8	Other specified condition involving the integument of fetus and newborn
794.15	Nonspecific abnormal auditory function studies
795.4	Other nonspecific abnormal histological findings
796.4	Other abnormal clinical finding
*V01.8	Contact with or exposure to other communicable diseases
V05.3	Need for prophylactic vaccination and inoculation against viral hepatitis
V05.4	Need for prophylactic vaccination and inoculation against varicella
V05.8	Need for prophylactic vaccination and inoculation against other specified disease
V20.1	Health supervision of other healthy infant or child receiving care
V20.2	Routine infant or child health check
*V29	Observation and evaluation of newborns and infants for suspected condition not found
V30.00	Single liveborn, born in hospital, delivered without mention of cesarean delivery
V30.01	Single liveborn, born in hospital, delivered by cesarean delivery
V30.1	Single liveborn, born before admission to hospital
V31.00	Twin, mate liveborn, born in hospital, delivered without mention of cesarean delivery
V31.01	Twin, mate liveborn, born in hospital, delivered by cesarean delivery
V31.1	Twin birth, mate liveborn, born before admission to hospital
V32.00	Twin, mate stillborn, born in hospital, delivered without mention of cesarean delivery
V32.01	Twin, mate stillborn, born in hospital, delivered by cesarean delivery
V32.1	Twin birth, mate stillborn, born before admission to hospital
V33.00	Twin, unspecified whether mate stillborn or liveborn, born in hospital, delivered without mention of cesarean delivery
V33.01	Twin, unspecified whether mate stillborn or liveborn, born in hospital, delivered by cesarean delivery
V33.1	Twin birth, unspecified whether mate liveborn or stillborn, born before admission to hospital
V34.00	Other multiple, mates all liveborn, born in hospital, delivered without mention of cesarean delivery
V34.01	Other multiple, mates all liveborn, born in hospital, delivered by cesarean delivery
V34.1	Other multiple birth (three or more), mates all liveborn, born before admission to hospital
V35.00	Other multiple, mates all stillborn, born in hospital, delivered without mention of cesarean delivery
V35.01	Other multiple, mates all stillborn, born in hospital, delivered by cesarean delivery
V35.1	Other multiple birth (three or more), mates all stillborn, born before admission to hospital

DRG 391 — continued

V36.00 Other multiple, mates liveborn and stillborn, born in hospital, delivered without mention of cesarean delivery
V36.01 Other multiple, mates liveborn and stillborn, born in hospital, delivered by cesarean delivery
V36.1 Other multiple birth (three or more), mates liveborn and stillborn, born before admission to hospital
V37.00 Other multiple, unspecified whether mates stillborn or liveborn, born in hospital, delivered without mention of cesarean delivery
V37.01 Other multiple, unspecified whether mates stillborn or liveborn, born in hospital, delivered by cesarean delivery
V37.1 Other multiple birth (three or more), unspecified whether mates liveborn or stillborn, born before admission to hospital
V39.00 Liveborn infant, unspecified whether single, twin, or multiple, born in hospital, delivered without mention of cesarean delivery
V39.01 Liveborn infant, unspecified whether single, twin, or multiple, born in hospital, delivered by cesarean
V39.1 Liveborn, unspecified whether single, twin or multiple, born before admission to hospital
V50.2 Routine or ritual circumcision
V70.3 Other general medical examination for administrative purposes
V72.1 Examination of ears and hearing
V77.3 Screening for phenylketonuria (PKU)

M DRG 469 Principal Diagnosis Invalid as Discharge Diagnosis

GMLOS 0.0 AMLOS 0.0 RW 0.0000

Principal diagnoses listed for MDC 15 considered invalid as discharge diagnosis

V30.2 Single liveborn, born outside hospital and not hospitalized
V31.2 Twin birth, mate liveborn, born outside hospital and not hospitalized
V32.2 Twin birth, mate stillborn, born outside hospital and not hospitalized
V33.2 Twin birth, unspecified whether mate liveborn or stillborn, born outside hospital and not hospitalized
V34.2 Other multiple birth (three or more), mates all liveborn, born outside hospital and not hospitalized
V35.2 Other multiple birth (three or more), mates all stillborn, born outside of hospital and not hospitalized
V36.2 Other multiple birth (three or more), mates liveborn and stillborn, born outside hospital and not hospitalized
V37.2 Other multiple birth (three or more), unspecified whether mates liveborn or stillborn, born outside of hospital
V39.2 Liveborn, unspecified whether single, twin or multiple, born outside hospital and not hospitalized

MDC 16
DISEASES AND DISORDERS OF THE BLOOD AND BLOOD-FORMING ORGANS AND IMMUNOLOGICAL DISORDERS

The complete and up-to-date listing of ICD-9-CM diagnosis codes assigned to this MDC can be found online at www.ingenixonline.com/content/drg/resources.asp.

SURGICAL

S DRG 392 Splenectomy, Age Greater than 17

GMLOS 6.5 AMLOS 9.2 RW 3.0459 ☑ A

Operating Room Procedures

41.2	Splenotomy
41.33	Open biopsy of spleen
*41.4	Excision or destruction of lesion or tissue of spleen
41.5	Total splenectomy
41.93	Excision of accessory spleen
41.94	Transplantation of spleen
41.95	Repair and plastic operations on spleen
41.99	Other operations on spleen

S DRG 393 Splenectomy, Age 0-17

GMLOS 9.1 AMLOS 9.1 RW 1.3645 ☑ A

Select operating room procedures listed under DRG 392

S DRG 394 Other O.R. Procedures of the Blood and Blood-Forming Organs

GMLOS 4.5 AMLOS 7.4 RW 1.9109

Operating Room Procedures

07.16	Biopsy of thymus
*07.8	Thymectomy
*07.9	Other operations on thymus
26.30	Sialoadenectomy, not otherwise specified
34.22	Mediastinoscopy
34.26	Open biopsy of mediastinum
38.7	Interruption of the vena cava
40.0	Incision of lymphatic structures
*40.1	Diagnostic procedures on lymphatic structures
*40.2	Simple excision of lymphatic structure
40.3	Regional lymph node excision
*40.4	Radical excision of cervical lymph nodes
*40.5	Radical excision of other lymph nodes
40.9	Other operations on lymphatic structures
50.12	Open biopsy of liver
50.19	Other diagnostic procedures on liver
54.11	Exploratory laparotomy
54.19	Other laparotomy
54.21	Laparoscopy
54.23	Biopsy of peritoneum
54.29	Other diagnostic procedures on abdominal region
55.24	Open biopsy of kidney
55.29	Other diagnostic procedures on kidney
77.49	Biopsy of other bone, except facial bones
83.21	Biopsy of soft tissue
86.06	Insertion of totally implantable infusion pump
86.22	Excisional debridement of wound, infection, or burn

MDC 16
DISEASES AND DISORDERS OF THE BLOOD AND BLOOD-FORMING ORGANS AND IMMUNOLOGICAL DISORDERS

The complete and up-to-date listing of ICD-9-CM diagnosis codes assigned to this MDC can be found online at www.ingenixonline.com/content/drg/resources.asp.

MEDICAL

[M] DRG 395 Red Blood Cell Disorders, Age Greater than 17

GMLOS 3.2 AMLOS 4.3 RW 0.8328 ☑ [T] [A]

Principal Diagnosis

*280	Iron deficiency anemias
*281	Other deficiency anemias
*282	Hereditary hemolytic anemias
283.0	Autoimmune hemolytic anemias
*283.1	Non-autoimmune hemolytic anemias
283.2	Hemoglobinuria due to hemolysis from external causes
283.9	Acquired hemolytic anemia, unspecified
*284	Aplastic anemia
*285	Other and unspecified anemias
289.7	Methemoglobinemia
*790.0	Abnormality of red blood cells
999.6	Abo incompatibility reaction, not elsewhere classified
999.7	Rh incompatibility reaction, not elsewhere classified
999.8	Other transfusion reaction, not elsewhere classified

[M] DRG 396 Red Blood Cell Disorders, Age 0-17

GMLOS 2.6 AMLOS 4.3 RW 0.8323 ☑ [A]

Select principal diagnosis listed under DRG 395

[M] DRG 397 Coagulation Disorders

GMLOS 3.7 AMLOS 5.1 RW 1.2986

Principal Diagnosis

*286	Coagulation defects
*287	Purpura and other hemorrhagic conditions
782.7	Spontaneous ecchymoses

[M] DRG 398 Reticuloendothelial and Immunity Disorders with CC

GMLOS 4.4 AMLOS 5.7 RW 1.2082 ☑ [CC]

Principal Diagnosis

*017.2	Tuberculosis of peripheral lymph nodes
*017.7	Tuberculosis of spleen
078.3	Cat-scratch disease
091.4	Adenopathy due to secondary syphilis
212.6	Benign neoplasm of thymus
228.1	Lymphangioma, any site
229.0	Benign neoplasm of lymph nodes
*254	Diseases of thymus gland
273.0	Polyclonal hypergammaglobulinemia
273.1	Monoclonal paraproteinemia
*279.0	Deficiency of humoral immunity
*279.1	Deficiency of cell-mediated immunity
279.2	Combined immunity deficiency
279.3	Unspecified immunity deficiency
279.8	Other specified disorders involving the immune mechanism

279.9	Unspecified disorder of immune mechanism
*288	Diseases of white blood cells
289.0	Polycythemia, secondary
289.1	Chronic lymphadenitis
289.3	Lymphadenitis, unspecified, except mesenteric
289.4	Hypersplenism
*289.5	Other diseases of spleen
289.6	Familial polycythemia
*289.8	Other specified diseases of blood and blood-forming organs
289.9	Unspecified diseases of blood and blood-forming organs
457.8	Other noninfectious disorders of lymphatic channels
457.9	Unspecified noninfectious disorder of lymphatic channels
683	Acute lymphadenitis
759.0	Congenital anomalies of spleen
785.6	Enlargement of lymph nodes
789.2	Splenomegaly
*795.7	Other nonspecific immunological findings
*865	Injury to spleen
996.85	Complications of bone marrow transplant
V42.81	Bone marrow replaced by transplant
V42.82	Peripheral stem cells replaced by transplant

M DRG 399 Reticuloendothelial and Immunity Disorders without CC

GMLOS 2.7 AMLOS 3.3 RW 0.6674 ☑

Select principal diagnosis listed under DRG 398

MDC 17
MYELOPROLIFERATIVE DISEASES AND DISORDERS AND POORLY DIFFERENTIATED NEOPLASMS

The complete and up-to-date listing of ICD-9-CM diagnosis codes assigned to this MDC can be found online at www.ingenixonline.com/content/drg/resources.asp.

SURGICAL

DRG 400 No Longer Valid

GMLOS 0.0 AMLOS 0.0 RW 0.0000

Omitted in the October 2003 grouper version

S DRG 401 Lymphoma and Nonacute Leukemia with Other O.R. Procedure with CC

GMLOS 8.0 AMLOS 11.3 RW 2.9678 T CC

Select principal diagnosis listed under DRG 539

Select any other operating room procedures not listed under DRG 539

OR

Nonoperating Room Procedures

*92.3	Stereotactic radiosurgery

S DRG 402 Lymphoma and Nonacute Leukemia with Other O.R. Procedure without CC

GMLOS 2.8 AMLOS 4.1 RW 1.1810 ☑ T

Select principal diagnosis listed under DRG 539

Select any other operating room procedures not listed under DRG 539

OR

Nonoperating Room Procedures

*92.3	Stereotactic radiosurgery

S DRG 406 Myeloproliferative Disorders or Poorly Differentiated Neoplasms with Major O.R. Procedures with CC

GMLOS 7.0 AMLOS 9.9 RW 2.7897 ☑ CC

Principal Diagnosis

158.0	Malignant neoplasm of retroperitoneum
164.0	Malignant neoplasm of thymus
195.4	Malignant neoplasm of upper limb
195.5	Malignant neoplasm of lower limb
195.8	Malignant neoplasm of other specified sites
198.89	Secondary malignant neoplasm of other specified sites
*199	Malignant neoplasm without specification of site
*202.5	Letterer-Siwe disease
229.8	Benign neoplasm of other specified sites
229.9	Benign neoplasm of unspecified site
234.8	Carcinoma in situ of other specified sites
234.9	Carcinoma in situ, site unspecified
238.8	Neoplasm of uncertain behavior of other specified sites
238.9	Neoplasm of uncertain behavior, site unspecified
239.8	Neoplasm of unspecified nature of other specified sites
239.9	Neoplasm of unspecified nature, site unspecified
273.8	Other disorders of plasma protein metabolism
273.9	Unspecified disorder of plasma protein metabolism
759.6	Other congenital hamartoses, not elsewhere classified
*V10	Personal history of malignant neoplasm

V58.0 Radiotherapy
*V58.1 Encounter for antineoplastic chemotherapy and immunotherapy
V67.1 Radiotherapy follow-up examination
V67.2 Chemotherapy follow-up examination
V71.1 Observation for suspected malignant neoplasm

Select operating room procedures listed under DRG 539

S DRG 407 Myeloproliferative Disorders or Poorly Differentiated Neoplasms with Major O.R. Procedures without CC

GMLOS 3.0 AMLOS 3.8 RW 1.2289 ☑

Select principal diagnosis listed under DRG 406 with operating room procedures listed under DRG 539

S DRG 408 Myeloproliferative Disorders or Poorly Differentiated Neoplasms with Other O.R. Procedures

GMLOS 4.8 AMLOS 8.2 RW 2.2460 ☑

Select principal diagnosis listed under DRG 406

Select any other operating room procedures not listed under DRG 539

OR

Nonoperating Room Procedure

*92.3 Stereotactic radiosurgery

S DRG 539 Lymphoma and Leukemia with Major O.R. Procedure with CC

GMLOS 7.0 AMLOS 10.8 RW 3.2782 CC

Principal Diagnosis

159.1 Malignant neoplasm of spleen, not elsewhere classified
176.5 Kaposi's sarcoma of lymph nodes
*196 Secondary and unspecified malignant neoplasm of lymph nodes
*200 Lymphosarcoma and reticulosarcoma
*201 Hodgkin's disease
*202.0 Nodular lymphoma
*202.1 Mycosis fungoides
*202.2 Sezary's disease
*202.3 Malignant histiocytosis
*202.4 Leukemic reticuloendotheliosis
*202.6 Malignant mast cell tumors
*202.8 Other malignant lymphomas
*202.9 Other and unspecified malignant neoplasms of lymphoid and histiocytic tissue
*203 Multiple myeloma and immunoproliferative neoplasms
*204 Lymphoid leukemia
*205 Myeloid leukemia
*206 Monocytic leukemia
*207 Other specified leukemia
*208 Leukemia of unspecified cell type
238.4 Neoplasm of uncertain behavior of polycythemia vera
238.5 Neoplasm of uncertain behavior of histiocytic and mast cells
238.6 Neoplasm of uncertain behavior of plasma cells
238.7 Neoplasm of uncertain behavior of other lymphatic and hematopoietic tissues
273.2 Other paraproteinemias
273.3 Macroglobulinemia

Operating Room Procedures

01.12 Open biopsy of cerebral meninges
01.14 Open biopsy of brain
01.18 Other diagnostic procedures on brain and cerebral meninges
01.22 Removal of intracranial neurostimulator lead(s)
01.23 Reopening of craniotomy site
01.24 Other craniotomy

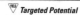

DRG 539 — continued

01.25	Other craniectomy
01.31	Incision of cerebral meninges
01.32	Lobotomy and tractotomy
01.39	Other incision of brain
*01.4	Operations on thalamus and globus pallidus
*01.5	Other excision or destruction of brain and meninges
01.6	Excision of lesion of skull
02.2	Ventriculostomy
*02.3	Extracranial ventricular shunt
02.42	Replacement of ventricular shunt
02.91	Lysis of cortical adhesions
02.93	Implantation or replacement of intracranial neurostimulator lead(s)
02.99	Other operations on skull, brain, and cerebral meninges
03.02	Reopening of laminectomy site
03.09	Other exploration and decompression of spinal canal
03.1	Division of intraspinal nerve root
*03.2	Chordotomy
03.32	Biopsy of spinal cord or spinal meninges
03.39	Other diagnostic procedures on spinal cord and spinal canal structures
03.4	Excision or destruction of lesion of spinal cord or spinal meninges
03.53	Repair of vertebral fracture
03.59	Other repair and plastic operations on spinal cord structures
03.6	Lysis of adhesions of spinal cord and nerve roots
*03.7	Shunt of spinal theca
03.93	Implantation or replacement of spinal neurostimulator lead(s)
03.97	Revision of spinal thecal shunt
03.99	Other operations on spinal cord and spinal canal structures
07.16	Biopsy of thymus
07.80	Thymectomy, not otherwise specified
07.81	Partial excision of thymus
07.82	Total excision of thymus
*07.9	Other operations on thymus
32.29	Other local excision or destruction of lesion or tissue of lung
33.28	Open biopsy of lung
34.02	Exploratory thoracotomy
34.22	Mediastinoscopy
34.26	Open biopsy of mediastinum
34.3	Excision or destruction of lesion or tissue of mediastinum
34.4	Excision or destruction of lesion of chest wall
34.51	Decortication of lung
34.6	Scarification of pleura
37.12	Pericardiotomy
37.24	Biopsy of pericardium
37.31	Pericardiectomy
37.91	Open chest cardiac massage
38.08	Incision of lower limb arteries
39.98	Control of hemorrhage, not otherwise specified
39.99	Other operations on vessels
40.3	Regional lymph node excision
*40.4	Radical excision of cervical lymph nodes
*40.5	Radical excision of other lymph nodes
40.9	Other operations on lymphatic structures
41.2	Splenotomy
41.33	Open biopsy of spleen
*41.4	Excision or destruction of lesion or tissue of spleen
41.5	Total splenectomy
41.93	Excision of accessory spleen
41.94	Transplantation of spleen
41.95	Repair and plastic operations on spleen
41.99	Other operations on spleen
*42.1	Esophagostomy
42.21	Operative esophagoscopy by incision

S Surgical   M Medical   CC CC Indicator   A Age Restriction   ● New DRG   ▲ Revised DRG Title

42.25	Open biopsy of esophagus
42.32	Local excision of other lesion or tissue of esophagus
42.39	Other destruction of lesion or tissue of esophagus
*42.4	Excision of esophagus
*42.5	Intrathoracic anastomosis of esophagus
*42.6	Antesternal anastomosis of esophagus
42.7	Esophagomyotomy
42.82	Suture of laceration of esophagus
42.83	Closure of esophagostomy
42.84	Repair of esophageal fistula, not elsewhere classified
42.85	Repair of esophageal stricture
42.86	Production of subcutaneous tunnel without esophageal anastomosis
42.87	Other graft of esophagus
42.89	Other repair of esophagus
43.0	Gastrotomy
43.5	Partial gastrectomy with anastomosis to esophagus
43.6	Partial gastrectomy with anastomosis to duodenum
43.7	Partial gastrectomy with anastomosis to jejunum
*43.8	Other partial gastrectomy
*43.9	Total gastrectomy
44.11	Transabdominal gastroscopy
*44.3	Gastroenterostomy without gastrectomy
44.63	Closure of other gastric fistula
45.02	Other incision of small intestine
45.03	Incision of large intestine
45.11	Transabdominal endoscopy of small intestine
45.31	Other local excision of lesion of duodenum
45.32	Other destruction of lesion of duodenum
45.33	Local excision of lesion or tissue of small intestine, except duodenum
45.34	Other destruction of lesion of small intestine, except duodenum
45.41	Excision of lesion or tissue of large intestine
45.49	Other destruction of lesion of large intestine
45.50	Isolation of intestinal segment, not otherwise specified
45.61	Multiple segmental resection of small intestine
45.62	Other partial resection of small intestine
45.63	Total removal of small intestine
45.71	Multiple segmental resection of large intestine
45.73	Right hemicolectomy
45.74	Resection of transverse colon
45.75	Left hemicolectomy
45.76	Sigmoidectomy
45.79	Other partial excision of large intestine
45.8	Total intra-abdominal colectomy
45.90	Intestinal anastomosis, not otherwise specified
45.91	Small-to-small intestinal anastomosis
45.92	Anastomosis of small intestine to rectal stump
45.93	Other small-to-large intestinal anastomosis
45.94	Large-to-large intestinal anastomosis
45.95	Anastomosis to anus
*46.0	Exteriorization of intestine
46.10	Colostomy, not otherwise specified
46.11	Temporary colostomy
46.13	Permanent colostomy
46.20	Ileostomy, not otherwise specified
46.21	Temporary ileostomy
46.22	Continent ileostomy
46.23	Other permanent ileostomy
46.40	Revision of intestinal stoma, not otherwise specified
46.41	Revision of stoma of small intestine
46.80	Intra-abdominal manipulation of intestine, not otherwise specified
46.81	Intra-abdominal manipulation of small intestine
46.82	Intra-abdominal manipulation of large intestine
46.97	Transplant of intestine

DRG 539 — continued

46.99	Other operations on intestines
*48.4	Pull-through resection of rectum
48.5	Abdominoperineal resection of rectum
*48.6	Other resection of rectum
50.12	Open biopsy of liver
50.19	Other diagnostic procedures on liver
*51.2	Cholecystectomy
*51.3	Anastomosis of gallbladder or bile duct
51.42	Common duct exploration for relief of other obstruction
51.43	Insertion of choledochohepatic tube for decompression
51.49	Incision of other bile ducts for relief of obstruction
51.59	Incision of other bile duct
51.93	Closure of other biliary fistula
51.94	Revision of anastomosis of biliary tract
51.95	Removal of prosthetic device from bile duct
51.99	Other operations on biliary tract
52.12	Open biopsy of pancreas
52.19	Other diagnostic procedures on pancreas
52.92	Cannulation of pancreatic duct
54.0	Incision of abdominal wall
54.11	Exploratory laparotomy
54.12	Reopening of recent laparotomy site
54.19	Other laparotomy
54.22	Biopsy of abdominal wall or umbilicus
54.29	Other diagnostic procedures on abdominal region
54.3	Excision or destruction of lesion or tissue of abdominal wall or umbilicus
54.4	Excision or destruction of peritoneal tissue
54.63	Other suture of abdominal wall
54.64	Suture of peritoneum
54.72	Other repair of abdominal wall
54.73	Other repair of peritoneum
54.74	Other repair of omentum
54.75	Other repair of mesentery
54.93	Creation of cutaneoperitoneal fistula
54.94	Creation of peritoneovascular shunt
54.95	Incision of peritoneum
55.24	Open biopsy of kidney
55.29	Other diagnostic procedures on kidney
*56.5	Cutaneous uretero-ileostomy
*56.6	Other external urinary diversion
56.71	Urinary diversion to intestine
56.72	Revision of ureterointestinal anastomosis
56.73	Nephrocystanastomosis, not otherwise specified
56.75	Transureteroureterostomy
56.83	Closure of ureterostomy
56.84	Closure of other fistula of ureter
57.18	Other suprapubic cystostomy
57.21	Vesicostomy
57.22	Revision or closure of vesicostomy
57.34	Open biopsy of bladder
57.39	Other diagnostic procedures on bladder
57.59	Open excision or destruction of other lesion or tissue of bladder
57.6	Partial cystectomy
*57.7	Total cystectomy
57.82	Closure of cystostomy
57.83	Repair of fistula involving bladder and intestine
57.84	Repair of other fistula of bladder
57.88	Other anastomosis of bladder
58.43	Closure of other fistula of urethra
59.00	Retroperitoneal dissection, not otherwise specified
59.02	Other lysis of perirenal or periureteral adhesions
59.03	Laparoscopic lysis of perirenal or periureteral adhesions

59.09	Other incision of perirenal or periureteral tissue
*59.1	Incision of perivesical tissue
*59.2	Diagnostic procedures on perirenal and perivesical tissue
59.91	Excision of perirenal or perivesical tissue
59.92	Other operations on perirenal or perivesical tissue
70.72	Repair of colovaginal fistula
70.73	Repair of rectovaginal fistula
70.74	Repair of other vaginoenteric fistula
70.75	Repair of other fistula of vagina

S DRG 540 Lymphoma and Leukemia with Major O.R. Procedure without CC

GMLOS 2.6 AMLOS 3.6 RW 1.1940 ☑

Select principal diagnosis listed under DRG 539 with operating room procedures listed under DRG 539

MDC 17
MYELOPROLIFERATIVE DISEASES AND DISORDERS AND POORLY DIFFERENTIATED NEOPLASMS

The complete and up-to-date listing of ICD-9-CM diagnosis codes assigned to this MDC can be found online at www.ingenixonline.com/content/drg/resources.asp.

MEDICAL

M DRG 403 Lymphoma and Nonacute Leukemia with CC
GMLOS 5.8 AMLOS 8.1 RW 1.8432 ☑ T CC

Select principal diagnosis listed under DRG 539

M DRG 404 Lymphoma and Nonacute Leukemia without CC
GMLOS 3.0 AMLOS 4.2 RW 0.9265 ☑ T

Select principal diagnosis listed under DRG 539

M DRG 405 Acute Leukemia without Major O.R. Procedure, Age 0-17
GMLOS 4.9 AMLOS 4.9 RW 1.9346 ☑ A

Principal Diagnosis

*204.0	Acute lymphoid leukemia
*205.0	Acute myeloid leukemia
*206.0	Acute monocytic leukemia
*207.0	Acute erythremia and erythroleukemia
*208.0	Acute leukemia of unspecified cell type

M DRG 409 Radiotherapy
GMLOS 4.3 AMLOS 5.8 RW 1.2074

Principal Diagnosis

V58.0	Radiotherapy
V67.1	Radiotherapy follow-up examination

M DRG 410 Chemotherapy without Acute Leukemia as Secondary Diagnosis
GMLOS 3.0 AMLOS 3.8 RW 1.1069 ☑

Principal Diagnosis

V67.2	Chemotherapy follow-up examination

M DRG 411 History of Malignancy without Endoscopy
GMLOS 2.5 AMLOS 3.3 RW 0.3635

Principal Diagnosis

*V10	Personal history of malignant neoplasm
V71.1	Observation for suspected malignant neoplasm

M DRG 412 History of Malignancy with Endoscopy
GMLOS 1.8 AMLOS 2.8 RW 0.8451

Principal Diagnosis

*V10	Personal history of malignant neoplasm
V71.1	Observation for suspected malignant neoplasm

AND

Nonoperating Room Procedures

21.21	Rhinoscopy
29.11	Pharyngoscopy
31.41	Tracheoscopy through artificial stoma

S *Surgical* M *Medical* CC *CC Indicator* A *Age Restriction* ● *New DRG* ▲ *Revised DRG Title*

31.42	Laryngoscopy and other tracheoscopy
31.43	Closed (endoscopic) biopsy of larynx
31.44	Closed (endoscopic) biopsy of trachea
32.01	Endoscopic excision or destruction of lesion or tissue of bronchus
32.28	Endoscopic excision or destruction of lesion or tissue of lung
33.21	Bronchoscopy through artificial stoma
33.22	Fiber-optic bronchoscopy
33.23	Other bronchoscopy
33.24	Closed (endoscopic) biopsy of bronchus
42.22	Esophagoscopy through artificial stoma
42.23	Other esophagoscopy
42.24	Closed (endoscopic) biopsy of esophagus
42.33	Endoscopic excision or destruction of lesion or tissue of esophagus
43.41	Endoscopic excision or destruction of lesion or tissue of stomach
44.12	Gastroscopy through artificial stoma
44.13	Other gastroscopy
44.14	Closed [endoscopic] biopsy of stomach
45.12	Endoscopy of small intestine through artificial stoma
45.13	Other endoscopy of small intestine
45.14	Closed [endoscopic] biopsy of small intestine
45.16	Esophagogastroduodenoscopy (EGD) with closed biopsy
45.22	Endoscopy of large intestine through artificial stoma
45.23	Colonoscopy
45.24	Flexible sigmoidoscopy
45.25	Closed [endoscopic] biopsy of large intestine
45.30	Endoscopic excision or destruction of lesion of duodenum
45.42	Endoscopic polypectomy of large intestine
45.43	Endoscopic destruction of other lesion or tissue of large intestine
48.22	Proctosigmoidoscopy through artificial stoma
48.23	Rigid proctosigmoidoscopy
48.24	Closed (endoscopic) biopsy of rectum
48.36	[Endoscopic] polypectomy of rectum
49.21	Anoscopy
49.31	Endoscopic excision or destruction of lesion or tissue of anus
51.10	Endoscopic retrograde cholangiopancreatography (ERCP)
51.11	Endoscopic retrograde cholangiography (ERC)
51.14	Other closed (endoscopic) biopsy of biliary duct or sphincter of Oddi
51.64	Endoscopic excision or destruction of lesion of biliary ducts or sphincter of Oddi
51.84	Endoscopic dilation of ampulla and biliary duct
51.85	Endoscopic sphincterotomy and papillotomy
51.86	Endoscopic insertion of nasobiliary drainage tube
51.87	Endoscopic insertion of stent (tube) into bile duct
52.13	Endoscopic retrograde pancreatography (ERP)
52.14	Closed (endoscopic) biopsy of pancreatic duct
52.21	Endoscopic excision or destruction of lesion or tissue of pancreatic duct
52.93	Endoscopic insertion of stent (tube) into pancreatic duct
52.97	Endoscopic insertion of nasopancreatic drainage tube
52.98	Endoscopic dilation of pancreatic duct
55.21	Nephroscopy
55.22	Pyeloscopy
56.31	Ureteroscopy
57.31	Cystoscopy through artificial stoma
57.32	Other cystoscopy
58.22	Other urethroscopy
68.12	Hysteroscopy
70.21	Vaginoscopy
70.22	Culdoscopy

M DRG 413 Other Myeloproliferative Disorders or Poorly Differentiated Neoplasm Diagnoses with CC

GMLOS 5.0 AMLOS 6.8 RW 1.3048 ☑ CC

Principal Diagnosis

158.0	Malignant neoplasm of retroperitoneum
164.0	Malignant neoplasm of thymus
195.4	Malignant neoplasm of upper limb
195.5	Malignant neoplasm of lower limb
195.8	Malignant neoplasm of other specified sites
198.89	Secondary malignant neoplasm of other specified sites
*199	Malignant neoplasm without specification of site
*202.5	Letterer-Siwe disease
229.8	Benign neoplasm of other specified sites
229.9	Benign neoplasm of unspecified site
234.8	Carcinoma in situ of other specified sites
234.9	Carcinoma in situ, site unspecified
238.8	Neoplasm of uncertain behavior of other specified sites
238.9	Neoplasm of uncertain behavior, site unspecified
239.8	Neoplasm of unspecified nature of other specified sites
239.9	Neoplasm of unspecified nature, site unspecified
273.8	Other disorders of plasma protein metabolism
273.9	Unspecified disorder of plasma protein metabolism
759.6	Other congenital hamartoses, not elsewhere classified

M DRG 414 Other Myeloproliferative Disorders or Poorly Differentiated Neoplasm Diagnoses without CC

GMLOS 3.0 AMLOS 4.0 RW 0.7788 ☑

Select principal diagnosis listed under DRG 413

M DRG 473 Acute Leukemia without Major O.R. Procedure, Age Greater than 17

GMLOS 7.4 AMLOS 12.7 RW 3.4231 A

Select principal diagnosis listed under DRG 405

M DRG 492 Chemotherapy with Acute Leukemia as Secondary Diagnosis or with Use of High-Dose Chemotherapy Agent

GMLOS 8.8 AMLOS 13.7 RW 3.5926

Principal Diagnosis

V67.2	Chemotherapy follow-up examination

AND

Secondary Diagnosis

*204.0	Acute lymphoid leukemia
*205.0	Acute myeloid leukemia
*206.0	Acute monocytic leukemia
*207.0	Acute erythremia and erythroleukemia
*208.0	Acute leukemia of unspecified cell type

OR

Nonoperating Room Procedure

00.15	High-dose infusion interleukin-2 [IL-2]

MDC 17: Myeloproliferative and Poorly Differentiated Neoplasms — Medical

MDC 18
INFECTIOUS AND PARASITIC DISEASES

The complete and up-to-date listing of ICD-9-CM diagnosis codes assigned to this MDC can be found online at www.ingenixonline.com/content/drg/resources.asp.

SURGICAL

S DRG 415 O.R. Procedure for Infectious and Parasitic Diseases

GMLOS 11.0 AMLOS 14.8 RW 3.9890 T

Select any operating room procedure

MDC 18
INFECTIOUS AND PARASITIC DISEASES

The complete and up-to-date listing of ICD-9-CM diagnosis codes assigned to this MDC can be found online at www.ingenixonline.com/content/drg/resources.asp.

MEDICAL

M DRG 416 Septicemia, Age Greater than 17
GMLOS 5.6 AMLOS 7.5 RW 1.6774 ☑ T ▽ A

Principal Diagnosis

003.1	Salmonella septicemia
020.2	Septicemic plague
022.3	Anthrax septicemia
036.2	Meningococcemia
036.3	Waterhouse-Friderichsen syndrome, meningococcal
036.89	Other specified meningococcal infections
036.9	Unspecified meningococcal infection
*038	Septicemia
054.5	Herpetic septicemia
785.52	Septic shock
785.59	Other shock without mention of trauma
790.7	Bacteremia
*995.9	Systemic inflammatory response syndrome (SIRS)

M DRG 417 Septicemia, Age 0-17
GMLOS 3.2 AMLOS 4.1 RW 1.1689 ☑ A

Select principal diagnosis listed under DRG 416

M DRG 418 Postoperative and Posttraumatic Infections
GMLOS 4.8 AMLOS 6.2 RW 1.0716 ☑ T

Principal Diagnosis

958.3	Posttraumatic wound infection not elsewhere classified
*998.5	Postoperative infection, not elsewhere classified

M DRG 419 Fever of Unknown Origin, Age Greater than 17 with CC
GMLOS 3.4 AMLOS 4.4 RW 0.8453 CC A

Principal Diagnosis

780.6	Fever

M DRG 420 Fever of Unknown Origin, Age Greater than 17 without CC
GMLOS 2.7 AMLOS 3.4 RW 0.6077 ☑ A

Select principal diagnosis listed under DRG 419

M DRG 421 Viral Illness, Age Greater than 17
GMLOS 3.1 AMLOS 4.1 RW 0.7664 A

Principal Diagnosis

*045.2	Acute nonparalytic poliomyelitis
*050	Smallpox
051.0	Cowpox
051.9	Unspecified paravaccinia
052.7	Chickenpox with other specified complications
052.8	Chickenpox with unspecified complication
052.9	Varicella without mention of complication
053.79	Other specified herpes zoster complications
053.8	Unspecified herpes zoster complication

054.79	Other specified herpes simplex complications
054.8	Unspecified herpes simplex complication
055.79	Other specified measles complications
055.8	Unspecified measles complication
055.9	Measles without mention of complication
056.79	Rubella with other specified complications
056.8	Unspecified rubella complications
056.9	Rubella without mention of complication
*057	Other viral exanthemata
*060	Yellow fever
061	Dengue
*065	Arthropod-borne hemorrhagic fever
066.0	Phlebotomus fever
066.1	Tick-borne fever
066.3	Other mosquito-borne fever
*066.4	West Nile fever
066.8	Other specified arthropod-borne viral diseases
066.9	Unspecified arthropod-borne viral disease
072.79	Mumps with other specified complications
072.8	Unspecified mumps complication
072.9	Mumps without mention of complication
073.7	Ornithosis with other specified complications
073.8	Ornithosis with unspecified complication
073.9	Unspecified ornithosis
074.3	Hand, foot, and mouth disease
074.8	Other specified diseases due to Coxsackievirus
075	Infectious mononucleosis
078.2	Sweating fever
078.4	Foot and mouth disease
078.5	Cytomegaloviral disease
078.7	Arenaviral hemorrhagic fever
078.88	Other specified diseases due to Chlamydiae
078.89	Other specified diseases due to viruses
*079	Viral and chlamydial infection in conditions classified elsewhere and of unspecified site
487.8	Influenza with other manifestations
790.8	Unspecified viremia
999.0	Generalized vaccinia as complication of medical care, not elsewhere classified
V08	Asymptomatic human immunodeficiency virus (HIV) infection status

M DRG 422 Viral Illness and Fever of Unknown Origin, Age 0-17

GMLOS 2.6 AMLOS 3.7 RW 0.6171 ☑ A

Select principal diagnosis listed under DRG 421 or principal diagnosis listed below

780.6	Fever

M DRG 423 Other Infectious and Parasitic Diseases Diagnoses

GMLOS 6.0 AMLOS 8.4 RW 1.9196 T

Principal Diagnosis

*002	Typhoid and paratyphoid fevers
003.20	Unspecified localized salmonella infection
003.29	Other localized salmonella infections
003.8	Other specified salmonella infections
003.9	Unspecified salmonella infection
005.1	Botulism
006.8	Amebic infection of other sites
006.9	Unspecified amebiasis
*017.9	Tuberculosis of other specified organs
*018.0	Acute miliary tuberculosis
*018.8	Other specified miliary tuberculosis
*018.9	Unspecified miliary tuberculosis
020.0	Bubonic plague

** Code Range* ☑ *Optimization Potential* *Targeted Potential* T *Transfer DRG* SP *Special Payment*

DRG 423 — continued

020.1	Cellulocutaneous plague
020.8	Other specified types of plague
020.9	Unspecified plague
021.0	Ulceroglandular tularemia
021.3	Oculoglandular tularemia
021.8	Other specified tularemia
021.9	Unspecified tularemia
022.8	Other specified manifestations of anthrax
022.9	Unspecified anthrax
*023	Brucellosis
024	Glanders
025	Melioidosis
*026	Rat-bite fever
*027	Other zoonotic bacterial diseases
*030	Leprosy
031.2	Disseminated diseases due to other mycobacteria
031.8	Other specified diseases due to other mycobacteria
031.9	Unspecified diseases due to mycobacteria
032.89	Other specified diphtheria
032.9	Unspecified diphtheria
034.1	Scarlet fever
037	Tetanus
039.8	Actinomycotic infection of other specified sites
039.9	Actinomycotic infection of unspecified site
040.0	Gas gangrene
040.1	Rhinoscleroma
040.3	Necrobacillosis
040.82	Toxic shock syndrome
040.89	Other specified bacterial diseases
*041	Bacterial infection in conditions classified elsewhere and of unspecified site
080	Louse-borne (epidemic) typhus
*081	Other typhus
*082	Tick-borne rickettsioses
*083	Other rickettsioses
*084	Malaria
085.0	Visceral leishmaniasis (kala-azar)
085.9	Unspecified leishmaniasis
*086	Trypanosomiasis
*087	Relapsing fever
*088	Other arthropod-borne diseases
090.0	Early congenital syphilis, symptomatic
090.1	Early congenital syphilis, latent
090.2	Unspecified early congenital syphilis
090.5	Other late congenital syphilis, symptomatic
090.6	Late congenital syphilis, latent
090.7	Late congenital syphilis, unspecified
090.9	Congenital syphilis, unspecified
091.2	Other primary syphilis
091.7	Early syphilis, secondary syphilis, relapse
091.89	Early syphilis, other forms of secondary syphilis
091.9	Early syphilis, unspecified secondary syphilis
*092	Early syphilis, latent
095.8	Other specified forms of late symptomatic syphilis
095.9	Unspecified late symptomatic syphilis
096	Late syphilis, latent
*097	Other and unspecified syphilis
098.89	Gonococcal infection of other specified sites
100.0	Leptospirosis icterohemorrhagica
100.9	Unspecified leptospirosis
102.7	Other manifestations due to yaws
102.8	Latent yaws
102.9	Unspecified yaws

103.2	Late lesions of pinta
103.9	Unspecified pinta
*104	Other spirochetal infection
112.5	Disseminated candidiasis
112.89	Other candidiasis of other specified sites
112.9	Candidiasis of unspecified site
114.3	Other forms of progressive coccidioidomycosis
114.9	Unspecified coccidioidomycosis
115.00	Histoplasma capsulatum, without mention of manifestation
115.09	Histoplasma capsulatum, with mention of other manifestation
115.10	Histoplasma duboisii, without mention of manifestation
115.19	Histoplasma duboisii with mention of other manifestation
115.90	Unspecified Histoplasmosis without mention of manifestation
115.99	Unspecified Histoplasmosis with mention of other manifestation
*116	Blastomycotic infection
*117	Other mycoses
118	Opportunistic mycoses
120.2	Schistosomiasis due to schistosoma japonicum
120.8	Other specified schistosomiasis
120.9	Unspecified schistosomiasis
121.5	Metagonimiasis
121.6	Heterophyiasis
121.8	Other specified trematode infections
121.9	Unspecified trematode infection
122.3	Other echinococcus granulosus infection
122.4	Unspecified echinococcus granulosus infection
122.6	Other echinococcus multilocularis infection
122.7	Unspecified echinococcus multilocularis infection
122.9	Other and unspecified echinococcosis
124	Trichinosis
*125	Filarial infection and dracontiasis
127.8	Mixed intestinal helminthiasis
*128	Other and unspecified helminthiases
130.7	Toxoplasmosis of other specified sites
130.8	Multisystemic disseminated toxoplasmosis
130.9	Unspecified toxoplasmosis
131.8	Trichomoniasis of other specified sites
131.9	Unspecified trichomoniasis
136.0	Ainhum
136.2	Specific infections by free-living amebae
136.4	Psorospermiasis
136.5	Sarcosporidiosis
136.8	Other specified infectious and parasitic diseases
136.9	Unspecified infectious and parasitic diseases
137.4	Late effects of tuberculosis of other specified organs
139.8	Late effects of other and unspecified infectious and parasitic diseases
*795.3	Nonspecific positive culture findings
999.3	Other infection due to medical care, not elsewhere classified
*V09	Infection with drug-resistent microorganisms

MDC 18: Infectious and Parasitic Diseases — Medical

MDC 19
MENTAL DISEASES AND DISORDERS

The complete and up-to-date listing of ICD-9-CM diagnosis codes assigned to this MDC can be found online at www.ingenixonline.com/content/drg/resources.asp.

SURGICAL

S DRG 424 O.R. Procedure with Principal Diagnosis of Mental Illness
GMLOS 7.3 AMLOS 12.4 RW 2.2773

Select any operating room procedure

MDC 19
MENTAL DISEASES AND DISORDERS

The complete and up-to-date listing of ICD-9-CM diagnosis codes assigned to this MDC can be found online at www.ingenixonline.com/content/drg/resources.asp.

MEDICAL

[M] DRG 425 Acute Adjustment Reactions and Psychosocial Dysfunction
GMLOS 2.6 AMLOS 3.5 RW 0.6191 ☑ [Targeted Potential]

Principal Diagnosis

293.0	Delirium due to conditions classified elsewhere
293.1	Subacute delirium
293.9	Unspecified transient mental disorder in conditions classified elsewhere
*300.0	Anxiety states
300.10	Hysteria, unspecified
300.11	Conversion disorder
300.12	Dissociative amnesia
300.13	Dissociative fugue
300.15	Dissociative disorder or reaction, unspecified
300.16	Factitious disorder with predominantly psychological signs and symptoms
300.19	Other and unspecified factitious illness
300.9	Unspecified nonpsychotic mental disorder
*308	Acute reaction to stress
780.1	Hallucinations
799.2	Nervousness
V62.84	Suicidal ideation
V71.01	Observation of adult antisocial behavior
V71.02	Observation of childhood or adolescent antisocial behavior

[M] DRG 426 Depressive Neuroses
GMLOS 3.0 AMLOS 4.1 RW 0.4656 ☑

Principal Diagnosis

300.4	Dysthymic disorder
301.12	Chronic depressive personality disorder
309.0	Adjustment disorder with depressed mood
309.1	Prolonged depressive reaction as adjustment reaction
311	Depressive disorder, not elsewhere classified

[M] DRG 427 Neuroses Except Depressive
GMLOS 3.2 AMLOS 4.7 RW 0.5135 ☑

Principal Diagnosis

*300.2	Phobic disorders
300.3	Obsessive-compulsive disorders
300.5	Neurasthenia
300.6	Depersonalization disorder
300.7	Hypochondriasis
*300.8	Somatoform disorders
306.7	Malfunction of organs of special sense arising from mental factors
306.9	Unspecified psychophysiological malfunction
307.53	Rumination disorder
307.54	Psychogenic vomiting
307.80	Psychogenic pain, site unspecified
307.89	Other pain disorder related to psychological factors
*309.2	Predominant disturbance of other emotions as adjustment reaction
309.3	Adjustment disorder with disturbance of conduct
309.4	Adjustment disorder with mixed disturbance of emotions and conduct

DRG 427 — continued

*309.8	Other specified adjustment reactions
309.9	Unspecified adjustment reaction
313.0	Overanxious disorder specific to childhood and adolescence
313.1	Misery and unhappiness disorder specific to childhood and adolescence

M DRG 428 Disorders of Personality and Impulse Control

GMLOS 4.6 AMLOS 7.3 RW 0.6981

Principal Diagnosis

300.14	Dissociative identity disorder
301.0	Paranoid personality disorder
301.10	Affective personality disorder, unspecified
301.11	Chronic hypomanic personality disorder
301.13	Cyclothymic disorder
*301.2	Schizoid personality disorder
301.3	Explosive personality disorder
301.4	Obsessive-compulsive personality disorder
*301.5	Histrionic personality disorder
301.6	Dependent personality disorder
301.7	Antisocial personality disorder
*301.8	Other personality disorders
301.9	Unspecified personality disorder
307.1	Anorexia nervosa
312.31	Pathological gambling
312.32	Kleptomania
312.34	Intermittent explosive disorder
312.35	Isolated explosive disorder
312.39	Other disorder of impulse control

M DRG 429 Organic Disturbances and Mental Retardation

GMLOS 4.3 AMLOS 5.6 RW 0.7919 T

Principal Diagnosis

*290	Dementias
*293.8	Other specified transient mental disorders due to conditions classified elsewhere
*294	Persistent mental disorders due to conditions classified elsewhere
*299.0	Autistic disorder
*299.1	Childhood disintegrative disorder
307.9	Other and unspecified special symptom or syndrome, not elsewhere classified
310.0	Frontal lobe syndrome
310.1	Personality change due to conditions classified elsewhere
310.8	Other specified nonpsychotic mental disorder following organic brain damage
310.9	Unspecified nonpsychotic mental disorder following organic brain damage
316	Psychic factors associated with diseases classified elsewhere
317	Mild mental retardation
*318	Other specified mental retardation
319	Unspecified mental retardation
758.0	Down's syndrome
758.1	Patau's syndrome
758.2	Edwards' syndrome
*758.3	Autosomal deletion syndromes
759.83	Fragile X syndrome
780.02	Transient alteration of awareness
797	Senility without mention of psychosis

M DRG 430 Psychoses

GMLOS 5.8 AMLOS 7.9 RW 0.6483 T

Principal Diagnosis

*295	Schizophrenic disorders
*296	Episodic mood disorders
*297	Delusional disorders

298.0	Depressive type psychosis
298.1	Excitative type psychosis
298.3	Acute paranoid reaction
298.4	Psychogenic paranoid psychosis
298.8	Other and unspecified reactive psychosis
298.9	Unspecified psychosis
*299.8	Other specified pervasive developmental disorders
*299.9	Unspecified pervasive developmental disorder

Ⓜ DRG 431 Childhood Mental Disorders

GMLOS 4.0 AMLOS 5.9 RW 0.5178

Principal Diagnosis

307.52	Pica
307.6	Enuresis
307.7	Encopresis
*312.0	Undersocialized conduct disorder, aggressive type
*312.1	Undersocialized conduct disorder, unaggressive type
*312.2	Socialized conduct disorder
312.30	Impulse control disorder, unspecified
312.33	Pyromania
312.4	Mixed disturbance of conduct and emotions
*312.8	Other specified disturbances of conduct, not elsewhere classified
312.9	Unspecified disturbance of conduct
*313.2	Sensitivity, shyness, and social withdrawal disorder specific to childhood and adolescence
313.3	Relationship problems specific to childhood and adolescence
*313.8	Other or mixed emotional disturbances of childhood or adolescence
313.9	Unspecified emotional disturbance of childhood or adolescence
*314	Hyperkinetic syndrome of childhood
*315	Specific delays in development
784.61	Alexia and dyslexia
784.69	Other symbolic dysfunction

Ⓜ DRG 432 Other Mental Disorder Diagnoses

GMLOS 2.9 AMLOS 4.3 RW 0.6282 ☑

Principal Diagnosis

298.2	Reactive confusion
*302	Sexual and gender identity disorders
306.8	Other specified psychophysiological malfunction
307.0	Stuttering
307.3	Stereotypic movement disorder
*307.4	Specific disorders of sleep of nonorganic origin
307.50	Eating disorder, unspecified
307.51	Bulimia nervosa
307.59	Other disorder of eating
*327.0	Organic disorders of initiating and maintaining sleep [Organic insomnia]
*327.1	Organic disorders of excessive somnolence [Organic hypersomnia]
780.50	Unspecified sleep disturbance
780.52	Insomnia, unspecified
780.54	Hypersomnia, unspecified
780.55	Disruption of 24 hour sleep wake cycle, unspecified
780.56	Dysfunctions associated with sleep stages or arousal from sleep
780.58	Sleep related movement disorder, unspecified
780.59	Other sleep disturbances
784.60	Symbolic dysfunction, unspecified
V71.09	Observation of other suspected mental condition

MDC 20
ALCOHOL/DRUG USE AND ALCOHOL/DRUG-INDUCED ORGANIC MENTAL DISORDERS

The complete and up-to-date listing of ICD-9-CM diagnosis codes assigned to this MDC can be found online at www.ingenixonline.com/content/drg/resources.asp.

MEDICAL

Ⓜ DRG 433 Alcohol/Drug Abuse or Dependence, Left Against Medical Advice

GMLOS 2.2 AMLOS 3.0 RW 0.2776

Discharge status of against medical advice (AMA)

DRG 434 No Longer Valid

GMLOS 0.0 AMLOS 0.0 RW 0.0000

Omitted in the October 2001 grouper version

DRG 435 No Longer Valid

GMLOS 0.0 AMLOS 0.0 RW 0.0000

Omitted in the October 2001 grouper version

DRG 436 No Longer Valid

GMLOS 0.0 AMLOS 0.0 RW 0.0000

Omitted in the October 2001 grouper version

DRG 437 No Longer Valid

GMLOS 0.0 AMLOS 0.0 RW 0.0000

Omitted in the October 2001 grouper version

DRG 438 No Longer Valid

GMLOS 0.0 AMLOS 0.0 RW 0.0000

Omitted in the May 1984 grouper revision

Ⓜ DRG 521 Alcohol/Drug Abuse or Dependence with CC

GMLOS 4.2 AMLOS 5.6 RW 0.6939 ☑ T CC

Principal Diagnosis

*291	Alcohol-induced mental disorders
*292	Drug-induced mental disorders
*303.0	Acute alcoholic intoxication
*303.9	Other and unspecified alcohol dependence
*304	Drug dependence
*305.0	Nondependent alcohol abuse
*305.2	Nondependent cannabis abuse
*305.3	Nondependent hallucinogen abuse
*305.4	Nondependent barbiturate and similarly acting sedative or hypnotic abuse
*305.5	Nondependent opioid abuse
*305.6	Nondependent cocaine abuse
*305.7	Nondependent amphetamine or related acting sympathomimetic abuse
*305.8	Nondependent antidepressant type abuse
*305.9	Other, mixed, or unspecified nondependent drug abuse
790.3	Excessive blood level of alcohol

Ⓜ DRG 522 Alcohol/Drug Abuse or Dependence with Rehabilitation Therapy without CC

GMLOS 7.7 AMLOS 9.6 RW 0.4794 ☑Ⓣ

Select principal diagnoses listed from DRG 521

AND

Nonoperating Room Procedures

94.61	Alcohol rehabilitation
94.63	Alcohol rehabilitation and detoxification
94.64	Drug rehabilitation
94.66	Drug rehabilitation and detoxification
94.67	Combined alcohol and drug rehabilitation
94.69	Combined alcohol and drug rehabilitation and detoxification

Ⓜ DRG 523 Alcohol/Drug Abuse or Dependence without Rehabilitation Therapy without CC

GMLOS 3.2 AMLOS 3.9 RW 0.3793 ☑

Select principal diagnoses listed from DRG 521

MDC 21
INJURY, POISONING AND TOXIC EFFECTS OF DRUGS

The complete and up-to-date listing of ICD-9-CM diagnosis codes assigned to this MDC can be found online at www.ingenixonline.com/content/drg/resources.asp.

SURGICAL

S DRG 439 Skin Grafts for Injuries
GMLOS 5.4 AMLOS 8.9 RW 1.9398

Operating Room Procedures

85.82	Split-thickness graft to breast
85.83	Full-thickness graft to breast
85.84	Pedicle graft to breast
86.60	Free skin graft, not otherwise specified
86.63	Full-thickness skin graft to other sites
86.65	Heterograft to skin
86.66	Homograft to skin
86.67	Dermal regenerative graft
86.69	Other skin graft to other sites
86.70	Pedicle or flap graft, not otherwise specified
86.71	Cutting and preparation of pedicle grafts or flaps
86.72	Advancement of pedicle graft
86.74	Attachment of pedicle or flap graft to other sites
86.75	Revision of pedicle or flap graft
86.93	Insertion of tissue expander

S DRG 440 Wound Debridements for Injuries
GMLOS 5.9 AMLOS 9.2 RW 1.9457 T

Operating Room Procedure

86.22	Excisional debridement of wound, infection, or burn

S DRG 441 Hand Procedures for Injuries
GMLOS 2.3 AMLOS 3.4 RW 0.9382 ☑

Operating Room Procedures

04.43	Release of carpal tunnel
77.04	Sequestrectomy of carpals and metacarpals
77.14	Other incision of carpals and metacarpals without division
77.24	Wedge osteotomy of carpals and metacarpals
77.34	Other division of carpals and metacarpals
77.44	Biopsy of carpals and metacarpals
77.64	Local excision of lesion or tissue of carpals and metacarpals
77.74	Excision of carpals and metacarpals for graft
77.84	Other partial ostectomy of carpals and metacarpals
77.94	Total ostectomy of carpals and metacarpals
78.04	Bone graft of carpals and metacarpals
78.14	Application of external fixator device, carpals and metacarpals
78.24	Limb shortening procedures, carpals and metacarpals
78.34	Limb lengthening procedures, carpals and metacarpals
78.44	Other repair or plastic operations on carpals and metacarpals
78.54	Internal fixation of carpals and metacarpals without fracture reduction
78.64	Removal of implanted device from carpals and metacarpals
78.74	Osteoclasis of carpals and metacarpals
78.84	Diagnostic procedures on carpals and metacarpals, not elsewhere classified
78.94	Insertion of bone growth stimulator into carpals and metacarpals
79.13	Closed reduction of fracture of carpals and metacarpals with internal fixation
79.14	Closed reduction of fracture of phalanges of hand with internal fixation
79.23	Open reduction of fracture of carpals and metacarpals without internal fixation
79.24	Open reduction of fracture of phalanges of hand without internal fixation

S *Surgical* M *Medical* CC *CC Indicator* A *Age Restriction* ● *New DRG* ▲ *Revised DRG Title*

79.33	Open reduction of fracture of carpals and metacarpals with internal fixation
79.34	Open reduction of fracture of phalanges of hand with internal fixation
79.63	Debridement of open fracture of carpals and metacarpals
79.64	Debridement of open fracture of phalanges of hand
79.83	Open reduction of dislocation of wrist
79.84	Open reduction of dislocation of hand and finger
79.93	Unspecified operation on bone injury of carpals and metacarpals
79.94	Unspecified operation on bone injury of phalanges of hand
80.03	Arthrotomy for removal of prosthesis of wrist
80.04	Arthrotomy for removal of prosthesis of hand and finger
80.13	Other arthrotomy of wrist
80.14	Other arthrotomy of hand and finger
80.43	Division of joint capsule, ligament, or cartilage of wrist
80.44	Division of joint capsule, ligament, or cartilage of hand and finger
80.73	Synovectomy of wrist
80.74	Synovectomy of hand and finger
80.83	Other local excision or destruction of lesion of wrist joint
80.84	Other local excision or destruction of lesion of joint of hand and finger
80.93	Other excision of wrist joint
80.94	Other excision of joint of hand and finger
81.25	Carporadial fusion
81.26	Metacarpocarpal fusion
81.27	Metacarpophalangeal fusion
81.28	Interphalangeal fusion
81.71	Arthroplasty of metacarpophalangeal and interphalangeal joint with implant
81.72	Arthroplasty of metacarpophalangeal and interphalangeal joint without implant
81.74	Arthroplasty of carpocarpal or carpometacarpal joint with implant
81.75	Arthroplasty of carpocarpal or carpometacarpal joint without implant
81.79	Other repair of hand, fingers, and wrist
82.01	Exploration of tendon sheath of hand
82.02	Myotomy of hand
82.03	Bursotomy of hand
82.09	Other incision of soft tissue of hand
*82.1	Division of muscle, tendon, and fascia of hand
*82.2	Excision of lesion of muscle, tendon, and fascia of hand
*82.3	Other excision of soft tissue of hand
*82.4	Suture of muscle, tendon, and fascia of hand
*82.5	Transplantation of muscle and tendon of hand
*82.6	Reconstruction of thumb
*82.7	Plastic operation on hand with graft or implant
*82.8	Other plastic operations on hand
82.91	Lysis of adhesions of hand
82.99	Other operations on muscle, tendon, and fascia of hand
84.01	Amputation and disarticulation of finger
84.02	Amputation and disarticulation of thumb
84.21	Thumb reattachment
84.22	Finger reattachment
86.61	Full-thickness skin graft to hand
86.62	Other skin graft to hand
86.73	Attachment of pedicle or flap graft to hand
86.85	Correction of syndactyly

S DRG 442 Other O.R. Procedures for Injuries with CC

GMLOS 6.0 AMLOS 8.9 RW 2.5660 ☑ T CC

Operating Room Procedures

00.61	Percutaneous angioplasty or atherectomy of precerebral (extracranial) vessel(s)
00.62	Percutaneous angioplasty or atherectomy of intracranial vessel(s)
00.70	Revision of hip replacement, both acetabular and femoral components
00.71	Revision of hip replacement, acetabular component
00.72	Revision of hip replacement, femoral component
00.73	Revision of hip replacement, acetabular liner and/or femoral head only
*00.8	Other knee procedures

** Code Range* ☑ *Optimization Potential* *Targeted Potential* T *Transfer DRG* SP *Special Payment*

DRG 442 — continued

01.18	Other diagnostic procedures on brain and cerebral meninges
01.19	Other diagnostic procedures on skull
01.23	Reopening of craniotomy site
01.24	Other craniotomy
01.25	Other craniectomy
*01.3	Incision of brain and cerebral meninges
01.41	Operations on thalamus
01.52	Hemispherectomy
01.53	Lobectomy of brain
01.59	Other excision or destruction of lesion or tissue of brain
*02.0	Cranioplasty
02.11	Simple suture of dura mater of brain
02.12	Other repair of cerebral meninges
02.13	Ligation of meningeal vessel
02.2	Ventriculostomy
*02.3	Extracranial ventricular shunt
02.42	Replacement of ventricular shunt
02.43	Removal of ventricular shunt
02.91	Lysis of cortical adhesions
02.92	Repair of brain
02.93	Implantation or replacement of intracranial neurostimulator lead(s)
02.94	Insertion or replacement of skull tongs or halo traction device
02.99	Other operations on skull, brain, and cerebral meninges
*03.0	Exploration and decompression of spinal canal structures
03.1	Division of intraspinal nerve root
*03.2	Chordotomy
03.53	Repair of vertebral fracture
03.59	Other repair and plastic operations on spinal cord structures
03.6	Lysis of adhesions of spinal cord and nerve roots
03.93	Implantation or replacement of spinal neurostimulator lead(s)
03.94	Removal of spinal neurostimulator lead(s)
03.97	Revision of spinal thecal shunt
03.98	Removal of spinal thecal shunt
03.99	Other operations on spinal cord and spinal canal structures
04.02	Division of trigeminal nerve
04.03	Division or crushing of other cranial and peripheral nerves
04.04	Other incision of cranial and peripheral nerves
04.05	Gasserian ganglionectomy
04.06	Other cranial or peripheral ganglionectomy
04.07	Other excision or avulsion of cranial and peripheral nerves
04.12	Open biopsy of cranial or peripheral nerve or ganglion
04.19	Other diagnostic procedures on cranial and peripheral nerves and ganglia
04.3	Suture of cranial and peripheral nerves
04.41	Decompression of trigeminal nerve root
04.42	Other cranial nerve decompression
04.44	Release of tarsal tunnel
04.49	Other peripheral nerve or ganglion decompression or lysis of adhesions
04.5	Cranial or peripheral nerve graft
04.6	Transposition of cranial and peripheral nerves
*04.7	Other cranial or peripheral neuroplasty
*04.9	Other operations on cranial and peripheral nerves
05.9	Other operations on nervous system
06.02	Reopening of wound of thyroid field
06.09	Other incision of thyroid field
06.92	Ligation of thyroid vessels
06.93	Suture of thyroid gland
07.43	Ligation of adrenal vessels
07.44	Repair of adrenal gland
07.45	Reimplantation of adrenal tissue
07.49	Other operations on adrenal glands, nerves, and vessels
*07.8	Thymectomy
07.91	Exploration of thymus field

07.92	Incision of thymus
07.93	Repair of thymus
08.11	Biopsy of eyelid
*08.2	Excision or destruction of lesion or tissue of eyelid
*08.3	Repair of blepharoptosis and lid retraction
*08.4	Repair of entropion or ectropion
*08.5	Other adjustment of lid position
*08.6	Reconstruction of eyelid with flaps or grafts
*08.7	Other reconstruction of eyelid
*08.9	Other operations on eyelids
09.11	Biopsy of lacrimal gland
09.19	Other diagnostic procedures on lacrimal system
09.21	Excision of lesion of lacrimal gland
09.22	Other partial dacryoadenectomy
09.23	Total dacryoadenectomy
09.3	Other operations on lacrimal gland
09.44	Intubation of nasolacrimal duct
09.52	Incision of lacrimal canaliculi
09.6	Excision of lacrimal sac and passage
*09.7	Repair of canaliculus and punctum
*09.8	Fistulization of lacrimal tract to nasal cavity
*09.9	Other operations on lacrimal system
10.0	Removal of embedded foreign body from conjunctiva by incision
*10.3	Excision or destruction of lesion or tissue of conjunctiva
*10.4	Conjunctivoplasty
10.6	Repair of laceration of conjunctiva
11.0	Magnetic removal of embedded foreign body from cornea
11.1	Incision of cornea
11.22	Biopsy of cornea
11.32	Excision of pterygium with corneal graft
11.42	Thermocauterization of corneal lesion
11.43	Cryotherapy of corneal lesion
11.49	Other removal or destruction of corneal lesion
*11.5	Repair of cornea
*11.6	Corneal transplant
*11.7	Other reconstructive and refractive surgery on cornea
*11.9	Other operations on cornea
*12.0	Removal of intraocular foreign body from anterior segment of eye
*12.1	Iridotomy and simple iridectomy
*12.2	Diagnostic procedures on iris, ciliary body, sclera, and anterior chamber
*12.3	Iridoplasty and coreoplasty
*12.4	Excision or destruction of lesion of iris and ciliary body
*12.5	Facilitation of intraocular circulation
*12.6	Scleral fistulization
*12.8	Operations on sclera
12.91	Therapeutic evacuation of anterior chamber
12.92	Injection into anterior chamber
12.97	Other operations on iris
12.98	Other operations on ciliary body
12.99	Other operations on anterior chamber
*13.0	Removal of foreign body from lens
13.72	Secondary insertion of intraocular lens prosthesis
13.8	Removal of implanted lens
13.9	Other operations on lens
*14.0	Removal of foreign body from posterior segment of eye
14.31	Repair of retinal tear by diathermy
*14.4	Repair of retinal detachment with scleral buckling and implant
*14.5	Other repair of retinal detachment
14.6	Removal of surgically implanted material from posterior segment of eye
*14.7	Operations on vitreous
14.9	Other operations on retina, choroid, and posterior chamber
15.7	Repair of injury of extraocular muscle
15.9	Other operations on extraocular muscles and tendons

**** Code Range*** ☑ ***Optimization Potential*** ▽ ***Targeted Potential*** 🅃 ***Transfer DRG*** SP ***Special Payment***

DRG 442 — continued

*16.0	Orbitotomy
16.1	Removal of penetrating foreign body from eye, not otherwise specified
*16.3	Evisceration of eyeball
*16.4	Enucleation of eyeball
*16.5	Exenteration of orbital contents
*16.6	Secondary procedures after removal of eyeball
*16.7	Removal of ocular or orbital implant
*16.8	Repair of injury of eyeball and orbit
16.92	Excision of lesion of orbit
16.93	Excision of lesion of eye, unspecified structure
16.98	Other operations on orbit
16.99	Other operations on eyeball
18.39	Other excision of external ear
18.6	Reconstruction of external auditory canal
*18.7	Other plastic repair of external ear
18.9	Other operations on external ear
21.04	Control of epistaxis by ligation of ethmoidal arteries
21.05	Control of epistaxis by (transantral) ligation of the maxillary artery
21.06	Control of epistaxis by ligation of the external carotid artery
21.07	Control of epistaxis by excision of nasal mucosa and skin grafting of septum and lateral nasal wall
21.09	Control of epistaxis by other means
21.4	Resection of nose
21.5	Submucous resection of nasal septum
21.62	Fracture of the turbinates
21.69	Other turbinectomy
21.72	Open reduction of nasal fracture
21.83	Total nasal reconstruction
21.84	Revision rhinoplasty
21.85	Augmentation rhinoplasty
21.86	Limited rhinoplasty
21.87	Other rhinoplasty
21.88	Other septoplasty
21.89	Other repair and plastic operations on nose
21.99	Other operations on nose
24.2	Gingivoplasty
24.5	Alveoloplasty
25.59	Other repair and plastic operations on tongue
*26.4	Repair of salivary gland or duct
27.0	Drainage of face and floor of mouth
27.49	Other excision of mouth
27.53	Closure of fistula of mouth
27.54	Repair of cleft lip
27.55	Full-thickness skin graft to lip and mouth
27.56	Other skin graft to lip and mouth
27.57	Attachment of pedicle or flap graft to lip and mouth
27.59	Other plastic repair of mouth
27.61	Suture of laceration of palate
27.92	Incision of mouth, unspecified structure
27.99	Other operations on oral cavity
28.7	Control of hemorrhage after tonsillectomy and adenoidectomy
28.91	Removal of foreign body from tonsil and adenoid by incision
29.0	Pharyngotomy
29.4	Plastic operation on pharynx
29.51	Suture of laceration of pharynx
29.53	Closure of other fistula of pharynx
29.59	Other repair of pharynx
29.99	Other operations on pharynx
30.1	Hemilaryngectomy
*30.2	Other partial laryngectomy
31.61	Suture of laceration of larynx
31.64	Repair of laryngeal fracture

31.69	Other repair of larynx
*31.7	Repair and plastic operations on trachea
31.92	Lysis of adhesions of trachea or larynx
31.99	Other operations on trachea
32.1	Other excision of bronchus
32.3	Segmental resection of lung
32.4	Lobectomy of lung
32.5	Complete pneumonectomy
32.9	Other excision of lung
33.0	Incision of bronchus
33.1	Incision of lung
*33.4	Repair and plastic operation on lung and bronchus
33.92	Ligation of bronchus
33.98	Other operations on bronchus
33.99	Other operations on lung
34.02	Exploratory thoracotomy
34.03	Reopening of recent thoracotomy site
34.1	Incision of mediastinum
34.21	Transpleural thoracoscopy
*34.5	Pleurectomy
34.6	Scarification of pleura
34.73	Closure of other fistula of thorax
34.79	Other repair of chest wall
34.82	Suture of laceration of diaphragm
34.83	Closure of fistula of diaphragm
34.84	Other repair of diaphragm
34.85	Implantation of diaphragmatic pacemaker
34.89	Other operations on diaphragm
34.93	Repair of pleura
34.99	Other operations on thorax
37.11	Cardiotomy
37.12	Pericardiotomy
37.31	Pericardiectomy
37.49	Other repair of heart and pericardium
37.74	Insertion or replacement of epicardial lead (electrode) into epicardium
37.75	Revision of lead (electrode)
37.76	Replacement of transvenous atrial and/or ventricular lead(s) (electrode(s))
37.77	Removal of lead(s) (electrodes) without replacement
37.79	Revision or relocation of cardiac device pocket
37.80	Insertion of permanent pacemaker, initial or replacement, type of device not specified
37.85	Replacement of any type of pacemaker device with single-chamber device, not specified as rate responsive
37.86	Replacement of any type of pacemaker device with single-chamber device, rate responsive
37.87	Replacement of any type of pacemaker device with dual-chamber device
37.89	Revision or removal of pacemaker device
37.91	Open chest cardiac massage
*38.0	Incision of vessel
38.10	Endarterectomy, unspecified site
38.12	Endarterectomy of other vessels of head and neck
38.13	Endarterectomy of upper limb vessels
38.14	Endarterectomy of aorta
38.15	Endarterectomy of other thoracic vessels
38.16	Endarterectomy of abdominal arteries
38.18	Endarterectomy of lower limb arteries
*38.3	Resection of vessel with anastomosis
*38.4	Resection of vessel with replacement
*38.6	Other excision of vessels
38.7	Interruption of the vena cava
*38.8	Other surgical occlusion of vessels
39.22	Aorta-subclavian-carotid bypass
39.23	Other intrathoracic vascular shunt or bypass
39.24	Aorta-renal bypass
39.25	Aorta-iliac-femoral bypass

*** Code Range** ☑ ***Optimization Potential*** ▽ ***Targeted Potential*** T ***Transfer DRG*** SP ***Special Payment***

DRG 442 — continued

39.26	Other intra-abdominal vascular shunt or bypass
39.27	Arteriovenostomy for renal dialysis
39.28	Extracranial-intracranial (EC-IC) vascular bypass
39.29	Other (peripheral) vascular shunt or bypass
*39.3	Suture of vessel
*39.4	Revision of vascular procedure
39.50	Angioplasty or atherectomy of other non-coronary vessel(s)
39.52	Other repair of aneurysm
39.56	Repair of blood vessel with tissue patch graft
39.57	Repair of blood vessel with synthetic patch graft
39.58	Repair of blood vessel with unspecified type of patch graft
39.59	Other repair of vessel
39.71	Endovascular implantation of graft in abdominal aorta
39.72	Endovascular repair or occlusion of head and neck vessels
39.73	Endovascular implantation of graft in thoracic aorta
39.79	Other endovascular repair (of aneurysm) of other vessels
39.91	Freeing of vessel
39.93	Insertion of vessel-to-vessel cannula
39.98	Control of hemorrhage, not otherwise specified
39.99	Other operations on vessels
40.29	Simple excision of other lymphatic structure
*40.6	Operations on thoracic duct
40.9	Other operations on lymphatic structures
41.2	Splenotomy
41.42	Excision of lesion or tissue of spleen
41.43	Partial splenectomy
41.5	Total splenectomy
41.93	Excision of accessory spleen
41.95	Repair and plastic operations on spleen
41.99	Other operations on spleen
42.09	Other incision of esophagus
*42.1	Esophagostomy
42.21	Operative esophagoscopy by incision
*42.4	Excision of esophagus
*42.5	Intrathoracic anastomosis of esophagus
*42.6	Antesternal anastomosis of esophagus
42.7	Esophagomyotomy
42.82	Suture of laceration of esophagus
42.83	Closure of esophagostomy
42.84	Repair of esophageal fistula, not elsewhere classified
42.85	Repair of esophageal stricture
42.86	Production of subcutaneous tunnel without esophageal anastomosis
42.87	Other graft of esophagus
42.89	Other repair of esophagus
43.0	Gastrotomy
43.5	Partial gastrectomy with anastomosis to esophagus
43.6	Partial gastrectomy with anastomosis to duodenum
43.7	Partial gastrectomy with anastomosis to jejunum
*43.8	Other partial gastrectomy
*43.9	Total gastrectomy
44.11	Transabdominal gastroscopy
44.5	Revision of gastric anastomosis
44.61	Suture of laceration of stomach
44.63	Closure of other gastric fistula
44.64	Gastropexy
44.65	Esophagogastroplasty
44.66	Other procedures for creation of esophagogastric sphincteric competence
44.67	Laparoscopic procedures for creation of esophagogastric sphincteric competence
44.68	Laparoscopic gastroplasty
44.69	Other repair of stomach
44.92	Intraoperative manipulation of stomach
44.99	Other operations on stomach

*45.0	Enterotomy
45.11	Transabdominal endoscopy of small intestine
45.21	Transabdominal endoscopy of large intestine
45.61	Multiple segmental resection of small intestine
45.62	Other partial resection of small intestine
45.63	Total removal of small intestine
*45.7	Partial excision of large intestine
45.8	Total intra-abdominal colectomy
*45.9	Intestinal anastomosis
*46.0	Exteriorization of intestine
46.10	Colostomy, not otherwise specified
46.11	Temporary colostomy
46.13	Permanent colostomy
46.20	Ileostomy, not otherwise specified
46.21	Temporary ileostomy
46.22	Continent ileostomy
46.23	Other permanent ileostomy
*46.4	Revision of intestinal stoma
*46.5	Closure of intestinal stoma
*46.7	Other repair of intestine
*46.8	Dilation and manipulation of intestine
46.93	Revision of anastomosis of small intestine
46.94	Revision of anastomosis of large intestine
46.97	Transplant of intestine
46.99	Other operations on intestines
*47.1	Incidental appendectomy
47.92	Closure of appendiceal fistula
48.0	Proctotomy
48.1	Proctostomy
48.21	Transabdominal proctosigmoidoscopy
48.49	Other pull-through resection of rectum
48.5	Abdominoperineal resection of rectum
*48.6	Other resection of rectum
*48.7	Repair of rectum
*48.8	Incision or excision of perirectal tissue or lesion
48.91	Incision of rectal stricture
*49.1	Incision or excision of anal fistula
49.71	Suture of laceration of anus
49.73	Closure of anal fistula
49.75	Implantation or revision of artificial anal sphincter
49.76	Removal of artificial anal sphincter
49.79	Other repair of anal sphincter
49.95	Control of (postoperative) hemorrhage of anus
49.99	Other operations on anus
50.0	Hepatotomy
50.12	Open biopsy of liver
50.19	Other diagnostic procedures on liver
50.22	Partial hepatectomy
50.3	Lobectomy of liver
50.4	Total hepatectomy
*50.6	Repair of liver
*51.2	Cholecystectomy
*51.3	Anastomosis of gallbladder or bile duct
51.42	Common duct exploration for relief of other obstruction
51.43	Insertion of choledochohepatic tube for decompression
51.59	Incision of other bile duct
51.61	Excision of cystic duct remnant
*51.7	Repair of bile ducts
51.81	Dilation of sphincter of Oddi
51.82	Pancreatic sphincterotomy
51.83	Pancreatic sphincteroplasty
51.89	Other operations on sphincter of Oddi
51.91	Repair of laceration of gallbladder

*** Code Range** ☑ ***Optimization Potential*** ▽ ***Targeted Potential*** 🅃 ***Transfer DRG*** SP ***Special Payment***

DRG 442 — continued

51.92	Closure of cholecystostomy
51.93	Closure of other biliary fistula
51.94	Revision of anastomosis of biliary tract
51.95	Removal of prosthetic device from bile duct
51.99	Other operations on biliary tract
52.12	Open biopsy of pancreas
52.19	Other diagnostic procedures on pancreas
*52.5	Partial pancreatectomy
52.6	Total pancreatectomy
52.7	Radical pancreaticoduodenectomy
52.92	Cannulation of pancreatic duct
52.95	Other repair of pancreas
52.96	Anastomosis of pancreas
52.99	Other operations on pancreas
53.49	Other umbilical herniorrhaphy
53.61	Incisional hernia repair with prosthesis
53.7	Repair of diaphragmatic hernia, abdominal approach
*53.8	Repair of diaphragmatic hernia, thoracic approach
54.0	Incision of abdominal wall
*54.1	Laparotomy
54.21	Laparoscopy
54.22	Biopsy of abdominal wall or umbilicus
54.29	Other diagnostic procedures on abdominal region
*54.5	Lysis of peritoneal adhesions
*54.6	Suture of abdominal wall and peritoneum
*54.7	Other repair of abdominal wall and peritoneum
54.92	Removal of foreign body from peritoneal cavity
54.93	Creation of cutaneoperitoneal fistula
54.95	Incision of peritoneum
*55.0	Nephrotomy and nephrostomy
55.11	Pyelotomy
55.12	Pyelostomy
55.24	Open biopsy of kidney
55.29	Other diagnostic procedures on kidney
55.31	Marsupialization of kidney lesion
55.4	Partial nephrectomy
55.51	Nephroureterectomy
55.52	Nephrectomy of remaining kidney
55.53	Removal of transplanted or rejected kidney
55.54	Bilateral nephrectomy
55.61	Renal autotransplantation
55.81	Suture of laceration of kidney
55.82	Closure of nephrostomy and pyelostomy
55.83	Closure of other fistula of kidney
55.84	Reduction of torsion of renal pedicle
55.86	Anastomosis of kidney
55.87	Correction of ureteropelvic junction
55.89	Other repair of kidney
55.97	Implantation or replacement of mechanical kidney
55.98	Removal of mechanical kidney
55.99	Other operations on kidney
56.0	Transurethral removal of obstruction from ureter and renal pelvis
56.1	Ureteral meatotomy
56.2	Ureterotomy
*56.4	Ureterectomy
*56.5	Cutaneous uretero-ileostomy
*56.6	Other external urinary diversion
*56.7	Other anastomosis or bypass of ureter
56.81	Lysis of intraluminal adhesions of ureter
56.82	Suture of laceration of ureter
56.83	Closure of ureterostomy
56.84	Closure of other fistula of ureter

56.86	Removal of ligature from ureter
56.89	Other repair of ureter
56.95	Ligation of ureter
56.99	Other operations on ureter
57.12	Lysis of intraluminal adhesions with incision into bladder
57.18	Other suprapubic cystostomy
57.19	Other cystotomy
57.21	Vesicostomy
57.22	Revision or closure of vesicostomy
57.39	Other diagnostic procedures on bladder
57.6	Partial cystectomy
57.79	Other total cystectomy
57.81	Suture of laceration of bladder
57.82	Closure of cystostomy
57.83	Repair of fistula involving bladder and intestine
57.84	Repair of other fistula of bladder
57.87	Reconstruction of urinary bladder
57.89	Other repair of bladder
57.93	Control of (postoperative) hemorrhage of bladder
57.99	Other operations on bladder
58.0	Urethrotomy
58.1	Urethral meatotomy
58.41	Suture of laceration of urethra
58.42	Closure of urethrostomy
58.43	Closure of other fistula of urethra
58.44	Reanastomosis of urethra
58.46	Other reconstruction of urethra
58.49	Other repair of urethra
58.5	Release of urethral stricture
58.93	Implantation of artificial urinary sphincter (AUS)
59.02	Other lysis of perirenal or periureteral adhesions
59.03	Laparoscopic lysis of perirenal or periureteral adhesions
59.09	Other incision of perirenal or periureteral tissue
*59.1	Incision of perivesical tissue
*59.2	Diagnostic procedures on perirenal and perivesical tissue
60.93	Repair of prostate
60.94	Control of (postoperative) hemorrhage of prostate
61.42	Repair of scrotal fistula
61.49	Other repair of scrotum and tunica vaginalis
61.99	Other operations on scrotum and tunica vaginalis
62.0	Incision of testis
62.3	Unilateral orchiectomy
*62.4	Bilateral orchiectomy
*62.6	Repair of testes
62.99	Other operations on testes
63.51	Suture of laceration of spermatic cord and epididymis
63.53	Transplantation of spermatic cord
63.59	Other repair of spermatic cord and epididymis
63.81	Suture of laceration of vas deferens and epididymis
63.82	Reconstruction of surgically divided vas deferens
63.89	Other repair of vas deferens and epididymis
63.94	Lysis of adhesions of spermatic cord
63.99	Other operations on spermatic card, epididymis, and vas deferens
64.41	Suture of laceration of penis
64.43	Construction of penis
64.44	Reconstruction of penis
64.45	Replantation of penis
64.49	Other repair of penis
*65.7	Repair of ovary
*65.8	Lysis of adhesions of ovary and fallopian tube
66.71	Simple suture of fallopian tube
66.79	Other repair of fallopian tube
67.51	Transabdominal cerclage of cervix

*** Code Range** ☑ ***Optimization Potential*** ▽ ***Targeted Potential*** 🅃 ***Transfer DRG*** 🅂🄿 ***Special Payment***

DRG 442 — continued

67.59	Other repair of cervical os
*67.6	Other repair of cervix
68.0	Hysterotomy
69.23	Vaginal repair of chronic inversion of uterus
69.29	Other repair of uterus and supporting structures
*69.4	Uterine repair
69.97	Removal of other penetrating foreign body from cervix
70.13	Lysis of intraluminal adhesions of vagina
70.62	Vaginal reconstruction
70.71	Suture of laceration of vagina
70.72	Repair of colovaginal fistula
70.73	Repair of rectovaginal fistula
70.74	Repair of other vaginoenteric fistula
70.75	Repair of other fistula of vagina
70.79	Other repair of vagina
71.01	Lysis of vulvar adhesions
71.71	Suture of laceration of vulva or perineum
71.72	Repair of fistula of vulva or perineum
71.79	Other repair of vulva and perineum
*76.0	Incision of facial bone without division
*76.1	Diagnostic procedures on facial bones and joints
76.2	Local excision or destruction of lesion of facial bone
*76.3	Partial ostectomy of facial bone
*76.4	Excision and reconstruction of facial bones
76.5	Temporomandibular arthroplasty
*76.6	Other facial bone repair and orthognathic surgery
76.70	Reduction of facial fracture, not otherwise specified
76.72	Open reduction of malar and zygomatic fracture
76.74	Open reduction of maxillary fracture
76.76	Open reduction of mandibular fracture
76.77	Open reduction of alveolar fracture
76.79	Other open reduction of facial fracture
76.91	Bone graft to facial bone
76.92	Insertion of synthetic implant in facial bone
76.94	Open reduction of temporomandibular dislocation
76.97	Removal of internal fixation device from facial bone
76.99	Other operations on facial bones and joints
*77.0	Sequestrectomy
*77.1	Other incision of bone without division
*77.2	Wedge osteotomy
*77.3	Other division of bone
77.58	Other excision, fusion, and repair of toes
*77.6	Local excision of lesion or tissue of bone
*77.7	Excision of bone for graft
*77.8	Other partial ostectomy
*77.9	Total ostectomy
78.00	Bone graft, unspecified site
78.01	Bone graft of scapula, clavicle, and thorax (ribs and sternum)
78.02	Bone graft of humerus
78.03	Bone graft of radius and ulna
78.05	Bone graft of femur
78.06	Bone graft of patella
78.07	Bone graft of tibia and fibula
78.08	Bone graft of tarsals and metatarsals
78.09	Bone graft of other bone, except facial bones
78.10	Application of external fixator device, unspecified site
78.11	Application of external fixator device, scapula, clavicle, and thorax [ribs and sternum]
78.12	Application of external fixator device, humerus
78.13	Application of external fixator device, radius and ulna
78.15	Application of external fixator device, femur
78.16	Application of external fixator device, patella
78.17	Application of external fixator device, tibia and fibula

78.18	Application of external fixator device, tarsals and metatarsals
78.19	Application of external fixator device, other
78.20	Limb shortening procedures, unspecified site
78.22	Limb shortening procedures, humerus
78.23	Limb shortening procedures, radius and ulna
78.25	Limb shortening procedures, femur
78.27	Limb shortening procedures, tibia and fibula
78.28	Limb shortening procedures, tarsals and metatarsals
78.29	Limb shortening procedures, other
78.30	Limb lengthening procedures, unspecified site
78.32	Limb lengthening procedures, humerus
78.33	Limb lengthening procedures, radius and ulna
78.35	Limb lengthening procedures, femur
78.37	Limb lengthening procedures, tibia and fibula
78.38	Limb lengthening procedures, tarsals and metatarsals
78.39	Other limb lengthening procedures
78.40	Other repair or plastic operations on bone, unspecified site
78.41	Other repair or plastic operations on scapula, clavicle, and thorax (ribs and sternum)
78.42	Other repair or plastic operation on humerus
78.43	Other repair or plastic operations on radius and ulna
78.45	Other repair or plastic operations on femur
78.46	Other repair or plastic operations on patella
78.47	Other repair or plastic operations on tibia and fibula
78.48	Other repair or plastic operations on tarsals and metatarsals
78.49	Other repair or plastic operations on other bone, except facial bones
78.50	Internal fixation of bone without fracture reduction, unspecified site
78.51	Internal fixation of scapula, clavicle, and thorax (ribs and sternum) without fracture reduction
78.52	Internal fixation of humerus without fracture reduction
78.53	Internal fixation of radius and ulna without fracture reduction
78.55	Internal fixation of femur without fracture reduction
78.56	Internal fixation of patella without fracture reduction
78.57	Internal fixation of tibia and fibula without fracture reduction
78.58	Internal fixation of tarsals and metatarsals without fracture reduction
78.59	Internal fixation of other bone, except facial bones, without fracture reduction
*78.6	Removal of implanted device from bone
*78.7	Osteoclasis
78.90	Insertion of bone growth stimulator, unspecified site
78.91	Insertion of bone growth stimulator into scapula, clavicle and thorax (ribs and sternum)
78.92	Insertion of bone growth stimulator into humerus
78.93	Insertion of bone growth stimulator into radius and ulna
78.95	Insertion of bone growth stimulator into femur
78.96	Insertion of bone growth stimulator into patella
78.97	Insertion of bone growth stimulator into tibia and fibula
78.98	Insertion of bone growth stimulator into tarsals and metatarsals
78.99	Insertion of bone growth stimulator into other bone
79.10	Closed reduction of fracture with internal fixation, unspecified site
79.11	Closed reduction of fracture of humerus with internal fixation
79.12	Closed reduction of fracture of radius and ulna with internal fixation
79.15	Closed reduction of fracture of femur with internal fixation
79.16	Closed reduction of fracture of tibia and fibula with internal fixation
79.17	Closed reduction of fracture of tarsals and metatarsals with internal fixation
79.18	Closed reduction of fracture of phalanges of foot with internal fixation
79.19	Closed reduction of fracture of other specified bone, except facial bones, with internal fixation
79.20	Open reduction of fracture without internal fixation, unspecified site
79.21	Open reduction of fracture of humerus without internal fixation
79.22	Open reduction of fracture of radius and ulna without internal fixation
79.25	Open reduction of fracture of femur without internal fixation
79.26	Open reduction of fracture of tibia and fibula without internal fixation
79.27	Open reduction of fracture of tarsals and metatarsals without internal fixation
79.28	Open reduction of fracture of phalanges of foot without internal fixation
79.29	Open reduction of fracture of other specified bone, except facial bones, without internal fixation
79.30	Open reduction of fracture with internal fixation, unspecified site

DRG 442 — continued

79.31	Open reduction of fracture of humerus with internal fixation
79.32	Open reduction of fracture of radius and ulna with internal fixation
79.35	Open reduction of fracture of femur with internal fixation
79.36	Open reduction of fracture of tibia and fibula with internal fixation
79.37	Open reduction of fracture of tarsals and metatarsals with internal fixation
79.38	Open reduction of fracture of phalanges of foot with internal fixation
79.39	Open reduction of fracture of other specified bone, except facial bones, with internal fixation
79.40	Closed reduction of separated epiphysis, unspecified site
79.41	Closed reduction of separated epiphysis of humerus
79.42	Closed reduction of separated epiphysis of radius and ulna
79.45	Closed reduction of separated epiphysis of femur
79.46	Closed reduction of separated epiphysis of tibia and fibula
79.49	Closed reduction of separated epiphysis of other specified bone
79.50	Open reduction of separated epiphysis, unspecified site
79.51	Open reduction of separated epiphysis of humerus
79.52	Open reduction of separated epiphysis of radius and ulna
79.55	Open reduction of separated epiphysis of femur
79.56	Open reduction of separated epiphysis of tibia and fibula
79.59	Open reduction of separated epiphysis of other specified bone
79.60	Debridement of open fracture, unspecified site
79.61	Debridement of open fracture of humerus
79.62	Debridement of open fracture of radius and ulna
79.65	Debridement of open fracture of femur
79.66	Debridement of open fracture of tibia and fibula
79.67	Debridement of open fracture of tarsals and metatarsals
79.68	Debridement of open fracture of phalanges of foot
79.69	Debridement of open fracture of other specified bone, except facial bones
79.80	Open reduction of dislocation of unspecified site
79.81	Open reduction of dislocation of shoulder
79.82	Open reduction of dislocation of elbow
79.85	Open reduction of dislocation of hip
79.86	Open reduction of dislocation of knee
79.87	Open reduction of dislocation of ankle
79.88	Open reduction of dislocation of foot and toe
79.89	Open reduction of dislocation of other specified site, except temporomandibular
79.90	Unspecified operation on bone injury, unspecified site
79.91	Unspecified operation on bone injury of humerus
79.92	Unspecified operation on bone injury of radius and ulna
79.95	Unspecified operation on bone injury of femur
79.96	Unspecified operation on bone injury of tibia and fibula
79.97	Unspecified operation on bone injury of tarsals and metatarsals
79.98	Unspecified operation on bone injury of phalanges of foot
79.99	Unspecified operation on bone injury of other specified bone
80.00	Arthrotomy for removal of prosthesis, unspecified site
80.01	Arthrotomy for removal of prosthesis of shoulder
80.02	Arthrotomy for removal of prosthesis of elbow
80.05	Arthrotomy for removal of prosthesis of hip
80.06	Arthrotomy for removal of prosthesis of knee
80.07	Arthrotomy for removal of prosthesis of ankle
80.08	Arthrotomy for removal of prosthesis of foot and toe
80.09	Arthrotomy for removal of prosthesis of other specified site
80.10	Other arthrotomy, unspecified site
80.11	Other arthrotomy of shoulder
80.12	Other arthrotomy of elbow
80.15	Other arthrotomy of hip
80.16	Other arthrotomy of knee
80.17	Other arthrotomy of ankle
80.18	Other arthrotomy of foot and toe
80.19	Other arthrotomy of other specified site
*80.2	Arthroscopy
80.40	Division of joint capsule, ligament, or cartilage, unspecified site
80.41	Division of joint capsule, ligament, or cartilage of shoulder

80.42	Division of joint capsule, ligament, or cartilage of elbow
80.45	Division of joint capsule, ligament, or cartilage of hip
80.46	Division of joint capsule, ligament, or cartilage of knee
80.47	Division of joint capsule, ligament, or cartilage of ankle
80.48	Division of joint capsule, ligament, or cartilage of foot and toe
80.49	Division of joint capsule, ligament, or cartilage of other specified site
80.50	Excision or destruction of intervertebral disc, unspecified
80.51	Excision of intervertebral disc
80.59	Other destruction of intervertebral disc
80.6	Excision of semilunar cartilage of knee
80.70	Synovectomy, unspecified site
80.71	Synovectomy of shoulder
80.72	Synovectomy of elbow
80.75	Synovectomy of hip
80.76	Synovectomy of knee
80.77	Synovectomy of ankle
80.78	Synovectomy of foot and toe
80.79	Synovectomy of other specified site
80.80	Other local excision or destruction of lesion of joint, unspecified site
80.81	Other local excision or destruction of lesion of shoulder joint
80.82	Other local excision or destruction of lesion of elbow joint
80.85	Other local excision or destruction of lesion of hip joint
80.86	Other local excision or destruction of lesion of knee joint
80.87	Other local excision or destruction of lesion of ankle joint
80.88	Other local excision or destruction of lesion of joint of foot and toe
80.89	Other local excision or destruction of lesion of joint of other specified site
80.90	Other excision of joint, unspecified site
80.91	Other excision of shoulder joint
80.92	Other excision of elbow joint
80.95	Other excision of hip joint
80.96	Other excision of knee joint
80.97	Other excision of ankle joint
80.98	Other excision of joint of foot and toe
80.99	Other excision of joint of other specified site
*81.0	Spinal fusion
*81.1	Arthrodesis and arthroereisis of foot and ankle
81.18	Subtalar joint arthroereisis
81.20	Arthrodesis of unspecified joint
81.21	Arthrodesis of hip
81.22	Arthrodesis of knee
81.23	Arthrodesis of shoulder
81.24	Arthrodesis of elbow
81.29	Arthrodesis of other specified joint
81.30	Refusion of spine, not otherwise specified
81.31	Refusion of Atlas-axis spine
81.32	Refusion of other cervical spine, anterior technique
81.33	Refusion of other cervical spine, posterior technique
81.34	Refusion of dorsal and dorsolumbar spine, anterior technique
81.35	Refusion of dorsal and dorsolumbar spine, posterior technique
81.36	Refusion of lumbar and lumbosacral spine, anterior technique
81.37	Refusion of lumbar and lumbosacral spine, lateral transverse process technique
81.38	Refusion of lumbar and lumbosacral spine, posterior technique
81.39	Refusion of spine, not elsewhere classified
*81.4	Other repair of joint of lower extremity
*81.5	Joint replacement of lower extremity
81.65	Vertebroplasty
81.66	Kyphoplasty
81.73	Total wrist replacement
81.80	Total shoulder replacement
81.81	Partial shoulder replacement
81.82	Repair of recurrent dislocation of shoulder
81.83	Other repair of shoulder
81.84	Total elbow replacement

***** Code Range** ☑ **Optimization Potential** ▽ **Targeted Potential** T **Transfer DRG** SP **Special Payment***

DRG 442 — continued

81.85	Other repair of elbow
81.93	Suture of capsule or ligament of upper extremity
81.94	Suture of capsule or ligament of ankle and foot
81.95	Suture of capsule or ligament of other lower extremity
81.96	Other repair of joint
81.97	Revision of joint replacement of upper extremity
81.98	Other diagnostic procedures on joint structures
81.99	Other operations on joint structures
*83.0	Incision of muscle, tendon, fascia, and bursa
*83.1	Division of muscle, tendon, and fascia
83.29	Other diagnostic procedures on muscle, tendon, fascia, and bursa, including that of hand
*83.3	Excision of lesion of muscle, tendon, fascia, and bursa
*83.4	Other excision of muscle, tendon, and fascia
83.5	Bursectomy
*83.6	Suture of muscle, tendon, and fascia
*83.7	Reconstruction of muscle and tendon
*83.8	Other plastic operations on muscle, tendon, and fascia
83.91	Lysis of adhesions of muscle, tendon, fascia, and bursa
83.92	Insertion or replacement of skeletal muscle stimulator
83.93	Removal of skeletal muscle stimulator
83.99	Other operations on muscle, tendon, fascia, and bursa
84.00	Upper limb amputation, not otherwise specified
84.03	Amputation through hand
84.04	Disarticulation of wrist
84.05	Amputation through forearm
84.06	Disarticulation of elbow
84.07	Amputation through humerus
84.08	Disarticulation of shoulder
84.09	Interthoracoscapular amputation
84.10	Lower limb amputation, not otherwise specified
84.11	Amputation of toe
84.12	Amputation through foot
84.13	Disarticulation of ankle
84.14	Amputation of ankle through malleoli of tibia and fibula
84.15	Other amputation below knee
84.16	Disarticulation of knee
84.17	Amputation above knee
84.18	Disarticulation of hip
84.19	Abdominopelvic amputation
84.23	Forearm, wrist, or hand reattachment
84.24	Upper arm reattachment
84.25	Toe reattachment
84.26	Foot reattachment
84.27	Lower leg or ankle reattachment
84.28	Thigh reattachment
84.29	Other reattachment of extremity
84.3	Revision of amputation stump
84.40	Implantation or fitting of prosthetic limb device, not otherwise specified
84.44	Implantation of prosthetic device of arm
84.48	Implantation of prosthetic device of leg
84.58	Implantation of interspinous process decompression device
84.59	Insertion of other spinal devices
*84.6	Replacement of spinal disc
84.91	Amputation, not otherwise specified
84.99	Other operations on musculoskeletal system
85.12	Open biopsy of breast
*85.2	Excision or destruction of breast tissue
*85.3	Reduction mammoplasty and subcutaneous mammectomy
*85.4	Mastectomy
85.50	Augmentation mammoplasty, not otherwise specified
85.53	Unilateral breast implant
85.54	Bilateral breast implant

85.6	Mastopexy
85.7	Total reconstruction of breast
85.85	Muscle flap graft to breast
85.86	Transposition of nipple
85.87	Other repair or reconstruction of nipple
85.89	Other mammoplasty
85.93	Revision of implant of breast
85.94	Removal of implant of breast
85.95	Insertion of breast tissue expander
85.96	Removal of breast tissue expander (s)
85.99	Other operations on the breast
86.06	Insertion of totally implantable infusion pump
86.21	Excision of pilonidal cyst or sinus
86.4	Radical excision of skin lesion
86.81	Repair for facial weakness
86.82	Facial rhytidectomy
86.83	Size reduction plastic operation
86.84	Relaxation of scar or web contracture of skin
86.86	Onychoplasty
86.89	Other repair and reconstruction of skin and subcutaneous tissue
86.91	Excision of skin for graft
92.27	Implantation or insertion of radioactive elements

OR

Any of the following procedure combinations

37.70	Initial insertion of lead (electrode), not otherwise specified
37.71	Initial insertion of transvenous lead (electrode) into ventricle
37.72	Initial insertion of transvenous leads (electrodes) into atrium and ventricle
37.73	Initial insertion of transvenous lead (electrode) into atrium
37.74	Insertion or replacement of epicardial lead (electrode) into epicardium
37.76	Replacement of transvenous atrial and/or ventricular lead(s) (electrode(s))

S DRG 443 Other O.R. Procedures for Injuries without CC

GMLOS 2.6 AMLOS 3.4 RW 0.9943 ☑ T

Select operating room procedure and combination procedures listed under DRG 442

MDC 21: Injury, Poisoning and Toxic Effects of Drugs — Surgical

MDC 21
INJURY, POISONING AND TOXIC EFFECTS OF DRUGS

The complete and up-to-date listing of ICD-9-CM diagnosis codes assigned to this MDC can be found online at www.ingenixonline.com/content/drg/resources.asp.

MEDICAL

M DRG 444 Traumatic Injury, Age Greater than 17 with CC

GMLOS 3.2 AMLOS 4.1 RW 0.7556 ☑ T CC A

Principal Diagnosis

*819	Multiple fractures involving both upper limbs, and upper limb with rib(s) and sternum
*828	Multiple fractures involving both lower limbs, lower with upper limb, and lower limb(s) with rib(s) and sternum
862.8	Injury to multiple and unspecified intrathoracic organs without mention of open wound into cavity
862.9	Injury to multiple and unspecified intrathoracic organs with open wound into cavity
868.09	Injury to other and multiple intra-abdominal organs without mention of open wound into cavity
868.19	Injury to other and multiple intra-abdominal organs, with open wound into cavity
*869	Internal injury to unspecified or ill-defined organs
875.1	Open wound of chest (wall), complicated
879.3	Open wound of abdominal wall, anterior, complicated
879.5	Open wound of abdominal wall, lateral, complicated
879.7	Open wound of other and unspecified parts of trunk, complicated
879.9	Open wound(s) (multiple) of unspecified site(s), complicated
*880.1	Open wound of shoulder and upper arm, complicated
*881.1	Open wound of elbow, forearm, and wrist, complicated
882.1	Open wound of hand except finger(s) alone, complicated
883.1	Open wound of finger(s), complicated
884.1	Multiple and unspecified open wound of upper limb, complicated
*885	Traumatic amputation of thumb (complete) (partial)
*886	Traumatic amputation of other finger(s) (complete) (partial)
*887	Traumatic amputation of arm and hand (complete) (partial)
890.1	Open wound of hip and thigh, complicated
891.1	Open wound of knee, leg (except thigh), and ankle, complicated
892.1	Open wound of foot except toe(s) alone, complicated
893.1	Open wound of toe(s), complicated
894.1	Multiple and unspecified open wound of lower limb, complicated
*895	Traumatic amputation of toe(s) (complete) (partial)
*896	Traumatic amputation of foot (complete) (partial)
*897	Traumatic amputation of leg(s) (complete) (partial)
*900	Injury to blood vessels of head and neck
*901	Injury to blood vessels of thorax
*902	Injury to blood vessels of abdomen and pelvis
*903	Injury to blood vessels of upper extremity
*904	Injury to blood vessels of lower extremity and unspecified sites
908.5	Late effect of foreign body in orifice
908.6	Late effect of certain complications of trauma
908.9	Late effect of unspecified injury
*925	Crushing injury of face, scalp, and neck
*926.1	Crushing injury of other specified sites of trunk
926.8	Crushing injury of multiple sites of trunk
926.9	Crushing injury of unspecified site of trunk
*927	Crushing injury of upper limb
*928	Crushing injury of lower limb
*929	Crushing injury of multiple and unspecified sites
*959	Injury, other and unspecified

M DRG 445 Traumatic Injury, Age Greater than 17 without CC

GMLOS 2.2 AMLOS 2.8 RW 0.5033 ☑ T A

Select principal diagnosis listed under DRG 444

M DRG 446 Traumatic Injury, Age 0-17

GMLOS 2.4 AMLOS 2.4 RW 0.2999 ☑ A

Select principal diagnosis listed under DRG 444

M DRG 447 Allergic Reactions, Age Greater than 17

GMLOS 1.9 AMLOS 2.6 RW 0.5569 ☑ A

Principal Diagnosis

995.0	Other anaphylactic shock not else where classifed
995.1	Angioneurotic edema not elsewhere classified
995.3	Allergy, unspecified not elsewhere classified
*995.6	Anaphylactic shock due to adverse food reaction
999.4	Anaphylactic shock due to serum, not elsewhere classified
999.5	Other serum reaction, not elsewhere classified

M DRG 448 Allergic Reactions, Age 0-17

GMLOS 2.9 AMLOS 2.9 RW 0.0987 ☑ A

Select principal diagnosis listed under DRG 447

M DRG 449 Poisoning and Toxic Effects of Drugs, Age Greater than 17 with CC

GMLOS 2.6 AMLOS 3.7 RW 0.8529 ☑ CC A

Principal Diagnosis

*960	Poisoning by antibiotics
*961	Poisoning by other anti-infectives
*962	Poisoning by hormones and synthetic substitutes
*963	Poisoning by primarily systemic agents
*964	Poisoning by agents primarily affecting blood constituents
*965	Poisoning by analgesics, antipyretics, and antirheumatics
*966	Poisoning by anticonvulsants and anti-Parkinsonism drugs
*967	Poisoning by sedatives and hypnotics
*968	Poisoning by other central nervous system depressants and anesthetics
*969	Poisoning by psychotropic agents
*970	Poisoning by central nervous system stimulants
*971	Poisoning by drugs primarily affecting the autonomic nervous system
*972	Poisoning by agents primarily affecting the cardiovascular system
*973	Poisoning by agents primarily affecting the gastrointestinal system
*974	Poisoning by water, mineral, and uric acid metabolism drugs
*975	Poisoning by agents primarily acting on the smooth and skeletal muscles and respiratory system
976.0	Poisoning by local anti-infectives and anti-inflammatory drugs
976.1	Poisoning by antipruritics
976.2	Poisoning by local astringents and local detergents
976.3	Poisoning by emollients, demulcents, and protectants
976.4	Poisoning by keratolytics, keratoplastics, other hair treatment drugs and preparations
976.6	Poisoning by anti-infectives and other drugs and preparations for ear, nose, and throat
976.7	Poisoning by dental drugs topically applied
976.8	Poisoning by other agents primarily affecting skin and mucous membrane
976.9	Poisoning by unspecified agent primarily affecting skin and mucous membrane
*977	Poisoning by other and unspecified drugs and medicinal substances
*978	Poisoning by bacterial vaccines
*979	Poisoning by other vaccines and biological substances
*980	Toxic effect of alcohol
981	Toxic effect of petroleum products
*982	Toxic effect of solvents other than petroleum-based
*983	Toxic effect of corrosive aromatics, acids, and caustic alkalis

** Code Range* ☑ *Optimization Potential* *Targeted Potential* T *Transfer DRG* SP *Special Payment*

DRG 449 — continued

*984	Toxic effect of lead and its compounds (including fumes)
*985	Toxic effect of other metals
986	Toxic effect of carbon monoxide
*987	Toxic effect of other gases, fumes, or vapors
*988	Toxic effect of noxious substances eaten as food
*989	Toxic effect of other substances, chiefly nonmedicinal as to source
995.2	Unspecified adverse effect of drug medicinal and biological substance, not elsewhere classified

M DRG 450 Poisoning and Toxic Effects of Drugs, Age Greater than 17 without CC

GMLOS 1.6 AMLOS 2.0 RW 0.4282 ☑ A

Select principal diagnosis listed under DRG 449

M DRG 451 Poisoning and Toxic Effects of Drugs, Age 0-17

GMLOS 2.1 AMLOS 2.1 RW 0.2663 ☑ A

Select principal diagnosis listed under DRG 449

M DRG 452 Complications of Treatment with CC

GMLOS 3.5 AMLOS 4.9 RW 1.0462 CC

Principal Diagnosis

996.52	Mechanical complication due to other tissue graft, not elsewhere classified
996.55	Mechanical complications due to artificial skin graft and decellularized allodermis
996.56	Mechanical complications due to peritoneal dialysis catheter
996.57	Mechanical complication, Due to insulin pump
996.59	Mechanical complication due to other implant and internal device, not elsewhere classified
996.60	Infection and inflammatory reaction due to unspecified device, implant, and graft
996.68	Infection and inflammatory reaction due to peritoneal dialysis catheter
996.69	Infection and inflammatory reaction due to other internal prosthetic device, implant, and graft
996.70	Other complications due to unspecified device, implant, and graft
996.79	Other complications due to other internal prosthetic device, implant, and graft
996.80	Complications of transplanted organ, unspecified site
996.87	Complications of transplanted organ, intestine
996.89	Complications of other transplanted organ
*997.9	Complications affecting other specified body systems, not elsewhere classified
998.0	Postoperative shock, not elsewhere classified
*998.1	Hemorrhage or hematoma or seroma complicating procedure, not elsewhere classified
998.2	Accidental puncture or laceration during procedure
*998.3	Disruption of operation wound
998.4	Foreign body accidentally left during procedure, not elsewhere classified
998.6	Persistent postoperative fistula, not elsewhere classified
998.7	Acute reaction to foreign substance accidentally left during procedure, not elsewhere classified
998.81	Emphysema (subcutaneous) (surgical) resulting from a procedure
998.83	Non-healing surgical wound
998.89	Other specified complications
998.9	Unspecified complication of procedure, not elsewhere classified
999.9	Other and unspecified complications of medical care, not elsewhere classified

M DRG 453 Complications of Treatment without CC

GMLOS 2.2 AMLOS 2.8 RW 0.5285 ☑

Select principal diagnosis listed under DRG 452

M DRG 454 Other Injury, Poisoning and Toxic Effect Diagnoses with CC

GMLOS 2.9 AMLOS 4.1 RW 0.8141 CC

Principal Diagnosis

796.0	Nonspecific abnormal toxicological findings
*909	Late effects of other and unspecified external causes
958.2	Secondary and recurrent hemorrhage as an early complication of trauma
958.4	Traumatic shock

S Surgical M Medical CC CC Indicator A Age Restriction ● New DRG ▲ Revised DRG Title

958.8	Other early complications of trauma
990	Effects of radiation, unspecified
*991	Effects of reduced temperature
*992	Effects of heat and light
993.2	Other and unspecified effects of high altitude
993.3	Caisson disease
993.4	Effects of air pressure caused by explosion
993.8	Other specified effects of air pressure
993.9	Unspecified effect of air pressure
994.0	Effects of lightning
994.1	Drowning and nonfatal submersion
994.2	Effects of hunger
994.3	Effects of thirst
994.4	Exhaustion due to exposure
994.5	Exhaustion due to excessive exertion
994.7	Asphyxiation and strangulation
994.8	Electrocution and nonfatal effects of electric current
994.9	Other effects of external causes
995.4	Shock due to anesthesia not elsewhere classified
*995.5	Child maltreatment syndrome
995.7	Other adverse food reactions, not elsewhere classified
*995.8	Other specified adverse effects, not elsewhere classified
V71.3	Observation following accident at work
V71.4	Observation following other accident
V71.6	Observation following other inflicted injury

M DRG 455 Other Injury, Poisoning and Toxic Effect Diagnoses without CC

GMLOS 1.7 **AMLOS 2.2** **RW 0.4725** ☑

Select principal diagnosis listed under DRG 454

MDC 22
BURNS

The complete and up-to-date listing of ICD-9-CM diagnosis codes assigned to this MDC can be found online at www.ingenixonline.com/content/drg/resources.asp.

SURGICAL

DRG 458 No Longer Valid
GMLOS 0.0 AMLOS 0.0 RW 0.0000

Omitted in October 1998 grouper version

DRG 459 No Longer Valid
GMLOS 0.0 AMLOS 0.0 RW 0.0000

Omitted in October 1998 grouper version

DRG 472 No Longer Valid
GMLOS 0.0 AMLOS 0.0 RW 0.0000

Omitted in October 1998 grouper version

▲ S DRG 504 Extensive Burns or Full Thickness Burns with Mechanical Ventilation 96+ Hours with Skin Graft
GMLOS 21.7 AMLOS 27.3 RW 11.8018

Principal or Secondary Diagnosis

948.21	Burn (any degree) involving 20-29% of body surface with third degree burn of 10-19%
948.22	Burn (any degree) involving 20-29% of body surface with third degree burn of 20-29%
948.31	Burn (any degree) involving 30-39% of body surface with third degree burn of 10-19%
948.32	Burn (any degree) involving 30-39% of body surface with third degree burn of 20-29%
948.33	Burn (any degree) involving 30-39% of body surface with third degree burn of 30-39%
948.41	Burn (any degree) involving 40-49% of body surface with third degree burn of 10-19%
948.42	Burn (any degree) involving 40-49% of body surface with third degree burn of 20-29%
948.43	Burn (any degree) involving 40-49% of body surface with third degree burn of 30-39%
948.44	Burn (any degree) involving 40-49% of body surface with third degree burn of 40-49%
948.51	Burn (any degree) involving 50-59% of body surface with third degree burn of 10-19%
948.52	Burn (any degree) involving 50-59% of body surface with third degree burn of 20-29%
948.53	Burn (any degree) involving 50-59% of body surface with third degree burn of 30-39%
948.54	Burn (any degree) involving 50-59% of body surface with third degree burn of 40-49%
948.55	Burn (any degree) involving 50-59% of body surface with third degree burn of 50-59%
948.61	Burn (any degree) involving 60-69% of body surface with third degree burn of 10-19%
948.62	Burn (any degree) involving 60-69% of body surface with third degree burn of 20-29%
948.63	Burn (any degree) involving 60-69% of body surface with third degree burn of 30-39%
948.64	Burn (any degree) involving 60-69% of body surface with third degree burn of 40-49%
948.65	Burn (any degree) involving 60-69% of body surface with third degree burn of 50-59%
948.66	Burn (any degree) involving 60-69% of body surface with third degree burn of 60-69%
948.71	Burn (any degree) involving 70-79% of body surface with third degree burn of 10-19%
948.72	Burn (any degree) involving 70-79% of body surface with third degree burn of 20-29%
948.73	Burn (any degree) involving 70-79% of body surface with third degree burn of 30-39%
948.74	Burn (any degree) involving 70-79% of body surface with third degree burn of 40-49%
948.75	Burn (any degree) involving 70-79% of body surface with third degree burn of 50-59%
948.76	Burn (any degree) involving 70-79% of body surface with third degree burn of 60-69%
948.77	Burn (any degree) involving 70-79% of body surface with third degree burn of 70-79%
948.81	Burn (any degree) involving 80-89% of body surface with third degree burn of 10-19%
948.82	Burn (any degree) involving 80-89% of body surface with third degree burn of 20-29%
948.83	Burn (any degree) involving 80-89% of body surface with third degree burn of 30-39%
948.84	Burn (any degree) involving 80-89% of body surface with third degree burn of 40-49%
948.85	Burn (any degree) involving 80-89% of body surface with third degree burn of 50-59%
948.86	Burn (any degree) involving 80-89% of body surface with third degree burn of 60-69%
948.87	Burn (any degree) involving 80-89% of body surface with third degree burn of 70-79%

948.88	Burn (any degree) involving 80-89% of body surface with third degree burn of 80-89%
948.91	Burn (any degree) involving 90% or more of body surface with third degree burn of 10-19%
948.92	Burn (any degree) involving 90% or more of body surface with third degree burn of 20-29%
948.93	Burn (any degree) involving 90% or more of body surface with third degree burn of 30-39%
948.94	Burn (any degree) involving 90% or more of body surface with third degree burn of 40-49%
948.95	Burn (any degree) involving 90% or more of body surface with third degree burn of 50-59%
948.96	Burn (any degree) involving 90% or more of body surface with third degree burn of 60-69%
948.97	Burn (any degree) involving 90% or more of body surface with third degree burn of 70-79%
948.98	Burn (any degree) involving 90% or more of body surface with third degree burn of 80-89%
948.99	Burn (any degree) involving 90% or more of body surface with third degree burn of 90% or more of body surface

OR

Principal or Secondary Diagnosis

*941.3	Full-thickness skin loss due to burn (third degree nos) of face, head, and neck
*941.4	Deep necrosis of underlying tissues due to burn (deep third degree) of face, head, and neck without mention of loss of a body part
*941.5	Deep necrosis of underlying tissues due to burn (deep third degree) of face, head, and neck with loss of a body part
*942.3	Full-thickness skin loss due to burn (third degree nos) of trunk
*942.4	Deep necrosis of underlying tissues due to burn (deep third degree) of trunk without mention of loss of a body part
*942.5	Deep necrosis of underlying tissues due to burn (deep third degree) of trunk with loss of a body part
*943.3	Full-thickness skin loss due to burn (third degree nos) of upper limb, except wrist and hand
*943.4	Deep necrosis of underlying tissues due to burn (deep third degree) of upper limb, except wrist and hand, without mention of loss of a body part
*943.5	Deep necrosis of underlying tissues due to burn (deep third degree) of upper limb, except wrist and hand, with loss of a body part
*944.3	Full-thickness skin loss due to burn (third degree nos) of wrist(s) and hand(s)
*944.4	Deep necrosis of underlying tissues due to burn (deep third degree) of wrist(s) and hand(s), without mention of loss of a body part
*944.5	Deep necrosis of underlying tissues due to burn (deep third degree) of wrist(s) and hand(s), with loss of a body part
*945.3	Full-thickness skin loss due to burn (third degree nos) of lower limb(s)
*945.4	Deep necrosis of underlying tissues due to burn (deep third degree) of lower limb(s) without mention of loss of a body part
*945.5	Deep necrosis of underlying tissues due to burn (deep third degree) of lower limb(s) with loss of a body part
946.3	Full-thickness skin loss due to burn (third degree nos) of multiple specified sites
946.4	Deep necrosis of underlying tissues due to burn (deep third degree) of multiple specified sites, without mention of loss of a body part
946.5	Deep necrosis of underlying tissues due to burn (deep third degree) of multiple specified sites, with loss of a body part
948.11	Burn (any degree) involving 10-19% of body surface with third degree burn of 10-19%
949.3	Full-thickness skin loss due to burn (third degree nos), unspecified site
949.4	Deep necrosis of underlying tissue due to burn (deep third degree), unspecified site without mention of loss of body part
949.5	Deep necrosis of underlying tissues due to burn (deep third degree, unspecified site with loss of body part

WITH

Nonoperating Room Procedure

96.72	Continuous mechanical ventilation for 96 consecutive hours or more

AND

Operating Room Procedures

85.82	Split-thickness graft to breast
85.83	Full-thickness graft to breast
85.84	Pedicle graft to breast
86.60	Free skin graft, not otherwise specified
86.61	Full-thickness skin graft to hand
86.62	Other skin graft to hand

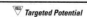

DRG 504 — continued

86.63 Full-thickness skin graft to other sites
86.65 Heterograft to skin
86.66 Homograft to skin
86.67 Dermal regenerative graft
86.69 Other skin graft to other sites
*86.7 Pedicle grafts or flaps
86.93 Insertion of tissue expander

S DRG 506 Full Thickness Burn with Skin Graft or Inhalation Injury with CC or Significant Trauma

GMLOS 11.2 AMLOS 15.9 RW 4.0939 ☑CC

Select principal or secondary diagnosis listed below in addition to either a secondary diagnosis code from the standard CC condition list or any significant trauma diagnosis code listed under DRG 487

Principal or Secondary Diagnosis

*941.3 Full-thickness skin loss due to burn (third degree nos) of face, head, and neck
*941.4 Deep necrosis of underlying tissues due to burn (deep third degree) of face, head, and neck without mention of loss of a body part
*941.5 Deep necrosis of underlying tissues due to burn (deep third degree) of face, head, and neck with loss of a body part
*942.3 Full-thickness skin loss due to burn (third degree nos) of trunk
*942.4 Deep necrosis of underlying tissues due to burn (deep third degree) of trunk without mention of loss of a body part
*942.5 Deep necrosis of underlying tissues due to burn (deep third degree) of trunk with loss of a body part
*943.3 Full-thickness skin loss due to burn (third degree nos) of upper limb, except wrist and hand
*943.4 Deep necrosis of underlying tissues due to burn (deep third degree) of upper limb, except wrist and hand, without mention of loss of a body part
*943.5 Deep necrosis of underlying tissues due to burn (deep third degree) of upper limb, except wrist and hand, with loss of a body part
*944.3 Full-thickness skin loss due to burn (third degree nos) of wrist(s) and hand(s)
*944.4 Deep necrosis of underlying tissues due to burn (deep third degree) of wrist(s) and hand(s), without mention of loss of a body part
*944.5 Deep necrosis of underlying tissues due to burn (deep third degree) of wrist(s) and hand(s), with loss of a body part
*945.3 Full-thickness skin loss due to burn (third degree nos) of lower limb(s)
*945.4 Deep necrosis of underlying tissues due to burn (deep third degree) of lower limb(s) without mention of loss of a body part
*945.5 Deep necrosis of underlying tissues due to burn (deep third degree) of lower limb(s) with loss of a body part
946.3 Full-thickness skin loss due to burn (third degree nos) of multiple specified sites
946.4 Deep necrosis of underlying tissues due to burn (deep third degree) of multiple specified sites, without mention of loss of a body part
946.5 Deep necrosis of underlying tissues due to burn (deep third degree) of multiple specified sites, with loss of a body part
948.11 Burn (any degree) involving 10-19% of body surface with third degree burn of 10-19%
949.3 Full-thickness skin loss due to burn (third degree nos), unspecified site
949.4 Deep necrosis of underlying tissue due to burn (deep third degree), unspecified site without mention of loss of body part
949.5 Deep necrosis of underlying tissues due to burn (deep third degree, unspecified site with loss of body part

AND

Operating Room Procedures

85.82 Split-thickness graft to breast
85.83 Full-thickness graft to breast
85.84 Pedicle graft to breast
86.60 Free skin graft, not otherwise specified
86.61 Full-thickness skin graft to hand
86.62 Other skin graft to hand

MDC 22: Burns — Surgical

86.63	Full-thickness skin graft to other sites
86.65	Heterograft to skin
86.66	Homograft to skin
86.67	Dermal regenerative graft
86.69	Other skin graft to other sites
*86.7	Pedicle grafts or flaps
86.93	Insertion of tissue expander

OR

Secondary Diagnosis

518.5	Pulmonary insufficiency following trauma and surgery
518.81	Acute respiratory failure
518.84	Acute and chronic respiratory failure
947.1	Burn of larynx, trachea, and lung
987.9	Toxic effect of unspecified gas, fume, or vapor

S DRG 507 Full Thickness Burn with Skin Graft or Inhalation Injury without CC or Significant Trauma

GMLOS 5.8 AMLOS 8.5 RW 1.7369 ☑

Select principal or secondary diagnosis and operating room procedure or secondary diagnosis listed under DRG 506

Select principal or secondary diagnosis in combination with secondary diagnosis of inhalation injury and operating room procedures listed under DRG 506

MDC 22
BURNS

The complete and up-to-date listing of ICD-9-CM diagnosis codes assigned to this MDC can be found online at www.ingenixonline.com/content/drg/resources.asp.

MEDICAL

DRG 456 No Longer Valid
GMLOS 0.0 AMLOS 0.0 RW 0.0000

Omitted in October 1998 grouper version

DRG 457 No Longer Valid
GMLOS 0.0 AMLOS 0.0 RW 0.0000

Omitted in October 1998 grouper version

DRG 460 No Longer Valid
GMLOS 0.0 AMLOS 0.0 RW 0.0000

Omitted in October 1998 grouper version

M DRG 505 Extensive Burns or Full Thickness Burns with Mechanical Ventilation 96+ Hours without Skin Graft
GMLOS 2.4 AMLOS 4.6 RW 2.2953 ☑

Principal or Secondary Diagnosis

948.21	Burn (any degree) involving 20-29% of body surface with third degree burn of 10-19%
948.22	Burn (any degree) involving 20-29% of body surface with third degree burn of 20-29%
948.31	Burn (any degree) involving 30-39% of body surface with third degree burn of 10-19%
948.32	Burn (any degree) involving 30-39% of body surface with third degree burn of 20-29%
948.33	Burn (any degree) involving 30-39% of body surface with third degree burn of 30-39%
948.41	Burn (any degree) involving 40-49% of body surface with third degree burn of 10-19%
948.42	Burn (any degree) involving 40-49% of body surface with third degree burn of 20-29%
948.43	Burn (any degree) involving 40-49% of body surface with third degree burn of 30-39%
948.44	Burn (any degree) involving 40-49% of body surface with third degree burn of 40-49%
948.51	Burn (any degree) involving 50-59% of body surface with third degree burn of 10-19%
948.52	Burn (any degree) involving 50-59% of body surface with third degree burn of 20-29%
948.53	Burn (any degree) involving 50-59% of body surface with third degree burn of 30-39%
948.54	Burn (any degree) involving 50-59% of body surface with third degree burn of 40-49%
948.55	Burn (any degree) involving 50-59% of body surface with third degree burn of 50-59%
948.61	Burn (any degree) involving 60-69% of body surface with third degree burn of 10-19%
948.62	Burn (any degree) involving 60-69% of body surface with third degree burn of 20-29%
948.63	Burn (any degree) involving 60-69% of body surface with third degree burn of 30-39%
948.64	Burn (any degree) involving 60-69% of body surface with third degree burn of 40-49%
948.65	Burn (any degree) involving 60-69% of body surface with third degree burn of 50-59%
948.66	Burn (any degree) involving 60-69% of body surface with third degree burn of 60-69%
948.71	Burn (any degree) involving 70-79% of body surface with third degree burn of 10-19%
948.72	Burn (any degree) involving 70-79% of body surface with third degree burn of 20-29%
948.73	Burn (any degree) involving 70-79% of body surface with third degree burn of 30-39%
948.74	Burn (any degree) involving 70-79% of body surface with third degree burn of 40-49%
948.75	Burn (any degree) involving 70-79% of body surface with third degree burn of 50-59%
948.76	Burn (any degree) involving 70-79% of body surface with third degree burn of 60-69%
948.77	Burn (any degree) involving 70-79% of body surface with third degree burn of 70-79%
948.81	Burn (any degree) involving 80-89% of body surface with third degree burn of 10-19%
948.82	Burn (any degree) involving 80-89% of body surface with third degree burn of 20-29%
948.83	Burn (any degree) involving 80-89% of body surface with third degree burn of 30-39%
948.84	Burn (any degree) involving 80-89% of body surface with third degree burn of 40-49%
948.85	Burn (any degree) involving 80-89% of body surface with third degree burn of 50-59%
948.86	Burn (any degree) involving 80-89% of body surface with third degree burn of 60-69%
948.87	Burn (any degree) involving 80-89% of body surface with third degree burn of 70-79%

948.88	Burn (any degree) involving 80-89% of body surface with third degree burn of 80-89%
948.91	Burn (any degree) involving 90% or more of body surface with third degree burn of 10-19%
948.92	Burn (any degree) involving 90% or more of body surface with third degree burn of 20-29%
948.93	Burn (any degree) involving 90% or more of body surface with third degree burn of 30-39%
948.94	Burn (any degree) involving 90% or more of body surface with third degree burn of 40-49%
948.95	Burn (any degree) involving 90% or more of body surface with third degree burn of 50-59%
948.96	Burn (any degree) involving 90% or more of body surface with third degree burn of 60-69%
948.97	Burn (any degree) involving 90% or more of body surface with third degree burn of 70-79%
948.98	Burn (any degree) involving 90% or more of body surface with third degree burn of 80-89%
948.99	Burn (any degree) involving 90% or more of body surface with third degree burn of 90% or more of body surface

OR

Principal or Secondary Diagnosis

*941.3	Full-thickness skin loss due to burn (third degree nos) of face, head, and neck
*941.4	Deep necrosis of underlying tissues due to burn (deep third degree) of face, head, and neck without mention of loss of a body part
*941.5	Deep necrosis of underlying tissues due to burn (deep third degree) of face, head, and neck with loss of a body part
*942.3	Full-thickness skin loss due to burn (third degree nos) of trunk
*942.4	Deep necrosis of underlying tissues due to burn (deep third degree) of trunk without mention of loss of a body part
*942.5	Deep necrosis of underlying tissues due to burn (deep third degree) of trunk with loss of a body part
*943.3	Full-thickness skin loss due to burn (third degree nos) of upper limb, except wrist and hand
*943.4	Deep necrosis of underlying tissues due to burn (deep third degree) of upper limb, except wrist and hand, without mention of loss of a body part
*943.5	Deep necrosis of underlying tissues due to burn (deep third degree) of upper limb, except wrist and hand, with loss of a body part
*944.3	Full-thickness skin loss due to burn (third degree nos) of wrist(s) and hand(s)
*944.4	Deep necrosis of underlying tissues due to burn (deep third degree) of wrist(s) and hand(s), without mention of loss of a body part
*944.5	Deep necrosis of underlying tissues due to burn (deep third degree) of wrist(s) and hand(s), with loss of a body part
*945.3	Full-thickness skin loss due to burn (third degree nos) of lower limb(s)
*945.4	Deep necrosis of underlying tissues due to burn (deep third degree) of lower limb(s) without mention of loss of a body part
*945.5	Deep necrosis of underlying tissues due to burn (deep third degree) of lower limb(s) with loss of a body part
946.3	Full-thickness skin loss due to burn (third degree nos) of multiple specified sites
946.4	Deep necrosis of underlying tissues due to burn (deep third degree) of multiple specified sites, without mention of loss of a body part
946.5	Deep necrosis of underlying tissues due to burn (deep third degree) of multiple specified sites, with loss of a body part
948.11	Burn (any degree) involving 10-19% of body surface with third degree burn of 10-19%
949.3	Full-thickness skin loss due to burn (third degree nos), unspecified site
949.4	Deep necrosis of underlying tissue due to burn (deep third degree), unspecified site without mention of loss of body part
949.5	Deep necrosis of underlying tissues due to burn (deep third degree, unspecified site with loss of body part

WITH

Nonoperating Room Procedure

96.72	Continuous mechanical ventilation for 96 consecutive hours or more

MDC 22: Burns — Medical

Ⓜ DRG 508 Full Thickness Burn without Skin Graft or Inhalation Injury with CC or Significant Trauma

GMLOS 5.1 AMLOS 7.4 RW 1.2767 ☑ CC

Select principal diagnosis listed below in addition to either a secondary diagnosis code from the standard CC condition list or any significant trauma diagnosis code listed under DRG 487

Principal or Secondary Diagnosis

*941.3	Full-thickness skin loss due to burn (third degree nos) of face, head, and neck
*941.4	Deep necrosis of underlying tissues due to burn (deep third degree) of face, head, and neck without mention of loss of a body part
*941.5	Deep necrosis of underlying tissues due to burn (deep third degree) of face, head, and neck with loss of a body part
*942.3	Full-thickness skin loss due to burn (third degree nos) of trunk
*942.4	Deep necrosis of underlying tissues due to burn (deep third degree) of trunk without mention of loss of a body part
*942.5	Deep necrosis of underlying tissues due to burn (deep third degree) of trunk with loss of a body part
*943.3	Full-thickness skin loss due to burn (third degree nos) of upper limb, except wrist and hand
*943.4	Deep necrosis of underlying tissues due to burn (deep third degree) of upper limb, except wrist and hand, without mention of loss of a body part
*943.5	Deep necrosis of underlying tissues due to burn (deep third degree) of upper limb, except wrist and hand, with loss of a body part
*944.3	Full-thickness skin loss due to burn (third degree nos) of wrist(s) and hand(s)
*944.4	Deep necrosis of underlying tissues due to burn (deep third degree) of wrist(s) and hand(s), without mention of loss of a body part
*944.5	Deep necrosis of underlying tissues due to burn (deep third degree) of wrist(s) and hand(s), with loss of a body part
*945.3	Full-thickness skin loss due to burn (third degree nos) of lower limb(s)
*945.4	Deep necrosis of underlying tissues due to burn (deep third degree) of lower limb(s) without mention of loss of a body part
*945.5	Deep necrosis of underlying tissues due to burn (deep third degree) of lower limb(s) with loss of a body part
946.3	Full-thickness skin loss due to burn (third degree nos) of multiple specified sites
946.4	Deep necrosis of underlying tissues due to burn (deep third degree) of multiple specified sites, without mention of loss of a body part
946.5	Deep necrosis of underlying tissues due to burn (deep third degree) of multiple specified sites, with loss of a body part
948.11	Burn (any degree) involving 10-19% of body surface with third degree burn of 10-19%
949.3	Full-thickness skin loss due to burn (third degree nos), unspecified site
949.4	Deep necrosis of underlying tissue due to burn (deep third degree), unspecified site without mention of loss of body part
949.5	Deep necrosis of underlying tissues due to burn (deep third degree, unspecified site with loss of body part

Ⓜ DRG 509 Full Thickness Burn without Skin Graft or Inhalation Injury without CC or Significant Trauma

GMLOS 3.6 AMLOS 5.2 RW 0.8217 ☑

Select principal diagnosis listed under DRG 508

Ⓜ DRG 510 Nonextensive Burns with CC or Significant Trauma

GMLOS 4.4 AMLOS 6.4 RW 1.1817 ☑ CC

Select principal diagnosis listed below in addition to either a secondary diagnosis code from the standard CC condition list or any significant trauma diagnosis code listed under DRG 487

Principal or Secondary Diagnosis

941.00	Burn of unspecified degree of unspecified site of face and head
941.01	Burn of unspecified degree of ear (any part)
941.03	Burn of unspecified degree of lip(s)
941.04	Burn of unspecified degree of chin

S *Surgical* M *Medical* CC *CC Indicator* A *Age Restriction* ● *New DRG* ▲ *Revised DRG Title*

941.05	Burn of unspecified degree of nose (septum)
941.06	Burn of unspecified degree of scalp (any part)
941.07	Burn of unspecified degree of forehead and cheek
941.08	Burn of unspecified degree of neck
941.09	Burn of unspecified degree of multiple sites (except with eye) of face, head, and neck
941.10	Erythema due to burn (first degree) of unspecified site of face and head
941.11	Erythema due to burn (first degree) of ear (any part)
941.13	Erythema due to burn (first degree) of lip(s)
941.14	Erythema due to burn (first degree) of chin
941.15	Erythema due to burn (first degree) of nose (septum)
941.16	Erythema due to burn (first degree) of scalp (any part)
941.17	Erythema due to burn (first degree) of forehead and cheek
941.18	Erythema due to burn (first degree) of neck
941.19	Erythema due to burn (first degree) of multiple sites (except with eye) of face, head, and neck
941.20	Blisters, with epidermal loss due to burn (second degree) of face and head, unspecified site
941.21	Blisters, with epidermal loss due to burn (second degree) of ear (any part)
941.23	Blisters, with epidermal loss due to burn (second degree) of lip(s)
941.24	Blisters, with epidermal loss due to burn (second degree) of chin
941.25	Blisters, with epidermal loss due to burn (second degree) of nose (septum)
941.26	Blisters, with epidermal loss due to burn (second degree) of scalp (any part)
941.27	Blisters, with epidermal loss due to burn (second degree) of forehead and cheek
941.28	Blisters, with epidermal loss due to burn (second degree) of neck
941.29	Blisters, with epidermal loss due to burn (second degree) of multiple sites (except with eye) of face, head, and neck
*942.0	Burn of trunk, unspecified degree
*942.1	Erythema due to burn (first degree) of trunk
*942.2	Blisters with epidermal loss due to burn (second degree) of trunk
*943.0	Burn of upper limb, except wrist and hand, unspecified degree
*943.1	Erythema due to burn (first degree) of upper limb, except wrist and hand
*943.2	Blisters with epidermal loss due to burn (second degree) of upper limb, except wrist and hand
*944.0	Burn of wrist(s) and hand(s), unspecified degree
*944.1	Erythema due to burn (first degree) of wrist(s) and hand(s)
*944.2	Blisters with epidermal loss due to burn (second degree) of wrist(s) and hand(s)
*945.0	Burn of lower limb(s), unspecified degree
*945.1	Erythema due to burn (first degree) of lower limb(s)
*945.2	Blisters with epidermal loss due to burn (second degree) of lower limb(s)
946.0	Burns of multiple specified sites, unspecified degree
946.1	Erythema due to burn (first degree) of multiple specified sites
946.2	Blisters with epidermal loss due to burn (second degree) of multiple specified sites
947.8	Burn of other specified sites of internal organs
947.9	Burn of internal organs, unspecified site
948.00	Burn (any degree) involving less than 10% of body surface with third degree burn of less than 10% or unspecified amount
948.10	Burn (any degree) involving 10-19% of body surface with third degree burn of less than 10% or unspecified amount
948.20	Burn (any degree) involving 20-29% of body surface with third degree burn of less than 10% or unspecified amount
948.30	Burn (any degree) involving 30-39% of body surface with third degree burn of less than 10% or unspecified amount
948.40	Burn (any degree) involving 40-49% of body surface with third degree burn of less than 10% or unspecified amount
948.50	Burn (any degree) involving 50-59% of body surface with third degree burn of less than 10% or unspecified amount
948.60	Burn (any degree) involving 60-69% of body surface with third degree burn of less than 10% or unspecified amount
948.70	Burn (any degree) involving 70-79% of body surface with third degree burn of less than 10% or unspecified amount
948.80	Burn (any degree) involving 80-89% of body surface with third degree burn of less than 10% or unspecified amount
948.90	Burn (any degree) involving 90% or more of body surface with third degree burn of less than 10% or unspecified amount

DRG 510 — continued

949.0	Burn of unspecified site, unspecified degree
949.1	Erythema due to burn (first degree), unspecified site
949.2	Blisters with epidermal loss due to burn (second degree), unspecified site

M DRG 511 Nonextensive Burns without CC or Significant Trauma

GMLOS 2.6 AMLOS 4.1 RW 0.7424 ☑

Select principal diagnosis listed under DRG 510

MDC 23
FACTORS INFLUENCING HEALTH STATUS AND OTHER CONTACTS WITH HEALTH SERVICES

The complete and up-to-date listing of ICD-9-CM diagnosis codes assigned to this MDC can be found online at www.ingenixonline.com/content/drg/resources.asp.

SURGICAL

S DRG 461 O.R. Procedure with Diagnosis of Other Contact with Health Services

GMLOS 3.0 AMLOS 5.1 RW 1.3974

Select any operating room procedure

MDC 23
FACTORS INFLUENCING HEALTH STATUS AND OTHER CONTACTS WITH HEALTH SERVICES

The complete and up-to-date listing of ICD-9-CM diagnosis codes assigned to this MDC can be found online at www.ingenixonline.com/content/drg/resources.asp.

MEDICAL

M DRG 462 Rehabilitation
GMLOS 8.9 AMLOS 10.8 RW 0.8700 T

Principal Diagnosis

V52.8	Fitting and adjustment of other specified prosthetic device
V52.9	Fitting and adjustment of unspecified prosthetic device
V57.1	Other physical therapy
*V57.2	Occupational therapy and vocational rehabilitation
V57.3	Speech therapy
V57.89	Other specified rehabilitation procedure
V57.9	Unspecified rehabilitation procedure

M DRG 463 Signs and Symptoms with CC
GMLOS 3.1 AMLOS 3.9 RW 0.6960 ☑ T CC

Principal Diagnosis

*780.7	Malaise and fatigue
*780.9	Other general symptoms
782.3	Edema
782.5	Cyanosis
*782.6	Pallor and flushing
789.5	Ascites
790.1	Elevated sedimentation rate
790.4	Nonspecific elevation of levels of transaminase or lactic acid dehydrogenase (LDH)
790.5	Other nonspecific abnormal serum enzyme levels
790.6	Other abnormal blood chemistry
*790.9	Other nonspecific findings on examination of blood
791.3	Myoglobinuria
792.5	Cloudy (hemodialysis) (peritoneal) dialysis affluent
792.9	Other nonspecific abnormal finding in body substances
793.9	Nonspecific abnormal findings on radiological and other examination of other site of body
795.4	Other nonspecific abnormal histological findings
796.4	Other abnormal clinical finding
796.6	Nonspecific abnormal findings on neonatal screening
796.9	Other nonspecific abnormal finding
799.3	Unspecified debility
799.4	Cachexia

M DRG 464 Signs and Symptoms without CC
GMLOS 2.4 AMLOS 2.9 RW 0.5055 ☑ T

Select principal diagnosis listed under DRG 463

M DRG 465 Aftercare with History of Malignancy as Secondary Diagnosis
GMLOS 2.4 AMLOS 3.8 RW 0.6224

Principal Diagnosis

*V58.4	Other aftercare following surgery
V58.5	Orthodontics aftercare
*V58.6	Encounter for long-term (current) drug use
*V58.7	Aftercare following surgery to specified body systems, not elsewhere classified

*V58.8	Other specified aftercare
V58.9	Unspecified aftercare
*V67.0	Surgery follow-up examination
V67.4	Treatment of healed fracture follow-up examination

AND

Secondary Diagnosis

*V10	Personal history of malignant neoplasm
V71.1	Observation for suspected malignant neoplasm

M DRG 466 Aftercare without History of Malignancy as Secondary Diagnosis

GMLOS 2.8 AMLOS 5.3 RW 0.7806

Select principal diagnosis listed under DRG 465 excluding secondary diagnoses listed under DRG 465

M DRG 467 Other Factors Influencing Health Status

GMLOS 2.0 AMLOS 2.7 RW 0.4803 ☑

Principal Diagnosis

305.1	Nondependent tobacco use disorder
758.4	Balanced autosomal translocation in normal individual
758.5	Other conditions due to autosomal anomalies
758.9	Conditions due to anomaly of unspecified chromosome
759.9	Unspecified congenital anomaly
795.2	Nonspecific abnormal findings on chromosomal analysis
798.9	Unattended death
*799.8	Other ill-defined conditions
799.9	Other unknown and unspecified cause of morbidity or mortality
*V01	Contact with or exposure to communicable diseases
V02.0	Carrier or suspected carrier of cholera
V02.1	Carrier or suspected carrier of typhoid
V02.2	Carrier or suspected carrier of amebiasis
V02.3	Carrier or suspected carrier of other gastrointestinal pathogens
V02.4	Carrier or suspected carrier of diphtheria
*V02.5	Carrier or suspected carrier of other specified bacterial diseases
V02.7	Carrier or suspected carrier of gonorrhea
V02.8	Carrier or suspected carrier of other venereal diseases
V02.9	Carrier or suspected carrier of other specified infectious organism
*V03	Need for prophylactic vaccination and inoculation against bacterial diseases
*V04	Need for prophylactic vaccination and inoculation against certain viral diseases
*V05	Need for other prophylactic vaccination and inoculation against single diseases
*V06	Need for prophylactic vaccination and inoculation against combinations of diseases
*V07	Need for isolation and other prophylactic measures
*V11	Personal history of mental disorder
*V12	Personal history of certain other diseases
*V13	Personal history of other diseases
*V14	Personal history of allergy to medicinal agents
*V15	Other personal history presenting hazards to health
*V16	Family history of malignant neoplasm
*V17	Family history of certain chronic disabling diseases
*V18	Family history of certain other specific conditions
*V19	Family history of other conditions
*V20	Health supervision of infant or child
*V21	Constitutional states in development
*V22	Normal pregnancy
V24.1	Postpartum care and examination of lactating mother
V24.2	Routine postpartum follow-up
*V25.0	General counseling and advice for contraceptive management
V25.1	Insertion of intrauterine contraceptive device
*V25.4	Surveillance of previously prescribed contraceptive methods
V25.5	Insertion of implantable subdermal contraceptive

MDC 23: Factors Influencing Health Status — Medical

DRG 467 — continued

V25.8	Other specified contraceptive management
V25.9	Unspecified contraceptive management
V26.1	Artificial insemination
*V26.2	Investigation and testing for procreation management
*V26.3	Genetic counseling and testing
V26.4	General counseling and advice for procreative management
*V26.5	Sterilization status
V26.8	Other specified procreative management
V26.9	Unspecified procreative management
*V27	Outcome of delivery
V28.3	Antenatal screening for malformation using ultrasonics
V28.4	Antenatal screening for fetal growth retardation using ultrasonics
V28.5	Antenatal screening for isoimmunization
V28.6	Screening of Streptococcus B
V28.8	Other specified antenatal screening
V28.9	Unspecified antenatal screening
*V29	Observation and evaluation of newborns and infants for suspected condition not found
*V40	Mental and behavioral problems
*V41	Problems with special senses and other special functions
V42.84	Organ or tissue replaced by transplant, intestines
V42.89	Other organ or tissue replaced by transplant
V42.9	Unspecified organ or tissue replaced by transplant
*V43.8	Other organ or tissue replaced by other means
*V44	Artificial opening status
*V45.0	Postsurgical cardiac pacemaker in situ
V45.1	Renal dialysis status
V45.2	Presence of cerebrospinal fluid drainage device
V45.3	Intestinal bypass or anastomosis status
V45.4	Arthrodesis status
*V45.5	Presence of contraceptive device
V45.61	Cataract extraction status
V45.69	Other states following surgery of eye and adnexa
V45.71	Acquired absence of breast
V45.72	Acquired absence of intestine (large) (small)
V45.73	Acquired absence of kidney
V45.75	Acquired absence of organ, stomach
V45.79	Other acquired absence of organ
V45.81	Postsurgical aortocoronary bypass status
V45.82	Postsurgical percutaneous transluminal coronary angioplasty status
V45.83	Breast implant removal status
V45.84	Dental restoration status
V45.85	Insulin pump status
V45.89	Other postsurgical status
*V46	Other dependence on machines
*V47	Other problems with internal organs
*V48	Problems with head, neck, and trunk
*V49	Problems with limbs and other problems
V50.49	Other prophylactic gland removal
V50.8	Other elective surgery for purposes other than remedying health states
V50.9	Unspecified elective surgery for purposes other than remedying health states
V52.2	Fitting and adjustment of artificial eye
V52.3	Fitting and adjustment of dental prosthetic device
V52.4	Fitting and adjustment of breast prosthesis and implant
V53.1	Fitting and adjustment of spectacles and contact lenses
V53.2	Fitting and adjustment of hearing aid
V53.4	Fitting and adjustment of orthodontic devices
V53.8	Fitting and adjustment of wheelchair
*V53.9	Fitting and adjustment of other and unspecified device
V55.8	Attention to other specified artificial opening
V55.9	Attention to unspecified artificial opening
V57.0	Care involving breathing exercises
V57.4	Orthoptic training

V57.81	Orthotic training
V58.2	Blood transfusion, without reported diagnosis
V58.3	Attention to surgical dressings and sutures
*V59.0	Blood donor
V59.3	Bone marrow donor
V59.5	Cornea donor
*V59.7	Egg (oocyte) (ovum) Donor
V59.8	Donor of other specified organ or tissue
V59.9	Donor of unspecified organ or tissue
*V60	Housing, household, and economic circumstances
*V61	Other family circumstances
*V62	Other psychosocial circumstances
*V63	Unavailability of other medical facilities for care
*V64	Persons encountering health services for specific procedures, not carried out
*V65	Other persons seeking consultation without complaint or sickness
*V66	Convalescence and palliative care
V67.3	Psychotherapy and other treatment for mental disorder follow-up examination
*V67.5	Other follow-up examination
V67.6	Combined treatment follow-up examination
V67.9	Unspecified follow-up examination
*V68	Encounters for administrative purposes
*V69	Problems related to lifestyle
*V70	General medical examination
V71.5	Observation following alleged rape or seduction
*V71.8	Observation and evaluation for other specified suspected conditions
V71.9	Observation for unspecified suspected condition
*V72	Special investigations and examinations
*V73	Special screening examination for viral and chlamydial diseases
*V74	Special screening examination for bacterial and spirochetal diseases
*V75	Special screening examination for other infectious diseases
*V76	Special screening for malignant neoplasms
*V77	Special screening for endocrine, nutritional, metabolic, and immunity disorders
*V78	Special screening for disorders of blood and blood-forming organs
*V79	Special screening for mental disorders and developmental handicaps
*V80	Special screening for neurological, eye, and ear diseases
*V81	Special screening for cardiovascular, respiratory, and genitourinary diseases
*V82	Special screening for other condition
V83.01	Asymptomatic hemophilia A carrier
V83.02	Symptomatic hemophilia A carrier
*V83.8	Other genetic carrier status
*V84.0	Genetic susceptibility to malignant neoplasm
V84.8	Genetic susceptibility to other disease
*V85	Body Mass Index

MDC 24
MULTIPLE SIGNIFICANT TRAUMA

The complete and up-to-date listing of ICD-9-CM diagnosis codes assigned to this MDC can be found online at www.ingenixonline.com/content/drg/resources.asp.

SURGICAL

S DRG 484 Craniotomy for Multiple Significant Trauma
GMLOS 9.3 AMLOS 12.8 RW 5.1438

Select the principal diagnosis from the Trauma Diagnosis List located in DRG 487

AND

At least two different diagnoses from two different Significant Trauma Body Site Categories located in DRG 487

AND

Operating Room Procedure

01.21	Incision and drainage of cranial sinus
01.23	Reopening of craniotomy site
01.24	Other craniotomy
01.25	Other craniectomy
01.31	Incision of cerebral meninges
01.32	Lobotomy and tractotomy
01.39	Other incision of brain
01.41	Operations on thalamus
01.42	Operations on globus pallidus
01.51	Excision of lesion or tissue of cerebral meninges
01.52	Hemispherectomy
01.53	Lobectomy of brain
01.59	Other excision or destruction of lesion or tissue of brain
01.6	Excision of lesion of skull
02.01	Opening of cranial suture
02.02	Elevation of skull fracture fragments
02.03	Formation of cranial bone flap
02.04	Bone graft to skull
02.05	Insertion of skull plate
02.06	Other cranial osteoplasty
02.11	Simple suture of dura mater of brain
02.12	Other repair of cerebral meninges
02.13	Ligation of meningeal vessel
02.14	Choroid plexectomy
02.2	Ventriculostomy
02.92	Repair of brain
02.94	Insertion or replacement of skull tongs or halo traction device
02.99	Other operations on skull, brain, and cerebral meninges
04.41	Decompression of trigeminal nerve root
38.81	Other surgical occlusion of intracranial vessels

OR

Select a principal diagnosis from one Significant Trauma Body Site Category located in DRG 487

AND

Two or more significant trauma diagnoses from different Significant Trauma Body Site Categories located in DRG 487

AND

Any operating room procedure listed above

S DRG 485 Limb Reattachment, Hip and Femur Procedures for Multiple Significant Trauma

GMLOS 8.4 AMLOS 10.2 RW 3.4952 ☑ T

Select principal diagnosis from Trauma Diagnosis List located in DRG 487

AND

At least two different diagnoses from two different Significant Trauma Body Site Categories located in DRG 487

AND

Operating Room Procedure

00.70	Revision of hip replacement, both acetabular and femoral components
00.71	Revision of hip replacement, acetabular component
00.72	Revision of hip replacement, femoral component
00.73	Revision of hip replacement, acetabular liner and/or femoral head only
*00.8	Other knee procedures
77.05	Sequestrectomy of femur
77.25	Wedge osteotomy of femur
77.35	Other division of femur
77.85	Other partial ostectomy of femur
77.95	Total ostectomy of femur
78.05	Bone graft of femur
78.15	Application of external fixator device, femur
78.25	Limb shortening procedures, femur
78.35	Limb lengthening procedures, femur
78.45	Other repair or plastic operations on femur
78.55	Internal fixation of femur without fracture reduction
78.75	Osteoclasis of femur
78.95	Insertion of bone growth stimulator into femur
79.15	Closed reduction of fracture of femur with internal fixation
79.25	Open reduction of fracture of femur without internal fixation
79.35	Open reduction of fracture of femur with internal fixation
79.45	Closed reduction of separated epiphysis of femur
79.55	Open reduction of separated epiphysis of femur
79.65	Debridement of open fracture of femur
79.85	Open reduction of dislocation of hip
79.95	Unspecified operation on bone injury of femur
80.05	Arthrotomy for removal of prosthesis of hip
80.15	Other arthrotomy of hip
80.45	Division of joint capsule, ligament, or cartilage of hip
80.95	Other excision of hip joint
81.21	Arthrodesis of hip
81.40	Repair of hip, not elsewhere classified
81.51	Total hip replacement
81.52	Partial hip replacement
81.53	Revision of hip replacement, not otherwise specified
83.12	Adductor tenotomy of hip
84.23	Forearm, wrist, or hand reattachment
84.24	Upper arm reattachment
84.26	Foot reattachment
84.27	Lower leg or ankle reattachment
84.28	Thigh reattachment

OR

Select a principal diagnosis from one Significant Trauma Body Site Category located in DRG 487

AND

Two or more significant trauma diagnoses from different Significant Trauma Body Site Categories located in DRG 487

AND

Operating room procedure listed above

MDC 24: Multiple Significant Trauma — Surgical

Ⓢ DRG 486 Other O.R. Procedures for Multiple Significant Trauma

GMLOS 8.5 AMLOS 12.5 RW 4.7323 ☑

Select principal diagnosis from Trauma Diagnosis List located in DRG 487

AND

At least two different diagnoses from two different Significant Trauma Body Site Categories located in DRG 487

AND

Any operating room procedure from MDC 21

EXCLUDING

Pacemaker leads and devices

All procedure listed under DRGs 484 and 485

OR

Select a principal diagnosis from one Significant Trauma Body Site Category located in DRG 487

AND

Two or more significant trauma diagnoses from different Significant Trauma Body Site Categories located in DRG 487

AND

Any operating room procedure from MDC 21

EXCLUDING

Pacemaker leads and devices

All procedures listed under DRGs 484 and 485

MDC 24
MULTIPLE SIGNIFICANT TRAUMA

The complete and up-to-date listing of ICD-9-CM diagnosis codes assigned to this MDC can be found online at www.ingenixonline.com/content/drg/resources.asp.

MEDICAL

M DRG 487 Other Multiple Significant Trauma

GMLOS 5.3 AMLOS 7.3 RW 1.9459 ☑ T

Select principal diagnosis from list of the Trauma Diagnosis List located below

WITH

At least two different diagnoses from two different Significant Trauma Body Site Categories located in DRG 487

OR

Select a principal diagnosis from one Significant Trauma Body Site Category

AND

Two or more significant trauma diagnoses from different Significant Trauma Body Site Categories located in DRG 487

Trauma Diagnosis

*800.0	Closed fracture of vault of skull without mention of intracranial injury
*800.1	Closed fracture of vault of skull with cerebral laceration and contusion
*800.2	Closed fracture of vault of skull with subarachnoid, subdural, and extradural hemorrhage
*800.3	Closed fracture of vault of skull with other and unspecified intracranial hemorrhage
*800.4	Closed fracture of vault of skull with intercranial injury of other and unspecified nature
*800.5	Open fracture of vault of skull without mention of intracranial injury
*800.6	Open fracture of vault of skull with cerebral laceration and contusion
*800.7	Open fracture of vault of skull with subarachnoid, subdural, and extradural hemorrhage
*800.8	Open fracture of vault of skull with other and unspecified intracranial hemorrhage
*800.9	Open fracture of vault of skull with intracranial injury of other and unspecified nature
*801.0	Closed fracture of base of skull without mention of intracranial injury
*801.1	Closed fracture of base of skull with cerebral laceration and contusion
*801.2	Closed fracture of base of skull with subarachnoid, subdural, and extradural hemorrhage
*801.3	Closed fracture of base of skull with other and unspecified intracranial hemorrhage
*801.4	Closed fracture of base of skull with intracranial injury of other and unspecified nature
*801.5	Open fracture of base of skull without mention of intracranial injury
*801.6	Open fracture of base of skull with cerebral laceration and contusion
*801.7	Open fracture of base of skull with subarachnoid, subdural, and extradural hemorrhage
*801.8	Open fracture of base of skull with other and unspecified intracranial hemorrhage
*801.9	Open fracture of base of skull with intracranial injury of other and unspecified nature
802.0	Nasal bones, closed fracture
802.1	Nasal bones, open fracture
*802.2	Mandible, closed fracture
*802.3	Mandible, open fracture
802.4	Malar and maxillary bones, closed fracture
802.5	Malar and maxillary bones, open fracture
802.6	Orbital floor (blow-out), closed fracture
802.7	Orbital floor (blow-out), open fracture
802.8	Other facial bones, closed fracture
802.9	Other facial bones, open fracture
*803.0	Other closed skull fracture without mention of intracranial injury
*803.1	Other closed skull fracture with cerebral laceration and contusion
*803.2	Other closed skull fracture with subarachnoid, subdural, and extradural hemorrhage
*803.3	Closed skull fracture with other and unspecified intracranial hemorrhage
*803.4	Other closed skull fracture with intracranial injury of other and unspecified nature
*803.5	Other open skull fracture without mention of intracranial injury
*803.6	Other open skull fracture with cerebral laceration and contusion
*803.7	Other open skull fracture with subarachnoid, subdural, and extradural hemorrhage

*** Code Range** ☑ **Optimization Potential** ▽ **Targeted Potential** T **Transfer DRG** SP **Special Payment**

DRG 487 — continued

*803.8	Other open skull fracture with other and unspecified intracranial hemorrhage
*803.9	Other open skull fracture with intracranial injury of other and unspecified nature
*804.0	Closed fractures involving skull or face with other bones, without mention of intracranial injury
*804.1	Closed fractures involving skull or face with other bones, with cerebral laceration and contusion
*804.2	Closed fractures involving skull or face with other bones with subarachnoid, subdural, and extradural hemorrhage
*804.3	Closed fractures involving skull or face with other bones, with other and unspecified intracranial hemorrhage
*804.4	Closed fractures involving skull or face with other bones, with intracranial injury of other and unspecified nature
*804.5	Open fractures involving skull or face with other bones, without mention of intracranial injury
*804.6	Open fractures involving skull or face with other bones, with cerebral laceration and contusion
*804.7	Open fractures involving skull or face with other bones with subarachnoid, subdural, and extradural hemorrhage
*804.8	Open fractures involving skull or face with other bones, with other and unspecified intracranial hemorrhage
*804.9	Open fractures involving skull or face with other bones, with intracranial injury of other and unspecified nature
*805.0	Closed fracture of cervical vertebra without mention of spinal cord injury
*805.1	Open fracture of cervical vertebra without mention of spinal cord injury
805.2	Closed fracture of dorsal (thoracic) vertebra without mention of spinal cord injury
805.3	Open fracture of dorsal (thoracic) vertebra without mention of spinal cord injury
805.4	Closed fracture of lumbar vertebra without mention of spinal cord injury
805.5	Open fracture of lumbar vertebra without mention of spinal cord injury
805.6	Closed fracture of sacrum and coccyx without mention of spinal cord injury
805.7	Open fracture of sacrum and coccyx without mention of spinal cord injury
805.8	Closed fracture of unspecified part of vertebral column without mention of spinal cord injury
805.9	Open fracture of unspecified part of vertebral column without mention of spinal cord injury
*806.0	Closed fracture of cervical vertebra with spinal cord injury
*806.1	Open fracture of cervical vertebra with spinal cord injury
*806.2	Closed fracture of dorsal (thoracic) vertebra with spinal cord injury
*806.3	Open fracture of dorsal vertebra with spinal cord injury
806.4	Closed fracture of lumbar spine with spinal cord injury
806.5	Open fracture of lumbar spine with spinal cord injury
*806.6	Closed fracture of sacrum and coccyx with spinal cord injury
*806.7	Open fracture of sacrum and coccyx with spinal cord injury
806.8	Closed fracture of unspecified vertebra with spinal cord injury
806.9	Open fracture of unspecified vertebra with spinal cord injury
*807.0	Closed fracture of rib(s)
*807.1	Open fracture of rib(s)
807.2	Closed fracture of sternum
807.3	Open fracture of sternum
807.4	Flail chest
807.5	Closed fracture of larynx and trachea
807.6	Open fracture of larynx and trachea
808.0	Closed fracture of acetabulum
808.1	Open fracture of acetabulum
808.2	Closed fracture of pubis
808.3	Open fracture of pubis
*808.4	Closed fracture of other specified part of pelvis
*808.5	Open fracture of other specified part of pelvis
808.8	Unspecified closed fracture of pelvis
808.9	Unspecified open fracture of pelvis
809.0	Fracture of bones of trunk, closed
809.1	Fracture of bones of trunk, open
*810.0	Closed fracture of clavicle
*810.1	Open fracture of clavicle
*811.0	Closed fracture of scapula
*811.1	Open fracture of scapula
*812.0	Closed fracture of upper end of humerus

*812.1	Open fracture of upper end of humerus
*812.2	Closed fracture of shaft or unspecified part of humerus
*812.3	Open fracture of shaft or unspecified part of humerus
*812.4	Closed fracture of lower end of humerus
*812.5	Open fracture of lower end of humerus
*813.0	Closed fracture of upper end of radius and ulna
*813.1	Open fracture of upper end of radius and ulna
*813.2	Closed fracture of shaft of radius and ulna
*813.3	Open fracture of shaft of radius and ulna
*813.4	Closed fracture of lower end of radius and ulna
*813.5	Open fracture of lower end of radius and ulna
*813.8	Closed fracture of unspecified part of radius with ulna
*813.9	Open fracture of unspecified part of radius with ulna
*814.0	Closed fractures of carpal bones
*814.1	Open fractures of carpal bones
*815.0	Closed fracture of metacarpal bones
*815.1	Open fracture of metacarpal bones
*816.0	Closed fracture of one or more phalanges of hand
*816.1	Open fracture of one or more phalanges of hand
817.0	Multiple closed fractures of hand bones
817.1	Multiple open fractures of hand bones
818.0	Ill-defined closed fractures of upper limb
818.1	Ill-defined open fractures of upper limb
819.0	Multiple closed fractures involving both upper limbs, and upper limb with rib(s) and sternum
819.1	Multiple open fractures involving both upper limbs, and upper limb with rib(s) and sternum
*820.0	Closed transcervical fracture
*820.1	Open transcervical fracture
*820.2	Closed pertrochanteric fracture of femur
*820.3	Open pertrochanteric fracture of femur
820.8	Closed fracture of unspecified part of neck of femur
820.9	Open fracture of unspecified part of neck of femur
*821.0	Closed fracture of shaft or unspecified part of femur
*821.1	Open fracture of shaft or unspecified part of femur
*821.2	Closed fracture of lower end of femur
*821.3	Open fracture of lower end of femur
822.0	Closed fracture of patella
822.1	Open fracture of patella
*823.0	Closed fracture of upper end of tibia and fibula
*823.1	Open fracture of upper end of tibia and fibula
*823.2	Closed fracture of shaft of tibia and fibula
*823.3	Open fracture of shaft of tibia and fibula
*823.4	Torus fracture of tibia and fibula
*823.8	Closed fracture of unspecified part of tibia and fibula
*823.9	Open fracture of unspecified part of tibia and fibula
824.0	Closed fracture of medial malleolus
824.1	Open fracture of medial malleolus
824.2	Closed fracture of lateral malleolus
824.3	Open fracture of lateral malleolus
824.4	Closed bimalleolar fracture
824.5	Open bimalleolar fracture
824.6	Closed trimalleolar fracture
824.7	Open trimalleolar fracture
824.8	Unspecified closed fracture of ankle
824.9	Unspecified open fracture of ankle
825.0	Closed fracture of calcaneus
825.1	Open fracture of calcaneus
*825.2	Closed fracture of other tarsal and metatarsal bones
*825.3	Open fracture of other tarsal and metatarsal bones
826.0	Closed fracture of one or more phalanges of foot
826.1	Open fracture of one or more phalanges of foot
827.0	Other, multiple and ill-defined closed fractures of lower limb
827.1	Other, multiple and ill-defined open fractures of lower limb

DRG 487 — continued

828.0	Multiple closed fractures involving both lower limbs, lower with upper limb, and lower limb(s) with rib(s) and sternum
828.1	Multiple fractures involving both lower limbs, lower with upper limb, and lower limb(s) with rib(s) and sternum, open
829.0	Closed fracture of unspecified bone
829.1	Open fracture of unspecified bone
830.0	Closed dislocation of jaw
830.1	Open dislocation of jaw
*831.0	Closed dislocation of shoulder, unspecified
*831.1	Open dislocation of shoulder
*832.0	Closed dislocation of elbow
*832.1	Open dislocation of elbow
*833.0	Closed dislocation of wrist
*833.1	Open dislocation of wrist
*834.0	Closed dislocation of finger
*834.1	Open dislocation of finger
*835.0	Closed dislocation of hip
*835.1	Open dislocation of hip
836.0	Tear of medial cartilage or meniscus of knee, current
836.1	Tear of lateral cartilage or meniscus of knee, current
836.2	Other tear of cartilage or meniscus of knee, current
836.3	Closed dislocation of patella
836.4	Open dislocation of patella
*836.5	Other closed dislocation of knee
*836.6	Other open dislocation of knee
837.0	Closed dislocation of ankle
837.1	Open dislocation of ankle
*838.0	Closed dislocation of foot
*838.1	Open dislocation of foot
*839.0	Closed dislocation, cervical vertebra
*839.1	Open dislocation, cervical vertebra
*839.2	Closed dislocation, thoracic and lumbar vertebra
*839.3	Open dislocation, thoracic and lumbar vertebra
*839.4	Closed dislocation, other vertebra
*839.5	Open dislocation, other vertebra
*839.6	Closed dislocation, other location
839.71	Open dislocation, sternum
839.79	Open dislocation, other location
839.8	Closed dislocation, multiple and ill-defined sites
839.9	Open dislocation, multiple and ill-defined sites
840.0	Acromioclavicular (joint) (ligament) sprain and strain
840.1	Coracoclavicular (ligament) sprain and strain
840.2	Coracohumeral (ligament) sprain and strain
840.3	Infraspinatus (muscle) (tendon) sprain and strain
840.4	Rotator cuff (capsule) sprain and strain
840.5	Subscapularis (muscle) sprain and strain
840.6	Supraspinatus (muscle) (tendon) sprain and strain
840.7	Superior glenoid labrum lesions (SLAP)
840.8	Sprain and strain of other specified sites of shoulder and upper arm
840.9	Sprain and strain of unspecified site of shoulder and upper arm
*841	Sprains and strains of elbow and forearm
*842	Sprains and strains of wrist and hand
*843	Sprains and strains of hip and thigh
*844	Sprains and strains of knee and leg
*845	Sprains and strains of ankle and foot
*846	Sprains and strains of sacroiliac region
*847	Sprains and strains of other and unspecified parts of back
*848	Other and ill-defined sprains and strains
850.0	Concussion with no loss of consciousness
*850.1	Concussion with brief (less than one hour) loss of consciousness
850.2	Concussion with moderate (1-24 hours) loss of consciousness

850.3	Concussion with prolonged (more than 24 hours) loss of consciousness and return to pre-existing conscious level
850.4	Concussion with prolonged (more than 24 hours) loss of consciousness, without return to pre-existing conscious level
850.5	Concussion with loss of consciousness of unspecified duration
850.9	Unspecified concussion
*851.0	Cortex (cerebral) contusion without mention of open intracranial wound
*851.1	Cortex (cerebral) contusion with open intracranial wound
*851.2	Cortex (cerebral) laceration without mention of open intracranial wound
*851.3	Cortex (cerebral) laceration with open intracranial wound
*851.4	Cerebellar or brain stem contusion without mention of open intracranial wound
*851.5	Cerebellar or brain stem contusion with open intracranial wound
*851.6	Cerebellar or brain stem laceration without mention of open intracranial wound
*851.7	Cerebellar or brain stem laceration with open intracranial wound
*851.8	Other and unspecified cerebral laceration and contusion, without mention of open intracranial wound
*851.9	Other and unspecified cerebral laceration and contusion, with open intracranial wound
*852	Subarachnoid, subdural, and extradural hemorrhage, following injury
*853	Other and unspecified intracranial hemorrhage following injury
*854	Intracranial injury of other and unspecified nature
*860	Traumatic pneumothorax and hemothorax
*861	Injury to heart and lung
*862	Injury to other and unspecified intrathoracic organs
863.0	Stomach injury without mention of open wound into cavity
863.1	Stomach injury with open wound into cavity
*863.2	Small intestine injury without mention of open wound into cavity
*863.3	Small intestine injury with open wound into cavity
*863.4	Colon or rectal injury without mention of open wound into cavity
*863.5	Injury to colon or rectum with open wound into cavity
*863.8	Injury to other and unspecified gastrointestinal sites without mention of open wound into cavity
*863.9	Injury to other and unspecified gastrointestinal sites, with open wound into cavity
*864.0	Liver injury without mention of open wound into cavity
*864.1	Liver injury with open wound into cavity
*865	Injury to spleen
*866	Injury to kidney
*867	Injury to pelvic organs
*868.0	Injury to other intra-abdominal organs without mention of open wound into cavity
*868.1	Injury to other intra-abdominal organs with open wound into cavity
*869	Internal injury to unspecified or ill-defined organs
*870	Open wound of ocular adnexa
*871	Open wound of eyeball
*872	Open wound of ear
*873	Other open wound of head
*874.0	Open wound of larynx and trachea, without mention of complication
*874.1	Open wound of larynx and trachea, complicated
874.2	Open wound of thyroid gland, without mention of complication
874.3	Open wound of thyroid gland, complicated
874.4	Open wound of pharynx, without mention of complication
874.5	Open wound of pharynx, complicated
874.8	Open wound of other and unspecified parts of neck, without mention of complication
874.9	Open wound of other and unspecified parts of neck, complicated
*875	Open wound of chest (wall)
*876	Open wound of back
*877	Open wound of buttock
*878	Open wound of genital organs (external), including traumatic amputation
*879	Open wound of other and unspecified sites, except limbs
*880	Open wound of shoulder and upper arm
*881	Open wound of elbow, forearm, and wrist
*882	Open wound of hand except finger(s) alone
*883	Open wound of finger(s)
*884	Multiple and unspecified open wound of upper limb
*885	Traumatic amputation of thumb (complete) (partial)

DRG 487 — continued

*886	Traumatic amputation of other finger(s) (complete) (partial)
*887	Traumatic amputation of arm and hand (complete) (partial)
*890	Open wound of hip and thigh
*891	Open wound of knee, leg (except thigh), and ankle
*892	Open wound of foot except toe(s) alone
*893	Open wound of toe(s)
*894	Multiple and unspecified open wound of lower limb
*895	Traumatic amputation of toe(s) (complete) (partial)
*896	Traumatic amputation of foot (complete) (partial)
*897	Traumatic amputation of leg(s) (complete) (partial)
*900.0	Injury to carotid artery
900.1	Internal jugular vein injury
*900.8	Injury to other specified blood vessels of head and neck
901.0	Thoracic aorta injury
901.1	Innominate and subclavian artery injury
901.2	Superior vena cava injury
901.3	Innominate and subclavian vein injury
*901.4	Pulmonary blood vessel injury
*901.8	Injury to other specified blood vessels of thorax
901.9	Injury to unspecified blood vessel of thorax
*902	Injury to blood vessels of abdomen and pelvis
*903	Injury to blood vessels of upper extremity
904.0	Common femoral artery injury
904.1	Superficial femoral artery injury
904.2	Femoral vein injury
904.3	Saphenous vein injury
*904.4	Popliteal blood vessel vein
*904.5	Tibial blood vessel(s) injury
904.6	Deep plantar blood vessels injury
904.7	Injury to specified blood vessels of lower extremity, other
904.8	Injury to unspecified blood vessel of lower extremity
904.9	Injury to blood vessels, unspecified site
*910	Superficial injury of face, neck, and scalp, except eye
*911	Superficial injury of trunk
*912	Superficial injury of shoulder and upper arm
*913	Superficial injury of elbow, forearm, and wrist
*914	Superficial injury of hand(s) except finger(s) alone
*915	Superficial injury of finger(s)
*916	Superficial injury of hip, thigh, leg, and ankle
*917	Superficial injury of foot and toe(s)
*918	Superficial injury of eye and adnexa
*919	Superficial injury of other, multiple, and unspecified sites
920	Contusion of face, scalp, and neck except eye(s)
*921	Contusion of eye and adnexa
*922	Contusion of trunk
*923	Contusion of upper limb
*924	Contusion of lower limb and of other and unspecified sites
*925	Crushing injury of face, scalp, and neck
926.0	Crushing injury of external genitalia
*926.1	Crushing injury of other specified sites of trunk
926.8	Crushing injury of multiple sites of trunk
926.9	Crushing injury of unspecified site of trunk
*927.0	Crushing injury of shoulder and upper arm
*927.1	Crushing injury of elbow and forearm
*927.2	Crushing injury of wrist and hand(s), except finger(s) alone
927.3	Crushing injury of finger(s)
927.8	Crushing injury of multiple sites of upper limb
927.9	Crushing injury of unspecified site of upper limb
*928.0	Crushing injury of hip and thigh
*928.1	Crushing injury of knee and lower leg
*928.2	Crushing injury of ankle and foot, excluding toe(s) alone
928.3	Crushing injury of toe(s)

S *Surgical* M *Medical* CC *CC Indicator* A *Age Restriction* ● *New DRG* ▲ *Revised DRG Title*

928.8	Crushing injury of multiple sites of lower limb
928.9	Crushing injury of unspecified site of lower limb
*929	Crushing injury of multiple and unspecified sites
*950	Injury to optic nerve and pathways
*951	Injury to other cranial nerve(s)
*952	Spinal cord injury without evidence of spinal bone injury
*953	Injury to nerve roots and spinal plexus
953.1	Injury to dorsal nerve root
953.2	Injury to lumbar nerve root
953.3	Injury to sacral nerve root
953.4	Injury to brachial plexus
953.5	Injury to lumbosacral plexus
953.8	Injury to multiple sites of nerve roots and spinal plexus
953.9	Injury to unspecified site of nerve roots and spinal plexus
954.0	Injury to cervical sympathetic nerve, excluding shoulder and pelvic girdles
954.1	Injury to other sympathetic nerve, excluding shoulder and pelvic girdles
954.8	Injury to other specified nerve(s) of trunk, excluding shoulder and pelvic girdles
954.9	Injury to unspecified nerve of trunk, excluding shoulder and pelvic girdles
955.0	Injury to axillary nerve
955.1	Injury to median nerve
955.2	Injury to ulnar nerve
955.3	Injury to radial nerve
955.4	Injury to musculocutaneous nerve
955.5	Injury to cutaneous sensory nerve, upper limb
955.6	Injury to digital nerve, upper limb
955.7	Injury to other specified nerve(s) of shoulder girdle and upper limb
955.8	Injury to multiple nerves of shoulder girdle and upper limb
955.9	Injury to unspecified nerve of shoulder girdle and upper limb
956.0	Injury to sciatic nerve
956.1	Injury to femoral nerve
956.2	Injury to posterior tibial nerve
956.3	Injury to peroneal nerve
956.4	Injury to cutaneous sensory nerve, lower limb
956.5	Injury to other specified nerve(s) of pelvic girdle and lower limb
956.8	Injury to multiple nerves of pelvic girdle and lower limb
956.9	Injury to unspecified nerve of pelvic girdle and lower limb
*957	Injury to other and unspecified nerves
958.0	Air embolism as an early complication of trauma
958.1	Fat embolism as an early complication of trauma
958.2	Secondary and recurrent hemorrhage as an early complication of trauma
958.3	Posttraumatic wound infection not elsewhere classified
958.4	Traumatic shock
958.5	Traumatic anuria
958.6	Volkmann's ischemic contracture
958.7	Traumatic subcutaneous emphysema
958.8	Other early complications of trauma
*959.0	Injury, other and unspecified, head, face, and neck
*959.1	Injury, other and unspecified, trunk
959.2	Injury, other and unspecified, shoulder and upper arm
959.3	Injury, other and unspecified, elbow, forearm, and wrist
959.4	Injury, other and unspecified, hand, except finger
959.5	Injury, other and unspecified, finger
959.6	Injury, other and unspecified, hip and thigh
959.7	Injury, other and unspecified, knee, leg, ankle, and foot
959.8	Injury, other and unspecified, other specified sites, including multiple
959.9	Injury, other and unspecified, unspecified site

Significant Trauma Body Site Category 1—Head

800.02	Closed fracture of vault of skull without mention of intracranial injury, brief (less than one hour) loss of consciousness
800.03	Closed fracture of vault of skull without mention of intracranial injury, moderate (1-24 hours) loss of consciousness

DRG 487 — continued

800.04	Closed fracture of vault of skull without mention of intracranial injury, prolonged (more than 24 hours) loss of consciousness and return to pre-existing conscious level
800.05	Closed fracture of vault of skull without mention of intracranial injury, prolonged (more than 24 hours) loss of consciousness, without return to pre-existing conscious level
800.10	Closed fracture of vault of skull with cerebral laceration and contusion, unspecified state of consciousness
800.12	Closed fracture of vault of skull with cerebral laceration and contusion, brief (less than one hour) loss of consciousness
800.13	Closed fracture of vault of skull with cerebral laceration and contusion, moderate (1-24 hours) loss of consciousness
800.14	Closed fracture of vault of skull with cerebral laceration and contusion, prolonged (more than 24 hours) loss of consciousness and return to pre-existing conscious level
800.15	Closed fracture of vault of skull with cerebral laceration and contusion, prolonged (more than 24 hours) loss of consciousness, without return to pre-existing conscious level
800.16	Closed fracture of vault of skull with cerebral laceration and contusion, loss of consciousness of unspecified duration
800.19	Closed fracture of vault of skull with cerebral laceration and contusion, unspecified concussion
800.20	Closed fracture of vault of skull with subarachnoid, subdural, and extradural hemorrhage, unspecified state of consciousness
800.22	Closed fracture of vault of skull with subarachnoid, subdural, and extradural hemorrhage, brief (less than one hour) loss of consciousness
800.23	Closed fracture of vault of skull with subarachnoid, subdural, and extradural hemorrhage, moderate (1-24 hours) loss of consciousness
800.24	Closed fracture of vault of skull with subarachnoid, subdural, and extradural hemorrhage, prolonged (more than 24 hours) loss of consciousness and return to pre-existing conscious level
800.25	Closed fracture of vault of skull with subarachnoid, subdural, and extradural hemorrhage, prolonged (more than 24 hours) loss of consciousness, without return to pre-existing conscious level
800.26	Closed fracture of vault of skull with subarachnoid, subdural, and extradural hemorrhage, loss of consciousness of unspecified duration
800.29	Closed fracture of vault of skull with subarachnoid, subdural, and extradural hemorrhage, unspecified concussion
800.30	Closed fracture of vault of skull with other and unspecified intracranial hemorrhage, unspecified state of consciousness
800.32	Closed fracture of vault of skull with other and unspecified intracranial hemorrhage, brief (less than one hour) loss of consciousness
800.33	Closed fracture of vault of skull with other and unspecified intracranial hemorrhage, moderate (1-24 hours) loss of consciousness
800.34	Closed fracture of vault of skull with other and unspecified intracranial hemorrhage, prolonged (more than 24 hours) loss of consciousness and return to pre-existing conscious level
800.35	Closed fracture of vault of skull with other and unspecified intracranial hemorrhage, prolonged (more than 24 hours) loss of consciousness, without return to pre-existing conscious level
800.36	Closed fracture of vault of skull with other and unspecified intracranial hemorrhage, loss of consciousness of unspecified duration
800.39	Closed fracture of vault of skull with other and unspecified intracranial hemorrhage, unspecified concussion
800.40	Closed fracture of vault of skull with intracranial injury of other and unspecified nature, unspecified state of consciousness
800.42	Closed fracture of vault of skull with intracranial injury of other and unspecified nature, brief (less than one hour) loss of consciousness
800.43	Closed fracture of vault of skull with intracranial injury of other and unspecified nature, moderate (1-24 hours) loss of consciousness
800.44	Closed fracture of vault of skull with intracranial injury of other and unspecified nature, prolonged (more than 24 hours) loss of consciousness and return to pre-existing conscious level
800.45	Closed fracture of vault of skull with intracranial injury of other and unspecified nature, prolonged (more than 24 hours) loss of consciousness, without return to pre-existing conscious level
800.46	Closed fracture of vault of skull with intracranial injury of other and unspecified nature, loss of consciousness of unspecified duration

800.49	Closed fracture of vault of skull with intracranial injury of other and unspecified nature, unspecified concussion
800.52	Open fracture of vault of skull without mention of intracranial injury, brief (less than one hour) loss of consciousness
800.53	Open fracture of vault of skull without mention of intracranial injury, moderate (1-24 hours) loss of consciousness
800.54	Open fracture of vault of skull without mention of intracranial injury, prolonged (more than 24 hours) loss of consciousness and return to pre-existing conscious level
800.55	Open fracture of vault of skull without mention of intracranial injury, prolonged (more than 24 hours) loss of consciousness, without return to pre-existing conscious level
*800.6	Open fracture of vault of skull with cerebral laceration and contusion
*800.7	Open fracture of vault of skull with subarachnoid, subdural, and extradural hemorrhage
*800.8	Open fracture of vault of skull with other and unspecified intracranial hemorrhage
*800.9	Open fracture of vault of skull with intracranial injury of other and unspecified nature
801.02	Closed fracture of base of skull without mention of intracranial injury, brief (less than one hour) loss of consciousness
801.03	Closed fracture of base of skull without mention of intracranial injury, moderate (1-24 hours) loss of consciousness
801.04	Closed fracture of base of skull without mention of intracranial injury, prolonged (more than 24 hours) loss of consciousness and return to pre-existing conscious level
801.05	Closed fracture of base of skull without mention of intracranial injury, prolonged (more than 24 hours) loss of consciousness, without return to pre-existing conscious level
*801.1	Closed fracture of base of skull with cerebral laceration and contusion
*801.2	Closed fracture of base of skull with subarachnoid, subdural, and extradural hemorrhage
*801.3	Closed fracture of base of skull with other and unspecified intracranial hemorrhage
*801.4	Closed fracture of base of skull with intracranial injury of other and unspecified nature
801.52	Open fracture of base of skull without mention of intracranial injury, brief (less than one hour) loss of consciousness
801.53	Open fracture of base of skull without mention of intracranial injury, moderate (1-24 hours) loss of consciousness
801.54	Open fracture of base of skull without mention of intracranial injury, prolonged (more than 24 hours) loss of consciousness and return to pre-existing conscious level
801.55	Open fracture of base of skull without mention of intracranial injury, prolonged (more than 24 hours) loss of consciousness, without return to pre-existing conscious level
*801.6	Open fracture of base of skull with cerebral laceration and contusion
*801.7	Open fracture of base of skull with subarachnoid, subdural, and extradural hemorrhage
*801.8	Open fracture of base of skull with other and unspecified intracranial hemorrhage
*801.9	Open fracture of base of skull with intracranial injury of other and unspecified nature
803.02	Other closed skull fracture without mention of intracranial injury, brief (less than one hour) loss of consciousness
803.03	Other closed skull fracture without mention of intracranial injury, moderate (1-24 hours) loss of consciousness
803.04	Other closed skull fracture without mention of intracranial injury, prolonged (more than 24 hours) loss of consciousness and return to pre-existing conscious level
803.05	Other closed skull fracture without mention of intracranial injury, prolonged (more than 24 hours) loss of consciousness, without return to pre-existing conscious level
*803.1	Other closed skull fracture with cerebral laceration and contusion
*803.2	Other closed skull fracture with subarachnoid, subdural, and extradural hemorrhage
*803.3	Closed skull fracture with other and unspecified intracranial hemorrhage
*803.4	Other closed skull fracture with intracranial injury of other and unspecified nature
803.52	Other open skull fracture without mention of intracranial injury, brief (less than one hour) loss of consciousness
803.53	Other open skull fracture without mention of intracranial injury, moderate (1-24 hours) loss of consciousness
803.54	Other open skull fracture without mention of intracranial injury, prolonged (more than 24 hours) loss of consciousness and return to pre-existing conscious level
803.55	Other open skull fracture without mention of intracranial injury, prolonged (more than 24 hours) loss of consciousness, without return to pre-existing conscious level
*803.6	Other open skull fracture with cerebral laceration and contusion
*803.7	Other open skull fracture with subarachnoid, subdural, and extradural hemorrhage
*803.8	Other open skull fracture with other and unspecified intracranial hemorrhage
*803.9	Other open skull fracture with intracranial injury of other and unspecified nature

DRG 487 — continued

804.02	Closed fractures involving skull or face with other bones, without mention of intracranial injury, brief (less than one hour) loss of consciousness
804.03	Closed fractures involving skull or face with other bones, without mention of intracranial injury, moderate (1-24 hours) loss of consciousness
804.04	Closed fractures involving skull or face with other bones, without mention or intracranial injury, prolonged (more than 24 hours) loss of consciousness and return to pre-existing conscious level
804.05	Closed fractures involving skull of face with other bones, without mention of intracranial injury, prolonged (more than 24 hours) loss of consciousness, without return to pre-existing conscious level
804.06	Closed fractures involving skull of face with other bones, without mention of intracranial injury, loss of consciousness of unspecified duration
*804.1	Closed fractures involving skull or face with other bones, with cerebral laceration and contusion
*804.2	Closed fractures involving skull or face with other bones with subarachnoid, subdural, and extradural hemorrhage
*804.3	Closed fractures involving skull or face with other bones, with other and unspecified intracranial hemorrhage
804.40	Closed fractures involving skull or face with other bones, with intracranial injury of other and unspecified nature, unspecified state of consciousness
804.41	Closed fractures involving skull or face with other bones, with intracranial injury of other and unspecified nature, no loss of consciousness
804.42	Closed fractures involving skull or face with other bones, with intracranial injury of other and unspecified nature, brief (less than one hour) loss of consciousness
804.43	Closed fractures involving skull or face with other bones, with intracranial injury of other and unspecified nature, moderate (1-24 hours) loss of consciousness
804.44	Closed fractures involving skull or face with other bones, with intracranial injury of other and unspecified nature, prolonged (more than 24 hours) loss of consciousness and return to pre-existing conscious level
804.45	Closed fractures involving skull or face with other bones, with intracranial injury of other and unspecified nature, prolonged (more than 24 hours) loss of consciousness, without return to pre-existing conscious level
804.46	Closed fractures involving skull or face with other bones, with intracranial injury of other and unspecified nature, loss of consciousness of unspecified duration
804.52	Open fractures involving skull or face with other bones, without mention of intracranial injury, brief (less than one hour) loss of consciousness
804.53	Open fractures involving skull or face with other bones, without mention of intracranial injury, moderate (1-24 hours) loss of consciousness
804.54	Open fractures involving skull or face with other bones, without mention of intracranial injury, prolonged (more than 24 hours) loss of consciousness and return to pre-existing conscious level
804.55	Open fractures involving skull or face with other bones, without mention of intracranial injury, prolonged (more than 24 hours) loss of consciousness, without return to pre-existing conscious level
804.60	Open fractures involving skull or face with other bones, with cerebral laceration and contusion, unspecified state of consciousness
804.61	Open fractures involving skull or face with other bones, with cerebral laceration and contusion, no loss of consciousness
804.62	Open fractures involving skull or face with other bones, with cerebral laceration and contusion, brief (less than one hour) loss of consciousness
804.63	Open fractures involving skull or face with other bones, with cerebral laceration and contusion, moderate (1-24 hours) loss of consciousness
804.64	Open fractures involving skull or face with other bones, with cerebral laceration and contusion, prolonged (more than 24 hours) loss of consciousness and return to pre-existing conscious level
804.65	Open fractures involving skull or face with other bones, with cerebral laceration and contusion, prolonged (more than 24 hours) loss of consciousness, without return to pre-existing conscious level
804.66	Open fractures involving skull or face with other bones, with cerebral laceration and contusion, loss of consciousness of unspecified duration
*804.7	Open fractures involving skull or face with other bones with subarachnoid, subdural, and extradural hemorrhage

*804.8	Open fractures involving skull or face with other bones, with other and unspecified intracranial hemorrhage
*804.9	Open fractures involving skull or face with other bones, with intracranial injury of other and unspecified nature
850.2	Concussion with moderate (1-24 hours) loss of consciousness
850.3	Concussion with prolonged (more than 24 hours) loss of consciousness and return to pre-existing conscious level
850.4	Concussion with prolonged (more than 24 hours) loss of consciousness, without return to pre-existing conscious level
851.00	Cortex (cerebral) contusion without mention of open intracranial wound, state of consciousness unspecified
851.01	Cortex (cerebral) contusion without mention of open intracranial wound, no loss of consciousness
851.02	Cortex (cerebral) contusion without mention of open intracranial wound, brief (less than 1 hour) loss of consciousness
851.03	Cortex (cerebral) contusion without mention of open intracranial wound, moderate (1-24 hours) loss of consciousness
851.04	Cortex (cerebral) contusion without mention of open intracranial wound, prolonged (more than 24 hours) loss of consciousness and return to pre-exisiting conscious level
851.05	Cortex (cerebral) contusion without mention of open intracranial wound, prolonged (more than 24 hours) loss of consciousness, without return to pre-existing conscious level
851.06	Cortex (cerebral) contusion without mention of open intracranial wound, loss of consciousness of unspecified duration
851.09	Cortex (cerebral) contusion without mention of open intracranial wound, unspecified concussion
*851.1	Cortex (cerebral) contusion with open intracranial wound
*851.2	Cortex (cerebral) laceration without mention of open intracranial wound
*851.3	Cortex (cerebral) laceration with open intracranial wound
*851.4	Cerebellar or brain stem contusion without mention of open intracranial wound
*851.5	Cerebellar or brain stem contusion with open intracranial wound
*851.6	Cerebellar or brain stem laceration without mention of open intracranial wound
*851.7	Cerebellar or brain stem laceration with open intracranial wound
*851.8	Other and unspecified cerebral laceration and contusion, without mention of open intracranial wound
*851.9	Other and unspecified cerebral laceration and contusion, with open intracranial wound
*852	Subarachnoid, subdural, and extradural hemorrhage, following injury
*853	Other and unspecified intracranial hemorrhage following injury
*854	Intracranial injury of other and unspecified nature
900.01	Common carotid artery injury
900.02	External carotid artery injury
900.03	Internal carotid artery injury
900.1	Internal jugular vein injury
900.81	External jugular vein injury
900.82	Injury to multiple blood vessels of head and neck
925.1	Crushing injury of face and scalp
925.2	Crushing injury of neck
959.01	Head injury, unspecified
959.09	Injury of face and neck, other and unspecified

Significant Trauma Body Site Category 2—Chest

807.07	Closed fracture of seven ribs
807.08	Closed fracture of eight or more ribs
807.14	Open fracture of four ribs
807.15	Open fracture of five ribs
807.16	Open fracture of six ribs
807.17	Open fracture of seven ribs
807.18	Open fracture of eight or more ribs
807.19	Open fracture of multiple ribs, unspecified
807.3	Open fracture of sternum
807.4	Flail chest
807.5	Closed fracture of larynx and trachea
807.6	Open fracture of larynx and trachea
819.1	Multiple open fractures involving both upper limbs, and upper limb with rib(s) and sternum

** Code Range* ☑ *Optimization Potential* *Targeted Potential* T *Transfer DRG* SP *Special Payment*

DRG 487 — continued

839.71	Open dislocation, sternum
*860	Traumatic pneumothorax and hemothorax
*861	Injury to heart and lung
*862	Injury to other and unspecified intrathoracic organs
874.10	Open wound of larynx with trachea, complicated
874.11	Open wound of larynx, complicated
874.12	Open wound of trachea, complicated
901.0	Thoracic aorta injury
901.1	Innominate and subclavian artery injury
901.2	Superior vena cava injury
901.3	Innominate and subclavian vein injury
*901.4	Pulmonary blood vessel injury
901.83	Injury to multiple blood vessels of thorax
901.89	Injury to specified blood vessels of thorax, other
901.9	Injury to unspecified blood vessel of thorax
927.01	Crushing injury of scapular region
958.0	Air embolism as an early complication of trauma
958.1	Fat embolism as an early complication of trauma

Significant Trauma Body Site Category 3—Abdomen

863.0	Stomach injury without mention of open wound into cavity
863.1	Stomach injury with open wound into cavity
*863.2	Small intestine injury without mention of open wound into cavity
*863.3	Small intestine injury with open wound into cavity
*863.4	Colon or rectal injury without mention of open wound into cavity
*863.5	Injury to colon or rectum with open wound into cavity
863.81	Pancreas head injury without mention of open wound into cavity
863.82	Pancreas body injury without mention of open wound into cavity
863.83	Pancreas tail injury without mention of open wound into cavity
863.84	Pancreas injury, multiple and unspecified sites, without mention of open wound into cavity
863.85	Appendix injury without mention of open wound into cavity
863.89	Injury to other and unspecified gastrointestinal sites without mention of open wound into cavity
*863.9	Injury to other and unspecified gastrointestinal sites, with open wound into cavity
*864	Injury to liver
*865	Injury to spleen
868.02	Bile duct and gallbladder injury without mention of open wound into cavity
868.09	Injury to other and multiple intra-abdominal organs without mention of open wound into cavity
868.12	Bile duct and gallbladder injury, with open wound into cavity
868.13	Peritoneum injury with open wound into cavity
868.14	Retroperitoneum injury with open wound into cavity
868.19	Injury to other and multiple intra-abdominal organs, with open wound into cavity
*902	Injury to blood vessels of abdomen and pelvis

Significant Trauma Body Site Category 4—Kidney

*866	Injury to kidney
868.01	Adrenal gland injury without mention of open wound into cavity
868.11	Adrenal gland injury, with open wound into cavity

Significant Trauma Body Site Category 5—Urinary

*867	Injury to pelvic organs

Significant Trauma Body Site Category 6—Pelvis and Spine

805.6	Closed fracture of sacrum and coccyx without mention of spinal cord injury
805.7	Open fracture of sacrum and coccyx without mention of spinal cord injury
*806.0	Closed fracture of cervical vertebra with spinal cord injury
*806.1	Open fracture of cervical vertebra with spinal cord injury
*806.2	Closed fracture of dorsal (thoracic) vertebra with spinal cord injury
*806.3	Open fracture of dorsal vertebra with spinal cord injury
806.4	Closed fracture of lumbar spine with spinal cord injury
806.5	Open fracture of lumbar spine with spinal cord injury
806.60	Closed fracture of sacrum and coccyx with unspecified spinal cord injury

*806.7	Open fracture of sacrum and coccyx with spinal cord injury
806.8	Closed fracture of unspecified vertebra with spinal cord injury
806.9	Open fracture of unspecified vertebra with spinal cord injury
*808	Fracture of pelvis
809.1	Fracture of bones of trunk, open
*839.0	Closed dislocation, cervical vertebra
*839.1	Open dislocation, cervical vertebra
839.52	Open dislocation, sacrum
839.59	Open dislocation, other vertebra
868.03	Peritoneum injury without mention of open wound into cavity
868.04	Retroperitoneum injury without mention of open wound into cavity
926.11	Crushing injury of back
926.19	Crushing injury of other specified sites of trunk
926.8	Crushing injury of multiple sites of trunk
926.9	Crushing injury of unspecified site of trunk
*952	Spinal cord injury without evidence of spinal bone injury
953.5	Injury to lumbosacral plexus
953.8	Injury to multiple sites of nerve roots and spinal plexus
954.8	Injury to other specified nerve(s) of trunk, excluding shoulder and pelvic girdles
954.9	Injury to unspecified nerve of trunk, excluding shoulder and pelvic girdles

Significant Trauma Body Site Category 7—Upper Limb

*812.1	Open fracture of upper end of humerus
812.30	Open fracture of unspecified part of humerus
812.31	Open fracture of shaft of humerus
*812.5	Open fracture of lower end of humerus
*813.1	Open fracture of upper end of radius and ulna
*813.3	Open fracture of shaft of radius and ulna
*813.5	Open fracture of lower end of radius and ulna
*813.9	Open fracture of unspecified part of radius with ulna
818.1	Ill-defined open fractures of upper limb
*831.1	Open dislocation of shoulder
*832.1	Open dislocation of elbow
*887	Traumatic amputation of arm and hand (complete) (partial)
*903	Injury to blood vessels of upper extremity
*927.0	Crushing injury of shoulder and upper arm
*927.1	Crushing injury of elbow and forearm
927.8	Crushing injury of multiple sites of upper limb
927.9	Crushing injury of unspecified site of upper limb
953.4	Injury to brachial plexus
955.0	Injury to axillary nerve
955.1	Injury to median nerve
955.2	Injury to ulnar nerve
955.3	Injury to radial nerve
955.8	Injury to multiple nerves of shoulder girdle and upper limb
958.6	Volkmann's ischemic contracture

Significant Trauma Body Site Category 8—Lower Limb

*820	Fracture of neck of femur
*821	Fracture of other and unspecified parts of femur
*823.1	Open fracture of upper end of tibia and fibula
*823.3	Open fracture of shaft of tibia and fibula
*823.9	Open fracture of unspecified part of tibia and fibula
*828	Multiple fractures involving both lower limbs, lower with upper limb, and lower limb(s) with rib(s) and sternum
*835.1	Open dislocation of hip
*836.6	Other open dislocation of knee
837.1	Open dislocation of ankle
*896	Traumatic amputation of foot (complete) (partial)
*897	Traumatic amputation of leg(s) (complete) (partial)
904.0	Common femoral artery injury
904.1	Superficial femoral artery injury
904.2	Femoral vein injury
*904.4	Popliteal blood vessel vein

DRG 487 — continued

*904.5	Tibial blood vessel(s) injury
904.7	Injury to specified blood vessels of lower extremity, other
926.12	Crushing injury of buttock
*928.0	Crushing injury of hip and thigh
*928.1	Crushing injury of knee and lower leg
928.8	Crushing injury of multiple sites of lower limb
928.9	Crushing injury of unspecified site of lower limb
956.0	Injury to sciatic nerve
956.1	Injury to femoral nerve
956.2	Injury to posterior tibial nerve
956.3	Injury to peroneal nerve
956.8	Injury to multiple nerves of pelvic girdle and lower limb
956.9	Injury to unspecified nerve of pelvic girdle and lower limb

MDC 25
HUMAN IMMUNODEFICIENCY VIRUS INFECTIONS

The complete and up-to-date listing of ICD-9-CM diagnosis codes assigned to this MDC can be found online at www.ingenixonline.com/content/drg/resources.asp.

SURGICAL

[S] DRG 488 HIV with Extensive O.R. Procedure
GMLOS 11.8 AMLOS 16.4 RW 4.4353

Principal Diagnosis

042 Human immunodeficiency virus [HIV]

AND

Any operating room procedures excluding nonextensive operating room procedures (those procedures assigned to DRG 477)

OR

Secondary Diagnosis

042 Human immunodeficiency virus [HIV]

WITH

Principal Diagnosis

Any major or significant HIV-related condition listed in DRG 489 or DRG 490

AND

Any operating room procedures excluding nonextensive operating room procedures (those procedures assigned to DRG 477)

MDC 25
HUMAN IMMUNODEFICIENCY VIRUS INFECTIONS

The complete and up-to-date listing of ICD-9-CM diagnosis codes assigned to this MDC can be found online at www.ingenixonline.com/content/drg/resources.asp.

MEDICAL

M DRG 489 HIV with Major Related Condition

GMLOS 5.9 AMLOS 8.4 RW 1.8058 ☑

Principal Diagnosis

042 Human immunodeficiency virus [HIV]

AND

Major HIV-related Secondary Diagnosis

003.1	Salmonella septicemia
*003.2	Localized salmonella infections
003.8	Other specified salmonella infections
003.9	Unspecified salmonella infection
007.2	Coccidiosis
*010	Primary tuberculous infection
*011	Pulmonary tuberculosis
*012	Other respiratory tuberculosis
*013	Tuberculosis of meninges and central nervous system
*014	Tuberculosis of intestines, peritoneum, and mesenteric glands
*015	Tuberculosis of bones and joints
*016	Tuberculosis of genitourinary system
*017	Tuberculosis of other organs
*018	Miliary tuberculosis
031.2	Disseminated diseases due to other mycobacteria
031.8	Other specified diseases due to other mycobacteria
031.9	Unspecified diseases due to mycobacteria
*038	Septicemia
*039	Actinomycotic infections
046.3	Progressive multifocal leukoencephalopathy
046.8	Other specified slow virus infection of central nervous system
046.9	Unspecified slow virus infection of central nervous system
049.8	Other specified non-arthropod-borne viral diseases of central nervous system
049.9	Unspecified non-arthropod-borne viral disease of central nervous system
*053	Herpes zoster
*054	Herpes simplex
078.5	Cytomegaloviral disease
112.0	Candidiasis of mouth
112.3	Candidiasis of skin and nails
112.4	Candidiasis of lung
112.5	Disseminated candidiasis
*112.8	Candidiasis of other specified sites
112.9	Candidiasis of unspecified site
*114	Coccidioidomycosis
*115	Histoplasmosis
117.5	Cryptococcosis
118	Opportunistic mycoses
127.2	Strongyloidiasis
*130	Toxoplasmosis
136.3	Pneumocystosis
136.8	Other specified infectious and parasitic diseases
*176	Kaposi's sarcoma
*200.0	Reticulosarcoma
*200.2	Burkitt's tumor or lymphoma
*200.8	Other named variants of lymphosarcoma and reticulosarcoma

*202.8	Other malignant lymphomas
*290.1	Presenile dementia
294.9	Unspecified persistent mental disorders due to conditions classified elsewhere
298.9	Unspecified psychosis
310.9	Unspecified nonpsychotic mental disorder following organic brain damage
323.8	Other causes of encephalitis
323.9	Unspecified cause of encephalitis
336.9	Unspecified disease of spinal cord
341.9	Unspecified demyelinating disease of central nervous system
*348.3	Unspecified encephalopathy
348.9	Unspecified condition of brain
349.9	Unspecified disorders of nervous system
421.0	Acute and subacute bacterial endocarditis
421.9	Unspecified acute endocarditis
*422.9	Other and unspecified acute myocarditis
480.3	Pneumonia due to SARS-associated coronavirus
480.8	Pneumonia due to other virus not elsewhere classified
480.9	Unspecified viral pneumonia
481	Pneumococcal pneumonia (streptococcus pneumoniae pneumonia)
*482	Other bacterial pneumonia
486	Pneumonia, organism unspecified

OR

Principal Diagnosis

Any major HIV-related diagnosis listed above

AND

Secondary Diagnosis

042	Human immunodeficiency virus [HIV]

M DRG 490 HIV with or without Other Related Condition

GMLOS 3.8 AMLOS 5.4 RW 1.0639 ☑

Principal Diagnosis

042	Human immunodeficiency virus [HIV]

AND

Nonmajor HIV-related secondary diagnosis

*009	Ill-defined intestinal infections
047.9	Unspecified viral meningitis
*079.9	Unspecified viral and chlamydial infections, in conditions classified elsewhere and of unspecified site
*110	Dermatophytosis
*111	Dermatomycosis, other and unspecified
260	Kwashiorkor
261	Nutritional marasmus
262	Other severe protein-calorie malnutrition
*263	Other and unspecified protein-calorie malnutrition
*264	Vitamin A deficiency
*265	Thiamine and niacin deficiency states
*266	Deficiency of B-complex components
267	Ascorbic acid deficiency
*268	Vitamin D deficiency
*269	Other nutritional deficiencies
*276	Disorders of fluid, electrolyte, and acid-base balance
*279	Disorders involving the immune mechanism
*280	Iron deficiency anemias
*281	Other deficiency anemias
*283	Acquired hemolytic anemias
284.8	Other specified aplastic anemias
284.9	Unspecified aplastic anemia
285.9	Unspecified anemia
287.4	Secondary thrombocytopenia

DRG 490 — continued

287.5	Unspecified thrombocytopenia
288.0	Agranulocytosis
289.4	Hypersplenism
289.9	Unspecified diseases of blood and blood-forming organs
357.0	Acute infective polyneuritis
*357.8	Other inflammatory and toxic neuropathy
357.9	Unspecified inflammatory and toxic neuropathy
*362.1	Other background retinopathy and retinal vascular changes
*369	Blindness and low vision
425.9	Unspecified secondary cardiomyopathy
516.8	Other specified alveolar and parietoalveolar pneumonopathies
527.9	Unspecified disease of the salivary glands
528.6	Leukoplakia of oral mucosa, including tongue
*558	Other noninfectious gastroenteritis and colitis
579.9	Unspecified intestinal malabsorption
*580	Acute glomerulonephritis
*581	Nephrotic syndrome
*582	Chronic glomerulonephritis
*583	Nephritis and nephropathy, not specified as acute or chronic
683	Acute lymphadenitis
709.9	Unspecified disorder of skin and subcutaneous tissue
*711.0	Pyogenic arthritis
*711.9	Unspecified infective arthritis
*716.9	Unspecified arthropathy
729.2	Unspecified neuralgia, neuritis, and radiculitis
780.6	Fever
*780.7	Malaise and fatigue
780.8	Generalized hyperhidrosis
782.1	Rash and other nonspecific skin eruption
*783.2	Abnormal loss of weight
*783.4	Lack of expected normal physiological development
785.6	Enlargement of lymph nodes
*786.0	Dyspnea and respiratory abnormalities
789.1	Hepatomegaly
789.2	Splenomegaly
799.4	Cachexia

OR

Principal Diagnosis

Any principal diagnosis of nonmajor HIV-related condition

AND

Secondary Diagnosis

042	Human immunodeficiency virus [HIV]

DRGs Associated with All MDCs and Pre-MDC

DRGs Associated with All MDCs

[S] DRG 469 Principal Diagnosis Invalid as Discharge Diagnosis

GMLOS 0.0 AMLOS 0.0 RW 0.0000

Discharges with diagnosis not precise enough to assign case to a clinically coherent DRG

[S] DRG 470 Ungroupable

GMLOS 0.0 AMLOS 0.0 RW 0.0000

Discharges with invalid ICD-9-CM principal diagnosis or age, sex, or discharge status both invalid and necessary for DRG assignment

Unrelated Operating Room Procedures

SURGICAL

[S] DRG 468 Extensive O.R. Procedure Unrelated to Principal Diagnosis

GMLOS 9.7 AMLOS 13.2 RW 4.0031 [T]

Discharges with all operating room procedures not listed for DRG 476 and DRG 477 that are unrelated to principal diagnosis

[S] DRG 476 Prostatic O.R. Procedure Unrelated to Principal Diagnosis

GMLOS 7.4 AMLOS 10.5 RW 2.1822

Operating Room Procedures

60.0	Incision of prostate
60.12	Open biopsy of prostate
60.15	Biopsy of periprostatic tissue
60.18	Other diagnostic procedures on prostate and periprostatic tissue
*60.2	Transurethral prostatectomy
60.61	Local excision of lesion of prostate
60.69	Other prostatectomy
*60.8	Incision or excision of periprostatic tissue
60.93	Repair of prostate
60.94	Control of (postoperative) hemorrhage of prostate
60.95	Transurethral balloon dilation of the prostatic urethra
60.96	Transurethral destruction of prostate tissue by microwave thermotherapy
60.97	Other transurethral destruction of prostate tissue by other thermotherapy
60.99	Other operations on prostate

With or without operating room procedures listed under DRG 477

[S] DRG 477 Nonextensive O.R. Procedure Unrelated to Principal Diagnosis

GMLOS 5.8 AMLOS 8.7 RW 2.0607 ☑[T]

Operating Room Procedures

04.07	Other excision or avulsion of cranial and peripheral nerves
*04.4	Lysis of adhesions and decompression of cranial and peripheral nerves
05.23	Lumbar sympathectomy
06.02	Reopening of wound of thyroid field
08.11	Biopsy of eyelid
*08.2	Excision or destruction of lesion or tissue of eyelid
*08.3	Repair of blepharoptosis and lid retraction
*08.4	Repair of entropion or ectropion
*08.5	Other adjustment of lid position
*08.6	Reconstruction of eyelid with flaps or grafts

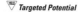

DRG 477 — continued

*08.7	Other reconstruction of eyelid
*08.9	Other operations on eyelids
09.0	Incision of lacrimal gland
*09.1	Diagnostic procedures on lacrimal system
*09.2	Excision of lesion or tissue of lacrimal gland
09.3	Other operations on lacrimal gland
*09.4	Manipulation of lacrimal passage
*09.5	Incision of lacrimal sac and passages
09.6	Excision of lacrimal sac and passage
*09.7	Repair of canaliculus and punctum
*09.8	Fistulization of lacrimal tract to nasal cavity
*09.9	Other operations on lacrimal system
10.0	Removal of embedded foreign body from conjunctiva by incision
10.1	Other incision of conjunctiva
*10.2	Diagnostic procedures on conjunctiva
*10.3	Excision or destruction of lesion or tissue of conjunctiva
*10.4	Conjunctivoplasty
10.5	Lysis of adhesions of conjunctiva and eyelid
10.6	Repair of laceration of conjunctiva
*10.9	Other operations on conjunctiva
11.0	Magnetic removal of embedded foreign body from cornea
11.1	Incision of cornea
*11.2	Diagnostic procedures on cornea
*11.3	Excision of pterygium
*11.4	Excision or destruction of tissue or other lesion of cornea
*11.5	Repair of cornea
*11.6	Corneal transplant
*11.7	Other reconstructive and refractive surgery on cornea
*11.9	Other operations on cornea
*12.0	Removal of intraocular foreign body from anterior segment of eye
*12.1	Iridotomy and simple iridectomy
*12.2	Diagnostic procedures on iris, ciliary body, sclera, and anterior chamber
*12.3	Iridoplasty and coreoplasty
*12.4	Excision or destruction of lesion of iris and ciliary body
*12.5	Facilitation of intraocular circulation
*12.6	Scleral fistulization
*12.7	Other procedures for relief of elevated intraocular pressure
*12.8	Operations on sclera
*12.9	Other operations on iris, ciliary body, and anterior chamber
*13.0	Removal of foreign body from lens
*13.1	Intracapsular extraction of lens
13.2	Extracapsular extraction of lens by linear extraction technique
13.3	Extracapsular extraction of lens by simple aspiration (and irrigation) technique
*13.4	Extracapsular extraction of lens by fragmentation and aspiration technique
*13.5	Other extracapsular extraction of lens
*13.6	Other cataract extraction
13.70	Insertion of pseudophakos, not otherwise specified
13.71	Insertion of intraocular lens prosthesis at time of cataract extraction, one-stage
13.72	Secondary insertion of intraocular lens prosthesis
13.8	Removal of implanted lens
13.9	Other operations on lens
*14.0	Removal of foreign body from posterior segment of eye
*14.1	Diagnostic procedures on retina, choroid, vitreous, and posterior chamber
14.21	Destruction of chorioretinal lesion by diathermy
14.22	Destruction of chorioretinal lesion by cryotherapy
14.26	Destruction of chorioretinal lesion by radiation therapy
14.27	Destruction of chorioretinal lesion by implantation of radiation source
14.29	Other destruction of chorioretinal lesion
14.31	Repair of retinal tear by diathermy
14.32	Repair of retinal tear by cryotherapy
14.39	Other repair of retinal tear
*14.4	Repair of retinal detachment with scleral buckling and implant

*14.5	Other repair of retinal detachment
14.6	Removal of surgically implanted material from posterior segment of eye
*14.7	Operations on vitreous
14.9	Other operations on retina, choroid, and posterior chamber
*15.0	Diagnostic procedures on extraocular muscles or tendons
*15.1	Operations on one extraocular muscle involving temporary detachment from globe
*15.2	Other operations on one extraocular muscle
15.3	Operations on two or more extraocular muscles involving temporary detachment from globe, one or both eyes
15.4	Other operations on two or more extraocular muscles, one or both eyes
15.5	Transposition of extraocular muscles
15.6	Revision of extraocular muscle surgery
15.7	Repair of injury of extraocular muscle
15.9	Other operations on extraocular muscles and tendons
*16.0	Orbitotomy
16.1	Removal of penetrating foreign body from eye, not otherwise specified
16.22	Diagnostic aspiration of orbit
16.23	Biopsy of eyeball and orbit
16.29	Other diagnostic procedures on orbit and eyeball
*16.3	Evisceration of eyeball
*16.4	Enucleation of eyeball
*16.5	Exenteration of orbital contents
*16.6	Secondary procedures after removal of eyeball
*16.7	Removal of ocular or orbital implant
*16.8	Repair of injury of eyeball and orbit
16.92	Excision of lesion of orbit
16.93	Excision of lesion of eye, unspecified structure
16.98	Other operations on orbit
16.99	Other operations on eyeball
18.21	Excision of preauricular sinus
18.31	Radical excision of lesion of external ear
18.39	Other excision of external ear
18.5	Surgical correction of prominent ear
18.6	Reconstruction of external auditory canal
18.71	Construction of auricle of ear
18.72	Reattachment of amputated ear
18.79	Other plastic repair of external ear
18.9	Other operations on external ear
*19.1	Stapedectomy
19.4	Myringoplasty
19.9	Other repair of middle ear
20.01	Myringotomy with insertion of tube
*20.2	Incision of mastoid and middle ear
20.32	Biopsy of middle and inner ear
20.39	Other diagnostic procedures on middle and inner ear
20.51	Excision of lesion of middle ear
21.09	Control of epistaxis by other means
21.5	Submucous resection of nasal septum
21.62	Fracture of the turbinates
21.69	Other turbinectomy
21.72	Open reduction of nasal fracture
21.82	Closure of nasal fistula
21.83	Total nasal reconstruction
21.84	Revision rhinoplasty
21.85	Augmentation rhinoplasty
21.86	Limited rhinoplasty
21.87	Other rhinoplasty
21.88	Other septoplasty
21.89	Other repair and plastic operations on nose
21.99	Other operations on nose
22.63	Ethmoidectomy
24.4	Excision of dental lesion of jaw
24.5	Alveoloplasty

DRG 477 — continued

25.1	Excision or destruction of lesion or tissue of tongue
26.12	Open biopsy of salivary gland or duct
*26.2	Excision of lesion of salivary gland
*26.3	Sialoadenectomy
27.21	Biopsy of bony palate
27.22	Biopsy of uvula and soft palate
*27.3	Excision of lesion or tissue of bony palate
27.42	Wide excision of lesion of lip
27.43	Other excision of lesion or tissue of lip
27.49	Other excision of mouth
27.53	Closure of fistula of mouth
27.54	Repair of cleft lip
27.55	Full-thickness skin graft to lip and mouth
27.56	Other skin graft to lip and mouth
27.57	Attachment of pedicle or flap graft to lip and mouth
27.59	Other plastic repair of mouth
*27.7	Operations on uvula
27.92	Incision of mouth, unspecified structure
27.99	Other operations on oral cavity
28.11	Biopsy of tonsils and adenoids
28.2	Tonsillectomy without adenoidectomy
29.4	Plastic operation on pharynx
30.09	Other excision or destruction of lesion or tissue of larynx
31.98	Other operations on larynx
33.27	Closed endoscopic biopsy of lung
34.3	Excision or destruction of lesion or tissue of mediastinum
34.4	Excision or destruction of lesion of chest wall
37.89	Revision or removal of pacemaker device
38.00	Incision of vessel, unspecified site
38.09	Incision of lower limb veins
38.21	Biopsy of blood vessel
38.59	Ligation and stripping of lower limb varicose veins
38.86	Other surgical occlusion of abdominal arteries
39.94	Replacement of vessel-to-vessel cannula
40.0	Incision of lymphatic structures
*40.1	Diagnostic procedures on lymphatic structures
40.21	Excision of deep cervical lymph node
40.23	Excision of axillary lymph node
40.24	Excision of inguinal lymph node
40.29	Simple excision of other lymphatic structure
40.3	Regional lymph node excision
43.49	Other destruction of lesion or tissue of stomach
44.15	Open biopsy of stomach
44.67	Laparoscopic procedures for creation of esophagogastric sphincteric competence
44.68	Laparoscopic gastroplasty
44.95	Laparoscopic gastric restrictive procedure
44.96	Laparoscopic revision of gastric restrictive procedure
44.97	Laparoscopic removal of gastric restrictive device(s)
44.98	(Laparoscopic) adjustment of size of adjustable gastric restrictive device
45.11	Transabdominal endoscopy of small intestine
45.21	Transabdominal endoscopy of large intestine
45.26	Open biopsy of large intestine
45.31	Other local excision of lesion of duodenum
45.32	Other destruction of lesion of duodenum
45.33	Local excision of lesion or tissue of small intestine, except duodenum
45.34	Other destruction of lesion of small intestine, except duodenum
45.41	Excision of lesion or tissue of large intestine
45.49	Other destruction of lesion of large intestine
46.41	Revision of stoma of small intestine
46.43	Other revision of stoma of large intestine
46.52	Closure of stoma of large intestine
48.25	Open biopsy of rectum

48.35	Local excision of rectal lesion or tissue
*48.8	Incision or excision of perirectal tissue or lesion
*49.1	Incision or excision of anal fistula
49.39	Other local excision or destruction of lesion or tissue of anus
49.44	Destruction of hemorrhoids by cryotherapy
49.45	Ligation of hemorrhoids
49.46	Excision of hemorrhoids
49.49	Other procedures on hemorrhoids
*49.5	Division of anal sphincter
49.6	Excision of anus
49.79	Other repair of anal sphincter
51.23	Laparoscopic cholecystectomy
51.99	Other operations on biliary tract
*53.0	Unilateral repair of inguinal hernia
*53.1	Bilateral repair of inguinal hernia
*53.2	Unilateral repair of femoral hernia
*53.3	Bilateral repair of femoral hernia
*53.4	Repair of umbilical hernia
53.51	Incisional hernia repair
*53.6	Repair of other hernia of anterior abdominal wall with graft or prosthesis
54.21	Laparoscopy
54.22	Biopsy of abdominal wall or umbilicus
54.29	Other diagnostic procedures on abdominal region
54.3	Excision or destruction of lesion or tissue of abdominal wall or umbilicus
54.4	Excision or destruction of peritoneal tissue
54.64	Suture of peritoneum
55.12	Pyelostomy
56.0	Transurethral removal of obstruction from ureter and renal pelvis
56.1	Ureteral meatotomy
56.2	Ureterotomy
56.39	Other diagnostic procedures on ureter
56.52	Revision of cutaneous uretero-ileostomy
57.22	Revision or closure of vesicostomy
57.33	Closed (transurethral) biopsy of bladder
57.39	Other diagnostic procedures on bladder
57.49	Other transurethral excision or destruction of lesion or tissue of bladder
57.59	Open excision or destruction of other lesion or tissue of bladder
57.82	Closure of cystostomy
57.91	Sphincterotomy of bladder
57.97	Replacement of electronic bladder stimulator
57.98	Removal of electronic bladder stimulator
58.0	Urethrotomy
58.1	Urethral meatotomy
58.5	Release of urethral stricture
58.99	Other operations on urethra and periurethral tissue
59.79	Other repair of urinary stress incontinence
61.2	Excision of hydrocele (of tunica vaginalis)
63.09	Other diagnostic procedures on spermatic cord, epididymis, and vas deferens
63.1	Excision of varicocele and hydrocele of spermatic cord
63.2	Excision of cyst of epididymis
63.3	Excision of other lesion or tissue of spermatic cord and epididymis
64.0	Circumcision
64.11	Biopsy of penis
64.2	Local excision or destruction of lesion of penis
64.49	Other repair of penis
64.92	Incision of penis
64.93	Division of penile adhesions
64.95	Insertion or replacement of non-inflatable penile prosthesis
64.96	Removal of internal prosthesis of penis
64.97	Insertion or replacement of inflatable penile prosthesis
64.98	Other operations on penis
64.99	Other operations on male genital organs
65.61	Other removal of both ovaries and tubes at same operative episode

***** Code Range** ☑ **Optimization Potential** **Targeted Potential** **T Transfer DRG** **SP Special Payment**

DRG 477 — continued

*66.2	Bilateral endoscopic destruction or occlusion of fallopian tubes
*66.3	Other bilateral destruction or occlusion of fallopian tubes
66.92	Unilateral destruction or occlusion of fallopian tube
*67.1	Diagnostic procedures on cervix
67.2	Conization of cervix
*67.3	Other excision or destruction of lesion or tissue of cervix
68.15	Closed biopsy of uterine ligaments
68.16	Closed biopsy of uterus
68.29	Other excision or destruction of lesion of uterus
*68.5	Vaginal hysterectomy
69.01	Dilation and curettage for termination of pregnancy
69.09	Other dilation and curettage of uterus
69.51	Aspiration curettage of uterus for termination of pregnancy
69.52	Aspiration curettage following delivery or abortion
69.95	Incision of cervix
70.14	Other vaginotomy
70.23	Biopsy of cul-de-sac
70.24	Vaginal biopsy
70.29	Other diagnostic procedures on vagina and cul-de-sac
*70.3	Local excision or destruction of vagina and cul-de-sac
70.76	Hymenorrhaphy
71.09	Other incision of vulva and perineum
*71.1	Diagnostic procedures on vulva
71.22	Incision of Bartholin's gland (cyst)
71.23	Marsupialization of Bartholin's gland (cyst)
71.24	Excision or other destruction of Bartholin's gland (cyst)
71.29	Other operations on Bartholin's gland
71.3	Other local excision or destruction of vulva and perineum
71.4	Operations on clitoris
71.71	Suture of laceration of vulva or perineum
71.79	Other repair of vulva and perineum
76.11	Biopsy of facial bone
76.2	Local excision or destruction of lesion of facial bone
77.38	Other division of tarsals and metatarsals
*77.4	Biopsy of bone
*77.5	Excision and repair of bunion and other toe deformities
*77.6	Local excision of lesion or tissue of bone
77.88	Other partial ostectomy of tarsals and metatarsals
77.98	Total ostectomy of tarsals and metatarsals
78.03	Bone graft of radius and ulna
*78.6	Removal of implanted device from bone
79.12	Closed reduction of fracture of radius and ulna with internal fixation
80.16	Other arthrotomy of knee
80.18	Other arthrotomy of foot and toe
80.26	Arthroscopy of knee
80.46	Division of joint capsule, ligament, or cartilage of knee
80.6	Excision of semilunar cartilage of knee
*80.7	Synovectomy
80.86	Other local excision or destruction of lesion of knee joint
80.88	Other local excision or destruction of lesion of joint of foot and toe
80.98	Other excision of joint of foot and toe
81.57	Replacement of joint of foot and toe
81.83	Other repair of shoulder
82.01	Exploration of tendon sheath of hand
82.09	Other incision of soft tissue of hand
82.11	Tenotomy of hand
82.21	Excision of lesion of tendon sheath of hand
82.29	Excision of other lesion of soft tissue of hand
82.41	Suture of tendon sheath of hand
82.45	Other suture of other tendon of hand
82.46	Suture of muscle or fascia of hand
*83.0	Incision of muscle, tendon, fascia, and bursa

83.13	Other tenotomy
83.19	Other division of soft tissue
83.21	Biopsy of soft tissue
83.32	Excision of lesion of muscle
83.39	Excision of lesion of other soft tissue
83.5	Bursectomy
*83.6	Suture of muscle, tendon, and fascia
84.01	Amputation and disarticulation of finger
85.12	Open biopsy of breast
85.20	Excision or destruction of breast tissue, not otherwise specified
85.21	Local excision of lesion of breast
85.23	Subtotal mastectomy
85.50	Augmentation mammoplasty, not otherwise specified
85.53	Unilateral breast implant
85.54	Bilateral breast implant
85.93	Revision of implant of breast
85.94	Removal of implant of breast
85.95	Insertion of breast tissue expander
85.96	Removal of breast tissue expander (s)
85.99	Other operations on the breast
86.21	Excision of pilonidal cyst or sinus
86.25	Dermabrasion
86.4	Radical excision of skin lesion
86.60	Free skin graft, not otherwise specified
86.62	Other skin graft to hand
86.65	Heterograft to skin
86.82	Facial rhytidectomy
86.83	Size reduction plastic operation
86.84	Relaxation of scar or web contracture of skin
86.89	Other repair and reconstruction of skin and subcutaneous tissue
87.53	Intraoperative cholangiogram
92.27	Implantation or insertion of radioactive elements
95.04	Eye examination under anesthesia

Pre-MDC

SURGICAL

S DRG 103 Heart Transplant or Implant of Heart Assist System

GMLOS 23.7 AMLOS 37.7 RW 18.5617

Operating Room Procedures

33.6	Combined heart-lung transplantation
37.51	Heart transplantation
37.66	Insertion of implantable heart assist system

OR

37.65	Implant of external heart assist system

AND

37.64	Removal of heart assist system

S DRG 480 Liver Transplant and/or Intestinal Transplant

GMLOS 13.7 AMLOS 18.0 RW 8.9693

Operating Room Procedure

46.97	Transplant of intestine
50.51	Auxiliary liver transplant
50.59	Other transplant of liver

** Code Range* ☑ *Optimization Potential* *Targeted Potential* T *Transfer DRG* SP *Special Payment*

S DRG 481 Bone Marrow Transplant

GMLOS 18.2 AMLOS 21.7 RW 6.2321

Operating Room Procedure

41.00 Bone marrow transplant, not otherwise specified
41.01 Autologous bone marrow transplant without purging
41.02 Allogeneic bone marrow transplant with purging
41.03 Allogeneic bone marrow transplant without purging
41.04 Autologous hematopoietic stem cell transplant without purging
41.05 Allogeneic hematopoietic stem cell transplant without purging
41.06 Cord blood stem cell transplant
41.07 Autologous hematopoietic stem cell transplant with purging
41.08 Allogeneic hematopoietic stem cell transplant with purging
41.09 Autologous bone marrow transplant with purging

S DRG 482 Tracheostomy for Face, Mouth and Neck Diagnoses

GMLOS 9.6 AMLOS 12.1 RW 3.3387 ☑ T

Principal Diagnosis

*012.3 Tuberculous laryngitis
032.0 Faucial diphtheria
032.1 Nasopharyngeal diphtheria
032.2 Anterior nasal diphtheria
032.3 Laryngeal diphtheria
034.0 Streptococcal sore throat
054.2 Herpetic gingivostomatitis
074.0 Herpangina
098.6 Gonococcal infection of pharynx
099.51 Chlamydia trachomatis infection of pharynx
101 Vincent's angina
102.5 Gangosa due to yaws
112.0 Candidiasis of mouth
*140 Malignant neoplasm of lip
*141 Malignant neoplasm of tongue
*142 Malignant neoplasm of major salivary glands
*143 Malignant neoplasm of gum
*144 Malignant neoplasm of floor of mouth
*145 Malignant neoplasm of other and unspecified parts of mouth
*146 Malignant neoplasm of oropharynx
*147 Malignant neoplasm of nasopharynx
*148 Malignant neoplasm of hypopharynx
*149 Malignant neoplasm of other and ill-defined sites within the lip, oral cavity, and pharynx
*160 Malignant neoplasm of nasal cavities, middle ear, and accessory sinuses
*161 Malignant neoplasm of larynx
165.0 Malignant neoplasm of upper respiratory tract, part unspecified
170.1 Malignant neoplasm of mandible
173.0 Other malignant neoplasm of skin of lip
176.2 Kaposi's sarcoma of palate
193 Malignant neoplasm of thyroid gland
195.0 Malignant neoplasm of head, face, and neck
196.0 Secondary and unspecified malignant neoplasm of lymph nodes of head, face, and neck
200.01 Reticulosarcoma of lymph nodes of head, face, and neck
200.11 Lymphosarcoma of lymph nodes of head, face, and neck
200.21 Burkitt's tumor or lymphoma of lymph nodes of head, face, and neck
200.81 Other named variants of lymphosarcoma and reticulosarcoma of lymph nodes of head, face, and neck
201.01 Hodgkin's paragranuloma of lymph nodes of head, face, and neck
201.11 Hodgkin's granuloma of lymph nodes of head, face, and neck
201.21 Hodgkin's sarcoma of lymph nodes of head, face, and neck
201.41 Hodgkin's disease, lymphocytic-histiocytic predominance of lymph nodes of head, face, and neck
201.51 Hodgkin's disease, nodular sclerosis, of lymph nodes of head, face, and neck
201.61 Hodgkin's disease, mixed cellularity, involving lymph nodes of head, face, and neck

S *Surgical* M *Medical* CC *CC Indicator* A *Age Restriction* ● *New DRG* ▲ *Revised DRG Title*

201.71	Hodgkin's disease, lymphocytic depletion, of lymph nodes of head, face, and neck
201.91	Hodgkin's disease, unspecified type, of lymph nodes of head, face, and neck
202.01	Nodular lymphoma of lymph nodes of head, face, and neck
202.11	Mycosis fungoides of lymph nodes of head, face, and neck
202.21	Sezary's disease of lymph nodes of head, face, and neck
202.31	Malignant histiocytosis of lymph nodes of head, face, and neck
202.41	Leukemic reticuloendotheliosis of lymph nodes of head, face, and neck
202.51	Letterer-Siwe disease of lymph nodes of head, face, and neck
202.61	Malignant mast cell tumors of lymph nodes of head, face, and neck
202.81	Other malignant lymphomas of lymph nodes of head, face, and neck
202.91	Other and unspecified malignant neoplasms of lymphoid and histiocytic tissue of lymph nodes of head, face, and neck
*210	Benign neoplasm of lip, oral cavity, and pharynx
212.0	Benign neoplasm of nasal cavities, middle ear, and accessory sinuses
212.1	Benign neoplasm of larynx
213.0	Benign neoplasm of bones of skull and face
213.1	Benign neoplasm of lower jaw bone
226	Benign neoplasm of thyroid glands
228.00	Hemangioma of unspecified site
228.01	Hemangioma of skin and subcutaneous tissue
228.09	Hemangioma of other sites
230.0	Carcinoma in situ of lip, oral cavity, and pharynx
231.0	Carcinoma in situ of larynx
235.0	Neoplasm of uncertain behavior of major salivary glands
235.1	Neoplasm of uncertain behavior of lip, oral cavity, and pharynx
235.6	Neoplasm of uncertain behavior of larynx
*242	Thyrotoxicosis with or without goiter
*245	Thyroiditis
246.2	Cyst of thyroid
246.3	Hemorrhage and infarction of thyroid
246.8	Other specified disorders of thyroid
246.9	Unspecified disorder of thyroid
*327.2	Organic sleep apnea
*327.3	Circadian rhythm sleep disorder
*327.4	Organic parasomnia
*327.5	Organic sleep related movement disorders
327.8	Other organic sleep disorders
460	Acute nasopharyngitis (common cold)
462	Acute pharyngitis
463	Acute tonsillitis
464.00	Acute laryngitis, without mention of obstruction
464.01	Acute laryngitis, with obstruction
*464.2	Acute laryngotracheitis
*464.3	Acute epiglottitis
464.4	Croup
464.50	Unspecified supraglottis, without mention of obstruction
464.51	Unspecified supraglottis, with obstruction
*465	Acute upper respiratory infections of multiple or unspecified sites
470	Deviated nasal septum
472.1	Chronic pharyngitis
472.2	Chronic nasopharyngitis
*474	Chronic disease of tonsils and adenoids
475	Peritonsillar abscess
476.0	Chronic laryngitis
476.1	Chronic laryngotracheitis
*478.2	Other diseases of pharynx, not elsewhere classified
*478.3	Paralysis of vocal cords or larynx
478.4	Polyp of vocal cord or larynx
478.5	Other diseases of vocal cords
478.6	Edema of larynx
*478.7	Other diseases of larynx, not elsewhere classified
478.8	Upper respiratory tract hypersensitivity reaction, site unspecified
478.9	Other and unspecified diseases of upper respiratory tract

Code Range ☑ ***Optimization Potential*** ***Targeted Potential*** ***Transfer DRG*** ***Special Payment***

DRG 482 — continued

*519.0	Tracheostomy complications
519.1	Other diseases of trachea and bronchus, not elsewhere classified
*520	Disorders of tooth development and eruption
*521	Diseases of hard tissues of teeth
*522	Diseases of pulp and periapical tissues
*523	Gingival and periodontal diseases
*524	Dentofacial anomalies, including malocclusion
*525	Other diseases and conditions of the teeth and supporting structures
*526	Diseases of the jaws
*527	Diseases of the salivary glands
*528	Diseases of the oral soft tissues, excluding lesions specific for gingiva and tongue
*529	Diseases and other conditions of the tongue
682.0	Cellulitis and abscess of face
682.1	Cellulitis and abscess of neck
748.2	Congenital web of larynx
748.3	Other congenital anomaly of larynx, trachea, and bronchus
*749.0	Cleft palate
*749.1	Cleft lip
*749.2	Cleft palate with cleft lip
750.0	Tongue tie
*750.1	Other congenital anomalies of tongue
750.21	Congenital absence of salivary gland
750.22	Congenital accessory salivary gland
750.23	Congenital atresia, salivary duct
750.24	Congenital fistula of salivary gland
750.25	Congenital fistula of lip
750.26	Other specified congenital anomalies of mouth
750.27	Congenital diverticulum of pharynx
750.29	Other specified congenital anomaly of pharynx
784.8	Hemorrhage from throat
*802.2	Mandible, closed fracture
*802.3	Mandible, open fracture
802.4	Malar and maxillary bones, closed fracture
802.5	Malar and maxillary bones, open fracture
802.6	Orbital floor (blow-out), closed fracture
802.7	Orbital floor (blow-out), open fracture
802.8	Other facial bones, closed fracture
802.9	Other facial bones, open fracture
807.5	Closed fracture of larynx and trachea
807.6	Open fracture of larynx and trachea
*830	Dislocation of jaw
*873.2	Open wound of nose, without mention of complication
*873.3	Open wound of nose, complicated
873.40	Open wound of face, unspecified site, without mention of complication
873.41	Open wound of cheek, without mention of complication
873.43	Open wound of lip, without mention of complication
873.44	Open wound of jaw, without mention of complication
873.50	Open wound of face, unspecified site, complicated
873.51	Open wound of cheek, complicated
873.53	Open wound of lip, complicated
873.54	Open wound of jaw, complicated
*873.6	Open wound of internal structures of mouth, without mention of complication
*873.7	Open wound of internal structure of mouth, complicated
874.00	Open wound of larynx with trachea, without mention of complication
874.01	Open wound of larynx, without mention of complication
874.02	Open wound of trachea, without mention of complication
874.10	Open wound of larynx with trachea, complicated
874.11	Open wound of larynx, complicated
874.12	Open wound of trachea, complicated
874.2	Open wound of thyroid gland, without mention of complication
874.3	Open wound of thyroid gland, complicated
874.4	Open wound of pharynx, without mention of complication

874.5 Open wound of pharynx, complicated
874.8 Open wound of other and unspecified parts of neck, without mention of complication
874.9 Open wound of other and unspecified parts of neck, complicated
900.82 Injury to multiple blood vessels of head and neck
900.89 Injury to other specified blood vessels of head and neck
900.9 Injury to unspecified blood vessel of head and neck
*925 Crushing injury of face, scalp, and neck
*933 Foreign body in pharynx and larynx
935.0 Foreign body in mouth
947.0 Burn of mouth and pharynx
*959.0 Injury, other and unspecified, head, face, and neck
V10.01 Personal history of malignant neoplasm of tongue
V10.02 Personal history of malignant neoplasm of other and unspecified parts of oral cavity and pharynx
V10.21 Personal history of malignant neoplasm of larynx

AND

Operating Room Procedures

31.21 Mediastinal tracheostomy
31.29 Other permanent tracheostomy

OR

Nonoperating Room Procedure

31.1 Temporary tracheostomy

OR

Any principal diagnosis

AND

Operating Room Procedures

30.3 Complete laryngectomy
30.4 Radical laryngectomy

DRG 483 No Longer Valid

GMLOS 0.0 AMLOS 0.0 RW 0.0000

Omitted in October 2004 grouper version

[S] DRG 495 Lung Transplant

GMLOS 14.0 AMLOS 17.3 RW 8.5736 ☑

Operating Room Procedure

*33.5 Lung transplant

[S] DRG 512 Simultaneous Pancreas/Kidney Transplant

GMLOS 10.7 AMLOS 12.8 RW 5.3660

Principal or Secondary Diabetes Mellitus Diagnosis

*250.0 Diabetes mellitus without mention of complication
*250.1 Diabetes with ketoacidosis
*250.2 Diabetes with hyperosmolarity
*250.3 Diabetes with other coma
*250.4 Diabetes with renal manifestations
*250.5 Diabetes with ophthalmic manifestations
*250.6 Diabetes with neurological manifestations
*250.7 Diabetes with peripheral circulatory disorders
*250.8 Diabetes with other specified manifestations
*250.9 Diabetes with unspecified complication

Principal or Secondary Diagnosis

403.01 Hypertensive kidney disease, malignant, with chronic kidney disease
403.11 Hypertensive kidney disease, benign, with chronic kidney disease
403.91 Hypertensive kidney disease, unspecified, with chronic kidney disease
404.02 Hypertensive heart and kidney disease, malignant, with chronic kidney disease

DRG 512 — continued

404.03	Hypertensive heart and kidney disease, malignant, with heart failure and chronic kidney disease
404.12	Hypertensive heart and kidney disease, benign, with chronic kidney disease
404.13	Hypertensive heart and kidney disease, benign, with heart failure and chronic kidney disease
404.92	Hypertensive heart and kidney disease, unspecified, with chronic kidney disease
404.93	Hypertensive heart and kidney disease, unspecified, with heart failure and chronic kidney disease
*585	Chronic kidney disease (CKD)
V42.0	Kidney replaced by transplant
V43.89	Other organ or tissue replaced by other means

AND

Any of the following procedure combinations

52.80	Pancreatic transplant, not otherwise specified
55.69	Other kidney transplantation

OR

52.82	Homotransplant of pancreas
55.69	Other kidney transplantation

S DRG 513 Pancreas Transplant

GMLOS 8.9 AMLOS 9.9 RW 5.9669

Principal or Secondary Diabetes Mellitus Diagnosis

*250.0	Diabetes mellitus without mention of complication
*250.1	Diabetes with ketoacidosis
*250.2	Diabetes with hyperosmolarity
*250.3	Diabetes with other coma
*250.4	Diabetes with renal manifestations
*250.5	Diabetes with ophthalmic manifestations
*250.6	Diabetes with neurological manifestations
*250.7	Diabetes with peripheral circulatory disorders
*250.8	Diabetes with other specified manifestations
*250.9	Diabetes with unspecified complication

AND

Principal or Secondary Diagnosis

403.01	Hypertensive kidney disease, malignant, with chronic kidney disease
403.11	Hypertensive kidney disease, benign, with chronic kidney disease
403.91	Hypertensive kidney disease, unspecified, with chronic kidney disease
404.02	Hypertensive heart and kidney disease, malignant, with chronic kidney disease
404.03	Hypertensive heart and kidney disease, malignant, with heart failure and chronic kidney disease
404.12	Hypertensive heart and kidney disease, benign, with chronic kidney disease
404.13	Hypertensive heart and kidney disease, benign, with heart failure and chronic kidney disease
404.92	Hypertensive heart and kidney disease, unspecified, with chronic kidney disease
404.93	Hypertensive heart and kidney disease, unspecified, with heart failure and chronic kidney disease
*585	Chronic kidney disease (CKD)
V42.0	Kidney replaced by transplant
V43.89	Other organ or tissue replaced by other means

AND

Operating Room Procedures

52.80	Pancreatic transplant, not otherwise specified
52.82	Homotransplant of pancreas

▲ [S] DRG 541 ECMO or Tracheostomy with Mechanical Ventilation 96+ Hours or Principal Diagnosis Except Face, Mouth, and Neck with Major O.R.

GMLOS 38.1 AMLOS 45.7 RW 19.8038 [T]

Principal Diagnosis

Any diagnosis except mouth, larynx and pharynx disorders listed under DRG 482

AND

Operating Room Procedures

31.21 Mediastinal tracheostomy
31.29 Other permanent tracheostomy
39.65 Extracorporeal membrane oxygenation (ECMO)

OR

Nonoperating Room Procedure

31.1 Temporary tracheostomy

AND

Major Operating Room Procedure

Any O.R. procedure not listed under DRG 476 or DRG 477

OR

Any principal diagnosis

AND

Operating Room Procedures

31.21 Mediastinal tracheostomy
31.29 Other permanent tracheostomy
39.65 Extracorporeal membrane oxygenation (ECMO)

OR

Nonoperating Room Procedure

31.1 Temporary tracheostomy

AND

Nonoperating Room Procedure

96.72 Continuous mechanical ventilation for 96 consecutive hours or more

AND

Major Operating Room Procedure

Any O.R. procedure not listed under DRG 476 or DRG 477

▲ [S] DRG 542 Tracheostomy with Mechanical Ventilation 96+ Hours or Principal Diagnosis Except Face, Mouth, and Neck without Major O.R.

GMLOS 29.1 AMLOS 35.1 RW 12.8719 ☑[T]

Principal Diagnosis

Any diagnosis except mouth, larynx and pharynx disorders listed under DRG 482

AND

Operating Room Procedures

31.21 Mediastinal tracheostomy
31.29 Other permanent tracheostomy

OR

Nonoperating Room Procedure

31.1 Temporary tracheostomy

OR

Any principal diagnosis

** Code Range* ☑ *Optimization Potential* *Targeted Potential* [T] *Transfer DRG* [SP] *Special Payment*

DRG 542 — continued

AND

Operating Room Procedures

31.21	Mediastinal tracheostomy
31.29	Other permanent tracheostomy

OR

Nonoperating Room Procedure

31.1	Temporary tracheostomy

AND

Nonoperating Room Procedure

96.72	Continuous mechanical ventilation for 96 consecutive hours or more

Alphabetic Index to Diseases

Code	Narrative	Page
786.7	Abnormal chest sounds	46
*795.0	Abnormal findings, nonspecific, pap smear, cervix and cervical HPV	177, 184
796.6	Abnormal findings, other nonspecific, neonatal screening	286
781.0	Abnormal involuntary movements	16
781.92	Abnormal posture	16
*388.4	Abnormal, auditory perception	36
791.7	Abnormal, findings, cells and casts, urine	164
792.5	Abnormal, findings, cloudy dialysis effluent	286
*795.3	Abnormal, findings, culture, nonspecific positive	249
792.3	Abnormal, findings, nonspecific, amniotic fluid	210
792.0	Abnormal, findings, nonspecific, cerebrospinal fluid	16
793.6	Abnormal, findings, nonspecific, radiological and other examination, abdominal area, including retroperitoneum	103
793.3	Abnormal, findings, nonspecific, radiological and other examination, biliary tract	111
793.89	Abnormal, findings, nonspecific, radiological and other examination, breast	143
793.4	Abnormal, findings, nonspecific, radiological and other examination, gastrointestinal tract	103
793.5	Abnormal, findings, nonspecific, radiological and other examination, genitourinary organs	164
793.2	Abnormal, findings, nonspecific, radiological and other examination, intrathoracic organ	87
793.1	Abnormal, findings, nonspecific, radiological and other examination, lung field	46
793.7	Abnormal, findings, nonspecific, radiological and other examination, musculoskeletal system	135
793.9	Abnormal, findings, nonspecific, radiological and other examination, other body site	286
793.0	Abnormal, findings, nonspecific, radiological and other examination, skull and head	16
792.4	Abnormal, findings, nonspecific, saliva	37
792.2	Abnormal, findings, nonspecific, semen	173
792.1	Abnormal, findings, nonspecific, stool contents	103
796.9	Abnormal, findings, other nonspecific	286

Code	Narrative	Page
796.5	Abnormal, findings, other nonspecific, antenatal screening	210
796.2	Abnormal, findings, other nonspecific, blood pressure, elevated without diagnosis of hypertension	91
796.3	Abnormal, findings, other nonspecific, blood pressure, low	91
796.4	Abnormal, findings, other nonspecific, clinical	231, 286
796.1	Abnormal, findings, other nonspecific, reflex	16
796.0	Abnormal, findings, other nonspecific, toxicological	274
791.9	Abnormal, findings, other nonspecific, urine	164
648.83	Abnormal, glucose tolerance, maternal, complicating pregnancy, childbirth, or the puerperium, antepartum condition or complication	207, 211
648.81	Abnormal, glucose tolerance, maternal, complicating pregnancy, childbirth, or the puerperium, delivered, with or without mention of antepartum condition	186, 198
648.82	Abnormal, glucose tolerance, maternal, complicating pregnancy, childbirth, or the puerperium, delivered, with mention of postpartum complication	186, 198
648.84	Abnormal, glucose tolerance, maternal, complicating pregnancy, childbirth, or the puerperium, postpartum condition or complication	204
648.80	Abnormal, glucose tolerance, maternal, complicating pregnancy, childbirth, or the puerperium, unspecified as to episode of care	212
793.80	Abnormal, mammogram, unspecified	143
795.2	Abnormal, nonspecific, findings, chromosomal analysis	287
794.31	Abnormal, nonspecific, findings, electrocardiogram [ECG] [EKG]	91
794.17	Abnormal, nonspecific, findings, electromyogram [EMG]	135
794.12	Abnormal, nonspecific, findings, electrooculogram	25
794.15	Abnormal, nonspecific, findings, function studies, auditory	37, 231
794.7	Abnormal, nonspecific, findings, function studies, basal metabolic rate	156
794.6	Abnormal, nonspecific, findings, function studies, endocrine	156
794.4	Abnormal, nonspecific, findings, function studies, kidney	164

Code	Narrative	Page
794.8	Abnormal, nonspecific, findings, function studies, liver	111
794.19	Abnormal, nonspecific, findings, function studies, nervous system, peripheral	16
794.9	Abnormal, nonspecific, findings, function studies, not elsewhere classified	164
794.14	Abnormal, nonspecific, findings, function studies, oculomotor	25
794.39	Abnormal, nonspecific, findings, function studies, other, cardiovascular	91
794.2	Abnormal, nonspecific, findings, function studies, pulmonary	47
794.11	Abnormal, nonspecific, findings, function studies, retinal	25
794.5	Abnormal, nonspecific, findings, function studies, thyroid	156
794.30	Abnormal, nonspecific, findings, function studies, unspecified, cardiovascular	91
794.16	Abnormal, nonspecific, findings, function studies, vestibular	37
795.4	Abnormal, nonspecific, findings, histological, other	231, 286
795.1	Abnormal, nonspecific, findings, pap smear, other site	43
794.13	Abnormal, nonspecific, findings, visually evoked potential	25
794.10	Abnormal, nonspecific, response to nerve stimulation, unspecified	16
*794.0	Abnormal, nonspecific, results, function studies, brain and central nervous system	16
792.9	Abnormal, other findings, nonspecific, body substances	286
785.3	Abnormal, other, heart sounds	91
631	Abnormal, other, product of conception	206
379.40	Abnormal, pupillary function, unspecified	22
786.4	Abnormal, sputum	46
*783.2	Abnormal, weight loss and underweight	310
654.03	Abnormalities, congenital, uterus, complicating pregnancy, childbirth, or the puerperium, antepartum condition or complication	207
654.01	Abnormalities, congenital, uterus, complicating pregnancy, childbirth, or the puerperium, delivered, with or without mention of antepartum condition	187, 199
654.02	Abnormalities, congenital, uterus, complicating pregnancy, childbirth, or the puerperium, delivered, with mention of postpartum complication	187, 199
654.04	Abnormalities, congenital, uterus, complicating pregnancy, childbirth, or the puerperium, postpartum condition or complication	204
654.00	Abnormalities, congenital, uterus, complicating pregnancy, childbirth, or the puerperium, unspecified as to episode of care	213
654.43	Abnormalities, other, shape or position, gravis uterus and neighboring structures, antepartum condition or complication	207
654.42	Abnormalities, other, shape or position, gravis uterus and neighboring structures, delivered, with mention of postpartum complication	187, 199
654.41	Abnormalities, other, shape or position, gravis uterus and neighboring structures, delivered, with or without mention of antepartum condition	187, 199
654.44	Abnormalities, other, shape or position, gravis uterus and neighboring structures, postpartum condition or complication	204
654.40	Abnormalities, other, shape or position, gravis uterus and neighboring structures, unspecified as to episode of care	213
655.13	Abnormality, chromosomal, fetus, affecting management of mother, antepartum condition or complication	208
655.11	Abnormality, chromosomal, fetus, affecting management of mother, delivered, with or without mention of antepartum condition	187, 199
655.10	Abnormality, chromosomal, fetus, affecting management of mother, unspecified as to episode of care	213
659.73	Abnormality, fetal heart rate or rhythm, antepartum condition or complication	208
659.71	Abnormality, fetal heart rate or rhythm, delivered, with or without mention of antepartum condition	188, 200
659.70	Abnormality, fetal heart rate or rhythm, unspecified as to episode of care or not applicable	188, 200
655.80	Abnormality, fetal, other known or suspected, not elsewhere classified, affecting management of mother, unspecified as to episode of care	213
655.81	Abnormality, fetal, other known or suspected, not elsewhere classified, affecting management of mother, delivered, with or without mention of antepartum condition	187, 199
655.83	Abnormality, fetal, other known or suspected, not elsewhere classified, affecting management of mother, antepartum condition or complication	208

 * Code Range

Code	Narrative	Page
655.93	Abnormality, fetal, unspecified, affecting management of mother, antepartum condition or complication	208
655.91	Abnormality, fetal, unspecified, affecting management of mother, delivered, with or without mention of antepartum condition	187, 199
655.90	Abnormality, fetal, unspecified, affecting management of mother, unspecified as to episode of care	213
781.2	Abnormality, gait	16
654.90	Abnormality, other and unspecified, organs and soft tissues, pelvis, complicating pregnancy, childbirth, or the puerperium, unspecified as to episode of care	213
654.91	Abnormality, other and unspecified, organs and soft tissues, pelvis, complicating pregnancy, childbirth, or the puerperium, delivered, with or without mention of antepartum condition	187, 199
654.92	Abnormality, other and unspecified, organs and soft tissues, pelvis, complicating pregnancy, childbirth, or the puerperium, delivered, with mention of postpartum complication	187, 199
654.93	Abnormality, other and unspecified, organs and soft tissues, pelvis, complicating pregnancy, childbirth, or the puerperium, antepartum condition or complication	207
654.94	Abnormality, other and unspecified, organs and soft tissues, pelvis, complicating pregnancy, childbirth, or the puerperium, postpartum condition or complication	204
654.60	Abnormality, other, congenital or acquired, cervix, complicating pregnancy, childbirth, or the puerperium, unspecified as to episode of care	213
654.61	Abnormality, other, congenital or acquired, cervix, complicating pregnancy, childbirth, or the puerperium, delivered, with or without mention of antepartum condition	187, 199
654.62	Abnormality, other, congenital or acquired, cervix, complicating pregnancy, childbirth, or the puerperium, delivered, with mention of postpartum complication	187, 199
654.63	Abnormality, other, congenital or acquired, cervix, complicating pregnancy, childbirth, or the puerperium, antepartum condition or complication	207
654.64	Abnormality, other, congenital or acquired, cervix, complicating pregnancy, childbirth, or the puerperium, postpartum condition or complication	204
654.70	Abnormality, other, congenital or acquired, vagina, complicating pregnancy, childbirth, or the puerperium, unspecified as to episode of care	213
654.71	Abnormality, other, congenital or acquired, vagina, complicating pregnancy, childbirth, or the puerperium, delivered, with or without mention of antepartum condition	187, 199
654.72	Abnormality, other, congenital or acquired, vagina, complicating pregnancy, childbirth, or the puerperium, delivered, with mention of postpartum complication	187, 199
654.73	Abnormality, other, congenital or acquired, vagina, complicating pregnancy, childbirth, or the puerperium, antepartum condition or complication	207
654.74	Abnormality, other, congenital or acquired, vagina, complicating pregnancy, childbirth, or the puerperium, postpartum condition or complication	204
654.80	Abnormality, other, congenital or acquired, vulva, complicating pregnancy, childbirth, or the puerperium, unspecified as to episode of care	213
654.81	Abnormality, other, congenital or acquired, vulva, complicating pregnancy, childbirth, or the puerperium, delivered, with or without mention of antepartum condition	187, 199
654.82	Abnormality, other, congenital or acquired, vulva, complicating pregnancy, childbirth, or the puerperium, delivered, with mention of postpartum complication	187, 199
654.83	Abnormality, other, congenital or acquired, vulva, complicating pregnancy, childbirth, or the puerperium, antepartum condition or complication	207
654.84	Abnormality, other, congenital or acquired, vulva, complicating pregnancy, childbirth, or the puerperium, postpartum condition or complication	204
653.73	Abnormality, other, fetal, causing disproportion, antepartum condition or complication	207
653.71	Abnormality, other, fetal, causing disproportion, delivered, with or without mention of antepartum condition	187, 199

Alphabetic Index to Diseases

Code	Narrative	Page
653.70	Abnormality, other, fetal, causing disproportion, unspecified as to episode of care	213
*788.6	Abnormality, other, urination	164
*790.0	Abnormality, red blood cells	234
251.5	Abnormality, secretion of gastrin	100
251.4	Abnormality, secretion of glucagon	156
661.93	Abnormality, unspecified, labor, antepartum condition or complication	208
661.91	Abnormality, unspecified, labor, delivered, with or without mention of antepartum condition	189, 201
661.90	Abnormality, unspecified, labor, unspecified as to episode of care	189, 201
*638	Abortion, failed attempted	206
*636	Abortion, induced, illegally	206
*635	Abortion, induced, legally	206
632	Abortion, missed	206
*634	Abortion, spontaneous	206
640.03	Abortion, threatened, antepartum condition or complication	205
640.01	Abortion, threatened, delivered, with or without mention of antepartum condition	185, 197
640.00	Abortion, threatened, unspecified as to episode of care	205
*637	Abortion, unspecified	206
006.3	Abscess, amebic, liver	110
006.4	Abscess, amebic, lung	42
566	Abscess, anal and rectal regions	104, 220, 227
675.13	Abscess, breast, associated with childbirth, antepartum condition or complication	209
675.12	Abscess, breast, associated with childbirth, delivered, with mention of postpartum complication	192, 197
675.11	Abscess, breast, associated with childbirth, delivered, with or without mention of antepartum condition	192, 197
675.14	Abscess, breast, associated with childbirth, postpartum condition or complication	205
675.10	Abscess, breast, associated with childbirth, unspecified as to episode of care	214
370.55	Abscess, corneal	21
616.3	Abscess, gland, Bartholin's	177, 183
569.5	Abscess, intestine	104
*324	Abscess, intracranial and intraspinal	8, 13, 218, 225
326	Abscess, intracranial, late effect of	15
572.0	Abscess, liver	220, 227
*572	Abscess, liver and sequela of chronic liver disease	111
*513	Abscess, lung, mediastinum	43, 220, 227
616.4	Abscess, other, vulva	177, 183

Code	Narrative	Page
478.22	Abscess, parapharyngeal	34, 219, 226
475	Abscess, peritonsillar	34, 319
590.2	Abscess, renal and perinephric	221, 228
478.24	Abscess, retropharyngeal	34, 219, 226
383.01	Abscess, subperiosteal, mastoid	218, 225
254.1	Abscess, thymus	218, 225
597.0	Abscess, urethral	221, 228
360.04	Abscess, vitreous	21
V45.71	Absence, acquired, breast	288
V45.78	Absence, acquired, eye	26
V45.77	Absence, acquired, genital organs	173, 178, 184
V45.72	Absence, acquired, intestine	288
V45.73	Absence, acquired, kidney	288
V45.76	Absence, acquired, lung	47
V45.79	Absence, acquired, organ, other	288
V45.75	Absence, acquired, stomach	288
V45.74	Absence, acquired, urinary tract, other parts	165
750.21	Absence, congenital, salivary gland	36, 320
756.13	Absence, congenital, vertebra	129
747.5	Absence, hypoplasia, congenital, umbilical artery	87
*305.0	Abuse, nondependent, alcohol	254
*305.7	Abuse, nondependent, amphetamine or related acting sympathomimetic	254
*305.8	Abuse, nondependent, antidepressant	254
*305.2	Abuse, nondependent, cannabis	254
*305.6	Abuse, nondependent, cocaine	254
*305.4	Abuse, nondependent, drug, sedative, hypnotic or anxiolytic	254
*305.3	Abuse, nondependent, hallucinogen	254
*305.5	Abuse, nondependent, opioid	254
*305.9	Abuse, nondependent, other, mixed or unspecified drug	254
305.1	Abuse, nondependent, tobacco	287
*133	Acariasis	146
750.22	Accessory, congenital, salivary gland	36, 320
791.6	Acetonuria	154
530.0	Achalasia and cardiospasm	102
536.0	Achlorhydia	102
368.54	Achromatopsia	24
775.7	Acidosis, metabolic, late, newborn	216, 223
428.41	Acute combined systolic and diastolic heart failure	59, 62, 64, 73, 77, 79
428.31	Acute diastolic heart failure	59, 61, 64, 73, 77, 79
420.91	Acute idiopathic pericarditis	59, 61, 63, 73, 76, 79

 *** Code Range***

Code	Narrative	Page
428.43	Acute on chronic combined systolic and diastolic heart failure	59, 62, 64, 73, 77, 79
428.33	Acute on chronic diastolic heart failure	59, 61, 64, 73, 77, 79
428.23	Acute on chronic systolic heart failure	59, 61, 64, 73, 77, 79
428.21	Acute systolic heart failure	59, 61, 64, 73, 77, 79
474.02	Adenoiditis and tonsillitis, chronic	34
474.01	Adenoiditis, chronic	34
091.4	Adenopathy, due to secondary syphilis	234
*364.7	Adhesions, disruptions, iris, ciliary body	23
614.6	Adhesions, peritoneal, pelvic, female	183
309.0	Adjustment disorder, with depressed mood	251
309.3	Adjustment disorder, with disturbance of conduct	251
309.4	Adjustment disorder, with mixed disturbance of emotions and conduct	251
*255	Adrenal gland disorders	156
726.2	Affections, other, not elsewhere classified, shoulder region	131
V58.2	Aftercare, blood transfusion, without reported diagnosis	289
*V58.7	Aftercare, following surgery	286
*V54.2	Aftercare, for healing fracture, pathologic	131
*V54.1	Aftercare, for healing fracture, traumatic	131
V51	Aftercare, involving use of plastic surgery	148
V58.5	Aftercare, orthodontics	286
*V54.0	Aftercare, orthopedic, involving removal, fracture plate, other internal fixation device	131
*V54.8	Aftercare, orthopedic, other	131
V54.9	Aftercare, orthopedic, unspecified	131
*V58.4	Aftercare, other, following surgery	286
*V58.8	Aftercare, procedures, other specified	287
V58.3	Aftercare, surgical dressings and sutures	289
V58.9	Aftercare, unspecified	287
748.5	Agenesis, hypoplasia, and dysplasia, congenital, lung	47
288.0	Agranulocytosis	310
136.0	Ainhum	249
784.61	Alexia and dyslexia	253
733.7	Algoneurodystrophy	134
117.6	Allescheriosis, petriellidosis	218, 225
091.82	Alopecia, syphilitic, secondary, early	146
780.09	Alteration, other, consciousness	13
780.02	Alteration, transient, awareness	252
*495	Alveolitis, extrinsic allergic	45

Code	Narrative	Page
*368.0	Amblyopia ex anopsia	24
006.1	Amebiasis, intestinal, chronic, without mention of abscess	102
006.9	Amebiasis, unspecified	247
006.5	Amebic brain abscess	7, 12
300.12	Amnesia, dissociative	251
437.7	Amnesia, transient global	11
*887	Amputation, traumatic, complete, partial, arm and hand	272, 298, 305
*896	Amputation, traumatic, complete, partial, foot	272, 298, 305
*897	Amputation, traumatic, complete, partial, leg(s)	272, 298, 305
*886	Amputation, traumatic, complete, partial, other finger(s)	272, 298
*885	Amputation, traumatic, complete, partial, thumb	272, 297
*895	Amputation, traumatic, complete, partial, toe(s)	272, 298
277.3	Amyloidosis	128
*126	Ancylostomiasis, necatoriasis	102
*284	Anemia, aplastic	234
284.8	Anemia, aplastic, other specified	309
284.9	Anemia, aplastic, unspecified	309
*283	Anemia, hemolytic, acquired	309
283.9	Anemia, hemolytic, acquired, unspecified	218, 225, 234
283.0	Anemia, hemolytic, autoimmune	234
*282	Anemia, hemolytic, hereditary	234
*283.1	Anemia, hemolytic, non-autoimmune	218, 225, 234
648.23	Anemia, maternal, complicating pregnancy, childbirth, or the puerperium, antepartum condition or complication	207, 210
648.22	Anemia, maternal, complicating pregnancy, childbirth, or the puerperium, delivered, with mention of postpartum complication	186, 198
648.21	Anemia, maternal, complicating pregnancy, childbirth, or the puerperium, delivered, with or without mention of antepartum condition	186, 198
648.24	Anemia, maternal, complicating pregnancy, childbirth, or the puerperium, postpartum condition or complication	204
648.20	Anemia, maternal, complicating pregnancy, childbirth, or the puerperium, unspecified as to episode of care	212
776.6	Anemia, of prematurity	216, 223
285.1	Anemia, posthemorrhagic, acute	218, 225
285.9	Anemia, unspecified	309
*285	Anemias, other and unspecified	234
414.11	Aneurysm of coronary vessels	58, 61, 63, 73, 76, 79

Alphabetic Index to Diseases

Code	Narrative	Page
093.0	Aneurysm, aorta, specified as syphilitic	88
442.3	Aneurysm, artery, extremity, lower	86
442.0	Aneurysm, artery, extremity, upper	86
442.2	Aneurysm, artery, iliac	86
*442.8	Aneurysm, artery, other specified	86
442.1	Aneurysm, artery, renal	165
442.9	Aneurysm, artery, unspecified site	86
*441.0	Aneurysm, dissecting, aorta	83, 86
*414.1	Aneurysm, heart	82, 91
414.10	Aneurysm, heart	58, 61, 63, 73, 76, 79, 219, 226
437.3	Aneurysm, nonruptured, brain	16
094.87	Aneurysm, ruptured cerebral, syphilitic	5, 15
441.3	Aneurysm, ruptured, aorta, abdominal	59, 62, 64, 73, 77, 79, 86
441.1	Aneurysm, ruptured, aorta, thoracic	59, 62, 64, 73, 77, 79, 86
441.6	Aneurysm, ruptured, aorta, thoracoabdominal	59, 62, 64, 73, 77, 79, 86
441.5	Aneurysm, ruptured, aorta, unspecified site	59, 62, 64, 73, 77, 79, 86
441.4	Aneurysm, without rupture, aorta, abdominal	86
441.2	Aneurysm, without rupture, aorta, thoracic	86
441.7	Aneurysm, without rupture, aorta, thoracoabdominal	86
441.9	Aneurysm, without rupture, aorta, unspecified site	86
*446.2	Angiitis, hypersensitivity	128
413.0	Angina, decubitus	89
413.9	Angina, other, unspecified	89
413.1	Angina, prinzmetal	89
101	Angina, Vincent's	34, 318
569.85	Angiodysplasia, intestine, with hemorrhage	100
569.84	Angiodysplasia, intestine, without hemorrhage	104
537.83	Angiodysplasia, stomach and duodenum, with hemorrhage	100
537.82	Angiodysplasia, stomach and duodenum, without hemorrhage	102
127.1	Anisakiasis	102
379.41	Anisocoria	22
*367.3	Anisometropia, aniseikonia	24
*718.5	Ankylosis, joint	130
*740	Anomalies, anencephalus and similar	16, 221, 228
744.1	Anomalies, congenital, accessory auricle	36, 230
*744.0	Anomalies, congenital, ear, causing impairment of hearing	36
*743	Anomalies, congenital, eye	25
*752.1	Anomalies, congenital, fallopian tubes, broad ligaments	183
*747.4	Anomalies, congenital, great veins	89
*752.6	Anomalies, congenital, hypospadias, epispadias, and other penile	173
751.4	Anomalies, congenital, intestinal, fixation	104
759.7	Anomalies, congenital, multiple, so described	135
759.89	Anomalies, congenital, other specified	135
750.4	Anomalies, congenital, other specified, esophagus	104
*752.8	Anomalies, congenital, other specified, genital organs	173
752.89	Anomalies, congenital, other specified, genital organs	177, 183
750.26	Anomalies, congenital, other specified, mouth	37, 320
*756.8	Anomalies, congenital, other specified, muscle, tendon, fascia, and connective tissue	135
750.29	Anomalies, congenital, other specified, pharynx	36, 320
750.7	Anomalies, congenital, other specified, stomach	104
750.8	Anomalies, congenital, other specified, upper alimentary tract	104
745.8	Anomalies, congenital, other, bulbus cordis and cardiac septal closure	88
751.69	Anomalies, congenital, other, gallbladder, bile ducts, and liver	111
*755	Anomalies, congenital, other, limb	135
*750.1	Anomalies, congenital, other, tongue	37, 320
752.0	Anomalies, congenital, ovaries	177, 183
751.7	Anomalies, congenital, pancreas	110
747.3	Anomalies, congenital, pulmonary artery	89
*746.0	Anomalies, congenital, pulmonary valve	88
756.0	Anomalies, congenital, skull and face bones	135
759.9	Anomalies, congenital, unspecified	287
752.10	Anomalies, congenital, unspecified, fallopian tubes, broad ligaments	177
748.60	Anomalies, congenital, unspecified, lung	47
750.9	Anomalies, congenital, unspecified, upper alimentary tract	104
*753	Anomalies, congenital, urinary system	165
757.2	Anomalies, dermatoglyphic	148
746.84	Anomalies, obstructive, congenital, not elsewhere classified, heart	88
*744.2	Anomalies, other specified, congenital, ear	36

Alphabetic Index to Diseases

* Code Range

Code	Narrative	Page
426.7	Anomaly, atrioventricular excitation	219, 226
747.83	Anomaly, circulatory system, persistent fetal circulation	215, 222
*756.7	Anomaly, congenital, abdominal wall	105
759.1	Anomaly, congenital, adrenal gland	156
758.5	Anomaly, congenital, autosomal, other conditions due to	287
747.81	Anomaly, congenital, cerebrovascular system	16
*752.4	Anomaly, congenital, cervix, vagina and external female genitalia	183
758.4	Anomaly, congenital, chromosomal, translocation, autosomal, balanced, normal individual	287
*749.1	Anomaly, congenital, cleft lip	320
*749.0	Anomaly, congenital, cleft palate	320
*749	Anomaly, congenital, cleft palate and cleft lip	37
*749.2	Anomaly, congenital, cleft palate with cleft lip	320
*747.1	Anomaly, congenital, coarctation, aorta	89
745.3	Anomaly, congenital, common ventricle	88
759.4	Anomaly, congenital, conjoined twins	105, 221, 228
746.82	Anomaly, congenital, cor triatriatum	88
746.85	Anomaly, congenital, coronary artery	88
748.4	Anomaly, congenital, cystic lung	47
756.6	Anomaly, congenital, diaphragm	47
751.0	Anomaly, congenital, diverticulum, Meckel's	101
759.2	Anomaly, congenital, endocrine glands, other	156
756.15	Anomaly, congenital, fusion, spine, vertebra	129
759.6	Anomaly, congenital, harmartosis, other, not elsewhere classified	236, 244
746.86	Anomaly, congenital, heart block	89
756.14	Anomaly, congenital, hemivertebra	129
752.42	Anomaly, congenital, imperforate hymen	177
752.7	Anomaly, congenital, indeterminate sex and pseudohermaphroditism	173, 177, 183
746.87	Anomaly, congenital, malposition, heart and cardiac apex	88
756.9	Anomaly, congenital, other and unspecified, musculoskeletal system	135
747.89	Anomaly, congenital, other specified, circulatory system	87
751.8	Anomaly, congenital, other specified, digestive system	104
746.89	Anomaly, congenital, other specified, heart	88
757.8	Anomaly, congenital, other specified, integument	148
754.89	Anomaly, congenital, other specified, nonteratogenic	135
748.8	Anomaly, congenital, other specified, respiratory system	47
757.39	Anomaly, congenital, other specified, skin	148, 231
*747.2	Anomaly, congenital, other, aorta	89
752.49	Anomaly, congenital, other, cervix, vagina and external female genitalia	177
752.19	Anomaly, congenital, other, fallopian tubes and broad ligaments	177
751.5	Anomaly, congenital, other, intestine	104
748.3	Anomaly, congenital, other, larynx, trachea, and bronchus	36, 320
748.69	Anomaly, congenital, other, lung	47
748.1	Anomaly, congenital, other, nose	36
*747.6	Anomaly, congenital, other, peripheral vascular system	87
756.3	Anomaly, congenital, other, ribs and sternum	47
756.19	Anomaly, congenital, other, spine	129
752.3	Anomaly, congenital, other, uterine	177, 183
747.0	Anomaly, congenital, patent ductus arteriosus	88
754.82	Anomaly, congenital, pectus carinatum	47
754.81	Anomaly, congenital, pectus excavatum	47
757.33	Anomaly, congenital, pigmentation, skin	148, 231
756.2	Anomaly, congenital, rib, cervical	135
759.5	Anomaly, congenital, sclerosis, tuberculous	16
759.3	Anomaly, congenital, situs inversus	105
757.6	Anomaly, congenital, specified, breast	143
757.4	Anomaly, congenital, specified, hair	148
757.5	Anomaly, congenital, specified, nails	148
756.10	Anomaly, congenital, spine, unspecified	129
759.0	Anomaly, congenital, spleen	235
756.12	Anomaly, congenital, spondylolisthesis	129
756.11	Anomaly, congenital, spondylolysis, lumbosacral region	129
750.0	Anomaly, congenital, tongue tie	37, 320
*745.1	Anomaly, congenital, transposition, great vessels	88
745.0	Anomaly, congenital, truncus, common	88
*752.5	Anomaly, congenital, undescended and retractile, testicle	172, 231

Alphabetic Index to Diseases

* Code Range

Code	Narrative	Page
752.40	Anomaly, congenital, unspecified, cervix, vagina and external female genitalia	177
747.9	Anomaly, congenital, unspecified, circulatory system	87
751.9	Anomaly, congenital, unspecified, digestive system	104
751.60	Anomaly, congenital, unspecified, gallbladder, bile ducts, and liver	111
752.9	Anomaly, congenital, unspecified, genital organs	173, 177, 183
746.9	Anomaly, congenital, unspecified, heart	88
757.9	Anomaly, congenital, unspecified, integument	148
748.9	Anomaly, congenital, unspecified, respiratory system	47
747.82	Anomaly, congenital, vessel, spinal	16
*524	Anomaly, dentofacial, including malocclusion	37, 320
378.85	Anomaly, divergence, binocular eye movement	25
746.2	Anomaly, Ebstein's	88
*742	Anomaly, other congenital, nervous system	16, 221, 228
744.89	Anomaly, other specified, congenital, face and neck	36
379.49	Anomaly, other, pupillary function	22
744.3	Anomaly, unspecified, congenital, ear	36
744.9	Anomaly, unspecified, congenital, face and neck	148
307.1	Anorexia nervosa	252
022.0	Anthrax, cutaneous	146
022.2	Anthrax, gastrointestinal	103
022.8	Anthrax, other specified manifestations	248
022.1	Anthrax, pulmonary	42
022.3	Anthrax, septicemia,	246
022.9	Anthrax, unspecified	248
*300.0	Anxiety states	251
093.1	Aortitis, syphilitic	88
*379.3	Aphakia, other disorders, lens	25
784.3	Aphasia	16
327.27	Apnea, sleep, organic, central, in conditions classifiable elsewhere	15
*327.2	Apnea, sleep, organic	319
327.23	Apnea, sleep, organic, obstructive, (adult) (pediatric)	35
327.29	Apnea, sleep, organic, other	35
327.21	Apnea, sleep, organic, primary central	15
327.20	Apnea, sleep, organic, unspecified	35
780.57	Apnea, sleep, unspecified	16
*540	Appendicitis, acute	104
540.1	Appendicitis, acute, with peritoneal abscess	96
540.0	Appendicitis, acute, with peritonitis, generalized	96
542	Appendicitis, other	104
541	Appendicitis, unqualified	104
379.45	Argyll-Robertson pupil, atypical	10
327.41	Arousals, confusional	15
427.5	Arrest, cardiac	59, 61, 63, 73, 77, 79, 82, 84, 86, 219, 226
733.91	Arrest, development or growth, bone	134
799.1	Arrest, respiratory	47, 221, 228
440.1	Arteriosclerosis, renal artery	165
437.4	Arteritis, cerebral	13
446.5	Arteritis, giant cell	128
447.6	Arteritis, unspecified	128
*716.2	Arthritis, allergic	130
*711.1	Arthritis, associated with Reiter's disease and nonspecific urethriti	128
*716.3	Arthritis, climacteric	130
056.71	Arthritis, due to rubella	129
098.50	Arthritis, gonococcal	128
*711.9	Arthritis, infective, unspecified	128, 310
*711.0	Arthritis, pyogenic	128, 310
711.06	Arthritis, pyogenic, lower leg	123
714.0	Arthritis, rheumatoid	128
714.2	Arthritis, rheumatoid with visceral or systemic involvement	128
003.23	Arthritis, Salmonella	128
*712	Arthropathies, crystal	129
*713	Arthropathy, associated with disorders, other, classified elsewhere	129
*711.7	Arthropathy, associated with helminthiasis	128
*711.8	Arthropathy, associated with infectious, parasitic diseases, other	128
*711.6	Arthropathy, associated with mycoses	128
*711.4	Arthropathy, associated with other bacterial diseases	128
*711.5	Arthropathy, associated with other viral diseases	129
274.0	Arthropathy, gouty	129
*711.2	Arthropathy, in Behcet's syndrome	128
036.82	Arthropathy, meningococcal	128, 217, 224
*716.8	Arthropathy, other specified	130
*711.3	Arthropathy, postdysenteric	129
714.4	Arthropathy, postrheumatic, rheumatic	129
*716.4	Arthropathy, transient	130
*716.1	Arthropathy, traumatic	129
*716.9	Arthropathy, unspecified	130, 310
501	Asbestosis	45
127.0	Ascariasis	102
789.5	Ascites	286

*Code Range

Code	Narrative	Page
117.3	Aspergillosis	218, 225
518.6	Aspergillosis, allergic bronchopulmonary	45
*799.0	Asphyxia and hypoxemia	47
768.6	Asphyxia, mild or moderate, newborn	230, 231
768.5	Asphyxia, severe, newborn	216, 223
*770.1	Aspiration, fetal and newborn	216, 221, 223
493.20	Asthma, chronic, obstructive, unspecified	44
493.22	Asthma, chronic, obstructive, with (acute) exacerbation	44
493.21	Asthma, chronic, obstructive, with status asthmaticus	44
*493.0	Asthma, extrinsic	46
493.01	Asthma, extrinsic, with status asthmaticus	219, 227
*493.1	Asthma, intrinsic	46
493.11	Asthma, intrinsic, with status asthmaticus	220, 227
*493.8	Asthma, other forms	46
*493.9	Asthma, unspecified	46
493.91	Asthma, unspecified, with status asthmaticus	220, 227
*367.2	Astigmatism	24
331.89	Ataxia, cerebral	10
770.4	Atelectasis, primary, fetus or newborn	216, 223
*445.0	Atheroembolism, extremities	86
445.81	Atheroembolism, kidney	60, 62, 65, 74, 78, 80, 165
445.89	Atheroembolism, other site	86
440.0	Atherosclerosis, aorta	86
440.8	Atherosclerosis, arteries, other specified	86
*440.3	Atherosclerosis, bypass graft, extremities	86
437.0	Atherosclerosis, cerebral	11
*414.0	Atherosclerosis, coronary	87
440.9	Atherosclerosis, generalized and unspecified	86
*440.2	Atherosclerosis, native arteries, extremities	86
440.24	Atherosclerosis, native arteries, extremities, with gangrene	219, 226
596.4	Atony, bladder	221, 228
751.2	Atresia and stenosis, congenital, large intestine, rectum, anal canal	104
751.1	Atresia and stenosis, congenital, small intestine	104
746.1	Atresia and stenosis, congenital, tricuspid	88
751.61	Atresia, congenital, biliary	111
748.0	Atresia, congenital, choanal	36
750.23	Atresia, congenital, salivary duct	36, 320
377.16	Atrophy, hereditary, optic	22

Code	Narrative	Page
356.1	Atrophy, muscle, peroneal	11
377.14	Atrophy, optic disc, cupping, glaucomatous	25
377.13	Atrophy, optic, associated with retinal dystrophies	25
094.84	Atrophy, optic, syphilitic	22
377.10	Atrophy, optic, unspecified	22
377.15	Atrophy, partial, optic	22
377.12	Atrophy, postinflammatory, optic	22
377.11	Atrophy, primary, optic	22
608.3	Atrophy, testis	172
333.93	Attacks, shuddering, benign	15
V55.3	Attention, openings, artificial, colostomy	105
V55.5	Attention, openings, artificial, cystostomy	165
V55.4	Attention, openings, artificial, digestive tract	105
V55.1	Attention, openings, artificial, gastrostomy	105
V55.2	Attention, openings, artificial, ileostomy	105
V55.8	Attention, openings, artificial, other specified	288
V55.0	Attention, openings, artificial, tracheostomy	47
V55.9	Attention, openings, artificial, unspecified	288
V55.6	Attention, openings, artificial, urinary tract	165
V55.7	Attention, openings, artificial, vagina	178, 184
*299.0	Autistic disorder	252
790.7	Bacteremia	221, 228, 246
607.81	Balanitis xerotica obliterans	172
607.1	Balanoposthitis	172
993.0	Barotrauma, otitic	34
993.1	Barotrauma, sinus	34
530.85	Barrett's esophagus	100
136.1	Behcet's syndrome	128
791.4	Biliuria	111
921.0	Black eye, unspecified	25
116.0	Blastomycosis	218, 225
492.0	Bleb, emphysematous	44
374.34	Blepharochalasis	24
374.46	Blepharophimosis	24
333.81	Blepharospasm	23
*369	Blindness, low vision	24, 310
*368.6	Blindness, night	24
426.52	Block, bundle branch, right, and left fascicular block, anterior	82
426.51	Block, bundle branch, right, and left fascicular block, posterior	82
426.0	Block, complete, atrioventricular	59, 61, 73, 76, 79, 82, 219, 226

Code	Narrative	Page
426.12	Block, Mobitz, type II, atrioventricular	82
426.13	Block, other second-degree, atrioventricular	82
426.53	Block, other, bundle branch, bilateral	59, 61, 73, 76, 79, 82, 219, 226
426.3	Block, other, bundle branch, left	82
426.54	Block, trifascicular	59, 61, 73, 77, 79, 82, 219, 226
426.10	Block, unspecified, atrioventricular	82
*V85	Body Mass Index	289
V85.4	Body Mass Index, 40 and over, adult	154
005.1	Botulism	247
754.42	Bowing, congenital, femur	135
754.44	Bowing, congenital, long bones of leg, unspecified	135
754.43	Bowing, congenital, tibia and fibula	135
669.61	Breech extraction, without mention of indication, delivered, with or without mention of antepartum condition	191, 202
669.60	Breech extraction, without mention of indication, unspecified as to episode of care	191, 202
652.13	Breech or other malpresentation, converted to cephalic presentation, antepartum condition or complication	207
652.11	Breech or other malpresentation, converted to cephalic presentation, delivered, with or without mention of antepartum condition	187, 198
652.10	Breech or other malpresentation, converted to cephalic presentation, unspecified as to episode of care	212
*494	Bronchiectasis	44
748.61	Bronchiectasis, congenital	45
*466	Bronchitis and bronchiolitis, acute	46
506.0	Bronchitis and pneumonitis due to fumes, vapors, chemical	47
491.1	Bronchitis, chronic, mucopurulent	44
*491.2	Bronchitis, chronic, obstructive	44
491.8	Bronchitis, chronic, other	44
491.0	Bronchitis, chronic, simple	46
491.9	Bronchitis, chronic, unspecified	44
490	Bronchitis, not specified as acute or chronic	46
485	Bronchopneumonia, organism unspecified	45, 83, 219, 226
*023	Brucellosis	248
307.51	Bulimia nervosa	253
727.1	Bunion	134
*200.2	Burkitt's tumor or lymphoma	308
200.21	Burkitt's tumor or lymphoma, lymph nodes, head, face, and neck	318

Code	Narrative	Page
948.11	Burn, any degree, 10-19% of body surface, with 10-19% third degree	277, 278, 281, 282
948.10	Burn, any degree, 10-19% of body surface, with less than 10% third degree or unspecified	283
948.21	Burn, any degree, 20-29% of body surface, with 10-19% third degree	276, 280
948.22	Burn, any degree, 20-29% of body surface, with 20-29% third degree	276, 280
948.20	Burn, any degree, 20-29% of body surface, with less than 10% third degree or unspecified	283
948.31	Burn, any degree, 30-39% of body surface, with 10-19% third degree	276, 280
948.32	Burn, any degree, 30-39% of body surface, with 20-29% third degree	276, 280
948.33	Burn, any degree, 30-39% of body surface, with 30-39% third degree	276, 280
948.30	Burn, any degree, 30-39% of body surface, with less than 10% third degree or unspecified	283
948.41	Burn, any degree, 40-49% of body surface, with 10-19% third degree	276, 280
948.42	Burn, any degree, 40-49% of body surface, with 20-29% third degree	276, 280
948.43	Burn, any degree, 40-49% of body surface, with 30-39% third degree	276, 280
948.44	Burn, any degree, 40-49% of body surface, with 40-49% third degree	276, 280
948.40	Burn, any degree, 40-49% of body surface, with less than 10% third degree or unspecified	283
948.51	Burn, any degree, 50-59% of body surface, with 10-19% third degree	276, 280
948.52	Burn, any degree, 50-59% of body surface, with 20-29% third degree	276, 280
948.53	Burn, any degree, 50-59% of body surface, with 30-39% third degree	276, 280
948.54	Burn, any degree, 50-59% of body surface, with 40-49% third degree	276, 280
948.55	Burn, any degree, 50-59% of body surface, with 50-59% third degree	276, 280
948.50	Burn, any degree, 50-59% of body surface, with less than 10% third degree or unspecified	283
948.61	Burn, any degree, 60-69% of body surface, with 10-19% third degree	276, 280
948.62	Burn, any degree, 60-69% of body surface, with 20-29% third degree	276, 280
948.63	Burn, any degree, 60-69% of body surface, with 30-39% third degree	276, 280
948.64	Burn, any degree, 60-69% of body surface, with 40-49% third degree	276, 280
948.65	Burn, any degree, 60-69% of body surface, with 50-59% third degree	276, 280
948.66	Burn, any degree, 60-69% of body surface, with 60-69% third degree	276, 280
948.60	Burn, any degree, 60-69% of body surface, with less than 10% third degree or unspecified	283
948.71	Burn, any degree, 70-79% of body surface, with 10-19% third degree	276, 280

** Code Range*

Code	Narrative	Page
948.72	Burn, any degree, 70-79% of body surface, with 20-29% third degree	276, 280
948.73	Burn, any degree, 70-79% of body surface, with 30-39% third degree	276, 280
948.74	Burn, any degree, 70-79% of body surface, with 40-49% third degree	276, 280
948.75	Burn, any degree, 70-79% of body surface, with 50-59% third degree	276, 280
948.76	Burn, any degree, 70-79% of body surface, with 60-69% third degree	276, 280
948.77	Burn, any degree, 70-79% of body surface, with 70-79% third degree	276, 280
948.70	Burn, any degree, 70-79% of body surface, with less than 10% third degree or unspecified	283
948.81	Burn, any degree, 80-89% of body surface, with 10-19% third degree	276, 280
948.82	Burn, any degree, 80-89% of body surface, with 20-29% third degree	276, 280
948.83	Burn, any degree, 80-89% of body surface, with 30-39% third degree	276, 280
948.84	Burn, any degree, 80-89% of body surface, with 40-49% third degree	276, 280
948.85	Burn, any degree, 80-89% of body surface, with 50-59% third degree	276, 280
948.86	Burn, any degree, 80-89% of body surface, with 60-69% third degree	276, 280
948.87	Burn, any degree, 80-89% of body surface, with 70-79% third degree	276, 280
948.88	Burn, any degree, 80-89% of body surface, with 80-89% third degree	277, 281
948.80	Burn, any degree, 80-89% of body surface, with less than 10% third degree or unspecified	283
948.91	Burn, any degree, 90% or more of body surface, with 10-19% third degree	277, 281
948.92	Burn, any degree, 90% or more of body surface, with 20-29% third degree	277, 281
948.93	Burn, any degree, 90% or more of body surface, with 30-39% third degree	277, 281
948.94	Burn, any degree, 90% or more of body surface, with 40-49% third degree	277, 281
948.95	Burn, any degree, 90% or more of body surface, with 50-59% third degree	277, 281
948.96	Burn, any degree, 90% or more of body surface, with 60-69% third degree	277, 281
948.97	Burn, any degree, 90% or more of body surface, with 70-79% third degree	277, 281
948.98	Burn, any degree, 90% or more of body surface, with 80-89% third degree	277, 281
948.99	Burn, any degree, 90% or more of body surface, with 90% or more third degree	277, 281
948.90	Burn, any degree, 90% or more of body surface, with less than 10% third degree or unspecified	283
948.00	Burn, any degree, less than 10% of body surface, with less than 10% third degree or unspecified	283
941.24	Burn, blisters, epidermal loss [second degree], chin	283
941.21	Burn, blisters, epidermal loss [second degree], ear (any part)	283
941.22	Burn, blisters, epidermal loss [second degree], eye (with other parts of face, head, and neck)	26
941.29	Burn, blisters, epidermal loss [second degree], face, head and neck multiple sites (except eye)	283
941.20	Burn, blisters, epidermal loss [second degree], face, head, and neck, unspecified site	283
941.27	Burn, blisters, epidermal loss [second degree], forehead and cheek	283
941.23	Burn, blisters, epidermal loss [second degree], lip(s)	283
*945.2	Burn, blisters, epidermal loss [second degree], lower limb	283
946.2	Burn, blisters, epidermal loss [second degree], multiple, specified sites	283
949.2	Burn, blisters, epidermal loss [second degree], multiple, unspecified sites	284
941.28	Burn, blisters, epidermal loss [second degree], neck	283
941.25	Burn, blisters, epidermal loss [second degree], nose (septum)	283
941.26	Burn, blisters, epidermal loss [second degree], scalp	283
*942.2	Burn, blisters, epidermal loss [second degree], trunk	283
*943.2	Burn, blisters, epidermal loss [second degree], upper limb, except wrist and hand	283
*944.2	Burn, blisters, epidermal loss, [second degree], wrist(s) and hand(s)	283
*940	Burn, confined to eye and adnexa	26
*945.5	Burn, deep necrosis [deep third degree] with loss body part, lower limb	277, 278, 281, 282
946.5	Burn, deep necrosis [deep third degree] with loss body part, multiple, specified sites	277, 278, 281, 282
949.5	Burn, deep necrosis [deep third degree] with loss body part, multiple, unspecified sites	277, 278, 281, 282
*943.5	Burn, deep necrosis [deep third degree] with loss body part, upper limb, except wrist and hand	277, 278, 281, 282
*944.5	Burn, deep necrosis [deep third degree] with loss body part, wrist(s) and hand(s)	277, 278, 281, 282
*945.4	Burn, deep necrosis [deep third degree] without loss body part, lower limb	277, 278, 281, 282

Alphabetic Index to Diseases

*** Code Range**

Code	Narrative	Page
946.4	Burn, deep necrosis [deep third degree] without loss body part, multiple, specified sites	277, 278, 281, 282
949.4	Burn, deep necrosis [deep third degree] without loss body part, multiple, unspecified sites	277, 278, 281, 282
*943.4	Burn, deep necrosis [deep third degree] without loss body part, upper limb, except wrist and hand	277, 278, 281, 282
*944.4	Burn, deep necrosis [deep third degree] without loss body part, wrist(s) and hand(s)	277, 278, 281, 282
941.52	Burn, deep necrosis [deep third degree], with loss body part, eye (with other parts of face, head, and neck)	26
*941.5	Burn, deep necrosis [deep third degree], with loss body part, face, head, and neck	277, 278, 281, 282
*942.5	Burn, deep necrosis [deep third degree], with loss body part, trunk	277, 278, 281, 282
941.42	Burn, deep necrosis [deep third degree], without loss body part, eye (with other parts of face, head, and neck)	26
*941.4	Burn, deep necrosis [deep third degree], without loss body part, face, head, and neck	277, 278, 281, 282
*942.4	Burn, deep necrosis [deep third degree], without loss body part, trunk	277, 278, 281, 282
941.14	Burn, erythema [first degree], chin	283
941.11	Burn, erythema [first degree], ear (any part)	283
941.12	Burn, erythema [first degree], eye (with other parts of face, head, and neck)	26
941.19	Burn, erythema [first degree], face, head and neck multiple sites (except eye)	283
941.10	Burn, erythema [first degree], face, head, and neck, unspecified site	283
941.17	Burn, erythema [first degree], forehead and cheek	283
941.13	Burn, erythema [first degree], lip(s)	283
*945.1	Burn, erythema [first degree], lower limb	283
946.1	Burn, erythema [first degree], multiple, specified sites	283
949.1	Burn, erythema [first degree], multiple, unspecified sites	284
941.18	Burn, erythema [first degree], neck	283
941.15	Burn, erythema [first degree], nose (septum)	283
941.16	Burn, erythema [first degree], scalp	283
*942.1	Burn, erythema [first degree], trunk	283
*943.1	Burn, erythema [first degree], upper limb, except wrist and hand	283
*944.1	Burn, erythema [first degree], wrist(s) and hand(s)	283
947.2	Burn, esophagus	105
947.3	Burn, gastrointestinal tract	105

Code	Narrative	Page
947.1	Burn, larynx, trachea and lung	47, 279
947.0	Burn, mouth and pharynx	37, 321
947.8	Burn, organs, internal, other specified sites	283
947.9	Burn, organs, internal, unspecified sites	283
941.32	Burn, skin loss, full-thickness [third degree NOS], eye (with other parts of face, head, and neck)	26
*941.3	Burn, skin loss, full-thickness [third degree NOS], face, head, and neck	277, 278, 281, 282
*945.3	Burn, skin loss, full-thickness [third degree NOS], lower limb	277, 278, 281, 282
946.3	Burn, skin loss, full-thickness [third degree NOS], multiple, specified sites	277, 278, 281, 282
949.3	Burn, skin loss, full-thickness [third degree NOS], multiple, unspecified sites	277, 278, 281, 282
*942.3	Burn, skin loss, full-thickness [third degree NOS], trunk	277, 278, 281, 282
*943.3	Burn, skin loss, full-thickness [third degree NOS], upper limb, except wrist and hand	277, 278, 281, 282
*944.3	Burn, skin loss, full-thickness [third degree NOS], wrist(s) and hand(s)	277, 278, 281, 282
941.04	Burn, unspecified degree, chin	282
941.01	Burn, unspecified degree, ear (any part)	282
941.02	Burn, unspecified degree, eye (with other parts of face, head, and neck)	26
941.09	Burn, unspecified degree, face, head and neck multiple sites (except eye)	283
941.00	Burn, unspecified degree, face, head, and neck, unspecified site	282
941.07	Burn, unspecified degree, forehead and cheek	283
941.03	Burn, unspecified degree, lip(s)	282
*945.0	Burn, unspecified degree, lower limb	283
946.0	Burn, unspecified degree, multiple, specified sites	283
949.0	Burn, unspecified degree, multiple, unspecified sites	284
941.08	Burn, unspecified degree, neck	283
941.05	Burn, unspecified degree, nose (septum)	283
941.06	Burn, unspecified degree, scalp	283
*942.0	Burn, unspecified degree, trunk	283
*943.0	Burn, unspecified degree, upper limb, except wrist and hand	283
*944.0	Burn, unspecified degree, wrist(s) and hand(s)	283
947.4	Burn, vagina and uterus	178, 184
098.52	Bursitis, gonococcal	128
727.3	Bursitis, other	131
727.2	Bursitis, specific, occupational origin	131

*Code Range

Code	Narrative	Page
726.71	Bursitis, tendinitis, Achilles	131
799.4	Cachexia	286, 310
594.0	Calculus, bladder, diverticulum	165
*592	Calculus, kidney and ureter	163
594.1	Calculus, other, bladder	163
594.2	Calculus, urethra	163
594.8	Calculus, urinary tract, lower, specified site	163
594.9	Calculus, urinary tract, lower, unspecified	163
375.31	Canaliculitis, acute, lacrimal	21
112.5	Candidiasis, disseminated	217, 224, 249, 308
112.84	Candidiasis, esophagus	102, 217, 224
112.85	Candidiasis, intestine	102, 217, 224
112.4	Candidiasis, lung	42, 217, 224, 308
112.0	Candidiasis, mouth	37, 308, 318
*112.8	Candidiasis, other specified sites	308
112.89	Candidiasis, other specified sites	249
112.2	Candidiasis, other urogenital sites	172, 176, 182
112.3	Candidiasis, skin and nails	146, 308
112.9	Candidiasis, unspecified site	249, 308
112.1	Candidiasis, vulvovaginitis	176, 182
127.5	Capillariasis	102
726.0	Capsulitis, adhesive, shoulder	131
*680	Carbuncle and furuncle	143
230.5	Carcinoma in situ, anal sphincter	99
230.6	Carcinoma in situ, anus, unspecified	99
233.7	Carcinoma in situ, bladder	157, 162
233.0	Carcinoma in situ, breast	136, 142
231.2	Carcinoma in situ, bronchus and lung	43
233.1	Carcinoma in situ, cervix uteri	174, 179
230.3	Carcinoma in situ, colon	99
230.9	Carcinoma in situ, digestive organs, other and unspecified	99
232.2	Carcinoma in situ, ear and external auditory canal	147
230.1	Carcinoma in situ, esophagus	99
234.0	Carcinoma in situ, eye	23
233.3	Carcinoma in situ, female genital organs, other and unspecified	174, 179
230.7	Carcinoma in situ, intestine, other and unspecified	99
231.0	Carcinoma in situ, larynx	33, 319
230.0	Carcinoma in situ, lip, oral cavity, pharynx	33, 319
230.8	Carcinoma in situ, liver and biliary system	108, 110
233.6	Carcinoma in situ, male genital organs, other and unspecified	167, 169, 171

Code	Narrative	Page
234.8	Carcinoma in situ, other specified sites	236, 244
233.5	Carcinoma in situ, penis	167, 169, 171
233.4	Carcinoma in situ, prostate	167, 169, 171
230.4	Carcinoma in situ, rectum	99
231.8	Carcinoma in situ, respiratory system other specified parts	43
231.9	Carcinoma in situ, respiratory system, part unspecified	43
232.4	Carcinoma in situ, scalp and skin of neck	147
234.9	Carcinoma in situ, site unspecified	236, 244
232.1	Carcinoma in situ, skin of eyelid, including canthus	22
232.3	Carcinoma in situ, skin of face, other and unspecified parts	147
232.0	Carcinoma in situ, skin of lip	147
232.7	Carcinoma in situ, skin of lower limb	147
232.5	Carcinoma in situ, skin of trunk, except scrotum	147
232.6	Carcinoma in situ, skin of upper limb	147
232.8	Carcinoma in situ, skin, other specified sites	147
232.9	Carcinoma in situ, skin, site unspecified	147
230.2	Carcinoma in situ, stomach	99
231.1	Carcinoma in situ, trachea	43
233.9	Carcinoma in situ, urinary organs, other and unspecified	157, 162
233.2	Carcinoma in situ, uterus, other and unspecified parts	174, 179
429.3	Cardiomegaly	87
*425	Cardiomyopathy	91
425.5	Cardiomyopathy, alcoholic	84
425.7	Cardiomyopathy, nutritional and metabolic, classified elsewhere	84
425.2	Cardiomyopathy, obscure, of Africa	84
425.8	Cardiomyopathy, other diseases classified elsewhere	84, 219, 226
425.4	Cardiomyopathy, other, primary	84
674.53	Cardiomyopathy, peripartum, antepartum condition or complication	209
674.52	Cardiomyopathy, peripartum, delivered, with mention of postpartum condition	192
674.51	Cardiomyopathy, peripartum, delivered, with or without mention of antepartum condition	192
674.54	Cardiomyopathy, peripartum, postpartum condition or complication	205
674.50	Cardiomyopathy, peripartum, unspecified as to episode of care or not applicable	214
425.9	Cardiomyopathy, secondary, unspecified	84, 310

*** Code Range**

Code	Narrative	Page
074.20	Carditis, Coxsackie, unspecified	90
*036.4	Carditis, meningococcal	217, 224
036.40	Carditis, meningococcal, unspecified	90
V57.0	Care, involving, rehabilitation procedures, breathing exercises	288
V57.4	Care, involving, rehabilitation procedures, orthoptic training	288
V57.81	Care, involving, rehabilitation procedures, orthotic training	289
V57.89	Care, involving, rehabilitation procedures, other specified	286
V57.1	Care, involving, rehabilitation procedures, physical therapy	286
V57.3	Care, involving, rehabilitation procedures, speech therapy	286
V57.9	Care, involving, rehabilitation procedures, unspecified	286
V02.2	Carrier or suspected carrier, amebiasis	287
*V02.5	Carrier or suspected carrier, bacterial diseases, other specified	287
V02.0	Carrier or suspected carrier, cholera	287
V02.4	Carrier or suspected carrier, diphtheria	287
V02.3	Carrier or suspected carrier, gastrointestinal pathogens, other	287
V02.7	Carrier or suspected carrier, gonorrhea	287
V02.9	Carrier or suspected carrier, infectious organism, other specified	287
V02.1	Carrier or suspected carrier, typhoid	287
V02.8	Carrier or suspected carrier, venereal diseases, other	287
*V02.6	Carrier or suspected carrier, viral hepatitis	111
599.3	Caruncle, urethral	165
*347	Cataplexy, narcolepsy	15
*366	Cataract	23
738.7	Cauliflower ear	36
682.0	Cellulitis and abscess, face	320
*681	Cellulitis and abscess, finger, toe	137, 143
682.1	Cellulitis and abscess, neck	320
*682	Cellulitis and abscess, other	137, 143, 221, 228
478.71	Cellulitis and perichondritis, larynx	34
376.01	Cellulitis, orbital	21
478.21	Cellulitis, pharynx or nasopharynx	34
723.1	Cervicalgia	129
616.0	Cervicitis and endocervicitis	177, 183
098.15	Cervicitis, gonococcal, acute	176, 182
098.35	Cervicitis, gonococcal, chronic	176, 182
654.23	Cesarean section, previous, complicating pregnancy, childbirth, or the puerperium, antepartum condition or complication	207
654.21	Cesarean section, previous, complicating pregnancy, childbirth, or the puerperium, delivered, with or without mention of antepartum condition	187, 199
654.20	Cesarean section, previous, complicating pregnancy, childbirth, or the puerperium, unspecified as to episode of care	213
086.0	Chagas' disease, with heart involvement	90
099.0	Chancroid	172, 176, 182
310.1	Change, personality, due to conditions classified elsewhere	252
*375.6	Changes, other, lacrimal passages	25
782.8	Changes, skin texture	148
V20.2	Check, health, routine, infant or child	231
*052	Chickenpox	217, 224
052.7	Chickenpox, other specified complications	246
052.8	Chickenpox, unspecified complications	246
576.1	Cholangitis	220, 227
*574	Cholelithiasis	111
*001	Cholera	101
380.03	Chondritis, pinna	134
756.4	Chondrodystrophy	135
733.92	Chondromalacia	130
717.7	Chondromalacia, patella	132
333.4	Chorea, Huntington's	10
333.5	Chorea, other	10
*392	Chorea, rheumatic	90
049.0	Choriomeningitis, lymphocytic	13
130.2	Chorioretinitis, due to toxoplasmosis	22, 218, 225
428.42	Chronic combined systolic and diastolic heart failure	59, 62, 64, 73, 77, 79
428.32	Chronic diastolic heart failure	59, 61, 64, 73, 77, 79
*585	Chronic kidney disease (CKD)	161, 162, 322
428.22	Chronic systolic heart failure	59, 61, 64, 73, 77, 79
791.1	Chyluria	164, 221, 228
571.6	Cirrhosis, biliary	110
571.0	Cirrhosis, fatty, alcoholic	111
571.2	Cirrhosis, liver, alcoholic	110
571.5	Cirrhosis, liver, without mention of alcohol	110
736.74	Claw foot, acquired	12
736.06	Claw hand, acquired	12
121.1	Clonorchiasis	111
736.07	Club hand, acquired	12
781.5	Clubbing, fingers	47

Code Range

Code	Narrative	Page
776.2	Coagulation, disseminated, intravascular, neonatal	216, 223
*114	Coccidioidomycosis	308
114.1	Coccidioidomycosis, extrapulmonary, primary	146
114.3	Coccidioidomycosis, progressive, other forms	217, 224, 249
114.4	Coccidioidomycosis, pulmonary, chronic	42
114.0	Coccidioidomycosis, pulmonary, primary	42
114.5	Coccidioidomycosis, pulmonary, unspecified	42
114.9	Coccidioidomycosis, unspecified	249
007.2	Coccidiosis	308
788.0	Colic, renal	163
006.2	Colitis, amebic, nondysenteric	102
518.0	Collapse, pulmonary	47, 83, 220, 227
377.23	Coloboma, optic disc	25
780.01	Coma	13, 221, 228
572.2	Coma, hepatic	220, 227
251.0	Coma, hypoglycemic	154, 218, 225
*639	Complication, abortion or ectopic and molar pregnancies	203
*997.6	Complication, amputation stump	135
996.85	Complication, bone marrow transplant	235
*536.4	Complication, gastrostomy	104
996.68	Complication, infection and inflammatory reaction, peritoneal dialysis catheter	274
996.61	Complication, infection, inflammatory reaction, cardiac device, implant and graft	59, 62, 64, 74, 77, 80, 91
996.60	Complication, infection, inflammatory reaction, device, implant, and graft, unspecified	274
996.65	Complication, infection, inflammatory reaction, genitourinary device, implant and graft, other	165
996.64	Complication, infection, inflammatory reaction, indwelling urinary catheter	165
996.66	Complication, infection, inflammatory reaction, internal joint prosthesis	124, 131
996.67	Complication, infection, inflammatory reaction, internal orthopedic device, implant, and graft, other	124, 131
996.69	Complication, infection, inflammatory reaction, internal prosthetic device, implant, and graft, other	274
996.63	Complication, infection, inflammatory reaction, nervous system device, implant, and graft	16
996.62	Complication, infection, inflammatory reaction, vascular device, implant and graft, other	59, 62, 64, 74, 77, 80, 83, 91
763.9	Complication, labor and delivery, fetus or newborn affected by, unspecified complication	229, 231
996.55	Complication, mechanical, artificial skin graft and decellularized allodermis	274
996.04	Complication, mechanical, automatic implantable cardiac defibrillator	89
996.54	Complication, mechanical, breast prosthesis	143
996.09	Complication, mechanical, cardiac device, implant and graft, other	91
996.00	Complication, mechanical, cardiac device, implant and graft, unspecified	91
996.01	Complication, mechanical, cardiac pacemaker electrode	89
996.51	Complication, mechanical, corneal graft	26
996.03	Complication, mechanical, coronary bypass graft	91
530.87	Complication, mechanical, esophagostomy	104
996.39	Complication, mechanical, genitourinary device, implant or graft, other,	165
996.30	Complication, mechanical, genitourinary device, implant or graft, unspecified	165
996.52	Complication, mechanical, graft, other tissue, not elsewhere classified	274
996.02	Complication, mechanical, heart valve prosthesis	89
996.59	Complication, mechanical, implant and internal device, other	274
996.57	Complication, mechanical, insulin pump	274
*996.4	Complication, mechanical, internal orthopedic device, implant and graft	131
996.32	Complication, mechanical, intrauterine contraceptive device	178, 184
996.2	Complication, mechanical, nervous system device, implant and graft	16
996.53	Complication, mechanical, ocular lens prosthesis	26
996.56	Complication, mechanical, peritoneal dialysis catheter	274
996.31	Complication, mechanical, urethral indwelling catheter	165
349.1	Complication, nervous system, from device surgically implanted	15, 218, 225
996.72	Complication, other, cardiac device, implant and graft, other	60, 62, 64, 74, 77, 80, 83, 91
996.70	Complication, other, device, implant, and graft, unspecified	274

*Code Range

Code	Narrative	Page
996.76	Complication, other, genitourinary device, implant, and graft	165
996.71	Complication, other, heart valve prosthesis	91
996.77	Complication, other, internal joint prosthesis	131
996.78	Complication, other, internal orthopedic device, implant, and graft	131
996.79	Complication, other, internal prosthetic device, implant, and graft, other	274
996.75	Complication, other, nervous system device, implant, and graft	16
996.73	Complication, other, renal dialysis device, implant and graft	91
996.74	Complication, other, vascular device, implant and graft, other	91
*996.9	Complication, reattached extremity or body part	131
*519.0	Complication, tracheostomy	47, 320
996.83	Complication, transplanted heart	60, 62, 64, 74, 77, 80, 91
996.87	Complication, transplanted intestine	274
996.81	Complication, transplanted kidney	165
996.82	Complication, transplanted liver	111
996.84	Complication, transplanted lung	47
996.89	Complication, transplanted organ, other,	274
996.80	Complication, transplanted organ, unspecified	274
996.86	Complication, transplanted pancreas	110
997.71	Complication, vascular, artery, mesenteric	105, 222, 229
997.72	Complication, vascular, artery, renal	165, 222, 229
997.79	Complication, vascular, other vessels	87, 222, 229
*383.3	Complications following mastoidectomy	36
*997.9	Complications, affecting other specified body system, not elsewhere classified	274
668.13	Complications, cardiac, of anesthetic or other sedation, labor and delivery, antepartum condition or complication	209
668.12	Complications, cardiac, of anesthetic or other sedation, labor and delivery, delivered, with mention of postpartum complication	190, 196
668.11	Complications, cardiac, of anesthetic or other sedation, labor and delivery, delivered, with or without mention of antepartum condition	190, 196
668.14	Complications, cardiac, of anesthetic or other sedation, labor and delivery, postpartum condition or complication	204
668.10	Complications, cardiac, of anesthetic or other sedation, labor and delivery, unspecified as to episode of care	190, 202
668.23	Complications, central nervous system, of anesthetic or other sedation, labor and delivery, antepartum condition or complication	209
668.21	Complications, central nervous system, of anesthetic or other sedation, labor and delivery, delivered, with or without mention of antepartum condition	190, 196
668.22	Complications, central nervous system, of anesthetic or other sedation, labor and delivery, delivered, with mention of postpartum complication	190, 196
668.24	Complications, central nervous system, of anesthetic or other sedation, labor and delivery, postpartum condition or complication	204
668.20	Complications, central nervous system, of anesthetic or other sedation, labor and delivery, unspecified as to episode of care	190, 202
*569.6	Complications, colostomy and enterostomy	104
958.5	Complications, early, trauma, anuria	161, 162, 222, 229, 299
958.6	Complications, early, trauma, contracture, Volkmann's ischemic	135, 299, 305
958.0	Complications, early, trauma, embolism, air	42, 222, 229, 299, 304
958.1	Complications, early, trauma, embolism, fat	42, 222, 229, 299, 304
958.7	Complications, early, trauma, emphysema, subcutaneous	46, 222, 229, 299
958.2	Complications, early, trauma, hemorrhage, secondary and recurrent	222, 229, 274, 299
958.3	Complications, early, trauma, infection, not elsewhere classified, wound	222, 229, 246, 299
958.8	Complications, early, trauma, other	275, 299
958.4	Complications, early, trauma, shock	222, 229, 274, 299
762.5	Complications, fetus or newborn affected by, compression of umbilical cord, other	229, 231
762.6	Complications, fetus or newborn affected by, conditions of umbilical cord, other and unspecified	229, 231
762.4	Complications, fetus or newborn affected by, prolapsed cord	229, 231

Alphabetic Index to Diseases

* Code Range

Code	Narrative	Page
763.0	Complications, labor and delivery, fetus or newborn affected by, breech delivery and extraction	229, 231
763.4	Complications, labor and delivery, fetus or newborn affected by, cesarean delivery	215, 222
763.3	Complications, labor and delivery, fetus or newborn affected by, delivery by vacuum extractor	229, 231
763.2	Complications, labor and delivery, fetus or newborn affected by, forceps delivery	229, 231
763.1	Complications, labor and delivery, fetus or newborn affected by, malpresentation, malposition, and disproportion, other	229, 231
763.6	Complications, labor and delivery, fetus or newborn affected by, precipitate delivery	229, 231
996.1	Complications, mechanical, vascular device, implant and graft	91
997.1	Complications, not elsewhere classified, cardiac	91, 222, 229
997.4	Complications, not elsewhere classified, digestive system	105, 222, 229
999.1	Complications, not elsewhere classified, embolism, air	42, 222, 229
999.3	Complications, not elsewhere classified, infection, other	222, 229, 249
*997.0	Complications, not elsewhere classified, nervous system	16, 222, 229
999.9	Complications, not elsewhere classified, other and unspecified,	274
997.2	Complications, not elsewhere classified, peripheral vascular	87, 222, 229
999.6	Complications, not elsewhere classified, reaction, incompatibility ABO	222, 229, 234
999.7	Complications, not elsewhere classified, reaction, incompatibility Rh	222, 229, 234
999.5	Complications, not elsewhere classified, reaction, serum, other	222, 229, 273
999.8	Complications, not elsewhere classified, Reaction, transfusion, other	222, 229, 234
997.3	Complications, not elsewhere classified, respiratory	47, 222, 229
999.4	Complications, not elsewhere classified, shock, anaphylactic, due to serum	222, 229, 273
997.5	Complications, not elsewhere classified, urinary	165, 222, 229
999.0	Complications, not elsewhere classified, vaccinia, generalized	247
999.2	Complications, not elsewhere classified, vascular, other	91, 222, 229
998.89	Complications, other specified, not elsewhere classified, procedures	274
*998	Complications, other, not elsewhere classified, procedures	222, 229

Code	Narrative	Page
669.43	Complications, other, obstetrical, surgery and procedures, antepartum condition or complication	209
669.42	Complications, other, obstetrical, surgery and procedures, delivered, with mention of postpartum complication	191, 196
669.41	Complications, other, obstetrical, surgery and procedures, delivered, with or without mention of antepartum condition	191, 196
669.44	Complications, other, obstetrical, surgery and procedures, postpartum condition or complication	205
669.40	Complications, other, obstetrical, surgery and procedures, unspecified as to episode of care	191, 202
668.83	Complications, other, of anesthetic or other sedation, labor and delivery, antepartum condition or complication	209
668.82	Complications, other, of anesthetic or other sedation, labor and delivery, delivered, with mention of postpartum complication	190, 196
668.81	Complications, other, of anesthetic or other sedation, labor and delivery, delivered, with or without mention of antepartum condition	190, 196
668.84	Complications, other, of anesthetic or other sedation, labor and delivery, postpartum condition or complication	204
668.80	Complications, other, of anesthetic or other sedation, labor and delivery, unspecified as to episode of care	190, 202
669.83	Complications, other, of labor and delivery, antepartum condition or complication	209
669.82	Complications, other, of labor and delivery, delivered, with mention of postpartum complication	191, 202
669.81	Complications, other, of labor and delivery, delivered, with or without mention of antepartum condition	191, 202
669.84	Complications, other, of labor and delivery, postpartum condition or complication	205
669.80	Complications, other, of labor and delivery, unspecified as to episode of care	191, 202
674.82	Complications, other, of puerperium, delivered, with mention of postpartum complication	192, 197
674.84	Complications, other, of puerperium, postpartum condition or complication	205
674.80	Complications, other, of puerperium, unspecified as to episode of care	214

*** Code Range**

Code	Narrative	Page
663.83	Complications, other, unbilical cord, during labor and delivery, antepartum condition or complication	209
663.81	Complications, other, unbilical cord, during labor and delivery, delivered, with or without mention of antepartum condition	189, 201
663.80	Complications, other, unbilical cord, during labor and delivery, unspecified as to episode of care	189, 201
674.32	Complications, other, wounds, obstetrical surgical, delivered, with mention of postpartum complication	192, 197
674.34	Complications, other, wounds, obstetrical surgical, postpartum condition or complication	205
674.30	Complications, other, wounds, obstetrical surgical, unspecified as to episode of care	214
998.9	Complications, procedures,	274
998.7	Complications, procedures, acute reaction, foreign substance accidentally left,	274
*998.3	Complications, procedures, disruption, wound, operative	274
998.81	Complications, procedures, emphysema, subcutaneous	274
998.6	Complications, procedures, fistula, persistent, postoperative	274
998.4	Complications, procedures, foreign body, accidentally left	274
998.82	Complications, procedures, fragments, cataract, in eye	26
*998.1	Complications, procedures, hemorrhage, hematoma, seroma, complicating a procedure	274
*998.5	Complications, procedures, infection, postoperative	246
998.2	Complications, procedures, laceration or puncture, accidental	274
998.0	Complications, procedures, shock, postoperative	274
998.83	Complications, procedures, wound, surgical, nonhealing	274
668.03	Complications, pulmonary, of anesthetic or other sedation, labor and delivery, antepartum condition or complication	209
668.02	Complications, pulmonary, of anesthetic or other sedation, labor and delivery, delivered, with mention of postpartum complication	190, 196
668.01	Complications, pulmonary, of anesthetic or other sedation, labor and delivery, delivered, with or without mention of antepartum condition	190, 196
668.04	Complications, pulmonary, of anesthetic or other sedation, labor and delivery, postpartum condition or complication	204
668.00	Complications, pulmonary, of anesthetic or other sedation, labor and delivery, unspecified as to episode of care	190, 202
668.93	Complications, unspecified, of anesthetic or other sedation, labor and delivery, antepartum condition or complication	209
668.92	Complications, unspecified, of anesthetic or other sedation, labor and delivery, delivered, with mention of postpartum complication	191, 196
668.91	Complications, unspecified, of anesthetic or other sedation, labor and delivery, delivered, with or without mention of antepartum condition	191, 196
668.94	Complications, unspecified, of anesthetic or other sedation, labor and delivery, postpartum condition or complication	205
668.90	Complications, unspecified, of anesthetic or other sedation, labor and delivery, unspecified as to episode of care	191, 202
669.93	Complications, unspecified, of labor and delivery, antepartum condition or complication	209
669.92	Complications, unspecified, of labor and delivery, delivered, with mention of postpartum complication	191, 202
669.91	Complications, unspecified, of labor and delivery, delivered, with or without mention of antepartum condition	191, 202
669.94	Complications, unspecified, of labor and delivery, postpartum condition or complication	205
669.90	Complications, unspecified, of labor and delivery, unspecified as to episode of care	191, 202
674.92	Complications, unspecified, of puerperium, delivered, with mention of postpartum complication	192, 203
674.94	Complications, unspecified, of puerperium, postpartum condition or complication	205
674.90	Complications, unspecified, of puerperium, unspecified as to episode of care	214
663.93	Complications, unspecified, unbilical cord, during labor and delivery, antepartum condition or complication	209
663.91	Complications, unspecified, unbilical cord, during labor and delivery, delivered, with or without mention of antepartum condition	189, 201
663.90	Complications, unspecified, unbilical cord, during labor and delivery, unspecified as to episode of care	189, 201

*Code Range

Code	Narrative	Page
671.83	Complications, venous, other, in pregnancy and puerperium, antepartum condition or complication	209
671.82	Complications, venous, other, in pregnancy and puerperium, delivered, with mention of postpartum complication	191, 202
671.81	Complications, venous, other, in pregnancy and puerperium, delivered, with or without antepartum condition	191, 202
671.84	Complications, venous, other, in pregnancy and puerperium, postpartum condition or complication	205
671.80	Complications, venous, other, in pregnancy and puerperium, unspecified as to episode of care	214
671.93	Complications, venous, unspecified, in pregnancy and puerperium, antepartum condition or complication	209
671.92	Complications, venous, unspecified, in pregnancy and puerperium, delivered, with mention of postpartum complication	191, 203
671.91	Complications, venous, unspecified, in pregnancy and puerperium, delivered, with or without antepartum condition	191, 203
671.94	Complications, venous, unspecified, in pregnancy and puerperium, postpartum condition or complication	205
671.90	Complications, venous, unspecified, in pregnancy and puerperium, unspecified as to episode of care	214
348.4	Compression, brain	13
663.13	Compression, cord around neck, complicating labor and delivery, antepartum condition or complication	209
663.11	Compression, cord around neck, complicating labor and delivery, delivered, with or without mention of antepartum condition	189, 201
663.10	Compression, cord around neck, complicating labor and delivery, unspecified as to episode of care	189, 201
663.33	Compression, cord, other and unspecified, complicating labor and delivery, antepartum condition or complication	209
663.31	Compression, cord, other and unspecified, complicating labor and delivery, delivered, with or without mention of antepartum condition	189, 201
663.30	Compression, cord, other and unspecified, complicating labor and delivery, unspecified as to episode of care	189, 201
459.2	Compression, vein	87

Code	Narrative	Page
*850	Concussion	14, 15
850.9	Concussion, unspecified	297
*850.1	Concussion, with brief loss of consciousness	296
850.5	Concussion, with loss of consciousness of unspecified duration	297
850.2	Concussion, with moderate loss of consciousness	296, 303
850.0	Concussion, with no loss of consciousness	296
850.3	Concussion, with prolonged loss of consciousness and return to preexisting conscious level	297, 303
850.4	Concussion, with prolonged loss of consciousness, without return to preexisting conscious level	297, 303
508.0	Condition, respiratory, acute, due to radiation	47, 220, 227
508.1	Condition, respiratory, chronic, other, due to radiation	45
508.8	Condition, respiratory, due to other specified agents, external	47
508.9	Condition, respiratory, due to unspecified agent, external	47
758.9	Conditions, due to chromosome anomalies, unspecified	287
778.8	Conditions, other specified, integument, fetus and newborn	230, 231
648.93	Conditions, other, current, maternal, complicating pregnancy, childbirth, or the puerperium, antepartum condition or complication	207, 211
648.91	Conditions, other, current, maternal, complicating pregnancy, childbirth, or the puerperium, delivered, with or without mention of antepartum condition	186, 198
648.92	Conditions, other, current, maternal, complicating pregnancy, childbirth, or the puerperium, delivered, with mention of postpartum complication	186, 198
648.94	Conditions, other, current, maternal, complicating pregnancy, childbirth, or the puerperium, postpartum condition or complication	204
648.90	Conditions, other, current, maternal, complicating pregnancy, childbirth, or the puerperium, unspecified as to episode of care	212
*758.8	Conditions, other, due to chromosome anomalies	173, 177, 183
*V49	Conditions, other, influencing health	288
656.73	Conditions, other, placental, affecting management of mother, antepartum condition or complication	208

Alphabetic Index to Diseases

Code	Narrative	Page
656.71	Conditions, other, placental, affecting management of mother, delivered, with or without mention of antepartum condition	188, 199
656.70	Conditions, other, placental, affecting management of mother, unspecified as to episode of care	213
506.4	Conditions, respiratory, chronic, due to fumes, vapors	44
506.3	Conditions, respiratory, other acute, subacute, due to fumes, vapors	47
506.9	Conditions, respiratory, unspecified, due to fumes, vapors	45
514	Congestion, lung, hypostatic	44
130.1	Conjunctivitis, due to toxoplasmosis	22, 218, 225
*564.0	Constipation	103
*V01	Contact with or exposure to, communicable diseases	287
*V01.8	Contact with or exposure, communicable diseases, other	231
653.13	Contracted pelvis in pregnancy, antepartum condition or complication	207
653.11	Contracted pelvis in pregnancy, delivered, with or without mention of antepartum condition	187, 198
653.10	Contracted pelvis in pregnancy, unspecified as to episode of care	212
368.45	Contraction, constriction, generalized, visual field	21
653.23	Contraction, inlet, pelvis in pregnancy, antepartum condition or complication	207
653.21	Contraction, inlet, pelvis in pregnancy, delivered, with or without mention of antepartum condition	187, 199
653.20	Contraction, inlet, pelvis in pregnancy, unspecified as to episode of care	212
653.33	Contraction, outlet, pelvis in pregnancy, antepartum condition or complication	207
653.31	Contraction, outlet, pelvis in pregnancy, delivered, with or without mention of antepartum condition	187, 199
653.30	Contraction, outlet, pelvis in pregnancy, unspecified as to episode of care	212
*718.4	Contracture, joint	134
922.2	Contusion, abdominal wall	145
*922.3	Contusion, back	145
922.0	Contusion, breast	145
*851.5	Contusion, cerebellar or brain stem, with open intracranial wound	8, 297, 303
*851.4	Contusion, cerebellar or brain stem, without open intracranial wound	297, 303
*851.1	Contusion, cerebral cortex, with open intracranial wound	8, 297, 303
*851.0	Contusion, cerebral cortex, without open intracranial wound	297
851.02	Contusion, cerebral cortex, without open intracranial wound, brief loss of consciousness	303
851.03	Contusion, cerebral cortex, without open intracranial wound, moderate loss of consciousness	303
851.01	Contusion, cerebral cortex, without open intracranial wound, no loss of consciousness	303
851.04	Contusion, cerebral cortex, without open intracranial wound, prolonged loss of consciousness and return to preexisting conscious level	303
851.05	Contusion, cerebral cortex, without open intracranial wound, prolonged loss of consciousness, without return to preexisting conscious level	303
851.00	Contusion, cerebral cortex, without open intracranial wound, unspecified state of consciousness	303
851.09	Contusion, cerebral cortex, without open intracranial wound, with concussion, unspecified	303
851.06	Contusion, cerebral cortex, without open intracranial wound, with loss of consciousness, unspecified duration	303
922.1	Contusion, chest wall	145
*921	Contusion, eye and adnexa	298
921.9	Contusion, eye, unspecified	26
921.3	Contusion, eyeball	21
921.1	Contusion, eyelids and periocular area	21
920	Contusion, face, scalp and neck, except eye(s)	145, 298
922.4	Contusion, genital organs	173, 177, 184
*924	Contusion, lower limb and other and unspecified sites	145, 298
861.31	Contusion, lung, with open wound into thorax	47
861.21	Contusion, lung, without open wound into thorax	47
921.2	Contusion, orbital tissues	25
*922	Contusion, trunk	298
922.8	Contusion, trunk, multiple sites	145
922.9	Contusion, trunk, unspecified part	145
*923	Contusion, upper limb	145, 298
*V66	Convalescence, palliative care	289
*780.3	Convulsions	13, 221, 228
779.0	Convulsions, newborn	216, 223
415.0	Cor pulmonale, acute	59, 61, 63, 73, 76, 79, 84, 91
700	Corns and callosities	147
786.2	Cough	46

* Code Range

Code	Narrative	Page
*V26.3	Counseling and testing, genetic	288
051.0	Cowpox	246
676.13	Cracked nipple, associated with childbirth, antepartum condition or complication	209
676.12	Cracked nipple, associated with childbirth, delivered, with mention of postpartum complication	192, 203
676.11	Cracked nipple, associated with childbirth, delivered, with or without mention of antepartum condition	192, 203
676.14	Cracked nipple, associated with childbirth, postpartum condition or complication	205
676.10	Cracked nipple, associated with childbirth, unspecified as to episode of care	214
729.82	Cramp, limb	130
333.84	Cramp, writer's, organic	15
464.4	Croup	35, 319
117.5	Cryptococcosis	218, 225, 308
736.01	Cubitus valgus (acquired)	134
736.02	Cubitus varus (acquired)	134
*737	Curvature, spine	129
782.5	Cyanosis	286
577.2	Cyst and pseudocyst, pancreas	220, 227
*744.4	Cyst or fistula, congenital, branchial cleft, preauricular sinus	36
593.2	Cyst, acquired, kidney	165
*733.2	Cyst, bone	130
348.0	Cyst, brain	15
752.41	Cyst, congenital, embryonic, cervix, vagina, and external female genitalia	177
752.11	Cyst, embryonic, fallopian tubes and broad ligaments	177
616.2	Cyst, gland or duct, Bartholin's	177, 183
*364.6	Cyst, iris, ciliary body, anterior chamber	23
376.81	Cyst, orbital	25
478.26	Cyst, pharynx or nasopharynx	36
*685	Cyst, pilonidal	143
246.2	Cyst, thyroid	319
277.03	Cystic fibrosis, with gastrointestinal manifestations	104
277.01	Cystic fibrosis, with meconium ileus	215, 218, 222
277.09	Cystic fibrosis, with other manifestations	154
277.02	Cystic fibrosis, with pulmonary manifestations	42
277.00	Cystic fibrosis, without mention of meconium ileus	154
595.0	Cystitis, acute	163, 221, 228
595.2	Cystitis, chronic, other	163
595.81	Cystitis, cystica	163, 221, 228
098.11	Cystitis, gonococcal, acute	163
098.31	Cystitis, gonococcal, chronic	163
595.4	Cystitis, in diseases classified elsewhere	163, 221, 228
595.1	Cystitis, interstitial, chronic	163
595.82	Cystitis, irradiation	165
595.89	Cystitis, other specified types	163, 221, 228
595.9	Cystitis, unspecified	163, 221, 228
078.5	Cytomegaloviral disease	247, 308
375.01	Dacryoadenitis, acute	21
375.02	Dacryoadenitis, chronic	24
375.00	Dacryoadenitis, unspecified	24
375.32	Dacryocystitis, acute	21
375.33	Dacryocystitis, phlegmonous	25
375.30	Dacryocystitis, unspecified	25
348.1	Damage, brain, anoxic	15, 218, 225
571.3	Damage, liver, alcoholic, unspecified	110
665.61	Damage, obstetrical, pelvic joints and ligaments, delivered, with or without mention of antepartum condition	190, 202
665.64	Damage, obstetrical, pelvic joints and ligaments, postpartum condition or complication	204
665.60	Damage, obstetrical, pelvic joints and ligaments, unspecified as to episode of care	190, 202
655.53	Damage, suspected, fetal, from drugs, affecting management of mother, antepartum condition or complication	208
655.51	Damage, suspected, fetal, from drugs, affecting management of mother, delivered, with or without mention of antepartum condition	187, 199
655.50	Damage, suspected, fetal, from drugs, affecting management of mother, unspecified as to episode of care	213
655.63	Damage, suspected, fetal, from radiation, affecting management of mother, antepartum condition or complication	208
655.61	Damage, suspected, fetal, from radiation, affecting management of mother, delivered, with or without mention of antepartum condition	187, 199
655.60	Damage, suspected, fetal, from radiation, affecting management of mother, unspecified as to episode of care	213
656.43	Death, fetal intrauterine, affecting management of mother, antepartum condition or complication	208

*** Code Range**

Code	Narrative	Page
656.41	Death, fetal intrauterine, affecting management of mother, delivered, with or without mention of antepartum condition	188, 199
656.40	Death, fetal intrauterine, affecting management of mother, unspecified as to episode of care	188, 199
798.1	Death, instantaneous	86
798.2	Death, occurring in less than 24 hours, from onset of symptoms, cause unknown	86
798.9	Death, unattended	287
799.3	Debility, unspecified	286
655.73	Decreased, movements, fetal, antepartum condition or complication	208
655.71	Decreased, movements, fetal, delivered, with or without mention of antepartum condition	187, 199
655.70	Decreased, movements, fetal, unspecified as to episode of care	213
429.71	Defect, acquired, cardiac septal	59, 62, 64, 73, 77, 79, 84, 91
745.5	Defect, congenital, atrial septal, ostium secundum type	88
745.7	Defect, congenital, cor biloculare	88
745.61	Defect, congenital, ostium primum	88
745.69	Defect, congenital, other, endocardial cushion	88
745.9	Defect, congenital, unspecified, septal closure	88
745.4	Defect, congenital, ventricular septal	88, 221, 228
*361.3	Defect, retinal, without detachment	23
368.52	Defect, vision, color, deutan	24
368.51	Defect, vision, color, protan	24
368.53	Defect, vision, color, tritan	24
368.47	Defect, visual field, heteronymous, bilateral	21
368.46	Defect, visual field, homonymous, bilateral	21
368.44	Defect, visual field, localized, other	21
368.43	Defect, visual field, sector or arcuate	21
368.40	Defect, visual field, unspecified	21
*286	Defects, coagulation	234
666.32	Defects, coagulation, postpartum, delivered, with mention of postpartum complication	190, 196
666.34	Defects, coagulation, postpartum, postpartum condition or complication	204
666.30	Defects, coagulation, postpartum, unspecified as to episode of care	213
745.60	Defects, congenital, unspecified type, endocardial cushion	88
286.6	Defibrination syndrome	218, 225
*269	Deficiencies, nutritional, other	154, 309
*281	Deficiency anemias, other	234, 309

Code	Narrative	Page
267	Deficiency, ascorbic acid	154, 309
*266	Deficiency, B complex components	154, 309
368.55	Deficiency, color vision, acquired	21
368.59	Deficiency, color vision, other	24
277.6	Deficiency, enzymes circulating, other	155
279.8	Deficiency, immune mechanism, other specified	234
279.9	Deficiency, immune mechanism, unspecified	235
*279.1	Deficiency, immunity, cell-mediated	234
279.2	Deficiency, immunity, combined	234
*279.0	Deficiency, immunity, humoral	234
279.3	Deficiency, immunity, unspecified	234
271.3	Deficiency, intestinal, disaccharidase and disaccharide, malabsorption	102
*280	Deficiency, iron, anemia	234, 309
*265	Deficiency, thiamine and niacin	154, 309
*264	Deficiency, vitamin A	309
264.0	Deficiency, vitamin A, conjunctival xerosis	23
264.1	Deficiency, vitamin A, conjunctival xerosis, Bitot's spot	23
264.3	Deficiency, vitamin A, corneal ulceration, xerosis	23
264.2	Deficiency, vitamin A, corneal xerosis	23
264.4	Deficiency, vitamin A, keratomalacia	23
264.5	Deficiency, vitamin A, night blindness	23
264.8	Deficiency, vitamin A, other manifestations	154
264.7	Deficiency, vitamin A, other ocular manifestations	23
264.9	Deficiency, vitamin A, unspecified	154
264.6	Deficiency, vitamin A, xerophthalmic scars, cornea	23
*268	Deficiency, vitamin D	309
268.9	Deficiency, vitamin D, unspecified	154
*736.3	Deformities, acquired, hip	134
754.0	Deformities, congenital, musculoskeletal, skull, face and jaw	135
754.2	Deformities, congenital, musculoskeletal, spine	135
754.1	Deformities, congenital, musculoskeletal, sternocleidomastoid muscle	135
*754.7	Deformities, congenital, other, feet	135
754.61	Deformities, congenital, pes planus	231
*754.5	Deformities, congenital, varus, feet	135
*736.2	Deformities, other, acquired, finger	134
736.00	Deformities, unspecified, acquired, forearm, excluding fingers	134
738.3	Deformity, acquired, chest and rib	135
736.71	Deformity, acquired, equinovarus	134

** Code Range*

Code	Narrative	Page
736.75	Deformity, acquired, foot, cavovarus	134
736.73	Deformity, acquired, foot, cavus	134
736.72	Deformity, acquired, foot, equinus	134
736.9	Deformity, acquired, limb, site unspecified	135
738.2	Deformity, acquired, neck	135
738.0	Deformity, acquired, nose	35
*736.8	Deformity, acquired, other parts of limbs	134
738.6	Deformity, acquired, pelvis	135
738.8	Deformity, acquired, specified site, other	135
738.9	Deformity, acquired, unspecified site	135
*754.6	Deformity, congenital, valgus, feet	135
*376.4	Deformity, orbit	25
736.79	Deformity, other, acquired, ankle and foot	134
738.5	Deformity, other, acquired, back or spine	129
736.76	Deformity, other, acquired, foot, calcaneus	134
736.09	Deformity, other, acquired, forearm, excluding fingers	134
*738.1	Deformity, other, acquired, head	135
736.6	Deformity, other, acquired, knee	134
*735	Deformity, toe, acquired	134
736.70	Deformity, unspecified, acquired, ankle and foot	134
736.03	Deformity, valgus, acquired, wrist	134
736.04	Deformity, varus, acquired, wrist	134
333.0	Degeneration, basal ganglia, other	10
331.7	Degeneration, brain, in disease classified elsewhere	10
331.2	Degeneration, brain, senile	10
331.9	Degeneration, brain, unspecified	10
*330	Degeneration, brain, usually manifested in childhood	10
336.2	Degeneration, combined, spinal cord, subacute, in other diseases classified elsewhere	15
*360.4	Degeneration, globe	23
*364.5	Degeneration, iris and ciliary body	23
*362.5	Degeneration, macula, retina, posterior pole	23
429.1	Degeneration, myocardial	91
*362.6	Degeneration, retinal, peripheral	23
662.33	Delayed delivery of second twin, triplet, etc., antepartum condition or complication	209
662.31	Delayed delivery of second twin, triplet, etc., delivered, with or without mention of antepartum condition	189, 201
662.30	Delayed delivery of second twin, triplet, etc., unspecified as to episode of care	189, 201
779.83	Delayed separation, umbilical cord	230
*315	Delays, specific, development	253
293.0	Delirium, due to conditions classified elsewhere, transient	251
293.1	Delirium, subacute, psychotic	251
669.71	Delivery, cesarean, without mention of indication, delivered, with or without mention of antepartum condition	191, 202
669.70	Delivery, cesarean, without mention of indication, unspecified as to episode of care	191, 202
659.83	Delivery, complicated by indications for care or intervention, specified, antepartum condition or complication	208
659.81	Delivery, complicated by indications for care or intervention, specified, delivered, with or without mention of antepartum condition	188, 200
659.80	Delivery, complicated by indications for care or intervention, specified, unspecified as to episode of care, other	188, 200
659.93	Delivery, complicated by indications for care or intervention, unspecified, antepartum condition or complication	208
659.91	Delivery, complicated by indications for care or intervention, unspecified, delivered, with or without mention of antepartum condition	188, 200
659.90	Delivery, complicated by indications for care or intervention, unspecified, unspecified as to episode of care	188, 200
660.23	Delivery, complicated by obstructed labor due to abnormal pelvic soft tissues, antepartum condition or complication	208
660.21	Delivery, complicated by obstructed labor due to abnormal pelvic soft tissues, delivered, with or without mention of antepartum condition	188, 200
660.20	Delivery, complicated by obstructed labor due to abnormal pelvic soft tissues, unspecified as to episode of care	188, 200
660.13	Delivery, complicated by obstructed labor due to bony pelvis, antepartum condition or complication	208
660.11	Delivery, complicated by obstructed labor due to bony pelvis, delivered, with or without mention of antepartum condition	188, 200
660.10	Delivery, complicated by obstructed labor due to bony pelvis, unspecified as to episode of care	188, 200
660.30	Delivery, complicated by obstructed labor due to deep transverse arrest and persistant occipitoposterior position, unspecified as to episode of care	188, 200

Alphabetic Index to Diseases

* Code Range

Code	Narrative	Page
717.3	Derangement, meniscus, medial, other, unspecified,	132
717.2	Derangement, meniscus, medial, posterior horn	132
717.5	Derangement, meniscus, not elsewhere classified	132
*718.8	Derangement, other, joint	134
*718.9	Derangement, unspecified, joint	134
717.9	Derangement, unspecified, knee, internal	132
*691	Dermatitis, atopic, and related conditions	147
*692	Dermatitis, contact, and other eczema	147
051.2	Dermatitis, contagious, pustular	146
693.0	Dermatitis, due to drugs and medicine taken internally	221, 228
*693	Dermatitis, due to substances taken internally	147
698.4	Dermatitis, factitia, (artefacta)	147
694.0	Dermatitis, herpetiformis	147
694.2	Dermatitis, herpetiformis, juvenile	147
*111	Dermatomycosis, other, unspecified	146, 309
*110	Dermatophytosis	146, 309
*702	Dermatoses, other	147
694.8	Dermatosis, bullous, other specified	142
694.9	Dermatosis, bullous, unspecified	142
*690	Dermatosis, erythematosquamous	147
694.1	Dermatosis, pustular, subcorneal	147
*361.0	Detachment, retina, with retinal defect	23
*361.8	Detachment, retinal, other forms	23
361.2	Detachment, retinal, serous	23
361.9	Detachment, retinal, unspecified	23
*V21	Development, constitutional states	287
470	Deviated, septum, nasal	35, 319
378.87	Deviation, other dissociated, eye movements	22
253.5	Diabetes insipidus	218, 225
648.03	Diabetes mellitus, maternal, complicating pregnancy, childbirth, or the puerperium, antepartum condition or complication	207, 210
648.01	Diabetes mellitus, maternal, complicating pregnancy, childbirth, or the puerperium, delivered, with or without mention of antepartum condition	186, 195
648.02	Diabetes mellitus, maternal, complicating pregnancy, childbirth, or the puerperium, delivered, with mention of postpartum complication	186, 195
648.04	Diabetes mellitus, maternal, complicating pregnancy, childbirth, or the puerperium, postpartum condition or complication	204
648.00	Diabetes mellitus, maternal, complicating pregnancy, childbirth, or the puerperium, unspecified as to episode of care	212
775.1	Diabetes mellitus, neonatal	216, 223
*250.0	Diabetes mellitus, without mention of complication	154, 321, 322
*250.3	Diabetes, coma, other	154, 321, 322
*250.2	Diabetes, hyperosmolarity	154, 321, 322
*250.1	Diabetes, ketoacidosis	154, 321, 322
*250.6	Diabetes, neurological manifestations	11, 321, 322
*250.5	Diabetes, ophthalmic manifestations	23, 321, 322
*250.8	Diabetes, other specified manifestations	154, 321, 322
*250.7	Diabetes, peripheral circulatory disorders	86, 321, 322
*250.4	Diabetes, renal manifestations	164, 321, 322
*250.9	Diabetes, unspecified complications	154, 321, 322
564.5	Diarrhea, functional	103
564.4	Diarrhea, functional, following gastrointestinal surgery	103
569.86	Dieulafoy lesion (hemorrhagic), intestine	104
537.84	Dieulafoy lesion (hemorrhagic), stomach and duodenum	100
719.7	Difficulty, walking	130
536.1	Dilation, stomach, acute	102, 220, 227
032.2	Diphtheria, anterior nasal	35, 318
032.81	Diphtheria, conjunctival	22
032.85	Diphtheria, cutaneous	146
032.84	Diphtheria, cystitis	163
032.0	Diphtheria, faucial	35, 318
032.3	Diphtheria, laryngeal	35, 318
032.82	Diphtheria, myocarditis	90
032.1	Diphtheria, nasopharyngeal	35, 318
032.89	Diphtheria, other	248
032.83	Diphtheria, peritonitis	103
032.9	Diphtheria, unspecified	248
344.2	Diplegia, upper limbs	9
343.0	Diplegic, congenital	9
368.2	Diplopia	21
788.7	Discharge, urethral	164
368.13	Discomfort, visual	24
436	Disease, acute, but ill-defined, cerebrovascular	11, 60, 62, 65, 74, 78, 80, 83, 219, 226
331.0	Disease, Alzheimer's	10

Alphabetic Index to Diseases

Code	Narrative	Page
279.4	Disease, autoimmune, not elsewhere classified	128
040.89	Disease, bacterial, other	248
348.8	Disease, brain, other, calcification, fungus	11
348.9	Disease, brain, unspecified	11, 309
993.3	Disease, caisson	275
429.2	Disease, cardiovascular, unspecified	87
078.3	Disease, cat scratch	234
049.8	Disease, central nervous system, nonarthropod-borne viral, other specified	12, 308
049.9	Disease, central nervous system, nonarthropod-borne, unspecified	12, 308
*474	Disease, chronic, tonsils and adenoids	319
751.62	Disease, congenital, cystic, liver	111
031.1	Disease, cutaneous, due to other mycobacteria	146
*341	Disease, demyelinating, central nervous system	10
341.9	Disease, demyelinating, central nervous system, unspecified	309
078.88	Disease, due to Chlamydia, other specified,	247
031.2	Disease, due to disseminated mycobacterium avium-intracellulare complex (DMAC)	248, 308
031.9	Disease, due to mycobacteria, unspecified	248, 308
078.89	Disease, due to viruses, other specified	247
048	Disease, enterovirus, other, central nervous system	13
333.90	Disease, extrapyramidal, unspecified, and abnormal movement disorders	10
078.4	Disease, foot and mouth	247
*704	Disease, hair and hair follicles	147
074.3	Disease, hand, foot and mouth	247
*411	Disease, heart, ischemic, acute and subacute forms, other	84
411.89	Disease, heart, ischemic, acute and subacute forms, other	89
414.8	Disease, heart, ischemic, other specified forms, chronic	87
414.9	Disease, heart, ischemic, unspecified, chronic	87
398.99	Disease, heart, other and unspecified, rheumatic	90
098.85	Disease, heart, other gonococcal	90
*415	Disease, heart, pulmonary, acute	219, 226
*416	Disease, heart, pulmonary, chronic	91
391.8	Disease, heart, rheumatic, acute, other	90
391.9	Disease, heart, rheumatic, acute, unspecified	90
398.90	Disease, heart, rheumatic, unspecified	90
429.9	Disease, heart, unspecified	87
773.2	Disease, hemolytic, due to isoimmunization, other and unspecified, fetus or newborn	216, 223
776.0	Disease, hemorrhagic, newborn	216, 223
655.23	Disease, hereditary, possibly affecting fetus, affecting management of mother, antepartum condition or complication	208
655.21	Disease, hereditary, possibly affecting fetus, affecting management of mother, delivered, with or without mention of antepartum condition	187, 199
655.20	Disease, hereditary, possibly affecting fetus, affecting management of mother, unspecified as to episode of care	213
751.3	Disease, Hirschsprung's, and disorders, congenital, other, functional colon	104
*335	Disease, horn cell, anterior	10
042	Disease, human immunodeficiency virus (HIV)	307, 308, 309, 310
429.82	Disease, hyperkinetic, heart	84, 91, 219, 226
136.8	Disease, infectious and parasitic, other	249, 308
647.80	Disease, infectious and parasitic, other, maternal, classifiable elsewhere, complicating pregnancy, childbirth, or the puerperium, unspecified as to episode of care	212
647.81	Disease, infectious and parasitic, other, maternal, classifiable elsewhere, complicating pregnancy, childbirth, or the puerperium, delivered, with or without mention of antepartum condition	186, 195
647.82	Disease, infectious and parasitic, other, maternal, classifiable elsewhere, complicating pregnancy, childbirth, or the puerperium, delivered, with mention of postpartum complication	186, 195
647.83	Disease, infectious and parasitic, other, maternal, classifiable elsewhere, complicating pregnancy, childbirth, or the puerperium, antepartum condition or complication	207, 210
647.84	Disease, infectious and parasitic, other, maternal, classifiable elsewhere, complicating pregnancy, childbirth, or the puerperium, postpartum condition or complication	204
136.9	Disease, infectious and parasitic, unspecified	249

Code Range

Code	Narrative	Page
647.90	Disease, infectious and parasitic, unspecified, maternal, classifiable elsewhere, complicating pregnancy, childbirth, or the puerperium, unspecified as to episode of care	212
647.91	Disease, infectious and parasitic, unspecified, maternal, classifiable elsewhere, complicating pregnancy, childbirth, or the puerperium, delivered, with or without mention of antepartum condition	186, 195
647.92	Disease, infectious and parasitic, unspecified, maternal, classifiable elsewhere, complicating pregnancy, childbirth, or the puerperium, delivered, with mention of postpartum complication	186, 195
647.93	Disease, infectious and parasitic, unspecified, maternal, classifiable elsewhere, complicating pregnancy, childbirth, or the puerperium, antepartum condition or complication	207, 210
647.94	Disease, infectious and parasitic, unspecified, maternal, classifiable elsewhere, complicating pregnancy, childbirth, or the puerperium, postpartum condition or complication	204
*614	Disease, inflammatory, of ovary, fallopian tube, pelvic cellular tissue and peritoneum	177
*615	Disease, inflammatory, uterus, except cervix	177, 183
*007	Disease, intestinal, protozoal, other	102
*716.0	Disease, Kaschin-Beck	129
*438	Disease, late effects, cerebrovascular	10
571.8	Disease, liver, chronic, nonalcoholic, other	111
571.9	Disease, liver, chronic, without mention of alcohol, unspecified	111
*386.0	Disease, Meniere's	33
437.5	Disease, Moyamoya	16
031.8	Disease, mycobacterial, other	248, 308
616.8	Disease, other specified, inflammatory, cervix, vagina, vulva	177, 183
*543	Disease, other, appendix	104
*088	Disease, other, arthropod-borne	248
437.8	Disease, other, cerebrovascular	11
474.8	Disease, other, chronic, tonsils and adenoids	36
*077	Disease, other, conjunctiva, due to viruses and Chlamydiae	22
074.8	Disease, other, due to Coxsackie virus	247
437.1	Disease, other, general, ischemic, cerebrovascular	17
429.89	Disease, other, ill-defined, heart	87
655.43	Disease, other, maternal, suspected fetal damage, affecting management of mother, antepartum condition or complication	208
655.41	Disease, other, maternal, suspected fetal damage, affecting management of mother, delivered, with or without mention of antepartum condition	187, 199
655.40	Disease, other, maternal, suspected fetal damage, affecting management of mother, unspecified as to episode of care	213
519.3	Disease, other, mediastinum	47
518.89	Disease, other, not elsewhere classified, lung	47
478.29	Disease, other, pharynx or nasopharynx	36
519.1	Disease, other, trachea, bronchus	46, 320
448.9	Disease, other, unspecified, capillary	86
066.8	Disease, other, viral, specified arthropod-borne	247
*332	Disease, Parkinson's	10
614.8	Disease, pelvic, inflammatory, female, other	183
614.9	Disease, pelvic, inflammatory, female, unspecified	183
*523	Disease, periodontal	37, 320
607.85	Disease, Peyronie's	172
031.0	Disease, pulmonary, due to Mycobacterium avium, intracellulare, kansasii	42
356.3	Disease, Refsum's	15
099.3	Disease, Reiter's	128
770.7	Disease, respiratory, chronic, arising in the perinatal period	45
519.9	Disease, respiratory, unspecified	47
695.81	Disease, Ritter's	142
*527	Disease, salivary glands	36, 320
*706	Disease, sebaceous glands	147
336.9	Disease, spinal cord, unspecified	15, 309
*334	Disease, spinocerebellar	10
446.7	Disease, Takayasu's	128
733.6	Disease, Tietze's	47
*522	Disease, tooth, pulp, periapical tissues	37, 320
289.9	Disease, unspecified, blood and blood-forming organs	235, 310
437.9	Disease, unspecified, cerebrovascular	11
474.9	Disease, unspecified, chronic, tonsils and adenoids	36
616.9	Disease, unspecified, inflammatory, cervix, vagina, vulva	177, 183
478.70	Disease, unspecified, larynx	36
478.20	Disease, unspecified, pharynx	36
443.9	Disease, vascular, peripheral, unspecified type	86

Code	Narrative	Page
099.52	Disease, venereal, due to Chlamydia trachomatis, anus and rectum	103
099.53	Disease, venereal, due to Chlamydia trachomatis, lower genitourinary sites	172, 176, 182
099.54	Disease, venereal, due to Chlamydia trachomatis, other genitourinary sites	163
099.59	Disease, venereal, due to Chlamydia trachomatis, other specified sites	172, 176, 182
099.56	Disease, venereal, due to Chlamydia trachomatis, peritoneum	103
099.51	Disease, venereal, due to Chlamydia trachomatis, pharynx	34, 318
099.55	Disease, venereal, due to Chlamydia trachomatis, unspecified genitourinary sites	172, 176, 182
099.50	Disease, venereal, due to Chlamydia trachomatis, unspecified site	172, 176, 182
099.8	Disease, venereal, other specified	172, 176, 182
099.9	Disease, venereal, unspecified	172, 176, 182
066.9	Disease, viral, arthropod-borne, unspecified	247
655.33	Disease, viral, maternal, suspected fetal damage, affecting management of mother, antepartum condition or complication	208
655.31	Disease, viral, maternal, suspected fetal damage, affecting management of mother, delivered, with or without mention of antepartum condition	187, 199
655.30	Disease, viral, maternal, suspected fetal damage, affecting management of mother, unspecified as to episode of care	213
647.60	Disease, viral, other, maternal, classifiable elsewhere, complicating pregnancy, childbirth, or the puerperium, unspecified as to episode of care	212
647.61	Disease, viral, other, maternal, classifiable elsewhere, complicating pregnancy, childbirth, or the puerperium, delivered, with or without mention of antepartum condition	186, 195
647.62	Disease, viral, other, maternal, classifiable elsewhere, complicating pregnancy, childbirth, or the puerperium, delivered, with mention of postpartum complication	186, 195
647.63	Disease, viral, other, maternal, classifiable elsewhere, complicating pregnancy, childbirth, or the puerperium, antepartum condition or complication	207, 210
647.64	Disease, viral, other, maternal, classifiable elsewhere, complicating pregnancy, childbirth, or the puerperium, postpartum condition or complication	204
040.2	Disease, Whipple's	103
*288	Disease, white blood cells	235
*027	Disease, zoonotic bacterial, other	248
*395	Diseases, aortic valve	88
648.63	Diseases, cardiovascular, other, maternal, complicating pregnancy, childbirth, or the puerperium, antepartum condition or complication	207, 210
648.61	Diseases, cardiovascular, other, maternal, complicating pregnancy, childbirth, or the puerperium, delivered, with or without mention of antepartum condition	186, 196
648.62	Diseases, cardiovascular, other, maternal, complicating pregnancy, childbirth, or the puerperium, delivered, with mention of postpartum complication	186, 196
648.64	Diseases, cardiovascular, other, maternal, complicating pregnancy, childbirth, or the puerperium, postpartum condition or complication	204
648.60	Diseases, cardiovascular, other, maternal, complicating pregnancy, childbirth, or the puerperium, unspecified as to episode of care	212
*525	Diseases, conditions, other, teeth, supporting structures	37, 320
*529	Diseases, conditions, other, tongue	37, 320
*710	Diseases, diffuse, connective tissue	128
*397	Diseases, endocardial structures, other	88
*526	Diseases, jaw	37, 320
*396	Diseases, mitral and aortic valves	88
*394	Diseases, mitral valve	88
*703	Diseases, nail	147
478.9	Diseases, other and unspecified, upper respiratory tract	34, 319
*289.8	Diseases, other specified, blood and blood-forming organs	235
*424	Diseases, other, endocardium	88
478.79	Diseases, other, larynx	36
*478.7	Diseases, other, larynx, not elsewhere classified	319
478.1	Diseases, other, nasal cavity and sinuses	36, 230
*423	Diseases, other, pericardium	91
*478.2	Diseases, other, pharynx, not elsewhere classified	319
*417	Diseases, other, pulmonary circulation	91
519.8	Diseases, other, respiratory system	47

*** Code Range**

Code	Narrative	Page
*289.5	Diseases, other, spleen,	235
478.5	Diseases, other, vocal cords	36, 319
*577	Diseases, pancreas	110
*528	Diseases, soft tissues, oral, excluding lesions specific for gingiva, tongue	37, 320
*521	Diseases, tooth, hard tissue	37, 320
527.9	Diseases, unspecified, salivary glands	310
*443.8	Diseases, vascular, peripheral, specified type	86
647.20	Diseases, venereal, other, maternal, classifiable elsewhere, complicating pregnancy, childbirth, or the puerperium, unspecified as to episode of care	211
647.21	Diseases, venereal, other, maternal, classifiable elsewhere, complicating pregnancy, childbirth, or the puerperium, delivered, with or without mention of antepartum condition	186, 195
647.22	Diseases, venereal, other, maternal, classifiable elsewhere, complicating pregnancy, childbirth, or the puerperium, delivered, with mention of postpartum complication	186, 195
647.23	Diseases, venereal, other, maternal, classifiable elsewhere, complicating pregnancy, childbirth, or the puerperium, antepartum condition or complication	207, 210
647.24	Diseases, venereal, other, maternal, classifiable elsewhere, complicating pregnancy, childbirth, or the puerperium, postpartum condition or complication	204
*837	Dislocation, ankle	133
837.0	Dislocation, closed, ankle	296
*832.0	Dislocation, closed, elbow	296
*834.0	Dislocation, closed, finger	296
*838.0	Dislocation, closed, foot	296
*835.0	Dislocation, closed, hip	296
830.0	Dislocation, closed, jaw	296
839.8	Dislocation, closed, multiple and ill-defined	132, 296
*839.6	Dislocation, closed, other location	296
*836.5	Dislocation, closed, other, knee	296
839.69	Dislocation, closed, other, multiple and ill-defined, other location	132
836.3	Dislocation, closed, patella	296
*831.0	Dislocation, closed, shoulder	296
839.61	Dislocation, closed, sternum	44
*839.4	Dislocation, closed, vertebra, other	129, 296
*839.2	Dislocation, closed, vertebra, thoracic and lumbar	129, 296
*833.0	Dislocation, closed, wrist	296
*754.3	Dislocation, congenital, hip	135
754.41	Dislocation, congenital, knee, with genu recurvatum	133
*718.7	Dislocation, developmental, joint	134
*832	Dislocation, elbow	133
*834	Dislocation, finger	132
*838	Dislocation, foot	132
*835	Dislocation, hip	127
*830	Dislocation, jaw	38, 320
*836	Dislocation, knee	133
836.1	Dislocation, knee, tear of cartilage meniscus, lateral, current	296
836.0	Dislocation, knee, tear of cartilage meniscus, medial, current	296
836.2	Dislocation, knee, tear of cartilage meniscus, other, current	296
837.1	Dislocation, open, ankle	296, 305
*832.1	Dislocation, open, elbow	296, 305
*834.1	Dislocation, open, finger	296
*838.1	Dislocation, open, foot	296
*835.1	Dislocation, open, hip	296, 305
830.1	Dislocation, open, jaw	296
839.9	Dislocation, open, multiple and ill-defined	132, 296
*836.6	Dislocation, open, other, knee	296, 305
839.79	Dislocation, open, other, multiple and ill-defined, other location	132, 296
836.4	Dislocation, open, patella	296
*831.1	Dislocation, open, shoulder	296, 305
839.71	Dislocation, open, sternum	44, 296, 304
*839.5	Dislocation, open, vertebra, other	129, 296
839.59	Dislocation, open, vertebra, other	305
839.52	Dislocation, open, vertebra, sacrum	305
*839.3	Dislocation, open, vertebra, thoracic and lumbar	129, 296
*833.1	Dislocation, open, wrist	296
718.27	Dislocation, pathological, ankle and foot	133
718.23	Dislocation, pathological, forearm	132
718.24	Dislocation, pathological, hand	132
718.26	Dislocation, pathological, lower leg	133
718.29	Dislocation, pathological, multiple sites	134
718.28	Dislocation, pathological, other specified sites	134
718.25	Dislocation, pathological, pelvic region and thich	134
718.21	Dislocation, pathological, shoulder region	133
718.20	Dislocation, pathological, site unspecified	132
718.22	Dislocation, pathological, upper arm	133
718.37	Dislocation, recurrent, joint, ankle and foot	133
718.33	Dislocation, recurrent, joint, forearm	132

Code	Narrative	Page
718.34	Dislocation, recurrent, joint, hand	132
718.36	Dislocation, recurrent, joint, lower leg	133
718.39	Dislocation, recurrent, joint, multiple sites	134
718.38	Dislocation, recurrent, joint, other specified sites	134
718.35	Dislocation, recurrent, joint, pelvic region and thich	134
718.31	Dislocation, recurrent, joint, shoulder region	133
718.30	Dislocation, recurrent, joint, site unspecified	134
718.32	Dislocation, recurrent, joint, upper arm	133
*831	Dislocation, shoulder	133
*833	Dislocation, wrist	132
*839.0	Dislocations, closed, other, multiple, ill-defined, vertebra, cervical	129, 296, 305
*839.1	Dislocations, open, other, multiple, ill-defined, vertebra, cervical	129, 296, 305
*367.8	Disorder, accommodation, refraction, other	24
277.4	Disorder, bilirubin excretion	111
*596	Disorder, bladder	165
*275.4	Disorder, calcium metabolism	154
271.8	Disorder, carbohydrate transport and metabolism, other specified	155
271.9	Disorder, carbohydrate transport and metabolism, unspecified	155
718.07	Disorder, cartilage, articular, ankle and foot	133
718.03	Disorder, cartilage, articular, forearm	132
718.04	Disorder, cartilage, articular, hand	132
718.09	Disorder, cartilage, articular, multiple sites	134
718.08	Disorder, cartilage, articular, other specified sites	134
718.05	Disorder, cartilage, articular, pelvic region and thigh	134
718.01	Disorder, cartilage, articular, shoulder region	132
718.00	Disorder, cartilage, articular, site unspecified	134
718.02	Disorder, cartilage, articular, upper arm	133
*299.1	Disorder, childhood, disintegrative	252
*312.8	Disorder, conduct, other, not elsewhere classified	253
*312.2	Disorder, conduct, socialized	253
*312.0	Disorder, conduct, undersocialized, aggressive type	253
426.89	Disorder, conduction, other specified	219, 226
275.1	Disorder, copper metabolism	155
300.6	Disorder, depersonalization	251
311	Disorder, depressive, other	251
*299.8	Disorder, developmental, pervasive, other specified	253
*299.9	Disorder, developmental, pervasive, unspecified	253
*722	Disorder, disc, intervertebral	129
300.4	Disorder, dysthymic	251
307.50	Disorder, eating, unspecified	253
*259	Disorder, endocrine, other	156
300.16	Disorder, factitious, with predominantly psychological signs and symptoms	251
307.59	Disorder, feeding, psychogenic, other	253
*276	Disorder, fluid, electrolyte and acid-base balance	154, 218, 225, 309
536.9	Disorder, function, stomach, unspecified	102
*360.2	Disorder, globe, degenerative	23
312.34	Disorder, impulse control, explosive, intermittent	252
312.35	Disorder, impulse control, explosive, isolated	252
312.31	Disorder, impulse control, gambling, pathological	252
312.32	Disorder, impulse control, kleptomania	252
312.39	Disorder, impulse control, other	252
312.33	Disorder, impulse control, pyromania	253
569.89	Disorder, intestine, other	104
569.9	Disorder, intestine, unspecified	104
275.0	Disorder, iron metabolism	155
*375.1	Disorder, lacrimal gland, other	24
*272	Disorder, lipoid metabolism	155
*766.2	Disorder, long gestation, postterm, infant, not heavy-for-dates	230, 231
275.2	Disorder, magnesium metabolism	154
*626	Disorder, menstruation, abnormal bleeding, genital tract, female	177, 183
292.0	Disorder, mental, drug-induced, drug withdrawal	218, 225
294.9	Disorder, mental, due to conditions classified elsewhere, persistent, unspecified	309
*293.8	Disorder, mental, due to conditions classified elsewhere, transient, other	252
293.9	Disorder, mental, due to conditions classified elsewhere, transient, unspecified	251
310.8	Disorder, mental, other specified nonpsychotic, following organic brain damage	252
310.9	Disorder, mental, unspecified nonpsychotic, following organic brain damage	252, 309
273.4	Disorder, metabolism, plasma protein, alpha-1-antitrypsin deficiency	155
273.8	Disorder, metabolism, plasma protein, other	236, 244

*Code Range

Code	Narrative	Page
273.2	Disorder, metabolism, plasma protein, other paraproteinemias	237
277.9	Disorder, metabolism, unspecified	155
275.8	Disorder, mineral metabolism, other specified	155
275.9	Disorder, mineral metabolism, unspecified	155
313.1	Disorder, misery and unhappiness, childhood, adolescence	252
*327.5	Disorder, movement, sleep related, organic	319
327.53	Disorder, movement, sleep related, organic, bruxism	35
327.52	Disorder, movement, sleep related, organic, leg cramps	15
327.59	Disorder, movement, sleep related, organic, other	35
327.51	Disorder, movement, sleep related, organic, periodic limb	15
780.58	Disorder, movement, sleep related, unspecified	253
307.3	Disorder, movement, stereotypic	253
358.2	Disorder, myoneural toxic	11
358.8	Disorder, myoneural, other specified	12
358.9	Disorder, myoneural, unspecified	12
*353	Disorder, nerve root, plexus	11
388.5	Disorder, nerve, acoustic	36
*352	Disorder, nerve, other cranial	11
*337	Disorder, nervous system, autonomic	11
349.9	Disorder, nervous system, unspecified	11, 309
300.9	Disorder, nonpsychotic mental, unspecified	251
301.4	Disorder, obsessive-compulsive personality	252
*377.5	Disorder, optic chiasm	16
676.33	Disorder, other and unspecified, breast, associated with childbirth, antepartum condition or complication	209
676.32	Disorder, other and unspecified, breast, associated with childbirth, delivered, with mention of postpartum complication	192, 203
676.31	Disorder, other and unspecified, breast, associated with childbirth, delivered, with or without mention of antepartum condition	192, 203
676.34	Disorder, other and unspecified, breast, associated with childbirth, postpartum condition or complication	205
676.30	Disorder, other and unspecified, breast, associated with childbirth, unspecified as to episode of care	214
374.56	Disorder, other degenerative, skin affecting eyelid	24
*719.8	Disorder, other specified, joint	130
623.8	Disorder, other specified, noninflammatory, vagina	230
607.89	Disorder, other specified, penis	172
537.89	Disorder, other specified, stomach and duodenum	102
733.99	Disorder, other, bone and cartilage	134
776.3	Disorder, other, coagulation, transient, neonatal	216, 223
530.89	Disorder, other, esophagus	102
*380.8	Disorder, other, external ear	35
*374.8	Disorder, other, eyelid	24
*375.8	Disorder, other, lacrimal system	25
676.83	Disorder, other, lactation, antepartum condition or complication	209
676.82	Disorder, other, lactation, delivered, with mention of postpartum complication	193, 203
676.81	Disorder, other, lactation, delivered, with or without mention of antepartum condition	193, 203
676.84	Disorder, other, lactation, postpartum condition or complication	205
676.80	Disorder, other, lactation, unspecified as to episode of care	214
376.89	Disorder, other, orbital	25
*602	Disorder, other, prostate	172
313.0	Disorder, overanxious, childhood, adolescence	252
*568	Disorder, peritoneum, other	104
301.10	Disorder, personality, affective, unspecified	252
301.7	Disorder, personality, antisocial	252
301.12	Disorder, personality, chronic depressive	251
301.11	Disorder, personality, chronic hypomanic,	252
301.13	Disorder, personality, cyclothymic	252
301.6	Disorder, personality, dependent	252
301.3	Disorder, personality, explosive	252
*301.5	Disorder, personality, histrionic	252
*301.8	Disorder, personality, other	252
301.0	Disorder, personality, paranoid	252
*301.2	Disorder, personality, schizoid	252
301.9	Disorder, personality, unspecified	252
275.3	Disorder, phosphorus metabolism	155
273.9	Disorder, plasma protein metabolism, unspecified	236, 244
277.1	Disorder, porphyrin metabolism	155
277.2	Disorder, purine and pyrimidine metabolism, other	155
327.42	Disorder, REM sleep behavior	35
362.9	Disorder, retina, unspecified	23
*327.3	Disorder, sleep, circadian rhythm	15, 319
*307.4	Disorder, sleep, nonorganic origin	253
327.8	Disorder, sleep, organic, other	35, 319
327.22	Disorder, sleep, periodic breathing, high altitude	46

Code	Narrative	Page
*300.8	Disorder, somatoform	251
367.9	Disorder, unspecified, accommodation, refraction, other	24
733.90	Disorder, unspecified, bone and cartilage	134
459.9	Disorder, unspecified, circulatory system	87
388.9	Disorder, unspecified, ear	36
530.9	Disorder, unspecified, esophagus	102
380.9	Disorder, unspecified, external ear	35
378.9	Disorder, unspecified, eye movements	25
*379.9	Disorder, unspecified, eye, adnexa	25
374.9	Disorder, unspecified, eyelid	24
608.9	Disorder, unspecified, genital organs, male	172
360.9	Disorder, unspecified, globe	23
364.9	Disorder, unspecified, iris, ciliary body	23
*719.9	Disorder, unspecified, joint	130
593.9	Disorder, unspecified, kidney and ureter	165
375.9	Disorder, unspecified, lacrimal system	25
676.93	Disorder, unspecified, lactation, antepartum condition or complication	210
676.92	Disorder, unspecified, lactation, delivered, with mention of postpartum complication	193, 203
676.91	Disorder, unspecified, lactation, delivered, with or without mention of antepartum condition	193, 203
676.94	Disorder, unspecified, lactation, postpartum condition or complication	205
676.90	Disorder, unspecified, lactation, unspecified as to episode of care	214
377.9	Disorder, unspecified, optic nerve, visual pathways	16
376.9	Disorder, unspecified, orbital	25
607.9	Disorder, unspecified, penis	172
698.9	Disorder, unspecified, Pruritic	147
709.9	Disorder, unspecified, skin and subcutaneous tissue	310
537.9	Disorder, unspecified, stomach and duodenum	102
727.9	Disorder, unspecified, synovium, tendon and bursa	131
384.9	Disorder, unspecified, tympanic membrane	36
*599.8	Disorder, urethra and urinary tract, other specified	165
607.82	Disorder, vascular, penis	172
*368.3	Disorder, vision, binocular	24
*588	Disorders from impairment, function, renal disorders	165
*270	Disorders, amino-acid transport and metabolism	155

Code	Narrative	Page
648.70	Disorders, bone and joint, back, pelvis, lower limbs, maternal, complicating pregnancy, childbirth, or the puerperium, unspecified as to episode of care	212
648.71	Disorders, bone and joint, back, pelvis, lower limbs, maternal, complicating pregnancy, childbirth, or the puerperium, delivered, with or without mention of antepartum condition	186, 198
648.72	Disorders, bone and joint, back, pelvis, lower limbs, maternal, complicating pregnancy, childbirth, or the puerperium, delivered, with mention of postpartum complication	186, 198
648.73	Disorders, bone and joint, back, pelvis, lower limbs, maternal, complicating pregnancy, childbirth, or the puerperium, antepartum condition or complication	207, 211
648.74	Disorders, bone and joint, back, pelvis, lower limbs, maternal, complicating pregnancy, childbirth, or the puerperium, postpartum condition or complication	204
648.50	Disorders, cardiovascular, congenital, maternal, complicating pregnancy, childbirth, or the puerperium, unspecified as to episode of care	212
648.51	Disorders, cardiovascular, congenital, maternal, complicating pregnancy, childbirth, or the puerperium, delivered, with or without mention of antepartum condition	186, 195
648.52	Disorders, cardiovascular, congenital, maternal, complicating pregnancy, childbirth, or the puerperium, delivered, with mention of postpartum complication	186, 196
648.53	Disorders, cardiovascular, congenital, maternal, complicating pregnancy, childbirth, or the puerperium, antepartum condition or complication	207, 210
648.54	Disorders, cardiovascular, congenital, maternal, complicating pregnancy, childbirth, or the puerperium, postpartum condition or complication	204
674.03	Disorders, cerebrovascular, in the puerperium, antepartum condition or complication	209
674.02	Disorders, cerebrovascular, in the puerperium, delivered, with mention of postpartum complication	192, 197
674.01	Disorders, cerebrovascular, in the puerperium, delivered, with or without mention of antepartum condition	192, 197

* Code Range

Code	Narrative	Page
674.04	Disorders, cerebrovascular, in the puerperium, postpartum condition or complication	205
674.00	Disorders, cerebrovascular, in the puerperium, unspecified as to episode of care	214
*426	Disorders, conduction, heart	89
*372	Disorders, conjunctiva	24
*388.0	Disorders, degenerative, vascular, ear	36
519.4	Disorders, diaphragm	47
766.1	Disorders, high birthweight, heavy-for-dates, other, infant	229, 231
*279	Disorders, immune mechanism	309
312.30	Disorders, impulse control, unspecified	253
*376.1	Disorders, inflammatory, chronic, orbit	25
766.0	Disorders, long gestation, large baby, exceptionally	229, 231
349.2	Disorders, meninges, not elsewhere classified	15
*627	Disorders, menopausal and postmenopausal	177, 183
*291	Disorders, mental, alcohol-induced	254
*292	Disorders, mental, drug-induced	254
*294	Disorders, mental, due to conditions classified elsewhere, persistent	252
648.43	Disorders, mental, maternal, complicating pregnancy, childbirth, or the puerperium, antepartum condition or complication	207, 210
648.41	Disorders, mental, maternal, complicating pregnancy, childbirth, or the puerperium, delivered, with or without mention of antepartum condition	186, 198
648.42	Disorders, mental, maternal, complicating pregnancy, childbirth, or the puerperium, delivered, with mention of postpartum complication	186, 198
648.44	Disorders, mental, maternal, complicating pregnancy, childbirth, or the puerperium, postpartum condition or complication	204
648.40	Disorders, mental, maternal, complicating pregnancy, childbirth, or the puerperium, unspecified as to episode of care	212
*277.8	Disorders, metabolism, other specified	155
*296	Disorders, mood, episodic	252
*728	Disorders, muscle, ligament and fascia	131
723.9	Disorders, musculoskeletal, unspecified, and symptoms referable to neck	129
*351	Disorders, nerve, facial	11
*350	Disorders, nerve, trigeminal	11
349.89	Disorders, nervous system, other	11
457.8	Disorders, noninfectious, other, lymphatic channels	235
*380.3	Disorders, noninfectious, pinna	35
457.9	Disorders, noninfectious, unspecified, lymphatic channels	235
*622	Disorders, noninflammatory, cervix	177, 183
*620	Disorders, noninflammatory, ovary, fallopian tube, broad ligament	177, 183
*623	Disorders, noninflammatory, vagina	177, 183
*624	Disorders, noninflammatory, vulva and perineum	177, 183
300.3	Disorders, obsessive compulsive	251
*724	Disorders, other and unspecified, back	129
729.9	Disorders, other and unspecified, soft tissue	130
364.8	Disorders, other iris, ciliary body	23
447.8	Disorders, other specified, arteries and arterioles	86
459.89	Disorders, other specified, circulatory system	87
379.8	Disorders, other specified, eye, adnexa	25
*608.8	Disorders, other specified, genital organs, male	172
*593.8	Disorders, other specified, kidney and ureter	165
*569.4	Disorders, other specified, rectum and anus	104
*384.8	Disorders, other specified, tympanic membrane	36
*576	Disorders, other, biliary tract	111
*611	Disorders, other, breast	143
388.8	Disorders, other, ear	36
*381.8	Disorders, other, Eustachian tube	36
*575	Disorders, other, gallbladder	111
*629	Disorders, other, genital organs, female	177, 183
*360.8	Disorders, other, globe	23
386.8	Disorders, other, labyrinth	33
*573	Disorders, other, liver	111
*383.8	Disorders, other, mastoid	36
*385	Disorders, other, middle ear and mastoid	36
*377.4	Disorders, other, optic nerve	22
429.81	Disorders, other, papillary muscle	59, 62, 64, 73, 77, 79, 83, 84, 88, 219, 226
*379.1	Disorders, other, sclera	25
374.45	Disorders, other, sensorimotor, eyelid	22
*709	Disorders, other, skin and subcutaneous tissue	148, 230
*727.8	Disorders, other, synovium, tendon and bursa	131
*300.2	Disorders, phobic	251
*362.8	Disorders, retinal, other	23

Code	Narrative	Page
*295	Disorders, schizophrenic	252
*313.2	Disorders, sensitivity , shyness, social withdrawal, childhood or adolescence	253
374.44	Disorders, sensory, eyelid	24
*302	Disorders, sexual and gender identity	253
*327.0	Disorders, sleep, organic, initiating and maintaining sleep	253
*705	Disorders, sweat glands	147
*520	Disorders, tooth development, eruption	37, 320
447.9	Disorders, unspecified, arteries and arterioles	86
374.50	Disorders, unspecified, degenerative, eyelid	24
381.9	Disorders, unspecified, Eustachian tube	36
599.9	Disorders, unspecified, urethra and urinary tract	165
*621	Disorders, uterus, not elsewhere classified	177, 183
*377.7	Disorders, visual cortex	16
*377.6	Disorders, visual pathways, other	16
*379.2	Disorders, vitreous body	25
376.36	Displacement, lateral, globe	22
653.03	Disproportion, abnormality, major, bony pelvis, not further specified, in pregnancy, antepartum condition or complication	207
653.01	Disproportion, abnormality, major, bony pelvis, not further specified, in pregnancy, delivered, with or without mention of antepartum condition	187, 198
653.00	Disproportion, abnormality, major, bony pelvis, not further specified, in pregnancy, unspecified as to episode of care	212
653.43	Disproportion, fetopelvic, antepartum condition or complication	207
653.41	Disproportion, fetopelvic, delivered, with or without mention of antepartum condition	187, 199
653.40	Disproportion, fetopelvic, unspecified as to episode of care	212
653.83	Disproportion, other origin, fetal, antepartum condition or complication	207
653.81	Disproportion, other origin, fetal, delivered, with or without mention of antepartum condition	187, 199
653.80	Disproportion, other origin, fetal, unspecified as to episode of care	213
653.93	Disproportion, unspecified, fetal, antepartum condition or complication	207
653.91	Disproportion, unspecified, fetal, delivered, with or without mention of antepartum condition	187, 199
653.90	Disproportion, unspecified, fetal, unspecified as to episode of care	213
780.55	Disruption, of 24 hour sleep wake cycles, unspecified	253
674.12	Disruption, wound, cesarean, delivered, with mention of postpartum complication	192, 197
674.14	Disruption, wound, cesarean, postpartum condition or complication	205
674.10	Disruption, wound, cesarean, unspecified as to episode of care	214
674.22	Disruption, wound, perineal, obstetrical, delivered, with mention of postpartum complication	192, 197
674.24	Disruption, wound, perineal, obstetrical, postpartum condition or complication	205
674.20	Disruption, wound, perineal, obstetrical, unspecified as to episode of care	214
441.02	Dissecting aortic aneurysm (any part), abdominal	59, 62, 64, 73, 77, 79
441.01	Dissecting aortic aneurysm (any part), thoracic	59, 62, 64, 73, 77, 79
441.03	Dissecting aortic aneurysm (any part), thoracoabdominal	59, 62, 64, 73, 77, 79
441.00	Dissecting aortic aneurysm (any part), unspecified site	59, 62, 64, 73, 77, 79
414.12	Dissection of coronary artery	58, 61, 63, 73, 76, 79
443.21	Dissection, carotid artery	86
443.22	Dissection, iliac artery	59, 62, 64, 73, 77, 79, 86
443.29	Dissection, other artery	59, 62, 64, 73, 77, 80, 86
443.23	Dissection, renal artery	165
443.24	Dissection, vertebral artery	86
368.15	Distortion, visual, entoptic phenomena, other	24
368.14	Distortion, visual, shape, size	24
656.33	Distress, fetal, affecting management of mother, antepartum condition or complication	208
656.31	Distress, fetal, affecting management of mother, delivered, with or without mention of antepartum condition	188, 199
656.30	Distress, fetal, affecting management of mother, unspecified as to episode of care	188, 199
669.03	Distress, maternal, antepartum condition or complication	209
669.02	Distress, maternal, delivered, with mention of postpartum complication	191, 202
669.01	Distress, maternal, delivered, with or without mention of antepartum condition	191, 202
669.04	Distress, maternal, postpartum condition or complication	205

Code	Narrative	Page
669.00	Distress, maternal, unspecified as to episode of care	191, 202
769	Distress, syndrome, respiratory, newborn	215
312.4	Disturbance, conduct, mixed with emotions	253
*312.1	Disturbance, conduct, undersocialized, unaggressive type	253
312.9	Disturbance, conduct, unspecified	253
*313.8	Disturbance, emotional, other or mixed, childhood or adolescence	253
313.9	Disturbance, emotional, unspecified, childhood or adolescence	253
429.4	Disturbance, heart, functional, following cardiac surgery	84, 91, 219, 226
784.5	Disturbance, other, speech	16
782.0	Disturbance, sensation, skin	16
781.1	Disturbance, sensation, smell and taste	16
780.50	Disturbance, unspecified, sleep	253
368.8	Disturbance, visual, other specified	24
368.16	Disturbance, visual, psychophysical	24
368.10	Disturbance, visual, subjective, unspecified	24
368.9	Disturbance, visual, unspecified	24
*784.4	Disturbance, voice	36
520.6	Disturbances, tooth eruption	230
562.13	Diverticulitis, colon, with hemorrhage	100
562.11	Diverticulitis, colon, without hemorrhage	103
562.03	Diverticulitis, small intestine, with hemorrhage	100
562.01	Diverticulitis, small intestine, without hemorrhage	103
562.12	Diverticulosis, colon, with hemorrhage	100
562.10	Diverticulosis, colon, without hemorrhage	103
562.02	Diverticulosis, small intestine, with hemorrhage	100
562.00	Diverticulosis, small intestine, without hemorrhage	103
750.27	Diverticulum, congenital, pharynx	36, 320
530.6	Diverticulum, esophagus, acquired	102
537.1	Diverticulum, gastric	102
599.2	Diverticulum, urethral	165
780.4	Dizziness and giddiness	33
*V59.0	Donor, blood	289
V59.2	Donor, bone	135
V59.3	Donor, bone marrow	289
V59.5	Donor, cornea	289
*V59.7	Donor, egg (oocyte) (ovum)	289
V59.4	Donor, kidney	165
V59.6	Donor, liver	111
V59.8	Donor, organ or tissue, other specified	289
V59.9	Donor, organ or tissue, unspecified	289
V59.1	Donor, skin	148
752.2	Doubling, congenital, uterus	177, 183
736.05	Drop wrist, acquired	12
377.21	Drusen, optic disc	22
535.61	Duodenitis, with hemorrhage	100
535.60	Duodenitis, without hemorrhage	102
006.0	Dysentery, amebic, acute, without mention of abscess	101
780.56	Dysfunction, associated with sleep stages or arousal from sleep	253
*386.5	Dysfunction, labyrinthine	33
*256	Dysfunction, ovarian	176, 183
*258	Dysfunction, polyglandular, related disorders	156
784.69	Dysfunction, symbolic, other	253
784.60	Dysfunction, symbolic, unspecified	253
*257	Dysfunction, testicular	156
648.13	Dysfunction, thyroid, maternal, complicating pregnancy, childbirth, or the puerperium, antepartum condition or complication	207, 210
648.11	Dysfunction, thyroid, maternal, complicating pregnancy, childbirth, or the puerperium, delivered, with or without mention of antepartum condition	186, 198
648.12	Dysfunction, thyroid, maternal, complicating pregnancy, childbirth, or the puerperium, delivered, with mention of postpartum complication	186, 198
648.14	Dysfunction, thyroid, maternal, complicating pregnancy, childbirth, or the puerperium, postpartum condition or complication	204
648.10	Dysfunction, thyroid, maternal, complicating pregnancy, childbirth, or the puerperium, unspecified as to episode of care	212
758.6	Dysgenesis, gonadal	173, 177, 183
530.5	Dyskinesia, esophagus	102
333.82	Dyskinesia, orofacial	15
277.7	Dysmetabolic syndrome X	155
536.8	Dyspepsia and disorders of function, other specified, stomach	102
*610	Dysplasia, benign , mammary	143
757.31	Dysplasia, congenital, ectodermal	148
*786.0	Dyspnea, respiratory abnormalities	46, 310
*427.8	Dysrhythmia, other specified, cardiac	89
427.9	Dysrhythmia, unspecified, cardiac	89
333.89	Dystonia, torsion, fragments, other	15
333.6	Dystonia, torsion, idiopathic	10
333.7	Dystonia, torsion, symptomatic	10

Alphabetic Index to Diseases

Code	Narrative	Page
*362.7	Dystrophy, hereditary, retinal	23
*359	Dystrophy, muscular, other myopathies	16
788.1	Dysuria	164
782.7	Ecchymoses, spontaneous	234
122.2	Echinococcosis granulosus, thyroid	155
122.9	Echinococcosis, other and unspecified	249
122.0	Echinococcus granulosus, liver	111
122.1	Echinococcus granulosus, lung	42
122.3	Echinococcus granulosus, other	249
122.4	Echinococcus granulosus, unspecified	249
122.5	Echinococcus multilocularis, liver	111
122.6	Echinococcus multilocularis, other	249
122.7	Echinococcus multilocularis, unspecified	249
122.8	Echinococcus, liver, unspecified	111
642.63	Eclampsia, complicating pregnancy, childbirth, and the puerperium, antepartum condition or complication	206, 210
642.62	Eclampsia, complicating pregnancy, childbirth, and the puerperium, delivered, with mention of postpartum complication	185, 195
642.61	Eclampsia, complicating pregnancy, childbirth, and the puerperium, delivered, with or without mention of antepartum condition	185, 195
642.64	Eclampsia, complicating pregnancy, childbirth, and the puerperium, postpartum complication	203
642.60	Eclampsia, complicating pregnancy, childbirth, and the puerperium, unspecified as to episode of care	210, 211
*374.1	Ectropion	24
054.0	Eczema, herpeticum	146, 217, 224
782.3	Edema	286
646.13	Edema or excessive weight gain in pregnancy, without hypertension, antepartum condition or complication	206, 210
646.12	Edema or excessive weight gain in pregnancy, without hypertension, with delivery, with current postpartum complication	185, 198
646.11	Edema or excessive weight gain in pregnancy, without hypertension, with delivery, with or without mention of antepartum complication	185, 198
646.14	Edema or excessive weight gain in pregnancy, without hypertension, with delivery, with postpartum condition or complication	203
348.5	Edema, brain	13
646.10	Edema, excessive weight gain in pregnancy, without hypertension, unspecified as to episode of care	210, 211
757.0	Edema, hereditary, legs	148
478.6	Edema, larynx	36, 319
518.4	Edema, lung, acute, unspecified	44, 220, 227
376.33	Edema, orbital	25
607.83	Edema, penis	172
478.25	Edema, pharynx or nasopharynx	36
506.1	Edema, pulmonary, acute, due to fumes, vapors	44
905.9	Effect, late, amputation, traumatic	131
908.6	Effect, late, certain complications of trauma	272
905.6	Effect, late, dislocation	132
*909	Effect, late, external causes, other and unspecified	274
908.5	Effect, late, foreign body in orifice	272
905.0	Effect, late, fracture, bone, skull and face	16
905.5	Effect, late, fracture, bones, multiple and unspecified	131
905.4	Effect, late, fracture, lower extremities	131
905.3	Effect, late, fracture, neck of femur	131
905.2	Effect, late, fracture, upper extremities	131
905.1	Effect, late, fracture, without spinal cord lesion, spine and trunk	129
*906	Effect, late, injuries, skin and subcutaneous tissues	145
908.3	Effect, late, injury, blood vessel, head, neck and extremities	87
908.4	Effect, late, injury, blood vessel, thorax, abdomen, and pelvis	87
908.0	Effect, late, injury, internal, chest	47
908.1	Effect, late, injury, internal, intraabdominal organs	105
907.0	Effect, late, injury, intracranial, without mention of skull fracture	16
907.3	Effect, late, injury, nerve root(s), spinal plexus(es), and other nerves, trunk	16
907.1	Effect, late, injury, nerve, cranial	16
907.9	Effect, late, injury, nerve, other and unspecified	16
907.5	Effect, late, injury, peripheral nerve, pelvic girdle and lower limb	16
907.4	Effect, late, injury, peripheral nerve, shoulder girdle and upper limb	16
907.2	Effect, late, injury, spinal cord	9
905.8	Effect, late, injury, tendon	131
908.2	Effect, late, internal injury, internal organs, other	173, 177, 184
905.7	Effect, late, sprain and strain, without mention of tendon injury	132
908.9	Effect, late, unspecified injury	272

* Code Range

Code	Narrative	Page
*388.1	Effect, noise, on inner ear	36
*980	Effect, toxic, alcohol	273
986	Effect, toxic, carbon monoxide	274
*983	Effect, toxic, corrosive aromatics, acids, and caustic alkalis	273
987.9	Effect, toxic, gas, fume, or vapor, unspecified	279
*987	Effect, toxic, gases, fumes, or vapors, other	274
*984	Effect, toxic, lead and its compounds (including fumes)	274
*988	Effect, toxic, noxious substances eaten as food	274
*985	Effect, toxic, other metals	274
*989	Effect, toxic, other substances, chiefly nonmedicinal as to source	274
981	Effect, toxic, petroleum products	273
*982	Effect, toxic, solvents other than petroleum-based	273
995.1	Effects, adverse, dema, angioneurotic, not elsewhere classified	273
995.3	Effects, adverse, not elsewhere classified allergy, unspecified	273
995.4	Effects, adverse, not elsewhere classified shock, due to anesthesia	222, 229, 275
*995.8	Effects, adverse, other specified, not elsewhere classified	275
995.0	Effects, adverse, shock, anaphylactic, other, not elsewhere classifed	273
995.2	Effects, adverse, unspecified, drug, medicinal and biological substances, not elsewhere classified	222, 229, 274
993.4	Effects, air pressure caused by explosion	275
994.7	Effects, asphyxiation and strangulation	275
994.1	Effects, drowning and nonfatal submersion	275
994.8	Effects, electrocution and nonfatal effects of electric current	275
994.5	Effects, exhaustion due to excessive exertion	275
994.4	Effects, exhaustion due to exposure	275
*992	Effects, heat and light	275
994.2	Effects, hunger	275
994.0	Effects, lightning	275
994.6	Effects, motion	33
993.2	Effects, other and unspecified, high altitude	275
993.8	Effects, other specified air pressure,	275
994.9	Effects, other, external causes	275
990	Effects, radiation, unspecified	275
*991	Effects, reduced temperature	275
994.3	Effects, thirst	275
993.9	Effects, unspecified air pressure	275
*719.0	Effusion, joint	134
511.9	Effusion, pleural, unspecified	44, 220, 227
*415.1	Embolism and infarction, pulmonary	42, 83, 85
*444	Embolism and thrombosis, arterial	219, 226
444.0	Embolism and thrombosis, arterial, aorta, abdominal	59, 62, 64, 73, 77, 80, 86
444.1	Embolism and thrombosis, arterial, aorta, thoracic	59, 62, 64, 73, 77, 80, 86
*444.2	Embolism and thrombosis, arterial, extremities	86
*444.8	Embolism and thrombosis, arterial, other specified artery	86
444.9	Embolism and thrombosis, arterial, unspecified	86
453.8	Embolism and thrombosis, other specified veins	87
453.3	Embolism and thrombosis, renal vein	165
453.9	Embolism and thrombosis, vein, unspecified site	87
453.2	Embolism and thrombosis, vena cava	59, 62, 64, 73, 77, 80, 86, 219, 226
*453.4	Embolism and thrombosis, venous, deep vessels, lower extremity	87
673.03	Embolism, air, pulmonary, obstetrical, antepartum condition or complication	209
673.02	Embolism, air, pulmonary, obstetrical, delivered, with mention of postpartum complication	192, 196
673.01	Embolism, air, pulmonary, obstetrical, delivered, with or without mention of antepartum condition	192, 196
673.04	Embolism, air, pulmonary, obstetrical, postpartum condition or complication	205
673.00	Embolism, air, pulmonary, obstetrical, unspecified as to episode of care	214
673.13	Embolism, amniotic fluid, pulmonary, obstetrical, antepartum condition or complication	209
673.12	Embolism, amniotic fluid, pulmonary, obstetrical, delivered, with mention of postpartum complication	192, 196
673.11	Embolism, amniotic fluid, pulmonary, obstetrical, delivered, with or without mention of antepartum condition	192, 196
673.14	Embolism, amniotic fluid, pulmonary, obstetrical, postpartum condition or complication	205
673.10	Embolism, amniotic fluid, pulmonary, obstetrical, unspecified as to episode of care	214

Alphabetic Index to Diseases

*** Code Range**

Code	Narrative	Page
673.23	Embolism, blood-clot, pulmonary, obstetrical, antepartum condition or complication	209
673.22	Embolism, blood-clot, pulmonary, obstetrical, delivered, with mention of postpartum complication	192, 196
673.21	Embolism, blood-clot, pulmonary, obstetrical, delivered, with or without mention of antepartum condition	192, 196
673.24	Embolism, blood-clot, pulmonary, obstetrical, postpartum condition or complication	205
673.20	Embolism, blood-clot, pulmonary, obstetrical, unspecified as to episode of care	214
673.83	Embolism, other, pulmonary, obstetrical, antepartum condition or complication	209
673.82	Embolism, other, pulmonary, obstetrical, delivered, with mention of postpartum complication	192, 197
673.81	Embolism, other, pulmonary, obstetrical, delivered, with or without mention of antepartum condition	192, 197
673.84	Embolism, other, pulmonary, obstetrical, postpartum condition or complication	205
673.80	Embolism, other, pulmonary, obstetrical, unspecified as to episode of care	214
673.33	Embolism, pyemic and septic, pulmonary, obstetrical, antepartum condition or complication	209
673.32	Embolism, pyemic and septic, pulmonary, obstetrical, delivered, with mention of postpartum complication	192, 196
673.31	Embolism, pyemic and septic, pulmonary, obstetrical, delivered, with or without mention of antepartum condition	192, 196
673.34	Embolism, pyemic and septic, pulmonary, obstetrical, postpartum condition or complication	205
673.30	Embolism, pyemic and septic, pulmonary, obstetrical, unspecified as to episode of care	214
434.11	Embolism, with cerebral infarction, arteries, cerebral	8, 10, 17, 60, 62, 65, 74, 78, 80
434.10	Embolism, without mention of cerebral infarction, arteries, cerebral	11, 60, 62, 64, 74, 78, 80
518.2	Emphysema, compensatory	47
518.1	Emphysema, interstitial	46, 220, 227
770.2	Emphysema, interstitial, related conditions, fetus or newborn	216, 223
492.8	Emphysema, other	44
*510	Empyema	43, 220, 227
036.1	Encephalitis, meningococcal	7, 12

Code	Narrative	Page
323.8	Encephalitis, other causes	8, 13, 309
323.4	Encephalitis, other, due to infection classified elsewhere	8, 13
323.5	Encephalitis, postimmunization	8, 13
323.6	Encephalitis, postinfection, in conditions classified elsewhere	8, 13
055.0	Encephalitis, postmeasles	7, 12, 217, 224
052.0	Encephalitis, postvaricella	12
323.2	Encephalitis, protozoal diseases classified elsewhere	8, 13
323.1	Encephalitis, rickettsial diseases classified elsewhere	8, 13
094.81	Encephalitis, syphilitic	8, 12
323.7	Encephalitis, toxic	8, 15
323.9	Encephalitis, unspecified cause	8, 13, 309
323.0	Encephalitis, viral diseases elsewhere classified	8, 13
*062	Encephalitis, viral, mosquito-borne	7, 12
*063	Encephalitis, viral, tick-borne	7, 12
064	Encephalitis, viral, transmitted by other and unspecified arthropods	7, 12
056.01	Encephalomyelitis, due to rubella	12
437.2	Encephalopathy, hypertensive	13
349.82	Encephalopathy, toxic	15, 218, 225
*348.3	Encephalopathy, unspecified	11, 309
307.7	Encopresis, nonorganic	253
*V68	Encounter, administrative purposes	289
*V61	Encounter, circumstances, family, other	289
*V60	Encounter, circumstances, housing, household and economic	289
*V62	Encounter, circumstances, psychosocial, other	289
*V65	Encounter, consultation, without complaint or sickness	289
*V56	Encounter, dialysis and dialysis catheter care	162
*V58.6	Encounter, drug use, long-term (current)	286
*V70	Encounter, examination, medical, general	289
V70.3	Encounter, examination, other medical, for administrative purposes	232
V61.5	Encounter, multiparity	178, 184
*V57.2	Encounter, occupational therapy, vocational rehabilitation	286
V61.6	Encounter, pregnancy, illegitimate	210
V61.7	Encounter, pregnancy, other, unwanted	206
*V69	Encounter, problems, lifestyle	289
*V58.1	Encounter, procedure, antineoplastic chemotherapy and immunotherapy	237
V58.0	Encounter, procedure, radiotherapy	237, 242

* Code Range

Code	Narrative	Page
*V64	Encounter, specific procedures, services, not carried out	289
093.20	Endocarditis of valve, unspecified, syphilitic	85
*421	Endocarditis, acute, subacute	84, 219, 226
421.9	Endocarditis, acute, unspecified	59, 61, 63, 73, 76, 79, 85, 309
093.22	Endocarditis, aortic valve, syphilitic	88
421.0	Endocarditis, bacterial, acute or subacute	59, 61, 63, 73, 76, 79, 85, 309
112.81	Endocarditis, candidal	85, 217, 224
074.22	Endocarditis, Coxsackie	88
098.84	Endocarditis, gonococcal	85
424.91	Endocarditis, in diseases classified elsewhere	84
421.1	Endocarditis, infective, acute, subacute, in diseases classified elsewhere	59, 61, 63, 73, 76, 79, 85
036.42	Endocarditis, meningococcal	85
093.21	Endocarditis, mitral valve, syphilitic	88
093.24	Endocarditis, pulmonary valve, syphilitic	88
391.1	Endocarditis, rheumatic, acute	88
093.23	Endocarditis, tricuspid valve, syphilitic	88
*424.9	Endocarditis, valve unspecified	219, 226
424.90	Endocarditis, valve unspecified, unspecified cause	59, 61, 63, 73, 76, 79, 84
617.2	Endometriosis, fallopian tube	177, 183
617.5	Endometriosis, intestinal	103
617.1	Endometriosis, ovary	177, 183
617.3	Endometriosis, pelvic peritoneum	177, 183
617.8	Endometriosis, site, other specified	177, 183
617.9	Endometriosis, site, unspecified	177, 183
617.6	Endometriosis, skin scar	147
617.0	Endometriosis, uterus	177, 183
617.4	Endometriosis, vaginal	177, 183
098.16	Endometritis, gonococcal, acute	176, 182
098.36	Endometritis, gonococcal, chronic	176, 182
360.01	Endophthalmitis, acute	21
360.03	Endophthalmitis, chronic	23
360.19	Endophthalmitis, other	21
360.13	Endophthalmitis, parasitic, unspecified	21
360.00	Endophthalmitis, purulent, unspecified	21
676.23	Engorgement, breast, associated with childbirth, antepartum condition or complication	209
676.22	Engorgement, breast, associated with childbirth, delivered, with mention of postpartum complication	192, 203
676.21	Engorgement, breast, associated with childbirth, delivered, with or without mention of antepartum condition	192, 203
676.24	Engorgement, breast, associated with childbirth, postpartum condition or complication	205
676.20	Engorgement, breast, associated with childbirth, unspecified as to episode of care	214
375.03	Enlargement, chronic, lacrimal gland	24
785.6	Enlargement, lymph nodes	235, 310
*376.5	Enophthalmos	25
663.23	Entanglement, compression, cord, other and unspecified, complicating labor and delivery, antepartum condition or complication	209
663.21	Entanglement, compression, cord, other and unspecified, complicating labor and delivery, delivered, with or without mention of antepartum condition	189, 201
663.20	Entanglement, compression, cord, other and unspecified, complicating labor and delivery, unspecified as to episode of care	189, 201
*555	Enteritis, regional	101
127.4	Enterobiasis	102
777.5	Enterocolitis, necrotizing, in fetus or newborn	216, 223
*556	Enterocolitis, ulcerative	101
*726.3	Enthesopathy, elbow region	131
726.5	Enthesopathy, hip region	131
*726.6	Enthesopathy, knee	131
726.79	Enthesopathy, other, ankle and tarsus	131
726.8	Enthesopathy, other, peripheral	131
720.1	Enthesopathy, spinal	129
*726.9	Enthesopathy, unspecified	131
726.70	Enthesopathy, unspecified, ankle and tarsus	131
726.4	Enthesopathy, wrist and carpus	131
*374.0	Entropion and trichiasis, eyelid	24
307.6	Enuresis, nonorganic	253
518.3	Eosinophilia, pulmonary	45
098.13	Epididymoorchitis, gonococcal, acute	171
098.33	Epididymoorchitis, gonococcal, chronic	171
*464.3	Epiglottitis, acute	33, 319
*345	Epilepsy	13
*375.2	Epiphora	25
095.0	Episcleritis, syphilitic	22
784.7	Epistaxis	33
035	Erysipelas	143
695.1	Erythema multiforme	142
695.2	Erythema nodosum	142

Alphabetic Index to Diseases

Code	Narrative	Page
695.89	Erythema, generalized, other specified	147
695.9	Erythema, generalized, unspecified	147
695.0	Erythema, toxic	142, 221, 228
*207.0	Erythremia and erythroleukemia, acute	242, 244
*530.1	Esophagitis	102
*378.0	Esotropia	25
V24.0	Examination and care, postpartum, immediately after delivery	205
V24.1	Examination and care, postpartum, lactating mother	287
V24.2	Examination and care, postpartum, routine, follow-up	287
V72.1	Examination, ears, hearing	232
V67.2	Examination, follow-up, following chemotherapy	237, 242, 244
V67.6	Examination, follow-up, following combined treatment	289
*V67.5	Examination, follow-up, following other treatment	289
V67.3	Examination, follow-up, following psychotherapy and other treatment for mental disorder	289
V67.1	Examination, follow-up, following radiotherapy	237, 242
V67.4	Examination, follow-up, following treatment, healed fracture	287
*V67.0	Examination, follow-up, surgery	287
V67.9	Examination, follow-up, unspecified	289
*V74	Examination, screening, diseases, bacterial and spirochetal	289
*V75	Examination, screening, diseases, infectious, other	289
*V73	Examination, screening, special, for viral diseases	289
*057	Exanthemata, viral, other	247
378.84	Excess, convergence or spasm, binocular eye movement	25
376.31	Exophthalmos, constant	25
*376.2	Exophthalmos, endocrine	25
376.34	Exophthalmos, intermittent	22
376.35	Exophthalmos, pulsating	22
376.30	Exophthalmos, unspecified	25
*378.1	Exotropia	25
788.8	Extravasation, urine	164
428.0	Failure, congestive, heart, unspecified	57, 59, 61, 63, 73, 77, 79, 219, 226
*428	Failure, heart	82, 84, 85
*428.4	Failure, heart, combined systolic and diastolic	57, 219, 226
398.91	Failure, heart, congestive, rheumatic	56, 58, 61, 63, 72, 76, 78, 82, 84, 85, 218, 225
*428.3	Failure, heart, diastolic	57, 219, 226
428.1	Failure, heart, left	57, 59, 61, 63, 73, 77, 79, 219, 226
*428.2	Failure, heart, systolic	57, 219, 226
428.9	Failure, heart, unspecified	57, 59, 62, 64, 73, 77, 79, 219, 226
676.43	Failure, lactation, antepartum condition or complication	209
676.42	Failure, lactation, delivered, with mention of postpartum complication	192, 203
676.41	Failure, lactation, delivered, with or without mention of antepartum condition	192, 203
676.44	Failure, lactation, postpartum condition or complication	205
676.40	Failure, lactation, unspecified as to episode of care	214
*584	Failure, renal, acute	221, 228
669.32	Failure, renal, acute, following labor and delivery, delivered with mention of postpartum complication	191, 196
669.34	Failure, renal, acute, following labor and delivery, postpartum condition or complication	205
669.30	Failure, renal, acute, following labor and delivery, unspecified as to episode of care	191, 202
584.9	Failure, renal, acute, unspecified	83, 161, 162
584.6	Failure, renal, acute, with lesion of necrosis, cortical	83, 161, 162
584.7	Failure, renal, acute, with lesion of necrosis, medullary	83, 161, 162
584.5	Failure, renal, acute, with lesion of tubular necrosis	83, 161, 162
584.8	Failure, renal, acute, with other specified pathological lesion	83, 161, 162
586	Failure, renal, unspecified	161, 162
518.81	Failure, respiratory, acute	44, 83, 279
518.84	Failure, respiratory, acute and chronic	44, 83, 279
518.83	Failure, respiratory, chronic	44, 83
770.84	Failure, respiratory, newborn	216, 223
729.4	Fasciitis, unspecified	131
121.3	Fascioliasis	111
121.4	Fasciolopsiasis	111
780.6	Fever	246, 247, 310

 * Code Range

Code	Narrative	Page
078.7	Fever, arenaviral hemorrhagic	247
*065	Fever, hemorrhagic, arthropod-borne	247
066.3	Fever, other, mosquito-borne	247
066.0	Fever, phlebotomus	247
*087	Fever, relapsing	248
390	Fever, rheumatic, without mention of heart involvement	128
078.2	Fever, sweating	247
066.1	Fever, tick-borne	247
066.2	Fever, Venezuelan equine	7, 12
*066.4	Fever, West Nile	247
*060	Fever, yellow	247
*427.3	Fibrillation and flutter, atrial	82, 89, 219, 226
*427.4	Fibrillation and flutter, ventricular	82, 89, 219, 226
425.3	Fibroelastosis, endocardial	84
515	Fibrosis, lung, postinflammatory	45
*790.2	Findings, nonspecific, abnormal glucose	154
790.3	Findings, nonspecific, alcohol blood level	254
*795.7	Findings, nonspecific, other immunological	235
790.6	Findings, nonspecific, other, chemistry, blood	286
790.1	Findings, nonspecific, sedimentation rate, elevated	286
790.5	Findings, nonspecific, serum enzyme levels	286
790.4	Findings, nonspecific, transaminase or lactic acid dehydrogenase levels	286
*790.9	Findings, other nonspecific, examination of blood	286
795.6	Findings, serological for syphilis, false positive	128
*565	Fissure and fistula, anal	104
447.0	Fistula, acquired, arteriovenous	86
750.25	Fistula, congenital, lip	37, 320
750.24	Fistula, congenital, salivary gland	36, 320
750.3	Fistula, congenital, tracheoesophageal	104
619.1	Fistula, digestive-genital tract, female	104, 221, 228
569.81	Fistula, intestine, excluding rectum and anus	104
596.1	Fistula, intestinovesical	221, 228
*386.4	Fistula, labyrinthine	36
619.8	Fistula, other specified, genital tract, female	177, 183, 221, 228
383.81	Fistula, postauricular	218, 225
619.2	Fistula, skin-genital tract, female	177, 183
537.4	Fistula, stomach or duodenum	102
530.84	Fistula, tracheoesophageal	102, 220, 227
619.9	Fistula, unspecified, genital tract, female	177, 183
599.1	Fistula, urethral	165
619.0	Fistula, urinary-genital tract, female	177, 183
596.2	Fistula, vesical, NEC	221, 228
V52.0	Fitting, adjustment, artificial arm	131
V52.2	Fitting, adjustment, artificial eye	288
V52.1	Fitting, adjustment, artificial leg	131
*V53.3	Fitting, adjustment, device, cardiac	91
*V53.9	Fitting, adjustment, device, other and unspecified	288
V53.4	Fitting, adjustment, devices, orthodontic	288
V53.7	Fitting, adjustment, devices, orthopedic	131
*V53.0	Fitting, adjustment, devices, related to nervous system and special senses	16
V53.6	Fitting, adjustment, devices, urinary	165
V53.2	Fitting, adjustment, hearing aid	288
V53.5	Fitting, adjustment, intestinal appliance, other	105
V52.4	Fitting, adjustment, prosthesis, implant, breast	288
V52.3	Fitting, adjustment, prosthetic device, dental	288
V52.8	Fitting, adjustment, prosthetic device, other specified	286
V52.9	Fitting, adjustment, prosthetic device, unspecified	286
V53.1	Fitting, adjustment, spectacles and contact lenses	288
V53.8	Fitting, adjustment, wheelchair	288
807.4	Flail chest	44, 294, 303
734	Flat foot	134
937	Foreign body, anus and rectum	105
939.0	Foreign body, bladder and urethra	165
938	Foreign body, digestive system, unspecified	105
931	Foreign body, ear	37
935.1	Foreign body, esophagus	105
*930	Foreign body, external eye	26
939.9	Foreign body, genitourinary tract, unspecified site	165
936	Foreign body, intestine and colon	105
*360.5	Foreign body, magnetic, retained, old, intraocular	23
934.1	Foreign body, main bronchus	47
935.0	Foreign body, mouth	38, 321
*360.6	Foreign body, nonmagnetic, retained, old, intraocular	23
932	Foreign body, nose	35
939.3	Foreign body, penis	173
*933	Foreign body, pharynx and larynx	37, 321
729.6	Foreign body, residual, soft tissue	134

Code	Narrative	Page
934.9	Foreign body, respiratory tree, unspecified	47
376.6	Foreign body, retained, old, following penetrating wound, orbit	25
935.2	Foreign body, stomach	105
934.0	Foreign body, trachea	47
934.8	Foreign body, trachea, bronchus, and lung, other specified parts	47
939.1	Foreign body, uterus, any part	178, 184
939.2	Foreign body, vulva and vagina	178, 184
*824	Fracture, ankle	133
*829	Fracture, bones, unspecified	132
*814	Fracture, carpal bone(s)	132
*810	Fracture, clavicle	133
808.0	Fracture, closed, acetabulum	294
824.0	Fracture, closed, ankle	295
824.4	Fracture, closed, ankle, bimalleolar	295
824.2	Fracture, closed, ankle, lateral malleolus	295
824.6	Fracture, closed, ankle, trimalleolar	295
824.8	Fracture, closed, ankle, unspecified	295
829.0	Fracture, closed, bones, unspecified	296
825.0	Fracture, closed, calcaneus	133, 295
*814.0	Fracture, closed, carpal bone(s)	295
*805.0	Fracture, closed, cervical vertebra, without mention of spinal cord injury	294
*810.0	Fracture, closed, clavicle	294
*821.2	Fracture, closed, femur, lower end	295
820.8	Fracture, closed, femur, neck, unspecified part	295
*821.0	Fracture, closed, femur, shaft or unspecified part	221, 228, 295
826.0	Fracture, closed, foot, one or more phalanges	295
*812.4	Fracture, closed, humerus, lower end	295
*812.2	Fracture, closed, humerus, shaft or unspecified part	295
*812.0	Fracture, closed, humerus, upper end	294
809.0	Fracture, closed, ill-defined, bones of trunk	135, 294
818.0	Fracture, closed, ill-defined, upper limb	295
807.5	Fracture, closed, larynx and trachea	37, 294, 303, 320
802.4	Fracture, closed, malar and maxillary bones	37, 293, 320
*802.2	Fracture, closed, mandible	37, 293, 320
*815.0	Fracture, closed, metacarpal bone(s)	295
817.0	Fracture, closed, multiple, hand bones	295
828.0	Fracture, closed, multiple, involving both lower limbs, lower with upper limb and lower limb with rib and sternum	296
819.0	Fracture, closed, multiple, involving both upper limbs, upper limbs with rib(s), sternum	295
*804.1	Fracture, closed, multiple, involving skull or face with other bones, with cerebral laceration and contusion	294, 302
*804.2	Fracture, closed, multiple, involving skull or face with other bones, with hemorrhage, subarachnoid, subdural, and extradural	294, 302
*804.3	Fracture, closed, multiple, involving skull or face with other bones, with other and unspecified intracranial hemorrhage	294, 302
804.40	Fracture, closed, multiple, involving skull or face with other bones, with other and unspecified intracranial injury, unspecified state of consciousness	302
804.41	Fracture, closed, multiple, involving skull or face with other bones, with other and unspecified intracranial injury, no loss of consciousness	302
804.42	Fracture, closed, multiple, involving skull or face with other bones, with other and unspecified intracranial injury, brief loss of consciousness	302
804.43	Fracture, closed, multiple, involving skull or face with other bones, with other and unspecified intracranial injury, moderate loss of consciousness	302
804.44	Fracture, closed, multiple, involving skull or face with other bones, with other and unspecified intracranial injury, prolonged loss of consciousness, return to preexisting conscious level	302
804.45	Fracture, closed, multiple, involving skull or face with other bones, with other and unspecified intracranial injury, prolonged loss of consciousness, without return to preexisting conscious level	302
804.46	Fracture, closed, multiple, involving skull or face with other bones, with other and unspecified intracranial injury, loss of consciousness, unspecified duration	302
*804.4	Fracture, closed, multiple, involving skull or face with other bones, with with other and unspecified intracranial injury	294
*804.0	Fracture, closed, multiple, involving skull or face with other bones, without mention of intracranial injury	294
804.02	Fracture, closed, multiple, involving skull or face with other bones, without mention of intracranial injury, brief loss of consciousness	302

** Code Range*

Code	Narrative	Page
804.03	Fracture, closed, multiple, involving skull or face with other bones, without mention of intracranial injury, moderate loss of consciousness	302
804.04	Fracture, closed, multiple, involving skull or face with other bones, without mention of intracranial injury, prolonged loss of consciousness, return to preexisting conscious level	302
804.05	Fracture, closed, multiple, involving skull or face with other bones, without mention of intracranial injury, prolonged loss of consciousness, without return to preexisting conscious level	302
804.06	Fracture, closed, multiple, involving skull or face with other bones, without mention of intracranial injury, loss of consciousness, unspecified duration	302
802.0	Fracture, closed, nasal bones	35, 293
802.6	Fracture, closed, orbital floor, blow-out	25, 293, 320
802.8	Fracture, closed, other facial bones	135, 293, 320
827.0	Fracture, closed, other, multiple and ill-defined, lower limb	295
822.0	Fracture, closed, patella	295
*808.4	Fracture, closed, pelvis, other specified part	294
808.8	Fracture, closed, pelvis, unspecified	294
*820.2	Fracture, closed, pertrochanteric, femur	295
*816.0	Fracture, closed, phalanges, one or more, hand	295
808.2	Fracture, closed, pubis	294
*813.4	Fracture, closed, radius and ulna, lower end	295
*813.2	Fracture, closed, radius and ulna, shaft	295
*813.8	Fracture, closed, radius and ulna, unspecified part	295
*813.0	Fracture, closed, radius and ulna, upper end	295
*807.0	Fracture, closed, rib(s)	294
807.08	Fracture, closed, rib(s), eight or more	44, 303
807.05	Fracture, closed, rib(s), five	43
807.04	Fracture, closed, rib(s), four	43
807.09	Fracture, closed, rib(s), multiple, unspecified	44
807.01	Fracture, closed, rib(s), one	47
807.07	Fracture, closed, rib(s), seven s	43, 303
807.06	Fracture, closed, rib(s), six	43
807.03	Fracture, closed, rib(s), three	43
807.02	Fracture, closed, rib(s), two	47
807.00	Fracture, closed, rib(s), unspecified	47
*811.0	Fracture, closed, scapula	294
811.01	Fracture, closed, scapula, acromial process	133
811.02	Fracture, closed, scapula, coracoid process	133
811.03	Fracture, closed, scapula, glenoid cavity and neck	133
811.09	Fracture, closed, scapula, other	135
811.00	Fracture, closed, scapula, unspecified part	133
*801.1	Fracture, closed, skull, base, with cerebral laceration and contusion,	293, 301
*801.2	Fracture, closed, skull, base, with hemorrhage, subarachnoid, subdural, and extradural	293, 301
*801.3	Fracture, closed, skull, base, with other and unspecified intracranial hemorrhage	293, 301
*801.4	Fracture, closed, skull, base, with with other and unspecified intracranial injury	293, 301
*801.0	Fracture, closed, skull, base, without mention of intracranial injury	293
801.02	Fracture, closed, skull, base, without mention of intracranial injury, brief loss of consciousness	301
801.03	Fracture, closed, skull, base, without mention of intracranial injury, moderate loss of consciousness	301
801.04	Fracture, closed, skull, base, without mention of intracranial injury, prolonged loss of consciousness, return to preexisting conscious level	301
801.05	Fracture, closed, skull, base, without mention of intracranial injury, prolonged loss of consciousness, without return to preexisting conscious level	301
*803.1	Fracture, closed, skull, other and unqualified, with cerebral laceration and contusion	293, 301
*803.6	Fracture, closed, skull, other and unqualified, with cerebral laceration and contusion	293, 301
*803.2	Fracture, closed, skull, other and unqualified, with hemorrhage, subarachnoid, subdural, and extradural	293, 301
*803.3	Fracture, closed, skull, other and unqualified, with other and unspecified intracranial hemorrhage	293, 301
*803.4	Fracture, closed, skull, other and unqualified, with with other and unspecified intracranial injury	293, 301
*803.0	Fracture, closed, skull, other and unqualified, without mention of intracranial injury	293
803.02	Fracture, closed, skull, other and unqualified, without mention of intracranial injury, brief loss of consciousness	301

Code	Narrative	Page
803.03	Fracture, closed, skull, other and unqualified, without mention of intracranial injury, moderate loss of consciousness	301
803.04	Fracture, closed, skull, other and unqualified, without mention of intracranial injury, prolonged loss of consciousness, return to preexisting conscious level	301
803.05	Fracture, closed, skull, other and unqualified, without mention of intracranial injury, prolonged loss of consciousness, without return to preexisting conscious level	301
*800.1	Fracture, closed, skull, vault, with cerebral laceration and contusion,	293
800.12	Fracture, closed, skull, vault, with cerebral laceration and contusion, brief loss of consciousness	300
800.16	Fracture, closed, skull, vault, with cerebral laceration and contusion, loss of consciousness, unspecified duration	300
800.13	Fracture, closed, skull, vault, with cerebral laceration and contusion, moderate loss of consciousness	300
800.14	Fracture, closed, skull, vault, with cerebral laceration and contusion, prolonged loss of consciousness, return to preexisting conscious level	300
800.15	Fracture, closed, skull, vault, with cerebral laceration and contusion, prolonged loss of consciousness, without return to preexisting conscious level	300
800.10	Fracture, closed, skull, vault, with cerebral laceration and contusion, unspecified state of consciousness	300
800.19	Fracture, closed, skull, vault, with cerebral laceration and contusion, with concussion, unspecified	300
*800.2	Fracture, closed, skull, vault, with hemorrhage, subarachnoid, subdural, and extradural	293
800.22	Fracture, closed, skull, vault, with hemorrhage, subarachnoid, subdural, and extradural, brief loss of consciousness	300
800.26	Fracture, closed, skull, vault, with hemorrhage, subarachnoid, subdural, and extradural, loss of consciousness, unspecified duration	300
800.23	Fracture, closed, skull, vault, with hemorrhage, subarachnoid, subdural, and extradural, moderate loss of consciousness	300
800.24	Fracture, closed, skull, vault, with hemorrhage, subarachnoid, subdural, and extradural, prolonged loss of consciousness, return to preexisting conscious level	300
800.25	Fracture, closed, skull, vault, with hemorrhage, subarachnoid, subdural, and extradural, prolonged loss of consciousness, without return to preexisting conscious level	300
800.20	Fracture, closed, skull, vault, with hemorrhage, subarachnoid, subdural, and extradural, unspecified state of consciousness	300
800.29	Fracture, closed, skull, vault, with hemorrhage, subarachnoid, subdural, and extradural, with concussion, unspecified	300
*800.3	Fracture, closed, skull, vault, with other and unspecified intracranial hemorrhage	293
800.32	Fracture, closed, skull, vault, with other and unspecified intracranial hemorrhage, brief loss of consciousness	300
800.36	Fracture, closed, skull, vault, with other and unspecified intracranial hemorrhage, loss of consciousness, unspecified duration	300
800.33	Fracture, closed, skull, vault, with other and unspecified intracranial hemorrhage, moderate loss of consciousness	300
800.34	Fracture, closed, skull, vault, with other and unspecified intracranial hemorrhage, prolonged loss of consciousness, return to preexisting conscious level	300
800.35	Fracture, closed, skull, vault, with other and unspecified intracranial hemorrhage, prolonged loss of consciousness, without return to preexisting conscious level	300
800.30	Fracture, closed, skull, vault, with other and unspecified intracranial hemorrhage, unspecified state of consciousness	300
800.39	Fracture, closed, skull, vault, with other and unspecified intracranial hemorrhage, with concussion, unspecified	300
800.42	Fracture, closed, skull, vault, with other and unspecified intracranial injury, brief loss of consciousness	300
800.46	Fracture, closed, skull, vault, with other and unspecified intracranial injury, loss of consciousness, unspecified duration	300
800.43	Fracture, closed, skull, vault, with other and unspecified intracranial injury, moderate loss of consciousness	300
800.44	Fracture, closed, skull, vault, with other and unspecified intracranial injury, prolonged loss of consciousness, return to preexisting conscious level	300

*** Code Range**

Code	Narrative	Page
800.45	Fracture, closed, skull, vault, with other and unspecified intracranial injury, prolonged loss of consciousness, without return to preexisting conscious level	300
800.40	Fracture, closed, skull, vault, with other and unspecified intracranial injury, unspecified state of consciousness	300
800.49	Fracture, closed, skull, vault, with other and unspecified intracranial injury, with concussion, unspecified	301
*800.4	Fracture, closed, skull, vault, with with other and unspecified intracranial injury	293
*800.0	Fracture, closed, skull, vault, without mention of intracranial injury	293
800.02	Fracture, closed, skull, vault, without mention of intracranial injury, brief loss of consciousness	299
800.03	Fracture, closed, skull, vault, without mention of intracranial injury, moderate loss of consciousness	299
800.04	Fracture, closed, skull, vault, without mention of intracranial injury, prolonged loss of consciousness, return to preexisting conscious level	300
800.05	Fracture, closed, skull, vault, without mention of intracranial injury, prolonged loss of consciousness, without return to preexisting conscious level	300
807.2	Fracture, closed, sternum	44, 294
*825.2	Fracture, closed, tarsal and metatarsal bones, other	132, 295
*823.2	Fracture, closed, tibia and fibula, shaft	295
*823.8	Fracture, closed, tibia and fibula, unspecified part	295
*823.0	Fracture, closed, tibia and fibula, upper end	295
*820.0	Fracture, closed, transcervical	295
*806.0	Fracture, closed, vertebral column, cervical, with spinal cord injury	294, 304
*806.2	Fracture, closed, vertebral column, dorsal [thoracic], with spinal cord injury	294, 304
805.2	Fracture, closed, vertebral column, dorsal [thoracic], without mention of spinal cord injury	294
806.4	Fracture, closed, vertebral column, lumbar, with spinal cord injury	294, 304
805.4	Fracture, closed, vertebral column, lumbar, without mention of spinal cord injury	294
*806.6	Fracture, closed, vertebral column, sacrum and coccyx, with spinal cord injury	294
806.60	Fracture, closed, vertebral column, sacrum and coccyx, with spinal cord injury, unspecified	304
805.6	Fracture, closed, vertebral column, sacrum and coccyx, without mention of spinal cord injury	294, 304
806.8	Fracture, closed, vertebral column, unspecified, with spinal cord injury	294, 305
805.8	Fracture, closed, vertebral column, unspecified, without mention of spinal cord injury	294
*820	Fracture, femur, neck	127, 221, 228, 305
*821	Fracture, femur, other and unspecified parts	127, 305
*826	Fracture, foot, one or more phalanges	132
*812	Fracture, humerus	133
*815	Fracture, metacarpal bone(s)	132
*804	Fracture, multiple, involving skull or face with other bones	14
808.1	Fracture, open, acetabulum	294
824.5	Fracture, open, ankle, bimalleolar	295
824.3	Fracture, open, ankle, lateral malleolus	295
824.1	Fracture, open, ankle, medial malleolus	295
824.7	Fracture, open, ankle, trimalleolar	295
824.9	Fracture, open, ankle, unspecified	295
829.1	Fracture, open, bones, unspecified	296
825.1	Fracture, open, calcaneus	133, 295
*814.1	Fracture, open, carpal bone(s)	295
*805.1	Fracture, open, cervical vertebra, without mention of spinal cord injury	294
*810.1	Fracture, open, clavicle	294
*821.3	Fracture, open, femur, lower end	295
820.9	Fracture, open, femur, neck, unspecified part	295
*821.1	Fracture, open, femur, shaft or unspecified part	221, 228, 295
826.1	Fracture, open, foot, one or more phalanges	295
*812.5	Fracture, open, humerus, lower end	295, 305
812.31	Fracture, open, humerus, shaft	305
*812.3	Fracture, open, humerus, shaft or unspecified part	295
812.30	Fracture, open, humerus, unspecified part	305
*812.1	Fracture, open, humerus, upper end	295, 305
809.1	Fracture, open, ill-defined, bones of trunk	135, 294, 305
818.1	Fracture, open, ill-defined, upper limb	295, 305
807.6	Fracture, open, larynx and trachea	37, 294, 303, 320
802.5	Fracture, open, malar and maxillary bones	37, 293, 320
*802.3	Fracture, open, mandible	37, 293, 320

*** Code Range**

Code	Narrative	Page
*815.1	Fracture, open, metacarpal bone(s)	295
817.1	Fracture, open, multiple, hand bones	295
828.1	Fracture, open, multiple, involving both lower limbs, lower with upper limb and lower limb with rib and sternum	296
819.1	Fracture, open, multiple, involving both upper limbs, upper limbs with rib(s), sternum	295, 303
*804.6	Fracture, open, multiple, involving skull or face with other bones, with cerebral laceration and contusion,	294
804.60	Fracture, open, multiple, involving skull or face with other bones, with cerebral laceration and contusion, unspecified state of consciousness	302
804.61	Fracture, open, multiple, involving skull or face with other bones, with cerebral laceration and contusion, no loss of consciousness	302
804.62	Fracture, open, multiple, involving skull or face with other bones, with cerebral laceration and contusion, brief loss of consciousness	302
804.63	Fracture, open, multiple, involving skull or face with other bones, with cerebral laceration and contusion, moderate loss of consciousness	302
804.64	Fracture, open, multiple, involving skull or face with other bones, with cerebral laceration and contusion, prolonged loss of consciousness, return to preexisting conscious level	302
804.65	Fracture, open, multiple, involving skull or face with other bones, with cerebral laceration and contusion, prolonged loss of consciousness, without return to preexisting conscious level	302
804.66	Fracture, open, multiple, involving skull or face with other bones, with cerebral laceration and contusion, loss of consciousness, unspecified duration	302
*804.7	Fracture, open, multiple, involving skull or face with other bones, with hemorrhage, subarachnoid, subdural, and extradural	294, 302
*804.8	Fracture, open, multiple, involving skull or face with other bones, with other and unspecified intracranial hemorrhage	294, 303
*804.9	Fracture, open, multiple, involving skull or face with other bones, with with other and unspecified intracranial injury	294, 303
*804.5	Fracture, open, multiple, involving skull or face with other bones, without mention of intracranial injury	294

Code	Narrative	Page
804.52	Fracture, open, multiple, involving skull or face with other bones, without mention of intracranial injury, brief loss of consciousness	302
804.53	Fracture, open, multiple, involving skull or face with other bones, without mention of intracranial injury, moderate loss of consciousness	302
804.54	Fracture, open, multiple, involving skull or face with other bones, without mention of intracranial injury, prolonged loss of consciousness, return to preexisting conscious level	302
804.55	Fracture, open, multiple, involving skull or face with other bones, without mention of intracranial injury, prolonged loss of consciousness, without return to preexisting conscious level	302
802.1	Fracture, open, nasal bones	35, 293
802.7	Fracture, open, orbital floor, blow-out	25, 293, 320
802.9	Fracture, open, other facial bones	135, 293, 320
827.1	Fracture, open, other, multiple and ill-defined, lower limb	295
822.1	Fracture, open, patella	295
*808.5	Fracture, open, pelvis, other specified part	294
808.9	Fracture, open, pelvis, unspecified	294
*820.3	Fracture, open, pertrochanteric, femur	295
*816.1	Fracture, open, phalanges, one or more, hand	295
808.3	Fracture, open, pubis	294
*813.5	Fracture, open, radius and ulna, lower end	295, 305
*813.3	Fracture, open, radius and ulna, shaft	295, 305
*813.9	Fracture, open, radius and ulna, unspecified part	295, 305
*813.1	Fracture, open, radius and ulna, upper end	295, 305
*807.1	Fracture, open, rib(s)	44, 294
807.18	Fracture, open, rib(s), eight or more	303
807.15	Fracture, open, rib(s), five	303
807.14	Fracture, open, rib(s), four	303
807.19	Fracture, open, rib(s), multiple, unspecified	303
807.17	Fracture, open, rib(s), seven s	303
807.16	Fracture, open, rib(s), six	303
*811.1	Fracture, open, scapula	294
811.11	Fracture, open, scapula, acromial process	133
811.12	Fracture, open, scapula, coracoid process	133
811.13	Fracture, open, scapula, glenoid cavity and neck	133
811.19	Fracture, open, scapula, other	135

Alphabetic Index to Diseases

* Code Range

Code	Narrative	Page
811.10	Fracture, open, scapula, unspecified part	133
*801.6	Fracture, open, skull, base, with cerebral laceration and contusion,	293, 301
*801.7	Fracture, open, skull, base, with hemorrhage, subarachnoid, subdural, and extradural	293, 301
*801.8	Fracture, open, skull, base, with other and unspecified intracranial hemorrhage	293, 301
*801.9	Fracture, open, skull, base, with with other and unspecified intracranial injury	293, 301
*801.5	Fracture, open, skull, base, without mention of intracranial injury	293
801.52	Fracture, open, skull, base, without mention of intracranial injury, brief loss of consciousness	301
801.53	Fracture, open, skull, base, without mention of intracranial injury, moderate loss of consciousness	301
801.54	Fracture, open, skull, base, without mention of intracranial injury, prolonged loss of consciousness, return to preexisting conscious level	301
801.55	Fracture, open, skull, base, without mention of intracranial injury, prolonged loss of consciousness, without return to preexisting conscious level	301
*803.7	Fracture, open, skull, other and unqualified, with hemorrhage, subarachnoid, subdural, and extradural	293, 301
*803.8	Fracture, open, skull, other and unqualified, with other and unspecified intracranial hemorrhage	294, 301
*803.9	Fracture, open, skull, other and unqualified, with with other and unspecified intracranial injury	294, 301
*803.5	Fracture, open, skull, other and unqualified, without mention of intracranial injury	293
803.52	Fracture, open, skull, other and unqualified, without mention of intracranial injury, brief loss of consciousness	301
803.53	Fracture, open, skull, other and unqualified, without mention of intracranial injury, moderate loss of consciousness	301
803.54	Fracture, open, skull, other and unqualified, without mention of intracranial injury, prolonged loss of consciousness, return to preexisting conscious level	301
803.55	Fracture, open, skull, other and unqualified, without mention of intracranial injury, prolonged loss of consciousness, without return to preexisting conscious level	301
*800.6	Fracture, open, skull, vault, with cerebral laceration and contusion,	293, 301
*800.7	Fracture, open, skull, vault, with hemorrhage, subarachnoid, subdural, and extradural	293, 301
*800.8	Fracture, open, skull, vault, with other and unspecified intracranial hemorrhage	293, 301
*800.9	Fracture, open, skull, vault, with with other and unspecified intracranial injury	293, 301
*800.5	Fracture, open, skull, vault, without mention of intracranial injury	293
800.52	Fracture, open, skull, vault, without mention of intracranial injury, brief loss of consciousness	301
800.53	Fracture, open, skull, vault, without mention of intracranial injury, moderate loss of consciousness	301
800.54	Fracture, open, skull, vault, without mention of intracranial injury, prolonged loss of consciousness, return to preexisting conscious level	301
800.55	Fracture, open, skull, vault, without mention of intracranial injury, prolonged loss of consciousness, without return to preexisting conscious level	301
807.3	Fracture, open, sternum	44, 294, 303
*825.3	Fracture, open, tarsal and metatarsal bones, other	132, 295
*823.3	Fracture, open, tibia and fibula, shaft	295, 305
*823.9	Fracture, open, tibia and fibula, unspecified part	295, 305
*823.1	Fracture, open, tibia and fibula, upper end	295, 305
*820.1	Fracture, open, transcervical	295
*806.1	Fracture, open, vertebral column, cervical, with spinal cord injury	294, 304
*806.3	Fracture, open, vertebral column, dorsal [thoracic], with spinal cord injury	294, 304
805.3	Fracture, open, vertebral column, dorsal [thoracic], without mention of spinal cord injury	294
806.5	Fracture, open, vertebral column, lumbar, with spinal cord injury	294, 304
805.5	Fracture, open, vertebral column, lumbar, without mention of spinal cord injury	294
*806.7	Fracture, open, vertebral column, sacrum and coccyx, with spinal cord injury	294, 305
805.7	Fracture, open, vertebral column, sacrum and coccyx, without mention of spinal cord injury	294, 304
806.9	Fracture, open, vertebral column, unspecified, with spinal cord injury	294, 305
805.9	Fracture, open, vertebral column, unspecified, without mention of spinal cord injury	294
*827	Fracture, other, multiple and ill-defined, lower limb	133

* Code Range

Code	Narrative	Page
*822	Fracture, patella	133
*733.1	Fracture, pathologic	127, 221, 228
*808	Fracture, pelvis	127, 305
*816	Fracture, phalanges, one or more, hand	132
*813	Fracture, radius and ulna	132
*801	Fracture, skull, base	14
*803	Fracture, skull, other and unqualified	14
*800	Fracture, skull, vault	14
733.94	Fracture, stress, metatarsals	128
733.95	Fracture, stress, other bone	128
733.93	Fracture, stress, tibia or fibula	128
*823	Fracture, tibia and fibula	133
*823.4	Fracture, torus, tibia and fibula	295
*806	Fracture, vertebral column, with spinal cord injury	9
*805	Fracture, vertebral column, without mention of spinal cord injury	129
*818	Fractures, ill-defined, upper limb	133
*817	Fractures, multiple, hand bones	132
*828	Fractures, multiple, involving both lower limbs, lower with upper limb and lower limb with rib and sternum	272, 305
*819	Fractures, multiple, involving both upper limbs, upper limbs with rib(s), sternum	272
*788.4	Frequency, urination and polyuria	164
300.13	Fugue, dissociative	251
676.63	Galactorrhea, associated with childbirth, antepartum condition or complication	209
676.62	Galactorrhea, associated with childbirth, delivered, with mention of postpartum complication	192, 203
676.61	Galactorrhea, associated with childbirth, delivered, with or without mention of antepartum condition	192, 203
676.64	Galactorrhea, associated with childbirth, postpartum condition or complication	205
676.60	Galactorrhea, associated with childbirth, unspecified as to episode of care	214
271.1	Galactosemia	155
*727.4	Ganglion and cyst, synovium, tendon and bursa	131
102.5	Gangosa	35, 318
785.4	Gangrene	87, 221, 228
040.0	Gangrene, gas	217, 224, 248
535.51	Gastritis and gastroduodenitis, unspecified, with hemorrhage	100
535.50	Gastritis and gastroduodenitis, unspecified, without hemorrhage	102
535.01	Gastritis, acute, with hemorrhage	100

Code	Narrative	Page
535.00	Gastritis, acute, without hemorrhage	102
535.31	Gastritis, alcoholic, with hemorrhage	100
535.30	Gastritis, alcoholic, without hemorrhage	102
535.11	Gastritis, atrophic, with hemorrhage	100
535.10	Gastritis, atrophic, without hemorrhage	102
535.41	Gastritis, other specified, with hemorrhage	100
535.40	Gastritis, other specified, without hemorrhage	102
558.3	Gastroenteritis and colitis, allergic	102
558.1	Gastroenteritis and colitis, due to radiation	104
558.9	Gastroenteritis and colitis, noninfectious, other and unspecified	102
*558	Gastroenteritis and colitis, other, noninfectious	310
558.2	Gastroenteritis and colitis, toxic	104, 220, 227
003.0	Gastroenteritis, Salmonella	101
536.3	Gastroparesis	102
537.5	Gastroptosis	102
736.5	Genu recurvatum, acquired	134
754.40	Genu recurvatum, congenital	135
*736.4	Genu valgum or varum, acquired	134
765.22	Gestation, 24 completed weeks of gestation	215
765.23	Gestation, 25-26 completed weeks of gestation	215
765.24	Gestation, 27-28 completed weeks of gestation	215, 222
765.25	Gestation, 29-30 completed weeks of gestation	215, 222
765.26	Gestation, 31-32 completed weeks of gestation	215, 222
765.27	Gestation, 33-34 completed weeks of gestation	215, 222
765.28	Gestation, 35-36 completed weeks of gestation	215, 222
765.29	Gestation, 37 or more completed weeks of gestation	229, 231
765.21	Gestation, less than 24 completed weeks of gestation	215
652.63	Gestation, multiple with malpresentation, one fetus or more, antepartum condition or complication	207
652.61	Gestation, multiple with malpresentation, one fetus or more, delivered, with or without mention of antepartum condition	187, 198
652.60	Gestation, multiple with malpresentation, one fetus or more, unspecified as to episode of care	212

Code	Narrative	Page
651.73	Gestation, multiple, following (elective) fetal reduction, antepartum condition or complication	207
651.71	Gestation, multiple, following (elective) fetal reduction, delivered, with or without mention of antepartum condition	186, 198
651.70	Gestation, multiple, following (elective) fetal reduction, unspecified as to episode of care	212
651.83	Gestation, multiple, other specified, antepartum condition or complication	207
651.81	Gestation, multiple, other specified, delivered, with or without mention of antepartum condition	187, 198
651.80	Gestation, multiple, other specified, unspecified as to episode of care	212
651.93	Gestation, multiple, unspecified, antepartum condition or complication	207
651.91	Gestation, multiple, unspecified, delivered, with or without mention of antepartum condition	187, 198
651.90	Gestation, multiple, unspecified, unspecified as to episode of care	212
765.20	Gestation, unspecified weeks of gestation	229, 231
024	Glanders	248
*365.2	Glaucoma, angle-closure, primary	23
*365.4	Glaucoma, associated with congenital anomalies, dystrophies, systemic syndromes	23
*365.5	Glaucoma, associated with lens disorders	23
*365.6	Glaucoma, associated with ocular disorders, other	23
*365.0	Glaucoma, borderline	23
365.14	Glaucoma, childhood	23
*365.3	Glaucoma, corticosteroid induced	23
365.12	Glaucoma, low tension	21
365.11	Glaucoma, open angle, primary	23
365.15	Glaucoma, open angle, residual stage	23
365.10	Glaucoma, open-angle, unspecified	23
*365.8	Glaucoma, other specified forms	23
365.13	Glaucoma, pigmentary	23
365.9	Glaucoma, unspecified	23
*580	Glomerulonephritis, acute	165, 221, 228, 310
*582	Glomerulonephritis, chronic	165, 310
271.0	Glycogenosis	155
791.5	Glycosuria	154
271.4	Glycosuria, renal	155
*241	Goiter, nontoxic, nodular	156
*240	Goiter, simple and unspecified	155
647.10	Gonorrhea, maternal, classifiable elsewhere, complicating pregnancy, childbirth, or the puerperium, unspecified as to episode of care	211
647.11	Gonorrhea, maternal, classifiable elsewhere, complicating pregnancy, childbirth, or the puerperium, delivered, with or without mention of antepartum condition	186, 195
647.12	Gonorrhea, maternal, classifiable elsewhere, complicating pregnancy, childbirth, or the puerperium, delivered, with mention of postpartum complication	186, 195
647.13	Gonorrhea, maternal, classifiable elsewhere, complicating pregnancy, childbirth, or the puerperium, antepartum condition or complication	207, 210
647.14	Gonorrhea, maternal, classifiable elsewhere, complicating pregnancy, childbirth, or the puerperium, postpartum condition or complication	204
*274.8	Gout, other specified manifestations	129
274.9	Gout, unspecified	129
099.2	Granuloma, inguinale	172, 176, 182
446.3	Granuloma, lethal, midline	127
446.4	Granulomatosis, Wegener's	127
656.63	Growth, excessive, fetal, affecting management of mother, antepartum condition or complication	208
656.61	Growth, excessive, fetal, affecting management of mother, delivered, with or without mention of antepartum condition	188, 199
656.60	Growth, excessive, fetal, affecting management of mother, unspecified as to episode of care	213
656.53	Growth, poor, fetal, affecting management of mother, antepartum condition or complication	208
656.51	Growth, poor, fetal, affecting management of mother, delivered, with or without mention of antepartum condition	188, 199
656.50	Growth, poor, fetal, affecting management of mother, unspecified as to episode of care	213
780.1	Hallucinations	251
757.32	Hamartoma, congenital, vascular	148
784.0	Headache	13
307.81	Headache, tension	13
861.11	Heart contusion with open wound into thorax	59, 62, 64, 74, 77, 80

Alphabetic Index to Diseases

Code	Narrative	Page
861.13	Heart laceration with penetration of heart chambers and open wound into thorax	59, 62, 64, 74, 77, 80
861.03	Heart laceration with penetration of heart chambers, without mention of open wound into thorax	59, 62, 64, 74, 77, 80
861.02	Heart laceration without penetration of heart chambers or mention of open wound into thorax	59, 62, 64, 73, 77, 80
861.12	Heart laceration without penetration of heart chambers, with open wound into thorax	59, 62, 64, 74, 77, 80
127.8	Helminthiasis, intestinal, mixed	249
127.7	Helminthiasis, intestinal, other, specified	102
127.9	Helminthiasis, intestinal, unspecified	102
*128	Helminthiasis, other and specified	249
228.04	Hemangioma, intra-abdominal structures	102
228.02	Hemangioma, intracranial structures	15
228.09	Hemangioma, other site	90, 319
228.03	Hemangioma, retina	22
228.01	Hemangioma, skin and subcutaneous tissue	147, 319
228.00	Hemangioma, unspecifed site	90, 319
*719.1	Hemarthrosis	130
620.7	Hematoma, broad ligament	221, 228
665.72	Hematoma, obstetrical, pelvic, delivered, with mention of postpartum complication	190, 202
665.71	Hematoma, obstetrical, pelvic, delivered, with or without mention of antepartum condition	190, 202
665.74	Hematoma, obstetrical, pelvic, postpartum condition or complication	204
665.70	Hematoma, obstetrical, pelvic, unspecified as to episode of care	190, 202
664.51	Hematoma, vulvar and perineal, during delivery, delivered, with or without mention of antepartum condition	190, 201
664.54	Hematoma, vulvar and perineal, during delivery, postpartum condition or complication	204
664.50	Hematoma, vulvar and perineal, during delivery, unspecified as to episode of care	190, 201
599.7	Hematuria	164, 221, 228
*342	Hemiplegia and hemiparesis	10
343.4	Hemiplegia, infantile	9
343.1	Hemiplegic, congenital	9
791.2	Hemoglobinuria	164
283.2	Hemoglobinuria, due to hemolysis, external causes	218, 225, 234
423.0	Hemopericardium	59, 61, 63, 73, 76, 79, 84, 219, 226
568.81	Hemoperitoneum, nontraumatic	220, 227
786.3	Hemoptysis	46
246.3	Hemorrhage and infarction, thyroid	319
772.5	Hemorrhage, adrenal, fetal and neonatal	216, 223
641.33	Hemorrhage, antepartum, coagulation defects, antepartum complication	206, 210
641.31	Hemorrhage, antepartum, coagulation defects, delivered, with or without mention of antepartum condition	185, 195
641.30	Hemorrhage, antepartum, coagulation defects, unspecified as to episode of care	210, 211
641.83	Hemorrhage, antepartum, other, antepartum complication	206
641.81	Hemorrhage, antepartum, other, delivered, with or without mention of antepartum condition	185, 195
641.80	Hemorrhage, antepartum, other, unspecified as to episode of care	211
641.93	Hemorrhage, antepartum, unspecified, antepartum complication	206
641.91	Hemorrhage, antepartum, unspecified, delivered, with or without mention of antepartum condition	185, 195
641.90	Hemorrhage, antepartum, unspecified, unspecified as to episode of care	211
772.6	Hemorrhage, cutaneous, fetal and neonatal	230, 231
666.22	Hemorrhage, delayed and secondary, postpartum, delivered, with mention of postpartum condition	190, 196
666.24	Hemorrhage, delayed and secondary, postpartum, postpartum condition or complication	204
666.20	Hemorrhage, delayed and secondary, postpartum, unspecified as to episode of care	213
530.82	Hemorrhage, esophageal	99
432.0	Hemorrhage, extradural, nontraumatic	60, 62, 64, 74, 77, 80, 83
656.03	Hemorrhage, fetal-maternal, affecting management of mother, antepartum condition or complication	208
656.01	Hemorrhage, fetal-maternal, affecting management of mother, delivered, with or without mention of antepartum condition	188, 199
656.00	Hemorrhage, fetal-maternal, affecting management of mother, unspecified as to episode of care	213

** Code Range*

Code	Narrative	Page
*578	Hemorrhage, gastrointestinal	100, 221, 228
772.4	Hemorrhage, gastrointestinal, fetal and neonatal	216, 223
596.7	Hemorrhage, into bladder wall	221, 228
431	Hemorrhage, intracerebral	5, 8, 10, 60, 62, 64, 74, 77, 80, 83, 219, 226
*432	Hemorrhage, intracranial, other and unspecified	5, 10, 219, 226
*854.1	Hemorrhage, intracranial, other and unspecified nature, with open intracranial wound	8
*853	Hemorrhage, intracranial, other and unspecified, following injury	14, 297, 303
*853.1	Hemorrhage, intracranial, other and unspecified, following injury, with open intracranial wound	8
*853.0	Hemorrhage, intracranial, other and unspecified, following injury, without mention of open intracranial wound	8
432.9	Hemorrhage, intracranial, unspecified	8, 60, 62, 64, 74, 77, 80, 83
*772.1	Hemorrhage, intraventricular, fetal and neonatal	216, 223
376.32	Hemorrhage, orbital	25
640.83	Hemorrhage, other specified, early pregnancy, antepartum condition or complication	205
640.81	Hemorrhage, other specified, early pregnancy, delivered, with or without mention of antepartum condition	185, 197
640.80	Hemorrhage, other specified, early pregnancy, unspecified as to episode of care	205
666.12	Hemorrhage, other, immediate, postpartum, delivered, with mention of postpartum condition	190, 196
666.14	Hemorrhage, other, immediate, postpartum, postpartum condition or complication	204
666.10	Hemorrhage, other, immediate, postpartum, unspecified as to episode of care	213
770.3	Hemorrhage, pulmonary, fetus or newborn	216, 223
569.3	Hemorrhage, rectum and anus	100, 220, 227
430	Hemorrhage, subarachnoid	5, 8, 10, 60, 62, 64, 74, 77, 80, 83, 219, 226
772.2	Hemorrhage, subarachnoid, fetal and neonatal	216, 223
*852.1	Hemorrhage, subarachnoid, following injury with open intracranial wound	8
*852.0	Hemorrhage, subarachnoid, following injury without mention of open intracranial wound	8
*852	Hemorrhage, subarachnoid, subdural and extradural, following injury	14, 297, 303
432.1	Hemorrhage, subdural	60, 62, 64, 74, 77, 80, 83
767.0	Hemorrhage, subdural and cerebral, trauma, birth	216, 223
*852.3	Hemorrhage, subdural, following injury with open intracranial wound	8
666.02	Hemorrhage, third-stage, postpartum, delivered, with mention of postpartum condition	190, 196
666.04	Hemorrhage, third-stage, postpartum, postpartum condition or complication	204
666.00	Hemorrhage, third-stage, postpartum, unspecified as to episode of care	213
784.8	Hemorrhage, throat	37, 320
459.0	Hemorrhage, unspecified	91, 219, 226
640.93	Hemorrhage, unspecified, early pregnancy, antepartum condition or complication	206
640.91	Hemorrhage, unspecified, early pregnancy, delivered, with or without mention of antepartum condition	185, 197
640.90	Hemorrhage, unspecified, early pregnancy, unspecified as to episode of care	206
*455	Hemorrhoid	104
571.1	Hepatitis, acute, alcoholic	110
*070.2	Hepatitis, B, viral, hepatic coma	217, 224
*070.3	Hepatitis, B, viral, without mention of hepatic coma	217, 224
*571.4	Hepatitis, chronic	111
130.5	Hepatitis, due to toxoplasmosis	111, 218, 225
091.62	Hepatitis, secondary syphilitic, early	110
573.3	Hepatitis, unspecified	220, 227
*070	Hepatitis, viral	110
*070.4	Hepatitis, viral, with hepatic coma, other specified	217, 224
070.6	Hepatitis, viral, with hepatic coma, unspecified	217, 224
*070.5	Hepatitis, viral, without hepatic coma, other specified	217, 224
070.9	Hepatitis, viral, without hepatic coma, unspecified	217, 224
789.1	Hepatomegaly	111, 310
553.8	Hernia, abdominal cavity, without mention of obstruction or gangrene, other specified sites	104
553.9	Hernia, abdominal cavity, without mention of obstruction or gangrene, unspecified site	104

*** Code Range**

Code	Narrative	Page
750.6	Hernia, congenital, hiatus	104
553.3	Hernia, diaphragmatic	102
551.3	Hernia, diaphragmatic, with gangrene	220, 227
552.3	Hernia, diaphragmatic, with obstruction	102, 220, 227
*553.0	Hernia, femoral	104
551.02	Hernia, femoral, with gangrene, bilateral, not specified as recurrent	220, 227
551.00	Hernia, femoral, with gangrene, unilateral or unspecified, not specified as recurrent	220, 227
*552.0	Hernia, femoral, with obstruction	104
552.02	Hernia, femoral, with obstruction, bilateral, not specified as recurrent	220, 227
552.00	Hernia, femoral, with obstruction, unilateral or unspecified, not specified as recurrent	220, 227
*550	Hernia, inguinal	104
550.02	Hernia, inguinal, with gangrene, bilateral, not specified as recurrent	220, 227
550.00	Hernia, inguinal, with gangrene, unilateral or unspecified, not specified as recurrent	220, 227
550.12	Hernia, inguinal, with obstruction, without mention of gangrene, bilateral, not specified as recurrent	220, 227
550.10	Hernia, inguinal, with obstruction, without mention of gangrene, unilateral or unspecified, not specified as recurrent	220, 227
551.8	Hernia, other specified sites, with gangrene	220, 227
552.8	Hernia, other specified sites, with obstruction	104, 220, 227
*551	Hernia, other, abdominal cavity, with gangrene	104
553.1	Hernia, umbilical	104
551.1	Hernia, umbilical, with gangrene	220, 227
552.1	Hernia, umbilical, with obstruction	104, 220, 227
551.9	Hernia, unspecified site, with gangrene	220, 227
552.9	Hernia, unspecified site, with obstruction	104, 220, 227
*551.2	Hernia, ventral, with gangrene	220, 227
*552.2	Hernia, ventral, with obstruction	104, 220, 227
*553.2	Hernia, ventral, without mention of obstruction or gangrene	104
074.0	Herpangina	34, 318
*054	Herpes simplex	308
054.19	Herpes, genital, other	171, 176, 182
054.10	Herpes, genital, unspecified	171, 176, 182
054.2	Herpes, gingivostomatitis	37, 217, 224, 318
054.13	Herpes, infection, penis	171
054.3	Herpes, meningoencephalitis	7, 12, 217, 224
054.5	Herpes, septicemia	217, 224, 246
054.72	Herpes, simplex, meningitis	7, 13
054.79	Herpes, simplex, other specified complications	247
054.73	Herpes, simplex, otitis externa	35
054.8	Herpes, simplex, unspecified complication	217, 224, 247
054.71	Herpes, simplex, visceral	103
*054.4	Herpes, simplex, with opthalmic complications	22, 217, 224
*054.7	Herpes, simplex, with other specified complications	217, 224
054.9	Herpes, simplex, without mention of complication	146
054.12	Herpes, vulva	176, 182
054.11	Herpes, vulvovaginitis	176, 182
054.6	Herpes, whitlow	146
*053	Herpes, zoster	217, 224, 308
053.11	Herpes, zoster, geniculate	11
053.79	Herpes, zoster, other specified complications	246
053.19	Herpes, zoster, other, with nervous system complications	11
053.71	Herpes, zoster, otitis externa	35
053.8	Herpes, zoster, unspecified complication	246
053.0	Herpes, zoster, with meningitis	13
*053.2	Herpes, zoster, with opthalmic complications	22
053.10	Herpes, zoster, with unspecified nervous system complications	11
053.9	Herpes, zoster, without mention of complication	142
*378.4	Heterophoria	25
121.6	Heterophyiasis	249
*378.2	Heterotropia, intermittent	25
*378.3	Heterotropia, other and unspecified	25
786.8	Hiccough	46
652.53	High fetal head at term, antepartum condition or complication	207
652.51	High fetal head at term, delivered, with or without mention of antepartum condition	187, 198
652.50	High fetal head at term, unspecified as to episode of care	212
*202.3	Histiocytosis, malignant	237
202.31	Histiocytosis, malignant, lymph nodes, head, face, and neck	319
*115	Histoplasmosis	308
115.04	Histoplasmosis, due to Histoplasma capsulatum, endocarditis	85, 217, 224

Alphabetic Index to Diseases

* Code Range

Code	Narrative	Page
115.01	Histoplasmosis, due to histoplasma capsulatum, meningitis	8, 13, 217, 224
115.09	Histoplasmosis, due to Histoplasma capsulatum, other	249
115.03	Histoplasmosis, due to Histoplasma capsulatum, pericarditis	90, 217, 224
115.05	Histoplasmosis, due to Histoplasma capsulatum, pneumonia	42, 217, 224
115.02	Histoplasmosis, due to Histoplasma capsulatum, retinitis	22, 217, 224
115.00	Histoplasmosis, due to Histoplasma capsulatum, without mention of manifestation	249
115.14	Histoplasmosis, due to Histoplasma duboisii, endocarditis	85, 217, 224
115.11	Histoplasmosis, due to histoplasma duboisii, meningitis	8, 13, 217, 224
115.19	Histoplasmosis, due to Histoplasma duboisii, other	249
115.13	Histoplasmosis, due to Histoplasma duboisii, pericarditis	90, 217, 224
115.15	Histoplasmosis, due to Histoplasma duboisii, pneumonia	42, 217, 224
115.12	Histoplasmosis, due to Histoplasma duboisii, retinitis	22, 217, 224
115.10	Histoplasmosis, due to Histoplasma duboisii, without mention of manifestation	249
115.94	Histoplasmosis, endocarditis, unspecified	85, 218, 225
115.91	Histoplasmosis, meningitis, unspecified	8, 13, 217, 225
115.99	Histoplasmosis, other, unspecified	249
115.93	Histoplasmosis, pericarditis, unspecified	90, 218, 225
115.95	Histoplasmosis, pneumonia, unspecified	42, 218, 225
115.92	Histoplasmosis, retinitis, unspecified	22, 218, 225
115.90	Histoplasmosis, without mention of manifestation, unspecified	249
*V17	History, family, certain chronic disabling diseases	287
*V18	History, family, certain other specific conditions	287
*V16	History, family, malignant neoplasm	287
*V19	History, family, other conditions	287
*V14	History, personal, allergy to medicinal agents	287
*V12	History, personal, certain other diseases	287
*V10	History, personal, malignant neoplasm	236, 242, 287
V10.21	History, personal, malignant neoplasm, larynx	321
V10.02	History, personal, malignant neoplasm, oral cavity and pharynx, other and unspecified	321
V10.01	History, personal, malignant neoplasm, tongue	321
*V11	History, personal, mental disorder	287
*V13	History, personal, other diseases	287
*V15	History, personal, other, presenting hazards to health	287
*201	Hodgkin's disease	237
201.71	Hodgkin's disease, lymphocytic depletion, lymph nodes, head, face, and neck	319
201.41	Hodgkin's disease, lymphocytic-histiocytic predominance, lymph nodes, head, face, and neck	318
201.61	Hodgkin's disease, mixed cellularity, lymph nodes, head, face, and neck	318
201.51	Hodgkin's disease, nodular sclerosis, lymph nodes, head, face, and neck	318
201.91	Hodgkin's disease, unspecified, lymph nodes, head, face, and neck	319
201.11	Hodgkin's granuloma, lymph nodes, head, face, and neck	318
201.01	Hodgkin's paragranuloma, lymph nodes, head, face, and neck	318
201.21	Hodgkin's sarcoma, lymph nodes, head, face, and neck	318
377.22	Holes, crater-like, optic disc	25
603.0	Hydrocele, encysted	172
603.1	Hydrocele, infected	172
603.8	Hydrocele, other specified types	172
603.9	Hydrocele, unspecified	172
653.63	Hydrocephalic, fetus, causing disproportion, antepartum condition or complication	207
653.61	Hydrocephalic, fetus, causing disproportion, delivered, with or without mention of antepartum condition	187, 199
653.60	Hydrocephalic, fetus, causing disproportion, unspecified as to episode of care	212
331.3	Hydrocephalus, communicating	10
331.4	Hydrocephalus, obstructive	10
591	Hydronephrosis	163, 221, 228
778.0	Hydrops fetalis not due to isoimmunization	216, 223
773.3	Hydrops fetalis, due to isoimmunization, fetus or newborn	216, 223
593.5	Hydroureter	163, 221, 228
643.03	Hyperemesis, gravidarum, mild, antepartum complication	206, 210
643.01	Hyperemesis, gravidarum, mild, delivered, with or without mention of antepartum condition	185, 197
643.00	Hyperemesis, gravidarum, mild, unspecified as to episode of care	210, 211

Alphabetic Index to Diseases

Code	Narrative	Page
643.13	Hyperemesis, gravidarum, with metabolic disturbance, antepartum complication	206, 210
643.11	Hyperemesis, gravidarum, with metabolic disturbance, delivered, with or without mention of antepartum condition	185, 197
643.10	Hyperemesis, gravidarum, with metabolic disturbance, unspecified as to episode of care	210, 211
273.0	Hypergammaglobinemia, polyclonal	234
780.8	Hyperhidrosis, generalized	148, 310
367.0	Hypermetropia	23
733.3	Hyperostosis, skull	134
374.52	Hyperpigmentation, eyelid	24
*600	Hyperplasia, prostate	171
447.3	Hyperplasia, renal artery	165
478.8	Hypersensitivity, reaction, upper respiratory tract, site unspecified	34, 319
*327.1	Hypersomnia, organic	253
780.54	Hypersomnia, unspecified	253
780.53	Hypersomnia, with sleep apnea, unspecified	16
289.4	Hypersplenism	235, 310
642.03	Hypertension, benign essential, complicating pregnancy, childbirth, and the puerperium, antepartum condition or complication	206, 210
642.01	Hypertension, benign essential, complicating pregnancy, childbirth, and the puerperium, delivered, with or without mention of antepartum condition	185, 195
642.02	Hypertension, benign essential, complicating pregnancy, childbirth, and the puerperium, delivered, with mention of postpartum complication	185, 195
642.04	Hypertension, benign essential, complicating pregnancy, childbirth, and the puerperium, postpartum complication	203
642.00	Hypertension, benign essential, complicating pregnancy, childbirth, and the puerperium, unspecified as to episode of care	211
401.1	Hypertension, essential, benign	87
401.0	Hypertension, essential, malignant	87
401.9	Hypertension, essential, unspecified	88
348.2	Hypertension, intracranial, benign	13
642.23	Hypertension, other pre-existing, complicating pregnancy, childbirth, and the puerperium, antepartum condition or complication	206, 210
642.21	Hypertension, other pre-existing, complicating pregnancy, childbirth, and the puerperium, delivered, with or without mention of antepartum condition	185, 195
642.22	Hypertension, other pre-existing, complicating pregnancy, childbirth, and the puerperium, delivered, with mention of postpartum complication	185, 195
642.24	Hypertension, other pre-existing, complicating pregnancy, childbirth, and the puerperium, postpartum complication	203
642.20	Hypertension, other pre-existing, complicating pregnancy, childbirth, and the puerperium, unspecified as to episode of care	211
416.0	Hypertension, pulmonary, primary	82
*405	Hypertension, secondary	88
642.13	Hypertension, secondary to renal disease, complicating pregnancy, childbirth, and the puerperium, antepartum condition or complication	206, 210
642.11	Hypertension, secondary to renal disease, complicating pregnancy, childbirth, and the puerperium, delivered, with or without mention of antepartum condition	185, 195
642.12	Hypertension, secondary to renal disease, complicating pregnancy, childbirth, and the puerperium, delivered, with mention of postpartum complication	185, 195
642.14	Hypertension, secondary to renal disease, complicating pregnancy, childbirth, and the puerperium, postpartum complication	203
642.10	Hypertension, secondary to renal disease, complicating pregnancy, childbirth, and the puerperium, unspecified as to episode of care	211
642.33	Hypertension, transient, complicating pregnancy, childbirth, and the puerperium, antepartum condition or complication	206
642.32	Hypertension, transient, complicating pregnancy, childbirth, and the puerperium, delivered, with mention of postpartum complication	185, 197
642.31	Hypertension, transient, complicating pregnancy, childbirth, and the puerperium, delivered, with or without mention of antepartum condition	185, 197
642.34	Hypertension, transient, complicating pregnancy, childbirth, and the puerperium, postpartum complication	203
642.30	Hypertension, transient, complicating pregnancy, childbirth, and the puerperium, unspecified as to episode of care	211
642.93	Hypertension, unspecified, complicating pregnancy, childbirth, and the puerperium, antepartum condition or complication	206, 210

Code	Narrative	Page
642.92	Hypertension, unspecified, complicating pregnancy, childbirth, and the puerperium, delivered, with mention of postpartum complication	185, 195
642.91	Hypertension, unspecified, complicating pregnancy, childbirth, and the puerperium, delivered, with or without mention of antepartum condition	185, 195
642.94	Hypertension, unspecified, complicating pregnancy, childbirth, and the puerperium, postpartum complication	203
642.90	Hypertension, unspecified, complicating pregnancy, childbirth, and the puerperium, unspecified as to episode of care	211
*459.3	Hypertension, venous, chronic (idiopathic)	87
404.12	Hypertensive heart and kidney disease, benign, with chronic kidney disease	161, 162, 322
404.11	Hypertensive heart and kidney disease, benign, with heart failure	57, 58, 61, 63, 72, 76, 78, 82, 84, 85, 219, 226
404.13	Hypertensive heart and kidney disease, benign, with heart failure and chronic kidney disease	57, 58, 61, 63, 72, 76, 78, 82, 84, 85, 219, 226, 322
404.10	Hypertensive heart and kidney disease, benign, without heart failure or chronic kidney disease	88
404.02	Hypertensive heart and kidney disease, malignant, with chronic kidney disease	161, 162, 321, 322
404.01	Hypertensive heart and kidney disease, malignant, with heart failure	56, 58, 61, 63, 72, 76, 78, 82, 84, 85, 218, 225
404.03	Hypertensive heart and kidney disease, malignant, with heart failure and chronic kidney disease	57, 58, 61, 63, 72, 76, 78, 82, 84, 85, 219, 226, 322
404.00	Hypertensive heart and kidney disease, malignant, without heart failure or chronic kidney disease	88
404.92	Hypertensive heart and kidney disease, unspecified, with chronic kidney disease	161, 162, 322
404.91	Hypertensive heart and kidney disease, unspecified, with heart failure	57, 58, 61, 63, 72, 76, 78, 82, 84, 85, 219, 226
404.93	Hypertensive heart and kidney disease, unspecified, with heart failure and chronic kidney disease	57, 58, 61, 63, 72, 76, 79, 82, 84, 85, 219, 226, 322
404.90	Hypertensive heart and kidney disease, unspecified, without heart failure or chronic kidney disease	88
402.11	Hypertensive heart disease, benign, with heart failure	56, 58, 61, 63, 72, 76, 78, 82, 84, 85, 218, 225
402.10	Hypertensive heart disease, benign, without heart failure	88
402.01	Hypertensive heart disease, malignant, with heart failure	56, 58, 61, 63, 72, 76, 78, 82, 84, 85, 218, 225
402.00	Hypertensive heart disease, malignant, without heart failure	88
402.91	Hypertensive heart disease, unspecified, with heart failure	56, 58, 61, 63, 72, 76, 78, 82, 84, 85, 218, 225
402.90	Hypertensive heart disease, unspecified, without heart failure	88
403.11	Hypertensive kidney disease, benign, with chronic kidney disease	161, 162, 321, 322
403.10	Hypertensive kidney disease, benign, without chronic kidney disease	165
403.01	Hypertensive kidney disease, malignant, with chronic kidney disease	161, 162, 321, 322
403.00	Hypertensive kidney disease, malignant, without chronic kidney disease	165
403.91	Hypertensive kidney disease, unspecified, with chronic kidney disease	161, 162, 321, 322
403.90	Hypertensive kidney disease, unspecified, without chronic kidney disease	165
661.43	Hypertonic, incoordinate, or prolonged uterine contractions, antepartum condition or complication	208
661.41	Hypertonic, incoordinate, or prolonged uterine contractions, delivered, with or without mention of antepartum condition	189, 201
661.40	Hypertonic, incoordinate, or prolonged uterine contractions, unspecified as to episode of care	189, 201
374.54	Hypertrichosis, eyelid	24
*701	Hypertrophy and atrophy, skin conditions, other	147
535.21	Hypertrophy, gastric mucosal, with hemorrhage	100
535.20	Hypertrophy, gastric mucosal, without hemorrhage	102
593.1	Hypertrophy, kidney	165
478.0	Hypertrophy, nasal turbinates	36
*474.1	Hypertrophy, tonsils and adenoids	36
364.41	Hyphema	21

Alphabetic Index to Diseases

*** Code Range**

Code	Narrative	Page
775.4	Hypocalcemia and hypomagnesemia, neonatal	216, 223
300.7	Hypochondriasis	251
775.6	Hypoglycemia, neonatal	216, 223
251.1	Hypoglycemia, other specified	156
251.2	Hypoglycemia, unspecified	154
251.3	Hypoinsulinemia, postsurgical	154
252.1	Hypoparathyroidism	218, 225
374.53	Hypopigmentation, eyelid	24
458.1	Hypotension, chronic	91
*458.2	Hypotension, iatrogenic	89
458.0	Hypotension, orthostatic	89
458.8	Hypotension, other specified	83, 91
458.9	Hypotension, unspecified	83, 91
*244	Hypothyroidism, acquired	156
243	Hypothyroidism, congenital	156
*360.3	Hypotony, eye	23
374.55	Hypotrichosis, eyelid	24
327.24	Hypoventilation, sleep related, idiopathic, nonobstructive alveolar	35
327.26	Hypoventilation, sleep related, in conditions classifiable elsewhere	35
300.11	Hysteria, conversion disorder	251
300.15	Hysteria, dissociative type, unspecified	251
300.10	Hysteria, unspecified	251
415.11	Iatrogenic pulmonary embolism and infarction	60, 62, 64, 74, 77, 80
757.1	Ichthyosis congenita	148
V62.84	Ideation, suicidal	251
300.14	Identity disorder, dissociative	252
537.2	Ileus, duodenal, chronic	102
560.1	Ileus, paralytic	220, 227
300.19	Illness, factitious, other and unspecified	251
775.5	Imbalance, electrolytes, transitory, neonatal	216, 223
765.04	Immaturity, extreme, fetal, 1,000-1,249 grams	215
765.05	Immaturity, extreme, fetal, 1,250-1,499 grams	215
765.06	Immaturity, extreme, fetal, 1,500-1,749 grams	215, 222
765.07	Immaturity, extreme, fetal, 1,750-1,999 grams	215, 222
765.08	Immaturity, extreme, fetal, 2,000-2,499 grams	215, 222
765.02	Immaturity, extreme, fetal, 500-749 grams	215
765.03	Immaturity, extreme, fetal, 750-999 grams	215
765.01	Immaturity, extreme, fetal, less than 500 grams	215
765.00	Immaturity, extreme, fetal, unspecified (weight)	215, 222
380.4	Impacted cerumen	35
560.39	Impaction, intestine, other	220, 227
560.30	Impaction, intestine, unspecified	220, 227
684	Impetigo	143
694.3	Impetigo, herpetiformis	147
607.84	Impotence, organic origin	172
654.53	Incompetence, cervical, antepartum condition or complication	207
654.52	Incompetence, cervical, delivered, with mention of postpartum complication	187, 199
654.51	Incompetence, cervical, delivered, with or without mention of antepartum condition	187, 199
654.54	Incompetence, cervical, postpartum condition or complication	204
654.50	Incompetence, cervical, unspecified as to episode of care	213
*788.3	Incontinence, urine	164
659.03	Induction labor, failed, mechanical, antepartum condition or complication	208
659.01	Induction labor, failed, mechanical, delivered, with or without mention of antepartum condition	188, 200
659.00	Induction labor, failed, mechanical, unspecified as to episode of care	188, 200
659.13	Induction labor, failed, medical or unspecified, antepartum condition or complication	208
659.11	Induction labor, failed, medical or unspecified, delivered, with or without mention of antepartum condition	188, 200
659.10	Induction labor, failed, medical or unspecified, unspecified as to episode of care	188, 200
661.23	Inertia, other and unspecified, uterine, antepartum condition or complication	208
661.21	Inertia, other and unspecified, uterine, delivered, with or without mention of antepartum condition	189, 200
661.20	Inertia, other and unspecified, uterine, unspecified as to episode of care	189, 200
661.03	Inertia, primary, uterine, antepartum condition or complication	208
661.01	Inertia, primary, uterine, delivered, with or without mention of antepartum condition	189, 200
661.00	Inertia, primary, uterine, unspecified as to episode of care	189, 200
661.13	Inertia, secondary, uterine, antepartum condition or complication	208
661.11	Inertia, secondary, uterine, delivered, with or without mention of antepartum condition	189, 200
661.10	Inertia, secondary, uterine, unspecified as to episode of care	189, 200

* Code Range

Code	Narrative	Page
410.11	Infarction, acute, myocardial, anterior wall, other, initial episode of care	57, 58, 61, 63, 72, 76, 79, 82, 83, 84
410.12	Infarction, acute, myocardial, anterior wall, other, subsequent episode of care	90
410.10	Infarction, acute, myocardial, anterior wall, other, unspecified episode of care	90
410.01	Infarction, acute, myocardial, anterolateral wall, initial episode of care	57, 58, 61, 63, 72, 76, 79, 82, 83, 84
410.02	Infarction, acute, myocardial, anterolateral wall, subsequent episode of care	90
410.00	Infarction, acute, myocardial, anterolateral wall, unspecified episode of care	90
410.41	Infarction, acute, myocardial, inferior wall, other, initial episode of care	57, 58, 61, 63, 72, 76, 79, 82, 83, 84
410.42	Infarction, acute, myocardial, inferior wall, other, subsequent episode of care	90
410.40	Infarction, acute, myocardial, inferior wall, other, unspecified episode of care	90
410.21	Infarction, acute, myocardial, inferolateral wall, initial episode of care	57, 58, 61, 63, 72, 76, 79, 82, 83, 84
410.22	Infarction, acute, myocardial, inferolateral wall, subsequent episode of care	90
410.20	Infarction, acute, myocardial, inferolateral wall, unspecified episode of care	90
410.31	Infarction, acute, myocardial, inferoposterior wall, initial episode of care	57, 58, 61, 63, 72, 76, 79, 82, 83, 84
410.32	Infarction, acute, myocardial, inferoposterior wall, subsequent episode of care	90
410.30	Infarction, acute, myocardial, inferoposterior wall, unspecified episode of care	90
410.51	Infarction, acute, myocardial, lateral wall, other, initial episode of care	57, 58, 61, 63, 72, 76, 79, 82, 83, 84
410.52	Infarction, acute, myocardial, lateral wall, other, subsequent episode of care	90
410.50	Infarction, acute, myocardial, lateral wall, other, unspecified episode of care	90
410.81	Infarction, acute, myocardial, other specified sites, initial episode of care	57, 58, 61, 63, 73, 76, 79, 82, 83, 84
410.82	Infarction, acute, myocardial, other specified sites, subsequent episode of care	91
410.80	Infarction, acute, myocardial, other specified sites, unspecified episode of care	91
410.61	Infarction, acute, myocardial, posterior wall, true, initial episode of care	57, 58, 61, 63, 73, 76, 79, 82, 83, 84
410.62	Infarction, acute, myocardial, posterior wall, true, subsequent episode of care	90
410.60	Infarction, acute, myocardial, posterior wall, true, unspecified episode of care	90
410.71	Infarction, acute, myocardial, subendocardial, initial episode of care	57, 58, 61, 63, 73, 76, 79, 82, 83, 84
410.72	Infarction, acute, myocardial, subendocardial, subsequent episode of care	91
410.70	Infarction, acute, myocardial, subendocardial, unspecified episode of care	90
410.91	Infarction, acute, myocardial, unspecified sites, initial episode of care	57, 58, 61, 63, 73, 76, 79, 82, 83, 84
410.92	Infarction, acute, myocardial, unspecified sites, subsequent episode of care	91
410.90	Infarction, acute, myocardial, unspecified sites, unspecified episode of care	91
573.4	Infarction, hepatic	220, 227
412	Infarction, myocardial, old	87
658.43	Infection of amniotic cavity, antepartum condition or complication	208
658.41	Infection of amniotic cavity, delivered, with or without mention of antepartum condition	188, 200
658.40	Infection of amniotic cavity, unspecified as to episode of care	188, 200
*039	Infection, actinomycotic	308
039.2	Infection, actinomycotic, abdominal	103
039.3	Infection, actinomycotic, cervicofacial	146
039.0	Infection, actinomycotic, cutaneous	146
039.8	Infection, actinomycotic, other specified sites	248
039.1	Infection, actinomycotic, pulmonary	42
039.9	Infection, actinomycotic, unspecified site	248
006.8	Infection, amebic, other sites	247
*041	Infection, bacterial, in conditions classified elsewhere	248
*116	Infection, blastomycotic	249

Code	Narrative	Page
*123	Infection, cestode, other	102
771.1	Infection, congenital, cytomegalovirus	216, 223
530.86	Infection, esophagostomy	104
659.33	Infection, generalized, during labor, antepartum condition or complication	208
659.31	Infection, generalized, during labor, unspecified, delivered, with or without mention of antepartum condition	188, 196
659.30	Infection, generalized, during labor, unspecified, unspecified as to episode of care	188, 200
098.7	Infection, gonococcal, anus and rectum	103
*098.4	Infection, gonococcal, eye	22
098.59	Infection, gonococcal, joint, other	128
098.0	Infection, gonococcal, lower genitourinary tract, acute	171, 176, 182
098.2	Infection, gonococcal, lower genitourinary tract, chronic	171, 176, 182
098.89	Infection, gonococcal, other specified sites	248
098.6	Infection, gonococcal, pharynx	34, 318
098.39	Infection, gonococcal, upper genitourinary tract, other, chronic	172, 176, 182
098.10	Infection, gonococcal, upper genitourinary tract, site unspecified, acute	171, 176, 182
098.30	Infection, gonococcal, upper genitourinary tract, site unspecified, chronic	163
098.19	Infection, gonococcal, upper genitourinary, other, acute	171, 176, 182
*008	Infection, intestinal, due to other organisms	102
*009	Infection, intestinal, ill-defined	102, 309
590.9	Infection, kidney, unspecified	221, 228
*100.8	Infection, leptospiral, other specified	8, 12
036.89	Infection, meningococcal, other, specified	246
036.9	Infection, meningococcal, unspecified	246
675.83	Infection, other specified, breast and nipple, associated with childbirth, antepartum condition or complication	209
675.82	Infection, other specified, breast and nipple, associated with childbirth, delivered, with mention of postpartum complication	192, 203
675.81	Infection, other specified, breast and nipple, associated with childbirth, delivered, with or without mention of antepartum condition	192, 203
675.84	Infection, other specified, breast and nipple, associated with childbirth, postpartum condition or complication	205
675.80	Infection, other specified, breast and nipple, associated with childbirth, unspecified as to episode of care	214
*730.8	Infection, other, bone, in diseases classified elsewhere	127
*686	Infection, other, skin and subcutaneous tissue, local	143
*771.8	Infection, other, specific to perinatal period	216, 223
670.02	Infection, puerperal, major, delivered, with mention of postpartum complication	191, 196
670.04	Infection, puerperal, major, postpartum condition or complication	205
670.00	Infection, puerperal, major, unspecified as to episode of care	213
*003.2	Infection, Salmonella, localized	308
003.29	Infection, Salmonella, localized, other	247
003.20	Infection, Salmonella, localized, unspecified	247
003.8	Infection, Salmonella, other	247, 308
003.9	Infection, Salmonella, unspecified	247, 308
*046	Infection, slow virus, central nervous system	9
136.2	Infection, specific, by free-living amebae	249
*104	Infection, spirochetal, other	249
121.8	Infection, trematode, other	249
121.9	Infection, trematode, unspecified	249
*730.9	Infection, unspecified, bone	127
675.93	Infection, unspecified, breast and nipple, associated with childbirth, antepartum condition or complication	209
675.92	Infection, unspecified, breast and nipple, associated with childbirth, delivered, with mention of postpartum complication	192, 203
675.91	Infection, unspecified, breast and nipple, associated with childbirth, delivered, with or without mention of antepartum condition	192, 203
675.94	Infection, unspecified, breast and nipple, associated with childbirth, postpartum condition or complication	205
675.90	Infection, unspecified, breast and nipple, associated with childbirth, unspecified as to episode of care	214
599.0	Infection, urinary tract, site not specified	163, 221, 228
*079.9	Infection, viral and chlamydial, in conditions classified elsewhere and of unspecified site, unspecified	309
*079	Infection, viral, in conditions classified elsewhere, unspecified site	247
046.8	Infection, viral, slow, central nervous system, other specified	308

*** Code Range**

Code	Narrative	Page
046.9	Infection, viral, slow, central nervous system, unspecified	308
*465	Infections, acute, respiratory, upper, multiple or unspecified sites	34, 319
*590	Infections, kidney	163
675.03	Infections, nipple, associated with childbirth, antepartum condition or complication	209
675.02	Infections, nipple, associated with childbirth, delivered, with mention of postpartum complication	192, 197
675.01	Infections, nipple, associated with childbirth, delivered, with or without mention of antepartum condition	192, 197
675.04	Infections, nipple, associated with childbirth, postpartum condition or complication	205
675.00	Infections, nipple, associated with childbirth, unspecified as to episode of care	214
771.2	Infections, other, congenital	216, 223
*567.3	Infections, retroperitoneal	215, 222
686.9	Infections, unspecified, skin and subcutaneous tissue, local	230
*628	Infertility, female	177, 183
*606	Infertility, male	172
*125	Infestation, filarial, dracontiasis	249
*134	Infestation, parasitic, other	146
376.00	Inflammation, acute, unspecified, orbit	25
*375.4	Inflammation, chronic, lacrimal passages	25
*373	Inflammation, eyelid	24
608.4	Inflammation, genital organs, male	172
607.2	Inflammation, penis	172
*601	Inflammation, prostate	172
506.2	Inflammation, upper respiratory, due to fumes, vapors	47
*363	Inflammations, scars, and other disorders, choroid	23
487.8	Influenza with other manifestations	247
487.0	Influenza, with pneumonia	45, 83
487.1	Influenza, with respiratory manifestations	34
868.11	Injury, adrenal gland, with open wound into cavity	156, 304
868.01	Injury, adrenal gland, without open wound into cavity	156, 304
863.95	Injury, appendix, with open wound into cavity	105
863.85	Injury, appendix, without open wound into cavity	105, 304
868.12	Injury, bile duct and gallbladder, with open wound into cavity	111, 304
868.02	Injury, bile duct and gallbladder, without open wound into cavity	111, 304
867.1	Injury, bladder and urethra, with open wound into cavity	165
867.0	Injury, bladder and urethra, without open wound into cavity	165
*902	Injury, blood vessels, abdomen and pelvis	272, 298, 304
902.0	Injury, blood vessels, aorta, abdominal	222, 229
901.0	Injury, blood vessels, aorta, thoracic	221, 228, 298, 304
901.1	Injury, blood vessels, arteries, innominate and subclavian	221, 228, 298, 304
*900.0	Injury, blood vessels, artery, carotid	221, 228, 298
900.01	Injury, blood vessels, artery, carotid, common	303
900.02	Injury, blood vessels, artery, carotid, external	303
900.03	Injury, blood vessels, artery, carotid, internal	303
904.0	Injury, blood vessels, artery, femoral, common	298, 305
904.1	Injury, blood vessels, artery, femoral, superficial	298, 305
901.41	Injury, blood vessels, artery, pulmonary	222, 229
*900	Injury, blood vessels, head and neck	272
*904	Injury, blood vessels, lower extremity and unspecified sites	272
900.82	Injury, blood vessels, multiple, head and neck	303, 321
901.83	Injury, blood vessels, multiple, thorax	304
*900.8	Injury, blood vessels, other specified, head and neck	298
904.7	Injury, blood vessels, other specified, lower extremity	298, 306
*901.8	Injury, blood vessels, other specified, thorax	298
900.89	Injury, blood vessels, other, head and neck	321
901.89	Injury, blood vessels, other, thorax	304
904.6	Injury, blood vessels, plantar, deep	298
*904.4	Injury, blood vessels, popliteal	298, 305
*901.4	Injury, blood vessels, pulmonary	298, 304
*901	Injury, blood vessels, thorax	272
*904.5	Injury, blood vessels, tibial	298, 306
904.9	Injury, blood vessels, unspecified site	298
900.9	Injury, blood vessels, unspecified, head and neck	321
904.8	Injury, blood vessels, unspecified, lower extremity	298
901.9	Injury, blood vessels, unspecified, thorax	298, 304
*903	Injury, blood vessels, upper extremity	272, 298, 305
900.81	Injury, blood vessels, vein, jugular, external	221, 228, 303
900.1	Injury, blood vessels, vein, jugular, internal	221, 228, 298, 303

* Code Range

Code	Narrative	Page
901.42	Injury, blood vessels, vein, pulmonary	222, 229
904.2	Injury, blood vessels, veins, femoral	298, 305
901.3	Injury, blood vessels, veins, innominate and subclavian	222, 229, 298, 304
904.3	Injury, blood vessels, veins, saphenous	298
902.10	Injury, blood vessels, vena cava, inferior, unspecified	222, 229
901.2	Injury, blood vessels, vena cava, superior	222, 229, 298, 304
862.31	Injury, bronchus, with open wound into cavity	44
862.21	Injury, bronchus, without open wound into cavity	44
*863.5	Injury, colon or rectum, with open wound into cavity	105, 297, 304
*863.4	Injury, colon or rectum, without open wound into cavity	105, 297, 304
767.7	Injury, cranial and peripheral nerve, other, trauma, birth	216, 223
*928.2	Injury, crushing, ankle and foot, excluding toe(s) alone	298
926.11	Injury, crushing, back	305
926.12	Injury, crushing, buttock	306
*927.1	Injury, crushing, elbow and forearm	298, 305
926.0	Injury, crushing, external genitalia	173, 178, 184, 298
925.1	Injury, crushing, face and scalp	303
*925	Injury, crushing, face, scalp, and neck	272, 298, 321
927.3	Injury, crushing, finger(s)	298
*928.0	Injury, crushing, hip and thigh	298, 306
*928.1	Injury, crushing, knee and lower leg	298, 306
*928	Injury, crushing, lower limb	272
*929	Injury, crushing, multiple and unspecified sites	272, 299
928.8	Injury, crushing, multiple sites, lower limb	299, 306
927.8	Injury, crushing, multiple sites, upper limb	298, 305
925.2	Injury, crushing, neck	303
927.01	Injury, crushing, scapular region	304
*927.0	Injury, crushing, shoulder and upper arm	298, 305
928.3	Injury, crushing, toe(s)	298
926.8	Injury, crushing, trunk, multiple sites	272, 298, 305
*926.1	Injury, crushing, trunk, other specified sites	272, 298
926.19	Injury, crushing, trunk, other specified sites	305
926.9	Injury, crushing, trunk, unspecified site	272, 298, 305
928.9	Injury, crushing, unspecified site, lower limb	299, 306
927.9	Injury, crushing, unspecified site, upper limb	298, 305
*927	Injury, crushing, upper limb	272
*927.2	Injury, crushing, wrist and hand(s), except finger(s) alone	298
862.1	Injury, diaphragm, with open wound into cavity	44
862.0	Injury, diaphragm, without open wound into cavity	44
862.32	Injury, esophagus, with open wound into cavity	105
862.22	Injury, esophagus, without open wound into cavity	105
*863.9	Injury, gastrointestinal sites, other and unspecified, with open wound into cavity	297, 304
*863.8	Injury, gastrointestinal sites, other and unspecified, without open wound into cavity	297
863.99	Injury, gastrointestinal sites, other, with open wound into cavity	105
863.89	Injury, gastrointestinal sites, other, without open wound into cavity	105, 304
863.90	Injury, gastrointestinal tract, unspecified site, with open wound into cavity	105
863.80	Injury, gastrointestinal tract, unspecified site, without open wound into cavity	105
959.01	Injury, head, unspecified	303
*861	Injury, heart and lung	297, 304
*861.1	Injury, heart, with open wound into thorax	91
*861.0	Injury, heart, without open wound into thorax	91
*869	Injury, internal, organ, ill-defined or unspecified	272, 297
868.10	Injury, intra-abdominal organ, unspecified, with open wound into cavity	105
868.00	Injury, intra-abdominal organ, unspecified, without open wound into cavity	105
*868.1	Injury, intra-abdominal organs, other, with open wound into cavity	297
*868.0	Injury, intra-abdominal organs, other, without open wound into cavity	297
868.19	Injury, intraabdominal organs, other and multiple, with open wound into cavity	272, 304
868.09	Injury, intraabdominal organs, other and multiple, without open wound into cavity	272, 304
*854	Injury, intracranial, other and unspecified nature	14, 297, 303
862.9	Injury, intrathoracic organs, multiple and unspecified, with mention of open wound into cavity	60, 62, 65, 74, 78, 80, 272
862.8	Injury, intrathoracic organs, multiple and unspecified, without mention of open wound into cavity	272

** Code Range*

Code	Narrative	Page
*862	Injury, intrathoracic organs, other and unspecified	297, 304
862.39	Injury, intrathoracic organs, other specified, with open wound into cavity	47
862.29	Injury, intrathoracic organs, other specified, without open wound into cavity	47
*866	Injury, kidney	165, 297, 304
*864	Injury, liver	111, 304
*864.1	Injury, liver, with open wound into cavity	297
*864.0	Injury, liver, without open wound into cavity	297
861.30	Injury, lung, unspecified, with open wound into thorax	47
861.20	Injury, lung, unspecified, without open wound into thorax	47
953.1	Injury, nerve root, dorsal	299
953.2	Injury, nerve root, lumbar	299
953.3	Injury, nerve root, sacral	299
*953	Injury, nerve roots and spinal plexus	12, 299
953.8	Injury, nerve roots and spinal plexus, multiple sites	299, 305
953.9	Injury, nerve roots and spinal plexus, unspecified site	299
951.3	Injury, nerve, abducens	12
951.6	Injury, nerve, accessory	12
951.5	Injury, nerve, acoustic	37
955.0	Injury, nerve, axillary	299, 305
951.9	Injury, nerve, cranial, unspecified	12
956.4	Injury, nerve, cutaneous sensory, lower limb	299
955.5	Injury, nerve, cutaneous sensory, upper limb	299
955.6	Injury, nerve, digital, shoulder girdle and upper limb	299
951.4	Injury, nerve, facial	12
956.1	Injury, nerve, femoral	299, 306
951.7	Injury, nerve, hypoglossal	12
955.1	Injury, nerve, median	299, 305
955.4	Injury, nerve, musculocutaneous	299
951.0	Injury, nerve, oculomotor	12
956.3	Injury, nerve, peroneal	299, 306
956.2	Injury, nerve, posterior tibial	299, 306
955.3	Injury, nerve, radial	299, 305
956.0	Injury, nerve, sciatic	299, 306
954.0	Injury, nerve, sympathetic, cervical	299
951.2	Injury, nerve, trigeminal	12
951.1	Injury, nerve, trochlear	12
955.2	Injury, nerve, ulnar	299, 305
956.9	Injury, nerve, unspecified site, pelvic girdle and lower limb	299, 306
955.9	Injury, nerve, unspecified, shoulder girdle and upper limb	299
954.9	Injury, nerve, unspecified, trunk	299, 305
*951	Injury, nerve(s), other cranial	299
956.5	Injury, nerve(s), other specified, pelvic girdle and lower limb	299
955.7	Injury, nerve(s), other specified, shoulder girdle and upper limb	299
954.8	Injury, nerve(s), other specified, trunk	299, 305
*954	Injury, nerve(s), other, trunk, excluding shoulder and pelvic girdles	12
*956	Injury, nerve(s), peripheral, pelvic girdle and lower limb	12
*955	Injury, nerve(s), peripheral, shoulder girdle and upper limb	12
954.1	Injury, nerve(s), sympathetic, other, trunk	299
951.8	Injury, nerves, cranial, other specified	12
956.8	Injury, nerves, multiple, pelvic girdle and lower limb	299, 306
955.8	Injury, nerves, multiple, shoulder girdle and upper limb	299, 305
*957	Injury, nerves, other and unspecified	12, 299
950.1	Injury, optic chiasm	16
950.0	Injury, optic nerve	26
*950	Injury, optic nerve and pathways	299
950.9	Injury, optic nerve and pathways, unspecified	16
950.2	Injury, optic pathways	16
*959	Injury, other and unspecified	272
959.3	Injury, other and unspecified, elbow, forearm, and wrist	299
*959.0	Injury, other and unspecified, face and neck	299, 321
959.09	Injury, other and unspecified, face and neck	303
959.5	Injury, other and unspecified, finger	299
959.4	Injury, other and unspecified, hand, except finger	299
959.6	Injury, other and unspecified, hip and thigh	299
959.7	Injury, other and unspecified, knee, leg, ankle, and foot	299
959.8	Injury, other and unspecified, other specified sites, including multiple	299
959.2	Injury, other and unspecified, shoulder and upper arm	299
*959.1	Injury, other and unspecified, trunk	299
959.9	Injury, other and unspecified, unspecified site	299
665.51	Injury, other, obstetrical, pelvic organs, delivered, with or without mention of antepartum condition	190, 202
665.54	Injury, other, obstetrical, pelvic organs, postpartum condition or complication	204

Alphabetic Index to Diseases

** Code Range*

Code	Narrative	Page
665.50	Injury, other, obstetrical, pelvic organs, unspecified as to episode of care	190, 202
863.92	Injury, pancreas, body, with open wound into cavity	110
863.82	Injury, pancreas, body, without open wound into cavity	110, 304
863.91	Injury, pancreas, head, with open wound into cavity	110
863.81	Injury, pancreas, head, without open wound into cavity	110, 304
863.94	Injury, pancreas, multiple and unspecified sites, with open wound into cavity	110
863.84	Injury, pancreas, multiple and unspecified sites, without open wound into cavity	110, 304
863.93	Injury, pancreas, tail, with open wound into cavity	110
863.83	Injury, pancreas, tail, without open wound into cavity	110, 304
*867	Injury, pelvic organs	297, 304
867.7	Injury, pelvic organs, other, with open wound into cavity	173, 177, 184
867.6	Injury, pelvic organs, other, without open wound into cavity	173, 177, 184
867.9	Injury, pelvic organs, unspecified, with open wound into cavity	173, 177, 184
867.8	Injury, pelvic organs, unspecified, without open wound into cavity	173, 177, 184
868.13	Injury, peritoneum, with open wound into cavity	105, 304
868.03	Injury, peritoneum, without open wound into cavity	105, 305
868.14	Injury, retroperitoneum, with open wound into cavity	165, 304
868.04	Injury, retroperitoneum, without open wound into cavity	165, 305
767.11	Injury, scalp, trauma, birth, epicranial subaponeurotic hemorrhage (massive)	216, 223
767.19	Injury, scalp, trauma, birth, other	230, 231
*863.3	Injury, small intestine, with open wound into cavity	105, 297, 304
*863.2	Injury, small intestine, without open wound into cavity	105, 297, 304
*952	Injury, spinal cord, without spinal bone injury	9, 299, 305
953.4	Injury, spinal plexus, brachial	222, 229, 299, 305
953.5	Injury, spinal plexus, lumbosacral	299, 305
767.4	Injury, spine and spinal cord, trauma, birth	216, 223
*865	Injury, spleen	221, 228, 235, 297, 304
863.1	Injury, stomach, with open wound into cavity	105, 297, 304
863.0	Injury, stomach, without open wound into cavity	105, 297, 304
913.1	Injury, superficial, abrasion or friction burn, infected, elbow, forearm and wrist	143
910.1	Injury, superficial, abrasion or friction burn, infected, face, neck and scalp, except eye	143
915.1	Injury, superficial, abrasion or friction burn, infected, finger(s)	143
917.1	Injury, superficial, abrasion or friction burn, infected, foot and toe(s)	144
914.1	Injury, superficial, abrasion or friction burn, infected, hand(s) except finger(s) alone	143
916.1	Injury, superficial, abrasion or friction burn, infected, hip, thigh, leg, and ankle	144
912.1	Injury, superficial, abrasion or friction burn, infected, shoulder and upper arm	143
919.1	Injury, superficial, abrasion or friction burn, infected, sites, other, multiple and unspecified	144
911.1	Injury, superficial, abrasion or friction burn, infected, trunk	143
913.0	Injury, superficial, abrasion or friction burn, without infection, elbow, forearm and wrist	145
915.0	Injury, superficial, abrasion or friction burn, without infection, finger(s)	145
917.0	Injury, superficial, abrasion or friction burn, without infection, foot and toe(s)	145
914.0	Injury, superficial, abrasion or friction burn, without infection, hand(s) except finger(s) alone	145
916.0	Injury, superficial, abrasion or friction burn, without infection, hip, thigh, leg, and ankle	145
912.0	Injury, superficial, abrasion or friction burn, without infection, shoulder and upper arm	145
919.0	Injury, superficial, abrasion or friction burn, without infection, sites, other, multiple and unspecified	145
911.0	Injury, superficial, abrasion or friction burn, without infection, trunk	145
910.0	Injury, superficial, abrasion, friction burn, without infection, face, neck and scalp except eye	145
913.3	Injury, superficial, blister, infected, elbow, forearm and wrist	143
910.3	Injury, superficial, blister, infected, face, neck and scalp, except eye	148
915.3	Injury, superficial, blister, infected, finger(s)	143
917.3	Injury, superficial, blister, infected, foot and toe(s)	144
914.3	Injury, superficial, blister, infected, hand(s) except finger(s) alone	143
916.3	Injury, superficial, blister, infected, hip, thigh, leg, and ankle	144

** Code Range*

Code	Narrative	Page
912.3	Injury, superficial, blister, infected, shoulder and upper arm	143
919.3	Injury, superficial, blister, infected, sites, other, multiple and unspecified	144
911.3	Injury, superficial, blister, infected, trunk	143
910.2	Injury, superficial, blister, without infection, face, neck and scalp, except eye	148
912.2	Injury, superficial, blister, without infection, shoulder or upper arm	145
913.2	Injury, superficial, blister, without infection, shoulder or upper arm	148
914.2	Injury, superficial, blister, without infection, shoulder or upper arm	148
915.2	Injury, superficial, blister, without infection, shoulder or upper arm	148
916.2	Injury, superficial, blister, without infection, shoulder or upper arm	148
917.2	Injury, superficial, blister, without infection, shoulder or upper arm	148
919.2	Injury, superficial, blister, without infection, shoulder or upper arm	148
911.2	Injury, superficial, blister, without infection, trunk	148
*913	Injury, superficial, elbow, forearm and wrist	298
*918	Injury, superficial, eye and adnexa	25, 298
*910	Injury, superficial, face, neck and scalp except eye	298
*915	Injury, superficial, finger(s)	298
*917	Injury, superficial, foot and toe(s)	298
913.6	Injury, superficial, foreign body (splinter), without major open wound or infection, elbow, forearm and wrist	145
913.7	Injury, superficial, foreign body (splinter), without major open wound, infected, elbow, forearm and wrist	143
910.6	Injury, superficial, foreign body, without major open wound or infection, face, neck and scalp except eye	145
915.6	Injury, superficial, foreign body, without major open wound or infection, finger(s)	145
917.6	Injury, superficial, foreign body, without major open wound or infection, foot and toe(s)	145
914.6	Injury, superficial, foreign body, without major open wound or infection, hand(s) except finger(s) alone	145
916.6	Injury, superficial, foreign body, without major open wound or infection, hip, thigh, leg, and ankle	145
912.6	Injury, superficial, foreign body, without major open wound or infection, shoulder and upper arm	145
919.6	Injury, superficial, foreign body, without major open wound or infection, sites, other, multiple and unspecified	145
911.6	Injury, superficial, foreign body, without major open wound or infection, trunk	145
910.7	Injury, superficial, foreign body, without major open wound, infected, face, neck and scalp except eye	143
915.7	Injury, superficial, foreign body, without major open wound, infected, finger(s)	144
917.7	Injury, superficial, foreign body, without major open wound, infected, foot and toe(s)	144
914.7	Injury, superficial, foreign body, without major open wound, infected, hand(s) except finger(s) alone	143
916.7	Injury, superficial, foreign body, without major open wound, infected, hip, thigh, leg, and ankle	144
912.7	Injury, superficial, foreign body, without major open wound, infected, shoulder and upper arm	143
919.7	Injury, superficial, foreign body, without major open wound, infected, sites, other, multiple and unspecified	144
911.7	Injury, superficial, foreign body, without major open wound, infected, trunk	143
*914	Injury, superficial, hand(s) except finger(s) alone	298
*916	Injury, superficial, hip, thigh, leg, and ankle	298
913.5	Injury, superficial, insect bite, nonvenomous, infected, elbow, forearm and wrist	143
910.5	Injury, superficial, insect bite, nonvenomous, infected, face, neck and scalp except eye	143
915.5	Injury, superficial, insect bite, nonvenomous, infected, finger(s)	143
917.5	Injury, superficial, insect bite, nonvenomous, infected, foot and toe(s)	144
914.5	Injury, superficial, insect bite, nonvenomous, infected, hand(s) except finger(s) alone	143
916.5	Injury, superficial, insect bite, nonvenomous, infected, hip, thigh, leg, and ankle	144
912.5	Injury, superficial, insect bite, nonvenomous, infected, shoulder and upper arm	143
919.5	Injury, superficial, insect bite, nonvenomous, infected, sites, other, multiple and unspecified	144
911.5	Injury, superficial, insect bite, nonvenomous, infected, trunk	143

*** Code Range**

Code	Narrative	Page
913.4	Injury, superficial, insect bite, nonvenomous, without infection, elbow, forearm and wrist	148
910.4	Injury, superficial, insect bite, nonvenomous, without infection, face, neck and scalp except eye	148
915.4	Injury, superficial, insect bite, nonvenomous, without infection, finger(s)	148
917.4	Injury, superficial, insect bite, nonvenomous, without infection, foot and toe(s)	148
914.4	Injury, superficial, insect bite, nonvenomous, without infection, hand(s) except finger(s) alone	148
916.4	Injury, superficial, insect bite, nonvenomous, without infection, hip, thigh, leg, and ankle	148
912.4	Injury, superficial, insect bite, nonvenomous, without infection, shoulder and upper arm	148
919.4	Injury, superficial, insect bite, nonvenomous, without infection, sites, other, multiple and unspecified	148
911.4	Injury, superficial, insect bite, nonvenomous, without infection, trunk	148
913.9	Injury, superficial, other and unspecified, infected, elbow, forearm and wrist	143
910.9	Injury, superficial, other and unspecified, infected, face, neck and scalp	143
915.9	Injury, superficial, other and unspecified, infected, finger(s)	144
917.9	Injury, superficial, other and unspecified, infected, foot and toe(s)	144
914.9	Injury, superficial, other and unspecified, infected, hand(s) except finger(s) alone	143
916.9	Injury, superficial, other and unspecified, infected, hip, thigh, leg, and ankle	144
912.9	Injury, superficial, other and unspecified, infected, shoulder and upper arm	143
919.9	Injury, superficial, other and unspecified, infected, sites, other, multiple and unspecified	144
911.9	Injury, superficial, other and unspecified, infected, trunk	143
913.8	Injury, superficial, other and unspecified, without infection, elbow, forearm and wrist	145
910.8	Injury, superficial, other and unspecified, without infection, face, neck and scalp	145
915.8	Injury, superficial, other and unspecified, without infection, finger(s)	145
917.8	Injury, superficial, other and unspecified, without infection, foot and toe(s)	145
914.8	Injury, superficial, other and unspecified, without infection, hand(s) except finger(s) alone	145
916.8	Injury, superficial, other and unspecified, without infection, hip, thigh, leg, and ankle	145
912.8	Injury, superficial, other and unspecified, without infection, shoulder and upper arm	145
919.8	Injury, superficial, other and unspecified, without infection, sites, other, multiple and unspecified	145
911.8	Injury, superficial, other and unspecified, without infection, trunk	145
*912	Injury, superficial, shoulder and upper arm	298
*919	Injury, superficial, sites, other, multiple and unspecified	298
*911	Injury, superficial, trunk	298
867.3	Injury, ureter, with open wound into cavity	165
867.2	Injury, ureter, without open wound into cavity	165
867.5	Injury, uterus, with open wound into cavity	177, 184
867.4	Injury, uterus, without open wound into cavity	177, 184
950.3	Injury, visual cortex	16
V25.5	Insertion, implantable contraceptive, subdermal	287
780.52	Insomnia, unspecified	253
780.51	Insomnia, with sleep apnea, unspecified	16
557.0	Insufficiency, acute, vascular, intestine	220, 227
746.4	Insufficiency, congenital, aortic valve	88
746.6	Insufficiency, congenital, mitralvalve	88
378.83	Insufficiency, convergence or palsy, binocular eye movement	25
518.5	Insufficiency, pulmonary, following trauma and surgery	44, 83, 220, 227, 279
518.82	Insufficiency, pulmonary, other	46
*557	Insufficiency, vascular, intestine	104
459.81	Insufficiency, venous, peripheral, unspecified	87
271.2	Intolerance, fructose, hereditary	102
*303.0	Intoxication, acute alcoholic	254
560.0	Intussusception	220, 227
665.22	Inversion, obstetrical, uterus, delivered, with mention of postpartum complication	190, 201
665.24	Inversion, obstetrical, uterus, postpartum condition or complication	204
665.20	Inversion, obstetrical, uterus, unspecified as to episode of care	190, 201
*V72	Investigation, examination, special	289

Alphabetic Index to Diseases

Code	Narrative	Page
517.8	Involvement, lung, in other diseases classified elsewhere	45
364.42	Iridis, rubeosis	23
*364.0	Iridocyclitis, acute, subacute	23
*364.2	Iridocyclitis, certain types	23
*364.1	Iridocyclitis, chronic	23
364.3	Iridocyclitis, unspecified	23
379.59	Irregularity, other, eye movements	25
779.1	Irritability, other and unspecified, cerebral, newborn	216, 223
*435	Ischemia, transient, cerebral	17
656.23	Isoimmunization, other and unspecified blood group, affecting management of mother, antepartum condition or complication	208
656.21	Isoimmunization, other and unspecified blood group, affecting management of mother, delivered, with or without mention of antepartum condition	188, 199
656.20	Isoimmunization, other and unspecified blood group, affecting management of mother, unspecified as to episode of care	213
656.13	Isoimmunization, rhesus, affecting management of mother, antepartum condition or complication	208
656.11	Isoimmunization, rhesus, affecting management of mother, delivered, with or without mention of antepartum condition	188, 199
656.10	Isoimmunization, rhesus, affecting management of mother, unspecified as to episode of care	213
*V07	Isolation need or other prophylactic measures	287
*774.3	Jaundice, neonatal, due to delayed conjugation	230, 231
774.4	Jaundice, perinatal, due to hepatocellular damage	216, 223
774.5	Jaundice, perinatal, from other causes	230, 231
774.6	Jaundice, unspecified, fetal and neonatal	230, 231
782.4	Jaundice, unspecified, not newborn	111
370.52	Keratitis, interstitial, diffuse	24
370.59	Keratitis, interstitial, other and deep	24
090.3	Keratitis, interstitial, syphilitic	22
370.50	Keratitis, interstitial, unspecified	24
370.8	Keratitis, other forms	24
370.54	Keratitis, sclerosing	24
*370.2	Keratitis, superficial, without conjunctivitis	24
370.9	Keratitis, unspecified	24
*370.3	Keratoconjunctivitis, certain types	24
*370.4	Keratoconjunctivitis, other, unspecified	24
098.81	Keratosis, blennorrhagica, gonococcal	22
773.4	Kernicterus, due to isoimmunization, fetus or newborn	216, 223
774.7	Kernicterus, not due to isoimmunization, fetus or newborn	216, 223
260	Kwashiorkor	154, 309
644.13	Labor, other, threatened, antepartum condition	206
644.10	Labor, other, threatened, unspecified as to episode of care	206
644.03	Labor, premature, threatened, antepartum condition	206
644.00	Labor, premature, threatened, unspecified as to episode of care	206
*386.3	Labyrinthitis	33
*851	Laceration and contusion, cerebral	14
*851.7	Laceration, cerebellar or brain stem, with open intracranial wound	8, 297, 303
*851.6	Laceration, cerebellar or brain stem, without mention of open intracranial wound	8, 297, 303
*851.3	Laceration, cerebral cortex, with open intracranial wound	8, 297, 303
*851.2	Laceration, cerebral cortex, without mention of open intracranial wound	8, 297, 303
*851.9	Laceration, contusion, cerebral, with open intracranial wound	8, 297, 303
*851.8	Laceration, contusion, cerebral, without mention of open intracranial wound	8, 297, 303
664.01	Laceration, first-degree, perineal, during delivery, degree, delivered with or without mention of antepartum condition	189, 201
664.04	Laceration, first-degree, perineal, during delivery, postpartum condition or complication	204
664.00	Laceration, first-degree, perineal, during delivery, unspecified as to episode of care	189, 201
664.31	Laceration, fourth-degree, perineal, during delivery, degree, delivered with or without mention of antepartum condition	189, 201
664.34	Laceration, fourth-degree, perineal, during delivery, postpartum condition or complication	204
664.30	Laceration, fourth-degree, perineal, during delivery, unspecified as to episode of care	189, 201
665.41	Laceration, high, vaginal, during and after labor, delivered, with or without mention of antepartum condition	190, 201
665.44	Laceration, high, vaginal, during and after labor, postpartum condition or complication	204
665.40	Laceration, high, vaginal, during and after labor, unspecified as to episode of care	190, 201

Alphabetic Index to Diseases

Code	Narrative	Page
861.32	Laceration, lung, with open wound into thorax	44
861.22	Laceration, lung, without open wound into thorax	44
665.31	Laceration, obstetrical, cervix, delivered, with or without mention of antepartum condition	190, 201
665.34	Laceration, obstetrical, cervix, postpartum condition or complication	204
665.30	Laceration, obstetrical, cervix, unspecified as to episode of care	190, 201
664.11	Laceration, second-degree, perineal, during delivery, degree, delivered with or without mention of antepartum condition	189, 201
664.14	Laceration, second-degree, perineal, during delivery, postpartum condition or complication	204
664.10	Laceration, second-degree, perineal, during delivery, unspecified as to episode of care	189, 201
664.21	Laceration, third-degree, perineal, during delivery, degree, delivered with or without mention of antepartum condition	189, 201
664.24	Laceration, third-degree, perineal, during delivery, postpartum condition or complication	204
664.20	Laceration, third-degree, perineal, during delivery, unspecified as to episode of care	189, 201
664.41	Laceration, unspecified, perineal, during delivery, degree, delivered with or without mention of antepartum condition	189, 201
664.44	Laceration, unspecified, perineal, during delivery, postpartum condition or complication	204
664.40	Laceration, unspecified, perineal, during delivery, unspecified as to episode of care	189, 201
781.3	Lack of coordination	16
*783.4	Lack, development, physiological in childhood	310
*374.2	Lagophthalmos	24
653.53	Large, unusually, fetus, causing disproportion, antepartum condition or complication	207
653.51	Large, unusually, fetus, causing disproportion, delivered, with or without mention of antepartum condition	187, 199
653.50	Large, unusually, fetus, causing disproportion, unspecified as to episode of care	212
*476	Laryngitis and laryngotracheitis, chronic	34
464.01	Laryngitis, acute, with obstruction	34, 319
464.00	Laryngitis, acute, without obstruction	34, 319
476.0	Laryngitis, chronic	319
*464.2	Laryngotracheitis, acute	35, 319
476.1	Laryngotracheitis, chronic	319
773.5	Late anemia, due to isoimmunization, fetus or newborn	216, 223
677	Late effect, complication, pregnancy, childbirth and puerperium	214
139.8	Late effect, other infectious and parasitic diseases	249
138	Late effect, poliomyelitis, acute	15
139.1	Late effect, trachoma	22
137.3	Late effect, tuberculosis, bones and joints	133
137.1	Late effect, tuberculosis, central nervous system	15
137.2	Late effect, tuberculosis, genitourinary	163
137.4	Late effect, tuberculosis, other	249
137.0	Late effect, tuberculosis, respiratory, unspecified	45
139.0	Late effect, viral encephalitis	15
*218	Leiomyoma, uterine	176, 183
085.4	Leishmaniasis, cutaneous, American	146
085.2	Leishmaniasis, cutaneous, Asian desert	146
085.3	Leishmaniasis, cutaneous, Ethiopian	146
085.1	Leishmaniasis, cutaneous, urban	146
085.5	Leishmaniasis, mucocutaneous, American	146
085.9	Leishmaniasis, unspecified	248
085.0	Leishmaniasis, visceral (kala-azar)	248
*030	Leprosy	248
100.0	Leptospirosis icterohemorrhagica	248
100.9	Leptospirosis, unspecified	248
739.9	Lesions, nonallopathic, not elsewhere classified, abdomen and other	130
739.1	Lesions, nonallopathic, not elsewhere classified, cervical region	129
739.0	Lesions, nonallopathic, not elsewhere classified, head region	130
739.6	Lesions, nonallopathic, not elsewhere classified, lower extremities	130
739.3	Lesions, nonallopathic, not elsewhere classified, lumbar region	129
739.5	Lesions, nonallopathic, not elsewhere classified, pelvic region	130
739.8	Lesions, nonallopathic, not elsewhere classified, rib cage	130
739.4	Lesions, nonallopathic, not elsewhere classified, sacral region	129
739.2	Lesions, nonallopathic, not elsewhere classified, thoracic region	129
739.7	Lesions, nonallopathic, not elsewhere classified, upper extremities	130

** Code Range*

Code	Narrative	Page
663.63	Lesions, vascular, cord, complicating labor and delivery, antepartum condition or complication	209
663.61	Lesions, vascular, cord, complicating labor and delivery, delivered, with or without mention of antepartum condition	189, 201
663.60	Lesions, vascular, cord, complicating labor and delivery, unspecified as to episode of care	189, 201
*202.5	Letterer-Siwe disease	236, 244
202.51	Letterer-Siwe disease, lymph nodes, head, face, and neck	319
*204	Leukemia, lymphoid	237
*204.0	Leukemia, lymphoid, acute	242, 244
*206	Leukemia, monocytic	237
*206.0	Leukemia, monocytic, acute	242, 244
*205	Leukemia, myeloid	237
*205.0	Leukemia, myeloid, acute	242, 244
*207	Leukemia, other specified	237
*208	Leukemia, unspecified cell type	237
*208.0	Leukemia, unspecified cell type, acute	242, 244
046.3	Leukoencephalopathy, multifocal, progressive	308
779.7	Leukomalacia, periventricular	16, 221, 228
530.83	Leukoplakia, esophageal	102
528.6	Leukoplakia, oral mucosa, including tongue	310
607.0	Leukoplakia, penis	172
*697	Lichen	147
698.3	Lichenification and lichen, simplex chronicus	147
764.14	Light-for-dates with malnutrition, fetal, 1,000-1,249 grams	216, 223
764.15	Light-for-dates with malnutrition, fetal, 1,250-1,499 grams	216, 223
764.16	Light-for-dates with malnutrition, fetal, 1,500-1,749 grams	216, 223
764.17	Light-for-dates with malnutrition, fetal, 1,750-1,999 grams	216, 223
764.18	Light-for-dates with malnutrition, fetal, 2,000-2,499 grams	216, 223
764.12	Light-for-dates with malnutrition, fetal, 500-749 grams	215, 222
764.13	Light-for-dates with malnutrition, fetal, 750-999 grams	215, 223
764.11	Light-for-dates with malnutrition, fetal, less than 500 grams	215, 222
764.08	Light-for-dates without malnutrition, fetal, 2,000-2,499 grams	229, 231
764.09	Light-for-dates without malnutrition, fetal, 2,500 or more grams	229, 231
214.3	Lipoma, intraabdominal organs	104
214.2	Lipoma, intrathoracic organs	43
214.8	Lipoma, other specified sites	147
214.0	Lipoma, skin and subcutaneous tissue, face	147
214.1	Lipoma, skin and subcutaneous tissue, other	147
214.4	Lipoma, spermatic cord	172
214.9	Lipoma, unspecified site	147
*718.1	Loose body, joint	134
717.6	Loose body, knee	134
781.91	Loss of height	16
772.0	Loss, blood, fetal	216, 223
*389	Loss, hearing	36
388.2	Loss, hearing, sudden, unspecified	36
368.11	Loss, visual, sudden	21
368.12	Loss, visual, transient	21
695.4	Lupus erythematosus	142
683	Lymphadenitis, acute	221, 228, 235, 310
289.1	Lymphadenitis, chronic	235
289.2	Lymphadenitis, mesenteric, nonspecific	104
289.3	Lymphadenitis, unspecified, except mesenteric	235
228.1	Lymphangioma, any site	234
457.2	Lymphangitis	143, 219, 226
457.1	Lymphedema, other	147
099.1	Lymphogranuloma, venereum	172, 176, 182
*202.8	Lymphoma, malignant, other	237, 309
202.81	Lymphoma, malignant, other, lymph nodes, head, face, and neck	319
*202.0	Lymphoma, nodular	237
202.01	Lymphoma, nodular, lymph nodes, head, face, and neck	319
*200	Lymphosarcoma and reticulosarcoma	237
*200.8	Lymphosarcoma and reticulosarcoma, other named variants	308
200.81	Lymphosarcoma and reticulosarcoma, other named variants, lymph nodes, head, face, and neck	318
200.11	Lymphosarcoma, lymph nodes, head, face, and neck	318
744.81	Macrocheilia	37
273.3	Macroglobulinemia	237
744.83	Macrostomia	37
039.4	Madura foot	146
*579	Malabsorption, intestinal	103
579.3	Malabsorption, postsurgical, other and unspecified	221, 228
579.9	Malabsorption, unspecified, intestinal	310
*780.7	Malaise, fatigue	286, 310
*084	Malaria	248

Code	Narrative	Page
647.43	Malaria, maternal, classifiable elsewhere, complicating pregnancy, childbirth, or the puerperium, antepartum condition or complication	207, 210
647.41	Malaria, maternal, classifiable elsewhere, complicating pregnancy, childbirth, or the puerperium, delivered, with or without mention of antepartum condition	186, 195
647.42	Malaria, maternal, classifiable elsewhere, complicating pregnancy, childbirth, or the puerperium, delivered, with mention of postpartum complication	186, 195
647.44	Malaria, maternal, classifiable elsewhere, complicating pregnancy, childbirth, or the puerperium, postpartum condition or complication	204
647.40	Malaria, maternal, classifiable elsewhere, complicating pregnancy, childbirth, or the puerperium, unspecified as to episode of care	211
655.03	Malformation, central nervous system, fetus, affecting management of mother, antepartum condition or complication	207
655.01	Malformation, central nervous system, fetus, affecting management of mother, delivered, with or without mention of antepartum condition	187, 199
655.00	Malformation, central nervous system, fetus, affecting management of mother, unspecified as to episode of care	213
306.3	Malfunction, physiological, from mental factors	147
306.2	Malfunction, physiological, from mental factors, cardiovascular	90
306.52	Malfunction, physiological, from mental factors, dysmenorrhea, psychogenic	176, 183
306.53	Malfunction, physiological, from mental factors, dysuria, psychogenic	165
306.6	Malfunction, physiological, from mental factors, endocrine	156
306.4	Malfunction, physiological, from mental factors, gastrointestinal	102
306.59	Malfunction, physiological, from mental factors, genitourinary other	165
306.50	Malfunction, physiological, from mental factors, genitourinary unspecified	164
306.0	Malfunction, physiological, from mental factors, musculoskeletal	131
306.8	Malfunction, physiological, from mental factors, other specified	253
306.1	Malfunction, physiological, from mental factors, respiratory	47

Code	Narrative	Page
306.7	Malfunction, physiological, from mental factors, special sense organs	251
306.9	Malfunction, physiological, from mental factors, unspecified	251
306.51	Malfunction, physiological, from mental factors, vaginismus, psychogenic	176, 183
*202.9	Malignant neoplasms, lymphoid and histiocytic tissue, other and unspecified	237
202.91	Malignant neoplasms, lymphoid and histiocytic tissue, other and unspecified, lymph nodes, head, face, and neck	319
736.1	Mallet finger	134
263.1	Malnutrition, degree, mild	218, 225
263.0	Malnutrition, degree, moderate	218, 225
764.24	Malnutrition, fetal, without mention of light-for-dates, 1,000-1,249 grams	216, 223
764.25	Malnutrition, fetal, without mention of light-for-dates, 1,250-1,499 grams	216, 223
764.26	Malnutrition, fetal, without mention of light-for-dates, 1,500-1,749 grams	216, 223
764.27	Malnutrition, fetal, without mention of light-for-dates, 1,750-1,999 grams	216, 223
764.28	Malnutrition, fetal, without mention of light-for-dates, 2,000-2,499 grams	216, 223
764.22	Malnutrition, fetal, without mention of light-for-dates, 500-749 grams	216, 223
764.23	Malnutrition, fetal, without mention of light-for-dates, 750-999 grams	216, 223
764.21	Malnutrition, fetal, without mention of light-for-dates, less than 500 grams	216, 223
263.8	Malnutrition, protein-calorie, other	218, 225
262	Malnutrition, protein-calorie, other severe	154, 218, 225, 309
*263	Malnutrition, protein-calorie, unspecified	154, 309
263.9	Malnutrition, protein-calorie, unspecified	218, 225
652.83	Malposition or malpresentation, other specified, fetus, antepartum condition or complication	207
652.81	Malposition or malpresentation, other specified, fetus, delivered, with or without mention of antepartum condition	187, 198
652.80	Malposition or malpresentation, other specified, fetus, unspecified as to episode of care	212
652.93	Malposition or malpresentation, unspecified, fetus, antepartum condition or complication	207
652.91	Malposition or malpresentation, unspecified, fetus, delivered, with or without mention of antepartum condition	187, 198

*** Code Range**

Code	Narrative	Page
652.90	Malposition or malpresentation, unspecified, fetus, unspecified as to episode of care	212
*733.8	Malunion and nonunion, fracture	134
V25.3	Management, contraceptive, extraction, menstrual	178, 184
*V25.0	Management, contraceptive, general counseling and advice	287
V25.1	Management, contraceptive, insertion, intrauterine contraceptive device	287
V25.8	Management, contraceptive, other specified	288
V25.2	Management, contraceptive, sterilization	172, 178, 184
V25.9	Management, contraceptive, unspecified	288
V26.4	Management, procreative, general counseling and advice	288
V26.1	Management, procreative, insemination, artificial	288
*V26.2	Management, procreative, investigation and testing	288
V26.8	Management, procreative, other specified	288
*V26.5	Management, procreative, sterilization status	288
V26.0	Management, procreative, tuboplasty or vasoplasty, after previous sterilization	173, 178, 184
V26.9	Management, procreative, unspecified	288
261	Marasmus, nutritional	154, 218, 225, 309
771.5	Mastitis, infective, neonatal	216, 223
675.23	Mastitis, nonpurulent, associated with childbirth, antepartum condition or complication	209
675.22	Mastitis, nonpurulent, associated with childbirth, delivered, with mention of postpartum complication	192, 197
675.21	Mastitis, nonpurulent, associated with childbirth, delivered, with or without mention of antepartum condition	192, 197
675.24	Mastitis, nonpurulent, associated with childbirth, postpartum condition or complication	205
675.20	Mastitis, nonpurulent, associated with childbirth, unspecified as to episode of care	214
*383.0	Mastoiditis, acute	34
383.1	Mastoiditis, chronic	34
383.9	Mastoiditis, unspecified	34
055.71	Measles, keratoconjunctivitis	22
055.79	Measles, other specified complications	247
055.8	Measles, unspecified complications	217, 224, 247
*055.7	Measles, with other specified complications	217, 224
055.9	Measles, without mention of complication	247
519.2	Mediastinitis	43, 220, 227
564.7	Megacolon, other than Hirschsprung's disease	104
172.2	Melanoma, ear and external auditory canal, malignant	142
172.1	Melanoma, eyelid, including canthus, malignant	22
172.3	Melanoma, face, other and unspecified parts, malignant	142
172.0	Melanoma, lip, malignant	142
172.7	Melanoma, lower limb, including hip, malignant	142
172.8	Melanoma, other specified sites, malignant	142
172.4	Melanoma, scalp and neck, malignant	142
172.9	Melanoma, skin, site unspecified, malignant	142
172.5	Melanoma, trunk, except scrotum, malignant	142
172.6	Melanoma, upper limb, including shoulder, malignant	142
025	Melioidosis	248
781.6	Meningismus	16
091.81	Meningitis, acute syphilitic, secondary, early	7, 12
*320	Meningitis, bacterial	8, 13, 218, 225
112.83	Meningitis, candidal	8, 13, 217, 224
114.2	Meningitis, coccidioidal	8, 13, 217, 224
321.0	Meningitis, cryptococcal	8
049.1	Meningitis, due to adenovirus	13
*047	Meningitis, due to enterovirus	13
321.3	Meningitis, due to trypanosomiasis	8
321.2	Meningitis, due to viruses, not elsewhere classified	8
322.1	Meningitis, eosinophilic	218, 225
098.82	Meningitis, gonococcal	8, 12
036.0	Meningitis, meningococcal	7, 12
322.0	Meningitis, nonpyogenic	218, 225
321.1	Meningitis, other fungal diseases	8
*321	Meningitis, other organisms	13, 218, 225
094.2	Meningitis, syphilitic	8, 12
322.9	Meningitis, unspecified	218, 225
*322	Meningitis, unspecified cause	13
047.9	Meningitis,viral, unspecified	309
036.2	Meningococcemia	246
130.0	Meningoencephalitis, due to toxoplasmosis	8, 13, 218, 225
121.5	Metagonimiasis	249
289.7	Methemoglobinemia	234
446.6	Microangiopathy, thrombotic	128

Code	Narrative	Page
793.81	Microcalcification, mammographic	143
744.82	Microcheilia	37
744.84	Microstomia	37
*346	Migraine	13
379.42	Miosis, persistent, not due to miotics	22
630	Mole, hydatidiform	206
078.0	Molluscum contagiosum	146
*716.6	Monoarthritis, unspecified	130
*355	Mononeuritis, lower limb	11
*354	Mononeuritis, upper limb and multiplex	11
075	Mononucleosis, infectious	247
*344.3	Monoplegia, lower limb	15
344.5	Monoplegia, unspecified	15
*344.4	Monoplegia, upper limb	15
343.3	Monoplegic	15
*799.8	Morbidity and mortality, causes, other and ill-defined conditions	287
799.9	Morbidity and mortality, causes, other unknown and unspecified	287
277.5	Mucopolysaccharidosis	155
659.63	Multigravida, elderly, antepartum condition or complication	208
659.61	Multigravida, elderly, delivered, with or without mention of antepartum condition	188, 200
659.60	Multigravida, elderly, unspecified as to episode of care	188, 200
659.43	Multiparity, grand, with current pregnancy, antepartum condition or complication	208
659.41	Multiparity, grand, with current pregnancy, delivered, with or without mention of antepartum condition	188, 200
659.40	Multiparity, grand, with current pregnancy, unspecified as to episode of care	213
072.2	Mumps, encephalitis	7, 12, 217, 224
072.71	Mumps, hepatitis	110
072.1	Mumps, meningitis	7, 13, 217, 224
072.0	Mumps, orchitis	171, 217, 224
072.79	Mumps, other specified complications	247
072.3	Mumps, pancreatitis	110, 217, 224
072.72	Mumps, polyneuropathy	11
072.8	Mumps, unspecified complication	217, 224, 247
*072.7	Mumps, with other specified complications	217, 224
072.9	Mumps, without mention of complication	247
785.2	Murmurs, cardiac, functional, undiagnosed	89
729.1	Myalgia and myositis, unspecified	130
*358.0	Myasthenia gravis	10
775.2	Myasthenia gravis, neonatal	216, 223
117.4	Mycetomas, mycotic	218, 225
*202.1	Mycosis fungoides	237
202.11	Mycosis fungoides, lymph nodes, head, face, and neck	319
118	Mycosis, opportunistic	218, 225, 249, 308
*117	Mycosis, other	249
379.43	Mydriasis, persistent, not due to mydriatics	22
*203	Myeloma, multiple, and immunoproliferative neoplasms	237
336.8	Myelopathy, other, drug or radiation induced	15
336.3	Myelopathy, spinal cord, in other diseases classified elsewhere	15
336.1	Myelopathy, vascular	15
*422	Myocarditis, acute	84, 91
422.0	Myocarditis, acute, in diseases classified elsewhere	219, 226
*422.9	Myocarditis, acute, other and unspecified	309
074.23	Myocarditis, Coxsackie	90
130.3	Myocarditis, due to toxoplasmosis	90, 218, 225
036.43	Myocarditis, meningococcal	90
398.0	Myocarditis, rheumatic	90
391.2	Myocarditis, rheumatic, acute	90
422.92	Myocarditis, septic	59, 61, 63, 73, 76, 79, 219, 226
429.0	Myocarditis, unspecified	91
333.2	Myoclonus	15
791.3	Myoglobinuria	286
376.82	Myopathy, extraocular muscles	22
367.1	Myopia	24
*384.0	Myringitis, acute, without mention of otitis media	34
384.1	Myringitis, chronic, without mention of otitis media	34
460	Nasopharyngitis, acute, common cold	34, 319
472.2	Nasopharyngitis, chronic	319
040.3	Necrobacillosis	248
447.5	Necrosis, artery	86
*733.4	Necrosis, aseptic, bone	130
570	Necrosis, liver, acute and subacute	111, 220, 227
195.2	Neoplasm, abdomen, malignant	99
194.0	Neoplasm, adrenal gland, malignant	155
198.7	Neoplasm, adrenal gland, secondary, malignant	155
164.2	Neoplasm, anterior mediastinum, malignant	43

Alphabetic Index to Diseases

* Code Range

Code	Narrative	Page
194.6	Neoplasm, aortic body and other paraganglia, malignant	9
210.5	Neoplasm, benign tonsil	35
227.0	Neoplasm, benign, adrenal gland	155
227.6	Neoplasm, benign, aortic body, other paraganglia	9
213.9	Neoplasm, benign, bone and articular cartilage, site unspecified	133
213.1	Neoplasm, benign, bone, lower jaw	37, 319
213.0	Neoplasm, benign, bones, skull and face	133, 319
*225	Neoplasm, benign, brain, other parts of nervous system	9
217	Neoplasm, benign, breast	147
212.3	Neoplasm, benign, bronchus and lung	43
227.5	Neoplasm, benign, carotid body	9
211.3	Neoplasm, benign, colon	103
211.9	Neoplasm, benign, digestive system, other and unspecified site	104
211.2	Neoplasm, benign, duodenum, jejunum and ileum	103
216.2	Neoplasm, benign, ear and external auditory canal	147
227.9	Neoplasm, benign, endocrine gland, site unspecified	155
227.8	Neoplasm, benign, endocrine glands, related structures, other	155
211.0	Neoplasm, benign, esophagus	103
*224	Neoplasm, benign, eye	22
*221	Neoplasm, benign, female genital organs, other	176, 183
210.3	Neoplasm, benign, floor of mouth	37
212.7	Neoplasm, benign, heart	90
210.8	Neoplasm, benign, hypopharynx	35
211.7	Neoplasm, benign, islets of Langerhans	155
*223	Neoplasm, benign, kidney and other urinary organs	157, 162
212.1	Neoplasm, benign, larynx	35, 319
210.0	Neoplasm, benign, lip	37
*210	Neoplasm, benign, lip, oral cavity and pharynx	319
211.5	Neoplasm, benign, liver and biliary passages	111
213.7	Neoplasm, benign, long bones, lower limb	133
229.0	Neoplasm, benign, lymph nodes	234
210.2	Neoplasm, benign, major salivary glands	35
*222	Neoplasm, benign, male genital organs	172
212.5	Neoplasm, benign, mediastinum	43
212.0	Neoplasm, benign, nasal cavities, middle ear and accessory sinuses	35, 319
210.7	Neoplasm, benign, nasopharynx	35
210.6	Neoplasm, benign, oropharynx, other parts	35
229.8	Neoplasm, benign, other specified sites	236, 244
220	Neoplasm, benign, ovary	176, 183
211.6	Neoplasm, benign, pancreas except islets of Langerhans	110
227.1	Neoplasm, benign, parathyroid gland	155
210.4	Neoplasm, benign, parts of mouth, other and unspecified	37
213.6	Neoplasm, benign, pelvic bones, sacrum and coccyx	133
210.9	Neoplasm, benign, pharynx, unspecified	35
227.4	Neoplasm, benign, pineal gland	9
227.3	Neoplasm, benign, pituitary gland, craniopharyngeal duct	155
212.4	Neoplasm, benign, pleura	43
211.4	Neoplasm, benign, rectum and anal canal	103
212.8	Neoplasm, benign, respiratory and intrathoracic organs, other specified sites	43
212.9	Neoplasm, benign, respiratory and intrathoracic organs, site unspecified	43
211.8	Neoplasm, benign, retroperitoneum and peritoneum	103
213.3	Neoplasm, benign, ribs, sternum, clavicle	43
216.4	Neoplasm, benign, scalp and skin of neck	147
213.4	Neoplasm, benign, scapula and long bones, upper limb	133
213.8	Neoplasm, benign, short bones, lower limb	133
213.5	Neoplasm, benign, short bones, upper limb	133
229.9	Neoplasm, benign, site unspecified	236, 244
216.1	Neoplasm, benign, skin of eyelid, including canthus	22
216.3	Neoplasm, benign, skin of face, other and unspecified parts	147
216.0	Neoplasm, benign, skin of lip	147
216.7	Neoplasm, benign, skin of lower limb	147
216.5	Neoplasm, benign, skin of trunk, except scrotum	147
216.6	Neoplasm, benign, skin of upper limb	147
216.8	Neoplasm, benign, skin, other specified sites	147
216.9	Neoplasm, benign, skin, site unspecified	147
211.1	Neoplasm, benign, stomach,	103
212.6	Neoplasm, benign, thymus	234
226	Neoplasm, benign, thyroid glands	155, 319
210.1	Neoplasm, benign, tongue	37
212.2	Neoplasm, benign, trachea	43
213.2	Neoplasm, benign, vertebral column except sacrum and coccyx	133

Alphabetic Index to Diseases

*** Code Range**

Code	Narrative	Page
*188	Neoplasm, bladder, malignant	157, 162
*182	Neoplasm, body of uterus, malignant	174, 179
*170	Neoplasm, bone and articular cartilage, malignant	127
198.5	Neoplasm, bone and bone marrow, malignant, malignant	127
198.3	Neoplasm, brain and spinal cord, secondary, malignant	9
*191	Neoplasm, brain, malignant	9
198.81	Neoplasm, breast, secondary, malignant	136, 142
194.5	Neoplasm, carotid body, malignant	9
*180	Neoplasm, cervix uteri, malignant	174, 179
153.5	Neoplasm, colon, appendix, malignant	'96
*153	Neoplasm, colon, malignant	99
*171	Neoplasm, connective and other soft tissue, malignant	127
173.8	Neoplasm, contiguous or overlapping specified sites of skin, malignant	146
159.8	Neoplasm, digestive organs and contiguous sites with peritoneum/intraabdominal organs, other sites, malignant	99
159.9	Neoplasm, digestive organs and peritoneum, ill-defined, malignant	99
159.1	Neoplasm, digestive organs and peritoneum/spleen, other and ill-defined sites, malignant	237
194.9	Neoplasm, endocrine gland, site unspecified, malignant	155
*150	Neoplasm, esophagus, malignant	99
*190	Neoplasm, eye, malignant	22
*174	Neoplasm, female breast, malignant	136, 142
*184	Neoplasm, female genital organs,other and unspecified malignant	174, 179
*156	Neoplasm, gallbladder and extrahepatic bile duct, malignant	107, 110
198.82	Neoplasm, genital organs, secondary, malignant	167, 169, 171, 174, 179
*143	Neoplasm, gum, malignant	33, 318
195.0	Neoplasm, head, face and neck, malignant	33, 318
164.1	Neoplasm, heart, malignant	90
*148	Neoplasm, hypopharynx, malignant	33, 318
159.0	Neoplasm, intestinal tract, part unspecified, malignant	99
*189	Neoplasm, kidney and other unspecified urinary organs, malignant	157, 162
198.0	Neoplasm, kidney, secondary, malignant	157, 162
197.5	Neoplasm, large intestine and rectum, malignant, secondary	99
*161	Neoplasm, larynx, malignant	33, 318
*149	Neoplasm, lip and/or oral cavity and/or pharynx, contiguous sites, malignant	33, 318
*140	Neoplasm, lip, malignant	33, 318
*155	Neoplasm, liver and intrahepatic bile duct, malignant	107, 110
197.7	Neoplasm, liver, malignant, secondary	108, 110
195.5	Neoplasm, lower limb, malignant	236, 244
197.0	Neoplasm, lung, malignant, secondary	43
196.0	Neoplasm, lymph nodes, head, face and neck, secondary and unspecified, malignant	318
*196	Neoplasm, lymph nodes, secondary and unspecified, malignant	237
*142	Neoplasm, major salivary glands, malignant	33, 318
*175	Neoplasm, male breast, malignant	136, 142
170.1	Neoplasm, mandible, malignant	318
197.1	Neoplasm, mediastinum, malignant, secondary	43
164.9	Neoplasm, mediastinum, part unspecified, malignant	43
*144	Neoplasm, mouth, floor, malignant	33, 318
*145	Neoplasm, mouth, other and unspecified parts, malignant	33, 318
*160	Neoplasm, nasal cavities, middle ear, accessory sinuses, malignant	33, 318
*147	Neoplasm, nasopharynx, malignant	33, 318
*146	Neoplasm, oropharynx, malignant	33, 318
*192	Neoplasm, other and unspecified parts of nervous system, malignant	9
*215	Neoplasm, other benign, connective and other soft tissue	134
*219	Neoplasm, other benign, uterus	176, 183
197.8	Neoplasm, other digestive organs and spleen, malignant, secondary	99
194.8	Neoplasm, other endocrine glands and related structures, malignant	155
198.4	Neoplasm, other parts of nervous system, secondary, malignant	9
197.3	Neoplasm, other respiratory organs, malignant, secondary	43
195.8	Neoplasm, other specified sites, malignant	236, 244
198.89	Neoplasm, other specified sites, secondary, malignant	236, 244
198.1	Neoplasm, other urinary organs, malignant, secondary, malignant	157, 162
*183	Neoplasm, ovary and other uterine adnexa, malignant	175, 179
198.6	Neoplasm, ovary, secondary, malignant	175, 179
*157	Neoplasm, pancreas, malignant	107, 110
194.1	Neoplasm, parathyroid gland, malignant	155

 ** Code Range*

Code	Narrative	Page
195.3	Neoplasm, pelvis, malignant	167, 169, 171, 174, 179
*187	Neoplasm, penis and other male genital organs, malignant	167, 169, 171
158.9	Neoplasm, peritoneum, unspecified, malignant	99
194.4	Neoplasm, pineal gland, malignant	9
194.3	Neoplasm, pituitary gland and craniopharyngeal duct, malignant	155
181	Neoplasm, placenta, malignant	174, 179
*163	Neoplasm, pleura, malignant	43
197.2	Neoplasm, pleura, malignant, secondary	43
164.3	Neoplasm, posterior mediastinum, malignant	43
185	Neoplasm, prostate, malignant	167, 169, 171
*154	Neoplasm, rectum, rectosigmoid junction and anus, malignant	99
165.8	Neoplasm, respiratory system and intrathoracic organs, contiguous or overlapping site, malignant	43
165.9	Neoplasm, respiratory tract, unspecified, malignant	43
158.8	Neoplasm, retroperitoneum and peritoneum, contiguous or overlapping sites, specified parts, malignant	99
197.6	Neoplasm, retroperitoneum and peritoneum, malignant, secondary	99
158.0	Neoplasm, retroperitoneum, malignant	236, 244
173.4	Neoplasm, scalp and skin of neck, malignant	146
173.2	Neoplasm, skin of ear and external auditory canal, malignant	146
173.1	Neoplasm, skin of eyelid and canthus, malignant	22
173.3	Neoplasm, skin of face, other and unspecified parts, malignant	146
173.0	Neoplasm, skin of lip, malignant	146, 318
173.7	Neoplasm, skin of lower limb including hip, malignant	146
173.9	Neoplasm, skin of site unspecified, malignant	146
173.5	Neoplasm, skin of trunk except scrotum, malignant	146
173.6	Neoplasm, skin of upper limb, including shoulder, malignant	146
198.2	Neoplasm, skin, secondary, malignant	136, 142
197.4	Neoplasm, small intestine including duodenum, malignant, secondary	99
*152	Neoplasm, small intestine, including duodenum, malignant	99
*151	Neoplasm, stomach, malignant	99
*186	Neoplasm, testes, malignant	167, 169, 171
195.1	Neoplasm, thorax, malignant	43
164.8	Neoplasm, thymus, heart and mediastinum of contiguous or overlapping sites, other, malignant	43
164.0	Neoplasm, thymus, malignant	236, 244
193	Neoplasm, thyroid gland, malignant	155, 318
*141	Neoplasm, tongue, malignant	33, 318
*162	Neoplasm, trachea, bronchus and lung, malignant	43
237.2	Neoplasm, uncertain behavior, adrenal gland	155
236.7	Neoplasm, uncertain behavior, bladder	157, 162
238.0	Neoplasm, uncertain behavior, bone and articular cartilage	127
237.5	Neoplasm, uncertain behavior, brain and spinal cord	9
238.3	Neoplasm, uncertain behavior, breast	136, 142
238.1	Neoplasm, uncertain behavior, connective and other soft tissue	134
235.5	Neoplasm, uncertain behavior, digestive organs, other and unspecified	99
237.4	Neoplasm, uncertain behavior, endocrine glands, other and unspecified	155
236.3	Neoplasm, uncertain behavior, female genital organs, other and unspecified	174, 180
238.5	Neoplasm, uncertain behavior, histiocytic and mast cells	237
235.6	Neoplasm, uncertain behavior, larynx	33, 319
235.1	Neoplasm, uncertain behavior, lip, oral cavity, pharynx	33, 319
235.3	Neoplasm, uncertain behavior, liver, biliary passages	108, 110
238.7	Neoplasm, uncertain behavior, lymphatic and hematopoietic tissues	237
235.0	Neoplasm, uncertain behavior, major salivary glands	33, 319
236.6	Neoplasm, uncertain behavior, male genital organs, other and unspecified	167, 169, 171
237.6	Neoplasm, uncertain behavior, meninges	9
237.9	Neoplasm, uncertain behavior, nervous system, other and unspecified parts	9
238.8	Neoplasm, uncertain behavior, other specified sites	236, 244
236.2	Neoplasm, uncertain behavior, ovary	175, 179
237.3	Neoplasm, uncertain behavior, paraganglia	9
237.1	Neoplasm, uncertain behavior, pineal gland	9
237.0	Neoplasm, uncertain behavior, pituitary gland, craniopharyngeal duct	155

Code	Narrative	Page
236.1	Neoplasm, uncertain behavior, placenta	174, 179
238.6	Neoplasm, uncertain behavior, plasma cells	237
235.8	Neoplasm, uncertain behavior, pleura, thymus, mediastinum	43
236.5	Neoplasm, uncertain behavior, prostate	167, 169, 171
235.9	Neoplasm, uncertain behavior, respiratory organs, other and unspecified	43
235.4	Neoplasm, uncertain behavior, retroperitoneum, peritoneum	99
238.9	Neoplasm, uncertain behavior, site unspecified	236, 244
238.2	Neoplasm, uncertain behavior, skin	147
235.2	Neoplasm, uncertain behavior, stomach, intestines, rectum	99
236.4	Neoplasm, uncertain behavior, testis	167, 169, 171
235.7	Neoplasm, uncertain behavior, trachea, bronchus and lung	43
*236.9	Neoplasm, uncertain behavior, urinary organs, other and unspecified	157, 162
236.0	Neoplasm, uncertain behavior, uterus	174, 179
195.4	Neoplasm, upper limb, malignant	236, 244
165.0	Neoplasm, upper respiratory tract, part unspecified, malignant	33, 318
179	Neoplasm, uterus, unspecified, malignant	174, 179
*199	Neoplasm, without specification of site, malignant	236, 244
239.4	Neoplasms, unspecified nature, bladder	157, 162
239.2	Neoplasms, unspecified nature, bone, soft tissue and skin	134
239.6	Neoplasms, unspecified nature, brain	9
239.3	Neoplasms, unspecified nature, breast	143
239.0	Neoplasms, unspecified nature, digestive system	99
239.7	Neoplasms, unspecified nature, endocrine glands and other nervous system parts	155
239.5	Neoplasms, unspecified nature, genitourinary organs	157, 162
239.1	Neoplasms, unspecified nature, respiratory system	43
239.9	Neoplasms, unspecified nature, site unspecified	236, 244
239.8	Neoplasms, unspecified nature, specified sites, other	236, 244
*370.6	Neovascularization, corneal	24
*583	Nephritis and nephropathy, not specified as acute or chronic	165, 310
274.11	Nephrolithiasis, uric acid	163
274.19	Nephropathy, gouty, other	164
274.10	Nephropathy, gouty, unspecified	164
593.0	Nephroptosis	165
078.6	Nephrosonephritis, hemorrhagic	163
799.2	Nervousness	251
729.2	Neuralgia, neuritis and radiculitis, unspecified	12, 310
053.12	Neuralgia, postherpetic, trigeminal	11
300.5	Neurasthenia	251
723.4	Neuritis or radiculitis, brachial, unspecified	12
094.86	Neuritis, acoustic, syphilitic	35
036.81	Neuritis, meningococcal, optic	21, 217, 224
*377.3	Neuritis, optic	22
094.85	Neuritis, retrobulbar, syphilitic	9
237.71	Neurofibromatosis, type 1 [von Recklinghausen's disease]	15
237.72	Neurofibromatosis, type 2 [acoustic neurofibromatosis]	15
237.70	Neurofibromatosis, unspecified	15
356.9	Neuropathy, hereditary and peripheral, unspecified	11
*357.8	Neuropathy, inflammatory, toxic, other	11, 310
357.9	Neuropathy, inflammatory, toxic, unspecified	11, 310
356.0	Neuropathy, peripheral hereditary	11
356.2	Neuropathy, sensory, hereditary	11
356.8	Neuropathy, specified, idiopathic, peripheral, supranuclear paralysis	11
094.3	Neurosyphilis, asymptomatic	12
*090.4	Neurosyphilis, juvenile	12
094.89	Neurosyphilis, other specified	9
094.9	Neurosyphilis, unspecified	10
448.1	Nevus, nonneoplastic	147
V30.1	Newborn, liveborn, before admission to hospital, single	230, 231
V30.01	Newborn, liveborn, in hospital, delivered by cesarean delivery, single	230, 231
V30.00	Newborn, liveborn, in hospital, delivered without mention of cesarean delivery, single	230, 231
V30.2	Newborn, liveborn, outside hospital and not hospitalized, single	232
V34.1	Newborn, other multiple, mates all liveborn, before admission to hospital	230, 231
V34.01	Newborn, other multiple, mates all liveborn, in hospital, delivered by cesarean delivery	230, 231
V34.00	Newborn, other multiple, mates all liveborn, in hospital, delivered without mention of cesarean delivery	230, 231
V34.2	Newborn, other multiple, mates all liveborn, outside hospital and not hospitalized	232

*** Code Range**

Code	Narrative	Page
V35.1	Newborn, other multiple, mates all stillborn, before admission to hospital	230, 231
V35.01	Newborn, other multiple, mates all stillborn, in hospital, delivered by cesarean delivery	230, 231
V35.00	Newborn, other multiple, mates all stillborn, in hospital, delivered without mention of cesarean delivery	230, 231
V35.2	Newborn, other multiple, mates all stillborn, outside hospital and not hospitalized	232
V36.1	Newborn, other multiple, mates live and stillborn, before admission to hospital	230, 232
V36.00	Newborn, other multiple, mates live and stillborn, in hospital, delivered without mention of cesarean delivery	230, 232
V36.2	Newborn, other multiple, mates live and stillborn, outside hospital and not hospitalized	232
V36.01	Newborn, other multiple, mates live- and stillborn, in hospital, delivered by cesarean delivery	230, 232
V37.1	Newborn, other multiple, unspecified, before admission to hospital	230, 232
V37.01	Newborn, other multiple, unspecified, in hospital, delivered by cesarean delivery	230, 232
V37.00	Newborn, other multiple, unspecified, in hospital, delivered without mention of cesarean delivery	230, 232
V37.2	Newborn, other multiple, unspecified, outside hospital and not hospitalized	232
V31.1	Newborn, twin, mate liveborn, before admission to hospital	230, 231
V31.01	Newborn, twin, mate liveborn, in hospital, delivered by cesarean delivery	230, 231
V31.00	Newborn, twin, mate liveborn, in hospital, delivered without mention of cesarean delivery	230, 231
V31.2	Newborn, twin, mate liveborn, outside hospital and not hospitalized	232
V32.1	Newborn, twin, mate stillborn, before admission to hospital	230, 231
V32.01	Newborn, twin, mate stillborn, in hospital, delivered by cesarean delivery	230, 231
V32.00	Newborn, twin, mate stillborn, in hospital, delivered without mention of cesarean delivery	230, 231
V32.2	Newborn, twin, mate stillborn, outside hospital and not hospitalized	232
V33.1	Newborn, twin, unspecified whether mate liveborn or stillborn, before admission to hospital	230, 231
V33.2	Newborn, twin, unspecified whether mate liveborn or stillborn, outside hospital and not hospitalized	232
V33.01	Newborn, twin, unspecified, in hospital, delivered by cesarean delivery	230, 231
V33.00	Newborn, twin, unspecified, in hospital, delivered without mention of cesarean delivery	230, 231
V39.1	Newborn, unspecified whether single, twin, or multiple, before admission to hospital	230, 232
V39.01	Newborn, unspecified whether single, twin, or multiple, in hospital, delivered by cesarean delivery	230, 232
V39.00	Newborn, unspecified whether single, twin, or multiple, in hospital, delivered without mention of cesarean delivery	230, 232
V39.2	Newborn, unspecified whether single, twin, or multiple, outside hospital and not hospitalized	232
379.54	Nystagmus, associated with disorders of the vestibular system	22
379.51	Nystagmus, congenital	25
379.55	Nystagmus, dissociated	22
379.52	Nystagmus, latent	22
379.56	Nystagmus, other forms	25
379.50	Nystagmus, unspecified	22
379.53	Nystagmus, visual deprivation	25
379.57	Nystagmus, with deficiency, saccadic eye movements	22
379.58	Nystagmus, with deficiency, smooth pursuit movements	22
V71.7	Observation suspected cardiovascular disease	90
V71.01	Observation, evaluation, behavior, antisocial, adult, not found	251
V71.02	Observation, evaluation, behavior, antisocial, childhood or adolescent, not found	251
*V29	Observation, evaluation, newborn, infant, suspected condition not found	231, 288
V71.09	Observation, evaluation, suspected mental condition, other, not found	253
V71.3	Observation, following accident at work	275
V71.5	Observation, following alleged rape or seduction	289
V71.4	Observation, following other accident	275
V71.6	Observation, following other inflicted injury	275
*V71.8	Observation, suspected conditions, other specified	289
V71.9	Observation, suspected conditions, unspecified	289
V71.1	Observation, suspected malignant neoplasm	237, 242, 287

* Code Range

Code	Narrative	Page
V71.2	Observation, suspected tuberculosis	43
660.93	Obstructed labor, unspecified, antepartum condition or complication	208
660.91	Obstructed labor, unspecified, delivered, with or without mention of antepartum condition	189, 200
660.90	Obstructed labor, unspecified, unspecified as to episode of care	189, 200
*599.6	Obstruction, urinary	165, 221, 228
496	Obstruction, airway, chronic, not elsewhere classified	44
596.0	Obstruction, bladder neck	221, 228
537.3	Obstruction, duodenum, other	101
*381.6	Obstruction, Eustachian tube	35
777.2	Obstruction, intestinal, due to inspissated milk, newborn	216, 223
560.89	Obstruction, intestinal, other specified	220, 227
560.9	Obstruction, intestinal, unspecified	220, 227
*560	Obstruction, intestinal, without mention of hernia	101
660.03	Obstruction, labor, at onset, caused by malposition of fetus, antepartum condition or complication	208
660.01	Obstruction, labor, at onset, caused by malposition of fetus, delivered, with or without mention of antepartum condition	188, 200
660.00	Obstruction, labor, at onset, caused by malposition of fetus, unspecified as to episode of care	188, 200
777.1	Obstruction, meconium, fetal and newborn	216, 223
593.4	Obstruction, other, ureteric	163
*434	Occlusion, arteries, cerebral	83, 219, 226
411.81	Occlusion, coronary, acute, without myocardial infarction	63, 89
433.31	Occlusion, stenosis, with cerebral infarction, arteries, multiple and bilateral, precerebral	8, 10, 17, 60, 62, 64, 74, 78, 80, 83, 219, 226
433.81	Occlusion, stenosis, with cerebral infarction, arteries, other specified, precerebral	8, 10, 17, 60, 62, 64, 74, 78, 80, 83, 219, 226
433.91	Occlusion, stenosis, with cerebral infarction, arteries, unspecified, precerebral	8, 10, 17, 60, 62, 64, 74, 78, 80, 83, 219, 226
433.01	Occlusion, stenosis, with cerebral infarction, artery, basilar	8, 10, 17, 60, 62, 64, 74, 77, 80, 83, 219, 226
433.11	Occlusion, stenosis, with cerebral infarction, artery, carotid	8, 10, 17, 60, 62, 64, 74, 77, 80, 83, 219, 226
433.21	Occlusion, stenosis, with cerebral infarction, artery, vertebral	8, 10, 17, 60, 62, 64, 74, 77, 80, 83, 219, 226
433.30	Occlusion, stenosis, without mention of cerebral infarction, arteries, multiple and bilateral, precerebral	10
433.80	Occlusion, stenosis, without mention of cerebral infarction, arteries, other specified, precerebral	11
433.90	Occlusion, stenosis, without mention of cerebral infarction, arteries, unspecified, precerebral	11
433.00	Occlusion, stenosis, without mention of cerebral infarction, artery, basilar	10
433.10	Occlusion, stenosis, without mention of cerebral infarction, artery, carotid	10
433.20	Occlusion, stenosis, without mention of cerebral infarction, artery, vertebral	10
434.91	Occlusion, unspecified, with cerebral infarction, arteries, cerebral	8, 10, 17, 60, 62, 65, 74, 78, 80
434.90	Occlusion, unspecified, without mention of cerebral infarction, arteries, cerebral	11, 60, 62, 65, 74, 78, 80
*362.3	Occlusion, vascular, retinal	21
658.03	Oligohydramnios, antepartum condition or complication	208
658.01	Oligohydramnios, delivered, with or without mention of antepartum condition	188, 200
658.00	Oligohydramnios, unspecified as to episode of care	213
788.5	Oliguria and anuria	161, 162
771.4	Omphalitis, newborn	216, 223
*371	Opacity, other disorders, corneal	24
360.14	Ophthalmia, nodosa	23
367.52	Ophthalmoplegia, internal, total or complete	21
378.86	Ophthalmoplegia, internuclear	16
378.72	Ophthalmoplegia, progressive, external	22
121.0	Opisthorchiasis	110
*604	Orchitis and epididymitis	172
073.7	Ornithosis, with other specified complications	247
073.0	Ornithosis, with pneumonia	42
073.9	Ornithosis, with unspecified	247
073.8	Ornithosis, with unspecified complication	247

Alphabetic Index to Diseases

* Code Range

Code	Narrative	Page
723.7	Ossification, ligament, posterior longitudinal in cervical region	129
733.5	Osteitis condensans	130
*731	Osteitis deformans and osteopathies, associated with other disorders, classified elsewhere	130
*715	Osteoarthrosis and allied disorders	129
*732	Osteochondropathies	130
*756.5	Osteodystrophy, congenital	135
268.2	Osteomalacia, unspecified	129
*730.0	Osteomyelitis, acute	127
730.06	Osteomyelitis, acute, lower leg	123
*730.1	Osteomyelitis, chronic	127
730.16	Osteomyelitis, chronic, lower leg	123
376.03	Osteomyelitis, orbital	21
003.24	Osteomyelitis, Salmonella	127
*730.2	Osteomyelitis, unspecified	127
730.26	Osteomyelitis, unspecified, lower leg	124
*730.7	Osteopathy from poliomyelitis	134
*733.0	Osteoporosis	130
*388.7	Otalgia	36
420.99	Other acute pericarditis	59, 61, 63, 73, 76, 79
414.19	Other aneurysm of heart	59, 61, 63, 73, 76, 79
415.19	Other pulmonary embolism and infarction	60, 62, 64, 74, 77, 80
*567.8	Other specified peritonitis	215, 222
*567.2	Other suppurative peritonitis	215, 222
112.82	Otitis externa, candidal	35, 217, 224
*380.1	Otitis externa, infective	35
*380.2	Otitis externa, other	35
*381.0	Otitis media, acute, nonsuppurative	34
*381.2	Otitis media, chronic, mucoid	34
*381.1	Otitis media, chronic, serous	34
381.4	Otitis media, nonsuppurative, not specified as acute or chronic	34
381.3	Otitis media, other and unspecified, chronic, nonsuppurative	34
055.2	Otitis media, postmeasles	34, 217, 224
*382	Otitis media, suppurative and unspecified	34
388.61	Otorrhea, cerebrospinal fluid	16
388.69	Otorrhea, other	36
388.60	Otorrhea, unspecified	36
*387	Otosclerosis	36
*V27	Outcome of delivery	288
*278	Overweight, obesity, other hyperalimentation	154
*789.0	Pain, abdominal	103
786.59	Pain, chest, other	90
786.50	Pain, chest, unspecified	90
*719.4	Pain, joint	130
729.5	Pain, limb	130
*625	Pain, other symptoms, genital organs, female	177, 183
786.51	Pain, precordial	90
307.80	Pain, psychogenic, site unspecified	251
307.89	Pain, related to psychological factors, other	251
784.1	Pain, throat	36
786.52	Painful, respiration	46
*782.6	Pallor, flushing	286
785.1	Palpitations	89
343.8	Palsy, cerebral, infantile, other specified	15
343.9	Palsy, cerebral, infantile, unspecified	15
378.81	Palsy, conjugate gaze	25
251.8	Pancreatic internal secretion disorder, other specified	156
251.9	Pancreatic internal secretion disorder, unspecified	156
577.0	Pancreatitis, acute	220, 227
046.2	Panencephalitis, subacute, sclerosing	217, 224
723.6	Panniculitis, neck	148
*729.3	Panniculitis, unspecified	148
360.02	Panophthalmitis	21
360.12	Panuveitis	23
377.02	Papilledema, associated with decreased ocular pressure	25, 218, 225
377.01	Papilledema, associated with increased intracranial pressure	16, 218, 225
377.03	Papilledema, associated with retinal disorder	25
377.00	Papilledema, unspecified	16, 218, 225
646.03	Papyraceous fetus, antepartum condition or complication	206
646.01	Papyraceous fetus, delivered, with or without mention of antepartum condition	185, 198
646.00	Papyraceous fetus, unspecified as to episode of care	185, 198
116.1	Paracoccidioidomycosis	218, 225
121.2	Paragonimiasis	42
327.43	Paralysis, isolated sleep, recurrent	15
781.4	Paralysis, transient, limb	16
344.9	Paralysis, unspecified	15
*478.3	Paralysis, vocal cords or larynx	36, 219, 226, 319
614.3	Parametritis, acute	182
614.4	Parametritis, chronic	183
344.1	Paraplegia, unspecified	9
273.1	Paraproteinemia, monoclonal	234
696.2	Parapsoriasis	142

*** Code Range**

Alphabetic Index to Diseases

Code	Narrative	Page
129	Parasitism, intestinal, unspecified	102
*327.4	Parasomnia, organic	319
327.44	Parasomnia, organic, in conditions classified elsewhere	35
327.49	Parasomnia, organic, other	35
327.40	Parasomnia, organic, unspecified	35
*252	Parathyroid gland disorder	156
051.9	Paravaccinia, unspecified	246
367.51	Paresis, accommodation	24
094.1	Paresis, general	9
094.82	Parkinsonism, syphilitic	9
599.4	Passage, false, urethral	165
381.7	Patulous, Eustachian tube	36
*132	Pediculosis and phthirus infestation	146
694.5	Pemphigoid	142
694.61	Pemphigoid, benign, mucous membrane with ocular involvement	25
694.60	Pemphigoid, benign, mucous membrane, without mention of ocular involvement	142
694.4	Pemphigus	142
530.4	Perforation, esophagus	102, 220, 227
777.6	Perforation, intestinal, perinatal	216, 223
569.83	Perforation, intestine	104, 220, 227
*384.2	Perforation, tympanic membrane	36
*420	Pericarditis, acute	91
420.0	Pericarditis, acute, in diseases classified elsewhere	59, 61, 63, 73, 76, 79, 84, 219, 226
*420.9	Pericarditis, acute, other, unspecified	84
074.21	Pericarditis, Coxsackie	90
098.83	Pericarditis, gonococcal	90
036.41	Pericarditis, meningococcal	90
391.0	Pericarditis, rheumatic, acute	90
393	Pericarditis, rheumatic, chronic	90
380.01	Perichondritis, acute, pinna	134
380.02	Perichondritis, chronic, pinna	134
380.00	Perichondritis, unspecified, pinna	34
730.37	Periostitis without osteomyelitis, ankle and foot	134
730.33	Periostitis without osteomyelitis, forearm	130
730.34	Periostitis without osteomyelitis, hand	130
730.36	Periostitis without osteomyelitis, lower leg	130
730.39	Periostitis without osteomyelitis, multiple sites	134
730.38	Periostitis without osteomyelitis, other specified sites	134
730.35	Periostitis without osteomyelitis, pelvic region and thich	130
730.31	Periostitis without osteomyelitis, shoulder region	130
730.30	Periostitis without osteomyelitis, site unspecified	130
730.32	Periostitis without osteomyelitis, upper arm	130
376.02	Periostitis, orbital	21
091.61	Periostitis, secondary syphilitic, early	127
*567	Peritonitis and retroperitoneal infections	104, 220, 227
614.5	Peritonitis, acute, pelvic, female	183
614.7	Peritonitis, chronic, pelvic, female	183
098.86	Peritonitis, gonococcal	103
095.2	Peritonitis, syphilitic	103
*383.2	Petrositis	34
*472	Pharyngitis and nasopharyngitis, chronic	34
462	Pharyngitis, acute	34, 319
472.1	Pharyngitis, chronic	319
451.83	Phlebitis and thrombophlebitis, deep veins, upper extremities	87
*451.1	Phlebitis and thrombophlebitis, deep vessels, lower extremities	86, 219, 226
451.2	Phlebitis and thrombophlebitis, deep vessels, unspecified, lower extremities	86, 219, 226
451.81	Phlebitis and thrombophlebitis, iliac vein	86, 219, 226
451.89	Phlebitis and thrombophlebitis, other sites	87
451.82	Phlebitis and thrombophlebitis, superficial veins, upper extremities	87
451.0	Phlebitis and thrombophlebitis, superficial vessels, lower extremities	87
451.9	Phlebitis and thrombophlebitis, unspecified site	87
451.84	Phlebitis and thrombophlebitis, unspecified, upper extremities	87
671.53	Phlebitis and thrombosis, other, complicating pregnancy and puerperium, antepartum condition or complication	209
671.52	Phlebitis and thrombosis, other, complicating pregnancy and puerperium, delivered, with mention of postpartum complication	191, 196
671.51	Phlebitis and thrombosis, other, complicating pregnancy and puerperium, delivered, with or without mention of antepartum condition	191, 196
671.54	Phlebitis and thrombosis, other, complicating pregnancy and puerperium, postpartum condition or complication	205
671.50	Phlebitis and thrombosis, other, complicating pregnancy and puerperium, unspecified as to episode of care	214

* Code Range

Code	Narrative	Page
325	Phlebitis, thrombophlebitis, intracranial sinuses, venous	8, 15
671.33	Phlebothrombosis, deep, antepartum, antepartum condition or complication	209
671.31	Phlebothrombosis, deep, antepartum, delivered, with or without mention of antepartum condition	191, 196
671.30	Phlebothrombosis, deep, antepartum, unspecified as to episode of care	214
671.42	Phlebothrombosis, deep, postpartum, delivered, with mention of postpartum condition	191, 196
671.44	Phlebothrombosis, deep, postpartum, postpartum condition or complication	205
671.40	Phlebothrombosis, deep, postpartum, unspecified as to episode of care	214
307.52	Pica	253
103.1	Pinta, intermediate lesions	146
103.2	Pinta, late lesions	249
103.3	Pinta, mixed lesions	146
103.0	Pinta, primary lesions	146
103.9	Pinta, unspecified	249
*253	Pituitary gland and hypothalamic control disorders	156
696.5	Pityriasis, other and unspecified	147
696.3	Pityriasis, rosea	147
696.4	Pityriasis, rubra pilaris	147
641.13	Placenta previa, hemorrhage, antepartum complication	206
641.11	Placenta previa, hemorrhage, delivered, with or without mention of antepartum condition	185, 195
641.10	Placenta previa, hemorrhage, unspecified as to episode of care	211
641.03	Placenta previa, without hemorrhage, antepartum complication	206
641.01	Placenta previa, without hemorrhage, delivered, with or without mention of antepartum condition	185, 195
641.00	Placenta previa, without hemorrhage, unspecified as to episode of care	211
020.0	Plague, bubonic	247
020.1	Plague, cellulocutaneous	248
020.8	Plague, other specified types	248
020.3	Plague, pneumonic, primary	42
020.4	Plague, pneumonic, secondary	42
020.5	Plague, pneumonic, unspecified	42
020.9	Plague, unspecified	248
511.8	Pleurisy, effusion, other specified forms, except tuberculosis	44, 220, 227
511.1	Pleurisy, with effusion, bacterial, nontuberculous	43, 220, 227
511.0	Pleurisy, without mention of effusion, current tuberculosis	45
074.1	Pleurodynia, epidemic	45
500	Pneumoconiosis, coal worker's	45
503	Pneumoconiosis, due to dust, inorganic, other	45
504	Pneumoconiosis, due to inhalation of dust, other	45
502	Pneumoconiosis, due to silica or silicates, other	45
505	Pneumoconiosis, unspecified	45
136.3	Pneumocystosis	42, 218, 225, 308
482.2	Pneumonia, bacterial, due to Hemophilus influenzae	45
482.0	Pneumonia, bacterial, due to Klebsiella pneumoniae	42
482.1	Pneumonia, bacterial, due to Pseudomonas	42
*482.3	Pneumonia, bacterial, due to Streptococcus	45
*482.8	Pneumonia, bacterial, other specified	42
*482.4	Pneumonia, bacterial, Staphylococcus	42
482.9	Pneumonia, bacterial, unspecified	45
770.0	Pneumonia, congenital	216, 223
*483	Pneumonia, due to other specified organism	45, 83, 219, 226
*484	Pneumonia, in infectious diseases classified elsewhere	42, 83
486	Pneumonia, organism unspecified	45, 83, 219, 226, 309
*482	Pneumonia, other, bacterial	83, 219, 226, 309
481	Pneumonia, pneumococcal	45, 83, 219, 226, 309
055.1	Pneumonia, postmeasles	42, 217, 224
517.1	Pneumonia, rheumatic, conditions classified elsewhere	45
003.22	Pneumonia, Salmonella	42
*480	Pneumonia, viral	45
480.8	Pneumonia, viral, due to other specified virus	309
480.3	Pneumonia, viral, due to SARS-associated coronavirus	309
480.9	Pneumonia, viral, unspecified	309
507.0	Pneumonitis, due to inhalation, food, vomitus	220, 227
507.8	Pneumonitis, due to inhalation, other solids, liquids	220, 227
*507	Pneumonitis, due to inhalation, solids, liquids	42, 83
130.4	Pneumonitis, due to toxoplasmosis	42, 218, 225
052.1	Pneumonitis, varicella, hemorrhagic	42

*** Code Range**

Code	Narrative	Page
516.8	Pneumonopathies, alveolar and parietoalveolar, other specified	310
*516	Pneumopathy, other, alveolar and parietoalveolar	45
*860	Pneumothorax and hemothorax, traumatic	46, 221, 228, 297, 304
512.1	Pneumothorax, iatrogenic	46
512.8	Pneumothorax, other spontaneous	46
512.0	Pneumothorax, spontaneous tension	46
976.9	Poisoning, agent, unspecified, primarily affecting skin and mucous membrane	273
976.8	Poisoning, agents, other, primarily affecting skin and mucous membrane	273
*975	Poisoning, agents, primarily acting on the smooth and skeletal muscles and respiratory system	273
*964	Poisoning, agents, primarily affecting blood constituents	273
*972	Poisoning, agents, primarily affecting the cardiovascular system	273
*973	Poisoning, agents, primarily affecting the gastrointestinal system	273
*963	Poisoning, agents, primarily systemic	273
*969	Poisoning, agents, psychotropic	273
*965	Poisoning, analgesics, antipyretics, and antirheumatics	273
976.6	Poisoning, anti-infectives and drugs, other, and preparations for ear, nose, and throat	273
*961	Poisoning, anti-infectives, other	273
*960	Poisoning, antibiotics	273
976.1	Poisoning, antipruritics	273
*968	Poisoning, central nervous system depressants and anesthetics, other	273
*970	Poisoning, central nervous system stimulants	273
976.7	Poisoning, dental drugs topically applied	273
*977	Poisoning, drugs and medicinal substances, other and unspecified	273
*966	Poisoning, drugs, anticonvulsants and anti-Parkinsonism	273
*971	Poisoning, drugs, primarily affecting the autonomic nervous system	273
976.3	Poisoning, emollients, demulcents, and protectants	273
976.5	Poisoning, eye anti-infectives and other eye drugs	26
005.2	Poisoning, food, due to Clostridium perfringens [C Welchii]	101
005.3	Poisoning, food, due to other Clostridia	101
005.4	Poisoning, food, due to Vibrio parahaemolyticus	101
*005.8	Poisoning, food, other bacteria	101
005.0	Poisoning, food, staphylococcal	101
005.9	Poisoning, food, unspecified	101
*962	Poisoning, hormones and synthetic substitutes	273
976.4	Poisoning, keratolytics, keratoplastics, other hair treatment drugs and preparations	273
976.0	Poisoning, local anti-infectives and anti-inflammatory drugs	273
976.2	Poisoning, local, astringents and detergents	273
*967	Poisoning, sedatives and hypnotics	273
*978	Poisoning, vaccines, bacterial	273
*979	Poisoning, vaccines, other, and biological substances	273
*974	Poisoning, water, mineral, and uric acid metabolism drugs	273
*045.0	Poliomyelitis, acute paralytic, specified as bulbar	7, 12
*045.2	Poliomyelitis, acute, nonparalytic	246
*045.9	Poliomyelitis, acute, unspecified	7, 12
*045.1	Poliomyelitis, acute, with other paralysis	7, 12
446.0	Polyarteritis nodosa	128
*714.3	Polyarthritis, juvenile chronic	128
714.89	Polyarthropathies, inflammatory, other, specified	128
*716.5	Polyarthropathy or polyarthritis, unspecified	130
714.9	Polyarthropathy, inflammatory, unspecified	129
238.4	Polycythemia vera	237
289.6	Polycythemia, familial	235
289.0	Polycythemia, secondary	235
657.03	Polyhydramnios, antepartum condition or complication	208
657.01	Polyhydramnios, delivered, with or without mention of antepartum condition	188, 199
657.00	Polyhydramnios, unspecified as to episode of care	213
725	Polymyalgia rheumatica	128
357.0	Polyneuritis, acute infective	13, 310
357.5	Polyneuropathy, alcoholic	11
357.6	Polyneuropathy, due to drugs	11
357.7	Polyneuropathy, due to other toxic agents	11
356.4	Polyneuropathy, idiopathic, progressive	11
357.1	Polyneuropathy, in collagen vascular disease	11
357.2	Polyneuropathy, in diabetes	11
357.3	Polyneuropathy, in malignant disease	11

* Code Range

Code	Narrative	Page
357.4	Polyneuropathy, in other diseases classified elsewhere	11
053.13	Polyneuropathy, postherpetic	11
569.0	Polyp, anal and rectal	104
674.42	Polyp, placental, delivered with mention of postpartum complication	192, 203
674.44	Polyp, placental, postpartum condition or complication	205
674.40	Polyp, placental, unspecified as to episode of care	214
478.4	Polyp, vocal cord or larynx	36, 319
*471	Polyps, nasal	36
642.70	Pre-eclampsia or eclampsia, with pre-existing hypertension, complicating pregnancy, childbirth, and the puerperium, unspecified as to episode of care	210, 211
642.71	Pre-eclampsia or eclampsia, with pre-existing hypertension, complicating pregnancy, childbirth, and the puerperium, delivered, with or without mention of antepartum condition	185, 195
642.72	Pre-eclampsia or eclampsia, with pre-existing hypertension, complicating pregnancy, childbirth, and the puerperium, delivered, with mention of postpartum complication	185, 195
642.73	Pre-eclampsia or eclampsia, with pre-existing hypertension, complicating pregnancy, childbirth, and the puerperium, antepartum condition or complication	206, 210
642.74	Pre-eclampsia or eclampsia, with pre-existing hypertension, complicating pregnancy, childbirth, and the puerperium, postpartum complication	203
642.43	Pre-eclampsia, mild or unspecified, complicating pregnancy, childbirth, and the puerperium, antepartum condition or complication	206, 210
642.41	Pre-eclampsia, mild or unspecified, complicating pregnancy, childbirth, and the puerperium, delivered, with or without mention of antepartum condition	185, 195
642.42	Pre-eclampsia, mild or unspecified, complicating pregnancy, childbirth, and the puerperium, delivered, with mention of postpartum complication	185, 195
642.44	Pre-eclampsia, mild or unspecified, complicating pregnancy, childbirth, and the puerperium, postpartum complication	203
642.40	Pre-eclampsia, mild or unspecified, complicating pregnancy, childbirth, and the puerperium, unspecified as to episode of care	211
642.53	Pre-eclampsia, severe, complicating pregnancy, childbirth, and the puerperium, antepartum condition or complication	206, 210
642.52	Pre-eclampsia, severe, complicating pregnancy, childbirth, and the puerperium, delivered, with mention of postpartum complication	185, 195
642.51	Pre-eclampsia, severe, complicating pregnancy, childbirth, and the puerperium, delivered, with or without mention of antepartum condition	185, 195
642.54	Pre-eclampsia, severe, complicating pregnancy, childbirth, and the puerperium, postpartum complication	203
642.50	Pre-eclampsia, severe, complicating pregnancy, childbirth, and the puerperium, unspecified as to episode of care	210, 211
661.33	Precipitate labor, antepartum condition or complication	208
661.31	Precipitate labor, delivered, with or without mention of antepartum condition	189, 201
661.30	Precipitate labor, unspecified as to episode of care	189, 200
646.33	Pregnancy complicated, habitual aborter, antepartum condition or complication	206
646.31	Pregnancy complicated, habitual aborter, delivered, with or without mention of antepartum condition	185, 198
646.30	Pregnancy complicated, habitual aborter, unspecified as to episode of care	211
646.53	Pregnancy, complicated by bacteriuria, asymptomatic, antepartum condition or complication	206
646.52	Pregnancy, complicated by bacteriuria, asymptomatic, delivered, with mention of postpartum complication	185, 198
646.51	Pregnancy, complicated by bacteriuria, asymptomatic, delivered, with or without mention of antepartum condition	185, 198
646.54	Pregnancy, complicated by bacteriuria, asymptomatic, postpartum condition or complication	203
646.50	Pregnancy, complicated by bacteriuria, asymptomatic, unspecified as to episode of care	211
646.70	Pregnancy, complicated by disorder, liver, unspecified as to episode of care	210, 211

Code	Narrative	Page
646.73	Pregnancy, complicated by disorders, liver, antepartum condition or complication	206, 210
646.71	Pregnancy, complicated by disorders, liver, delivered, with or without mention of antepartum condition	186, 198
646.60	Pregnancy, complicated by infection, genitourinary tract, unspecified as to episode of care	210, 211
646.63	Pregnancy, complicated by infections, genitourinary tract, antepartum complication	206, 210
646.61	Pregnancy, complicated by infections, genitourinary tract, delivered, with or without mention of antepartum condition	186, 198
646.62	Pregnancy, complicated by infections, genitourinary tract, delivered, with or without mention of postpartum complication	186, 198
646.64	Pregnancy, complicated by infections, genitourinary tract, postpartum condition or complication	203
646.43	Pregnancy, complicated by peripheral neuritis, antepartum condition or complication	206, 210
646.42	Pregnancy, complicated by peripheral neuritis, delivered, with mention of postpartum complication	185, 198
646.41	Pregnancy, complicated by peripheral neuritis, delivered, with or without mention of antepartum condition	185, 198
646.44	Pregnancy, complicated by peripheral neuritis, postpartum condition or complication	203
646.40	Pregnancy, complicated by peripheral neuritis, unspecified as to episode of care	211
646.23	Pregnancy, complicated by renal disease, unspecified, without hypertension, antepartum condition or complication	206, 210
646.22	Pregnancy, complicated by renal disease, unspecified, without hypertension, delivered, with mention of postpartum complication	185, 198
646.21	Pregnancy, complicated by renal disease, unspecified, without hypertension, delivered, with or without mention of antepartum condition	185, 198
646.24	Pregnancy, complicated by renal disease, unspecified, without hypertension, postpartum condition or complication	203
646.20	Pregnancy, complicated by renal disease, unspecified, without hypertension, unspecified as to episode of care	210, 211
646.83	Pregnancy, complication, other specified, antepartum complication	206, 210
646.82	Pregnancy, complication, other specified, delivered, with mention of postpartum condition	186, 198
646.81	Pregnancy, complication, other specified, delivered, with or without mention of antepartum condition	186, 198
646.84	Pregnancy, complication, other specified, postpartum condition or complication	203
646.80	Pregnancy, complication, other specified, unspecified as to episode of care	210, 211
646.93	Pregnancy, complication, unspecified, delivered, with mention of postpartum condition	207
646.91	Pregnancy, complication, unspecified, delivered, with or without mention of antepartum condition	186, 198
646.90	Pregnancy, complication, unspecified, unspecified as to episode of care	211
*633	Pregnancy, ectopic	205
651.63	Pregnancy, multiple, other, fetal loss and retention of one or more fetus(es), antepartum condition or complication	207
651.61	Pregnancy, multiple, other, fetal loss and retention of one or more fetus(es), delivered, with or without mention of antepartum condition	186, 198
651.60	Pregnancy, multiple, other, fetal loss and retention of one or more fetus(es), unspecified as to episode of care	212
*V22	Pregnancy, normal	287
645.13	Pregnancy, post-term, antepartum condition or complication	206
645.11	Pregnancy, post-term, delivered, with or without mention of antepartum condition	185, 197
645.10	Pregnancy, post-term, unspecified as to episode of care	211
645.23	Pregnancy, prolonged, antepartum condition or complication	206
645.21	Pregnancy, prolonged, delivered, with or without mention of antepartum condition	185, 198
645.20	Pregnancy, prolonged, unspecified as to episode of care	211
651.23	Pregnancy, quadruplet, antepartum condition or complication	207
651.21	Pregnancy, quadruplet, delivered, with or without mention of antepartum condition	186, 198
651.53	Pregnancy, quadruplet, fetal loss and retention of one or more fetus(es), antepartum condition or complication	207
651.51	Pregnancy, quadruplet, fetal loss and retention of one or more fetus(es), delivered, with or without mention of antepartum condition	186, 198

* Code Range

Code	Narrative	Page
651.50	Pregnancy, quadruplet, fetal loss and retention of one or more fetus(es), unspecified as to episode of care	212
651.20	Pregnancy, quadruplet, unspecified as to episode of care	212
651.13	Pregnancy, triplet, antepartum condition or complication	207
651.11	Pregnancy, triplet, delivered, with or without mention of antepartum condition	186, 198
651.43	Pregnancy, triplet, fetal loss and retention of one or more fetus(es), antepartum condition or complication	207
651.41	Pregnancy, triplet, fetal loss and retention of one or more fetus(es), delivered, with or without mention of antepartum condition	186, 198
651.40	Pregnancy, triplet, fetal loss and retention of one or more fetus(es), unspecified as to episode of care	212
651.10	Pregnancy, triplet, unspecified as to episode of care	212
651.03	Pregnancy, twin, antepartum condition or complication	207
651.01	Pregnancy, twin, delivered, with or without mention of antepartum condition	186, 198
651.33	Pregnancy, twin, fetal loss and retention of one fetus, antepartum condition or complication	207
651.31	Pregnancy, twin, fetal loss and retention of one fetus, delivered, with or without mention of antepartum condition	186, 198
651.30	Pregnancy, twin, fetal loss and retention of one fetus, unspecified as to episode of care	212
651.00	Pregnancy, twin, unspecified as to episode of care	212
*427.6	Premature beats	89
367.4	Presbyopia	24
652.23	Presentation, breech without mention of version, antepartum condition or complication	207
652.21	Presentation, breech without mention of version, delivered, with or without mention of antepartum condition	187, 198
652.20	Presentation, breech without mention of version, unspecified as to episode of care	212
652.43	Presentation, face or brow, fetal, antepartum condition or complication	207
652.41	Presentation, face or brow, fetal, delivered, with or without mention of antepartum condition	187, 198
652.40	Presentation, face or brow, fetal, unspecified as to episode of care	212
652.33	Presentation, transverse or oblique, fetus, antepartum condition or complication	207
652.31	Presentation, transverse or oblique, fetus, delivered, with or without mention of antepartum condition	187, 198
652.30	Presentation, transverse or oblique, fetus, unspecified as to episode of care	212
*765.1	Preterm, other, infants	215, 222
607.3	Priapism	172
659.53	Primigravida, elderly, antepartum condition or complication	208
659.51	Primigravida, elderly, delivered, with or without mention of antepartum condition	188, 200
659.50	Primigravida, elderly, unspecified as to episode of care	188, 200
779.3	Problems, feeding, newborn	230
*V40	Problems, mental and behavioral	288
656.83	Problems, other specified, fetal and placental, affecting management of mother, antepartum condition or complication	208
656.81	Problems, other specified, fetal and placental, affecting management of mother, delivered, with or without mention of antepartum condition	188, 199
656.80	Problems, other specified, fetal and placental, affecting management of mother, unspecified as to episode of care	213
658.83	Problems, other, with amniotic cavity and membranes, antepartum condition or complication	208
658.81	Problems, other, with amniotic cavity and membranes, delivered, with or without mention of antepartum condition	188, 200
658.80	Problems, other, with amniotic cavity and membranes, unspecified as to episode of care	213
*V47	Problems, other, with internal organs	288
313.3	Problems, relationship, childhood, adolescence	253
*V41	Problems, special senses and other special functions	288
656.93	Problems, unspecified, fetal and placental, affecting management of mother, antepartum condition or complication	208
656.91	Problems, unspecified, fetal and placental, affecting management of mother, delivered, with or without mention of antepartum condition	188, 199
656.90	Problems, unspecified, fetal and placental, affecting management of mother, unspecified as to episode of care	213

Code	Narrative	Page
658.93	Problems, unspecified, with amniotic cavity and membranes, antepartum condition or complication	208
658.91	Problems, unspecified, with amniotic cavity and membranes, delivered, with or without mention of antepartum condition	188, 200
658.90	Problems, unspecified, with amniotic cavity and membranes, unspecified as to episode of care	213
*V48	Problems, with head, neck and trunk	288
663.03	Prolapse, cord, complicating labor and delivery, antepartum condition or complication	209
663.01	Prolapse, cord, complicating labor and delivery, delivered, with or without mention of antepartum condition	189, 201
663.00	Prolapse, cord, complicating labor and delivery, unspecified as to episode of care	189, 201
*618	Prolapse, genital	177, 183
599.5	Prolapse, mucosa, urethral	165
569.1	Prolapse, rectal	104
652.73	Prolapsed arm, fetus, antepartum condition or complication	207
652.71	Prolapsed arm, fetus, delivered, with or without mention of antepartum condition	187, 198
652.70	Prolapsed arm, fetus, unspecified as to episode of care	212
662.03	Prolonged first stage, labor, antepartum condition or complication	209
662.01	Prolonged first stage, labor, delivered, with or without mention of antepartum condition	189, 201
662.00	Prolonged first stage, labor, unspecified as to episode of care	189, 201
662.13	Prolonged labor, unspecified, antepartum condition or complication	209
662.11	Prolonged labor, unspecified, delivered, with or without mention of antepartum condition	189, 201
662.10	Prolonged labor, unspecified, unspecified as to episode of care	189, 201
662.23	Prolonged second stage, labor, antepartum condition or complication	209
662.21	Prolonged second stage, labor, delivered, with or without mention of antepartum condition	189, 201
662.20	Prolonged second stage, labor, unspecified as to episode of care	189, 201
098.12	Prostatitis, gonococcal, acute	171
098.32	Prostatitis, gonococcal, chronic	171
791.0	Proteinuria	164
593.6	Proteinuria, postural	165

Code	Narrative	Page
718.65	Protrusion, unspecified, intrapelvic, acetabulumm, pelvic region and thigh	134
718.60	Protrusion, unspecified, intrapelvic, acetabulumm, site unspecified	134
698.2	Prurigo	147
698.8	Pruritis, other specified	147
698.0	Pruritus ani	147
698.1	Pruritus, genital organs	172, 177, 183
051.1	Pseudocowpox	146
377.24	Pseudopapilledema	22
696.0	Psoriasis, arthropathic	128
696.1	Psoriasis, other	142
696.8	Psoriasis, other and similar disorders	147
136.4	Psorospermiasis	249
316	Psychic factors, associated with diseases classified elsewhere	252
298.0	Psychosis, depressive type, nonorganic	253
298.1	Psychosis, excitative type, nonorganic	253
298.9	Psychosis, nonorganic, unspecified	253, 309
298.3	Psychosis, paranoid reaction, acute	253
298.4	Psychosis, paranoid, psychogenic	253
298.2	Psychosis, reactive, confusion	253
298.8	Psychosis, reactive, other and unspecified	253
374.33	Ptosis, mechanical	24
374.32	Ptosis, myogenic	21
374.31	Ptosis, paralytic	21
374.30	Ptosis, unspecified, eyelid	21
*287	Purpura, other hemorrhagic conditions	234
*590.1	Pyelonephritis, acute	221, 228
*590.8	Pyelonephritis, pyelonephrosis, other, not specified as acute or chronic	221, 228
590.3	Pyeloureteritis cystica	221, 228
572.1	Pyemia, portal	220, 227
537.81	Pylorospasm	102
040.81	Pyomyositis, tropical	131
659.23	Pyrexia, maternal, during labor, antepartum condition or complication	208
659.21	Pyrexia, maternal, during labor, unspecified, delivered, with or without mention of antepartum condition	188, 196
659.20	Pyrexia, maternal, during labor, unspecified, unspecified as to episode of care	188, 200

** Code Range*

Code	Narrative	Page
672.02	Pyrexia, unknown origin, during puerperium, delivered, with mention of postpartum complication	192, 196
672.04	Pyrexia, unknown origin, during puerperium, postpartum condition of complication	205
672.00	Pyrexia, unknown origin, during puerperium, unspecified as to episode of care	214
*344.0	Quadriplegia and quadriparesis	9
343.2	Quadriplegia, congenital	9
071	Rabies	7, 12
691.0	Rash, diaper or napkin	230
782.1	Rash, other nonspecific skin eruption	148, 310
*026	Rat-bite fever	248
779.4	Reaction and intoxication, drugs, specific to newborn	217, 224
*308	Reaction to stress, acute	251
*309.8	Reaction, adjustment, other specified	252
309.9	Reaction, adjustment, unspecified	252
*309.2	Reaction, adjustment, with predominant disturbance of other emotions	251
995.7	Reaction, adverse, food, not elsewhere classified	275
309.1	Reaction, depressive, prolonged	251
795.5	Reaction, nonspecific, tuberculin skin test, without active tuberculosis	43
349.0	Reaction, spinal or lumbar puncture	13, 218, 225
379.46	Reaction, tonic pupillary	22
605	Redundant, prepuce and phimosis	172, 230
530.81	Reflux, esophageal	102
*593.7	Reflux, vesicoureteral	165
667.04	Retained placenta without hemorrhage, postpartum condition or complication	204
667.00	Retained placenta without hemorrhage, unspecified as to episode of care	213
667.02	Retained placenta without hemorrhage, with delivery, with mention of postpartum complication	190, 196
667.12	Retained portions, placenta or membranes, without hemorrhage, delivered, with mention of postpartum complication	190, 196
667.14	Retained portions, placenta or membranes, without hemorrhage, postpartum condition or complication	204
667.10	Retained portions, placenta or membranes, without hemorrhage, unspecified as to episode of care	213
764.98	Retardation, growth, unspecified, fetal, 2,000-2,499 grams	229, 231

Code	Narrative	Page
764.99	Retardation, growth, unspecified, fetal, 2,500 or more grams	229, 231
317	Retardation, mental, mild	252
*318	Retardation, mental, specified	252
319	Retardation, mental, unspecified	252
*788.2	Retention, urine	164, 221, 228
202.41	Reticuloendotheliosis, leukemic, lymph nodes, head, face, and neck	319
*202.4	Reticuloendotheliosis. leukemic	237
*200.0	Reticulosarcoma	308
200.01	Reticulosarcoma, lymph nodes, head, face, and neck	318
094.83	Retinochoroiditis, syphilitic, disseminated	22
*362.0	Retinopathy, diabetic, classified elsewhere	23
*362.1	Retinopathy, other background, retinal vascular changes	23, 310
*362.2	Retinopathy, other proliferative	23
*361.1	Retinoschisis, retinal cysts	23
676.03	Retracted nipple, associated with childbirth, antepartum condition or complication	209
676.02	Retracted nipple, associated with childbirth, delivered, with mention of postpartum complication	192, 203
676.01	Retracted nipple, associated with childbirth, delivered, with or without mention of antepartum condition	192, 203
676.04	Retracted nipple, associated with childbirth, postpartum condition or complication	205
676.00	Retracted nipple, associated with childbirth, unspecified as to episode of care	214
374.41	Retraction, lag, eyelid	24
654.33	Retroverted, incarcerated, gravid uterus, antepartum condition or complication	207
654.32	Retroverted, incarcerated, gravid uterus, delivered, with mention of postpartum complication	187, 199
654.31	Retroverted, incarcerated, gravid uterus, delivered, with or without mention of antepartum condition	187, 199
654.34	Retroverted, incarcerated, gravid uterus, postpartum condition or complication	204
654.30	Retroverted, incarcerated, gravid uterus, unspecified as to episode of care	213
*719.3	Rheumatism, palindromic	130
729.0	Rheumatism, unspecified, and fibrositis	130
714.81	Rheumatoid lung	45
*477	Rhinitis, allergic	34
349.81	Rhinorrhea, cerebral spinal fluid	15, 218, 225
040.1	Rhinoscleroma	248

Alphabetic Index to Diseases

Code	Narrative	Page
268.0	Rickets, active	129
268.1	Rickets, late effect	129
*083	Rickettsiosis, other	248
*082	Rickettsiosis, tick-borne	248
*789.4	Rigidity, abdominal	105
695.3	Rosacea	147
771.0	Rubella, congenital	216, 223
647.53	Rubella, maternal, classifiable elsewhere, complicating pregnancy, childbirth, or the puerperium, antepartum condition or complication	207, 210
647.51	Rubella, maternal, classifiable elsewhere, complicating pregnancy, childbirth, or the puerperium, delivered, with or without mention of antepartum condition	186, 195
647.52	Rubella, maternal, classifiable elsewhere, complicating pregnancy, childbirth, or the puerperium, delivered, with mention of postpartum complication	186, 195
647.54	Rubella, maternal, classifiable elsewhere, complicating pregnancy, childbirth, or the puerperium, postpartum condition or complication	204
647.50	Rubella, maternal, classifiable elsewhere, complicating pregnancy, childbirth, or the puerperium, unspecified as to episode of care	212
*056.0	Rubella, with neurological complications	217, 224
056.09	Rubella, with other neurological complications	12
*056.7	Rubella, with other specified complications	217, 224
056.79	Rubella, with other specified complications	247
056.8	Rubella, with unspecified complications	217, 224, 247
056.00	Rubella, with unspecified neurological complication	11
056.9	Rubella, without mention of complication	247
307.53	Rumination disorder	251
447.2	Rupture, artery	86
658.33	Rupture, artificial, membranes in pregnancy, delivery delayed, antepartum condition or complication	208
658.31	Rupture, artificial, membranes in pregnancy, delivery delayed, delivered, with or without mention of antepartum condition	188, 200
658.30	Rupture, artificial, membranes in pregnancy, delivery delayed, unspecified as to episode of care	188, 200
429.5	Rupture, chordae tendinae	59, 62, 64, 73, 77, 79, 82, 84, 88
596.6	Rupture, nontraumatic, bladder	221, 228
*727.6	Rupture, nontraumatic, tendon	131
429.6	Rupture, papillary muscle	59, 62, 64, 73, 77, 79, 82, 84, 88
658.13	Rupture, premature, membranes in pregnancy, antepartum condition or complication	208
658.11	Rupture, premature, membranes in pregnancy, delivered, with or without mention of antepartum condition	188, 200
658.10	Rupture, premature, membranes in pregnancy, unspecified as to episode of care	188, 200
658.23	Rupture, spontaneous or unspecified, membranes in pregnancy, delivery delayed, antepartum condition or complication	208
658.21	Rupture, spontaneous or unspecified, membranes in pregnancy, delivery delayed, delivered, with or without mention of antepartum condition	188, 200
658.20	Rupture, spontaneous or unspecified, membranes in pregnancy, delivery delayed, unspecified as to episode of care	188, 200
*727.5	Rupture, synovium	131
665.03	Rupture, uterus, before onset of labor, antepartum condition or complication	209
665.01	Rupture, uterus, before onset of labor, delivered, with or without mention of antepartum condition	190, 201
665.00	Rupture, uterus, before onset of labor, unspecified as to episode of care	190, 201
665.11	Rupture, uterus, during and after labor, delivered, with or without mention of antepartum condition	190, 201
665.10	Rupture, uterus, during and after labor, unspecified as to episode of care	190, 201
720.2	Sacroiliitis, not elsewhere classified	129
003.21	Salmonella meningitis	7, 12
*381.5	Salpingitis, Eustachian	34
098.17	Salpingitis, gonococcal, acute	176, 182
098.37	Salpingitis, gonococcal, chronic	176, 182
614.0	Salpingo-oophoritis, acute	182
614.1	Salpingo-oophoritis, chronic	182
614.2	Salpingo-oophoritis, unspecified	182
135	Sarcoidosis	45
*176	Sarcoma, Kaposi's	308
176.3	Sarcoma, Kaposi's, gastrointestinal sites	99
176.4	Sarcoma, Kaposi's, lung	43

Alphabetic Index to Diseases

* Code Range

Code	Narrative	Page
176.5	Sarcoma, Kaposi's, lymph node	237
176.8	Sarcoma, Kaposi's, other specified site	147
176.2	Sarcoma, Kaposi's, palate	33, 318
176.0	Sarcoma, Kaposi's, skin	146
176.1	Sarcoma, Kaposi's, soft tissue	147
176.9	Sarcoma, Kaposi's, unspecified site	147
136.5	Sarcosporidiosis	249
034.1	Scarlet fever	248
120.0	Schistosoma, haematobium	163
120.2	Schistosoma, japonicum	249
120.1	Schistosoma, mansoni	110
120.3	Schistosomiasis [bilharziasis] cutaneous	146
120.8	Schistosomiasis, other	249
120.9	Schistosomiasis, unspecified	249
*379.0	Scleritis, episcleritis	25
340	Sclerosis, multiple	10
517.2	Sclerosis, systemic, lung involvement, conditions classified elsewhere	45
587	Sclerosis, unspecified, renal	165
368.42	Scotoma, blind spot area	24
368.41	Scotoma, involving central area	21
V28.1	Screening amniotic fluid, chromosomal anomalies, raised alpha-fetoprotein levels, antenatal	210
V28.0	Screening, amniocentesis, chromosomal anomalies, antenatal	210
V28.5	Screening, isoimmunization, antenatal	288
V28.8	Screening, other specified, antenatal	288
V28.2	Screening, other, based on amniocentesis, antenatal	210
*V82	Screening, special, conditions, other	289
*V81	Screening, special, diseases, cardiovascular, respiratory, and genitourinary	289
*V80	Screening, special, diseases, neurological, eye and ear	289
*V78	Screening, special, disorders, blood, blood-forming organs	289
*V77	Screening, special, disorders, endocrine, nutritional, metabolic and immunity	289
*V76	Screening, special, malignant neoplasms	289
*V79	Screening, special, mental disorders and developmental handicaps	289
V77.3	Screening, special, phenylketonuria (PKU)	232
V28.6	Screening, Streptococcus B, antenatal	288
V28.4	Screening, ultrasonics, fetal growth retardation, antenatal	288
V28.3	Screening, ultrasonics, malformation, antenatal	288
V28.9	Screening, unspecified, antenatal	288
797	Senility, without mention of psychosis	252
641.23	Separation, premature, placenta, antepartum complication	206
641.21	Separation, premature, placenta, delivered, with or without mention of antepartum condition	185, 195
641.20	Separation, premature, placenta, unspecified as to episode of care	211
*362.4	Separation, retinal layers	23
*038	Septicemia	217, 224, 246, 308
020.2	Septicemia, plague	246
003.1	Septicemia, Salmonella	246, 308
429.79	Sequelae, other, of myocardial infarction, not elsewhere classified	59, 62, 64, 73, 77, 79, 84, 91
*202.2	Sezary's disease	237
202.21	Sezary's disease, lymph nodes, head, face, and neck	319
*004	Shigellosis	101
669.13	Shock during or following labor and delivery, antepartum condition or complication	209
669.12	Shock during or following labor and delivery, delivered, with mention of postpartum complication	191, 196
669.11	Shock during or following labor and delivery, delivered, with or without mention of antepartum condition	191, 196
669.14	Shock during or following labor and delivery, postpartum condition or complication	205
669.10	Shock during or following labor and delivery, unspecified as to episode of care	191, 202
*995.6	Shock, anaphylactic, due to foods	273
785.51	Shock, cardiogenic	57, 59, 62, 64, 73, 77, 80, 83, 84, 85
785.52	Shock, septic	246
785.50	Shock, unspecified, without mention of trauma	57, 59, 62, 64, 73, 77, 80, 83, 84, 85, 221, 228
785.59	Shock, without mention of trauma, other	246
663.43	Short cord complicating labor and delivery, antepartum condition or complication	209
663.41	Short cord complicating labor and delivery, delivered, with or without mention of antepartum condition	189, 201

* Code Range

Code	Narrative	Page
663.40	Short cord complicating labor and delivery, unspecified as to episode of care	189, 201
*461	Sinusitis, acute	34
*473	Sinusitis, chronic	34
780.59	Sleep disturbance, other	253
*589	Small kidney, unknown cause	165
*050	Smallpox	246
034.0	Sore throat, streptococcal	34, 318
367.53	Spasm, accommodation	24
564.6	Spasm, anal	103
378.82	Spasm, conjugate gaze	25
478.75	Spasm, laryngeal	36, 219, 226
728.85	Spasm, muscle	130
608.1	Spermatocele	172
*741	Spina bifida	16, 221, 228
756.17	Spina bifida, occulta	16
789.2	Splenomegaly	235, 310
720.0	Spondylitis, ankylosing	128
098.53	Spondylitis, gonococcal	127
738.4	Spondylolisthesis, acquired	129
720.9	Spondylopathies, unspecified, inflammatory	129
*720.8	Spondylopathy, other, inflammatory	129
*721	Spondylosis and allied disorders	129
840.0	Sprains and strains, acromioclavicular (joint) (ligament)	296
*845.0	Sprains and strains, ankle	133
*845	Sprains and strains, ankle and foot	296
*847	Sprains and strains, back, other and unspecified parts	129, 296
840.1	Sprains and strains, coracoclavicular (ligament)	296
840.2	Sprains and strains, coracohumeral (ligament)	296
*841	Sprains and strains, elbow and forearm	132, 296
*845.1	Sprains and strains, foot	132
*843	Sprains and strains, hip and thigh	127, 296
840.3	Sprains and strains, infraspinatus (muscle) (tendon)	296
848.1	Sprains and strains, jaw	38
*844	Sprains and strains, knee and leg	133, 296
848.0	Sprains and strains, nose, septal cartilage	135
*848	Sprains and strains, other and ill-defined	296
848.8	Sprains and strains, other specified sites	132
848.5	Sprains and strains, pelvis	127
848.3	Sprains and strains, ribs	47
840.4	Sprains and strains, rotator cuff (capsule)	296
*846	Sprains and strains, sacroiliac region	129, 296
*840	Sprains and strains, shoulder and upper arm	133
840.8	Sprains and strains, shoulder and upper arm, other specified sites	296
840.9	Sprains and strains, shoulder and upper arm, unspecified site	296
*848.4	Sprains and strains, sternum	47
840.5	Sprains and strains, subscapularis (muscle)	296
840.7	Sprains and strains, superior glenoid labrum lesions (SLAP)	296
840.6	Sprains and strains, supraspinatus (muscle) (tendon)	296
848.2	Sprains and strains, thyroid region	135
848.9	Sprains and strains, unspecified sites	132
*842	Sprains and strains, wrist and hand	132, 296
726.73	Spur, calcaneal	134
780.03	State, vegetative, persistent	13, 221, 228
V45.69	States, other, following surgery, eye and adnexa	288
*V45.0	States, postprocedural, device, cardiac in situ	288
V45.4	Status, arthrodesis	288
*V44	Status, artificial opening	288
V45.3	Status, bypass or anastomosis, intestinal	288
*V83.8	Status, carrier, genetic	289
V83.02	Status, carrier, genetic, hemophilia A symptomatic	289
V83.01	Status, carrier, genetic, hemophilia A, asymptomatic	289
V45.61	Status, cataract extraction	288
V08	Status, infection, asymptomatic, human immunodeficiency virus [HIV]	247
*V09	Status, infection, microorganisms, drug resistant	249
V43.5	Status, organ or tissue replaced by other means, bladder	165
V43.4	Status, organ or tissue replaced by other means, blood vessel	91
V43.0	Status, organ or tissue replaced by other means, eye globe	26
*V43.2	Status, organ or tissue replaced by other means, heart	91
V43.3	Status, organ or tissue replaced by other means, heart valve	91
*V43.6	Status, organ or tissue replaced by other means, joint	135
V43.1	Status, organ or tissue replaced by other means, lens	26
V43.7	Status, organ or tissue replaced by other means, limb	135
*V43.8	Status, organ or tissue replaced by other means, other	288

** Code Range*

Code	Narrative	Page
V43.89	Status, organ or tissue replaced by other means, other means	322
V42.4	Status, organ or tissue replaced by transplant, bone	135
V42.81	Status, organ or tissue replaced by transplant, bone marrow	235
V42.5	Status, organ or tissue replaced by transplant, cornea	26
V42.1	Status, organ or tissue replaced by transplant, heart	91
V42.2	Status, organ or tissue replaced by transplant, heart valve	91
V42.84	Status, organ or tissue replaced by transplant, intestines	288
V42.0	Status, organ or tissue replaced by transplant, kidney	165, 322
V42.7	Status, organ or tissue replaced by transplant, liver	111
V42.6	Status, organ or tissue replaced by transplant, lung	47
V42.89	Status, organ or tissue replaced by transplant, other	288
V42.83	Status, organ or tissue replaced by transplant, pancreas	110
V42.3	Status, organ or tissue replaced by transplant, skin	148
V42.82	Status, organ or tissue replaced by transplant, stem cells, peripheral	235
V42.9	Status, organ or tissue replaced by transplant, unspecified	288
V45.82	Status, postprocedural, angioplasty, percutaneous transluminal coronary	288
V45.81	Status, postprocedural, aortocoronary bypass	288
V45.84	Status, postprocedural, dental restoration	288
V45.85	Status, postprocedural, insulin pump	288
V45.89	Status, postprocedural, other	288
V45.83	Status, postprocedural, removal, implant, breast	288
*V45.5	Status, presence of device, contraceptive	288
V45.2	Status, presence of device, drainage, cerebrospinal fluid	288
V45.1	Status, renal dialysis	288
*380.5	Stenosis, acquired, external ear canal	35
746.3	Stenosis, congenital, aortic valve	88
750.5	Stenosis, congenital, hypertrophic, pyloric	104
746.83	Stenosis, congenital, infundibulum cardiac	88
746.5	Stenosis, congenital, mitral valve	88
746.81	Stenosis, congenital, subaortic	88
*375.5	Stenosis, insufficiency, lacrimal passages	25
478.74	Stenosis, larynx	36
537.0	Stenosis, pyloric, acquired, hypertrophic	101
569.2	Stenosis, rectum and anus	104
723.0	Stenosis, spinal, cervical region	129
*719.5	Stiffness, joint, not elsewhere classified	130
378.73	Strabismus, in other neuromuscular disorders	22
*378.6	Strabismus, mechanical	25
*378.5	Strabismus, paralytic	22
530.3	Stricture and stenosis, esophagus	102
593.3	Stricture or kinking, ureter	163
537.6	Stricture or stenosis, hourglass, stomach	102
447.1	Stricture, artery	86
*598	Stricture, urethral	164
786.1	Stridor	46
127.2	Strongyloidiasis	102, 308
307.0	Stuttering	253
*V20	Supervision, health, infant or child	287
V20.1	Supervision, health, other healthy infant or child receiving care	231
V23.7	Supervision, pregnancy, high-risk, affected by insufficient prenatal care	214
*V23.4	Supervision, pregnancy, high-risk, affected by poor obstetric history	214
V23.3	Supervision, pregnancy, high-risk, grand multiparity	214
V23.0	Supervision, pregnancy, high-risk, history of infertility	214
V23.2	Supervision, pregnancy, high-risk, history of previous abortion	214
V23.1	Supervision, pregnancy, high-risk, history of trophoblastic disease	214
*V23.8	Supervision, pregnancy, high-risk, other	214
V23.5	Supervision, pregnancy, high-risk, poor reproductive history	214
V23.9	Supervision, pregnancy, high-risk, unspecified	214
676.53	Suppressed, lactation, antepartum condition or complication	209
676.52	Suppressed, lactation, delivered, with mention of postpartum complication	192, 203
676.51	Suppressed, lactation, delivered, with or without mention of antepartum condition	192, 203
676.54	Suppressed, lactation, postpartum condition or complication	205
676.50	Suppressed, lactation, unspecified as to episode of care	214
464.51	Supraglottitis, unspecified, with obstruction	34, 319
464.50	Supraglottitis, unspecified, without obstruction	34, 319
V50.41	Surgery, elective, breast removal, prophylactic	143
V50.2	Surgery, elective, circumcision, routine or ritual	172, 232

Code Range

Code	Narrative	Page
V50.49	Surgery, elective, organ removal, other, prophylactic	288
V50.8	Surgery, elective, other, purposes other than remedying health states	288
V50.42	Surgery, elective, ovary removal, prophylactic	178, 184
V50.1	Surgery, elective, plastic, unacceptable cosmetic appearance	148
V50.0	Surgery, elective, transplant, hair	148
V50.9	Surgery, elective, unspecified, purposes other than remedying health states	288
*V25.4	Surveillance, previously prescribed contraceptive	287
V84.8	Susceptibility, genetic, to diseases, other	289
*V84.0	Susceptibility, genetic, to malignant neoplasm	289
782.2	Swelling mass or lump, superficial, localized	148
729.81	Swelling, limb	130
*789.3	Swelling, mass or lump, abdominal or pelvic	103
784.2	Swelling, mass, or lump in head and neck	148
786.6	Swelling, mass, or lump, chest	46
307.9	Symptom or syndrome, special, other and unspecified	252
*780.9	Symptom, other general	286
785.9	Symptom, other, involving cardiovascular system	91
784.9	Symptom, other, involving head, neck	37
782.9	Symptom, other, involving skin, integumentary tissue	148
729.89	Symptom, other, musculoskeletal, referable to limbs	130
*719.6	Symptom, other, referable to joint	130
*783	Symptoms concerning, nutrition, metabolism and development	154
*787	Symptoms, digestive system	103
789.9	Symptoms, other, involving abdomen, pelvis	103
788.9	Symptoms, other, involving urinary system	164
781.99	Symptoms, other, nervous and musculoskeletal systems	16
786.9	Symptoms, other, respiratory system, chest	46
780.2	Syncope, collapse	89
374.43	Syndrome, abnormal innervation, eyelid	24
517.3	Syndrome, acute chest	45
*758.3	Syndrome, autosomal deletion	252
453.0	Syndrome, Budd-Chiari	111
344.61	Syndrome, cauda equina, with neurogenic bladder	165
344.60	Syndrome, cauda equina, without mention of neurogenic bladder	11
447.4	Syndrome, celiac, artery compression	102
723.3	Syndrome, cervicobrachial, diffuse	12
723.2	Syndrome, cervicocranial	12
*995.5	Syndrome, child maltreatment	275
327.25	Syndrome, congenital central alveolar hypoventilation	15
758.0	Syndrome, Down's	252
378.71	Syndrome, Duane's	25
758.2	Syndrome, Edwards'	252
714.1	Syndrome, Felty's	128
377.04	Syndrome, Foster-Kennedy	16
759.83	Syndrome, Fragile X	252
310.0	Syndrome, frontal lobe	252
*564.8	Syndrome, functional, bowel, other, specified	103
564.9	Syndrome, functional, bowel, unspecified	103
530.7	Syndrome, gastroesophageal, laceration, hemorrhage	99
572.4	Syndrome, hepatorenal	220, 227
*314	Syndrome, hyperkinetic, childhood	253
746.7	Syndrome, hypoplastic left heart	88
669.23	Syndrome, hypotension, maternal, antepartum condition or complication	209
669.22	Syndrome, hypotension, maternal, delivered, with mention of postpartum complication	191, 202
669.21	Syndrome, hypotension, maternal, delivered, with or without mention of antepartum condition	191, 202
669.24	Syndrome, hypotension, maternal, postpartum condition or complication	205
669.20	Syndrome, hypotension, maternal, unspecified as to episode of care	191, 202
411.1	Syndrome, intermediate coronary	63, 89
564.1	Syndrome, irritable bowel	103
758.7	Syndrome, Klinefelter's	173
756.16	Syndrome, Klippel-Feil	135
759.82	Syndrome, Marfan	89
446.1	Syndrome, mucocutaneous lymph node (MCLS), acute, febrile	128
358.1	Syndrome, myasthenic, diseases classified elsewhere	10
*581	Syndrome, nephrotic	165, 310
333.92	Syndrome, neuroleptic, malignant	15
781.8	Syndrome, neurologic neglect	16
723.8	Syndrome, other, affecting cervical region	129
*344.8	Syndrome, paralytic, other specified	15
758.1	Syndrome, Patau's	252
310.2	Syndrome, postconcussion	13
564.2	Syndrome, postgastric surgery	103
457.0	Syndrome, postmastectomy lymphedema	143

* Code Range

Code	Narrative	Page
411.0	Syndrome, postmyocardial infarction	58, 61, 63, 73, 76, 79, 82, 91
*459.1	Syndrome, postphlebitic	87
759.81	Syndrome, Prader-Willi	135
443.0	Syndrome, Raynaud's	128
333.99	Syndrome, restless legs	10
331.81	Syndrome, Reye's	15
*726.1	Syndrome, rotator cuff, shoulder, and allied disorders	131
333.91	Syndrome, stiff-man	15
798.0	Syndrome, sudden infant death	16
040.82	Syndrome, toxic shock	248
386.9	Syndrome, vertiginous, labyrinthine disorders, unspecified	33
036.3	Syndrome, Waterhouse-Friderichsen, meningococcal	217, 224, 246
779.5	Syndrome, withdrawal, drug, in newborn	217, 224
098.51	Synovitis and tenosynovitis, gonococcal	128
727.01	Synovitis and tenosynovitis, in disease classified elsewhere	131
727.09	Synovitis and tenosynovitis, other	131
727.00	Synovitis and tenosynovitis, unspecified	131
*719.2	Synovitis, villonodular	130
095.5	Syphilis, bone	127
*093.8	Syphilis, cardiovascular	90
093.9	Syphilis, cardiovascular, unspecified	90
090.9	Syphilis, congenital, unspecified	248
090.1	Syphilis, early congenital, latent	248
090.0	Syphilis, early congenital, symptomatic	248
090.2	Syphilis, early congenital, unspecified	248
*092	Syphilis, early, latent	248
095.4	Syphilis, kidney	163
090.6	Syphilis, late congenital, latent	248
090.7	Syphilis, late congenital, unspecified	248
095.8	Syphilis, late symptomatic, other specified forms	248
095.9	Syphilis, late symptomatic, unspecified	248
096	Syphilis, late, latent	248
095.3	Syphilis, liver	110
095.1	Syphilis, lung	42
647.03	Syphilis, maternal, classifiable elsewhere, complicating pregnancy, childbirth, or the puerperium, antepartum condition or complication	207, 210
647.01	Syphilis, maternal, classifiable elsewhere, complicating pregnancy, childbirth, or the puerperium, delivered, with or without mention of antepartum condition	186, 195
647.02	Syphilis, maternal, classifiable elsewhere, complicating pregnancy, childbirth, or the puerperium, delivered, with mention of postpartum complication	186, 195
647.04	Syphilis, maternal, classifiable elsewhere, complicating pregnancy, childbirth, or the puerperium, postpartum condition or complication	204
647.00	Syphilis, maternal, classifiable elsewhere, complicating pregnancy, childbirth, or the puerperium, unspecified as to episode of care	211
095.6	Syphilis, muscle	131
*097	Syphilis, other and unspecified	248
090.5	Syphilis, other late congenital, symptomatic	248
091.1	Syphilis, primary, anal	103
091.0	Syphilis, primary, genital	171, 176, 182
091.2	Syphilis, primary, other	248
091.89	Syphilis, secondary, early, other	248
091.9	Syphilis, secondary, early, unspecified	248
091.69	Syphilis, secondary, early, viscera, other	103
091.3	Syphilis, secondary, skin or mucous membranes	146
091.7	Syphilis, secondary,early, relapse	248
095.7	Syphilis, synovium, tendon and bursa	131
336.0	Syringobulbia or syringomyelia	10
*995.9	Systemic inflammatory response syndrome (SIRS)	246
094.0	Tabes dorsalis	9
427.0	Tachycardia, paroxysmal, supraventricular	82, 89
427.2	Tachycardia, paroxysmal, unspecified	82, 89
427.1	Tachycardia, paroxysmal, ventricular	59, 61, 63, 73, 77, 79, 82, 84, 89, 219, 226
785.0	Tachycardia, unspecified	89, 221, 228
717.0	Tear, meniscus, medial, bucket handle	132
448.0	Telangiectasis, hereditary, hemorrhagic	86
*789.6	Tenderness, abdominal	103
726.72	Tendinitis, tibialis	131
376.04	Tenonitis	21

Alphabetic Index to Diseases

Code	Narrative	Page
727.06	Tenosynovitis, foot and ankle	131
727.05	Tenosynovitis, other, hand and wrist	131
727.04	Tenosynovitis, radial styloid	131
037	Tetanus	217, 224, 248
781.7	Tetany	154, 221, 228
745.2	Tetralogy of Fallot	88
*282.4	Thalassemias	218, 225
443.1	Thrombangiitis obliterans, Buerger's disease	86
287.4	Thrombocytopenia, secondary	218, 225, 309
776.1	Thrombocytopenia, transient, neonatal	216, 223
287.5	Thrombocytopenia, unspecified	310
453.1	Thrombophlebitis migrans	87
671.20	Thrombophlebitis, superficial complicating pregnancy and puerperium, unspecified as to episode of care	214
671.23	Thrombophlebitis, superficial, complicating pregnancy and puerperium, antepartum condition or complication	209
671.22	Thrombophlebitis, superficial, complicating pregnancy and puerperium, delivered, with mention of postpartum complication	191, 202
671.21	Thrombophlebitis, superficial, complicating pregnancy and puerperium, delivered, with or without mention of antepartum condition	191, 202
671.24	Thrombophlebitis, superficial, complicating pregnancy and puerperium, postpartum condition or complication	205
437.6	Thrombosis, nonpyogenic, intracranial venous sinus	16
452	Thrombosis, portal vein	111
434.01	Thrombosis, with cerebral infarction, arteries, cerebral	8, 10, 17, 60, 62, 64, 74, 78, 80
434.00	Thrombosis, without mention of cerebral infarction, arteries, cerebral	11, 60, 62, 64, 74, 78, 80
*254	Thymus gland diseases	234
246.9	Thyroid disorder, unspecified	319
*246	Thyroid disorders, other	156
246.8	Thyroid disorders, other specified	319
*245	Thyroiditis	156, 319
775.3	Thyrotoxicosis, neonatal	216, 223
*242	Thyrotoxicosis, with or without goiter	156, 319
333.3	Tic, organic origin	15
*307.2	Tics	15
*388.3	Tinnitus	36
463	Tonsillitis, acute	34, 319
474.00	Tonsillitis, chronic	34
608.2	Torsion, testis	172
781.93	Torticollis, ocular	129
333.83	Torticollis, spasmodic	15
723.5	Torticollis, unspecified	129
*130	Toxoplasmosis	308
130.8	Toxoplasmosis, multisystemic, disseminated	218, 225, 249
130.7	Toxoplasmosis, other specified sites	218, 225, 249
130.9	Toxoplasmosis, unspecified	249
*464.1	Tracheitis, acute	46
*076	Trachoma	22
665.83	Trauma, obstetrical, other specified, antepartum condition or complication	209
665.82	Trauma, obstetrical, other specified, delivered, with mention of postpartum complication	190, 202
665.81	Trauma, obstetrical, other specified, delivered, with or without mention of antepartum condition	190, 202
665.84	Trauma, obstetrical, other specified, postpartum condition or complication	204
665.80	Trauma, obstetrical, other specified, unspecified as to episode of care	190, 202
665.93	Trauma, obstetrical, unspecified, antepartum condition or complication	209
665.92	Trauma, obstetrical, unspecified, delivered, with mention of postpartum complication	190, 202
665.91	Trauma, obstetrical, unspecified, delivered, with or without mention of antepartum condition	190, 202
665.94	Trauma, obstetrical, unspecified, postpartum condition or complication	204
665.90	Trauma, obstetrical, unspecified, unspecified as to episode of care	190, 202
664.81	Trauma, other specified, perineum and vulva, during delivery, delivered, with or without mention of antepartum condition	190, 201
664.84	Trauma, other specified, perineum and vulva, during delivery, postpartum condition or complication	204
664.80	Trauma, other specified, perineum and vulva, during delivery, unspecified as to episode of care	190, 201
664.91	Trauma, unspecified, perineum and vulva, during delivery, delivered, with or without mention of antepartum condition	190, 201
664.94	Trauma, unspecified, perineum and vulva, during delivery, postpartum condition or complication	204

* Code Range

Code	Narrative	Page
664.90	Trauma, unspecified, perineum and vulva, during delivery, unspecified as to episode of care	190, 201
333.1	Tremor, essential, specified forms	15
124	Trichinosis	249
131.8	Trichomoniasis, other specified sites	249
131.03	Trichomoniasis, prostatitis	172
131.9	Trichomoniasis, unspecified	249
131.02	Trichomoniasis, urethritis	172, 176, 182
131.09	Trichomoniasis, urogenital, other	172, 176, 182
131.00	Trichomoniasis, urogenital, unspecified	172, 176, 182
131.01	Trichomoniasis, vaginitis	176, 182
127.6	Trichostrongyliasis	102
127.3	Trichuriasis	102
727.03	Trigger finger, acquired	131
595.3	Trigonitis	163
*086	Trypanosomiasis	248
*017.6	Tuberculosis, adrenal gland	155
*016.1	Tuberculosis, bladder	163
*015.7	Tuberculosis, bone, other specified	127
*015	Tuberculosis, bones and joints	308
*015.9	Tuberculosis, bones and joints, unspecified	128
*017.4	Tuberculosis, ear	35
*016.4	Tuberculosis, epididymis	171
*017.1	Tuberculosis, erythema nodosum with hypersensitivity reaction	142
*017.8	Tuberculosis, esophagus	103
*017.3	Tuberculosis, eye	22
*016.5	Tuberculosis, genital organs, male, other	171
*016	Tuberculosis, genitourinary system	308
*016.9	Tuberculosis, genitourinary, unspecified	163
*015.1	Tuberculosis, hip	128
*014	Tuberculosis, intestines, peritoneum and mesenteric glands	103, 308
*012.1	Tuberculosis, intrathoracic lymph nodes	42
*015.8	Tuberculosis, joint, other specified	128
*016.0	Tuberculosis, kidney	163
*015.2	Tuberculosis, knee	128
*012.3	Tuberculosis, laryngitis	35, 318
*015.5	Tuberculosis, limb bones	127
*015.6	Tuberculosis, mastoid	35
647.30	Tuberculosis, maternal, classifiable elsewhere, complicating pregnancy, childbirth, or the puerperium, unspecified as to episode of care	211
647.31	Tuberculosis, maternal, classifiable elsewhere, complicating pregnancy, childbirth, or the puerperium, delivered, with or without mention of antepartum condition	186, 195
647.32	Tuberculosis, maternal, classifiable elsewhere, complicating pregnancy, childbirth, or the puerperium, delivered, with mention of postpartum complication	186, 195
647.33	Tuberculosis, maternal, classifiable elsewhere, complicating pregnancy, childbirth, or the puerperium, antepartum condition or complication	207, 210
647.34	Tuberculosis, maternal, classifiable elsewhere, complicating pregnancy, childbirth, or the puerperium, postpartum condition or complication	204
*013	Tuberculosis, meninges and central nervous system	7, 12, 308
*018	Tuberculosis, miliary	308
*018.0	Tuberculosis, miliary, acute	247
*018.8	Tuberculosis, miliary, other specified	247
*018.9	Tuberculosis, miliary, unspecified	247
*017.9	Tuberculosis, organs, other specified	247
*017	Tuberculosis, other organs	308
*016.7	Tuberculosis, other, female genital organs	176, 182
*017.2	Tuberculosis, peripheral lymph nodes	234
*012.0	Tuberculosis, pleurisy	42
*010	Tuberculosis, primary	42, 308
*011	Tuberculosis, pulmonary	42, 308
*012	Tuberculosis, respiratory, other	308
*012.8	Tuberculosis, respiratory, other specified	42
*017.0	Tuberculosis, skin and subcutaneous cellular tissue	146
*017.7	Tuberculosis, spleen	234
*017.5	Tuberculosis, thyroid gland	155
*012.2	Tuberculosis, tracheobronchial, isolated	42
*016.2	Tuberculosis, ureter	163
*016.3	Tuberculosis, urinary organs, other	163
*015.0	Tuberculosis, vertebral column	127
*016.6	Tuberculous oophoritis and salpingitis	176, 182
021.1	Tularemia, enteric	103
021.3	Tularemia, oculoglandular	248
021.8	Tularemia, other specified	248
021.2	Tularemia, pulmonary	42
021.0	Tularemia, ulceroglandular	248
021.9	Tularemia, unspecified	248
727.02	Tumor, giant cell, tendon sheath	134

** Code Range*

Code	Narrative	Page
*202.6	Tumor, mast cell, malignant	237
202.61	Tumor, mast cell, malignant, lymph nodes, head, face, and neck	319
654.13	Tumors, body of pregnant uterus, complicating pregnancy, childbirth, or the puerperium, antepartum condition or complication	207
654.11	Tumors, body of pregnant uterus, complicating pregnancy, childbirth, or the puerperium, delivered, with or without mention of antepartum condition	187, 199
654.12	Tumors, body of pregnant uterus, complicating pregnancy, childbirth, or the puerperium, delivered, with mention of postpartum complication	187, 199
654.14	Tumors, body of pregnant uterus, complicating pregnancy, childbirth, or the puerperium, postpartum condition or complication	204
654.10	Tumors, body of pregnant uterus, complicating pregnancy, childbirth, or the puerperium, unspecified as to episode of care	213
*002	Typhoid and parathyphoid fevers	247
080	Typhus, louse-borne	248
*081	Typhus, other	248
*707	Ulcer, chronic, skin	137, 142
370.03	Ulcer, corneal, central	21
370.01	Ulcer, corneal, marginal	24
370.05	Ulcer, corneal, mycotic	21
370.06	Ulcer, corneal, perforated	21
370.02	Ulcer, corneal, ring	24
370.00	Ulcer, corneal, unspecified	21
*707.0	Ulcer, decubitus	83
*532.0	Ulcer, duodenal, acute, with hemorrhage	99
*532.2	Ulcer, duodenal, acute, with hemorrhage and perforation	99
*532.1	Ulcer, duodenal, acute, with perforation	100
532.31	Ulcer, duodenal, acute, without mention of hemorrhage and perforation, with obstruction	100
532.30	Ulcer, duodenal, acute, without mention of hemorrhage and perforation, without mention of obstruction	101
*532.4	Ulcer, duodenal, chronic or unspecified, with hemorrhage	99
*532.6	Ulcer, duodenal, chronic or unspecified, with hemorrhage and perforation	100
*532.5	Ulcer, duodenal, chronic or unspecified, with perforation	100
532.71	Ulcer, duodenal, chronic, without mention of hemorrhage and perforation, with obstruction	100
532.70	Ulcer, duodenal, chronic, without mention of hemorrhage, perforation or obstruction	101
532.91	Ulcer, duodenal, unspecified as acute or chronic, without mention of hemorrhage or perforation, with obstruction	100
532.90	Ulcer, duodenal, unspecified as acute or chronic, without mention of hemorrhage, perforation or obstruction	101
*530.2	Ulcer, esophagus	100
*531.0	Ulcer, gastric, acute, with hemorrhage	99
*531.2	Ulcer, gastric, acute, with hemorrhage and perforation	99
*531.1	Ulcer, gastric, acute, with perforation	100
531.31	Ulcer, gastric, acute, without mention of hemorrhage and perforation, with obstruction	100
531.30	Ulcer, gastric, acute, without mention of hemorrhage and perforation, without mention of obstruction	101
*531.4	Ulcer, gastric, chronic or unspecified, with hemorrhage	99
*531.6	Ulcer, gastric, chronic or unspecified, with hemorrhage and perforation	99
*531.5	Ulcer, gastric, chronic or unspecified, with perforation	100
531.71	Ulcer, gastric, chronic, without mention of hemorrhage and perforation, with obstruction	100
531.70	Ulcer, gastric, chronic, without mention of hemorrhage, perforation or obstruction	101
531.91	Ulcer, gastric, unspecified as acute or chronic, without mention of hemorrhage or perforation, with obstruction	100
531.90	Ulcer, gastric, unspecified as acute or chronic, without mention of hemorrhage, perforation or obstruction	101
*534.0	Ulcer, gastrojejunal, acute, with hemorrhage	100
*534.2	Ulcer, gastrojejunal, acute, with hemorrhage and perforation	100
*534.1	Ulcer, gastrojejunal, acute, with perforation	100
*534.3	Ulcer, gastrojejunal, acute, without mention of hemorrhage and perforation	100
*534.4	Ulcer, gastrojejunal, chronic or unspecified, with hemorrhage	100
*534.6	Ulcer, gastrojejunal, chronic or unspecified, with hemorrhage and perforation	100
*534.5	Ulcer, gastrojejunal, chronic or unspecified, with perforation	100
*534.7	Ulcer, gastrojejunal, chronic, without mention of hemorrhage and perforation	100
*534.9	Ulcer, gastrojejunal, unspecified as acute or chronic, without mention of hemorrhage or perforation	101

* Code Range

Code	Narrative	Page
370.04	Ulcer, hypopyon	21
370.07	Ulcer, Mooren's	24
*533.0	Ulcer, peptic, site unspecified, acute, with hemorrhage	100
*533.2	Ulcer, peptic, site unspecified, acute, with hemorrhage and perforation	100
*533.1	Ulcer, peptic, site unspecified, acute, with perforation	100
533.31	Ulcer, peptic, site unspecified, acute, without mention of hemorrhage and perforation, with obstruction	100
533.30	Ulcer, peptic, site unspecified, acute, without mention of hemorrhage and perforation, without mention of obstruction	101
*533.4	Ulcer, peptic, site unspecified, chronic or unspecified, with hemorrhage	100
*533.6	Ulcer, peptic, site unspecified, chronic or unspecified, with hemorrhage and perforation	100
*533.5	Ulcer, peptic, site unspecified, chronic or unspecified, with perforation	100
533.71	Ulcer, peptic, site unspecified, chronic, without mention of hemorrhage and perforation, with obstruction	100
533.70	Ulcer, peptic, site unspecified, chronic, without mention of hemorrhage, perforation or obstruction	101
533.91	Ulcer, peptic, site unspecified, unspecified as acute or chronic, without mention of hemorrhage or perforation, with obstruction	100
533.90	Ulcer, peptic, site unspecified, unspecified as acute or chronic, without mention of hemorrhage, perforation or obstruction	101
006.6	Ulceration, amebic, skin	146
569.82	Ulceration, intestine	104
*616.5	Ulceration, vulva	177, 183
*V63	Unavailability, medical facilities for care	289
420.90	Unspecified acute pericarditis	59, 61, 63, 73, 76, 79
428.40	Unspecified combined systolic and diastolic heart failure	59, 61, 64, 73, 77, 79
428.30	Unspecified diastolic heart failure	59, 61, 64, 73, 77, 79
861.10	Unspecified injury to heart with open wound into thorax	59, 62, 64, 74, 77, 80
428.20	Unspecified systolic heart failure	59, 61, 63, 73, 77, 79
652.03	Unstable lie, fetus, antepartum condition or complication	207
652.01	Unstable lie, fetus, delivered, with or without mention of antepartum condition	187, 198
652.00	Unstable lie, fetus, unspecified as to episode of care	212
*099.4	Urethritis, nongonococcal, other	172, 176, 182
*597	Urethritis, not sexually transmitted, urethral syndrome	163
*708	Urticaria	147
708.0	Urticaria, allergic	221, 228
*091.5	Uveitis, due to secondary syphilis, early	22
360.11	Uveitis, sympathetic	23
*V04	Vaccination and inoculation need, against certain viral diseases	287
V05.4	Vaccination and inoculation need, against prophylactic, varicella	231
*V03	Vaccination and inoculation need, prophylactic, against bacterial diseases	287
*V06	Vaccination and inoculation need, prophylactic, against combinations of diseases	287
V05.8	Vaccination and inoculation need, prophylactic, against other specified disease	231
*V05	Vaccination and inoculation need, prophylactic, against other, single diseases	287
V05.3	Vaccination and inoculation need, prophylactic, against viral hepatitis	231
*616.1	Vaginitis and vulvovaginitis	177, 183
052.9	Varicella, without mention of complication	246
*456.2	Varices, esophageal, in diseases classified elsewhere	104
456.0	Varices, esophageal, with bleeding	99
456.1	Varices, esophageal, without bleeding	104
456.8	Varices, other sites	87
456.5	Varices, pelvic	172, 176, 183
456.4	Varices, scrotal	172
456.3	Varices, sublingual	87
456.6	Varices, vulva	176, 183
671.02	Varicose veins of legs, complicating pregnancy and puerperium, delivered, with mention of postpartum complication	191, 202
454.9	Varicose veins, asymptomatic	87
671.00	Varicose veins, legs complicating pregnancy and puerperium, unspecified as to episode of care	213
671.03	Varicose veins, legs, complicating pregnancy and puerperium, antepartum condition or complication	209
671.01	Varicose veins, legs, complicating pregnancy and puerperium, delivered, with or without mention of antepartum condition	191, 202

** Code Range*

Code	Narrative	Page
671.04	Varicose veins, legs, complicating pregnancy and puerperium, postpartum condition or complication	205
454.1	Varicose veins, lower extremities, with inflammation	87
454.0	Varicose veins, lower extremities, with ulcer	87
454.2	Varicose veins, lower extremities, with ulcer and inflammation	87
671.10	Varicose veins, vulva complicating pregnancy and puerperium, unspecified as to episode of care	214
671.13	Varicose veins, vulva, complicating pregnancy and puerperium, antepartum condition or complication	209
671.12	Varicose veins, vulva, complicating pregnancy and puerperium, delivered, with mention of postpartum complication	191, 202
671.11	Varicose veins, vulva, complicating pregnancy and puerperium, delivered, with or without mention of antepartum condition	191, 202
671.14	Varicose veins, vulva, complicating pregnancy and puerperium, postpartum condition or complication	205
454.8	Varicose, veins, lower extremities, with other complications	87
663.53	Vasa previa complicating labor and delivery, antepartum condition or complication	209
663.51	Vasa previa complicating labor and delivery, delivered, with or without mention of antepartum condition	189, 201
663.50	Vasa previa complicating labor and delivery, unspecified as to episode of care	189, 201
474.2	Vegetations, adenoid	36
427.41	Ventricular fibrillation	59, 61, 63, 73, 77, 79
386.2	Vertigo, central origin	33
078.81	Vertigo, epidemic	15
*386.1	Vertigo, peripheral, other and unspecified	33
098.34	Vesiculitis, gonococcal, seminal, chronic	172
608.0	Vesiculitis, seminal	172
098.14	Vesiculitis, seminal, acute, gonococcal	171
790.8	Viremia, unspecified	247
079.6	Virus, respiratory syncytial (RSV)	217, 224
560.2	Volvulus	220, 227
078.82	Vomiting syndrome, epidemic	102
564.3	Vomiting, bilious following gastrointestinal surgery	103
643.23	Vomiting, late, in pregnancy, antepartum complication	206, 210
643.21	Vomiting, late, in pregnancy, delivered, with or without mention of antepartum condition	185, 197
643.20	Vomiting, late, in pregnancy, unspecified as to episode of care	210, 211
643.83	Vomiting, other, complicating pregnancy, antepartum complication	206, 210
643.81	Vomiting, other, complicating pregnancy, delivered, with or without mention of antepartum condition	185, 197
643.80	Vomiting, other, complicating pregnancy, unspecified as to episode of care	210, 211
536.2	Vomiting, persistent	102
307.54	Vomiting, psychogenic	251
643.93	Vomiting, unspecified, in pregnancy, antepartum complication	206, 210
643.91	Vomiting, unspecified, in pregnancy, delivered, with or without mention of antepartum condition	185, 197
643.90	Vomiting, unspecified, in pregnancy, unspecified as to episode of care	210, 211
*078.1	Warts, viral	146
781.94	Weakness, facial	16
728.87	Weakness, muscle (generalized)	130
748.2	Web, congenital, larynx	36, 320
744.5	Webbing, congenital, neck	148
*033	Whooping cough	46
879.3	Wound, open, abdominal wall, anterior, complicated	272
879.2	Wound, open, abdominal wall, anterior, without complication	144
879.5	Wound, open, abdominal wall, lateral, complicated	272
879.4	Wound, open, abdominal wall, lateral, without complication	144
*876	Wound, open, back	144, 297
879.1	Wound, open, breast, complicated	144
879.0	Wound, open, breast, without complication	144
*877	Wound, open, buttock	144, 297
873.51	Wound, open, cheek, complicated	144, 320
873.41	Wound, open, cheek, without complication	144, 320
*875	Wound, open, chest (wall)	297
875.1	Wound, open, chest wall, complicated	272
875.0	Wound, open, chest wall, without complication	144
*872	Wound, open, ear	37, 297
*881.1	Wound, open, elbow, forearm and wrist, complicated	272
*881.0	Wound, open, elbow, forearm and wrist, without complication	144
*881	Wound, open, elbow, forearm, and wrist	297
*871	Wound, open, eyeball	25, 297

** Code Range*

Code	Narrative	Page
873.59	Wound, open, face, other and multiple sites, complicated	144
873.49	Wound, open, face, other and multiple sites, without complication	144
873.50	Wound, open, face, unspecified site, complicated	144, 320
873.40	Wound, open, face, unspecified site, without complication	144, 320
*883	Wound, open, finger(s)	297
883.1	Wound, open, finger(s), complicated	272
883.0	Wound, open, finger(s), without complication	144
892.1	Wound, open, foot except toe(s, alone, complicated	272
*892	Wound, open, foot except toe(s), alone	298
892.0	Wound, open, foot except toe(s), alone, without complication	145
873.52	Wound, open, forehead, complicated	144
873.42	Wound, open, forehead, without complication	144
*882	Wound, open, hand except finger(s) alone	297
882.1	Wound, open, hand, except finger(s), alone, complicated	272
882.0	Wound, open, hand, except finger(s), alone, without complication	144
*890	Wound, open, hip and thigh	298
890.1	Wound, open, hip and thigh, complicated	272
890.0	Wound, open, hip and thigh, without complication	145
*878	Wound, open, including traumatic amputation, genital organs (external)	297
878.9	Wound, open, including traumatic amputation, genital organs, other and unspecified parts, complicated	173, 177, 184
878.8	Wound, open, including traumatic amputation, genital organs, other and unspecified parts, without complication	173, 177, 184
878.1	Wound, open, including traumatic amputation, penis, complicated	173
878.0	Wound, open, including traumatic amputation, penis, without complication	173
878.3	Wound, open, including traumatic amputation, scrotum and testes, complicated	173
878.2	Wound, open, including traumatic amputation, scrotum and testes, without complication	173
878.5	Wound, open, including traumatic amputation, vulva, complicated	177, 184
878.4	Wound, open, including traumatic amputation, vulva, without complication	177, 184
873.54	Wound, open, jaw, complicated	38, 320
873.44	Wound, open, jaw, without complication	38, 320
*891	Wound, open, knee, leg [except thigh], and ankle	298
891.1	Wound, open, knee, leg [except thigh], and ankle, complicated	272
891.0	Wound, open, knee, leg [except thigh], and ankle, without complication	145
*874.1	Wound, open, larynx and trachea, complicated	297
*874.0	Wound, open, larynx and trachea, without complication	297
874.10	Wound, open, larynx with trachea, complicated	37, 304, 320
874.00	Wound, open, larynx with trachea, without complication	37, 320
874.11	Wound, open, larynx, complicated	37, 304, 320
874.01	Wound, open, larynx, without complication	37, 320
873.53	Wound, open, lip, complicated	38, 320
873.43	Wound, open, lip, without complication	38, 320
*873.7	Wound, open, mouth, internal structures, complicated	38, 320
*873.6	Wound, open, mouth, internal structures, without complication	38, 320
*894	Wound, open, multiple and unspecified, lower limb	298
894.1	Wound, open, multiple and unspecified, lower limb, complicated	272
894.0	Wound, open, multiple and unspecified, lower limb, without complication	145
*884	Wound, open, multiple and unspecified, upper limb	297
884.1	Wound, open, multiple and unspecified, upper limb, complicated	272
884.0	Wound, open, multiple and unspecified, upper limb, without complication	145
879.9	Wound, open, multiple, unspecified site(s), complicated	272
879.8	Wound, open, multiple, unspecified site(s), without complication	144
873.22	Wound, open, nasal cavity, without complication	37
873.21	Wound, open, nasal septum, without complication	37
873.23	Wound, open, nasal sinus, without complication	37
874.9	Wound, open, neck, other and unspecified parts, complicated	144, 297, 321
874.8	Wound, open, neck, other and unspecified parts, without complication	144, 297, 321
*873.3	Wound, open, nose, complicated	37, 320
873.29	Wound, open, nose, multiple sites, without complication	37

Code	Narrative	Page
873.20	Wound, open, nose, unspecified site, without complication	35
*873.2	Wound, open, nose, without complication	320
*870	Wound, open, ocular adnexa	25, 297
*879	Wound, open, other and unspecified sites, except limbs	297
873.9	Wound, open, other and unspecified, head, complicated	144
873.8	Wound, open, other and unspecified, head, without mention of complication	144
*873	Wound, open, other, head	297
874.5	Wound, open, pharynx, complicated	37, 297, 321
874.4	Wound, open, pharynx, without complication	37, 297, 320
873.1	Wound, open, scalp, complicated	144
873.0	Wound, open, scalp, without complication	144
*880	Wound, open, shoulder and upper arm	297
*880.1	Wound, open, shoulder and upper arm, complicated	272
*880.0	Wound, open, shoulder and upper arm, without complication	144
*881.2	Wound, open, tendon involvement, elbow, forearm and wrist, complicated	135
883.2	Wound, open, tendon involvement, finger(s),	135
892.2	Wound, open, tendon involvement, foot except toe(s), alone	135
882.2	Wound, open, tendon involvement, hand, except finger(s), alone	135
890.2	Wound, open, tendon involvement, hip and thigh	135
891.2	Wound, open, tendon involvement, knee, leg [except thigh], and ankle	135
894.2	Wound, open, tendon involvement, multiple and unspecified, lower limb	135
884.2	Wound, open, tendon involvement, multiple and unspecified, upper limb, complicated	135
*880.2	Wound, open, tendon involvement, shoulder and upper arm	135
893.2	Wound, open, tendon involvement, toe(s)	135
874.3	Wound, open, thyroid gland, complicated	156, 297, 320
874.2	Wound, open, thyroid gland, without complication	156, 297, 320
*893	Wound, open, toe(s)	298
893.1	Wound, open, toe(s), complicated	272
893.0	Wound, open, toe(s), without complication	145
874.12	Wound, open, trachea, complicated	44, 304, 320
874.02	Wound, open, trachea, without complication	44, 320
879.7	Wound, open, trunk, other and unspecified parts, complicated	272
879.6	Wound, open, trunk, other and unspecified, parts, without complication	144
878.7	Wound, open, vagina, complicated	177, 184
878.6	Wound, open, vagina, without complication	177, 184
374.51	Xanthelasma	147
102.4	Yaws, gummata and ulcers	146
102.3	Yaws, hyperkeratosis	146
102.0	Yaws, initial lesions	146
102.8	Yaws, latent	248
102.6	Yaws, lesions, bone or joint	128
102.1	Yaws, multiple papillomata and wet crab yaws	146
102.2	Yaws, other early skin lesions	146
102.7	Yaws, other manifestations	248
102.9	Yaws, unspecified	248
117.7	Zygomycosis, phycomycosis or mucormycosis	218, 225

Code Range

Numeric Index to Diseases

Code	Narrative	Page
*001	Cholera	101
*002	Typhoid and parathyphoid fevers	247
003.0	Gastroenteritis, Salmonella	101
003.1	Septicemia, Salmonella	246, 308
*003.2	Infection, Salmonella, localized	308
003.20	Infection, Salmonella, localized, unspecified	247
003.21	Salmonella meningitis	7, 12
003.22	Pneumonia, Salmonella	42
003.23	Arthritis, Salmonella	128
003.24	Osteomyelitis, Salmonella	127
003.29	Infection, Salmonella, localized, other	247
003.8	Infection, Salmonella, other	247, 308
003.9	Infection, Salmonella, unspecified	247, 308
*004	Shigellosis	101
005.0	Poisoning, food, staphylococcal	101
005.1	Botulism	247
005.2	Poisoning, food, due to Clostridium perfringens [C Welchii]	101
005.3	Poisoning, food, due to other Clostridia	101
005.4	Poisoning, food, due to Vibrio parahaemolyticus	101
*005.8	Poisoning, food, other bacteria	101
005.9	Poisoning, food, unspecified	101
006.0	Dysentery, amebic, acute, without mention of abscess	101
006.1	Amebiasis, intestinal, chronic, without mention of abscess	102
006.2	Colitis, amebic, nondysenteric	102
006.3	Abscess, amebic, liver	110
006.4	Abscess, amebic, lung	42
006.5	Amebic brain abscess	7, 12
006.6	Ulceration, amebic, skin	146
006.8	Infection, amebic, other sites	247
006.9	Amebiasis, unspecified	247
*007	Disease, intestinal, protozoal, other	102
007.2	Coccidiosis	308
*008	Infection, intestinal, due to other organisms	102
*009	Infection, intestinal, ill-defined	102, 309
*010	Tuberculosis, primary	42, 308
*011	Tuberculosis, pulmonary	42, 308
*012	Tuberculosis, respiratory, other	308
*012.0	Tuberculosis, pleurisy	42
*012.1	Tuberculosis, intrathoracic lymph nodes	42
*012.2	Tuberculosis, tracheobronchial, isolated	42
*012.3	Tuberculosis, laryngitis	35, 318
*012.8	Tuberculosis, respiratory, other specified	42
*013	Tuberculosis, meninges and central nervous system	7, 12, 308
*014	Tuberculosis, intestines, peritoneum and mesenteric glands	103, 308
*015	Tuberculosis, bones and joints	308
*015.0	Tuberculosis, vertebral column	127
*015.1	Tuberculosis, hip	128
*015.2	Tuberculosis, knee	128
*015.5	Tuberculosis, limb bones	127
*015.6	Tuberculosis, mastoid	35
*015.7	Tuberculosis, bone, other specified	127
*015.8	Tuberculosis, joint, other specified	128
*015.9	Tuberculosis, bones and joints, unspecified	128
*016	Tuberculosis, genitourinary system	308
*016.0	Tuberculosis, kidney	163
*016.1	Tuberculosis, bladder	163
*016.2	Tuberculosis, ureter	163
*016.3	Tuberculosis, urinary organs, other	163
*016.4	Tuberculosis, epididymis	171
*016.5	Tuberculosis, genital organs, male, other	171
*016.6	Tuberculous oophoritis and salpingitis	176, 182
*016.7	Tuberculosis, other, female genital organs	176, 182
*016.9	Tuberculosis, genitourinary, unspecified	163
*017	Tuberculosis, other organs	308
*017.0	Tuberculosis, skin and subcutaneous cellular tissue	146
*017.1	Tuberculosis, erythema nodosum with hypersensitivity reaction	142
*017.2	Tuberculosis, peripheral lymph nodes	234
*017.3	Tuberculosis, eye	22
*017.4	Tuberculosis, ear	35
*017.5	Tuberculosis, thyroid gland	155
*017.6	Tuberculosis, adrenal gland	155
*017.7	Tuberculosis, spleen	234
*017.8	Tuberculosis, esophagus	103
*017.9	Tuberculosis, organs, other specified	247
*018	Tuberculosis, miliary	308
*018.0	Tuberculosis, miliary, acute	247
*018.8	Tuberculosis, miliary, other specified	247
*018.9	Tuberculosis, miliary, unspecified	247
020.0	Plague, bubonic	247
020.1	Plague, cellulocutaneous	248
020.2	Septicemia, plague	246

*** Code Range**

Code	Narrative	Page
020.3	Plague, pneumonic, primary	42
020.4	Plague, pneumonic, secondary	42
020.5	Plague, pneumonic, unspecified	42
020.8	Plague, other specified types	248
020.9	Plague, unspecified	248
021.0	Tularemia, ulceroglandular	248
021.1	Tularemia, enteric	103
021.2	Tularemia, pulmonary	42
021.3	Tularemia, oculoglandular	248
021.8	Tularemia, other specified	248
021.9	Tularemia, unspecified	248
022.0	Anthrax, cutaneous	146
022.1	Anthrax, pulmonary	42
022.2	Anthrax, gastrointestinal	103
022.3	Anthrax, septicemia,	246
022.8	Anthrax, other specified manifestations	248
022.9	Anthrax, unspecified	248
*023	Brucellosis	248
024	Glanders	248
025	Melioidosis	248
*026	Rat-bite fever	248
*027	Disease, zoonotic bacterial, other	248
*030	Leprosy	248
031.0	Disease, pulmonary, due to Mycobacterium avium, intracellulare, kansasii	42
031.1	Disease, cutaneous, due to other mycobacteria	146
031.2	Disease, due to disseminated mycobacterium avium-intracellulare complex (DMAC)	248, 308
031.8	Disease, mycobacterial, other	248, 308
031.9	Disease, due to mycobacteria, unspecified	248, 308
032.0	Diphtheria, faucial	35, 318
032.1	Diphtheria, nasopharyngeal	35, 318
032.2	Diphtheria, anterior nasal	35, 318
032.3	Diphtheria, laryngeal	35, 318
032.81	Diphtheria, conjunctival	22
032.82	Diphtheria, myocarditis	90
032.83	Diphtheria, peritonitis	103
032.84	Diphtheria, cystitis	163
032.85	Diphtheria, cutaneous	146
032.89	Diphtheria, other	248
032.9	Diphtheria, unspecified	248
*033	Whooping cough	46
034.0	Sore throat, streptococcal	34, 318
034.1	Scarlet fever	248
035	Erysipelas	143
036.0	Meningitis, meningococcal	7, 12
036.1	Encephalitis, meningococcal	7, 12
036.2	Meningococcemia	246
036.3	Syndrome, Waterhouse-Friderichsen, meningococcal	217, 224, 246
*036.4	Carditis, meningococcal	217, 224
036.40	Carditis, meningococcal, unspecified	90
036.41	Pericarditis, meningococcal	90
036.42	Endocarditis, meningococcal	85
036.43	Myocarditis, meningococcal	90
036.81	Neuritis, meningococcal, optic	21, 217, 224
036.82	Arthropathy, meningococcal	128, 217, 224
036.89	Infection, meningococcal, other, specified	246
036.9	Infection, meningococcal, unspecified	246
037	Tetanus	217, 224, 248
*038	Septicemia	217, 224, 246, 308
*039	Infection, actinomycotic	308
039.0	Infection, actinomycotic, cutaneous	146
039.1	Infection, actinomycotic, pulmonary	42
039.2	Infection, actinomycotic, abdominal	103
039.3	Infection, actinomycotic, cervicofacial	146
039.4	Madura foot	146
039.8	Infection, actinomycotic, other specified sites	248
039.9	Infection, actinomycotic, unspecified site	248
040.0	Gangrene, gas	217, 224, 248
040.1	Rhinoscleroma	248
040.2	Disease, Whipple's	103
040.3	Necrobacillosis	248
040.81	Pyomyositis, tropical	131
040.82	Syndrome, toxic shock	248
040.89	Disease, bacterial, other	248
*041	Infection, bacterial, in conditions classified elsewhere	248
042	Disease, human immunodeficiency virus (HIV)	307, 308, 309, 310
*045.0	Poliomyelitis, acute paralytic, specified as bulbar	7, 12
*045.1	Poliomyelitis, acute, with other paralysis	7, 12
*045.2	Poliomyelitis, acute, nonparalytic	246
*045.9	Poliomyelitis, acute, unspecified	7, 12
*046	Infection, slow virus, central nervous system	9
046.2	Panencephalitis, subacute, sclerosing	217, 224
046.3	Leukoencephalopathy, multifocal, progressive	308

 * Code Range

Code	Narrative	Page
046.8	Infection, viral, slow, central nervous system, other specified	308
046.9	Infection, viral, slow, central nervous system, unspecified	308
*047	Meningitis, due to enterovirus	13
047.9	Meningitis,viral, unspecified	309
048	Disease, enterovirus, other, central nervous system	13
049.0	Choriomeningitis, lymphocytic	13
049.1	Meningitis, due to adenovirus	13
049.8	Disease, central nervous system, nonarthropod-borne viral, other specified	12, 308
049.9	Disease, central nervous system, nonarthropod-borne, unspecified	12, 308
*050	Smallpox	246
051.0	Cowpox	246
051.1	Pseudocowpox	146
051.2	Dermatitis, contagious, pustular	146
051.9	Paravaccinia, unspecified	246
*052	Chickenpox	217, 224
052.0	Encephalitis, postvaricella	12
052.1	Pneumonitis, varicella, hemorrhagic	42
052.7	Chickenpox, other specified complications	246
052.8	Chickenpox, unspecified complications	246
052.9	Varicella, without mention of complication	246
*053	Herpes, zoster	217, 224, 308
053.0	Herpes, zoster, with meningitis	13
053.10	Herpes, zoster, with unspecified nervous system complications	11
053.11	Herpes, zoster, geniculate	11
053.12	Neuralgia, postherpetic, trigeminal	11
053.13	Polyneuropathy, postherpetic	11
053.19	Herpes, zoster, other, with nervous system complications	11
*053.2	Herpes, zoster, with opthalmic complications	22
053.71	Herpes, zoster, otitis externa	35
053.79	Herpes, zoster, other specified complications	246
053.8	Herpes, zoster, unspecified complication	246
053.9	Herpes, zoster, without mention of complication	142
*054	Herpes simplex	308
054.0	Eczema, herpeticum	146, 217, 224
054.10	Herpes, genital, unspecified	171, 176, 182
054.11	Herpes, vulvovaginitis	176, 182
054.12	Herpes, vulva	176, 182
054.13	Herpes, infection, penis	171
054.19	Herpes, genital, other	171, 176, 182
054.2	Herpes, gingivostomatitis	37, 217, 224, 318
054.3	Herpes, meningoencephalitis	7, 12, 217, 224
*054.4	Herpes, simplex, with opthalmic complications	22, 217, 224
054.5	Herpes, septicemia	217, 224, 246
054.6	Herpes, whitlow	146
*054.7	Herpes, simplex, with other specified complications	217, 224
054.71	Herpes, simplex, visceral	103
054.72	Herpes, simplex, meningitis	7, 13
054.73	Herpes, simplex, otitis externa	35
054.79	Herpes, simplex, other specified complications	247
054.8	Herpes, simplex, unspecified complication	217, 224, 247
054.9	Herpes, simplex, without mention of complication	146
055.0	Encephalitis, postmeasles	7, 12, 217, 224
055.1	Pneumonia, postmeasles	42, 217, 224
055.2	Otitis media, postmeasles	34, 217, 224
*055.7	Measles, with other specified complications	217, 224
055.71	Measles, keratoconjunctivitis	22
055.79	Measles, other specified complications	247
055.8	Measles, unspecified complications	217, 224, 247
055.9	Measles, without mention of complication	247
*056.0	Rubella, with neurological complications	217, 224
056.00	Rubella, with unspecified neurological complication	11
056.01	Encephalomyelitis, due to rubella	12
056.09	Rubella, with other neurological complications	12
*056.7	Rubella, with other specified complications	217, 224
056.71	Arthritis, due to rubella	129
056.79	Rubella, with other specified complications	247
056.8	Rubella, with unspecified complications	217, 224, 247
056.9	Rubella, without mention of complication	247
*057	Exanthemata, viral, other	247
*060	Fever, yellow	247
061	Dengue	247
*062	Encephalitis, viral, mosquito-borne	7, 12
*063	Encephalitis, viral, tick-borne	7, 12

Code	Narrative	Page
064	Encephalitis, viral, transmitted by other and unspecified arthropods	7, 12
*065	Fever, hemorrhagic, arthropod-borne	247
066.0	Fever, phlebotomus	247
066.1	Fever, tick-borne	247
066.2	Fever, Venezuelan equine	7, 12
066.3	Fever, other, mosquito-borne	247
*066.4	Fever, West Nile	247
066.8	Disease, other, viral, specified arthropod-borne	247
066.9	Disease, viral, arthropod-borne, unspecified	247
*070	Hepatitis, viral	110
*070.2	Hepatitis, B, viral, hepatic coma	217, 224
*070.3	Hepatitis, B, viral, without mention of hepatic coma	217, 224
*070.4	Hepatitis, viral, with hepatic coma, other specified	217, 224
*070.5	Hepatitis, viral, without hepatic coma, other specified	217, 224
070.6	Hepatitis, viral, with hepatic coma, unspecified	217, 224
070.9	Hepatitis, viral, without hepatic coma, unspecified	217, 224
071	Rabies	7, 12
072.0	Mumps, orchitis	171, 217, 224
072.1	Mumps, meningitis	7, 13, 217, 224
072.2	Mumps, encephalitis	7, 12, 217, 224
072.3	Mumps, pancreatitis	110, 217, 224
*072.7	Mumps, with other specified complications	217, 224
072.71	Mumps, hepatitis	110
072.72	Mumps, polyneuropathy	11
072.79	Mumps, other specified complications	247
072.8	Mumps, unspecified complication	217, 224, 247
072.9	Mumps, without mention of complication	247
073.0	Ornithosis, with pneumonia	42
073.7	Ornithosis, with other specified complications	247
073.8	Ornithosis, with unspecified complication	247
073.9	Ornithosis, with unspecified	247
074.0	Herpangina	34, 318
074.1	Pleurodynia, epidemic	45
074.20	Carditis, Coxsackie, unspecified	90
074.21	Pericarditis, Coxsackie	90
074.22	Endocarditis, Coxsackie	88
074.23	Myocarditis, Coxsackie	90
074.3	Disease, hand, foot and mouth	247
074.8	Disease, other, due to Coxsackie virus	247
075	Mononucleosis, infectious	247
*076	Trachoma	22
*077	Disease, other, conjunctiva, due to viruses and Chlamydiae	22
078.0	Molluscum contagiosum	146
*078.1	Warts, viral	146
078.2	Fever, sweating	247
078.3	Disease, cat scratch	234
078.4	Disease, foot and mouth	247
078.5	Cytomegaloviral disease	247, 308
078.6	Nephrosonephritis, hemorrhagic	163
078.7	Fever, arenaviral hemorrhagic	247
078.81	Vertigo, epidemic	15
078.82	Vomiting syndrome, epidemic	102
078.88	Disease, due to Chlamydia, other specified,	247
078.89	Disease, due to viruses, other specified	247
*079	Infection, viral, in conditions classified elsewhere, unspecified site	247
079.6	Virus, respiratory syncytial (RSV)	217, 224
*079.9	Infection, viral and chlamydial, in conditions classified elsewhere and of unspecified site, unspecified	309
080	Typhus, louse-borne	248
*081	Typhus, other	248
*082	Rickettsiosis, tick-borne	248
*083	Rickettsiosis, other	248
*084	Malaria	248
085.0	Leishmaniasis, visceral (kala-azar)	248
085.1	Leishmaniasis, cutaneous, urban	146
085.2	Leishmaniasis, cutaneous, Asian desert	146
085.3	Leishmaniasis, cutaneous, Ethiopian	146
085.4	Leishmaniasis, cutaneous, American	146
085.5	Leishmaniasis, mucocutaneous, American	146
085.9	Leishmaniasis, unspecified	248
*086	Trypanosomiasis	248
086.0	Chagas' disease, with heart involvement	90
*087	Fever, relapsing	248
*088	Disease, other, arthropod-borne	248
090.0	Syphilis, early congenital, symptomatic	248
090.1	Syphilis, early congenital, latent	248
090.2	Syphilis, early congenital, unspecified	248
090.3	Keratitis, interstitial, syphilitic	22
*090.4	Neurosyphilis, juvenile	12

Numeric Index to Diseases

*Code Range

Code	Narrative	Page
090.5	Syphilis, other late congenital, symptomatic	248
090.6	Syphilis, late congenital, latent	248
090.7	Syphilis, late congenital, unspecified	248
090.9	Syphilis, congenital, unspecified	248
091.0	Syphilis, primary, genital	171, 176, 182
091.1	Syphilis, primary, anal	103
091.2	Syphilis, primary, other	248
091.3	Syphilis, secondary, skin or mucous membranes	146
091.4	Adenopathy, due to secondary syphilis	234
*091.5	Uveitis, due to secondary syphilis, early	22
091.61	Periostitis, secondary syphilitic, early	127
091.62	Hepatitis, secondary syphilitic, early	110
091.69	Syphilis, secondary, early, viscera, other	103
091.7	Syphilis, secondary,early, relapse	248
091.81	Meningitis, acute syphilitic, secondary, early	7, 12
091.82	Alopecia, syphilitic, secondary, early	146
091.89	Syphilis, secondary, early, other	248
091.9	Syphilis, secondary, early, unspecified	248
*092	Syphilis, early, latent	248
093.0	Aneurysm, aorta, specified as syphilitic	88
093.1	Aortitis, syphilitic	88
093.20	Endocarditis of valve, unspecified, syphilitic	85
093.21	Endocarditis, mitral valve, syphilitic	88
093.22	Endocarditis, aortic valve, syphilitic	88
093.23	Endocarditis, tricuspid valve, syphilitic	88
093.24	Endocarditis, pulmonary valve, syphilitic	88
*093.8	Syphilis, cardiovascular	90
093.9	Syphilis, cardiovascular, unspecified	90
094.0	Tabes dorsalis	9
094.1	Paresis, general	9
094.2	Meningitis, syphilitic	8, 12
094.3	Neurosyphilis, asymptomatic	12
094.81	Encephalitis, syphilitic	8, 12
094.82	Parkinsonism, syphilitic	9
094.83	Retinochoroiditis, syphilitic, disseminated	22
094.84	Atrophy, optic, syphilitic	22
094.85	Neuritis, retrobulbar, syphilitic	9
094.86	Neuritis, acoustic, syphilitic	35
094.87	Aneurysm, ruptured cerebral, syphilitic	5, 15
094.89	Neurosyphilis, other specified	9
094.9	Neurosyphilis, unspecified	10
095.0	Episcleritis, syphilitic	22
095.1	Syphilis, lung	42
095.2	Peritonitis, syphilitic	103
095.3	Syphilis, liver	110
095.4	Syphilis, kidney	163
095.5	Syphilis, bone	127
095.6	Syphilis, muscle	131
095.7	Syphilis, synovium, tendon and bursa	131
095.8	Syphilis, late symptomatic, other specified forms	248
095.9	Syphilis, late symptomatic, unspecified	248
096	Syphilis, late, latent	248
*097	Syphilis, other and unspecified	248
098.0	Infection, gonococcal, lower genitourinary tract, acute	171, 176, 182
098.10	Infection, gonococcal, upper genitourinary tract, site unspecified, acute	171, 176, 182
098.11	Cystitis, gonococcal, acute	163
098.12	Prostatitis, gonococcal, acute	171
098.13	Epididymoorchitis, gonococcal, acute	171
098.14	Vesiculitis, seminal, acute, gonococcal	171
098.15	Cervicitis, gonococcal, acute	176, 182
098.16	Endometritis, gonococcal, acute	176, 182
098.17	Salpingitis, gonococcal, acute	176, 182
098.19	Infection, gonococcal, upper genitourinary, other, acute	171, 176, 182
098.2	Infection, gonococcal, lower genitourinary tract, chronic	171, 176, 182
098.30	Infection, gonococcal, upper genitourinary tract, site unspecified, chronic	163
098.31	Cystitis, gonococcal, chronic	163
098.32	Prostatitis, gonococcal, chronic	171
098.33	Epididymoorchitis, gonococcal, chronic	171
098.34	Vesiculitis, gonococcal, seminal, chronic	172
098.35	Cervicitis, gonococcal, chronic	176, 182
098.36	Endometritis, gonococcal, chronic	176, 182
098.37	Salpingitis, gonococcal, chronic	176, 182
098.39	Infection, gonococcal, upper genitourinary tract, other, chronic	172, 176, 182
*098.4	Infection, gonococcal, eye	22
098.50	Arthritis, gonococcal	128
098.51	Synovitis and tenosynovitis, gonococcal	128
098.52	Bursitis, gonococcal	128
098.53	Spondylitis, gonococcal	127
098.59	Infection, gonococcal, joint, other	128

Code	Narrative	Page
098.6	Infection, gonococcal, pharynx	34, 318
098.7	Infection, gonococcal, anus and rectum	103
098.81	Keratosis, blennorrhagica, gonococcal	22
098.82	Meningitis, gonococcal	8, 12
098.83	Pericarditis, gonococcal	90
098.84	Endocarditis, gonococcal	85
098.85	Disease, heart, other gonococcal	90
098.86	Peritonitis, gonococcal	103
098.89	Infection, gonococcal, other specified sites	248
099.0	Chancroid	172, 176, 182
099.1	Lymphogranuloma, venereum	172, 176, 182
099.2	Granuloma, inguinale	172, 176, 182
099.3	Disease, Reiter's	128
*099.4	Urethritis, nongonococcal, other	172, 176, 182
099.50	Disease, venereal, due to Chlamydia trachomatis, unspecified site	172, 176, 182
099.51	Disease, venereal, due to Chlamydia trachomatis, pharynx	34, 318
099.52	Disease, venereal, due to Chlamydia trachomatis, anus and rectum	103
099.53	Disease, venereal, due to Chlamydia trachomatis, lower genitourinary sites	172, 176, 182
099.54	Disease, venereal, due to Chlamydia trachomatis, other genitourinary sites	163
099.55	Disease, venereal, due to Chlamydia trachomatis, unspecified genitourinary sites	172, 176, 182
099.56	Disease, venereal, due to Chlamydia trachomatis, peritoneum	103
099.59	Disease, venereal, due to Chlamydia trachomatis, other specified sites	172, 176, 182
099.8	Disease, venereal, other specified	172, 176, 182
099.9	Disease, venereal, unspecified	172, 176, 182
100.0	Leptospirosis icterohemorrhagica	248
*100.8	Infection, leptospiral, other specified	8, 12
100.9	Leptospirosis, unspecified	248
101	Angina, Vincent's	34, 318
102.0	Yaws, initial lesions	146
102.1	Yaws, multiple papillomata and wet crab yaws	146
102.2	Yaws, other early skin lesions	146
102.3	Yaws, hyperkeratosis	146
102.4	Yaws, gummata and ulcers	146
102.5	Gangosa	35, 318
102.6	Yaws, lesions, bone or joint	128
102.7	Yaws, other manifestations	248
102.8	Yaws, latent	248
102.9	Yaws, unspecified	248
103.0	Pinta, primary lesions	146
103.1	Pinta, intermediate lesions	146
103.2	Pinta, late lesions	249
103.3	Pinta, mixed lesions	146
103.9	Pinta, unspecified	249
*104	Infection, spirochetal, other	249
*110	Dermatophytosis	146, 309
*111	Dermatomycosis, other, unspecified	146, 309
112.0	Candidiasis, mouth	37, 308, 318
112.1	Candidiasis, vulvovaginitis	176, 182
112.2	Candidiasis, other urogenital sites	172, 176, 182
112.3	Candidiasis, skin and nails	146, 308
112.4	Candidiasis, lung	42, 217, 224, 308
112.5	Candidiasis, disseminated	217, 224, 249, 308
*112.8	Candidiasis, other specified sites	308
112.81	Endocarditis, candidal	85, 217, 224
112.82	Otitis externa, candidal	35, 217, 224
112.83	Meningitis, candidal	8, 13, 217, 224
112.84	Candidiasis, esophagus	102, 217, 224
112.85	Candidiasis, intestine	102, 217, 224
112.89	Candidiasis, other specified sites	249
112.9	Candidiasis, unspecified site	249, 308
*114	Coccidioidomycosis	308
114.0	Coccidioidomycosis, pulmonary, primary	42
114.1	Coccidioidomycosis, extrapulmonary, primary	146
114.2	Meningitis, coccidioidal	8, 13, 217, 224
114.3	Coccidioidomycosis, progressive, other forms	217, 224, 249
114.4	Coccidioidomycosis, pulmonary, chronic	42
114.5	Coccidioidomycosis, pulmonary, unspecified	42
114.9	Coccidioidomycosis, unspecified	249
*115	Histoplasmosis	308
115.00	Histoplasmosis, due to Histoplasma capsulatum, without mention of manifestation	249
115.01	Histoplasmosis, due to histoplasma capsulatum, meningitis	8, 13, 217, 224

*** Code Range**

Code	Narrative	Page
115.02	Histoplasmosis, due to Histoplasma capsulatum, retinitis	22, 217, 224
115.03	Histoplasmosis, due to Histoplasma capsulatum, pericarditis	90, 217, 224
115.04	Histoplasmosis, due to Histoplasma capsulatum, endocarditis	85, 217, 224
115.05	Histoplasmosis, due to Histoplasma capsulatum, pneumonia	42, 217, 224
115.09	Histoplasmosis, due to Histoplasma capsulatum, other	249
115.10	Histoplasmosis, due to Histoplasma duboisii, without mention of manifestation	249
115.11	Histoplasmosis, due to histoplasma duboisii, meningitis	8, 13, 217, 224
115.12	Histoplasmosis, due to Histoplasma duboisii, retinitis	22, 217, 224
115.13	Histoplasmosis, due to Histoplasma duboisii, pericarditis	90, 217, 224
115.14	Histoplasmosis, due to Histoplasma duboisii, endocarditis	85, 217, 224
115.15	Histoplasmosis, due to Histoplasma duboisii, pneumonia	42, 217, 224
115.19	Histoplasmosis, due to Histoplasma duboisii, other	249
115.90	Histoplasmosis, without mention of manifestation, unspecified	249
115.91	Histoplasmosis, meningitis, unspecified	8, 13, 217, 225
115.92	Histoplasmosis, retinitis, unspecified	22, 218, 225
115.93	Histoplasmosis, pericarditis, unspecified	90, 218, 225
115.94	Histoplasmosis, endocarditis, unspecified	85, 218, 225
115.95	Histoplasmosis, pneumonia, unspecified	42, 218, 225
115.99	Histoplasmosis, other, unspecified	249
*116	Infection, blastomycotic	249
116.0	Blastomycosis	218, 225
116.1	Paracoccidioidomycosis	218, 225
*117	Mycosis, other	249
117.3	Aspergillosis	218, 225
117.4	Mycetomas, mycotic	218, 225
117.5	Cryptococcosis	218, 225, 308
117.6	Allescheriosis, petriellidosis	218, 225
117.7	Zygomycosis, phycomycosis or mucormycosis	218, 225
118	Mycosis, opportunistic	218, 225, 249, 308
120.0	Schistosoma, haematobium	163
120.1	Schistosoma, mansoni	110
120.2	Schistosoma, japonicum	249
120.3	Schistosomiasis [bilharziasis] cutaneous	146
120.8	Schistosomiasis, other	249
120.9	Schistosomiasis, unspecified	249
121.0	Opisthorchiasis	110
121.1	Clonorchiasis	111
121.2	Paragonimiasis	42
121.3	Fascioliasis	111
121.4	Fasciolopsiasis	111
121.5	Metagonimiasis	249
121.6	Heterophyiasis	249
121.8	Infection, trematode, other	249
121.9	Infection, trematode, unspecified	249
122.0	Echinococcus granulosus, liver	111
122.1	Echinococcus granulosus, lung	42
122.2	Echinococcosis granulosus, thyroid	155
122.3	Echinococcus granulosus, other	249
122.4	Echinococcus granulosus, unspecified	249
122.5	Echinococcus multilocularis, liver	111
122.6	Echinococcus multilocularis, other	249
122.7	Echinococcus multilocularis, unspecified	249
122.8	Echinococcus, liver, unspecified	111
122.9	Echinococcosis, other and unspecified	249
*123	Infection, cestode, other	102
124	Trichinosis	249
*125	Infestation, filarial, dracontiasis	249
*126	Ancylostomiasis, necatoriasis	102
127.0	Ascariasis	102
127.1	Anisakiasis	102
127.2	Strongyloidiasis	102, 308
127.3	Trichuriasis	102
127.4	Enterobiasis	102
127.5	Capillariasis	102
127.6	Trichostrongyliasis	102
127.7	Helminthiasis, intestinal, other, specified	102
127.8	Helminthiasis, intestinal, mixed	249
127.9	Helminthiasis, intestinal, unspecified	102
*128	Helminthiasis, other and specified	249
129	Parasitism, intestinal, unspecified	102
*130	Toxoplasmosis	308
130.0	Meningoencephalitis, due to toxoplasmosis	8, 13, 218, 225
130.1	Conjunctivitis, due to toxoplasmosis	22, 218, 225
130.2	Chorioretinitis, due to toxoplasmosis	22, 218, 225
130.3	Myocarditis, due to toxoplasmosis	90, 218, 225
130.4	Pneumonitis, due to toxoplasmosis	42, 218, 225

** Code Range*

Code	Narrative	Page
130.5	Hepatitis, due to toxoplasmosis	111, 218, 225
130.7	Toxoplasmosis, other specified sites	218, 225, 249
130.8	Toxoplasmosis, multisystemic, disseminated	218, 225, 249
130.9	Toxoplasmosis, unspecified	249
131.00	Trichomoniasis, urogenital, unspecified	172, 176, 182
131.01	Trichomoniasis, vaginitis	176, 182
131.02	Trichomoniasis, urethritis	172, 176, 182
131.03	Trichomoniasis, prostatitis	172
131.09	Trichomoniasis, urogenital, other	172, 176, 182
131.8	Trichomoniasis, other specified sites	249
131.9	Trichomoniasis, unspecified	249
*132	Pediculosis and phthirus infestation	146
*133	Acariasis	146
*134	Infestation, parasitic, other	146
135	Sarcoidosis	45
136.0	Ainhum	249
136.1	Behcet's syndrome	128
136.2	Infection, specific, by free-living amebae	249
136.3	Pneumocystosis	42, 218, 225, 308
136.4	Psorospermiasis	249
136.5	Sarcosporidiosis	249
136.8	Disease, infectious and parasitic, other	249, 308
136.9	Disease, infectious and parasitic, unspecified	249
137.0	Late effect, tuberculosis, respiratory, unspecified	45
137.1	Late effect, tuberculosis, central nervous system	15
137.2	Late effect, tuberculosis, genitourinary	163
137.3	Late effect, tuberculosis, bones and joints	133
137.4	Late effect, tuberculosis, other	249
138	Late effect, poliomyelitis, acute	15
139.0	Late effect, viral encephalitis	15
139.1	Late effect, trachoma	22
139.8	Late effect, other infectious and parasitic diseases	249
*140	Neoplasm, lip, malignant	33, 318
*141	Neoplasm, tongue, malignant	33, 318
*142	Neoplasm, major salivary glands, malignant	33, 318
*143	Neoplasm, gum, malignant	33, 318
*144	Neoplasm, mouth, floor, malignant	33, 318
*145	Neoplasm, mouth, other and unspecified parts, malignant	33, 318
*146	Neoplasm, oropharynx, malignant	33, 318

Code	Narrative	Page
*147	Neoplasm, nasopharynx, malignant	33, 318
*148	Neoplasm, hypopharynx, malignant	33, 318
*149	Neoplasm, lip and/or oral cavity and/or pharynx, contiguous sites, malignant	33, 318
*150	Neoplasm, esophagus, malignant	99
*151	Neoplasm, stomach, malignant	99
*152	Neoplasm, small intestine, including duodenum, malignant	99
*153	Neoplasm, colon, malignant	99
153.5	Neoplasm, colon, appendix, malignant	96
*154	Neoplasm, rectum, rectosigmoid junction and anus, malignant	99
*155	Neoplasm, liver and intrahepatic bile duct, malignant	107, 110
*156	Neoplasm, gallbladder and extrahepatic bile duct, malignant	107, 110
*157	Neoplasm, pancreas, malignant	107, 110
158.0	Neoplasm, retroperitoneum, malignant	236, 244
158.8	Neoplasm, retroperitoneum and peritoneum, contiguous or overlapping sites, specified parts, malignant	99
158.9	Neoplasm, peritoneum, unspecified, malignant	99
159.0	Neoplasm, intestinal tract, part unspecified, malignant	99
159.1	Neoplasm, digestive organs and peritoneum/spleen, other and ill-defined sites, malignant	237
159.8	Neoplasm, digestive organs and contiguous sites with peritoneum/intraabdominal organs, other sites, malignant	99
159.9	Neoplasm, digestive organs and peritoneum, ill-defined, malignant	99
*160	Neoplasm, nasal cavities, middle ear, accessory sinuses, malignant	33, 318
*161	Neoplasm, larynx, malignant	33, 318
*162	Neoplasm, trachea, bronchus and lung, malignant	43
*163	Neoplasm, pleura, malignant	43
164.0	Neoplasm, thymus, malignant	236, 244
164.1	Neoplasm, heart, malignant	90
164.2	Neoplasm, anterior mediastinum, malignant	43
164.3	Neoplasm, posterior mediastinum, malignant	43
164.8	Neoplasm, thymus, heart and mediastinum of contiguous or overlapping sites, other, malignant	43
164.9	Neoplasm, mediastinum, part unspecified, malignant	43
165.0	Neoplasm, upper respiratory tract, part unspecified, malignant	33, 318
165.8	Neoplasm, respiratory system and intrathoracic organs, contiguous or overlapping site, malignant	43

Numeric Index to Diseases

* Code Range

Code	Narrative	Page
165.9	Neoplasm, respiratory tract, unspecified, malignant	43
*170	Neoplasm, bone and articular cartilage, malignant	127
170.1	Neoplasm, mandible, malignant	318
*171	Neoplasm, connective and other soft tissue, malignant	127
172.0	Melanoma, lip, malignant	142
172.1	Melanoma, eyelid, including canthus, malignant	22
172.2	Melanoma, ear and external auditory canal, malignant	142
172.3	Melanoma, face, other and unspecified parts, malignant	142
172.4	Melanoma, scalp and neck, malignant	142
172.5	Melanoma, trunk, except scrotum, malignant	142
172.6	Melanoma, upper limb, including shoulder, malignant	142
172.7	Melanoma, lower limb, including hip, malignant	142
172.8	Melanoma, other specified sites, malignant	142
172.9	Melanoma, skin, site unspecified, malignant	142
173.0	Neoplasm, skin of lip, malignant	146, 318
173.1	Neoplasm, skin of eyelid and canthus, malignant	22
173.2	Neoplasm, skin of ear and external auditory canal, malignant	146
173.3	Neoplasm, skin of face, other and unspecified parts, malignant	146
173.4	Neoplasm, scalp and skin of neck, malignant	146
173.5	Neoplasm, skin of trunk except scrotum, malignant	146
173.6	Neoplasm, skin of upper limb, including shoulder, malignant	146
173.7	Neoplasm, skin of lower limb including hip, malignant	146
173.8	Neoplasm, contiguous or overlapping specified sites of skin, malignant	146
173.9	Neoplasm, skin of site unspecified, malignant	146
*174	Neoplasm, female breast, malignant	136, 142
*175	Neoplasm, male breast, malignant	136, 142
*176	Sarcoma, Kaposi's	308
176.0	Sarcoma, Kaposi's, skin	146
176.1	Sarcoma, Kaposi's, soft tissue	147
176.2	Sarcoma, Kaposi's, palate	33, 318
176.3	Sarcoma, Kaposi's, gastrointestinal sites	99
176.4	Sarcoma, Kaposi's, lung	43
176.5	Sarcoma, Kaposi's, lymph node	237
176.8	Sarcoma, Kaposi's, other specified site	147
176.9	Sarcoma, Kaposi's, unspecified site	147

Code	Narrative	Page
179	Neoplasm, uterus, unspecified, malignant	174, 179
*180	Neoplasm, cervix uteri, malignant	174, 179
181	Neoplasm, placenta, malignant	174, 179
*182	Neoplasm, body of uterus, malignant	174, 179
*183	Neoplasm, ovary and other uterine adnexa, malignant	175, 179
*184	Neoplasm, female genital organs,other and unspecified malignant	174, 179
185	Neoplasm, prostate, malignant	167, 169, 171
*186	Neoplasm, testes, malignant	167, 169, 171
*187	Neoplasm, penis and other male genital organs, malignant	167, 169, 171
*188	Neoplasm, bladder, malignant	157, 162
*189	Neoplasm, kidney and other unspecified urinary organs, malignant	157, 162
*190	Neoplasm, eye, malignant	22
*191	Neoplasm, brain, malignant	9
*192	Neoplasm, other and unspecified parts of nervous system, malignant	9
193	Neoplasm, thyroid gland, malignant	155, 318
194.0	Neoplasm, adrenal gland, malignant	155
194.1	Neoplasm, parathyroid gland, malignant	155
194.3	Neoplasm, pituitary gland and craniopharyngeal duct, malignant	155
194.4	Neoplasm, pineal gland, malignant	9
194.5	Neoplasm, carotid body, malignant	9
194.6	Neoplasm, aortic body and other paraganglia, malignant	9
194.8	Neoplasm, other endocrine glands and related structures, malignant	155
194.9	Neoplasm, endocrine gland, site unspecified, malignant	155
195.0	Neoplasm, head, face and neck, malignant	33, 318
195.1	Neoplasm, thorax, malignant	43
195.2	Neoplasm, abdomen, malignant	99
195.3	Neoplasm, pelvis, malignant	167, 169, 171, 174, 179
195.4	Neoplasm, upper limb, malignant	236, 244
195.5	Neoplasm, lower limb, malignant	236, 244
195.8	Neoplasm, other specified sites, malignant	236, 244
*196	Neoplasm, lymph nodes, secondary and unspecified, malignant	237
196.0	Neoplasm, lymph nodes, head, face and neck, secondary and unspecified, malignant	318

*** Code Range**

Code	Narrative	Page
197.0	Neoplasm, lung, malignant, secondary	43
197.1	Neoplasm, mediastinum, malignant, secondary	43
197.2	Neoplasm, pleura, malignant, secondary	43
197.3	Neoplasm, other respiratory organs, malignant, secondary	43
197.4	Neoplasm, small intestine including duodenum, malignant, secondary	99
197.5	Neoplasm, large intestine and rectum, malignant, secondary	99
197.6	Neoplasm, retroperitoneum and peritoneum, malignant, secondary	99
197.7	Neoplasm, liver, malignant, secondary	108, 110
197.8	Neoplasm, other digestive organs and spleen, malignant, secondary	99
198.0	Neoplasm, kidney, secondary, malignant	157, 162
198.1	Neoplasm, other urinary organs, malignant, secondary, malignant	157, 162
198.2	Neoplasm, skin, secondary, malignant	136, 142
198.3	Neoplasm, brain and spinal cord, secondary, malignant	9
198.4	Neoplasm, other parts of nervous system, secondary, malignant	9
198.5	Neoplasm, bone and bone marrow, malignant, malignant	127
198.6	Neoplasm, ovary, secondary, malignant	175, 179
198.7	Neoplasm, adrenal gland, secondary, malignant	155
198.81	Neoplasm, breast, secondary, malignant	136, 142
198.82	Neoplasm, genital organs, secondary, malignant	167, 169, 171, 174, 179
198.89	Neoplasm, other specified sites, secondary, malignant	236, 244
*199	Neoplasm, without specification of site, malignant	236, 244
*200	Lymphosarcoma and reticulosarcoma	237
*200.0	Reticulosarcoma	308
200.01	Reticulosarcoma, lymph nodes, head, face, and neck	318
200.11	Lymphosarcoma, lymph nodes, head, face, and neck	318
*200.2	Burkitt's tumor or lymphoma	308
200.21	Burkitt's tumor or lymphoma, lymph nodes, head, face, and neck	318
*200.8	Lymphosarcoma and reticulosarcoma, other named variants	308
200.81	Lymphosarcoma and reticulosarcoma, other named variants, lymph nodes, head, face, and neck	318
*201	Hodgkin's disease	237
201.01	Hodgkin's paragranuloma, lymph nodes, head, face, and neck	318
201.11	Hodgkin's granuloma, lymph nodes, head, face, and neck	318
201.21	Hodgkin's sarcoma, lymph nodes, head, face, and neck	318
201.41	Hodgkin's disease, lymphocytic-histiocytic predominance, lymph nodes, head, face, and neck	318
201.51	Hodgkin's disease, nodular sclerosis, lymph nodes, head, face, and neck	318
201.61	Hodgkin's disease, mixed cellularity, lymph nodes, head, face, and neck	318
201.71	Hodgkin's disease, lymphocytic depletion, lymph nodes, head, face, and neck	319
201.91	Hodgkin's disease, unspecified, lymph nodes, head, face, and neck	319
*202.0	Lymphoma, nodular	237
202.01	Lymphoma, nodular, lymph nodes, head, face, and neck	319
*202.1	Mycosis fungoides	237
202.11	Mycosis fungoides, lymph nodes, head, face, and neck	319
*202.2	Sezary's disease	237
202.21	Sezary's disease, lymph nodes, head, face, and neck	319
*202.3	Histiocytosis, malignant	237
202.31	Histiocytosis, malignant, lymph nodes, head, face, and neck	319
*202.4	Reticuloendotheliosis. leukemic	237
202.41	Reticuloendotheliosis, leukemic, lymph nodes, head, face, and neck	319
*202.5	Letterer-Siwe disease	236, 244
202.51	Letterer-Siwe disease, lymph nodes, head, face, and neck	319
*202.6	Tumor, mast cell, malignant	237
202.61	Tumor, mast cell, malignant, lymph nodes, head, face, and neck	319
*202.8	Lymphoma, malignant, other	237, 309
202.81	Lymphoma, malignant, other, lymph nodes, head, face, and neck	319
*202.9	Malignant neoplasms, lymphoid and histiocytic tissue, other and unspecified	237
202.91	Malignant neoplasms, lymphoid and histiocytic tissue, other and unspecified, lymph nodes, head, face, and neck	319
*203	Myeloma, multiple, and immunoproliferative neoplasms	237
*204	Leukemia, lymphoid	237
*204.0	Leukemia, lymphoid, acute	242, 244
*205	Leukemia, myeloid	237
*205.0	Leukemia, myeloid, acute	242, 244
*206	Leukemia, monocytic	237
*206.0	Leukemia, monocytic, acute	242, 244
*207	Leukemia, other specified	237

Code	Narrative	Page
*207.0	Erythremia and erythroleukemia, acute	242, 244
*208	Leukemia, unspecified cell type	237
*208.0	Leukemia, unspecified cell type, acute	242, 244
*210	Neoplasm, benign, lip, oral cavity and pharynx	319
210.0	Neoplasm, benign, lip	37
210.1	Neoplasm, benign, tongue	37
210.2	Neoplasm, benign, major salivary glands	35
210.3	Neoplasm, benign, floor of mouth	37
210.4	Neoplasm, benign, parts of mouth, other and unspecified	37
210.5	Neoplasm, benign tonsil	35
210.6	Neoplasm, benign, oropharynx, other parts	35
210.7	Neoplasm, benign, nasopharynx	35
210.8	Neoplasm, benign, hypopharynx	35
210.9	Neoplasm, benign, pharynx, unspecified	35
211.0	Neoplasm, benign, esophagus	103
211.1	Neoplasm, benign, stomach,	103
211.2	Neoplasm, benign, duodenum, jejunum and ileum	103
211.3	Neoplasm, benign, colon	103
211.4	Neoplasm, benign, rectum and anal canal	103
211.5	Neoplasm, benign, liver and biliary passages	111
211.6	Neoplasm, benign, pancreas except islets of Langerhans	110
211.7	Neoplasm, benign, islets of Langerhans	155
211.8	Neoplasm, benign, retroperitoneum and peritoneum	103
211.9	Neoplasm, benign, digestive system, other and unspecified site	104
212.0	Neoplasm, benign, nasal cavities, middle ear and accessory sinuses	35, 319
212.1	Neoplasm, benign, larynx	35, 319
212.2	Neoplasm, benign, trachea	43
212.3	Neoplasm, benign, bronchus and lung	43
212.4	Neoplasm, benign, pleura	43
212.5	Neoplasm, benign, mediastinum	43
212.6	Neoplasm, benign, thymus	234
212.7	Neoplasm, benign, heart	90
212.8	Neoplasm, benign, respiratory and intrathoracic organs, other specified sites	43
212.9	Neoplasm, benign, respiratory and intrathoracic organs, site unspecified	43
213.0	Neoplasm, benign, bones, skull and face	133, 319
213.1	Neoplasm, benign, bone, lower jaw	37, 319
213.2	Neoplasm, benign, vertebral column except sacrum and coccyx	133
213.3	Neoplasm, benign, ribs, sternum, clavicle	43
213.4	Neoplasm, benign, scapula and long bones, upper limb	133
213.5	Neoplasm, benign, short bones, upper limb	133
213.6	Neoplasm, benign, pelvic bones, sacrum and coccyx	133
213.7	Neoplasm, benign, long bones, lower limb	133
213.8	Neoplasm, benign, short bones, lower limb	133
213.9	Neoplasm, benign, bone and articular cartilage, site unspecified	133
214.0	Lipoma, skin and subcutaneous tissue, face	147
214.1	Lipoma, skin and subcutaneous tissue, other	147
214.2	Lipoma, intrathoracic organs	43
214.3	Lipoma, intraabdominal organs	104
214.4	Lipoma, spermatic cord	172
214.8	Lipoma, other specified sites	147
214.9	Lipoma, unspecified site	147
*215	Neoplasm, other benign, connective and other soft tissue	134
216.0	Neoplasm, benign, skin of lip	147
216.1	Neoplasm, benign, skin of eyelid, including canthus	22
216.2	Neoplasm, benign, ear and external auditory canal	147
216.3	Neoplasm, benign, skin of face, other and unspecified parts	147
216.4	Neoplasm, benign, scalp and skin of neck	147
216.5	Neoplasm, benign, skin of trunk, except scrotum	147
216.6	Neoplasm, benign, skin of upper limb	147
216.7	Neoplasm, benign, skin of lower limb	147
216.8	Neoplasm, benign, skin, other specified sites	147
216.9	Neoplasm, benign, skin, site unspecified	147
217	Neoplasm, benign, breast	147
*218	Leiomyoma, uterine	176, 183
*219	Neoplasm, other benign, uterus	176, 183
220	Neoplasm, benign, ovary	176, 183
*221	Neoplasm, benign, female genital organs, other	176, 183
*222	Neoplasm, benign, male genital organs	172
*223	Neoplasm, benign, kidney and other urinary organs	157, 162
*224	Neoplasm, benign, eye	22
*225	Neoplasm, benign, brain, other parts of nervous system	9
226	Neoplasm, benign, thyroid glands	155, 319
227.0	Neoplasm, benign, adrenal gland	155

*Code Range

Code	Narrative	Page
227.1	Neoplasm, benign, parathyroid gland	155
227.3	Neoplasm, benign, pituitary gland, craniopharyngeal duct	155
227.4	Neoplasm, benign, pineal gland	9
227.5	Neoplasm, benign, carotid body	9
227.6	Neoplasm, benign, aortic body, other paraganglia	9
227.8	Neoplasm, benign, endocrine glands, related structures, other	155
227.9	Neoplasm, benign, endocrine gland, site unspecified	155
228.00	Hemangioma, unspecifed site	90, 319
228.01	Hemangioma, skin and subcutaneous tissue	147, 319
228.02	Hemangioma, intracranial structures	15
228.03	Hemangioma, retina	22
228.04	Hemangioma, intra-abdominal structures	102
228.09	Hemangioma, other site	90, 319
228.1	Lymphangioma, any site	234
229.0	Neoplasm, benign, lymph nodes	234
229.8	Neoplasm, benign, other specified sites	236, 244
229.9	Neoplasm, benign, site unspecified	236, 244
230.0	Carcinoma in situ, lip, oral cavity, pharynx	33, 319
230.1	Carcinoma in situ, esophagus	99
230.2	Carcinoma in situ, stomach	99
230.3	Carcinoma in situ, colon	99
230.4	Carcinoma in situ, rectum	99
230.5	Carcinoma in situ, anal sphincter	99
230.6	Carcinoma in situ, anus, unspecified	99
230.7	Carcinoma in situ, intestine, other and unspecified	99
230.8	Carcinoma in situ, liver and biliary system	108, 110
230.9	Carcinoma in situ, digestive organs, other and unspecified	99
231.0	Carcinoma in situ, larynx	33, 319
231.1	Carcinoma in situ, trachea	43
231.2	Carcinoma in situ, bronchus and lung	43
231.8	Carcinoma in situ, respiratory system other specified parts	43
231.9	Carcinoma in situ, respiratory system, part unspecified	43
232.0	Carcinoma in situ, skin of lip	147
232.1	Carcinoma in situ, skin of eyelid, including canthus	22
232.2	Carcinoma in situ, ear and external auditory canal	147
232.3	Carcinoma in situ, skin of face, other and unspecified parts	147
232.4	Carcinoma in situ, scalp and skin of neck	147
232.5	Carcinoma in situ, skin of trunk, except scrotum	147
232.6	Carcinoma in situ, skin of upper limb	147
232.7	Carcinoma in situ, skin of lower limb	147
232.8	Carcinoma in situ, skin, other specified sites	147
232.9	Carcinoma in situ, skin, site unspecified	147
233.0	Carcinoma in situ, breast	136, 142
233.1	Carcinoma in situ, cervix uteri	174, 179
233.2	Carcinoma in situ, uterus, other and unspecified parts	174, 179
233.3	Carcinoma in situ, female genital organs, other and unspecified	174, 179
233.4	Carcinoma in situ, prostate	167, 169, 171
233.5	Carcinoma in situ, penis	167, 169, 171
233.6	Carcinoma in situ, male genital organs, other and unspecified	167, 169, 171
233.7	Carcinoma in situ, bladder	157, 162
233.9	Carcinoma in situ, urinary organs, other and unspecified	157, 162
234.0	Carcinoma in situ, eye	23
234.8	Carcinoma in situ, other specified sites	236, 244
234.9	Carcinoma in situ, site unspecified	236, 244
235.0	Neoplasm, uncertain behavior, major salivary glands	33, 319
235.1	Neoplasm, uncertain behavior, lip, oral cavity, pharynx	33, 319
235.2	Neoplasm, uncertain behavior, stomach, intestines, rectum	99
235.3	Neoplasm, uncertain behavior, liver, biliary passages	108, 110
235.4	Neoplasm, uncertain behavior, retroperitoneum, peritoneum	99
235.5	Neoplasm, uncertain behavior, digestive organs, other and unspecified	99
235.6	Neoplasm, uncertain behavior, larynx	33, 319
235.7	Neoplasm, uncertain behavior, trachea, bronchus and lung	43
235.8	Neoplasm, uncertain behavior, pleura, thymus, mediastinum	43
235.9	Neoplasm, uncertain behavior, respiratory organs, other and unspecified	43
236.0	Neoplasm, uncertain behavior, uterus	174, 179
236.1	Neoplasm, uncertain behavior, placenta	174, 179
236.2	Neoplasm, uncertain behavior, ovary	175, 179
236.3	Neoplasm, uncertain behavior, female genital organs, other and unspecified	174, 180
236.4	Neoplasm, uncertain behavior, testis	167, 169, 171

*** Code Range**

Code	Narrative	Page
236.5	Neoplasm, uncertain behavior, prostate	167, 169, 171
236.6	Neoplasm, uncertain behavior, male genital organs, other and unspecified	167, 169, 171
236.7	Neoplasm, uncertain behavior, bladder	157, 162
*236.9	Neoplasm, uncertain behavior, urinary organs, other and unspecified	157, 162
237.0	Neoplasm, uncertain behavior, pituitary gland, craniopharyngeal duct	155
237.1	Neoplasm, uncertain behavior, pineal gland	9
237.2	Neoplasm, uncertain behavior, adrenal gland	155
237.3	Neoplasm, uncertain behavior, paraganglia	9
237.4	Neoplasm, uncertain behavior, endocrine glands, other and unspecified	155
237.5	Neoplasm, uncertain behavior, brain and spinal cord	9
237.6	Neoplasm, uncertain behavior, meninges	9
237.70	Neurofibromatosis, unspecified	15
237.71	Neurofibromatosis, type 1 [von Recklinghausen's disease]	15
237.72	Neurofibromatosis, type 2 [acoustic neurofibromatosis]	15
237.9	Neoplasm, uncertain behavior, nervous system, other and unspecified parts	9
238.0	Neoplasm, uncertain behavior, bone and articular cartilage	127
238.1	Neoplasm, uncertain behavior, connective and other soft tissue	134
238.2	Neoplasm, uncertain behavior, skin	147
238.3	Neoplasm, uncertain behavior, breast	136, 142
238.4	Polycythemia vera	237
238.5	Neoplasm, uncertain behavior, histiocytic and mast cells	237
238.6	Neoplasm, uncertain behavior, plasma cells	237
238.7	Neoplasm, uncertain behavior, lymphatic and hematopoietic tissues	237
238.8	Neoplasm, uncertain behavior, other specified sites	236, 244
238.9	Neoplasm, uncertain behavior, site unspecified	236, 244
239.0	Neoplasms, unspecified nature, digestive system	99
239.1	Neoplasms, unspecified nature, respiratory system	43
239.2	Neoplasms, unspecified nature, bone, soft tissue and skin	134
239.3	Neoplasms, unspecified nature, breast	143
239.4	Neoplasms, unspecified nature, bladder	157, 162
239.5	Neoplasms, unspecified nature, genitourinary organs	157, 162
239.6	Neoplasms, unspecified nature, brain	9
239.7	Neoplasms, unspecified nature, endocrine glands and other nervous system parts	155
239.8	Neoplasms, unspecified nature, specified sites, other	236, 244
239.9	Neoplasms, unspecified nature, site unspecified	236, 244
*240	Goiter, simple and unspecified	155
*241	Goiter, nontoxic, nodular	156
*242	Thyrotoxicosis, with or without goiter	156, 319
243	Hypothyroidism, congenital	156
*244	Hypothyroidism, acquired	156
*245	Thyroiditis	156, 319
*246	Thyroid disorders, other	156
246.2	Cyst, thyroid	319
246.3	Hemorrhage and infarction, thyroid	319
246.8	Thyroid disorders, other specified	319
246.9	Thyroid disorder, unspecified	319
*250.0	Diabetes mellitus, without mention of complication	154, 321, 322
*250.1	Diabetes, ketoacidosis	154, 321, 322
*250.2	Diabetes, hyperosmolarity	154, 321, 322
*250.3	Diabetes, coma, other	154, 321, 322
*250.4	Diabetes, renal manifestations	164, 321, 322
*250.5	Diabetes, ophthalmic manifestations	23, 321, 322
*250.6	Diabetes, neurological manifestations	11, 321, 322
*250.7	Diabetes, peripheral circulatory disorders	86, 321, 322
*250.8	Diabetes, other specified manifestations	154, 321, 322
*250.9	Diabetes, unspecified complications	154, 321, 322
251.0	Coma, hypoglycemic	154, 218, 225
251.1	Hypoglycemia, other specified	156
251.2	Hypoglycemia, unspecified	154
251.3	Hypoinsulinemia, postsurgical	154
251.4	Abnormality, secretion of glucagon	156
251.5	Abnormality, secretion of gastrin	100
251.8	Pancreatic internal secretion disorder, other specified	156
251.9	Pancreatic internal secretion disorder, unspecified	156
*252	Parathyroid gland disorder	156
252.1	Hypoparathyroidism	218, 225

Numeric Index to Diseases

*** Code Range**

Code	Narrative	Page
*253	Pituitary gland and hypothalamic control disorders	156
253.5	Diabetes insipidus	218, 225
*254	Thymus gland diseases	234
254.1	Abscess, thymus	218, 225
*255	Adrenal gland disorders	156
*256	Dysfunction, ovarian	176, 183
*257	Dysfunction, testicular	156
*258	Dysfunction, polyglandular, related disorders	156
*259	Disorder, endocrine, other	156
260	Kwashiorkor	154, 309
261	Marasmus, nutritional	154, 218, 225, 309
262	Malnutrition, protein-calorie, other severe	154, 218, 225, 309
*263	Malnutrition, protein-calorie, unspecified	154, 309
263.0	Malnutrition, degree, moderate	218, 225
263.1	Malnutrition, degree, mild	218, 225
263.8	Malnutrition, protein-calorie, other	218, 225
263.9	Malnutrition, protein-calorie, unspecified	218, 225
*264	Deficiency, vitamin A	309
264.0	Deficiency, vitamin A, conjunctival xerosis	23
264.1	Deficiency, vitamin A, conjunctival xerosis, Bitot's spot	23
264.2	Deficiency, vitamin A, corneal xerosis	23
264.3	Deficiency, vitamin A, corneal ulceration, xerosis	23
264.4	Deficiency, vitamin A, keratomalacia	23
264.5	Deficiency, vitamin A, night blindness	23
264.6	Deficiency, vitamin A, xerophthalmic scars, cornea	23
264.7	Deficiency, vitamin A, other ocular manifestations	23
264.8	Deficiency, vitamin A, other manifestations	154
264.9	Deficiency, vitamin A, unspecified	154
*265	Deficiency, thiamine and niacin	154, 309
*266	Deficiency, B complex components	154, 309
267	Deficiency, ascorbic acid	154, 309
*268	Deficiency, vitamin D	309
268.0	Rickets, active	129
268.1	Rickets, late effect	129
268.2	Osteomalacia, unspecified	129
268.9	Deficiency, vitamin D, unspecified	154
*269	Deficiencies, nutritional, other	154, 309
*270	Disorders, amino-acid transport and metabolism	155
271.0	Glycogenosis	155
271.1	Galactosemia	155
271.2	Intolerance, fructose, hereditary	102
271.3	Deficiency, intestinal, disaccharidase and disaccharide, malabsorption	102
271.4	Glycosuria, renal	155
271.8	Disorder, carbohydrate transport and metabolism, other specified	155
271.9	Disorder, carbohydrate transport and metabolism, unspecified	155
*272	Disorder, lipoid metabolism	155
273.0	Hypergammaglobinemia, polyclonal	234
273.1	Paraproteinemia, monoclonal	234
273.2	Disorder, metabolism, plasma protein, other paraproteinemias	237
273.3	Macroglobulinemia	237
273.4	Disorder, metabolism, plasma protein, alpha-1-antitrypsin deficiency	155
273.8	Disorder, metabolism, plasma protein, other	236, 244
273.9	Disorder, plasma protein metabolism, unspecified	236, 244
274.0	Arthropathy, gouty	129
274.10	Nephropathy, gouty, unspecified	164
274.11	Nephrolithiasis, uric acid	163
274.19	Nephropathy, gouty, other	164
*274.8	Gout, other specified manifestations	129
274.9	Gout, unspecified	129
275.0	Disorder, iron metabolism	155
275.1	Disorder, copper metabolism	155
275.2	Disorder, magnesium metabolism	154
275.3	Disorder, phosphorus metabolism	155
*275.4	Disorder, calcium metabolism	154
275.8	Disorder, mineral metabolism, other specified	155
275.9	Disorder, mineral metabolism, unspecified	155
*276	Disorder, fluid, electrolyte and acid-base balance	154, 218, 225, 309
*276.5	Depletion, volume	215
277.00	Cystic fibrosis, without mention of meconium ileus	154
277.01	Cystic fibrosis, with meconium ileus	215, 218, 222
277.02	Cystic fibrosis, with pulmonary manifestations	42
277.03	Cystic fibrosis, with gastrointestinal manifestations	104
277.09	Cystic fibrosis, with other manifestations	154
277.1	Disorder, porphyrin metabolism	155
277.2	Disorder, purine and pyrimidine metabolism, other	155
277.3	Amyloidosis	128
277.4	Disorder, bilirubin excretion	111
277.5	Mucopolysaccharidosis	155
277.6	Deficiency, enzymes circulating, other	155

Numeric Index to Diseases

* Code Range

Code	Narrative	Page
277.7	Dysmetabolic syndrome X	155
*277.8	Disorders, metabolism, other specified	155
277.9	Disorder, metabolism, unspecified	155
*278	Overweight, obesity, other hyperalimentation	154
*279	Disorders, immune mechanism	309
*279.0	Deficiency, immunity, humoral	234
*279.1	Deficiency, immunity, cell-mediated	234
279.2	Deficiency, immunity, combined	234
279.3	Deficiency, immunity, unspecified	234
279.4	Disease, autoimmune, not elsewhere classified	128
279.8	Deficiency, immune mechanism, other specified	234
279.9	Deficiency, immune mechanism, unspecified	235
*280	Deficiency, iron, anemia	234, 309
*281	Deficiency anemias, other	234, 309
*282	Anemia, hemolytic, hereditary	234
*282.4	Thalassemias	218, 225
*283	Anemia, hemolytic, acquired	309
283.0	Anemia, hemolytic, autoimmune	234
*283.1	Anemia, hemolytic, non-autoimmune	218, 225, 234
283.2	Hemoglobinuria, due to hemolysis, external causes	218, 225, 234
283.9	Anemia, hemolytic, acquired, unspecified	218, 225, 234
*284	Anemia, aplastic	234
284.8	Anemia, aplastic, other specified	309
284.9	Anemia, aplastic, unspecified	309
*285	Anemias, other and unspecified	234
285.1	Anemia, posthemorrhagic, acute	218, 225
285.9	Anemia, unspecified	309
*286	Defects, coagulation	234
286.6	Defibrination syndrome	218, 225
*287	Purpura, other hemorrhagic conditions	234
287.4	Thrombocytopenia, secondary	218, 225, 309
287.5	Thrombocytopenia, unspecified	310
*288	Disease, white blood cells	235
288.0	Agranulocytosis	310
289.0	Polycythemia, secondary	235
289.1	Lymphadenitis, chronic	235
289.2	Lymphadenitis, mesenteric, nonspecific	104
289.3	Lymphadenitis, unspecified, except mesenteric	235
289.4	Hypersplenism	235, 310
*289.5	Diseases, other, spleen,	235
289.6	Polycythemia, familial	235
289.7	Methemoglobinemia	234
*289.8	Diseases, other specified, blood and blood-forming organs	235
289.9	Disease, unspecified, blood and blood-forming organs	235, 310
*290	Dementias	252
*290.1	Dementia, presenile	309
*291	Disorders, mental, alcohol-induced	254
*292	Disorders, mental, drug-induced	254
292.0	Disorder, mental, drug-induced, drug withdrawal	218, 225
293.0	Delirium, due to conditions classified elsewhere, transient	251
293.1	Delirium, subacute, psychotic	251
*293.8	Disorder, mental, due to conditions classified elsewhere, transient, other	252
293.9	Disorder, mental, due to conditions classified elsewhere, transient, unspecified	251
*294	Disorders, mental, due to conditions classified elsewhere, persistent	252
294.9	Disorder, mental, due to conditions classified elsewhere, persistent, unspecified	309
*295	Disorders, schizophrenic	252
*296	Disorders, mood, episodic	252
*297	Delusional disorders	252
298.0	Psychosis, depressive type, nonorganic	253
298.1	Psychosis, excitative type, nonorganic	253
298.2	Psychosis, reactive, confusion	253
298.3	Psychosis, paranoid reaction, acute	253
298.4	Psychosis, paranoid, psychogenic	253
298.8	Psychosis, reactive, other and unspecified	253
298.9	Psychosis, nonorganic, unspecified	253, 309
*299.0	Autistic disorder	252
*299.1	Disorder, childhood, disintegrative	252
*299.8	Disorder, developmental, pervasive, other specified	253
*299.9	Disorder, developmental, pervasive, unspecified	253
*300.0	Anxiety states	251
300.10	Hysteria, unspecified	251
300.11	Hysteria, conversion disorder	251
300.12	Amnesia, dissociative	251
300.13	Fugue, dissociative	251
300.14	Identity disorder, dissociative	252
300.15	Hysteria, dissociative type, unspecified	251
300.16	Disorder, factitious, with predominantly psychological signs and symptoms	251
300.19	Illness, factitious, other and unspecified	251
*300.2	Disorders, phobic	251
300.3	Disorders, obsessive compulsive	251

Numeric Index to Diseases

* Code Range

Code	Narrative	Page
300.4	Disorder, dysthymic	251
300.5	Neurasthenia	251
300.6	Disorder, depersonalization	251
300.7	Hypochondriasis	251
*300.8	Disorder, somatoform	251
300.9	Disorder, nonpsychotic mental, unspecified	251
301.0	Disorder, personality, paranoid	252
301.10	Disorder, personality, affective, unspecified	252
301.11	Disorder, personality, chronic hypomanic,	252
301.12	Disorder, personality, chronic depressive	251
301.13	Disorder, personality, cyclothymic	252
*301.2	Disorder, personality, schizoid	252
301.3	Disorder, personality, explosive	252
301.4	Disorder, obsessive-compulsive personality	252
*301.5	Disorder, personality, histrionic	252
301.6	Disorder, personality, dependent	252
301.7	Disorder, personality, antisocial	252
*301.8	Disorder, personality, other	252
301.9	Disorder, personality, unspecified	252
*302	Disorders, sexual and gender identity	253
*303.0	Intoxication, acute alcoholic	254
*303.9	Dependence, alcohol, other, unspecified	254
*304	Dependence, drug	254
*305.0	Abuse, nondependent, alcohol	254
305.1	Abuse, nondependent, tobacco	287
*305.2	Abuse, nondependent, cannabis	254
*305.3	Abuse, nondependent, hallucinogen	254
*305.4	Abuse, nondependent, drug, sedative, hypnotic or anxiolytic	254
*305.5	Abuse, nondependent, opioid	254
*305.6	Abuse, nondependent, cocaine	254
*305.7	Abuse, nondependent, amphetamine or related acting sympathomimetic	254
*305.8	Abuse, nondependent, antidepressant	254
*305.9	Abuse, nondependent, other, mixed or unspecified drug	254
306.0	Malfunction, physiological, from mental factors, musculoskeletal	131
306.1	Malfunction, physiological, from mental factors, respiratory	47
306.2	Malfunction, physiological, from mental factors, cardiovascular	90
306.3	Malfunction, physiological, from mental factors	147
306.4	Malfunction, physiological, from mental factors, gastrointestinal	102
306.50	Malfunction, physiological, from mental factors, genitourinary unspecified	164
306.51	Malfunction, physiological, from mental factors, vaginismus, psychogenic	176, 183
306.52	Malfunction, physiological, from mental factors, dysmenorrhea, psychogenic	176, 183
306.53	Malfunction, physiological, from mental factors, dysuria, psychogenic	165
306.59	Malfunction, physiological, from mental factors, genitourinary other	165
306.6	Malfunction, physiological, from mental factors, endocrine	156
306.7	Malfunction, physiological, from mental factors, special sense organs	251
306.8	Malfunction, physiological, from mental factors, other specified	253
306.9	Malfunction, physiological, from mental factors, unspecified	251
307.0	Stuttering	253
307.1	Anorexia nervosa	252
*307.2	Tics	15
307.3	Disorder, movement, stereotypic	253
*307.4	Disorder, sleep, nonorganic origin	253
307.50	Disorder, eating, unspecified	253
307.51	Bulimia nervosa	253
307.52	Pica	253
307.53	Rumination disorder	251
307.54	Vomiting, psychogenic	251
307.59	Disorder, feeding, psychogenic, other	253
307.6	Enuresis, nonorganic	253
307.7	Encopresis, nonorganic	253
307.80	Pain, psychogenic, site unspecified	251
307.81	Headache, tension	13
307.89	Pain, related to psychological factors, other	251
307.9	Symptom or syndrome, special, other and unspecified	252
*308	Reaction to stress, acute	251
309.0	Adjustment disorder, with depressed mood	251
309.1	Reaction, depressive, prolonged	251
*309.2	Reaction, adjustment, with predominant disturbance of other emotions	251
309.3	Adjustment disorder, with disturbance of conduct	251
309.4	Adjustment disorder, with mixed disturbance of emotions and conduct	251
*309.8	Reaction, adjustment, other specified	252
309.9	Reaction, adjustment, unspecified	252
310.0	Syndrome, frontal lobe	252

* Code Range

Code	Narrative	Page
310.1	Change, personality, due to conditions classified elsewhere	252
310.2	Syndrome, postconcussion	13
310.8	Disorder, mental, other specified nonpsychotic, following organic brain damage	252
310.9	Disorder, mental, unspecified nonpsychotic, following organic brain damage	252, 309
311	Disorder, depressive, other	251
*312.0	Disorder, conduct, undersocialized, aggressive type	253
*312.1	Disturbance, conduct, undersocialized, unaggressive type	253
*312.2	Disorder, conduct, socialized	253
312.30	Disorders, impulse control, unspecified	253
312.31	Disorder, impulse control, gambling, pathological	252
312.32	Disorder, impulse control, kleptomania	252
312.33	Disorder, impulse control, pyromania	253
312.34	Disorder, impulse control, explosive, intermittent	252
312.35	Disorder, impulse control, explosive, isolated	252
312.39	Disorder, impulse control, other	252
312.4	Disturbance, conduct, mixed with emotions	253
*312.8	Disorder, conduct, other, not elsewhere classified	253
312.9	Disturbance, conduct, unspecified	253
313.0	Disorder, overanxious, childhood, adolescence	252
313.1	Disorder, misery and unhappiness, childhood, adolescence	252
*313.2	Disorders, sensitivity , shyness, social withdrawal, childhood or adolescence	253
313.3	Problems, relationship, childhood, adolescence	253
*313.8	Disturbance, emotional, other or mixed, childhood or adolescence	253
313.9	Disturbance, emotional, unspecified, childhood or adolescence	253
*314	Syndrome, hyperkinetic, childhood	253
*315	Delays, specific, development	253
316	Psychic factors, associated with diseases classified elsewhere	252
317	Retardation, mental, mild	252
*318	Retardation, mental, specified	252
319	Retardation, mental, unspecified	252
*320	Meningitis, bacterial	8, 13, 218, 225
*321	Meningitis, other organisms	13, 218, 225
321.0	Meningitis, cryptococcal	8
321.1	Meningitis, other fungal diseases	8
321.2	Meningitis, due to viruses, not elsewhere classified	8
321.3	Meningitis, due to trypanosomiasis	8
*322	Meningitis, unspecified cause	13
322.0	Meningitis, nonpyogenic	218, 225
322.1	Meningitis, eosinophilic	218, 225
322.9	Meningitis, unspecified	218, 225
323.0	Encephalitis, viral diseases elsewhere classified	8, 13
323.1	Encephalitis, rickettsial diseases classified elsewhere	8, 13
323.2	Encephalitis, protozoal diseases classified elsewhere	8, 13
323.4	Encephalitis, other, due to infection classified elsewhere	8, 13
323.5	Encephalitis, postimmunization	8, 13
323.6	Encephalitis, postinfection, in conditions classified elsewhere	8, 13
323.7	Encephalitis, toxic	8, 15
323.8	Encephalitis, other causes	8, 13, 309
323.9	Encephalitis, unspecified cause	8, 13, 309
*324	Abscess, intracranial and intraspinal	8, 13, 218, 225
325	Phlebitis, thrombophlebitis, intracranial sinuses, venous	8, 15
326	Abscess, intracranial, late effect of	15
*327.0	Disorders, sleep, organic, initiating and maintaining sleep	253
*327.1	Hypersomnia, organic	253
*327.2	Apnea, sleep, organic	319
327.20	Apnea, sleep, organic, unspecified	35
327.21	Apnea, sleep, organic, primary central	15
327.22	Disorder, sleep, periodic breathing, high altitude	46
327.23	Apnea, sleep, organic, obstructive, (adult) (pediatric)	35
327.24	Hypoventilation, sleep related, idiopathic, nonobstructive alveolar	35
327.25	Syndrome, congenital central alveolar hypoventilation	15
327.26	Hypoventilation, sleep related, in conditions classifiable elsewhere	35
327.27	Apnea, sleep, organic, central, in conditions classifiable elsewhere	15
327.29	Apnea, sleep, organic, other	35
*327.3	Disorder, sleep, circadian rhythm	15, 319
*327.4	Parasomnia, organic	319
327.40	Parasomnia, organic, unspecified	35
327.41	Arousals, confusional	15
327.42	Disorder, REM sleep behavior	35
327.43	Paralysis, isolated sleep, recurrent	15
327.44	Parasomnia, organic, in conditions classified elsewhere	35
327.49	Parasomnia, organic, other	35
*327.5	Disorder, movement, sleep related, organic	319

Numeric Index to Diseases

Code	Narrative	Page
327.51	Disorder, movement, sleep related, organic, periodic limb	15
327.52	Disorder, movement, sleep related, organic, leg cramps	15
327.53	Disorder, movement, sleep related, organic, bruxism	35
327.59	Disorder, movement, sleep related, organic, other	35
327.8	Disorder, sleep, organic, other	35, 319
*330	Degeneration, brain, usually manifested in childhood	10
331.0	Disease, Alzheimer's	10
*331.1	Dementia, frontotemporal	10
331.2	Degeneration, brain, senile	10
331.3	Hydrocephalus, communicating	10
331.4	Hydrocephalus, obstructive	10
331.7	Degeneration, brain, in disease classified elsewhere	10
331.81	Syndrome, Reye's	15
331.82	Dementia, with Lewy bodies	10
331.89	Ataxia, cerebral	10
331.9	Degeneration, brain, unspecified	10
*332	Disease, Parkinson's	10
333.0	Degeneration, basal ganglia, other	10
333.1	Tremor, essential, specified forms	15
333.2	Myoclonus	15
333.3	Tic, organic origin	15
333.4	Chorea, Huntington's	10
333.5	Chorea, other	10
333.6	Dystonia, torsion, idiopathic	10
333.7	Dystonia, torsion, symptomatic	10
333.81	Blepharospasm	23
333.82	Dyskinesia, orofacial	15
333.83	Torticollis, spasmodic	15
333.84	Cramp, writer's, organic	15
333.89	Dystonia, torsion, fragments, other	15
333.90	Disease, extrapyramidal, unspecified, and abnormal movement disorders	10
333.91	Syndrome, stiff-man	15
333.92	Syndrome, neuroleptic, malignant	15
333.93	Attacks, shuddering, benign	15
333.99	Syndrome, restless legs	10
*334	Disease, spinocerebellar	10
*335	Disease, horn cell, anterior	10
336.0	Syringobulbia or syringomyelia	10
336.1	Myelopathy, vascular	15
336.2	Degeneration, combined, spinal cord, subacute, in other diseases classified elsewhere	15
336.3	Myelopathy, spinal cord, in other diseases classified elsewhere	15
336.8	Myelopathy, other, drug or radiation induced	15
336.9	Disease, spinal cord, unspecified	15, 309
*337	Disorder, nervous system, autonomic	11
340	Sclerosis, multiple	10
*341	Disease, demyelinating, central nervous system	10
341.9	Disease, demyelinating, central nervous system, unspecified	309
*342	Hemiplegia and hemiparesis	10
343.0	Diplegic, congenital	9
343.1	Hemiplegic, congenital	9
343.2	Quadriplegia, congenital	9
343.3	Monoplegic	15
343.4	Hemiplegia, infantile	9
343.8	Palsy, cerebral, infantile, other specified	15
343.9	Palsy, cerebral, infantile, unspecified	15
*344.0	Quadriplegia and quadriparesis	9
344.1	Paraplegia, unspecified	9
344.2	Diplegia, upper limbs	9
*344.3	Monoplegia, lower limb	15
*344.4	Monoplegia, upper limb	15
344.5	Monoplegia, unspecified	15
344.60	Syndrome, cauda equina, without mention of neurogenic bladder	11
344.61	Syndrome, cauda equina, with neurogenic bladder	165
*344.8	Syndrome, paralytic, other specified	15
344.9	Paralysis, unspecified	15
*345	Epilepsy	13
*346	Migraine	13
*347	Cataplexy, narcolepsy	15
348.0	Cyst, brain	15
348.1	Damage, brain, anoxic	15, 218, 225
348.2	Hypertension, intracranial, benign	13
*348.3	Encephalopathy, unspecified	11, 309
348.4	Compression, brain	13
348.5	Edema, brain	13
348.8	Disease, brain, other, calcification, fungus	11
348.9	Disease, brain, unspecified	11, 309
349.0	Reaction, spinal or lumbar puncture	13, 218, 225
349.1	Complication, nervous system, from device surgically implanted	15, 218, 225
349.2	Disorders, meninges, not elsewhere classified	15
349.81	Rhinorrhea, cerebral spinal fluid	15, 218, 225
349.82	Encephalopathy, toxic	15, 218, 225
349.89	Disorders, nervous system, other	11
349.9	Disorder, nervous system, unspecified	11, 309
*350	Disorders, nerve, trigeminal	11

Code	Narrative	Page
*351	Disorders, nerve, facial	11
*352	Disorder, nerve, other cranial	11
*353	Disorder, nerve root, plexus	11
*354	Mononeuritis, upper limb and multiplex	11
*355	Mononeuritis, lower limb	11
356.0	Neuropathy, peripheral hereditary	11
356.1	Atrophy, muscle, peroneal	11
356.2	Neuropathy, sensory, hereditary	11
356.3	Disease, Refsum's	15
356.4	Polyneuropathy, idiopathic, progressive	11
356.8	Neuropathy, specified, idiopathic, peripheral, supranuclear paralysis	11
356.9	Neuropathy, hereditary and peripheral, unspecified	11
357.0	Polyneuritis, acute infective	13, 310
357.1	Polyneuropathy, in collagen vascular disease	11
357.2	Polyneuropathy, in diabetes	11
357.3	Polyneuropathy, in malignant disease	11
357.4	Polyneuropathy, in other diseases classified elsewhere	11
357.5	Polyneuropathy, alcoholic	11
357.6	Polyneuropathy, due to drugs	11
357.7	Polyneuropathy, due to other toxic agents	11
*357.8	Neuropathy, inflammatory, toxic, other	11, 310
357.9	Neuropathy, inflammatory, toxic, unspecified	11, 310
*358.0	Myasthenia gravis	10
358.1	Syndrome, myasthenic, diseases classified elsewhere	10
358.2	Disorder, myoneural toxic	11
358.8	Disorder, myoneural, other specified	12
358.9	Disorder, myoneural, unspecified	12
*359	Dystrophy, muscular, other myopathies	16
360.00	Endophthalmitis, purulent, unspecified	21
360.01	Endophthalmitis, acute	21
360.02	Panophthalmitis	21
360.03	Endophthalmitis, chronic	23
360.04	Abscess, vitreous	21
360.11	Uveitis, sympathetic	23
360.12	Panuveitis	23
360.13	Endophthalmitis, parasitic, unspecified	21
360.14	Ophthalmia, nodosa	23
360.19	Endophthalmitis, other	21
*360.2	Disorder, globe, degenerative	23
*360.3	Hypotony, eye	23
*360.4	Degeneration, globe	23
*360.5	Foreign body, magnetic, retained, old, intraocular	23
*360.6	Foreign body, nonmagnetic, retained, old, intraocular	23
*360.8	Disorders, other, globe	23
360.9	Disorder, unspecified, globe	23
*361.0	Detachment, retina, with retinal defect	23
*361.1	Retinoschisis, retinal cysts	23
361.2	Detachment, retinal, serous	23
*361.3	Defect, retinal, without detachment	23
*361.8	Detachment, retinal, other forms	23
361.9	Detachment, retinal, unspecified	23
*362.0	Retinopathy, diabetic, classified elsewhere	23
*362.1	Retinopathy, other background, retinal vascular changes	23, 310
*362.2	Retinopathy, other proliferative	23
*362.3	Occlusion, vascular, retinal	21
*362.4	Separation, retinal layers	23
*362.5	Degeneration, macula, retina, posterior pole	23
*362.6	Degeneration, retinal, peripheral	23
*362.7	Dystrophy, hereditary, retinal	23
*362.8	Disorders, retinal, other	23
362.9	Disorder, retina, unspecified	23
*363	Inflammations, scars, and other disorders, choroid	23
*364.0	Iridocyclitis, acute, subacute	23
*364.1	Iridocyclitis, chronic	23
*364.2	Iridocyclitis, certain types	23
364.3	Iridocyclitis, unspecified	23
364.41	Hyphema	21
364.42	Iridis, rubeosis	23
*364.5	Degeneration, iris and ciliary body	23
*364.6	Cyst, iris, ciliary body, anterior chamber	23
*364.7	Adhesions, disruptions, iris, ciliary body	23
364.8	Disorders, other iris, ciliary body	23
364.9	Disorder, unspecified, iris, ciliary body	23
*365.0	Glaucoma, borderline	23
365.10	Glaucoma, open-angle, unspecified	23
365.11	Glaucoma, open angle, primary	23
365.12	Glaucoma, low tension	21
365.13	Glaucoma, pigmentary	23
365.14	Glaucoma, childhood	23
365.15	Glaucoma, open angle, residual stage	23
*365.2	Glaucoma, angle-closure, primary	23
*365.3	Glaucoma, corticosteroid induced	23
*365.4	Glaucoma, associated with congenital anomalies, dystrophies, systemic syndromes	23

Code	Narrative	Page
*365.5	Glaucoma, associated with lens disorders	23
*365.6	Glaucoma, associated with ocular disorders, other	23
*365.8	Glaucoma, other specified forms	23
365.9	Glaucoma, unspecified	23
*366	Cataract	23
367.0	Hypermetropia	23
367.1	Myopia	24
*367.2	Astigmatism	24
*367.3	Anisometropia, aniseikonia	24
367.4	Presbyopia	24
367.51	Paresis, accommodation	24
367.52	Ophthalmoplegia, internal, total or complete	21
367.53	Spasm, accommodation	24
*367.8	Disorder, accommodation, refraction, other	24
367.9	Disorder, unspecified, accommodation, refraction, other	24
*368.0	Amblyopia ex anopsia	24
368.10	Disturbance, visual, subjective, unspecified	24
368.11	Loss, visual, sudden	21
368.12	Loss, visual, transient	21
368.13	Discomfort, visual	24
368.14	Distortion, visual, shape, size	24
368.15	Distortion, visual, entoptic phenomena, other	24
368.16	Disturbance, visual, psychophysical	24
368.2	Diplopia	21
*368.3	Disorder, vision, binocular	24
368.40	Defect, visual field, unspecified	21
368.41	Scotoma, involving central area	21
368.42	Scotoma, blind spot area	24
368.43	Defect, visual field, sector or arcuate	21
368.44	Defect, visual field, localized, other	21
368.45	Contraction, constriction, generalized, visual field	21
368.46	Defect, visual field, homonymous, bilateral	21
368.47	Defect, visual field, heteronymous, bilateral	21
368.51	Defect, vision, color, protan	24
368.52	Defect, vision, color, deutan	24
368.53	Defect, vision, color, tritan	24
368.54	Achromatopsia	24
368.55	Deficiency, color vision, acquired	21
368.59	Deficiency, color vision, other	24
*368.6	Blindness, night	24
368.8	Disturbance, visual, other specified	24
368.9	Disturbance, visual, unspecified	24
*369	Blindness, low vision	24, 310
370.00	Ulcer, corneal, unspecified	21
370.01	Ulcer, corneal, marginal	24
370.02	Ulcer, corneal, ring	24
370.03	Ulcer, corneal, central	21
370.04	Ulcer, hypopyon	21
370.05	Ulcer, corneal, mycotic	21
370.06	Ulcer, corneal, perforated	21
370.07	Ulcer, Mooren's	24
*370.2	Keratitis, superficial, without conjunctivitis	24
*370.3	Keratoconjunctivitis, certain types	24
*370.4	Keratoconjunctivitis, other, unspecified	24
370.50	Keratitis, interstitial, unspecified	24
370.52	Keratitis, interstitial, diffuse	24
370.54	Keratitis, sclerosing	24
370.55	Abscess, corneal	21
370.59	Keratitis, interstitial, other and deep	24
*370.6	Neovascularization, corneal	24
370.8	Keratitis, other forms	24
370.9	Keratitis, unspecified	24
*371	Opacity, other disorders, corneal	24
*372	Disorders, conjunctiva	24
*373	Inflammation, eyelid	24
*374.0	Entropion and trichiasis, eyelid	24
*374.1	Ectropion	24
*374.2	Lagophthalmos	24
374.30	Ptosis, unspecified, eyelid	21
374.31	Ptosis, paralytic	21
374.32	Ptosis, myogenic	21
374.33	Ptosis, mechanical	24
374.34	Blepharochalasis	24
374.41	Retraction, lag, eyelid	24
374.43	Syndrome, abnormal innervation, eyelid	24
374.44	Disorders, sensory, eyelid	24
374.45	Disorders, other, sensorimotor, eyelid	22
374.46	Blepharophimosis	24
374.50	Disorders, unspecified, degenerative, eyelid	24
374.51	Xanthelasma	147
374.52	Hyperpigmentation, eyelid	24
374.53	Hypopigmentation, eyelid	24
374.54	Hypertrichosis, eyelid	24
374.55	Hypotrichosis, eyelid	24
374.56	Disorder, other degenerative, skin affecting eyelid	24
*374.8	Disorder, other, eyelid	24
374.9	Disorder, unspecified, eyelid	24
375.00	Dacryoadenitis, unspecified	24
375.01	Dacryoadenitis, acute	21
375.02	Dacryoadenitis, chronic	24

** Code Range*

Code	Narrative	Page
375.03	Enlargement, chronic, lacrimal gland	24
*375.1	Disorder, lacrimal gland, other	24
*375.2	Epiphora	25
375.30	Dacryocystitis, unspecified	25
375.31	Canaliculitis, acute, lacrimal	21
375.32	Dacryocystitis, acute	21
375.33	Dacryocystitis, phlegmonous	25
*375.4	Inflammation, chronic, lacrimal passages	25
*375.5	Stenosis, insufficiency, lacrimal passages	25
*375.6	Changes, other, lacrimal passages	25
*375.8	Disorder, other, lacrimal system	25
375.9	Disorder, unspecified, lacrimal system	25
376.00	Inflammation, acute, unspecified, orbit	25
376.01	Cellulitis, orbital	21
376.02	Periostitis, orbital	21
376.03	Osteomyelitis, orbital	21
376.04	Tenonitis	21
*376.1	Disorders, inflammatory, chronic, orbit	25
*376.2	Exophthalmos, endocrine	25
376.30	Exophthalmos, unspecified	25
376.31	Exophthalmos, constant	25
376.32	Hemorrhage, orbital	25
376.33	Edema, orbital	25
376.34	Exophthalmos, intermittent	22
376.35	Exophthalmos, pulsating	22
376.36	Displacement, lateral, globe	22
*376.4	Deformity, orbit	25
*376.5	Enophthalmos	25
376.6	Foreign body, retained, old, following penetrating wound, orbit	25
376.81	Cyst, orbital	25
376.82	Myopathy, extraocular muscles	22
376.89	Disorder, other, orbital	25
376.9	Disorder, unspecified, orbital	25
377.00	Papilledema, unspecified	16, 218, 225
377.01	Papilledema, associated with increased intracranial pressure	16, 218, 225
377.02	Papilledema, associated with decreased ocular pressure	25, 218, 225
377.03	Papilledema, associated with retinal disorder	25
377.04	Syndrome, Foster-Kennedy	16
377.10	Atrophy, optic, unspecified	22
377.11	Atrophy, primary, optic	22
377.12	Atrophy, postinflammatory, optic	22
377.13	Atrophy, optic, associated with retinal dystrophies	25
377.14	Atrophy, optic disc, cupping, glaucomatous	25
377.15	Atrophy, partial, optic	22
377.16	Atrophy, hereditary, optic	22
377.21	Drusen, optic disc	22
377.22	Holes, crater-like, optic disc	25
377.23	Coloboma, optic disc	25
377.24	Pseudopapilledema	22
*377.3	Neuritis, optic	22
*377.4	Disorders, other, optic nerve	22
*377.5	Disorder, optic chiasm	16
*377.6	Disorders, visual pathways, other	16
*377.7	Disorders, visual cortex	16
377.9	Disorder, unspecified, optic nerve, visual pathways	16
*378.0	Esotropia	25
*378.1	Exotropia	25
*378.2	Heterotropia, intermittent	25
*378.3	Heterotropia, other and unspecified	25
*378.4	Heterophoria	25
*378.5	Strabismus, paralytic	22
*378.6	Strabismus, mechanical	25
378.71	Syndrome, Duane's	25
378.72	Ophthalmoplegia, progressive, external	22
378.73	Strabismus, in other neuromuscular disorders	22
378.81	Palsy, conjugate gaze	25
378.82	Spasm, conjugate gaze	25
378.83	Insufficiency, convergence or palsy, binocular eye movement	25
378.84	Excess, convergence or spasm, binocular eye movement	25
378.85	Anomaly, divergence, binocular eye movement	25
378.86	Ophthalmoplegia, internuclear	16
378.87	Deviation, other dissociated, eye movements	22
378.9	Disorder, unspecified, eye movements	25
*379.0	Scleritis, episcleritis	25
*379.1	Disorders, other, sclera	25
*379.2	Disorders, vitreous body	25
*379.3	Aphakia, other disorders, lens	25
379.40	Abnormal, pupillary function, unspecified	22
379.41	Anisocoria	22
379.42	Miosis, persistent, not due to miotics	22
379.43	Mydriasis, persistent, not due to mydriatics	22
379.45	Argyll-Robertson pupil, atypical	10
379.46	Reaction, tonic pupillary	22
379.49	Anomaly, other, pupillary function	22
379.50	Nystagmus, unspecified	22
379.51	Nystagmus, congenital	25
379.52	Nystagmus, latent	22

Numeric Index to Diseases

Code	Narrative	Page
379.53	Nystagmus, visual deprivation	25
379.54	Nystagmus, associated with disorders of the vestibular system	22
379.55	Nystagmus, dissociated	22
379.56	Nystagmus, other forms	25
379.57	Nystagmus, with deficiency, saccadic eye movements	22
379.58	Nystagmus, with deficiency, smooth pursuit movements	22
379.59	Irregularity, other, eye movements	25
379.8	Disorders, other specified, eye, adnexa	25
*379.9	Disorder, unspecified, eye, adnexa	25
380.00	Perichondritis, unspecified, pinna	34
380.01	Perichondritis, acute, pinna	134
380.02	Perichondritis, chronic, pinna	134
380.03	Chondritis, pinna	134
*380.1	Otitis externa, infective	35
*380.2	Otitis externa, other	35
*380.3	Disorders, noninfectious, pinna	35
380.4	Impacted cerumen	35
*380.5	Stenosis, acquired, external ear canal	35
*380.8	Disorder, other, external ear	35
380.9	Disorder, unspecified, external ear	35
*381.0	Otitis media, acute, nonsuppurative	34
*381.1	Otitis media, chronic, serous	34
*381.2	Otitis media, chronic, mucoid	34
381.3	Otitis media, other and unspecified, chronic, nonsuppurative	34
381.4	Otitis media, nonsuppurative, not specified as acute or chronic	34
*381.5	Salpingitis, Eustachian	34
*381.6	Obstruction, Eustachian tube	35
381.7	Patulous, Eustachian tube	36
*381.8	Disorders, other, Eustachian tube	36
381.9	Disorders, unspecified, Eustachian tube	36
*382	Otitis media, suppurative and unspecified	34
*383.0	Mastoiditis, acute	34
383.01	Abscess, subperiosteal, mastoid	218, 225
383.1	Mastoiditis, chronic	34
*383.2	Petrositis	34
*383.3	Complications following mastoidectomy	36
*383.8	Disorders, other, mastoid	36
383.81	Fistula, postauricular	218, 225
383.9	Mastoiditis, unspecified	34
*384.0	Myringitis, acute, without mention of otitis media	34
384.1	Myringitis, chronic, without mention of otitis media	34
*384.2	Perforation, tympanic membrane	36
*384.8	Disorders, other specified, tympanic membrane	36
384.9	Disorder, unspecified, tympanic membrane	36
*385	Disorders, other, middle ear and mastoid	36
*386.0	Disease, Meniere's	33
*386.1	Vertigo, peripheral, other and unspecified	33
386.2	Vertigo, central origin	33
*386.3	Labyrinthitis	33
*386.4	Fistula, labyrinthine	36
*386.5	Dysfunction, labyrinthine	33
386.8	Disorders, other, labyrinth	33
386.9	Syndrome, vertiginous, labyrinthine disorders, unspecified	33
*387	Otosclerosis	36
*388.0	Disorders, degenerative, vascular, ear	36
*388.1	Effect, noise, on inner ear	36
388.2	Loss, hearing, sudden, unspecified	36
*388.3	Tinnitus	36
*388.4	Abnormal, auditory perception	36
388.5	Disorder, nerve, acoustic	36
388.60	Otorrhea, unspecified	36
388.61	Otorrhea, cerebrospinal fluid	16
388.69	Otorrhea, other	36
*388.7	Otalgia	36
388.8	Disorders, other, ear	36
388.9	Disorder, unspecified, ear	36
*389	Loss, hearing	36
390	Fever, rheumatic, without mention of heart involvement	128
391.0	Pericarditis, rheumatic, acute	90
391.1	Endocarditis, rheumatic, acute	88
391.2	Myocarditis, rheumatic, acute	90
391.8	Disease, heart, rheumatic, acute, other	90
391.9	Disease, heart, rheumatic, acute, unspecified	90
*392	Chorea, rheumatic	90
393	Pericarditis, rheumatic, chronic	90
*394	Diseases, mitral valve	88
*395	Diseases, aortic valve	88
*396	Diseases, mitral and aortic valves	88
*397	Diseases, endocardial structures, other	88
398.0	Myocarditis, rheumatic	90
398.90	Disease, heart, rheumatic, unspecified	90
398.91	Failure, heart, congestive, rheumatic	56, 58, 61, 63, 72, 76, 78, 82, 84, 85, 218, 225
398.99	Disease, heart, other and unspecified, rheumatic	90

Numeric Index to Diseases

Code	Narrative	Page
401.0	Hypertension, essential, malignant	87
401.1	Hypertension, essential, benign	87
401.9	Hypertension, essential, unspecified	88
402.00	Hypertensive heart disease, malignant, without heart failure	88
402.01	Hypertensive heart disease, malignant, with heart failure	56, 58, 61, 63, 72, 76, 78, 82, 84, 85, 218, 225
402.10	Hypertensive heart disease, benign, without heart failure	88
402.11	Hypertensive heart disease, benign, with heart failure	56, 58, 61, 63, 72, 76, 78, 82, 84, 85, 218, 225
402.90	Hypertensive heart disease, unspecified, without heart failure	88
402.91	Hypertensive heart disease, unspecified, with heart failure	56, 58, 61, 63, 72, 76, 78, 82, 84, 85, 218, 225
403.00	Hypertensive kidney disease, malignant, without chronic kidney disease	165
403.01	Hypertensive kidney disease, malignant, with chronic kidney disease	161, 162, 321, 322
403.10	Hypertensive kidney disease, benign, without chronic kidney disease	165
403.11	Hypertensive kidney disease, benign, with chronic kidney disease	161, 162, 321, 322
403.90	Hypertensive kidney disease, unspecified, without chronic kidney disease	165
403.91	Hypertensive kidney disease, unspecified, with chronic kidney disease	161, 162, 321, 322
404.00	Hypertensive heart and kidney disease, malignant, without heart failure or chronic kidney disease	88
404.01	Hypertensive heart and kidney disease, malignant, with heart failure	56, 58, 61, 63, 72, 76, 78, 82, 84, 85, 218, 225
404.02	Hypertensive heart and kidney disease, malignant, with chronic kidney disease	161, 162, 321, 322
404.03	Hypertensive heart and kidney disease, malignant, with heart failure and chronic kidney disease	57, 58, 61, 63, 72, 76, 78, 82, 84, 85, 219, 226, 322
404.10	Hypertensive heart and kidney disease, benign, without heart failure or chronic kidney disease	88
404.11	Hypertensive heart and kidney disease, benign, with heart failure	57, 58, 61, 63, 72, 76, 78, 82, 84, 85, 219, 226
404.12	Hypertensive heart and kidney disease, benign, with chronic kidney disease	161, 162, 322
404.13	Hypertensive heart and kidney disease, benign, with heart failure and chronic kidney disease	57, 58, 61, 63, 72, 76, 78, 82, 84, 85, 219, 226, 322
404.90	Hypertensive heart and kidney disease, unspecified, without heart failure or chronic kidney disease	88
404.91	Hypertensive heart and kidney disease, unspecified, with heart failure	57, 58, 61, 63, 72, 76, 78, 82, 84, 85, 219, 226
404.92	Hypertensive heart and kidney disease, unspecified, with chronic kidney disease	161, 162, 322
404.93	Hypertensive heart and kidney disease, unspecified, with heart failure and chronic kidney disease	57, 58, 61, 63, 72, 76, 79, 82, 84, 85, 219, 226, 322
*405	Hypertension, secondary	88
410.00	Infarction, acute, myocardial, anterolateral wall, unspecified episode of care	90
410.01	Infarction, acute, myocardial, anterolateral wall, initial episode of care	57, 58, 61, 63, 72, 76, 79, 82, 83, 84
410.02	Infarction, acute, myocardial, anterolateral wall, subsequent episode of care	90
410.10	Infarction, acute, myocardial, anterior wall, other, unspecified episode of care	90
410.11	Infarction, acute, myocardial, anterior wall, other, initial episode of care	57, 58, 61, 63, 72, 76, 79, 82, 83, 84
410.12	Infarction, acute, myocardial, anterior wall, other, subsequent episode of care	90
410.20	Infarction, acute, myocardial, inferolateral wall, unspecified episode of care	90
410.21	Infarction, acute, myocardial, inferolateral wall, initial episode of care	57, 58, 61, 63, 72, 76, 79, 82, 83, 84
410.22	Infarction, acute, myocardial, inferolateral wall, subsequent episode of care	90
410.30	Infarction, acute, myocardial, inferoposterior wall, unspecified episode of care	90

* Code Range

Code	Narrative	Page
410.31	Infarction, acute, myocardial, inferoposterior wall, initial episode of care	57, 58, 61, 63, 72, 76, 79, 82, 83, 84
410.32	Infarction, acute, myocardial, inferoposterior wall, subsequent episode of care	90
410.40	Infarction, acute, myocardial, inferior wall, other, unspecified episode of care	90
410.41	Infarction, acute, myocardial, inferior wall, other, initial episode of care	57, 58, 61, 63, 72, 76, 79, 82, 83, 84
410.42	Infarction, acute, myocardial, inferior wall, other, subsequent episode of care	90
410.50	Infarction, acute, myocardial, lateral wall, other, unspecified episode of care	90
410.51	Infarction, acute, myocardial, lateral wall, other, initial episode of care	57, 58, 61, 63, 72, 76, 79, 82, 83, 84
410.52	Infarction, acute, myocardial, lateral wall, other, subsequent episode of care	90
410.60	Infarction, acute, myocardial, posterior wall, true, unspecified episode of care	90
410.61	Infarction, acute, myocardial, posterior wall, true, initial episode of care	57, 58, 61, 63, 73, 76, 79, 82, 83, 84
410.62	Infarction, acute, myocardial, posterior wall, true, subsequent episode of care	90
410.70	Infarction, acute, myocardial, subendocardial, unspecified episode of care	90
410.71	Infarction, acute, myocardial, subendocardial, initial episode of care	57, 58, 61, 63, 73, 76, 79, 82, 83, 84
410.72	Infarction, acute, myocardial, subendocardial, subsequent episode of care	91
410.80	Infarction, acute, myocardial, other specified sites, unspecified episode of care	91
410.81	Infarction, acute, myocardial, other specified sites, initial episode of care	57, 58, 61, 63, 73, 76, 79, 82, 83, 84
410.82	Infarction, acute, myocardial, other specified sites, subsequent episode of care	91
410.90	Infarction, acute, myocardial, unspecified sites, unspecified episode of care	91
410.91	Infarction, acute, myocardial, unspecified sites, initial episode of care	57, 58, 61, 63, 73, 76, 79, 82, 83, 84
410.92	Infarction, acute, myocardial, unspecified sites, subsequent episode of care	91
*411	Disease, heart, ischemic, acute and subacute forms, other	84
411.0	Syndrome, postmyocardial infarction	58, 61, 63, 73, 76, 79, 82, 91
411.1	Syndrome, intermediate coronary	63, 89
411.81	Occlusion, coronary, acute, without myocardial infarction	63, 89
411.89	Disease, heart, ischemic, acute and subacute forms, other	89
412	Infarction, myocardial, old	87
413.0	Angina, decubitus	89
413.1	Angina, prinzmetal	89
413.9	Angina, other, unspecified	89
*414.0	Atherosclerosis, coronary	87
*414.1	Aneurysm, heart	82, 91
414.10	Aneurysm, heart	58, 61, 63, 73, 76, 79, 219, 226
414.11	Aneurysm of coronary vessels	58, 61, 63, 73, 76, 79
414.12	Dissection of coronary artery	58, 61, 63, 73, 76, 79
414.19	Other aneurysm of heart	59, 61, 63, 73, 76, 79
414.8	Disease, heart, ischemic, other specified forms, chronic	87
414.9	Disease, heart, ischemic, unspecified, chronic	87
*415	Disease, heart, pulmonary, acute	219, 226
415.0	Cor pulmonale, acute	59, 61, 63, 73, 76, 79, 84, 91
*415.1	Embolism and infarction, pulmonary	42, 83, 85
415.11	Iatrogenic pulmonary embolism and infarction	60, 62, 64, 74, 77, 80
415.19	Other pulmonary embolism and infarction	60, 62, 64, 74, 77, 80
*416	Disease, heart, pulmonary, chronic	91
416.0	Hypertension, pulmonary, primary	82
*417	Diseases, other, pulmonary circulation	91
*420	Pericarditis, acute	91
420.0	Pericarditis, acute, in diseases classified elsewhere	59, 61, 63, 73, 76, 79, 84, 219, 226
*420.9	Pericarditis, acute, other, unspecified	84
420.90	Unspecified acute pericarditis	59, 61, 63, 73, 76, 79
420.91	Acute idiopathic pericarditis	59, 61, 63, 73, 76, 79
420.99	Other acute pericarditis	59, 61, 63, 73, 76, 79

** Code Range*

Code	Narrative	Page
*421	Endocarditis, acute, subacute	84, 219, 226
421.0	Endocarditis, bacterial, acute or subacute	59, 61, 63, 73, 76, 79, 85, 309
421.1	Endocarditis, infective, acute, subacute, in diseases classified elsewhere	59, 61, 63, 73, 76, 79, 85
421.9	Endocarditis, acute, unspecified	59, 61, 63, 73, 76, 79, 85, 309
*422	Myocarditis, acute	84, 91
422.0	Myocarditis, acute, in diseases classified elsewhere	219, 226
*422.9	Myocarditis, acute, other and unspecified	309
422.92	Myocarditis, septic	59, 61, 63, 73, 76, 79, 219, 226
*423	Diseases, other, pericardium	91
423.0	Hemopericardium	59, 61, 63, 73, 76, 79, 84, 219, 226
*424	Diseases, other, endocardium	88
*424.9	Endocarditis, valve unspecified	219, 226
424.90	Endocarditis, valve unspecified, unspecified cause	59, 61, 63, 73, 76, 79, 84
424.91	Endocarditis, in diseases classified elsewhere	84
*425	Cardiomyopathy	91
425.2	Cardiomyopathy, obscure, of Africa	84
425.3	Fibroelastosis, endocardial	84
425.4	Cardiomyopathy, other, primary	84
425.5	Cardiomyopathy, alcoholic	84
425.7	Cardiomyopathy, nutritional and metabolic, classified elsewhere	84
425.8	Cardiomyopathy, other diseases classified elsewhere	84, 219, 226
425.9	Cardiomyopathy, secondary, unspecified	84, 310
*426	Disorders, conduction, heart	89
426.0	Block, complete, atrioventricular	59, 61, 73, 76, 79, 82, 219, 226
426.10	Block, unspecified, atrioventricular	82
426.12	Block, Mobitz, type II, atrioventricular	82
426.13	Block, other second-degree, atrioventricular	82
426.3	Block, other, bundle branch, left	82
426.51	Block, bundle branch, right, and left fascicular block, posterior	82
426.52	Block, bundle branch, right, and left fascicular block, anterior	82
426.53	Block, other, bundle branch, bilateral	59, 61, 73, 76, 79, 82, 219, 226
426.54	Block, trifascicular	59, 61, 73, 77, 79, 82, 219, 226
426.7	Anomaly, atrioventricular excitation	219, 226
426.89	Disorder, conduction, other specified	219, 226
427.0	Tachycardia, paroxysmal, supraventricular	82, 89
427.1	Tachycardia, paroxysmal, ventricular	59, 61, 63, 73, 77, 79, 82, 84, 89, 219, 226
427.2	Tachycardia, paroxysmal, unspecified	82, 89
*427.3	Fibrillation and flutter, atrial	82, 89, 219, 226
*427.4	Fibrillation and flutter, ventricular	82, 89, 219, 226
427.41	Ventricular fibrillation	59, 61, 63, 73, 77, 79
427.5	Arrest, cardiac	59, 61, 63, 73, 77, 79, 82, 84, 86, 219, 226
*427.6	Premature beats	89
*427.8	Dysrhythmia, other specified, cardiac	89
427.9	Dysrhythmia, unspecified, cardiac	89
*428	Failure, heart	82, 84, 85
428.0	Failure, congestive, heart, unspecified	57, 59, 61, 63, 73, 77, 79, 219, 226
428.1	Failure, heart, left	57, 59, 61, 63, 73, 77, 79, 219, 226
*428.2	Failure, heart, systolic	57, 219, 226
428.20	Unspecified systolic heart failure	59, 61, 63, 73, 77, 79
428.21	Acute systolic heart failure	59, 61, 64, 73, 77, 79
428.22	Chronic systolic heart failure	59, 61, 64, 73, 77, 79
428.23	Acute on chronic systolic heart failure	59, 61, 64, 73, 77, 79
*428.3	Failure, heart, diastolic	57, 219, 226
428.30	Unspecified diastolic heart failure	59, 61, 64, 73, 77, 79
428.31	Acute diastolic heart failure	59, 61, 64, 73, 77, 79
428.32	Chronic diastolic heart failure	59, 61, 64, 73, 77, 79
428.33	Acute on chronic diastolic heart failure	59, 61, 64, 73, 77, 79
*428.4	Failure, heart, combined systolic and diastolic	57, 219, 226
428.40	Unspecified combined systolic and diastolic heart failure	59, 61, 64, 73, 77, 79

*** Code Range**

Code	Narrative	Page
428.41	Acute combined systolic and diastolic heart failure	59, 62, 64, 73, 77, 79
428.42	Chronic combined systolic and diastolic heart failure	59, 62, 64, 73, 77, 79
428.43	Acute on chronic combined systolic and diastolic heart failure	59, 62, 64, 73, 77, 79
428.9	Failure, heart, unspecified	57, 59, 62, 64, 73, 77, 79, 219, 226
429.0	Myocarditis, unspecified	91
429.1	Degeneration, myocardial	91
429.2	Disease, cardiovascular, unspecified	87
429.3	Cardiomegaly	87
429.4	Disturbance, heart, functional, following cardiac surgery	84, 91, 219, 226
429.5	Rupture, chordae tendinae	59, 62, 64, 73, 77, 79, 82, 84, 88
429.6	Rupture, papillary muscle	59, 62, 64, 73, 77, 79, 82, 84, 88
429.71	Defect, acquired, cardiac septal	59, 62, 64, 73, 77, 79, 84, 91
429.79	Sequelae, other, of myocardial infarction, not elsewhere classified	59, 62, 64, 73, 77, 79, 84, 91
429.81	Disorders, other, papillary muscle	59, 62, 64, 73, 77, 79, 83, 84, 88, 219, 226
429.82	Disease, hyperkinetic, heart	84, 91, 219, 226
429.89	Disease, other, ill-defined, heart	87
429.9	Disease, heart, unspecified	87
430	Hemorrhage, subarachnoid	5, 8, 10, 60, 62, 64, 74, 77, 80, 83, 219, 226
431	Hemorrhage, intracerebral	5, 8, 10, 60, 62, 64, 74, 77, 80, 83, 219, 226
*432	Hemorrhage, intracranial, other and unspecified	5, 10, 219, 226
432.0	Hemorrhage, extradural, nontraumatic	60, 62, 64, 74, 77, 80, 83
432.1	Hemorrhage, subdural	60, 62, 64, 74, 77, 80, 83
432.9	Hemorrhage, intracranial, unspecified	8, 60, 62, 64, 74, 77, 80, 83
433.00	Occlusion, stenosis, without mention of cerebral infarction, artery, basilar	10
433.01	Occlusion, stenosis, with cerebral infarction, artery, basilar	8, 10, 17, 60, 62, 64, 74, 77, 80, 83, 219, 226
433.10	Occlusion, stenosis, without mention of cerebral infarction, artery, carotid	10
433.11	Occlusion, stenosis, with cerebral infarction, artery, carotid	8, 10, 17, 60, 62, 64, 74, 77, 80, 83, 219, 226
433.20	Occlusion, stenosis, without mention of cerebral infarction, artery, vertebral	10
433.21	Occlusion, stenosis, with cerebral infarction, artery, vertebral	8, 10, 17, 60, 62, 64, 74, 77, 80, 83, 219, 226
433.30	Occlusion, stenosis, without mention of cerebral infarction, arteries, multiple and bilateral, precerebral	10
433.31	Occlusion, stenosis, with cerebral infarction, arteries, multiple and bilateral, precerebral	8, 10, 17, 60, 62, 64, 74, 78, 80, 83, 219, 226
433.80	Occlusion, stenosis, without mention of cerebral infarction, arteries, other specified, precerebral	11
433.81	Occlusion, stenosis, with cerebral infarction, arteries, other specified, precerebral	8, 10, 17, 60, 62, 64, 74, 78, 80, 83, 219, 226
433.90	Occlusion, stenosis, without mention of cerebral infarction, arteries, unspecified, precerebral	11
433.91	Occlusion, stenosis, with cerebral infarction, arteries, unspecified, precerebral	8, 10, 17, 60, 62, 64, 74, 78, 80, 83, 219, 226
*434	Occlusion, arteries, cerebral	83, 219, 226
434.00	Thrombosis, without mention of cerebral infarction, arteries, cerebral	11, 60, 62, 64, 74, 78, 80
434.01	Thrombosis, with cerebral infarction, arteries, cerebral	8, 10, 17, 60, 62, 64, 74, 78, 80
434.10	Embolism, without mention of cerebral infarction, arteries, cerebral	11, 60, 62, 64, 74, 78, 80
434.11	Embolism, with cerebral infarction, arteries, cerebral	8, 10, 17, 60, 62, 65, 74, 78, 80
434.90	Occlusion, unspecified, without mention of cerebral infarction, arteries, cerebral	11, 60, 62, 65, 74, 78, 80

* Code Range

Code	Narrative	Page
434.91	Occlusion, unspecified, with cerebral infarction, arteries, cerebral	8, 10, 17, 60, 62, 65, 74, 78, 80
*435	Ischemia, transient, cerebral	17
436	Disease, acute, but ill-defined, cerebrovascular	11, 60, 62, 65, 74, 78, 80, 83, 219, 226
437.0	Atherosclerosis, cerebral	11
437.1	Disease, other, general, ischemic, cerebrovascular	17
437.2	Encephalopathy, hypertensive	13
437.3	Aneurysm, nonruptured, brain	16
437.4	Arteritis, cerebral	13
437.5	Disease, Moyamoya	16
437.6	Thrombosis, nonpyogenic, intracranial venous sinus	16
437.7	Amnesia, transient global	11
437.8	Disease, other, cerebrovascular	11
437.9	Disease, unspecified, cerebrovascular	11
*438	Disease, late effects, cerebrovascular	10
440.0	Atherosclerosis, aorta	86
440.1	Arteriosclerosis, renal artery	165
*440.2	Atherosclerosis, native arteries, extremities	86
440.24	Atherosclerosis, native arteries, extremities, with gangrene	219, 226
*440.3	Atherosclerosis, bypass graft, extremities	86
440.8	Atherosclerosis, arteries, other specified	86
440.9	Atherosclerosis, generalized and unspecified	86
*441.0	Aneurysm, dissecting, aorta	83, 86
441.00	Dissecting aortic aneurysm (any part), unspecified site	59, 62, 64, 73, 77, 79
441.01	Dissecting aortic aneurysm (any part), thoracic	59, 62, 64, 73, 77, 79
441.02	Dissecting aortic aneurysm (any part), abdominal	59, 62, 64, 73, 77, 79
441.03	Dissecting aortic aneurysm (any part), thoracoabdominal	59, 62, 64, 73, 77, 79
441.1	Aneurysm, ruptured, aorta, thoracic	59, 62, 64, 73, 77, 79, 86
441.2	Aneurysm, without rupture, aorta, thoracic	86
441.3	Aneurysm, ruptured, aorta, abdominal	59, 62, 64, 73, 77, 79, 86
441.4	Aneurysm, without rupture, aorta, abdominal	86
441.5	Aneurysm, ruptured, aorta, unspecified site	59, 62, 64, 73, 77, 79, 86
441.6	Aneurysm, ruptured, aorta, thoracoabdominal	59, 62, 64, 73, 77, 79, 86
441.7	Aneurysm, without rupture, aorta, thoracoabdominal	86
441.9	Aneurysm, without rupture, aorta, unspecified site	86
442.0	Aneurysm, artery, extremity, upper	86
442.1	Aneurysm, artery, renal	165
442.2	Aneurysm, artery, iliac	86
442.3	Aneurysm, artery, extremity, lower	86
*442.8	Aneurysm, artery, other specified	86
442.9	Aneurysm, artery, unspecified site	86
443.0	Syndrome, Raynaud's	128
443.1	Thrombangiitis obliterans, Buerger's disease	86
443.21	Dissection, carotid artery	86
443.22	Dissection, iliac artery	59, 62, 64, 73, 77, 79, 86
443.23	Dissection, renal artery	165
443.24	Dissection, vertebral artery	86
443.29	Dissection, other artery	59, 62, 64, 73, 77, 80, 86
*443.8	Diseases, vascular, peripheral, specified type	86
443.9	Disease, vascular, peripheral, unspecified type	86
*444	Embolism and thrombosis, arterial	219, 226
444.0	Embolism and thrombosis, arterial, aorta, abdominal	59, 62, 64, 73, 77, 80, 86
444.1	Embolism and thrombosis, arterial, aorta, thoracic	59, 62, 64, 73, 77, 80, 86
*444.2	Embolism and thrombosis, arterial, extremities	86
*444.8	Embolism and thrombosis, arterial, other specified artery	86
444.9	Embolism and thrombosis, arterial, unspecified	86
*445.0	Atheroembolism, extremities	86
445.81	Atheroembolism, kidney	60, 62, 65, 74, 78, 80, 165
445.89	Atheroembolism, other site	86
446.0	Polyarteritis nodosa	128
446.1	Syndrome, mucocutaneous lymph node (MCLS), acute, febrile	128
*446.2	Angiitis, hypersensitivity	128
446.3	Granuloma, lethal, midline	127
446.4	Granulomatosis, Wegener's	127
446.5	Arteritis, giant cell	128
446.6	Microangiopathy, thrombotic	128
446.7	Disease, Takayasu's	128
447.0	Fistula, acquired, arteriovenous	86
447.1	Stricture, artery	86
447.2	Rupture, artery	86
447.3	Hyperplasia, renal artery	165

** Code Range*

Code	Narrative	Page
447.4	Syndrome, celiac, artery compression	102
447.5	Necrosis, artery	86
447.6	Arteritis, unspecified	128
447.8	Disorders, other specified, arteries and arterioles	86
447.9	Disorders, unspecified, arteries and arterioles	86
448.0	Telangiectasis, hereditary, hemorrhagic	86
448.1	Nevus, nonneoplastic	147
448.9	Disease, other, unspecified, capillary	86
451.0	Phlebitis and thrombophlebitis, superficial vessels, lower extremities	87
*451.1	Phlebitis and thrombophlebitis, deep vessels, lower extremities	86, 219, 226
451.2	Phlebitis and thrombophlebitis, deep vessels, unspecified, lower extremities	86, 219, 226
451.81	Phlebitis and thrombophlebitis, iliac vein	86, 219, 226
451.82	Phlebitis and thrombophlebitis, superficial veins, upper extremities	87
451.83	Phlebitis and thrombophlebitis, deep veins, upper extremities	87
451.84	Phlebitis and thrombophlebitis, unspecified, upper extremities	87
451.89	Phlebitis and thrombophlebitis, other sites	87
451.9	Phlebitis and thrombophlebitis, unspecified site	87
452	Thrombosis, portal vein	111
453.0	Syndrome, Budd-Chiari	111
453.1	Thrombophlebitis migrans	87
453.2	Embolism and thrombosis, vena cava	59, 62, 64, 73, 77, 80, 86, 219, 226
453.3	Embolism and thrombosis, renal vein	165
*453.4	Embolism and thrombosis, venous, deep vessels, lower extremity	87
453.8	Embolism and thrombosis, other specified veins	87
453.9	Embolism and thrombosis, vein, unspecified site	87
454.0	Varicose veins, lower extremities, with ulcer	87
454.1	Varicose veins, lower extremities, with inflammation	87
454.2	Varicose veins, lower extremities, with ulcer and inflammation	87
454.8	Varicose, veins, lower extremities, with other complications	87
454.9	Varicose veins, asymptomatic	87
*455	Hemorrhoid	104
456.0	Varices, esophageal, with bleeding	99
456.1	Varices, esophageal, without bleeding	104
*456.2	Varices, esophageal, in diseases classified elsewhere	104
456.3	Varices, sublingual	87
456.4	Varices, scrotal	172
456.5	Varices, pelvic	172, 176, 183
456.6	Varices, vulva	176, 183
456.8	Varices, other sites	87
457.0	Syndrome, postmastectomy lymphedema	143
457.1	Lymphedema, other	147
457.2	Lymphangitis	143, 219, 226
457.8	Disorders, noninfectious, other, lymphatic channels	235
457.9	Disorders, noninfectious, unspecified, lymphatic channels	235
458.0	Hypotension, orthostatic	89
458.1	Hypotension, chronic	91
*458.2	Hypotension, iatrogenic	89
458.8	Hypotension, other specified	83, 91
458.9	Hypotension, unspecified	83, 91
459.0	Hemorrhage, unspecified	91, 219, 226
*459.1	Syndrome, postphlebitic	87
459.2	Compression, vein	87
*459.3	Hypertension, venous, chronic (idiopathic)	87
459.81	Insufficiency, venous, peripheral, unspecified	87
459.89	Disorders, other specified, circulatory system	87
459.9	Disorder, unspecified, circulatory system	87
460	Nasopharyngitis, acute, common cold	34, 319
*461	Sinusitis, acute	34
462	Pharyngitis, acute	34, 319
463	Tonsillitis, acute	34, 319
464.00	Laryngitis, acute, without obstruction	34, 319
464.01	Laryngitis, acute, with obstruction	34, 319
*464.1	Tracheitis, acute	46
*464.2	Laryngotracheitis, acute	35, 319
*464.3	Epiglottitis, acute	33, 319
464.4	Croup	35, 319
464.50	Supraglottitis, unspecified, without obstruction	34, 319
464.51	Supraglottitis, unspecified, with obstruction	34, 319
*465	Infections, acute, respiratory, upper, multiple or unspecified sites	34, 319
*466	Bronchitis and bronchiolitis, acute	46
470	Deviated, septum, nasal	35, 319
*471	Polyps, nasal	36
*472	Pharyngitis and nasopharyngitis, chronic	34

*Code Range

Code	Narrative	Page
472.1	Pharyngitis, chronic	319
472.2	Nasopharyngitis, chronic	319
*473	Sinusitis, chronic	34
*474	Disease, chronic, tonsils and adenoids	319
474.00	Tonsillitis, chronic	34
474.01	Adenoiditis, chronic	34
474.02	Adenoiditis and tonsillitis, chronic	34
*474.1	Hypertrophy, tonsils and adenoids	36
474.2	Vegetations, adenoid	36
474.8	Disease, other, chronic, tonsils and adenoids	36
474.9	Disease, unspecified, chronic, tonsils and adenoids	36
475	Abscess, peritonsillar	34, 319
*476	Laryngitis and laryngotracheitis, chronic	34
476.0	Laryngitis, chronic	319
476.1	Laryngotracheitis, chronic	319
*477	Rhinitis, allergic	34
478.0	Hypertrophy, nasal turbinates	36
478.1	Diseases, other, nasal cavity and sinuses	36, 230
*478.2	Diseases, other, pharynx, not elsewhere classified	319
478.20	Disease, unspecified, pharynx	36
478.21	Cellulitis, pharynx or nasopharynx	34
478.22	Abscess, parapharyngeal	34, 219, 226
478.24	Abscess, retropharyngeal	34, 219, 226
478.25	Edema, pharynx or nasopharynx	36
478.26	Cyst, pharynx or nasopharynx	36
478.29	Disease, other, pharynx or nasopharynx	36
*478.3	Paralysis, vocal cords or larynx	36, 219, 226, 319
478.4	Polyp, vocal cord or larynx	36, 319
478.5	Diseases, other, vocal cords	36, 319
478.6	Edema, larynx	36, 319
*478.7	Diseases, other, larynx, not elsewhere classified	319
478.70	Disease, unspecified, larynx	36
478.71	Cellulitis and perichondritis, larynx	34
478.74	Stenosis, larynx	36
478.75	Spasm, laryngeal	36, 219, 226
478.79	Diseases, other, larynx	36
478.8	Hypersensitivity, reaction, upper respiratory tract, site unspecified	34, 319
478.9	Diseases, other and unspecified, upper respiratory tract	34, 319
*480	Pneumonia, viral	45
480.3	Pneumonia, viral, due to SARS-associated coronavirus	309
480.8	Pneumonia, viral, due to other specified virus	309
480.9	Pneumonia, viral, unspecified	309
481	Pneumonia, pneumococcal	45, 83, 219, 226, 309
*482	Pneumonia, other, bacterial	83, 219, 226, 309
482.0	Pneumonia, bacterial, due to Klebsiella pneumoniae	42
482.1	Pneumonia, bacterial, due to Pseudomonas	42
482.2	Pneumonia, bacterial, due to Hemophilus influenzae	45
*482.3	Pneumonia, bacterial, due to Streptococcus	45
*482.4	Pneumonia, bacterial, Staphylococcus	42
*482.8	Pneumonia, bacterial, other specified	42
482.9	Pneumonia, bacterial, unspecified	45
*483	Pneumonia, due to other specified organism	45, 83, 219, 226
*484	Pneumonia, in infectious diseases classified elsewhere	42, 83
485	Bronchopneumonia, organism unspecified	45, 83, 219, 226
486	Pneumonia, organism unspecified	45, 83, 219, 226, 309
487.0	Influenza, with pneumonia	45, 83
487.1	Influenza, with respiratory manifestations	34
487.8	Influenza with other manifestations	247
490	Bronchitis, not specified as acute or chronic	46
491.0	Bronchitis, chronic, simple	46
491.1	Bronchitis, chronic, mucopurulent	44
*491.2	Bronchitis, chronic, obstructive	44
491.8	Bronchitis, chronic, other	44
491.9	Bronchitis, chronic, unspecified	44
492.0	Bleb, emphysematous	44
492.8	Emphysema, other	44
*493.0	Asthma, extrinsic	46
493.01	Asthma, extrinsic, with status asthmaticus	219, 227
*493.1	Asthma, intrinsic	46
493.11	Asthma, intrinsic, with status asthmaticus	220, 227
493.20	Asthma, chronic, obstructive, unspecified	44
493.21	Asthma, chronic, obstructive, with status asthmaticus	44
493.22	Asthma, chronic, obstructive, with (acute) exacerbation	44
*493.8	Asthma, other forms	46
*493.9	Asthma, unspecified	46
493.91	Asthma, unspecified, with status asthmaticus	220, 227
*494	Bronchiectasis	44
*495	Alveolitis, extrinsic allergic	45

* Code Range

Code	Narrative	Page
496	Obstruction, airway, chronic, not elsewhere classified	44
500	Pneumoconiosis, coal worker's	45
501	Asbestosis	45
502	Pneumoconiosis, due to silica or silicates, other	45
503	Pneumoconiosis, due to dust, inorganic, other	45
504	Pneumoconiosis, due to inhalation of dust, other	45
505	Pneumoconiosis, unspecified	45
506.0	Bronchitis and pneumonitis due to fumes, vapors, chemical	47
506.1	Edema, pulmonary, acute, due to fumes, vapors	44
506.2	Inflammation, upper respiratory, due to fumes, vapors	47
506.3	Conditions, respiratory, other acute, subacute, due to fumes, vapors	47
506.4	Conditions, respiratory, chronic, due to fumes, vapors	44
506.9	Conditions, respiratory, unspecified, due to fumes, vapors	45
*507	Pneumonitis, due to inhalation, solids, liquids	42, 83
507.0	Pneumonitis, due to inhalation, food, vomitus	220, 227
507.8	Pneumonitis, due to inhalation, other solids, liquids	220, 227
508.0	Condition, respiratory, acute, due to radiation	47, 220, 227
508.1	Condition, respiratory, chronic, other, due to radiation	45
508.8	Condition, respiratory, due to other specified agents, external	47
508.9	Condition, respiratory, due to unspecified agent, external	47
*510	Empyema	43, 220, 227
511.0	Pleurisy, without mention of effusion, current tuberculosis	45
511.1	Pleurisy, with effusion, bacterial, nontuberculous	43, 220, 227
511.8	Pleurisy, effusion, other specified forms, except tuberculosis	44, 220, 227
511.9	Effusion, pleural, unspecified	44, 220, 227
512.0	Pneumothorax, spontaneous tension	46
512.1	Pneumothorax, iatrogenic	46
512.8	Pneumothorax, other spontaneous	46
*513	Abscess, lung, mediastinum	43, 220, 227
514	Congestion, lung, hypostatic	44
515	Fibrosis, lung, postinflammatory	45
*516	Pneumopathy, other, alveolar and parietoalveolar	45
516.8	Pneumonopathies, alveolar and parietoalveolar, other specified	310

Code	Narrative	Page
517.1	Pneumonia, rheumatic, conditions classified elsewhere	45
517.2	Sclerosis, systemic, lung involvement, conditions classified elsewhere	45
517.3	Syndrome, acute chest	45
517.8	Involvement, lung, in other diseases classified elsewhere	45
518.0	Collapse, pulmonary	47, 83, 220, 227
518.1	Emphysema, interstitial	46, 220, 227
518.2	Emphysema, compensatory	47
518.3	Eosinophilia, pulmonary	45
518.4	Edema, lung, acute, unspecified	44, 220, 227
518.5	Insufficiency, pulmonary, following trauma and surgery	44, 83, 220, 227, 279
518.6	Aspergillosis, allergic bronchopulmonary	45
518.81	Failure, respiratory, acute	44, 83, 279
518.82	Insufficiency, pulmonary, other	46
518.83	Failure, respiratory, chronic	44, 83
518.84	Failure, respiratory, acute and chronic	44, 83, 279
518.89	Disease, other, not elsewhere classified, lung	47
*519.0	Complication, tracheostomy	47, 320
519.1	Disease, other, trachea, bronchus	46, 320
519.2	Mediastinitis	43, 220, 227
519.3	Disease, other, mediastinum	47
519.4	Disorders, diaphragm	47
519.8	Diseases, other, respiratory system	47
519.9	Disease, respiratory, unspecified	47
*520	Disorders, tooth development, eruption	37, 320
520.6	Disturbances, tooth eruption	230
*521	Diseases, tooth, hard tissue	37, 320
*522	Disease, tooth, pulp, periapical tissues	37, 320
*523	Disease, periodontal	37, 320
*524	Anomaly, dentofacial, including malocclusion	37, 320
*525	Diseases, conditions, other, teeth, supporting structures	37, 320
*526	Diseases, jaw	37, 320
*527	Disease, salivary glands	36, 320
527.9	Diseases, unspecified, salivary glands	310
*528	Diseases, soft tissues, oral, excluding lesions specific for gingiva, tongue	37, 320
528.6	Leukoplakia, oral mucosa, including tongue	310
*529	Diseases, conditions, other, tongue	37, 320

Numeric Index to Diseases

*Code Range

Code	Narrative	Page
530.0	Achalasia and cardiospasm	102
*530.1	Esophagitis	102
*530.2	Ulcer, esophagus	100
530.3	Stricture and stenosis, esophagus	102
530.4	Perforation, esophagus	102, 220, 227
530.5	Dyskinesia, esophagus	102
530.6	Diverticulum, esophagus, acquired	102
530.7	Syndrome, gastroesophageal, laceration, hemorrhage	99
530.81	Reflux, esophageal	102
530.82	Hemorrhage, esophageal	99
530.83	Leukoplakia, esophageal	102
530.84	Fistula, tracheoesophageal	102, 220, 227
530.85	Barrett's esophagus	100
530.86	Infection, esophagostomy	104
530.87	Complication, mechanical, esophagostomy	104
530.89	Disorder, other, esophagus	102
530.9	Disorder, unspecified, esophagus	102
*531.0	Ulcer, gastric, acute, with hemorrhage	99
*531.1	Ulcer, gastric, acute, with perforation	100
*531.2	Ulcer, gastric, acute, with hemorrhage and perforation	99
531.30	Ulcer, gastric, acute, without mention of hemorrhage and perforation, without mention of obstruction	101
531.31	Ulcer, gastric, acute, without mention of hemorrhage and perforation, with obstruction	100
*531.4	Ulcer, gastric, chronic or unspecified, with hemorrhage	99
*531.5	Ulcer, gastric, chronic or unspecified, with perforation	100
*531.6	Ulcer, gastric, chronic or unspecified, with hemorrhage and perforation	99
531.70	Ulcer, gastric, chronic, without mention of hemorrhage, perforation or obstruction	101
531.71	Ulcer, gastric, chronic, without mention of hemorrhage and perforation, with obstruction	100
531.90	Ulcer, gastric, unspecified as acute or chronic, without mention of hemorrhage, perforation or obstruction	101
531.91	Ulcer, gastric, unspecified as acute or chronic, without mention of hemorrhage or perforation, with obstruction	100
*532.0	Ulcer, duodenal, acute, with hemorrhage	99
*532.1	Ulcer, duodenal, acute, with perforation	100
*532.2	Ulcer, duodenal, acute, with hemorrhage and perforation	99
532.30	Ulcer, duodenal, acute, without mention of hemorrhage and perforation, without mention of obstruction	101
532.31	Ulcer, duodenal, acute, without mention of hemorrhage and perforation, with obstruction	100
*532.4	Ulcer, duodenal, chronic or unspecified, with hemorrhage	99
*532.5	Ulcer, duodenal, chronic or unspecified, with perforation	100
*532.6	Ulcer, duodenal, chronic or unspecified, with hemorrhage and perforation	100
532.70	Ulcer, duodenal, chronic, without mention of hemorrhage, perforation or obstruction	101
532.71	Ulcer, duodenal, chronic, without mention of hemorrhage and perforation, with obstruction	100
532.90	Ulcer, duodenal, unspecified as acute or chronic, without mention of hemorrhage, perforation or obstruction	101
532.91	Ulcer, duodenal, unspecified as acute or chronic, without mention of hemorrhage or perforation, with obstruction	100
*533.0	Ulcer, peptic, site unspecified, acute, with hemorrhage	100
*533.1	Ulcer, peptic, site unspecified, acute, with perforation	100
*533.2	Ulcer, peptic, site unspecified, acute, with hemorrhage and perforation	100
533.30	Ulcer, peptic, site unspecified, acute, without mention of hemorrhage and perforation, without mention of obstruction	101
533.31	Ulcer, peptic, site unspecified, acute, without mention of hemorrhage and perforation, with obstruction	100
*533.4	Ulcer, peptic, site unspecified, chronic or unspecified, with hemorrhage	100
*533.5	Ulcer, peptic, site unspecified, chronic or unspecified, with perforation	100
*533.6	Ulcer, peptic, site unspecified, chronic or unspecified, with hemorrhage and perforation	100
533.70	Ulcer, peptic, site unspecified, chronic, without mention of hemorrhage, perforation or obstruction	101
533.71	Ulcer, peptic, site unspecified, chronic, without mention of hemorrhage and perforation, with obstruction	100
533.90	Ulcer, peptic, site unspecified, unspecified as acute or chronic, without mention of hemorrhage, perforation or obstruction	101

*** Code Range**

Code	Narrative	Page
533.91	Ulcer, peptic, site unspecified, unspecified as acute or chronic, without mention of hemorrhage or perforation, with obstruction	100
*534.0	Ulcer, gastrojejunal, acute, with hemorrhage	100
*534.1	Ulcer, gastrojejunal, acute, with perforation	100
*534.2	Ulcer, gastrojejunal, acute, with hemorrhage and perforation	100
*534.3	Ulcer, gastrojejunal, acute, without mention of hemorrhage and perforation	100
*534.4	Ulcer, gastrojejunal, chronic or unspecified, with hemorrhage	100
*534.5	Ulcer, gastrojejunal, chronic or unspecified, with perforation	100
*534.6	Ulcer, gastrojejunal, chronic or unspecified, with hemorrhage and perforation	100
*534.7	Ulcer, gastrojejunal, chronic, without mention of hemorrhage and perforation	100
*534.9	Ulcer, gastrojejunal, unspecified as acute or chronic, without mention of hemorrhage or perforation	101
535.00	Gastritis, acute, without hemorrhage	102
535.01	Gastritis, acute, with hemorrhage	100
535.10	Gastritis, atrophic, without hemorrhage	102
535.11	Gastritis, atrophic, with hemorrhage	100
535.20	Hypertrophy, gastric mucosal, without hemorrhage	102
535.21	Hypertrophy, gastric mucosal, with hemorrhage	100
535.30	Gastritis, alcoholic, without hemorrhage	102
535.31	Gastritis, alcoholic, with hemorrhage	100
535.40	Gastritis, other specified, without hemorrhage	102
535.41	Gastritis, other specified, with hemorrhage	100
535.50	Gastritis and gastroduodenitis, unspecified, without hemorrhage	102
535.51	Gastritis and gastroduodenitis, unspecified, with hemorrhage	100
535.60	Duodenitis, without hemorrhage	102
535.61	Duodenitis, with hemorrhage	100
536.0	Achlorhydia	102
536.1	Dilation, stomach, acute	102, 220, 227
536.2	Vomiting, persistent	102
536.3	Gastroparesis	102
*536.4	Complication, gastrostomy	104
536.8	Dyspepsia and disorders of function, other specified, stomach	102
536.9	Disorder, function, stomach, unspecified	102
537.0	Stenosis, pyloric, acquired, hypertrophic	101
537.1	Diverticulum, gastric	102
537.2	Ileus, duodenal, chronic	102
537.3	Obstruction, duodenum, other	101
537.4	Fistula, stomach or duodenum	102
537.5	Gastroptosis	102
537.6	Stricture or stenosis, hourglass, stomach	102
537.81	Pylorospasm	102
537.82	Angiodysplasia, stomach and duodenum, without hemorrhage	102
537.83	Angiodysplasia, stomach and duodenum, with hemorrhage	100
537.84	Dieulafoy lesion (hemorrhagic), stomach and duodenum	100
537.89	Disorder, other specified, stomach and duodenum	102
537.9	Disorder, unspecified, stomach and duodenum	102
*540	Appendicitis, acute	104
540.0	Appendicitis, acute, with peritonitis, generalized	96
540.1	Appendicitis, acute, with peritoneal abscess	96
541	Appendicitis, unqualified	104
542	Appendicitis, other	104
*543	Disease, other, appendix	104
*550	Hernia, inguinal	104
550.00	Hernia, inguinal, with gangrene, unilateral or unspecified, not specified as recurrent	220, 227
550.02	Hernia, inguinal, with gangrene, bilateral, not specified as recurrent	220, 227
550.10	Hernia, inguinal, with obstruction, without mention of gangrene, unilateral or unspecified, not specified as recurrent	220, 227
550.12	Hernia, inguinal, with obstruction, without mention of gangrene, bilateral, not specified as recurrent	220, 227
*551	Hernia, other, abdominal cavity, with gangrene	104
551.00	Hernia, femoral, with gangrene, unilateral or unspecified, not specified as recurrent	220, 227
551.02	Hernia, femoral, with gangrene, bilateral, not specified as recurrent	220, 227
551.1	Hernia, umbilical, with gangrene	220, 227
*551.2	Hernia, ventral, with gangrene	220, 227
551.3	Hernia, diaphragmatic, with gangrene	220, 227
551.8	Hernia, other specified sites, with gangrene	220, 227
551.9	Hernia, unspecified site, with gangrene	220, 227
*552.0	Hernia, femoral, with obstruction	104
552.00	Hernia, femoral, with obstruction, unilateral or unspecified, not specified as recurrent	220, 227

** Code Range*

Code	Narrative	Page
552.02	Hernia, femoral, with obstruction, bilateral, not specified as recurrent	220, 227
552.1	Hernia, umbilical, with obstruction	104, 220, 227
*552.2	Hernia, ventral, with obstruction	104, 220, 227
552.3	Hernia, diaphragmatic, with obstruction	102, 220, 227
552.8	Hernia, other specified sites, with obstruction	104, 220, 227
552.9	Hernia, unspecified site, with obstruction	104, 220, 227
*553.0	Hernia, femoral	104
553.1	Hernia, umbilical	104
*553.2	Hernia, ventral, without mention of obstruction or gangrene	104
553.3	Hernia, diaphragmatic	102
553.8	Hernia, abdominal cavity, without mention of obstruction or gangrene, other specified sites	104
553.9	Hernia, abdominal cavity, without mention of obstruction or gangrene, unspecified site	104
*555	Enteritis, regional	101
*556	Enterocolitis, ulcerative	101
*557	Insufficiency, vascular, intestine	104
557.0	Insufficiency, acute, vascular, intestine	220, 227
*558	Gastroenteritis and colitis, other, noninfectious	310
558.1	Gastroenteritis and colitis, due to radiation	104
558.2	Gastroenteritis and colitis, toxic	104, 220, 227
558.3	Gastroenteritis and colitis, allergic	102
558.9	Gastroenteritis and colitis, noninfectious, other and unspecified	102
*560	Obstruction, intestinal, without mention of hernia	101
560.0	Intussusception	220, 227
560.1	Ileus, paralytic	220, 227
560.2	Volvulus	220, 227
560.30	Impaction, intestine, unspecified	220, 227
560.39	Impaction, intestine, other	220, 227
560.89	Obstruction, intestinal, other specified	220, 227
560.9	Obstruction, intestinal, unspecified	220, 227
562.00	Diverticulosis, small intestine, without hemorrhage	103
562.01	Diverticulitis, small intestine, without hemorrhage	103
562.02	Diverticulosis, small intestine, with hemorrhage	100
562.03	Diverticulitis, small intestine, with hemorrhage	100
562.10	Diverticulosis, colon, without hemorrhage	103
562.11	Diverticulitis, colon, without hemorrhage	103
562.12	Diverticulosis, colon, with hemorrhage	100
562.13	Diverticulitis, colon, with hemorrhage	100
*564.0	Constipation	103
564.1	Syndrome, irritable bowel	103
564.2	Syndrome, postgastric surgery	103
564.3	Vomiting, bilious following gastrointestinal surgery	103
564.4	Diarrhea, functional, following gastrointestinal surgery	103
564.5	Diarrhea, functional	103
564.6	Spasm, anal	103
564.7	Megacolon, other than Hirschsprung's disease	104
*564.8	Syndrome, functional, bowel, other, specified	103
564.9	Syndrome, functional, bowel, unspecified	103
*565	Fissure and fistula, anal	104
566	Abscess, anal and rectal regions	104, 220, 227
*567	Peritonitis and retroperitoneal infections	104, 220, 227
*567.2	Other suppurative peritonitis	215, 222
*567.3	Infections, retroperitoneal	215, 222
*567.8	Other specified peritonitis	215, 222
*568	Disorder, peritoneum, other	104
568.81	Hemoperitoneum, nontraumatic	220, 227
569.0	Polyp, anal and rectal	104
569.1	Prolapse, rectal	104
569.2	Stenosis, rectum and anus	104
569.3	Hemorrhage, rectum and anus	100, 220, 227
*569.4	Disorders, other specified, rectum and anus	104
569.5	Abscess, intestine	104
*569.6	Complications, colostomy and enterostomy	104
569.81	Fistula, intestine, excluding rectum and anus	104
569.82	Ulceration, intestine	104
569.83	Perforation, intestine	104, 220, 227
569.84	Angiodysplasia, intestine, without hemorrhage	104
569.85	Angiodysplasia, intestine, with hemorrhage	100
569.86	Dieulafoy lesion (hemorrhagic), intestine	104
569.89	Disorder, intestine, other	104
569.9	Disorder, intestine, unspecified	104
570	Necrosis, liver, acute and subacute	111, 220, 227
571.0	Cirrhosis, fatty, alcoholic	111
571.1	Hepatitis, acute, alcoholic	110

*** Code Range**

Code	Narrative	Page
571.2	Cirrhosis, liver, alcoholic	110
571.3	Damage, liver, alcoholic, unspecified	110
*571.4	Hepatitis, chronic	111
571.5	Cirrhosis, liver, without mention of alcohol	110
571.6	Cirrhosis, biliary	110
571.8	Disease, liver, chronic, nonalcoholic, other	111
571.9	Disease, liver, chronic, without mention of alcohol, unspecified	111
*572	Abscess, liver and sequela of chronic liver disease	111
572.0	Abscess, liver	220, 227
572.1	Pyemia, portal	220, 227
572.2	Coma, hepatic	220, 227
572.4	Syndrome, hepatorenal	220, 227
*573	Disorders, other, liver	111
573.3	Hepatitis, unspecified	220, 227
573.4	Infarction, hepatic	220, 227
*574	Cholelithiasis	111
*575	Disorders, other, gallbladder	111
*576	Disorders, other, biliary tract	111
576.1	Cholangitis	220, 227
*577	Diseases, pancreas	110
577.0	Pancreatitis, acute	220, 227
577.2	Cyst and pseudocyst, pancreas	220, 227
*578	Hemorrhage, gastrointestinal	100, 221, 228
*579	Malabsorption, intestinal	103
579.3	Malabsorption, postsurgical, other and unspecified	221, 228
579.9	Malabsorption, unspecified, intestinal	310
*580	Glomerulonephritis, acute	165, 221, 228, 310
*581	Syndrome, nephrotic	165, 310
*582	Glomerulonephritis, chronic	165, 310
*583	Nephritis and nephropathy, not specified as acute or chronic	165, 310
*584	Failure, renal, acute	221, 228
584.5	Failure, renal, acute, with lesion of tubular necrosis	83, 161, 162
584.6	Failure, renal, acute, with lesion of necrosis, cortical	83, 161, 162
584.7	Failure, renal, acute, with lesion of necrosis, medullary	83, 161, 162
584.8	Failure, renal, acute, with other specified pathological lesion	83, 161, 162
584.9	Failure, renal, acute, unspecified	83, 161, 162
*585	Chronic kidney disease (CKD)	161, 162, 322
586	Failure, renal, unspecified	161, 162
587	Sclerosis, unspecified, renal	165
*588	Disorders from impairment, function, renal disorders	165
*589	Small kidney, unknown cause	165
*590	Infections, kidney	163
*590.1	Pyelonephritis, acute	221, 228
590.2	Abscess, renal and perinephric	221, 228
590.3	Pyeloureteritis cystica	221, 228
*590.8	Pyelonephritis, pyelonephrosis, other, not specified as acute or chronic	221, 228
590.9	Infection, kidney, unspecified	221, 228
591	Hydronephrosis	163, 221, 228
*592	Calculus, kidney and ureter	163
593.0	Nephroptosis	165
593.1	Hypertrophy, kidney	165
593.2	Cyst, acquired, kidney	165
593.3	Stricture or kinking, ureter	163
593.4	Obstruction, other, ureteric	163
593.5	Hydroureter	163, 221, 228
593.6	Proteinuria, postural	165
*593.7	Reflux, vesicoureteral	165
*593.8	Disorders, other specified, kidney and ureter	165
593.9	Disorder, unspecified, kidney and ureter	165
594.0	Calculus, bladder, diverticulum	165
594.1	Calculus, other, bladder	163
594.2	Calculus, urethra	163
594.8	Calculus, urinary tract, lower, specified site	163
594.9	Calculus, urinary tract, lower, unspecified	163
595.0	Cystitis, acute	163, 221, 228
595.1	Cystitis, interstitial, chronic	163
595.2	Cystitis, chronic, other	163
595.3	Trigonitis	163
595.4	Cystitis, in diseases classified elsewhere	163, 221, 228
595.81	Cystitis, cystica	163, 221, 228
595.82	Cystitis, irradiation	165
595.89	Cystitis, other specified types	163, 221, 228
595.9	Cystitis, unspecified	163, 221, 228
*596	Disorder, bladder	165
596.0	Obstruction, bladder neck	221, 228
596.1	Fistula, intestinovesical	221, 228
596.2	Fistula, vesical, NEC	221, 228
596.4	Atony, bladder	221, 228
596.6	Rupture, nontraumatic, bladder	221, 228
596.7	Hemorrhage, into bladder wall	221, 228
*597	Urethritis, not sexually transmitted, urethral syndrome	163
597.0	Abscess, urethral	221, 228

*** Code Range**

Code	Narrative	Page
*598	Stricture, urethral	164
599.0	Infection, urinary tract, site not specified	163, 221, 228
599.1	Fistula, urethral	165
599.2	Diverticulum, urethral	165
599.3	Caruncle, urethral	165
599.4	Passage, false, urethral	165
599.5	Prolapse, mucosa, urethral	165
*599.6	Obstruction, urinary	165, 221, 228
599.7	Hematuria	164, 221, 228
*599.8	Disorder, urethra and urinary tract, other specified	165
599.9	Disorders, unspecified, urethra and urinary tract	165
*600	Hyperplasia, prostate	171
*601	Inflammation, prostate	172
*602	Disorder, other, prostate	172
603.0	Hydrocele, encysted	172
603.1	Hydrocele, infected	172
603.8	Hydrocele, other specified types	172
603.9	Hydrocele, unspecified	172
*604	Orchitis and epididymitis	172
605	Redundant, prepuce and phimosis	172, 230
*606	Infertility, male	172
607.0	Leukoplakia, penis	172
607.1	Balanoposthitis	172
607.2	Inflammation, penis	172
607.3	Priapism	172
607.81	Balanitis xerotica obliterans	172
607.82	Disorder, vascular, penis	172
607.83	Edema, penis	172
607.84	Impotence, organic origin	172
607.85	Disease, Peyronie's	172
607.89	Disorder, other specified, penis	172
607.9	Disorder, unspecified, penis	172
608.0	Vesiculitis, seminal	172
608.1	Spermatocele	172
608.2	Torsion, testis	172
608.3	Atrophy, testis	172
608.4	Inflammation, genital organs, male	172
*608.8	Disorders, other specified, genital organs, male	172
608.9	Disorder, unspecified, genital organs, male	172
*610	Dysplasia, benign , mammary	143
*611	Disorders, other, breast	143
*614	Disease, inflammatory, of ovary, fallopian tube, pelvic cellular tissue and peritoneum	177
614.0	Salpingo-oophoritis, acute	182
614.1	Salpingo-oophoritis, chronic	182
614.2	Salpingo-oophoritis, unspecified	182
614.3	Parametritis, acute	182
614.4	Parametritis, chronic	183
614.5	Peritonitis, acute, pelvic, female	183
614.6	Adhesions, peritoneal, pelvic, female	183
614.7	Peritonitis, chronic, pelvic, female	183
614.8	Disease, pelvic, inflammatory, female, other	183
614.9	Disease, pelvic, inflammatory, female, unspecified	183
*615	Disease, inflammatory, uterus, except cervix	177, 183
616.0	Cervicitis and endocervicitis	177, 183
*616.1	Vaginitis and vulvovaginitis	177, 183
616.2	Cyst, gland or duct, Bartholin's	177, 183
616.3	Abscess, gland, Bartholin's	177, 183
616.4	Abscess, other, vulva	177, 183
*616.5	Ulceration, vulva	177, 183
616.8	Disease, other specified, inflammatory, cervix, vagina, vulva	177, 183
616.9	Disease, unspecified, inflammatory, cervix, vagina, vulva	177, 183
617.0	Endometriosis, uterus	177, 183
617.1	Endometriosis, ovary	177, 183
617.2	Endometriosis, fallopian tube	177, 183
617.3	Endometriosis, pelvic peritoneum	177, 183
617.4	Endometriosis, vaginal	177, 183
617.5	Endometriosis, intestinal	103
617.6	Endometriosis, skin scar	147
617.8	Endometriosis, site, other specified	177, 183
617.9	Endometriosis, site, unspecified	177, 183
*618	Prolapse, genital	177, 183
619.0	Fistula, urinary-genital tract, female	177, 183
619.1	Fistula, digestive-genital tract, female	104, 221, 228
619.2	Fistula, skin-genital tract, female	177, 183
619.8	Fistula, other specified, genital tract, female	177, 183, 221, 228
619.9	Fistula, unspecified, genital tract, female	177, 183
*620	Disorders, noninflammatory, ovary, fallopian tube, broad ligament	177, 183
620.7	Hematoma, broad ligament	221, 228
*621	Disorders, uterus, not elsewhere classified	177, 183
*622	Disorders, noninflammatory, cervix	177, 183
*623	Disorders, noninflammatory, vagina	177, 183
623.8	Disorder, other specified, noninflammatory, vagina	230
*624	Disorders, noninflammatory, vulva and perineum	177, 183
*625	Pain, other symptoms, genital organs, female	177, 183
*626	Disorder, menstruation, abnormal bleeding, genital tract, female	177, 183

Numeric Index to Diseases

Code	Narrative	Page
*627	Disorders, menopausal and postmenopausal	177, 183
*628	Infertility, female	177, 183
*629	Disorders, other, genital organs, female	177, 183
630	Mole, hydatidiform	206
631	Abnormal, other, product of conception	206
632	Abortion, missed	206
*633	Pregnancy, ectopic	205
*634	Abortion, spontaneous	206
*635	Abortion, induced, legally	206
*636	Abortion, induced, illegally	206
*637	Abortion, unspecified	206
*638	Abortion, failed attempted	206
*639	Complication, abortion or ectopic and molar pregnancies	203
640.00	Abortion, threatened, unspecified as to episode of care	205
640.01	Abortion, threatened, delivered, with or without mention of antepartum condition	185, 197
640.03	Abortion, threatened, antepartum condition or complication	205
640.80	Hemorrhage, other specified, early pregnancy, unspecified as to episode of care	205
640.81	Hemorrhage, other specified, early pregnancy, delivered, with or without mention of antepartum condition	185, 197
640.83	Hemorrhage, other specified, early pregnancy, antepartum condition or complication	205
640.90	Hemorrhage, unspecified, early pregnancy, unspecified as to episode of care	206
640.91	Hemorrhage, unspecified, early pregnancy, delivered, with or without mention of antepartum condition	185, 197
640.93	Hemorrhage, unspecified, early pregnancy, antepartum condition or complication	206
641.00	Placenta previa, without hemorrhage, unspecified as to episode of care	211
641.01	Placenta previa, without hemorrhage, delivered, with or without mention of antepartum condition	185, 195
641.03	Placenta previa, without hemorrhage, antepartum complication	206
641.10	Placenta previa, hemorrhage, unspecified as to episode of care	211
641.11	Placenta previa, hemorrhage, delivered, with or without mention of antepartum condition	185, 195
641.13	Placenta previa, hemorrhage, antepartum complication	206
641.20	Separation, premature, placenta, unspecified as to episode of care	211
641.21	Separation, premature, placenta, delivered, with or without mention of antepartum condition	185, 195
641.23	Separation, premature, placenta, antepartum complication	206
641.30	Hemorrhage, antepartum, coagulation defects, unspecified as to episode of care	210, 211
641.31	Hemorrhage, antepartum, coagulation defects, delivered, with or without mention of antepartum condition	185, 195
641.33	Hemorrhage, antepartum, coagulation defects, antepartum complication	206, 210
641.80	Hemorrhage, antepartum, other, unspecified as to episode of care	211
641.81	Hemorrhage, antepartum, other, delivered, with or without mention of antepartum condition	185, 195
641.83	Hemorrhage, antepartum, other, antepartum complication	206
641.90	Hemorrhage, antepartum, unspecified, unspecified as to episode of care	211
641.91	Hemorrhage, antepartum, unspecified, delivered, with or without mention of antepartum condition	185, 195
641.93	Hemorrhage, antepartum, unspecified, antepartum complication	206
642.00	Hypertension, benign essential, complicating pregnancy, childbirth, and the puerperium, unspecified as to episode of care	211
642.01	Hypertension, benign essential, complicating pregnancy, childbirth, and the puerperium, delivered, with or without mention of antepartum condition	185, 195
642.02	Hypertension, benign essential, complicating pregnancy, childbirth, and the puerperium, delivered, with mention of postpartum complication	185, 195
642.03	Hypertension, benign essential, complicating pregnancy, childbirth, and the puerperium, antepartum condition or complication	206, 210
642.04	Hypertension, benign essential, complicating pregnancy, childbirth, and the puerperium, postpartum complication	203
642.10	Hypertension, secondary to renal disease, complicating pregnancy, childbirth, and the puerperium, unspecified as to episode of care	211
642.11	Hypertension, secondary to renal disease, complicating pregnancy, childbirth, and the puerperium, delivered, with or without mention of antepartum condition	185, 195

** Code Range*

Numeric Index to Diseases

Code	Narrative	Page
642.70	Pre-eclampsia or eclampsia, with pre-existing hypertension, complicating pregnancy, childbirth, and the puerperium, unspecified as to episode of care	210, 211
642.71	Pre-eclampsia or eclampsia, with pre-existing hypertension, complicating pregnancy, childbirth, and the puerperium, delivered, with or without mention of antepartum condition	185, 195
642.72	Pre-eclampsia or eclampsia, with pre-existing hypertension, complicating pregnancy, childbirth, and the puerperium, delivered, with mention of postpartum complication	185, 195
642.73	Pre-eclampsia or eclampsia, with pre-existing hypertension, complicating pregnancy, childbirth, and the puerperium, antepartum condition or complication	206, 210
642.74	Pre-eclampsia or eclampsia, with pre-existing hypertension, complicating pregnancy, childbirth, and the puerperium, postpartum complication	203
642.90	Hypertension, unspecified, complicating pregnancy, childbirth, and the puerperium, unspecified as to episode of care	211
642.91	Hypertension, unspecified, complicating pregnancy, childbirth, and the puerperium, delivered, with or without mention of antepartum condition	185, 195
642.92	Hypertension, unspecified, complicating pregnancy, childbirth, and the puerperium, delivered, with mention of postpartum complication	185, 195
642.93	Hypertension, unspecified, complicating pregnancy, childbirth, and the puerperium, antepartum condition or complication	206, 210
642.94	Hypertension, unspecified, complicating pregnancy, childbirth, and the puerperium, postpartum complication	203
643.00	Hyperemesis, gravidarum, mild, unspecified as to episode of care	210, 211
643.01	Hyperemesis, gravidarum, mild, delivered, with or without mention of antepartum condition	185, 197
643.03	Hyperemesis, gravidarum, mild, antepartum complication	206, 210
643.10	Hyperemesis, gravidarum, with metabolic disturbance, unspecified as to episode of care	210, 211
643.11	Hyperemesis, gravidarum, with metabolic disturbance, delivered, with or without mention of antepartum condition	185, 197
643.13	Hyperemesis, gravidarum, with metabolic disturbance, antepartum complication	206, 210
643.20	Vomiting, late, in pregnancy, unspecified as to episode of care	210, 211
643.21	Vomiting, late, in pregnancy, delivered, with or without mention of antepartum condition	185, 197
643.23	Vomiting, late, in pregnancy, antepartum complication	206, 210
643.80	Vomiting, other, complicating pregnancy, unspecified as to episode of care	210, 211
643.81	Vomiting, other, complicating pregnancy, delivered, with or without mention of antepartum condition	185, 197
643.83	Vomiting, other, complicating pregnancy, antepartum complication	206, 210
643.90	Vomiting, unspecified, in pregnancy, unspecified as to episode of care	210, 211
643.91	Vomiting, unspecified, in pregnancy, delivered, with or without mention of antepartum condition	185, 197
643.93	Vomiting, unspecified, in pregnancy, antepartum complication	206, 210
644.00	Labor, premature, threatened, unspecified as to episode of care	206
644.03	Labor, premature, threatened, antepartum condition	206
644.10	Labor, other, threatened, unspecified as to episode of care	206
644.13	Labor, other, threatened, antepartum condition	206
644.20	Delivery, early onset, unspecified as to episode of care	206
644.21	Delivery, early onset, with or without mention of antepartum condition	185, 197
645.10	Pregnancy, post-term, unspecified as to episode of care	211
645.11	Pregnancy, post-term, delivered, with or without mention of antepartum condition	185, 197
645.13	Pregnancy, post-term, antepartum condition or complication	206
645.20	Pregnancy, prolonged, unspecified as to episode of care	211
645.21	Pregnancy, prolonged, delivered, with or without mention of antepartum condition	185, 198
645.23	Pregnancy, prolonged, antepartum condition or complication	206
646.00	Papyraceous fetus, unspecified as to episode of care	185, 198
646.01	Papyraceous fetus, delivered, with or without mention of antepartum condition	185, 198
646.03	Papyraceous fetus, antepartum condition or complication	206
646.10	Edema, excessive weight gain in pregnancy, without hypertension, unspecified as to episode of care	210, 211

Code	Narrative	Page
646.11	Edema or excessive weight gain in pregnancy, without hypertension, with delivery, with or without mention of antepartum complication	185, 198
646.12	Edema or excessive weight gain in pregnancy, without hypertension, with delivery, with current postpartum complication	185, 198
646.13	Edema or excessive weight gain in pregnancy, without hypertension, antepartum condition or complication	206, 210
646.14	Edema or excessive weight gain in pregnancy, without hypertension, with delivery, with postpartum condition or complication	203
646.20	Pregnancy, complicated by renal disease, unspecified, without hypertension, unspecified as to episode of care	210, 211
646.21	Pregnancy, complicated by renal disease, unspecified, without hypertension, delivered, with or without mention of antepartum condition	185, 198
646.22	Pregnancy, complicated by renal disease, unspecified, without hypertension, delivered, with mention of postpartum complication	185, 198
646.23	Pregnancy, complicated by renal disease, unspecified, without hypertension, antepartum condition or complication	206, 210
646.24	Pregnancy, complicated by renal disease, unspecified, without hypertension, postpartum condition or complication	203
646.30	Pregnancy complicated, habitual aborter, unspecified as to episode of care	211
646.31	Pregnancy complicated, habitual aborter, delivered, with or without mention of antepartum condition	185, 198
646.33	Pregnancy complicated, habitual aborter, antepartum condition or complication	206
646.40	Pregnancy, complicated by peripheral neuritis, unspecified as to episode of care	211
646.41	Pregnancy, complicated by peripheral neuritis, delivered, with or without mention of antepartum condition	185, 198
646.42	Pregnancy, complicated by peripheral neuritis, delivered, with mention of postpartum complication	185, 198
646.43	Pregnancy, complicated by peripheral neuritis, antepartum condition or complication	206, 210
646.44	Pregnancy, complicated by peripheral neuritis, postpartum condition or complication	203
646.50	Pregnancy, complicated by bacteriuria, asymptomatic, unspecified as to episode of care	211
646.51	Pregnancy, complicated by bacteriuria, asymptomatic, delivered, with or without mention of antepartum condition	185, 198
646.52	Pregnancy, complicated by bacteriuria, asymptomatic, delivered, with mention of postpartum complication	185, 198
646.53	Pregnancy, complicated by bacteriuria, asymptomatic, antepartum condition or complication	206
646.54	Pregnancy, complicated by bacteriuria, asymptomatic, postpartum condition or complication	203
646.60	Pregnancy, complicated by infection, genitourinary tract, unspecified as to episode of care	210, 211
646.61	Pregnancy, complicated by infections, genitourinary tract, delivered, with or without mention of antepartum condition	186, 198
646.62	Pregnancy, complicated by infections, genitourinary tract, delivered, with or without mention of postpartum complication	186, 198
646.63	Pregnancy, complicated by infections, genitourinary tract, antepartum complication	206, 210
646.64	Pregnancy, complicated by infections, genitourinary tract, postpartum condition or complication	203
646.70	Pregnancy, complicated by disorder, liver, unspecified as to episode of care	210, 211
646.71	Pregnancy, complicated by disorders, liver, delivered, with or without mention of antepartum condition	186, 198
646.73	Pregnancy, complicated by disorders, liver, antepartum condition or complication	206, 210
646.80	Pregnancy, complication, other specified, unspecified as to episode of care	210, 211
646.81	Pregnancy, complication, other specified, delivered, with or without mention of antepartum condition	186, 198
646.82	Pregnancy, complication, other specified, delivered, with mention of postpartum condition	186, 198
646.83	Pregnancy, complication, other specified, antepartum complication	206, 210
646.84	Pregnancy, complication, other specified, postpartum condition or complication	203
646.90	Pregnancy, complication, unspecified, unspecified as to episode of care	211

Code	Narrative	Page
646.91	Pregnancy, complication, unspecified, delivered, with or without mention of antepartum condition	186, 198
646.93	Pregnancy, complication, unspecified, delivered, with mention of postpartum condition	207
647.00	Syphilis, maternal, classifiable elsewhere, complicating pregnancy, childbirth, or the puerperium, unspecified as to episode of care	211
647.01	Syphilis, maternal, classifiable elsewhere, complicating pregnancy, childbirth, or the puerperium, delivered, with or without mention of antepartum condition	186, 195
647.02	Syphilis, maternal, classifiable elsewhere, complicating pregnancy, childbirth, or the puerperium, delivered, with mention of postpartum complication	186, 195
647.03	Syphilis, maternal, classifiable elsewhere, complicating pregnancy, childbirth, or the puerperium, antepartum condition or complication	207, 210
647.04	Syphilis, maternal, classifiable elsewhere, complicating pregnancy, childbirth, or the puerperium, postpartum condition or complication	204
647.10	Gonorrhea, maternal, classifiable elsewhere, complicating pregnancy, childbirth, or the puerperium, unspecified as to episode of care	211
647.11	Gonorrhea, maternal, classifiable elsewhere, complicating pregnancy, childbirth, or the puerperium, delivered, with or without mention of antepartum condition	186, 195
647.12	Gonorrhea, maternal, classifiable elsewhere, complicating pregnancy, childbirth, or the puerperium, delivered, with mention of postpartum complication	186, 195
647.13	Gonorrhea, maternal, classifiable elsewhere, complicating pregnancy, childbirth, or the puerperium, antepartum condition or complication	207, 210
647.14	Gonorrhea, maternal, classifiable elsewhere, complicating pregnancy, childbirth, or the puerperium, postpartum condition or complication	204
647.20	Diseases, venereal, other, maternal, classifiable elsewhere, complicating pregnancy, childbirth, or the puerperium, unspecified as to episode of care	211
647.21	Diseases, venereal, other, maternal, classifiable elsewhere, complicating pregnancy, childbirth, or the puerperium, delivered, with or without mention of antepartum condition	186, 195
647.22	Diseases, venereal, other, maternal, classifiable elsewhere, complicating pregnancy, childbirth, or the puerperium, delivered, with mention of postpartum complication	186, 195
647.23	Diseases, venereal, other, maternal, classifiable elsewhere, complicating pregnancy, childbirth, or the puerperium, antepartum condition or complication	207, 210
647.24	Diseases, venereal, other, maternal, classifiable elsewhere, complicating pregnancy, childbirth, or the puerperium, postpartum condition or complication	204
647.30	Tuberculosis, maternal, classifiable elsewhere, complicating pregnancy, childbirth, or the puerperium, unspecified as to episode of care	211
647.31	Tuberculosis, maternal, classifiable elsewhere, complicating pregnancy, childbirth, or the puerperium, delivered, with or without mention of antepartum condition	186, 195
647.32	Tuberculosis, maternal, classifiable elsewhere, complicating pregnancy, childbirth, or the puerperium, delivered, with mention of postpartum complication	186, 195
647.33	Tuberculosis, maternal, classifiable elsewhere, complicating pregnancy, childbirth, or the puerperium, antepartum condition or complication	207, 210
647.34	Tuberculosis, maternal, classifiable elsewhere, complicating pregnancy, childbirth, or the puerperium, postpartum condition or complication	204
647.40	Malaria, maternal, classifiable elsewhere, complicating pregnancy, childbirth, or the puerperium, unspecified as to episode of care	211
647.41	Malaria, maternal, classifiable elsewhere, complicating pregnancy, childbirth, or the puerperium, delivered, with or without mention of antepartum condition	186, 195
647.42	Malaria, maternal, classifiable elsewhere, complicating pregnancy, childbirth, or the puerperium, delivered, with mention of postpartum complication	186, 195

Code	Narrative	Page
647.43	Malaria, maternal, classifiable elsewhere, complicating pregnancy, childbirth, or the puerperium, antepartum condition or complication	207, 210
647.44	Malaria, maternal, classifiable elsewhere, complicating pregnancy, childbirth, or the puerperium, postpartum condition or complication	204
647.50	Rubella, maternal, classifiable elsewhere, complicating pregnancy, childbirth, or the puerperium, unspecified as to episode of care	212
647.51	Rubella, maternal, classifiable elsewhere, complicating pregnancy, childbirth, or the puerperium, delivered, with or without mention of antepartum condition	186, 195
647.52	Rubella, maternal, classifiable elsewhere, complicating pregnancy, childbirth, or the puerperium, delivered, with mention of postpartum complication	186, 195
647.53	Rubella, maternal, classifiable elsewhere, complicating pregnancy, childbirth, or the puerperium, antepartum condition or complication	207, 210
647.54	Rubella, maternal, classifiable elsewhere, complicating pregnancy, childbirth, or the puerperium, postpartum condition or complication	204
647.60	Disease, viral, other, maternal, classifiable elsewhere, complicating pregnancy, childbirth, or the puerperium, unspecified as to episode of care	212
647.61	Disease, viral, other, maternal, classifiable elsewhere, complicating pregnancy, childbirth, or the puerperium, delivered, with or without mention of antepartum condition	186, 195
647.62	Disease, viral, other, maternal, classifiable elsewhere, complicating pregnancy, childbirth, or the puerperium, delivered, with mention of postpartum complication	186, 195
647.63	Disease, viral, other, maternal, classifiable elsewhere, complicating pregnancy, childbirth, or the puerperium, antepartum condition or complication	207, 210
647.64	Disease, viral, other, maternal, classifiable elsewhere, complicating pregnancy, childbirth, or the puerperium, postpartum condition or complication	204
647.80	Disease, infectious and parasitic, other, maternal, classifiable elsewhere, complicating pregnancy, childbirth, or the puerperium, unspecified as to episode of care	212
647.81	Disease, infectious and parasitic, other, maternal, classifiable elsewhere, complicating pregnancy, childbirth, or the puerperium, delivered, with or without mention of antepartum condition	186, 195
647.82	Disease, infectious and parasitic, other, maternal, classifiable elsewhere, complicating pregnancy, childbirth, or the puerperium, delivered, with mention of postpartum complication	186, 195
647.83	Disease, infectious and parasitic, other, maternal, classifiable elsewhere, complicating pregnancy, childbirth, or the puerperium, antepartum condition or complication	207, 210
647.84	Disease, infectious and parasitic, other, maternal, classifiable elsewhere, complicating pregnancy, childbirth, or the puerperium, postpartum condition or complication	204
647.90	Disease, infectious and parasitic, unspecified, maternal, classifiable elsewhere, complicating pregnancy, childbirth, or the puerperium, unspecified as to episode of care	212
647.91	Disease, infectious and parasitic, unspecified, maternal, classifiable elsewhere, complicating pregnancy, childbirth, or the puerperium, delivered, with or without mention of antepartum condition	186, 195
647.92	Disease, infectious and parasitic, unspecified, maternal, classifiable elsewhere, complicating pregnancy, childbirth, or the puerperium, delivered, with mention of postpartum complication	186, 195
647.93	Disease, infectious and parasitic, unspecified, maternal, classifiable elsewhere, complicating pregnancy, childbirth, or the puerperium, antepartum condition or complication	207, 210
647.94	Disease, infectious and parasitic, unspecified, maternal, classifiable elsewhere, complicating pregnancy, childbirth, or the puerperium, postpartum condition or complication	204
648.00	Diabetes mellitus, maternal, complicating pregnancy, childbirth, or the puerperium, unspecified as to episode of care	212

 * Code Range

Code	Narrative	Page
648.60	Diseases, cardiovascular, other, maternal, complicating pregnancy, childbirth, or the puerperium, unspecified as to episode of care	212
648.61	Diseases, cardiovascular, other, maternal, complicating pregnancy, childbirth, or the puerperium, delivered, with or without mention of antepartum condition	186, 196
648.62	Diseases, cardiovascular, other, maternal, complicating pregnancy, childbirth, or the puerperium, delivered, with mention of postpartum complication	186, 196
648.63	Diseases, cardiovascular, other, maternal, complicating pregnancy, childbirth, or the puerperium, antepartum condition or complication	207, 210
648.64	Diseases, cardiovascular, other, maternal, complicating pregnancy, childbirth, or the puerperium, postpartum condition or complication	204
648.70	Disorders, bone and joint, back, pelvis, lower limbs, maternal, complicating pregnancy, childbirth, or the puerperium, unspecified as to episode of care	212
648.71	Disorders, bone and joint, back, pelvis, lower limbs, maternal, complicating pregnancy, childbirth, or the puerperium, delivered, with or without mention of antepartum condition	186, 198
648.72	Disorders, bone and joint, back, pelvis, lower limbs, maternal, complicating pregnancy, childbirth, or the puerperium, delivered, with mention of postpartum complication	186, 198
648.73	Disorders, bone and joint, back, pelvis, lower limbs, maternal, complicating pregnancy, childbirth, or the puerperium, antepartum condition or complication	207, 211
648.74	Disorders, bone and joint, back, pelvis, lower limbs, maternal, complicating pregnancy, childbirth, or the puerperium, postpartum condition or complication	204
648.80	Abnormal, glucose tolerance, maternal, complicating pregnancy, childbirth, or the puerperium, unspecified as to episode of care	212
648.81	Abnormal, glucose tolerance, maternal, complicating pregnancy, childbirth, or the puerperium, delivered, with or without mention of antepartum condition	186, 198
648.82	Abnormal, glucose tolerance, maternal, complicating pregnancy, childbirth, or the puerperium, delivered, with mention of postpartum complication	186, 198
648.83	Abnormal, glucose tolerance, maternal, complicating pregnancy, childbirth, or the puerperium, antepartum condition or complication	207, 211
648.84	Abnormal, glucose tolerance, maternal, complicating pregnancy, childbirth, or the puerperium, postpartum condition or complication	204
648.90	Conditions, other, current, maternal, complicating pregnancy, childbirth, or the puerperium, unspecified as to episode of care	212
648.91	Conditions, other, current, maternal, complicating pregnancy, childbirth, or the puerperium, delivered, with or without mention of antepartum condition	186, 198
648.92	Conditions, other, current, maternal, complicating pregnancy, childbirth, or the puerperium, delivered, with mention of postpartum complication	186, 198
648.93	Conditions, other, current, maternal, complicating pregnancy, childbirth, or the puerperium, antepartum condition or complication	207, 211
648.94	Conditions, other, current, maternal, complicating pregnancy, childbirth, or the puerperium, postpartum condition or complication	204
650	Delivery, normal	186, 198
651.00	Pregnancy, twin, unspecified as to episode of care	212
651.01	Pregnancy, twin, delivered, with or without mention of antepartum condition	186, 198
651.03	Pregnancy, twin, antepartum condition or complication	207
651.10	Pregnancy, triplet, unspecified as to episode of care	212
651.11	Pregnancy, triplet, delivered, with or without mention of antepartum condition	186, 198
651.13	Pregnancy, triplet, antepartum condition or complication	207
651.20	Pregnancy, quadruplet, unspecified as to episode of care	212
651.21	Pregnancy, quadruplet, delivered, with or without mention of antepartum condition	186, 198
651.23	Pregnancy, quadruplet, antepartum condition or complication	207
651.30	Pregnancy, twin, fetal loss and retention of one fetus, unspecified as to episode of care	212
651.31	Pregnancy, twin, fetal loss and retention of one fetus, delivered, with or without mention of antepartum condition	186, 198

Code	Narrative	Page
651.33	Pregnancy, twin, fetal loss and retention of one fetus, antepartum condition or complication	207
651.40	Pregnancy, triplet, fetal loss and retention of one or more fetus(es), unspecified as to episode of care	212
651.41	Pregnancy, triplet, fetal loss and retention of one or more fetus(es), delivered, with or without mention of antepartum condition	186, 198
651.43	Pregnancy, triplet, fetal loss and retention of one or more fetus(es), antepartum condition or complication	207
651.50	Pregnancy, quadruplet, fetal loss and retention of one or more fetus(es), unspecified as to episode of care	212
651.51	Pregnancy, quadruplet, fetal loss and retention of one or more fetus(es), delivered, with or without mention of antepartum condition	186, 198
651.53	Pregnancy, quadruplet, fetal loss and retention of one or more fetus(es), antepartum condition or complication	207
651.60	Pregnancy, multiple, other, fetal loss and retention of one or more fetus(es), unspecified as to episode of care	212
651.61	Pregnancy, multiple, other, fetal loss and retention of one or more fetus(es), delivered, with or without mention of antepartum condition	186, 198
651.63	Pregnancy, multiple, other, fetal loss and retention of one or more fetus(es), antepartum condition or complication	207
651.70	Gestation, multiple, following (elective) fetal reduction, unspecified as to episode of care	212
651.71	Gestation, multiple, following (elective) fetal reduction, delivered, with or without mention of antepartum condition	186, 198
651.73	Gestation, multiple, following (elective) fetal reduction, antepartum condition or complication	207
651.80	Gestation, multiple, other specified, unspecified as to episode of care	212
651.81	Gestation, multiple, other specified, delivered, with or without mention of antepartum condition	187, 198
651.83	Gestation, multiple, other specified, antepartum condition or complication	207
651.90	Gestation, multiple, unspecified, unspecified as to episode of care	212
651.91	Gestation, multiple, unspecified, delivered, with or without mention of antepartum condition	187, 198
651.93	Gestation, multiple, unspecified, antepartum condition or complication	207

Code	Narrative	Page
652.00	Unstable lie, fetus, unspecified as to episode of care	212
652.01	Unstable lie, fetus, delivered, with or without mention of antepartum condition	187, 198
652.03	Unstable lie, fetus, antepartum condition or complication	207
652.10	Breech or other malpresentation, converted to cephalic presentation, unspecified as to episode of care	212
652.11	Breech or other malpresentation, converted to cephalic presentation, delivered, with or without mention of antepartum condition	187, 198
652.13	Breech or other malpresentation, converted to cephalic presentation, antepartum condition or complication	207
652.20	Presentation, breech without mention of version, unspecified as to episode of care	212
652.21	Presentation, breech without mention of version, delivered, with or without mention of antepartum condition	187, 198
652.23	Presentation, breech without mention of version, antepartum condition or complication	207
652.30	Presentation, transverse or oblique, fetus, unspecified as to episode of care	212
652.31	Presentation, transverse or oblique, fetus, delivered, with or without mention of antepartum condition	187, 198
652.33	Presentation, transverse or oblique, fetus, antepartum condition or complication	207
652.40	Presentation, face or brow, fetal, unspecified as to episode of care	212
652.41	Presentation, face or brow, fetal, delivered, with or without mention of antepartum condition	187, 198
652.43	Presentation, face or brow, fetal, antepartum condition or complication	207
652.50	High fetal head at term, unspecified as to episode of care	212
652.51	High fetal head at term, delivered, with or without mention of antepartum condition	187, 198
652.53	High fetal head at term, antepartum condition or complication	207
652.60	Gestation, multiple with malpresentation, one fetus or more, unspecified as to episode of care	212
652.61	Gestation, multiple with malpresentation, one fetus or more, delivered, with or without mention of antepartum condition	187, 198

Code	Narrative	Page
652.63	Gestation, multiple with malpresentation, one fetus or more, antepartum condition or complication	207
652.70	Prolapsed arm, fetus, unspecified as to episode of care	212
652.71	Prolapsed arm, fetus, delivered, with or without mention of antepartum condition	187, 198
652.73	Prolapsed arm, fetus, antepartum condition or complication	207
652.80	Malposition or malpresentation, other specified, fetus, unspecified as to episode of care	212
652.81	Malposition or malpresentation, other specified, fetus, delivered, with or without mention of antepartum condition	187, 198
652.83	Malposition or malpresentation, other specified, fetus, antepartum condition or complication	207
652.90	Malposition or malpresentation, unspecified, fetus, unspecified as to episode of care	212
652.91	Malposition or malpresentation, unspecified, fetus, delivered, with or without mention of antepartum condition	187, 198
652.93	Malposition or malpresentation, unspecified, fetus, antepartum condition or complication	207
653.00	Disproportion, abnormality, major, bony pelvis, not further specified, in pregnancy, unspecified as to episode of care	212
653.01	Disproportion, abnormality, major, bony pelvis, not further specified, in pregnancy, delivered, with or without mention of antepartum condition	187, 198
653.03	Disproportion, abnormality, major, bony pelvis, not further specified, in pregnancy, antepartum condition or complication	207
653.10	Contracted pelvis in pregnancy, unspecified as to episode of care	212
653.11	Contracted pelvis in pregnancy, delivered, with or without mention of antepartum condition	187, 198
653.13	Contracted pelvis in pregnancy, antepartum condition or complication	207
653.20	Contraction, inlet, pelvis in pregnancy, unspecified as to episode of care	212
653.21	Contraction, inlet, pelvis in pregnancy, delivered, with or without mention of antepartum condition	187, 199
653.23	Contraction, inlet, pelvis in pregnancy, antepartum condition or complication	207
653.30	Contraction, outlet, pelvis in pregnancy, unspecified as to episode of care	212
653.31	Contraction, outlet, pelvis in pregnancy, delivered, with or without mention of antepartum condition	187, 199
653.33	Contraction, outlet, pelvis in pregnancy, antepartum condition or complication	207
653.40	Disproportion, fetopelvic, unspecified as to episode of care	212
653.41	Disproportion, fetopelvic, delivered, with or without mention of antepartum condition	187, 199
653.43	Disproportion, fetopelvic, antepartum condition or complication	207
653.50	Large, unusually, fetus, causing disproportion, unspecified as to episode of care	212
653.51	Large, unusually, fetus, causing disproportion, delivered, with or without mention of antepartum condition	187, 199
653.53	Large, unusually, fetus, causing disproportion, antepartum condition or complication	207
653.60	Hydrocephalic, fetus, causing disproportion, unspecified as to episode of care	212
653.61	Hydrocephalic, fetus, causing disproportion, delivered, with or without mention of antepartum condition	187, 199
653.63	Hydrocephalic, fetus, causing disproportion, antepartum condition or complication	207
653.70	Abnormality, other, fetal, causing disproportion, unspecified as to episode of care	213
653.71	Abnormality, other, fetal, causing disproportion, delivered, with or without mention of antepartum condition	187, 199
653.73	Abnormality, other, fetal, causing disproportion, antepartum condition or complication	207
653.80	Disproportion, other origin, fetal, unspecified as to episode of care	213
653.81	Disproportion, other origin, fetal, delivered, with or without mention of antepartum condition	187, 199
653.83	Disproportion, other origin, fetal, antepartum condition or complication	207
653.90	Disproportion, unspecified, fetal, unspecified as to episode of care	213
653.91	Disproportion, unspecified, fetal, delivered, with or without mention of antepartum condition	187, 199
653.93	Disproportion, unspecified, fetal, antepartum condition or complication	207
654.00	Abnormalities, congenital, uterus, complicating pregnancy, childbirth, or the puerperium, unspecified as to episode of care	213

Code	Narrative	Page
654.01	Abnormalities, congenital, uterus, complicating pregnancy, childbirth, or the puerperium, delivered, with or without mention of antepartum condition	187, 199
654.02	Abnormalities, congenital, uterus, complicating pregnancy, childbirth, or the puerperium, delivered, with mention of postpartum complication	187, 199
654.03	Abnormalities, congenital, uterus, complicating pregnancy, childbirth, or the puerperium, antepartum condition or complication	207
654.04	Abnormalities, congenital, uterus, complicating pregnancy, childbirth, or the puerperium, postpartum condition or complication	204
654.10	Tumors, body of pregnant uterus, complicating pregnancy, childbirth, or the puerperium, unspecified as to episode of care	213
654.11	Tumors, body of pregnant uterus, complicating pregnancy, childbirth, or the puerperium, delivered, with or without mention of antepartum condition	187, 199
654.12	Tumors, body of pregnant uterus, complicating pregnancy, childbirth, or the puerperium, delivered, with mention of postpartum complication	187, 199
654.13	Tumors, body of pregnant uterus, complicating pregnancy, childbirth, or the puerperium, antepartum condition or complication	207
654.14	Tumors, body of pregnant uterus, complicating pregnancy, childbirth, or the puerperium, postpartum condition or complication	204
654.20	Cesarean section, previous, complicating pregnancy, childbirth, or the puerperium, unspecified as to episode of care	213
654.21	Cesarean section, previous, complicating pregnancy, childbirth, or the puerperium, delivered, with or without mention of antepartum condition	187, 199
654.23	Cesarean section, previous, complicating pregnancy, childbirth, or the puerperium, antepartum condition or complication	207
654.30	Retroverted, incarcerated, gravid uterus, unspecified as to episode of care	213
654.31	Retroverted, incarcerated, gravid uterus, delivered, with or without mention of antepartum condition	187, 199
654.32	Retroverted, incarcerated, gravid uterus, delivered, with mention of postpartum complication	187, 199
654.33	Retroverted, incarcerated, gravid uterus, antepartum condition or complication	207

Code	Narrative	Page
654.34	Retroverted, incarcerated, gravid uterus, postpartum condition or complication	204
654.40	Abnormalities, other, shape or position, gravis uterus and neighboring structures, unspecified as to episode of care	213
654.41	Abnormalities, other, shape or position, gravis uterus and neighboring structures, delivered, with or without mention of antepartum condition	187, 199
654.42	Abnormalities, other, shape or position, gravis uterus and neighboring structures, delivered, with mention of postpartum complication	187, 199
654.43	Abnormalities, other, shape or position, gravis uterus and neighboring structures, antepartum condition or complication	207
654.44	Abnormalities, other, shape or position, gravis uterus and neighboring structures, postpartum condition or complication	204
654.50	Incompetence, cervical, unspecified as to episode of care	213
654.51	Incompetence, cervical, delivered, with or without mention of antepartum condition	187, 199
654.52	Incompetence, cervical, delivered, with mention of postpartum complication	187, 199
654.53	Incompetence, cervical, antepartum condition or complication	207
654.54	Incompetence, cervical, postpartum condition or complication	204
654.60	Abnormality, other, congenital or acquired, cervix, complicating pregnancy, childbirth, or the puerperium, unspecified as to episode of care	213
654.61	Abnormality, other, congenital or acquired, cervix, complicating pregnancy, childbirth, or the puerperium, delivered, with or without mention of antepartum condition	187, 199
654.62	Abnormality, other, congenital or acquired, cervix, complicating pregnancy, childbirth, or the puerperium, delivered, with mention of postpartum complication	187, 199
654.63	Abnormality, other, congenital or acquired, cervix, complicating pregnancy, childbirth, or the puerperium, antepartum condition or complication	207

Code	Narrative	Page
654.64	Abnormality, other, congenital or acquired, cervix, complicating pregnancy, childbirth, or the puerperium, postpartum condition or complication	204
654.70	Abnormality, other, congenital or acquired, vagina, complicating pregnancy, childbirth, or the puerperium, unspecified as to episode of care	213
654.71	Abnormality, other, congenital or acquired, vagina, complicating pregnancy, childbirth, or the puerperium, delivered, with or without mention of antepartum condition	187, 199
654.72	Abnormality, other, congenital or acquired, vagina, complicating pregnancy, childbirth, or the puerperium, delivered, with mention of postpartum complication	187, 199
654.73	Abnormality, other, congenital or acquired, vagina, complicating pregnancy, childbirth, or the puerperium, antepartum condition or complication	207
654.74	Abnormality, other, congenital or acquired, vagina, complicating pregnancy, childbirth, or the puerperium, postpartum condition or complication	204
654.80	Abnormality, other, congenital or acquired, vulva, complicating pregnancy, childbirth, or the puerperium, unspecified as to episode of care	213
654.81	Abnormality, other, congenital or acquired, vulva, complicating pregnancy, childbirth, or the puerperium, delivered, with or without mention of antepartum condition	187, 199
654.82	Abnormality, other, congenital or acquired, vulva, complicating pregnancy, childbirth, or the puerperium, delivered, with mention of postpartum complication	187, 199
654.83	Abnormality, other, congenital or acquired, vulva, complicating pregnancy, childbirth, or the puerperium, antepartum condition or complication	207
654.84	Abnormality, other, congenital or acquired, vulva, complicating pregnancy, childbirth, or the puerperium, postpartum condition or complication	204
654.90	Abnormality, other and unspecified, organs and soft tissues, pelvis, complicating pregnancy, childbirth, or the puerperium, unspecified as to episode of care	213
654.91	Abnormality, other and unspecified, organs and soft tissues, pelvis, complicating pregnancy, childbirth, or the puerperium, delivered, with or without mention of antepartum condition	187, 199
654.92	Abnormality, other and unspecified, organs and soft tissues, pelvis, complicating pregnancy, childbirth, or the puerperium, delivered, with mention of postpartum complication	187, 199
654.93	Abnormality, other and unspecified, organs and soft tissues, pelvis, complicating pregnancy, childbirth, or the puerperium, antepartum condition or complication	207
654.94	Abnormality, other and unspecified, organs and soft tissues, pelvis, complicating pregnancy, childbirth, or the puerperium, postpartum condition or complication	204
655.00	Malformation, central nervous system, fetus, affecting management of mother, unspecified as to episode of care	213
655.01	Malformation, central nervous system, fetus, affecting management of mother, delivered, with or without mention of antepartum condition	187, 199
655.03	Malformation, central nervous system, fetus, affecting management of mother, antepartum condition or complication	207
655.10	Abnormality, chromosomal, fetus, affecting management of mother, unspecified as to episode of care	213
655.11	Abnormality, chromosomal, fetus, affecting management of mother, delivered, with or without mention of antepartum condition	187, 199
655.13	Abnormality, chromosomal, fetus, affecting management of mother, antepartum condition or complication	208
655.20	Disease, hereditary, possibly affecting fetus, affecting management of mother, unspecified as to episode of care	213
655.21	Disease, hereditary, possibly affecting fetus, affecting management of mother, delivered, with or without mention of antepartum condition	187, 199
655.23	Disease, hereditary, possibly affecting fetus, affecting management of mother, antepartum condition or complication	208

Code	Narrative	Page
655.30	Disease, viral, maternal, suspected fetal damage, affecting management of mother, unspecified as to episode of care	213
655.31	Disease, viral, maternal, suspected fetal damage, affecting management of mother, delivered, with or without mention of antepartum condition	187, 199
655.33	Disease, viral, maternal, suspected fetal damage, affecting management of mother, antepartum condition or complication	208
655.40	Disease, other, maternal, suspected fetal damage, affecting management of mother, unspecified as to episode of care	213
655.41	Disease, other, maternal, suspected fetal damage, affecting management of mother, delivered, with or without mention of antepartum condition	187, 199
655.43	Disease, other, maternal, suspected fetal damage, affecting management of mother, antepartum condition or complication	208
655.50	Damage, suspected, fetal, from drugs, affecting management of mother, unspecified as to episode of care	213
655.51	Damage, suspected, fetal, from drugs, affecting management of mother, delivered, with or without mention of antepartum condition	187, 199
655.53	Damage, suspected, fetal, from drugs, affecting management of mother, antepartum condition or complication	208
655.60	Damage, suspected, fetal, from radiation, affecting management of mother, unspecified as to episode of care	213
655.61	Damage, suspected, fetal, from radiation, affecting management of mother, delivered, with or without mention of antepartum condition	187, 199
655.63	Damage, suspected, fetal, from radiation, affecting management of mother, antepartum condition or complication	208
655.70	Decreased, movements, fetal, unspecified as to episode of care	213
655.71	Decreased, movements, fetal, delivered, with or without mention of antepartum condition	187, 199
655.73	Decreased, movements, fetal, antepartum condition or complication	208
655.80	Abnormality, fetal, other known or suspected, not elsewhere classified, affecting management of mother, unspecified as to episode of care	213
655.81	Abnormality, fetal, other known or suspected, not elsewhere classified, affecting management of mother, delivered, with or without mention of antepartum condition	187, 199
655.83	Abnormality, fetal, other known or suspected, not elsewhere classified, affecting management of mother, antepartum condition or complication	208
655.90	Abnormality, fetal, unspecified, affecting management of mother, unspecified as to episode of care	213
655.91	Abnormality, fetal, unspecified, affecting management of mother, delivered, with or without mention of antepartum condition	187, 199
655.93	Abnormality, fetal, unspecified, affecting management of mother, antepartum condition or complication	208
656.00	Hemorrhage, fetal-maternal, affecting management of mother, unspecified as to episode of care	213
656.01	Hemorrhage, fetal-maternal, affecting management of mother, delivered, with or without mention of antepartum condition	188, 199
656.03	Hemorrhage, fetal-maternal, affecting management of mother, antepartum condition or complication	208
656.10	Isoimmunization, rhesus, affecting management of mother, unspecified as to episode of care	213
656.11	Isoimmunization, rhesus, affecting management of mother, delivered, with or without mention of antepartum condition	188, 199
656.13	Isoimmunization, rhesus, affecting management of mother, antepartum condition or complication	208
656.20	Isoimmunization, other and unspecified blood group, affecting management of mother, unspecified as to episode of care	213
656.21	Isoimmunization, other and unspecified blood group, affecting management of mother, delivered, with or without mention of antepartum condition	188, 199
656.23	Isoimmunization, other and unspecified blood group, affecting management of mother, antepartum condition or complication	208
656.30	Distress, fetal, affecting management of mother, unspecified as to episode of care	188, 199
656.31	Distress, fetal, affecting management of mother, delivered, with or without mention of antepartum condition	188, 199

** Code Range*

Code	Narrative	Page
656.33	Distress, fetal, affecting management of mother, antepartum condition or complication	208
656.40	Death, fetal intrauterine, affecting management of mother, unspecified as to episode of care	188, 199
656.41	Death, fetal intrauterine, affecting management of mother, delivered, with or without mention of antepartum condition	188, 199
656.43	Death, fetal intrauterine, affecting management of mother, antepartum condition or complication	208
656.50	Growth, poor, fetal, affecting management of mother, unspecified as to episode of care	213
656.51	Growth, poor, fetal, affecting management of mother, delivered, with or without mention of antepartum condition	188, 199
656.53	Growth, poor, fetal, affecting management of mother, antepartum condition or complication	208
656.60	Growth, excessive, fetal, affecting management of mother, unspecified as to episode of care	213
656.61	Growth, excessive, fetal, affecting management of mother, delivered, with or without mention of antepartum condition	188, 199
656.63	Growth, excessive, fetal, affecting management of mother, antepartum condition or complication	208
656.70	Conditions, other, placental, affecting management of mother, unspecified as to episode of care	213
656.71	Conditions, other, placental, affecting management of mother, delivered, with or without mention of antepartum condition	188, 199
656.73	Conditions, other, placental, affecting management of mother, antepartum condition or complication	208
656.80	Problems, other specified, fetal and placental, affecting management of mother, unspecified as to episode of care	213
656.81	Problems, other specified, fetal and placental, affecting management of mother, delivered, with or without mention of antepartum condition	188, 199
656.83	Problems, other specified, fetal and placental, affecting management of mother, antepartum condition or complication	208
656.90	Problems, unspecified, fetal and placental, affecting management of mother, unspecified as to episode of care	213
656.91	Problems, unspecified, fetal and placental, affecting management of mother, delivered, with or without mention of antepartum condition	188, 199
656.93	Problems, unspecified, fetal and placental, affecting management of mother, antepartum condition or complication	208
657.00	Polyhydramnios, unspecified as to episode of care	213
657.01	Polyhydramnios, delivered, with or without mention of antepartum condition	188, 199
657.03	Polyhydramnios, antepartum condition or complication	208
658.00	Oligohydramnios, unspecified as to episode of care	213
658.01	Oligohydramnios, delivered, with or without mention of antepartum condition	188, 200
658.03	Oligohydramnios, antepartum condition or complication	208
658.10	Rupture, premature, membranes in pregnancy, unspecified as to episode of care	188, 200
658.11	Rupture, premature, membranes in pregnancy, delivered, with or without mention of antepartum condition	188, 200
658.13	Rupture, premature, membranes in pregnancy, antepartum condition or complication	208
658.20	Rupture, spontaneous or unspecified, membranes in pregnancy, delivery delayed, unspecified as to episode of care	188, 200
658.21	Rupture, spontaneous or unspecified, membranes in pregnancy, delivery delayed, delivered, with or without mention of antepartum condition	188, 200
658.23	Rupture, spontaneous or unspecified, membranes in pregnancy, delivery delayed, antepartum condition or complication	208
658.30	Rupture, artificial, membranes in pregnancy, delivery delayed, unspecified as to episode of care	188, 200
658.31	Rupture, artificial, membranes in pregnancy, delivery delayed, delivered, with or without mention of antepartum condition	188, 200
658.33	Rupture, artificial, membranes in pregnancy, delivery delayed, antepartum condition or complication	208
658.40	Infection of amniotic cavity, unspecified as to episode of care	188, 200
658.41	Infection of amniotic cavity, delivered, with or without mention of antepartum condition	188, 200
658.43	Infection of amniotic cavity, antepartum condition or complication	208

Code	Narrative	Page
658.80	Problems, other, with amniotic cavity and membranes, unspecified as to episode of care	213
658.81	Problems, other, with amniotic cavity and membranes, delivered, with or without mention of antepartum condition	188, 200
658.83	Problems, other, with amniotic cavity and membranes, antepartum condition or complication	208
658.90	Problems, unspecified, with amniotic cavity and membranes, unspecified as to episode of care	213
658.91	Problems, unspecified, with amniotic cavity and membranes, delivered, with or without mention of antepartum condition	188, 200
658.93	Problems, unspecified, with amniotic cavity and membranes, antepartum condition or complication	208
659.00	Induction labor, failed, mechanical, unspecified as to episode of care	188, 200
659.01	Induction labor, failed, mechanical, delivered, with or without mention of antepartum condition	188, 200
659.03	Induction labor, failed, mechanical, antepartum condition or complication	208
659.10	Induction labor, failed, medical or unspecified, unspecified as to episode of care	188, 200
659.11	Induction labor, failed, medical or unspecified, delivered, with or without mention of antepartum condition	188, 200
659.13	Induction labor, failed, medical or unspecified, antepartum condition or complication	208
659.20	Pyrexia, maternal, during labor, unspecified, unspecified as to episode of care	188, 200
659.21	Pyrexia, maternal, during labor, unspecified, delivered, with or without mention of antepartum condition	188, 196
659.23	Pyrexia, maternal, during labor, antepartum condition or complication	208
659.30	Infection, generalized, during labor, unspecified, unspecified as to episode of care	188, 200
659.31	Infection, generalized, during labor, unspecified, delivered, with or without mention of antepartum condition	188, 196
659.33	Infection, generalized, during labor, antepartum condition or complication	208
659.40	Multiparity, grand, with current pregnancy, unspecified as to episode of care	213
659.41	Multiparity, grand, with current pregnancy, delivered, with or without mention of antepartum condition	188, 200
659.43	Multiparity, grand, with current pregnancy, antepartum condition or complication	208
659.50	Primigravida, elderly, unspecified as to episode of care	188, 200
659.51	Primigravida, elderly, delivered, with or without mention of antepartum condition	188, 200
659.53	Primigravida, elderly, antepartum condition or complication	208
659.60	Multigravida, elderly, unspecified as to episode of care	188, 200
659.61	Multigravida, elderly, delivered, with or without mention of antepartum condition	188, 200
659.63	Multigravida, elderly, antepartum condition or complication	208
659.70	Abnormality, fetal heart rate or rhythm, unspecified as to episode of care or not applicable	188, 200
659.71	Abnormality, fetal heart rate or rhythm, delivered, with or without mention of antepartum condition	188, 200
659.73	Abnormality, fetal heart rate or rhythm, antepartum condition or complication	208
659.80	Delivery, complicated by indications for care or intervention, specified, unspecified as to episode of care, other	188, 200
659.81	Delivery, complicated by indications for care or intervention, specified, delivered, with or without mention of antepartum condition	188, 200
659.83	Delivery, complicated by indications for care or intervention, specified, antepartum condition or complication	208
659.90	Delivery, complicated by indications for care or intervention, unspecified, unspecified as to episode of care	188, 200
659.91	Delivery, complicated by indications for care or intervention, unspecified, delivered, with or without mention of antepartum condition	188, 200
659.93	Delivery, complicated by indications for care or intervention, unspecified, antepartum condition or complication	208
660.00	Obstruction, labor, at onset, caused by malposition of fetus, unspecified as to episode of care	188, 200
660.01	Obstruction, labor, at onset, caused by malposition of fetus, delivered, with or without mention of antepartum condition	188, 200
660.03	Obstruction, labor, at onset, caused by malposition of fetus, antepartum condition or complication	208

Numeric Index to Diseases

Code	Narrative	Page
660.10	Delivery, complicated by obstructed labor due to bony pelvis, unspecified as to episode of care	188, 200
660.11	Delivery, complicated by obstructed labor due to bony pelvis, delivered, with or without mention of antepartum condition	188, 200
660.13	Delivery, complicated by obstructed labor due to bony pelvis, antepartum condition or complication	208
660.20	Delivery, complicated by obstructed labor due to abnormal pelvic soft tissues, unspecified as to episode of care	188, 200
660.21	Delivery, complicated by obstructed labor due to abnormal pelvic soft tissues, delivered, with or without mention of antepartum condition	188, 200
660.23	Delivery, complicated by obstructed labor due to abnormal pelvic soft tissues, antepartum condition or complication	208
660.30	Delivery, complicated by obstructed labor due to deep transverse arrest and persistant occipitoposterior position, unspecified as to episode of care	188, 200
660.31	Delivery, complicated by obstructed labor due to deep transverse arrest and persistent occipitoposterior position, delivered, with or without mention of antepartum condition	188, 200
660.33	Delivery, complicated by obstructed labor due to deep transverse arrest, antepartum condition or complication	208
660.40	Delivery, complicated by obstructed labor due to shoulder dystocia, unspecified as to episode of care	188, 200
660.41	Delivery, complicated by obstructed labor due to shoulder dystocia, delivered, with or without mention of antepartum condition	188, 200
660.43	Delivery, complicated by obstructed labor due to shoulder dystocia, antepartum condition or complication	208
660.50	Delivery, complicated by obstructed labor due to locked twins, unspecified as to episode of care	188, 200
660.51	Delivery, complicated by obstructed labor due to locked twins, delivered, with or without mention of antepartum condition	189, 200
660.53	Delivery, complicated by obstructed labor due to locked twins, antepartum condition or complication	208
660.60	Delivery, complicated by obstructed labor due to failed trial of labor, unspecified, unspecified as to episode of care	189, 200
660.61	Delivery, complicated by obstructed labor due to failed trial of labor, unspecified, delivered, with or without mention of antepartum condition	189, 200
660.63	Delivery, complicated by obstructed labor due to trial labor, failed, unspecified, antepartum condition or complication	208
660.70	Delivery, complicated by obstructed labor due to failed forceps or vacuum extractor, unspecified, unspecified as to episode of care	189, 200
660.71	Delivery, complicated by obstructed labor due to failed forceps or vacuum extractor, unspecified, delivered, with or without mention of antepartum condition	189, 200
660.73	Delivery, complicated by obstructed labor due to failed forceps or vacuum extractor, unspecified, antepartum condition or complication	208
660.80	Delivery, complicated by obstructed labor, other causes, unspecified as to episode of care	189, 200
660.81	Delivery, complicated by obstructed labor, other causes, delivered, with or without mention of antepartum condition	189, 200
660.83	Delivery, complicated by obstructed labor, other causes, antepartum condition or complication	208
660.90	Obstructed labor, unspecified, unspecified as to episode of care	189, 200
660.91	Obstructed labor, unspecified, delivered, with or without mention of antepartum condition	189, 200
660.93	Obstructed labor, unspecified, antepartum condition or complication	208
661.00	Inertia, primary, uterine, unspecified as to episode of care	189, 200
661.01	Inertia, primary, uterine, delivered, with or without mention of antepartum condition	189, 200
661.03	Inertia, primary, uterine, antepartum condition or complication	208
661.10	Inertia, secondary, uterine, unspecified as to episode of care	189, 200
661.11	Inertia, secondary, uterine, delivered, with or without mention of antepartum condition	189, 200
661.13	Inertia, secondary, uterine, antepartum condition or complication	208

Code	Narrative	Page
661.20	Inertia, other and unspecified, uterine, unspecified as to episode of care	189, 200
661.21	Inertia, other and unspecified, uterine, delivered, with or without mention of antepartum condition	189, 200
661.23	Inertia, other and unspecified, uterine, antepartum condition or complication	208
661.30	Precipitate labor, unspecified as to episode of care	189, 200
661.31	Precipitate labor, delivered, with or without mention of antepartum condition	189, 201
661.33	Precipitate labor, antepartum condition or complication	208
661.40	Hypertonic, incoordinate, or prolonged uterine contractions, unspecified as to episode of care	189, 201
661.41	Hypertonic, incoordinate, or prolonged uterine contractions, delivered, with or without mention of antepartum condition	189, 201
661.43	Hypertonic, incoordinate, or prolonged uterine contractions, antepartum condition or complication	208
661.90	Abnormality, unspecified, labor, unspecified as to episode of care	189, 201
661.91	Abnormality, unspecified, labor, delivered, with or without mention of antepartum condition	189, 201
661.93	Abnormality, unspecified, labor, antepartum condition or complication	208
662.00	Prolonged first stage, labor, unspecified as to episode of care	189, 201
662.01	Prolonged first stage, labor, delivered, with or without mention of antepartum condition	189, 201
662.03	Prolonged first stage, labor, antepartum condition or complication	209
662.10	Prolonged labor, unspecified, unspecified as to episode of care	189, 201
662.11	Prolonged labor, unspecified, delivered, with or without mention of antepartum condition	189, 201
662.13	Prolonged labor, unspecified, antepartum condition or complication	209
662.20	Prolonged second stage, labor, unspecified as to episode of care	189, 201
662.21	Prolonged second stage, labor, delivered, with or without mention of antepartum condition	189, 201
662.23	Prolonged second stage, labor, antepartum condition or complication	209
662.30	Delayed delivery of second twin, triplet, etc., unspecified as to episode of care	189, 201
662.31	Delayed delivery of second twin, triplet, etc., delivered, with or without mention of antepartum condition	189, 201
662.33	Delayed delivery of second twin, triplet, etc., antepartum condition or complication	209
663.00	Prolapse, cord, complicating labor and delivery, unspecified as to episode of care	189, 201
663.01	Prolapse, cord, complicating labor and delivery, delivered, with or without mention of antepartum condition	189, 201
663.03	Prolapse, cord, complicating labor and delivery, antepartum condition or complication	209
663.10	Compression, cord around neck, complicating labor and delivery, unspecified as to episode of care	189, 201
663.11	Compression, cord around neck, complicating labor and delivery, delivered, with or without mention of antepartum condition	189, 201
663.13	Compression, cord around neck, complicating labor and delivery, antepartum condition or complication	209
663.20	Entanglement, compression, cord, other and unspecified, complicating labor and delivery, unspecified as to episode of care	189, 201
663.21	Entanglement, compression, cord, other and unspecified, complicating labor and delivery, delivered, with or without mention of antepartum condition	189, 201
663.23	Entanglement, compression, cord, other and unspecified, complicating labor and delivery, antepartum condition or complication	209
663.30	Compression, cord, other and unspecified, complicating labor and delivery, unspecified as to episode of care	189, 201
663.31	Compression, cord, other and unspecified, complicating labor and delivery, delivered, with or without mention of antepartum condition	189, 201
663.33	Compression, cord, other and unspecified, complicating labor and delivery, antepartum condition or complication	209
663.40	Short cord complicating labor and delivery, unspecified as to episode of care	189, 201
663.41	Short cord complicating labor and delivery, delivered, with or without mention of antepartum condition	189, 201
663.43	Short cord complicating labor and delivery, antepartum condition or complication	209

Code	Narrative	Page
663.50	Vasa previa complicating labor and delivery, unspecified as to episode of care	189, 201
663.51	Vasa previa complicating labor and delivery, delivered, with or without mention of antepartum condition	189, 201
663.53	Vasa previa complicating labor and delivery, antepartum condition or complication	209
663.60	Lesions, vascular, cord, complicating labor and delivery, unspecified as to episode of care	189, 201
663.61	Lesions, vascular, cord, complicating labor and delivery, delivered, with or without mention of antepartum condition	189, 201
663.63	Lesions, vascular, cord, complicating labor and delivery, antepartum condition or complication	209
663.80	Complications, other, unbilical cord, during labor and delivery, unspecified as to episode of care	189, 201
663.81	Complications, other, unbilical cord, during labor and delivery, delivered, with or without mention of antepartum condition	189, 201
663.83	Complications, other, unbilical cord, during labor and delivery, antepartum condition or complication	209
663.90	Complications, unspecified, unbilical cord, during labor and delivery, unspecified as to episode of care	189, 201
663.91	Complications, unspecified, unbilical cord, during labor and delivery, delivered, with or without mention of antepartum condition	189, 201
663.93	Complications, unspecified, unbilical cord, during labor and delivery, antepartum condition or complication	209
664.00	Laceration, first-degree, perineal, during delivery, unspecified as to episode of care	189, 201
664.01	Laceration, first-degree, perineal, during delivery, degree, delivered with or without mention of antepartum condition	189, 201
664.04	Laceration, first-degree, perineal, during delivery, postpartum condition or complication	204
664.10	Laceration, second-degree, perineal, during delivery, unspecified as to episode of care	189, 201
664.11	Laceration, second-degree, perineal, during delivery, degree, delivered with or without mention of antepartum condition	189, 201
664.14	Laceration, second-degree, perineal, during delivery, postpartum condition or complication	204
664.20	Laceration, third-degree, perineal, during delivery, unspecified as to episode of care	189, 201
664.21	Laceration, third-degree, perineal, during delivery, degree, delivered with or without mention of antepartum condition	189, 201
664.24	Laceration, third-degree, perineal, during delivery, postpartum condition or complication	204
664.30	Laceration, fourth-degree, perineal, during delivery, unspecified as to episode of care	189, 201
664.31	Laceration, fourth-degree, perineal, during delivery, degree, delivered with or without mention of antepartum condition	189, 201
664.34	Laceration, fourth-degree, perineal, during delivery, postpartum condition or complication	204
664.40	Laceration, unspecified, perineal, during delivery, unspecified as to episode of care	189, 201
664.41	Laceration, unspecified, perineal, during delivery, degree, delivered with or without mention of antepartum condition	189, 201
664.44	Laceration, unspecified, perineal, during delivery, postpartum condition or complication	204
664.50	Hematoma, vulvar and perineal, during delivery, unspecified as to episode of care	190, 201
664.51	Hematoma, vulvar and perineal, during delivery, delivered, with or without mention of antepartum condition	190, 201
664.54	Hematoma, vulvar and perineal, during delivery, postpartum condition or complication	204
664.80	Trauma, other specified, perineum and vulva, during delivery, unspecified as to episode of care	190, 201
664.81	Trauma, other specified, perineum and vulva, during delivery, delivered, with or without mention of antepartum condition	190, 201
664.84	Trauma, other specified, perineum and vulva, during delivery, postpartum condition or complication	204
664.90	Trauma, unspecified, perineum and vulva, during delivery, unspecified as to episode of care	190, 201
664.91	Trauma, unspecified, perineum and vulva, during delivery, delivered, with or without mention of antepartum condition	190, 201
664.94	Trauma, unspecified, perineum and vulva, during delivery, postpartum condition or complication	204
665.00	Rupture, uterus, before onset of labor, unspecified as to episode of care	190, 201

Code	Narrative	Page
665.01	Rupture, uterus, before onset of labor, delivered, with or without mention of antepartum condition	190, 201
665.03	Rupture, uterus, before onset of labor, antepartum condition or complication	209
665.10	Rupture, uterus, during and after labor, unspecified as to episode of care	190, 201
665.11	Rupture, uterus, during and after labor, delivered, with or without mention of antepartum condition	190, 201
665.20	Inversion, obstetrical, uterus, unspecified as to episode of care	190, 201
665.22	Inversion, obstetrical, uterus, delivered, with mention of postpartum complication	190, 201
665.24	Inversion, obstetrical, uterus, postpartum condition or complication	204
665.30	Laceration, obstetrical, cervix, unspecified as to episode of care	190, 201
665.31	Laceration, obstetrical, cervix, delivered, with or without mention of antepartum condition	190, 201
665.34	Laceration, obstetrical, cervix, postpartum condition or complication	204
665.40	Laceration, high, vaginal, during and after labor, unspecified as to episode of care	190, 201
665.41	Laceration, high, vaginal, during and after labor, delivered, with or without mention of antepartum condition	190, 201
665.44	Laceration, high, vaginal, during and after labor, postpartum condition or complication	204
665.50	Injury, other, obstetrical, pelvic organs, unspecified as to episode of care	190, 202
665.51	Injury, other, obstetrical, pelvic organs, delivered, with or without mention of antepartum condition	190, 202
665.54	Injury, other, obstetrical, pelvic organs, postpartum condition or complication	204
665.60	Damage, obstetrical, pelvic joints and ligaments, unspecified as to episode of care	190, 202
665.61	Damage, obstetrical, pelvic joints and ligaments, delivered, with or without mention of antepartum condition	190, 202
665.64	Damage, obstetrical, pelvic joints and ligaments, postpartum condition or complication	204
665.70	Hematoma, obstetrical, pelvic, unspecified as to episode of care	190, 202
665.71	Hematoma, obstetrical, pelvic, delivered, with or without mention of antepartum condition	190, 202
665.72	Hematoma, obstetrical, pelvic, delivered, with mention of postpartum complication	190, 202
665.74	Hematoma, obstetrical, pelvic, postpartum condition or complication	204
665.80	Trauma, obstetrical, other specified, unspecified as to episode of care	190, 202
665.81	Trauma, obstetrical, other specified, delivered, with or without mention of antepartum condition	190, 202
665.82	Trauma, obstetrical, other specified, delivered, with mention of postpartum complication	190, 202
665.83	Trauma, obstetrical, other specified, antepartum condition or complication	209
665.84	Trauma, obstetrical, other specified, postpartum condition or complication	204
665.90	Trauma, obstetrical, unspecified, unspecified as to episode of care	190, 202
665.91	Trauma, obstetrical, unspecified, delivered, with or without mention of antepartum condition	190, 202
665.92	Trauma, obstetrical, unspecified, delivered, with mention of postpartum complication	190, 202
665.93	Trauma, obstetrical, unspecified, antepartum condition or complication	209
665.94	Trauma, obstetrical, unspecified, postpartum condition or complication	204
666.00	Hemorrhage, third-stage, postpartum, unspecified as to episode of care	213
666.02	Hemorrhage, third-stage, postpartum, delivered, with mention of postpartum condition	190, 196
666.04	Hemorrhage, third-stage, postpartum, postpartum condition or complication	204
666.10	Hemorrhage, other, immediate, postpartum, unspecified as to episode of care	213
666.12	Hemorrhage, other, immediate, postpartum, delivered, with mention of postpartum condition	190, 196
666.14	Hemorrhage, other, immediate, postpartum, postpartum condition or complication	204
666.20	Hemorrhage, delayed and secondary, postpartum, unspecified as to episode of care	213
666.22	Hemorrhage, delayed and secondary, postpartum, delivered, with mention of postpartum condition	190, 196
666.24	Hemorrhage, delayed and secondary, postpartum, postpartum condition or complication	204
666.30	Defects, coagulation, postpartum, unspecified as to episode of care	213

Numeric Index to Diseases

* Code Range

Code	Narrative	Page
666.32	Defects, coagulation, postpartum, delivered, with mention of postpartum complication	190, 196
666.34	Defects, coagulation, postpartum, postpartum condition or complication	204
667.00	Retained placenta without hemorrhage, unspecified as to episode of care	213
667.02	Retained placenta without hemorrhage, with delivery, with mention of postpartum complication	190, 196
667.04	Retained placenta without hemorrhage, postpartum condition or complication	204
667.10	Retained portions, placenta or membranes, without hemorrhage, unspecified as to episode of care	213
667.12	Retained portions, placenta or membranes, without hemorrhage, delivered, with mention of postpartum complication	190, 196
667.14	Retained portions, placenta or membranes, without hemorrhage, postpartum condition or complication	204
668.00	Complications, pulmonary, of anesthetic or other sedation, labor and delivery, unspecified as to episode of care	190, 202
668.01	Complications, pulmonary, of anesthetic or other sedation, labor and delivery, delivered, with or without mention of antepartum condition	190, 196
668.02	Complications, pulmonary, of anesthetic or other sedation, labor and delivery, delivered, with mention of postpartum complication	190, 196
668.03	Complications, pulmonary, of anesthetic or other sedation, labor and delivery, antepartum condition or complication	209
668.04	Complications, pulmonary, of anesthetic or other sedation, labor and delivery, postpartum condition or complication	204
668.10	Complications, cardiac, of anesthetic or other sedation, labor and delivery, unspecified as to episode of care	190, 202
668.11	Complications, cardiac, of anesthetic or other sedation, labor and delivery, delivered, with or without mention of antepartum condition	190, 196
668.12	Complications, cardiac, of anesthetic or other sedation, labor and delivery, delivered, with mention of postpartum complication	190, 196
668.13	Complications, cardiac, of anesthetic or other sedation, labor and delivery, antepartum condition or complication	209
668.14	Complications, cardiac, of anesthetic or other sedation, labor and delivery, postpartum condition or complication	204
668.20	Complications, central nervous system, of anesthetic or other sedation, labor and delivery, unspecified as to episode of care	190, 202
668.21	Complications, central nervous system, of anesthetic or other sedation, labor and delivery, delivered, with or without mention of antepartum condition	190, 196
668.22	Complications, central nervous system, of anesthetic or other sedation, labor and delivery, delivered, with mention of postpartum complication	190, 196
668.23	Complications, central nervous system, of anesthetic or other sedation, labor and delivery, antepartum condition or complication	209
668.24	Complications, central nervous system, of anesthetic or other sedation, labor and delivery, postpartum condition or complication	204
668.80	Complications, other, of anesthetic or other sedation, labor and delivery, unspecified as to episode of care	190, 202
668.81	Complications, other, of anesthetic or other sedation, labor and delivery, delivered, with or without mention of antepartum condition	190, 196
668.82	Complications, other, of anesthetic or other sedation, labor and delivery, delivered, with mention of postpartum complication	190, 196
668.83	Complications, other, of anesthetic or other sedation, labor and delivery, antepartum condition or complication	209
668.84	Complications, other, of anesthetic or other sedation, labor and delivery, postpartum condition or complication	204
668.90	Complications, unspecified, of anesthetic or other sedation, labor and delivery, unspecified as to episode of care	191, 202
668.91	Complications, unspecified, of anesthetic or other sedation, labor and delivery, delivered, with or without mention of antepartum condition	191, 196
668.92	Complications, unspecified, of anesthetic or other sedation, labor and delivery, delivered, with mention of postpartum complication	191, 196

Numeric Index to Diseases

Code	Narrative	Page
668.93	Complications, unspecified, of anesthetic or other sedation, labor and delivery, antepartum condition or complication	209
668.94	Complications, unspecified, of anesthetic or other sedation, labor and delivery, postpartum condition or complication	205
669.00	Distress, maternal, unspecified as to episode of care	191, 202
669.01	Distress, maternal, delivered, with or without mention of antepartum condition	191, 202
669.02	Distress, maternal, delivered, with mention of postpartum complication	191, 202
669.03	Distress, maternal, antepartum condition or complication	209
669.04	Distress, maternal, postpartum condition or complication	205
669.10	Shock during or following labor and delivery, unspecified as to episode of care	191, 202
669.11	Shock during or following labor and delivery, delivered, with or without mention of antepartum condition	191, 196
669.12	Shock during or following labor and delivery, delivered, with mention of postpartum complication	191, 196
669.13	Shock during or following labor and delivery, antepartum condition or complication	209
669.14	Shock during or following labor and delivery, postpartum condition or complication	205
669.20	Syndrome, hypotension, maternal, unspecified as to episode of care	191, 202
669.21	Syndrome, hypotension, maternal, delivered, with or without mention of antepartum condition	191, 202
669.22	Syndrome, hypotension, maternal, delivered, with mention of postpartum complication	191, 202
669.23	Syndrome, hypotension, maternal, antepartum condition or complication	209
669.24	Syndrome, hypotension, maternal, postpartum condition or complication	205
669.30	Failure, renal, acute, following labor and delivery, unspecified as to episode of care	191, 202
669.32	Failure, renal, acute, following labor and delivery, delivered with mention of postpartum complication	191, 196
669.34	Failure, renal, acute, following labor and delivery, postpartum condition or complication	205
669.40	Complications, other, obstetrical, surgery and procedures, unspecified as to episode of care	191, 202
669.41	Complications, other, obstetrical, surgery and procedures, delivered, with or without mention of antepartum condition	191, 196
669.42	Complications, other, obstetrical, surgery and procedures, delivered, with mention of postpartum complication	191, 196
669.43	Complications, other, obstetrical, surgery and procedures, antepartum condition or complication	209
669.44	Complications, other, obstetrical, surgery and procedures, postpartum condition or complication	205
669.50	Delivery, forceps or vacuum extractor, without mention of indication, unspecified as to episode of care	191, 202
669.51	Delivery, forceps or vacuum extractor, without mention of indication, delivered, with or without mention of antepartum condition	191, 202
669.60	Breech extraction, without mention of indication, unspecified as to episode of care	191, 202
669.61	Breech extraction, without mention of indication, delivered, with or without mention of antepartum condition	191, 202
669.70	Delivery, cesarean, without mention of indication, unspecified as to episode of care	191, 202
669.71	Delivery, cesarean, without mention of indication, delivered, with or without mention of antepartum condition	191, 202
669.80	Complications, other, of labor and delivery, unspecified as to episode of care	191, 202
669.81	Complications, other, of labor and delivery, delivered, with or without mention of antepartum condition	191, 202
669.82	Complications, other, of labor and delivery, delivered, with mention of postpartum complication	191, 202
669.83	Complications, other, of labor and delivery, antepartum condition or complication	209
669.84	Complications, other, of labor and delivery, postpartum condition or complication	205
669.90	Complications, unspecified, of labor and delivery, unspecified as to episode of care	191, 202
669.91	Complications, unspecified, of labor and delivery, delivered, with or without mention of antepartum condition	191, 202
669.92	Complications, unspecified, of labor and delivery, delivered, with mention of postpartum complication	191, 202

 ** Code Range*

Code	Narrative	Page
669.93	Complications, unspecified, of labor and delivery, antepartum condition or complication	209
669.94	Complications, unspecified, of labor and delivery, postpartum condition or complication	205
670.00	Infection, puerperal, major, unspecified as to episode of care	213
670.02	Infection, puerperal, major, delivered, with mention of postpartum complication	191, 196
670.04	Infection, puerperal, major, postpartum condition or complication	205
671.00	Varicose veins, legs complicating pregnancy and puerperium, unspecified as to episode of care	213
671.01	Varicose veins, legs, complicating pregnancy and puerperium, delivered, with or without mention of antepartum condition	191, 202
671.02	Varicose veins of legs, complicating pregnancy and puerperium, delivered, with mention of postpartum complication	191, 202
671.03	Varicose veins, legs, complicating pregnancy and puerperium, antepartum condition or complication	209
671.04	Varicose veins, legs, complicating pregnancy and puerperium, postpartum condition or complication	205
671.10	Varicose veins, vulva complicating pregnancy and puerperium, unspecified as to episode of care	214
671.11	Varicose veins, vulva, complicating pregnancy and puerperium, delivered, with or without mention of antepartum condition	191, 202
671.12	Varicose veins, vulva, complicating pregnancy and puerperium, delivered, with mention of postpartum complication	191, 202
671.13	Varicose veins, vulva, complicating pregnancy and puerperium, antepartum condition or complication	209
671.14	Varicose veins, vulva, complicating pregnancy and puerperium, postpartum condition or complication	205
671.20	Thrombophlebitis, superficial complicating pregnancy and puerperium, unspecified as to episode of care	214
671.21	Thrombophlebitis, superficial, complicating pregnancy and puerperium, delivered, with or without mention of antepartum condition	191, 202
671.22	Thrombophlebitis, superficial, complicating pregnancy and puerperium, delivered, with mention of postpartum complication	191, 202
671.23	Thrombophlebitis, superficial, complicating pregnancy and puerperium, antepartum condition or complication	209
671.24	Thrombophlebitis, superficial, complicating pregnancy and puerperium, postpartum condition or complication	205
671.30	Phlebothrombosis, deep, antepartum, unspecified as to episode of care	214
671.31	Phlebothrombosis, deep, antepartum, delivered, with or without mention of antepartum condition	191, 196
671.33	Phlebothrombosis, deep, antepartum, antepartum condition or complication	209
671.40	Phlebothrombosis, deep, postpartum, unspecified as to episode of care	214
671.42	Phlebothrombosis, deep, postpartum, delivered, with mention of postpartum condition	191, 196
671.44	Phlebothrombosis, deep, postpartum, postpartum condition or complication	205
671.50	Phlebitis and thrombosis, other, complicating pregnancy and puerperium, unspecified as to episode of care	214
671.51	Phlebitis and thrombosis, other, complicating pregnancy and puerperium, delivered, with or without mention of antepartum condition	191, 196
671.52	Phlebitis and thrombosis, other, complicating pregnancy and puerperium, delivered, with mention of postpartum complication	191, 196
671.53	Phlebitis and thrombosis, other, complicating pregnancy and puerperium, antepartum condition or complication	209
671.54	Phlebitis and thrombosis, other, complicating pregnancy and puerperium, postpartum condition or complication	205
671.80	Complications, venous, other, in pregnancy and puerperium, unspecified as to episode of care	214
671.81	Complications, venous, other, in pregnancy and puerperium, delivered, with or without antepartum condition	191, 202
671.82	Complications, venous, other, in pregnancy and puerperium, delivered, with mention of postpartum complication	191, 202

** Code Range*

Code	Narrative	Page
671.83	Complications, venous, other, in pregnancy and puerperium, antepartum condition or complication	209
671.84	Complications, venous, other, in pregnancy and puerperium, postpartum condition or complication	205
671.90	Complications, venous, unspecified, in pregnancy and puerperium, unspecified as to episode of care	214
671.91	Complications, venous, unspecified, in pregnancy and puerperium, delivered, with or without antepartum condition	191, 203
671.92	Complications, venous, unspecified, in pregnancy and puerperium, delivered, with mention of postpartum complication	191, 203
671.93	Complications, venous, unspecified, in pregnancy and puerperium, antepartum condition or complication	209
671.94	Complications, venous, unspecified, in pregnancy and puerperium, postpartum condition or complication	205
672.00	Pyrexia, unknown origin, during puerperium, unspecified as to episode of care	214
672.02	Pyrexia, unknown origin, during puerperium, delivered, with mention of postpartum complication	192, 196
672.04	Pyrexia, unknown origin, during puerperium, postpartum condition of complication	205
673.00	Embolism, air, pulmonary, obstetrical, unspecified as to episode of care	214
673.01	Embolism, air, pulmonary, obstetrical, delivered, with or without mention of antepartum condition	192, 196
673.02	Embolism, air, pulmonary, obstetrical, delivered, with mention of postpartum complication	192, 196
673.03	Embolism, air, pulmonary, obstetrical, antepartum condition or complication	209
673.04	Embolism, air, pulmonary, obstetrical, postpartum condition or complication	205
673.10	Embolism, amniotic fluid, pulmonary, obstetrical, unspecified as to episode of care	214
673.11	Embolism, amniotic fluid, pulmonary, obstetrical, delivered, with or without mention of antepartum condition	192, 196
673.12	Embolism, amniotic fluid, pulmonary, obstetrical, delivered, with mention of postpartum complication	192, 196

Code	Narrative	Page
673.13	Embolism, amniotic fluid, pulmonary, obstetrical, antepartum condition or complication	209
673.14	Embolism, amniotic fluid, pulmonary, obstetrical, postpartum condition or complication	205
673.20	Embolism, blood-clot, pulmonary, obstetrical, unspecified as to episode of care	214
673.21	Embolism, blood-clot, pulmonary, obstetrical, delivered, with or without mention of antepartum condition	192, 196
673.22	Embolism, blood-clot, pulmonary, obstetrical, delivered, with mention of postpartum complication	192, 196
673.23	Embolism, blood-clot, pulmonary, obstetrical, antepartum condition or complication	209
673.24	Embolism, blood-clot, pulmonary, obstetrical, postpartum condition or complication	205
673.30	Embolism, pyemic and septic, pulmonary, obstetrical, unspecified as to episode of care	214
673.31	Embolism, pyemic and septic, pulmonary, obstetrical, delivered, with or without mention of antepartum condition	192, 196
673.32	Embolism, pyemic and septic, pulmonary, obstetrical, delivered, with mention of postpartum complication	192, 196
673.33	Embolism, pyemic and septic, pulmonary, obstetrical, antepartum condition or complication	209
673.34	Embolism, pyemic and septic, pulmonary, obstetrical, postpartum condition or complication	205
673.80	Embolism, other, pulmonary, obstetrical, unspecified as to episode of care	214
673.81	Embolism, other, pulmonary, obstetrical, delivered, with or without mention of antepartum condition	192, 197
673.82	Embolism, other, pulmonary, obstetrical, delivered, with mention of postpartum complication	192, 197
673.83	Embolism, other, pulmonary, obstetrical, antepartum condition or complication	209
673.84	Embolism, other, pulmonary, obstetrical, postpartum condition or complication	205
674.00	Disorders, cerebrovascular, in the puerperium, unspecified as to episode of care	214
674.01	Disorders, cerebrovascular, in the puerperium, delivered, with or without mention of antepartum condition	192, 197
674.02	Disorders, cerebrovascular, in the puerperium, delivered, with mention of postpartum complication	192, 197

*** Code Range**

Code	Narrative	Page
674.03	Disorders, cerebrovascular, in the puerperium, antepartum condition or complication	209
674.04	Disorders, cerebrovascular, in the puerperium, postpartum condition or complication	205
674.10	Disruption, wound, cesarean, unspecified as to episode of care	214
674.12	Disruption, wound, cesarean, delivered, with mention of postpartum complication	192, 197
674.14	Disruption, wound, cesarean, postpartum condition or complication	205
674.20	Disruption, wound, perineal, obstetrical, unspecified as to episode of care	214
674.22	Disruption, wound, perineal, obstetrical, delivered, with mention of postpartum complication	192, 197
674.24	Disruption, wound, perineal, obstetrical, postpartum condition or complication	205
674.30	Complications, other, wounds, obstetrical surgical, unspecified as to episode of care	214
674.32	Complications, other, wounds, obstetrical surgical, delivered, with mention of postpartum complication	192, 197
674.34	Complications, other, wounds, obstetrical surgical, postpartum condition or complication	205
674.40	Polyp, placental, unspecified as to episode of care	214
674.42	Polyp, placental, delivered with mention of postpartum complication	192, 203
674.44	Polyp, placental, postpartum condition or complication	205
674.50	Cardiomyopathy, peripartum, unspecified as to episode of care or not applicable	214
674.51	Cardiomyopathy, peripartum, delivered, with or without mention of antepartum condition	192
674.52	Cardiomyopathy, peripartum, delivered, with mention of postpartum condition	192
674.53	Cardiomyopathy, peripartum, antepartum condition or complication	209
674.54	Cardiomyopathy, peripartum, postpartum condition or complication	205
674.80	Complications, other, of puerperium, unspecified as to episode of care	214
674.82	Complications, other, of puerperium, delivered, with mention of postpartum complication	192, 197
674.84	Complications, other, of puerperium, postpartum condition or complication	205
674.90	Complications, unspecified, of puerperium, unspecified as to episode of care	214
674.92	Complications, unspecified, of puerperium, delivered, with mention of postpartum complication	192, 203
674.94	Complications, unspecified, of puerperium, postpartum condition or complication	205
675.00	Infections, nipple, associated with childbirth, unspecified as to episode of care	214
675.01	Infections, nipple, associated with childbirth, delivered, with or without mention of antepartum condition	192, 197
675.02	Infections, nipple, associated with childbirth, delivered, with mention of postpartum complication	192, 197
675.03	Infections, nipple, associated with childbirth, antepartum condition or complication	209
675.04	Infections, nipple, associated with childbirth, postpartum condition or complication	205
675.10	Abscess, breast, associated with childbirth, unspecified as to episode of care	214
675.11	Abscess, breast, associated with childbirth, delivered, with or without mention of antepartum condition	192, 197
675.12	Abscess, breast, associated with childbirth, delivered, with mention of postpartum complication	192, 197
675.13	Abscess, breast, associated with childbirth, antepartum condition or complication	209
675.14	Abscess, breast, associated with childbirth, postpartum condition or complication	205
675.20	Mastitis, nonpurulent, associated with childbirth, unspecified as to episode of care	214
675.21	Mastitis, nonpurulent, associated with childbirth, delivered, with or without mention of antepartum condition	192, 197
675.22	Mastitis, nonpurulent, associated with childbirth, delivered, with mention of postpartum complication	192, 197
675.23	Mastitis, nonpurulent, associated with childbirth, antepartum condition or complication	209
675.24	Mastitis, nonpurulent, associated with childbirth, postpartum condition or complication	205
675.80	Infection, other specified, breast and nipple, associated with childbirth, unspecified as to episode of care	214

Code	Narrative	Page
675.81	Infection, other specified, breast and nipple, associated with childbirth, delivered, with or without mention of antepartum condition	192, 203
675.82	Infection, other specified, breast and nipple, associated with childbirth, delivered, with mention of postpartum complication	192, 203
675.83	Infection, other specified, breast and nipple, associated with childbirth, antepartum condition or complication	209
675.84	Infection, other specified, breast and nipple, associated with childbirth, postpartum condition or complication	205
675.90	Infection, unspecified, breast and nipple, associated with childbirth, unspecified as to episode of care	214
675.91	Infection, unspecified, breast and nipple, associated with childbirth, delivered, with or without mention of antepartum condition	192, 203
675.92	Infection, unspecified, breast and nipple, associated with childbirth, delivered, with mention of postpartum complication	192, 203
675.93	Infection, unspecified, breast and nipple, associated with childbirth, antepartum condition or complication	209
675.94	Infection, unspecified, breast and nipple, associated with childbirth, postpartum condition or complication	205
676.00	Retracted nipple, associated with childbirth, unspecified as to episode of care	214
676.01	Retracted nipple, associated with childbirth, delivered, with or without mention of antepartum condition	192, 203
676.02	Retracted nipple, associated with childbirth, delivered, with mention of postpartum complication	192, 203
676.03	Retracted nipple, associated with childbirth, antepartum condition or complication	209
676.04	Retracted nipple, associated with childbirth, postpartum condition or complication	205
676.10	Cracked nipple, associated with childbirth, unspecified as to episode of care	214
676.11	Cracked nipple, associated with childbirth, delivered, with or without mention of antepartum condition	192, 203
676.12	Cracked nipple, associated with childbirth, delivered, with mention of postpartum complication	192, 203
676.13	Cracked nipple, associated with childbirth, antepartum condition or complication	209
676.14	Cracked nipple, associated with childbirth, postpartum condition or complication	205
676.20	Engorgement, breast, associated with childbirth, unspecified as to episode of care	214
676.21	Engorgement, breast, associated with childbirth, delivered, with or without mention of antepartum condition	192, 203
676.22	Engorgement, breast, associated with childbirth, delivered, with mention of postpartum complication	192, 203
676.23	Engorgement, breast, associated with childbirth, antepartum condition or complication	209
676.24	Engorgement, breast, associated with childbirth, postpartum condition or complication	205
676.30	Disorder, other and unspecified, breast, associated with childbirth, unspecified as to episode of care	214
676.31	Disorder, other and unspecified, breast, associated with childbirth, delivered, with or without mention of antepartum condition	192, 203
676.32	Disorder, other and unspecified, breast, associated with childbirth, delivered, with mention of postpartum complication	192, 203
676.33	Disorder, other and unspecified, breast, associated with childbirth, antepartum condition or complication	209
676.34	Disorder, other and unspecified, breast, associated with childbirth, postpartum condition or complication	205
676.40	Failure, lactation, unspecified as to episode of care	214
676.41	Failure, lactation, delivered, with or without mention of antepartum condition	192, 203
676.42	Failure, lactation, delivered, with mention of postpartum complication	192, 203
676.43	Failure, lactation, antepartum condition or complication	209
676.44	Failure, lactation, postpartum condition or complication	205
676.50	Suppressed, lactation, unspecified as to episode of care	214
676.51	Suppressed, lactation, delivered, with or without mention of antepartum condition	192, 203
676.52	Suppressed, lactation, delivered, with mention of postpartum complication	192, 203
676.53	Suppressed, lactation, antepartum condition or complication	209
676.54	Suppressed, lactation, postpartum condition or complication	205

Code	Narrative	Page
676.60	Galactorrhea, associated with childbirth, unspecified as to episode of care	214
676.61	Galactorrhea, associated with childbirth, delivered, with or without mention of antepartum condition	192, 203
676.62	Galactorrhea, associated with childbirth, delivered, with mention of postpartum complication	192, 203
676.63	Galactorrhea, associated with childbirth, antepartum condition or complication	209
676.64	Galactorrhea, associated with childbirth, postpartum condition or complication	205
676.80	Disorder, other, lactation, unspecified as to episode of care	214
676.81	Disorder, other, lactation, delivered, with or without mention of antepartum condition	193, 203
676.82	Disorder, other, lactation, delivered, with mention of postpartum complication	193, 203
676.83	Disorder, other, lactation, antepartum condition or complication	209
676.84	Disorder, other, lactation, postpartum condition or complication	205
676.90	Disorder, unspecified, lactation, unspecified as to episode of care	214
676.91	Disorder, unspecified, lactation, delivered, with or without mention of antepartum condition	193, 203
676.92	Disorder, unspecified, lactation, delivered, with mention of postpartum complication	193, 203
676.93	Disorder, unspecified, lactation, antepartum condition or complication	210
676.94	Disorder, unspecified, lactation, postpartum condition or complication	205
677	Late effect, complication, pregnancy, childbirth and puerperium	214
*680	Carbuncle and furuncle	143
*681	Cellulitis and abscess, finger, toe	137, 143
*682	Cellulitis and abscess, other	137, 143, 221, 228
682.0	Cellulitis and abscess, face	320
682.1	Cellulitis and abscess, neck	320
683	Lymphadenitis, acute	221, 228, 235, 310
684	Impetigo	143
*685	Cyst, pilonidal	143
*686	Infection, other, skin and subcutaneous tissue, local	143
686.9	Infections, unspecified, skin and subcutaneous tissue, local	230
*690	Dermatosis, erythematosquamous	147
*691	Dermatitis, atopic, and related conditions	147
691.0	Rash, diaper or napkin	230
*692	Dermatitis, contact, and other eczema	147
*693	Dermatitis, due to substances taken internally	147
693.0	Dermatitis, due to drugs and medicine taken internally	221, 228
694.0	Dermatitis, herpetiformis	147
694.1	Dermatosis, pustular, subcorneal	147
694.2	Dermatitis, herpetiformis, juvenile	147
694.3	Impetigo, herpetiformis	147
694.4	Pemphigus	142
694.5	Pemphigoid	142
694.60	Pemphigoid, benign, mucous membrane, without mention of ocular involvement	142
694.61	Pemphigoid, benign, mucous membrane with ocular involvement	25
694.8	Dermatosis, bullous, other specified	142
694.9	Dermatosis, bullous, unspecified	142
695.0	Erythema, toxic	142, 221, 228
695.1	Erythema multiforme	142
695.2	Erythema nodosum	142
695.3	Rosacea	147
695.4	Lupus erythematosus	142
695.81	Disease, Ritter's	142
695.89	Erythema, generalized, other specified	147
695.9	Erythema, generalized, unspecified	147
696.0	Psoriasis, arthropathic	128
696.1	Psoriasis, other	142
696.2	Parapsoriasis	142
696.3	Pityriasis, rosea	147
696.4	Pityriasis, rubra pilaris	147
696.5	Pityriasis, other and unspecified	147
696.8	Psoriasis, other and similar disorders	147
*697	Lichen	147
698.0	Pruritus ani	147
698.1	Pruritus, genital organs	172, 177, 183
698.2	Prurigo	147
698.3	Lichenification and lichen, simplex chronicus	147
698.4	Dermatitis, factitia, (artefacta)	147
698.8	Pruritis, other specified	147
698.9	Disorder, unspecified, Pruritic	147
700	Corns and callosities	147
*701	Hypertrophy and atrophy, skin conditions, other	147
*702	Dermatoses, other	147

* Code Range

Code	Narrative	Page
*703	Diseases, nail	147
*704	Disease, hair and hair follicles	147
*705	Disorders, sweat glands	147
*706	Disease, sebaceous glands	147
*707	Ulcer, chronic, skin	137, 142
*707.0	Ulcer, decubitus	83
*708	Urticaria	147
708.0	Urticaria, allergic	221, 228
*709	Disorders, other, skin and subcutaneous tissue	148, 230
709.9	Disorder, unspecified, skin and subcutaneous tissue	310
*710	Diseases, diffuse, connective tissue	128
*711.0	Arthritis, pyogenic	128, 310
711.06	Arthritis, pyogenic, lower leg	123
*711.1	Arthritis, associated with Reiter's disease and nonspecific urethriti	128
*711.2	Arthropathy, in Behcet's syndrome	128
*711.3	Arthropathy, postdysenteric	129
*711.4	Arthropathy, associated with other bacterial diseases	128
*711.5	Arthropathy, associated with other viral diseases	129
*711.6	Arthropathy, associated with mycoses	128
*711.7	Arthropathy, associated with helminthiasis	128
*711.8	Arthropathy, associated with infectious, parasitic diseases, other	128
*711.9	Arthritis, infective, unspecified	128, 310
*712	Arthropathies, crystal	129
*713	Arthropathy, associated with disorders, other, classified elsewhere	129
714.0	Arthritis, rheumatoid	128
714.1	Syndrome, Felty's	128
714.2	Arthritis, rheumatoid with visceral or systemic involvement	128
*714.3	Polyarthritis, juvenile chronic	128
714.4	Arthropathy, postrheumatic, rheumatic	129
714.81	Rheumatoid lung	45
714.89	Polyarthropathies, inflammatory, other, specified	128
714.9	Polyarthropathy, inflammatory, unspecified	129
*715	Osteoarthrosis and allied disorders	129
*716.0	Disease, Kaschin-Beck	129
*716.1	Arthropathy, traumatic	129
*716.2	Arthritis, allergic	130
*716.3	Arthritis, climacteric	130
*716.4	Arthropathy, transient	130
*716.5	Polyarthropathy or polyarthritis, unspecified	130
*716.6	Monoarthritis, unspecified	130
*716.8	Arthropathy, other specified	130
*716.9	Arthropathy, unspecified	130, 310
717.0	Tear, meniscus, medial, bucket handle	132
717.1	Derangement, meniscus, medial, anterior horn	132
717.2	Derangement, meniscus, medial, posterior horn	132
717.3	Derangement, meniscus, medial, other, unspecified,	132
*717.4	Derangement, meniscus, lateral	132
717.5	Derangement, meniscus, not elsewhere classified	132
717.6	Loose body, knee	134
717.7	Chondromalacia, patella	132
*717.8	Derangement, knee, other, internal	132
717.9	Derangement, unspecified, knee, internal	132
718.00	Disorder, cartilage, articular, site unspecified	134
718.01	Disorder, cartilage, articular, shoulder region	132
718.02	Disorder, cartilage, articular, upper arm	133
718.03	Disorder, cartilage, articular, forearm	132
718.04	Disorder, cartilage, articular, hand	132
718.05	Disorder, cartilage, articular, pelvic region and thigh	134
718.07	Disorder, cartilage, articular, ankle and foot	133
718.08	Disorder, cartilage, articular, other specified sites	134
718.09	Disorder, cartilage, articular, multiple sites	134
*718.1	Loose body, joint	134
718.20	Dislocation, pathological, site unspecified	132
718.21	Dislocation, pathological, shoulder region	133
718.22	Dislocation, pathological, upper arm	133
718.23	Dislocation, pathological, forearm	132
718.24	Dislocation, pathological, hand	132
718.25	Dislocation, pathological, pelvic region and thich	134
718.26	Dislocation, pathological, lower leg	133
718.27	Dislocation, pathological, ankle and foot	133
718.28	Dislocation, pathological, other specified sites	134
718.29	Dislocation, pathological, multiple sites	134
718.30	Dislocation, recurrent, joint, site unspecified	134
718.31	Dislocation, recurrent, joint, shoulder region	133
718.32	Dislocation, recurrent, joint, upper arm	133
718.33	Dislocation, recurrent, joint, forearm	132

 ** Code Range*

Code	Narrative	Page
718.34	Dislocation, recurrent, joint, hand	132
718.35	Dislocation, recurrent, joint, pelvic region and thich	134
718.36	Dislocation, recurrent, joint, lower leg	133
718.37	Dislocation, recurrent, joint, ankle and foot	133
718.38	Dislocation, recurrent, joint, other specified sites	134
718.39	Dislocation, recurrent, joint, multiple sites	134
*718.4	Contracture, joint	134
*718.5	Ankylosis, joint	130
718.60	Protrusion, unspecified, intrapelvic, acetabulumm, site unspecified	134
718.65	Protrusion, unspecified, intrapelvic, acetabulumm, pelvic region and thigh	134
*718.7	Dislocation, developmental, joint	134
*718.8	Derangement, other, joint	134
*718.9	Derangement, unspecified, joint	134
*719.0	Effusion, joint	134
*719.1	Hemarthrosis	130
*719.2	Synovitis, villonodular	130
*719.3	Rheumatism, palindromic	130
*719.4	Pain, joint	130
*719.5	Stiffness, joint, not elsewhere classified	130
*719.6	Symptom, other, referable to joint	130
719.7	Difficulty, walking	130
*719.8	Disorder, other specified, joint	130
*719.9	Disorder, unspecified, joint	130
720.0	Spondylitis, ankylosing	128
720.1	Enthesopathy, spinal	129
720.2	Sacroiliitis, not elsewhere classified	129
*720.8	Spondylopathy, other, inflammatory	129
720.9	Spondylopathies, unspecified, inflammatory	129
*721	Spondylosis and allied disorders	129
*722	Disorder, disc, intervertebral	129
723.0	Stenosis, spinal, cervical region	129
723.1	Cervicalgia	129
723.2	Syndrome, cervicocranial	12
723.3	Syndrome, cervicobrachial, diffuse	12
723.4	Neuritis or radiculitis, brachial, unspecified	12
723.5	Torticollis, unspecified	129
723.6	Panniculitis, neck	148
723.7	Ossification, ligament, posterior longitudinal in cervical region	129
723.8	Syndrome, other, affecting cervical region	129
723.9	Disorders, musculoskeletal, unspecified, and symptoms referable to neck	129
*724	Disorders, other and unspecified, back	129
725	Polymyalgia rheumatica	128
726.0	Capsulitis, adhesive, shoulder	131
*726.1	Syndrome, rotator cuff, shoulder, and allied disorders	131
726.2	Affections, other, not elsewhere classified, shoulder region	131
*726.3	Enthesopathy, elbow region	131
726.4	Enthesopathy, wrist and carpus	131
726.5	Enthesopathy, hip region	131
*726.6	Enthesopathy, knee	131
726.70	Enthesopathy, unspecified, ankle and tarsus	131
726.71	Bursitis, tendinitis, Achilles	131
726.72	Tendinitis, tibialis	131
726.73	Spur, calcaneal	134
726.79	Enthesopathy, other, ankle and tarsus	131
726.8	Enthesopathy, other, peripheral	131
*726.9	Enthesopathy, unspecified	131
727.00	Synovitis and tenosynovitis, unspecified	131
727.01	Synovitis and tenosynovitis, in disease classified elsewhere	131
727.02	Tumor, giant cell, tendon sheath	134
727.03	Trigger finger, acquired	131
727.04	Tenosynovitis, radial styloid	131
727.05	Tenosynovitis, other, hand and wrist	131
727.06	Tenosynovitis, foot and ankle	131
727.09	Synovitis and tenosynovitis, other	131
727.1	Bunion	134
727.2	Bursitis, specific, occupational origin	131
727.3	Bursitis, other	131
*727.4	Ganglion and cyst, synovium, tendon and bursa	131
*727.5	Rupture, synovium	131
*727.6	Rupture, nontraumatic, tendon	131
*727.8	Disorders, other, synovium, tendon and bursa	131
727.9	Disorder, unspecified, synovium, tendon and bursa	131
*728	Disorders, muscle, ligament and fascia	131
728.85	Spasm, muscle	130
728.87	Weakness, muscle (generalized)	130
729.0	Rheumatism, unspecified, and fibrositis	130
729.1	Myalgia and myositis, unspecified	130
729.2	Neuralgia, neuritis and radiculitis, unspecified	12, 310
*729.3	Panniculitis, unspecified	148

Numeric Index to Diseases

*** Code Range**

Code	Narrative	Page
729.4	Fasciitis, unspecified	131
729.5	Pain, limb	130
729.6	Foreign body, residual, soft tissue	134
729.81	Swelling, limb	130
729.82	Cramp, limb	130
729.89	Symptom, other, musculoskeletal, referable to limbs	130
729.9	Disorders, other and unspecified, soft tissue	130
*730.0	Osteomyelitis, acute	127
730.06	Osteomyelitis, acute, lower leg	123
*730.1	Osteomyelitis, chronic	127
730.16	Osteomyelitis, chronic, lower leg	123
*730.2	Osteomyelitis, unspecified	127
730.26	Osteomyelitis, unspecified, lower leg	124
730.30	Periostitis without osteomyelitis, site unspecified	130
730.31	Periostitis without osteomyelitis, shoulder region	130
730.32	Periostitis without osteomyelitis, upper arm	130
730.33	Periostitis without osteomyelitis, forearm	130
730.34	Periostitis without osteomyelitis, hand	130
730.35	Periostitis without osteomyelitis, pelvic region and thich	130
730.36	Periostitis without osteomyelitis, lower leg	130
730.37	Periostitis without osteomyelitis, ankle and foot	134
730.38	Periostitis without osteomyelitis, other specified sites	134
730.39	Periostitis without osteomyelitis, multiple sites	134
*730.7	Osteopathy from poliomyelitis	134
*730.8	Infection, other, bone, in diseases classified elsewhere	127
*730.9	Infection, unspecified, bone	127
*731	Osteitis deformans and osteopathies, associated with other disorders, classified elsewhere	130
*732	Osteochondropathies	130
*733.0	Osteoporosis	130
*733.1	Fracture, pathologic	127, 221, 228
*733.2	Cyst, bone	130
733.3	Hyperostosis, skull	134
*733.4	Necrosis, aseptic, bone	130
733.5	Osteitis condensans	130
733.6	Disease, Tietze's	47
733.7	Algoneurodystrophy	134
*733.8	Malunion and nonunion, fracture	134
733.90	Disorder, unspecified, bone and cartilage	134
733.91	Arrest, development or growth, bone	134
733.92	Chondromalacia	130
733.93	Fracture, stress, tibia or fibula	128
733.94	Fracture, stress, metatarsals	128
733.95	Fracture, stress, other bone	128
733.99	Disorder, other, bone and cartilage	134
734	Flat foot	134
*735	Deformity, toe, acquired	134
736.00	Deformities, unspecified, acquired, forearm, excluding fingers	134
736.01	Cubitus valgus (acquired)	134
736.02	Cubitus varus (acquired)	134
736.03	Deformity, valgus, acquired, wrist	134
736.04	Deformity, varus, acquired, wrist	134
736.05	Drop wrist, acquired	12
736.06	Claw hand, acquired	12
736.07	Club hand, acquired	12
736.09	Deformity, other, acquired, forearm, excluding fingers	134
736.1	Mallet finger	134
*736.2	Deformities, other, acquired, finger	134
*736.3	Deformities, acquired, hip	134
*736.4	Genu valgum or varum, acquired	134
736.5	Genu recurvatum, acquired	134
736.6	Deformity, other, acquired, knee	134
736.70	Deformity, unspecified, acquired, ankle and foot	134
736.71	Deformity, acquired, equinovarus	134
736.72	Deformity, acquired, foot, equinus	134
736.73	Deformity, acquired, foot, cavus	134
736.74	Claw foot, acquired	12
736.75	Deformity, acquired, foot, cavovarus	134
736.76	Deformity, other, acquired, foot, calcaneus	134
736.79	Deformity, other, acquired, ankle and foot	134
*736.8	Deformity, acquired, other parts of limbs	134
736.9	Deformity, acquired, limb, site unspecified	135
*737	Curvature, spine	129
738.0	Deformity, acquired, nose	35
*738.1	Deformity, other, acquired, head	135
738.2	Deformity, acquired, neck	135
738.3	Deformity, acquired, chest and rib	135
738.4	Spondylolisthesis, acquired	129
738.5	Deformity, other, acquired, back or spine	129
738.6	Deformity, acquired, pelvis	135
738.7	Cauliflower ear	36
738.8	Deformity, acquired, specified site, other	135
738.9	Deformity, acquired, unspecified site	135

*** Code Range**

Code	Narrative	Page
739.0	Lesions, nonallopathic, not elsewhere classified, head region	130
739.1	Lesions, nonallopathic, not elsewhere classified, cervical region	129
739.2	Lesions, nonallopathic, not elsewhere classified, thoracic region	129
739.3	Lesions, nonallopathic, not elsewhere classified, lumbar region	129
739.4	Lesions, nonallopathic, not elsewhere classified, sacral region	129
739.5	Lesions, nonallopathic, not elsewhere classified, pelvic region	130
739.6	Lesions, nonallopathic, not elsewhere classified, lower extremities	130
739.7	Lesions, nonallopathic, not elsewhere classified, upper extremities	130
739.8	Lesions, nonallopathic, not elsewhere classified, rib cage	130
739.9	Lesions, nonallopathic, not elsewhere classified, abdomen and other	130
*740	Anomalies, anencephalus and similar	16, 221, 228
*741	Spina bifida	16, 221, 228
*742	Anomaly, other congenital, nervous system	16, 221, 228
*743	Anomalies, congenital, eye	25
*744.0	Anomalies, congenital, ear, causing impairment of hearing	36
744.1	Anomalies, congenital, accessory auricle	36, 230
*744.2	Anomalies, other specified, congenital, ear	36
744.3	Anomaly, unspecified, congenital, ear	36
*744.4	Cyst or fistula, congenital, branchial cleft, preauricular sinus	36
744.5	Webbing, congenital, neck	148
744.81	Macrocheilia	37
744.82	Microcheilia	37
744.83	Macrostomia	37
744.84	Microstomia	37
744.89	Anomaly, other specified, congenital, face and neck	36
744.9	Anomaly, unspecified, congenital, face and neck	148
745.0	Anomaly, congenital, truncus, common	88
*745.1	Anomaly, congenital, transposition, great vessels	88
745.2	Tetralogy of Fallot	88
745.3	Anomaly, congenital, common ventricle	88
745.4	Defect, congenital, ventricular septal	88, 221, 228
745.5	Defect, congenital, atrial septal, ostium secundum type	88
745.60	Defects, congenital, unspecified type, endocardial cushion	88
745.61	Defect, congenital, ostium primum	88
745.69	Defect, congenital, other, endocardial cushion	88
745.7	Defect, congenital, cor biloculare	88
745.8	Anomalies, congenital, other, bulbus cordis and cardiac septal closure	88
745.9	Defect, congenital, unspecified, septal closure	88
*746.0	Anomalies, congenital, pulmonary valve	88
746.1	Atresia and stenosis, congenital, tricuspid	88
746.2	Anomaly, Ebstein's	88
746.3	Stenosis, congenital, aortic valve	88
746.4	Insufficiency, congenital, aortic valve	88
746.5	Stenosis, congenital, mitral valve	88
746.6	Insufficiency, congenital, mitralvalve	88
746.7	Syndrome, hypoplastic left heart	88
746.81	Stenosis, congenital, subaortic	88
746.82	Anomaly, congenital, cor triatriatum	88
746.83	Stenosis, congenital, infundibulum cardiac	88
746.84	Anomalies, obstructive, congenital, not elsewhere classified, heart	88
746.85	Anomaly, congenital, coronary artery	88
746.86	Anomaly, congenital, heart block	89
746.87	Anomaly, congenital, malposition, heart and cardiac apex	88
746.89	Anomaly, congenital, other specified, heart	88
746.9	Anomaly, congenital, unspecified, heart	88
747.0	Anomaly, congenital, patent ductus arteriosus	88
*747.1	Anomaly, congenital, coarctation, aorta	89
*747.2	Anomaly, congenital, other, aorta	89
747.3	Anomalies, congenital, pulmonary artery	89
*747.4	Anomalies, congenital, great veins	89
747.5	Absence, hypoplasia, congenital, umbilical artery	87
*747.6	Anomaly, congenital, other, peripheral vascular system	87
747.81	Anomaly, congenital, cerebrovascular system	16
747.82	Anomaly, congenital, vessel, spinal	16
747.83	Anomaly, circulatory system, persistent fetal circulation	215, 222
747.89	Anomaly, congenital, other specified, circulatory system	87

Code	Narrative	Page
747.9	Anomaly, congenital, unspecified, circulatory system	87
748.0	Atresia, congenital, choanal	36
748.1	Anomaly, congenital, other, nose	36
748.2	Web, congenital, larynx	36, 320
748.3	Anomaly, congenital, other, larynx, trachea, and bronchus	36, 320
748.4	Anomaly, congenital, cystic lung	47
748.5	Agenesis, hypoplasia, and dysplasia, congenital, lung	47
748.60	Anomalies, congenital, unspecified, lung	47
748.61	Bronchiectasis, congenital	45
748.69	Anomaly, congenital, other, lung	47
748.8	Anomaly, congenital, other specified, respiratory system	47
748.9	Anomaly, congenital, unspecified, respiratory system	47
*749	Anomaly, congenital, cleft palate and cleft lip	37
*749.0	Anomaly, congenital, cleft palate	320
*749.1	Anomaly, congenital, cleft lip	320
*749.2	Anomaly, congenital, cleft palate with cleft lip	320
750.0	Anomaly, congenital, tongue tie	37, 320
*750.1	Anomalies, congenital, other, tongue	37, 320
750.21	Absence, congenital, salivary gland	36, 320
750.22	Accessory, congenital, salivary gland	36, 320
750.23	Atresia, congenital, salivary duct	36, 320
750.24	Fistula, congenital, salivary gland	36, 320
750.25	Fistula, congenital, lip	37, 320
750.26	Anomalies, congenital, other specified, mouth	37, 320
750.27	Diverticulum, congenital, pharynx	36, 320
750.29	Anomalies, congenital, other specified, pharynx	36, 320
750.3	Fistula, congenital, tracheoesophageal	104
750.4	Anomalies, congenital, other specified, esophagus	104
750.5	Stenosis, congenital, hypertrophic, pyloric	104
750.6	Hernia, congenital, hiatus	104
750.7	Anomalies, congenital, other specified, stomach	104
750.8	Anomalies, congenital, other specified, upper alimentary tract	104
750.9	Anomalies, congenital, unspecified, upper alimentary tract	104
751.0	Anomaly, congenital, diverticulum, Meckel's	101
751.1	Atresia and stenosis, congenital, small intestine	104
751.2	Atresia and stenosis, congenital, large intestine, rectum, anal canal	104
751.3	Disease, Hirschsprung's, and disorders, congenital, other, functional colon	104
751.4	Anomalies, congenital, intestinal, fixation	104
751.5	Anomaly, congenital, other, intestine	104
751.60	Anomaly, congenital, unspecified, gallbladder, bile ducts, and liver	111
751.61	Atresia, congenital, biliary	111
751.62	Disease, congenital, cystic, liver	111
751.69	Anomalies, congenital, other, gallbladder, bile ducts, and liver	111
751.7	Anomalies, congenital, pancreas	110
751.8	Anomaly, congenital, other specified, digestive system	104
751.9	Anomaly, congenital, unspecified, digestive system	104
752.0	Anomalies, congenital, ovaries	177, 183
*752.1	Anomalies, congenital, fallopian tubes, broad ligaments	183
752.10	Anomalies, congenital, unspecified, fallopian tubes, broad ligaments	177
752.11	Cyst, embryonic, fallopian tubes and broad ligaments	177
752.19	Anomaly, congenital, other, fallopian tubes and broad ligaments	177
752.2	Doubling, congenital, uterus	177, 183
752.3	Anomaly, congenital, other, uterine	177, 183
*752.4	Anomaly, congenital, cervix, vagina and external female genitalia	183
752.40	Anomaly, congenital, unspecified, cervix, vagina and external female genitalia	177
752.41	Cyst, congenital, embryonic, cervix, vagina, and external female genitalia	177
752.42	Anomaly, congenital, imperforate hymen	177
752.49	Anomaly, congenital, other, cervix, vagina and external female genitalia	177
*752.5	Anomaly, congenital, undescended and retractile, testicle	172, 231
*752.6	Anomalies, congenital, hypospadias, epispadias, and other penile	173
752.7	Anomaly, congenital, indeterminate sex and pseudohermaphroditism	173, 177, 183
*752.8	Anomalies, congenital, other specified, genital organs	173
752.89	Anomalies, congenital, other specified, genital organs	177, 183
752.9	Anomaly, congenital, unspecified, genital organs	173, 177, 183
*753	Anomalies, congenital, urinary system	165

* Code Range

Code	Narrative	Page
754.0	Deformities, congenital, musculoskeletal, skull, face and jaw	135
754.1	Deformities, congenital, musculoskeletal, sternocleidomastoid muscle	135
754.2	Deformities, congenital, musculoskeletal, spine	135
*754.3	Dislocation, congenital, hip	135
754.40	Genu recurvatum, congenital	135
754.41	Dislocation, congenital, knee, with genu recurvatum	133
754.42	Bowing, congenital, femur	135
754.43	Bowing, congenital, tibia and fibula	135
754.44	Bowing, congenital, long bones of leg, unspecified	135
*754.5	Deformities, congenital, varus, feet	135
*754.6	Deformity, congenital, valgus, feet	135
754.61	Deformities, congenital, pes planus	231
*754.7	Deformities, congenital, other, feet	135
754.81	Anomaly, congenital, pectus excavatum	47
754.82	Anomaly, congenital, pectus carinatum	47
754.89	Anomaly, congenital, other specified, nonteratogenic	135
*755	Anomalies, congenital, other, limb	135
756.0	Anomalies, congenital, skull and face bones	135
756.10	Anomaly, congenital, spine, unspecified	129
756.11	Anomaly, congenital, spondylolysis, lumbosacral region	129
756.12	Anomaly, congenital, spondylolisthesis	129
756.13	Absence, congenital, vertebra	129
756.14	Anomaly, congenital, hemivertebra	129
756.15	Anomaly, congenital, fusion, spine, vertebra	129
756.16	Syndrome, Klippel-Feil	135
756.17	Spina bifida, occulta	16
756.19	Anomaly, congenital, other, spine	129
756.2	Anomaly, congenital, rib, cervical	135
756.3	Anomaly, congenital, other, ribs and sternum	47
756.4	Chondrodystrophy	135
*756.5	Osteodystrophy, congenital	135
756.6	Anomaly, congenital, diaphragm	47
*756.7	Anomaly, congenital, abdominal wall	105
*756.8	Anomalies, congenital, other specified, muscle, tendon, fascia, and connective tissue	135
756.9	Anomaly, congenital, other and unspecified, musculoskeletal system	135
757.0	Edema, hereditary, legs	148
757.1	Ichthyosis congenita	148
757.2	Anomalies, dermatoglyphic	148
757.31	Dysplasia, congenital, ectodermal	148
757.32	Hamartoma, congenital, vascular	148
757.33	Anomaly, congenital, pigmentation, skin	148, 231
757.39	Anomaly, congenital, other specified, skin	148, 231
757.4	Anomaly, congenital, specified, hair	148
757.5	Anomaly, congenital, specified, nails	148
757.6	Anomaly, congenital, specified, breast	143
757.8	Anomaly, congenital, other specified, integument	148
757.9	Anomaly, congenital, unspecified, integument	148
758.0	Syndrome, Down's	252
758.1	Syndrome, Patau's	252
758.2	Syndrome, Edwards'	252
*758.3	Syndrome, autosomal deletion	252
758.4	Anomaly, congenital, chromosomal, translocation, autosomal, balanced, normal individual	287
758.5	Anomaly, congenital, autosomal, other conditions due to	287
758.6	Dysgenesis, gonadal	173, 177, 183
758.7	Syndrome, Klinefelter's	173
*758.8	Conditions, other, due to chromosome anomalies	173, 177, 183
758.9	Conditions, due to chromosome anomalies, unspecified	287
759.0	Anomaly, congenital, spleen	235
759.1	Anomaly, congenital, adrenal gland	156
759.2	Anomaly, congenital, endocrine glands, other	156
759.3	Anomaly, congenital, situs inversus	105
759.4	Anomaly, congenital, conjoined twins	105, 221, 228
759.5	Anomaly, congenital, sclerosis, tuberculous	16
759.6	Anomaly, congenital, harmartosis, other, not elsewhere classified	236, 244
759.7	Anomalies, congenital, multiple, so described	135
759.81	Syndrome, Prader-Willi	135
759.82	Syndrome, Marfan	89
759.83	Syndrome, Fragile X	252
759.89	Anomalies, congenital, other specified	135
759.9	Anomalies, congenital, unspecified	287
762.4	Complications, fetus or newborn affected by, prolapsed cord	229, 231
762.5	Complications, fetus or newborn affected by, compression of umbilical cord, other	229, 231

Code	Narrative	Page
762.6	Complications, fetus or newborn affected by, conditions of umbilical cord, other and unspecified	229, 231
763.0	Complications, labor and delivery, fetus or newborn affected by, breech delivery and extraction	229, 231
763.1	Complications, labor and delivery, fetus or newborn affected by, malpresentation, malposition, and disproportion, other	229, 231
763.2	Complications, labor and delivery, fetus or newborn affected by, forceps delivery	229, 231
763.3	Complications, labor and delivery, fetus or newborn affected by, delivery by vacuum extractor	229, 231
763.4	Complications, labor and delivery, fetus or newborn affected by, cesarean delivery	215, 222
763.6	Complications, labor and delivery, fetus or newborn affected by, precipitate delivery	229, 231
763.9	Complication, labor and delivery, fetus or newborn affected by, unspecified complication	229, 231
764.08	Light-for-dates without malnutrition, fetal, 2,000-2,499 grams	229, 231
764.09	Light-for-dates without malnutrition, fetal, 2,500 or more grams	229, 231
764.11	Light-for-dates with malnutrition, fetal, less than 500 grams	215, 222
764.12	Light-for-dates with malnutrition, fetal, 500-749 grams	215, 222
764.13	Light-for-dates with malnutrition, fetal, 750-999 grams	215, 223
764.14	Light-for-dates with malnutrition, fetal, 1,000-1,249 grams	216, 223
764.15	Light-for-dates with malnutrition, fetal, 1,250-1,499 grams	216, 223
764.16	Light-for-dates with malnutrition, fetal, 1,500-1,749 grams	216, 223
764.17	Light-for-dates with malnutrition, fetal, 1,750-1,999 grams	216, 223
764.18	Light-for-dates with malnutrition, fetal, 2,000-2,499 grams	216, 223
764.21	Malnutrition, fetal, without mention of light-for-dates, less than 500 grams	216, 223
764.22	Malnutrition, fetal, without mention of light-for-dates, 500-749 grams	216, 223
764.23	Malnutrition, fetal, without mention of light-for-dates, 750-999 grams	216, 223
764.24	Malnutrition, fetal, without mention of light-for-dates, 1,000-1,249 grams	216, 223
764.25	Malnutrition, fetal, without mention of light-for-dates, 1,250-1,499 grams	216, 223
764.26	Malnutrition, fetal, without mention of light-for-dates, 1,500-1,749 grams	216, 223
764.27	Malnutrition, fetal, without mention of light-for-dates, 1,750-1,999 grams	216, 223
764.28	Malnutrition, fetal, without mention of light-for-dates, 2,000-2,499 grams	216, 223
764.98	Retardation, growth, unspecified, fetal, 2,000-2,499 grams	229, 231
764.99	Retardation, growth, unspecified, fetal, 2,500 or more grams	229, 231
765.00	Immaturity, extreme, fetal, unspecified (weight)	215, 222
765.01	Immaturity, extreme, fetal, less than 500 grams	215
765.02	Immaturity, extreme, fetal, 500-749 grams	215
765.03	Immaturity, extreme, fetal, 750-999 grams	215
765.04	Immaturity, extreme, fetal, 1,000-1,249 grams	215
765.05	Immaturity, extreme, fetal, 1,250-1,499 grams	215
765.06	Immaturity, extreme, fetal, 1,500-1,749 grams	215, 222
765.07	Immaturity, extreme, fetal, 1,750-1,999 grams	215, 222
765.08	Immaturity, extreme, fetal, 2,000-2,499 grams	215, 222
*765.1	Preterm, other, infants	215, 222
765.20	Gestation, unspecified weeks of gestation	229, 231
765.21	Gestation, less than 24 completed weeks of gestation	215
765.22	Gestation, 24 completed weeks of gestation	215
765.23	Gestation, 25-26 completed weeks of gestation	215
765.24	Gestation, 27-28 completed weeks of gestation	215, 222
765.25	Gestation, 29-30 completed weeks of gestation	215, 222
765.26	Gestation, 31-32 completed weeks of gestation	215, 222
765.27	Gestation, 33-34 completed weeks of gestation	215, 222
765.28	Gestation, 35-36 completed weeks of gestation	215, 222
765.29	Gestation, 37 or more completed weeks of gestation	229, 231
766.0	Disorders, long gestation, large baby, exceptionally	229, 231
766.1	Disorders, high birthweight, heavy-for-dates, other, infant	229, 231
*766.2	Disorder, long gestation, postterm, infant, not heavy-for-dates	230, 231
767.0	Hemorrhage, subdural and cerebral, trauma, birth	216, 223
767.11	Injury, scalp, trauma, birth, epicranial subaponeurotic hemorrhage (massive)	216, 223
767.19	Injury, scalp, trauma, birth, other	230, 231
767.4	Injury, spine and spinal cord, trauma, birth	216, 223

** Code Range*

Code	Narrative	Page
767.7	Injury, cranial and peripheral nerve, other, trauma, birth	216, 223
768.5	Asphyxia, severe, newborn	216, 223
768.6	Asphyxia, mild or moderate, newborn	230, 231
769	Distress, syndrome, respiratory, newborn	215
770.0	Pneumonia, congenital	216, 223
*770.1	Aspiration, fetal and newborn	216, 221, 223
770.2	Emphysema, interstitial, related conditions, fetus or newborn	216, 223
770.3	Hemorrhage, pulmonary, fetus or newborn	216, 223
770.4	Atelectasis, primary, fetus or newborn	216, 223
770.7	Disease, respiratory, chronic, arising in the perinatal period	45
770.84	Failure, respiratory, newborn	216, 223
771.0	Rubella, congenital	216, 223
771.1	Infection, congenital, cytomegalovirus	216, 223
771.2	Infections, other, congenital	216, 223
771.4	Omphalitis, newborn	216, 223
771.5	Mastitis, infective, neonatal	216, 223
*771.8	Infection, other, specific to perinatal period	216, 223
772.0	Loss, blood, fetal	216, 223
*772.1	Hemorrhage, intraventricular, fetal and neonatal	216, 223
772.2	Hemorrhage, subarachnoid, fetal and neonatal	216, 223
772.4	Hemorrhage, gastrointestinal, fetal and neonatal	216, 223
772.5	Hemorrhage, adrenal, fetal and neonatal	216, 223
772.6	Hemorrhage, cutaneous, fetal and neonatal	230, 231
773.2	Disease, hemolytic, due to isoimmunization, other and unspecified, fetus or newborn	216, 223
773.3	Hydrops fetalis, due to isoimmunization, fetus or newborn	216, 223
773.4	Kernicterus, due to isoimmunization, fetus or newborn	216, 223
773.5	Late anemia, due to isoimmunization, fetus or newborn	216, 223
*774.3	Jaundice, neonatal, due to delayed conjugation	230, 231
774.4	Jaundice, perinatal, due to hepatocellular damage	216, 223
774.5	Jaundice, perinatal, from other causes	230, 231
774.6	Jaundice, unspecified, fetal and neonatal	230, 231
774.7	Kernicterus, not due to isoimmunization, fetus or newborn	216, 223
775.1	Diabetes mellitus, neonatal	216, 223
775.2	Myasthenia gravis, neonatal	216, 223
775.3	Thyrotoxicosis, neonatal	216, 223
775.4	Hypocalcemia and hypomagnesemia, neonatal	216, 223
775.5	Imbalance, electrolytes, transitory, neonatal	216, 223
775.6	Hypoglycemia, neonatal	216, 223
775.7	Acidosis, metabolic, late, newborn	216, 223
776.0	Disease, hemorrhagic, newborn	216, 223
776.1	Thrombocytopenia, transient, neonatal	216, 223
776.2	Coagulation, disseminated, intravascular, neonatal	216, 223
776.3	Disorder, other, coagulation, transient, neonatal	216, 223
776.6	Anemia, of prematurity	216, 223
777.1	Obstruction, meconium, fetal and newborn	216, 223
777.2	Obstruction, intestinal, due to inspissated milk, newborn	216, 223
777.5	Enterocolitis, necrotizing, in fetus or newborn	216, 223
777.6	Perforation, intestinal, perinatal	216, 223
778.0	Hydrops fetalis not due to isoimmunization	216, 223
778.8	Conditions, other specified, integument, fetus and newborn	230, 231
779.0	Convulsions, newborn	216, 223
779.1	Irritability, other and unspecified, cerebral, newborn	216, 223
779.2	Depression, cerebral, coma, other abnormal cerebral signs, newborn	216, 223
779.3	Problems, feeding, newborn	230
779.4	Reaction and intoxication, drugs, specific to newborn	217, 224
779.5	Syndrome, withdrawal, drug, in newborn	217, 224
779.7	Leukomalacia, periventricular	16, 221, 228
779.83	Delayed separation, umbilical cord	230
780.01	Coma	13, 221, 228
780.02	Alteration, transient, awareness	252
780.03	State, vegetative, persistent	13, 221, 228
780.09	Alteration, other, consciousness	13
780.1	Hallucinations	251
780.2	Syncope, collapse	89
*780.3	Convulsions	13, 221, 228
780.4	Dizziness and giddiness	33
780.50	Disturbance, unspecified, sleep	253
780.51	Insomnia, with sleep apnea, unspecified	16
780.52	Insomnia, unspecified	253
780.53	Hypersomnia, with sleep apnea, unspecified	16
780.54	Hypersomnia, unspecified	253
780.55	Disruption, of 24 hour sleep wake cycles, unspecified	253

Numeric Index to Diseases

Numeric Index to Diseases

Code	Narrative	Page
780.56	Dysfunction, associated with sleep stages or arousal from sleep	253
780.57	Apnea, sleep, unspecified	16
780.58	Disorder, movement, sleep related, unspecified	253
780.59	Sleep disturbance, other	253
780.6	Fever	246, 247, 310
*780.7	Malaise, fatigue	286, 310
780.8	Hyperhidrosis, generalized	148, 310
*780.9	Symptom, other general	286
781.0	Abnormal involuntary movements	16
781.1	Disturbance, sensation, smell and taste	16
781.2	Abnormality, gait	16
781.3	Lack of coordination	16
781.4	Paralysis, transient, limb	16
781.5	Clubbing, fingers	47
781.6	Meningismus	16
781.7	Tetany	154, 221, 228
781.8	Syndrome, neurologic neglect	16
781.91	Loss of height	16
781.92	Abnormal posture	16
781.93	Torticollis, ocular	129
781.94	Weakness, facial	16
781.99	Symptoms, other, nervous and musculoskeletal systems	16
782.0	Disturbance, sensation, skin	16
782.1	Rash, other nonspecific skin eruption	148, 310
782.2	Swelling mass or lump, superficial, localized	148
782.3	Edema	286
782.4	Jaundice, unspecified, not newborn	111
782.5	Cyanosis	286
*782.6	Pallor, flushing	286
782.7	Ecchymoses, spontaneous	234
782.8	Changes, skin texture	148
782.9	Symptom, other, involving skin, integumentary tissue	148
*783	Symptoms concerning, nutrition, metabolism and development	154
*783.2	Abnormal, weight loss and underweight	310
*783.4	Lack, development, physiological in childhood	310
784.0	Headache	13
784.1	Pain, throat	36
784.2	Swelling, mass, or lump in head and neck	148
784.3	Aphasia	16
*784.4	Disturbance, voice	36
784.5	Disturbance, other, speech	16
784.60	Dysfunction, symbolic, unspecified	253
784.61	Alexia and dyslexia	253
784.69	Dysfunction, symbolic, other	253
784.7	Epistaxis	33
784.8	Hemorrhage, throat	37, 320
784.9	Symptom, other, involving head, neck	37
785.0	Tachycardia, unspecified	89, 221, 228
785.1	Palpitations	89
785.2	Murmurs, cardiac, functional, undiagnosed	89
785.3	Abnormal, other, heart sounds	91
785.4	Gangrene	87, 221, 228
785.50	Shock, unspecified, without mention of trauma	57, 59, 62, 64, 73, 77, 80, 83, 84, 85, 221, 228
785.51	Shock, cardiogenic	57, 59, 62, 64, 73, 77, 80, 83, 84, 85
785.52	Shock, septic	246
785.59	Shock, without mention of trauma, other	246
785.6	Enlargement, lymph nodes	235, 310
785.9	Symptom, other, involving cardiovascular system	91
*786.0	Dyspnea, respiratory abnormalities	46, 310
786.1	Stridor	46
786.2	Cough	46
786.3	Hemoptysis	46
786.4	Abnormal, sputum	46
786.50	Pain, chest, unspecified	90
786.51	Pain, precordial	90
786.52	Painful, respiration	46
786.59	Pain, chest, other	90
786.6	Swelling, mass, or lump, chest	46
786.7	Abnormal chest sounds	46
786.8	Hiccough	46
786.9	Symptoms, other, respiratory system, chest	46
*787	Symptoms, digestive system	103
788.0	Colic, renal	163
788.1	Dysuria	164
*788.2	Retention, urine	164, 221, 228
*788.3	Incontinence, urine	164
*788.4	Frequency, urination and polyuria	164
788.5	Oliguria and anuria	161, 162
*788.6	Abnormality, other, urination	164
788.7	Discharge, urethral	164
788.8	Extravasation, urine	164
788.9	Symptoms, other, involving urinary system	164

* Code Range

Code	Narrative	Page
*789.0	Pain, abdominal	103
789.1	Hepatomegaly	111, 310
789.2	Splenomegaly	235, 310
*789.3	Swelling, mass or lump, abdominal or pelvic	103
*789.4	Rigidity, abdominal	105
789.5	Ascites	286
*789.6	Tenderness, abdominal	103
789.9	Symptoms, other, involving abdomen, pelvis	103
*790.0	Abnormality, red blood cells	234
790.1	Findings, nonspecific, sedimentation rate, elevated	286
*790.2	Findings, nonspecific, abnormal glucose	154
790.3	Findings, nonspecific, alcohol blood level	254
790.4	Findings, nonspecific, transaminase or lactic acid dehydrogenase levels	286
790.5	Findings, nonspecific, serum enzyme levels	286
790.6	Findings, nonspecific, other, chemistry, blood	286
790.7	Bacteremia	221, 228, 246
790.8	Viremia, unspecified	247
*790.9	Findings, other nonspecific, examination of blood	286
791.0	Proteinuria	164
791.1	Chyluria	164, 221, 228
791.2	Hemoglobinuria	164
791.3	Myoglobinuria	286
791.4	Biliuria	111
791.5	Glycosuria	154
791.6	Acetonuria	154
791.7	Abnormal, findings, cells and casts, urine	164
791.9	Abnormal, findings, other nonspecific, urine	164
792.0	Abnormal, findings, nonspecific, cerebrospinal fluid	16
792.1	Abnormal, findings, nonspecific, stool contents	103
792.2	Abnormal, findings, nonspecific, semen	173
792.3	Abnormal, findings, nonspecific, amniotic fluid	210
792.4	Abnormal, findings, nonspecific, saliva	37
792.5	Abnormal, findings, cloudy dialysis effluent	286
792.9	Abnormal, other findings, nonspecific, body substances	286
793.0	Abnormal, findings, nonspecific, radiological and other examination, skull and head	16

Code	Narrative	Page
793.1	Abnormal, findings, nonspecific, radiological and other examination, lung field	46
793.2	Abnormal, findings, nonspecific, radiological and other examination, intrathoracic organ	87
793.3	Abnormal, findings, nonspecific, radiological and other examination, biliary tract	111
793.4	Abnormal, findings, nonspecific, radiological and other examination, gastrointestinal tract	103
793.5	Abnormal, findings, nonspecific, radiological and other examination, genitourinary organs	164
793.6	Abnormal, findings, nonspecific, radiological and other examination, abdominal area, including retroperitoneum	103
793.7	Abnormal, findings, nonspecific, radiological and other examination, musculoskeletal system	135
793.80	Abnormal, mammogram, unspecified	143
793.81	Microcalcification, mammographic	143
793.89	Abnormal, findings, nonspecific, radiological and other examination, breast	143
793.9	Abnormal, findings, nonspecific, radiological and other examination, other body site	286
*794.0	Abnormal, nonspecific, results, function studies, brain and central nervous system	16
794.10	Abnormal, nonspecific, response to nerve stimulation, unspecified	16
794.11	Abnormal, nonspecific, findings, function studies, retinal	25
794.12	Abnormal, nonspecific, findings, electrooculogram	25
794.13	Abnormal, nonspecific, findings, visually evoked potential	25
794.14	Abnormal, nonspecific, findings, function studies, oculomotor	25
794.15	Abnormal, nonspecific, findings, function studies, auditory	37, 231
794.16	Abnormal, nonspecific, findings, function studies, vestibular	37
794.17	Abnormal, nonspecific, findings, electromyogram [EMG]	135
794.19	Abnormal, nonspecific, findings, function studies, nervous system, peripheral	16
794.2	Abnormal, nonspecific, findings, function studies, pulmonary	47
794.30	Abnormal, nonspecific, findings, function studies, unspecified, cardiovascular	91
794.31	Abnormal, nonspecific, findings, electrocardiogram [ECG] [EKG]	91
794.39	Abnormal, nonspecific, findings, function studies, other, cardiovascular	91

Numeric Index to Diseases

* *Code Range*

Code	Narrative	Page
794.4	Abnormal, nonspecific, findings, function studies, kidney	164
794.5	Abnormal, nonspecific, findings, function studies, thyroid	156
794.6	Abnormal, nonspecific, findings, function studies, endocrine	156
794.7	Abnormal, nonspecific, findings, function studies, basal metabolic rate	156
794.8	Abnormal, nonspecific, findings, function studies, liver	111
794.9	Abnormal, nonspecific, findings, function studies, not elsewhere classified	164
*795.0	Abnormal findings, nonspecific, pap smear, cervix and cervical HPV	177, 184
795.1	Abnormal, nonspecific, findings, pap smear, other site	43
795.2	Abnormal, nonspecific, findings, chromosomal analysis	287
*795.3	Abnormal, findings, culture, nonspecific positive	249
795.4	Abnormal, nonspecific, findings, histological, other	231, 286
795.5	Reaction, nonspecific, tuberculin skin test, without active tuberculosis	43
795.6	Findings, serological for syphilis, false positive	128
*795.7	Findings, nonspecific, other immunological	235
796.0	Abnormal, findings, other nonspecific, toxicological	274
796.1	Abnormal, findings, other nonspecific, reflex	16
796.2	Abnormal, findings, other nonspecific, blood pressure, elevated without diagnosis of hypertension	91
796.3	Abnormal, findings, other nonspecific, blood pressure, low	91
796.4	Abnormal, findings, other nonspecific, clinical	231, 286
796.5	Abnormal, findings, other nonspecific, antenatal screening	210
796.6	Abnormal findings, other nonspecific, neonatal screening	286
796.9	Abnormal, findings, other nonspecific	286
797	Senility, without mention of psychosis	252
798.0	Syndrome, sudden infant death	16
798.1	Death, instantaneous	86
798.2	Death, occurring in less than 24 hours, from onset of symptoms, cause unknown	86
798.9	Death, unattended	287
*799.0	Asphyxia and hypoxemia	47
799.1	Arrest, respiratory	47, 221, 228
799.2	Nervousness	251

Code	Narrative	Page
799.3	Debility, unspecified	286
799.4	Cachexia	286, 310
*799.8	Morbidity and mortality, causes, other and ill-defined conditions	287
799.9	Morbidity and mortality, causes, other unknown and unspecified	287
*800	Fracture, skull, vault	14
*800.0	Fracture, closed, skull, vault, without mention of intracranial injury	293
800.02	Fracture, closed, skull, vault, without mention of intracranial injury, brief loss of consciousness	299
800.03	Fracture, closed, skull, vault, without mention of intracranial injury, moderate loss of consciousness	299
800.04	Fracture, closed, skull, vault, without mention of intracranial injury, prolonged loss of consciousness, return to preexisting conscious level	300
800.05	Fracture, closed, skull, vault, without mention of intracranial injury, prolonged loss of consciousness, without return to preexisting conscious level	300
*800.1	Fracture, closed, skull, vault, with cerebral laceration and contusion,	293
800.10	Fracture, closed, skull, vault, with cerebral laceration and contusion, unspecified state of consciousness	300
800.12	Fracture, closed, skull, vault, with cerebral laceration and contusion, brief loss of consciousness	300
800.13	Fracture, closed, skull, vault, with cerebral laceration and contusion, moderate loss of consciousness	300
800.14	Fracture, closed, skull, vault, with cerebral laceration and contusion, prolonged loss of consciousness, return to preexisting conscious level	300
800.15	Fracture, closed, skull, vault, with cerebral laceration and contusion, prolonged loss of consciousness, without return to preexisting conscious level	300
800.16	Fracture, closed, skull, vault, with cerebral laceration and contusion, loss of consciousness, unspecified duration	300
800.19	Fracture, closed, skull, vault, with cerebral laceration and contusion, with concussion, unspecified	300
*800.2	Fracture, closed, skull, vault, with hemorrhage, subarachnoid, subdural, and extradural	293
800.20	Fracture, closed, skull, vault, with hemorrhage, subarachnoid, subdural, and extradural, unspecified state of consciousness	300

* Code Range

Code	Narrative	Page
800.22	Fracture, closed, skull, vault, with hemorrhage, subarachnoid, subdural, and extradural, brief loss of consciousness	300
800.23	Fracture, closed, skull, vault, with hemorrhage, subarachnoid, subdural, and extradural, moderate loss of consciousness	300
800.24	Fracture, closed, skull, vault, with hemorrhage, subarachnoid, subdural, and extradural, prolonged loss of consciousness, return to preexisting conscious level	300
800.25	Fracture, closed, skull, vault, with hemorrhage, subarachnoid, subdural, and extradural, prolonged loss of consciousness, without return to preexisting conscious level	300
800.26	Fracture, closed, skull, vault, with hemorrhage, subarachnoid, subdural, and extradural, loss of consciousness, unspecified duration	300
800.29	Fracture, closed, skull, vault, with hemorrhage, subarachnoid, subdural, and extradural, with concussion, unspecified	300
*800.3	Fracture, closed, skull, vault, with other and unspecified intracranial hemorrhage	293
800.30	Fracture, closed, skull, vault, with other and unspecified intracranial hemorrhage, unspecified state of consciousness	300
800.32	Fracture, closed, skull, vault, with other and unspecified intracranial hemorrhage, brief loss of consciousness	300
800.33	Fracture, closed, skull, vault, with other and unspecified intracranial hemorrhage, moderate loss of consciousness	300
800.34	Fracture, closed, skull, vault, with other and unspecified intracranial hemorrhage, prolonged loss of consciousness, return to preexisting conscious level	300
800.35	Fracture, closed, skull, vault, with other and unspecified intracranial hemorrhage, prolonged loss of consciousness, without return to preexisting conscious level	300
800.36	Fracture, closed, skull, vault, with other and unspecified intracranial hemorrhage, loss of consciousness, unspecified duration	300
800.39	Fracture, closed, skull, vault, with other and unspecified intracranial hemorrhage, with concussion, unspecified	300
*800.4	Fracture, closed, skull, vault, with with other and unspecified intracranial injury	293

Code	Narrative	Page
800.40	Fracture, closed, skull, vault, with other and unspecified intracranial injury, unspecified state of consciousness	300
800.42	Fracture, closed, skull, vault, with other and unspecified intracranial injury, brief loss of consciousness	300
800.43	Fracture, closed, skull, vault, with other and unspecified intracranial injury, moderate loss of consciousness	300
800.44	Fracture, closed, skull, vault, with other and unspecified intracranial injury, prolonged loss of consciousness, return to preexisting conscious level	300
800.45	Fracture, closed, skull, vault, with other and unspecified intracranial injury, prolonged loss of consciousness, without return to preexisting conscious level	300
800.46	Fracture, closed, skull, vault, with other and unspecified intracranial injury, loss of consciousness, unspecified duration	300
800.49	Fracture, closed, skull, vault, with other and unspecified intracranial injury, with concussion, unspecified	301
*800.5	Fracture, open, skull, vault, without mention of intracranial injury	293
800.52	Fracture, open, skull, vault, without mention of intracranial injury, brief loss of consciousness	301
800.53	Fracture, open, skull, vault, without mention of intracranial injury, moderate loss of consciousness	301
800.54	Fracture, open, skull, vault, without mention of intracranial injury, prolonged loss of consciousness, return to preexisting conscious level	301
800.55	Fracture, open, skull, vault, without mention of intracranial injury, prolonged loss of consciousness, without return to preexisting conscious level	301
*800.6	Fracture, open, skull, vault, with cerebral laceration and contusion,	293, 301
*800.7	Fracture, open, skull, vault, with hemorrhage, subarachnoid, subdural, and extradural	293, 301
*800.8	Fracture, open, skull, vault, with other and unspecified intracranial hemorrhage	293, 301
*800.9	Fracture, open, skull, vault, with with other and unspecified intracranial injury	293, 301
*801	Fracture, skull, base	14
*801.0	Fracture, closed, skull, base, without mention of intracranial injury	293
801.02	Fracture, closed, skull, base, without mention of intracranial injury, brief loss of consciousness	301

Numeric Index to Diseases

*** Code Range**

Code	Narrative	Page
801.03	Fracture, closed, skull, base, without mention of intracranial injury, moderate loss of consciousness	301
801.04	Fracture, closed, skull, base, without mention of intracranial injury, prolonged loss of consciousness, return to preexisting conscious level	301
801.05	Fracture, closed, skull, base, without mention of intracranial injury, prolonged loss of consciousness, without return to preexisting conscious level	301
*801.1	Fracture, closed, skull, base, with cerebral laceration and contusion,	293, 301
*801.2	Fracture, closed, skull, base, with hemorrhage, subarachnoid, subdural, and extradural	293, 301
*801.3	Fracture, closed, skull, base, with other and unspecified intracranial hemorrhage	293, 301
*801.4	Fracture, closed, skull, base, with with other and unspecified intracranial injury	293, 301
*801.5	Fracture, open, skull, base, without mention of intracranial injury	293
801.52	Fracture, open, skull, base, without mention of intracranial injury, brief loss of consciousness	301
801.53	Fracture, open, skull, base, without mention of intracranial injury, moderate loss of consciousness	301
801.54	Fracture, open, skull, base, without mention of intracranial injury, prolonged loss of consciousness, return to preexisting conscious level	301
801.55	Fracture, open, skull, base, without mention of intracranial injury, prolonged loss of consciousness, without return to preexisting conscious level	301
*801.6	Fracture, open, skull, base, with cerebral laceration and contusion,	293, 301
*801.7	Fracture, open, skull, base, with hemorrhage, subarachnoid, subdural, and extradural	293, 301
*801.8	Fracture, open, skull, base, with other and unspecified intracranial hemorrhage	293, 301
*801.9	Fracture, open, skull, base, with with other and unspecified intracranial injury	293, 301
802.0	Fracture, closed, nasal bones	35, 293
802.1	Fracture, open, nasal bones	35, 293
*802.2	Fracture, closed, mandible	37, 293, 320
*802.3	Fracture, open, mandible	37, 293, 320
802.4	Fracture, closed, malar and maxillary bones	37, 293, 320
802.5	Fracture, open, malar and maxillary bones	37, 293, 320
802.6	Fracture, closed, orbital floor, blow-out	25, 293, 320
802.7	Fracture, open, orbital floor, blow-out	25, 293, 320
802.8	Fracture, closed, other facial bones	135, 293, 320
802.9	Fracture, open, other facial bones	135, 293, 320
*803	Fracture, skull, other and unqualified	14
*803.0	Fracture, closed, skull, other and unqualified, without mention of intracranial injury	293
803.02	Fracture, closed, skull, other and unqualified, without mention of intracranial injury, brief loss of consciousness	301
803.03	Fracture, closed, skull, other and unqualified, without mention of intracranial injury, moderate loss of consciousness	301
803.04	Fracture, closed, skull, other and unqualified, without mention of intracranial injury, prolonged loss of consciousness, return to preexisting conscious level	301
803.05	Fracture, closed, skull, other and unqualified, without mention of intracranial injury, prolonged loss of consciousness, without return to preexisting conscious level	301
*803.1	Fracture, closed, skull, other and unqualified, with cerebral laceration and contusion	293, 301
*803.2	Fracture, closed, skull, other and unqualified, with hemorrhage, subarachnoid, subdural, and extradural	293, 301
*803.3	Fracture, closed, skull, other and unqualified, with other and unspecified intracranial hemorrhage	293, 301
*803.4	Fracture, closed, skull, other and unqualified, with with other and unspecified intracranial injury	293, 301
*803.5	Fracture, open, skull, other and unqualified, without mention of intracranial injury	293
803.52	Fracture, open, skull, other and unqualified, without mention of intracranial injury, brief loss of consciousness	301
803.53	Fracture, open, skull, other and unqualified, without mention of intracranial injury, moderate loss of consciousness	301
803.54	Fracture, open, skull, other and unqualified, without mention of intracranial injury, prolonged loss of consciousness, return to preexisting conscious level	301

* Code Range

Code	Narrative	Page
803.55	Fracture, open, skull, other and unqualified, without mention of intracranial injury, prolonged loss of consciousness, without return to preexisting conscious level	301
*803.6	Fracture, closed, skull, other and unqualified, with cerebral laceration and contusion	293, 301
*803.7	Fracture, open, skull, other and unqualified, with hemorrhage, subarachnoid, subdural, and extradural	293, 301
*803.8	Fracture, open, skull, other and unqualified, with other and unspecified intracranial hemorrhage	294, 301
*803.9	Fracture, open, skull, other and unqualified, with with other and unspecified intracranial injury	294, 301
*804	Fracture, multiple, involving skull or face with other bones	14
*804.0	Fracture, closed, multiple, involving skull or face with other bones, without mention of intracranial injury	294
804.02	Fracture, closed, multiple, involving skull or face with other bones, without mention of intracranial injury, brief loss of consciousness	302
804.03	Fracture, closed, multiple, involving skull or face with other bones, without mention of intracranial injury, moderate loss of consciousness	302
804.04	Fracture, closed, multiple, involving skull or face with other bones, without mention of intracranial injury, prolonged loss of consciousness, return to preexisting conscious level	302
804.05	Fracture, closed, multiple, involving skull or face with other bones, without mention of intracranial injury, prolonged loss of consciousness, without return to preexisting conscious level	302
804.06	Fracture, closed, multiple, involving skull or face with other bones, without mention of intracranial injury, loss of consciousness, unspecified duration	302
*804.1	Fracture, closed, multiple, involving skull or face with other bones, with cerebral laceration and contusion	294, 302
*804.2	Fracture, closed, multiple, involving skull or face with other bones, with hemorrhage, subarachnoid, subdural, and extradural	294, 302
*804.3	Fracture, closed, multiple, involving skull or face with other bones, with other and unspecified intracranial hemorrhage	294, 302
*804.4	Fracture, closed, multiple, involving skull or face with other bones, with with other and unspecified intracranial injury	294
804.40	Fracture, closed, multiple, involving skull or face with other bones, with other and unspecified intracranial injury, unspecified state of consciousness	302
804.41	Fracture, closed, multiple, involving skull or face with other bones, with other and unspecified intracranial injury, no loss of consciousness	302
804.42	Fracture, closed, multiple, involving skull or face with other bones, with other and unspecified intracranial injury, brief loss of consciousness	302
804.43	Fracture, closed, multiple, involving skull or face with other bones, with other and unspecified intracranial injury, moderate loss of consciousness	302
804.44	Fracture, closed, multiple, involving skull or face with other bones, with other and unspecified intracranial injury, prolonged loss of consciousness, return to preexisting conscious level	302
804.45	Fracture, closed, multiple, involving skull or face with other bones, with other and unspecified intracranial injury, prolonged loss of consciousness, without return to preexisting conscious level	302
804.46	Fracture, closed, multiple, involving skull or face with other bones, with other and unspecified intracranial injury, loss of consciousness, unspecified duration	302
*804.5	Fracture, open, multiple, involving skull or face with other bones, without mention of intracranial injury	294
804.52	Fracture, open, multiple, involving skull or face with other bones, without mention of intracranial injury, brief loss of consciousness	302
804.53	Fracture, open, multiple, involving skull or face with other bones, without mention of intracranial injury, moderate loss of consciousness	302
804.54	Fracture, open, multiple, involving skull or face with other bones, without mention of intracranial injury, prolonged loss of consciousness, return to preexisting conscious level	302
804.55	Fracture, open, multiple, involving skull or face with other bones, without mention of intracranial injury, prolonged loss of consciousness, without return to preexisting conscious level	302
*804.6	Fracture, open, multiple, involving skull or face with other bones, with cerebral laceration and contusion,	294
804.60	Fracture, open, multiple, involving skull or face with other bones, with cerebral laceration and contusion, unspecified state of consciousness	302

Numeric Index to Diseases

Code	Narrative	Page
804.61	Fracture, open, multiple, involving skull or face with other bones, with cerebral laceration and contusion, no loss of consciousness	302
804.62	Fracture, open, multiple, involving skull or face with other bones, with cerebral laceration and contusion, brief loss of consciousness	302
804.63	Fracture, open, multiple, involving skull or face with other bones, with cerebral laceration and contusion, moderate loss of consciousness	302
804.64	Fracture, open, multiple, involving skull or face with other bones, with cerebral laceration and contusion, prolonged loss of consciousness, return to preexisting conscious level	302
804.65	Fracture, open, multiple, involving skull or face with other bones, with cerebral laceration and contusion, prolonged loss of consciousness, without return to preexisting conscious level	302
804.66	Fracture, open, multiple, involving skull or face with other bones, with cerebral laceration and contusion, loss of consciousness, unspecified duration	302
*804.7	Fracture, open, multiple, involving skull or face with other bones, with hemorrhage, subarachnoid, subdural, and extradural	294, 302
*804.8	Fracture, open, multiple, involving skull or face with other bones, with other and unspecified intracranial hemorrhage	294, 303
*804.9	Fracture, open, multiple, involving skull or face with other bones, with with other and unspecified intracranial injury	294, 303
*805	Fracture, vertebral column, without mention of spinal cord injury	129
*805.0	Fracture, closed, cervical vertebra, without mention of spinal cord injury	294
*805.1	Fracture, open, cervical vertebra, without mention of spinal cord injury	294
805.2	Fracture, closed, vertebral column, dorsal [thoracic], without mention of spinal cord injury	294
805.3	Fracture, open, vertebral column, dorsal [thoracic], without mention of spinal cord injury	294
805.4	Fracture, closed, vertebral column, lumbar, without mention of spinal cord injury	294
805.5	Fracture, open, vertebral column, lumbar, without mention of spinal cord injury	294
805.6	Fracture, closed, vertebral column, sacrum and coccyx, without mention of spinal cord injury	294, 304
805.7	Fracture, open, vertebral column, sacrum and coccyx, without mention of spinal cord injury	294, 304
805.8	Fracture, closed, vertebral column, unspecified, without mention of spinal cord injury	294
805.9	Fracture, open, vertebral column, unspecified, without mention of spinal cord injury	294
*806	Fracture, vertebral column, with spinal cord injury	9
*806.0	Fracture, closed, vertebral column, cervical, with spinal cord injury	294, 304
*806.1	Fracture, open, vertebral column, cervical, with spinal cord injury	294, 304
*806.2	Fracture, closed, vertebral column, dorsal [thoracic], with spinal cord injury	294, 304
*806.3	Fracture, open, vertebral column, dorsal [thoracic], with spinal cord injury	294, 304
806.4	Fracture, closed, vertebral column, lumbar, with spinal cord injury	294, 304
806.5	Fracture, open, vertebral column, lumbar, with spinal cord injury	294, 304
*806.6	Fracture, closed, vertebral column, sacrum and coccyx, with spinal cord injury	294
806.60	Fracture, closed, vertebral column, sacrum and coccyx, with spinal cord injury, unspecified	304
*806.7	Fracture, open, vertebral column, sacrum and coccyx, with spinal cord injury	294, 305
806.8	Fracture, closed, vertebral column, unspecified, with spinal cord injury	294, 305
806.9	Fracture, open, vertebral column, unspecified, with spinal cord injury	294, 305
*807.0	Fracture, closed, rib(s)	294
807.00	Fracture, closed, rib(s), unspecified	47
807.01	Fracture, closed, rib(s), one	47
807.02	Fracture, closed, rib(s), two	47
807.03	Fracture, closed, rib(s), three	43
807.04	Fracture, closed, rib(s), four	43
807.05	Fracture, closed, rib(s), five	43
807.06	Fracture, closed, rib(s), six	43
807.07	Fracture, closed, rib(s), seven s	43, 303
807.08	Fracture, closed, rib(s), eight or more	44, 303
807.09	Fracture, closed, rib(s), multiple, unspecified	44
*807.1	Fracture, open, rib(s)	44, 294
807.14	Fracture, open, rib(s), four	303
807.15	Fracture, open, rib(s), five	303
807.16	Fracture, open, rib(s), six	303
807.17	Fracture, open, rib(s), seven s	303
807.18	Fracture, open, rib(s), eight or more	303
807.19	Fracture, open, rib(s), multiple, unspecified	303

Code	Narrative	Page
807.2	Fracture, closed, sternum	44, 294
807.3	Fracture, open, sternum	44, 294, 303
807.4	Flail chest	44, 294, 303
807.5	Fracture, closed, larynx and trachea	37, 294, 303, 320
807.6	Fracture, open, larynx and trachea	37, 294, 303, 320
*808	Fracture, pelvis	127, 305
808.0	Fracture, closed, acetabulum	294
808.1	Fracture, open, acetabulum	294
808.2	Fracture, closed, pubis	294
808.3	Fracture, open, pubis	294
*808.4	Fracture, closed, pelvis, other specified part	294
*808.5	Fracture, open, pelvis, other specified part	294
808.8	Fracture, closed, pelvis, unspecified	294
808.9	Fracture, open, pelvis, unspecified	294
809.0	Fracture, closed, ill-defined, bones of trunk	135, 294
809.1	Fracture, open, ill-defined, bones of trunk	135, 294, 305
*810	Fracture, clavicle	133
*810.0	Fracture, closed, clavicle	294
*810.1	Fracture, open, clavicle	294
*811.0	Fracture, closed, scapula	294
811.00	Fracture, closed, scapula, unspecified part	133
811.01	Fracture, closed, scapula, acromial process	133
811.02	Fracture, closed, scapula, coracoid process	133
811.03	Fracture, closed, scapula, glenoid cavity and neck	133
811.09	Fracture, closed, scapula, other	135
*811.1	Fracture, open, scapula	294
811.10	Fracture, open, scapula, unspecified part	133
811.11	Fracture, open, scapula, acromial process	133
811.12	Fracture, open, scapula, coracoid process	133
811.13	Fracture, open, scapula, glenoid cavity and neck	133
811.19	Fracture, open, scapula, other	135
*812	Fracture, humerus	133
*812.0	Fracture, closed, humerus, upper end	294
*812.1	Fracture, open, humerus, upper end	295, 305
*812.2	Fracture, closed, humerus, shaft or unspecified part	295
*812.3	Fracture, open, humerus, shaft or unspecified part	295
812.30	Fracture, open, humerus, unspecified part	305
812.31	Fracture, open, humerus, shaft	305
*812.4	Fracture, closed, humerus, lower end	295
*812.5	Fracture, open, humerus, lower end	295, 305
*813	Fracture, radius and ulna	132
*813.0	Fracture, closed, radius and ulna, upper end	295
*813.1	Fracture, open, radius and ulna, upper end	295, 305
*813.2	Fracture, closed, radius and ulna, shaft	295
*813.3	Fracture, open, radius and ulna, shaft	295, 305
*813.4	Fracture, closed, radius and ulna, lower end	295
*813.5	Fracture, open, radius and ulna, lower end	295, 305
*813.8	Fracture, closed, radius and ulna, unspecified part	295
*813.9	Fracture, open, radius and ulna, unspecified part	295, 305
*814	Fracture, carpal bone(s)	132
*814.0	Fracture, closed, carpal bone(s)	295
*814.1	Fracture, open, carpal bone(s)	295
*815	Fracture, metacarpal bone(s)	132
*815.0	Fracture, closed, metacarpal bone(s)	295
*815.1	Fracture, open, metacarpal bone(s)	295
*816	Fracture, phalanges, one or more, hand	132
*816.0	Fracture, closed, phalanges, one or more, hand	295
*816.1	Fracture, open, phalanges, one or more, hand	295
*817	Fractures, multiple, hand bones	132
817.0	Fracture, closed, multiple, hand bones	295
817.1	Fracture, open, multiple, hand bones	295
*818	Fractures, ill-defined, upper limb	133
818.0	Fracture, closed, ill-defined, upper limb	295
818.1	Fracture, open, ill-defined, upper limb	295, 305
*819	Fractures, multiple, involving both upper limbs, upper limbs with rib(s), sternum	272
819.0	Fracture, closed, multiple, involving both upper limbs, upper limbs with rib(s), sternum	295
819.1	Fracture, open, multiple, involving both upper limbs, upper limbs with rib(s), sternum	295, 303
*820	Fracture, femur, neck	127, 221, 228, 305
*820.0	Fracture, closed, transcervical	295
*820.1	Fracture, open, transcervical	295
*820.2	Fracture, closed, pertrochanteric, femur	295

Numeric Index to Diseases

Code	Narrative	Page
*820.3	Fracture, open, pertrochanteric, femur	295
820.8	Fracture, closed, femur, neck, unspecified part	295
820.9	Fracture, open, femur, neck, unspecified part	295
*821	Fracture, femur, other and unspecified parts	127, 305
*821.0	Fracture, closed, femur, shaft or unspecified part	221, 228, 295
*821.1	Fracture, open, femur, shaft or unspecified part	221, 228, 295
*821.2	Fracture, closed, femur, lower end	295
*821.3	Fracture, open, femur, lower end	295
*822	Fracture, patella	133
822.0	Fracture, closed, patella	295
822.1	Fracture, open, patella	295
*823	Fracture, tibia and fibula	133
*823.0	Fracture, closed, tibia and fibula, upper end	295
*823.1	Fracture, open, tibia and fibula, upper end	295, 305
*823.2	Fracture, closed, tibia and fibula, shaft	295
*823.3	Fracture, open, tibia and fibula, shaft	295, 305
*823.4	Fracture, torus, tibia and fibula	295
*823.8	Fracture, closed, tibia and fibula, unspecified part	295
*823.9	Fracture, open, tibia and fibula, unspecified part	295, 305
*824	Fracture, ankle	133
824.0	Fracture, closed, ankle	295
824.1	Fracture, open, ankle, medial malleolus	295
824.2	Fracture, closed, ankle, lateral malleolus	295
824.3	Fracture, open, ankle, lateral malleolus	295
824.4	Fracture, closed, ankle, bimalleolar	295
824.5	Fracture, open, ankle, bimalleolar	295
824.6	Fracture, closed, ankle, trimalleolar	295
824.7	Fracture, open, ankle, trimalleolar	295
824.8	Fracture, closed, ankle, unspecified	295
824.9	Fracture, open, ankle, unspecified	295
825.0	Fracture, closed, calcaneus	133, 295
825.1	Fracture, open, calcaneus	133, 295
*825.2	Fracture, closed, tarsal and metatarsal bones, other	132, 295
*825.3	Fracture, open, tarsal and metatarsal bones, other	132, 295
*826	Fracture, foot, one or more phalanges	132
826.0	Fracture, closed, foot, one or more phalanges	295
826.1	Fracture, open, foot, one or more phalanges	295

Code	Narrative	Page
*827	Fracture, other, multiple and ill-defined, lower limb	133
827.0	Fracture, closed, other, multiple and ill-defined, lower limb	295
827.1	Fracture, open, other, multiple and ill-defined, lower limb	295
*828	Fractures, multiple, involving both lower limbs, lower with upper limb and lower limb with rib and sternum	272, 305
828.0	Fracture, closed, multiple, involving both lower limbs, lower with upper limb and lower limb with rib and sternum	296
828.1	Fracture, open, multiple, involving both lower limbs, lower with upper limb and lower limb with rib and sternum	296
*829	Fracture, bones, unspecified	132
829.0	Fracture, closed, bones, unspecified	296
829.1	Fracture, open, bones, unspecified	296
*830	Dislocation, jaw	38, 320
830.0	Dislocation, closed, jaw	296
830.1	Dislocation, open, jaw	296
*831	Dislocation, shoulder	133
*831.0	Dislocation, closed, shoulder	296
*831.1	Dislocation, open, shoulder	296, 305
*832	Dislocation, elbow	133
*832.0	Dislocation, closed, elbow	296
*832.1	Dislocation, open, elbow	296, 305
*833	Dislocation, wrist	132
*833.0	Dislocation, closed, wrist	296
*833.1	Dislocation, open, wrist	296
*834	Dislocation, finger	132
*834.0	Dislocation, closed, finger	296
*834.1	Dislocation, open, finger	296
*835	Dislocation, hip	127
*835.0	Dislocation, closed, hip	296
*835.1	Dislocation, open, hip	296, 305
*836	Dislocation, knee	133
836.0	Dislocation, knee, tear of cartilage meniscus, medial, current	296
836.1	Dislocation, knee, tear of cartilage meniscus, lateral, current	296
836.2	Dislocation, knee, tear of cartilage meniscus, other, current	296
836.3	Dislocation, closed, patella	296
836.4	Dislocation, open, patella	296
*836.5	Dislocation, closed, other, knee	296
*836.6	Dislocation, open, other, knee	296, 305
*837	Dislocation, ankle	133
837.0	Dislocation, closed, ankle	296
837.1	Dislocation, open, ankle	296, 305
*838	Dislocation, foot	132
*838.0	Dislocation, closed, foot	296
*838.1	Dislocation, open, foot	296

* Code Range

Code	Narrative	Page
*839.0	Dislocations, closed, other, multiple, ill-defined, vertebra, cervical	129, 296, 305
*839.1	Dislocations, open, other, multiple, ill-defined, vertebra, cervical	129, 296, 305
*839.2	Dislocation, closed, vertebra, thoracic and lumbar	129, 296
*839.3	Dislocation, open, vertebra, thoracic and lumbar	129, 296
*839.4	Dislocation, closed, vertebra, other	129, 296
*839.5	Dislocation, open, vertebra, other	129, 296
839.52	Dislocation, open, vertebra, sacrum	305
839.59	Dislocation, open, vertebra, other	305
*839.6	Dislocation, closed, other location	296
839.61	Dislocation, closed, sternum	44
839.69	Dislocation, closed, other, multiple and ill-defined, other location	132
839.71	Dislocation, open, sternum	44, 296, 304
839.79	Dislocation, open, other, multiple and ill-defined, other location	132, 296
839.8	Dislocation, closed, multiple and ill-defined	132, 296
839.9	Dislocation, open, multiple and ill-defined	132, 296
*840	Sprains and strains, shoulder and upper arm	133
840.0	Sprains and strains, acromioclavicular (joint) (ligament)	296
840.1	Sprains and strains, coracoclavicular (ligament)	296
840.2	Sprains and strains, coracohumeral (ligament)	296
840.3	Sprains and strains, infraspinatus (muscle) (tendon)	296
840.4	Sprains and strains, rotator cuff (capsule)	296
840.5	Sprains and strains, subscapularis (muscle)	296
840.6	Sprains and strains, supraspinatus (muscle) (tendon)	296
840.7	Sprains and strains, superior glenoid labrum lesions (SLAP)	296
840.8	Sprains and strains, shoulder and upper arm, other specified sites	296
840.9	Sprains and strains, shoulder and upper arm, unspecified site	296
*841	Sprains and strains, elbow and forearm	132, 296
*842	Sprains and strains, wrist and hand	132, 296
*843	Sprains and strains, hip and thigh	127, 296
*844	Sprains and strains, knee and leg	133, 296
*845	Sprains and strains, ankle and foot	296
*845.0	Sprains and strains, ankle	133
*845.1	Sprains and strains, foot	132
*846	Sprains and strains, sacroiliac region	129, 296
*847	Sprains and strains, back, other and unspecified parts	129, 296
*848	Sprains and strains, other and ill-defined	296
848.0	Sprains and strains, nose, septal cartilage	135
848.1	Sprains and strains, jaw	38
848.2	Sprains and strains, thyroid region	135
848.3	Sprains and strains, ribs	47
*848.4	Sprains and strains, sternum	47
848.5	Sprains and strains, pelvis	127
848.8	Sprains and strains, other specified sites	132
848.9	Sprains and strains, unspecified sites	132
*850	Concussion	14, 15
850.0	Concussion, with no loss of consciousness	296
*850.1	Concussion, with brief loss of consciousness	296
850.2	Concussion, with moderate loss of consciousness	296, 303
850.3	Concussion, with prolonged loss of consciousness and return to preexisting conscious level	297, 303
850.4	Concussion, with prolonged loss of consciousness, without return to preexisting conscious level	297, 303
850.5	Concussion, with loss of consciousness of unspecified duration	297
850.9	Concussion, unspecified	297
*851	Laceration and contusion, cerebral	14
*851.0	Contusion, cerebral cortex, without open intracranial wound	297
851.00	Contusion, cerebral cortex, without open intracranial wound, unspecified state of consciousness	303
851.01	Contusion, cerebral cortex, without open intracranial wound, no loss of consciousness	303
851.02	Contusion, cerebral cortex, without open intracranial wound, brief loss of consciousness	303
851.03	Contusion, cerebral cortex, without open intracranial wound, moderate loss of consciousness	303
851.04	Contusion, cerebral cortex, without open intracranial wound, prolonged loss of consciousness and return to preexisting conscious level	303
851.05	Contusion, cerebral cortex, without open intracranial wound, prolonged loss of consciousness, without return to preexisting conscious level	303
851.06	Contusion, cerebral cortex, without open intracranial wound, with loss of consciousness, unspecified duration	303

Code	Narrative	Page
851.09	Contusion, cerebral cortex, without open intracranial wound, with concussion, unspecified	303
*851.1	Contusion, cerebral cortex, with open intracranial wound	8, 297, 303
*851.2	Laceration, cerebral cortex, without mention of open intracranial wound	8, 297, 303
*851.3	Laceration, cerebral cortex, with open intracranial wound	8, 297, 303
*851.4	Contusion, cerebellar or brain stem, without open intracranial wound	297, 303
*851.5	Contusion, cerebellar or brain stem, with open intracranial wound	8, 297, 303
*851.6	Laceration, cerebellar or brain stem, without mention of open intracranial wound	8, 297, 303
*851.7	Laceration, cerebellar or brain stem, with open intracranial wound	8, 297, 303
*851.8	Laceration, contusion, cerebral, without mention of open intracranial wound	8, 297, 303
*851.9	Laceration, contusion, cerebral, with open intracranial wound	8, 297, 303
*852	Hemorrhage, subarachnoid, subdural and extradural, following injury	14, 297, 303
*852.0	Hemorrhage, subarachnoid, following injury without mention of open intracranial wound	8
*852.1	Hemorrhage, subarachnoid, following injury with open intracranial wound	8
*852.3	Hemorrhage, subdural, following injury with open intracranial wound	8
*853	Hemorrhage, intracranial, other and unspecified, following injury	14, 297, 303
*853.0	Hemorrhage, intracranial, other and unspecified, following injury, without mention of open intracranial wound	8
*853.1	Hemorrhage, intracranial, other and unspecified, following injury, with open intracranial wound	8
*854	Injury, intracranial, other and unspecified nature	14, 297, 303
*854.1	Hemorrhage, intracranial, other and unspecified nature, with open intracranial wound	8
*860	Pneumothorax and hemothorax, traumatic	46, 221, 228, 297, 304
*861	Injury, heart and lung	297, 304
*861.0	Injury, heart, without open wound into thorax	91
861.02	Heart laceration without penetration of heart chambers or mention of open wound into thorax	59, 62, 64, 73, 77, 80
861.03	Heart laceration with penetration of heart chambers, without mention of open wound into thorax	59, 62, 64, 74, 77, 80
*861.1	Injury, heart, with open wound into thorax	91
861.10	Unspecified injury to heart with open wound into thorax	59, 62, 64, 74, 77, 80
861.11	Heart contusion with open wound into thorax	59, 62, 64, 74, 77, 80
861.12	Heart laceration without penetration of heart chambers, with open wound into thorax	59, 62, 64, 74, 77, 80
861.13	Heart laceration with penetration of heart chambers and open wound into thorax	59, 62, 64, 74, 77, 80
861.20	Injury, lung, unspecified, without open wound into thorax	47
861.21	Contusion, lung, without open wound into thorax	47
861.22	Laceration, lung, without open wound into thorax	44
861.30	Injury, lung, unspecified, with open wound into thorax	47
861.31	Contusion, lung, with open wound into thorax	47
861.32	Laceration, lung, with open wound into thorax	44
*862	Injury, intrathoracic organs, other and unspecified	297, 304
862.0	Injury, diaphragm, without open wound into cavity	44
862.1	Injury, diaphragm, with open wound into cavity	44
862.21	Injury, bronchus, without open wound into cavity	44
862.22	Injury, esophagus, without open wound into cavity	105
862.29	Injury, intrathoracic organs, other specified, without open wound into cavity	47
862.31	Injury, bronchus, with open wound into cavity	44
862.32	Injury, esophagus, with open wound into cavity	105
862.39	Injury, intrathoracic organs, other specified, with open wound into cavity	47
862.8	Injury, intrathoracic organs, multiple and unspecified, without mention of open wound into cavity	272
862.9	Injury, intrathoracic organs, multiple and unspecified, with mention of open wound into cavity	60, 62, 65, 74, 78, 80, 272
863.0	Injury, stomach, without open wound into cavity	105, 297, 304
863.1	Injury, stomach, with open wound into cavity	105, 297, 304
*863.2	Injury, small intestine, without open wound into cavity	105, 297, 304
*863.3	Injury, small intestine, with open wound into cavity	105, 297, 304
*863.4	Injury, colon or rectum, without open wound into cavity	105, 297, 304
*863.5	Injury, colon or rectum, with open wound into cavity	105, 297, 304
*863.8	Injury, gastrointestinal sites, other and unspecified, without open wound into cavity	297

*** Code Range**

Code	Narrative	Page
863.80	Injury, gastrointestinal tract, unspecified site, without open wound into cavity	105
863.81	Injury, pancreas, head, without open wound into cavity	110, 304
863.82	Injury, pancreas, body, without open wound into cavity	110, 304
863.83	Injury, pancreas, tail, without open wound into cavity	110, 304
863.84	Injury, pancreas, multiple and unspecified sites, without open wound into cavity	110, 304
863.85	Injury, appendix, without open wound into cavity	105, 304
863.89	Injury, gastrointestinal sites, other, without open wound into cavity	105, 304
*863.9	Injury, gastrointestinal sites, other and unspecified, with open wound into cavity	297, 304
863.90	Injury, gastrointestinal tract, unspecified site, with open wound into cavity	105
863.91	Injury, pancreas, head, with open wound into cavity	110
863.92	Injury, pancreas, body, with open wound into cavity	110
863.93	Injury, pancreas, tail, with open wound into cavity	110
863.94	Injury, pancreas, multiple and unspecified sites, with open wound into cavity	110
863.95	Injury, appendix, with open wound into cavity	105
863.99	Injury, gastrointestinal sites, other, with open wound into cavity	105
*864	Injury, liver	111, 304
*864.0	Injury, liver, without open wound into cavity	297
*864.1	Injury, liver, with open wound into cavity	297
*865	Injury, spleen	221, 228, 235, 297, 304
*866	Injury, kidney	165, 297, 304
*867	Injury, pelvic organs	297, 304
867.0	Injury, bladder and urethra, without open wound into cavity	165
867.1	Injury, bladder and urethra, with open wound into cavity	165
867.2	Injury, ureter, without open wound into cavity	165
867.3	Injury, ureter, with open wound into cavity	165
867.4	Injury, uterus, without open wound into cavity	177, 184
867.5	Injury, uterus, with open wound into cavity	177, 184
867.6	Injury, pelvic organs, other, without open wound into cavity	173, 177, 184
867.7	Injury, pelvic organs, other, with open wound into cavity	173, 177, 184
867.8	Injury, pelvic organs, unspecified, without open wound into cavity	173, 177, 184
867.9	Injury, pelvic organs, unspecified, with open wound into cavity	173, 177, 184
*868.0	Injury, intra-abdominal organs, other, without open wound into cavity	297
868.00	Injury, intra-abdominal organ, unspecified, without open wound into cavity	105
868.01	Injury, adrenal gland, without open wound into cavity	156, 304
868.02	Injury, bile duct and gallbladder, without open wound into cavity	111, 304
868.03	Injury, peritoneum, without open wound into cavity	105, 305
868.04	Injury, retroperitoneum, without open wound into cavity	165, 305
868.09	Injury, intraabdominal organs, other and multiple, without open wound into cavity	272, 304
*868.1	Injury, intra-abdominal organs, other, with open wound into cavity	297
868.10	Injury, intra-abdominal organ, unspecified, with open wound into cavity	105
868.11	Injury, adrenal gland, with open wound into cavity	156, 304
868.12	Injury, bile duct and gallbladder, with open wound into cavity	111, 304
868.13	Injury, peritoneum, with open wound into cavity	105, 304
868.14	Injury, retroperitoneum, with open wound into cavity	165, 304
868.19	Injury, intraabdominal organs, other and multiple, with open wound into cavity	272, 304
*869	Injury, internal, organ, ill-defined or unspecified	272, 297
*870	Wound, open, ocular adnexa	25, 297
*871	Wound, open, eyeball	25, 297
*872	Wound, open, ear	37, 297
*873	Wound, open, other, head	297
873.0	Wound, open, scalp, without complication	144
873.1	Wound, open, scalp, complicated	144
*873.2	Wound, open, nose, without complication	320
873.20	Wound, open, nose, unspecified site, without complication	35
873.21	Wound, open, nasal septum, without complication	37
873.22	Wound, open, nasal cavity, without complication	37
873.23	Wound, open, nasal sinus, without complication	37
873.29	Wound, open, nose, multiple sites, without complication	37
*873.3	Wound, open, nose, complicated	37, 320
873.40	Wound, open, face, unspecified site, without complication	144, 320

Code	Narrative	Page
873.41	Wound, open, cheek, without complication	144, 320
873.42	Wound, open, forehead, without complication	144
873.43	Wound, open, lip, without complication	38, 320
873.44	Wound, open, jaw, without complication	38, 320
873.49	Wound, open, face, other and multiple sites, without complication	144
873.50	Wound, open, face, unspecified site, complicated	144, 320
873.51	Wound, open, cheek, complicated	144, 320
873.52	Wound, open, forehead, complicated	144
873.53	Wound, open, lip, complicated	38, 320
873.54	Wound, open, jaw, complicated	38, 320
873.59	Wound, open, face, other and multiple sites, complicated	144
*873.6	Wound, open, mouth, internal structures, without complication	38, 320
*873.7	Wound, open, mouth, internal structures, complicated	38, 320
873.8	Wound, open, other and unspecified, head, without mention of complication	144
873.9	Wound, open, other and unspecified, head, complicated	144
*874.0	Wound, open, larynx and trachea, without complication	297
874.00	Wound, open, larynx with trachea, without complication	37, 320
874.01	Wound, open, larynx, without complication	37, 320
874.02	Wound, open, trachea, without complication	44, 320
*874.1	Wound, open, larynx and trachea, complicated	297
874.10	Wound, open, larynx with trachea, complicated	37, 304, 320
874.11	Wound, open, larynx, complicated	37, 304, 320
874.12	Wound, open, trachea, complicated	44, 304, 320
874.2	Wound, open, thyroid gland, without complication	156, 297, 320
874.3	Wound, open, thyroid gland, complicated	156, 297, 320
874.4	Wound, open, pharynx, without complication	37, 297, 320
874.5	Wound, open, pharynx, complicated	37, 297, 321
874.8	Wound, open, neck, other and unspecified parts, without complication	144, 297, 321
874.9	Wound, open, neck, other and unspecified parts, complicated	144, 297, 321
*875	Wound, open, chest (wall)	297
875.0	Wound, open, chest wall, without complication	144
875.1	Wound, open, chest wall, complicated	272
*876	Wound, open, back	144, 297
*877	Wound, open, buttock	144, 297
*878	Wound, open, including traumatic amputation, genital organs (external)	297
878.0	Wound, open, including traumatic amputation, penis, without complication	173
878.1	Wound, open, including traumatic amputation, penis, complicated	173
878.2	Wound, open, including traumatic amputation, scrotum and testes, without complication	173
878.3	Wound, open, including traumatic amputation, scrotum and testes, complicated	173
878.4	Wound, open, including traumatic amputation, vulva, without complication	177, 184
878.5	Wound, open, including traumatic amputation, vulva, complicated	177, 184
878.6	Wound, open, vagina, without complication	177, 184
878.7	Wound, open, vagina, complicated	177, 184
878.8	Wound, open, including traumatic amputation, genital organs, other and unspecified parts, without complication	173, 177, 184
878.9	Wound, open, including traumatic amputation, genital organs, other and unspecified parts, complicated	173, 177, 184
*879	Wound, open, other and unspecified sites, except limbs	297
879.0	Wound, open, breast, without complication	144
879.1	Wound, open, breast, complicated	144
879.2	Wound, open, abdominal wall, anterior, without complication	144
879.3	Wound, open, abdominal wall, anterior, complicated	272
879.4	Wound, open, abdominal wall, lateral, without complication	144
879.5	Wound, open, abdominal wall, lateral, complicated	272
879.6	Wound, open, trunk, other and unspecified, parts, without complication	144
879.7	Wound, open, trunk, other and unspecified parts, complicated	272
879.8	Wound, open, multiple, unspecified site(s), without complication	144
879.9	Wound, open, multiple, unspecified site(s), complicated	272
*880	Wound, open, shoulder and upper arm	297
*880.0	Wound, open, shoulder and upper arm, without complication	144
*880.1	Wound, open, shoulder and upper arm, complicated	272
*880.2	Wound, open, tendon involvement, shoulder and upper arm	135

*** Code Range**

Code	Narrative	Page
*881	Wound, open, elbow, forearm, and wrist	297
*881.0	Wound, open, elbow, forearm and wrist, without complication	144
*881.1	Wound, open, elbow, forearm and wrist, complicated	272
*881.2	Wound, open, tendon involvement, elbow, forearm and wrist, complicated	135
*882	Wound, open, hand except finger(s) alone	297
882.0	Wound, open, hand, except finger(s), alone, without complication	144
882.1	Wound, open, hand, except finger(s), alone, complicated	272
882.2	Wound, open, tendon involvement, hand, except finger(s), alone	135
*883	Wound, open, finger(s)	297
883.0	Wound, open, finger(s), without complication	144
883.1	Wound, open, finger(s), complicated	272
883.2	Wound, open, tendon involvement, finger(s),	135
*884	Wound, open, multiple and unspecified, upper limb	297
884.0	Wound, open, multiple and unspecified, upper limb, without complication	145
884.1	Wound, open, multiple and unspecified, upper limb, complicated	272
884.2	Wound, open, tendon involvement, multiple and unspecified, upper limb, complicated	135
*885	Amputation, traumatic, complete, partial, thumb	272, 297
*886	Amputation, traumatic, complete, partial, other finger(s)	272, 298
*887	Amputation, traumatic, complete, partial, arm and hand	272, 298, 305
*890	Wound, open, hip and thigh	298
890.0	Wound, open, hip and thigh, without complication	145
890.1	Wound, open, hip and thigh, complicated	272
890.2	Wound, open, tendon involvement, hip and thigh	135
*891	Wound, open, knee, leg [except thigh], and ankle	298
891.0	Wound, open, knee, leg [except thigh], and ankle, without complication	145
891.1	Wound, open, knee, leg [except thigh], and ankle, complicated	272
891.2	Wound, open, tendon involvement, knee, leg [except thigh], and ankle	135
*892	Wound, open, foot except toe(s), alone	298
892.0	Wound, open, foot except toe(s), alone, without complication	145
892.1	Wound, open, foot except toe(s, alone, complicated	272
892.2	Wound, open, tendon involvement, foot except toe(s), alone	135
*893	Wound, open, toe(s)	298
893.0	Wound, open, toe(s), without complication	145
893.1	Wound, open, toe(s), complicated	272
893.2	Wound, open, tendon involvement, toe(s)	135
*894	Wound, open, multiple and unspecified, lower limb	298
894.0	Wound, open, multiple and unspecified, lower limb, without complication	145
894.1	Wound, open, multiple and unspecified, lower limb, complicated	272
894.2	Wound, open, tendon involvement, multiple and unspecified, lower limb	135
*895	Amputation, traumatic, complete, partial, toe(s)	272, 298
*896	Amputation, traumatic, complete, partial, foot	272, 298, 305
*897	Amputation, traumatic, complete, partial, leg(s)	272, 298, 305
*900	Injury, blood vessels, head and neck	272
*900.0	Injury, blood vessels, artery, carotid	221, 228, 298
900.01	Injury, blood vessels, artery, carotid, common	303
900.02	Injury, blood vessels, artery, carotid, external	303
900.03	Injury, blood vessels, artery, carotid, internal	303
900.1	Injury, blood vessels, vein, jugular, internal	221, 228, 298, 303
*900.8	Injury, blood vessels, other specified, head and neck	298
900.81	Injury, blood vessels, vein, jugular, external	221, 228, 303
900.82	Injury, blood vessels, multiple, head and neck	303, 321
900.89	Injury, blood vessels, other, head and neck	321
900.9	Injury, blood vessels, unspecified, head and neck	321
*901	Injury, blood vessels, thorax	272
901.0	Injury, blood vessels, aorta, thoracic	221, 228, 298, 304
901.1	Injury, blood vessels, arteries, innominate and subclavian	221, 228, 298, 304
901.2	Injury, blood vessels, vena cava, superior	222, 229, 298, 304
901.3	Injury, blood vessels, veins, innominate and subclavian	222, 229, 298, 304
*901.4	Injury, blood vessels, pulmonary	298, 304
901.41	Injury, blood vessels, artery, pulmonary	222, 229

Code	Narrative	Page
901.42	Injury, blood vessels, vein, pulmonary	222, 229
*901.8	Injury, blood vessels, other specified, thorax	298
901.83	Injury, blood vessels, multiple, thorax	304
901.89	Injury, blood vessels, other, thorax	304
901.9	Injury, blood vessels, unspecified, thorax	298, 304
*902	Injury, blood vessels, abdomen and pelvis	272, 298, 304
902.0	Injury, blood vessels, aorta, abdominal	222, 229
902.10	Injury, blood vessels, vena cava, inferior, unspecified	222, 229
*903	Injury, blood vessels, upper extremity	272, 298, 305
*904	Injury, blood vessels, lower extremity and unspecified sites	272
904.0	Injury, blood vessels, artery, femoral, common	298, 305
904.1	Injury, blood vessels, artery, femoral, superficial	298, 305
904.2	Injury, blood vessels, veins, femoral	298, 305
904.3	Injury, blood vessels, veins, saphenous	298
*904.4	Injury, blood vessels, popliteal	298, 305
*904.5	Injury, blood vessels, tibial	298, 306
904.6	Injury, blood vessels, plantar, deep	298
904.7	Injury, blood vessels, other specified, lower extremity	298, 306
904.8	Injury, blood vessels, unspecified, lower extremity	298
904.9	Injury, blood vessels, unspecified site	298
905.0	Effect, late, fracture, bone, skull and face	16
905.1	Effect, late, fracture, without spinal cord lesion, spine and trunk	129
905.2	Effect, late, fracture, upper extremities	131
905.3	Effect, late, fracture, neck of femur	131
905.4	Effect, late, fracture, lower extremities	131
905.5	Effect, late, fracture, bones, multiple and unspecified	131
905.6	Effect, late, dislocation	132
905.7	Effect, late, sprain and strain, without mention of tendon injury	132
905.8	Effect, late, injury, tendon	131
905.9	Effect, late, amputation, traumatic	131
*906	Effect, late, injuries, skin and subcutaneous tissues	145
907.0	Effect, late, injury, intracranial, without mention of skull fracture	16
907.1	Effect, late, injury, nerve, cranial	16
907.2	Effect, late, injury, spinal cord	9
907.3	Effect, late, injury, nerve root(s), spinal plexus(es), and other nerves, trunk	16
907.4	Effect, late, injury, peripheral nerve, shoulder girdle and upper limb	16
907.5	Effect, late, injury, peripheral nerve, pelvic girdle and lower limb	16
907.9	Effect, late, injury, nerve, other and unspecified	16
908.0	Effect, late, injury, internal, chest	47
908.1	Effect, late, injury, internal, intraabdominal organs	105
908.2	Effect, late, internal injury, internal organs, other	173, 177, 184
908.3	Effect, late, injury, blood vessel, head, neck and extremities	87
908.4	Effect, late, injury, blood vessel, thorax, abdomen, and pelvis	87
908.5	Effect, late, foreign body in orifice	272
908.6	Effect, late, certain complications of trauma	272
908.9	Effect, late, unspecified injury	272
*909	Effect, late, external causes, other and unspecified	274
*910	Injury, superficial, face, neck and scalp except eye	298
910.0	Injury, superficial, abrasion, friction burn, without infection, face, neck and scalp except eye	145
910.1	Injury, superficial, abrasion or friction burn, infected, face, neck and scalp, except eye	143
910.2	Injury, superficial, blister, without infection, face, neck and scalp, except eye	148
910.3	Injury, superficial, blister, infected, face, neck and scalp, except eye	148
910.4	Injury, superficial, insect bite, nonvenomous, without infection, face, neck and scalp except eye	148
910.5	Injury, superficial, insect bite, nonvenomous, infected, face, neck and scalp except eye	143
910.6	Injury, superficial, foreign body, without major open wound or infection, face, neck and scalp except eye	145
910.7	Injury, superficial, foreign body, without major open wound, infected, face, neck and scalp except eye	143
910.8	Injury, superficial, other and unspecified, without infection, face, neck and scalp	145
910.9	Injury, superficial, other and unspecified, infected, face, neck and scalp	143
*911	Injury, superficial, trunk	298
911.0	Injury, superficial, abrasion or friction burn, without infection, trunk	145

* Code Range

Code	Narrative	Page
911.1	Injury, superficial, abrasion or friction burn, infected, trunk	143
911.2	Injury, superficial, blister, without infection, trunk	148
911.3	Injury, superficial, blister, infected, trunk	143
911.4	Injury, superficial, insect bite, nonvenomous, without infection, trunk	148
911.5	Injury, superficial, insect bite, nonvenomous, infected, trunk	143
911.6	Injury, superficial, foreign body, without major open wound or infection, trunk	145
911.7	Injury, superficial, foreign body, without major open wound, infected, trunk	143
911.8	Injury, superficial, other and unspecified, without infection, trunk	145
911.9	Injury, superficial, other and unspecified, infected, trunk	143
*912	Injury, superficial, shoulder and upper arm	298
912.0	Injury, superficial, abrasion or friction burn, without infection, shoulder and upper arm	145
912.1	Injury, superficial, abrasion or friction burn, infected, shoulder and upper arm	143
912.2	Injury, superficial, blister, without infection, shoulder or upper arm	145
912.3	Injury, superficial, blister, infected, shoulder and upper arm	143
912.4	Injury, superficial, insect bite, nonvenomous, without infection, shoulder and upper arm	148
912.5	Injury, superficial, insect bite, nonvenomous, infected, shoulder and upper arm	143
912.6	Injury, superficial, foreign body, without major open wound or infection, shoulder and upper arm	145
912.7	Injury, superficial, foreign body, without major open wound, infected, shoulder and upper arm	143
912.8	Injury, superficial, other and unspecified, without infection, shoulder and upper arm	145
912.9	Injury, superficial, other and unspecified, infected, shoulder and upper arm	143
*913	Injury, superficial, elbow, forearm and wrist	298
913.0	Injury, superficial, abrasion or friction burn, without infection, elbow, forearm and wrist	145
913.1	Injury, superficial, abrasion or friction burn, infected, elbow, forearm and wrist	143
913.2	Injury, superficial, blister, without infection, shoulder or upper arm	148
913.3	Injury, superficial, blister, infected, elbow, forearm and wrist	143
913.4	Injury, superficial, insect bite, nonvenomous, without infection, elbow, forearm and wrist	148
913.5	Injury, superficial, insect bite, nonvenomous, infected, elbow, forearm and wrist	143
913.6	Injury, superficial, foreign body (splinter), without major open wound or infection, elbow, forearm and wrist	145
913.7	Injury, superficial, foreign body (splinter), without major open wound, infected, elbow, forearm and wrist	143
913.8	Injury, superficial, other and unspecified, without infection, elbow, forearm and wrist	145
913.9	Injury, superficial, other and unspecified, infected, elbow, forearm and wrist	143
*914	Injury, superficial, hand(s) except finger(s) alone	298
914.0	Injury, superficial, abrasion or friction burn, without infection, hand(s) except finger(s) alone	145
914.1	Injury, superficial, abrasion or friction burn, infected, hand(s) except finger(s) alone	143
914.2	Injury, superficial, blister, without infection, shoulder or upper arm	148
914.3	Injury, superficial, blister, infected, hand(s) except finger(s) alone	143
914.4	Injury, superficial, insect bite, nonvenomous, without infection, hand(s) except finger(s) alone	148
914.5	Injury, superficial, insect bite, nonvenomous, infected, hand(s) except finger(s) alone	143
914.6	Injury, superficial, foreign body, without major open wound or infection, hand(s) except finger(s) alone	145
914.7	Injury, superficial, foreign body, without major open wound, infected, hand(s) except finger(s) alone	143
914.8	Injury, superficial, other and unspecified, without infection, hand(s) except finger(s) alone	145
914.9	Injury, superficial, other and unspecified, infected, hand(s) except finger(s) alone	143
*915	Injury, superficial, finger(s)	298
915.0	Injury, superficial, abrasion or friction burn, without infection, finger(s)	145
915.1	Injury, superficial, abrasion or friction burn, infected, finger(s)	143
915.2	Injury, superficial, blister, without infection, shoulder or upper arm	148
915.3	Injury, superficial, blister, infected, finger(s)	143
915.4	Injury, superficial, insect bite, nonvenomous, without infection, finger(s)	148

Code	Narrative	Page
915.5	Injury, superficial, insect bite, nonvenomous, infected, finger(s)	143
915.6	Injury, superficial, foreign body, without major open wound or infection, finger(s)	145
915.7	Injury, superficial, foreign body, without major open wound, infected, finger(s)	144
915.8	Injury, superficial, other and unspecified, without infection, finger(s)	145
915.9	Injury, superficial, other and unspecified, infected, finger(s)	144
*916	Injury, superficial, hip, thigh, leg, and ankle	298
916.0	Injury, superficial, abrasion or friction burn, without infection, hip, thigh, leg, and ankle	145
916.1	Injury, superficial, abrasion or friction burn, infected, hip, thigh, leg, and ankle	144
916.2	Injury, superficial, blister, without infection, shoulder or upper arm	148
916.3	Injury, superficial, blister, infected, hip, thigh, leg, and ankle	144
916.4	Injury, superficial, insect bite, nonvenomous, without infection, hip, thigh, leg, and ankle	148
916.5	Injury, superficial, insect bite, nonvenomous, infected, hip, thigh, leg, and ankle	144
916.6	Injury, superficial, foreign body, without major open wound or infection, hip, thigh, leg, and ankle	145
916.7	Injury, superficial, foreign body, without major open wound, infected, hip, thigh, leg, and ankle	144
916.8	Injury, superficial, other and unspecified, without infection, hip, thigh, leg, and ankle	145
916.9	Injury, superficial, other and unspecified, infected, hip, thigh, leg, and ankle	144
*917	Injury, superficial, foot and toe(s)	298
917.0	Injury, superficial, abrasion or friction burn, without infection, foot and toe(s)	145
917.1	Injury, superficial, abrasion or friction burn, infected, foot and toe(s)	144
917.2	Injury, superficial, blister, without infection, shoulder or upper arm	148
917.3	Injury, superficial, blister, infected, foot and toe(s)	144
917.4	Injury, superficial, insect bite, nonvenomous, without infection, foot and toe(s)	148
917.5	Injury, superficial, insect bite, nonvenomous, infected, foot and toe(s)	144
917.6	Injury, superficial, foreign body, without major open wound or infection, foot and toe(s)	145
917.7	Injury, superficial, foreign body, without major open wound, infected, foot and toe(s)	144
917.8	Injury, superficial, other and unspecified, without infection, foot and toe(s)	145
917.9	Injury, superficial, other and unspecified, infected, foot and toe(s)	144
*918	Injury, superficial, eye and adnexa	25, 298
*919	Injury, superficial, sites, other, multiple and unspecified	298
919.0	Injury, superficial, abrasion or friction burn, without infection, sites, other, multiple and unspecified	145
919.1	Injury, superficial, abrasion or friction burn, infected, sites, other, multiple and unspecified	144
919.2	Injury, superficial, blister, without infection, shoulder or upper arm	148
919.3	Injury, superficial, blister, infected, sites, other, multiple and unspecified	144
919.4	Injury, superficial, insect bite, nonvenomous, without infection, sites, other, multiple and unspecified	148
919.5	Injury, superficial, insect bite, nonvenomous, infected, sites, other, multiple and unspecified	144
919.6	Injury, superficial, foreign body, without major open wound or infection, sites, other, multiple and unspecified	145
919.7	Injury, superficial, foreign body, without major open wound, infected, sites, other, multiple and unspecified	144
919.8	Injury, superficial, other and unspecified, without infection, sites, other, multiple and unspecified	145
919.9	Injury, superficial, other and unspecified, infected, sites, other, multiple and unspecified	144
920	Contusion, face, scalp and neck, except eye(s)	145, 298
*921	Contusion, eye and adnexa	298
921.0	Black eye, unspecified	25
921.1	Contusion, eyelids and periocular area	21
921.2	Contusion, orbital tissues	25
921.3	Contusion, eyeball	21
921.9	Contusion, eye, unspecified	26
*922	Contusion, trunk	298
922.0	Contusion, breast	145
922.1	Contusion, chest wall	145
922.2	Contusion, abdominal wall	145
*922.3	Contusion, back	145
922.4	Contusion, genital organs	173, 177, 184

Numeric Index to Diseases

* Code Range

Code	Narrative	Page
922.8	Contusion, trunk, multiple sites	145
922.9	Contusion, trunk, unspecified part	145
*923	Contusion, upper limb	145, 298
*924	Contusion, lower limb and other and unspecified sites	145, 298
*925	Injury, crushing, face, scalp, and neck	272, 298, 321
925.1	Injury, crushing, face and scalp	303
925.2	Injury, crushing, neck	303
926.0	Injury, crushing, external genitalia	173, 178, 184, 298
*926.1	Injury, crushing, trunk, other specified sites	272, 298
926.11	Injury, crushing, back	305
926.12	Injury, crushing, buttock	306
926.19	Injury, crushing, trunk, other specified sites	305
926.8	Injury, crushing, trunk, multiple sites	272, 298, 305
926.9	Injury, crushing, trunk, unspecified site	272, 298, 305
*927	Injury, crushing, upper limb	272
*927.0	Injury, crushing, shoulder and upper arm	298, 305
927.01	Injury, crushing, scapular region	304
*927.1	Injury, crushing, elbow and forearm	298, 305
*927.2	Injury, crushing, wrist and hand(s), except finger(s) alone	298
927.3	Injury, crushing, finger(s)	298
927.8	Injury, crushing, multiple sites, upper limb	298, 305
927.9	Injury, crushing, unspecified site, upper limb	298, 305
*928	Injury, crushing, lower limb	272
*928.0	Injury, crushing, hip and thigh	298, 306
*928.1	Injury, crushing, knee and lower leg	298, 306
*928.2	Injury, crushing, ankle and foot, excluding toe(s) alone	298
928.3	Injury, crushing, toe(s)	298
928.8	Injury, crushing, multiple sites, lower limb	299, 306
928.9	Injury, crushing, unspecified site, lower limb	299, 306
*929	Injury, crushing, multiple and unspecified sites	272, 299
*930	Foreign body, external eye	26
931	Foreign body, ear	37
932	Foreign body, nose	35
*933	Foreign body, pharynx and larynx	37, 321
934.0	Foreign body, trachea	47
934.1	Foreign body, main bronchus	47
934.8	Foreign body, trachea, bronchus, and lung, other specified parts	47
934.9	Foreign body, respiratory tree, unspecified	47
935.0	Foreign body, mouth	38, 321
935.1	Foreign body, esophagus	105
935.2	Foreign body, stomach	105
936	Foreign body, intestine and colon	105
937	Foreign body, anus and rectum	105
938	Foreign body, digestive system, unspecified	105
939.0	Foreign body, bladder and urethra	165
939.1	Foreign body, uterus, any part	178, 184
939.2	Foreign body, vulva and vagina	178, 184
939.3	Foreign body, penis	173
939.9	Foreign body, genitourinary tract, unspecified site	165
*940	Burn, confined to eye and adnexa	26
941.00	Burn, unspecified degree, face, head, and neck, unspecified site	282
941.01	Burn, unspecified degree, ear (any part)	282
941.02	Burn, unspecified degree, eye (with other parts of face, head, and neck)	26
941.03	Burn, unspecified degree, lip(s)	282
941.04	Burn, unspecified degree, chin	282
941.05	Burn, unspecified degree, nose (septum)	283
941.06	Burn, unspecified degree, scalp	283
941.07	Burn, unspecified degree, forehead and cheek	283
941.08	Burn, unspecified degree, neck	283
941.09	Burn, unspecified degree, face, head and neck multiple sites (except eye)	283
941.10	Burn, erythema [first degree], face, head, and neck, unspecified site	283
941.11	Burn, erythema [first degree], ear (any part)	283
941.12	Burn, erythema [first degree], eye (with other parts of face, head, and neck)	26
941.13	Burn, erythema [first degree], lip(s)	283
941.14	Burn, erythema [first degree], chin	283
941.15	Burn, erythema [first degree], nose (septum)	283
941.16	Burn, erythema [first degree], scalp	283
941.17	Burn, erythema [first degree], forehead and cheek	283
941.18	Burn, erythema [first degree], neck	283
941.19	Burn, erythema [first degree], face, head and neck multiple sites (except eye)	283
941.20	Burn, blisters, epidermal loss [second degree], face, head, and neck, unspecified site	283
941.21	Burn, blisters, epidermal loss [second degree], ear (any part)	283
941.22	Burn, blisters, epidermal loss [second degree], eye (with other parts of face, head, and neck)	26
941.23	Burn, blisters, epidermal loss [second degree], lip(s)	283

Code	Narrative	Page
941.24	Burn, blisters, epidermal loss [second degree], chin	283
941.25	Burn, blisters, epidermal loss [second degree], nose (septum)	283
941.26	Burn, blisters, epidermal loss [second degree], scalp	283
941.27	Burn, blisters, epidermal loss [second degree], forehead and cheek	283
941.28	Burn, blisters, epidermal loss [second degree], neck	283
941.29	Burn, blisters, epidermal loss [second degree], face, head and neck multiple sites (except eye)	283
*941.3	Burn, skin loss, full-thickness [third degree NOS], face, head, and neck	277, 278, 281, 282
941.32	Burn, skin loss, full-thickness [third degree NOS], eye (with other parts of face, head, and neck)	26
*941.4	Burn, deep necrosis [deep third degree], without loss body part, face, head, and neck	277, 278, 281, 282
941.42	Burn, deep necrosis [deep third degree], without loss body part, eye (with other parts of face, head, and neck)	26
*941.5	Burn, deep necrosis [deep third degree], with loss body part, face, head, and neck	277, 278, 281, 282
941.52	Burn, deep necrosis [deep third degree], with loss body part, eye (with other parts of face, head, and neck)	26
*942.0	Burn, unspecified degree, trunk	283
*942.1	Burn, erythema [first degree], trunk	283
*942.2	Burn, blisters, epidermal loss [second degree], trunk	283
*942.3	Burn, skin loss, full-thickness [third degree NOS], trunk	277, 278, 281, 282
*942.4	Burn, deep necrosis [deep third degree], without loss body part, trunk	277, 278, 281, 282
*942.5	Burn, deep necrosis [deep third degree], with loss body part, trunk	277, 278, 281, 282
*943.0	Burn, unspecified degree, upper limb, except wrist and hand	283
*943.1	Burn, erythema [first degree], upper limb, except wrist and hand	283
*943.2	Burn, blisters, epidermal loss [second degree], upper limb, except wrist and hand	283
*943.3	Burn, skin loss, full-thickness [third degree NOS], upper limb, except wrist and hand	277, 278, 281, 282
*943.4	Burn, deep necrosis [deep third degree] without loss body part, upper limb, except wrist and hand	277, 278, 281, 282
*943.5	Burn, deep necrosis [deep third degree] with loss body part, upper limb, except wrist and hand	277, 278, 281, 282
*944.0	Burn, unspecified degree, wrist(s) and hand(s)	283
*944.1	Burn, erythema [first degree], wrist(s) and hand(s)	283
*944.2	Burn, blisters, epidermal loss, [second degree], wrist(s) and hand(s)	283
*944.3	Burn, skin loss, full-thickness [third degree NOS], wrist(s) and hand(s)	277, 278, 281, 282
*944.4	Burn, deep necrosis [deep third degree] without loss body part, wrist(s) and hand(s)	277, 278, 281, 282
*944.5	Burn, deep necrosis [deep third degree] with loss body part, wrist(s) and hand(s)	277, 278, 281, 282
*945.0	Burn, unspecified degree, lower limb	283
*945.1	Burn, erythema [first degree], lower limb	283
*945.2	Burn, blisters, epidermal loss [second degree], lower limb	283
*945.3	Burn, skin loss, full-thickness [third degree NOS], lower limb	277, 278, 281, 282
*945.4	Burn, deep necrosis [deep third degree] without loss body part, lower limb	277, 278, 281, 282
*945.5	Burn, deep necrosis [deep third degree] with loss body part, lower limb	277, 278, 281, 282
946.0	Burn, unspecified degree, multiple, specified sites	283
946.1	Burn, erythema [first degree], multiple, specified sites	283
946.2	Burn, blisters, epidermal loss [second degree], multiple, specified sites	283
946.3	Burn, skin loss, full-thickness [third degree NOS], multiple, specified sites	277, 278, 281, 282
946.4	Burn, deep necrosis [deep third degree] without loss body part, multiple, specified sites	277, 278, 281, 282
946.5	Burn, deep necrosis [deep third degree] with loss body part, multiple, specified sites	277, 278, 281, 282
947.0	Burn, mouth and pharynx	37, 321
947.1	Burn, larynx, trachea and lung	47, 279
947.2	Burn, esophagus	105
947.3	Burn, gastrointestinal tract	105
947.4	Burn, vagina and uterus	178, 184
947.8	Burn, organs, internal, other specified sites	283
947.9	Burn, organs, internal, unspecified sites	283
948.00	Burn, any degree, less than 10% of body surface, with less than 10% third degree or unspecified	283
948.10	Burn, any degree, 10-19% of body surface, with less than 10% third degree or unspecified	283
948.11	Burn, any degree, 10-19% of body surface, with 10-19% third degree	277, 278, 281, 282
948.20	Burn, any degree, 20-29% of body surface, with less than 10% third degree or unspecified	283

* Code Range

Code	Narrative	Page
948.21	Burn, any degree, 20-29% of body surface, with 10-19% third degree	276, 280
948.22	Burn, any degree, 20-29% of body surface, with 20-29% third degree	276, 280
948.30	Burn, any degree, 30-39% of body surface, with less than 10% third degree or unspecified	283
948.31	Burn, any degree, 30-39% of body surface, with 10-19% third degree	276, 280
948.32	Burn, any degree, 30-39% of body surface, with 20-29% third degree	276, 280
948.33	Burn, any degree, 30-39% of body surface, with 30-39% third degree	276, 280
948.40	Burn, any degree, 40-49% of body surface, with less than 10% third degree or unspecified	283
948.41	Burn, any degree, 40-49% of body surface, with 10-19% third degree	276, 280
948.42	Burn, any degree, 40-49% of body surface, with 20-29% third degree	276, 280
948.43	Burn, any degree, 40-49% of body surface, with 30-39% third degree	276, 280
948.44	Burn, any degree, 40-49% of body surface, with 40-49% third degree	276, 280
948.50	Burn, any degree, 50-59% of body surface, with less than 10% third degree or unspecified	283
948.51	Burn, any degree, 50-59% of body surface, with 10-19% third degree	276, 280
948.52	Burn, any degree, 50-59% of body surface, with 20-29% third degree	276, 280
948.53	Burn, any degree, 50-59% of body surface, with 30-39% third degree	276, 280
948.54	Burn, any degree, 50-59% of body surface, with 40-49% third degree	276, 280
948.55	Burn, any degree, 50-59% of body surface, with 50-59% third degree	276, 280
948.60	Burn, any degree, 60-69% of body surface, with less than 10% third degree or unspecified	283
948.61	Burn, any degree, 60-69% of body surface, with 10-19% third degree	276, 280
948.62	Burn, any degree, 60-69% of body surface, with 20-29% third degree	276, 280
948.63	Burn, any degree, 60-69% of body surface, with 30-39% third degree	276, 280
948.64	Burn, any degree, 60-69% of body surface, with 40-49% third degree	276, 280
948.65	Burn, any degree, 60-69% of body surface, with 50-59% third degree	276, 280
948.66	Burn, any degree, 60-69% of body surface, with 60-69% third degree	276, 280
948.70	Burn, any degree, 70-79% of body surface, with less than 10% third degree or unspecified	283
948.71	Burn, any degree, 70-79% of body surface, with 10-19% third degree	276, 280
948.72	Burn, any degree, 70-79% of body surface, with 20-29% third degree	276, 280
948.73	Burn, any degree, 70-79% of body surface, with 30-39% third degree	276, 280
948.74	Burn, any degree, 70-79% of body surface, with 40-49% third degree	276, 280
948.75	Burn, any degree, 70-79% of body surface, with 50-59% third degree	276, 280
948.76	Burn, any degree, 70-79% of body surface, with 60-69% third degree	276, 280
948.77	Burn, any degree, 70-79% of body surface, with 70-79% third degree	276, 280
948.80	Burn, any degree, 80-89% of body surface, with less than 10% third degree or unspecified	283
948.81	Burn, any degree, 80-89% of body surface, with 10-19% third degree	276, 280
948.82	Burn, any degree, 80-89% of body surface, with 20-29% third degree	276, 280
948.83	Burn, any degree, 80-89% of body surface, with 30-39% third degree	276, 280
948.84	Burn, any degree, 80-89% of body surface, with 40-49% third degree	276, 280
948.85	Burn, any degree, 80-89% of body surface, with 50-59% third degree	276, 280
948.86	Burn, any degree, 80-89% of body surface, with 60-69% third degree	276, 280
948.87	Burn, any degree, 80-89% of body surface, with 70-79% third degree	276, 280
948.88	Burn, any degree, 80-89% of body surface, with 80-89% third degree	277, 281
948.90	Burn, any degree, 90% or more of body surface, with less than 10% third degree or unspecified	283
948.91	Burn, any degree, 90% or more of body surface, with 10-19% third degree	277, 281
948.92	Burn, any degree, 90% or more of body surface, with 20-29% third degree	277, 281
948.93	Burn, any degree, 90% or more of body surface, with 30-39% third degree	277, 281
948.94	Burn, any degree, 90% or more of body surface, with 40-49% third degree	277, 281
948.95	Burn, any degree, 90% or more of body surface, with 50-59% third degree	277, 281
948.96	Burn, any degree, 90% or more of body surface, with 60-69% third degree	277, 281
948.97	Burn, any degree, 90% or more of body surface, with 70-79% third degree	277, 281
948.98	Burn, any degree, 90% or more of body surface, with 80-89% third degree	277, 281
948.99	Burn, any degree, 90% or more of body surface, with 90% or more third degree	277, 281
949.0	Burn, unspecified degree, multiple, unspecified sites	284
949.1	Burn, erythema [first degree], multiple, unspecified sites	284
949.2	Burn, blisters, epidermal loss [second degree], multiple, unspecified sites	284

Numeric Index to Diseases

*** Code Range**

Code	Narrative	Page
949.3	Burn, skin loss, full-thickness [third degree NOS], multiple, unspecified sites	277, 278, 281, 282
949.4	Burn, deep necrosis [deep third degree] without loss body part, multiple, unspecified sites	277, 278, 281, 282
949.5	Burn, deep necrosis [deep third degree] with loss body part, multiple, unspecified sites	277, 278, 281, 282
*950	Injury, optic nerve and pathways	299
950.0	Injury, optic nerve	26
950.1	Injury, optic chiasm	16
950.2	Injury, optic pathways	16
950.3	Injury, visual cortex	16
950.9	Injury, optic nerve and pathways, unspecified	16
*951	Injury, nerve(s), other cranial	299
951.0	Injury, nerve, oculomotor	12
951.1	Injury, nerve, trochlear	12
951.2	Injury, nerve, trigeminal	12
951.3	Injury, nerve, abducens	12
951.4	Injury, nerve, facial	12
951.5	Injury, nerve, acoustic	37
951.6	Injury, nerve, accessory	12
951.7	Injury, nerve, hypoglossal	12
951.8	Injury, nerves, cranial, other specified	12
951.9	Injury, nerve, cranial, unspecified	12
*952	Injury, spinal cord, without spinal bone injury	9, 299, 305
*953	Injury, nerve roots and spinal plexus	12, 299
953.1	Injury, nerve root, dorsal	299
953.2	Injury, nerve root, lumbar	299
953.3	Injury, nerve root, sacral	299
953.4	Injury, spinal plexus, brachial	222, 229, 299, 305
953.5	Injury, spinal plexus, lumbosacral	299, 305
953.8	Injury, nerve roots and spinal plexus, multiple sites	299, 305
953.9	Injury, nerve roots and spinal plexus, unspecified site	299
*954	Injury, nerve(s), other, trunk, excluding shoulder and pelvic girdles	12
954.0	Injury, nerve, sympathetic, cervical	299
954.1	Injury, nerve(s), sympathetic, other, trunk	299
954.8	Injury, nerve(s), other specified, trunk	299, 305
954.9	Injury, nerve, unspecified, trunk	299, 305
*955	Injury, nerve(s), peripheral, shoulder girdle and upper limb	12
955.0	Injury, nerve, axillary	299, 305
955.1	Injury, nerve, median	299, 305
955.2	Injury, nerve, ulnar	299, 305
955.3	Injury, nerve, radial	299, 305
955.4	Injury, nerve, musculocutaneous	299
955.5	Injury, nerve, cutaneous sensory, upper limb	299
955.6	Injury, nerve, digital, shoulder girdle and upper limb	299
955.7	Injury, nerve(s), other specified, shoulder girdle and upper limb	299
955.8	Injury, nerves, multiple, shoulder girdle and upper limb	299, 305
955.9	Injury, nerve, unspecified, shoulder girdle and upper limb	299
*956	Injury, nerve(s), peripheral, pelvic girdle and lower limb	12
956.0	Injury, nerve, sciatic	299, 306
956.1	Injury, nerve, femoral	299, 306
956.2	Injury, nerve, posterior tibial	299, 306
956.3	Injury, nerve, peroneal	299, 306
956.4	Injury, nerve, cutaneous sensory, lower limb	299
956.5	Injury, nerve(s), other specified, pelvic girdle and lower limb	299
956.8	Injury, nerves, multiple, pelvic girdle and lower limb	299, 306
956.9	Injury, nerve, unspecified site, pelvic girdle and lower limb	299, 306
*957	Injury, nerves, other and unspecified	12, 299
958.0	Complications, early, trauma, embolism, air	42, 222, 229, 299, 304
958.1	Complications, early, trauma, embolism, fat	42, 222, 229, 299, 304
958.2	Complications, early, trauma, hemorrhage, secondary and recurrent	222, 229, 274, 299
958.3	Complications, early, trauma, infection, not elsewhere classified, wound	222, 229, 246, 299
958.4	Complications, early, trauma, shock	222, 229, 274, 299
958.5	Complications, early, trauma, anuria	161, 162, 222, 229, 299
958.6	Complications, early, trauma, contracture, Volkmann's ischemic	135, 299, 305
958.7	Complications, early, trauma, emphysema, subcutaneous	46, 222, 229, 299
958.8	Complications, early, trauma, other	275, 299
*959	Injury, other and unspecified	272
*959.0	Injury, other and unspecified, face and neck	299, 321
959.01	Injury, head, unspecified	303
959.09	Injury, other and unspecified, face and neck	303
*959.1	Injury, other and unspecified, trunk	299
959.2	Injury, other and unspecified, shoulder and upper arm	299
959.3	Injury, other and unspecified, elbow, forearm, and wrist	299

*** Code Range**

Code	Narrative	Page
959.4	Injury, other and unspecified, hand, except finger	299
959.5	Injury, other and unspecified, finger	299
959.6	Injury, other and unspecified, hip and thigh	299
959.7	Injury, other and unspecified, knee, leg, ankle, and foot	299
959.8	Injury, other and unspecified, other specified sites, including multiple	299
959.9	Injury, other and unspecified, unspecified site	299
*960	Poisoning, antibiotics	273
*961	Poisoning, anti-infectives, other	273
*962	Poisoning, hormones and synthetic substitutes	273
*963	Poisoning, agents, primarily systemic	273
*964	Poisoning, agents, primarily affecting blood constituents	273
*965	Poisoning, analgesics, antipyretics, and antirheumatics	273
*966	Poisoning, drugs, anticonvulsants and anti-Parkinsonism	273
*967	Poisoning, sedatives and hypnotics	273
*968	Poisoning, central nervous system depressants and anesthetics, other	273
*969	Poisoning, agents, psychotropic	273
*970	Poisoning, central nervous system stimulants	273
*971	Poisoning, drugs, primarily affecting the autonomic nervous system	273
*972	Poisoning, agents, primarily affecting the cardiovascular system	273
*973	Poisoning, agents, primarily affecting the gastrointestinal system	273
*974	Poisoning, water, mineral, and uric acid metabolism drugs	273
*975	Poisoning, agents, primarily acting on the smooth and skeletal muscles and respiratory system	273
976.0	Poisoning, local anti-infectives and anti-inflammatory drugs	273
976.1	Poisoning, antipruritics	273
976.2	Poisoning, local, astringents and detergents	273
976.3	Poisoning, emollients, demulcents, and protectants	273
976.4	Poisoning, keratolytics, keratoplastics, other hair treatment drugs and preparations	273
976.5	Poisoning, eye anti-infectives and other eye drugs	26
976.6	Poisoning, anti-infectives and drugs, other, and preparations for ear, nose, and throat	273
976.7	Poisoning, dental drugs topically applied	273
976.8	Poisoning, agents, other, primarily affecting skin and mucous membrane	273
976.9	Poisoning, agent, unspecified, primarily affecting skin and mucous membrane	273
*977	Poisoning, drugs and medicinal substances, other and unspecified	273
*978	Poisoning, vaccines, bacterial	273
*979	Poisoning, vaccines, other, and biological substances	273
*980	Effect, toxic, alcohol	273
981	Effect, toxic, petroleum products	273
*982	Effect, toxic, solvents other than petroleum-based	273
*983	Effect, toxic, corrosive aromatics, acids, and caustic alkalis	273
*984	Effect, toxic, lead and its compounds (including fumes)	274
*985	Effect, toxic, other metals	274
986	Effect, toxic, carbon monoxide	274
*987	Effect, toxic, gases, fumes, or vapors, other	274
987.9	Effect, toxic, gas, fume, or vapor, unspecified	279
*988	Effect, toxic, noxious substances eaten as food	274
*989	Effect, toxic, other substances, chiefly nonmedicinal as to source	274
990	Effects, radiation, unspecified	275
*991	Effects, reduced temperature	275
*992	Effects, heat and light	275
993.0	Barotrauma, otitic	34
993.1	Barotrauma, sinus	34
993.2	Effects, other and unspecified, high altitude	275
993.3	Disease, caisson	275
993.4	Effects, air pressure caused by explosion	275
993.8	Effects, other specified air pressure,	275
993.9	Effects, unspecified air pressure	275
994.0	Effects, lightning	275
994.1	Effects, drowning and nonfatal submersion	275
994.2	Effects, hunger	275
994.3	Effects, thirst	275
994.4	Effects, exhaustion due to exposure	275
994.5	Effects, exhaustion due to excessive exertion	275
994.6	Effects, motion	33
994.7	Effects, asphyxiation and strangulation	275
994.8	Effects, electrocution and nonfatal effects of electric current	275
994.9	Effects, other, external causes	275

Numeric Index to Diseases

*** Code Range**

Code	Narrative	Page
995.0	Effects, adverse, shock, anaphylactic, other, not elsewhere classifed	273
995.1	Effects, adverse, dema, angioneurotic, not elsewhere classified	273
995.2	Effects, adverse, unspecified, drug, medicinal and biological substances, not elsewhere classified	222, 229, 274
995.3	Effects, adverse, not elsewhere classified allergy, unspecified	273
995.4	Effects, adverse, not elsewhere classified shock, due to anesthesia	222, 229, 275
*995.5	Syndrome, child maltreatment	275
*995.6	Shock, anaphylactic, due to foods	273
995.7	Reaction, adverse, food, not elsewhere classified	275
*995.8	Effects, adverse, other specified, not elsewhere classified	275
*995.9	Systemic inflammatory response syndrome (SIRS)	246
996.00	Complication, mechanical, cardiac device, implant and graft, unspecified	91
996.01	Complication, mechanical, cardiac pacemaker electrode	89
996.02	Complication, mechanical, heart valve prosthesis	89
996.03	Complication, mechanical, coronary bypass graft	91
996.04	Complication, mechanical, automatic implantable cardiac defibrillator	89
996.09	Complication, mechanical, cardiac device, implant and graft, other	91
996.1	Complications, mechanical, vascular device, implant and graft	91
996.2	Complication, mechanical, nervous system device, implant and graft	16
996.30	Complication, mechanical, genitourinary device, implant or graft, unspecified	165
996.31	Complication, mechanical, urethral indwelling catheter	165
996.32	Complication, mechanical, intrauterine contraceptive device	178, 184
996.39	Complication, mechanical, genitourinary device, implant or graft, other,	165
*996.4	Complication, mechanical, internal orthopedic device, implant and graft	131
996.51	Complication, mechanical, corneal graft	26
996.52	Complication, mechanical, graft, other tissue, not elsewhere classified	274
996.53	Complication, mechanical, ocular lens prosthesis	26
996.54	Complication, mechanical, breast prosthesis	143

Code	Narrative	Page
996.55	Complication, mechanical, artificial skin graft and decellularized allodermis	274
996.56	Complication, mechanical, peritoneal dialysis catheter	274
996.57	Complication, mechanical, insulin pump	274
996.59	Complication, mechanical, implant and internal device, other	274
996.60	Complication, infection, inflammatory reaction, device, implant, and graft, unspecified	274
996.61	Complication, infection, inflammatory reaction, cardiac device, implant and graft	59, 62, 64, 74, 77, 80, 91
996.62	Complication, infection, inflammatory reaction, vascular device, implant and graft, other	59, 62, 64, 74, 77, 80, 83, 91
996.63	Complication, infection, inflammatory reaction, nervous system device, implant, and graft	16
996.64	Complication, infection, inflammatory reaction, indwelling urinary catheter	165
996.65	Complication, infection, inflammatory reaction, genitourinary device, implant and graft, other	165
996.66	Complication, infection, inflammatory reaction, internal joint prosthesis	124, 131
996.67	Complication, infection, inflammatory reaction, internal orthopedic device, implant, and graft, other	124, 131
996.68	Complication, infection and inflammatory reaction, peritoneal dialysis catheter	274
996.69	Complication, infection, inflammatory reaction, internal prosthetic device, implant, and graft, other	274
996.70	Complication, other, device, implant, and graft, unspecified	274
996.71	Complication, other, heart valve prosthesis	91
996.72	Complication, other, cardiac device, implant and graft, other	60, 62, 64, 74, 77, 80, 83, 91
996.73	Complication, other, renal dialysis device, implant and graft	91
996.74	Complication, other, vascular device, implant and graft, other	91
996.75	Complication, other, nervous system device, implant, and graft	16
996.76	Complication, other, genitourinary device, implant, and graft	165
996.77	Complication, other, internal joint prosthesis	131
996.78	Complication, other, internal orthopedic device, implant, and graft	131

* Code Range

Code	Narrative	Page
996.79	Complication, other, internal prosthetic device, implant, and graft, other	274
996.80	Complication, transplanted organ, unspecified	274
996.81	Complication, transplanted kidney	165
996.82	Complication, transplanted liver	111
996.83	Complication, transplanted heart	60, 62, 64, 74, 77, 80, 91
996.84	Complication, transplanted lung	47
996.85	Complication, bone marrow transplant	235
996.86	Complication, transplanted pancreas	110
996.87	Complication, transplanted intestine	274
996.89	Complication, transplanted organ, other,	274
*996.9	Complication, reattached extremity or body part	131
*997.0	Complications, not elsewhere classified, nervous system	16, 222, 229
997.1	Complications, not elsewhere classified, cardiac	91, 222, 229
997.2	Complications, not elsewhere classified, peripheral vascular	87, 222, 229
997.3	Complications, not elsewhere classified, respiratory	47, 222, 229
997.4	Complications, not elsewhere classified, digestive system	105, 222, 229
997.5	Complications, not elsewhere classified, urinary	165, 222, 229
*997.6	Complication, amputation stump	135
997.71	Complication, vascular, artery, mesenteric	105, 222, 229
997.72	Complication, vascular, artery, renal	165, 222, 229
997.79	Complication, vascular, other vessels	87, 222, 229
*997.9	Complications, affecting other specified body system, not elsewhere classified	274
*998	Complications, other, not elsewhere classified, procedures	222, 229
998.0	Complications, procedures, shock, postoperative	274
*998.1	Complications, procedures, hemorrhage, hematoma, seroma, complicating a procedure	274
998.2	Complications, procedures, laceration or puncture, accidental	274
*998.3	Complications, procedures, disruption, wound, operative	274
998.4	Complications, procedures, foreign body, accidentally left	274
*998.5	Complications, procedures, infection, postoperative	246
998.6	Complications, procedures, fistula, persistent, postoperative	274
998.7	Complications, procedures, acute reaction, foreign substance accidentally left,	274
998.81	Complications, procedures, emphysema, subcutaneous	274
998.82	Complications, procedures, fragments, cataract, in eye	26
998.83	Complications, procedures, wound, surgical, nonhealing	274
998.89	Complications, other specified, not elsewhere classified, procedures	274
998.9	Complications, procedures,	274
999.0	Complications, not elsewhere classified, vaccinia, generalized	247
999.1	Complications, not elsewhere classified, embolism, air	42, 222, 229
999.2	Complications, not elsewhere classified, vascular, other	91, 222, 229
999.3	Complications, not elsewhere classified, infection, other	222, 229, 249
999.4	Complications, not elsewhere classified, shock, anaphylactic, due to serum	222, 229, 273
999.5	Complications, not elsewhere classified, reaction, serum, other	222, 229, 273
999.6	Complications, not elsewhere classified, reaction, incompatibility ABO	222, 229, 234
999.7	Complications, not elsewhere classified, reaction, incompatibility Rh	222, 229, 234
999.8	Complications, not elsewhere classified, Reaction, transfusion, other	222, 229, 234
999.9	Complications, not elsewhere classified, other and unspecified,	274
*V01	Contact with or exposure to, communicable diseases	287
*V01.8	Contact with or exposure, communicable diseases, other	231
V02.0	Carrier or suspected carrier, cholera	287
V02.1	Carrier or suspected carrier, typhoid	287
V02.2	Carrier or suspected carrier, amebiasis	287
V02.3	Carrier or suspected carrier, gastrointestinal pathogens, other	287
V02.4	Carrier or suspected carrier, diphtheria	287
*V02.5	Carrier or suspected carrier, bacterial diseases, other specified	287
*V02.6	Carrier or suspected carrier, viral hepatitis	111
V02.7	Carrier or suspected carrier, gonorrhea	287
V02.8	Carrier or suspected carrier, venereal diseases, other	287
V02.9	Carrier or suspected carrier, infectious organism, other specified	287

*** Code Range**

Code	Narrative	Page
*V03	Vaccination and inoculation need, prophylactic, against bacterial diseases	287
*V04	Vaccination and inoculation need, against certain viral diseases	287
*V05	Vaccination and inoculation need, prophylactic, against other, single diseases	287
V05.3	Vaccination and inoculation need, prophylactic, against viral hepatitis	231
V05.4	Vaccination and inoculation need, against prophylactic, varicella	231
V05.8	Vaccination and inoculation need, prophylactic, against other specified disease	231
*V06	Vaccination and inoculation need, prophylactic, against combinations of diseases	287
*V07	Isolation need or other prophylactic measures	287
V08	Status, infection, asymptomatic, human immunodeficiency virus [HIV]	247
*V09	Status, infection, microorganisms, drug resistant	249
*V10	History, personal, malignant neoplasm	236, 242, 287
V10.01	History, personal, malignant neoplasm, tongue	321
V10.02	History, personal, malignant neoplasm, oral cavity and pharynx, other and unspecified	321
V10.21	History, personal, malignant neoplasm, larynx	321
*V11	History, personal, mental disorder	287
*V12	History, personal, certain other diseases	287
*V13	History, personal, other diseases	287
*V14	History, personal, allergy to medicinal agents	287
*V15	History, personal, other, presenting hazards to health	287
*V16	History, family, malignant neoplasm	287
*V17	History, family, certain chronic disabling diseases	287
*V18	History, family, certain other specific conditions	287
*V19	History, family, other conditions	287
*V20	Supervision, health, infant or child	287
V20.1	Supervision, health, other healthy infant or child receiving care	231
V20.2	Check, health, routine, infant or child	231
*V21	Development, constitutional states	287
*V22	Pregnancy, normal	287
V23.0	Supervision, pregnancy, high-risk, history of infertility	214
V23.1	Supervision, pregnancy, high-risk, history of trophoblastic disease	214
V23.2	Supervision, pregnancy, high-risk, history of previous abortion	214
V23.3	Supervision, pregnancy, high-risk, grand multiparity	214
*V23.4	Supervision, pregnancy, high-risk, affected by poor obstetric history	214
V23.5	Supervision, pregnancy, high-risk, poor reproductive history	214
V23.7	Supervision, pregnancy, high-risk, affected by insufficient prenatal care	214
*V23.8	Supervision, pregnancy, high-risk, other	214
V23.9	Supervision, pregnancy, high-risk, unspecified	214
V24.0	Examination and care, postpartum, immediately after delivery	205
V24.1	Examination and care, postpartum, lactating mother	287
V24.2	Examination and care, postpartum, routine, follow-up	287
*V25.0	Management, contraceptive, general counseling and advice	287
V25.1	Management, contraceptive, insertion, intrauterine contraceptive device	287
V25.2	Management, contraceptive, sterilization	172, 178, 184
V25.3	Management, contraceptive, extraction, menstrual	178, 184
*V25.4	Surveillance, previously prescribed contraceptive	287
V25.5	Insertion, implantable contraceptive, subdermal	287
V25.8	Management, contraceptive, other specified	288
V25.9	Management, contraceptive, unspecified	288
V26.0	Management, procreative, tuboplasty or vasoplasty, after previous sterilization	173, 178, 184
V26.1	Management, procreative, insemination, artificial	288
*V26.2	Management, procreative, investigation and testing	288
*V26.3	Counseling and testing, genetic	288
V26.4	Management, procreative, general counseling and advice	288
*V26.5	Management, procreative, sterilization status	288
V26.8	Management, procreative, other specified	288
V26.9	Management, procreative, unspecified	288
*V27	Outcome of delivery	288
V28.0	Screening, amniocentesis, chromosomal anomalies, antenatal	210
V28.1	Screening amniotic fluid, chromosomal anomalies, raised alpha-fetoprotein levels, antenatal	210
V28.2	Screening, other, based on amniocentesis, antenatal	210

* Code Range

Code	Narrative	Page
V28.3	Screening, ultrasonics, malformation, antenatal	288
V28.4	Screening, ultrasonics, fetal growth retardation, antenatal	288
V28.5	Screening, isoimmunization, antenatal	288
V28.6	Screening, Streptococcus B, antenatal	288
V28.8	Screening, other specified, antenatal	288
V28.9	Screening, unspecified, antenatal	288
*V29	Observation, evaluation, newborn, infant, suspected condition not found	231, 288
V30.00	Newborn, liveborn, in hospital, delivered without mention of cesarean delivery, single	230, 231
V30.01	Newborn, liveborn, in hospital, delivered by cesarean delivery, single	230, 231
V30.1	Newborn, liveborn, before admission to hospital, single	230, 231
V30.2	Newborn, liveborn, outside hospital and not hospitalized, single	232
V31.00	Newborn, twin, mate liveborn, in hospital, delivered without mention of cesarean delivery	230, 231
V31.01	Newborn, twin, mate liveborn, in hospital, delivered by cesarean delivery	230, 231
V31.1	Newborn, twin, mate liveborn, before admission to hospital	230, 231
V31.2	Newborn, twin, mate liveborn, outside hospital and not hospitalized	232
V32.00	Newborn, twin, mate stillborn, in hospital, delivered without mention of cesarean delivery	230, 231
V32.01	Newborn, twin, mate stillborn, in hospital, delivered by cesarean delivery	230, 231
V32.1	Newborn, twin, mate stillborn, before admission to hospital	230, 231
V32.2	Newborn, twin, mate stillborn, outside hospital and not hospitalized	232
V33.00	Newborn, twin, unspecified, in hospital, delivered without mention of cesarean delivery	230, 231
V33.01	Newborn, twin, unspecified, in hospital, delivered by cesarean delivery	230, 231
V33.1	Newborn, twin, unspecified whether mate liveborn or stillborn, before admission to hospital	230, 231
V33.2	Newborn, twin, unspecified whether mate liveborn or stillborn, outside hospital and not hospitalized	232
V34.00	Newborn, other multiple, mates all liveborn, in hospital, delivered without mention of cesarean delivery	230, 231
V34.01	Newborn, other multiple, mates all liveborn, in hospital, delivered by cesarean delivery	230, 231
V34.1	Newborn, other multiple, mates all liveborn, before admission to hospital	230, 231
V34.2	Newborn, other multiple, mates all liveborn, outside hospital and not hospitalized	232
V35.00	Newborn, other multiple, mates all stillborn, in hospital, delivered without mention of cesarean delivery	230, 231
V35.01	Newborn, other multiple, mates all stillborn, in hospital, delivered by cesarean delivery	230, 231
V35.1	Newborn, other multiple, mates all stillborn, before admission to hospital	230, 231
V35.2	Newborn, other multiple, mates all stillborn, outside hospital and not hospitalized	232
V36.00	Newborn, other multiple, mates live and stillborn, in hospital, delivered without mention of cesarean delivery	230, 232
V36.01	Newborn, other multiple, mates live- and stillborn, in hospital, delivered by cesarean delivery	230, 232
V36.1	Newborn, other multiple, mates live and stillborn, before admission to hospital	230, 232
V36.2	Newborn, other multiple, mates live and stillborn, outside hospital and not hospitalized	232
V37.00	Newborn, other multiple, unspecified, in hospital, delivered without mention of cesarean delivery	230, 232
V37.01	Newborn, other multiple, unspecified, in hospital, delivered by cesarean delivery	230, 232
V37.1	Newborn, other multiple, unspecified, before admission to hospital	230, 232
V37.2	Newborn, other multiple, unspecified, outside hospital and not hospitalized	232
V39.00	Newborn, unspecified whether single, twin, or multiple, in hospital, delivered without mention of cesarean delivery	230, 232
V39.01	Newborn, unspecified whether single, twin, or multiple, in hospital, delivered by cesarean delivery	230, 232
V39.1	Newborn, unspecified whether single, twin, or multiple, before admission to hospital	230, 232
V39.2	Newborn, unspecified whether single, twin, or multiple, outside hospital and not hospitalized	232
*V40	Problems, mental and behavioral	288
*V41	Problems, special senses and other special functions	288

*** Code Range**

Code	Narrative	Page
V42.0	Status, organ or tissue replaced by transplant, kidney	165, 322
V42.1	Status, organ or tissue replaced by transplant, heart	91
V42.2	Status, organ or tissue replaced by transplant, heart valve	91
V42.3	Status, organ or tissue replaced by transplant, skin	148
V42.4	Status, organ or tissue replaced by transplant, bone	135
V42.5	Status, organ or tissue replaced by transplant, cornea	26
V42.6	Status, organ or tissue replaced by transplant, lung	47
V42.7	Status, organ or tissue replaced by transplant, liver	111
V42.81	Status, organ or tissue replaced by transplant, bone marrow	235
V42.82	Status, organ or tissue replaced by transplant, stem cells, peripheral	235
V42.83	Status, organ or tissue replaced by transplant, pancreas	110
V42.84	Status, organ or tissue replaced by transplant, intestines	288
V42.89	Status, organ or tissue replaced by transplant, other	288
V42.9	Status, organ or tissue replaced by transplant, unspecified	288
V43.0	Status, organ or tissue replaced by other means, eye globe	26
V43.1	Status, organ or tissue replaced by other means, lens	26
*V43.2	Status, organ or tissue replaced by other means, heart	91
V43.3	Status, organ or tissue replaced by other means, heart valve	91
V43.4	Status, organ or tissue replaced by other means, blood vessel	91
V43.5	Status, organ or tissue replaced by other means, bladder	165
*V43.6	Status, organ or tissue replaced by other means, joint	135
V43.7	Status, organ or tissue replaced by other means, limb	135
*V43.8	Status, organ or tissue replaced by other means, other	288
V43.89	Status, organ or tissue replaced by other means, other means	322
*V44	Status, artificial opening	288
*V45.0	States, postprocedural, device, cardiac in situ	288
V45.1	Status, renal dialysis	288
V45.2	Status, presence of device, drainage, cerebrospinal fluid	288
V45.3	Status, bypass or anastomosis, intestinal	288
V45.4	Status, arthrodesis	288
*V45.5	Status, presence of device, contraceptive	288
V45.61	Status, cataract extraction	288
V45.69	States, other, following surgery, eye and adnexa	288
V45.71	Absence, acquired, breast	288
V45.72	Absence, acquired, intestine	288
V45.73	Absence, acquired, kidney	288
V45.74	Absence, acquired, urinary tract, other parts	165
V45.75	Absence, acquired, stomach	288
V45.76	Absence, acquired, lung	47
V45.77	Absence, acquired, genital organs	173, 178, 184
V45.78	Absence, acquired, eye	26
V45.79	Absence, acquired, organ, other	288
V45.81	Status, postprocedural, aortocoronary bypass	288
V45.82	Status, postprocedural, angioplasty, percutaneous transluminal coronary	288
V45.83	Status, postprocedural, removal, implant, breast	288
V45.84	Status, postprocedural, dental restoration	288
V45.85	Status, postprocedural, insulin pump	288
V45.89	Status, postprocedural, other	288
*V46	Dependence, other, on machines	288
*V47	Problems, other, with internal organs	288
*V48	Problems, with head, neck and trunk	288
*V49	Conditions, other, influencing health	288
V50.0	Surgery, elective, transplant, hair	148
V50.1	Surgery, elective, plastic, unacceptable cosmetic appearance	148
V50.2	Surgery, elective, circumcision, routine or ritual	172, 232
V50.41	Surgery, elective, breast removal, prophylactic	143
V50.42	Surgery, elective, ovary removal, prophylactic	178, 184
V50.49	Surgery, elective, organ removal, other, prophylactic	288
V50.8	Surgery, elective, other, purposes other than remedying health states	288
V50.9	Surgery, elective, unspecified, purposes other than remedying health states	288
V51	Aftercare, involving use of plastic surgery	148
V52.0	Fitting, adjustment, artificial arm	131
V52.1	Fitting, adjustment, artificial leg	131
V52.2	Fitting, adjustment, artificial eye	288
V52.3	Fitting, adjustment, prosthetic device, dental	288
V52.4	Fitting, adjustment, prosthesis, implant, breast	288
V52.8	Fitting, adjustment, prosthetic device, other specified	286
V52.9	Fitting, adjustment, prosthetic device, unspecified	286

*** Code Range***

Code	Narrative	Page
*V53.0	Fitting, adjustment, devices, related to nervous system and special senses	16
V53.1	Fitting, adjustment, spectacles and contact lenses	288
V53.2	Fitting, adjustment, hearing aid	288
*V53.3	Fitting, adjustment, device, cardiac	91
V53.4	Fitting, adjustment, devices, orthodontic	288
V53.5	Fitting, adjustment, intestinal appliance, other	105
V53.6	Fitting, adjustment, devices, urinary	165
V53.7	Fitting, adjustment, devices, orthopedic	131
V53.8	Fitting, adjustment, wheelchair	288
*V53.9	Fitting, adjustment, device, other and unspecified	288
*V54.0	Aftercare, orthopedic, involving removal, fracture plate, other internal fixation device	131
*V54.1	Aftercare, for healing fracture, traumatic	131
*V54.2	Aftercare, for healing fracture, pathologic	131
*V54.8	Aftercare, orthopedic, other	131
V54.9	Aftercare, orthopedic, unspecified	131
V55.0	Attention, openings, artificial, tracheostomy	47
V55.1	Attention, openings, artificial, gastrostomy	105
V55.2	Attention, openings, artificial, ileostomy	105
V55.3	Attention, openings, artificial, colostomy	105
V55.4	Attention, openings, artificial, digestive tract	105
V55.5	Attention, openings, artificial, cystostomy	165
V55.6	Attention, openings, artificial, urinary tract	165
V55.7	Attention, openings, artificial, vagina	178, 184
V55.8	Attention, openings, artificial, other specified	288
V55.9	Attention, openings, artificial, unspecified	288
*V56	Encounter, dialysis and dialysis catheter care	162
V57.0	Care, involving, rehabilitation procedures, breathing exercises	288
V57.1	Care, involving, rehabilitation procedures, physical therapy	286
*V57.2	Encounter, occupational therapy, vocational rehabilitation	286
V57.3	Care, involving, rehabilitation procedures, speech therapy	286
V57.4	Care, involving, rehabilitation procedures, orthoptic training	288
V57.81	Care, involving, rehabilitation procedures, orthotic training	289
V57.89	Care, involving, rehabilitation procedures, other specified	286
V57.9	Care, involving, rehabilitation procedures, unspecified	286
V58.0	Encounter, procedure, radiotherapy	237, 242
*V58.1	Encounter, procedure, antineoplastic chemotherapy and immunotherapy	237
V58.2	Aftercare, blood transfusion, without reported diagnosis	289
V58.3	Aftercare, surgical dressings and sutures	289
*V58.4	Aftercare, other, following surgery	286
V58.5	Aftercare, orthodontics	286
*V58.6	Encounter, drug use, long-term (current)	286
*V58.7	Aftercare, following surgery	286
*V58.8	Aftercare, procedures, other specified	287
V58.9	Aftercare, unspecified	287
*V59.0	Donor, blood	289
V59.1	Donor, skin	148
V59.2	Donor, bone	135
V59.3	Donor, bone marrow	289
V59.4	Donor, kidney	165
V59.5	Donor, cornea	289
V59.6	Donor, liver	111
*V59.7	Donor, egg (oocyte) (ovum)	289
V59.8	Donor, organ or tissue, other specified	289
V59.9	Donor, organ or tissue, unspecified	289
*V60	Encounter, circumstances, housing, household and economic	289
*V61	Encounter, circumstances, family, other	289
V61.5	Encounter, multiparity	178, 184
V61.6	Encounter, pregnancy, illegitimate	210
V61.7	Encounter, pregnancy, other, unwanted	206
*V62	Encounter, circumstances, psychosocial, other	289
V62.84	Ideation, suicidal	251
*V63	Unavailability, medical facilities for care	289
*V64	Encounter, specific procedures, services, not carried out	289
*V65	Encounter, consultation, without complaint or sickness	289
*V66	Convalescence, palliative care	289
*V67.0	Examination, follow-up, surgery	287
V67.1	Examination, follow-up, following radiotherapy	237, 242
V67.2	Examination, follow-up, following chemotherapy	237, 242, 244
V67.3	Examination, follow-up, following psychotherapy and other treatment for mental disorder	289

Code	Narrative	Page
V67.4	Examination, follow-up, following treatment, healed fracture	287
*V67.5	Examination, follow-up, following other treatment	289
V67.6	Examination, follow-up, following combined treatment	289
V67.9	Examination, follow-up, unspecified	289
*V68	Encounter, administrative purposes	289
*V69	Encounter, problems, lifestyle	289
*V70	Encounter, examination, medical, general	289
V70.3	Encounter, examination, other medical, for administrative purposes	232
V71.01	Observation, evaluation, behavior, antisocial, adult, not found	251
V71.02	Observation, evaluation, behavior, antisocial, childhood or adolescent, not found	251
V71.09	Observation, evaluation, suspected mental condition, other, not found	253
V71.1	Observation, suspected malignant neoplasm	237, 242, 287
V71.2	Observation, suspected tuberculosis	43
V71.3	Observation, following accident at work	275
V71.4	Observation, following other accident	275
V71.5	Observation, following alleged rape or seduction	289
V71.6	Observation, following other inflicted injury	275
V71.7	Observation suspected cardiovascular disease	90
*V71.8	Observation, suspected conditions, other specified	289
V71.9	Observation, suspected conditions, unspecified	289
*V72	Investigation, examination, special	289
V72.1	Examination, ears, hearing	232
*V73	Examination, screening, special, for viral diseases	289
*V74	Examination, screening, diseases, bacterial and spirochetal	289
*V75	Examination, screening, diseases, infectious, other	289
*V76	Screening, special, malignant neoplasms	289
*V77	Screening, special, disorders, endocrine, nutritional, metabolic and immunity	289
V77.3	Screening, special, phenylketonuria (PKU)	232
*V78	Screening, special, disorders, blood, blood-forming organs	289
*V79	Screening, special, mental disorders and developmental handicaps	289
*V80	Screening, special, diseases, neurological, eye and ear	289
*V81	Screening, special, diseases, cardiovascular, respiratory, and genitourinary	289
*V82	Screening, special, conditions, other	289
V83.01	Status, carrier, genetic, hemophilia A, asymptomatic	289
V83.02	Status, carrier, genetic, hemophilia A symptomatic	289
*V83.8	Status, carrier, genetic	289
*V84.0	Susceptibility, genetic, to malignant neoplasm	289
V84.8	Susceptibility, genetic, to diseases, other	289
*V85	Body Mass Index	289
V85.4	Body Mass Index, 40 and over, adult	154

*** Code Range**

Alphabetic Index to Procedures

Code	Narrative	Page
68.23	Ablation, endometrial	175, 176, 178
83.11	Achillotenotomy	117
28.6	Adenoidectomy, without tonsillectomy	29
*08.5	Adjstment, other, lid position	3, 19, 138, 259, 311
44.98	Adjustment, size of adjustable gastric restrictive device, laparoscopic	150, 314
07.3	Adrenalectomy, bilateral	139, 149
*07.2	Adrenalectomy, partial	149
07.22	Adrenalectomy, unilateral	139
86.72	Advancement, pedicle graft	4, 31, 54, 98, 114, 149, 256
83.71	Advancement, tendon, except hand	140
52.85	Allotransplantation, cells of islet of Langerhans	161
24.5	Alveoloplasty	32, 260, 313
84.17	Amputation above knee	4, 51, 113, 149, 270
84.01	Amputation and disarticulation, finger	118, 257, 317
84.02	Amputation and disarticulation, thumb	119, 257
84.19	Amputation, abdominopelvic	51, 113, 270
84.14	Amputation, ankle, through malleoli tibia and fibula	4, 51, 113, 149, 270
67.4	Amputation, cervix	178
84.09	Amputation, interthoracoscapular	113, 270
*84.1	Amputation, lower limb	140
84.10	Amputation, lower limb, unspecified	51, 113, 149, 270
84.15	Amputation, other, below knee	4, 51, 113, 149, 270
64.3	Amputation, penis	168
84.12	Amputation, through foot	4, 51, 113, 149, 270
84.05	Amputation, through forearm	113, 270
84.03	Amputation, through hand	113, 270
84.07	Amputation, through humerus	113, 270
84.11	Amputation, toe	4, 52, 117, 149, 270
84.91	Amputation, unspecified	51, 113, 140, 270
*84.0	Amputation, upper limb	52, 140
84.00	Amputation, upper limb, unspecified	113, 270
*56.7	Anastomosis or bypass, other, ureter	157, 264
04.73	Anastomosis, accessory, hypoglossal	30
*42.6	Anastomosis, antesternal, esophagus	31, 94, 239, 262
57.88	Anastomosis, bladder, other	158, 170, 240
39.21	Anastomosis, cavalpulmonary artery	51
*42.5	Anastomosis, esophagus, intrathoracic	31, 94, 239, 262
04.72	Anastomosis, face, accessory	30
04.71	Anastomosis, face, hypoglossal	30
*51.3	Anastomosis, gallbladder or bile duct	97, 106, 240, 263
*45.9	Anastomosis, intestinal	92, 263
45.90	Anastomosis, intestinal, unspecified	150, 239
45.95	Anastomosis, intestine, large-to-anus	239
45.94	Anastomosis, intestine, large-to-large	152, 239
45.93	Anastomosis, intestine, small-to-large, other	53, 152, 239
45.92	Anastomosis, intestine, small-to-rectal stump	239
45.91	Anastomosis, intestine, small-to-small	150, 239
55.86	Anastomosis, kidney	264
04.74	Anastomosis, other, cranial or peripheral nerve	30
52.96	Anastomosis, pancreas	106, 264
58.44	Anastomosis, urethra	265
39.1	Anastomosis, venous, intraabdominal	51, 94, 106
88.53	Angiocardiogram, left heart	49, 58, 60, 85
88.54	Angiocardiogram, right and left heart	49, 58, 60, 85
88.52	Angiocardiogram, right heart	49, 58, 60, 85
39.50	Angioplasty or atherectomy, noncoronary vessel(s), other	6, 40, 55, 75, 76, 97, 108, 120, 139, 151, 160, 262
00.62	Angioplasty or atherectomy, percutaneous, intracranial vessel(s)	6, 54, 74, 75, 257
00.61	Angioplasty or atherectomy, percutaneous, precerebral (extracranial) vessel(s)	6, 54, 74, 75, 257
36.03	Angioplasty, coronary, chest, open	50
35.33	Annuloplasty	49
49.21	Anoscopy	243
88.55	Anteriogram, coronary, one catheter	49, 58, 60, 85

** Code Range*

Code	Narrative	Page
88.57	Anteriogram, coronary, other	49, 58, 60, 61, 85
88.56	Anteriogram, coronary, two catheters	49, 58, 60, 85
*22.3	Antrotomy, external maxillary	28
*47.0	Appendectomy	96
*47.1	Appendectomy, incidental	180, 263
47.09	Appendectomy, other	53
47.91	Appendicostomy	93
78.14	Application, external fixation device, carpals and metacarpals	118, 256
78.15	Application, external fixation device, femur	112, 266, 291
78.12	Application, external fixation device, humerus	114, 266
78.19	Application, external fixation device, other	121, 267
78.16	Application, external fixation device, patella	124, 266
78.13	Application, external fixation device, radius and ulna	115, 121, 266
78.11	Application, external fixation device, scapula, clavicle and thorax	41, 121, 266
78.18	Application, external fixation device, tarsals and metatarsals	116, 267
78.17	Application, external fixation device, tibia and fibula	114, 266
78.10	Application, external fixation device, unspecified site	121, 266
39.27	Arteriovenostomy, for renal dialysis	53, 97, 151, 160, 262
81.25	Arthrodesis, carporadial	118, 257
81.24	Arthrodesis, elbow	115, 269
*81.1	Arthrodesis, foot and ankle	269
81.21	Arthrodesis, hip	112, 269, 291
81.28	Arthrodesis, interphalangeal	118, 257
81.22	Arthrodesis, knee	124, 269
81.26	Arthrodesis, metacarpocarpal	118, 257
81.27	Arthrodesis, metacarpophalangeal	118, 257
81.29	Arthrodesis, other specified joints	121, 269
81.23	Arthrodesis, shoulder	115, 152, 269
81.12	Arthrodesis, triple	115
81.20	Arthrodesis, unspecified joints	121, 269
*81.7	Arthroplasty, hand, fingers, and wrist	119
81.85	Arthroplasty, other, elbow	115, 270
81.83	Arthroplasty, other, shoulder	115, 269, 316
81.82	Arthroplasty, shoulder, recurrent dislocation	116, 269
76.5	Arthroplasty, temporomandibular	31, 120, 266
81.74	Arthroplasty, with implant, carpocarpal or carpometacarpal joint, with implant	3, 257
81.71	Arthroplasty, with implant, metacarpophalangeal and interphalangeal joint, with implant	3, 257
81.75	Arthroplasty, without implant, carpocarpal or carpometacarpal joint, without implant	3, 257
81.72	Arthroplasty, without implant, metacarpophalangeal and interphalangeal joint, without implant	3, 257
*80.2	Arthroscopy	119, 268
80.26	Arthroscopy, knee	152, 316
80.07	Arthrotomy, for removal of prosthesis, ankle	125, 268
80.02	Arthrotomy, for removal of prosthesis, elbow	125, 268
80.08	Arthrotomy, for removal of prosthesis, foot and toe	125, 268
80.04	Arthrotomy, for removal of prosthesis, hand and finger	125, 257
80.05	Arthrotomy, for removal of prosthesis, hip	112, 268, 291
80.06	Arthrotomy, for removal of prosthesis, knee	125, 268
80.09	Arthrotomy, for removal of prosthesis, other	125, 268
80.01	Arthrotomy, for removal of prosthesis, shoulder	125, 268
80.00	Arthrotomy, for removal of prosthesis, unspecified site	125, 268
80.03	Arthrotomy, for removal of prosthesis, wrist	125, 257
80.17	Arthrotomy, other, ankle	115, 268
80.12	Arthrotomy, other, elbow	115, 152, 268
80.18	Arthrotomy, other, foot and toe	117, 268, 316
80.14	Arthrotomy, other, hand and finger	119, 257
80.15	Arthrotomy, other, hip	112, 268, 291
80.16	Arthrotomy, other, knee	124, 152, 268, 316
80.19	Arthrotomy, other, other specified sites	121, 268
80.11	Arthrotomy, other, shoulder	115, 268
80.10	Arthrotomy, other, unspecified site	121, 152, 268
80.13	Arthrotomy, other, wrist	119, 257
69.52	Aspiration curettage, following delivery or abortion	193, 194, 316
69.51	Aspiration curettage, uterus, for termination of pregnancy	194, 316
12.21	Aspiration, diagnostic, eye, anterior chamber,	20
16.22	Aspiration, diagnostic, orbit	18, 313
86.73	Attachment, pedicle or flap graft to hand	119, 257
27.57	Attachment, pedicle or flap graft, to lip and mouth	32, 139, 260, 314

Alphabetic Index to Procedures

* Code Range

Code	Narrative	Page
86.74	Attachment, pedicle or flap graft, to other sites	4, 31, 54, 98, 114, 149, 256
52.84	Autotransplantation, cells of islet of Langerhans	161
55.61	Autotransplantation, kidney	157, 264
54.22	Biopsy, abdominal wall or umbilicus	98, 140, 240, 264, 315
07.12	Biopsy, adrenal gland, open	149
38.21	Biopsy, blood vessel	3, 19, 30, 40, 54, 74, 75, 120, 151, 160, 314
*77.4	Biopsy, bone	113, 140, 152, 160, 170, 316
77.44	Biopsy, bone, carpals and metacarpals	118, 256
77.49	Biopsy, bone, other	31, 41, 233
77.41	Biopsy, bone, scapula, clavicle and thorax	40
77.40	Biopsy, bone, unspecified site	31
27.21	Biopsy, bony palate	32, 314
33.27	Biopsy, closed endoscopic, lung	40, 53, 314
33.24	Biopsy, closed, endoscopic, bronchus	243
44.14	Biopsy, closed, endoscopic, gastric	243
31.43	Biopsy, closed, endoscopic, larynx	243
31.44	Biopsy, closed, endoscopic, trachea	243
45.25	Biopsy, closed, large bowel	243
45.14	Biopsy, closed, small bowel	243
57.33	Biopsy, closed, transurethral, bladder	159, 169, 180, 315
68.15	Biopsy, closed, uterine ligament	179, 316
68.16	Biopsy, closed, uterus	180, 316
11.22	Biopsy, cornea	259
70.22	Biopsy, cul-de-sac	243
70.23	Biopsy, cul-de-sac	179, 194, 316
34.27	Biopsy, diaphragm	39
42.24	Biopsy, esophagus, closed, endoscopic	243
42.25	Biopsy, esophagus, open	31, 94, 239
16.23	Biopsy, eyeball and orbit	18, 313
08.11	Biopsy, eyelid	19, 259, 311
76.11	Biopsy, facial bone	316
45.26	Biopsy, intestine, large, open	93, 314
45.15	Biopsy, intestine, small, open	93
12.22	Biopsy, iris	18
09.11	Biopsy, lacrimal gland	259
09.12	Biopsy, lacrimal sac	28
40.11	Biopsy, lymphatic structure	3, 40, 108, 160, 180
34.26	Biopsy, mediastinum, open	40, 53, 151, 233, 238
20.32	Biopsy, middle ear and inner ear	28, 313
22.12	Biopsy, nasal sinus, open	28
57.34	Biopsy, open, bladder	158, 169, 180, 240
01.14	Biopsy, open, brain	1, 2, 6, 237
85.12	Biopsy, open, breast	136, 137, 152, 270, 317
33.25	Biopsy, open, bronchus	39
01.12	Biopsy, open, cerebral meninges	1, 2, 6, 237
04.12	Biopsy, open, cranial or peripheral nerve or ganglion	3, 30, 119, 258
51.13	Biopsy, open, gallbladder or bile duct	97, 108
55.24	Biopsy, open, kidney	120, 157, 233, 240, 264
31.45	Biopsy, open, larynx or trachea	28, 40
50.12	Biopsy, open, liver	31, 40, 53, 97, 108, 120, 140, 152, 160, 169, 180, 233, 240, 263
33.28	Biopsy, open, lung	39, 53, 120, 160, 238
60.12	Biopsy, open, prostate	159, 170, 311
48.25	Biopsy, open, rectum	53, 93, 314
60.14	Biopsy, open, seminal vesicles	170
44.15	Biopsy, open, stomach	94, 314
62.12	Biopsy, open, testes	168
56.34	Biopsy, open, ureter	157
68.14	Biopsy, open, uterine ligaments, open	175, 176, 178
68.13	Biopsy, open, uterus	174, 176, 178
51.14	Biopsy, other closed (endoscopic), biliary duct or sphincter of Oddi	243
52.12	Biopsy, pancreas, open	97, 108, 152, 240, 264
52.14	Biopsy, pancreatic duct, closed (endoscopic)	243
06.13	Biopsy, parathyroid gland	120, 150
64.11	Biopsy, penis	140, 168, 315
37.24	Biopsy, pericardium	39, 50, 238
60.15	Biopsy, periprostatic tissue	170, 311
54.23	Biopsy, peritoneum	98, 108, 180, 233
07.17	Biopsy, pineal gland	1, 2, 7, 149
07.13	Biopsy, pituitary gland, transfrontal approach	1, 2, 7, 149

* Code Range

Code	Narrative	Page
07.14	Biopsy, pituitary gland, transphenoidal approach	1, 2, 7, 149
07.15	Biopsy, pituitary gland, unspecified approach	1, 2, 7, 149
48.24	Biopsy, rectal, closed, endoscopic	243
26.12	Biopsy, salivary gland or duct, open	27, 314
01.15	Biopsy, skull	1, 2, 6, 113, 150
83.21	Biopsy, soft tissue	4, 41, 140, 233, 317
03.32	Biopsy, spinal cord or spinal meninges	6, 123, 238
41.33	Biopsy, spleen, open	233, 238
07.16	Biopsy, thymus	39, 150, 233, 238
06.12	Biopsy, thyroid gland, open	150
28.11	Biopsy, tonsils, adenoids	314
27.22	Biopsy, uvula and soft palate	32, 314
70.24	Biopsy, vagina	140, 179, 197, 316
25.02	Biopsy, wedge, tongue, open	32
33.22	Bronchoscopy, fiberoptic	243
33.23	Bronchoscopy, other	243
33.21	Bronchoscopy, through artificial stoma	243
14.49	Buckling, scleral, other	151
83.5	Bursectomy, except hand	117, 270, 317
82.03	Bursotomy, hand	118, 257
66.97	Burying, fimbriae in uterine wall	174, 175, 178, 193
*36.1	Bypass, aortocoronary	49, 60, 63
39.25	Bypass, vascular, aorto-iliac-femoral	51, 139, 151, 261
39.22	Bypass, vascular, aorto-subclavian-carotid	6, 51, 261
39.28	Bypass, vascular, extracranial-intracranial (EC-IC)	1, 2, 5, 7, 262
39.26	Bypass, vascular, intraabdominal	51, 97, 108, 157, 262
39.23	Bypass, vascular, intrathoracic	51, 261
39.29	Bypass, vascular, peripheral artery	6, 40, 54, 75, 108, 139, 151, 262
39.24	Bypass, vascular, renal artery	51, 157, 261
52.92	Cannulation, pancreatic duct	97, 106, 240, 264
88.58	Cardiogram, negative-contrast	49, 58, 60, 61, 85
37.11	Cardiotomy	50, 261
37.23	Catheterization, cardiac, combined right and left heart	49, 58, 60, 85
37.22	Catheterization, cardiac, left heart	49, 58, 60, 85
37.21	Catheterization, cardiac, right heart	49, 58, 60, 85
45.72	Cecectomy	53
49.72	Cerclage, anal	95, 140
67.51	Cerclage, cervix, transabdominal	178, 197, 265
74.0	Cesarean section, classical	193
74.2	Cesarean section, extraperitoneal	193
74.1	Cesarean section, low cervical	193
74.4	Cesarean section, other specified type	193
74.99	Cesarean section, unspecified type	193
83.85	Change, length, other, in muscle or tendon, except hand	4, 117
87.53	Cholangiogram, intraoperative	108, 317
51.11	Cholangiography, retrograde, endoscopic (ERC)	243
51.10	Cholangiopancreatography (ERCP), endoscopic retrograde	243
*51.2	Cholecystectomy	107, 240, 263
51.22	Cholecystectomy	97, 107
51.23	Cholecystectomy, laparoscopic	97, 109, 315
51.24	Cholecystectomy, laparoscopic, partial	109
51.21	Cholecystectomy, partial other	107
51.03	Cholecystostomy, other	97, 106
51.02	Cholecystostomy, trocar	106
51.04	Cholecystotomy, other	106
*03.2	Chordotomy	5, 108, 238, 258
64.0	Circumcision	160, 169, 315
39.51	Clipping, aneurysm	1, 2, 5, 7, 55, 75, 76
51.92	Closure, cholecystostomy	107, 264
57.82	Closure, cystostomy	158, 170, 180, 240, 265, 315
54.62	Closure, delayed, abdominal wall, granulating wound	108, 180
42.83	Closure, esophagostomy	31, 94, 239, 262
49.73	Closure, fistula, anal	95, 140, 263
47.92	Closure, fistula, appendix	92, 263
51.93	Closure, fistula, biliary tract, other	107, 240, 264
29.52	Closure, fistula, branchial cleft	139
34.83	Closure, fistula, diaphragm	261
46.72	Closure, fistula, duodenum	94
46.76	Closure, fistula, large intestine	92
27.53	Closure, fistula, mouth	32, 260, 314
44.63	Closure, fistula, other, gastric	94, 108, 239, 262

*** Code Range**

Code	Narrative	Page
55.83	Closure, fistula, other, kidney	264
29.53	Closure, fistula, pharynx, other	260
48.73	Closure, fistula, rectal	95, 139, 178
46.74	Closure, fistula, small intestine except duodenum	92
56.84	Closure, fistula, ureter, other	93, 169, 180, 240, 264
58.43	Closure, fistula, urethra, other	168, 180, 240, 265
69.42	Closure, fistula, uterine	93
50.61	Closure, laceration, liver	106
21.82	Closure, nasal fistula	28, 313
55.82	Closure, nephrostomy and pyelostomy	264
34.73	Closure, other fistula, thorax	39, 261
31.73	Closure, other fistula, trachea	39, 93
48.72	Closure, proctostomy	92
*46.5	Closure, stoma, intestinal	93, 263
46.52	Closure, stoma, large intestine	314
31.72	Closure, tracheostomy	40, 53, 139
56.83	Closure, ureterostomy	169, 180, 240, 264
58.42	Closure, urethrostomy	265
45.8	Colectomy, total, intraabdominal	53, 92, 239, 263
33.39	Collapse, surgical, unspecified, lung	39
45.23	Colonoscopy, fiberoptic, flexible	243
46.13	Colostomy, other, permanent	53, 92, 239, 263
46.11	Colostomy, temporary	92, 239, 263
46.10	Colostomy, unspecified	92, 239, 263
67.2	Conization, cervix	180, 193, 316
*10.4	Conjunctivoplasty	259, 312
18.71	Construction, auricle of ear	138, 313
64.43	Construction, penis	265
21.07	Control, epistaxis, by excision, nasal mucosa and skin grafting, septum and lateral nasal wall	30, 53, 260
21.04	Control, epistaxis, by ligation, ethmoidal arteries	30, 53, 260
21.06	Control, epistaxis, by ligation, external carotid artery	30, 53, 260
21.09	Control, epistaxis, by other means	30, 53, 260, 313
21.05	Control, epistaxis, by transantral ligation, maxillary artery	30, 53, 260
28.7	Control, hemorrhage, after tonsillectomy, adenoidectomy	29, 260
57.93	Control, hemorrhage, bladder, postoperative	159, 265
39.41	Control, hemorrhage, postvascular surgery	54, 75, 76, 151
60.94	Control, hemorrhage, prostate	170, 265, 311
39.98	Control, hemorrhage, unspecified	30, 40, 53, 97, 108, 120, 139, 151, 160, 169, 180, 193, 238, 262
49.95	Control, postoperative, hemorrhage, anus	263
30.22	Cordectomy, vocal	28
12.35	Coreoplasty	20
27.62	Correction, cleft palate	3, 27
75.36	Correction, fetal defect	194
08.38	Correction, lid retraction	138, 151
75.93	Correction, surgical, inverted uterus	194
18.5	Correction, surgical, prominent ear	28, 138, 313
86.85	Correction, syndactyly	119, 138, 257
55.87	Correction, ureteropelvic junction	264
02.01	Craniectomy, linear	290
01.25	Craniectomy, other	119, 238, 258, 290
*02.0	Cranioplasty	1, 2, 7, 119, 258
*01.2	Craniotomy and craniectomy	1, 2, 7
01.24	Craniotomy, other	237, 258, 290
35.94	Creation, conduit, between atrium and pulmonary artery	50
35.93	Creation, conduit, between left ventricle and aorta	50
35.92	Creation, conduit, between right ventricle and pulmonary artery	50
44.67	Creation, laparoscopic, esophagogastric sphincteric competence	94, 262, 314
35.42	Creation, septal defect, heart	50
11.43	Cryotherapy, corneal lesion	259
70.12	Culdotomy	181, 194
86.71	Cutting, pedicle grafts or flaps	4, 31, 54, 98, 114, 149, 256
12.72	Cyclocryotherapy	151
12.55	Cyclodialysis	18
57.79	Cystectomy, other, total	265
57.6	Cystectomy, partial	158, 167, 180, 240, 265
*57.7	Cystectomy, total	158, 167, 180, 240
57.32	Cystoscopy, other	243
57.31	Cystoscopy, through stoma, artificial	243
57.19	Cystostomy, other	158, 265

Alphabetic Index to Procedures

* Code Range

Code	Narrative	Page
57.18	Cystostomy, other, suprapubic	158, 169, 178, 240, 265
57.85	Cystourethroplasty and plastic repair, bladder neck	158, 175
09.22	Dacryoadenectomy, other, partial	259
09.23	Dacryoadenectomy, total	259
09.81	Dacryocystorhinostomy	28
79.63	Debridement, open fracture, carpals and metacarpals	118, 257
79.65	Debridement, open fracture, femur	112, 268, 291
79.61	Debridement, open fracture, humerus	114, 268
79.69	Debridement, open fracture, other specified bone	31, 121, 268
79.68	Debridement, open fracture, phalanges of foot	116, 268
79.64	Debridement, open fracture, phalanges of hand	118, 257
79.62	Debridement, open fracture, radius and ulna	116, 268
79.67	Debridement, open fracture, tarsals and metatarsals	116, 268
79.66	Debridement, open fracture, tibia and fibula	114, 268
79.60	Debridement, open fracture, unspecified site	121, 268
86.22	Debridement, wound, infection or burn	4, 19, 31, 41, 53, 98, 109, 114, 137, 149, 160, 170, 181, 233, 256
55.91	Decapsulation, kidney	53, 157
04.42	Decompression, other, cranial nerve	3, 30, 258
04.41	Decompression, trigeminal nerve root	1, 2, 7, 30, 258, 290
34.51	Decortication, lung	238
69.3	Denervation, paracervical uterine	175, 176, 178
86.25	Dermabrasion	138, 317
*66.2	Destruction or occlusion, endoscopic, fallopian tubes, bilateral	179, 193, 316
*66.3	Destruction or occlusion, other, fallopian tubes, bilateral	179, 193, 316
14.22	Destruction, by cryotherapy, lesion, chorioretinal	18, 312
14.21	Destruction, by diathermy, lesion, chorioretinal	18, 312
14.27	Destruction, by implantation of radiation source, chorioretinal lesion	18, 312
14.26	Destruction, by radiation therapy, chorioretinal lesion	18, 312
45.43	Destruction, endoscopic, other lesion, large intestine	243
49.44	Destruction, hemorrhoids by cryotherapy	95, 315
32.09	Destruction, lesion, bronchus, other	39
42.39	Destruction, lesion, esophagus	31, 94, 239
08.25	Destruction, lesion, eyelid	139
66.61	Destruction, lesion, fallopian tube	174, 175, 178
50.29	Destruction, lesion, liver, other	97, 106
12.43	Destruction, lesion, nonexcisional, ciliary body	20
12.41	Destruction, lesion, nonexcisional, iris	18
68.29	Destruction, lesion, other, uterine	175, 176, 178, 316
14.29	Destruction, other, chorioretinal lesion	18, 312
80.59	Destruction, other, intervertebral disc	6, 123, 269
43.49	Destruction, other, lesion or tissue, stomach	94, 314
45.32	Destruction, other, lesion, duodenum	94, 108, 239, 314
45.49	Destruction, other, lesion, large intestine	93, 239, 314
45.34	Destruction, other, lesion, small intestine except duodenum	93, 239, 314
60.96	Destruction, transurethral, microwave thermotherapy, prostate tissue	158, 167, 311
60.97	Destruction, transurethral, other thermotherapy, prostate tissue	158, 167, 311
69.02	Dilation and curettage, following delivery or abortion	193
69.09	Dilation and curettage, other	180, 193, 316
*69.0	Dilation and curettage, uterus	194
69.01	Dilation, curettage, uterus, termination of pregnancy	316
51.84	Dilation, endoscopic, ampulla and biliary duct	243
52.98	Dilation, endoscopic, pancreatic duct	243
66.96	Dilation, fallopian tube	174, 175, 178
44.21	Dilation, pylorus, by incision	94
51.81	Dilation, sphincter of Oddi	97, 106, 263
60.95	Dilation, transurethral balloon, prostatic urethra	159, 170, 311
84.13	Disarticulation, ankle	4, 51, 113, 149, 270
84.06	Disarticulation, elbow	113, 270
84.18	Disarticulation, hip	51, 113, 270
84.16	Disarticulation, knee	4, 51, 113, 149, 270
84.08	Disarticulation, shoulder	113, 270
84.04	Disarticulation, wrist	113, 270
40.54	Dissection, groin, radical	120, 157, 167, 174

Alphabetic Index to Procedures

*** Code Range**

Code	Narrative	Page
40.42	Dissection, neck, radical, bilateral	27
40.41	Dissection, neck, radical, unilateral	27
40.40	Dissection, neck, radical, unspecified	27
32.6	Dissection, radical, thoracic structure	39
59.00	Dissection, retroperitoneal, unspecified	120, 140, 158, 167, 181, 240
*56.6	Diversion, urinary, other, external	157, 169, 180, 240, 264
56.71	Diversion, urinary, ureter to intestine	169, 180, 240
04.03	Division or crushing, other, cranial and peripheral nerves	3, 119, 258
64.93	Division, adhesions, penile	168, 315
*77.3	Division, bone, other (except carpals and metacarpals 77.34)	266
77.34	Division, bone, other, carpals and metacarpals	118, 256
77.39	Division, bone, other, except facial bones	121
77.35	Division, bone, other, femur, other	112, 291
77.32	Division, bone, other, humerus	114
77.36	Division, bone, other, patella	124
77.33	Division, bone, other, radius and ulna	115
77.31	Division, bone, other, scapula, clavicle and thorax, ribs and sternum, other	40, 121
77.38	Division, bone, other, tarsals and metatarsals, other	116, 152, 316
77.37	Division, bone, other, tibia and fibula	114
77.30	Division, bone, unspecified site	31, 120
03.1	Division, intraspinal nerve root	5, 123, 238, 258
80.47	Division, joint capsule, ligament or cartilage, ankle	115, 269
80.42	Division, joint capsule, ligament or cartilage, elbow	116, 269
80.48	Division, joint capsule, ligament or cartilage, foot and toe	117, 269
80.44	Division, joint capsule, ligament or cartilage, hand and finger	118, 257
80.45	Division, joint capsule, ligament or cartilage, hip	112, 269, 291
80.46	Division, joint capsule, ligament or cartilage, knee	124, 269, 316
80.49	Division, joint capsule, ligament or cartilage, other specified sites	121, 269
80.41	Division, joint capsule, ligament or cartilage, shoulder	116, 268
80.40	Division, joint capsule, ligament or cartilage, unspecified site	121, 268
80.43	Division, joint capsule, ligament or cartilage, wrist	118, 257
*83.1	Division, muscle, tendon and fascia, except hand	270
*82.1	Division, muscle, tendon and fascia, hand	118, 257
29.92	Division, nerve, glossopharyngeal	1, 2, 7, 30
31.91	Division, nerve, laryngeal	28, 40
83.19	Division, other, soft tissue, except hand	4, 117, 317
*49.5	Division, sphincter, anal	95, 315
05.0	Division, sympathetic nerve or ganglion	3, 52
68.21	Division, synechiae, endometrial	180
06.91	Division, thyroid isthmus	150
04.02	Division, trigeminal nerve	3, 258
47.2	Drainage, abscess, appendix	96
52.4	Drainage, cyst, pancreas, internal	106
27.0	Drainage, face and floor, mouth	32, 139, 260
02.02	Elevation, fragments, fracture, skull	290
38.16	Endarterectomy, abdominal arteries	50, 97, 160, 261
38.14	Endarterectomy, aorta	50, 97, 261
38.11	Endarterectomy, intracranial vessels	1, 2, 5, 7
38.18	Endarterectomy, lower limbs arteries	54, 74, 75, 151, 261
38.15	Endarterectomy, other thoracic vessels	39, 50, 261
38.12	Endarterectomy, other, vessels, head, neck	6, 30, 54, 74, 75, 151, 261
38.10	Endarterectomy, unspecified site	6, 54, 74, 75, 261
38.13	Endarterectomy, upper limb vessels	54, 74, 75, 151, 261
45.22	Endoscopy, intestine, large, through stoma, artificial	243
45.13	Endoscopy, intestine, small, other	243
45.12	Endoscopy, intestine, small, through stoma, artificial	243
45.11	Endoscopy, intestine, small, transabdominal	93, 239, 263, 314
45.21	Endoscopy, transabdominal, intestine, large	93, 263, 314
39.73	Endovascular implantation of graft in thoracic aorta	51, 160, 262
*45.0	Enterotomy	263
*16.4	Enucleation, eyeball	18, 260, 313
63.4	Epididymectomy	168
63.92	Epididymotomy	168
63.83	Epididymovasostomy	168
30.21	Epiglottidectomy	30
11.76	Epikeratophakia	19
45.16	Esophagogastroduodenoscopy, with closed biopsy	243
44.65	Esophagogastroplasty	94, 262
42.7	Esophagomyotomy	31, 94, 239, 262

* Code Range

Code	Narrative	Page
42.21	Esophagoscopy, by incision, operative	31, 94, 238, 262
42.23	Esophagoscopy, other	243
42.22	Esophagoscopy, through stoma, artificial	243
*42.1	Esophagostomy	31, 94, 238, 262
22.63	Ethmoidectomy	313
12.91	Evacuation, therapeutic, anterior chamber	19, 20, 259
*16.3	Evisceration, eyeball	18, 260, 313
68.8	Evisceration, pelvic	92, 174
95.04	Examination, eye, under anesthesia	19, 317
*76.4	Excision and reconstruction, facial bones	120, 266
*77.5	Excision and repair, bunion and other toe deformities	116, 316
82.29	Excision lesion, hand, other soft tissue	140, 316
04.07	Excision or avulsion, other, cranial and peripheral nerve	3, 119, 258, 311
85.20	Excision or destruction, breast tissue, unspecified	137, 317
80.50	Excision or destruction, intervertebral disc, unspecified	6, 123, 269
54.3	Excision or destruction, lesion or tissue, abdominal wall or umbilicus	98, 117, 140, 152, 240, 315
*27.3	Excision or destruction, lesion or tissue, bony palate	314
*10.3	Excision or destruction, lesion or tissue, conjunctiva	259, 312
*08.2	Excision or destruction, lesion or tissue, eyelid	19, 259, 311
*30.0	Excision or destruction, lesion or tissue, larynx	28
30.09	Excision or destruction, lesion or tissue, larynx	40, 314
34.3	Excision or destruction, lesion or tissue, mediastinum	39, 151, 238, 314
*41.4	Excision or destruction, lesion or tissue, spleen	233, 238
25.1	Excision or destruction, lesion or tissue, tongue	32, 53, 314
34.4	Excision or destruction, lesion, chest wall	40, 125, 139, 151, 238, 314
70.32	Excision or destruction, lesion, cul-de-sac	194
49.31	Excision or destruction, lesion, endoscopic, anus	243
51.64	Excision or destruction, lesion, endoscopic, biliary ducts or sphincter of Oddi	243
32.01	Excision or destruction, lesion, endoscopic, bronchus	243
45.30	Excision or destruction, lesion, endoscopic, duodenum	243
42.33	Excision or destruction, lesion, endoscopic, esophagus	243
32.28	Excision or destruction, lesion, endoscopic, lung	243
52.21	Excision or destruction, lesion, endoscopic, pancreatic duct	243
43.41	Excision or destruction, lesion, endoscopic, stomach	243
80.88	Excision or destruction, lesion, foot and toe	117, 152, 269, 316
*12.4	Excision or destruction, lesion, iris and ciliary body	259, 312
80.87	Excision or destruction, lesion, joint, ankle	115, 269
80.82	Excision or destruction, lesion, joint, elbow	125, 152, 269
80.84	Excision or destruction, lesion, joint, hand and finger	118, 257
80.85	Excision or destruction, lesion, joint, hip	119, 269
80.86	Excision or destruction, lesion, joint, knee	125, 269, 316
80.89	Excision or destruction, lesion, joint, other specified sites	125, 269
80.81	Excision or destruction, lesion, joint, shoulder	125, 269
80.80	Excision or destruction, lesion, joint, unspecified sites	125, 269
80.83	Excision or destruction, lesion, joint, wrist, other	118, 140, 257
12.84	Excision or destruction, lesion, sclera	19
03.4	Excision or destruction, lesion, spinal cord or spinal meninges	6, 123, 238
62.2	Excision or destruction, lesion, testicular	168
*29.3	Excision or destruction, lesion, tissue, pharynx	30, 93
70.33	Excision or destruction, lesion, vagina	140, 197
27.31	Excision or destruction, local, lesion or tissue, bony palate	32
*55.3	Excision or destruction, local, lesion or tissue, kidney	157
76.2	Excision or destruction, local, lesion, facial bone	31, 125, 266, 316
64.2	Excision or destruction, local, lesion, penis	140, 168, 315
31.5	Excision or destruction, local, lesion, tissue, trachea	28, 40
42.31	Excision or destruction, local, other lesion, tissue, esophagus	31, 94
71.3	Excision or destruction, local, other, vulva or perineum	140, 179, 197, 316
37.33	Excision or destruction, open approach, other lesion or tissue, heart	50
57.59	Excision or destruction, open, lesion or tissues, bladder, other	240, 315
37.34	Excision or destruction, other approach, other lesion or tissue, heart	56, 78, 80, 81
52.22	Excision or destruction, other lesion pancreas or pancreatic duct	106, 152

* Code Range

Code	Narrative	Page
49.39	Excision or destruction, other local lesion, anus	95, 138, 315
71.24	Excision or destruction, other, Bartholin's gland cyst	140, 179, 194, 316
*01.5	Excision or destruction, other, brain and meninges	1, 2, 7, 238
01.59	Excision or destruction, other, lesion or tissue, brain	258, 290
01.51	Excision or destruction, other, lesion or tissue, cerebral meninges	290
*67.3	Excision or destruction, other, lesion or tissue, cervix	178, 193, 316
67.39	Excision or destruction, other, lesion or tissue, cervix	140
57.49	Excision or destruction, other, lesion or tissue, transurethral bladder	169, 315
86.3	Excision or destruction, other, local, lesion or tissue, skin and subcutaneous tissue	141
54.4	Excision or destruction, peritoneal tissue	98, 108, 152, 180, 240, 315
*11.4	Excision or destruction, tissue or other lesion, cornea	19, 312
27.32	Excision or destruction, wide, lesion or tissue, bony palate	27
51.62	Excision, ampulla of Vater, with reimplantation of common duct	97, 106
49.6	Excision, anus	95, 315
51.69	Excision, bile duct, other	97, 106
*77.7	Excision, bone for graft (except carpals and metacarpals 77.74)	266
77.74	Excision, bone for graft, carpals and metacarpals	118, 256
77.75	Excision, bone for graft, femur	119
77.72	Excision, bone for graft, humerus	125
77.79	Excision, bone for graft, other	31, 125
77.76	Excision, bone for graft, patella	125
77.73	Excision, bone for graft, radius and ulna	125
77.71	Excision, bone for graft, scapula, clavicle and thorax, ribs and sternum	41, 125
77.78	Excision, bone for graft, tarsals and metatarsals	116
77.77	Excision, bone for graft, tibia and fibula	125
77.70	Excision, bone for graft, unspecified site	125
29.2	Excision, branchial cleft cyst, vestige	30, 139
85.24	Excision, breast, ectopic tissue	137
32.1	Excision, bronchus	39, 261
80.6	Excision, cartilage of knee, semilunar	124, 152, 269, 316
51.63	Excision, common duct, other	97, 106
63.2	Excision, cyst, epididymis	168, 315
*42.4	Excision, esophagus	31, 94, 239, 262

Code	Narrative	Page
77.58	Excision, fusion, and repair of toes, other	266
37.32	Excision, heart, aneurysm	50
49.46	Excision, hemorrhoids	95, 193, 315
61.2	Excision, hydrocele, tunica vaginalis	168, 315
80.51	Excision, intervertebral disc	6, 123, 269
45.79	Excision, intestine, large, other partial	53, 239
*45.7	Excision, intestine, large, partial	92, 263
*45.6	Excision, intestine, small	92
09.6	Excision, lacrimal sac and passage	259, 312
*09.2	Excision, lesion or tissue, lacrimal gland	312
45.41	Excision, lesion or tissue, large intestine	95, 152, 239, 314
41.42	Excision, lesion or tissue, spleen	262
12.44	Excision, lesion, ciliary body	20
24.4	Excision, lesion, dental, jaw	32, 313
16.93	Excision, lesion, eye, unspecified structure	19, 139, 260, 313
*82.2	Excision, lesion, hand, muscle, tendon and fascia	118, 257
82.21	Excision, lesion, hand, tendon sheath	140, 152, 316
12.42	Excision, lesion, iris	18
09.21	Excision, lesion, lacrimal gland	259
32.29	Excision, lesion, lung	39, 238
22.62	Excision, lesion, maxillary sinus, with other approach	120
20.51	Excision, lesion, middle ear	313
83.32	Excision, lesion, muscle, except hand	140, 317
*83.3	Excision, lesion, muscle, tendon, fascia and bursa, except hand	117, 270
16.92	Excision, lesion, orbit	18, 260, 313
83.39	Excision, lesion, other soft tissue, except hand	31, 140, 152, 317
*38.6	Excision, lesion, other vessels	261
38.60	Excision, lesion, other vessels, unspecified site	54, 74, 75, 151
38.66	Excision, lesion, other, abdominal arteries	51, 97, 160
38.61	Excision, lesion, other, intracranial vessels	1, 2, 5, 7
38.65	Excision, lesion, other, thoracic vessels	39, 51, 93
38.63	Excision, lesion, other, upper limb vessels	54, 75, 151
38.64	Excision, lesion, other, vessels, aorta	51, 97
38.62	Excision, lesion, other, vessels, head, neck	6, 30, 54, 74, 75
*26.2	Excision, lesion, salivary gland	27, 314

*** Code Range**

Code	Narrative	Page
01.6	Excision, lesion, skull	1, 2, 7, 125, 238, 290
83.31	Excision, lesion, tendon sheath, except hand	152
34.81	Excision, lesion, tissue, diaphragm	120
61.92	Excision, lesion, tunica vaginalis other than hydrocele	168
06.6	Excision, lingual thyroid	30, 150
28.5	Excision, lingual tonsil	29
42.32	Excision, local, esophagus	31, 94, 239
*77.6	Excision, local, lesion or tissue, bone	266, 316
77.64	Excision, local, lesion or tissue, bone, carpals and metacarpals	118, 256
77.65	Excision, local, lesion or tissue, bone, femur	119
77.62	Excision, local, lesion or tissue, bone, humerus	125
77.69	Excision, local, lesion or tissue, bone, other	31, 125, 152
77.66	Excision, local, lesion or tissue, bone, patella	125
77.63	Excision, local, lesion or tissue, bone, radius and ulna	125
77.61	Excision, local, lesion or tissue, bone, scapula, clavicle and thorax, ribs and sternum	41, 125, 152
77.68	Excision, local, lesion or tissue, bone, tarsals and metatarsals	116, 152
77.67	Excision, local, lesion or tissue, bone, tibia and fibula	125
77.60	Excision, local, lesion or tissue, bone, unspecified site	125
45.33	Excision, local, lesion or tissue, small intestine except duodenum	95, 239, 314
85.21	Excision, local, lesion, breast	137, 152, 317
60.61	Excision, local, lesion, prostate	170, 311
43.42	Excision, local, other lesion or tissue, stomach	94, 108, 151
45.31	Excision, local, other, lesion, duodenum	94, 108, 239, 314
48.35	Excision, local, rectal lesion, tissue	53, 95, 139, 315
*70.3	Excision, local, vagina and cul-de-sac	179, 316
32.9	Excision, lung, other	39, 261
40.23	Excision, lymph node, axillary	30, 40, 53, 97, 120, 314
40.51	Excision, lymph node, axillary, radical	120
40.21	Excision, lymph node, cervical, deep	30, 40, 53, 97, 120, 151, 314
40.53	Excision, lymph node, iliac, radical	120, 151, 157, 167, 174
40.24	Excision, lymph node, inguinal	40, 53, 97, 120, 160, 169, 180, 193, 314
40.22	Excision, lymph node, internal mammary	40
40.52	Excision, lymph node, periaortic, radical	40, 120, 151, 157, 167, 174
*40.5	Excision, lymph node, radical, other	97, 139, 233, 238
40.50	Excision, lymph node, radical, unspecified	27, 40, 160, 169, 174
40.3	Excision, lymph node, regional	30, 40, 53, 97, 120, 139, 151, 160, 169, 180, 193, 233, 238, 314
*40.4	Excision, lymph nodes, cervical, radical	40, 139, 151, 233, 238
08.24	Excision, major lesion, eyelid, full-thickness	139
08.23	Excision, major lesion, eyelid, partial-thickness	139
83.43	Excision, muscle or fascia for graft, except hand	4
85.25	Excision, nipple	137
63.3	Excision, other lesion or tissue, spermatic cord and epididymis	168, 315
40.59	Excision, other lymph nodes, radical	27, 40, 120, 157, 167, 174
40.29	Excision, other lymphatic structure, simple	30, 40, 53, 97, 120, 151, 160, 169, 180, 262, 314
08.22	Excision, other minor lesion, eyelid	139
*57.5	Excision, other, bladder tissue	158, 169, 180
*18.3	Excision, other, external ear	28, 139
18.39	Excision, other, external ear	260, 313
*82.3	Excision, other, hand, soft tissue	118, 257
82.39	Excision, other, hand, soft tissue	140
80.97	Excision, other, joint, ankle	115, 269
80.92	Excision, other, joint, elbow	116, 269
80.98	Excision, other, joint, foot and toe	117, 152, 269, 316
80.94	Excision, other, joint, hand and finger	118, 257
80.95	Excision, other, joint, hip	112, 269, 291
80.96	Excision, other, joint, knee	124, 269
80.99	Excision, other, joint, other specified sites	115, 269
80.91	Excision, other, joint, shoulder	116, 269

* Code Range

Code	Narrative	Page
80.90	Excision, other, joint, unspecified site	121, 269
80.93	Excision, other, joint, wrist	118, 257
27.43	Excision, other, lesion or tissue, lip	32, 139, 314
38.67	Excision, other, lesion, abdominal veins	51, 97, 160
38.68	Excision, other, lesion, lower limb arteries	54, 75, 151
38.69	Excision, other, lesion, lower limb veins	52
*20.5	Excision, other, middle ear	28
27.49	Excision, other, mouth	32, 260, 314
*83.4	Excision, other, muscle, tendon and fascia, except hand	117, 270
49.04	Excision, other, perianal tissue	95, 138
83.49	Excision, other, soft tissue, except hand	4, 31, 140
69.19	Excision, other, uterine ligaments	175, 176, 178
07.63	Excision, partial, pituitary gland, unspecified approach	139
07.81	Excision, partial, thymus	238
59.91	Excision, perirenal or perivesical tissue	159, 170, 241
58.92	Excision, periurethral tissue	159
86.21	Excision, pilonidal cyst or sinus	138, 271, 317
18.21	Excision, preauricular sinus	28, 139, 313
*11.3	Excision, pterygium	19, 312
18.31	Excision, radical, lesion, external ear	313
51.61	Excision, remnant, cystic duct	106, 263
60.73	Excision, seminal vesicle	170
*40.2	Excision, simple, lymphatic structures	139, 233
86.91	Excision, skin for graft	4, 32, 54, 137, 149, 271
86.4	Excision, skin, radical	4, 19, 31, 53, 117, 137, 271, 317
41.93	Excision, spleen, accessory	233, 238, 262
83.41	Excision, tendon for graft, except hand	4
06.7	Excision, thyroglossal duct or tract	30, 150
*85.2	Excision, tissue, breast	136, 270
28.4	Excision, tonsil tag	29
07.68	Excision, total, pituitary gland, other specified approach	139
07.64	Excision, total, pituitary gland, transfrontal approach	139
07.65	Excision, total, pituitary gland, transsphenoidal approach	139
07.69	Excision, total, pituitary gland, unspecified approach	139
07.82	Excision, total, thymus	238
*57.4	Excision, transurethral, bladder tissue	159
63.1	Excision, varicocele and hydrocele, spermatic cord	168, 315
27.42	Excision, wide, lesion, lip	32, 139, 314
11.32	Excision, with corneal graft, pterygium	259
16.51	Exenteration, orbit, with removal of adjacent structures	120
16.52	Exenteration, orbit, with therapeutic removal of orbital bone	30
*16.5	Exenteration, orbital contents	18, 260, 313
16.59	Exenteration, other, orbit	120
03.09	Exploration and decompression, other, spinal canal	123, 238
*03.0	Exploration and decompression, spinal canal structures	5, 258
*07.0	Exploration, adrenal gland	149
51.42	Exploration, common bile duct for relief of other obstruction	107, 240, 263
51.41	Exploration, common bile duct for removal of calculus	107
51.51	Exploration, common duct	107
82.01	Exploration, tendon sheath, hand	118, 257, 316
07.91	Exploration, thymus	258
*46.0	Exteriorization, intestine	92, 239, 263
46.03	Exteriorization, intestine, large	53
39.65	Extracorporeal membrane oxygenation [ECMO]	323
98.51	Extracorporeal shockwave lithotripsy [ESWL], kidney, ureter and/or bladder	163
*13.6	Extraction, cataract, other	312
*13.4	Extraction, extracapsular, fragmentation and aspiration technique, lens	312
13.2	Extraction, extracapsular, linear extraction technique, lens	312
*13.5	Extraction, extracapsular, other, lens	312
13.3	Extraction, extracapsular, simple aspiration and irrigation technique, lens	312
*13.1	Extraction, intracapsular, lens	151, 312
13.59	Extraction, other extracapsular, lens	151
*23	Extraction, restoration, tooth	38
*12.5	Facilitation, intraocular circulation	259, 312
12.59	Facilitation, other, intraocular circulation	18
83.44	Fasciectomy, other, except hand	140
83.14	Fasciotomy, except hand	4, 117, 140
*20.6	Fenestration, inner ear	28
49.12	Fistulectomy, anal	139

Code	Narrative	Page
*09.8	Fistulization, lacrimal tract to nasal cavity	259, 312
*12.6	Fistulization, scleral	20, 259, 312
49.11	Fistulotomy, anal	138
*49.1	Fistulotomy, fistulectomy, anal	95, 263, 315
78.54	Fixation, bone, internal, without fracture reduction, carpals and metacarpals	118, 256
78.55	Fixation, bone, internal, without fracture reduction, femur	112, 267, 291
78.52	Fixation, bone, internal, without fracture reduction, humerus	114, 267
78.59	Fixation, bone, internal, without fracture reduction, other	121, 267
78.56	Fixation, bone, internal, without fracture reduction, patella	124, 267
78.53	Fixation, bone, internal, without fracture reduction, radius and ulna	115, 267
78.51	Fixation, bone, internal, without fracture reduction, scapula, clavicle and thorax (ribs and sternum)	41, 121, 267
78.58	Fixation, bone, internal, without fracture reduction, tarsals and metatarsals	116, 267
78.57	Fixation, bone, internal, without fracture reduction, tibia and fibula	114, 267
78.50	Fixation, bone, internal, without fracture reduction, unspecified site	121, 267
*46.6	Fixation, intestine	93
54.93	Formation, fistula, cutaneoperitoneal	53, 98, 109, 160, 240, 264
02.03	Formation, flap, cranial	290
54.94	Formation, shunt, peritoneovascular	98, 106, 240
42.86	Formation, subcutaneous tunnel, without esophageal anastomosis	31, 94, 239, 262
21.62	Fracture, turbinates	260, 313
39.91	Freeing, vessel	55, 75, 76, 97, 151, 262
81.04	Fusion, anterior, dorsal/ dorsolumbar	122, 123, 126
81.06	Fusion, anterior, lumbar/ lumbosacral	122, 123, 126
81.02	Fusion, anterior, other cervical	122, 124
81.01	Fusion, Atlas-axis	124
81.11	Fusion, joint, ankle	115, 152
81.16	Fusion, joint, metatarsophalangeal	117
81.14	Fusion, joint, midtarsal	117
81.13	Fusion, joint, subtalar	117
81.15	Fusion, joint, tarsometatarsal	117
81.07	Fusion, lateral, lumbar/ lumbosacral	122, 123, 126
81.17	Fusion, other, foot	117
81.05	Fusion, posterior, dorsal/ dorsolumbar	122, 123, 126
81.08	Fusion, posterior, lumbar/ lumbosacral	122, 123, 126
81.03	Fusion, posterior, other cervical	122, 124
*81.0	Fusion, spinal	6, 269
81.00	Fusion, spinal, NOS	123, 126
04.05	Ganglionectomy, gasserian	3, 258
04.06	Ganglionectomy, other, cranial or peripheral	3, 119, 258
05.21	Ganglionectomy, sphenopalatine	30
*43.8	Gastrectomy, partial, other	94, 239, 262
43.89	Gastrectomy, partial, other	53
43.6	Gastrectomy, partial, with anastomosis to duodenum	53, 94, 239, 262
43.5	Gastrectomy, partial, with anastomosis to esophagus	94, 239, 262
43.7	Gastrectomy, partial, with anastomosis to jejunum	53, 94, 152, 239, 262
*43.9	Gastrectomy, total	94, 239, 262
43.99	Gastrectomy, total	53
44.39	Gastroenterostomy	108
44.38	Gastroenterostomy, laparoscopic	53, 108
*44.3	Gastroenterostomy, without gastrectomy	94, 150, 239
44.32	Gastrojejunostomy, percutaneous (endoscopic)	108
44.64	Gastropexy	94, 262
44.68	Gastroplasty, laparoscopic	94, 150, 262, 314
44.13	Gastroscopy, other	243
44.12	Gastroscopy, through stoma, artificial	243
44.11	Gastroscopy, transabdominal	94, 108, 239, 262
43.0	Gastrotomy	94, 108, 151, 239, 262
24.2	Gingivoplasty	32, 260
25.3	Glossectomy, complete	27
25.2	Glossectomy, partial	32
25.4	Glossectomy, radical	27
25.94	Glossotomy, other	32
12.51	Goniopuncture, without goniotomy	20
12.53	Goniotomy, with goniopuncture	20
12.52	Goniotomy, without goniopuncture	20
78.04	Graft, bone, carpals and metacarpals	118, 256
78.05	Graft, bone, femur	112, 266, 291
78.02	Graft, bone, humerus	114, 266
78.09	Graft, bone, other except facial bones	121, 266
78.06	Graft, bone, patella	124, 266
78.03	Graft, bone, radius and ulna	115, 266, 316

Code	Narrative	Page
78.01	Graft, bone, scapula, clavicle and thorax (ribs and sternum)	41, 121, 266
02.04	Graft, bone, skull	290
78.08	Graft, bone, tarsals and metatarsals	116, 266
78.07	Graft, bone, tibia and fibula	114, 266
76.91	Graft, bone, to facial bone	18, 31, 120, 266
78.00	Graft, bone, unspecified site	121, 266
86.67	Graft, dermal regenerative	4, 31, 54, 98, 114, 137, 149, 256, 278, 279
42.87	Graft, esophagus, other	31, 94, 239, 262
86.60	Graft, free skin, unspecified	4, 54, 98, 114, 137, 149, 256, 277, 278, 317
27.55	Graft, full-thickness skin, lip and mouth	32, 138, 260, 314
83.82	Graft, muscle or fascia, except hand	4, 117, 140
04.5	Graft, nerve, cranial or peripheral	3, 258
27.56	Graft, other skin, lip and mouth	32, 138, 260, 314
86.69	Graft, other, skin to other sites	4, 31, 41, 54, 98, 114, 137, 149, 256, 278, 279
86.62	Graft, other, skin, to hand	4, 54, 119, 137, 257, 277, 278, 317
*86.7	Graft, pedicle or flap	137, 278, 279
86.70	Graft, pedicle or flap, unspecified	4, 31, 54, 98, 114, 149, 256
16.65	Graft, secondary, to exenteration cavity	30
85.83	Graft, skin, full-thickness, to breast	137, 256, 277, 278
86.61	Graft, skin, full-thickness, to hand	4, 54, 119, 137, 257, 277, 278
86.63	Graft, skin, full-thickness, to other sites	4, 31, 54, 98, 114, 137, 149, 256, 278, 279
86.65	Graft, skin, heterograft	4, 54, 98, 114, 137, 256, 278, 279, 317
86.66	Graft, skin, homograft	4, 31, 54, 98, 114, 137, 256, 278, 279

Code	Narrative	Page
85.85	Graft, skin, muscle flap, to breast	137, 271
85.84	Graft, skin, pedicle, to breast	137, 256, 277, 278
85.82	Graft, split-thickness, to breast	137, 256, 277, 278
83.81	Graft, tendon, except hand	4, 117
45.75	Hemicolectomy, left	53, 152, 239
45.73	Hemicolectomy, right	53, 239
30.1	Hemilaryngectomy	27, 40, 260
01.52	Hemispherectomy	258, 290
50.22	Hepatectomy, partial	106, 263
50.4	Hepatectomy, total	106, 263
50.0	Hepatotomy	106, 263
70.31	Hymenectomy	197
70.76	Hymenorrhaphy	179, 316
*07.6	Hypophysectomy	1, 2, 7, 149
68.6	Hysterectomy, abdominal, radical	174, 193
68.9	Hysterectomy, other and unspecified	175, 176, 178, 193
*68.3	Hysterectomy, subtotal, abdominal	175, 176, 178, 193
68.4	Hysterectomy, total, abdominal	175, 176, 178, 193
*68.5	Hysterectomy, vaginal	175, 176, 178, 193, 316
68.7	Hysterectomy, vaginal, radical	174, 193
68.12	Hysteroscopy	243
68.0	Hysterotomy	174, 175, 178, 193, 266
74.91	Hysterotomy, to terminate pregnancy	194
46.22	Ileostomy, continent	92, 239, 263
46.23	Ileostomy, other, permanent	92, 239, 263
46.21	Ileostomy, temporary	92, 239, 263
46.20	Ileostomy, unspecified	92, 239, 263
85.54	Implant, breast, bilateral	136, 137, 270, 317
85.53	Implant, breast, unilateral	136, 137, 270, 317
37.65	Implant, heart assist system, external	56, 317
66.93	Implant, prosthesis, fallopian tube	174, 175, 178
37.61	Implant, pulsation balloon	50
84.58	Implantation of interspinous process decompression device	6, 123, 270
84.40	Implantation or fitting, prosthetic limb device, unspecified	122, 270

Code	Narrative	Page
92.27	Implantation or insertion, radioactive elements	4, 32, 41, 54, 78, 98, 141, 152, 161, 170, 180, 271, 317
00.54	Implantation or replacement, cardiac resynchronization defibrillator, pulse generator only [CRT-D]	55, 57, 68
00.53	Implantation or replacement, cardiac resynchronization pacemaker, pulse generator only [CRT-P]	52, 65, 66, 67, 68, 69, 70, 71, 72
20.98	Implantation or replacement, cochlear prosthetic device, multiple-channel	27
20.97	Implantation or replacement, cochlear prosthetic device, single-channel	27
02.93	Implantation or replacement, neurostimulator lead(s), intracranial	1, 2, 7, 238, 258
04.92	Implantation or replacement, neurostimulator lead(s), peripheral	30, 119, 160, 169, 180
03.93	Implantation or replacement, neurostimulator lead(s), spinal	6, 123, 160, 169, 180, 238, 258
00.52	Implantation or replacement, transvenous lead (electrode) into left ventricular coronary venous system	55, 57, 65, 68, 69
49.75	Implantation or revision, anal sphincter, artificial	92, 138, 263
58.93	Implantation, artificial urinary sphincter [AUS]	159, 265
00.51	Implantation, cardiac resynchronization defibrillator, total system [CRT-D]	55, 57
00.50	Implantation, cardiac resynchronization pacemaker, without mention of defibrillation, total system [CRT-P]	65, 69
37.67	Implantation, cardiomyostimulation system	50
37.94	Implantation, cardioverter/ defibrillator, automatic	55, 57
37.95	Implantation, cardioverter/ defibrillator, lead(s), only	55, 57, 68
37.96	Implantation, cardioverter/ defibrillator, pulse generator	55, 57, 68
00.10	Implantation, chemotherapeutic agent	7
20.96	Implantation, cochlear prosthetic device, unspecified	27
34.85	Implantation, diaphragmatic pacemaker	261
20.95	Implantation, electromagnetic hearing aid	28
57.96	Implantation, electronic stimulator, bladder	159
56.92	Implantation, electronic ureteral stimulator	158
84.44	Implantation, prosthetic device, arm	116, 270
84.48	Implantation, prosthetic device, leg	115, 270
37.52	Implantation, total replacement heart system	56
01.21	Incision and drainage, cranial sinus	290
28.0	Incision and drainage, tonsil and peritonsillar structures	29
68.22	Incision or excision, septum of uterus, congenital	180
*48.8	Incision or excision, tissue or lesion, perirectal	95, 139, 263, 315
54.0	Incision, abdominal wall	53, 98, 108, 140, 160, 240, 264
49.01	Incision, abscess, perianal	95, 138
*49.9	Incision, anal, other	95
71.22	Incision, Bartholin's gland cyst	179, 194, 316
51.59	Incision, bile duct, other	97, 106, 240, 263
*76.0	Incision, bone, facial, without division	31, 266
77.19	Incision, bone, without division	31, 125
*77.1	Incision, bone, without division (except carpals and metacarpals 77.14)	266
77.14	Incision, bone, without division, carpals and metacarpals	118, 256
77.15	Incision, bone, without division, femur	119
77.12	Incision, bone, without division, humerus	125
77.16	Incision, bone, without division, patella	125
77.13	Incision, bone, without division, radius and ulna	125
77.11	Incision, bone, without division, scapula, clavicle and thorax	40, 125
77.18	Incision, bone, without division, tarsals and metatarsals	116
77.17	Incision, bone, without division, tibia and fibula	125
77.10	Incision, bone, without division, unspecified site	125
*01.3	Incision, brain and cerebral meninges	1, 2, 7, 258
33.0	Incision, bronchus	39, 261
01.31	Incision, cerebral meninges	238, 290
69.95	Incision, cervix	178, 194, 316
11.1	Incision, cornea	19, 259, 312
*04.0	Incision, division and excision, cranial and peripheral nerves	30
45.01	Incision, duodenum	94, 108
42.01	Incision, esophageal web	94

Alphabetic Index to Procedures

** Code Range*

Code	Narrative	Page
*42.0	Incision, esophagus	30
42.09	Incision, esophagus	94, 262
*20.7	Incision, excision and destruction, inner ear	28
37.10	Incision, heart, unspecified	50
45.03	Incision, intestine, large	93, 239
45.00	Incision, intestine, NOS	93
45.02	Incision, intestine, small	93, 239
38.01	Incision, intracranial vessels	1, 2, 5, 7
09.52	Incision, lacrimal canaliculus	259
09.0	Incision, lacrimal gland	312
*09.5	Incision, lacrimal sac and passages	312
33.1	Incision, lung	39, 261
40.0	Incision, lymphatic structures	139, 233, 314
20.21	Incision, mastoid	27
*20.2	Incision, mastoid and middle ear	313
34.1	Incision, mediastinum	40, 53, 261
20.23	Incision, middle ear	28
27.92	Incision, mouth, unspecified structure	32, 139, 260, 314
*83.0	Incision, muscle, tendon, fascia and bursa, except hand	117, 270, 316
51.49	Incision, other bile ducts for relief of obstruction	106, 240
01.39	Incision, other, brain	238, 290
10.1	Incision, other, conjunctiva	312
04.04	Incision, other, cranial and peripheral nerves	3, 119, 258
76.09	Incision, other, facial bone	125
31.3	Incision, other, larynx, trachea	28, 40
49.02	Incision, other, perianal tissue	95, 138
59.09	Incision, other, perirenal or periureteral tissue	158, 170, 181, 241, 265
86.09	Incision, other, skin and subcutaneous tissue	141
83.09	Incision, other, soft tissue, except hand	140
82.09	Incision, other, soft tissue, hand	118, 140, 257, 316
06.09	Incision, other, thyroid field	28, 139, 150, 258
27.1	Incision, palate	32
64.92	Incision, penis	168, 315
*60.8	Incision, periprostatic tissue	170, 311
54.95	Incision, peritoneum	3, 53, 98, 109, 160, 240, 264
58.91	Incision, periurethral tissue	159
*59.1	Incision, perivesical tissue	159, 170, 181, 241, 265
20.22	Incision, petrous pyramid air cells	27
07.72	Incision, pituitary gland	139
60.0	Incision, prostate	170, 311
48.91	Incision, rectal stricture	263
60.72	Incision, seminal vesicle	170
63.93	Incision, spermatic cord	168
62.0	Incision, testes	168, 265
07.92	Incision, thymus	259
*38.0	Incision, vessel	261
38.06	Incision, vessel, abdominal arteries	50, 97, 160
38.07	Incision, vessel, abdominal veins	50, 97, 160
38.04	Incision, vessel, aorta	50, 97
38.02	Incision, vessel, head, neck	3, 30, 54, 74, 75, 151
38.08	Incision, vessel, lower limb arteries	54, 74, 75, 151, 238
38.09	Incision, vessel, lower limb veins	52, 314
38.05	Incision, vessel, other thoracic	39, 50, 93
38.00	Incision, vessel, unspecified site	30, 54, 74, 75, 151, 314
38.03	Incision, vessel, upper limb	54, 74, 75, 151
71.09	Incision, vulva and perineum, other	140, 316
35.34	Infundibulectomy	50
99.10	Injection or infusion of thrombolytic agent	17
00.15	Injection or infusion, high-dose infusion interleukin-2 (IL-2)	244
12.92	Injection, into anterior chamber	19, 20, 259
39.92	Injection, sclerosing agent into vein	6, 52
86.98	Insertion or replacement of dual array rechargeable neurostimulator pulse generator	4
86.97	Insertion or replacement of single array rechargeable neurostimulator pulse generator	4
83.92	Insertion or replacement, electric stimulator, skeletal muscle, except hand	4, 117, 270
37.74	Insertion or replacement, epicardial pacemaker lead [electrode], into epicardium (must be in combination with 37.80, 37.81, 37.82, 37.83, 37.85, 37.86 or 37.87)	3, 5, 52, 67, 68, 71, 72, 261, 271
86.95	Insertion or replacement, neurostimulator pulse generator, dual array	4
86.96	Insertion or replacement, neurostimulator pulse generator, other	4
86.94	Insertion or replacement, neurostimulator pulse generator, single array	4
02.94	Insertion or replacement, skull tongs or halo traction device	1, 2, 7, 119, 258, 290
39.93	Insertion, cannula, vessel-to-vessel	53, 151, 160, 262

 *Code Range

Code	Narrative	Page
51.43	Insertion, choledochohepatic tube for decompression	106, 240, 263
36.06	Insertion, coronary artery stent(s), nondrug-eluting	78
36.07	Insertion, coronary artery stents(s), drug-eluting	80, 81
37.90	Insertion, device, left atrial appendage	56
37.83	Insertion, dual-chamber device, initial	66, 67, 70, 71
51.86	Insertion, endoscopic, nasobiliary drainage tube	243
52.97	Insertion, endoscopic, nasopancreatic drainage tube	243
51.87	Insertion, endoscopic, stent (tube) into bile duct	243
37.66	Insertion, heart assist system, implantable	317
37.62	Insertion, heart assist system, non-implantable	56
76.92	Insertion, implant, facial bone, synthetic	18, 31, 120, 266
86.06	Insertion, infusion pump, totally implantable	4, 41, 53, 98, 109, 122, 140, 152, 160, 170, 181, 233, 271
37.70	Insertion, initial pacemaker lead [electrode], other (must be in combination with 37.80, 37.81, 37.82, 37.85, 37.86 or 37.87)	4, 65, 69, 271
37.73	Insertion, initial, transvenous pacemaker lead [electrode], into atrium (must be in combination with 37.80, 37.81, 37.82, 37.85, 37.86 or 37.87)	4, 66, 67, 70, 71, 271
37.72	Insertion, initial, transvenous pacemaker lead [electrode], into atrium and ventricle (must be in combination with 37.80 or 37.83)	4, 66, 70, 271
37.71	Insertion, initial, transvenous pacemaker lead [electrode], into ventricle (must be in combination with 37.80, 37.81, 37.82, 37.85, 37.86 or 37.87)	4, 66, 69, 70, 271
37.68	Insertion, percutaneous, heart assist device, external	49
37.80	Insertion, permanent pacemaker, initial or replacement, type device not specified	3, 52, 65, 66, 67, 68, 69, 70, 71, 72, 261
02.05	Insertion, plate, skull	290
13.71	Insertion, prosthesis, intraocular lens	312
64.97	Insertion, prosthesis, penile, inflatable	160, 169, 315
64.95	Insertion, prosthesis, penis, noninflatable	160, 169, 315
62.7	Insertion, prosthesis, testicular	152, 168
13.70	Insertion, pseudophakos, NOS	312
13.72	Insertion, secondary, prosthesis, intraocular lens	259, 312
37.81	Insertion, single-chamber device, initial, not specified as rate-responsive	65, 66, 67, 69, 70, 71
37.82	Insertion, single-chamber device, initial, rate-responsive	65, 66, 67, 69, 70, 71
84.59	Insertion, spinal devices, other	6, 123, 270
52.93	Insertion, stent (tube), endoscopic, pancreatic duct	243
78.94	Insertion, stimulator for bone growth, carpals and metacarpals	118, 256
78.95	Insertion, stimulator for bone growth, femur	112, 267, 291
78.92	Insertion, stimulator for bone growth, humerus	114, 267
78.99	Insertion, stimulator for bone growth, other	121, 267
78.96	Insertion, stimulator for bone growth, patella	124, 267
78.93	Insertion, stimulator for bone growth, radius and ulna	116, 267
78.91	Insertion, stimulator for bone growth, scapula, clavicle and thorax (ribs and sternum)	41, 121, 267
78.98	Insertion, stimulator for bone growth, tarsals and metatarsals	116, 267
78.97	Insertion, stimulator for bone growth, tibia and fibula	114, 267
78.90	Insertion, stimulator for bone growth, unspecified site	121, 267
86.93	Insertion, tissue expander	4, 32, 54, 98, 114, 137, 149, 256, 278, 279
85.95	Insertion, tissue expander, breast	136, 137, 271, 317
63.95	Insertion, valve, vas deferens	168
86.07	Insertion, vascular access device, totally implantable	141, 161
66.95	Insufflation, therapeutic agent into fallopian tubes	181
38.7	Interruption, vena cava	3, 40, 54, 75, 97, 108, 120, 151, 160, 169, 180, 193, 233, 261
09.44	Intubation, nasolacrimal duct	28, 259
*12.3	Iridoplasty and coreoplasty	259, 312
12.39	Iridoplasty, other	20
*12.1	Iridotomy, simple iridectomy	18, 259, 312
*45.5	Isolation, intestinal segment	92
45.50	Isolation, intestinal segment, unspecified	239
11.71	Keratomeleusis	19
11.72	Keratophakia	19
11.62	Keratoplasty, lamellar, other	19
11.61	Keratoplasty, lamellar, with autograft	19

** Code Range*

Code	Narrative	Page
11.64	Keratoplasty, penetrating, other	20
11.63	Keratoplasty, penetrating, with autograft	20
11.73	Keratoprosthesis	20
11.75	Keratotomy, radial	20
81.66	Kyphoplasty	121, 269
54.21	Laparoscopy, abdomen	98, 108, 140, 160, 179, 193, 233, 264, 315
*54.1	Laparotomy	98, 160, 180, 264
54.19	Laparotomy	53, 108, 233, 240
54.11	Laparotomy, exploratory	40, 53, 108, 140, 152, 167, 193, 233, 240
30.3	Laryngectomy, complete	321
*30.2	Laryngectomy, other, partial	40, 260
30.29	Laryngectomy, other, partial	27
30.4	Laryngectomy, radical	321
31.42	Laryngoscopy, other tracheoscopy	243
78.34	Lengthening, bone, carpals and metacarpals	118, 256
78.35	Lengthening, bone, femur	112, 267, 291
78.32	Lengthening, bone, humerus	114, 267
78.39	Lengthening, bone, other	121, 267
78.33	Lengthening, bone, radius and ulna	115, 267
78.38	Lengthening, bone, tarsals and metatarsals	116, 267
78.37	Lengthening, bone, tibia and fibula	114, 267
78.30	Lengthening, bone, unspecified site	121, 267
38.57	Ligation and stripping, varicose veins, abdominal veins	54, 74, 75, 97
38.51	Ligation and stripping, varicose veins, intracranial vessel	1, 2, 5, 7
38.59	Ligation and stripping, varicose veins, lower limb veins	52, 314
38.55	Ligation and stripping, varicose veins, other thoracic vessels	39, 51, 151
38.52	Ligation and stripping, varicose veins, other vessels, head, neck	54, 74, 75
38.50	Ligation and stripping, varicose veins, unspecified site	52
38.53	Ligation and stripping, varicose veins, upper limb vessels	52
07.43	Ligation, adrenal vessel	258
33.92	Ligation, bronchus	39, 261
38.85	Ligation, division, other thoracic vessels	39, 51, 93
38.86	Ligation, division, other, abdominal arteries	51, 97, 160, 314
38.87	Ligation, division, other, abdominal veins	51, 97, 160
38.81	Ligation, division, other, intracranial vessels	1, 2, 5, 7, 290
38.88	Ligation, division, other, lower limb arteries	54, 75, 151
38.89	Ligation, division, other, lower limb veins	52
38.82	Ligation, division, other, other vessels, head, neck	3, 30, 54, 75
38.83	Ligation, division, other, upper limb vessels	54, 75, 151
*38.8	Ligation, division, other, vessels	261
38.84	Ligation, division, other, vessels, aorta	51, 97
38.80	Ligation, division, other, vessels, unspecified site	54, 75
42.91	Ligation, esophageal varices	94, 108
66.92	Ligation, fallopian tube, unilateral	174, 175, 178, 193, 316
44.91	Ligation, gastric, varices	94, 108
49.45	Ligation, hemorrhoids	95, 315
02.13	Ligation, meningeal vessel	5, 258, 290
06.92	Ligation, thyroid vessels	150, 258
56.95	Ligation, ureter	158, 265
01.53	Lobectomy, brain	258, 290
50.3	Lobectomy, liver	106, 263
32.4	Lobectomy, lung	39, 261
06.2	Lobectomy, unilateral, thyroid	150
01.32	Lobotomy and tractotomy	238, 290
*04.4	Lysis, adhesions and decompression, cranial and peripheral nerves	311
04.49	Lysis, adhesions and decompression, other, peripheral nerve or ganglion	3, 30, 119, 258
57.12	Lysis, adhesions, bladder, intraluminal	158, 265
10.5	Lysis, adhesions, conjunctiva and eyelid	312
12.34	Lysis, adhesions, corneovitreal	20
02.91	Lysis, adhesions, cortical	1, 2, 7, 238, 258
82.91	Lysis, adhesions, hand	118, 140, 257
83.91	Lysis, adhesions, muscle, tendon, fascia and bursa, except hand	117, 270
*65.8	Lysis, adhesions, ovary and fallopian tube	265
*54.5	Lysis, adhesions, peritoneal	93, 108, 160, 180, 264
63.94	Lysis, adhesions, spermatic cord	168, 265
03.6	Lysis, adhesions, spinal cord and nerve roots	6, 123, 238, 258
31.92	Lysis, adhesions, trachea, larynx	30, 40, 261
56.81	Lysis, adhesions, ureter, intraluminal	264

Code	Narrative	Page
70.13	Lysis, adhesions, vagina, intraluminal	179, 197, 266
71.01	Lysis, adhesions, vulvar	266
12.32	Lysis, anterior synechiae, other	18
12.31	Lysis, goniosynechiae	18
59.03	Lysis, laparoscopic, adhesions, perirenal or periureteral	158, 170, 181, 240, 265
59.02	Lysis, other, adhesions, perirenal or periureteral	158, 170, 181, 240, 265
54.59	Lysis, other, adhesions, peritoneal	152
12.33	Lysis, posterior synechiae	18
85.50	Mammoplasty, augmentation, unspecified	136, 137, 270, 317
85.32	Mammoplasty, bilateral reduction	150
85.89	Mammoplasty, other	136, 137, 271
*85.3	Mammoplasty, reduction and subcutaneous mammectomy	136, 137, 270
85.31	Mammoplasty, unilateral reduction	150
76.42	Mandibulectomy, other, total	27
76.31	Mandibulectomy, partial	27, 120
76.41	Mandibulectomy, total, with synchronous reconstruction	27
46.80	Manipulation, bowel, intrabdominal	92, 108, 239
*46.8	Manipulation, intestine, intraabdominal	263
44.92	Manipulation, intraoperative, stomach	94, 108, 152, 262
*09.4	Manipulation, lacrimal passage	312
46.82	Manipulation, large bowel, intraabdominal	92, 108, 239
46.81	Manipulation, small bowel, intraabdominal	92, 108, 239
37.27	Mapping, cardiac	56, 78, 80, 81
71.23	Marsupialization, Bartholin's gland cyst	179, 194, 316
55.31	Marsupialization, cyst, kidney	264
55.4	Marsupialization, cyst, kidney	157, 264
30.01	Marsupialization, cyst, laryngeal	40
52.3	Marsupialization, cyst, pancreas	106
50.21	Marsupialization, lesion, liver	106
37.91	Massage, cardiac, open chest	39, 50, 238, 261
*85.4	Mastectomy	136, 137, 270
85.23	Mastectomy, subtotal	137, 317
*20.4	Mastoidectomy	27
85.6	Mastopexy	136, 137, 271
58.47	Meatoplasty, urethral	170
56.1	Meatotomy, ureteral	157, 264, 315
58.1	Meatotomy, urethral	159, 170, 265, 315
34.22	Mediastinoscopy	30, 40, 53, 233, 238
83.45	Myectomy, other, except hand	4, 140
46.92	Myotomy, colon, other parts	92
46.91	Myotomy, colon, sigmoid	92
83.02	Myotomy, except hand	31, 140
82.02	Myotomy, hand	118, 257
19.4	Myringoplasty	313
20.01	Myringotomy, with insertion of tube	29, 313
55.54	Nephrectomy, bilateral	264
*55.5	Nephrectomy, complete	157
55.52	Nephrectomy, remaining kidney	264
56.73	Nephrocystanastomosis, unspecified	169, 180, 240
55.7	Nephropexy	157
55.21	Nephroscopy	243
*55.0	Nephrostomy and nephrotomy	157, 264
55.51	Nephroureterectomy	264
*04.7	Neuroplasty, other, cranial or peripheral	3, 258
04.01	Neurotomy, acoustic	1, 2, 7
70.4	Obliteration, vagina	175
70.8	Obliteration, vaginal vault	175
86.86	Onychoplasty	141, 271
*65.5	Oophorectomy, bilateral	140
49.99	Operation, anus, other	263
47.99	Operation, appendix, other	96
73.99	Operation, assisting delivery, other	197
51.99	Operation, biliary tract, other	107, 240, 264, 315
57.99	Operation, bladder, other	159, 265
39.8	Operation, carotid body, other vascular bodies	6, 40, 55, 75, 76
69.99	Operation, cervix and uterus, other	181
35.32	Operation, chordae tendineae	49
71.4	Operation, clitoris	179, 316
*10	Operation, conjunctiva	19
*34.8	Operation, diaphragm	39
*15	Operation, extraocular muscle	19
66.99	Operation, fallopian tube, other	174, 175, 178
71.9	Operation, female genital organs, other	181
01.42	Operation, globus pallidus	290
55.99	Operation, kidney, other	157, 264
*09	Operation, lacrimal system	19
*13	Operation, lens	19
40.9	Operation, lymphatic structures, other	30, 97, 139, 160, 169, 233, 238, 262
*15.1	Operation, muscle, one extraocular	313

 *** Code Range**

Code	Narrative	Page
75.99	Operation, obstetric, other	194
*07.4	Operation, other, adrenal glands, nerves and vessels	149
07.49	Operation, other, adrenal glands, nerves and vessels	258
12.99	Operation, other, anterior chamber	20, 259
71.29	Operation, other, Bartholin's gland	179, 194, 316
85.99	Operation, other, breast	136, 137, 271, 317
33.98	Operation, other, bronchus	39, 261
12.98	Operation, other, ciliary body	20, 259
*10.9	Operation, other, conjunctiva	312
*11.9	Operation, other, cornea	259, 312
11.99	Operation, other, cornea	20
*04.9	Operation, other, cranial and peripheral nerves	3, 258
04.99	Operation, other, cranial and peripheral nerves	30, 120
34.89	Operation, other, diaphragm	261
18.9	Operation, other, external ear	28, 139, 260, 313
*15.2	Operation, other, extraocular muscle, one	313
15.9	Operation, other, extraocular muscles, tendons	259, 313
15.4	Operation, other, extraocular muscles, two or more, one or both eyes	313
16.99	Operation, other, eyeball	19, 151, 260, 313
*08.9	Operation, other, eyelids	19, 259, 312
08.99	Operation, other, eyelids	139
76.99	Operation, other, facial bones and joints	31, 120, 266
64.99	Operation, other, genital organs, male	169, 315
82.99	Operation, other, hand, muscle, tendon and fascia	118, 257
37.99	Operation, other, heart, pericardium	50
*07.7	Operation, other, hypophysis	1, 2, 7, 149
07.79	Operation, other, hypophysis	139
46.99	Operation, other, intestines	92, 108, 240, 263
12.97	Operation, other, iris	18, 259
*12.9	Operation, other, iris, ciliary body, and anterior chamber	312
81.99	Operation, other, joint structures	121, 270
09.3	Operation, other, lacrimal gland	259, 312
*09.9	Operation, other, lacrimal system	259, 312
09.99	Operation, other, lacrimal system	28
31.98	Operation, other, larynx	28, 40, 314
13.9	Operation, other, lens	259, 312
33.99	Operation, other, lung	39, 261
20.99	Operation, other, middle ear and inner ear	28
83.99	Operation, other, muscle, tendon, fascia and bursa, except hand	117, 270
84.99	Operation, other, musculoskeletal system	122, 270
05.9	Operation, other, nervous system	3, 258
21.99	Operation, other, nose	28, 138, 260, 313
22.9	Operation, other, on nasal sinuses	28
27.99	Operation, other, oral cavity	32, 260, 314
16.98	Operation, other, orbit	18, 30, 260, 313
*52.8	Operation, other, pancreas	106
52.99	Operation, other, pancreas	97, 106, 264
06.99	Operation, other, parathyroid glands	150
64.98	Operation, other, penis	169, 315
59.92	Operation, other, perirenal or perivesical tissue	159, 170, 241
29.99	Operation, other, pharynx	30, 260
60.99	Operation, other, prostate	170, 311
14.9	Operation, other, retina, choroid, and posterior chamber	18, 259, 313
26.99	Operation, other, salivary gland or duct	27
12.89	Operation, other, sclera	19
61.99	Operation, other, scrotum and tunica vaginalis	168, 265
60.79	Operation, other, seminal vesicles	170
35.98	Operation, other, septa of heart	50
64.5	Operation, other, sex transformation	168, 175
02.99	Operation, other, skull, brain and cerebral meninges	1, 2, 7, 119, 238, 258, 290
03.99	Operation, other, spinal cord and spinal canal structures	6, 123, 238, 258
41.99	Operation, other, spleen	233, 238, 262
*05.8	Operation, other, sympathetic nerves or ganglia	3
05.89	Operation, other, sympathetic nerves or ganglia	53
62.99	Operation, other, testes	168, 265
34.99	Operation, other, thorax	40, 261
*07.9	Operation, other, thymus	39, 151, 233, 238
06.98	Operation, other, thyroid glands	150
25.99	Operation, other, tongue	32
31.99	Operation, other, trachea	30, 40, 261
56.99	Operation, other, ureter	158, 265
58.99	Operation, other, urethra and periurethral tissue	159, 170, 181, 315
35.99	Operation, other, valves of heart	50

* Code Range

Alphabetic Index to Procedures

Code	Narrative	Page
39.99	Operation, other, vessels	30, 40, 55, 75, 76, 97, 193, 238, 262
*36.9	Operation, other, vessels, heart	50
*65	Operation, ovary	174, 175, 178
35.31	Operation, papillary muscle	49
*07.5	Operation, pineal gland	1, 2, 7, 149
29.4	Operation, plastic, pharynx	3, 30, 260, 314
86.83	Operation, plastic, size reduction	138, 150, 271, 317
*48.9	Operation, rectum and perirectal tissue, other	95
39.54	Operation, reentry, aorta	39, 51
*12.8	Operation, sclera	259, 312
59.4	Operation, sling, suprapubic	159, 175
63.99	Operation, spermatic cord, epididymis and vas deferens, other	168, 265
51.89	Operation, sphincter of Oddi, other	107, 263
44.99	Operation, stomach, other	94, 150, 262
35.39	Operation, structures adjacent to heart valves, other	50
01.41	Operation, thalamus	258, 290
*01.4	Operation, thalamus and globus pallidus	1, 2, 7, 238
*40.6	Operation, thoracic duct	40, 262
35.35	Operation, trabeculae carneae cordis	50
79.93	Operation, unspecified, bone injury, carpals and metacarpals	118, 257
79.95	Operation, unspecified, bone injury, femur	112, 268, 291
79.91	Operation, unspecified, bone injury, humerus	115, 268
79.99	Operation, unspecified, bone injury, other specified bone	121, 268
79.98	Operation, unspecified, bone injury, phalanges of foot	116, 268
79.94	Operation, unspecified, bone injury, phalanges of hand	118, 257
79.92	Operation, unspecified, bone injury, radius and ulna	116, 268
79.97	Operation, unspecified, bone injury, tarsals and metatarsals	115, 268
79.96	Operation, unspecified, bone injury, tibia and fibula	115, 268
79.90	Operation, unspecified, bone injury, unspecified site	121, 268
69.98	Operation, uterus, other, supporting structures	175
*27.7	Operation, uvula	32, 314
*14.7	Operation, vitreous	19, 20, 259, 313
*71.0	Operation, vulva and perineum	179, 197
71.8	Operation, vulva, other	179

Code	Narrative	Page
15.3	Operations, other, involving temporary detachment from globe, extraocular muscle, two or more, one or both eyes	313
*70.9	Operations, other, vagina and cul-de-sac	179
*28.9	Operations, tonsils and adenoids	29
*16.0	Orbitotomy	18, 260, 313
*62.4	Orchiectomy, bilateral	168, 265
62.41	Orchiectomy, bilateral, same operative episode	120
62.3	Orchiectomy, unilateral	168, 265
62.5	Orchiopexy	168
77.89	Ostectomy, other partial	31, 121, 152
*77.8	Ostectomy, other partial (except carpals and metacarpals 77.84)	266
77.84	Ostectomy, other partial, carpals and metacarpals	118, 256
77.85	Ostectomy, other partial, femur	112, 291
77.82	Ostectomy, other partial, humerus	114
77.86	Ostectomy, other partial, patella	124
77.83	Ostectomy, other partial, radius and ulna	115
77.88	Ostectomy, other partial, tarsals and metatarsals	116, 152, 316
77.87	Ostectomy, other partial, tibia and fibula	114
77.80	Ostectomy, other partial, unspecified site	121
77.81	Ostectomy, other, partial, scapula, clavicle and thorax, ribs and sternum	6, 41, 121
*76.3	Ostectomy, partial, facial bone	266
76.39	Ostectomy, partial, other facial bone	31, 120
77.23	Ostectomy, radius and ulna, wedge	115
*77.9	Ostectomy, total (except carpals and metacarpals 77.94)	266
77.96	Ostectomy, total patella	124
77.94	Ostectomy, total, carpals and metacarpals	118, 256
76.45	Ostectomy, total, facial bone	31
76.44	Ostectomy, total, facial with reconstruction	31
77.95	Ostectomy, total, femur, other	112, 291
77.92	Ostectomy, total, humerus	114
77.99	Ostectomy, total, other	31, 121
77.93	Ostectomy, total, radius and ulna	115
77.91	Ostectomy, total, scapula, clavicle and thorax, ribs and sternum	6, 41, 121
77.98	Ostectomy, total, tarsals and metatarsals	116, 316
77.97	Ostectomy, total, tibia and fibula	114
77.90	Ostectomy, total, unspecified site	121
*78.7	Osteoclasis (except carpals and metacarpals 78.74)	267

* Code Range

Code	Narrative	Page
78.74	Osteoclasis, carpals and metacarpals	118, 256
78.75	Osteoclasis, femur	112, 291
78.72	Osteoclasis, humerus	114
78.79	Osteoclasis, other	121
78.76	Osteoclasis, patella	124
78.73	Osteoclasis, radius and ulna	116
78.71	Osteoclasis, scapula, clavicle and thorax (ribs and sternum)	41, 121
78.78	Osteoclasis, tarsals and metatarsals	116
78.77	Osteoclasis, tibia and fibula	114
78.70	Osteoclasis, unspecified site	121
78.44	Osteoplasty, carpals and metacarpals	118, 256
*76.6	Osteoplasty, facial bone	31, 120, 266
78.45	Osteoplasty, femur	112, 267, 291
78.47	Osteoplasty, fibula	114, 267
78.42	Osteoplasty, humerus	114, 267
78.49	Osteoplasty, other	121, 267
02.06	Osteoplasty, other, cranial	290
78.46	Osteoplasty, patella	124, 267
78.43	Osteoplasty, radius and ulna	115, 267
78.41	Osteoplasty, scapula, clavicle and thorax	41, 121, 267
78.48	Osteoplasty, tarsals and metatarsals	116, 267
78.40	Osteoplasty, unspecified	121, 267
77.24	Osteotomy, carpals and metacarpals, wedge	118, 256
77.25	Osteotomy, femur, wedge	112, 291
77.22	Osteotomy, humerus, wedge	114
77.29	Osteotomy, other, wedge	120
77.26	Osteotomy, patella, wedge	124
77.21	Osteotomy, scapula, clavicle and thorax, ribs and sternum, wedge	40, 120
77.28	Osteotomy, tarsals and metatarsals, wedge	116, 140
77.27	Osteotomy, tibia and fibula, wedge	114, 152
77.20	Osteotomy, unspecified site, wedge	120
*77.2	Osteotomy, wedge (except carpals and metacarpals 77.24)	266
*00.7	Other hip procedures	122, 150
*00.8	Other knee procedures	122, 126, 257, 291
37.49	Other repair of heart and pericardium	261
*52.5	Pancreatectomy, partial	106, 152, 264
52.6	Pancreatectomy, total	106, 264
52.7	Pancreaticoduodenectomy, radical	94, 106, 264
52.13	Pancreatography, endoscopic, retrograde (ERP)	243
*52.0	Pancreatotomy	106
*06.8	Parathyroidectomy	150, 160
00.66	Percutaneous transluminal coronary angioplasty [PTCA] or coronary atherectomy	49, 56, 78, 80, 81
37.31	Pericardiectomy	39, 50, 238, 261
37.12	Pericardiotomy	39, 50, 238, 261
29.11	Pharyngoscopy	242
29.0	Pharyngotomy	30, 260
*38.3	Phlebectomy, with anastomosis	261
38.36	Phlebectomy, with anastomosis, abdominal arteries	51, 97, 160
38.37	Phlebectomy, with anastomosis, abdominal veins	51, 97, 160
38.34	Phlebectomy, with anastomosis, aorta	50, 97
38.31	Phlebectomy, with anastomosis, intracranial vessels	1, 2, 5, 7
38.38	Phlebectomy, with anastomosis, lower limb arteries	54, 74, 75, 151
38.39	Phlebectomy, with anastomosis, lower limb veins	52
38.35	Phlebectomy, with anastomosis, other thoracic vessels	39, 50, 93
38.32	Phlebectomy, with anastomosis, other vessels, head, neck	6, 30, 54, 74, 75
38.30	Phlebectomy, with anastomosis, unspecified site	54, 74, 75, 151
38.33	Phlebectomy, with anastomosis, upper limb vessels	54, 74, 75, 151
*38.4	Phlebectomy, with graft replacement	261
38.46	Phlebectomy, with graft replacement, abdominal arteries	51, 97, 160
38.47	Phlebectomy, with graft replacement, abdominal veins	51, 97, 160
38.41	Phlebectomy, with graft replacement, intracranial vessels	1, 2, 5, 7
38.48	Phlebectomy, with graft replacement, lower limb arteries	54, 74, 75, 151
38.49	Phlebectomy, with graft replacement, lower limb veins	52
38.42	Phlebectomy, with graft replacement, other, vessels, head, neck	3, 30, 54, 74, 75
38.40	Phlebectomy, with graft replacement, unspecified site	54, 74, 75
38.43	Phlebectomy, with graft replacement, upper limb vessels	54, 74, 75, 151
*34.5	Pleurectomy	39, 261
02.14	Plexectomy, choroid	290
32.21	Plication, bleb, emphysematous	39
59.3	Plication, urethrovesical junction	159
32.5	Pneumonectomy, complete	39, 261
48.36	Polypectomy (endoscopic), rectum	243
45.42	Polypectomy, endoscopic, large intestine	243

Code	Narrative	Page
09.43	Probing, nasolacrimal duct	30
*67.1	Procedure, diagnostic, cervix	140, 180, 193, 316
*11.2	Procedure, diagnostic, cornea	19, 312
*15.0	Procedure, diagnostic, extraocular, muscles, tendons	313
*76.1	Procedure, diagnostic, facial bones and joints	31, 113, 266
*66.1	Procedure, diagnostic, fallopian tubes	174, 175, 178
*12.2	Procedure, diagnostic, iris, ciliary body, sclera and anterior chamber	259, 312
*09.1	Procedure, diagnostic, lacrimal system	312
*40.1	Procedure, diagnostic, lymphatic structure	30, 53, 97, 120, 139, 151, 169, 233, 314
*83.2	Procedure, diagnostic, muscle, tendon, fascia and bursa, including that of hand	117
78.89	Procedure, diagnostic, NEC, bone, other	113
78.80	Procedure, diagnostic, NEC, bone, unspecified site	113
78.84	Procedure, diagnostic, NEC, carpals and metacarpals	118, 256
78.85	Procedure, diagnostic, NEC, femur	113
78.82	Procedure, diagnostic, NEC, humerus	113
78.86	Procedure, diagnostic, NEC, patella	113
78.83	Procedure, diagnostic, NEC, radius and ulna	113
78.81	Procedure, diagnostic, NEC, scapula, clavicle, and thorax, ribs and sternum	41, 113
78.88	Procedure, diagnostic, NEC, tarsals and metatarsals	116
78.87	Procedure, diagnostic, NEC, tibia and fibula	113
*10.2	Procedure, diagnostic, on conjunctiva	312
54.29	Procedure, diagnostic, other, abdominal region	98, 108, 180, 233, 240, 264, 315
07.19	Procedure, diagnostic, other, adrenal gland, pineal gland and thymus	3, 149
51.19	Procedure, diagnostic, other, biliary tract	97, 108
57.39	Procedure, diagnostic, other, bladder	158, 169, 240, 265, 315
38.29	Procedure, diagnostic, other, blood vessels	54, 74, 75, 151
01.18	Procedure, diagnostic, other, brain and cerebral meninges	1, 2, 7, 237, 258
34.28	Procedure, diagnostic, other, chest wall, pleura, diaphragm	40
04.19	Procedure, diagnostic, other, cranial and peripheral nerves and ganglia	3, 30, 119, 258
12.29	Procedure, diagnostic, other, iris, ciliary body, sclera and anterior chamber	20
81.98	Procedure, diagnostic, other, joint structures	113, 270
55.29	Procedure, diagnostic, other, kidney	157, 233, 240, 264
09.19	Procedure, diagnostic, other, lacrimal system	28, 259
50.19	Procedure, diagnostic, other, liver	97, 108, 140, 160, 233, 240, 263
33.29	Procedure, diagnostic, other, lung, bronchus	40
40.19	Procedure, diagnostic, other, lymphatic structures	40, 160
34.29	Procedure, diagnostic, other, mediastinum	40, 53
20.39	Procedure, diagnostic, other, middle and inner ear	28, 313
83.29	Procedure, diagnostic, other, muscle, tendon, fascia and bursa, including that of hand	270
16.29	Procedure, diagnostic, other, orbit and eyeball	18, 313
52.19	Procedure, diagnostic, other, pancreas	97, 108, 152, 240, 264
60.18	Procedure, diagnostic, other, prostate and periprostatic tissue	170, 311
60.19	Procedure, diagnostic, other, seminal vesicles	170
01.19	Procedure, diagnostic, other, skull	1, 2, 7, 113, 258
63.09	Procedure, diagnostic, other, spermatic cord, epididymis and vas deferens	168, 315
03.39	Procedure, diagnostic, other, spinal cord and spinal canal structures	6, 123, 238
62.19	Procedure, diagnostic, other, testes	168
06.19	Procedure, diagnostic, other, thyroid and parathyroid gland	120, 150
68.19	Procedure, diagnostic, other, uterus and adnexa	175, 176, 178
70.29	Procedure, diagnostic, other, vagina and cul-de-sac	179, 194, 316
*59.2	Procedure, diagnostic, perirenal and perivesical tissue	159, 170, 241, 265
*14.1	Procedure, diagnostic, retina, choroid, vitreous and posterior chamber	20, 312
*05.1	Procedure, diagnostic, sympathetic nerves or ganglia	3
*28.1	Procedure, diagnostic, tonsils and adenoids	29
56.39	Procedure, diagnostic, ureter, other	157, 315

Alphabetic Index to Procedures

** Code Range*

Code	Narrative	Page
*71.1	Procedure, diagnostic, vulva	140, 179, 197, 316
44.95	Procedure, gastric restrictive, laparoscopic	150, 314
12.79	Procedure, glaucoma, other	151
49.49	Procedure, hemorrhoids, other	95, 315
*12.7	Procedure, other, for relief of intraocular pressure	18, 312
48.75	Proctopexy, abdominal	92
48.76	Proctopexy, other	93
48.23	Proctosigmoidoscopy, other	243
48.22	Proctosigmoidoscopy, through stoma, artificial	243
48.21	Proctosigmoidoscopy, transabdominal	93, 263
48.1	Proctostomy	92, 263
48.0	Proctotomy	93, 263
60.69	Prostatectomy, other	158, 167, 311
60.62	Prostatectomy, perineal	158, 167
60.5	Prostatectomy, radical	158, 167
60.4	Prostatectomy, retropubic	158, 167
60.3	Prostatectomy, suprapubic	158, 167
*60.2	Prostatectomy, transurethral	158, 167, 311
73.94	Pubiotomy, to assist delivery	194
33.93	Puncture, lung	40
55.22	Pyeloscopy	243
55.12	Pyelostomy	264, 315
55.11	Pyelotomy	264
*55.1	Pyelotomy and pyelostomy	157
43.3	Pyloromyotomy	94
44.29	Pyloroplasty, other	94
83.86	Quadricepsplasty	117
*92.3	Radiosurgery, stereotactic	5, 152, 236, 237
18.72	Reattachment, amputated ear	313
84.22	Reattachment, finger	119, 257
84.26	Reattachment, foot	126, 270, 291
84.23	Reattachment, forearm, wrist or hand	122, 270, 291
84.27	Reattachment, lower leg or ankle	126, 270, 291
84.29	Reattachment, other, extremity	121, 270
64.45	Reattachment, penis	265
84.28	Reattachment, thigh	126, 270, 291
84.21	Reattachment, thumb	119, 257
84.25	Reattachment, toe	117, 270
84.24	Reattachment, upper arm	122, 270, 291
54.61	Reclosure, postoperative disruption, abdominal wall	108, 180
*70.6	Reconstruction and construction, vaginal	175
85.7	Reconstruction, breast, total	136, 137, 271
18.6	Reconstruction, external auditory canal	28, 138, 260, 313
76.46	Reconstruction, facial bone, other	18, 31
76.43	Reconstruction, mandible, other	31, 140
*83.7	Reconstruction, muscle and tendon, except hand	4, 117, 270
*08.7	Reconstruction, other, eyelid	19, 138, 259, 312
11.79	Reconstruction, other, surgery, cornea	20
64.44	Reconstruction, penis	265
83.83	Reconstruction, tendon pulley on muscle, tendon, and fascia, except hand	4, 117
*82.6	Reconstruction, thumb	3, 119, 257
21.83	Reconstruction, total, nasal	29, 120, 138, 260, 313
31.75	Reconstruction, trachea, construction, artificial larynx	39
08.70	Reconstruction, unspecified, eyelid	151
58.46	Reconstruction, urethra, other	168, 265
57.87	Reconstruction, urinary bladder	158, 265
70.62	Reconstruction, vaginal	266
63.82	Reconstruction, vas deferens, surgically divided	168, 265
*08.6	Reconstruction, with flaps or grafts, eyelid	19, 138, 259, 311
*11.7	Reconstructive, surgery, other, cornea	259, 312
48.74	Rectorectostomy	92
79.87	Reduction, dislocation, open, ankle	115, 268
79.82	Reduction, dislocation, open, elbow	116, 268
79.88	Reduction, dislocation, open, foot and toe	116, 268
79.84	Reduction, dislocation, open, hand and finger	118, 257
79.85	Reduction, dislocation, open, hip	112, 268, 291
79.86	Reduction, dislocation, open, knee	124, 268
79.89	Reduction, dislocation, open, other specified bone	121, 268
79.81	Reduction, dislocation, open, shoulder	116, 268
76.94	Reduction, dislocation, open, temporomandibular	31, 120, 266
79.80	Reduction, dislocation, open, unspecified site	121, 268
79.83	Reduction, dislocation, open, wrist	118, 257
79.33	Reduction, fracture, carpals and metacarpals, open, with internal fixation, carpals and metacarpals	118, 257
79.13	Reduction, fracture, closed, with internal fixation, carpals and metacarpals	118, 256
79.15	Reduction, fracture, closed, with internal fixation, femur	112, 267, 291

Alphabetic Index to Procedures

** Code Range*

Code	Narrative	Page
81.38	Refusion, posterior, lumbar/lumbosacral	122, 123, 126, 269
81.33	Refusion, posterior, other cervical	122, 124, 269
*81.3	Refusion, spinal	6, 126
81.39	Refusion, spinal, NEC	123, 126, 269
81.30	Refusion, spinal, NOS	123, 126, 269
94.61	Rehabilitation, alcohol	255
94.67	Rehabilitation, combination alcohol and drug	255
94.64	Rehabilitation, drug	255
94.63	Rehabilitation/detoxification, alcohol	255
94.69	Rehabilitation/detoxification, alcohol and drug combination	255
94.66	Rehabilitation/detoxification, drug	255
07.45	Reimplantation, adrenal tissue	258
06.95	Reimplantation, parathyroid tissue	150
39.55	Reimplantation, renal vessel, aberrant	55, 75, 76, 157
06.94	Reimplantation, thyroid tissue	150
12.88	Reinforcement, other, scleral	19
12.87	Reinforcement, scleral, with graft	19
04.43	Release, carpal tunnel	2, 118, 256
83.84	Release, clubfoot, other	117
86.84	Release, scar or web contraction, skin	32, 138, 271, 317
04.44	Release, tarsal tunnel	3, 116, 258
58.5	Release, urethral stricture	159, 168, 180, 265, 315
12.93	Removal or destruction, epithelial downgrowth from anterior chamber	20
11.49	Removal or destruction, other, corneal lesion	259
49.76	Removal, anal sphincter, artificial	92, 138, 263
39.43	Removal, arteriovenous shunt for renal dialysis	53, 160
11.92	Removal, artificial implant from cornea	20
85.94	Removal, breast implant	136, 137, 271, 317
78.60	Removal, devices implanted, bone, unspecified site	125
83.93	Removal, electric stimulator, skeletal muscle, except hand	4, 117, 270
57.98	Removal, electronic stimulator, bladder	159, 315
56.94	Removal, electronic stimulator, ureter	158
08.20	Removal, eyelid, lesion, unspecified	139, 151
*78.6	Removal, fixation device, internal (except carpals and metacarpals 78.64)	267, 316
78.64	Removal, fixation device, internal, carpals and metacarpals	125, 256
78.65	Removal, fixation device, internal, femur	119, 152
76.97	Removal, fixation device, internal, from facial bone	31, 125, 266
78.62	Removal, fixation device, internal, humerus	125
78.69	Removal, fixation device, internal, other	125
78.66	Removal, fixation device, internal, patella	125
78.63	Removal, fixation device, internal, radius and ulna	125
78.61	Removal, fixation device, internal, scapula, clavicle and thorax (ribs and sternum)	41, 125
78.68	Removal, fixation device, internal, tarsals and metatarsals	125
78.67	Removal, fixation device, internal, tibia and fibula	125
10.0	Removal, foreign body, embedded, by incision from conjunctiva	259, 312
69.97	Removal, foreign body, from cervix, other penetrating	179, 266
*14.0	Removal, foreign body, from posterior segment, eye	20, 259, 312
28.91	Removal, foreign body, from tonsil or adenoid, by incision	260
*13.0	Removal, foreign body, lens	259, 312
54.92	Removal, foreign body, peritoneal cavity	98, 160, 264
56.0	Removal, foreign body, ureter and renal pelvis, transurethral	159, 264, 315
44.97	Removal, gastric restrictive device(s), laparoscopic	150, 314
37.64	Removal, heart-assist system	50, 317
*16.7	Removal, implant, ocular or orbital	18, 260, 313
13.8	Removal, implanted lens	259, 312
01.22	Removal, intracranial neurostimulator lead(s)	237
*12.0	Removal, intraocular foreign body, anterior segment of eye	19, 259, 312
74.3	Removal, intraperitone, ectopic fetusal	194
55.98	Removal, kidney, mechanical	157, 264
55.53	Removal, kidney, transplanted or rejected	264
65.63	Removal, laparoscopic, tubes and ovaries, both	140
37.77	Removal, lead(s) [electrode] without replacement	3, 52, 261
12.40	Removal, lesion, anterior segment, eye, unspecified	18
56.86	Removal, ligature, ureter	265
11.0	Removal, magnetic, embedded foreign body, cornea	19, 259, 312
04.93	Removal, neurostimulator lead(s), peripheral	30, 119, 169, 180
03.94	Removal, neurostimulator lead(s), spinal	6, 123, 160, 169, 180, 258

Code	Narrative	Page
36.09	Removal, obstruction, coronary artery, other specified	56, 78, 80, 81
65.61	Removal, other, same operative episode tubes and ovaries, both	140, 315
14.72	Removal, other, vitreous	151
16.1	Removal, penetrating foreign body, from eye NOS	20, 260, 313
51.95	Removal, prosthesis from bile duct	107, 240, 264
66.94	Removal, prosthesis, fallopian tube	174, 175, 178
03.98	Removal, spinal thecal shunt	6, 123, 258
14.6	Removal, surgically implanted material, from posterior segment of eye	19, 151, 259, 313
85.96	Removal, tissue expander, breast	136, 137, 271, 317
63.85	Removal, valve, vas deferens	168
02.43	Removal, ventricular shunt	2, 5, 258
64.96	Removal, without replacement, prosthesis, penile	160, 169, 315
01.23	Reopening, craniotomy site	237, 258, 290
03.02	Reopening, laminectomy site	123, 238
54.12	Reopening, recent laparotomy site	108, 240
34.03	Reopening, thoracotomy site, recent	39, 53, 261
06.02	Reopening, wound, thyroid field	150, 258, 311
*33.4	Repair and plastic operation, lung, bronchus	39, 261
21.89	Repair and plastic operation, other, nose	28, 120, 138, 260, 313
03.59	Repair and plastic operation, other, spinal cord structures	123, 238, 258
31.79	Repair and plastic operation, other, trachea	39
41.95	Repair and plastic operation, spleen	233, 238, 262
*64.4	Repair and plastic operations, penis	168
86.89	Repair and reconstruction, other, skin and subcutaneous tissue	32, 138, 150, 271, 317
35.52	Repair of atrial septal defect with prosthesis, closed technique	56
35.51	Repair of atrial septal defect with prosthesis, open technique	50
35.54	Repair of endocardial cushion defect with prosthesis	50
35.50	Repair of unspecified septal defect of heart with prosthesis	50
35.53	Repair of ventricular septal defect with prosthesis	50
39.72	Repair or occlusion, endovascular, head and neck vessels	1, 2, 5, 7, 51, 160, 262
85.87	Repair or reconstruction, other, nipple	136, 137, 271
53.7	Repair, abdominal approach, hernia, diaphragmatic	40, 94, 264
54.72	Repair, abdominal wall	95, 96, 108, 140, 240
07.44	Repair, adrenal gland	258
*51.7	Repair, bile ducts, other	106, 263
75.61	Repair, bladder and urethra, obstetric laceration, current	197
57.86	Repair, bladder exstrophy	158
57.89	Repair, bladder, other	159, 180, 265
*08.3	Repair, blepharoptosis and lid retraction	19, 259, 311
39.57	Repair, blood vessel, patch graft synthetic	6, 55, 75, 76, 151, 160, 262
39.56	Repair, blood vessel, patch graft tissue	6, 55, 75, 76, 151, 160, 262
39.58	Repair, blood vessel, patch graft, unspecified type	6, 55, 75, 76, 151, 160, 262
02.92	Repair, brain	1, 2, 7, 258, 290
69.23	Repair, by vaginal approach, inverted uterus	266
09.73	Repair, canaliculus	139
*09.7	Repair, canaliculus and punctum	259, 312
*02.1	Repair, cerebral meninges	1, 2, 7
75.51	Repair, cervix, obstetric laceration, current	197
*67.6	Repair, cervix, other	178, 266
67.69	Repair, cervix, other	197
27.54	Repair, cleft lip	27, 139, 260, 314
*11.5	Repair, cornea	19, 259, 312
75.52	Repair, corpus uteri, obstetric laceration, current	194
70.51	Repair, cystocele	159
*70.5	Repair, cystocele and rectocele	175
70.50	Repair, cystocele and rectocele	98, 159
39.71	Repair, endovascular graft implantation, aneurysm, abdominal aorta	51, 160, 262
39.79	Repair, endovascular, other (of aneurysm), other vessels	1, 2, 5, 7, 51, 160, 262
*08.4	Repair, entropion or ectropion	19, 259, 311
08.44	Repair, entropion or ectropion with lid reconstruction	139
42.85	Repair, esophageal stricture	94, 239, 262
42.89	Repair, esophagus, other	31, 94, 239, 262
86.81	Repair, facial weakness	4, 32, 117, 138, 271

*** Code Range**

Code	Narrative	Page
*66.7	Repair, fallopian tube	174, 175, 178
66.79	Repair, fallopian tube, other	265
57.83	Repair, fistula involving bladder and intestine	93, 158, 170, 180, 240, 265
39.53	Repair, fistula, arteriovenous	1, 2, 5, 7, 55, 75, 76
67.62	Repair, fistula, cervix	193
70.72	Repair, fistula, colovaginal	93, 179, 241, 266
42.84	Repair, fistula, esophageal, other	31, 94, 239, 262
70.73	Repair, fistula, rectovaginal	93, 179, 241, 266
12.82	Repair, fistula, sclera	20
61.42	Repair, fistula, scrotal	168, 265
70.75	Repair, fistula, vagina, other	93, 179, 241, 266
70.74	Repair, fistula, vaginoenteric, other	93, 179, 241, 266
71.72	Repair, fistula, vulva or perineum	93, 266
44.66	Repair, for creation of esophagogastric sphincteric competence, stomach	94, 262
54.71	Repair, gastroschisis	95, 96
*37.4	Repair, heart and pericardium	50
37.63	Repair, heart assist system	56
*53.3	Repair, hernia, femoral, bilateral	96, 315
*53.2	Repair, hernia, femoral, unilateral	96, 315
*53.1	Repair, hernia, inguinal, bilateral	96, 315
*53.0	Repair, hernia, inguinal, unilateral	96, 315
*53.4	Repair, hernia, umbilical	95, 96, 315
81.40	Repair, hip, NEC	112, 291
58.45	Repair, hypospadias or epispadias	168
15.7	Repair, injury, extraocular muscle	259, 313
*16.8	Repair, injury, eyeball and orbit	18, 260, 313
67.59	Repair, internal cervical os, other	178, 197, 266
46.79	Repair, intestine, other	92
81.42	Repair, knee, five-in-one	124
81.43	Repair, knee, triad	124
10.6	Repair, laceration, conjunctiva	259, 312
51.91	Repair, laceration, gallbladder	107, 263
*31.6	Repair, larynx	28, 40
31.64	Repair, larynx fracture	260
59.71	Repair, levator muscle operation, urethrovesical suspension, stress incontinence	159, 175
*50.6	Repair, liver	263
50.69	Repair, liver, other	106
54.75	Repair, mesentery	98, 109, 240
*22.7	Repair, nasal sinus	28
75.50	Repair, NOS, uterus, obstetric laceration, current	197
04.76	Repair, old traumatic injury, cranial and peripheral nerves	30
54.74	Repair, omentum	98, 109, 240
*54.7	Repair, other, abdominal wall and peritoneum	264
39.52	Repair, other, aneurysm	1, 2, 5, 7, 51, 160, 262
81.49	Repair, other, ankle	115
39.59	Repair, other, blood vessel	6, 55, 75, 76, 139, 151, 160, 262
02.12	Repair, other, cerebral meninges	258, 290
34.79	Repair, other, chest wall	40, 120, 139, 261
34.84	Repair, other, diaphragm	261
18.79	Repair, other, external ear, plastic	138, 313
83.89	Repair, other, fascia, except hand	4, 117, 140
57.84	Repair, other, fistula, bladder	158, 170, 180, 240, 265
*82.8	Repair, other, hand	3, 118, 257
82.89	Repair, other, hand	138
81.79	Repair, other, hand, fingers and wrist	3, 257
53.9	Repair, other, hernia	95, 96
53.49	Repair, other, hernia, umbilical	264
*46.7	Repair, other, intestine	263
81.96	Repair, other, joint	121, 270
*81.4	Repair, other, joint of lower extremity	269
*55.8	Repair, other, kidney	157
55.89	Repair, other, kidney	264
81.47	Repair, other, knee	124
31.69	Repair, other, larynx	261
81.46	Repair, other, ligaments, collateral	124
81.45	Repair, other, ligaments, cruciate	124
19.9	Repair, other, middle ear	313
83.87	Repair, other, muscle, except hand	4, 117, 140
*83.8	Repair, other, muscle, tendon, fascia and bursa, except hand	270
52.95	Repair, other, pancreas	106, 264
64.49	Repair, other, penis	140, 265, 315
*29.5	Repair, other, pharynx	30, 62
29.59	Repair, other, pharynx	3, 260
27.59	Repair, other, plastic, mouth	32, 139, 260, 314
*14.5	Repair, other, retinal detachment	18, 259, 313
14.39	Repair, other, retinal tear	18, 312
12.86	Repair, other, scleral staphyloma	20

 ** Code Range*

Code	Narrative	Page
61.49	Repair, other, scrotum and tunica vaginalis	168, 265
63.59	Repair, other, spermatic cord and epididymis	168, 265
44.69	Repair, other, stomach	94, 150, 262
83.88	Repair, other, tendon, except hand	4, 117, 140
56.89	Repair, other, ureter	265
58.49	Repair, other, urethra, other	168, 180, 265
59.79	Repair, other, urinary stress incontinence	159, 175, 315
69.49	Repair, other, uterine	194
69.29	Repair, other, uterine ligaments	266
70.79	Repair, other, vagina	179, 197, 266
63.89	Repair, other, vas deferens and epididymis	168, 265
20.93	Repair, oval and round windows	28
*65.7	Repair, ovary	265
34.74	Repair, pectus deformity	39, 120
54.73	Repair, peritoneum	98, 109, 240
25.59	Repair, plastic operations, other, tongue	32, 260
*31.7	Repair, plastic operations, trachea	30, 261
*18.7	Repair, plastic, other, external ear	28, 260
27.69	Repair, plastic, other, palate	3, 27, 138
34.93	Repair, pleura	39, 261
60.93	Repair, prostate	170, 265, 311
*19	Repair, reconstructive, middle ear	28
70.52	Repair, rectocele	93
*48.7	Repair, rectum	263
48.79	Repair, rectum, other	95, 193
*14.4	Repair, retinal detachment, with scleral buckling and implant	18, 259, 312
14.32	Repair, retinal tear, by cryotherapy	18, 312
14.31	Repair, retinal tear, by diathermy	18, 259, 312
83.63	Repair, rotator cuff	116
*26.4	Repair, salivary gland or duct	27, 260
12.85	Repair, scleral staphyloma, with graft	20
*35.6	Repair, septa, atrial and ventricular	50
*35.7	Repair, septa, atrial, ventricular, unspecified	50
49.79	Repair, sphincter, anal, other	95, 138, 263, 315
*03.5	Repair, spinal cord structures	6
*62.6	Repair, testes	168, 265
*53.8	Repair, thoracic approach, hernia, diaphragmatic	40, 94, 264
07.93	Repair, thymus	259
*35.8	Repair, total, certain congenital cardiac anomalies	50
*56.8	Repair, ureter	158
*58.4	Repair, urethra	159
*69.4	Repair, uterine	175, 176, 178, 266
*69.2	Repair, uterine ligaments	175
03.53	Repair, vertebral fracture	123, 238, 258
*71.7	Repair, vulva and perineum	179
71.79	Repair, vulva and perineum, other	197, 266, 316
82.72	Repair, with graft of muscle or fascia, hand	140
*82.7	Repair, with graft or implant, hand	3, 118, 257
82.79	Repair, with graft or implant, hand	140
*53.6	Repair, with graft or prosthesis hernia, anterior abdominal wall	95, 96, 315
53.61	Repair, with graft or prosthesis, incisional, hernia, anterior abdominal wall	264
14.54	Repair, with laser photocoagulation, retinal detachment	151
*53.5	Repair, without graft or prosthesis, hernia, anterior abdominal wall	95, 96
53.51	Repair, without graft or prosthesis, incisional, hernia, anterior abdominal wall	315
37.54	Replacement or repair, other implantable component of total replacement heart system	56
37.53	Replacement or repair, thoracic unit of total replacement heart system	56
81.56	Replacement, ankle, total	122, 126
37.87	Replacement, any type pacemaker device, with dual-chamber device	3, 52, 65, 66, 67, 68, 69, 70, 71, 72, 261
37.85	Replacement, any type pacemaker, with single-chamber device, not specified as rate-responsive	3, 52, 65, 66, 67, 68, 69, 70, 71, 72, 261
37.86	Replacement, any type pacemaker, with single-chamber device, rate-responsive	3, 52, 65, 66, 67, 68, 69, 70, 71, 72, 261
39.94	Replacement, cannula, vessel-to-vessel	55, 75, 76, 160, 314
37.97	Replacement, cardioverter/ defibrillator, lead(s)	55, 57, 58, 68
37.98	Replacement, cardioverter/ defibrillator, pulse generator	55, 58, 68
81.84	Replacement, elbow, total	122, 269
57.97	Replacement, electronic stimulator, bladder	159, 315
56.93	Replacement, electronic stimulator, ureter	158
37.51	Replacement, heart	317
*35.2	Replacement, heart, valve	49
81.52	Replacement, hip, partial	122, 126, 152, 291

*** Code Range***

Code	Narrative	Page
81.51	Replacement, hip, total	122, 126, 291
81.57	Replacement, joint of foot and toe	117, 316
*81.5	Replacement, joint, lower extremity	269
55.97	Replacement, kidney, mechanical	157, 264
81.54	Replacement, knee, total	122, 126
81.59	Replacement, other, total hip	121
81.81	Replacement, shoulder, partial	122, 269
81.80	Replacement, shoulder, total	122, 269
*84.6	Replacement, spinal disc	6, 123, 270
37.76	Replacement, transvenous atrial and/or ventricular pacemaker lead [electrode] (must be in combination with 37.80, 37.85, 37.86 or 37.87)	3, 5, 52, 68, 72, 261, 271
02.42	Replacement, ventricular shunt	2, 5, 238, 258
81.73	Replacement, wrist, total	122, 269
38.44	Resection, aorta, abdominal, with graft replacement	50, 51
85.22	Resection, breast quadrant	137
45.71	Resection, intestine, large, multiple segmental	239
45.61	Resection, intestine, small, multiple segmental	53, 239, 263
45.62	Resection, intestine, small, other partial	53, 152, 239, 263
45.63	Resection, intestine, small, total	239, 263
65.24	Resection, laparoscopic, ovarian wedge	152
21.4	Resection, nose	28, 139, 260
65.22	Resection, ovarian wedge	152
48.5	Resection, rectum, abdominoperineal	92, 240, 263
48.62	Resection, rectum, anterior with synchronous colostomy	53
48.63	Resection, rectum, anterior, other	53
*48.6	Resection, rectum, other	92, 240, 263
48.69	Resection, rectum, other	53, 167
*48.4	Resection, rectum, pull-through	92, 240
48.49	Resection, rectum, pull-through, other	263
32.3	Resection, segmental, lung	39, 261
21.5	Resection, submucous, nasal septum	28, 260, 313
38.45	Resection, thoracic vessel, with graft replacement	39, 50, 51, 93
45.74	Resection, transverse colon	53, 239
36.2	Revascularization, heart, by arterial implant	50
*36.3	Revascularization, other, heart	50
00.71	Revision of hip replacement, acetabular component	126, 257, 291
00.73	Revision of hip replacement, acetabular liner and/or femoral head only	126, 257, 291
00.70	Revision of hip replacement, both acetabular and femoral components	126, 257, 291
00.72	Revision of hip replacement, femoral component	126, 257, 291
57.22	Revision or closure, vesicostomy	180, 240, 265, 315
84.3	Revision, amputation stump	52, 113, 140, 149, 270
51.94	Revision, anastomosis, biliary tract	107, 240, 264
46.94	Revision, anastomosis, intestine, large	92, 263
46.93	Revision, anastomosis, intestine, small	92, 263
56.72	Revision, anastomosis, ureterointestinal	169, 180, 240
39.42	Revision, arteriovenous shunt for renal dialysis	53, 151, 160
85.93	Revision, breast implant	136, 137, 271, 317
27.63	Revision, cleft palate repair	27, 139
35.95	Revision, corrective procedure, heart	50
15.6	Revision, extraocular muscle, surgery	313
44.5	Revision, gastric anastomosis	94, 150, 262
44.96	Revision, gastric restrictive procedure, laparoscopic	150, 314
81.53	Revision, hip replacement	122, 126, 152, 291
81.97	Revision, joint replacement, upper extremity	121, 270
81.55	Revision, knee replacement	122, 126
37.75	Revision, lead [electrode]	3, 52, 261
20.92	Revision, mastoidectomy	28
12.83	Revision, operative wound, anterior segment, unspecified	20
16.66	Revision, other, exenteration cavity	30
39.49	Revision, other, vascular procedure	54, 75, 76, 97, 108, 151, 160
86.75	Revision, pedicle or flap graft	4, 32, 54, 98, 114, 149, 256
04.75	Revision, previous repair, cranial and peripheral nerves	30
37.79	Revision, relocation, pacemaker pocket	3, 52, 139, 261
37.89	Revision, removal, pacemaker device	3, 52, 261, 314
*16.6	Revision, secondary, after removal of eyeball	18, 260, 313
03.97	Revision, spinal thecal shunt	6, 123, 238, 258
*46.4	Revision, stoma, intestinal	95, 263
46.40	Revision, stoma, intestinal	239
46.43	Revision, stoma, large intestine	314

Code	Narrative	Page
46.41	Revision, stoma, small intestine	239, 314
31.74	Revision, tracheostomy	40, 53, 139
56.52	Revision, ureteroileostomy, cutaneous	315
*39.4	Revision, vascular procedure	262
21.85	Rhinoplasty, augmentation	29, 120, 138, 260, 313
21.86	Rhinoplasty, limited	29, 120, 138, 260, 313
21.87	Rhinoplasty, other	29, 120, 138, 260, 313
21.84	Rhinoplasty, revision	29, 120, 138, 260, 313
21.21	Rhinoscopy	242
86.82	Rhytidectomy, facial	32, 138, 271, 317
66.63	Salpingectomy, partial, bilateral, unspecified	179, 193
66.69	Salpingectomy, partial, other	174, 175, 178, 193
*66.5	Salpingectomy, total, bilateral	174, 175, 178, 193
66.4	Salpingectomy, unilateral, total	174, 175, 178, 193
66.62	Salpingectomy, with removal of tubal pregnancy	174, 175, 178, 193
*66.0	Salpingotomy and salpingostomy	174, 175, 178
34.6	Scarification, pleura	39, 238, 261
84.92	Separation, twins, equal conjoined	122
84.93	Separation, twins, unequal conjoined	122
21.88	Septoplasty, other	29, 120, 138, 260, 313
*77.0	Sequestrectomy (except carpals and metacarpals 77.04)	266
76.01	Sequestrectomy, bone, facial	120
77.04	Sequestrectomy, carpals and metacarpals	118, 256
77.05	Sequestrectomy, femur	112, 291
77.02	Sequestrectomy, humerus	114
77.09	Sequestrectomy, other	120
77.06	Sequestrectomy, patella	124
77.03	Sequestrectomy, radius and ulna	115
77.01	Sequestrectomy, scapula, clavicle and thorax, ribs and sternum	40, 120
77.08	Sequestrectomy, tarsals and metatarsals	116
77.07	Sequestrectomy, tibia and fibula	114
77.00	Sequestrectomy, unspecified site	120
78.24	Shortening, bone, carpals and metacarpals	118, 256
78.25	Shortening, bone, femur	112, 267, 291
78.22	Shortening, bone, humerus	114, 267
78.29	Shortening, bone, other	121, 267
78.23	Shortening, bone, radius and ulna	115, 267
78.28	Shortening, bone, tarsals and metatarsals	116, 267
78.27	Shortening, bone, tibia and fibula	114, 267
78.20	Shortening, bone, unspecified site	121, 267
*03.7	Shunt, spinal theca	6, 238
39.0	Shunt, systemic to pulmonary artery	51
*02.3	Shunt, ventricular, extracranial	2, 5, 238, 258
*26.3	Sialoadenectomy	27, 314
26.30	Sialoadenectomy, unspecified	233
45.76	Sigmoidectomy	239
45.24	Sigmoidoscopy, flexible	243
*22.6	Sinusectomy, other, nasal	28
*22.4	Sinusotomy and sinusectomy, frontal	28
*22.5	Sinusotomy, other, nasal	28
51.83	Sphincteroplasty, pancreatic	94, 106, 263
51.85	Sphincterotomy and papillotomy, endoscopic	243
49.59	Sphincterotomy, anal, other	197
57.91	Sphincterotomy, bladder	159, 315
51.82	Sphincterotomy, pancreatic	94, 106, 263
41.43	Splenectomy, partial	120, 262
41.5	Splenectomy, total	53, 97, 120, 233, 238, 262
41.2	Splenotomy	233, 238, 262
81.44	Stabilization, patellar	124
*19.1	Stapedectomy	313
37.26	Stimulator, cardiac, electrophysiologic	49, 55, 58, 78, 80, 81
81.18	Subtalar joint arthroereisis	121, 269
32.22	Surgery, lung volume reduction	39
70.77	Suspension and fixation, vagina	159, 175
59.6	Suspension, paraurethral	159, 175
59.5	Suspension, urethral, retropubic	159, 175
*54.6	Suture, abdominal wall and peritoneum	98, 264
39.31	Suture, artery	40, 54, 75, 76, 139, 151
*39.3	Suture, blood vessel	6, 262
39.30	Suture, blood vessel, unspecified	54, 75
04.3	Suture, cranial and peripheral nerves	3, 258
83.62	Suture, delayed, tendon, except hand	117

Alphabetic Index to Procedures

* Code Range

Code	Narrative	Page
*82.4	Suture, hand, muscle, tendon and fascia	118, 257
82.41	Suture, hand, tendon sheath	316
49.71	Suture, laceration, anus	95, 139, 263
57.81	Suture, laceration, bladder	158, 265
67.61	Suture, laceration, cervix	197
34.82	Suture, laceration, diaphragm	261
46.71	Suture, laceration, duodenum	94
42.82	Suture, laceration, esophagus	31, 94, 239, 262
55.81	Suture, laceration, kidney	264
46.75	Suture, laceration, large intestine	92
31.61	Suture, laceration, larynx	260
27.61	Suture, laceration, palate	32, 260
64.41	Suture, laceration, penis	265
29.51	Suture, laceration, pharynx	260
48.71	Suture, laceration, rectum	92, 197
12.81	Suture, laceration, sclera	20
46.73	Suture, laceration, small intestine except duodenum	92
63.51	Suture, laceration, spermatic cord and epididymis	168, 265
44.61	Suture, laceration, stomach	94, 262
56.82	Suture, laceration, ureter	264
58.41	Suture, laceration, urethra	265
69.41	Suture, laceration, uterine	193
70.71	Suture, laceration, vagina	140, 179, 197, 266
63.81	Suture, laceration, vas deferens and epididymis	168, 265
71.71	Suture, laceration, vulva or perineum	140, 197, 266, 316
81.94	Suture, ligament, ankle and foot	117, 270
81.95	Suture, ligament, other, lower extremity	117, 270
81.93	Suture, ligament, upper extremity	116, 270
82.46	Suture, muscle, hand	316
*83.6	Suture, muscle, tendon and fascia, except hand	270, 317
54.63	Suture, other, abdominal wall	140, 240
82.45	Suture, other, hand, tendon	140, 316
83.65	Suture, other, muscle or fascia, except hand	117, 140, 152
83.64	Suture, other, tendon, except hand	117
54.64	Suture, peritoneum	108, 240, 315
02.11	Suture, simple, dura mater, brain	258, 290
66.71	Suture, simple, fallopian tube	265
83.61	Suture, tendon sheath, except hand	117
06.93	Suture, thyroid gland	150, 258
31.71	Suture, trachea laceration	40
44.42	Suture, ulcer, duodenal	94
44.41	Suture, ulcer, gastric	94
44.40	Suture, ulcer, peptic	94
39.32	Suture, vein	52
*05.2	Sympathectomy	3, 52
05.22	Sympathectomy, cervical	30
05.23	Sympathectomy, lumbar	311
05.24	Sympathectomy, presacral	180
*80.7	Synovectomy	316
80.77	Synovectomy, ankle	115, 269
80.72	Synovectomy, elbow	116, 269
80.78	Synovectomy, foot and toe	117, 269
80.74	Synovectomy, hand and finger	118, 257
80.75	Synovectomy, hip	112, 269
80.76	Synovectomy, knee	124, 269
80.79	Synovectomy, other specified site	117, 269
80.71	Synovectomy, shoulder	116, 269
80.70	Synovectomy, unspecified site	117, 269
80.73	Synovectomy, wrist	118, 257
11.91	Tattooing, cornea	19
82.33	Tenonectomy, other, hand	152
83.12	Tenotomy, adductor, hip	112, 291
82.11	Tenotomy, hand	316
83.13	Tenotomy, other, except hand	3, 117, 152, 317
11.42	Thermocauterization, corneal lesion	259
11.74	Thermokeratoplasty	19
33.34	Thoracoplasty	39
34.21	Thoracoscopy, transpleural	40, 53, 261
34.02	Thoracotomy, exploratory	39, 53, 160, 238, 261
*07.8	Thymectomy	3, 39, 150, 233, 258
07.80	Thymectomy, unspecified	238
06.4	Thyroidectomy, complete	150
*06.3	Thyroidectomy, other, partial	150
*06.5	Thyroidectomy, substernal	150
28.3	Tonsillectomy, with adenoidectomy	29
28.2	Tonsillectomy, without adenoidectomy	29, 314
12.64	Trabeculectomy, ab externo	151
12.54	Trabeculotomy, ab externo	20
31.41	Tracheoscopy, through tracheostomy	242
31.21	Tracheostomy, mediastinal	321, 323, 324
31.29	Tracheostomy, permanent, other	321, 323, 324
31.1	Tracheostomy, temporary	321, 323, 324
50.51	Transplant, auxiliary, liver	317
50.59	Transplant, other, liver	317
83.75	Transplantation or transfer, tendon, except hand	152

Alphabetic Index to Procedures

** Code Range*

Code	Narrative	Page
41.02	Transplantation, allogeneic, with purging, bone marrow	318
41.08	Transplantation, allogeneic, with purging, hematopoietic stem cell	318
41.03	Transplantation, allogeneic, without purging, bone marrow	318
41.05	Transplantation, allogeneic, without purging, hematopoietic stem cell	318
41.09	Transplantation, autologous, with purging, bone marrow	318
41.07	Transplantation, autologous, with purging, hematopoietic stem cell	318
41.01	Transplantation, autologous, without purging, bone marrow	318
41.04	Transplantation, autologous, without purging, hematopoietic stem cell	318
33.6	Transplantation, combined heart-lung	317
*11.6	Transplantation, corneal	259, 312
11.69	Transplantation, corneal, other	20
11.60	Transplantation, corneal, unspecified	19
49.74	Transplantation, gracilis muscle, for anal incontinence	97
46.97	Transplantation, intestine	108, 239, 263, 317
*33.5	Transplantation, lung	321
*82.5	Transplantation, muscle and tendon, hand	3, 118, 257
41.00	Transplantation, NOS, bone marrow	318
55.69	Transplantation, other, kidney	157, 322
52.83	Transplantation, pancreas, heterotransplant	152
52.82	Transplantation, pancreas, homotransplant	152, 322
52.80	Transplantation, pancreas, unspecified	152, 322
63.53	Transplantation, spermatic cord	168, 265
41.94	Transplantation, spleen	233, 238
41.06	Transplantation, stem cell, cord blood	318
04.6	Transposition, cranial and peripheral nerves	3, 258
15.5	Transposition, extraocular muscles	313
35.91	Transposition, interatrial, venous return	50
83.79	Transposition, muscle, other, except hand	152
85.86	Transposition, nipple	136, 137, 271
56.75	Transureteroureterostomy	169, 180, 240
*21.6	Turbinectomy	28
21.69	Turbinectomy, other	260, 313
20.91	Tympanosympathectomy	28
*56.4	Ureterectomy	157, 264
56.41	Ureterectomy, partial	169, 180
*56.5	Ureteroileostomy, cutaneous	157, 169, 180, 240, 264
56.31	Ureteroscopy	243
56.2	Ureterotomy	157, 264, 315
58.22	Urethroscopy, other	243
58.0	Urethrotomy	159, 180, 265, 315
70.21	Vaginoscopy	243
70.14	Vaginotomy, other	179, 197, 316
*44.0	Vagotomy	94
44.00	Vagotomy, NOS	3
*35.0	Valvotomy, closed, heart	50
*35.1	Valvuloplasty, open, heart,	49
35.96	Valvuloplasty, percutaneous	49, 56, 78, 80, 81
*96.7	Ventilation, mechanical, continuous	48
96.72	Ventilation, mechanical, continuous, for 96 consecutive hours or more	277, 281, 323, 324
02.2	Ventriculostomy	1, 2, 7, 238, 258, 290
37.35	Ventriculotomy, partial	50
81.65	Vertebroplasty	121, 269
*57.2	Vesicostomy	158, 169
57.21	Vesicostomy	178, 240, 265
14.74	Vitrectomy, mechanical, other	151
71.62	Vulvectomy, bilateral	140
*71.6	Vulvectomy, other	179
71.5	Vulvectomy, radical	174

Alphabetic Index to Procedures

*Code Range

Numeric Index to Procedures

Code	Narrative	Page
00.10	Implantation, chemotherapeutic agent	7
00.15	Injection or infusion, high-dose infusion interleukin-2 (IL-2)	244
00.50	Implantation, cardiac resynchronization pacemaker, without mention of defibrillation, total system [CRT-P]	65, 69
00.51	Implantation, cardiac resynchronization defibrillator, total system [CRT-D]	55, 57
00.52	Implantation or replacement, transvenous lead (electrode) into left ventricular coronary venous system	55, 57, 65, 68, 69
00.53	Implantation or replacement, cardiac resynchronization pacemaker, pulse generator only [CRT-P]	52, 65, 66, 67, 68, 69, 70, 71, 72
00.54	Implantation or replacement, cardiac resynchronization defibrillator, pulse generator only [CRT-D]	55, 57, 68
00.61	Angioplasty or atherectomy, percutaneous, precerebral (extracranial) vessel(s)	6, 54, 74, 75, 257
00.62	Angioplasty or atherectomy, percutaneous, intracranial vessel(s)	6, 54, 74, 75, 257
00.66	Percutaneous transluminal coronary angioplasty [PTCA] or coronary atherectomy	49, 56, 78, 80, 81
*00.7	Other hip procedures	122, 150
00.70	Revision of hip replacement, both acetabular and femoral components	126, 257, 291
00.71	Revision of hip replacement, acetabular component	126, 257, 291
00.72	Revision of hip replacement, femoral component	126, 257, 291
00.73	Revision of hip replacement, acetabular liner and/or femoral head only	126, 257, 291
*00.8	Other knee procedures	122, 126, 257, 291
01.12	Biopsy, open, cerebral meninges	1, 2, 6, 237
01.14	Biopsy, open, brain	1, 2, 6, 237
01.15	Biopsy, skull	1, 2, 6, 113, 150
01.18	Procedure, diagnostic, other, brain and cerebral meninges	1, 2, 7, 237, 258
01.19	Procedure, diagnostic, other, skull	1, 2, 7, 113, 258
*01.2	Craniotomy and craniectomy	1, 2, 7
01.21	Incision and drainage, cranial sinus	290
01.22	Removal, intracranial neurostimulator lead(s)	237
01.23	Reopening, craniotomy site	237, 258, 290
01.24	Craniotomy, other	237, 258, 290
01.25	Craniectomy, other	119, 238, 258, 290
*01.3	Incision, brain and cerebral meninges	1, 2, 7, 258
01.31	Incision, cerebral meninges	238, 290
01.32	Lobotomy and tractotomy	238, 290
01.39	Incision, other, brain	238, 290
*01.4	Operation, thalamus and globus pallidus	1, 2, 7, 238
01.41	Operation, thalamus	258, 290
01.42	Operation, globus pallidus	290
*01.5	Excision or destruction, other, brain and meninges	1, 2, 7, 238
01.51	Excision or destruction, other, lesion or tissue, cerebral meninges	290
01.52	Hemispherectomy	258, 290
01.53	Lobectomy, brain	258, 290
01.59	Excision or destruction, other, lesion or tissue, brain	258, 290
01.6	Excision, lesion, skull	1, 2, 7, 125, 238, 290
*02.0	Cranioplasty	1, 2, 7, 119, 258
02.01	Craniectomy, linear	290
02.02	Elevation, fragments, fracture, skull	290
02.03	Formation, flap, cranial	290
02.04	Graft, bone, skull	290
02.05	Insertion, plate, skull	290
02.06	Osteoplasty, other, cranial	290
*02.1	Repair, cerebral meninges	1, 2, 7
02.11	Suture, simple, dura mater, brain	258, 290
02.12	Repair, other, cerebral meninges	258, 290
02.13	Ligation, meningeal vessel	5, 258, 290
02.14	Plexectomy, choroid	290
02.2	Ventriculostomy	1, 2, 7, 238, 258, 290
*02.3	Shunt, ventricular, extracranial	2, 5, 238, 258
02.42	Replacement, ventricular shunt	2, 5, 238, 258
02.43	Removal, ventricular shunt	2, 5, 258
02.91	Lysis, adhesions, cortical	1, 2, 7, 238, 258
02.92	Repair, brain	1, 2, 7, 258, 290

*** Code Range**

Code	Narrative	Page
02.93	Implantation or replacement, neurostimulator lead(s), intracranial	1, 2, 7, 238, 258
02.94	Insertion or replacement, skull tongs or halo traction device	1, 2, 7, 119, 258, 290
02.99	Operation, other, skull, brain and cerebral meninges	1, 2, 7, 119, 238, 258, 290
*03.0	Exploration and decompression, spinal canal structures	5, 258
03.02	Reopening, laminectomy site	123, 238
03.09	Exploration and decompression, other, spinal canal	123, 238
03.1	Division, intraspinal nerve root	5, 123, 238, 258
*03.2	Chordotomy	5, 108, 238, 258
03.32	Biopsy, spinal cord or spinal meninges	6, 123, 238
03.39	Procedure, diagnostic, other, spinal cord and spinal canal structures	6, 123, 238
03.4	Excision or destruction, lesion, spinal cord or spinal meninges	6, 123, 238
*03.5	Repair, spinal cord structures	6
03.53	Repair, vertebral fracture	123, 238, 258
03.59	Repair and plastic operation, other, spinal cord structures	123, 238, 258
03.6	Lysis, adhesions, spinal cord and nerve roots	6, 123, 238, 258
*03.7	Shunt, spinal theca	6, 238
03.93	Implantation or replacement, neurostimulator lead(s), spinal	6, 123, 160, 169, 180, 238, 258
03.94	Removal, neurostimulator lead(s), spinal	6, 123, 160, 169, 180, 258
03.97	Revision, spinal thecal shunt	6, 123, 238, 258
03.98	Removal, spinal thecal shunt	6, 123, 258
03.99	Operation, other, spinal cord and spinal canal structures	6, 123, 238, 258
*04.0	Incision, division and excision, cranial and peripheral nerves	30
04.01	Neurotomy, acoustic	1, 2, 7
04.02	Division, trigeminal nerve	3, 258
04.03	Division or crushing, other, cranial and peripheral nerves	3, 119, 258
04.04	Incision, other, cranial and peripheral nerves	3, 119, 258
04.05	Ganglionectomy, gasserian	3, 258
04.06	Ganglionectomy, other, cranial or peripheral	3, 119, 258
04.07	Excision or avulsion, other, cranial and peripheral nerve	3, 119, 258, 311
04.12	Biopsy, open, cranial or peripheral nerve or ganglion	3, 30, 119, 258
04.19	Procedure, diagnostic, other, cranial and peripheral nerves and ganglia	3, 30, 119, 258
04.3	Suture, cranial and peripheral nerves	3, 258
*04.4	Lysis, adhesions and decompression, cranial and peripheral nerves	311
04.41	Decompression, trigeminal nerve root	1, 2, 7, 30, 258, 290
04.42	Decompression, other, cranial nerve	3, 30, 258
04.43	Release, carpal tunnel	2, 118, 256
04.44	Release, tarsal tunnel	3, 116, 258
04.49	Lysis, adhesions and decompression, other, peripheral nerve or ganglion	3, 30, 119, 258
04.5	Graft, nerve, cranial or peripheral	3, 258
04.6	Transposition, cranial and peripheral nerves	3, 258
*04.7	Neuroplasty, other, cranial or peripheral	3, 258
04.71	Anastomosis, face, hypoglossal	30
04.72	Anastomosis, face, accessory	30
04.73	Anastomosis, accessory, hypoglossal	30
04.74	Anastomosis, other, cranial or peripheral nerve	30
04.75	Revision, previous repair, cranial and peripheral nerves	30
04.76	Repair, old traumatic injury, cranial and peripheral nerves	30
*04.9	Operation, other, cranial and peripheral nerves	3, 258
04.92	Implantation or replacement, neurostimulator lead(s), peripheral	30, 119, 160, 169, 180
04.93	Removal, neurostimulator lead(s), peripheral	30, 119, 169, 180
04.99	Operation, other, cranial and peripheral nerves	30, 120
05.0	Division, sympathetic nerve or ganglion	3, 52
*05.1	Procedure, diagnostic, sympathetic nerves or ganglia	3
*05.2	Sympathectomy	3, 52
05.21	Ganglionectomy, sphenopalatine	30
05.22	Sympathectomy, cervical	30
05.23	Sympathectomy, lumbar	311
05.24	Sympathectomy, presacral	180
*05.8	Operation, other, sympathetic nerves or ganglia	3
05.89	Operation, other, sympathetic nerves or ganglia	53
05.9	Operation, other, nervous system	3, 258
06.02	Reopening, wound, thyroid field	150, 258, 311
06.09	Incision, other, thyroid field	28, 139, 150, 258
06.12	Biopsy, thyroid gland, open	150

* Code Range

Code	Narrative	Page
06.13	Biopsy, parathyroid gland	120, 150
06.19	Procedure, diagnostic, other, thyroid and parathyroid gland	120, 150
06.2	Lobectomy, unilateral, thyroid	150
*06.3	Thyroidectomy, other, partial	150
06.4	Thyroidectomy, complete	150
*06.5	Thyroidectomy, substernal	150
06.6	Excision, lingual thyroid	30, 150
06.7	Excision, thyroglossal duct or tract	30, 150
*06.8	Parathyroidectomy	150, 160
06.91	Division, thyroid isthmus	150
06.92	Ligation, thyroid vessels	150, 258
06.93	Suture, thyroid gland	150, 258
06.94	Reimplantation, thyroid tissue	150
06.95	Reimplantation, parathyroid tissue	150
06.98	Operation, other, thyroid glands	150
06.99	Operation, other, parathyroid glands	150
*07.0	Exploration, adrenal gland	149
07.12	Biopsy, adrenal gland, open	149
07.13	Biopsy, pituitary gland, transfrontal approach	1, 2, 7, 149
07.14	Biopsy, pituitary gland, transphenoidal approach	1, 2, 7, 149
07.15	Biopsy, pituitary gland, unspecified approach	1, 2, 7, 149
07.16	Biopsy, thymus	39, 150, 233, 238
07.17	Biopsy, pineal gland	1, 2, 7, 149
07.19	Procedure, diagnostic, other, adrenal gland, pineal gland and thymus	3, 149
*07.2	Adrenalectomy, partial	149
07.22	Adrenalectomy, unilateral	139
07.3	Adrenalectomy, bilateral	139, 149
*07.4	Operation, other, adrenal glands, nerves and vessels	149
07.43	Ligation, adrenal vessel	258
07.44	Repair, adrenal gland	258
07.45	Reimplantation, adrenal tissue	258
07.49	Operation, other, adrenal glands, nerves and vessels	258
*07.5	Operation, pineal gland	1, 2, 7, 149
*07.6	Hypophysectomy	1, 2, 7, 149
07.63	Excision, partial, pituitary gland, unspecified approach	139
07.64	Excision, total, pituitary gland, transfrontal approach	139
07.65	Excision, total, pituitary gland, transsphenoidal approach	139
07.68	Excision, total, pituitary gland, other specified approach	139
07.69	Excision, total, pituitary gland, unspecified approach	139
*07.7	Operation, other, hypophysis	1, 2, 7, 149
07.72	Incision, pituitary gland	139
07.79	Operation, other, hypophysis	139
*07.8	Thymectomy	3, 39, 150, 233, 258
07.80	Thymectomy, unspecified	238
07.81	Excision, partial, thymus	238
07.82	Excision, total, thymus	238
*07.9	Operation, other, thymus	39, 151, 233, 238
07.91	Exploration, thymus	258
07.92	Incision, thymus	259
07.93	Repair, thymus	259
08.11	Biopsy, eyelid	19, 259, 311
*08.2	Excision or destruction, lesion or tissue, eyelid	19, 259, 311
08.20	Removal, eyelid, lesion, unspecified	139, 151
08.22	Excision, other minor lesion, eyelid	139
08.23	Excision, major lesion, eyelid, partial-thickness	139
08.24	Excision, major lesion, eyelid, full-thickness	139
08.25	Destruction, lesion, eyelid	139
*08.3	Repair, blepharoptosis and lid retraction	19, 259, 311
08.38	Correction, lid retraction	138, 151
*08.4	Repair, entropion or ectropion	19, 259, 311
08.44	Repair, entropion or ectropion with lid reconstruction	139
*08.5	Adjstment, other, lid position	3, 19, 138, 259, 311
*08.6	Reconstruction, with flaps or grafts, eyelid	19, 138, 259, 311
*08.7	Reconstruction, other, eyelid	19, 138, 259, 312
08.70	Reconstruction, unspecified, eyelid	151
*08.9	Operation, other, eyelids	19, 259, 312
08.99	Operation, other, eyelids	139
*09	Operation, lacrimal system	19
09.0	Incision, lacrimal gland	312
*09.1	Procedure, diagnostic, lacrimal system	312
09.11	Biopsy, lacrimal gland	259
09.12	Biopsy, lacrimal sac	28
09.19	Procedure, diagnostic, other, lacrimal system	28, 259
*09.2	Excision, lesion or tissue, lacrimal gland	312
09.21	Excision, lesion, lacrimal gland	259
09.22	Dacryoadenectomy, other, partial	259
09.23	Dacryoadenectomy, total	259
09.3	Operation, other, lacrimal gland	259, 312
*09.4	Manipulation, lacrimal passage	312
09.43	Probing, nasolacrimal duct	30

Numeric Index to Procedures

Code	Narrative	Page
09.44	Intubation, nasolacrimal duct	28, 259
*09.5	Incision, lacrimal sac and passages	312
09.52	Incision, lacrimal canaliculus	259
09.6	Excision, lacrimal sac and passage	259, 312
*09.7	Repair, canaliculus and punctum	259, 312
09.73	Repair, canaliculus	139
*09.8	Fistulization, lacrimal tract to nasal cavity	259, 312
09.81	Dacryocystorhinostomy	28
*09.9	Operation, other, lacrimal system	259, 312
09.99	Operation, other, lacrimal system	28
*10	Operation, conjunctiva	19
10.0	Removal, foreign body, embedded, by incision from conjunctiva	259, 312
10.1	Incision, other, conjunctiva	312
*10.2	Procedure, diagnostic, on conjunctiva	312
*10.3	Excision or destruction, lesion or tissue, conjunctiva	259, 312
*10.4	Conjunctivoplasty	259, 312
10.5	Lysis, adhesions, conjunctiva and eyelid	312
10.6	Repair, laceration, conjunctiva	259, 312
*10.9	Operation, other, conjunctiva	312
11.0	Removal, magnetic, embedded foreign body, cornea	19, 259, 312
11.1	Incision, cornea	19, 259, 312
*11.2	Procedure, diagnostic, cornea	19, 312
11.22	Biopsy, cornea	259
*11.3	Excision, pterygium	19, 312
11.32	Excision, with corneal graft, pterygium	259
*11.4	Excision or destruction, tissue or other lesion, cornea	19, 312
11.42	Thermocauterization, corneal lesion	259
11.43	Cryotherapy, corneal lesion	259
11.49	Removal or destruction, other, corneal lesion	259
*11.5	Repair, cornea	19, 259, 312
*11.6	Transplantation, corneal	259, 312
11.60	Transplantation, corneal, unspecified	19
11.61	Keratoplasty, lamellar, with autograft	19
11.62	Keratoplasty, lamellar, other	19
11.63	Keratoplasty, penetrating, with autograft	20
11.64	Keratoplasty, penetrating, other	20
11.69	Transplantation, corneal, other	20
*11.7	Reconstructive, surgery, other, cornea	259, 312
11.71	Keratomeleusis	19
11.72	Keratophakia	19

Code	Narrative	Page
11.73	Keratoprosthesis	20
11.74	Thermokeratoplasty	19
11.75	Keratotomy, radial	20
11.76	Epikeratophakia	19
11.79	Reconstruction, other, surgery, cornea	20
*11.9	Operation, other, cornea	259, 312
11.91	Tattooing, cornea	19
11.92	Removal, artificial implant from cornea	20
11.99	Operation, other, cornea	20
*12.0	Removal, intraocular foreign body, anterior segment of eye	19, 259, 312
*12.1	Iridotomy, simple iridectomy	18, 259, 312
*12.2	Procedure, diagnostic, iris, ciliary body, sclera and anterior chamber	259, 312
12.21	Aspiration, diagnostic, eye, anterior chamber,	20
12.22	Biopsy, iris	18
12.29	Procedure, diagnostic, other, iris, ciliary body, sclera and anterior chamber	20
*12.3	Iridoplasty and coreoplasty	259, 312
12.31	Lysis, goniosynechiae	18
12.32	Lysis, anterior synechiae, other	18
12.33	Lysis, posterior synechiae	18
12.34	Lysis, adhesions, corneovitreal	20
12.35	Coreoplasty	20
12.39	Iridoplasty, other	20
*12.4	Excision or destruction, lesion, iris and ciliary body	259, 312
12.40	Removal, lesion, anterior segment, eye, unspecified	18
12.41	Destruction, lesion, nonexcisional, iris	18
12.42	Excision, lesion, iris	18
12.43	Destruction, lesion, nonexcisional, ciliary body	20
12.44	Excision, lesion, ciliary body	20
*12.5	Facilitation, intraocular circulation	259, 312
12.51	Goniopuncture, without goniotomy	20
12.52	Goniotomy, without goniopuncture	20
12.53	Goniotomy, with goniopuncture	20
12.54	Trabeculotomy, ab externo	20
12.55	Cyclodialysis	18
12.59	Facilitation, other, intraocular circulation	18
*12.6	Fistulization, scleral	20, 259, 312
12.64	Trabeculectomy, ab externo	151
*12.7	Procedure, other, for relief of intraocular pressure	18, 312
12.72	Cyclocryotherapy	151
12.79	Procedure, glaucoma, other	151
*12.8	Operation, sclera	259, 312

*** Code Range***

Code	Narrative	Page
12.81	Suture, laceration, sclera	20
12.82	Repair, fistula, sclera	20
12.83	Revision, operative wound, anterior segment, unspecified	20
12.84	Excision or destruction, lesion, sclera	19
12.85	Repair, scleral staphyloma, with graft	20
12.86	Repair, other, scleral staphyloma	20
12.87	Reinforcement, scleral, with graft	19
12.88	Reinforcement, other, scleral	19
12.89	Operation, other, sclera	19
*12.9	Operation, other, iris, ciliary body, and anterior chamber	312
12.91	Evacuation, therapeutic, anterior chamber	19, 20, 259
12.92	Injection, into anterior chamber	19, 20, 259
12.93	Removal or destruction, epithelial downgrowth from anterior chamber	20
12.97	Operation, other, iris	18, 259
12.98	Operation, other, ciliary body	20, 259
12.99	Operation, other, anterior chamber	20, 259
*13	Operation, lens	19
*13.0	Removal, foreign body, lens	259, 312
*13.1	Extraction, intracapsular, lens	151, 312
13.2	Extraction, extracapsular, linear extraction technique, lens	312
13.3	Extraction, extracapsular, simple aspiration and irrigation technique, lens	312
*13.4	Extraction, extracapsular, fragmentation and aspiration technique, lens	312
*13.5	Extraction, extracapsular, other, lens	312
13.59	Extraction, other extracapsular, lens	151
*13.6	Extraction, cataract, other	312
13.70	Insertion, pseudophakos, NOS	312
13.71	Insertion, prosthesis, intraocular lens	312
13.72	Insertion, secondary, prosthesis, intraocular lens	259, 312
13.8	Removal, implanted lens	259, 312
13.9	Operation, other, lens	259, 312
*14.0	Removal, foreign body, from posterior segment, eye	20, 259, 312
*14.1	Procedure, diagnostic, retina, choroid, vitreous and posterior chamber	20, 312
14.21	Destruction, by diathermy, lesion, chorioretinal	18, 312
14.22	Destruction, by cryotherapy, lesion, chorioretinal	18, 312
14.26	Destruction, by radiation therapy, chorioretinal lesion	18, 312
14.27	Destruction, by implantation of radiation source, chorioretinal lesion	18, 312
14.29	Destruction, other, chorioretinal lesion	18, 312
14.31	Repair, retinal tear, by diathermy	18, 259, 312
14.32	Repair, retinal tear, by cryotherapy	18, 312
14.39	Repair, other, retinal tear	18, 312
*14.4	Repair, retinal detachment, with scleral buckling and implant	18, 259, 312
14.49	Buckling, scleral, other	151
*14.5	Repair, other, retinal detachment	18, 259, 313
14.54	Repair, with laser photocoagulation, retinal detachment	151
14.6	Removal, surgically implanted material, from posterior segment of eye	19, 151, 259, 313
*14.7	Operation, vitreous	19, 20, 259, 313
14.72	Removal, other, vitreous	151
14.74	Vitrectomy, mechanical, other	151
14.9	Operation, other, retina, choroid, and posterior chamber	18, 259, 313
*15	Operation, extraocular muscle	19
*15.0	Procedure, diagnostic, extraocular, muscles, tendons	313
*15.1	Operation, muscle, one extraocular	313
*15.2	Operation, other, extraocular muscle, one	313
15.3	Operations, other, involving temporary detachment from globe, extraocular muscle, two or more, one or both eyes	313
15.4	Operation, other, extraocular muscles, two or more, one or both eyes	313
15.5	Transposition, extraocular muscles	313
15.6	Revision, extraocular muscle, surgery	313
15.7	Repair, injury, extraocular muscle	259, 313
15.9	Operation, other, extraocular muscles, tendons	259, 313
*16.0	Orbitotomy	18, 260, 313
16.1	Removal, penetrating foreign body, from eye NOS	20, 260, 313
16.22	Aspiration, diagnostic, orbit	18, 313
16.23	Biopsy, eyeball and orbit	18, 313
16.29	Procedure, diagnostic, other, orbit and eyeball	18, 313
*16.3	Evisceration, eyeball	18, 260, 313
*16.4	Enucleation, eyeball	18, 260, 313
*16.5	Exenteration, orbital contents	18, 260, 313
16.51	Exenteration, orbit, with removal of adjacent structures	120
16.52	Exenteration, orbit, with therapeutic removal of orbital bone	30

Numeric Index to Procedures

Code	Narrative	Page
16.59	Exenteration, other, orbit	120
*16.6	Revision, secondary, after removal of eyeball	18, 260, 313
16.65	Graft, secondary, to exenteration cavity	30
16.66	Revision, other, exenteration cavity	30
*16.7	Removal, implant, ocular or orbital	18, 260, 313
*16.8	Repair, injury, eyeball and orbit	18, 260, 313
16.92	Excision, lesion, orbit	18, 260, 313
16.93	Excision, lesion, eye, unspecified structure	19, 139, 260, 313
16.98	Operation, other, orbit	18, 30, 260, 313
16.99	Operation, other, eyeball	19, 151, 260, 313
18.21	Excision, preauricular sinus	28, 139, 313
*18.3	Excision, other, external ear	28, 139
18.31	Excision, radical, lesion, external ear	313
18.39	Excision, other, external ear	260, 313
18.5	Correction, surgical, prominent ear	28, 138, 313
18.6	Reconstruction, external auditory canal	28, 138, 260, 313
*18.7	Repair, plastic, other, external ear	28, 260
18.71	Construction, auricle of ear	138, 313
18.72	Reattachment, amputated ear	313
18.79	Repair, other, external ear, plastic	138, 313
18.9	Operation, other, external ear	28, 139, 260, 313
*19	Repair, reconstructive, middle ear	28
*19.1	Stapedectomy	313
19.4	Myringoplasty	313
19.9	Repair, other, middle ear	313
20.01	Myringotomy, with insertion of tube	29, 313
*20.2	Incision, mastoid and middle ear	313
20.21	Incision, mastoid	27
20.22	Incision, petrous pyramid air cells	27
20.23	Incision, middle ear	28
20.32	Biopsy, middle ear and inner ear	28, 313
20.39	Procedure, diagnostic, other, middle and inner ear	28, 313
*20.4	Mastoidectomy	27
*20.5	Excision, other, middle ear	28
20.51	Excision, lesion, middle ear	313
*20.6	Fenestration, inner ear	28
*20.7	Incision, excision and destruction, inner ear	28
20.91	Tympanosympathectomy	28
20.92	Revision, mastoidectomy	28
20.93	Repair, oval and round windows	28
20.95	Implantation, electromagnetic hearing aid	28
20.96	Implantation, cochlear prosthetic device, unspecified	27
20.97	Implantation or replacement, cochlear prosthetic device, single-channel	27
20.98	Implantation or replacement, cochlear prosthetic device, multiple-channel	27
20.99	Operation, other, middle ear and inner ear	28
21.04	Control, epistaxis, by ligation, ethmoidal arteries	30, 53, 260
21.05	Control, epistaxis, by transantral ligation, maxillary artery	30, 53, 260
21.06	Control, epistaxis, by ligation, external carotid artery	30, 53, 260
21.07	Control, epistaxis, by excision, nasal mucosa and skin grafting, septum and lateral nasal wall	30, 53, 260
21.09	Control, epistaxis, by other means	30, 53, 260, 313
21.21	Rhinoscopy	242
21.4	Resection, nose	28, 139, 260
21.5	Resection, submucous, nasal septum	28, 260, 313
*21.6	Turbinectomy	28
21.62	Fracture, turbinates	260, 313
21.69	Turbinectomy, other	260, 313
21.72	Reduction, nasal fracture, open	28, 120, 139, 260, 313
21.82	Closure, nasal fistula	28, 313
21.83	Reconstruction, total, nasal	29, 120, 138, 260, 313
21.84	Rhinoplasty, revision	29, 120, 138, 260, 313
21.85	Rhinoplasty, augmentation	29, 120, 138, 260, 313
21.86	Rhinoplasty, limited	29, 120, 138, 260, 313
21.87	Rhinoplasty, other	29, 120, 138, 260, 313
21.88	Septoplasty, other	29, 120, 138, 260, 313
21.89	Repair and plastic operation, other, nose	28, 120, 138, 260, 313
21.99	Operation, other, nose	28, 138, 260, 313
22.12	Biopsy, nasal sinus, open	28
*22.3	Antrotomy, external maxillary	28

*** Code Range**

Code	Narrative	Page
*22.4	Sinusotomy and sinusectomy, frontal	28
*22.5	Sinusotomy, other, nasal	28
*22.6	Sinusectomy, other, nasal	28
22.62	Excision, lesion, maxillary sinus, with other approach	120
22.63	Ethmoidectomy	313
*22.7	Repair, nasal sinus	28
22.9	Operation, other, on nasal sinuses	28
*23	Extraction, restoration, tooth	38
24.2	Gingivoplasty	32, 260
24.4	Excision, lesion, dental, jaw	32, 313
24.5	Alveoloplasty	32, 260, 313
25.02	Biopsy, wedge, tongue, open	32
25.1	Excision or destruction, lesion or tissue, tongue	32, 53, 314
25.2	Glossectomy, partial	32
25.3	Glossectomy, complete	27
25.4	Glossectomy, radical	27
25.59	Repair, plastic operations, other, tongue	32, 260
25.94	Glossotomy, other	32
25.99	Operation, other, tongue	32
26.12	Biopsy, salivary gland or duct, open	27, 314
*26.2	Excision, lesion, salivary gland	27, 314
*26.3	Sialoadenectomy	27, 314
26.30	Sialoadenectomy, unspecified	233
*26.4	Repair, salivary gland or duct	27, 260
26.99	Operation, other, salivary gland or duct	27
27.0	Drainage, face and floor, mouth	32, 139, 260
27.1	Incision, palate	32
27.21	Biopsy, bony palate	32, 314
27.22	Biopsy, uvula and soft palate	32, 314
*27.3	Excision or destruction, lesion or tissue, bony palate	314
27.31	Excision or destruction, local, lesion or tissue, bony palate	32
27.32	Excision or destruction, wide, lesion or tissue, bony palate	27
27.42	Excision, wide, lesion, lip	32, 139, 314
27.43	Excision, other, lesion or tissue, lip	32, 139, 314
27.49	Excision, other, mouth	32, 260, 314
27.53	Closure, fistula, mouth	32, 260, 314
27.54	Repair, cleft lip	27, 139, 260, 314
27.55	Graft, full-thickness skin, lip and mouth	32, 138, 260, 314
27.56	Graft, other skin, lip and mouth	32, 138, 260, 314
27.57	Attachment, pedicle or flap graft, to lip and mouth	32, 139, 260, 314
27.59	Repair, other, plastic, mouth	32, 139, 260, 314
27.61	Suture, laceration, palate	32, 260
27.62	Correction, cleft palate	3, 27
27.63	Revision, cleft palate repair	27, 139
27.69	Repair, plastic, other, palate	3, 27, 138
*27.7	Operation, uvula	32, 314
27.92	Incision, mouth, unspecified structure	32, 139, 260, 314
27.99	Operation, other, oral cavity	32, 260, 314
28.0	Incision and drainage, tonsil and peritonsillar structures	29
*28.1	Procedure, diagnostic, tonsils and adenoids	29
28.11	Biopsy, tonsils, adenoids	314
28.2	Tonsillectomy, without adenoidectomy	29, 314
28.3	Tonsillectomy, with adenoidectomy	29
28.4	Excision, tonsil tag	29
28.5	Excision, lingual tonsil	29
28.6	Adenoidectomy, without tonsillectomy	29
28.7	Control, hemorrhage, after tonsillectomy, adenoidectomy	29, 260
*28.9	Operations, tonsils and adenoids	29
28.91	Removal, foreign body, from tonsil or adenoid, by incision	260
29.0	Pharyngotomy	30, 260
29.11	Pharyngoscopy	242
29.2	Excision, branchial cleft cyst, vestige	30, 139
*29.3	Excision or destruction, lesion, tissue, pharynx	30, 93
29.4	Operation, plastic, pharynx	3, 30, 260, 314
*29.5	Repair, other, pharynx	30, 62
29.51	Suture, laceration, pharynx	260
29.52	Closure, fistula, branchial cleft	139
29.53	Closure, fistula, pharynx, other	260
29.59	Repair, other, pharynx	3, 260
29.92	Division, nerve, glossopharyngeal	1, 2, 7, 30
29.99	Operation, other, pharynx	30, 260
*30.0	Excision or destruction, lesion or tissue, larynx	28
30.01	Marsupialization, cyst, laryngeal	40
30.09	Excision or destruction, lesion or tissue, larynx	40, 314
30.1	Hemilaryngectomy	27, 40, 260
*30.2	Laryngectomy, other, partial	40, 260
30.21	Epiglottidectomy	30
30.22	Cordectomy, vocal	28
30.29	Laryngectomy, other, partial	27
30.3	Laryngectomy, complete	321

Code	Narrative	Page
30.4	Laryngectomy, radical	321
31.1	Tracheostomy, temporary	321, 323, 324
31.21	Tracheostomy, mediastinal	321, 323, 324
31.29	Tracheostomy, permanent, other	321, 323, 324
31.3	Incision, other, larynx, trachea	28, 40
31.41	Tracheoscopy, through tracheostomy	242
31.42	Laryngoscopy, other tracheoscopy	243
31.43	Biopsy, closed, endoscopic, larynx	243
31.44	Biopsy, closed, endoscopic, trachea	243
31.45	Biopsy, open, larynx or trachea	28, 40
31.5	Excision or destruction, local, lesion, tissue, trachea	28, 40
*31.6	Repair, larynx	28, 40
31.61	Suture, laceration, larynx	260
31.64	Repair, larynx fracture	260
31.69	Repair, other, larynx	261
*31.7	Repair, plastic operations, trachea	30, 261
31.71	Suture, trachea laceration	40
31.72	Closure, tracheostomy	40, 53, 139
31.73	Closure, other fistula, trachea	39, 93
31.74	Revision, tracheostomy	40, 53, 139
31.75	Reconstruction, trachea, construction, artificial larynx	39
31.79	Repair and plastic operation, other, trachea	39
31.91	Division, nerve, laryngeal	28, 40
31.92	Lysis, adhesions, trachea, larynx	30, 40, 261
31.98	Operation, other, larynx	28, 40, 314
31.99	Operation, other, trachea	30, 40, 261
32.01	Excision or destruction, lesion, endoscopic, bronchus	243
32.09	Destruction, lesion, bronchus, other	39
32.1	Excision, bronchus	39, 261
32.21	Plication, bleb, emphysematous	39
32.22	Surgery, lung volume reduction	39
32.28	Excision or destruction, lesion, endoscopic, lung	243
32.29	Excision, lesion, lung	39, 238
32.3	Resection, segmental, lung	39, 261
32.4	Lobectomy, lung	39, 261
32.5	Pneumonectomy, complete	39, 261
32.6	Dissection, radical, thoracic structure	39
32.9	Excision, lung, other	39, 261
33.0	Incision, bronchus	39, 261
33.1	Incision, lung	39, 261
33.21	Bronchoscopy, through artificial stoma	243
33.22	Bronchoscopy, fiberoptic	243
33.23	Bronchoscopy, other	243
33.24	Biopsy, closed, endoscopic, bronchus	243
33.25	Biopsy, open, bronchus	39
33.27	Biopsy, closed endoscopic, lung	40, 53, 314
33.28	Biopsy, open, lung	39, 53, 120, 160, 238
33.29	Procedure, diagnostic, other, lung, bronchus	40
33.34	Thoracoplasty	39
33.39	Collapse, surgical, unspecified, lung	39
*33.4	Repair and plastic operation, lung, bronchus	39, 261
*33.5	Transplantation, lung	321
33.6	Transplantation, combined heart-lung	317
33.92	Ligation, bronchus	39, 261
33.93	Puncture, lung	40
33.98	Operation, other, bronchus	39, 261
33.99	Operation, other, lung	39, 261
34.02	Thoracotomy, exploratory	39, 53, 160, 238, 261
34.03	Reopening, thoracotomy site, recent	39, 53, 261
34.1	Incision, mediastinum	40, 53, 261
34.21	Thoracoscopy, transpleural	40, 53, 261
34.22	Mediastinoscopy	30, 40, 53, 233, 238
34.26	Biopsy, mediastinum, open	40, 53, 151, 233, 238
34.27	Biopsy, diaphragm	39
34.28	Procedure, diagnostic, other, chest wall, pleura, diaphragm	40
34.29	Procedure, diagnostic, other, mediastinum	40, 53
34.3	Excision or destruction, lesion or tissue, mediastinum	39, 151, 238, 314
34.4	Excision or destruction, lesion, chest wall	40, 125, 139, 151, 238, 314
*34.5	Pleurectomy	39, 261
34.51	Decortication, lung	238
34.6	Scarification, pleura	39, 238, 261
34.73	Closure, other fistula, thorax	39, 261
34.74	Repair, pectus deformity	39, 120
34.79	Repair, other, chest wall	40, 120, 139, 261
*34.8	Operation, diaphragm	39
34.81	Excision, lesion, tissue, diaphragm	120
34.82	Suture, laceration, diaphragm	261
34.83	Closure, fistula, diaphragm	261
34.84	Repair, other, diaphragm	261
34.85	Implantation, diaphragmatic pacemaker	261

*** Code Range**

Code	Narrative	Page
34.89	Operation, other, diaphragm	261
34.93	Repair, pleura	39, 261
34.99	Operation, other, thorax	40, 261
*35.0	Valvotomy, closed, heart	50
*35.1	Valvuloplasty, open, heart,	49
*35.2	Replacement, heart, valve	49
35.31	Operation, papillary muscle	49
35.32	Operation, chordae tendineae	49
35.33	Annuloplasty	49
35.34	Infundibulectomy	50
35.35	Operation, trabeculae carneae cordis	50
35.39	Operation, structures adjacent to heart valves, other	50
35.42	Creation, septal defect, heart	50
35.50	Repair of unspecified septal defect of heart with prosthesis	50
35.51	Repair of atrial septal defect with prosthesis, open technique	50
35.52	Repair of atrial septal defect with prosthesis, closed technique	56
35.53	Repair of ventricular septal defect with prosthesis	50
35.54	Repair of endocardial cushion defect with prosthesis	50
*35.6	Repair, septa, atrial and ventricular	50
*35.7	Repair, septa, atrial, ventricular, unspecified	50
*35.8	Repair, total, certain congenital cardiac anomalies	50
35.91	Transposition, interatrial, venous return	50
35.92	Creation, conduit, between right ventricle and pulmonary artery	50
35.93	Creation, conduit, between left ventricle and aorta	50
35.94	Creation, conduit, between atrium and pulmonary artery	50
35.95	Revision, corrective procedure, heart	50
35.96	Valvuloplasty, percutaneous	49, 56, 78, 80, 81
35.98	Operation, other, septa of heart	50
35.99	Operation, other, valves of heart	50
36.03	Angioplasty, coronary, chest, open	50
36.06	Insertion, coronary artery stent(s), nondrug-eluting	78
36.07	Insertion, coronary artery stents(s), drug-eluting	80, 81
36.09	Removal, obstruction, coronary artery, other specified	56, 78, 80, 81
*36.1	Bypass, aortocoronary	49, 60, 63
36.2	Revascularization, heart, by arterial implant	50
*36.3	Revascularization, other, heart	50
*36.9	Operation, other, vessels, heart	50
37.10	Incision, heart, unspecified	50
37.11	Cardiotomy	50, 261
37.12	Pericardiotomy	39, 50, 238, 261
37.21	Catheterization, cardiac, right heart	49, 58, 60, 85
37.22	Catheterization, cardiac, left heart	49, 58, 60, 85
37.23	Catheterization, cardiac, combined right and left heart	49, 58, 60, 85
37.24	Biopsy, pericardium	39, 50, 238
37.26	Stimulator, cardiac, electrophysiologic	49, 55, 58, 78, 80, 81
37.27	Mapping, cardiac	56, 78, 80, 81
37.31	Pericardiectomy	39, 50, 238, 261
37.32	Excision, heart, aneurysm	50
37.33	Excision or destruction, open approach, other lesion or tissue, heart	50
37.34	Excision or destruction, other approach, other lesion or tissue, heart	56, 78, 80, 81
37.35	Ventriculotomy, partial	50
*37.4	Repair, heart and pericardium	50
37.49	Other repair of heart and pericardium	261
37.51	Replacement, heart	317
37.52	Implantation, total replacement heart system	56
37.53	Replacement or repair, thoracic unit of total replacement heart system	56
37.54	Replacement or repair, other implantable component of total replacement heart system	56
37.61	Implant, pulsation balloon	50
37.62	Insertion, heart assist system, non-implantable	56
37.63	Repair, heart assist system	56
37.64	Removal, heart-assist system	50, 317
37.65	Implant, heart assist system, external	56, 317
37.66	Insertion, heart assist system, implantable	317
37.67	Implantation, cardiomyostimulation system	50
37.68	Insertion, percutaneous, heart assist device, external	49
37.70	Insertion, initial pacemaker lead [electrode], other (must be in combination with 37.80, 37.81, 37.82, 37.85, 37.86 or 37.87)	4, 65, 69, 271
37.71	Insertion, initial, transvenous pacemaker lead [electrode], into ventricle (must be in combination with 37.80, 37.81, 37.82, 37.85, 37.86 or 37.87)	4, 66, 69, 70, 271
37.72	Insertion, initial, transvenous pacemaker lead [electrode], into atrium and ventricle (must be in combination with 37.80 or 37.83)	4, 66, 70, 271

Code	Narrative	Page
37.73	Insertion, initial, transvenous pacemaker lead [electrode], into atrium (must be in combination with 37.80, 37.81, 37.82, 37.85, 37.86 or 37.87)	4, 66, 67, 70, 71, 271
37.74	Insertion or replacement, epicardial pacemaker lead [electrode], into epicardium (must be in combination with 37.80, 37.81, 37.82, 37.83, 37.85, 37.86 or 37.87)	3, 5, 52, 67, 68, 71, 72, 261, 271
37.75	Revision, lead [electrode]	3, 52, 261
37.76	Replacement, transvenous atrial and/or ventricular pacemaker lead [electrode] (must be in combination with 37.80, 37.85, 37.86 or 37.87)	3, 5, 52, 68, 72, 261, 271
37.77	Removal, lead(s) [electrode] without replacement	3, 52, 261
37.79	Revision, relocation, pacemaker pocket	3, 52, 139, 261
37.80	Insertion, permanent pacemaker, initial or replacement, type device not specified	3, 52, 65, 66, 67, 68, 69, 70, 71, 72, 261
37.81	Insertion, single-chamber device, initial, not specified as rate-responsive	65, 66, 67, 69, 70, 71
37.82	Insertion, single-chamber device, initial, rate-responsive	65, 66, 67, 69, 70, 71
37.83	Insertion, dual-chamber device, initial	66, 67, 70, 71
37.85	Replacement, any type pacemaker, with single-chamber device, not specified as rate-responsive	3, 52, 65, 66, 67, 68, 69, 70, 71, 72, 261
37.86	Replacement, any type pacemaker, with single-chamber device, rate-responsive	3, 52, 65, 66, 67, 68, 69, 70, 71, 72, 261
37.87	Replacement, any type pacemaker device, with dual-chamber device	3, 52, 65, 66, 67, 68, 69, 70, 71, 72, 261
37.89	Revision, removal, pacemaker device	3, 52, 261, 314
37.90	Insertion, device, left atrial appendage	56
37.91	Massage, cardiac, open chest	39, 50, 238, 261
37.94	Implantation, cardioverter/defibrillator, automatic	55, 57
37.95	Implantation, cardioverter/defibrillator, lead(s), only	55, 57, 68
37.96	Implantation, cardioverter/defibrillator, pulse generator	55, 57, 68
37.97	Replacement, cardioverter/defibrillator, lead(s)	55, 57, 58, 68
37.98	Replacement, cardioverter/defibrillator, pulse generator	55, 58, 68
37.99	Operation, other, heart, pericardium	50
*38.0	Incision, vessel	261
38.00	Incision, vessel, unspecified site	30, 54, 74, 75, 151, 314
38.01	Incision, intracranial vessels	1, 2, 5, 7
38.02	Incision, vessel, head, neck	3, 30, 54, 74, 75, 151
38.03	Incision, vessel, upper limb	54, 74, 75, 151
38.04	Incision, vessel, aorta	50, 97
38.05	Incision, vessel, other thoracic	39, 50, 93
38.06	Incision, vessel, abdominal arteries	50, 97, 160
38.07	Incision, vessel, abdominal veins	50, 97, 160
38.08	Incision, vessel, lower limb arteries	54, 74, 75, 151, 238
38.09	Incision, vessel, lower limb veins	52, 314
38.10	Endarterectomy, unspecified site	6, 54, 74, 75, 261
38.11	Endarterectomy, intracranial vessels	1, 2, 5, 7
38.12	Endarterectomy, other, vessels, head, neck	6, 30, 54, 74, 75, 151, 261
38.13	Endarterectomy, upper limb vessels	54, 74, 75, 151, 261
38.14	Endarterectomy, aorta	50, 97, 261
38.15	Endarterectomy, other thoracic vessels	39, 50, 261
38.16	Endarterectomy, abdominal arteries	50, 97, 160, 261
38.18	Endarterectomy, lower limbs arteries	54, 74, 75, 151, 261
38.21	Biopsy, blood vessel	3, 19, 30, 40, 54, 74, 75, 120, 151, 160, 314
38.29	Procedure, diagnostic, other, blood vessels	54, 74, 75, 151
*38.3	Phlebectomy, with anastomosis	261
38.30	Phlebectomy, with anastomosis, unspecified site	54, 74, 75, 151
38.31	Phlebectomy, with anastomosis, intracranial vessels	1, 2, 5, 7
38.32	Phlebectomy, with anastomosis, other vessels, head, neck	6, 30, 54, 74, 75
38.33	Phlebectomy, with anastomosis, upper limb vessels	54, 74, 75, 151
38.34	Phlebectomy, with anastomosis, aorta	50, 97
38.35	Phlebectomy, with anastomosis, other thoracic vessels	39, 50, 93
38.36	Phlebectomy, with anastomosis, abdominal arteries	51, 97, 160
38.37	Phlebectomy, with anastomosis, abdominal veins	51, 97, 160
38.38	Phlebectomy, with anastomosis, lower limb arteries	54, 74, 75, 151
38.39	Phlebectomy, with anastomosis, lower limb veins	52

*Code Range

Code	Narrative	Page
*38.4	Phlebectomy, with graft replacement	261
38.40	Phlebectomy, with graft replacement, unspecified site	54, 74, 75
38.41	Phlebectomy, with graft replacement, intracranial vessels	1, 2, 5, 7
38.42	Phlebectomy, with graft replacement, other, vessels, head, neck	3, 30, 54, 74, 75
38.43	Phlebectomy, with graft replacement, upper limb vessels	54, 74, 75, 151
38.44	Resection, aorta, abdominal, with graft replacement	50, 51
38.45	Resection, thoracic vessel, with graft replacement	39, 50, 51, 93
38.46	Phlebectomy, with graft replacement, abdominal arteries	51, 97, 160
38.47	Phlebectomy, with graft replacement, abdominal veins	51, 97, 160
38.48	Phlebectomy, with graft replacement, lower limb arteries	54, 74, 75, 151
38.49	Phlebectomy, with graft replacement, lower limb veins	52
38.50	Ligation and stripping, varicose veins, unspecified site	52
38.51	Ligation and stripping, varicose veins, intracranial vessel	1, 2, 5, 7
38.52	Ligation and stripping, varicose veins, other vessels, head, neck	54, 74, 75
38.53	Ligation and stripping, varicose veins, upper limb vessels	52
38.55	Ligation and stripping, varicose veins, other thoracic vessels	39, 51, 151
38.57	Ligation and stripping, varicose veins, abdominal veins	54, 74, 75, 97
38.59	Ligation and stripping, varicose veins, lower limb veins	52, 314
*38.6	Excision, lesion, other vessels	261
38.60	Excision, lesion, other vessels, unspecified site	54, 74, 75, 151
38.61	Excision, lesion, other, intracranial vessels	1, 2, 5, 7
38.62	Excision, lesion, other, vessels, head, neck	6, 30, 54, 74, 75
38.63	Excision, lesion, other, upper limb vessels	54, 75, 151
38.64	Excision, lesion, other, vessels, aorta	51, 97
38.65	Excision, lesion, other, thoracic vessels	39, 51, 93
38.66	Excision, lesion, other, abdominal arteries	51, 97, 160
38.67	Excision, other, lesion, abdominal veins	51, 97, 160
38.68	Excision, other, lesion, lower limb arteries	54, 75, 151
38.69	Excision, other, lesion, lower limb veins	52
38.7	Interruption, vena cava	3, 40, 54, 75, 97, 108, 120, 151, 160, 169, 180, 193, 233, 261
*38.8	Ligation, division, other, vessels	261
38.80	Ligation, division, other, vessels, unspecified site	54, 75
38.81	Ligation, division, other, intracranial vessels	1, 2, 5, 7, 290
38.82	Ligation, division, other, other vessels, head, neck	3, 30, 54, 75
38.83	Ligation, division, other, upper limb vessels	54, 75, 151
38.84	Ligation, division, other, vessels, aorta	51, 97
38.85	Ligation, division, other thoracic vessels	39, 51, 93
38.86	Ligation, division, other, abdominal arteries	51, 97, 160, 314
38.87	Ligation, division, other, abdominal veins	51, 97, 160
38.88	Ligation, division, other, lower limb arteries	54, 75, 151
38.89	Ligation, division, other, lower limb veins	52
39.0	Shunt, systemic to pulmonary artery	51
39.1	Anastomosis, venous, intraabdominal	51, 94, 106
39.21	Anastomosis, cavalpulmonary artery	51
39.22	Bypass, vascular, aorto-subclavian-carotid	6, 51, 261
39.23	Bypass, vascular, intrathoracic	51, 261
39.24	Bypass, vascular, renal artery	51, 157, 261
39.25	Bypass, vascular, aorto-iliac-femoral	51, 139, 151, 261
39.26	Bypass, vascular, intraabdominal	51, 97, 108, 157, 262
39.27	Arteriovenostomy, for renal dialysis	53, 97, 151, 160, 262
39.28	Bypass, vascular, extracranial-intracranial (EC-IC)	1, 2, 5, 7, 262
39.29	Bypass, vascular, peripheral artery	6, 40, 54, 75, 108, 139, 151, 262
*39.3	Suture, blood vessel	6, 262
39.30	Suture, blood vessel, unspecified	54, 75
39.31	Suture, artery	40, 54, 75, 76, 139, 151
39.32	Suture, vein	52
*39.4	Revision, vascular procedure	262

Numeric Index to Procedures

Code	Narrative	Page
39.41	Control, hemorrhage, postvascular surgery	54, 75, 76, 151
39.42	Revision, arteriovenous shunt for renal dialysis	53, 151, 160
39.43	Removal, arteriovenous shunt for renal dialysis	53, 160
39.49	Revision, other, vascular procedure	54, 75, 76, 97, 108, 151, 160
39.50	Angioplasty or atherectomy, noncoronary vessel(s), other	6, 40, 55, 75, 76, 97, 108, 120, 139, 151, 160, 262
39.51	Clipping, aneurysm	1, 2, 5, 7, 55, 75, 76
39.52	Repair, other, aneurysm	1, 2, 5, 7, 51, 160, 262
39.53	Repair, fistula, arteriovenous	1, 2, 5, 7, 55, 75, 76
39.54	Operation, reentry, aorta	39, 51
39.55	Reimplantation, renal vessel, aberrant	55, 75, 76, 157
39.56	Repair, blood vessel, patch graft tissue	6, 55, 75, 76, 151, 160, 262
39.57	Repair, blood vessel, patch graft synthetic	6, 55, 75, 76, 151, 160, 262
39.58	Repair, blood vessel, patch graft, unspecified type	6, 55, 75, 76, 151, 160, 262
39.59	Repair, other, blood vessel	6, 55, 75, 76, 139, 151, 160, 262
39.65	Extracorporeal membrane oxygenation [ECMO]	323
39.71	Repair, endovascular graft implantation, aneurysm, abdominal aorta	51, 160, 262
39.72	Repair or occlusion, endovascular, head and neck vessels	1, 2, 5, 7, 51, 160, 262
39.73	Endovascular implantation of graft in thoracic aorta	51, 160, 262
39.79	Repair, endovascular, other (of aneurysm), other vessels	1, 2, 5, 7, 51, 160, 262
39.8	Operation, carotid body, other vascular bodies	6, 40, 55, 75, 76
39.91	Freeing, vessel	55, 75, 76, 97, 151, 262
39.92	Injection, sclerosing agent into vein	6, 52
39.93	Insertion, cannula, vessel-to-vessel	53, 151, 160, 262
39.94	Replacement, cannula, vessel-to-vessel	55, 75, 76, 160, 314
39.98	Control, hemorrhage, unspecified	30, 40, 53, 97, 108, 120, 139, 151, 160, 169, 180, 193, 238, 262
39.99	Operation, other, vessels	30, 40, 55, 75, 76, 97, 193, 238, 262
40.0	Incision, lymphatic structures	139, 233, 314
*40.1	Procedure, diagnostic, lymphatic structure	30, 53, 97, 120, 139, 151, 169, 233, 314
40.11	Biopsy, lymphatic structure	3, 40, 108, 160, 180
40.19	Procedure, diagnostic, other, lymphatic structures	40, 160
*40.2	Excision, simple, lymphatic structures	139, 233
40.21	Excision, lymph node, cervical, deep	30, 40, 53, 97, 120, 151, 314
40.22	Excision, lymph node, internal mammary	40
40.23	Excision, lymph node, axillary	30, 40, 53, 97, 120, 314
40.24	Excision, lymph node, inguinal	40, 53, 97, 120, 160, 169, 180, 193, 314
40.29	Excision, other lymphatic structure, simple	30, 40, 53, 97, 120, 151, 160, 169, 180, 262, 314
40.3	Excision, lymph node, regional	30, 40, 53, 97, 120, 139, 151, 160, 169, 180, 193, 233, 238, 314
*40.4	Excision, lymph nodes, cervical, radical	40, 139, 151, 233, 238
40.40	Dissection, neck, radical, unspecified	27
40.41	Dissection, neck, radical, unilateral	27
40.42	Dissection, neck, radical, bilateral	27
*40.5	Excision, lymph node, radical, other	97, 139, 233, 238
40.50	Excision, lymph node, radical, unspecified	27, 40, 160, 169, 174
40.51	Excision, lymph node, axillary, radical	120

** Code Range*

Code	Narrative	Page
40.52	Excision, lymph node, periaortic, radical	40, 120, 151, 157, 167, 174
40.53	Excision, lymph node, iliac, radical	120, 151, 157, 167, 174
40.54	Dissection, groin, radical	120, 157, 167, 174
40.59	Excision, other lymph nodes, radical	27, 40, 120, 157, 167, 174
*40.6	Operation, thoracic duct	40, 262
40.9	Operation, lymphatic structures, other	30, 97, 139, 160, 169, 233, 238, 262
41.00	Transplantation, NOS, bone marrow	318
41.01	Transplantation, autologous, without purging, bone marrow	318
41.02	Transplantation, allogeneic, with purging, bone marrow	318
41.03	Transplantation, allogeneic, without purging, bone marrow	318
41.04	Transplantation, autologous, without purging, hematopoietic stem cell	318
41.05	Transplantation, allogeneic, without purging, hematopoietic stem cell	318
41.06	Transplantation, stem cell, cord blood	318
41.07	Transplantation, autologous, with purging, hematopoietic stem cell	318
41.08	Transplantation, allogeneic, with purging, hematopoietic stem cell	318
41.09	Transplantation, autologous, with purging, bone marrow	318
41.2	Splenotomy	233, 238, 262
41.33	Biopsy, spleen, open	233, 238
*41.4	Excision or destruction, lesion or tissue, spleen	233, 238
41.42	Excision, lesion or tissue, spleen	262
41.43	Splenectomy, partial	120, 262
41.5	Splenectomy, total	53, 97, 120, 233, 238, 262
41.93	Excision, spleen, accessory	233, 238, 262
41.94	Transplantation, spleen	233, 238
41.95	Repair and plastic operation, spleen	233, 238, 262
41.99	Operation, other, spleen	233, 238, 262
*42.0	Incision, esophagus	30
42.01	Incision, esophageal web	94
42.09	Incision, esophagus	94, 262
*42.1	Esophagostomy	31, 94, 238, 262
42.21	Esophagoscopy, by incision, operative	31, 94, 238, 262
42.22	Esophagoscopy, through stoma, artificial	243
42.23	Esophagoscopy, other	243
42.24	Biopsy, esophagus, closed, endoscopic	243
42.25	Biopsy, esophagus, open	31, 94, 239
42.31	Excision or destruction, local, other lesion, tissue, esophagus	31, 94
42.32	Excision, local, esophagus	31, 94, 239
42.33	Excision or destruction, lesion, endoscopic, esophagus	243
42.39	Destruction, lesion, esophagus	31, 94, 239
*42.4	Excision, esophagus	31, 94, 239, 262
*42.5	Anastomosis, esophagus, intrathoracic	31, 94, 239, 262
*42.6	Anastomosis, antesternal, esophagus	31, 94, 239, 262
42.7	Esophagomyotomy	31, 94, 239, 262
42.82	Suture, laceration, esophagus	31, 94, 239, 262
42.83	Closure, esophagostomy	31, 94, 239, 262
42.84	Repair, fistula, esophageal, other	31, 94, 239, 262
42.85	Repair, esophageal stricture	94, 239, 262
42.86	Formation, subcutaneous tunnel, without esophageal anastomosis	31, 94, 239, 262
42.87	Graft, esophagus, other	31, 94, 239, 262
42.89	Repair, esophagus, other	31, 94, 239, 262
42.91	Ligation, esophageal varices	94, 108
43.0	Gastrotomy	94, 108, 151, 239, 262
43.3	Pyloromyotomy	94
43.41	Excision or destruction, lesion, endoscopic, stomach	243
43.42	Excision, local, other lesion or tissue, stomach	94, 108, 151
43.49	Destruction, other, lesion or tissue, stomach	94, 314
43.5	Gastrectomy, partial, with anastomosis to esophagus	94, 239, 262
43.6	Gastrectomy, partial, with anastomosis to duodenum	53, 94, 239, 262
43.7	Gastrectomy, partial, with anastomosis to jejunum	53, 94, 152, 239, 262
*43.8	Gastrectomy, partial, other	94, 239, 262
43.89	Gastrectomy, partial, other	53
*43.9	Gastrectomy, total	94, 239, 262

* Code Range

Code	Narrative	Page
43.99	Gastrectomy, total	53
*44.0	Vagotomy	94
44.00	Vagotomy, NOS	3
44.11	Gastroscopy, transabdominal	94, 108, 239, 262
44.12	Gastroscopy, through stoma, artificial	243
44.13	Gastroscopy, other	243
44.14	Biopsy, closed, endoscopic, gastric	243
44.15	Biopsy, open, stomach	94, 314
44.21	Dilation, pylorus, by incision	94
44.29	Pyloroplasty, other	94
*44.3	Gastroenterostomy, without gastrectomy	94, 150, 239
44.32	Gastrojejunostomy, percutaneous (endoscopic)	108
44.38	Gastroenterostomy, laparoscopic	53, 108
44.39	Gastroenterostomy	108
44.40	Suture, ulcer, peptic	94
44.41	Suture, ulcer, gastric	94
44.42	Suture, ulcer, duodenal	94
44.5	Revision, gastric anastomosis	94, 150, 262
44.61	Suture, laceration, stomach	94, 262
44.63	Closure, fistula, other, gastric	94, 108, 239, 262
44.64	Gastropexy	94, 262
44.65	Esophagogastroplasty	94, 262
44.66	Repair, for creation of esophagogastric sphincteric competence, stomach	94, 262
44.67	Creation, laparoscopic, esophagogastric sphincteric competence	94, 262, 314
44.68	Gastroplasty, laparoscopic	94, 150, 262, 314
44.69	Repair, other, stomach	94, 150, 262
44.91	Ligation, gastric, varices	94, 108
44.92	Manipulation, intraoperative, stomach	94, 108, 152, 262
44.95	Procedure, gastric restrictive, laparoscopic	150, 314
44.96	Revision, gastric restrictive procedure, laparoscopic	150, 314
44.97	Removal, gastric restrictive device(s), laparoscopic	150, 314
44.98	Adjustment, size of adjustable gastric restrictive device, laparoscopic	150, 314
44.99	Operation, stomach, other	94, 150, 262
*45.0	Enterotomy	263
45.00	Incision, intestine, NOS	93
45.01	Incision, duodenum	94, 108
45.02	Incision, intestine, small	93, 239
45.03	Incision, intestine, large	93, 239
45.11	Endoscopy, intestine, small, transabdominal	93, 239, 263, 314
45.12	Endoscopy, intestine, small, through stoma, artificial	243
45.13	Endoscopy, intestine, small, other	243
45.14	Biopsy, closed, small bowel	243
45.15	Biopsy, intestine, small, open	93
45.16	Esophagogastroduodenoscopy, with closed biopsy	243
45.21	Endoscopy, transabdominal, intestine, large	93, 263, 314
45.22	Endoscopy, intestine, large, through stoma, artificial	243
45.23	Colonoscopy, fiberoptic, flexible	243
45.24	Sigmoidoscopy, flexible	243
45.25	Biopsy, closed, large bowel	243
45.26	Biopsy, intestine, large, open	93, 314
45.30	Excision or destruction, lesion, endoscopic, duodenum	243
45.31	Excision, local, other, lesion, duodenum	94, 108, 239, 314
45.32	Destruction, other, lesion, duodenum	94, 108, 239, 314
45.33	Excision, local, lesion or tissue, small intestine except duodenum	95, 239, 314
45.34	Destruction, other, lesion, small intestine except duodenum	93, 239, 314
45.41	Excision, lesion or tissue, large intestine	95, 152, 239, 314
45.42	Polypectomy, endoscopic, large intestine	243
45.43	Destruction, endoscopic, other lesion, large intestine	243
45.49	Destruction, other, lesion, large intestine	93, 239, 314
*45.5	Isolation, intestinal segment	92
45.50	Isolation, intestinal segment, unspecified	239
*45.6	Excision, intestine, small	92
45.61	Resection, intestine, small, multiple segmental	53, 239, 263
45.62	Resection, intestine, small, other partial	53, 152, 239, 263
45.63	Resection, intestine, small, total	239, 263
*45.7	Excision, intestine, large, partial	92, 263
45.71	Resection, intestine, large, multiple segmental	239
45.72	Cecectomy	53
45.73	Hemicolectomy, right	53, 239
45.74	Resection, transverse colon	53, 239
45.75	Hemicolectomy, left	53, 152, 239
45.76	Sigmoidectomy	239
45.79	Excision, intestine, large, other partial	53, 239
45.8	Colectomy, total, intraabdominal	53, 92, 239, 263
*45.9	Anastomosis, intestinal	92, 263

* Code Range

Code	Narrative	Page
45.90	Anastomosis, intestinal, unspecified	150, 239
45.91	Anastomosis, intestine, small-to-small	150, 239
45.92	Anastomosis, intestine, small-to-rectal stump	239
45.93	Anastomosis, intestine, small-to-large, other	53, 152, 239
45.94	Anastomosis, intestine, large-to-large	152, 239
45.95	Anastomosis, intestine, large-to-anus	239
*46.0	Exteriorization, intestine	92, 239, 263
46.03	Exteriorization, intestine, large	53
46.10	Colostomy, unspecified	92, 239, 263
46.11	Colostomy, temporary	92, 239, 263
46.13	Colostomy, other, permanent	53, 92, 239, 263
46.20	Ileostomy, unspecified	92, 239, 263
46.21	Ileostomy, temporary	92, 239, 263
46.22	Ileostomy, continent	92, 239, 263
46.23	Ileostomy, other, permanent	92, 239, 263
*46.4	Revision, stoma, intestinal	95, 263
46.40	Revision, stoma, intestinal	239
46.41	Revision, stoma, small intestine	239, 314
46.43	Revision, stoma, large intestine	314
*46.5	Closure, stoma, intestinal	93, 263
46.52	Closure, stoma, large intestine	314
*46.6	Fixation, intestine	93
*46.7	Repair, other, intestine	263
46.71	Suture, laceration, duodenum	94
46.72	Closure, fistula, duodenum	94
46.73	Suture, laceration, small intestine except duodenum	92
46.74	Closure, fistula, small intestine except duodenum	92
46.75	Suture, laceration, large intestine	92
46.76	Closure, fistula, large intestine	92
46.79	Repair, intestine, other	92
*46.8	Manipulation, intestine, intraabdominal	263
46.80	Manipulation, bowel, intrabdominal	92, 108, 239
46.81	Manipulation, small bowel, intraabdominal	92, 108, 239
46.82	Manipulation, large bowel, intraabdominal	92, 108, 239
46.91	Myotomy, colon, sigmoid	92
46.92	Myotomy, colon, other parts	92
46.93	Revision, anastomosis, intestine, small	92, 263
46.94	Revision, anastomosis, intestine, large	92, 263
46.97	Transplantation, intestine	108, 239, 263, 317
46.99	Operation, other, intestines	92, 108, 240, 263
*47.0	Appendectomy	96
47.09	Appendectomy, other	53
*47.1	Appendectomy, incidental	180, 263
47.2	Drainage, abscess, appendix	96
47.91	Appendicostomy	93
47.92	Closure, fistula, appendix	92, 263
47.99	Operation, appendix, other	96
48.0	Proctotomy	93, 263
48.1	Proctostomy	92, 263
48.21	Proctosigmoidoscopy, transabdominal	93, 263
48.22	Proctosigmoidoscopy, through stoma, artificial	243
48.23	Proctosigmoidoscopy, other	243
48.24	Biopsy, rectal, closed, endoscopic	243
48.25	Biopsy, open, rectum	53, 93, 314
48.35	Excision, local, rectal lesion, tissue	53, 95, 139, 315
48.36	Polypectomy (endoscopic), rectum	243
*48.4	Resection, rectum, pull-through	92, 240
48.49	Resection, rectum, pull-through, other	263
48.5	Resection, rectum, abdominoperineal	92, 240, 263
*48.6	Resection, rectum, other	92, 240, 263
48.62	Resection, rectum, anterior with synchronous colostomy	53
48.63	Resection, rectum, anterior, other	53
48.69	Resection, rectum, other	53, 167
*48.7	Repair, rectum	263
48.71	Suture, laceration, rectum	92, 197
48.72	Closure, proctostomy	92
48.73	Closure, fistula, rectal	95, 139, 178
48.74	Rectorectostomy	92
48.75	Proctopexy, abdominal	92
48.76	Proctopexy, other	93
48.79	Repair, rectum, other	95, 193
*48.8	Incision or excision, tissue or lesion, perirectal	95, 139, 263, 315
*48.9	Operation, rectum and perirectal tissue, other	95
48.91	Incision, rectal stricture	263
49.01	Incision, abscess, perianal	95, 138
49.02	Incision, other, perianal tissue	95, 138
49.04	Excision, other, perianal tissue	95, 138
*49.1	Fistulotomy, fistulectomy, anal	95, 263, 315
49.11	Fistulotomy, anal	138

Code	Narrative	Page
49.12	Fistulectomy, anal	139
49.21	Anoscopy	243
49.31	Excision or destruction, lesion, endoscopic, anus	243
49.39	Excision or destruction, other local lesion, anus	95, 138, 315
49.44	Destruction, hemorrhoids by cryotherapy	95, 315
49.45	Ligation, hemorrhoids	95, 315
49.46	Excision, hemorrhoids	95, 193, 315
49.49	Procedure, hemorrhoids, other	95, 315
*49.5	Division, sphincter, anal	95, 315
49.59	Sphincterotomy, anal, other	197
49.6	Excision, anus	95, 315
49.71	Suture, laceration, anus	95, 139, 263
49.72	Cerclage, anal	95, 140
49.73	Closure, fistula, anal	95, 140, 263
49.74	Transplantation, gracilis muscle, for anal incontinence	97
49.75	Implantation or revision, anal sphincter, artificial	92, 138, 263
49.76	Removal, anal sphincter, artificial	92, 138, 263
49.79	Repair, sphincter, anal, other	95, 138, 263, 315
*49.9	Incision, anal, other	95
49.95	Control, postoperative, hemorrhage, anus	263
49.99	Operation, anus, other	263
50.0	Hepatotomy	106, 263
50.12	Biopsy, open, liver	31, 40, 53, 97, 108, 120, 140, 152, 160, 169, 180, 233, 240, 263
50.19	Procedure, diagnostic, other, liver	97, 108, 140, 160, 233, 240, 263
50.21	Marsupialization, lesion, liver	106
50.22	Hepatectomy, partial	106, 263
50.29	Destruction, lesion, liver, other	97, 106
50.3	Lobectomy, liver	106, 263
50.4	Hepatectomy, total	106, 263
50.51	Transplant, auxiliary, liver	317
50.59	Transplant, other, liver	317
*50.6	Repair, liver	263
50.61	Closure, laceration, liver	106
50.69	Repair, liver, other	106
51.02	Cholecystostomy, trocar	106
51.03	Cholecystostomy, other	97, 106
51.04	Cholecystotomy, other	106
51.10	Cholangiopancreatography (ERCP), endoscopic retrograde	243
51.11	Cholangiography, retrograde, endoscopic (ERC)	243
51.13	Biopsy, open, gallbladder or bile duct	97, 108
51.14	Biopsy, other closed (endoscopic), biliary duct or sphincter of Oddi	243
51.19	Procedure, diagnostic, other, biliary tract	97, 108
*51.2	Cholecystectomy	107, 240, 263
51.21	Cholecystectomy, partial other	107
51.22	Cholecystectomy	97, 107
51.23	Cholecystectomy, laparoscopic	97, 109, 315
51.24	Cholecystectomy, laparoscopic, partial	109
*51.3	Anastomosis, gallbladder or bile duct	97, 106, 240, 263
51.41	Exploration, common bile duct for removal of calculus	107
51.42	Exploration, common bile duct for relief of other obstruction	107, 240, 263
51.43	Insertion, choledochohepatic tube for decompression	106, 240, 263
51.49	Incision, other bile ducts for relief of obstruction	106, 240
51.51	Exploration, common duct	107
51.59	Incision, bile duct, other	97, 106, 240, 263
51.61	Excision, remnant, cystic duct	106, 263
51.62	Excision, ampulla of Vater, with reimplantation of common duct	97, 106
51.63	Excision, common duct, other	97, 106
51.64	Excision or destruction, lesion, endoscopic, biliary ducts or sphincter of Oddi	243
51.69	Excision, bile duct, other	97, 106
*51.7	Repair, bile ducts, other	106, 263
51.81	Dilation, sphincter of Oddi	97, 106, 263
51.82	Sphincterotomy, pancreatic	94, 106, 263
51.83	Sphincteroplasty, pancreatic	94, 106, 263
51.84	Dilation, endoscopic, ampulla and biliary duct	243
51.85	Sphincterotomy and papillotomy, endoscopic	243
51.86	Insertion, endoscopic, nasobiliary drainage tube	243
51.87	Insertion, endoscopic, stent (tube) into bile duct	243
51.89	Operation, sphincter of Oddi, other	107, 263
51.91	Repair, laceration, gallbladder	107, 263
51.92	Closure, cholecystostomy	107, 264
51.93	Closure, fistula, biliary tract, other	107, 240, 264

* Code Range

Code	Narrative	Page
51.94	Revision, anastomosis, biliary tract	107, 240, 264
51.95	Removal, prosthesis from bile duct	107, 240, 264
51.99	Operation, biliary tract, other	107, 240, 264, 315
*52.0	Pancreatotomy	106
52.12	Biopsy, pancreas, open	97, 108, 152, 240, 264
52.13	Pancreatography, endoscopic, retrograde (ERP)	243
52.14	Biopsy, pancreatic duct, closed (endoscopic)	243
52.19	Procedure, diagnostic, other, pancreas	97, 108, 152, 240, 264
52.21	Excision or destruction, lesion, endoscopic, pancreatic duct	243
52.22	Excision or destruction, other lesion pancreas or pancreatic duct	106, 152
52.3	Marsupialization, cyst, pancreas	106
52.4	Drainage, cyst, pancreas, internal	106
*52.5	Pancreatectomy, partial	106, 152, 264
52.6	Pancreatectomy, total	106, 264
52.7	Pancreaticoduodenectomy, radical	94, 106, 264
*52.8	Operation, other, pancreas	106
52.80	Transplantation, pancreas, unspecified	152, 322
52.82	Transplantation, pancreas, homotransplant	152, 322
52.83	Transplantation, pancreas, heterotransplant	152
52.84	Autotransplantation, cells of islet of Langerhans	161
52.85	Allotransplantation, cells of islet of Langerhans	161
52.92	Cannulation, pancreatic duct	97, 106, 240, 264
52.93	Insertion, stent (tube), endoscopic, pancreatic duct	243
52.95	Repair, other, pancreas	106, 264
52.96	Anastomosis, pancreas	106, 264
52.97	Insertion, endoscopic, nasopancreatic drainage tube	243
52.98	Dilation, endoscopic, pancreatic duct	243
52.99	Operation, other, pancreas	97, 106, 264
*53.0	Repair, hernia, inguinal, unilateral	96, 315
*53.1	Repair, hernia, inguinal, bilateral	96, 315
*53.2	Repair, hernia, femoral, unilateral	96, 315
*53.3	Repair, hernia, femoral, bilateral	96, 315
*53.4	Repair, hernia, umbilical	95, 96, 315
53.49	Repair, other, hernia, umbilical	264
*53.5	Repair, without graft or prosthesis, hernia, anterior abdominal wall	95, 96
53.51	Repair, without graft or prosthesis, incisional, hernia, anterior abdominal wall	315
*53.6	Repair, with graft or prosthesis hernia, anterior abdominal wall	95, 96, 315
53.61	Repair, with graft or prosthesis, incisional, hernia, anterior abdominal wall	264
53.7	Repair, abdominal approach, hernia, diaphragmatic	40, 94, 264
*53.8	Repair, thoracic approach, hernia, diaphragmatic	40, 94, 264
53.9	Repair, other, hernia	95, 96
54.0	Incision, abdominal wall	53, 98, 108, 140, 160, 240, 264
*54.1	Laparotomy	98, 160, 180, 264
54.11	Laparotomy, exploratory	40, 53, 108, 140, 152, 167, 193, 233, 240
54.12	Reopening, recent laparotomy site	108, 240
54.19	Laparotomy	53, 108, 233, 240
54.21	Laparoscopy, abdomen	98, 108, 140, 160, 179, 193, 233, 264, 315
54.22	Biopsy, abdominal wall or umbilicus	98, 140, 240, 264, 315
54.23	Biopsy, peritoneum	98, 108, 180, 233
54.29	Procedure, diagnostic, other, abdominal region	98, 108, 180, 233, 240, 264, 315
54.3	Excision or destruction, lesion or tissue, abdominal wall or umbilicus	98, 117, 140, 152, 240, 315
54.4	Excision or destruction, peritoneal tissue	98, 108, 152, 180, 240, 315
*54.5	Lysis, adhesions, peritoneal	93, 108, 160, 180, 264
54.59	Lysis, other, adhesions, peritoneal	152
*54.6	Suture, abdominal wall and peritoneum	98, 264
54.61	Reclosure, postoperative disruption, abdominal wall	108, 180
54.62	Closure, delayed, abdominal wall, granulating wound	108, 180
54.63	Suture, other, abdominal wall	140, 240
54.64	Suture, peritoneum	108, 240, 315
*54.7	Repair, other, abdominal wall and peritoneum	264

Code	Narrative	Page
54.71	Repair, gastroschisis	95, 96
54.72	Repair, abdominal wall	95, 96, 108, 140, 240
54.73	Repair, peritoneum	98, 109, 240
54.74	Repair, omentum	98, 109, 240
54.75	Repair, mesentery	98, 109, 240
54.92	Removal, foreign body, peritoneal cavity	98, 160, 264
54.93	Formation, fistula, cutaneoperitoneal	53, 98, 109, 160, 240, 264
54.94	Formation, shunt, peritoneovascular	98, 106, 240
54.95	Incision, peritoneum	3, 53, 98, 109, 160, 240, 264
*55.0	Nephrostomy and nephrotomy	157, 264
*55.1	Pyelotomy and pyelostomy	157
55.11	Pyelotomy	264
55.12	Pyelostomy	264, 315
55.21	Nephroscopy	243
55.22	Pyeloscopy	243
55.24	Biopsy, open, kidney	120, 157, 233, 240, 264
55.29	Procedure, diagnostic, other, kidney	157, 233, 240, 264
*55.3	Excision or destruction, local, lesion or tissue, kidney	157
55.31	Marsupialization, cyst, kidney	264
55.4	Marsupialization, cyst, kidney	157, 264
*55.5	Nephrectomy, complete	157
55.51	Nephroureterectomy	264
55.52	Nephrectomy, remaining kidney	264
55.53	Removal, kidney, transplanted or rejected	264
55.54	Nephrectomy, bilateral	264
55.61	Autotransplantation, kidney	157, 264
55.69	Transplantation, other, kidney	157, 322
55.7	Nephropexy	157
*55.8	Repair, other, kidney	157
55.81	Suture, laceration, kidney	264
55.82	Closure, nephrostomy and pyelostomy	264
55.83	Closure, fistula, other, kidney	264
55.84	Reduction, torsion, kidney pedicle	264
55.86	Anastomosis, kidney	264
55.87	Correction, ureteropelvic junction	264
55.89	Repair, other, kidney	264
55.91	Decapsulation, kidney	53, 157
55.97	Replacement, kidney, mechanical	157, 264
55.98	Removal, kidney, mechanical	157, 264
55.99	Operation, kidney, other	157, 264
56.0	Removal, foreign body, ureter and renal pelvis, transurethral	159, 264, 315
56.1	Meatotomy, ureteral	157, 264, 315
56.2	Ureterotomy	157, 264, 315
56.31	Ureteroscopy	243
56.34	Biopsy, open, ureter	157
56.39	Procedure, diagnostic, ureter, other	157, 315
*56.4	Ureterectomy	157, 264
56.41	Ureterectomy, partial	169, 180
*56.5	Ureteroileostomy, cutaneous	157, 169, 180, 240, 264
56.52	Revision, ureteroileostomy, cutaneous	315
*56.6	Diversion, urinary, other, external	157, 169, 180, 240, 264
*56.7	Anastomosis or bypass, other, ureter	157, 264
56.71	Diversion, urinary, ureter to intestine	169, 180, 240
56.72	Revision, anastomosis, ureterointestinal	169, 180, 240
56.73	Nephrocystanastomosis, unspecified	169, 180, 240
56.75	Transureteroureterostomy	169, 180, 240
*56.8	Repair, ureter	158
56.81	Lysis, adhesions, ureter, intraluminal	264
56.82	Suture, laceration, ureter	264
56.83	Closure, ureterostomy	169, 180, 240, 264
56.84	Closure, fistula, ureter, other	93, 169, 180, 240, 264
56.86	Removal, ligature, ureter	265
56.89	Repair, other, ureter	265
56.92	Implantation, electronic ureteral stimulator	158
56.93	Replacement, electronic stimulator, ureter	158
56.94	Removal, electronic stimulator, ureter	158
56.95	Ligation, ureter	158, 265
56.99	Operation, other, ureter	158, 265
57.12	Lysis, adhesions, bladder, intraluminal	158, 265
57.18	Cystostomy, other, suprapubic	158, 169, 178, 240, 265
57.19	Cystostomy, other	158, 265
*57.2	Vesicostomy	158, 169
57.21	Vesicostomy	178, 240, 265

Numeric Index to Procedures

* Code Range

Code	Narrative	Page
57.22	Revision or closure, vesicostomy	180, 240, 265, 315
57.31	Cystoscopy, through stoma, artificial	243
57.32	Cystoscopy, other	243
57.33	Biopsy, closed, transurethral, bladder	159, 169, 180, 315
57.34	Biopsy, open, bladder	158, 169, 180, 240
57.39	Procedure, diagnostic, other, bladder	158, 169, 240, 265, 315
*57.4	Excision, transurethral, bladder tissue	159
57.49	Excision or destruction, other, lesion or tissue, transurethral bladder	169, 315
*57.5	Excision, other, bladder tissue	158, 169, 180
57.59	Excision or destruction, open, lesion or tissues, bladder, other	240, 315
57.6	Cystectomy, partial	158, 167, 180, 240, 265
*57.7	Cystectomy, total	158, 167, 180, 240
57.79	Cystectomy, other, total	265
57.81	Suture, laceration, bladder	158, 265
57.82	Closure, cystostomy	158, 170, 180, 240, 265, 315
57.83	Repair, fistula involving bladder and intestine	93, 158, 170, 180, 240, 265
57.84	Repair, other, fistula, bladder	158, 170, 180, 240, 265
57.85	Cystourethroplasty and plastic repair, bladder neck	158, 175
57.86	Repair, bladder exstrophy	158
57.87	Reconstruction, urinary bladder	158, 265
57.88	Anastomosis, bladder, other	158, 170, 240
57.89	Repair, bladder, other	159, 180, 265
57.91	Sphincterotomy, bladder	159, 315
57.93	Control, hemorrhage, bladder, postoperative	159, 265
57.96	Implantation, electronic stimulator, bladder	159
57.97	Replacement, electronic stimulator, bladder	159, 315
57.98	Removal, electronic stimulator, bladder	159, 315
57.99	Operation, bladder, other	159, 265
58.0	Urethrotomy	159, 180, 265, 315
58.1	Meatotomy, urethral	159, 170, 265, 315
58.22	Urethroscopy, other	243
*58.4	Repair, urethra	159
58.41	Suture, laceration, urethra	265
58.42	Closure, urethrostomy	265
58.43	Closure, fistula, urethra, other	168, 180, 240, 265
58.44	Anastomosis, urethra	265
58.45	Repair, hypospadias or epispadias	168
58.46	Reconstruction, urethra, other	168, 265
58.47	Meatoplasty, urethral	170
58.49	Repair, other, urethra, other	168, 180, 265
58.5	Release, urethral stricture	159, 168, 180, 265, 315
58.91	Incision, periurethral tissue	159
58.92	Excision, periurethral tissue	159
58.93	Implantation, artificial urinary sphincter [AUS]	159, 265
58.99	Operation, other, urethra and periurethral tissue	159, 170, 181, 315
59.00	Dissection, retroperitoneal, unspecified	120, 140, 158, 167, 181, 240
59.02	Lysis, other, adhesions, perirenal or periureteral	158, 170, 181, 240, 265
59.03	Lysis, laparoscopic, adhesions, perirenal or periureteral	158, 170, 181, 240, 265
59.09	Incision, other, perirenal or periureteral tissue	158, 170, 181, 241, 265
*59.1	Incision, perivesical tissue	159, 170, 181, 241, 265
*59.2	Procedure, diagnostic, perirenal and perivesical tissue	159, 170, 241, 265
59.3	Plication, urethrovesical junction	159
59.4	Operation, sling, suprapubic	159, 175
59.5	Suspension, urethral, retropubic	159, 175
59.6	Suspension, paraurethral	159, 175
59.71	Repair, levator muscle operation, urethrovesical suspension, stress incontinence	159, 175
59.79	Repair, other, urinary stress incontinence	159, 175, 315
59.91	Excision, perirenal or perivesical tissue	159, 170, 241
59.92	Operation, other, perirenal or perivesical tissue	159, 170, 241
60.0	Incision, prostate	170, 311
60.12	Biopsy, open, prostate	159, 170, 311
60.14	Biopsy, open, seminal vesicles	170
60.15	Biopsy, periprostatic tissue	170, 311
60.18	Procedure, diagnostic, other, prostate and periprostatic tissue	170, 311

Code	Narrative	Page
60.19	Procedure, diagnostic, other, seminal vesicles	170
*60.2	Prostatectomy, transurethral	158, 167, 311
60.3	Prostatectomy, suprapubic	158, 167
60.4	Prostatectomy, retropubic	158, 167
60.5	Prostatectomy, radical	158, 167
60.61	Excision, local, lesion, prostate	170, 311
60.62	Prostatectomy, perineal	158, 167
60.69	Prostatectomy, other	158, 167, 311
60.72	Incision, seminal vesicle	170
60.73	Excision, seminal vesicle	170
60.79	Operation, other, seminal vesicles	170
*60.8	Incision, periprostatic tissue	170, 311
60.93	Repair, prostate	170, 265, 311
60.94	Control, hemorrhage, prostate	170, 265, 311
60.95	Dilation, transurethral balloon, prostatic urethra	159, 170, 311
60.96	Destruction, transurethral, microwave thermotherapy, prostate tissue	158, 167, 311
60.97	Destruction, transurethral, other thermotherapy, prostate tissue	158, 167, 311
60.99	Operation, other, prostate	170, 311
61.2	Excision, hydrocele, tunica vaginalis	168, 315
61.42	Repair, fistula, scrotal	168, 265
61.49	Repair, other, scrotum and tunica vaginalis	168, 265
61.92	Excision, lesion, tunica vaginalis other than hydrocele	168
61.99	Operation, other, scrotum and tunica vaginalis	168, 265
62.0	Incision, testes	168, 265
62.12	Biopsy, open, testes	168
62.19	Procedure, diagnostic, other, testes	168
62.2	Excision or destruction, lesion, testicular	168
62.3	Orchiectomy, unilateral	168, 265
*62.4	Orchiectomy, bilateral	168, 265
62.41	Orchiectomy, bilateral, same operative episode	120
62.5	Orchiopexy	168
*62.6	Repair, testes	168, 265
62.7	Insertion, prosthesis, testicular	152, 168
62.99	Operation, other, testes	168, 265
63.09	Procedure, diagnostic, other, spermatic cord, epididymis and vas deferens	168, 315
63.1	Excision, varicocele and hydrocele, spermatic cord	168, 315
63.2	Excision, cyst, epididymis	168, 315
63.3	Excision, other lesion or tissue, spermatic cord and epididymis	168, 315
63.4	Epididymectomy	168
63.51	Suture, laceration, spermatic cord and epididymis	168, 265
63.53	Transplantation, spermatic cord	168, 265
63.59	Repair, other, spermatic cord and epididymis	168, 265
63.81	Suture, laceration, vas deferens and epididymis	168, 265
63.82	Reconstruction, vas deferens, surgically divided	168, 265
63.83	Epididymovasostomy	168
63.85	Removal, valve, vas deferens	168
63.89	Repair, other, vas deferens and epididymis	168, 265
63.92	Epididymotomy	168
63.93	Incision, spermatic cord	168
63.94	Lysis, adhesions, spermatic cord	168, 265
63.95	Insertion, valve, vas deferens	168
63.99	Operation, spermatic cord, epididymis and vas deferens, other	168, 265
64.0	Circumcision	160, 169, 315
64.11	Biopsy, penis	140, 168, 315
64.2	Excision or destruction, local, lesion, penis	140, 168, 315
64.3	Amputation, penis	168
*64.4	Repair and plastic operations, penis	168
64.41	Suture, laceration, penis	265
64.43	Construction, penis	265
64.44	Reconstruction, penis	265
64.45	Reattachment, penis	265
64.49	Repair, other, penis	140, 265, 315
64.5	Operation, other, sex transformation	168, 175
64.92	Incision, penis	168, 315
64.93	Division, adhesions, penile	168, 315
64.95	Insertion, prosthesis, penis, noninflatable	160, 169, 315
64.96	Removal, without replacement, prosthesis, penile	160, 169, 315
64.97	Insertion, prosthesis, penile, inflatable	160, 169, 315
64.98	Operation, other, penis	169, 315
64.99	Operation, other, genital organs, male	169, 315
*65	Operation, ovary	174, 175, 178
65.22	Resection, ovarian wedge	152
65.24	Resection, laparoscopic, ovarian wedge	152
*65.5	Oophorectomy, bilateral	140
65.61	Removal, other, same operative episode tubes and ovaries, both	140, 315
65.63	Removal, laparoscopic, tubes and ovaries, both	140

* Code Range

Code	Narrative	Page
*65.7	Repair, ovary	265
*65.8	Lysis, adhesions, ovary and fallopian tube	265
*66.0	Salpingotomy and salpingostomy	174, 175, 178
*66.1	Procedure, diagnostic, fallopian tubes	174, 175, 178
*66.2	Destruction or occlusion, endoscopic, fallopian tubes, bilateral	179, 193, 316
*66.3	Destruction or occlusion, other, fallopian tubes, bilateral	179, 193, 316
66.4	Salpingectomy, unilateral, total	174, 175, 178, 193
*66.5	Salpingectomy, total, bilateral	174, 175, 178, 193
66.61	Destruction, lesion, fallopian tube	174, 175, 178
66.62	Salpingectomy, with removal of tubal pregnancy	174, 175, 178, 193
66.63	Salpingectomy, partial, bilateral, unspecified	179, 193
66.69	Salpingectomy, partial, other	174, 175, 178, 193
*66.7	Repair, fallopian tube	174, 175, 178
66.71	Suture, simple, fallopian tube	265
66.79	Repair, fallopian tube, other	265
66.92	Ligation, fallopian tube, unilateral	174, 175, 178, 193, 316
66.93	Implant, prosthesis, fallopian tube	174, 175, 178
66.94	Removal, prosthesis, fallopian tube	174, 175, 178
66.95	Insufflation, therapeutic agent into fallopian tubes	181
66.96	Dilation, fallopian tube	174, 175, 178
66.97	Burying, fimbriae in uterine wall	174, 175, 178, 193
66.99	Operation, fallopian tube, other	174, 175, 178
*67.1	Procedure, diagnostic, cervix	140, 180, 193, 316
67.2	Conization, cervix	180, 193, 316
*67.3	Excision or destruction, other, lesion or tissue, cervix	178, 193, 316
67.39	Excision or destruction, other, lesion or tissue, cervix	140
67.4	Amputation, cervix	178
67.51	Cerclage, cervix, transabdominal	178, 197, 265
67.59	Repair, internal cervical os, other	178, 197, 266
*67.6	Repair, cervix, other	178, 266
67.61	Suture, laceration, cervix	197
67.62	Repair, fistula, cervix	193
67.69	Repair, cervix, other	197
68.0	Hysterotomy	174, 175, 178, 193, 266
68.12	Hysteroscopy	243
68.13	Biopsy, open, uterus	174, 176, 178
68.14	Biopsy, open, uterine ligaments, open	175, 176, 178
68.15	Biopsy, closed, uterine ligament	179, 316
68.16	Biopsy, closed, uterus	180, 316
68.19	Procedure, diagnostic, other, uterus and adnexa	175, 176, 178
68.21	Division, synechiae, endometrial	180
68.22	Incision or excision, septum of uterus, congenital	180
68.23	Ablation, endometrial	175, 176, 178
68.29	Destruction, lesion, other, uterine	175, 176, 178, 316
*68.3	Hysterectomy, subtotal, abdominal	175, 176, 178, 193
68.4	Hysterectomy, total, abdominal	175, 176, 178, 193
*68.5	Hysterectomy, vaginal	175, 176, 178, 193, 316
68.6	Hysterectomy, abdominal, radical	174, 193
68.7	Hysterectomy, vaginal, radical	174, 193
68.8	Evisceration, pelvic	92, 174
68.9	Hysterectomy, other and unspecified	175, 176, 178, 193
*69.0	Dilation and curettage, uterus	194
69.01	Dilation, curettage, uterus, termination of pregnancy	316
69.02	Dilation and curettage, following delivery or abortion	193
69.09	Dilation and curettage, other	180, 193, 316
69.19	Excision, other, uterine ligaments	175, 176, 178
*69.2	Repair, uterine ligaments	175
69.23	Repair, by vaginal approach, inverted uterus	266
69.29	Repair, other, uterine ligaments	266
69.3	Denervation, paracervical uterine	175, 176, 178
*69.4	Repair, uterine	175, 176, 178, 266
69.41	Suture, laceration, uterine	193
69.42	Closure, fistula, uterine	93
69.49	Repair, other, uterine	194
69.51	Aspiration curettage, uterus, for termination of pregnancy	194, 316
69.52	Aspiration curettage, following delivery or abortion	193, 194, 316
69.95	Incision, cervix	178, 194, 316

Code	Narrative	Page
69.97	Removal, foreign body, from cervix, other penetrating	179, 266
69.98	Operation, uterus, other, supporting structures	175
69.99	Operation, cervix and uterus, other	181
70.12	Culdotomy	181, 194
70.13	Lysis, adhesions, vagina, intraluminal	179, 197, 266
70.14	Vaginotomy, other	179, 197, 316
70.21	Vaginoscopy	243
70.22	Biopsy, cul-de-sac	243
70.23	Biopsy, cul-de-sac	179, 194, 316
70.24	Biopsy, vagina	140, 179, 197, 316
70.29	Procedure, diagnostic, other, vagina and cul-de-sac	179, 194, 316
*70.3	Excision, local, vagina and cul-de-sac	179, 316
70.31	Hymenectomy	197
70.32	Excision or destruction, lesion, cul-de-sac	194
70.33	Excision or destruction, lesion, vagina	140, 197
70.4	Obliteration, vagina	175
*70.5	Repair, cystocele and rectocele	175
70.50	Repair, cystocele and rectocele	98, 159
70.51	Repair, cystocele	159
70.52	Repair, rectocele	93
*70.6	Reconstruction and construction, vaginal	175
70.62	Reconstruction, vaginal	266
70.71	Suture, laceration, vagina	140, 179, 197, 266
70.72	Repair, fistula, colovaginal	93, 179, 241, 266
70.73	Repair, fistula, rectovaginal	93, 179, 241, 266
70.74	Repair, fistula, vaginoenteric, other	93, 179, 241, 266
70.75	Repair, fistula, vagina, other	93, 179, 241, 266
70.76	Hymenorrhaphy	179, 316
70.77	Suspension and fixation, vagina	159, 175
70.79	Repair, other, vagina	179, 197, 266
70.8	Obliteration, vaginal vault	175
*70.9	Operations, other, vagina and cul-de-sac	179
*71.0	Operation, vulva and perineum	179, 197
71.01	Lysis, adhesions, vulvar	266
71.09	Incision, vulva and perineum, other	140, 316
*71.1	Procedure, diagnostic, vulva	140, 179, 197, 316
71.22	Incision, Bartholin's gland cyst	179, 194, 316
71.23	Marsupialization, Bartholin's gland cyst	179, 194, 316
71.24	Excision or destruction, other, Bartholin's gland cyst	140, 179, 194, 316
71.29	Operation, other, Bartholin's gland	179, 194, 316
71.3	Excision or destruction, local, other, vulva or perineum	140, 179, 197, 316
71.4	Operation, clitoris	179, 316
71.5	Vulvectomy, radical	174
*71.6	Vulvectomy, other	179
71.62	Vulvectomy, bilateral	140
*71.7	Repair, vulva and perineum	179
71.71	Suture, laceration, vulva or perineum	140, 197, 266, 316
71.72	Repair, fistula, vulva or perineum	93, 266
71.79	Repair, vulva and perineum, other	197, 266, 316
71.8	Operation, vulva, other	179
71.9	Operation, female genital organs, other	181
73.94	Pubiotomy, to assist delivery	194
73.99	Operation, assisting delivery, other	197
74.0	Cesarean section, classical	193
74.1	Cesarean section, low cervical	193
74.2	Cesarean section, extraperitoneal	193
74.3	Removal, intraperitone, ectopic fetusal	194
74.4	Cesarean section, other specified type	193
74.91	Hysterotomy, to terminate pregnancy	194
74.99	Cesarean section, unspecified type	193
75.36	Correction, fetal defect	194
75.50	Repair, NOS, uterus, obstetric laceration, current	197
75.51	Repair, cervix, obstetric laceration, current	197
75.52	Repair, corpus uteri, obstetric laceration, current	194
75.61	Repair, bladder and urethra, obstetric laceration, current	197
75.93	Correction, surgical, inverted uterus	194
75.99	Operation, obstetric, other	194
*76.0	Incision, bone, facial, without division	31, 266
76.01	Sequestrectomy, bone, facial	120
76.09	Incision, other, facial bone	125
*76.1	Procedure, diagnostic, facial bones and joints	31, 113, 266
76.11	Biopsy, facial bone	316
76.2	Excision or destruction, local, lesion, facial bone	31, 125, 266, 316
*76.3	Ostectomy, partial, facial bone	266
76.31	Mandibulectomy, partial	27, 120

*** Code Range**

Code	Narrative	Page
76.39	Ostectomy, partial, other facial bone	31, 120
*76.4	Excision and reconstruction, facial bones	120, 266
76.41	Mandibulectomy, total, with synchronous reconstruction	27
76.42	Mandibulectomy, other, total	27
76.43	Reconstruction, mandible, other	31, 140
76.44	Ostectomy, total, facial with reconstruction	31
76.45	Ostectomy, total, facial bone	31
76.46	Reconstruction, facial bone, other	18, 31
76.5	Arthroplasty, temporomandibular	31, 120, 266
*76.6	Osteoplasty, facial bone	31, 120, 266
76.70	Reduction, fracture, facial, NOS	31, 120, 266
76.72	Reduction, fracture, open, facial, malar and zygomatic	31, 120, 266
76.74	Reduction, fracture, open, facial, maxillary	31, 120, 266
76.76	Reduction, fracture, open, facial, mandibular	31, 120, 266
76.77	Reduction, fracture, open, facial, alveolar	31, 120, 266
76.79	Reduction, fracture, open, facial, other	18, 31, 120, 266
76.91	Graft, bone, to facial bone	18, 31, 120, 266
76.92	Insertion, implant, facial bone, synthetic	18, 31, 120, 266
76.94	Reduction, dislocation, open, temporomandibular	31, 120, 266
76.97	Removal, fixation device, internal, from facial bone	31, 125, 266
76.99	Operation, other, facial bones and joints	31, 120, 266
*77.0	Sequestrectomy (except carpals and metacarpals 77.04)	266
77.00	Sequestrectomy, unspecified site	120
77.01	Sequestrectomy, scapula, clavicle and thorax, ribs and sternum	40, 120
77.02	Sequestrectomy, humerus	114
77.03	Sequestrectomy, radius and ulna	115
77.04	Sequestrectomy, carpals and metacarpals	118, 256
77.05	Sequestrectomy, femur	112, 291
77.06	Sequestrectomy, patella	124
77.07	Sequestrectomy, tibia and fibula	114
77.08	Sequestrectomy, tarsals and metatarsals	116
77.09	Sequestrectomy, other	120
*77.1	Incision, bone, without division (except carpals and metacarpals 77.14)	266
77.10	Incision, bone, without division, unspecified site	125
77.11	Incision, bone, without division, scapula, clavicle and thorax	40, 125
77.12	Incision, bone, without division, humerus	125
77.13	Incision, bone, without division, radius and ulna	125
77.14	Incision, bone, without division, carpals and metacarpals	118, 256
77.15	Incision, bone, without division, femur	119
77.16	Incision, bone, without division, patella	125
77.17	Incision, bone, without division, tibia and fibula	125
77.18	Incision, bone, without division, tarsals and metatarsals	116
77.19	Incision, bone, without division	31, 125
*77.2	Osteotomy, wedge (except carpals and metacarpals 77.24)	266
77.20	Osteotomy, unspecified site, wedge	120
77.21	Osteotomy, scapula, clavicle and thorax, ribs and sternum, wedge	40, 120
77.22	Osteotomy, humerus, wedge	114
77.23	Ostectomy, radius and ulna, wedge	115
77.24	Osteotomy, carpals and metacarpals, wedge	118, 256
77.25	Osteotomy, femur, wedge	112, 291
77.26	Osteotomy, patella, wedge	124
77.27	Osteotomy, tibia and fibula, wedge	114, 152
77.28	Osteotomy, tarsals and metatarsals, wedge	116, 140
77.29	Osteotomy, other, wedge	120
*77.3	Division, bone, other (except carpals and metacarpals 77.34)	266
77.30	Division, bone, unspecified site	31, 120
77.31	Division, bone, other, scapula, clavicle and thorax, ribs and sternum, other	40, 121
77.32	Division, bone, other, humerus	114
77.33	Division, bone, other, radius and ulna	115
77.34	Division, bone, other, carpals and metacarpals	118, 256
77.35	Division, bone, other, femur, other	112, 291
77.36	Division, bone, other, patella	124
77.37	Division, bone, other, tibia and fibula	114
77.38	Division, bone, other, tarsals and metatarsals, other	116, 152, 316
77.39	Division, bone, other, except facial bones	121
*77.4	Biopsy, bone	113, 140, 152, 160, 170, 316
77.40	Biopsy, bone, unspecified site	31
77.41	Biopsy, bone, scapula, clavicle and thorax	40

* Code Range

Code	Narrative	Page
77.44	Biopsy, bone, carpals and metacarpals	118, 256
77.49	Biopsy, bone, other	31, 41, 233
*77.5	Excision and repair, bunion and other toe deformities	116, 316
77.58	Excision, fusion, and repair of toes, other	266
*77.6	Excision, local, lesion or tissue, bone	266, 316
77.60	Excision, local, lesion or tissue, bone, unspecified site	125
77.61	Excision, local, lesion or tissue, bone, scapula, clavicle and thorax, ribs and sternum	41, 125, 152
77.62	Excision, local, lesion or tissue, bone, humerus	125
77.63	Excision, local, lesion or tissue, bone, radius and ulna	125
77.64	Excision, local, lesion or tissue, bone, carpals and metacarpals	118, 256
77.65	Excision, local, lesion or tissue, bone, femur	119
77.66	Excision, local, lesion or tissue, bone, patella	125
77.67	Excision, local, lesion or tissue, bone, tibia and fibula	125
77.68	Excision, local, lesion or tissue, bone, tarsals and metatarsals	116, 152
77.69	Excision, local, lesion or tissue, bone, other	31, 125, 152
*77.7	Excision, bone for graft (except carpals and metacarpals 77.74)	266
77.70	Excision, bone for graft, unspecified site	125
77.71	Excision, bone for graft, scapula, clavicle and thorax, ribs and sternum	41, 125
77.72	Excision, bone for graft, humerus	125
77.73	Excision, bone for graft, radius and ulna	125
77.74	Excision, bone for graft, carpals and metacarpals	118, 256
77.75	Excision, bone for graft, femur	119
77.76	Excision, bone for graft, patella	125
77.77	Excision, bone for graft, tibia and fibula	125
77.78	Excision, bone for graft, tarsals and metatarsals	116
77.79	Excision, bone for graft, other	31, 125
*77.8	Ostectomy, other partial (except carpals and metacarpals 77.84)	266
77.80	Ostectomy, other partial, unspecified site	121
77.81	Ostectomy, other, partial, scapula, clavicle and thorax, ribs and sternum	6, 41, 121
77.82	Ostectomy, other partial, humerus	114
77.83	Ostectomy, other partial, radius and ulna	115
77.84	Ostectomy, other partial, carpals and metacarpals	118, 256
77.85	Ostectomy, other partial, femur	112, 291
77.86	Ostectomy, other partial, patella	124
77.87	Ostectomy, other partial, tibia and fibula	114
77.88	Ostectomy, other partial, tarsals and metatarsals	116, 152, 316
77.89	Ostectomy, other partial	31, 121, 152
*77.9	Ostectomy, total (except carpals and metacarpals 77.94)	266
77.90	Ostectomy, total, unspecified site	121
77.91	Ostectomy, total, scapula, clavicle and thorax, ribs and sternum	6, 41, 121
77.92	Ostectomy, total, humerus	114
77.93	Ostectomy, total, radius and ulna	115
77.94	Ostectomy, total, carpals and metacarpals	118, 256
77.95	Ostectomy, total, femur, other	112, 291
77.96	Ostectomy, total patella	124
77.97	Ostectomy, total, tibia and fibula	114
77.98	Ostectomy, total, tarsals and metatarsals	116, 316
77.99	Ostectomy, total, other	31, 121
78.00	Graft, bone, unspecified site	121, 266
78.01	Graft, bone, scapula, clavicle and thorax (ribs and sternum)	41, 121, 266
78.02	Graft, bone, humerus	114, 266
78.03	Graft, bone, radius and ulna	115, 266, 316
78.04	Graft, bone, carpals and metacarpals	118, 256
78.05	Graft, bone, femur	112, 266, 291
78.06	Graft, bone, patella	124, 266
78.07	Graft, bone, tibia and fibula	114, 266
78.08	Graft, bone, tarsals and metatarsals	116, 266
78.09	Graft, bone, other except facial bones	121, 266
78.10	Application, external fixation device, unspecified site	121, 266
78.11	Application, external fixation device, scapula, clavicle and thorax	41, 121, 266
78.12	Application, external fixation device, humerus	114, 266
78.13	Application, external fixation device, radius and ulna	115, 121, 266
78.14	Application, external fixation device, carpals and metacarpals	118, 256
78.15	Application, external fixation device, femur	112, 266, 291
78.16	Application, external fixation device, patella	124, 266
78.17	Application, external fixation device, tibia and fibula	114, 266
78.18	Application, external fixation device, tarsals and metatarsals	116, 267

Numeric Index to Procedures

* Code Range

Code	Narrative	Page
78.19	Application, external fixation device, other	121, 267
78.20	Shortening, bone, unspecified site	121, 267
78.22	Shortening, bone, humerus	114, 267
78.23	Shortening, bone, radius and ulna	115, 267
78.24	Shortening, bone, carpals and metacarpals	118, 256
78.25	Shortening, bone, femur	112, 267, 291
78.27	Shortening, bone, tibia and fibula	114, 267
78.28	Shortening, bone, tarsals and metatarsals	116, 267
78.29	Shortening, bone, other	121, 267
78.30	Lengthening, bone, unspecified site	121, 267
78.32	Lengthening, bone, humerus	114, 267
78.33	Lengthening, bone, radius and ulna	115, 267
78.34	Lengthening, bone, carpals and metacarpals	118, 256
78.35	Lengthening, bone, femur	112, 267, 291
78.37	Lengthening, bone, tibia and fibula	114, 267
78.38	Lengthening, bone, tarsals and metatarsals	116, 267
78.39	Lengthening, bone, other	121, 267
78.40	Osteoplasty, unspecified	121, 267
78.41	Osteoplasty, scapula, clavicle and thorax	41, 121, 267
78.42	Osteoplasty, humerus	114, 267
78.43	Osteoplasty, radius and ulna	115, 267
78.44	Osteoplasty, carpals and metacarpals	118, 256
78.45	Osteoplasty, femur	112, 267, 291
78.46	Osteoplasty, patella	124, 267
78.47	Osteoplasty, fibula	114, 267
78.48	Osteoplasty, tarsals and metatarsals	116, 267
78.49	Osteoplasty, other	121, 267
78.50	Fixation, bone, internal, without fracture reduction, unspecified site	121, 267
78.51	Fixation, bone, internal, without fracture reduction, scapula, clavicle and thorax (ribs and sternum)	41, 121, 267
78.52	Fixation, bone, internal, without fracture reduction, humerus	114, 267
78.53	Fixation, bone, internal, without fracture reduction, radius and ulna	115, 267
78.54	Fixation, bone, internal, without fracture reduction, carpals and metacarpals	118, 256
78.55	Fixation, bone, internal, without fracture reduction, femur	112, 267, 291
78.56	Fixation, bone, internal, without fracture reduction, patella	124, 267
78.57	Fixation, bone, internal, without fracture reduction, tibia and fibula	114, 267
78.58	Fixation, bone, internal, without fracture reduction, tarsals and metatarsals	116, 267
78.59	Fixation, bone, internal, without fracture reduction, other	121, 267
*78.6	Removal, fixation device, internal (except carpals and metacarpals 78.64)	267, 316
78.60	Removal, devices implanted, bone, unspecified site	125
78.61	Removal, fixation device, internal, scapula, clavicle and thorax (ribs and sternum)	41, 125
78.62	Removal, fixation device, internal, humerus	125
78.63	Removal, fixation device, internal, radius and ulna	125
78.64	Removal, fixation device, internal, carpals and metacarpals	125, 256
78.65	Removal, fixation device, internal, femur	119, 152
78.66	Removal, fixation device, internal, patella	125
78.67	Removal, fixation device, internal, tibia and fibula	125
78.68	Removal, fixation device, internal, tarsals and metatarsals	125
78.69	Removal, fixation device, internal, other	125
*78.7	Osteoclasis (except carpals and metacarpals 78.74)	267
78.70	Osteoclasis, unspecified site	121
78.71	Osteoclasis, scapula, clavicle and thorax (ribs and sternum)	41, 121
78.72	Osteoclasis, humerus	114
78.73	Osteoclasis, radius and ulna	116
78.74	Osteoclasis, carpals and metacarpals	118, 256
78.75	Osteoclasis, femur	112, 291
78.76	Osteoclasis, patella	124
78.77	Osteoclasis, tibia and fibula	114
78.78	Osteoclasis, tarsals and metatarsals	116
78.79	Osteoclasis, other	121
78.80	Procedure, diagnostic, NEC, bone, unspecified site	113
78.81	Procedure, diagnostic, NEC, scapula, clavicle, and thorax, ribs and sternum	41, 113
78.82	Procedure, diagnostic, NEC, humerus	113
78.83	Procedure, diagnostic, NEC, radius and ulna	113
78.84	Procedure, diagnostic, NEC, carpals and metacarpals	118, 256
78.85	Procedure, diagnostic, NEC, femur	113
78.86	Procedure, diagnostic, NEC, patella	113
78.87	Procedure, diagnostic, NEC, tibia and fibula	113

Code	Narrative	Page
78.88	Procedure, diagnostic, NEC, tarsals and metatarsals	116
78.89	Procedure, diagnostic, NEC, bone, other	113
78.90	Insertion, stimulator for bone growth, unspecified site	121, 267
78.91	Insertion, stimulator for bone growth, scapula, clavicle and thorax (ribs and sternum)	41, 121, 267
78.92	Insertion, stimulator for bone growth, humerus	114, 267
78.93	Insertion, stimulator for bone growth, radius and ulna	116, 267
78.94	Insertion, stimulator for bone growth, carpals and metacarpals	118, 256
78.95	Insertion, stimulator for bone growth, femur	112, 267, 291
78.96	Insertion, stimulator for bone growth, patella	124, 267
78.97	Insertion, stimulator for bone growth, tibia and fibula	114, 267
78.98	Insertion, stimulator for bone growth, tarsals and metatarsals	116, 267
78.99	Insertion, stimulator for bone growth, other	121, 267
79.10	Reduction, fracture, closed, with internal fixation, unspecified site	121, 267
79.11	Reduction, fracture, closed, with internal fixation, humerus	114, 267
79.12	Reduction, fracture, closed, with internal fixation, radius and ulna	116, 267, 316
79.13	Reduction, fracture, closed, with internal fixation, carpals and metacarpals	118, 256
79.14	Reduction, fracture, with internal fixation, phalanges of hand, closed	118, 256
79.15	Reduction, fracture, closed, with internal fixation, femur	112, 267, 291
79.16	Reduction, fracture, closed, with internal fixation, tibia and fibula	114, 267
79.17	Reduction, fracture, closed, with internal fixation, tarsals and metatarsals	116, 267
79.18	Reduction, fracture, closed, with internal fixation, phalanges of foot	116, 267
79.19	Reduction, fracture, closed, with internal fixation, other specified bone	121, 267
79.20	Reduction, fracture, open, without internal fixation, unspecified site	121, 267
79.21	Reduction, fracture, open, without internal fixation, humerus	114, 267
79.22	Reduction, fracture, open, without internal fixation, radius and ulna	116, 267
79.23	Reduction, fracture, open, without internal fixation, carpals and metacarpals	118, 256
79.24	Reduction, fracture, open, without internal fixation, phalanges of hand	118, 256
79.25	Reduction, fracture, open, without internal fixation, femur	112, 267, 291
79.26	Reduction, fracture, open, without internal fixation, tibia and fibula	114, 267
79.27	Reduction, fracture, open, without internal fixation, tarsals and metatarsals	116, 267
79.28	Reduction, fracture, open, without internal fixation, phalanges of foot	116, 267
79.29	Reduction, fracture, open, without internal fixation, other specified bone	31, 121, 267
79.30	Reduction, fracture, open, with internal fixation, unspecified site	121, 267
79.31	Reduction, fracture, open, with internal fixation, humerus	114, 268
79.32	Reduction, fracture, open, with internal fixation, radius and ulna	116, 268
79.33	Reduction, fracture, carpals and metacarpals, open, with internal fixation, carpals and metacarpals	118, 257
79.34	Reduction, fracture, open, with internal fixation, phalanges of hand	118, 257
79.35	Reduction, fracture, open, with internal fixation, femur	112, 152, 268, 291
79.36	Reduction, fracture, open, with internal fixation, tibia and fibula	114, 268
79.37	Reduction, fracture, open, with internal fixation, tarsals and metatarsals	116, 268
79.38	Reduction, fracture, open, with internal fixation, phalanges of foot	116, 268
79.39	Reduction, fracture, open, with internal fixation, other specified bone	31, 121, 268
79.40	Reduction, separated epiphysis, closed, with or without internal fixation, unspecified site	121, 268
79.41	Reduction, separated epiphysis, closed, with or without internal fixation, humerus	114, 268
79.42	Reduction, separated epiphysis, closed, with or without internal fixation, radius and ulna	116, 268
79.45	Reduction, separated epiphysis, closed, separated epiphysis,, with or without internal fixation, femur	112, 268, 291
79.46	Reduction, separated epiphysis, closed, with or without internal fixation, tibia and fibula	114, 268
79.49	Reduction, separated epiphysis, closed, with or without internal fixation, other specified bone	121, 268
79.50	Reduction, separated epiphysis, open, with or without internal fixation, unspecified site	121, 268
79.51	Reduction, separated epiphysis, open, with or without internal fixation, humerus	114, 268
79.52	Reduction, separated epiphysis, open, with or without internal fixation, radius and ulna	116, 268
79.55	Reduction, separated epiphysis, open, with or without internal fixation, femur	112, 268, 291
79.56	Reduction, separated epiphysis, open, with or without internal fixation, tibia and fibula	114, 268

Code	Narrative	Page
79.59	Reduction, separated epiphysis, open, with or without internal fixation, other specified bone	121, 268
79.60	Debridement, open fracture, unspecified site	121, 268
79.61	Debridement, open fracture, humerus	114, 268
79.62	Debridement, open fracture, radius and ulna	116, 268
79.63	Debridement, open fracture, carpals and metacarpals	118, 257
79.64	Debridement, open fracture, phalanges of hand	118, 257
79.65	Debridement, open fracture, femur	112, 268, 291
79.66	Debridement, open fracture, tibia and fibula	114, 268
79.67	Debridement, open fracture, tarsals and metatarsals	116, 268
79.68	Debridement, open fracture, phalanges of foot	116, 268
79.69	Debridement, open fracture, other specified bone	31, 121, 268
79.80	Reduction, dislocation, open, unspecified site	121, 268
79.81	Reduction, dislocation, open, shoulder	116, 268
79.82	Reduction, dislocation, open, elbow	116, 268
79.83	Reduction, dislocation, open, wrist	118, 257
79.84	Reduction, dislocation, open, hand and finger	118, 257
79.85	Reduction, dislocation, open, hip	112, 268, 291
79.86	Reduction, dislocation, open, knee	124, 268
79.87	Reduction, dislocation, open, ankle	115, 268
79.88	Reduction, dislocation, open, foot and toe	116, 268
79.89	Reduction, dislocation, open, other specified bone	121, 268
79.90	Operation, unspecified, bone injury, unspecified site	121, 268
79.91	Operation, unspecified, bone injury, humerus	115, 268
79.92	Operation, unspecified, bone injury, radius and ulna	116, 268
79.93	Operation, unspecified, bone injury, carpals and metacarpals	118, 257
79.94	Operation, unspecified, bone injury, phalanges of hand	118, 257
79.95	Operation, unspecified, bone injury, femur	112, 268, 291
79.96	Operation, unspecified, bone injury, tibia and fibula	115, 268
79.97	Operation, unspecified, bone injury, tarsals and metatarsals	115, 268
79.98	Operation, unspecified, bone injury, phalanges of foot	116, 268
79.99	Operation, unspecified, bone injury, other specified bone	121, 268
80.00	Arthrotomy, for removal of prosthesis, unspecified site	125, 268
80.01	Arthrotomy, for removal of prosthesis, shoulder	125, 268
80.02	Arthrotomy, for removal of prosthesis, elbow	125, 268
80.03	Arthrotomy, for removal of prosthesis, wrist	125, 257
80.04	Arthrotomy, for removal of prosthesis, hand and finger	125, 257
80.05	Arthrotomy, for removal of prosthesis, hip	112, 268, 291
80.06	Arthrotomy, for removal of prosthesis, knee	125, 268
80.07	Arthrotomy, for removal of prosthesis, ankle	125, 268
80.08	Arthrotomy, for removal of prosthesis, foot and toe	125, 268
80.09	Arthrotomy, for removal of prosthesis, other	125, 268
80.10	Arthrotomy, other, unspecified site	121, 152, 268
80.11	Arthrotomy, other, shoulder	115, 268
80.12	Arthrotomy, other, elbow	115, 152, 268
80.13	Arthrotomy, other, wrist	119, 257
80.14	Arthrotomy, other, hand and finger	119, 257
80.15	Arthrotomy, other, hip	112, 268, 291
80.16	Arthrotomy, other, knee	124, 152, 268, 316
80.17	Arthrotomy, other, ankle	115, 268
80.18	Arthrotomy, other, foot and toe	117, 268, 316
80.19	Arthrotomy, other, other specified sites	121, 268
*80.2	Arthroscopy	119, 268
80.26	Arthroscopy, knee	152, 316
80.40	Division, joint capsule, ligament or cartilage, unspecified site	121, 268
80.41	Division, joint capsule, ligament or cartilage, shoulder	116, 268
80.42	Division, joint capsule, ligament or cartilage, elbow	116, 269
80.43	Division, joint capsule, ligament or cartilage, wrist	118, 257
80.44	Division, joint capsule, ligament or cartilage, hand and finger	118, 257
80.45	Division, joint capsule, ligament or cartilage, hip	112, 269, 291
80.46	Division, joint capsule, ligament or cartilage, knee	124, 269, 316
80.47	Division, joint capsule, ligament or cartilage, ankle	115, 269
80.48	Division, joint capsule, ligament or cartilage, foot and toe	117, 269
80.49	Division, joint capsule, ligament or cartilage, other specified sites	121, 269
80.50	Excision or destruction, intervertebral disc, unspecified	6, 123, 269
80.51	Excision, intervertebral disc	6, 123, 269

Numeric Index to Procedures

* Code Range

Code	Narrative	Page
80.59	Destruction, other, intervertebral disc	6, 123, 269
80.6	Excision, cartilage of knee, semilunar	124, 152, 269, 316
*80.7	Synovectomy	316
80.70	Synovectomy, unspecified site	117, 269
80.71	Synovectomy, shoulder	116, 269
80.72	Synovectomy, elbow	116, 269
80.73	Synovectomy, wrist	118, 257
80.74	Synovectomy, hand and finger	118, 257
80.75	Synovectomy, hip	112, 269
80.76	Synovectomy, knee	124, 269
80.77	Synovectomy, ankle	115, 269
80.78	Synovectomy, foot and toe	117, 269
80.79	Synovectomy, other specified site	117, 269
80.80	Excision or destruction, lesion, joint, unspecified sites	125, 269
80.81	Excision or destruction, lesion, joint, shoulder	125, 269
80.82	Excision or destruction, lesion, joint, elbow	125, 152, 269
80.83	Excision or destruction, lesion, joint, wrist, other	118, 140, 257
80.84	Excision or destruction, lesion, joint, hand and finger	118, 257
80.85	Excision or destruction, lesion, joint, hip	119, 269
80.86	Excision or destruction, lesion, joint, knee	125, 269, 316
80.87	Excision or destruction, lesion, joint, ankle	115, 269
80.88	Excision or destruction, lesion, foot and toe	117, 152, 269, 316
80.89	Excision or destruction, lesion, joint, other specified sites	125, 269
80.90	Excision, other, joint, unspecified site	121, 269
80.91	Excision, other, joint, shoulder	116, 269
80.92	Excision, other, joint, elbow	116, 269
80.93	Excision, other, joint, wrist	118, 257
80.94	Excision, other, joint, hand and finger	118, 257
80.95	Excision, other, joint, hip	112, 269, 291
80.96	Excision, other, joint, knee	124, 269
80.97	Excision, other, joint, ankle	115, 269
80.98	Excision, other, joint, foot and toe	117, 152, 269, 316
80.99	Excision, other, joint, other specified sites	115, 269
*81.0	Fusion, spinal	6, 269
81.00	Fusion, spinal, NOS	123, 126
81.01	Fusion, Atlas-axis	124
81.02	Fusion, anterior, other cervical	122, 124
81.03	Fusion, posterior, other cervical	122, 124
81.04	Fusion, anterior, dorsal/dorsolumbar	122, 123, 126
81.05	Fusion, posterior, dorsal/dorsolumbar	122, 123, 126
81.06	Fusion, anterior, lumbar/lumbosacral	122, 123, 126
81.07	Fusion, lateral, lumbar/lumbosacral	122, 123, 126
81.08	Fusion, posterior, lumbar/lumbosacral	122, 123, 126
*81.1	Arthrodesis, foot and ankle	269
81.11	Fusion, joint, ankle	115, 152
81.12	Arthrodesis, triple	115
81.13	Fusion, joint, subtalar	117
81.14	Fusion, joint, midtarsal	117
81.15	Fusion, joint, tarsometatarsal	117
81.16	Fusion, joint, metatarsophalangeal	117
81.17	Fusion, other, foot	117
81.18	Subtalar joint arthroereisis	121, 269
81.20	Arthrodesis, unspecified joints	121, 269
81.21	Arthrodesis, hip	112, 269, 291
81.22	Arthrodesis, knee	124, 269
81.23	Arthrodesis, shoulder	115, 152, 269
81.24	Arthrodesis, elbow	115, 269
81.25	Arthrodesis, carporadial	118, 257
81.26	Arthrodesis, metacarpocarpal	118, 257
81.27	Arthrodesis, metacarpophalangeal	118, 257
81.28	Arthrodesis, interphalangeal	118, 257
81.29	Arthrodesis, other specified joints	121, 269
*81.3	Refusion, spinal	6
81.30	Refusion, spinal, NOS	123, 126, 269
81.31	Refusion, Atlas-axis	124, 269
81.32	Refusion, anterior, other cervical	122, 124, 269
81.33	Refusion, posterior, other cervical	122, 124, 269
81.34	Refusion, anterior, dorsal/dorsolumbar	122, 123, 126, 269
81.35	Refusion, posterior, dorsal/dorsolumbar	122, 123, 126, 269
81.36	Refusion, anterior, lumbar/lumbosacral	122, 123, 126, 269
81.37	Refusion, lateral transverse, lumbar/lumbosacral	122, 123, 126, 269
81.38	Refusion, posterior, lumbar/lumbosacral	122, 123, 126, 269
81.39	Refusion, spinal, NEC	123, 126, 269
*81.4	Repair, other, joint of lower extremity	269
81.40	Repair, hip, NEC	112, 291
81.42	Repair, knee, five-in-one	124
81.43	Repair, knee, triad	124
81.44	Stabilization, patellar	124
81.45	Repair, other, ligaments, cruciate	124

 * Code Range

Code	Narrative	Page
81.46	Repair, other, ligaments, collateral	124
81.47	Repair, other, knee	124
81.49	Repair, other, ankle	115
*81.5	Replacement, joint, lower extremity	269
81.51	Replacement, hip, total	122, 126, 291
81.52	Replacement, hip, partial	122, 126, 152, 291
81.53	Revision, hip replacement	122, 126, 152, 291
81.54	Replacement, knee, total	122, 126
81.55	Revision, knee replacement	122, 126
81.56	Replacement, ankle, total	122, 126
81.57	Replacement, joint of foot and toe	117, 316
81.59	Replacement, other, total hip	121
81.65	Vertebroplasty	121, 269
81.66	Kyphoplasty	121, 269
*81.7	Arthroplasty, hand, fingers, and wrist	119
81.71	Arthroplasty, with implant, metacarpophalangeal and interphalangeal joint, with implant	3, 257
81.72	Arthroplasty, without implant, metacarpophalangeal and interphalangeal joint, without implant	3, 257
81.73	Replacement, wrist, total	122, 269
81.74	Arthroplasty, with implant, carpocarpal or carpometacarpal joint, with implant	3, 257
81.75	Arthroplasty, without implant, carpocarpal or carpometacarpal joint, without implant	3, 257
81.79	Repair, other, hand, fingers and wrist	3, 257
81.80	Replacement, shoulder, total	122, 269
81.81	Replacement, shoulder, partial	122, 269
81.82	Arthroplasty, shoulder, recurrent dislocation	116, 269
81.83	Arthroplasty, other, shoulder	115, 269, 316
81.84	Replacement, elbow, total	122, 269
81.85	Arthroplasty, other, elbow	115, 270
81.93	Suture, ligament, upper extremity	116, 270
81.94	Suture, ligament, ankle and foot	117, 270
81.95	Suture, ligament, other, lower extremity	117, 270
81.96	Repair, other, joint	121, 270
81.97	Revision, joint replacement, upper extremity	121, 270
81.98	Procedure, diagnostic, other, joint structures	113, 270
81.99	Operation, other, joint structures	121, 270
82.01	Exploration, tendon sheath, hand	118, 257, 316
82.02	Myotomy, hand	118, 257
82.03	Bursotomy, hand	118, 257
82.09	Incision, other, soft tissue, hand	118, 140, 257, 316
*82.1	Division, muscle, tendon and fascia, hand	118, 257
82.11	Tenotomy, hand	316
*82.2	Excision, lesion, hand, muscle, tendon and fascia	118, 257
82.21	Excision, lesion, hand, tendon sheath	140, 152, 316
82.29	Excision lesion, hand, other soft tissue	140, 316
*82.3	Excision, other, hand, soft tissue	118, 257
82.33	Tenonectomy, other, hand	152
82.39	Excision, other, hand, soft tissue	140
*82.4	Suture, hand, muscle, tendon and fascia	118, 257
82.41	Suture, hand, tendon sheath	316
82.45	Suture, other, hand, tendon	140, 316
82.46	Suture, muscle, hand	316
*82.5	Transplantation, muscle and tendon, hand	3, 118, 257
*82.6	Reconstruction, thumb	3, 119, 257
*82.7	Repair, with graft or implant, hand	3, 118, 257
82.72	Repair, with graft of muscle or fascia, hand	140
82.79	Repair, with graft or implant, hand	140
*82.8	Repair, other, hand	3, 118, 257
82.89	Repair, other, hand	138
82.91	Lysis, adhesions, hand	118, 140, 257
82.99	Operation, other, hand, muscle, tendon and fascia	118, 257
*83.0	Incision, muscle, tendon, fascia and bursa, except hand	117, 270, 316
83.02	Myotomy, except hand	31, 140
83.09	Incision, other, soft tissue, except hand	140
*83.1	Division, muscle, tendon and fascia, except hand	270
83.11	Achillotenotomy	117
83.12	Tenotomy, adductor, hip	112, 291
83.13	Tenotomy, other, except hand	3, 117, 152, 317
83.14	Fasciotomy, except hand	4, 117, 140
83.19	Division, other, soft tissue, except hand	4, 117, 317
*83.2	Procedure, diagnostic, muscle, tendon, fascia and bursa, including that of hand	117
83.21	Biopsy, soft tissue	4, 41, 140, 233, 317
83.29	Procedure, diagnostic, other, muscle, tendon, fascia and bursa, including that of hand	270
*83.3	Excision, lesion, muscle, tendon, fascia and bursa, except hand	117, 270
83.31	Excision, lesion, tendon sheath, except hand	152

Numeric Index to Procedures

Code	Narrative	Page
83.32	Excision, lesion, muscle, except hand	140, 317
83.39	Excision, lesion, other soft tissue, except hand	31, 140, 152, 317
*83.4	Excision, other, muscle, tendon and fascia, except hand	117, 270
83.41	Excision, tendon for graft, except hand	4
83.43	Excision, muscle or fascia for graft, except hand	4
83.44	Fasciectomy, other, except hand	140
83.45	Myectomy, other, except hand	4, 140
83.49	Excision, other, soft tissue, except hand	4, 31, 140
83.5	Bursectomy, except hand	117, 270, 317
*83.6	Suture, muscle, tendon and fascia, except hand	270, 317
83.61	Suture, tendon sheath, except hand	117
83.62	Suture, delayed, tendon, except hand	117
83.63	Repair, rotator cuff	116
83.64	Suture, other, tendon, except hand	117
83.65	Suture, other, muscle or fascia, except hand	117, 140, 152
*83.7	Reconstruction, muscle and tendon, except hand	4, 117, 270
83.71	Advancement, tendon, except hand	140
83.75	Transplantation or transfer, tendon, except hand	152
83.79	Transposition, muscle, other, except hand	152
*83.8	Repair, other, muscle, tendon, fascia and bursa, except hand	270
83.81	Graft, tendon, except hand	4, 117
83.82	Graft, muscle or fascia, except hand	4, 117, 140
83.83	Reconstruction, tendon pulley on muscle, tendon, and fascia, except hand	4, 117
83.84	Release, clubfoot, other	117
83.85	Change, length, other, in muscle or tendon, except hand	4, 117
83.86	Quadricepsplasty	117
83.87	Repair, other, muscle, except hand	4, 117, 140
83.88	Repair, other, tendon, except hand	4, 117, 140
83.89	Repair, other, fascia, except hand	4, 117, 140
83.91	Lysis, adhesions, muscle, tendon, fascia and bursa, except hand	117, 270
83.92	Insertion or replacement, electric stimulator, skeletal muscle, except hand	4, 117, 270
83.93	Removal, electric stimulator, skeletal muscle, except hand	4, 117, 270
83.99	Operation, other, muscle, tendon, fascia and bursa, except hand	117, 270
*84.0	Amputation, upper limb	52, 140
84.00	Amputation, upper limb, unspecified	113, 270
84.01	Amputation and disarticulation, finger	118, 257, 317
84.02	Amputation and disarticulation, thumb	119, 257
84.03	Amputation, through hand	113, 270
84.04	Disarticulation, wrist	113, 270
84.05	Amputation, through forearm	113, 270
84.06	Disarticulation, elbow	113, 270
84.07	Amputation, through humerus	113, 270
84.08	Disarticulation, shoulder	113, 270
84.09	Amputation, interthoracoscapular	113, 270
*84.1	Amputation, lower limb	140
84.10	Amputation, lower limb, unspecified	51, 113, 149, 270
84.11	Amputation, toe	4, 52, 117, 149, 270
84.12	Amputation, through foot	4, 51, 113, 149, 270
84.13	Disarticulation, ankle	4, 51, 113, 149, 270
84.14	Amputation, ankle, through malleoli tibia and fibula	4, 51, 113, 149, 270
84.15	Amputation, other, below knee	4, 51, 113, 149, 270
84.16	Disarticulation, knee	4, 51, 113, 149, 270
84.17	Amputation above knee	4, 51, 113, 149, 270
84.18	Disarticulation, hip	51, 113, 270
84.19	Amputation, abdominopelvic	51, 113, 270
84.21	Reattachment, thumb	119, 257
84.22	Reattachment, finger	119, 257
84.23	Reattachment, forearm, wrist or hand	122, 270, 291
84.24	Reattachment, upper arm	122, 270, 291
84.25	Reattachment, toe	117, 270
84.26	Reattachment, foot	126, 270, 291
84.27	Reattachment, lower leg or ankle	126, 270, 291
84.28	Reattachment, thigh	126, 270, 291
84.29	Reattachment, other, extremity	121, 270
84.3	Revision, amputation stump	52, 113, 140, 149, 270
84.40	Implantation or fitting, prosthetic limb device, unspecified	122, 270
84.44	Implantation, prosthetic device, arm	116, 270
84.48	Implantation, prosthetic device, leg	115, 270
84.58	Implantation of interspinous process decompression device	6, 123, 270

Numeric Index to Procedures

* Code Range

Code	Narrative	Page
84.59	Insertion, spinal devices, other	6, 123, 270
*84.6	Replacement, spinal disc	6, 123, 270
84.91	Amputation, unspecified	51, 113, 140, 270
84.92	Separation, twins, equal conjoined	122
84.93	Separation, twins, unequal conjoined	122
84.99	Operation, other, musculoskeletal system	122, 270
85.12	Biopsy, open, breast	136, 137, 152, 270, 317
*85.2	Excision, tissue, breast	136, 270
85.20	Excision or destruction, breast tissue, unspecified	137, 317
85.21	Excision, local, lesion, breast	137, 152, 317
85.22	Resection, breast quadrant	137
85.23	Mastectomy, subtotal	137, 317
85.24	Excision, breast, ectopic tissue	137
85.25	Excision, nipple	137
*85.3	Mammoplasty, reduction and subcutaneous mammectomy	136, 137, 270
85.31	Mammoplasty, unilateral reduction	150
85.32	Mammoplasty, bilateral reduction	150
*85.4	Mastectomy	136, 137, 270
85.50	Mammoplasty, augmentation, unspecified	136, 137, 270, 317
85.53	Implant, breast, unilateral	136, 137, 270, 317
85.54	Implant, breast, bilateral	136, 137, 270, 317
85.6	Mastopexy	136, 137, 271
85.7	Reconstruction, breast, total	136, 137, 271
85.82	Graft, split-thickness, to breast	137, 256, 277, 278
85.83	Graft, skin, full-thickness, to breast	137, 256, 277, 278
85.84	Graft, skin, pedicle, to breast	137, 256, 277, 278
85.85	Graft, skin, muscle flap, to breast	137, 271
85.86	Transposition, nipple	136, 137, 271
85.87	Repair or reconstruction, other, nipple	136, 137, 271
85.89	Mammoplasty, other	136, 137, 271
85.93	Revision, breast implant	136, 137, 271, 317
85.94	Removal, breast implant	136, 137, 271, 317
85.95	Insertion, tissue expander, breast	136, 137, 271, 317
85.96	Removal, tissue expander, breast	136, 137, 271, 317
85.99	Operation, other, breast	136, 137, 271, 317
86.06	Insertion, infusion pump, totally implantable	4, 41, 53, 98, 109, 122, 140, 152, 160, 170, 181, 233, 271
86.07	Insertion, vascular access device, totally implantable	141, 161
86.09	Incision, other, skin and subcutaneous tissue	141
86.21	Excision, pilonidal cyst or sinus	138, 271, 317
86.22	Debridement, wound, infection or burn	4, 19, 31, 41, 53, 98, 109, 114, 137, 149, 160, 170, 181, 233, 256
86.25	Dermabrasion	138, 317
86.3	Excision or destruction, other, local, lesion or tissue, skin and subcutaneous tissue	141
86.4	Excision, skin, radical	4, 19, 31, 53, 117, 137, 271, 317
86.60	Graft, free skin, unspecified	4, 54, 98, 114, 137, 149, 256, 277, 278, 317
86.61	Graft, skin, full-thickness, to hand	4, 54, 119, 137, 257, 277, 278
86.62	Graft, other, skin, to hand	4, 54, 119, 137, 257, 277, 278, 317
86.63	Graft, skin, full-thickness, to other sites	4, 31, 54, 98, 114, 137, 149, 256, 278, 279
86.65	Graft, skin, heterograft	4, 54, 98, 114, 137, 256, 278, 279, 317
86.66	Graft, skin, homograft	4, 31, 54, 98, 114, 137, 256, 278, 279
86.67	Graft, dermal regenerative	4, 31, 54, 98, 114, 137, 149, 256, 278, 279
86.69	Graft, other, skin to other sites	4, 31, 41, 54, 98, 114, 137, 149, 256, 278, 279

Code	Narrative	Page
*86.7	Graft, pedicle or flap	137, 278, 279
86.70	Graft, pedicle or flap, unspecified	4, 31, 54, 98, 114, 149, 256
86.71	Cutting, pedicle grafts or flaps	4, 31, 54, 98, 114, 149, 256
86.72	Advancement, pedicle graft	4, 31, 54, 98, 114, 149, 256
86.73	Attachment, pedicle or flap graft to hand	119, 257
86.74	Attachment, pedicle or flap graft, to other sites	4, 31, 54, 98, 114, 149, 256
86.75	Revision, pedicle or flap graft	4, 32, 54, 98, 114, 149, 256
86.81	Repair, facial weakness	4, 32, 117, 138, 271
86.82	Rhytidectomy, facial	32, 138, 271, 317
86.83	Operation, plastic, size reduction	138, 150, 271, 317
86.84	Release, scar or web contraction, skin	32, 138, 271, 317
86.85	Correction, syndactyly	119, 138, 257
86.86	Onychoplasty	141, 271
86.89	Repair and reconstruction, other, skin and subcutaneous tissue	32, 138, 150, 271, 317
86.91	Excision, skin for graft	4, 32, 54, 137, 149, 271
86.93	Insertion, tissue expander	4, 32, 54, 98, 114, 137, 149, 256, 278, 279
86.94	Insertion or replacement, neurostimulator pulse generator, single array	4
86.95	Insertion or replacement, neurostimulator pulse generator, dual array	4
86.96	Insertion or replacement, neurostimulator pulse generator, other	4
86.97	Insertion or replacement of single array rechargeable neurostimulator pulse generator	4
86.98	Insertion or replacement of dual array rechargeable neurostimulator pulse generator	4
87.53	Cholangiogram, intraoperative	108, 317
88.52	Angiocardiogram, right heart	49, 58, 60, 85
88.53	Angiocardiogram, left heart	49, 58, 60, 85
88.54	Angiocardiogram, right and left heart	49, 58, 60, 85
88.55	Anteriogram, coronary, one catheter	49, 58, 60, 85
88.56	Anteriogram, coronary, two catheters	49, 58, 60, 85
88.57	Anteriogram, coronary, other	49, 58, 60, 61, 85
88.58	Cardiogram, negative-contrast	49, 58, 60, 61, 85
92.27	Implantation or insertion, radioactive elements	4, 32, 41, 54, 78, 98, 141, 152, 161, 170, 180, 271, 317
*92.3	Radiosurgery, stereotactic	5, 152, 236, 237
94.61	Rehabilitation, alcohol	255
94.63	Rehabilitation/detoxification, alcohol	255
94.64	Rehabilitation, drug	255
94.66	Rehabilitation/detoxification, drug	255
94.67	Rehabilitation, combination alcohol and drug	255
94.69	Rehabilitation/detoxification, alcohol and drug combination	255
95.04	Examination, eye, under anesthesia	19, 317
*96.7	Ventilation, mechanical, continuous	48
96.72	Ventilation, mechanical, continuous, for 96 consecutive hours or more	277, 281, 323, 324
98.51	Extracorporeal shockwave lithotripsy [ESWL], kidney, ureter and/or bladder	163
99.10	Injection or infusion of thrombolytic agent	17

Numeric Index to Procedures

* Code Range

Appendix A — Invalid DRG Conversion Table

According to section 1886(d) (4) (C) of the Social Security Act, the Secretary of Health and Human Services is required to periodically adjust DRG classifications to account for changes in resource consumption, treatment patterns, technology and other factors that may change the relative use of hospital resources. These adjustments may require reclassification and resultant invalidation of some DRGs.

The following table lists the DRGs that have become invalid and provides information concerning the new DRG assignment for the procedures and diagnoses due to the reclassification.

The first section of the table is sorted by procedure ICD-9-CM codes. The information sorted by diagnosis codes follows that first procedure section.

Proc Code	INVL DRG	DRG Title	NEW DRG	DRG Title	Effec-tive
00.50	115	Perm Cardiac Pacemaker Impl W AMI, Heart Failure or Shock or AICD Lead or Gen Proc	551	Perm Cardiac Pacemaker Impl W MCV Dx or AICD Lead or Generator	2005
	116	Other Perm Cardiac Pacemaker Impl	552	Other Perm Cardiac Pacemaker Impl W/O MCV Dx	
00.51 & 37.94 00.52 & 00.54	514††	Card Defib Impl W Card Cath	535	Cardiac Defibrillator Implant W Cardiac Catheterization W Acute MI, Heart Failure or Shock	2003
			536	Cardiac Defibrillator Implant W Cardiac Catheterization W/O Acute MI, Heart Failure or Shock	
00.52 & 00.53	115	Perm Cardiac Pacemaker Impl W AMI, Heart Failure or Shock or AICD Lead or Gen Proc	551	Perm Cardiac Pacemaker Impl W MCV Dx or AICD Lead or Generator	2005
	116	Other Perm Cardiac Pacemaker Impl	552	Other Perm Cardiac Pacemaker Impl W/O MCV Dx	
00.54	115	Perm Cardiac Pacemaker Impl W AMI, Heart Failure or Shock or AICD Lead or Gen Proc	551	Perm Cardiac Pacemaker Impl W MCV Dx or AICD Lead or Generator	2005
00.61-00.62	478	Other Vascular Procs W CC	553	Other Vascular Procs W CC W MCV Dx	2005
			554	Other Vascular Procs W CC W/O MCV Dx	
01.12 01.14 01.18 01.22-01.25 01.31 01.32 01.39 *01.4 *01.5	400	Lymphoma & Leukemia W Major O.R. Procedures	539	Lymphoma & Leukemia W Major O.R. Procedures W CC	2003
			540	Lymphoma & Leukemia W Major O.R. Procedures W/O CC	
01.6	231	Local Excision & Removal of Int Fix Devices, Except Hip & Femur	537	Local Excision & Removal of Int Fix Devices, Except Hip & Femur W CC	2003
			538	Local Excision & Removal of Int Fix Devices, Except Hip & Femur W/O CC	

† DRG 109 was reactivated in October 1998 as Coronary Bypass without Cardiac Catheterization
†† DRG 514 became invalid effective October 1, 2003
††† DRG assignment October 1, 1984, through September 30, 2001, only
§ DRG 483 became invalid effective October 1, 2004

Proc Code	INVL DRG	DRG Title	NEW DRG	DRG Title	Effec-tive
01.6	400	Lymphoma & Leukemia W Major O.R. Procedures	539 540	Lymphoma & Leukemia W Major O.R. Procedures W CC Lymphoma & Leukemia W Major O.R. Procedures W/O CC	2003
02.2 *02.3 02.42 02.91 02.93 02.99	400	Lymphoma & Leukemia W Major O.R. Procedures	539 540	Lymphoma & Leukemia W Major O.R. Procedures W CC Lymphoma & Leukemia W Major O.R. Procedures W/O CC	2003
*03.0	004	Spinal Procedures	531 532	Spinal Procedures W CC Spinal Procedures W/O CC	2003
03.02	214 215	Back/Neck Procs W CC Back/Neck Procs W/O CC	499 500	Back/Neck Procs Exc Spin Fus W CC Back/Neck Procs Exc Spin Fus W/O CC	1997
03.02 03.09	400	Lymphoma & Leukemia W Major O.R. Procedures	539 540	Lymphoma & Leukemia W Major O.R. Procedures W CC Lymphoma & Leukemia W Major O.R. Procedures W/O CC	2003
03.1	004	Spinal Procedures	531 532	Spinal Procedures W CC Spinal Procedures W/O CC	2003
03.1	214 215	Back/Neck Procs W CC Back/Neck Procs W/O CC	499 500	Back/Neck Procs Exc Spin Fus W CC Back/Neck Procs Exc Spin Fus W/O CC	1997
03.1	400	Lymphoma & Leukemia W Major O.R. Procedures	539 540	Lymphoma & Leukemia W Major O.R. Procedures W CC Lymphoma & Leukemia W Major O.R. Procedures W/O CC	2003
*03.2	004	Spinal Procedures	531 532	Spinal Procedures W CC Spinal Procedures W/O CC	2003
*03.2	400	Lymphoma & Leukemia W Major O.R. Procedures	539 540	Lymphoma & Leukemia W Major O.R. Procedures W CC Lymphoma & Leukemia W Major O.R. Procedures W/O CC	2003
03.32	004	Spinal Procedures	531 532	Spinal Procedures W CC Spinal Procedures W/O CC	2003
03.32	214 215	Back/Neck Procs W CC Back/Neck Procs W/O CC	499 500	Back/Neck Procs Exc Spin Fus W CC Back/Neck Procs Exc Spin Fus W/O CC	1997
03.32	400	Lymphoma & Leukemia W Major O.R. Procedures	539 540	Lymphoma & Leukemia W Major O.R. Procedures W CC Lymphoma & Leukemia W Major O.R. Procedures W/O CC	2003
03.39	004	Spinal Procedures	531 532	Spinal Procedures W CC Spinal Procedures W/O CC	2003
03.39	214 215	Back/Neck Procs W CC Back/Neck Procs W/O CC	499 500	Back/Neck Procs Exc Spin Fus W CC Back/Neck Procs Exc Spin Fus W/O CC	1997
03.39	400	Lymphoma & Leukemia W Major O.R. Procedures	539 540	Lymphoma & Leukemia W Major O.R. Procedures W CC Lymphoma & Leukemia W Major O.R. Procedures W/O CC	2003
03.4	004	Spinal Procedures	531 532	Spinal Procedures W CC Spinal Procedures W/O CC	2003

† DRG 109 was reactivated in October 1998 as Coronary Bypass without Cardiac Catheterization
†† DRG 514 became invalid effective October 1, 2003
††† DRG assignment October 1, 1984, through September 30, 2001, only
§ DRG 483 became invalid effective October 1, 2004

 * Code Range

Proc Code	INVL DRG	DRG Title	NEW DRG	DRG Title	Effec-tive
03.4	214 215	Back/Neck Procs W CC Back/Neck Procs W/O CC	499 500	Back/Neck Procs Exc Spin Fus W CC Back/Neck Procs Exc Spin Fus W/O CC	1997
03.4	400	Lymphoma & Leukemia W Major O.R. Procedures	539 540	Lymphoma & Leukemia W Major O.R. Procedures W CC Lymphoma & Leukemia W Major O.R. Procedures W/O CC	2003
***03.5**	004	Spinal Procedures	531 532	Spinal Procedures W CC Spinal Procedures W/O CC	2003
03.53	214 215	Back/Neck Procs W CC Back/Neck Procs W/O CC	499 500	Back/Neck Procs Exc Spin Fus W CC Back/Neck Procs Exc Spin Fus W/O CC	1997
03.53	400	Lymphoma & Leukemia W Major O.R. Procedures	539 540	Lymphoma & Leukemia W Major O.R. Procedures W CC Lymphoma & Leukemia W Major O.R. Procedures W/O CC	2003
03.59	214 215	Back/Neck Procs W CC Back/Neck Procs W/O CC	499 500	Back/Neck Procs Exc Spin Fus W CC Back/Neck Procs Exc Spin Fus W/O CC	1997
03.59	400	Lymphoma & Leukemia W Major O.R. Procedures	539 540	Lymphoma & Leukemia W Major O.R. Procedures W CC Lymphoma & Leukemia W Major O.R. Procedures W/O CC	2003
03.6	004	Spinal Procedures	531 532	Spinal Procedures W CC Spinal Procedures W/O CC	2003
03.6	214 215	Back/Neck Procs W CC Back/Neck Procs W/O CC	499 500	Back/Neck Procs Exc Spin Fus W CC Back/Neck Procs Exc Spin Fus W/O CC	1997
03.6 ***03.7**	400	Lymphoma & Leukemia W Major O.R. Procedures	539 540	Lymphoma & Leukemia W Major O.R. Procedures W CC Lymphoma & Leukemia W Major O.R. Procedures W/O CC	2003
***03.7**	004	Spinal Procedures	531 532	Spinal Procedures W CC Spinal Procedures W/O CC	2003
03.93	004	Spinal Procedures	531 532	Spinal Procedures W CC Spinal Procedures W/O CC	2003
03.93	214 215	Back/Neck Procs W CC Back/Neck Procs W/O CC	499 500	Back/Neck Procs Exc Spin Fus W CC Back/Neck Procs Exc Spin Fus W/O CC	1997
03.93	400	Lymphoma & Leukemia W Major O.R. Procedures	539 540	Lymphoma & Leukemia W Major O.R. Procedures W CC Lymphoma & Leukemia W Major O.R. Procedures W/O CC	2003
03.94	004	Spinal Procedures	531 532	Spinal Procedures W CC Spinal Procedures W/O CC	2003
03.94 **03.97**	214 215	Back/Neck Procs W CC Back/Neck Procs W/O CC	499 500	Back/Neck Procs Exc Spin Fus W CC Back/Neck Procs Exc Spin Fus W/O CC	1997
03.97	400	Lymphoma & Leukemia W Major O.R. Procedures	539 540	Lymphoma & Leukemia W Major O.R. Procedures W CC Lymphoma & Leukemia W Major O.R. Procedures W/O CC	2003

† DRG 109 was reactivated in October 1998 as Coronary Bypass without Cardiac Catheterization
†† DRG 514 became invalid effective October 1, 2003
††† DRG assignment October 1, 1984, through September 30, 2001, only
§ DRG 483 became invalid effective October 1, 2004

**** Code Range***

Appendix A — Invalid DRG Conversion Table

Proc Code	INVL DRG	DRG Title	NEW DRG	DRG Title	Effec-tive
03.97-03.99	004	Spinal Procedures	531 532	Spinal Procedures W CC Spinal Procedures W/O CC	2003
03.98 03.99	214 215	Back/Neck Procs W CC Back/Neck Procs W/O CC	499 500	Back/Neck Procs Exc Spin Fus W CC Back/Neck Procs Exc Spin Fus W/O CC	1997
03.99 07.16 07.80-07.82 *07.9	400	Lymphoma & Leukemia W Major O.R. Procedures	539 540	Lymphoma & Leukemia W Major O.R. Procedures W CC Lymphoma & Leukemia W Major O.R. Procedures W/O CC	2003
31.1 31.21 31.29	474	Respir System Diag W Trach	482 483§	Trach W Mouth, Larynx or Pharynx Disorder Trach Exc Mouth, Larynx or Pharynx Disorder	1990
31.1 31.21 31.29	483§	Trach W Mech Vent 96+ Hrs or PDx Exc Face, Mouth & Neck Diag	541 542	Trach W MV 96+ Hrs or PDx Exc Face, Mth, & Neck Dx W Major O.R. Trach W MV 96+ Hrs or PDx Exc Face, Mth, & Neck Dx W/O Major O.R.	2004
32.29 33.28 34.02 34.22 34.26 34.3	400	Lymphoma & Leukemia W Major O.R. Procedures	539 540	Lymphoma & Leukemia W Major O.R. Procedures W CC Lymphoma & Leukemia W Major O.R. Procedures W/O CC	2003
34.4	231	Local Excision & Removal of Int Fix Devices, Except Hip & Femur	537 538	Local Excision & Removal of Int Fix Devices, Except Hip & Femur W CC Local Excision & Removal of Int Fix Devices, Except Hip & Femur W/O CC	2003
34.4 34.51 34.6	400	Lymphoma & Leukemia W Major O.R. Procedures	539 540	Lymphoma & Leukemia W Major O.R. Procedures W CC Lymphoma & Leukemia W Major O.R. Procedures W/O CC	2003
35.0	109†	Oth Cardiothor Procs W/O Pump	110 111	Maj Cardiovasc Procs W CC Maj Cardiovasc Procs W/O CC	1990
35.06 36.09	516 517 526 527	Percutaneous Cardiovascular Procs W AMI Percutaneous Cardiovascular Procs W Non Drug-Eluting Stent W/O AMI Percutaneous Cardiovascular Procs W Drug-Eluting Stent W AMI Percutaneous Cardiovascular Procs W Drug-Eluting Stent W/O AMI	555 556 557 558	Percutaneous Cardiovascular Procs W MCV Dx Percutaneous Cardiovascular Procs W Non Drug-Eluting Stent W/O MCV Dx Percutaneous Cardiovascular Procs W Drug-Eluting Stent W MCV Dx Percutaneous Cardiovascular Procs W Drug-Eluting Stent W/O MCV Dx	2005
*35.3 35.42 *35.5 *35.6 *35.7 *35.8 *35.9	109†	Oth Cardiothor Procs W/O Pump	108	Oth Cardiothor Procs	1990
35.96 36.01 36.02	112	Perc Cardiovasc Procs	516 517 518	Perc Cardiovasc Procs W AMI Cardiovasc Procs W/O AMI W Stent Impl Perc Cardiovasc Procs W/O AMI W/O Stent Impl	2001

† DRG 109 was reactivated in October 1998 as Coronary Bypass without Cardiac Catheterization
†† DRG 514 became invalid effective October 1, 2003
††† DRG assignment October 1, 1984, through September 30, 2001, only
§ DRG 483 became invalid effective October 1, 2004

* Code Range

Proc Code	INVL DRG	DRG Title	NEW DRG	DRG Title	Effec-tive
35.96	516 517 526 527	Percutaneous Cardiovascular Procs W AMI Percutaneous Cardiovascular Procs W Non Drug-Eluting Stent W/O AMI Percutaneous Cardiovascular Procs W Drug-Eluting Stent W AMI Percutaneous Cardiovascular Procs W Drug-Eluting Stent W/O AMI	555 556 557 558	Percutaneous Cardiovascular Procs W MCV Dx Percutaneous Cardiovascular Procs W Non Drug-Eluting Stent W/O MCV Dx Percutaneous Cardiovascular Procs W Drug-Eluting Stent W MCV Dx Percutaneous Cardiovascular Procs W Drug-Eluting Stent W/O MCV Dx	2005
36.01	516 517 526 527	Percutaneous Cardiovascular Procs W AMI Percutaneous Cardiovascular Procs W Non Drug-Eluting Stent W/O AMI Percutaneous Cardiovascular Procs W Drug-Eluting Stent W AMI Percutaneous Cardiovascular Procs W Drug-Eluting Stent W/O AMI	555 556 557 558	Percutaneous Cardiovascular Procs W MCV Dx Percutaneous Cardiovascular Procs W Non Drug-Eluting Stent W/O MCV Dx Percutaneous Cardiovascular Procs W Drug-Eluting Stent W MCV Dx Percutaneous Cardiovascular Procs W Drug-Eluting Stent W/O MCV Dx	2005
36.02	516 517 526 527	Percutaneous Cardiovascular Procs W AMI Percutaneous Cardiovascular Procs W Non Drug-Eluting Stent W/O AMI Percutaneous Cardiovascular Procs W Drug-Eluting Stent W AMI Percutaneous Cardiovascular Procs W Drug-Eluting Stent W/O AMI	555 556 557 558	Percutaneous Cardiovascular Procs W MCV Dx Percutaneous Cardiovascular Procs W Non Drug-Eluting Stent W/O MCV Dx Percutaneous Cardiovascular Procs W Drug-Eluting Stent W MCV Dx Percutaneous Cardiovascular Procs W Drug-Eluting Stent W/O MCV Dx	2005
36.03	109†	Oth Cardiothor Procs W/O Pump	108	Oth Cardiothor Procs	1990
36.05 **36.09**	112	Perc Cardiovasc Procs	516 517 518	Perc Cardiovasc Procs W AMI Cardiovasc Procs W/O AMI W Stent Impl Perc Cardiovasc Procs W/O AMI W/O Stent Impl	2001
36.06	517	Percutaneous Cardiovascular Procs W Non Drug-Eluting Stent WO AMI	556	Percutaneous Cardiovascular Procs W Non Drug-Eluting Stent W/O MCV	2005
36.07	526 527	Percutaneous Cardiovascular Procs W Drug-Eluting Stent W AMI Percutaneous Cardiovascular Procs W Drug-Eluting Stent W/O AM Dx	557 558	Percutaneous Cardiovascular Procs W Drug-Eluting Stent W MCV Dx Percutaneous Cardiovascular Procs W Drug-Eluting Stent W/O MCV Dx	2005
***36.1**	107 109	Coronary Bypass W Cardiac Cath Coronary Bypass W Cardiac Cath	547 548 549 550	Coronary Bypass W Cardiac Cath w MCV Dx Coronary Bypass W Cardiac Cath w/o MCV Dx Coronary Bypass W Cardiac Cath w MCV Dx Coronary Bypass W Cardiac Cath w/o MCV DX	2005

† DRG 109 was reactivated in October 1998 as Coronary Bypass without Cardiac Catheterization
†† DRG 514 became invalid effective October 1, 2003
††† DRG assignment October 1, 1984, through September 30, 2001, only
§ DRG 483 became invalid effective October 1, 2004

Proc Code	INVL DRG	DRG Title	NEW DRG	DRG Title	Effec-tive
36.2 36.3 *36.9 37.11	109†	Oth Cardiothor Procs W/O Pump	108	Oth Cardiothor Procs	1990
37.12	109†	Oth Cardiothor Procs W/O Pump	110 111	Maj Cardiovasc Procs W CC Maj Cardiovasc Procs W/O CC	1990
37.12	400	Lymphoma & Leukemia W Major O.R. Procedures	539 540	Lymphoma & Leukemia W Major O.R. Procedures W CC Lymphoma & Leukemia W Major O.R. Procedures W/O CC	2003
37.21-37.23	514††	Card Defib Impl W Card Cath	535 536	Cardiac Defibrillator Implant W Cardiac Catheterization W Acute MI, Heart Failure or Shock Cardiac Defibrillator Implant W Cardiac Catheterization W/O Acute MI, Heart Failure or Shock	2003
37.21-37.23	107	Coronary Bypass W Cardiac Cath	547 548	Coronary Bypass W Cardiac Cath W MCV Dx Coronary Bypass W Cardiac Cath W/O MCV Dx	2005
37.24	109†	Oth Cardiothor Procs W/O Pump	110 111	Maj Cardiovasc Procs W CC Maj Cardiovasc Procs W/O CC	1990
37.24	400	Lymphoma & Leukemia W Major O.R. Procedures	539 540	Lymphoma & Leukemia W Major O.R. Procedures W CC Lymphoma & Leukemia W Major O.R. Procedures W/O CC	2003
37.26	112	Perc Cardiovasc Procs	514†† 516 517 518	Card Defib Impl W Card Cath Perc Cardiovasc Procs W AMI Cardiovasc Procs W/O AMI W Stent Impl Perc Cardiovasc Procs W/O AMI W/O Stent Impl	2001
37.26	514††	Card Defib Impl W Card Cath	535 536	Cardiac Defibrillator Implant W Cardiac Catheterization W Acute MI, Heart Failure or Shock Cardiac Defibrillator Implant W Cardiac Catheterization W/O Acute MI, Heart Failure or Shock	2003
37.26 37.27	516 517 526 527	Percutaneous Cardiovascular Procs W AMI Percutaneous Cardiovascular Procs W Non Drug-Eluting Stent W/O AMI Percutaneous Cardiovascular Procs W Drug-Eluting Stent W AMI Percutaneous Cardiovascular Procs W Drug-Eluting Stent W/O AMI	555 556 557 558	Percutaneous Cardiovascular Procs W MCV Dx Percutaneous Cardiovascular Procs W Non Drug-Eluting Stent W/O MCV Dx Percutaneous Cardiovascular Procs W Drug-Eluting Stent W MCV Dx Percutaneous Cardiovascular Procs W Drug-Eluting Stent W/O MCV Dx	2005
37.27	112	Perc Cardiovasc Procs	516 517 518	Perc Cardiovasc Procs W AMI Cardiovasc Procs W/O AMI W Stent Impl Perc Cardiovasc Procs W/O AMI W/O Stent Impl	2001
37.31	109†	Oth Cardiothor Procs W/O Pump	110 111	Maj Cardiovasc Procs W CC Maj Cardiovasc Procs W/O CC	1990
37.31	400	Lymphoma & Leukemia W Major O.R. Procedures	539 540	Lymphoma & Leukemia W Major O.R. Procedures W CC Lymphoma & Leukemia W Major O.R. Procedures W/O CC	2003

† DRG 109 was reactivated in October 1998 as Coronary Bypass without Cardiac Catheterization
†† DRG 514 became invalid effective October 1, 2003
††† DRG assignment October 1, 1984, through September 30, 2001, only
§ DRG 483 became invalid effective October 1, 2004

 * Code Range

Proc Code	INVL DRG	DRG Title	NEW DRG	DRG Title	Effec-tive
37.32 **37.33**	109†	Oth Cardiothor Procs W/O Pump	108	Oth Cardiothor Procs	1990
37.34	112	Perc Cardiovasc Procs	516 517 518	Perc Cardiovasc Procs W AMI Cardiovasc Procs W/O AMI W Stent Impl Perc Cardiovasc Procs W/O AMI W/ O Stent Impl	2001
37.34	516 517 526 527	Percutaneous Cardiovascular Procs W AMI Percutaneous Cardiovascular Procs W Non Drug-Eluting Stent W/O AMI Percutaneous Cardiovascular Procs W Drug-Eluting Stent W AMI Percutaneous Cardiovascular Procs W Drug-Eluting Stent W/O AMI	555 556 557 558	Percutaneous Cardiovascular Procs W MCV Dx Percutaneous Cardiovascular Procs W Non Drug-Eluting Stent W/O MCV Dx Percutaneous Cardiovascular Procs W Drug-Eluting Stent W MCV Dx Percutaneous Cardiovascular Procs W Drug-Eluting Stent W/O MCV Dx	2005
37.4 **37.61-37.64** **37.91**	109†	Oth Cardiothor Procs W/O Pump	110 111	Maj Cardiovasc Procs W CC Maj Cardiovasc Procs W/O CC	1990
37.70 & 00.53	115 116	Perm Cardiac Pacemaker Impl W AMI, Heart Failure or Shock or AICD Lead or Gen Proc Other Perm Cardiac Pacemaker Impl	551 552	Perm Cardiac Pacemaker Impl W MCV Dx or AICD Lead or Generator Other Perm Cardiac Pacemaker Impl W/O MCV Dx	2005
37.70 & 37.80	115 116	Perm Cardiac Pacemaker Impl W AMI, Heart Failure or Shock or AICD Lead or Gen Proc Other Perm Cardiac Pacemaker Impl	551 552	Perm Cardiac Pacemaker Impl W MCV Dx or AICD Lead or Generator Other Perm Cardiac Pacemaker Impl W/O MCV Dx	2005
37.70 & 37.81	115 116	Perm Cardiac Pacemaker Impl W AMI, Heart Failure or Shock or AICD Lead or Gen Proc Other Perm Cardiac Pacemaker Impl	551 552	Perm Cardiac Pacemaker Impl W MCV Dx or AICD Lead or Generator Other Perm Cardiac Pacemaker Impl W/O MCV Dx	2005
37.70 & 37.82	115 116	Perm Cardiac Pacemaker Impl W AMI, Heart Failure or Shock or AICD Lead or Gen Proc Other Perm Cardiac Pacemaker Impl	551 552	Perm Cardiac Pacemaker Impl W MCV Dx or AICD Lead or Generator Other Perm Cardiac Pacemaker Impl W/O MCV Dx	2005
37.70 & 37.85	115 116	Perm Cardiac Pacemaker Impl W AMI, Heart Failure or Shock or AICD Lead or Gen Proc Other Perm Cardiac Pacemaker Impl	551 552	Perm Cardiac Pacemaker Impl W MCV Dx or AICD Lead or Generator Other Perm Cardiac Pacemaker Impl W/O MCV Dx	2005
37.70 & 37.86	115 116	Perm Cardiac Pacemaker Impl W AMI, Heart Failure or Shock or AICD Lead or Gen Proc Other Perm Cardiac Pacemaker Impl	551 552	Perm Cardiac Pacemaker Impl W MCV Dx or AICD Lead or Generator Other Perm Cardiac Pacemaker Impl W/O MCV Dx	2005

† DRG 109 was reactivated in October 1998 as Coronary Bypass without Cardiac Catheterization
†† DRG 514 became invalid effective October 1, 2003
††† DRG assignment October 1, 1984, through September 30, 2001, only
§ DRG 483 became invalid effective October 1, 2004

Proc Code	INVL DRG	DRG Title	NEW DRG	DRG Title	Effec-tive
37.70 & 37.87	115	Perm Cardiac Pacemaker Impl W AMI, Heart Failure or Shock or AICD Lead or Gen Proc	551	Perm Cardiac Pacemaker Impl W MCV Dx or AICD Lead or Generator	2005
	116	Other Perm Cardiac Pacemaker Impl	552	Other Perm Cardiac Pacemaker Impl W/O MCV Dx	
37.71 & 00.53	115	Perm Cardiac Pacemaker Impl W AMI, Heart Failure or Shock or AICD Lead or Gen Proc	551	Perm Cardiac Pacemaker Impl W MCV Dx or AICD Lead or Generator	2005
	116	Other Perm Cardiac Pacemaker Impl	552	Other Perm Cardiac Pacemaker Impl W/O MCV Dx	
37.71 & 37.80	115	Perm Cardiac Pacemaker Impl W AMI, Heart Failure or Shock or AICD Lead or Gen Proc	551	Perm Cardiac Pacemaker Impl W MCV Dx or AICD Lead or Generator	2005
	116	Other Perm Cardiac Pacemaker Impl	552	Other Perm Cardiac Pacemaker Impl W/O MCV Dx	
37.71 & 37.81	115	Perm Cardiac Pacemaker Impl W AMI, Heart Failure or Shock or AICD Lead or Gen Proc	551	Perm Cardiac Pacemaker Impl W MCV Dx or AICD Lead or Generator	2005
	116	Other Perm Cardiac Pacemaker Impl	552	Other Perm Cardiac Pacemaker Impl W/O MCV Dx	
37.71 & 37.82	115	Perm Cardiac Pacemaker Impl W AMI, Heart Failure or Shock or AICD Lead or Gen Proc	551	Perm Cardiac Pacemaker Impl W MCV Dx or AICD Lead or Generator	2005
	116	Other Perm Cardiac Pacemaker Impl	552	Other Perm Cardiac Pacemaker Impl W/O MCV Dx	
37.71 & 37.85	115	Perm Cardiac Pacemaker Impl W AMI, Heart Failure or Shock or AICD Lead or Gen Proc	551	Perm Cardiac Pacemaker Impl W MCV Dx or AICD Lead or Generator	2005
	116	Other Perm Cardiac Pacemaker Impl	552	Other Perm Cardiac Pacemaker Impl W/O MCV Dx	
37.71 & 37.86	115	Perm Cardiac Pacemaker Impl W AMI, Heart Failure or Shock or AICD Lead or Gen Proc	551	Perm Cardiac Pacemaker Impl W MCV Dx or AICD Lead or Generator	2005
	116	Other Perm Cardiac Pacemaker Impl	552	Other Perm Cardiac Pacemaker Impl W/O MCV Dx	
37.71 & 37.87	115	Perm Cardiac Pacemaker Impl W AMI, Heart Failure or Shock or AICD Lead or Gen Proc	551	Perm Cardiac Pacemaker Impl W MCV Dx or AICD Lead or Generator	2005
	116	Other Perm Cardiac Pacemaker Impl	552	Other Perm Cardiac Pacemaker Impl W/O MCV Dx	
37.72 & 00.53	115	Perm Cardiac Pacemaker Impl W AMI, Heart Failure or Shock or AICD Lead or Gen Proc	551	Perm Cardiac Pacemaker Impl W MCV Dx or AICD Lead or Generator	2005
	116	Other Perm Cardiac Pacemaker Impl	552	Other Perm Cardiac Pacemaker Impl W/O MCV Dx	
37.72 & 37.80	115	Perm Cardiac Pacemaker Impl W AMI, Heart Failure or Shock or AICD Lead or Gen Proc	551	Perm Cardiac Pacemaker Impl W MCV Dx or AICD Lead or Generator	2005
	116	Other Perm Cardiac Pacemaker Impl	552	Other Perm Cardiac Pacemaker Impl W/O MCV Dx	

† DRG 109 was reactivated in October 1998 as Coronary Bypass without Cardiac Catheterization
†† DRG 514 became invalid effective October 1, 2003
††† DRG assignment October 1, 1984, through September 30, 2001, only
§ DRG 483 became invalid effective October 1, 2004

* Code Range

Proc Code	INVL DRG	DRG Title	NEW DRG	DRG Title	Effective
37.72 & 37.83	115	Perm Cardiac Pacemaker Impl W AMI, Heart Failure or Shock or AICD Lead or Gen Proc	551	Perm Cardiac Pacemaker Impl W MCV Dx or AICD Lead or Generator	2005
	116	Other Perm Cardiac Pacemaker Impl	552	Other Perm Cardiac Pacemaker Impl W/O MCV Dx	
37.73 & 00.53	115	Perm Cardiac Pacemaker Impl W AMI, Heart Failure or Shock or AICD Lead or Gen Proc	551	Perm Cardiac Pacemaker Impl W MCV Dx or AICD Lead or Generator	2005
	116	Other Perm Cardiac Pacemaker Impl	552	Other Perm Cardiac Pacemaker Impl W/O MCV Dx	
37.73 & 37.80	115	Perm Cardiac Pacemaker Impl W AMI, Heart Failure or Shock or AICD Lead or Gen Proc	551	Perm Cardiac Pacemaker Impl W MCV Dx or AICD Lead or Generator	2005
	116	Other Perm Cardiac Pacemaker Impl	552	Other Perm Cardiac Pacemaker Impl W/O MCV Dx	
37.73 & 37.81	115	Perm Cardiac Pacemaker Impl W AMI, Heart Failure or Shock or AICD Lead or Gen Proc	551	Perm Cardiac Pacemaker Impl W MCV Dx or AICD Lead or Generator	2005
	116	Other Perm Cardiac Pacemaker Impl	552	Other Perm Cardiac Pacemaker Impl W/O MCV Dx	
37.73 & 37.82	115	Perm Cardiac Pacemaker Impl W AMI, Heart Failure or Shock or AICD Lead or Gen Proc	551	Perm Cardiac Pacemaker Impl W MCV Dx or AICD Lead or Generator	2005
	116	Other Perm Cardiac Pacemaker Impl	552	Other Perm Cardiac Pacemaker Impl W/O MCV Dx	
37.73 & 37.85	115	Perm Cardiac Pacemaker Impl W AMI, Heart Failure or Shock or AICD Lead or Gen Proc	551	Perm Cardiac Pacemaker Impl W MCV Dx or AICD Lead or Generator	2005
	116	Other Perm Cardiac Pacemaker Impl	552	Other Perm Cardiac Pacemaker Impl W/O MCV Dx	
37.73 & 37.86	115	Perm Cardiac Pacemaker Impl W AMI, Heart Failure or Shock or AICD Lead or Gen Proc	551	Perm Cardiac Pacemaker Impl W MCV Dx or AICD Lead or Generator	2005
	116	Other Perm Cardiac Pacemaker Impl	552	Other Perm Cardiac Pacemaker Impl W/O MCV Dx	
37.73 & 37.87	115	Perm Cardiac Pacemaker Impl W AMI, Heart Failure or Shock or AICD Lead or Gen Proc	551	Perm Cardiac Pacemaker Impl W MCV Dx or AICD Lead or Generator	2005
	116	Other Perm Cardiac Pacemaker Impl	552	Other Perm Cardiac Pacemaker Impl W/O MCV Dx	
37.74 & 00.53	115	Perm Cardiac Pacemaker Impl W AMI, Heart Failure or Shock or AICD Lead or Gen Proc	551	Perm Cardiac Pacemaker Impl W MCV Dx or AICD Lead or Generator	2005
	116	Other Perm Cardiac Pacemaker Impl	552	Other Perm Cardiac Pacemaker Impl W/O MCV Dx	
37.74 & 37.80	115	Perm Cardiac Pacemaker Impl W AMI, Heart Failure or Shock or AICD Lead or Gen Proc	551	Perm Cardiac Pacemaker Impl W MCV Dx or AICD Lead or Generator	2005
	116	Other Perm Cardiac Pacemaker Impl	552	Other Perm Cardiac Pacemaker Impl W/O MCV Dx	

† DRG 109 was reactivated in October 1998 as Coronary Bypass without Cardiac Catheterization
†† DRG 514 became invalid effective October 1, 2003
††† DRG assignment October 1, 1984, through September 30, 2001, only
§ DRG 483 became invalid effective October 1, 2004

Proc Code	INVL DRG	DRG Title	NEW DRG	DRG Title	Effec-tive
37.74 & 37.81	115	Perm Cardiac Pacemaker Impl W AMI, Heart Failure or Shock or AICD Lead or Gen Proc	551	Perm Cardiac Pacemaker Impl W MCV Dx or AICD Lead or Generator	2005
	116	Other Perm Cardiac Pacemaker Impl	552	Other Perm Cardiac Pacemaker Impl W/O MCV Dx	
37.74 & 37.82	115	Perm Cardiac Pacemaker Impl W AMI, Heart Failure or Shock or AICD Lead or Gen Proc	551	Perm Cardiac Pacemaker Impl W MCV Dx or AICD Lead or Generator	2005
	116	Other Perm Cardiac Pacemaker Impl	552	Other Perm Cardiac Pacemaker Impl W/O MCV Dx	
37.74 & 37.83	115	Perm Cardiac Pacemaker Impl W AMI, Heart Failure or Shock or AICD Lead or Gen Proc	551	Perm Cardiac Pacemaker Impl W MCV Dx or AICD Lead or Generator	2005
	116	Other Perm Cardiac Pacemaker Impl	552	Other Perm Cardiac Pacemaker Impl W/O MCV Dx	
37.74 & 37.85	115	Perm Cardiac Pacemaker Impl W AMI, Heart Failure or Shock or AICD Lead or Gen Proc	551	Perm Cardiac Pacemaker Impl W MCV Dx or AICD Lead or Generator	2005
	116	Other Perm Cardiac Pacemaker Impl	552	Other Perm Cardiac Pacemaker Impl W/O MCV Dx	
37.74 & 37.86	115	Perm Cardiac Pacemaker Impl W AMI, Heart Failure or Shock or AICD Lead or Gen Proc	551	Perm Cardiac Pacemaker Impl W MCV Dx or AICD Lead or Generator	2005
	116	Other Perm Cardiac Pacemaker Impl	552	Other Perm Cardiac Pacemaker Impl W/O MCV Dx	
37.74 & 37.87	115	Perm Cardiac Pacemaker Impl W AMI, Heart Failure or Shock or AICD Lead or Gen Proc	551	Perm Cardiac Pacemaker Impl W MCV Dx or AICD Lead or Generator	2005
	116	Other Perm Cardiac Pacemaker Impl	552	Other Perm Cardiac Pacemaker Impl W/O MCV Dx	
37.76 & 00.53	115	Perm Cardiac Pacemaker Impl W AMI, Heart Failure or Shock or AICD Lead or Gen Proc	551	Perm Cardiac Pacemaker Impl W MCV Dx or AICD Lead or Generator	2005
	116	Other Perm Cardiac Pacemaker Impl	552	Other Perm Cardiac Pacemaker Impl W/O MCV Dx	
37.76 & 37.80	115	Perm Cardiac Pacemaker Impl W AMI, Heart Failure or Shock or AICD Lead or Gen Proc	551	Perm Cardiac Pacemaker Impl W MCV Dx or AICD Lead or Generator	2005
	116	Other Perm Cardiac Pacemaker Impl	552	Other Perm Cardiac Pacemaker Impl W/O MCV Dx	
37.76 & 37.85	115	Perm Cardiac Pacemaker Impl W AMI, Heart Failure or Shock or AICD Lead or Gen Proc	551	Perm Cardiac Pacemaker Impl W MCV Dx or AICD Lead or Generator	2005
	116	Other Perm Cardiac Pacemaker Impl	552	Other Perm Cardiac Pacemaker Impl W/O MCV Dx	
37.76 & 37.86	115	Perm Cardiac Pacemaker Impl W AMI, Heart Failure or Shock or AICD Lead or Gen Proc	551	Perm Cardiac Pacemaker Impl W MCV Dx or AICD Lead or Generator	2005
	116	Other Perm Cardiac Pacemaker Impl	552	Other Perm Cardiac Pacemaker Impl W/O MCV Dx	

† DRG 109 was reactivated in October 1998 as Coronary Bypass without Cardiac Catheterization
†† DRG 514 became invalid effective October 1, 2003
††† DRG assignment October 1, 1984, through September 30, 2001, only
§ DRG 483 became invalid effective October 1, 2004

 * Code Range

Proc Code	INVL DRG	DRG Title	NEW DRG	DRG Title	Effec-tive
37.76 & 37.87	115 116	Perm Cardiac Pacemaker Impl W AMI, Heart Failure or Shock or AICD Lead or Gen Proc Other Perm Cardiac Pacemaker Impl	551 552	Perm Cardiac Pacemaker Impl W MCV Dx or AICD Lead or Generator Other Perm Cardiac Pacemaker Impl W/O MCV Dx	2005
37.91	400	Lymphoma & Leukemia W Major O.R. Procedures	539 540	Lymphoma & Leukemia W Major O.R. Procedures W CC Lymphoma & Leukemia W Major O.R. Procedures W/O CC	2003
37.94 & 00.51 **37.95 & 37.96** **37.97 & 37.98**	514††	Card Defib Impl W Card Cath	535 536	Cardiac Defibrillator Implant W Cardiac Catheterization W Acute MI, Heart Failure or Shock Cardiac Defibrillator Implant W Cardiac Catheterization W/O Acute MI, Heart Failure or Shock	2003
37.95-37.98	115	Perm Cardiac Pacemaker Impl W AMI, Heart Failure or Shock or AICD Lead or Gen Proc	551	Perm Cardiac Pacemaker Impl W MCV Dx or AICD Lead or Generator	2005
37.99 **38.05**	109†	Oth Cardiothor Procs W/O Pump	110 111	Maj Cardiovasc Procs W CC Maj Cardiovasc Procs W/O CC	1990
38.00 **38.02** **38.03**	478	Other Vascular Procs W CC	553 554	Other Vascular Procs W CC W MCV Dx Other Vascular Procs W CC W/O MCV Dx	2005
38.08	400	Lymphoma & Leukemia W Major O.R. Procedures	539 540	Lymphoma & Leukemia W Major O.R. Procedures W CC Lymphoma & Leukemia W Major O.R. Procedures W/O CC	2003
38.08	478	Other Vascular Procs W CC	553 554	Other Vascular Procs W CC W MCV Dx Other Vascular Procs W CC W/O MCV Dx	2005
38.10 **38.12**	005	Extracranial Vascular Procedures	533 534	Extracranial Vascular Procedures W CC Extracranial Vascular Procedures W/O CC	2003
38.10 **38.12** **38.13**	478	Other Vascular Procs W CC	553 554	Other Vascular Procs W CC W MCV Dx Other Vascular Procs W CC W/O MCV Dx	2005
38.15	109†	Oth Cardiothor Procs W/O Pump	110 111	Maj Cardiovasc Procs W CC Maj Cardiovasc Procs W/O CC	1990
38.18 **38.21** **38.29** **38.30**	478	Other Vascular Procs W CC	553 554	Other Vascular Procs W CC W MCV Dx Other Vascular Procs W CC W/O MCV Dx	2005
38.32	005	Extracranial Vascular Procedures	533 534	Extracranial Vascular Procedures W CC Extracranial Vascular Procedures W/O CC	2003
38.32 **38.33**	478	Other Vascular Procs W CC	553 554	Other Vascular Procs W CC W MCV Dx Other Vascular Procs W CC W/O MCV Dx	2005

† DRG 109 was reactivated in October 1998 as Coronary Bypass without Cardiac Catheterization
†† DRG 514 became invalid effective October 1, 2003
††† DRG assignment October 1, 1984, through September 30, 2001, only
§ DRG 483 became invalid effective October 1, 2004

Proc Code	INVL DRG	DRG Title	NEW DRG	DRG Title	Effec-tive
38.35 38.45 38.55	109†	Oth Cardiothor Procs W/O Pump	110 111	Maj Cardiovasc Procs W CC Maj Cardiovasc Procs W/O CC	1990
38.38 38.40 38.42 38.43 38.48 38.52 38.57 38.60	478	Other Vascular Procs W CC	553 554	Other Vascular Procs W CC W MCV Dx Other Vascular Procs W CC W/O MCV Dx	2005
38.62	005	Extracranial Vascular Procedures	533 534	Extracranial Vascular Procedures W CC Extracranial Vascular Procedures W/O CC	2003
38.62 38.63	478	Other Vascular Procs W CC	553 554	Other Vascular Procs W CC W MCV Dx Other Vascular Procs W CC W/O MCV Dx	2005
38.65 38.85 39.0 39.21	109†	Oth Cardiothor Procs W/O Pump	110 111	Maj Cardiovasc Procs W CC Maj Cardiovasc Procs W/O CC	1990
38.68 38.7 38.80 38.82 38.83 38.88	478	Other Vascular Procs W CC	553 554	Other Vascular Procs W CC W MCV Dx Other Vascular Procs W CC W/O MCV Dx	2005
39.22	005	Extracranial Vascular Procedures	533 534	Extracranial Vascular Procedures W CC Extracranial Vascular Procedures W/O CC	2003
39.23	109†	Oth Cardiothor Procs W/O Pump	110 111	Maj Cardiovasc Procs W CC Maj Cardiovasc Procs W/O CC	1990
39.29 *39.3 39.50 39.56- 39.59 39.8 39.92	005	Extracranial Vascular Procedures	533 534	Extracranial Vascular Procedures W CC Extracranial Vascular Procedures W/O CC	2003
39.29 39.30 39.31 39.41 39.49 39.50 39.51 39.53 39.55 39.56 39.57 39.58 39.59 39.8 39.91 39.94	478	Other Vascular Procs W CC	553 554	Other Vascular Procs W CC W MCV Dx Other Vascular Procs W CC W/O MCV Dx	2005

† DRG 109 was reactivated in October 1998 as Coronary Bypass without Cardiac Catheterization
†† DRG 514 became invalid effective October 1, 2003
††† DRG assignment October 1, 1984, through September 30, 2001, only
§ DRG 483 became invalid effective October 1, 2004

* Code Range

Proc Code	INVL DRG	DRG Title	NEW DRG	DRG Title	Effec-tive
39.98	400	Lymphoma & Leukemia W Major O.R. Procedures	539 540	Lymphoma & Leukemia W Major O.R. Procedures W CC Lymphoma & Leukemia W Major O.R. Procedures W/O CC	2003
39.99	400	Lymphoma & Leukemia W Major O.R. Procedures	539 540	Lymphoma & Leukemia W Major O.R. Procedures W CC Lymphoma & Leukemia W Major O.R. Procedures W/O CC	2003
39.99	478	Other Vascular Procs W CC	553 554	Other Vascular Procs W CC W MCV Dx Other Vascular Procs W CC W/O MCV Dx	2005
40.3	400	Lymphoma & Leukemia W Major O.R. Procedures	539 540	Lymphoma & Leukemia W Major O.R. Procedures W CC Lymphoma & Leukemia W Major O.R. Procedures W/O CC	2003
*40.4	400	Lymphoma & Leukemia W Major O.R. Procedures	539 540	Lymphoma & Leukemia W Major O.R. Procedures W CC Lymphoma & Leukemia W Major O.R. Procedures W/O CC	2003
*40.5	400	Lymphoma & Leukemia W Major O.R. Procedures	539 540	Lymphoma & Leukemia W Major O.R. Procedures W CC Lymphoma & Leukemia W Major O.R. Procedures W/O CC	2003
40.9	400	Lymphoma & Leukemia W Major O.R. Procedures	539 540	Lymphoma & Leukemia W Major O.R. Procedures W CC Lymphoma & Leukemia W Major O.R. Procedures W/O CC	2003
41.2	400	Lymphoma & Leukemia W Major O.R. Procedures	539 540	Lymphoma & Leukemia W Major O.R. Procedures W CC Lymphoma & Leukemia W Major O.R. Procedures W/O CC	2003
41.33	400	Lymphoma & Leukemia W Major O.R. Procedures	539 540	Lymphoma & Leukemia W Major O.R. Procedures W CC Lymphoma & Leukemia W Major O.R. Procedures W/O CC	2003
*41.4	400	Lymphoma & Leukemia W Major O.R. Procedures	539 540	Lymphoma & Leukemia W Major O.R. Procedures W CC Lymphoma & Leukemia W Major O.R. Procedures W/O CC	2003
41.5	400	Lymphoma & Leukemia W Major O.R. Procedures	539 540	Lymphoma & Leukemia W Major O.R. Procedures W CC Lymphoma & Leukemia W Major O.R. Procedures W/O CC	2003
41.93-41.95	400	Lymphoma & Leukemia W Major O.R. Procedures	539 540	Lymphoma & Leukemia W Major O.R. Procedures W CC Lymphoma & Leukemia W Major O.R. Procedures W/O CC	2003
41.99	400	Lymphoma & Leukemia W Major O.R. Procedures	539 540	Lymphoma & Leukemia W Major O.R. Procedures W CC Lymphoma & Leukemia W Major O.R. Procedures W/O CC	2003
*42.1	400	Lymphoma & Leukemia W Major O.R. Procedures	539 540	Lymphoma & Leukemia W Major O.R. Procedures W CC Lymphoma & Leukemia W Major O.R. Procedures W/O CC	2003

† DRG 109 was reactivated in October 1998 as Coronary Bypass without Cardiac Catheterization
†† DRG 514 became invalid effective October 1, 2003
††† DRG assignment October 1, 1984, through September 30, 2001, only
§ DRG 483 became invalid effective October 1, 2004

Proc Code	INVL DRG	DRG Title	NEW DRG	DRG Title	Effec-tive
42.21	400	Lymphoma & Leukemia W Major O.R. Procedures	539 540	Lymphoma & Leukemia W Major O.R. Procedures W CC Lymphoma & Leukemia W Major O.R. Procedures W/O CC	2003
42.25	400	Lymphoma & Leukemia W Major O.R. Procedures	539 540	Lymphoma & Leukemia W Major O.R. Procedures W CC Lymphoma & Leukemia W Major O.R. Procedures W/O CC	2003
42.32	400	Lymphoma & Leukemia W Major O.R. Procedures	539 540	Lymphoma & Leukemia W Major O.R. Procedures W CC Lymphoma & Leukemia W Major O.R. Procedures W/O CC	2003
42.39	400	Lymphoma & Leukemia W Major O.R. Procedures	539 540	Lymphoma & Leukemia W Major O.R. Procedures W CC Lymphoma & Leukemia W Major O.R. Procedures W/O CC	2003
*42.4	400	Lymphoma & Leukemia W Major O.R. Procedures	539 540	Lymphoma & Leukemia W Major O.R. Procedures W CC Lymphoma & Leukemia W Major O.R. Procedures W/O CC	2003
*42.5	400	Lymphoma & Leukemia W Major O.R. Procedures	539 540	Lymphoma & Leukemia W Major O.R. Procedures W CC Lymphoma & Leukemia W Major O.R. Procedures W/O CC	2003
*42.6	400	Lymphoma & Leukemia W Major O.R. Procedures	539 540	Lymphoma & Leukemia W Major O.R. Procedures W CC Lymphoma & Leukemia W Major O.R. Procedures W/O CC	2003
42.7	400	Lymphoma & Leukemia W Major O.R. Procedures	539 540	Lymphoma & Leukemia W Major O.R. Procedures W CC Lymphoma & Leukemia W Major O.R. Procedures W/O CC	2003
42.82-42.89	400	Lymphoma & Leukemia W Major O.R. Procedures	539 540	Lymphoma & Leukemia W Major O.R. Procedures W CC Lymphoma & Leukemia W Major O.R. Procedures W/O CC	2003
43.0	400	Lymphoma & Leukemia W Major O.R. Procedures	539 540	Lymphoma & Leukemia W Major O.R. Procedures W CC Lymphoma & Leukemia W Major O.R. Procedures W/O CC	2003
43.5-43.7	400	Lymphoma & Leukemia W Major O.R. Procedures	539 540	Lymphoma & Leukemia W Major O.R. Procedures W CC Lymphoma & Leukemia W Major O.R. Procedures W/O CC	2003
*43.8	400	Lymphoma & Leukemia W Major O.R. Procedures	539 540	Lymphoma & Leukemia W Major O.R. Procedures W CC Lymphoma & Leukemia W Major O.R. Procedures W/O CC	2003
*43.9	400	Lymphoma & Leukemia W Major O.R. Procedures	539 540	Lymphoma & Leukemia W Major O.R. Procedures W CC Lymphoma & Leukemia W Major O.R. Procedures W/O CC	2003
44.11	400	Lymphoma & Leukemia W Major O.R. Procedures	539 540	Lymphoma & Leukemia W Major O.R. Procedures W CC Lymphoma & Leukemia W Major O.R. Procedures W/O CC	2003

† DRG 109 was reactivated in October 1998 as Coronary Bypass without Cardiac Catheterization
†† DRG 514 became invalid effective October 1, 2003
††† DRG assignment October 1, 1984, through September 30, 2001, only
§ DRG 483 became invalid effective October 1, 2004

* Code Range

Proc Code	INVL DRG	DRG Title	NEW DRG	DRG Title	Effective
*44.3	400	Lymphoma & Leukemia W Major O.R. Procedures	539 540	Lymphoma & Leukemia W Major O.R. Procedures W CC Lymphoma & Leukemia W Major O.R. Procedures W/O CC	2003
44.63	400	Lymphoma & Leukemia W Major O.R. Procedures	539 540	Lymphoma & Leukemia W Major O.R. Procedures W CC Lymphoma & Leukemia W Major O.R. Procedures W/O CC	2003
45.02	400	Lymphoma & Leukemia W Major O.R. Procedures	539 540	Lymphoma & Leukemia W Major O.R. Procedures W CC Lymphoma & Leukemia W Major O.R. Procedures W/O CC	2003
45.03	400	Lymphoma & Leukemia W Major O.R. Procedures	539 540	Lymphoma & Leukemia W Major O.R. Procedures W CC Lymphoma & Leukemia W Major O.R. Procedures W/O CC	2003
45.11	400	Lymphoma & Leukemia W Major O.R. Procedures	539 540	Lymphoma & Leukemia W Major O.R. Procedures W CC Lymphoma & Leukemia W Major O.R. Procedures W/O CC	2003
45.31-45.34	400	Lymphoma & Leukemia W Major O.R. Procedures	539 540	Lymphoma & Leukemia W Major O.R. Procedures W CC Lymphoma & Leukemia W Major O.R. Procedures W/O CC	2003
45.41	400	Lymphoma & Leukemia W Major O.R. Procedures	539 540	Lymphoma & Leukemia W Major O.R. Procedures W CC Lymphoma & Leukemia W Major O.R. Procedures W/O CC	2003
45.49	400	Lymphoma & Leukemia W Major O.R. Procedures	539 540	Lymphoma & Leukemia W Major O.R. Procedures W CC Lymphoma & Leukemia W Major O.R. Procedures W/O CC	2003
45.50	400	Lymphoma & Leukemia W Major O.R. Procedures	539 540	Lymphoma & Leukemia W Major O.R. Procedures W CC Lymphoma & Leukemia W Major O.R. Procedures W/O CC	2003
45.61-45.63	400	Lymphoma & Leukemia W Major O.R. Procedures	539 540	Lymphoma & Leukemia W Major O.R. Procedures W CC Lymphoma & Leukemia W Major O.R. Procedures W/O CC	2003
45.71 45.73-45.76 45.79	400	Lymphoma & Leukemia W Major O.R. Procedures	539 540	Lymphoma & Leukemia W Major O.R. Procedures W CC Lymphoma & Leukemia W Major O.R. Procedures W/O CC	2003
45.8	400	Lymphoma & Leukemia W Major O.R. Procedures	539 540	Lymphoma & Leukemia W Major O.R. Procedures W CC Lymphoma & Leukemia W Major O.R. Procedures W/O CC	2003
45.90-45.95	400	Lymphoma & Leukemia W Major O.R. Procedures	539 540	Lymphoma & Leukemia W Major O.R. Procedures W CC Lymphoma & Leukemia W Major O.R. Procedures W/O CC	2003
*46.0	400	Lymphoma & Leukemia W Major O.R. Procedures	539 540	Lymphoma & Leukemia W Major O.R. Procedures W CC Lymphoma & Leukemia W Major O.R. Procedures W/O CC	2003

† DRG 109 was reactivated in October 1998 as Coronary Bypass without Cardiac Catheterization
†† DRG 514 became invalid effective October 1, 2003
††† DRG assignment October 1, 1984, through September 30, 2001, only
§ DRG 483 became invalid effective October 1, 2004

** Code Range*

Appendix A — Invalid DRG Conversion Table

Proc Code	INVL DRG	DRG Title	NEW DRG	DRG Title	Effec-tive
46.10-46.13	400	Lymphoma & Leukemia W Major O.R. Procedures	539 540	Lymphoma & Leukemia W Major O.R. Procedures W CC Lymphoma & Leukemia W Major O.R. Procedures W/O CC	2003
46.20-46.23	400	Lymphoma & Leukemia W Major O.R. Procedures	539 540	Lymphoma & Leukemia W Major O.R. Procedures W CC Lymphoma & Leukemia W Major O.R. Procedures W/O CC	2003
46.40	400	Lymphoma & Leukemia W Major O.R. Procedures	539 540	Lymphoma & Leukemia W Major O.R. Procedures W CC Lymphoma & Leukemia W Major O.R. Procedures W/O CC	2003
46.41	400	Lymphoma & Leukemia W Major O.R. Procedures	539 540	Lymphoma & Leukemia W Major O.R. Procedures W CC Lymphoma & Leukemia W Major O.R. Procedures W/O CC	2003
46.80-46.82	400	Lymphoma & Leukemia W Major O.R. Procedures	539 540	Lymphoma & Leukemia W Major O.R. Procedures W CC Lymphoma & Leukemia W Major O.R. Procedures W/O CC	2003
46.97	400	Lymphoma & Leukemia W Major O.R. Procedures	539 540	Lymphoma & Leukemia W Major O.R. Procedures W CC Lymphoma & Leukemia W Major O.R. Procedures W/O CC	2003
46.99	400	Lymphoma & Leukemia W Major O.R. Procedures	539 540	Lymphoma & Leukemia W Major O.R. Procedures W CC Lymphoma & Leukemia W Major O.R. Procedures W/O CC	2003
*48.4	400	Lymphoma & Leukemia W Major O.R. Procedures	539 540	Lymphoma & Leukemia W Major O.R. Procedures W CC Lymphoma & Leukemia W Major O.R. Procedures W/O CC	2003
48.5	400	Lymphoma & Leukemia W Major O.R. Procedures	539 540	Lymphoma & Leukemia W Major O.R. Procedures W CC Lymphoma & Leukemia W Major O.R. Procedures W/O CC	2003
*48.6	400	Lymphoma & Leukemia W Major O.R. Procedures	539 540	Lymphoma & Leukemia W Major O.R. Procedures W CC Lymphoma & Leukemia W Major O.R. Procedures W/O CC	2003
50.12	400	Lymphoma & Leukemia W Major O.R. Procedures	539 540	Lymphoma & Leukemia W Major O.R. Procedures W CC Lymphoma & Leukemia W Major O.R. Procedures W/O CC	2003
50.19	400	Lymphoma & Leukemia W Major O.R. Procedures	539 540	Lymphoma & Leukemia W Major O.R. Procedures W CC Lymphoma & Leukemia W Major O.R. Procedures W/O CC	2003
*51.2	400	Lymphoma & Leukemia W Major O.R. Procedures	539 540	Lymphoma & Leukemia W Major O.R. Procedures W CC Lymphoma & Leukemia W Major O.R. Procedures W/O CC	2003
*51.3	400	Lymphoma & Leukemia W Major O.R. Procedures	539 540	Lymphoma & Leukemia W Major O.R. Procedures W CC Lymphoma & Leukemia W Major O.R. Procedures W/O CC	2003

† DRG 109 was reactivated in October 1998 as Coronary Bypass without Cardiac Catheterization
†† DRG 514 became invalid effective October 1, 2003
††† DRG assignment October 1, 1984, through September 30, 2001, only
§ DRG 483 became invalid effective October 1, 2004

 * Code Range

Proc Code	INVL DRG	DRG Title	NEW DRG	DRG Title	Effec-tive
51.42-51.49	400	Lymphoma & Leukemia W Major O.R. Procedures	539 540	Lymphoma & Leukemia W Major O.R. Procedures W CC Lymphoma & Leukemia W Major O.R. Procedures W/O CC	2003
51.59	400	Lymphoma & Leukemia W Major O.R. Procedures	539 540	Lymphoma & Leukemia W Major O.R. Procedures W CC Lymphoma & Leukemia W Major O.R. Procedures W/O CC	2003
51.93-51.95	400	Lymphoma & Leukemia W Major O.R. Procedures	539 540	Lymphoma & Leukemia W Major O.R. Procedures W CC Lymphoma & Leukemia W Major O.R. Procedures W/O CC	2003
51.99	400	Lymphoma & Leukemia W Major O.R. Procedures	539 540	Lymphoma & Leukemia W Major O.R. Procedures W CC Lymphoma & Leukemia W Major O.R. Procedures W/O CC	2003
52.12	400	Lymphoma & Leukemia W Major O.R. Procedures	539 540	Lymphoma & Leukemia W Major O.R. Procedures W CC Lymphoma & Leukemia W Major O.R. Procedures W/O CC	2003
52.19	400	Lymphoma & Leukemia W Major O.R. Procedures	539 540	Lymphoma & Leukemia W Major O.R. Procedures W CC Lymphoma & Leukemia W Major O.R. Procedures W/O CC	2003
52.92	400	Lymphoma & Leukemia W Major O.R. Procedures	539 540	Lymphoma & Leukemia W Major O.R. Procedures W CC Lymphoma & Leukemia W Major O.R. Procedures W/O CC	2003
54.0	400	Lymphoma & Leukemia W Major O.R. Procedures	539 540	Lymphoma & Leukemia W Major O.R. Procedures W CC Lymphoma & Leukemia W Major O.R. Procedures W/O CC	2003
54.11-54.19	400	Lymphoma & Leukemia W Major O.R. Procedures	539 540	Lymphoma & Leukemia W Major O.R. Procedures W CC Lymphoma & Leukemia W Major O.R. Procedures W/O CC	2003
54.22	400	Lymphoma & Leukemia W Major O.R. Procedures	539 540	Lymphoma & Leukemia W Major O.R. Procedures W CC Lymphoma & Leukemia W Major O.R. Procedures W/O CC	2003
54.29	400	Lymphoma & Leukemia W Major O.R. Procedures	539 540	Lymphoma & Leukemia W Major O.R. Procedures W CC Lymphoma & Leukemia W Major O.R. Procedures W/O CC	2003
54.3	400	Lymphoma & Leukemia W Major O.R. Procedures	539 540	Lymphoma & Leukemia W Major O.R. Procedures W CC Lymphoma & Leukemia W Major O.R. Procedures W/O CC	2003
54.4	400	Lymphoma & Leukemia W Major O.R. Procedures	539 540	Lymphoma & Leukemia W Major O.R. Procedures W CC Lymphoma & Leukemia W Major O.R. Procedures W/O CC	2003
54.63	400	Lymphoma & Leukemia W Major O.R. Procedures	539 540	Lymphoma & Leukemia W Major O.R. Procedures W CC Lymphoma & Leukemia W Major O.R. Procedures W/O CC	2003

† DRG 109 was reactivated in October 1998 as Coronary Bypass without Cardiac Catheterization
†† DRG 514 became invalid effective October 1, 2003
††† DRG assignment October 1, 1984, through September 30, 2001, only
§ DRG 483 became invalid effective October 1, 2004

Proc Code	INVL DRG	DRG Title	NEW DRG	DRG Title	Effective
54.64	400	Lymphoma & Leukemia W Major O.R. Procedures	539 540	Lymphoma & Leukemia W Major O.R. Procedures W CC Lymphoma & Leukemia W Major O.R. Procedures W/O CC	2003
54.72-54.75	400	Lymphoma & Leukemia W Major O.R. Procedures	539 540	Lymphoma & Leukemia W Major O.R. Procedures W CC Lymphoma & Leukemia W Major O.R. Procedures W/O CC	2003
54.93-54.95	400	Lymphoma & Leukemia W Major O.R. Procedures	539 540	Lymphoma & Leukemia W Major O.R. Procedures W CC Lymphoma & Leukemia W Major O.R. Procedures W/O CC	2003
55.24	400	Lymphoma & Leukemia W Major O.R. Procedures	539 540	Lymphoma & Leukemia W Major O.R. Procedures W CC Lymphoma & Leukemia W Major O.R. Procedures W/O CC	2003
55.29	400	Lymphoma & Leukemia W Major O.R. Procedures	539 540	Lymphoma & Leukemia W Major O.R. Procedures W CC Lymphoma & Leukemia W Major O.R. Procedures W/O CC	2003
*56.5	400	Lymphoma & Leukemia W Major O.R. Procedures	539 540	Lymphoma & Leukemia W Major O.R. Procedures W CC Lymphoma & Leukemia W Major O.R. Procedures W/O CC	2003
*56.6	400	Lymphoma & Leukemia W Major O.R. Procedures	539 540	Lymphoma & Leukemia W Major O.R. Procedures W CC Lymphoma & Leukemia W Major O.R. Procedures W/O CC	2003
56.71-56.73	400	Lymphoma & Leukemia W Major O.R. Procedures	539 540	Lymphoma & Leukemia W Major O.R. Procedures W CC Lymphoma & Leukemia W Major O.R. Procedures W/O CC	2003
56.75	400	Lymphoma & Leukemia W Major O.R. Procedures	539 540	Lymphoma & Leukemia W Major O.R. Procedures W CC Lymphoma & Leukemia W Major O.R. Procedures W/O CC	2003
56.83	400	Lymphoma & Leukemia W Major O.R. Procedures	539 540	Lymphoma & Leukemia W Major O.R. Procedures W CC Lymphoma & Leukemia W Major O.R. Procedures W/O CC	2003
56.84	400	Lymphoma & Leukemia W Major O.R. Procedures	539 540	Lymphoma & Leukemia W Major O.R. Procedures W CC Lymphoma & Leukemia W Major O.R. Procedures W/O CC	2003
57.18	400	Lymphoma & Leukemia W Major O.R. Procedures	539 540	Lymphoma & Leukemia W Major O.R. Procedures W CC Lymphoma & Leukemia W Major O.R. Procedures W/O CC	2003
57.21	400	Lymphoma & Leukemia W Major O.R. Procedures	539 540	Lymphoma & Leukemia W Major O.R. Procedures W CC Lymphoma & Leukemia W Major O.R. Procedures W/O CC	2003
57.22	400	Lymphoma & Leukemia W Major O.R. Procedures	539 540	Lymphoma & Leukemia W Major O.R. Procedures W CC Lymphoma & Leukemia W Major O.R. Procedures W/O CC	2003

† DRG 109 was reactivated in October 1998 as Coronary Bypass without Cardiac Catheterization
†† DRG 514 became invalid effective October 1, 2003
††† DRG assignment October 1, 1984, through September 30, 2001, only
§ DRG 483 became invalid effective October 1, 2004

* Code Range

Proc Code	INVL DRG	DRG Title	NEW DRG	DRG Title	Effec-tive
57.34	400	Lymphoma & Leukemia W Major O.R. Procedures	539 540	Lymphoma & Leukemia W Major O.R. Procedures W CC Lymphoma & Leukemia W Major O.R. Procedures W/O CC	2003
57.39	400	Lymphoma & Leukemia W Major O.R. Procedures	539 540	Lymphoma & Leukemia W Major O.R. Procedures W CC Lymphoma & Leukemia W Major O.R. Procedures W/O CC	2003
57.59	400	Lymphoma & Leukemia W Major O.R. Procedures	539 540	Lymphoma & Leukemia W Major O.R. Procedures W CC Lymphoma & Leukemia W Major O.R. Procedures W/O CC	2003
57.6	400	Lymphoma & Leukemia W Major O.R. Procedures	539 540	Lymphoma & Leukemia W Major O.R. Procedures W CC Lymphoma & Leukemia W Major O.R. Procedures W/O CC	2003
***57.7**	400	Lymphoma & Leukemia W Major O.R. Procedures	539 540	Lymphoma & Leukemia W Major O.R. Procedures W CC Lymphoma & Leukemia W Major O.R. Procedures W/O CC	2003
57.82-57.84	400	Lymphoma & Leukemia W Major O.R. Procedures	539 540	Lymphoma & Leukemia W Major O.R. Procedures W CC Lymphoma & Leukemia W Major O.R. Procedures W/O CC	2003
57.88	400	Lymphoma & Leukemia W Major O.R. Procedures	539 540	Lymphoma & Leukemia W Major O.R. Procedures W CC Lymphoma & Leukemia W Major O.R. Procedures W/O CC	2003
58.43	400	Lymphoma & Leukemia W Major O.R. Procedures	539 540	Lymphoma & Leukemia W Major O.R. Procedures W CC Lymphoma & Leukemia W Major O.R. Procedures W/O CC	2003
***59.0**	400	Lymphoma & Leukemia W Major O.R. Procedures	539 540	Lymphoma & Leukemia W Major O.R. Procedures W CC Lymphoma & Leukemia W Major O.R. Procedures W/O CC	2003
***59.1**	400	Lymphoma & Leukemia W Major O.R. Procedures	539 540	Lymphoma & Leukemia W Major O.R. Procedures W CC Lymphoma & Leukemia W Major O.R. Procedures W/O CC	2003
***59.2**	400	Lymphoma & Leukemia W Major O.R. Procedures	539 540	Lymphoma & Leukemia W Major O.R. Procedures W CC Lymphoma & Leukemia W Major O.R. Procedures W/O CC	2003
59.91	400	Lymphoma & Leukemia W Major O.R. Procedures	539 540	Lymphoma & Leukemia W Major O.R. Procedures W CC Lymphoma & Leukemia W Major O.R. Procedures W/O CC	2003
59.92	400	Lymphoma & Leukemia W Major O.R. Procedures	539 540	Lymphoma & Leukemia W Major O.R. Procedures W CC Lymphoma & Leukemia W Major O.R. Procedures W/O CC	2003
70.72-70.75	400	Lymphoma & Leukemia W Major O.R. Procedures	539 540	Lymphoma & Leukemia W Major O.R. Procedures W CC Lymphoma & Leukemia W Major O.R. Procedures W/O CC	2003

† DRG 109 was reactivated in October 1998 as Coronary Bypass without Cardiac Catheterization
†† DRG 514 became invalid effective October 1, 2003
††† DRG assignment October 1, 1984, through September 30, 2001, only
§ DRG 483 became invalid effective October 1, 2004

*** Code Range**

Proc Code	INVL DRG	DRG Title	NEW DRG	DRG Title	Effec-tive
76.09 76.2 76.97	231	Local Excision & Removal of Int Fix Devices, Except Hip & Femur	537 538	Local Excision & Removal of Int Fix Devices, Except Hip & Femur W CC Local Excision & Removal of Int Fix Devices, Except Hip & Femur W/O CC	2003
77.06	221 222	Knee Procs W CC Knee Procs W/O CC	501 502 503	Knee Procs W PDx of Infect W CC Knee Procs W PDx of Infect W/O CC Knee Procs W/O PDx of Infect	1997
77.10-77.13 77.16 77.17 77.19	231	Local Excision & Removal of Int Fix Devices, Except Hip & Femur	537 538	Local Excision & Removal of Int Fix Devices, Except Hip & Femur W CC Local Excision & Removal of Int Fix Devices, Except Hip & Femur W/O CC	2003
77.26 77.36	221 222	Knee Procs W CC Knee Procs W/O CC	501 502 503	Knee Procs W PDx of Infect W CC Knee Procs W PDx of Infect W/O CC Knee Procs W/O PDx of Infect	1997
77.60 77.61-77.63 77.66-77.67 77.69 77.70-77.73 77.76 77.77 77.79	231	Local Excision & Removal of Int Fix Devices, Except Hip & Femur	537 538	Local Excision & Removal of Int Fix Devices, Except Hip & Femur W CC Local Excision & Removal of Int Fix Devices, Except Hip & Femur W/O CC	2003
77.81	004	Spinal Procedures	531 532	Spinal Procedures W CC Spinal Procedures W/O CC	2003
77.86	221 222	Knee Procs W CC Knee Procs W/O CC	501 502 503	Knee Procs W PDx of Infect W CC Knee Procs W PDx of Infect W/O CC Knee Procs W/O PDx of Infect	1997
77.91	004	Spinal Procedures	531 532	Spinal Procedures W CC Spinal Procedures W/O CC	2003
77.96 78.06 78.16 78.46 78.56	221 222	Knee Procs W CC Knee Procs W/O CC	501 502 503	Knee Procs W PDx of Infect W CC Knee Procs W PDx of Infect W/O CC Knee Procs W/O PDx of Infect	1997
78.60-78.64 78.66-78.69	231	Local Excision & Removal of Int Fix Devices, Except Hip & Femur	537 538	Local Excision & Removal of Int Fix Devices, Except Hip & Femur W CC Local Excision & Removal of Int Fix Devices, Except Hip & Femur W/O CC	2003
78.76 78.96 79.86	221 222	Knee Procs W CC Knee Procs W/O CC	501 502 503	Knee Procs W PDx of Infect W CC Knee Procs W PDx of Infect W/O CC Knee Procs W/O PDx of Infect	1997
*80.0	231	Local Excision & Removal of Int Fix Devices, Except Hip & Femur	537 538	Local Excision & Removal of Int Fix Devices, Except Hip & Femur W CC Local Excision & Removal of Int Fix Devices, Except Hip & Femur W/O CC	2003

† DRG 109 was reactivated in October 1998 as Coronary Bypass without Cardiac Catheterization
†† DRG 514 became invalid effective October 1, 2003
††† DRG assignment October 1, 1984, through September 30, 2001, only
§ DRG 483 became invalid effective October 1, 2004

* Code Range

Proc Code	INVL DRG	DRG Title	NEW DRG	DRG Title	Effec-tive
80.16 80.46	221 222	Knee Procs W CC Knee Procs W/O CC	501 502 503	Knee Procs W PDx of Infect W CC Knee Procs W PDx of Infect W/O CC Knee Procs W/O PDx of Infect	1997
80.50	004	Spinal Procedures	531 532	Spinal Procedures W CC Spinal Procedures W/O CC	2003
80.50	214 215	Back/Neck Procs W CC Back/Neck Procs W/O CC	499 500	Back/Neck Procs Exc Spin Fus W CC Back/Neck Procs Exc Spin Fus W/O CC	1997
80.51	004	Spinal Procedures	531 532	Spinal Procedures W CC Spinal Procedures W/O CC	2003
80.51	214 215	Back/Neck Procs W CC Back/Neck Procs W/O CC	499 500	Back/Neck Procs Exc Spin Fus W CC Back/Neck Procs Exc Spin Fus W/O CC	1997
80.59	004	Spinal Procedures	531 532	Spinal Procedures W CC Spinal Procedures W/O CC	2003
80.59	214 215	Back/Neck Procs W CC Back/Neck Procs W/O CC	499 500	Back/Neck Procs Exc Spin Fus W CC Back/Neck Procs Exc Spin Fus W/O CC	1997
80.6 80.76	221 222	Knee Procs W CC Knee Procs W/O CC	501 502 503	Knee Procs W PDx of Infect W CC Knee Procs W PDx of Infect W/O CC Knee Procs W/O PDx of Infect	1997
80.80-80.82 80.86 80.89	231	Local Excision & Removal of Int Fix Devices, Except Hip & Femur	537 538	Local Excision & Removal of Int Fix Devices, Except Hip & Femur W CC Local Excision & Removal of Int Fix Devices, Except Hip & Femur W/O CC	2003
80.96	221 222	Knee Procs W CC Knee Procs W/O CC	501 502 503	Knee Procs W PDx of Infect W CC Knee Procs W PDx of Infect W/O CC Knee Procs W/O PDx of Infect	1997
*81.0	004	Spinal Procedures	531 532	Spinal Procedures W CC Spinal Procedures W/O CC	2003
81.01 81.02	214 215	Back/Neck Procs W CC Back/Neck Procs W/O CC	497 498	Spin Fus W CC Spin Fus W/O CC	1997
81.02 & 81.03 81.02 & 81.05 81.02 & 81.08 81.04 & 81.03 81.04 & 81.05 81.04 & 81.08 81.06 & 81.03 81.06 & 81.05 81.06 & 81.08	214 215	Back/Neck Procs W CC Back/Neck Procs W/O CC	496	Comb Ant/Postr Spin Fus	1997

† DRG 109 was reactivated in October 1998 as Coronary Bypass without Cardiac Catheterization
†† DRG 514 became invalid effective October 1, 2003
††† DRG assignment October 1, 1984, through September 30, 2001, only
§ DRG 483 became invalid effective October 1, 2004

Proc Code	INVL DRG	DRG Title	NEW DRG	DRG Title	Effec-tive
81.03 81.04 81.05 81.06 81.07 81.08 81.09	214 215	Back/Neck Procs W CC Back/Neck Procs W/O CC	497 498	Spin Fus W CC Spin Fus W/O CC	1997
81.22	221 222	Knee Procs W CC Knee Procs W/O CC	501 502 503	Knee Procs W PDx of Infect W CC Knee Procs W PDx of Infect W/O CC Knee Procs W/O PDx of Infect	1997
*81.3	004	Spinal Procedures	531 532	Spinal Procedures W CC Spinal Procedures W/O CC	2003
81.42-81.47	221 222	Knee Procs W CC Knee Procs W/O CC	501 502 503	Knee Procs W PDx of Infect W CC Knee Procs W PDx of Infect W/O CC Knee Procs W/O PDx of Infect	1997
81.51-81.56	209	Maj Joint & Limb Reattachment Proc	544 545	Maj Joint Replcmnt or Reattachment of Lower Extremity Revision of Hip or Knee Replcmnt	2005
81.61	004	Spinal Procedures	531 532	Spinal Procedures W CC Spinal Procedures W/O CC	2003
84.26-84.28	209	Maj Joint & Limb Reattachment Proc	544 545	Maj Joint Replcmnt or Reattachment of Lower Extremity Revision of Hip or Knee Replcmnt	2005
85.82-85.84 86.60-86.63 86.65 86.66 86.69 *86.7 86.93	458	Non-Ext Brns W Sk Grft	504	Ext 3rd Degree Brns W Sk Grft	1998
88.52-88.58	514††	Card Defib Impl W Card Cath	535 536	Cardiac Defibrillator Implant W Cardiac Catheterization W Acute MI, Heart Failure or Shock Cardiac Defibrillator Implant W Cardiac Catheterization W/O Acute MI, Heart Failure or Shock	2003
88.52-88.58	107	Coronary Bypass W Cardiac Cath	547 548	Coronary Bypass W Cardiac Cath W MCV Dx Coronary Bypass W Cardiac Cath W/O MCV Dx	2005
92.27	517	Percutaneous Cardiovascular Procs W Non Drug-Eluting Stent W/O AMI	556	Percutaneous Cardiovascular Procs W Non Drug-Eluting Stent W/O MCV	2005
94.61	436	Alc/Drug Dep W Rehab Therapy	522	Alc/Drug Abuse or Dep, Detox or Oth Symp Tx W/O CC W Rehab Therapy	2001
94.63	437	Alc/Drug Dep W Comb Rehab & Detox Therapy	522	Alc/Drug Abuse or Dep, Detox or Oth Symp Tx W/O CC W Rehab Therapy	2001
94.64	436	Alc/Drug Dep W Rehab Therapy	522	Alc/Drug Abuse or Dep, Detox or Oth Symp Tx W/O CC W Rehab Therapy	2001

† DRG 109 was reactivated in October 1998 as Coronary Bypass without Cardiac Catheterization
†† DRG 514 became invalid effective October 1, 2003
††† DRG assignment October 1, 1984, through September 30, 2001, only
§ DRG 483 became invalid effective October 1, 2004

* Code Range

Proc Code	INVL DRG	DRG Title	NEW DRG	DRG Title	Effec-tive
94.66	437	Alc/Drug Dep W Comb Rehab & Detox Therapy	522	Alc/Drug Abuse or Dep, Detox or Oth Symp Tx W/O CC W Rehab Therapy	2001
94.67	436	Alc/Drug Dep W Rehab Therapy	522	Alc/Drug Abuse or Dep, Detox or Oth Symp Tx W/O CC W Rehab Therapy	2001
94.69	437	Alc/Drug Dep W Comb Rehab & Detox Therapy	522	Alc/Drug Abuse or Dep, Detox or Oth Symp Tx W/O CC W Rehab Therapy	2001
96.72	483§	Trach W Mech Vent 96+ Hrs or PDx Exc Face, Mouth & Neck Diag	541 542	Trach W MV 96+ Hrs or PDx Exc Face, Mth, & Neck Dx W Major O.R. Trach W MV 96+ Hrs or PDx Exc Face, Mth, & Neck Dx W/O Major O.R.	2004

Diag Code	INVL DRG	DRG Title	NEW DRG	DRG Title	Effec-tive
032.82, *036.4, *074.2, 086.0, *093, 098.83, 098.84, 098.85, 112.81, 115.03, 115.04, 115.13, 115.14, 115.93, 115.94, 130.3, 164.1	116	Other Perm Cardiac Pacemaker Impl	552	Other Perm Cardiac Pacemaker Impl W/O MCV Dx	2005
159.1 176.5 *196 *200 *201 *202 *203 *204 *205 *206 *207 *208 238.4-238.7 273.2 273.3	400	Lymphoma & Leukemia W Major O.R. Procedures	539 540	Lymphoma & Leukemia W Major O.R. Procedures W CC Lymphoma & Leukemia W Major O.R. Procedures W/O CC	2003
212.7, 228.00, 228.09, *250.7	116	Other Perm Cardiac Pacemaker Impl	552	Other Perm Cardiac Pacemaker Impl W/O MCV Dx	2005

† DRG 109 was reactivated in October 1998 as Coronary Bypass without Cardiac Catheterization
†† DRG 514 became invalid effective October 1, 2003
††† DRG assignment October 1, 1984, through September 30, 2001, only
§ DRG 483 became invalid effective October 1, 2004

Diag Code	INVL DRG	DRG Title	NEW DRG	DRG Title	Effective
*291 *292 *303.0 *303.9 *304	434††† 435††† 436††† 437†††	Alc/Drug Abuse or Dep, Detox or Oth Symp Tx W CC Alc/Drug Abuse or Dep, Detox or Oth Symp Tx W/O CC Alc/Drug Dep W Rehab Therapy Alc/Drug Dep W Comb Rehab & Detox Therapy	521 522 523	Alc/Drug Abuse or Dep W CC Alc/Drug Abuse or Dep, Detox or Oth Symp Tx W/O CC W Rehab Therapy Alc/Drug Abuse or Dep w/o Rehab Therapy w/o CC	2001
*305.0 *305.2 *305.3 *305.4 *305.5 *305.6 *305.7 *305.8 *305.9 709.3	434††† 435††† 436††† 437†††	Alc/Drug Abuse or Dep, Detox or Oth Symp Tx W CC Alc/Drug Abuse or Dep, Detox or Oth Symp Tx W/O CC Alc/Drug Dep W Rehab Therapy Alc/Drug Dep W Comb Rehab & Detox Therapy	521 522 523	Alc/Drug Abuse or Dep W CC Alc/Drug Abuse or Dep, Detox or Oth Symp Tx W/O CC W Rehab Therapy Alc/Drug Abuse or Dep w/o Rehab Therapy w/o CC	2001
306.2, *391, *392, 393, *394, *395, *396, *397, 398.0, 398.90, 398.91, 398.99	116	Perm Cardiac Pacemaker Impl W AMI, Heart Failure or Shock or AICD Lead or Gen Proc	552	Other Perm Cardiac Pacemaker Impl W/O MCV Dx	2005
398.91, 398.99, *401, 402.00, 402.01, 402.10, 402.11, 402.90, 402.91, 404.00, 404.01, 404.03, 404.10, 404.11, 404.13, 404.90, 404.91, 404.93, *405.0, *405.1, *405.9, 410.00, 410.01, 410.02, 410.10, 410.11, 410.12, 410.20, 410.21, 410.22	115 116	Perm Cardiac Pacemaker Impl W AMI, Heart Failure or Shock or AICD Lead or Gen Proc Other Perm Cardiac Pacemaker Impl	551 552	Perm Cardiac Pacemaker Impl W MCV Dx or AICD Lead or Generator Other Perm Cardiac Pacemaker Impl W/O MCV Dx	2005

† DRG 109 was reactivated in October 1998 as Coronary Bypass without Cardiac Catheterization
†† DRG 514 became invalid effective October 1, 2003
††† DRG assignment October 1, 1984, through September 30, 2001, only
§ DRG 483 became invalid effective October 1, 2004

* Code Range

Diag Code	INVL DRG	DRG Title	NEW DRG	DRG Title	Effec-tive
410.30, 410.31, 410.32, 410.40,	115	Perm Cardiac Pacemaker Impl W AMI, Heart Failure or Shock or AICD Lead or Gen Proc	551	Perm Cardiac Pacemaker Impl W MCV Dx or AICD Lead or Generator	2005
410.41, 410.42, 410.50, 410.51, 410.52, 410.60, 410.61, 410.62, 410.70, 410.71, 410.72, 410.80, 410.81, 410.82, 410.90, 410.91, 410.92, *411, 412, *413, *414, 415.0, *416, *417, *420, *421, *422, *423, *424, *425, *426, *427, +428, *429, 440.0, *440.2, *440.3, 440.8, 440.9, *441, 442.0, 442.2, 442.3, *442.8, 442.9, 443.1, 443.21, 443.22, 443.24, 443.29, *443.8, 443.9, *444, *445.0, 445.89	116	Other Perm Cardiac Pacemaker Impl	552	Other Perm Cardiac Pacemaker Impl W/O MCV Dx	

† DRG 109 was reactivated in October 1998 as Coronary Bypass without Cardiac Catheterization
†† DRG 514 became invalid effective October 1, 2003
††† DRG assignment October 1, 1984, through September 30, 2001, only
§ DRG 483 became invalid effective October 1, 2004

Diag Code	INVL DRG	DRG Title	NEW DRG	DRG Title	Effec-tive
447.0, 447.1, 447.2, 447.5, 447.8, 447.9, 448.0, 448.9, 451.0, *451.1, 451.2, *451.8, 451.9, 453.1, 453.2, *453.4, 453.8, 453.9, *454, 456.3, 456.8, *458, *459, *745, *746, 747.0, *747.1, *747.2, 747.3, *747.4, 747.5, *747.6, 747.89, 747.9, 759.82, 780.2, 785.0, 785.1, 785.2, 785.3, 785.4, 785.50, 785.51, 785.9, *786.5, 793.2, *794.3, 796.2, 796.3, 798.1, 798.2, *861.0, *861.1, 908.3, 908.4, *996.0, 996.1, 996.61, 996.62, *996.7, 996.83, 997.1, 997.2, 997.79	115	Perm Cardiac Pacemaker Impl W AMI, Heart Failure or Shock or AICD Lead or Gen Proc	551	Perm Cardiac Pacemaker Impl W MCV Dx or AICD Lead or Generator	2005
	116	Other Perm Cardiac Pacemaker Impl	552	Other Perm Cardiac Pacemaker Impl W/O MCV Dx	

† DRG 109 was reactivated in October 1998 as Coronary Bypass without Cardiac Catheterization
†† DRG 514 became invalid effective October 1, 2003
††† DRG assignment October 1, 1984, through September 30, 2001, only
§ DRG 483 became invalid effective October 1, 2004

* Code Range

Diag Code	INVL DRG	DRG Title	NEW DRG	DRG Title	Effec-tive
999.2, V42.1, V42.2, V43.21, V43.22, V43.3, V43.4, V53.31, V53.32, V53.39, V71.7	115 116	Perm Cardiac Pacemaker Impl W AMI, Heart Failure or Shock or AICD Lead or Gen Proc Other Perm Cardiac Pacemaker Impl	551 552	Perm Cardiac Pacemaker Impl W MCV Dx or AICD Lead or Generator Other Perm Cardiac Pacemaker Impl W/O MCV Dx	2005
*941.0	458 459	Non-Ext Brns W Sk Grft Non-Ext Brns W Wnd Debrid or Oth O.R. Proc	510 511	Non-Ext Brns W CC or Sig Trau Non-Ext Brns W/O CC or Sig Trau	1998
*941.1 *941.2	458 459 460	Non-Ext Brns W Sk Grft Non-Ext Brns W Wnd Debrid or Oth O.R. Proc Non-Ext Brns W/O O.R. Proc	510 511	Non-Ext Brns W CC or Sig Trau Non-Ext Brns W/O CC or Sig Trau	1998
*941.3 *941.4 *941.5	458 459 460	Non-Ext Brns W Sk Grft Non-Ext Brns W Wnd Debrid or Oth O.R. Proc Non-Ext Brns W/O O.R. Proc	506 507 508 509	3rd Deg Brns W Sk Grft/Inhal Inj W CC or Sig Trau Full Thick Brns W Sk Grft/Inhal Inj W /O CC or Sig Trau Full Thick Brns W/O Sk Grft/Inhal Inj W CC or Sig Trau Full ThickBrns W/O Sk Grft/Inhal Inj W/O CC or Sig Trau	1998
*942.0 *942.1 *942.2	458 459 460	Non-Ext Brns W Sk Grft Non-Ext Brns W Wnd Debrid or Oth O.R. Proc Non-Ext Brns W/O O.R. Proc	510 511	Non-Ext Brns W CC or Sig Trau Non-Ext Brns W/O CC or Sig Trau	1998
*942.3 *942.4 *942.5	458 459 460	Non-Ext Brns W Sk Grft Non-Ext Brns W Wnd Debrid or Oth O.R. Proc Non-Ext Brns W/O O.R. Proc	506 507 508 509	3rd Deg Brns W Sk Grft/Inhal Inj W CC or Sig Trau Full Thick Brns W Sk Grft/Inhal Inj W /O CC or Sig Trau Full Thick Brns W/O Sk Grft/Inhal Inj W CC or Sig Trau Full ThickBrns W/O Sk Grft/Inhal Inj W/O CC or Sig Trau	1998
*943.0 *943.1 *943.2	458 459 460	Non-Ext Brns W Sk Grft Non-Ext Brns W Wnd Debrid or Oth O.R. Proc Non-Ext Brns W/O O.R. Proc	510 511	Non-Ext Brns W CC or Sig Trau Non-Ext Brns W/O CC or Sig Trau	1998
*943.3 *943.4 *943.5	458 459 460	Non-Ext Brns W Sk Grft Non-Ext Brns W Wnd Debrid or Oth O.R. Proc Non-Ext Brns W/O O.R. Proc	506 507 508 509	3rd Deg Brns W Sk Grft/Inhal Inj W CC or Sig Trau Full Thick Brns W Sk Grft/Inhal Inj W /O CC or Sig Trau Full Thick Brns W/O Sk Grft/Inhal Inj W CC or Sig Trau Full ThickBrns W/O Sk Grft/Inhal Inj W/O CC or Sig Trau	1998
*944.0 *944.1 *944.2	458 459 460	Non-Ext Brns W Sk Grft Non-Ext Brns W Wnd Debrid or Oth O.R. Proc Non-Ext Brns W/O O.R. Proc	510 511	Non-Ext Brns W CC or Sig Trau Non-Ext Brns W/O CC or Sig Trau	1998

† DRG 109 was reactivated in October 1998 as Coronary Bypass without Cardiac Catheterization
†† DRG 514 became invalid effective October 1, 2003
††† DRG assignment October 1, 1984, through September 30, 2001, only
§ DRG 483 became invalid effective October 1, 2004

Diag Code	INVL DRG	DRG Title	NEW DRG	DRG Title	Effec-tive
*944.3 *944.4 *944.5	458 459 460	Non-Ext Brns W Sk Grft Non-Ext Brns W Wnd Debrid or Oth O.R. Proc Non-Ext Brns W/O O.R. Proc	506 507 508 509	3rd Deg Brns W Sk Grft/Inhal Inj W CC or Sig Trau Full Thick Brns W Sk Grft/Inhal Inj W /O CC or Sig Trau Full Thick Brns W/O Sk Grft/Inhal Inj W CC or Sig Trau Full ThickBrns W/O Sk Grft/Inhal Inj W/O CC or Sig Trau	1998
*945.0 *945.1 *945.2	458 459 460	Non-Ext Brns W Sk Grft Non-Ext Brns W Wnd Debrid or Oth O.R. Proc Non-Ext Brns W/O O.R. Proc	510 511	Non-Ext Brns W CC or Sig Trau Non-Ext Brns W/O CC or Sig Trau	1998
*945.3 *945.4	458 459 460	Non-Ext Brns W Sk Grft Non-Ext Brns W Wnd Debrid or Oth O.R. Proc Non-Ext Brns W/O O.R. Proc	506 507 508 509	3rd Deg Brns W Sk Grft/Inhal Inj W CC or Sig Trau Full Thick Brns W Sk Grft/Inhal Inj W /O CC or Sig Trau Full Thick Brns W/O Sk Grft/Inhal Inj W CC or Sig Trau Full ThickBrns W/O Sk Grft/Inhal Inj W/O CC or Sig Trau	1998
946.0- 946.2	458 459 460	Non-Ext Brns W Sk Grft Non-Ext Brns W Wnd Debrid or Oth O.R. Proc Non-Ext Brns W/O O.R. Proc	510 511	Non-Ext Brns W CC or Sig Trau Non-Ext Brns W/O CC or Sig Trau	1998
946.3- 946.5	458 459 460	Non-Ext Brns W Sk Grft Non-Ext Brns W Wnd Debrid or Oth O.R. Proc Non-Ext Brns W/O O.R. Proc	506 507 508 509	3rd Deg Brns W Sk Grft/Inhal Inj W CC or Sig Trau Full Thick Brns W Sk Grft/Inhal Inj W /O CC or Sig Trau Full Thick Brns W/O Sk Grft/Inhal Inj W CC or Sig Trau Full ThickBrns W/O Sk Grft/Inhal Inj W/O CC or Sig Trau	1998
947.8 947.9 948.00- 948.10	458 459 460	Non-Ext Brns W Sk Grft Non-Ext Brns W Wnd Debrid or Oth O.R. Proc Non-Ext Brns W/O O.R. Proc	510 511	Non-Ext Brns W CC or Sig Trau Non-Ext Brns W/O CC or Sig Trau	1998
948.11	458 459 460	Non-Ext Brns W Sk Grft Non-Ext Brns W Wnd Debrid or Oth O.R. Proc Non-Ext Brns W/O O.R. Proc	506 507 508 509	3rd Deg Brns W Sk Grft/Inhal Inj W CC or Sig Trau Full Thick Brns W Sk Grft/Inhal Inj W /O CC or Sig Trau Full Thick Brns W/O Sk Grft/Inhal Inj W CC or Sig Trau Full ThickBrns W/O Sk Grft/Inhal Inj W/O CC or Sig Trau	1998
948.20	458 459 460	Non-Ext Brns W Sk Grft Non-Ext Brns W Wnd Debrid or Oth O.R. Proc Non-Ext Brns W/O O.R. Proc	506 507 508 509	3rd Deg Brns W Sk Grft/Inhal Inj W CC or Sig Trau Full Thick Brns W Sk Grft/Inhal Inj W /O CC or Sig Trau Full Thick Brns W/O Sk Grft/Inhal Inj W CC or Sig Trau Full ThickBrns W/O Sk Grft/Inhal Inj W/O CC or Sig Trau	1999
948.21	458 459 460	Non-Ext Brns W Sk Grft Non-Ext Brns W Wnd Debrid or Oth O.R. Proc Non-Ext Brns W/O O.R. Proc	504 505	Ext 3rd Degree Brns W Sk Grft Ext 3rd Degree Brns W/O Sk Grft	1998
948.22	457	Ext Brns W/O O.R. Proc	504 505	Ext 3rd Degree Brns W Sk Grft Ext 3rd Degree Brns W/O Sk Grft	1998

† DRG 109 was reactivated in October 1998 as Coronary Bypass without Cardiac Catheterization
†† DRG 514 became invalid effective October 1, 2003
††† DRG assignment October 1, 1984, through September 30, 2001, only
§ DRG 483 became invalid effective October 1, 2004

* Code Range

Diag Code	INVL DRG	DRG Title	NEW DRG	DRG Title	Effec-tive
948.30 & 948.40	458 459 460	Non-Ext Brns W Sk Grft Non-Ext Brns W Wnd Debrid or Oth O.R. Proc Non-Ext Brns W/O O.R. Proc	510 511	Non-Ext Brns W CC or Sig Trau Non-Ext Brns W/O CC or Sig Trau	1998
948.31-948.41	458 459 460	Non-Ext Brns W Sk Grft Non-Ext Brns W Wnd Debrid or Oth O.R. Proc Non-Ext Brns W/O O.R. Proc	504 505	Ext 3rd Degree Brns W Sk Grft Ext 3rd Degree Brns W/O Sk Grft	1998
948.32 948.33 948.42-948.44	457	Ext Brns W/O O.R. Proc	504 505	Ext 3rd Degree Brns W Sk Grft Ext 3rd Degree Brns W/O Sk Grft	1998
948.50	457	Ext Brns W/O O.R. Proc	510 511	Non-Ext Brns W CC or Sig Trau Non-Ext Brns W/O CC or Sig Trau	1998
948.51-948.55	457	Ext Brns W/O O.R. Proc	504 505	Ext 3rd Degree Brns W Sk Grft Ext 3rd Degree Brns W/O Sk Grft	1998
948.60	457	Ext Brns W/O O.R. Proc	510 511	Non-Ext Brns W CC or Sig Trau Non-Ext Brns W/O CC or Sig Trau	1998
948.61-948.66	457	Ext Brns W/O O.R. Proc	504 505	Ext 3rd Degree Brns W Sk Grft Ext 3rd Degree Brns W/O Sk Grft	1998
948.70	457	Ext Brns W/O O.R. Proc	510 511	Non-Ext Brns W CC or Sig Trau Non-Ext Brns W/O CC or Sig Trau	1998
948.71-948.77	457	Ext Brns W/O O.R. Proc	504 505	Ext 3rd Degree Brns W Sk Grft Ext 3rd Degree Brns W/O Sk Grft	1998
948.80	457	Ext Brns W/O O.R. Proc	510 511	Non-Ext Brns W CC or Sig Trau Non-Ext Brns W/O CC or Sig Trau	1998
948.81-948.88	457	Ext Brns W/O O.R. Proc	504 505	Ext 3rd Degree Brns W Sk Grft Ext 3rd Degree Brns W/O Sk Grft	1998
948.90	457	Ext Brns W/O O.R. Proc	510 511	Non-Ext Brns W CC or Sig Trau Non-Ext Brns W/O CC or Sig Trau	1998
948.91-948.99	457	Ext Brns W/O O.R. Proc	504 505	Ext 3rd Degree Brns W Sk Grft Ext 3rd Degree Brns W/O Sk Grft	1998
949.0 949.1 949.2	458 459 460	Non-Ext Brns W Sk Grft Non-Ext Brns W Wnd Debrid or Oth O.R. Proc Non-Ext Brns W/O O.R. Proc	510 511	Non-Ext Brns W CC or Sig Trau Non-Ext Brns W/O CC or Sig Trau	1998
949.3 949.4 949.5	458 459 460	Non-Ext Brns W Sk Grft Non-Ext Brns W Wnd Debrid or Oth O.R. Proc Non-Ext Brns W/O O.R. Proc	506 507 508 509	3rd Deg Brns W Sk Grft/Inhal Inj W CC or Sig Trau Full Thick Brns W Sk Grft/Inhal Inj W /O CC or Sig Trau Full Thick Brns W/O Sk Grft/Inhal Inj W CC or Sig Trau Full ThickBrns W/O Sk Grft/Inhal Inj W/O CC or Sig Trau	1998

† DRG 109 was reactivated in October 1998 as Coronary Bypass without Cardiac Catheterization
†† DRG 514 became invalid effective October 1, 2003
††† DRG assignment October 1, 1984, through September 30, 2001, only
§ DRG 483 became invalid effective October 1, 2004

Diag Code	INVL DRG	DRG Title	NEW DRG	DRG Title	Effec-tive
*996.0, 996.1, 996.61, 996.62, 996.71, 996.72, 996.73, 996.74, 996.83, 997.1, 997.2, 997.79, 999.2, V42.1, V42.2, *V43.2, V43.3, V43.4, *V53.3, V71.7	116	Other Perm Cardiac Pacemaker Impl	552	Other Perm Cardiac Pacemaker Impl W/O MCV Dx	2005

† DRG 109 was reactivated in October 1998 as Coronary Bypass without Cardiac Catheterization
†† DRG 514 became invalid effective October 1, 2003
††† DRG assignment October 1, 1984, through September 30, 2001, only
§ DRG 483 became invalid effective October 1, 2004

* Code Range

Appendix B — DRG Surgical Hierarchy Table

The surgical hierarchy reflects the relative resources requirement of the various surgical procedures of each major diagnostic category (MDC). The hierarchy is based upon variables such as principal diagnosis, surgical class, age, complications and comorbidities.

Arranging the surgical DRGs in this manner allows for the assignment of patients with multiple procedures related to the principal diagnosis to a surgical DRG that best reflects the resources used in the care of that patient. Since patients can be assigned to only one surgical class for each inpatient stay, patients with multiple procedures related to the principal diagnosis are assigned to the highest surgical DRG in the MDC assigned according to principal diagnosis. (*Federal Register*, August 12, 2005).

Pre MDC

Heart transplant or implant of heart assist system	103
ECMO or tracheostomy w mechanical vent 96+ hrs or PDx except face, mouth & neck w major O.R. procedure	541
Tracheostomy w mechanical vent 96+ hrs or PDx except face, mouth & neck w/o major O.R. procedure	542
Liver transplant and/or intestinal transplant	480
Lung transplant	495
Simultaneous pancreas/kidney transplant	512
Pancreas transplant	513
Bone marrow transplant	481
Tracheostomy for face, mouth & neck diagnoses	482

MDC 1 DISEASES & DISORDERS OF THE NERVOUS SYSTEM

Craniotomy age 0-17	003
Intracranial vascular procedures w PDx hemorrhage	528
Craniotomy w implant of chemo agent or acute complex central nervous system PDx	543
Craniotomy age >17 w CC	001
Craniotomy age >17 w/o CC	002
Ventricular shunt procedure w CC	529
Ventricular shunt procedure w/o CC	530
Spinal procedure w CC	531
Spinal procedure w/o CC	532
Extacranial procedures w CC	533
Extacranial procedures w/o CC	534
Carpal tunnel release	006
Peripheral & cranial nerve and other O.R. nervous system procedures w CC	007
Peripheral & cranial nerve and other O.R. nervous system procedures w/o CC	008

MDC 2 DISEASES & DISORDERS OF THE EYE

Orbital procedure	037
Extraocular procedures excluding orbit age >17	040
Extraocular procedures excluding orbit age 0-17	041
Retinal procedures	036
Intraocular procedures excluding retina, iris & lens	042
Lens procedures	039
Primary iris procedures	038

MDC 3 DISEASES & DISORDERS OF THE EAR, NOSE, MOUTH & THROAT

Major head & neck procedures	049
Myringotomy w tube insertion age >17	061
Myringotomy w tube insertion age 0-17	062
Sinus & mastoid procedures age >17	053
Sinus & mastoid procedures age 0-17	054
Tonsil & adenoid procedures excluding tonsillectomy &/or adenoidectomy age >17	057
Tonsil & adenoid procedures excluding tonsillectomy &/or adenoidectomy age 0-17	058
Cleft lip & palate repair	052
Mouth procedures w CC	168
Mouth procedures w/o CC	169
Rhinoplasty	056
Sialoadenectomy	050
Salivary gland procedures excluding sialoadenectomy	051
Miscellaneous ear, nose, mouth & throat procedures	055
Tonsillectomy &/or adenoidectomy only age >17	059
Tonsillectomy &/or adenoidectomy only age 0-17	060
Other ear, nose, mouth & throat O.R. procedure	063

MDC 4 DISEASES & DISORDERS OF THE RESPIRATORY SYSTEM

Major chest procedures	075
Other respiratory system O.R. procedures w CC	076
Other respiratory system O.R. procedures w/o CC	077

MDC 5 DISEASES & DISORDERS OF THE CIRCULATORY SYSTEM

Other heart assist system implant	525
Cardiac valve and other major cardiothoracic procedures w cardiac cath	104
Cardiac valve and other major cardiothoracic procedures w/o cardiac cath	105
Cardiac defibrillator implant w cardiac cath w AMI, heart failure, or shock	535
Cardiac defibrillator implant w cardiac cath w/o AMI, heart failure, or shock	536
Cardiac defibrillator implant w/o cardiac cath	515
Other cardiothoracic procedures	108
Coronary bypass w PTCA	106
Coronary bypasss w cardiac cath with MCV dx	547
Coronary bypass w cardiac cath w/o MCV dx	548
Coronary bypass w/o cardiac cath w MCV dx	549
Coronary bypass w/o cardiac cath w/o MCV dx	550
Cardiovascular procedures w CC	110
Cardiovascular procedures w/o CC	111
Amputation excluding upper limb & toe	113
Permanent cardiac pacemaker implantation w MCV dx or AICD lead or generator	551
Other permanentcardiac pacemaker implantation w/o MCV dx	552
Percutaneous cardiovascular procedures w drug-eluting stent w MCV dx	557
Percutaneous cardiovascular procedures w MCV dx	555
Percutaneous cardiovascular procedures w drug-eluting stent w/o MCV dx	558
Percutaneous cardiovascular procedures w non drug-eluting stent w/o MCV dx	556
Percutaneous cardiovascular procedures w/o AMI w coronary art stent implant	518
Other vascular procedures w CC w MCV dx	553
Other vascular procedures w CC w/o MCV dx	554
Other vascular procedures w/o CC	479
Amputation upper limb & toe for circulatory system disorder	114
Cardiac pacemaker replacement &/or revision excluding device replacement	117
Cardiac pacemaker device replacement	118
Vein ligation & stripping	119
Other circulatory system O.R. procedure	120

MDC 6 DISEASES & DISORDERS OF THE DIGESTIVE SYSTEM

Stomach, esophageal & duodenal procedures age >17 w CC	154
Stomach, esophageal & duodenal procedures age >17 w/o CC	155
Stomach, esophageal & duodenal procedures age 0-17	156
Major small & large bowel procedures w CC	148
Major small & large bowel procedures w/o CC	149
Rectal resection w CC	146
Rectal resection w/o CC	147
Peritoneal adhesiolysis w CC	150
Peritoneal adhesiolysis w/o CC	151
Appendectomy w complicated principal diagnosis w CC	164
Appendectomy w complicated principal diagnosis w/o CC	165
Appendectomy w/o complicated principal diagnosis w CC	166
Appendectomy w/o complicated principal diagnosis w/o CC	167
Minor small & large bowel procedures w CC	152
Minor small & large bowel procedures w/o CC	153
Anal and stomal procedures w CC	157
Anal and stomal procedures w/o CC	158
Hernia procedures excluding inguinal & femoral >17 w CC	159
Hernia procedures excluding inguinal & femoral >17 w/o CC	160
Inguinal & femoral hernia procedures age >17 w CC	161
Inguinal & femoral hernia procedures age >17 w/o CC	162
Hernia procedures age 0-17	163
Other digestive system O.R. procedures w CC	170
Other digestive system O.R. procedures w/o CC	171

MDC 7 DISEASES & DISORDERS OF THE HEPATOBILIARY SYSTEM & PANCREAS

Pancreas, liver & shunt procedures w CC	191
Pancreas, liver & shunt procedures w/o CC	192
Biliary tract procedures excluding only cholecyst w or w/o C.D.E.w CC	193
Biliary tract procedures excluding only cholecyst w or w/o C.D.E.w/o CC	194
Cholecystectomy w C.D.E. w CC	195
Cholecystectomy w C.D.E. w/o CC	196
Cholecystectomy excluding by laparoscope w/o C.D.E. w CC	197
Cholecystectomy excluding by laparoscope w/o C.D.E. w/o CC	198
Laparoscopic cholecystectomy w/o C.D.E.w CC	493
Laparoscopic cholecystectomy w/o C.D.E.w/o CC	494
Hepatobiliary diagnostic procedures for malignancy	199
Hepatobiliary diagnostic procedures for non-malignancy	200
Other hepatobiliary & pancreas O.R. procedure	201

MDC 8 DISEASES & DISORDERS OF THE MUSCULOSKELETAL SYSTEM & CONNECTIVE TISSUE

Combined anterior/posterior spinal fusion	496
Spinal fusions except cervical w curvature of the spine or malignancy	546
Spinal fusion w CC	497
Spinal fusion w/o CC	498
Bilateral or multiple major joint procedures of the lower extremity	471
Wound debridement & skin graft excluding hand	217
Revision of hip or knee replacement	545
Major joint replacement or reattachment of lower extremity	544
Cervical spinal fusion w CC	519
Cervical spinal fusion w/o CC	520
Biopsies	216
Amputations	213
Hip and femur procedures excluding major joint age>17 w CC	210
Hip and femur procedures excluding major joint age>17 w/o CC	211
Hip and femur procedures excluding major joint age 0-17	212
Major joint & limb reattachment procedures of upper extremity	491
Knee procedures w pdx of infection w CC PDX	501
Knee procedures w pdx of infection w/o CC PDX	502
Knee procedures w/o pdx of infection PDX	503
Back & neck procedures excluding spinal fusion w CC	499
Back & neck procedures excluding spinal fusion w/o CC	500
Lower extremity & humerus procedures excluding hip, foot, femur age>17 w CC	218
Lower extremity & humerus procedures excluding hip, foot, femur age >17 w/o CC	219
Lower extremity & humerus procedures excluding hip, foot, femur age 0-17	220
Local excision & removal of internal fixation devices excluding hip & femur w CC	537
Local excision & removal of internal fixation devices excluding hip & femur w/o CC	538
Local excision & removal of internal fixation devices of hip & femur	230
Soft tissue procedures w CC	226
Soft tissue procedures w/o CC	227
Foot procedures	225
Major thumb or joint procedures or other hand or wrist procedures w CC	228
Major shoulder/elbow procedures or other upper extremity procedures w CC	223
Arthroscopy	232
Shoulder, elbow or forearm procedures excluding major joint procedures w/o CC	224
Hand or wrist procedures excluding major joint procedures w/o CC	229
Other musculoskeletal system & connective tissue O.R. procedures w CC	233
Other musculoskeletal system & connective tissue O.R. procedures w/o CC	234

MDC 9 DISEASES & DISORDERS OF THE SKIN, SUBCUTANEOUS TISSUE & BREAST

Skin grafts &/or debridements for skin ulcers or cellulitis w CC	263
Skin grafts &/or debridements for skin ulcers or cellulitis w/o CC	264
Skin grafts &/or debridements excluding for skin ulcers or cellulitis w CC	265
Skin grafts &/or debridements excluding for skin ulcers or cellulitis w/o CC	266
Skin, subcutaneous tissue & breast plastic procedures	268
Perianal & pilonidal procedures	267
Total mastectomy for malignancy w CC	257
Total mastectomy for malignancy w/o CC	258
Subtotal mastectomy for malignancy w CC	259
Subtotal mastectomy for malignancy w/o CC	260
Breast procedure for non-malignancy excluding biopsy & local excision	261
Breast procedure biopsy & local excision for non-malignancy	262
Other skin, subcutaneous tissue & breast O.R. procedures w CC	269
Other skin, subcutaneous tissue & breast O.R. procedures w/o CC	270

MDC 10 ENDOCRINE, NUTRITIONAL & METABOLIC DISEASES & DISORDERS

Adrenal & pituitary procedures	286
O.R. procedures for obesity	288
Amputation of lower limb	285
Skin graft & wound debridement	287
Parathyroid procedures	289
Thyroid procedures	290
Thyroglossal procedures	291
Other endocrine, nutritional & metabolic O.R. procedures w CC	292
Other endocrine, nutritional & metabolic O.R. procedures w/o CC	293

MDC 11 DISEASES & DISORDERS OF THE KIDNEY & URINARY TRACT

Kidney transplant	302
Kidney, ureter & major bladder procedures for neoplasm	303
Kidney, ureter & major bladder procedures for non-neoplasm w CC	304
Kidney, ureter & major bladder procedures for non-neoplasm w/o CC	305
Minor bladder procedures w CC	308
Minor bladder procedures w/o CC	309
Prostatectomy w CC	306
Prostatectomy w/o CC	307
Transurethral procedures w CC	310
Transurethral procedures w/o CC	311
Urethral procedures age>17 w CC	312
Urethral procedures age>17 w/o CC	313
Urethral procedures age 0-17	314
Other kidney & urinary tract O.R. procedures	315

MDC 12 DISEASES & DISORDERS OF THE MALE REPRODUCTIVE SYSTEM

Major male pelvic procedures w CC	334
Major male pelvic procedures w/o CC	335
Penis procedures	341
Testes procedures for malignancy	338
Testes procedures non-malignancy age>17	339
Testes procedures non-malignancy age 0-17	340
Circumcision age >17	342
Circumcision age 0-17	343
Transurethral prostatectomy w CC	336
Transurethral prostatectomy w/o CC	337
Other male reprod system O.R. procedures for malignancy	344
Other male reprod system O.R. procedures excluding for malignancy	345

MDC 13 DISEASES & DISORDERS OF THE FEMALE REPRODUCTIVE SYSTEM

Pelvic evisceration, radical hysterectomy & radical vulvectomy	353
Uterine, adnexa procedures for non-ovarian/adnexal malig w CC	354
Uterine, adnexa procedures for non-ovarian/adnexal malig w/o CC	355
Uterine & adnexal procedures for ovarian or adnexal malignancy	357
Uterine, adnexa procedures for non malignant w CC	358
Uterine, adnexa procedures for non-malignant w/o CC	359
Laparoscopy & incisional tubal interruption	361
Vagina, cervix and vulva procedures	360
Reconstructive procedures	356
D & C, conization & radioactive implant w CC	363
D & C, conization & radioactive implant w/o CC	364
Endoscopic tubal interruption	362
Other female reproductive system O.R. procedures	365

MDC 14 PREGNANCY, CHILDBIRTH, & THE PUERPERIUM

Cesarean section w CC	370
Cesarean section w/o CC	371
Sterilization & postpartum D & C	374
Other O.R. procedures for pregnancy and childbirth	375

MDC 15 NEWBORNS & OTHER NEONATES W CONDITIONS ORIGINATING IN THE PERINATAL PERIOD

None	

MDC 16 DISEASES & DISORDERS OF THE BLOOD AND BLOOD FORMING ORGANS & IMMUNOLOGICAL DISORDERS

Splenectomy age >17	392
Splenectomy age 0-17	393
Other O.R. procedures of the blood & blood forming organs	394

MDC 17 MYELOPROLIFERATIVE DISEASES & DISORDERS, POORLY DIFFERENTIATED NEOPLASMS FOR LYMPHOMA AND LEUKEMIA

Lymphoma & leukemia w major O.R. procedures w CC	539
Lymphoma & leukemia w major O.R. procedures w/o CC	540
Other O.R. procedures for lymphoma or leukemia w CC	401
Other O.R. procedures for lymphoma or leukemia w/o CC	402
Major procedures for myeloproliferative disease and poorly diff neoplasms w CC	406
Major procedures for myeloproliferative disease and poorly diff neoplasms w/o CC	407
Other O.R. procedures for myeloproliferative disease and poorly diff neoplasms	408

MDC 18 INFECTIOUS & PARASITIC DISEASES SYSTEMIC OR UNSPECIFIED SITES

Any O.R. procedure for infectious & parasitic diseases	415

MDC 19 MENTAL DISEASES & DISORDERS

Any O.R. procedure w principal diagnosis of mental illness	424

MDC 20 ALCOHOL/DRUG USE & ALCOHOL/DRUG INDUCED ORGANIC MENTAL DISORDERS

None	

MDC 21 INJURY, POISONING & TOXIC EFFECTS OF DRUGS

Wound debridements	440
Skin grafts	439
Hand procedures	441
Other O.R. procedures for injuries w CC	442
Other O.R. procedures for injuries w/o CC	443

MDC 22 BURNS

Extensive burns or full thickness burns w mechanical vent 96+ hours w skin graft	504
Full thickness burn w skin graft w CC or significant trauma	506
Full thickness burn w skin graft w/o CC or significant trauma	507

MDC 23 FACTORS INFLUENCING HEALTH STATUS ALL OTHER CONTACTS W HEALTH

Any O.R. procedures w diagnosis of other contact w health services	461

MDC 24 MULTIPLE SIGNIFICANT TRAUMA

Craniotomy for multiple significant trauma	484
Limb reattachment, hip and femur procedures for multiple significant trauma	485
Other O.R. procedures for multiple significant trauma	486

MDC 25 HUMAN IMMUNODEFICIENCY VIRUS INFECTIONS

HIV w extensive O.R. procedure	488

Appendix C — LTC-DRG Crosswalk

The Centers for Medicare and Medicaid Services (CMS) modified the DRGs for the LTCH prospective payment system by developing LTCH-specific relative weights to account for the fact that LTCHs generally treat patients with multiple medical problems. Therefore, CMS developed a crosswalk of IPPS DRG to LTC DRG data including relative weight (RW), geometric mean length of stay (GMLOS), and 5/6 GMLOS for short stay outlier payment adjustment.

Since LTCHs generally do not treat the full range of diagnoses that make up the inpatient DRG system, the low volume DRGs were grouped into quintiles for setting the relative weights and length of stay data. The following footnotes provide the information concerning the grouping of the individual DRGs.

1 Relative weights for these LTC-DRGs were determined by assigning these cases to low-volume quintile 1.
2 Relative weights for these LTC-DRGs were determined by assigning these cases to low-volume quintile 2.
3 Relative weights for these LTC-DRGs were determined by assigning these cases to low-volume quintile 3.
4 Relative weights for these LTC-DRGs were determined by assigning these cases to low-volume quintile 4.
5 Relative weights for these LTC-DRGs were determined by assigning these cases to low-volume quintile 5.
6 Relative weights for these LTC-DRGs were assigned a value of 0.0000.
7 Relative weights for these LTC-DRGs were determined after adjusting to account for nonmonotonicity.
8 Relative weights for these LTC-DRGs were determined by assigning these cases to the appropriate low volume quintile because they had no LTCH cases in the FY 2003 MedPAR file.

LTC-DRG	Description	RW	GMLOS	5/6 GMLOS
1	[5] CRANIOTOMY AGE >17 W CC	1.7034	38.5	32.1
2	[7] CRANIOTOMY AGE > 17 W/O CC	1.7034	38.5	32.1
3	[7] CRANIOTOMY AGE 0-17	1.7034	38.5	32.1
6	[7] CARPAL TUNNEL RELEASE	0.4499	19.0	15.8
7	PERIPH & CRANIAL NERVE & OTHER NERV SYST PROC W CC	1.3984	37.7	31.4
8	[3] PERIPH & CRANIAL NERVE & OTHER NERV SYST PROC W/O CC	0.7637	24.8	20.7
9	SPINAL DISORDERS & INJURIES	0.9720	33.7	28.1
10	NERVOUS SYSTEM NEOPLASMS W CC	0.7554	24.5	20.4
11	[2] NERVOUS SYSTEM NEOPLASMS W/O CC	0.5837	21.3	17.8
12	DEGENERATIVE NERVOUS SYSTEM DISORDERS	0.6851	25.5	21.3
13	MULTIPLE SCLEROSIS & CEREBELLAR ATAXIA	0.6531	23.1	19.3
14	INTERCRANIAL HEMORRHAGE OR STROKE WITH INFARCT	0.7783	26.0	21.7
15	NONSPECIFIC CVA & PRECEREBRAL OCCULUSION WITHOUT INFARCT	0.7314	26.8	22.3
16	NONSPECIFIC CEREBROVASCULAR DISORDERS W CC	0.7471	23.5	19.6
17	[1] NONSPECIFIC CEREBROVASCULAR DISORDERS W/O CC	0.4499	19.0	15.8
18	CRANIAL & PERIPHERAL NERVE DISORDERS W CC	0.7197	23.6	19.7

LTC-DRG	Description	RW	GMLOS	5/6 GMLOS
19	CRANIAL & PERIPHERAL NERVE DISORDERS W/O CC	0.4773	21.2	17.7
20	NERVOUS SYSTEM INFECTION EXCEPT VIRAL MENINGITIS	1.0277	27.2	22.7
21	[3] VIRAL MENINGITIS	0.7637	24.8	20.7
22	[4] HYPERTENSIVE ENCEPHALOPATHY	1.1820	29.6	24.7
23	NONTRAUMATIC STUPOR & COMA	0.8054	25.4	21.2
24	SEIZURE & HEADACHE AGE >17 W CC	0.6251	22.6	18.8
25	[1] SEIZURE & HEADACHE AGE >17 W/O CC	0.4499	19.0	15.8
26	[7] SEIZURE & HEADACHE AGE 0-17	0.4499	19.0	15.8
27	TRAUMATIC STUPOR & COMA, COMA >1 HR	0.9444	27.1	22.6
28	TRAUMATIC STUPOR & COMA, COMA <1 HR AGE >17 W CC	0.8890	30.2	25.2
29	[2] TRAUMATIC STUPOR & COMA, COMA <1 HR AGE >17 W/O CC	0.5837	21.3	17.8
30	[7] TRAUMATIC STUPOR & COMA, COMA <1 HR AGE 0-17	0.5837	21.3	17.8
31	[3] CONCUSSION AGE >17 W CC	0.7637	24.8	20.7
32	[7] CONCUSSION AGE >17 W/O CC	0.4499	19.0	15.8
33	[7] CONCUSSION AGE 0-17	0.4499	19.0	15.8
34	OTHER DISORDERS OF NERVOUS SYSTEM W CC	0.8004	25.3	21.1
35	OTHER DISORDERS OF NERVOUS SYSTEM W/O CC	0.5698	24.2	20.2
36	[7] RETINAL PROCEDURES	1.1820	29.6	24.7
37	[7] ORBITAL PROCEDURES	1.1820	29.6	24.7
38	[7] PRIMARY IRIS PROCEDURES	1.1820	29.6	24.7
39	[7] LENS PROCEDURES WITH OR WITHOUT VITRECTOMY	1.1820	29.6	24.7
40	[4] EXTRAOCULAR PROCEDURES EXCEPT ORBIT AGE >17	1.1820	29.6	24.7
41	[7] EXTRAOCULAR PROCEDURES EXCEPT ORBIT AGE 0-17	1.1820	29.6	24.7
42	[7] INTRAOCULAR PROCEDURES EXCEPT RETINA, IRIS & LENS	1.1820	29.6	24.7
43	[7] HYPHEMA	1.1820	29.6	24.7
44	[2] ACUTE MAJOR EYE INFECTIONS	0.5837	21.3	17.8
45	[7] NEUROLOGICAL EYE DISORDERS	1.1820	29.6	24.7
46	[2] OTHER DISORDERS OF THE EYE AGE >17 W CC	0.5837	21.3	17.8
47	[7] OTHER DISORDERS OF THE EYE AGE >17 W/O CC	1.1820	29.6	24.7
48	[7] OTHER DISORDERS OF THE EYE AGE 0-17	1.1820	29.6	24.7
49	[7] MAJOR HEAD & NECK PROCEDURES	1.1820	29.6	24.7
50	[7] S IALOADENECTOMY	1.1820	29.6	24.7
51	[7] SALIVARY GLAND PROCEDURES EXCEPT SIALOADENECTOMY	1.1820	29.6	24.7
52	[7] CLEFT LIP & PALATE REPAIR	1.1820	29.6	24.7
53	[7] SINUS & MASTOID PROCEDURES AGE >17	1.1820	29.6	24.7
54	[7] SINUS & MASTOID PROCEDURES AGE 0-17	1.1820	29.6	24.7

LTC-DRG	Description	RW	GMLOS	5/6 GMLOS
55	[7] MISCELLANEOUS EAR, NOSE, MOUTH & THROAT PROCEDURES	1.1820	29.6	24.7
56	[7] RHINOPLASTY	1.1820	29.6	24.7
57	[7] T&A PROC, EXCEPT TONSILLECTOMY &/OR ADENOIDECTOMY ONLY, AGE >17	0.4499	19.0	15.8
58	[7] T&A PROC, EXCEPT TONSILLECTOMY &/OR ADENOIDECTOMY ONLY, AGE 0-17	0.4499	19.0	15.8
59	[7] TONSILLECTOMY &/OR ADENOIDECTOMY ONLY, AGE >17	0.4499	19.0	15.8
60	[7] TONSILLECTOMY &/OR ADENOIDECTOMY ONLY, AGE 0-17	0.4499	19.0	15.8
61	[3] MYRINGOTOMY W TUBE INSERTION AGE >17	0.7637	24.8	20.7
62	[7] MYRINGOTOMY W TUBE INSERTION AGE 0-17	0.4499	19.0	15.8
63	[4] OTHER EAR, NOSE, MOUTH & THROAT O.R. PROCEDURES	1.1820	29.6	24.7
64	EAR, NOSE, MOUTH & THROAT MALIGNANCY	1.1480	26.2	21.8
65	[1] DYSEQUILIBRIUM	0.4499	19.0	15.8
66	[7] EPISTAXIS	0.4499	19.0	15.8
67	[3] EPIGLOTTITIS	0.7637	24.8	20.7
68	OTITIS MEDIA & URI AGE >17 W CC	0.5111	18.0	15.0
69	[1] OTITIS MEDIA & URI AGE >17 W/O CC	0.4499	19.0	15.8
70	[7] OTITIS MEDIA & URI AGE 0-17	0.4499	19.0	15.8
71	[7] LARYNGOTRACHEITIS	0.5837	21.3	17.8
72	[7] NASAL TRAUMA & DEFORMITY	0.7637	24.8	20.7
73	OTHER EAR, NOSE, MOUTH & THROAT DIAGNOSES AGE >17	0.7535	21.9	18.3
74	[7] OTHER EAR, NOSE, MOUTH & THROAT DIAGNOSES AGE 0-17	0.4499	19.0	15.8
75	[5] MAJOR CHEST PROCEDURES	1.7034	38.5	32.1
76	OTHER RESP SYSTEM O.R. PROCEDURES W CC	2.5523	43.9	36.6
77	[5] OTHER RESP SYSTEM O.R. PROCEDURES W/O CC	1.7034	38.5	32.1
78	PULMONARY EMBOLISM	0.6900	21.9	18.3
79	RESPIRATORY INFECTIONS & INFLAMMATIONS AGE >17 W CC	0.8280	22.9	19.1
80	RESPIRATORY INFECTIONS & INFLAMMATIONS AGE >17 W/O CC	0.5986	21.7	18.1
81	7 RESPIRATORY INFECTIONS & INFLAMMATIONS AGE 0-17	0.4499	19.0	15.8
82	RESPIRATORY NEOPLASMS	0.7174	20.1	16.8
83	[2] MAJOR CHEST TRAUMA W CC	0.5837	21.3	17.8
84	[7] MAJOR CHEST TRAUMA W/O CC	0.5837	21.3	17.8
85	PLEURAL EFFUSION W CC	0.7264	21.2	17.7
86	[1] PLEURAL EFFUSION W/O CC	0.4499	19.0	15.8
87	PULMONARY EDEMA & RESPIRATORY FAILURE	1.0816	25.4	21.2
88	CHRONIC OBSTRUCTIVE PULMONARY DISEASE	0.6585	19.6	16.3
89	SIMPLE PNEUMONIA & PLEURISY AGE >17 W CC	0.6987	20.8	17.3
90	SIMPLE PNEUMONIA & PLEURISY AGE >17 W/O CC	0.4970	17.8	14.8

LTC-DRG	Description	RW	GMLOS	5/6 GMLOS
91	[7] SIMPLE PNEUMONIA & PLEURISY AGE 0-17	0.4499	19.0	15.8
92	INTERSTITIAL LUNG DISEASE W CC	0.6704	20.2	16.8
93	[2] INTERSTITIAL LUNG DISEASE W/O CC	0.5837	21.3	17.8
94	PNEUMOTHORAX W CC	0.5880	17.0	14.2
95	[1] PNEUMOTHORAX W/O CC	0.4499	19.0	15.8
96	BRONCHITIS & ASTHMA AGE >17 W CC	0.6417	19.4	16.2
97	[2] BRONCHITIS & ASTHMA AGE >17 W/O CC	0.5837	21.3	17.8
98	[7] BRONCHITIS & ASTHMA AGE 0-17	0.5837	21.3	17.8
99	RESPIRATORY SIGNS & SYMPTOMS W CC	0.9219	23.2	19.3
100	[3] RESPIRATORY SIGNS & SYMPTOMS W/O CC	0.7637	24.8	20.7
101	OTHER RESPIRATORY SYSTEM DIAGNOSES W CC	0.8147	21.1	17.6
102	[1] OTHER RESPIRATORY SYSTEM DIAGNOSES W/O CC	0.4499	19.0	15.8
103	[6] HEART TRANSPLANT OR IMPLANT OF HEART ASSIST SYSTEM	0.0000	0.0	0.0
104	[7] CARDIAC VALVE & OTHER MAJOR CARDIOTHORACIC PROC W CARDIAC CATH	0.7637	24.8	20.7
105	[7] CARDIAC VALVE & OTHER MAJOR CARDIOTHORACIC PROC W/O CARDIAC CATH	0.7637	24.8	20.7
106	[7] CORONARY BYPASS W PTCA	0.7637	24.8	20.7
108	[7] OTHER CARDIOTHORACIC PROCEDURES	0.7637	24.8	20.7
110	[3] MAJOR CARDIOVASCULAR PROCEDURES W CC	0.7637	24.8	20.7
111	[7] MAJOR CARDIOVASCULAR PROCEDURES W/O CC	0.7637	24.8	20.7
113	AMPUTATION FOR CIRC SYSTEM DISORDERS EXCEPT UPPER LIMB & TOE	1.4887	39.3	32.8
114	UPPER LIMB & TOE AMPUTATION FOR CIRC SYSTEM DISORDERS	1.2389	33.2	27.7
117	[4] CARDIAC PACEMAKER REVISION EXCEPT DEVICE REPLACEMENT	1.1820	29.6	24.7
118	[4] CARDIAC PACEMAKER DEVICE REPLACEMENT	1.1820	29.6	24.7
119	[3] VEIN LIGATION & STRIPPING	0.7637	24.8	20.7
120	OTHER CIRCULATORY SYSTEM O.R. PROCEDURES	1.0979	31.7	26.4
121	CIRCULATORY DISORDERS W AMI & MAJOR COMP, DISCHARGED ALIVE	0.8429	23.2	19.3
122	[2] CIRCULATORY DISORDERS W AMI W/O MAJOR COMP, DISCHARGED ALIVE	0.5837	21.3	17.8
123	CIRCULATORY DISORDERS W AMI, EXPIRED	1.1811	20.4	17.0
124	[4] CIRCULATORY DISORDERS EXCEPT AMI, W CARD CATH & COMPLEX DIAG	1.1820	29.6	24.7
125	[3] CIRCULATORY DISORDERS EXCEPT AMI, W CARD CATH W/O COMPLEX DIAG	0.7637	24.8	20.7
126	ACUTE & SUBACUTE ENDOCARDITIS	0.8386	25.3	21.1
127	HEART FAILURE & SHOCK	0.6857	21.2	17.7
128	[2] DEEP VEIN THROMBOPHLEBITIS	0.5837	21.3	17.8
129	[7] CARDIAC ARREST, UNEXPLAINED	0.7637	24.8	20.7
130	PERIPHERAL VASCULAR DISORDERS W CC	0.6741	23.2	19.3
131	PERIPHERAL VASCULAR DISORDERS W/O CC	0.4675	20.4	17.0

LTC-DRG	Description	RW	GMLOS	5/6 GMLOS
132	ATHEROSCLEROSIS W CC	0.6565	21.8	18.2
133	[1] ATHEROSCLEROSIS W/O CC	0.4499	19.0	15.8
134	HYPERTENSION	0.6354	24.8	20.7
135	CARDIAC CONGENITAL & VALVULAR DISORDERS AGE >17 W CC	0.7211	23.7	19.8
136	[2] CARDIAC CONGENITAL & VALVULAR DISORDERS AGE >17 W/O CC	0.5837	21.3	17.8
137	[7] CARDIAC CONGENITAL & VALVULAR DISORDERS AGE 0-17	0.5837	21.3	17.8
138	CARDIAC ARRHYTHMIA & CONDUCTION DISORDERS W CC	0.6201	20.5	17.1
139	[2] CARDIAC ARRHYTHMIA & CONDUCTION DISORDERS W/O CC	0.5837	21.3	17.8
140	[1] ANGINA PECTORIS	0.4499	19.0	15.8
141	[8] SYNCOPE & COLLAPSE W CC	0.4271	18.3	15.3
142	[8] SYNCOPE & COLLAPSE W/O CC	0.4271	18.3	15.3
143	[1] CHEST PAIN	0.4499	19.0	15.8
144	OTHER CIRCULATORY SYSTEM DIAGNOSES W CC	0.7413	21.7	18.1
145	OTHER CIRCULATORY SYSTEM DIAGNOSES W/O CC	0.4568	18.2	15.2
146	[7] RECTAL RESECTION W CC	1.7034	38.5	32.1
147	[7] RECTAL RESECTION W/O CC	1.7034	38.5	32.1
148	MAJOR SMALL & LARGE BOWEL PROCEDURES W CC	1.8616	40.9	34.1
149	[7] MAJOR SMALL & LARGE BOWEL PROCEDURES W/O CC	0.7637	24.8	20.7
150	[4] PERITONEAL ADHESIOLYSIS W CC	1.1820	29.6	24.7
151	[2] PERITONEAL ADHESIOLYSIS W/O CC	0.5837	21.3	17.8
152	[3] MINOR SMALL & LARGE BOWEL PROCEDURES W CC	0.7637	24.8	20.7
153	[7] MINOR SMALL & LARGE BOWEL PROCEDURES W/O CC	0.7637	24.8	20.7
154	[5] STOMACH, ESOPHAGEAL & DUODENAL PROCEDURES AGE >17 W CC	1.7034	38.5	32.1
155	[7] STOMACH, ESOPHAGEAL & DUODENAL PROCEDURES AGE >17 W/O CC	1.7034	38.5	32.1
156	[7] STOMACH, ESOPHAGEAL & DUODENAL PROCEDURES AGE 0-17	1.7034	38.5	32.1
157	[4] ANAL & STOMAL PROCEDURES W CC	1.1820	29.6	24.7
158	[7] ANAL & STOMAL PROCEDURES W/O CC	1.1820	29.6	24.7
159	[7] HERNIA PROCEDURES EXCEPT INGUINAL & FEMORAL AGE >17 W CC	0.7637	24.8	20.7
160	[7] HERNIA PROCEDURES EXCEPT INGUINAL & FEMORAL AGE >17 W/O CC	0.7637	24.8	20.7
161	[5] INGUINAL & FEMORAL HERNIA PROCEDURES AGE >17 W CC	1.7034	38.5	32.1
162	[7] INGUINAL & FEMORAL HERNIA PROCEDURES AGE >17 W/O CC	0.7637	24.8	20.7
163	[7] HERNIA PROCEDURES AGE 0-17	0.7637	24.8	20.7

LTC-DRG	Description	RW	GMLOS	5/6 GMLOS
164	[1] APPENDECTOMY W COMPLICATED PRINCIPAL DIAG W CC	1.7034	38.5	32.1
165	[7] APPENDECTOMY W COMPLICATED PRINCIPAL DIAG W/O CC	1.7034	38.5	32.1
166	[7] APPENDECTOMY W/O COMPLICATED PRINCIPAL DIAG W CC	1.7034	38.5	32.1
167	[7] APPENDECTOMY W/O COMPLICATED PRINCIPAL DIAG W/O CC	1.7034	38.5	32.1
168	[4] MOUTH PROCEDURES W CC	1.1820	29.6	24.7
169	[7] MOUTH PROCEDURES W/O CC	0.7637	24.8	20.7
170	OTHER DIGESTIVE SYSTEM O.R. PROCEDURES W CC	1.6271	35.9	29.9
171	[1] OTHER DIGESTIVE SYSTEM O.R. PROCEDURES W/O CC	0.4499	19.0	15.8
172	DIGESTIVE MALIGNANCY W CC	0.8553	21.8	18.2
173	[2] DIGESTIVE MALIGNANCY W/O CC	0.5837	21.3	17.8
174	G.I. HEMORRHAGE W CC	0.7119	22.2	18.5
175	[1] G.I. HEMORRHAGE W/O CC	0.4499	19.0	15.8
176	COMPLICATED PEPTIC ULCER	0.8426	21.5	17.9
177	[3] UNCOMPLICATED PEPTIC ULCER W CC	0.7637	24.8	20.7
178	[3] UNCOMPLICATED PEPTIC ULCER W/O CC	0.7637	24.8	20.7
179	INFLAMMATORY BOWEL DISEASE	0.9675	24.0	20.0
180	G.I. OBSTRUCTION W CC	0.9375	23.5	19.6
181	[3] G.I. OBSTRUCTION W/O CC	0.7637	24.8	20.7
182	ESOPHAGITIS, GASTROENT & MISC DIGEST DISORDERS AGE >17 W CC	0.7745	22.6	18.8
183	ESOPHAGITIS, GASTROENT & MISC DIGEST DISORDERS AGE >17 W/O CC	0.3870	16.8	14.0
184	[7] ESOPHAGITIS, GASTROENT & MISC DIGEST DISORDERS AGE 0-17	0.4499	19.0	15.8
185	[3] DENTAL & ORAL DIS EXCEPT EXTRACTIONS & RESTORATIONS, AGE >17	0.7637	24.8	20.7
186	[7] DENTAL & ORAL DIS EXCEPT EXTRACTIONS & RESTORATIONS, AGE 0-17	0.7637	24.8	20.7
187	[7] DENTAL EXTRACTIONS & RESTORATIONS	0.7637	24.8	20.7
188	OTHER DIGESTIVE SYSTEM DIAGNOSES AGE >17 W CC	0.9952	24.0	20.0
189	OTHER DIGESTIVE SYSTEM DIAGNOSES AGE >17 W/O CC	0.4707	18.2	15.2
190	[7] OTHER DIGESTIVE SYSTEM DIAGNOSES AGE 0-17	0.4499	19.0	15.8
191	[4] PANCREAS, LIVER & SHUNT PROCEDURES W CC	1.1820	29.6	24.7
192	[7] PANCREAS, LIVER & SHUNT PROCEDURES W/O CC	1.1820	29.6	24.7
193	[3] BILIARY TRACT PROC EXCEPT ONLY CHOLECYST W OR W/O C.D.E. W CC	0.7637	24.8	20.7
194	[7] BILIARY TRACT PROC EXCEPT ONLY CHOLECYST W OR W/O C.D.E. W/O CC	0.7637	24.8	20.7
195	[3] CHOLECYSTECTOMY W C.D.E. W CC	0.7637	24.8	20.7
196	[7] CHOLECYSTECTOMY W C.D.E. W/O CC	0.7637	24.8	20.7

LTC-DRG	Description	RW	GMLOS	5/6 GMLOS
197	[3] CHOLECYSTECTOMY EXCEPT BY LAPAROSCOPE W/O C.D.E. W CC	0.7637	24.8	20.7
198	[7] CHOLECYSTECTOMY EXCEPT BY LAPAROSCOPE W/O C.D.E. W/O CC	0.7637	24.8	20.7
199	[7] HEPATOBILIARY DIAGNOSTIC PROCEDURE FOR MALIGNANCY	1.7034	38.5	32.1
200	[5] HEPATOBILIARY DIAGNOSTIC PROCEDURE FOR NON-MALIGNANCY	1.7034	38.5	32.1
201	OTHER HEPATOBILIARY OR PANCREAS O.R. PROCEDURES	2.0371	36.1	30.1
202	CIRRHOSIS & ALCOHOLIC HEPATITIS	0.6610	20.6	17.2
203	MALIGNANCY OF HEPATOBILIARY SYSTEM OR PANCREAS	0.7896	19.5	16.3
204	DISORDERS OF PANCREAS EXCEPT MALIGNANCY	0.9441	22.7	18.9
205	DISORDERS OF LIVER EXCEPT MALIG,CIRR,ALC HEPA W CC	0.6642	20.5	17.1
206	[2] DISORDERS OF LIVER EXCEPT MALIG,CIRR,ALC HEPA W/O CC	0.5837	21.3	17.8
207	DISORDERS OF THE BILIARY TRACT W CC	0.7570	21.5	17.9
208	[2] DISORDERS OF THE BILIARY TRACT W/O CC	0.5837	21.3	17.8
210	[5] HIP & FEMUR PROCEDURES EXCEPT MAJOR JOINT AGE >17 W CC	1.7034	38.5	32.1
211	[4] HIP & FEMUR PROCEDURES EXCEPT MAJOR JOINT AGE >17 W/O CC	1.1820	29.6	24.7
212	[7] HIP & FEMUR PROCEDURES EXCEPT MAJOR JOINT AGE 0-17	1.7034	38.5	32.1
213	AMPUTATION FOR MUSCULOSKELETAL SYSTEM & CONN TISSUE DISORDERS	1.1948	34.0	28.3
216	[4] BIOPSIES OF MUSCULOSKELETAL SYSTEM & CONNECTIVE TISSUE	1.1820	29.6	24.7
217	WND DEBRID & SKN GRFT EXCEPT HAND,FOR MUSCSKELET & CONN TISS DIS	1.2927	38.0	31.7
218	[5] LOWER EXTREM & HUMER PROC EXCEPT HIP,FOOT,FEMUR AGE >17 W CC	1.7034	38.5	32.1
219	[1] LOWER EXTREM & HUMER PROC EXCEPT HIP,FOOT,FEMUR AGE >17 W/O CC	0.4499	19.0	15.8
220	[7] LOWER EXTREM & HUMER PROC EXCEPT HIP,FOOT,FEMUR AGE 0-17	1.7034	38.5	32.1
223	[3] MAJOR SHOULDER/ELBOW PROC, OR OTHER UPPER EXTREMITY PROC W CC	0.7637	24.8	20.7
224	[7] SHOULDER,ELBOW OR FOREARM PROC,EXC MAJOR JOINT PROC, W/O CC	0.7637	24.8	20.7
225	FOOT PROCEDURES	0.9869	28.4	23.7
226	SOFT TISSUE PROCEDURES W CC	0.9443	29.5	24.6
227	[3] SOFT TISSUE PROCEDURES W/O CC	0.7637	24.8	20.7
228	[4] MAJOR THUMB OR JOINT PROC,OR OTH HAND OR WRIST PROC W CC	1.1820	29.6	24.7
229	[7] HAND OR WRIST PROC, EXCEPT MAJOR JOINT PROC, W/O CC	0.4499	19.0	15.8
230	[5] LOCAL EXCISION & REMOVAL OF INT FIX DEVICES OF HIP & FEMUR	1.7034	38.5	32.1

LTC-DRG	Description	RW	GMLOS	5/6 GMLOS
232	[7] ARTHROSCOPY	0.4499	19.0	15.8
233	OTHER MUSCULOSKELET SYS & CONN TISS O.R. PROC W CC	1.3522	34.6	28.8
234	[7] OTHER MUSCULOSKELET SYS & CONN TISS O.R. PROC W/O CC	0.4499	19.0	15.8
235	[3] FRACTURES OF FEMUR	0.7637	24.8	20.7
236	FRACTURES OF HIP & PELVIS	0.6531	25.2	21.0
237	[1] SPRAINS, STRAINS, & DISLOCATIONS OF HIP, PELVIS & THIGH	0.4499	19.0	15.8
238	OSTEOMYELITIS	0.8278	28.3	23.6
239	PATHOLOGICAL FRACTURES & MUSCULOSKELETAL & CONN TISS MALIGNANCY	0.6935	23.6	19.7
240	CONNECTIVE TISSUE DISORDERS W CC	0.7310	24.8	20.7
241	[1] CONNECTIVE TISSUE DISORDERS W/O CC	0.4499	19.0	15.8
242	SEPTIC ARTHRITIS	0.7864	26.5	22.1
243	MEDICAL BACK PROBLEMS	0.6061	23.4	19.5
244	BONE DISEASES & SPECIFIC ARTHROPATHIES W CC	0.5259	22.2	18.5
245	BONE DISEASES & SPECIFIC ARTHROPATHIES W/O CC	0.4635	20.4	17.0
246	[1] NON-SPECIFIC ARTHROPATHIES	0.4499	19.0	15.8
247	SIGNS & SYMPTOMS OF MUSCULOSKELETAL SYSTEM & CONN TISSUE	0.5548	21.9	18.3
248	TENDONITIS, MYOSITIS & BURSITIS	0.6574	22.6	18.8
249	AFTERCARE, MUSCULOSKELETAL SYSTEM & CONNECTIVE TISSUE	0.6577	24.7	20.6
250	[2] FX, SPRN, STRN & DISL OF FOREARM, HAND, FOOT AGE >17 W CC	0.5837	21.3	17.8
251	[1] FX, SPRN, STRN & DISL OF FOREARM, HAND, FOOT AGE >17 W/O CC	0.4499	19.0	15.8
252	[7] FX, SPRN, STRN & DISL OF FOREARM, HAND, FOOT AGE 0-17	0.7637	24.8	20.7
253	FX, SPRN, STRN & DISL OF UPARM,LOWLEG EX FOOT AGE >17 W CC	0.6802	26.3	21.9
254	[2] FX, SPRN, STRN & DISL OF UPARM,LOWLEG EX FOOT AGE >17 W/O CC	0.5837	21.3	17.8
255	[7] FX, SPRN, STRN & DISL OF UPARM,LOWLEG EX FOOT AGE 0-17	0.7637	24.8	20.7
256	OTHER MUSCULOSKELETAL SYSTEM & CONNECTIVE TISSUE DIAGNOSES	0.7924	25.3	21.1
257	[7] TOTAL MASTECTOMY FOR MALIGNANCY W CC	0.7637	24.8	20.7
258	[7] TOTAL MASTECTOMY FOR MALIGNANCY W/O CC	0.7637	24.8	20.7
259	[2] SUBTOTAL MASTECTOMY FOR MALIGNANCY W CC	0.5837	21.3	17.8
260	[7] SUBTOTAL MASTECTOMY FOR MALIGNANCY W/O CC	0.7637	24.8	20.7
261	[7] BREAST PROC FOR NON-MALIGNANCY EXCEPT BIOPSY & LOCAL EXCISION	0.7637	24.8	20.7
262	[1] BREAST BIOPSY & LOCAL EXCISION FOR NON-MALIGNANCY	0.4499	19.0	15.8

LTC-DRG	Description	RW	GMLOS	5/6 GMLOS
263	SKIN GRAFT &/OR DEBRID FOR SKN ULCER OR CELLULITIS W CC	1.3222	39.5	32.9
264	SKIN GRAFT &/OR DEBRID FOR SKN ULCER OR CELLULITIS W/O CC	0.9584	32.0	26.7
265	SKIN GRAFT &/OR DEBRID EXCEPT FOR SKIN ULCER OR CELLULITIS W CC	1.0398	33.1	27.6
266	[3] SKIN GRAFT &/OR DEBRID EXCEPT FOR SKIN ULCER OR CELLULITIS W/O CC	0.7637	24.8	20.7
267	[7] PERIANAL & PILONIDAL PROCEDURES	0.7637	24.8	20.7
268	[5] SKIN, SUBCUTANEOUS TISSUE & BREAST PLASTIC PROCEDURES	1.7034	38.5	32.1
269	OTHER SKIN, SUBCUT TISS & BREAST PROC W CC	1.3037	36.1	30.1
270	[3] OTHER SKIN, SUBCUT TISS & BREAST PROC W/O CC	0.7637	24.8	20.7
271	SKIN ULCERS	0.8720	27.7	23.1
272	MAJOR SKIN DISORDERS W CC	0.7420	22.6	18.8
273	[1] MAJOR SKIN DISORDERS W/O CC	0.4499	19.0	15.8
274	[3] MALIGNANT BREAST DISORDERS W CC	0.7637	24.8	20.7
275	[7] MALIGNANT BREAST DISORDERS W/O CC	0.7637	24.8	20.7
276	[2] NON-MALIGANT BREAST DISORDERS	0.5837	21.3	17.8
277	CELLULITIS AGE >17 W CC	0.6264	21.0	17.5
278	CELLULITIS AGE >17 W/O CC	0.4420	17.8	14.8
279	[7] CELLULITIS AGE 0-17	0.4499	19.0	15.8
280	TRAUMA TO THE SKIN, SUBCUT TISS & BREAST AGE >17 W CC	0.6698	24.3	20.3
281	[1] TRAUMA TO THE SKIN, SUBCUT TISS & BREAST AGE >17 W/O CC	0.4499	19.0	15.8
282	[7] TRAUMA TO THE SKIN, SUBCUT TISS & BREAST AGE 0-17	0.4499	19.0	15.8
283	MINOR SKIN DISORDERS W CC	0.6935	23.9	19.9
284	[1] MINOR SKIN DISORDERS W/O CC	0.4499	19.0	15.8
285	AMPUTAT OF LOWER LIMB FOR ENDOCRINE,NUTRIT,& METABOL DISORDERS	1.3501	35.6	29.7
286	[7] ADRENAL & PITUITARY PROCEDURES	1.7034	38.5	32.1
287	SKIN GRAFTS & WOUND DEBRID FOR ENDOC, NUTRIT & METAB DISORDERS	1.1387	33.9	28.3
288	[4] O.R. PROCEDURES FOR OBESITY	1.1820	29.6	24.7
289	[7] PARATHYROID PROCEDURES	1.1820	29.6	24.7
290	[5] THYROID PROCEDURES	1.7034	38.5	32.1
291	[7] THYROGLOSSAL PROCEDURES	1.1820	29.6	24.7
292	OTHER ENDOCRINE, NUTRIT & METAB O.R. PROC W CC	1.3409	31.7	26.4
293	[2] OTHER ENDOCRINE, NUTRIT & METAB O.R. PROC W/O CC	0.5837	21.3	17.8
294	DIABETES AGE >35	0.7293	25.0	20.8
295	[3] DIABETES AGE 0-35	0.7637	24.8	20.7
296	NUTRITIONAL & MISC METABOLIC DISORDERS AGE >17 W CC	0.7212	23.1	19.3
297	NUTRITIONAL & MISC METABOLIC DISORDERS AGE >17 W/O CC	0.5227	18.4	15.3

LTC-DRG	Description	RW	GMLOS	5/6 GMLOS
298	[7] NUTRITIONAL & MISC METABOLIC DISORDERS AGE 0-17	0.5837	21.3	17.8
299	[4] INBORN ERRORS OF METABOLISM	1.1820	29.6	24.7
300	ENDOCRINE DISORDERS W CC	0.6376	21.2	17.7
301	[1] ENDOCRINE DISORDERS W/O CC	0.4499	19.0	15.8
302	[6] KIDNEY TRANSPLANT	0.0000	0.0	0.0
303	[4] KIDNEY,URETER & MAJOR BLADDER PROCEDURES FOR NEOPLASM	1.1820	29.6	24.7
304	[5] KIDNEY,URETER & MAJOR BLADDER PROC FOR NON-NEOPL W CC	1.7034	38.5	32.1
305	[1] KIDNEY,URETER & MAJOR BLADDER PROC FOR NON-NEOPL W/O CC	0.4499	19.0	15.8
306	[2] PROSTATECTOMY W CC	0.5837	21.3	17.8
307	[7] PROSTATECTOMY W/O CC	0.5837	21.3	17.8
308	[3] MINOR BLADDER PROCEDURES W CC	0.7637	24.8	20.7
309	[7] MINOR BLADDER PROCEDURES W/O CC	0.7637	24.8	20.7
310	[4] TRANSURETHRAL PROCEDURES W CC	1.1820	29.6	24.7
311	[7] TRANSURETHRAL PROCEDURES W/O CC	1.1820	29.6	24.7
312	[1] URETHRAL PROCEDURES, AGE >17 W CC	0.4499	19.0	15.8
313	[7] URETHRAL PROCEDURES, AGE >17 W/O CC	0.4499	19.0	15.8
314	[7] URETHRAL PROCEDURES, AGE 0-17	0.4499	19.0	15.8
315	OTHER KIDNEY & URINARY TRACT O.R. PROCEDURES	1.4055	31.6	26.3
316	RENAL FAILURE	0.8219	22.7	18.9
317	ADMIT FOR RENAL DIALYSIS	0.9852	25.2	21.0
318	KIDNEY & URINARY TRACT NEOPLASMS W CC	0.7586	20.2	16.8
319	[1] KIDNEY & URINARY TRACT NEOPLASMS W/O CC	0.4499	19.0	15.8
320	KIDNEY & URINARY TRACT INFECTIONS AGE >17 W CC	0.6179	22.2	18.5
321	KIDNEY & URINARY TRACT INFECTIONS AGE >17 W/O CC	0.4792	19.0	15.8
322	[7] KIDNEY & URINARY TRACT INFECTIONS AGE 0-17	0.4499	19.0	15.8
323	[4] URINARY STONES W CC, &/OR ESW LITHOTRIPSY	1.1820	29.6	24.7
324	[7] URINARY STONES W/O CC	0.4499	19.0	15.8
325	[2] KIDNEY & URINARY TRACT SIGNS & SYMPTOMS AGE >17 W CC	0.5837	21.3	17.8
326	[7] KIDNEY & URINARY TRACT SIGNS & SYMPTOMS AGE >17 W/O CC	0.4499	19.0	15.8
327	[7] KIDNEY & URINARY TRACT SIGNS & SYMPTOMS AGE 0-17	0.4499	19.0	15.8
328	[1] URETHRAL STRICTURE AGE >17 W CC	0.4499	19.0	15.8
329	[7] URETHRAL STRICTURE AGE >17 W/O CC	0.4499	19.0	15.8
330	[7] URETHRAL STRICTURE AGE 0-17	0.4499	19.0	15.8
331	OTHER KIDNEY & URINARY TRACT DIAGNOSES AGE >17 W CC	0.8010	23.1	19.3

LTC-DRG	Description	RW	GMLOS	5/6 GMLOS
332	[2] OTHER KIDNEY & URINARY TRACT DIAGNOSES AGE >17 W/O CC	0.5837	21.3	17.8
333	[7] OTHER KIDNEY & URINARY TRACT DIAGNOSES AGE 0-17	0.5837	21.3	17.8
334	[2] MAJOR MALE PELVIC PROCEDURES W CC	0.5837	21.3	17.8
335	[7] MAJOR MALE PELVIC PROCEDURES W/O CC	1.7034	38.5	32.1
336	[2] TRANSURETHRAL PROSTATECTOMY W CC	0.5837	21.3	17.8
337	[7] TRANSURETHRAL PROSTATECTOMY W/O CC	0.5837	21.3	17.8
338	[7] TESTES PROCEDURES, FOR MALIGNANCY	0.5837	21.3	17.8
339	[4] TESTES PROCEDURES, NON-MALIGNANCY AGE >17	1.1820	29.6	24.7
340	[7] TESTES PROCEDURES, NON-MALIGNANCY AGE 0-17	1.1820	29.6	24.7
341	[4] PENIS PROCEDURES	1.1820	29.6	24.7
342	[7] CIRCUMCISION AGE >17	1.1820	29.6	24.7
343	[7] CIRCUMCISION AGE 0-17	1.1820	29.6	24.7
344	[1] OTHER MALE REPRODUCTIVE SYSTEM O.R. PROCEDURES FOR MALIGNANCY	0.4499	19.0	15.8
345	[5] OTHER MALE REPRODUCTIVE SYSTEM O.R. PROC EXCEPT FOR MALIGNANCY	1.7034	38.5	32.1
346	MALIGNANCY, MALE REPRODUCTIVE SYSTEM, W CC	0.6060	20.6	17.2
347	[2] MALIGNANCY, MALE REPRODUCTIVE SYSTEM, W/O CC	0.5837	21.3	17.8
348	[2] BENIGN PROSTATIC HYPERTROPHY W CC	0.5837	21.3	17.8
349	[7] BENIGN PROSTATIC HYPERTROPHY W/O CC	1.1820	29.6	24.7
350	INFLAMMATION OF THE MALE REPRODUCTIVE SYSTEM	0.6798	21.9	18.3
351	[7] STERILIZATION, MALE	1.1820	29.6	24.7
352	OTHER MALE REPRODUCTIVE SYSTEM DIAGNOSES	0.6375	23.4	19.5
353	[7] PELVIC EVISCERATION, RADICAL HYSTERECTOMY & RADICAL VULVECTOMY	1.1820	29.6	24.7
354	[7] UTERINE,ADNEXA PROC FOR NON-OVARIAN/ ADNEXAL MALIG W CC	1.1820	29.6	24.7
355	[7] UTERINE,ADNEXA PROC FOR NON-OVARIAN/ ADNEXAL MALIG W/O CC	1.1820	29.6	24.7
356	[7] FEMALE REPRODUCTIVE SYSTEM RECONSTRUCTIVE PROCEDURES	1.1820	29.6	24.7
357	[7] UTERINE & ADNEXA PROC FOR OVARIAN OR ADNEXAL MALIGNANCY	1.1820	29.6	24.7
358	[7] UTERINE & ADNEXA PROC FOR NON-MALIGNANCY W CC	1.1820	29.6	24.7
359	[7] UTERINE & ADNEXA PROC FOR NON-MALIGNANCY W/O CC	1.1820	29.6	24.7
360	[4] VAGINA, CERVIX & VULVA PROCEDURES	1.1820	29.6	24.7
361	[7] LAPAROSCOPY & INCISIONAL TUBAL INTERRUPTION	0.7637	24.8	20.7
362	[7] ENDOSCOPIC TUBAL INTERRUPTION	0.7637	24.8	20.7

LTC-DRG	Description	RW	GMLOS	5/6 GMLOS
363	[7] D&C, CONIZATION & RADIO-IMPLANT, FOR MALIGNANCY	0.7637	24.8	20.7
364	[5] D&C, CONIZATION EXCEPT FOR MALIGNANCY	1.7034	38.5	32.1
365	[5] OTHER FEMALE REPRODUCTIVE SYSTEM O.R. PROCEDURES	1.7034	38.5	32.1
366	MALIGNANCY, FEMALE REPRODUCTIVE SYSTEM W CC	0.7072	20.3	16.9
367	[7] MALIGNANCY, FEMALE REPRODUCTIVE SYSTEM W/O CC	0.7637	24.8	20.7
368	INFECTIONS, FEMALE REPRODUCTIVE SYSTEM	0.6416	20.7	17.3
369	[3] MENSTRUAL & OTHER FEMALE REPRODUCTIVE SYSTEM DISORDERS	0.7637	24.8	20.7
370	[7] CESAREAN SECTION W CC	0.7637	24.8	20.7
371	[7] CESAREAN SECTION W/O CC	0.5837	21.3	17.8
372	[7] VAGINAL DELIVERY W COMPLICATING DIAGNOSES	0.7637	24.8	20.7
373	[7] VAGINAL DELIVERY W/O COMPLICATING DIAGNOSES	0.7637	24.8	20.7
374	[7] VAGINAL DELIVERY W STERILIZATION &/OR D&C	0.7637	24.8	20.7
375	[7] VAGINAL DELIVERY W O.R. PROC EXCEPT STERIL &/OR D&C	0.7637	24.8	20.7
376	[7] POSTPARTUM & POST ABORTION DIAGNOSES W/O O.R. PROCEDURE	0.7637	24.8	20.7
377	[7] POSTPARTUM & POST ABORTION DIAGNOSES W O.R. PROCEDURE	0.7637	24.8	20.7
378	[7] ECTOPIC PREGNANCY	0.7637	24.8	20.7
379	[7] THREATENED ABORTION	0.7637	24.8	20.7
380	[7] ABORTION W/O D&C	0.7637	24.8	20.7
381	[7] ABORTION W D&C, ASPIRATION CURETTAGE OR HYSTEROTOMY	0.7637	24.8	20.7
382	[7] FALSE LABOR	0.7637	24.8	20.7
383	[7] OTHER ANTEPARTUM DIAGNOSES W MEDICAL COMPLICATIONS	0.7637	24.8	20.7
384	[7] OTHER ANTEPARTUM DIAGNOSES W/O MEDICAL COMPLICATIONS	0.7637	24.8	20.7
385	[7] NEONATES, DIED OR TRANSFERRED TO ANOTHER ACUTE CARE FACILITY	0.7637	24.8	20.7
386	[7] EXTREME IMMATURITY	1.1820	29.6	24.7
387	[7] PREMATURITY W MAJOR PROBLEMS	1.1820	29.6	24.7
388	[7] PREMATURITY W/O MAJOR PROBLEMS	0.7637	24.8	20.7
389	[7] FULL TERM NEONATE W MAJOR PROBLEMS	1.1820	29.6	24.7
390	[7] NEONATE W OTHER SIGNIFICANT PROBLEMS	1.1820	29.6	24.7
391	[7] NORMAL NEWBORN	0.7637	24.8	20.7
392	[7] SPLENECTOMY AGE >17	0.7637	24.8	20.7
393	[7] SPLENECTOMY AGE 0-17	0.7637	24.8	20.7
394	[5] OTHER O.R. PROCEDURES OF THE BLOOD AND BLOOD FORMING ORGANS	1.7034	38.5	32.1
395	RED BLOOD CELL DISORDERS AGE >17	0.6581	22.0	18.3

LTC-DRG	Description	RW	GMLOS	5/6 GMLOS
396	[7] RED BLOOD CELL DISORDERS AGE 0-17	0.5837	21.3	17.8
397	COAGULATION DISORDERS	0.8675	22.9	19.1
398	RETICULOENDOTHELIAL & IMMUNITY DISORDERS W CC	0.8240	23.7	19.8
399	[2] RETICULOENDOTHELIAL & IMMUNITY DISORDERS W/O CC	0.5837	21.3	17.8
401	[5] LYMPHOMA & NON-ACUTE LEUKEMIA W OTHER O.R. PROC W CC	1.7034	38.5	32.1
402	[7] LYMPHOMA & NON-ACUTE LEUKEMIA W OTHER O.R. PROC W/O CC	0.5837	21.3	17.8
403	LYMPHOMA & NON-ACUTE LEUKEMIA W CC	0.8757	21.3	17.8
404	[2] LYMPHOMA & NON-ACUTE LEUKEMIA W/O CC	0.5837	21.3	17.8
405	[7] ACUTE LEUKEMIA W/O MAJOR O.R. PROCEDURE AGE 0-17	0.5837	21.3	17.8
406	[4] MYELOPROLIF DISORD OR POORLY DIFF NEOPL W MAJ O.R.PROC W CC	1.1820	29.6	24.7
407	[7] MYELOPROLIF DISORD OR POORLY DIFF NEOPL W MAJ O.R.PROC W/O CC	1.1820	29.6	24.7
408	[4] MYELOPROLIF DISORD OR POORLY DIFF NEOPL W OTHER O.R.PROC	1.1820	29.6	24.7
409	RADIOTHERAPY	0.8642	23.5	19.6
410	CHEMOTHERAPY W/O ACUTE LEUKEMIA AS SECONDARY DIAGNOSIS	1.1684	26.4	22.0
411	[7] HISTORY OF MALIGNANCY W/O ENDOSCOPY	0.7637	24.8	20.7
412	[7] HISTORY OF MALIGNANCY W ENDOSCOPY	0.7637	24.8	20.7
413	OTHER MYELOPROLIF DIS OR POORLY DIFF NEOPL DIAG W CC	0.8920	20.5	17.1
414	[7] OTHER MYELOPROLIF DIS OR POORLY DIFF NEOPL DIAG W/O CC	0.5837	21.3	17.8
415	O.R. PROCEDURE FOR INFECTIOUS & PARASITIC DISEASES	1.4251	35.6	29.7
416	SEPTICEMIA AGE >17	0.8241	23.5	19.6
417	[7] SEPTICEMIA AGE 0-17	0.7637	24.8	20.7
418	POSTOPERATIVE & POST-TRAUMATIC INFECTIONS	0.8252	24.7	20.6
419	[4] FEVER OF UNKNOWN ORIGIN AGE >17 W CC	1.1820	29.6	24.7
420	[7] FEVER OF UNKNOWN ORIGIN AGE >17 W/O CC	1.1820	29.6	24.7
421	VIRAL ILLNESS AGE >17	0.9441	27.3	22.8
422	[7] VIRAL ILLNESS & FEVER OF UNKNOWN ORIGIN AGE 0-17	1.1820	29.6	24.7
423	OTHER INFECTIOUS & PARASITIC DISEASES DIAGNOSES	0.9505	21.8	18.2
424	[3] O.R. PROCEDURE W PRINCIPAL DIAGNOSES OF MENTAL ILLNESS	0.7637	24.8	20.7
425	[2] ACUTE ADJUSTMENT REACTION & PSYCHOLOGICAL DYSFUNCTION	0.5837	21.3	17.8
426	DEPRESSIVE NEUROSES	0.4113	20.7	17.3
427	NEUROSES EXCEPT DEPRESSIVE	0.4653	23.8	19.8
428	[1] DISORDERS OF PERSONALITY & IMPULSE CONTROL	0.4499	19.0	15.8
429	ORGANIC DISTURBANCES & MENTAL RETARDATION	0.5813	26.8	22.3

LTC-DRG	Description	RW	GMLOS	5/6 GMLOS
430	PSYCHOSES	0.4330	24.2	20.2
431	[1] CHILDHOOD MENTAL DISORDERS	0.4499	19.0	15.8
432	[2] OTHER MENTAL DISORDER DIAGNOSES	0.5837	21.3	17.8
433	[2] ALCOHOL/DRUG ABUSE OR DEPENDENCE, LEFT AMA	0.5837	21.3	17.8
439	SKIN GRAFTS FOR INJURIES	1.3677	35.6	29.7
440	WOUND DEBRIDEMENTS FOR INJURIES	1.3442	36.1	30.1
441	[1] HAND PROCEDURES FOR INJURIES	0.4499	19.0	15.8
442	OTHER O.R. PROCEDURES FOR INJURIES W CC	1.3937	33.4	27.8
443	[3] OTHER O.R. PROCEDURES FOR INJURIES W/O CC	0.7637	24.8	20.7
444	TRAUMATIC INJURY AGE >17 W CC	0.7584	26.3	21.9
445	[1] TRAUMATIC INJURY AGE >17 W/O CC	0.4499	19.0	15.8
446	[7] TRAUMATIC INJURY AGE 0-17	0.4499	19.0	15.8
447	[2] ALLERGIC REACTIONS AGE >17	0.5837	21.3	17.8
448	[7] ALLERGIC REACTIONS AGE 0-17	0.5837	21.3	17.8
449	[3] POISONING & TOXIC EFFECTS OF DRUGS AGE >17 W CC	0.7637	24.8	20.7
450	[7] POISONING & TOXIC EFFECTS OF DRUGS AGE >17 W/O CC	0.7637	24.8	20.7
451	[7] POISONING & TOXIC EFFECTS OF DRUGS AGE 0-17	0.7637	24.8	20.7
452	COMPLICATIONS OF TREATMENT W CC	0.9265	25.3	21.1
453	COMPLICATIONS OF TREATMENT W/O CC	0.5871	23.8	19.8
454	[3] OTHER INJURY, POISONING & TOXIC EFFECT DIAG W CC	0.7637	24.8	20.7
455	[7] OTHER INJURY, POISONING & TOXIC EFFECT DIAG W/O CC	0.7637	24.8	20.7
461	O.R. PROC W DIAGNOSES OF OTHER CONTACT W HEALTH SERVICES	1.2245	34.0	28.3
462	REHABILITATION	0.5787	22.4	18.7
463	SIGNS & SYMPTOMS W CC	0.6258	23.8	19.8
464	SIGNS & SYMPTOMS W/O CC	0.5554	24.1	20.1
465	AFTERCARE W HISTORY OF MALIGNANCY AS SECONDARY DIAGNOSIS	0.6958	21.9	18.3
466	AFTERCARE W/O HISTORY OF MALIGNANCY AS SECONDARY DIAGNOSIS	0.6667	21.9	18.3
467	[3] OTHER FACTORS INFLUENCING HEALTH STATUS	0.7637	24.8	20.7
468	EXTENSIVE O.R. PROCEDURE UNRELATED TO PRINCIPAL DIAGNOSIS	2.1478	40.2	33.5
469	[6] PRINCIPAL DIAGNOSIS INVALID AS DISCHARGE DIAGNOSIS	0.0000	0.0	0.0
470	[6] UNGROUPABLE	0.0000	0.0	0.0
471	[5] BILATERAL OR MULTIPLE MAJOR JOINT PROCS OF LOWER EXTREMITY	1.7034	38.5	32.1
473	ACUTE LEUKEMIA W/O MAJOR O.R. PROCEDURE AGE >17	0.8537	20.0	16.7
475	RESPIRATORY SYSTEM DIAGNOSIS WITH VENTILATOR SUPPORT	2.0831	34.6	28.8

LTC-DRG	Description	RW	GMLOS	5/6 GMLOS
476	[4] PROSTATIC O.R. PROCEDURE UNRELATED TO PRINCIPAL DIAGNOSIS	1.1820	29.6	24.7
477	NON-EXTENSIVE O.R. PROCEDURE UNRELATED TO PRINCIPAL DIAGNOSIS	1.5836	35.3	29.4
479	[7] OTHER VASCULAR PROCEDURES W/O CC	0.7637	24.8	20.7
480	[6] LIVER TRANSPLANT	0.0000	0.0	0.0
481	[7] BONE MARROW TRANSPLANT	1.7034	38.5	32.1
482	[5] TRACHEOSTOMY FOR FACE,MOUTH & NECK DIAGNOSES	1.7034	38.5	32.1
484	[2] CRANIOTOMY FOR MULTIPLE SIGNIFICANT TRAUMA	0.5837	21.3	17.8
485	[7] LIMB REATTACHMENT, HIP AND FEMUR PROC FOR MULTIPLE SIGNIFICANT TR	1.1820	29.6	24.7
486	[5] OTHER O.R. PROCEDURES FOR MULTIPLE SIGNIFICANT TRAUMA	1.7034	38.5	32.1
487	OTHER MULTIPLE SIGNIFICANT TRAUMA	0.8992	26.0	21.7
488	[5] HIV W EXTENSIVE O.R. PROCEDURE	1.7034	38.5	32.1
489	HIV W MAJOR RELATED CONDITION	0.8535	21.4	17.8
490	HIV W OR W/O OTHER RELATED CONDITION	0.4919	16.6	13.8
491	[5] MAJOR JOINT & LIMB REATTACHMENT PROCEDURES OF UPPER EXTREMITY	1.7034	38.5	32.1
492	[7] CHEMOTHERAPY W ACUTE LEUKEMIA AS SECONDARY DIAGNOSIS	1.1820	29.6	24.7
493	[5] LAPAROSCOPIC CHOLECYSTECTOMY W/O C.D.E. W CC	1.7034	38.5	32.1
494	[7] LAPAROSCOPIC CHOLECYSTECTOMY W/O C.D.E. W/O CC	1.7034	38.5	32.1
495	[6] LUNG TRANSPLANT	0.0000	0.0	0.0
496	[7] COMBINED ANTERIOR/POSTERIOR SPINAL FUSION	1.1820	29.6	24.7
497	[4] SPINAL FUSION W CC	1.1820	29.6	24.7
498	[7] SPINAL FUSION W/O CC	1.1820	29.6	24.7
499	[5] BACK & NECK PROCEDURES EXCEPT SPINAL FUSION W CC	1.7034	38.5	32.1
500	[4] BACK & NECK PROCEDURES EXCEPT SPINAL FUSION W/O CC	1.1820	29.6	24.7
501	[5] KNEE PROCEDURES W PDX OF INFECTION W CC	1.7034	38.5	32.1
502	[4] KNEE PROCEDURES W PDX OF INFECTION W/O CC	1.1820	29.6	24.7
503	[2] KNEE PROCEDURES W/O PDX OF INFECTION	0.5837	21.3	17.8
504	[7] EXTENSIVE BURN OR FULL THICKNESS BURNS WITH MECH VENT 96+ HOURS WITH SKIN GRAFT	1.7034	38.5	32.1
505	[4] EXTENSIVE BURN OR FULL THICKNESS BURNS WITH MECH VENT 96+ HOURS WITHOUT SKIN GRAFT	1.1820	29.6	24.7
506	[4] FULL THICKNESS BURN W SKIN GRAFT OR INHAL INJ W CC OR SIG TRAUMA	1.1820	29.6	24.7
507	[3] FULL THICKNESS BURN W SKIN GRFT OR INHAL INJ W/O CC OR SIG TRAUMA	0.7637	24.8	20.7

LTC-DRG	Description	RW	GMLOS	5/6 GMLOS
508	FULL THICKNESS BURN W/O SKIN GRFT OR INHAL INJ W CC OR SIG TRAUMA	0.8367	29.4	24.5
509	[1] FULL THICKNESS BURN W/O SKIN GRFT OR INH INJ W/O CC OR SIG TRAUMA	0.4499	19.0	15.8
510	NON-EXTENSIVE BURNS W CC OR SIGNIFICANT TRAUMA	0.7709	24.6	20.5
511	[1] NON-EXTENSIVE BURNS W/O CC OR SIGNIFICANT TRAUMA	0.4499	19.0	15.8
512	[6] SIMULTANEOUS PANCREAS/KIDNEY TRANSPLANT	0.0000	0.0	0.0
513	[6] PANCREAS TRANSPLANT	0.0000	0.0	0.0
515	[5] CARDIAC DEFIBRILATOR IMPLANT W/O CARDIAC CATH	1.7034	38.5	32.1
518	[7] PERCUTANEOUS CARDIVASCULAR PROC W/O CORONARY ARTERY STENT OR AMI	0.7637	24.8	20.7
519	[5] CERVICAL SPINAL FUSION W CC	1.7034	38.5	32.1
520	[7] CERVICAL SPINAL FUSION W/O CC	1.1820	29.6	24.7
521	ALCOHOL/DRUG ABUSE OR DEPENDENCE W CC	0.4457	19.4	16.2
522	[7] ALCOHOL/DRUG ABUSE OR DEPENDENCE W REHABILITATION THERAPY W/O CC	0.4499	19.0	15.8
523	[7] ALCOHOL/DRUG ABUSE OR DEPENDENCE W/O REHABILITATION THERAPY W/O CC	0.4499	19.0	15.8
524	TRANSIENT ISCHEMIA	0.5043	21.1	17.6
525	[7] OTHER HEART ASSIST SYSTEM IMPLANT	1.7034	38.5	32.1
528	[7] INTRACRANIAL VASCULAR PROC W PDX HEMORRHAGE	1.7034	38.5	32.1
529	[5] VENTRICULAR SHUNT PROCEDURES W CC	1.7034	38.5	32.1
530	[7] VENTRICULAR SHUNT PROCEDURES W/O CC	1.7034	38.5	32.1
531	[3] SPINAL PROCEDURES WITH CC	0.7637	24.8	20.7
532	[3] SPINAL PROCEDURES WITHOUT CC	0.7637	24.8	20.7
533	[5] EXTRACRANIAL VASCULAR PROCEDURES WITH CC	1.7034	38.5	32.1
534	[7] EXTRACRANIAL VASCULAR PROCEDURES WITHOUT CC	1.1820	29.6	24.7
535	[7] CARDIAC DEFIB IMPLANT W CARDIAC CATH W AMI/HF/SHOCK	1.7034	38.5	32.1
536	[7] CARDIAC DEFIB IMPLANT W CARDIAC CATH W/O AMI/HF/SHOCK	1.7034	38.5	32.1
537	LOCAL EXCISION AND REMOVAL OF INTERNAL FIXATION DEVICES EXCEPT HIP AND FEMUR WITH CC	1.1615	34.7	28.9
538	[7] LOCAL EXCISION AND REMOVAL OF INTERNAL FIXATION DEVICES EXCEPT HIP AND FEMUR WITHOUT CC	1.1820	29.6	24.7
539	[4] LYMPHOMA AND LEUKEMIA WITH MAJOR O.R. PROCEDURE WITH CC	1.1820	29.6	24.7
540	[7] LYMPHOMA AND LEUKEMIA WITH MAJOR O.R. PROCEDURE WITHOUT CC	0.5837	21.3	17.8
541	ECMO OR TRACH W MECH VENT 96+ HRS OR PDX EXCEPT FACE,MOUTH & NECK DIAG WITH MAJOR OR	4.2287	65.6	54.7

LTC-DRG	Description	RW	GMLOS	5/6 GMLOS
542	TRACH W MECH VENT 96+ HRS OR PDX EXCEPT FACE,MOUTH & NECK DIAG WITHOUT MAJOR OR	3.1869	48.2	40.2
543	[5] CRANIOTOMY W IMPLANT OF CHEMO AGENT OR ACUTE COMPLEX CNS PDX	1.7034	38.5	32.1
544	[5] MAJOR JOINT REPLACEMENT OR REATTACHMENT OF LOWER EXTREMITY	1.7034	38.5	32.1
545	[5] REVISION OF HIP OR KNEE REPLACEMENT	1.7034	38.5	32.1
546	[7] SPINAL FUSION EXCEPT CERVICAL WITH CURVATURE OF SPINE OR MALIGNANCY	1.7034	38.5	32.1
547	[7] CORONARY BYPASS WITH CARDIAC CATH WITH MAJOR CV DIAGNOSIS	1.7034	38.5	32.1
548	[7] CORONARY BYPASS WITH CARDIAC CATH WITHOUT MAJOR CV DIAGNOSIS	1.7034	38.5	32.1
549	[7] CORONARY BYPASS WITHOUT CARDIAC CATH WITH MAJOR CV DIAGNOSIS	1.7034	38.5	32.1
550	[7] CORONARY BYPASS WITHOUT CARDIAC CATH WITHOUT MAJOR CV DIAGNOSIS	1.7034	38.5	32.1
551	[4] PERMANENT CARDIAC PACEMAKER IMPLANT WITH MAJOR CV DIAGNOSIS OR AICD LEAD OR GNRTR	1.1820	29.6	24.7
552	[4] OTHER PERMANENT CARDIAC PACEMAKER IMPLANT WITHOUT MAJOR CV DIAGNOSIS	1.1820	29.6	24.7
553	[8] OTHER VASCULAR PROCEDURES WITH CC WITH MAJOR CV DIAGNOSIS	1.3255	30.6	25.5
554	[8] OTHER VASCULAR PROCEDURES WITH CC WITHOUT MAJOR CV DIAGNOSIS	1.3255	30.6	25.5
555	[4] PERCUTANEOUS CARDIOVASCULAR PROC WITH MAJOR CV DIAGNOSIS	1.1820	29.6	24.7
556	[8] PERCUTANEOUS CARDIOVASCULAR PROC WITH NON-DRUG-ELUTING STENT WITHOUT MAJOR CV DIAGNOSIS	1.1820	29.6	24.7
557	[8] PERCUTANEOUS CARDIOVASCULAR PROC WITH DRUG-ELUTING STENT WITH MAJOR CV DIAGNOSIS	1.1820	29.6	24.7
558	[7] PERCUTANEOUS CARDIOVASCULAR PROC WITH DRUG-ELUTING STENT WITHOUT MAJOR CV DIAGNOSIS	1.1820	29.6	24.7
559	[7] ACUTE ISCHEMIC STROKE WITH USE OF THROMBOLYTIC AGENT	0.7637	24.8	20.7

Appendix D — National Average Payment Table

The national average payment for each DRG is calculated by multiplying the current relative weight of the DRG by the ESTIMATED national average hospital Medicare base rate. That estimated average hospital base rate is adjusted annually using information gathered by Ingenix, Inc. and the information published in the *Federal Register* (Medicare Program: Changes to the Inpatient Prospective Payment Systems and Fiscal Year 2005 Rates; Final Rule). This information is provided as a benchmark reference only. There is no official publication of the average hospital base rate, therefore the national average payments provide in this table are approximate.

DRG	Description	MDC	Nat'l Avg Payment
001	Craniotomy, Age Greater than 17 with CC	1	$16,222.09
002	Craniotomy, Age Greater than 17 without CC	1	$9,250.94
003	Craniotomy, Age 0-17	1	$9,379.88
004	No Longer Valid	1	$0.00
005	No Longer Valid	1	$0.00
006	Carpal Tunnel Release	1	$3,720.78
007	Peripheral and Cranial Nerve and Other Nervous System Procedures with CC	1	$12,741.71
008	Peripheral and Cranial Nerve and Other Nervous System Procedures without CC	1	$7,384.41
009	Spinal Disorders and Injuries	1	$6,633.45
010	Nervous System Neoplasms with CC	1	$5,772.45
011	Nervous System Neoplasms without CC	1	$4,126.01
012	Degenerative Nervous System Disorders	1	$4,249.76
013	Multiple Sclerosis and Cerebellar Ataxia	1	$4,049.97
014	Intracranial Hemorrhage or Cerebral Infarction	1	$5,882.97
015	Nonspecific Cerebrovascular and Precerebral Occlusion without Infarction	1	$4,449.54
016	Nonspecific Cerebrovascular Disorders with CC	1	$6,305.68
017	Nonspecific Cerebrovascular Disorders without CC	1	$3,414.26
018	Cranial and Peripheral Nerve Disorders with CC	1	$4,677.19
019	Cranial and Peripheral Nerve Disorders without CC	1	$3,342.47
020	Nervous System Infection Except Viral Meningitis	1	$13,160.64
021	Viral Meningitis	1	$6,825.21
022	Hypertensive Encephalopathy	1	$5,338.88
023	Nontraumatic Stupor and Coma	1	$3,642.38
024	Seizure and Headache, Age Greater than 17 with CC	1	$4,708.83
025	Seizure and Headache, Age Greater than 17 without CC	1	$2,918.81
026	Seizure and Headache, Age 0-17	1	$8,591.61
027	Traumatic Stupor and Coma, Coma Greater than One Hour	1	$6,390.69
028	Traumatic Stupor and Coma, Coma Less than One Hour, Age Greater than 17 with CC	1	$6,306.62
029	Traumatic Stupor and Coma, Coma Less than One Hour, Age Greater than 17 without CC	1	$3,406.23
030	Traumatic Stupor and Coma, Coma Less than One Hour, Age 0-17	1	$1,586.46
031	Concussion, Age Greater than 17 with CC	1	$4,518.49
032	Concussion, Age Greater than 17 without CC	1	$2,925.43
033	Concussion, Age 0-17	1	$996.08
034	Other Disorders of Nervous System with CC	1	$4,752.28
035	Other Disorders of Nervous System without CC	1	$2,947.62
036	Retinal Procedures	2	$3,442.12
037	Orbital Procedures	2	$5,600.53

* *Calculated with an average hospital Medicare base rate of $4,733. Each hospital's base rate and corresponding payment will vary.*

DRG	Description	MDC	Nat'l Avg Payment
038	Primary Iris Procedures	2	$3,294.29
039	Lens Procedures with or without Vitrectomy	2	$3,357.11
040	Extraocular Procedures Except Orbit, Age Greater than 17	2	$4,546.83
041	Extraocular Procedures Except Orbit, Age 0-17	2	$1,614.79
042	Intraocular Procedures Except Retina, Iris and Lens	2	$3,708.50
043	Hyphema	2	$2,900.39
044	Acute Major Eye Infections	2	$3,246.59
045	Neurological Eye Disorders	2	$3,529.97
046	Other Disorders of the Eye, Age Greater than 17 with CC	2	$3,553.59
047	Other Disorders of the Eye, Age Greater than 17 without CC	2	$2,457.38
048	Other Disorders of the Eye, Age 0-17	2	$1,422.57
049	Major Head and Neck Procedures	3	$7,727.30
050	Sialoadenectomy	3	$4,104.29
051	Salivary Gland Procedures Except Sialoadenectomy	3	$4,160.49
052	Cleft Lip and Palate Repair	3	$3,942.76
053	Sinus and Mastoid Procedures, Age Greater than 17	3	$6,266.95
054	Sinus and Mastoid Procedures, Age 0-17	3	$2,305.77
055	Miscellaneous Ear, Nose, Mouth and Throat Procedures	3	$4,532.66
056	Rhinoplasty	3	$4,114.21
057	Tonsillectomy and Adenoidectomy Procedures Except Tonsillectomy and/or Adenoidectomy Only, Age Greater than 17	3	$4,925.14
058	Tonsillectomy and Adenoidectomy Procedures Except Tonsillectomy and/or Adenoidectomy Only, Age 0-17	3	$1,309.22
059	Tonsillectomy and/or Adenoidectomy Only, Age Greater than 17	3	$3,817.13
060	Tonsillectomy and/or Adenoidectomy Only, Age 0-17	3	$996.55
061	Myringotomy with Tube Insertion, Age Greater than 17	3	$6,077.08
062	Myringotomy with Tube Insertion, Age 0-17	3	$1,411.70
063	Other Ear, Nose, Mouth and Throat O.R. Procedures	3	$6,604.17
064	Ear, Nose, Mouth and Throat Malignancy	3	$5,508.43
065	Dysequilibrium	3	$2,829.55
066	Epistaxis	3	$2,813.96
067	Epiglottitis	3	$3,648.52
068	Otitis Media and URI, Age Greater than 17 with CC	3	$3,122.38
069	Otitis Media and URI, Age Greater than 17 without CC	3	$2,290.66
070	Otitis Media and URI, Age 0-17	3	$1,988.38
071	Laryngotracheitis	3	$3,553.59
072	Nasal Trauma and Deformity	3	$3,518.16
073	Other Ear, Nose, Mouth and Throat Diagnoses, Age Greater than 17	3	$4,027.30
074	Other Ear, Nose, Mouth and Throat Diagnoses, Age 0-17	3	$1,604.88
075	Major Chest Procedures	4	$14,514.72
076	Other Respiratory System O.R. Procedures with CC	4	$13,616.41
077	Other Respiratory System O.R. Procedures without CC	4	$5,600.06
078	Pulmonary Embolism	4	$5,869.27
079	Respiratory Infections and Inflammations, Age Greater than 17 with CC	4	$7,669.21
080	Respiratory Infections and Inflammations, Age Greater than 17 without CC	4	$4,225.67
081	Respiratory Infections and Inflammations, Age 0-17	4	$7,265.39
082	Respiratory Neoplasms	4	$6,581.97
083	Major Chest Trauma with CC	4	$4,641.76
084	Major Chest Trauma without CC	4	$2,738.87
085	Pleural Effusion with CC	4	$5,858.88
086	Pleural Effusion without CC	4	$3,293.82

** Calculated with an average hospital Medicare base rate of $4,733. Each hospital's base rate and corresponding payment will vary.*

DRG	Description	MDC	Nat'l Avg Payment
087	Pulmonary Edema and Respiratory Failure	4	$6,448.78
088	Chronic Obstructive Pulmonary Disease	4	$4,145.85
089	Simple Pneumonia and Pleurisy, Age Greater than 17 with CC	4	$4,874.14
090	Simple Pneumonia and Pleurisy, Age Greater than 17 without CC	4	$2,882.92
091	Simple Pneumonia and Pleurisy, Age 0-17	4	$3,836.97
092	Interstitial Lung Disease with CC	4	$5,598.17
093	Interstitial Lung Disease without CC	4	$3,376.95
094	Pneumothorax with CC	4	$5,362.49
095	Pneumothorax without CC	4	$2,850.33
096	Bronchitis and Asthma, Age Greater than 17 with CC	4	$3,449.21
097	Bronchitis and Asthma, Age Greater than 17 without CC	4	$2,533.42
098	Bronchitis and Asthma, Age 0-17	4	$2,625.99
099	Respiratory Signs and Symptoms with CC	4	$3,350.50
100	Respiratory Signs and Symptoms without CC	4	$2,541.92
101	Other Respiratory System Diagnoses with CC	4	$4,124.60
102	Other Respiratory System Diagnoses without CC	4	$2,551.36
103	Heart Transplant or Implant of Heart Assist System	Pre	$87,666.91
104	Cardiac Valve Procedures and Other Major Cardiothoracic Procedures with Cardiac Catheterization	5	$38,823.53
105	Cardiac Valve Procedures and Other Major Cardiothoracic Procedures without Cardiac Catheterization	5	$28,428.68
106	Coronary Bypass with PTCA	5	$33,224.42
107	No Longer Valid	5	$0.00
108	Other Cardiothoracic Procedures	5	$27,766.04
109	No Longer Valid	5	$0.00
110	Major Cardiovascular Procedures with CC	5	$18,144.35
111	Major Cardiovascular Procedures without CC	5	$11,731.93
112	No Longer Valid	5	$0.00
113	Amputation for Circulatory System Disorders Except Upper Limb and Toe	5	$14,963.41
114	Upper Limb and Toe Amputation for Circulatory System Disorders	5	$8,196.29
115	No Longer Valid	5	$0.00
116	No Longer Valid	5	$0.00
117	Cardiac Pacemaker Revision Except Device Replacement	5	$6,245.22
118	Cardiac Pacemaker Device Replacement	5	$7,736.27
119	Vein Ligation and Stripping	5	$6,355.27
120	Other Circulatory System O.R. Procedures	5	$11,265.77
121	Circulatory Disorders with Acute Myocardial Infarction and Major Complications, Discharged Alive	5	$7,621.03
122	Circulatory Disorders with Acute Myocardial Infarction without Major Complications, Discharged Alive	5	$4,650.74
123	Circulatory Disorders with Acute Myocardial Infarction, Expired	5	$7,276.73
124	Circulatory Disorders Except Acute Myocardial Infarction with Cardiac Catheterization and Complex Diagnosis	5	$6,812.93
125	Circulatory Disorders Except Acute Myocardial Infarction with Cardiac Catheterization without Complex Diagnosis	5	$5,170.74
126	Acute and Subacute Endocarditis	5	$12,959.91
127	Heart Failure and Shock	5	$4,885.94
128	Deep Vein Thrombophlebitis	5	$3,282.01
129	Cardiac Arrest, Unexplained	5	$4,913.81
130	Peripheral Vascular Disorders with CC	5	$4,451.43
131	Peripheral Vascular Disorders without CC	5	$2,628.82
132	Atherosclerosis with CC	5	$2,962.74

** Calculated with an average hospital Medicare base rate of $4,733. Each hospital's base rate and corresponding payment will vary.*

DRG	Description	MDC	Nat'l Avg Payment
133	Atherosclerosis without CC	5	$2,520.67
134	Hypertension	5	$2,865.92
135	Cardiac Congenital and Valvular Disorders, Age Greater than 17 with CC	5	$4,211.50
136	Cardiac Congenital and Valvular Disorders, Age Greater than 17 without CC	5	$2,934.87
137	Cardiac Congenital and Valvular Disorders, Age 0-17	5	$3,914.42
138	Cardiac Arrhythmia and Conduction Disorders with CC	5	$3,913.95
139	Cardiac Arrhythmia and Conduction Disorders without CC	5	$2,468.71
140	Angina Pectoris	5	$2,416.29
141	Syncope and Collapse with CC	5	$3,552.17
142	Syncope and Collapse without CC	5	$2,763.90
143	Chest Pain	5	$2,672.75
144	Other Circulatory System Diagnoses with CC	5	$6,027.02
145	Other Circulatory System Diagnoses without CC	5	$2,755.87
146	Rectal Resection with CC	6	$12,573.10
147	Rectal Resection without CC	6	$6,981.07
148	Major Small and Large Bowel Procedures with CC	6	$16,284.43
149	Major Small and Large Bowel Procedures without CC	6	$6,765.23
150	Peritoneal Adhesiolysis with CC	6	$13,253.21
151	Peritoneal Adhesiolysis without CC	6	$5,970.34
152	Minor Small and Large Bowel Procedures with CC	6	$8,871.21
153	Minor Small and Large Bowel Procedures without CC	6	$5,110.76
154	Stomach, Esophageal and Duodenal Procedures, Age Greater than 17 with CC	6	$19,080.45
155	Stomach, Esophageal and Duodenal Procedures, Age Greater than 17 without CC	6	$6,087.47
156	Stomach, Esophageal and Duodenal Procedures, Age 0-17	6	$4,031.08
157	Anal and Stomal Procedures with CC	6	$6,308.04
158	Anal and Stomal Procedures without CC	6	$3,144.10
159	Hernia Procedures Except Inguinal and Femoral, Age Greater than 17 with CC	6	$6,650.46
160	Hernia Procedures Except Inguinal and Femoral, Age Greater than 17 without CC	6	$3,981.96
161	Inguinal and Femoral Hernia Procedures, Age Greater than 17 with CC	6	$5,635.01
162	Inguinal and Femoral Hernia Procedures, Age Greater than 17 without CC	6	$3,204.56
163	Hernia Procedures, Age 0-17	6	$3,175.27
164	Appendectomy with Complicated Principal Diagnosis with CC	6	$10,615.41
165	Appendectomy with Complicated Principal Diagnosis without CC	6	$5,605.26
166	Appendectomy without Complicated Principal Diagnosis with CC	6	$6,858.27
167	Appendectomy without Complicated Principal Diagnosis without CC	6	$4,217.17
168	Mouth Procedures with CC	3	$5,980.26
169	Mouth Procedures without CC	3	$3,446.37
170	Other Digestive System O.R. Procedures with CC	6	$13,985.75
171	Other Digestive System O.R. Procedures without CC	6	$5,622.73
172	Digestive Malignancy with CC	6	$6,671.24
173	Digestive Malignancy without CC	6	$3,515.33
174	GI Hemorrhage with CC	6	$4,751.34
175	GI Hemorrhage without CC	6	$2,666.61
176	Complicated Peptic Ulcer	6	$5,311.49
177	Uncomplicated Peptic Ulcer with CC	6	$4,329.10
178	Uncomplicated Peptic Ulcer without CC	6	$3,312.24
179	Inflammatory Bowel Disease	6	$5,153.27
180	GI Obstruction with CC	6	$4,620.98
181	GI Obstruction without CC	6	$2,651.49

** Calculated with an average hospital Medicare base rate of $4,733. Each hospital's base rate and corresponding payment will vary.*

DRG	Description	MDC	Nat'l Avg Payment
182	Esophagitis, Gastroenteritis and Miscellaneous Digestive Disorders, Age Greater than 17 with CC	6	$3,973.46
183	Esophagitis, Gastroenteritis and Miscellaneous Digestive Disorders, Age Greater than 17 without CC	6	$2,762.01
184	Esophagitis, Gastroenteritis and Miscellaneous Digestive Disorders, Age 0-17	6	$2,674.63
185	Dental and Oral Diseases Except Extractions and Restorations, Age Greater than 17	3	$4,109.95
186	Dental and Oral Diseases Except Extractions and Restorations, Age 0-17	3	$1,536.39
187	Dental Extractions and Restorations	3	$3,949.84
188	Other Digestive System Diagnoses, Age Greater than 17 with CC	6	$5,332.27
189	Other Digestive System Diagnoses, Age Greater than 17 without CC	6	$2,864.03
190	Other Digestive System Diagnoses, Age 0-17	6	$2,918.34
191	Pancreas, Liver and Shunt Procedures with CC	7	$18,740.86
192	Pancreas, Liver and Shunt Procedures without CC	7	$7,931.33
193	Biliary Tract Procedures Except Only Cholecystectomy with or without Common Duct Exploration with CC	7	$15,499.94
194	Biliary Tract Procedures Except Only Cholecystectomy with or without Common Duct Exploration without CC	7	$7,437.78
195	Cholecystectomy with Common Duct Exploration with CC	7	$14,419.32
196	Cholecystectomy with Common Duct Exploration without CC	7	$7,571.44
197	Cholecystectomy Except by Laparoscope without Common Duct Exploration with CC	7	$12,008.23
198	Cholecystectomy Except by Laparoscope without Common Duct Exploration without CC	7	$5,480.57
199	Hepatobiliary Diagnostic Procedure for Malignancy	7	$11,369.68
200	Hepatobiliary Diagnostic Procedure for Nonmalignancy	7	$13,162.06
201	Other Hepatobiliary or Pancreas O.R. Procedures	7	$17,635.21
202	Cirrhosis and Alcoholic Hepatitis	7	$6,290.09
203	Malignancy of Hepatobiliary System or Pancreas	7	$6,400.61
204	Disorders of Pancreas Except Malignancy	7	$5,312.90
205	Disorders of Liver Except Malignancy, Cirrhosis and Alcoholic Hepatitis with CC	7	$5,695.47
206	Disorders of Liver Except Malignancy, Cirrhosis and Alcoholic Hepatitis without CC	7	$3,444.01
207	Disorders of the Biliary Tract with CC	7	$5,547.64
208	Disorders of the Biliary Tract without CC	7	$3,256.51
209	No Longer Valid	8	$0.00
210	Hip and Femur Procedures Except Major Joint Procedures, Age Greater than 17 with CC	8	$9,001.57
211	Hip and Femur Procedures Except Major Joint Procedures, Age Greater than 17 without CC	8	$5,993.49
212	Hip and Femur Procedures Except Major Joint Procedures, Age 0-17	8	$6,081.81
213	Amputation for Musculoskeletal System and Connective Tissue Disorders	8	$9,648.14
214	No Longer Valid	8	$0.00
215	No Longer Valid	8	$0.00
216	Biopsies of Musculoskeletal System and Connective Tissue	8	$9,035.57
217	Wound Debridement and Skin Graft Except Hand for Musculoskeletal and Connective Tissue Disorders	8	$14,450.49
218	Lower Extremity and Humerus Procedures Except Hip, Foot and Femur, Age Greater than 17 with CC	8	$7,862.85
219	Lower Extremity and Humerus Procedures Except Hip, Foot and Femur, Age Greater than 17 without CC	8	$4,932.23
220	Lower Extremity and Humerus Procedures Except Hip, Foot and Femur, Age 0-17	8	$2,792.71
221	No Longer Valid	8	$0.00

** Calculated with an average hospital Medicare base rate of $4,733. Each hospital's base rate and corresponding payment will vary.*

DRG	Description	MDC	Nat'l Avg Payment
222	No Longer Valid	8	$0.00
223	Major Shoulder/Elbow Procedures or Other Upper Extremity Procedures with CC	8	$5,272.76
224	Shoulder, Elbow or Forearm Procedures Except Major Joint Procedures without CC	8	$3,865.78
225	Foot Procedures	8	$5,786.15
226	Soft Tissue Procedures with CC	8	$7,502.01
227	Soft Tissue Procedures without CC	8	$3,925.29
228	Major Thumb or Joint Procedures or Other Hand or Wrist Procedures with CC	8	$5,412.09
229	Hand or Wrist Procedures Except Major Joint Procedures without CC	8	$3,294.76
230	Local Excision and Removal of Internal Fixation Devices of Hip and Femur	8	$6,222.08
231	No Longer Valid	8	$0.00
232	Arthroscopy	8	$4,582.25
233	Other Musculoskeletal System and Connective Tissue O.R. Procedures with CC	8	$9,060.60
234	Other Musculoskeletal System and Connective Tissue O.R. Procedures without CC	8	$5,771.03
235	Fractures of Femur	8	$3,668.83
236	Fractures of Hip and Pelvis	8	$3,498.33
237	Sprains, Strains and Dislocations of Hip, Pelvis and Thigh	8	$2,876.31
238	Osteomyelitis	8	$6,801.59
239	Pathological Fractures and Musculoskeletal and Connective Tissue Malignancy	8	$5,085.25
240	Connective Tissue Disorders with CC	8	$6,636.29
241	Connective Tissue Disorders without CC	8	$3,130.88
242	Septic Arthritis	8	$5,433.34
243	Medical Back Problems	8	$3,616.87
244	Bone Diseases and Specific Arthropathies with CC	8	$3,400.56
245	Bone Diseases and Specific Arthropathies without CC	8	$2,164.55
246	Nonspecific Arthropathies	8	$2,801.68
247	Signs and Symptoms of Musculoskeletal System and Connective Tissue	8	$2,736.98
248	Tendonitis, Myositis and Bursitis	8	$4,040.05
249	Aftercare, Musculoskeletal System and Connective Tissue	8	$3,350.97
250	Fractures, Sprains, Strains and Dislocations of Forearm, Hand and Foot, Age Greater than 17 with CC	8	$3,293.82
251	Fractures, Sprains, Strains and Dislocations of Forearm, Hand and Foot, Age Greater than 17 without CC	8	$2,242.95
252	Fractures, Sprains, Strains and Dislocations of Forearm, Hand and Foot, Age 0-17	8	$1,212.39
253	Fractures, Sprains, Strains and Dislocations of Upper Arm and Lower Leg Except Foot, Age Greater than 17 with CC	8	$3,658.91
254	Fractures, Sprains, Strains and Dislocations of Upper Arm and Lower Leg Except Foot, Age Greater than 17 without CC	8	$2,166.91
255	Fractures, Sprains, Strains and Dislocations of Upper Arm and Lower Leg Except Foot, Age 0-17	8	$1,412.18
256	Other Musculoskeletal System and Connective Tissue Diagnoses	8	$4,018.80
257	Total Mastectomy for Malignancy with CC	9	$4,235.11
258	Total Mastectomy for Malignancy without CC	9	$3,371.28
259	Subtotal Mastectomy for Malignancy with CC	9	$4,567.61
260	Subtotal Mastectomy for Malignancy without CC	9	$3,321.21
261	Breast Procedure for Nonmalignancy Except Biopsy and Local Excision	9	$4,596.42
262	Breast Biopsy and Local Excision for Nonmalignancy	9	$4,612.48
263	Skin Graft and/or Debridement for Skin Ulcer or Cellulitis with CC	9	$9,979.70
264	Skin Graft and/or Debridement for Skin Ulcer or Cellulitis without CC	9	$5,022.91
265	Skin Graft and/or Debridement Except for Skin Ulcer or Cellulitis with CC	9	$7,836.87

** Calculated with an average hospital Medicare base rate of $4,733. Each hospital's base rate and corresponding payment will vary.*

DRG	Description	MDC	Nat'l Avg Payment
266	Skin Graft and/or Debridement Except for Skin Ulcer or Cellulitis without CC	9	$4,079.26
267	Perianal and Pilonidal Procedures	9	$4,232.75
268	Skin, Subcutaneous Tissue and Breast Plastic Procedures	9	$5,349.27
269	Other Skin, Subcutaneous Tissue and Breast Procedures with CC	9	$8,667.65
270	Other Skin, Subcutaneous Tissue and Breast Procedures without CC	9	$3,926.23
271	Skin Ulcers	9	$4,815.10
272	Major Skin Disorders with CC	9	$4,656.88
273	Major Skin Disorders without CC	9	$2,616.07
274	Malignant Breast Disorders with CC	9	$5,334.16
275	Malignant Breast Disorders without CC	9	$2,522.08
276	Nonmalignant Breast Disorders	9	$3,255.09
277	Cellulitis, Age Greater than 17 with CC	9	$4,097.67
278	Cellulitis, Age Greater than 17 without CC	9	$2,546.17
279	Cellulitis, Age 0-17	9	$3,694.33
280	Trauma to Skin, Subcutaneous Tissue and Breast, Age Greater than 17 with CC	9	$3,453.93
281	Trauma to Skin, Subcutaneous Tissue and Breast, Age Greater than 17 without CC	9	$2,320.41
282	Trauma to Skin, Subcutaneous Tissue and Breast, Age 0-17	9	$1,227.98
283	Minor Skin Disorders with CC	9	$3,505.88
284	Minor Skin Disorders without CC	9	$2,155.10
285	Amputation of Lower Limb for Endocrine, Nutritional and Metabolic Disorders	10	$10,310.78
286	Adrenal and Pituitary Procedures	10	$9,157.90
287	Skin Grafts and Wound Debridement for Endocrine, Nutritional and Metabolic Disorders	10	$9,195.68
288	O.R. Procedures for Obesity	10	$9,627.36
289	Parathyroid Procedures	10	$4,399.47
290	Thyroid Procedures	10	$4,199.22
291	Thyroglossal Procedures	10	$5,137.21
292	Other Endocrine, Nutritional and Metabolic O.R. Procedures with CC	10	$12,466.36
293	Other Endocrine, Nutritional and Metabolic O.R. Procedures without CC	10	$6,362.83
294	Diabetes, Age Greater than 35	10	$3,614.04
295	Diabetes, Age 0-35	10	$3,432.20
296	Nutritional and Miscellaneous Metabolic Disorders, Age Greater than 17 with CC	10	$3,866.72
297	Nutritional and Miscellaneous Metabolic Disorders, Age Greater than 17 without CC	10	$2,304.35
298	Nutritional and Miscellaneous Metabolic Disorders, Age 0-17	10	$2,591.04
299	Inborn Errors of Metabolism	10	$4,878.39
300	Endocrine Disorders with CC	10	$5,158.46
301	Endocrine Disorders without CC	10	$2,889.53
302	Kidney Transplant	11	$14,961.99
303	Kidney, Ureter and Major Bladder Procedures for Neoplasm	11	$10,477.03
304	Kidney, Ureter and Major Bladder Procedures for Non-neoplasms with CC	11	$11,222.32
305	Kidney, Ureter and Major Bladder Procedures for Non-neoplasms without CC	11	$5,476.32
306	Prostatectomy with CC	11	$5,998.21
307	Prostatectomy without CC	11	$2,929.20
308	Minor Bladder Procedures with CC	11	$7,721.63
309	Minor Bladder Procedures without CC	11	$4,290.85
310	Transurethral Procedures with CC	11	$5,619.43
311	Transurethral Procedures without CC	11	$3,037.83
312	Urethral Procedures, Age Greater than 17 with CC	11	$5,270.40
313	Urethral Procedures, Age Greater than 17 without CC	11	$3,203.61

** Calculated with an average hospital Medicare base rate of $4,733. Each hospital's base rate and corresponding payment will vary.*

Appendix D — National Average Payment Table

DRG	Description	MDC	Nat'l Avg Payment
314	Urethral Procedures, Age 0-17	11	$2,367.17
315	Other Kidney and Urinary Tract O.R. Procedures	11	$9,834.70
316	Renal Failure	11	$5,994.43
317	Admission for Renal Dialysis	11	$3,751.01
318	Kidney and Urinary Tract Neoplasms with CC	11	$5,449.87
319	Kidney and Urinary Tract Neoplasms without CC	11	$3,015.64
320	Kidney and Urinary Tract Infections, Age Greater than 17 with CC	11	$4,089.17
321	Kidney and Urinary Tract Infections, Age Greater than 17 without CC	11	$2,669.44
322	Kidney and Urinary Tract Infections, Age 0-17	11	$2,596.71
323	Urinary Stones with CC and/or ESW Lithotripsy	11	$3,879.47
324	Urinary Stones without CC	11	$2,385.12
325	Kidney and Urinary Tract Signs and Symptoms, Age Greater than 17 with CC	11	$3,039.72
326	Kidney and Urinary Tract Signs and Symptoms, Age Greater than 17 without CC	11	$2,073.87
327	Kidney and Urinary Tract Signs and Symptoms, Age 0-17	11	$1,770.18
328	Urethral Stricture, Age Greater than 17 with CC	11	$3,343.41
329	Urethral Stricture, Age Greater than 17 without CC	11	$2,220.28
330	Urethral Stricture, Age 0-17	11	$1,524.11
331	Other Kidney and Urinary Tract Diagnoses, Age Greater than 17 with CC	11	$5,015.35
332	Other Kidney and Urinary Tract Diagnoses, Age Greater than 17 without CC	11	$2,909.37
333	Other Kidney and Urinary Tract Diagnoses, Age 0-17	11	$4,566.67
334	Major Male Pelvic Procedures with CC	12	$6,786.01
335	Major Male Pelvic Procedures without CC	12	$5,197.19
336	Transurethral Prostatectomy with CC	12	$3,979.13
337	Transurethral Prostatectomy without CC	12	$2,714.31
338	Testes Procedures for Malignancy	12	$6,504.52
339	Testes Procedures for Nonmalignancy, Age Greater than 17	12	$5,604.31
340	Testes Procedures for Nonmalignancy, Age 0-17	12	$1,354.56
341	Penis Procedures	12	$5,961.37
342	Circumcision, Age Greater than 17	12	$4,126.49
343	Circumcision, Age 0-17	12	$736.32
344	Other Male Reproductive System O.R. Procedures for Malignancy	12	$5,891.94
345	Other Male Reproductive System O.R. Procedures Except for Malignancy	12	$5,418.23
346	Malignancy of Male Reproductive System with CC	12	$4,931.28
347	Malignancy of Male Reproductive System without CC	12	$2,882.92
348	Benign Prostatic Hypertrophy with CC	12	$3,394.89
349	Benign Prostatic Hypertrophy without CC	12	$1,988.38
350	Inflammation of the Male Reproductive System	12	$3,442.59
351	Sterilization, Male	12	$1,129.74
352	Other Male Reproductive System Diagnoses	12	$3,476.13
353	Pelvic Evisceration, Radical Hysterectomy and Radical Vulvectomy	13	$8,739.44
354	Uterine and Adnexa Procedures for Nonovarian/Adnexal Malignancy with CC	13	$7,148.26
355	Uterine and Adnexa Procedures for Nonovarian/Adnexal Malignancy without CC	13	$4,167.58
356	Female Reproductive System Reconstructive Procedures	13	$3,508.24
357	Uterine and Adnexa Procedures for Ovarian or Adnexal Malignancy	13	$10,502.54
358	Uterine and Adnexa Procedures for Nonmalignancy with CC	13	$5,406.89
359	Uterine and Adnexa Procedures for Nonmalignancy without CC	13	$3,753.84
360	Vagina, Cervix and Vulva Procedures	13	$4,053.28
361	Laparoscopy and Incisional Tubal Interruption	13	$5,123.04
362	Endoscopic Tubal Interruption	13	$1,443.82
363	D and C, Conization and Radio-Implant for Malignancy	13	$4,594.53

** Calculated with an average hospital Medicare base rate of $4,733. Each hospital's base rate and corresponding payment will vary.*

DRG	Description	MDC	Nat'l Avg Payment
364	D and C, Conization Except for Malignancy	13	$4,113.26
365	Other Female Reproductive System O.R. Procedures	13	$9,638.70
366	Malignancy of Female Reproductive System with CC	13	$5,831.96
367	Malignancy of Female Reproductive System without CC	13	$2,705.33
368	Infections of Female Reproductive System	13	$5,518.35
369	Menstrual and Other Female Reproductive System Disorders	13	$2,980.21
370	Cesarean Section with CC	14	$4,238.42
371	Cesarean Section without CC	14	$2,864.97
372	Vaginal Delivery with Complicating Diagnoses	14	$2,374.25
373	Vaginal Delivery without Complicating Diagnoses	14	$1,679.50
374	Vaginal Delivery with Sterilization and/or D and C	14	$3,170.08
375	Vaginal Delivery with O.R. Procedure Except Sterilization and/or D and C	14	$2,756.82
376	Postpartum and Postabortion Diagnoses without O.R. Procedure	14	$2,475.80
377	Postpartum and Postabortion Diagnoses with O.R. Procedure	14	$8,027.21
378	Ectopic Pregnancy	14	$3,529.03
379	Threatened Abortion	14	$1,689.89
380	Abortion without D and C	14	$1,853.78
381	Abortion with D and C, Aspiration Curettage or Hysterotomy	14	$2,849.86
382	False Labor	14	$977.66
383	Other Antepartum Diagnoses with Medical Complications	14	$2,386.53
384	Other Antepartum Diagnoses without Medical Complications	14	$1,523.17
385	Neonates, Died or Transferred to Another Acute Care Facility	15	$6,579.14
386	Extreme Immaturity or Respiratory Distress Syndrome of Neonate	15	$21,695.10
387	Prematurity with Major Problems	15	$14,817.00
388	Prematurity without Major Problems	15	$8,940.17
389	Full Term Neonate with Major Problems	15	$15,220.34
390	Neonate with Other Significant Problems	15	$5,387.05
391	Normal Newborn	15	$729.23
392	Splenectomy, Age Greater than 17	16	$14,385.79
393	Splenectomy, Age 0-17	16	$6,444.53
394	Other O.R. Procedures of the Blood and Blood-Forming Organs	16	$9,025.18
395	Red Blood Cell Disorders, Age Greater than 17	16	$3,933.31
396	Red Blood Cell Disorders, Age 0-17	16	$3,930.95
397	Coagulation Disorders	16	$6,133.29
398	Reticuloendothelial and Immunity Disorders with CC	16	$5,706.33
399	Reticuloendothelial and Immunity Disorders without CC	16	$3,152.13
400	No Longer Valid	17	$0.00
401	Lymphoma and Nonacute Leukemia with Other O.R. Procedure with CC	17	$14,016.92
402	Lymphoma and Nonacute Leukemia with Other O.R. Procedure without CC	17	$5,577.86
403	Lymphoma and Nonacute Leukemia with CC	17	$8,705.43
404	Lymphoma and Nonacute Leukemia without CC	17	$4,375.86
405	Acute Leukemia without Major O.R. Procedure, Age 0-17	17	$9,137.12
406	Myeloproliferative Disorders or Poorly Differentiated Neoplasms with Major O.R. Procedures with CC	17	$13,175.75
407	Myeloproliferative Disorders or Poorly Differentiated Neoplasms with Major O.R. Procedures without CC	17	$5,804.09
408	Myeloproliferative Disorders or Poorly Differentiated Neoplasms with Other O.R. Procedures	17	$10,607.86
409	Radiotherapy	17	$5,702.55
410	Chemotherapy without Acute Leukemia as Secondary Diagnosis	17	$5,227.89
411	History of Malignancy without Endoscopy	17	$1,716.81

** Calculated with an average hospital Medicare base rate of $4,733. Each hospital's base rate and corresponding payment will vary.*

DRG	Description	MDC	Nat'l Avg Payment
412	History of Malignancy with Endoscopy	17	$3,991.41
413	Other Myeloproliferative Disorders or Poorly Differentiated Neoplasm Diagnoses with CC	17	$6,162.57
414	Other Myeloproliferative Disorders or Poorly Differentiated Neoplasm Diagnoses without CC	17	$3,678.27
415	O.R. Procedure for Infectious and Parasitic Diseases	18	$18,840.05
416	Septicemia, Age Greater than 17	18	$7,922.36
417	Septicemia, Age 0-17	18	$5,520.71
418	Postoperative and Posttraumatic Infections	18	$5,061.17
419	Fever of Unknown Origin, Age Greater than 17 with CC	18	$3,992.35
420	Fever of Unknown Origin, Age Greater than 17 without CC	18	$2,870.17
421	Viral Illness, Age Greater than 17	18	$3,619.71
422	Viral Illness and Fever of Unknown Origin, Age 0-17	18	$2,914.56
423	Other Infectious and Parasitic Diseases Diagnoses	18	$9,066.27
424	O.R. Procedure with Principal Diagnosis of Mental Illness	19	$10,755.69
425	Acute Adjustment Reactions and Psychosocial Dysfunction	19	$2,924.01
426	Depressive Neuroses	19	$2,199.03
427	Neuroses Except Depressive	19	$2,425.26
428	Disorders of Personality and Impulse Control	19	$3,297.13
429	Organic Disturbances and Mental Retardation	19	$3,740.14
430	Psychoses	19	$3,061.92
431	Childhood Mental Disorders	19	$2,445.57
432	Other Mental Disorder Diagnoses	19	$2,966.99
433	Alcohol/Drug Abuse or Dependence, Left Against Medical Advice	20	$1,311.10
434	No Longer Valid	20	$0.00
435	No Longer Valid	20	$0.00
436	No Longer Valid	20	$0.00
437	No Longer Valid	20	$0.00
438	No Longer Valid	20	$0.00
439	Skin Grafts for Injuries	21	$9,161.68
440	Wound Debridements for Injuries	21	$9,189.54
441	Hand Procedures for Injuries	21	$4,431.12
442	Other O.R. Procedures for Injuries with CC	21	$12,119.22
443	Other O.R. Procedures for Injuries without CC	21	$4,696.08
444	Traumatic Injury, Age Greater than 17 with CC	21	$3,568.70
445	Traumatic Injury, Age Greater than 17 without CC	21	$2,377.09
446	Traumatic Injury, Age 0-17	21	$1,416.43
447	Allergic Reactions, Age Greater than 17	21	$2,630.24
448	Allergic Reactions, Age 0-17	21	$466.16
449	Poisoning and Toxic Effects of Drugs, Age Greater than 17 with CC	21	$4,028.25
450	Poisoning and Toxic Effects of Drugs, Age Greater than 17 without CC	21	$2,022.39
451	Poisoning and Toxic Effects of Drugs, Age 0-17	21	$1,257.73
452	Complications of Treatment with CC	21	$4,941.20
453	Complications of Treatment without CC	21	$2,496.11
454	Other Injury, Poisoning and Toxic Effect Diagnoses with CC	21	$3,844.99
455	Other Injury, Poisoning and Toxic Effect Diagnoses without CC	21	$2,231.62
456	No Longer Valid	22	$0.00
457	No Longer Valid	22	$0.00
458	No Longer Valid	22	$0.00
459	No Longer Valid	22	$0.00
460	No Longer Valid	22	$0.00

** Calculated with an average hospital Medicare base rate of $4,733. Each hospital's base rate and corresponding payment will vary.*

DRG	Description	MDC	Nat'l Avg Payment
461	O.R. Procedure with Diagnosis of Other Contact with Health Services	23	$6,599.92
462	Rehabilitation	23	$4,109.01
463	Signs and Symptoms with CC	23	$3,287.21
464	Signs and Symptoms without CC	23	$2,387.48
465	Aftercare with History of Malignancy as Secondary Diagnosis	23	$2,939.60
466	Aftercare without History of Malignancy as Secondary Diagnosis	23	$3,686.77
467	Other Factors Influencing Health Status	23	$2,268.46
468	Extensive O.R. Procedure Unrelated to Principal Diagnosis	All	$18,906.64
469	Principal Diagnosis Invalid as Discharge Diagnosis	14	$0.00
469	Principal Diagnosis Invalid as Discharge Diagnosis	15	$0.00
469	Principal Diagnosis Invalid as Discharge Diagnosis	All	$0.00
470	Ungroupable	All	$0.00
471	Bilateral or Multiple Major Joint Procedures of Lower Extremity	8	$14,825.97
472	No Longer Valid	22	$0.00
473	Acute Leukemia without Major O.R. Procedure, Age Greater than 17	17	$16,167.30
474	No Longer Valid	4	$0.00
475	Respiratory System Diagnosis with Ventilator Support	4	$17,045.78
476	Prostatic O.R. Procedure Unrelated to Principal Diagnosis	All	$10,306.53
477	Nonextensive O.R. Procedure Unrelated to Principal Diagnosis	All	$9,732.69
478	No Longer Valid	5	$0.00
479	Other Vascular Procedures without CC	5	$6,817.18
480	Liver Transplant and/or Intestinal Transplant	Pre	$42,362.00
481	Bone Marrow Transplant	Pre	$29,434.21
482	Tracheostomy for Face, Mouth and Neck Diagnoses	Pre	$15,768.68
483	No Longer Valid	Pre	$0.00
484	Craniotomy for Multiple Significant Trauma	24	$24,294.17
485	Limb Reattachment, Hip and Femur Procedures for Multiple Significant Trauma	24	$16,507.83
486	Other O.R. Procedures for Multiple Significant Trauma	24	$22,350.65
487	Other Multiple Significant Trauma	24	$9,190.49
488	HIV with Extensive O.R. Procedure	25	$20,947.92
489	HIV with Major Related Condition	25	$8,528.79
490	HIV with or without Other Related Condition	25	$5,024.80
491	Major Joint and Limb Reattachment Procedures of Upper Extremity	8	$7,925.19
492	Chemotherapy with Acute Leukemia as Secondary Diagnosis or with Use of High-Dose Chemotherapy Agent	17	$16,967.85
493	Laparoscopic Cholecystectomy without Common Duct Exploration with CC	7	$8,658.68
494	Laparoscopic Cholecystectomy without Common Duct Exploration without CC	7	$4,857.61
495	Lung Transplant	Pre	$40,493.11
496	Combined Anterior/Posterior Spinal Fusion	8	$28,778.18
497	Spinal Fusion Except Cervical with CC	8	$17,108.60
498	Spinal Fusion Except Cervical without CC	8	$13,125.69
499	Back and Neck Procedures Except Spinal Fusion with CC	8	$6,532.38
500	Back and Neck Procedures Except Spinal Fusion without CC	8	$4,272.43
501	Knee Procedures with Principal Diagnosis of Infection with CC	8	$12,498.00
502	Knee Procedures with Principal Diagnosis of Infection without CC	8	$6,830.40
503	Knee Procedures without Principal Diagnosis of Infection	8	$5,685.55
504	Extensive Burns or Full Thickness Burns with Mechanical Ventilation 96+ Hours with Skin Graft	22	$55,739.90
505	Extensive Burns or Full Thickness Burns with Mechanical Ventilation 96+ Hours without Skin Graft	22	$10,840.70

** Calculated with an average hospital Medicare base rate of $4,733. Each hospital's base rate and corresponding payment will vary.*

DRG	Description	MDC	Nat'l Avg Payment
506	Full Thickness Burn with Skin Graft or Inhalation Injury with CC or Significant Trauma	22	$19,335.49
507	Full Thickness Burn with Skin Graft or Inhalation Injury without CC or Significant Trauma	22	$8,203.38
508	Full Thickness Burn without Skin Graft or Inhalation Injury with CC or Significant Trauma	22	$6,029.85
509	Full Thickness Burn without Skin Graft or Inhalation Injury without CC or Significant Trauma	22	$3,880.89
510	Nonextensive Burns with CC or Significant Trauma	22	$5,581.17
511	Nonextensive Burns without CC or Significant Trauma	22	$3,506.36
512	Simultaneous Pancreas/Kidney Transplant	Pre	$25,343.62
513	Pancreas Transplant	Pre	$28,181.67
514	No Longer Valid	5	$0.00
515	Cardiac Defibrillator Implant without Cardiac Catheterization	5	$26,073.32
516	No Longer Valid	5	$0.00
517	No Longer Valid	5	$0.00
518	Percutaneous Cardiovascular Procedures without Acute Myocardial Infarction without Coronary Artery Stent Implant	5	$7,813.73
519	Cervical Spinal Fusion with CC	8	$11,663.45
520	Cervical Spinal Fusion without CC	8	$7,928.97
521	Alcohol/Drug Abuse or Dependence with CC	20	$3,277.29
522	Alcohol/Drug Abuse or Dependence with Rehabilitation Therapy without CC	20	$2,264.21
523	Alcohol/Drug Abuse or Dependence without Rehabilitation Therapy without CC	20	$1,791.43
524	Transient Ischemia	1	$3,442.12
525	Other Heart Assist System Implant	5	$53,975.39
526	No Longer Valid	5	$0.00
527	No Longer Valid	5	$0.00
528	Intracranial Vascular Procedure with Principal Diagnosis of Hemorrhage	1	$33,299.51
529	Ventricular Shunt Procedures with CC	1	$10,938.47
530	Ventricular Shunt Procedures without CC	1	$5,686.96
531	Spinal Procedures with CC	1	$14,773.07
532	Spinal Procedures without CC	1	$6,704.30
533	Extracranial Vascular Procedures with CC	1	$7,446.75
534	Extracranial Vascular Procedures without CC	1	$4,817.93
535	Cardiac Defibrillator Implant with Cardiac Catheterization with Acute Myocardial Infarction, Heart Failure, or Shock	5	$37,660.26
536	Cardiac Defibrillator Implant with Cardiac Catheterization without Acute Myocardial Infarction, Heart Failure, or Shock	5	$32,656.71
537	Local Excision and Removal of Internal Fixation Devices Except Hip and Femur with CC	8	$8,671.43
538	Local Excision and Removal of Internal Fixation Devices Except Hip and Femur without CC	8	$4,644.13
539	Lymphoma and Leukemia with Major O.R. Procedure with CC	17	$15,482.94
540	Lymphoma and Leukemia with Major O.R. Procedure without CC	17	$5,639.26
541	ECMO or Tracheostomy with Mechanical Ventilation 96+ Hours or Principal Diagnosis Except Face, Mouth, and Neck with Major O.R.	Pre	$93,533.35
542	Tracheostomy with Mechanical Ventilation 96+ Hours or Principal Diagnosis Except Face, Mouth, and Neck without Major O.R.	Pre	$60,793.98
543	Craniotomy with Implantation of Chemotherapeutic Agent or Acute Complex Central Nervous System Principal Diagnosis	1	$20,868.10
544	Major Joint Replacement or Reattachment of Lower Extremity	8	$9,277.39
545	Revision of Hip or Knee Replacement	8	$11,725.79
546	Spinal Fusions Except Cervical With Curvature of the Spine or Malignancy	8	$23,964.03

** Calculated with an average hospital Medicare base rate of $4,733. Each hospital's base rate and corresponding payment will vary.*

DRG	Description	MDC	Nat'l Avg Payment
547	Coronary Bypass with Cardiac Catheterization with MCV Diagnosis	5	$29,258.04
548	Coronary Bypass with Cardiac Catheterization without MCV Diagnosis	5	$22,291.62
549	Coronary Bypass without Cardiac Catheterization with MCV Diagnosis	5	$24,077.85
550	Coronary Bypass without Cardiac Catheterization without MCV Diagnosis	5	$17,074.12
551	Permanent Cardiac Pacemaker Implant with MCV Diagnosis or AICD Lead or Generator	5	$14,644.61
552	Other Permanent Cardiac Pacemaker Implant without MCV Diagnosis	5	$9,916.41
553	Other Vascular Procedures with CC with MCV Diagnosis	5	$14,620.99
554	Other Vascular Procedures with CC without MCV Diagnosis	5	$9,786.53
555	Percutaneous Cardiovascular Procedure with MCV Diagnosis	5	$11,483.97
556	Percutaneous Cardiovascular Procedure with Non Drug-Eluting Stent without MCV Diagnosis	5	$9,036.04
557	Percutaneous Cardiovascular Procedure with Drug-Eluting Stent with MCV Diagnosis	5	$13,563.04
558	Percutaneous Cardiovascular Procedure with Drug-Eluting Stent without MCV Diagnosis	5	$10,441.61
559	Acute Ischemic Stroke with Use of Thrombolytic Agent	1	$10,614.00

** Calculated with an average hospital Medicare base rate of $4,733. Each hospital's base rate and corresponding payment will vary.*

Appendix D — National Average Payment Table